AP® EDITION

Understanding PSYCHOLOGY

Fourteenth Edition

Robert S. Feldman
University of Massachusetts Amherst

AP Contributors

Hollie Drake
Overland High School, Colorado

Jessica Flitter
West Bend East High School, Wisconsin

McGraw Hill

UNDERSTANDING PSYCHOLOGY, FOURTEENTH EDITION

2 3 4 5 6 7 8 9 LKV 26 25 24 23

Bound:
ISBN 978-0-07-686332-7
MHID 0-07-686332-8

Portfolio Manager: *Nancy Welcher*
Product Development Manager: *Dawn Groundwater*
Product Developer: *Cara Labell*
Marketing Manager: *Augustine Laferrera and Olivia Kaiser*
Content Project Managers: *Mary E. Powers* (Core), *Jodi Banowetz* (Assessment)
Buyer: *Sandy Ludovissy*
Design: *David W. Hash*
Content Licensing *Specialist: Melisa Seegmiller*
Cover Image: ANDRZEJ WOJCICKI/SCIENCE PHOTO LIBRARY/Getty Images
Compositor: *Aptara®, Inc.*

Library of Congress Cataloging-in-Publication Data

Names: Feldman, Robert S. (Robert Stephen), 1947- author.
Title: Understanding psychology / Robert S. Feldman, University of
  Massachusetts Amherst.
Description: Fourteenth Edition. | Dubuque : McGraw-Hill Education, [2018] |
  Revised edition of the author's Understanding psychology, [2017]
Identifiers: LCCN 2018015406| ISBN 9780076863327 (hard cover : alk. paper) |
  ISBN 0076863328 (hard cover : alk. paper)
Subjects: LCSH: Psychology.
Classification: LCC BF121 .F34 2018 | DDC 150—dc23 LC record available at
https://lccn.loc.gov/2018015406

www.mheducation.com/prek-12

Dedication

To

Jon, Leigh, Alex, Miles, Josh, Julie, Naomi,
Marina, Sarah, Jeff, Lilia, Rose, and Kathy

About the Authors

ROBERT S. FELDMAN is Professor of Psychological and Brain Sciences and Senior Advisor to the Chancellor at the University of Massachusetts Amherst. A recipient of the College Distinguished Teacher Award, he teaches psychology classes ranging in size from 15 to nearly 500 students. During the course of more than three decades as a college instructor, he has taught undergraduate and graduate courses at Mount Holyoke College, Wesleyan University, and Virginia Commonwealth University in addition to the University of Massachusetts.

Professor Feldman, who initiated the Minority Mentoring Program at the University of Massachusetts, also has served as a Hewlett Teaching Fellow and Senior Online Teaching Fellow. He initiated distance-learning courses in psychology at the University of Massachusetts.

A Fellow of the American Psychological Association, the Association for Psychological Science, and the American Association for the Advancement of Science, Professor Feldman received a BA with High Honors from Wesleyan University and an MS and PhD from the University of Wisconsin-Madison. He is a winner of a Fulbright Senior Research Scholar and Lecturer Award and the Distinguished Alumnus Award from Wesleyan. He is past President of the Federation of Associations in Behavioral and Brain Sciences (FABBS) Foundation, which advocates for the field of psychology, and is on the board of the Social Psychology Network (SPN).

He has written and edited more than 250 books, book chapters, and scientific articles. He has edited *Development of Nonverbal Behavior in Children, Applications of Nonverbal Behavioral Theory and Research*, and *Improving the First Year of College: Research and Practice*, and co-edited *Fundamentals of Nonverbal Behavior*. He is also author of *P.O.W.E.R. Learning: Strategies for Success in College and Life*. His textbooks, which have been used by more than 2 million students around the world, have been translated into Spanish, French, Portuguese, Dutch, German, Italian, Chinese, Korean, and Japanese. His research interests include deception and honesty in everyday life, work that he described in *The Liar in Your Life*, a trade book published in 2009. His research has been supported by grants from the National Institute of Mental Health and the National Institute on Disabilities and Rehabilitation Research.

Professor Feldman loves music, is an enthusiastic pianist, and enjoys cooking and traveling. He serves on the Executive Committee and Board of New England Public Radio. He and his wife, also a psychologist, live in western Massachusetts in a home overlooking the Holyoke mountain range.

HOLLIE DRAKE teaches at Overland High School in the Cherry Creek School District in Aurora, Colorado. She has been teaching the AP Psychology course since 2007. Hollie has served as a reader for the AP Psychology exam for the past five years. Early in 2018, Hollie served as a consultant for the 2019 AP Psychology Course and Exam Description Guide.
Hollie Drake
Overland High School
Aurora, Colorado

JESSICA FLITTER has been teaching AP Psychology since 2004. She has been involved with the AP Reading since 2013, serving as a reader, table leader, and rubric master. Jessica was awarded the 2015 APA TOPSS Charles T. Blair-Broeker Excellence in Teaching Award. She is also co-author of the review book *AP Psychology: All Access* and contributing author to the blog *Books for Psychology Class*.
Jessica Flitter
West Bend East High School
West Bend, WI

Brief Contents

Contents

©DGLimages/Shutterstock

©Uppercut/SuperStock

CHAPTER 4

Sensation and Perception 87

©Eugenio Marongiu/Shutterstock

©MJTH/Shutterstock

CHAPTER 6
Learning 167

©India Picture/Shutterstock

©Chris Nash/Photodisc/Getty Images

©Yasuyoshi Chiba/AFP/Getty Images

Sexuality and Gender 330

©Jade/Getty Images

©Nancy Mao Smith/Shutterstock

©santypan/Shutterstock

©Fancy Collection/SuperStock

CHAPTER 14

Health Psychology: Stress, Coping, and Well-Being 456

©urbancow/Getty Images

©Ingram Publishing/SuperStock

©Shutterstock/Rawpixel.com

Preface

Using *Understanding Psychology*: A Guide for Students

If you're reading this, you're taking an Advanced Placement Psychology course. Maybe you're studying psychology because you've always been interested in what makes people tick. Or perhaps you've had a friend or family member who has sought assistance for a psychological disorder. Or maybe you have no idea of what psychology is all about, but you know that taking AP Psychology will help you explore an unfamiliar subject area at the college level and possibly earn college credit.

Whatever your motivation for taking the course and reading this book, here's my commitment to you: by the time you finish this text, you will have a better understanding of why people–including you–behave the way they do. You will know how, and why, psychologists conduct research, and you'll understand the theories that guide their research. You will become acquainted with the breadth of the field, and you'll obtain practical, useful information. In short, you'll gain a wealth of knowledge that hopefully will excite your curiosity and increase your understanding of people's behavior. And you'll do well on the AP exam!

To meet this commitment, the AP edition of **Understanding Psychology** has been written with you, the student, in mind. At every step in the development of the book, students and teachers have been consulted extensively to identify the specific combination of learning tools that would maximize your ability to learn and retain the subject matter of psychology. The result is a book that contains content and features that will not only help you to understand psychology but will also help you to see the relevance of the discipline in your life.

Now it's your turn. You'll need to take several steps to maximize the effectiveness of the learning tools in the book. These steps include familiarizing yourself with the goals of the book and its scope and organization.

OVERVIEW OF *UNDERSTANDING PSYCHOLOGY*, AP EDITION

Understanding Psychology has seven main goals:

- To provide broad coverage of the field of psychology, introducing the theories, research, and applications that constitute the discipline.
- To arouse intellectual curiosity and build an appreciation of the relevance of psychology.
- To motivate and engage.
- To serve as an impetus for you to think critically about psychological phenomena, particularly those that have an impact on our everyday lives.
- To illustrate the substantial diversity both within the field of psychology and in society by presenting material that reflects the discipline's increasing concern with cultural, gender, racial, and ethnic issues.
- To provide learning that aligns with the AP course requirements, including how the AP Psychology Skills–Concept Understanding, Data Analysis, and Scientific Investigation–can be applied to the content.
- To maximize students' performance on the AP Psychology Exam.

The text includes extensive coverage of both the traditional areas of psychology and applied topics, including the biological bases of behavior; sensation and perception; states of consciousness; learning; memory; cognitive psychology; developmental psychology; motivation, emotion, and personality; clinical psychology; and social psychology. Moreover, it features more applied chapters, such as health psychology. Ultimately, the book reflects a combination of traditional core topics and contemporary applied subjects, providing a broad and exceptionally current view of the field of psychology.

THE SCOPE AND ORGANIZATION OF *UNDERSTANDING PSYCHOLOGY*

To get the most out of this textbook, there are several things you should do. Begin by reading the list of chapters and skimming the detailed Table of Contents. From this you will get a sense of the topics covered and the logic of the sequence of chapters.

Then take some time to flip through the book. Choose a chapter that sounds particularly interesting to you, skim it, and see how it is laid out.

The heart of each chapter consists of several self-contained modules that provide logical starting and stopping points for reading and studying. This allows you to absorb new information in manageable chunks and process your learning before moving on to another topic. You can plan your studying around the modules of each chapter. For instance, if your teacher assigns a chapter to read over the course of a week, you might plan to read and study one module each day and use later days in the week to review the material.

USING THE BUILT-IN LEARNING AIDS

Once you have acquired a broad overview of *Understanding Psychology*, you are ready to begin reading and learning about psychology. Each chapter contains these specific learning aids that will help you master the material.

- **Prologue.** Each chapter starts with an account of a real-life situation that demonstrates the relevance of basic principles and concepts of psychology to pertinent issues and problems.

- **Looking Ahead.** These sections follow each prologue, providing a preview of the key themes and issues discussed within the chapter.

- **AP Learning Targets.** Every module starts with learning objectives for the upcoming material. They are tied to what you need to know to succeed on the AP Psychology Exam.

- **Applying Psychology in the 21st Century.** These boxes–highlighting the relevance of psychology–illustrate applications of current psychological theory and research findings to real-world problems, focusing on current advances and future possibilities and include AP-specific questions.

- **Neuroscience in Your Life.** This AP feature emphasizes the importance of neuroscientific research within the various subfields of the discipline and in students' lives. Representative brain scans, with both caption and textual explanation, illustrate significant neuroscientific findings that increasingly influence the field of psychology and provide an understanding of the biological bases of behavior.

- **Exploring Diversity.** In addition to a substantial amount of material relevant to diversity integrated throughout the text, every chapter also includes at least one special section devoted to an aspect of racial, ethnic, gender, or cultural diversity. These sections highlight the way in which psychology informs (and is informed by) issues relating to the increasing multiculturalism of our global society.

- *Becoming an Informed Consumer of Psychology.* Every chapter includes material designed to make you a more informed consumer of psychological information by giving you the ability to evaluate critically what the field of psychology offers. These discussions also provide sound, useful guidance concerning common problems.

- *Study Alerts.* Throughout the text, marginal notes point out important and difficult concepts and topics. These Study Alerts offer suggestions for learning the material effectively and for studying for class tests as well as for the AP exam.

- *From the Perspective of . . .* Most chapters include questions to help you connect psychological concepts with career realities. Called "From the Perspective of . . .," this feature helps students understand how psychology relates to various career fields.

- *Running Glossary.* Key terms are highlighted in boldface type within the text where they are introduced and are defined in the margin of the page. There is also an end-of-book glossary.

- *Chapter Citations.* The text uses a reference citation style endorsed by the American Psychological Association (APA). Citations include a name and date, typically set off in parentheses at the end of a sentence specifying the author(s) of the work being cited and the year of publication. You can use the citations to learn more about a topical area by referring to the Reference list at the end of the book.

- *AP Summary, Key Terms, and Test Practice.* Every module ends with an AP Summary, a list of key terms, and an AP Test Practice section, offering you the opportunity to consolidate and test your knowledge of the material as it specifically relates to the AP course.

- *Looking Back Epilogue.* Each chapter ends with an epilogue summarizing the topics and concepts covered in that chapter.

- *Visual Summary.* Finally, a visual summary is included at the end of every chapter, providing an overview of the chapter content in graphical form. Seeing the material in a visual format will help you study and learn in a way that supplements the traditional written presentation of the material.

A FINAL WORD

I hope you enjoy this introduction to psychology. Psychology is an exciting field, and I am confident that by the time you finish this text you'll see how psychology is not only a vibrant science but one that has real relevance to your life. And if you conscientiously use the built-in study aids and actively engage with the material in the book, you'll maximize your chances of excelling on the AP exam.

Finally, I welcome your comments and suggestions about *Understanding Psychology.* You can write me at feldman@psych.umass.edu. I will write back!

Robert S. Feldman
University of Massachusetts Amherst

Student Tools: Mastering the Material

Student success in psychology means mastering the material at a deep level. Here are some of the features and tools that help students maximize their performance:

Concept Clips help students comprehend some of the most difficult ideas in introductory psychology. Colorful graphics and stimulating animations describe core concepts in a step-by-step manner, engaging students and aiding in retention. Concept Clips can be used as a presentation tool in the classroom or for student assessment. New in the 14th edition, Concept Clips are embedded in the ebook to offer an alternative presentation of these challenging topics.

Interactivities, assignable in the digital course, engage students with content through experiential activities. Activities include: Perspectives in Psychology; Correlations; Neurons; The Brain and Drugs; The Stages of Sleep; Levels of Processing; Maslow's Hierarchy of Needs; Naturalistic Observation; Observational Learning; Defense Mechanisms; Stereotypes and Prejudice; Heuristics; Personality Assessment; and First Impressions and Attraction.

Through the connection of psychology to students' own lives, concepts become more relevant and understandable. **NewsFlash** exercises tie current news stories to key psychological principles and learning objectives. After interacting with a contemporary news story, students are assessed on their ability to make the link between real life and research findings.

Psychology at Work videos, assignable and assessable within the digital course highlight nine careers in which knowledge of psychology is beneficial in the workplace. Each video introduces a person at work, which applies the content students are learning into real-world work contexts.

AP Teacher Manual

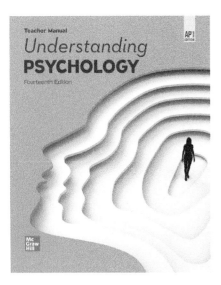

Our new **AP Teacher Manual** gives teachers the tools to help students navigate the AP Psychology course and succeed on the AP exam. The content supports and deepens understanding of the content covered in the Student Edition.

The Teacher Manual, available in print and digital format, provides:

- An AP Chapter Introduction that connects each chapter with AP Essential Questions and AP Learning Targets
- AP correlations for each module
- Module introductions that highlight critical concepts and key terms and people featured in each module
- Class discussion ideas to guide students in mastering AP content
- Activities that engage students in real-life applications of course material
- Additional readings and media to support both in-class and out-of-class learning
- Answers and rubrics for in-chapter features "Applying Psychology in the 21st Century" and "Neuroscience in Your Life" and the end-of-module and chapter AP Test Practice questions in the Student Edition

AP Features to Support Course and Exam Success

The AP edition of *Understanding Psychology* has been meticulously crafted to support student success with their coursework and on the Exam. AP-aligned content and concepts are reinforced in each chapter and module through visual call-outs that keep students intently focused on the critical skills and knowledge.

©Andrey_Popov/Shutterstock

CHAPTER 1
Introduction to Psychology

AP ESSENTIAL QUESTIONS ◄

- Why don't psychologists agree?

AP *Understanding Psychology* chapters pose Essential Questions and identify Learning Targets reflecting the AP curriculum framework for students to consider as they make their way through the concepts and topics in the chapter.

AP LEARNING TARGETS FOR CHAPTER 1 ◄

MODULE 1

- Describe and compare different theoretical approaches in explaining behavior.
- Distinguish the different domains of psychology.

PSYCHOLOGISTS AT WORK

The Subfields of Psychology: Psychology's Family Tree

Working at Psychology

AP MODULE 3: PSYCHOLOGY'S KEY ISSUES AND CONTROVERSIES

AP SUMMARY

- Recognize how philosophical and physiological perspectives shaped the development of psychological thought.
- Psychology's key issues and controversies center on how much of human behavior is a product of nature or

nurture, conscious or unconscious thoughts, observable actions or internal mental proces___ determinism, and individual diffe___ principles.

- Describe and compare different t___ in explaining behavior.

An **AP** focused Summary, AP Key Terms, and an AP Test Practice close each of the modules. The AP Test Practice consists of three multiple choice questions and a free response (essay) section emulating the actual AP Exam.

AP KEY TERMS ◄

free will   determinism

AP TEST PRACTICE ◄

Section I: Multiple Choice

1. In the debate known as nature versus nurture, advocates for nature support which of the following?
   A. Environment
   B. Heredity
   C. Unconscious
   D. Experience
   E. Free will

   C. Evolutionary
   D. Cognitive
   E. Psychodynamic

Section II: Free Response

Since the beginning of the discipline, psychology has had several key issues and controversies. Identify the following issues and connect them to the five major perspectives.

- Nature versus nurture
- Conscious versus unconscious
- Observable versus internal mental processes
- Free will versus determinism
- Individual differences versus universal principles

AP APPLYING PSYCHOLOGY IN THE 21ST CENTURY

SNIFFING OUT FLASH DRIVES

Sensation and perception tell us everything we know about the world around us. But as amazing as these processes are, they do have their limits. We can't see microbes or ultraviolet light, for example, nor can we detect radiation at all. Our ability to apprehend and respond to our environment diminishes greatly beyond the limits of our senses. Indeed, our very understanding of reality is largely bound by our limited sensory and perceptual abilities.

Many nonhuman animals have differe___ or greater sensory abilities___ Some insects can see ultravio___ can hear sounds at much hi___

The sense of smell in dogs is much better than that of humans, and their skill can even help detect illegal electronic equipment.
©Tengku Bahar/AFP/Getty Images

easily conceal in what would seem to be unlikely places—inside jewelry, in hollowed-out hiding spaces within walls or furnishings, or even inside more innocuous kinds of electronic devices. Finding these devices has become all but impossible for human investigators (Dienst, Schreiber, & Valiquette, 2016).

But not for Iris. Deception doesn't work on a dog. Not even the cleverest hiding spaces escape her outstanding canine senses. Her nose leads her right to them. A person would be hard pressed to detect the unique scent of a memory chip right under her own nose, but Iris can detect it at a distance—

detect a chemical commonly used on mem-   and quickly, too. She follows the scent trail ory chips and present in most electronic

AP SKILL: DEFINE AND/OR APPLY CONCEPT / EXPLAIN BEHAVIOR IN AUTHENTIC CONTEXT

1. Dogs detect smells that humans are not able to detect. What type of threshold is lower for dogs than humans?
2. How would your life change if you had an increased sense of smell like dogs?

AP Applying Psychology in the 21st Century presents students with issues that are relevant to their world today. Question sets infuse the rigor and practice of applying AP-specific skills, including **Concept Understanding, Data Analysis, and Scientific Investigation,** in the context of understanding these real-world theories and research findings to give students ample practice in demonstrating AP skill mastery required for the AP Exam.

AP Neuroscience in Your Life is an AP feature emphasizing the importance of neuroscientific research within the various subfields of the discipline and in students' lives. Representative brain scans, with both caption and textual explanation, illustrate significant neuroscientific findings that increasingly influence the field of psychology. For example, one of these features explains why people are so emotional when they don't get enough sleep. Throughout the text, students have the opportunity to check their grasp of **Concept Understanding, Data Analysis,** and **Scientific Investigation** by answering questions specific to each feature topic.

Recommended   May Be Appropriate

AP NEUROSCIENCE IN YOUR LIFE: WHY ARE WE SO EMOTIONAL WHEN WE DON'T GET ENOUGH SLEEP?

AP SKILL: DEFINE AND/OR APPLY CONCEPTS / SCIENTIFIC INVESTIGATION

1. What are some additional effects of sleep deprivation?

2. Describe the independent and dependent variables found in the experiment.

After a restless night, many people feel increased stress and overreact to events in their lives the next day. Recent research has now identified the neural basis for these reactions. For example, in one study, participants were kept awake all night and then asked to perform an experiment involving exposure to emotional and neutral images. Participants who were sleep deprived reacted to the neutral images as if they were emotional, and they had less connectivity between the amygdala (a region of the brain that processes emotion) and the anterior cingulate cortex (a region of frontal cortex important for emotional regulation). The green in the scan below shows the area of anterior cingulate that has greater connectivity to the amygdala for sleep-rested than sleep-deprived participants. These findings suggest that sleep loss increases emotional reactivity by interfering with our ability to control our emotions (Simon et al., 2015).

Source: Adapted from Simon, E. B., Oren, N., Sharon, H., Kirschner, A., Goldway, N., Okon-Singer, H., . . . Hendler, T. (2016). Losing neutrality: The neural basis of impaired emotional control without sleep. *Journal of Neuroscience, 35*(38), 13194-13205.

Keep in mind that professionals from a variety of occupations use the findings of psychologists. To understand how nonpsychologists use psychology, you will find a feature titled "From the perspective of . . ." throughout the text.

Chapters include questions to help students connect psychological concepts with career realities. Called "From the Perspective of . . .," this feature helps students understand how psychology relates to various career fields.

From the perspective of...

An Educator Imagine that a classroom teacher wants to improve the performance of a 10-year-old boy who is not doing well in math. What branches of psychology might she draw on to get ideas about how to help him?

©Andersen Ross/Blend Images/Getty Images

PSYCHOLOGISTS: A PORTRAIT

Although there is no "average" psychologist in terms of personal characteristics, we can draw a statistical portrait of the field. Some 360,000 active psychologists are working today in the United States . . .

Throughout, marginal notes point out important and difficult concepts and topics. These Study Alerts offer suggestions for learning the material effectively and for studying for tests.

tion of perception and thinking in a "whole" sense rather than on the individual elements of perception. (Module 2)

Study Alert
Knowing the basic outlines of the history of the field will help you understand how today's major perspectives have evolved.

Study Alert
Use Figure 2 to differentiate the five perspectives, which are important, because they provide a foundation for every topic covered throughout the text.

women to their graduate psychology programs in the early 1900s.

Despite the hurdles they faced, women made notable contributions to psychology, although their impact on the field was largely overlooked until recently. For example, Margaret Floy Washburn (1871-1939) was the first woman to receive a doctorate in psychology, and she did important work on animal behavior. Leta Stetter Hollingworth (1886-1939) was one of the first psychologists to focus on child development and on women's issues. She collected data to refute the view, popular in the early 1900s, that women's abilities periodically declined during parts of the menstrual cycle (Hollingworth, 1943/1990; Denmark & Fernandez, 1993; Furumoto & Scarborough, 2002).

Mary Calkins (1863-1930), who studied memory in the early part of the 20th century, became the first female president of the American Psychological Association. Karen Horney (pronounced "HORN-eye") (1885-1952) focused on the social and cultural factors behind personality; she also was the founder of the American Journal of Psychoanalysis. June Etta Downey (1875-1932) spearheaded the study of personality traits and became the first woman to head a psychology department at a state university. Anna Freud (1895-1982), the daughter of Sigmund Freud, also made notable contributions to the treatment of abnormal behavior, and Mamie Phipps Clark (1917-1983) carried out pioneering work on how children of color grew to recognize racial differences (Lal, 2002; Galdi, 2015).

Today's Five Major Perspectives

The men and women who laid the foundations of psychology shared a common goal: to explain and understand behavior using scientific methods. Seeking to achieve the same goal, the tens of thousands of psychologists who followed those early pioneers embraced—and often rejected—a variety of broad perspectives.

Student Learning: Content and Concepts

A major change in this new edition is an increased commitment to covering diversity. A new concluding module called "Epilogue: Diversity, Culture, Conflict, and Cooperation" addresses questions of how diversity affects individual behavior, how we observe and understand other people, and how our understandings (and misunderstandings) of our differences can lead to cooperation and/or conflict. Beyond the Epilogue, every chapter has a section called "Exploring Diversity," which examines how diversity affects psychology and vice-versa. These sections address ways to incorporate the concepts of diversity and culture across the curriculum as well as ways we can interact more effectively in this country and the world. In addition, the following information about new and revised topics and textual changes, provides a good indication of the content's currency and clarification for students.

Chapter 1–Introduction to Psychology
- Included new data on international versus U.S. psychologists
- Added a new figure on where psychologists work
- Clarified the concept of race
- Described race as a social construction
- Clarified the meaning of individual differences
- Clarified the meaning of universal principles
- Clarified introspection
- Redefined structuralism
- Redefined behavioral neuroscience
- Expanded the graphical timeline
- Noted discrepancies in salary and prestige between male and female psychologists
- Noted the impact of psychology on social policy

Chapter 2–Psychological Research
- Explained the use of Facebook in research
- Clarified the definition of theory
- Clarified the inability of correlational research to show causality
- Clarified experimental manipulation
- Clarified significant outcome
- Added a new example relating to the evaluation of research

Chapter 3–Neuroscience and Behavior
- Explained hydrogel-embedding methods of brain scanning
- Added new information on using computers to assist movement in quadriplegics
- Added research on cortical thickness and student income-level differences
- Clarified the definition of dendrite
- Redefined terminal button
- Clarified the process of neurotransmission
- Redefined neurotransmitter
- Added a new definition of reuptake

- Clarified the acetylcholine description
- Clarified the description of motor neurons
- Clarified transcranial magnetic stimulation
- Clarified reticular formation
- Added a new definition of neuroplasticity
- Reorganized the description of lateralization of hemispheres of brain
- Added information on brain-computer interface

Chapter 4–Sensation and Perception
- Clarified the description of light waves
- Clarified information on feature detection and specialization of receptors of visual information
- Clarified afterimage implications for trichromatic theory
- Clarified the place theory of hearing
- Clarified auditory neurons specialization
- Defined reflex sympathetic dystrophy syndrome
- Clarified gate–control theory
- Clarified biofeedback as a means to control pain
- Clarified synesthesia
- Redefined motion parallax
- Updated information on cognitive factors in pain perception
- Added a feature on the use of dogs' sensory capabilities for detection
- Enhanced the discussion of echolocation
- Updated statistics on chronic pain
- Introduced new synesthesia cases
- Introduced new information on inner speech and daydreaming

Chapter 5–States of Consciousness
- Included information on the opioid epidemic
- Added a new figure for sleep needs by age

- Discussed reverse learning and synaptic pruning as functions of sleep
- Clarified the definition of nightmares
- Added information on the frequency of nightmares
- Changed the stages of sleep from four to three, reflecting the American Academy of Sleep Medicine change
- Clarified the experience of waking consciousness while daydreaming
- Clarified changes in electrical activity during hypnosis
- Clarified the controversy regarding the nature of hypnosis
- Clarified the use of hypnosis in pain relief
- Discussed long-term effects of meditation on heart disease
- Clarified psychologists' motivation for studying consciousness
- Added an example of opioid addict whose addiction started with Percocet
- Discussed reasons for the increase in deaths due to opioid overdoses
- Clarified the difference between opioids and opiates
- Clarified reasons why people seek out drug highs
- Discussed Adderall use by college students
- Added new figure on drug use
- Clarified information on the use of cocaine and crack
- Clarified the definition of hallucinogens
- Discussed the expanded legalization of marijuana
- Clarified MDMA use

Chapter 6–Learning
- Added a feature on the use of learning principles by Uber and Lyft
- Added a new prologue on training dogs for medical purposes

- Clarified the classical conditioning figure
- Clarified neutral stimulus
- Clarified the description of classical conditioning
- Clarified the stimulus generalization definition
- Redefined operant conditioning
- Redefined the schedule of reinforcement
- Clarified continuous and partial reinforcement schedules
- Redefined the variable-ratio schedule
- Clarified the results of exposure to media aggression
- Noted that behavior modification can help students study more effectively
- Added APA task force findings on violent video game play

Chapter 7–Memory

- Discussed highly superior autobiographical memory (HSAM)
- Added information on the meaning of memories
- Enhanced the discussion of false memories
- Clarified the sensory memory explanation
- Redefined chunk
- Clarified the explanation of chunk
- Redefined mnemonics
- Clarified the description of memory stores in working memory
- Clarified procedural memory
- Added the term *implicit memory*
- Clarified the description of engram
- Clarified the flashbulb memory description
- Clarified similarities and differences between cultures in memory
- Clarified relearning and the importance of practice
- Refined the description of keyword technique
- Explained the value of forgetting regarding relearning
- Explained conditions under which eyewitness memories are accurate

Chapter 8–Cognition and Language

- Added information on the value of video gaming for cognitive skills
- Discussed attention span declines
- Included a new definition of reasoning
- Redefined familiarity heuristic, with a new example

- Clarified how we represent problems to ourselves
- Added a new definition of means-ends analysis
- Added a new definition of insight and clarified the presentation
- Added new examples of enhancing insight in humans
- Clarified the definition of functional fixedness
- Removed the term "mental set"
- Redefined divergent thinking
- Redefined cognitive complexity
- Added a new definition of convergent thinking
- Redefined semantics
- Clarified telegraphic speech
- Clarified overgeneralization
- Added new contrary evidence to the nativist approach
- Clarified the definition of interactionist approaches to language development
- Discussed the idea that language fosters reasoning
- Clarified the linguistic-relativity hypothesis
- Added new statistics on multilingual students
- Discussed the relevance of cognitive bias to other areas, such as prejudice
- Discussed behavioral economics
- Introduced information on artificial intelligence and Siri and Alexa
- Noted changes in creativity with aging

Chapter 9–Intelligence

- Redefined fluid intelligence
- Redefined crystallized intelligence
- Clarified Alfred Binet's role
- Added a new definition of reliability
- Added a new definition of validity
- Added a new definition of familial intellectual disability
- Redefined intellectual disability
- Clarified full inclusion
- Clarified the virtues of the intellectually gifted
- Added a feature on acquired savant syndrome
- Added a new prologue about a young, gifted genius

Chapter 10–Motivation and Emotion

- Added a feature regarding research on the biggest losers' inability to maintain their weight loss

- Added a new prologue on excessive weight loss and social media
- Clarified Maslow's view of esteem
- Clarified the self-determination theory
- Added a new definition of need for achievement
- Clarified the James-Lange theory of emotions
- Clarified the Schachter-Singer theory of emotions
- Updated the description of the facial-affect program
- Discussed the increase in obesity across the globe
- Discussed the heritability of eating disorders
- Included research on functional differences in the orbitofrontal cortex involved in eating disorders

Chapter 11–Sexuality and Gender

- Added statistics on sexting
- Augmented the discussion of gender identity choices
- Added new gender identity labels
- Discussed gender identities on Facebook and in the media
- Clarified gender roles
- Included new figures on sexual harassment
- Clarified statistics on women's earnings compared to men's
- Added new figures on the earnings gap between women and men
- Included data on the relationship between the frequency of sex and relationship satisfaction
- Clarified beliefs about gender equality in the workplace
- Clarified differences in nonverbal behavior between men and women
- Clarified the nature of sex differences in cognitive abilities
- Clarified the nature of evolutionary arguments about gender differences
- Expanded the explanation of the biosocial explanation of gender differences
- Clarified the use of gay and lesbian labels
- Clarified the biological and genetic causes of sexual orientation
- Redefined transgender
- Clarified the distinction between transgender and intersex persons
- Clarified the information on anger as a cause of rape

- Added a new definition of delayed ejaculation disorder
- Clarified the female orgasmic disorder
- Enhanced the discussion of the benefits of sex for relationship satisfaction
- Included information on the experience of rape as cause of frontal cortex impairment
- Added statistics on female genital cutting victims in the United States

Chapter 12–Development

- Discussed the use of mitochondria in in vitro fertilization
- Clarified the vision capabilities of neonates
- Updated information on the changes in cognitive abilities over the life span
- Clarified the benefits of play
- Clarified Erikson's trust-versus-mistrust stage
- Clarified Erikson's autonomy-versus-shame-and-doubt stage
- Clarified Erikson's industry-versus-inferiority stage
- Clarified the information processing approach
- Clarified Vygotsky's view of cognitive development
- Changed the presentation of scaffolding
- Clarified the presentation of puberty
- Clarified the discussion of spermarche
- Clarified Kohlberg's Level 2 morality
- Clarified Kohlberg's Level 3 morality
- Clarified adolescence as a period of relative tranquility
- Redefined personal fables
- Clarified the discussion of culture-specific rites of passage
- Clarified emerging adulthood
- Redefined genetic programming theories of aging
- Updated statistics on Alzheimer's disease
- Added new research on slowing the declines of Alzheimer's disease
- Added new statistics on Facebook use by adolescents
- Enhanced the discussion of mental health issues for early puberty
- Discussed cyberbullying as a cause of suicide

Chapter 13–Personality

- Add a new prologue on the Lance Armstrong case
- Discussed the stability of personality across generations

- Redefined ego
- Clarified the discussion of ego's mediating role
- Clarified the discussion of Freud's Oedipal conflict in boys and girls
- Added specificity to the description of psychoanalytic theory
- Added a new definition of inferiority complex
- Redefined the Allport cardinal trait
- Redefined the Allport central trait
- Refined factor analysis
- Clarified criticisms of trait theory
- Clarified the distinction between psychodynamic, trait, and learning theories
- Clarified the relationship harmony concept
- Clarified temporary reductions in self-esteem
- Clarified research studies on twins separated early in life
- Clarified Rogers' notion of self-concept
- Replaced the term *norm* with *test norm*
- Added a new definition of test norm
- Added a new definition of projective test
- Clarified projective test criticisms

Chapter 14–Health Psychology: Stress, Coping, and Well-Being

- Added the concept of posttraumatic growth
- Added a feature on training physicians to convey bad news effectively
- Added data on Facebook as a source of negative health outcomes
- Updated medical error death statistics
- Discussed nontraditional forms of PTSD for combat veterans
- Discussed e-health communication
- Added statistics on electronic-cigarette use
- Added discussion on e-cigarette use and its effect on quitting traditional cigarette smoking
- Discussed the link between social relationships and health
- Clarified the biological and psychological consequences of stress
- Clarified the critique of general adaption syndrome
- Clarified the effects of stress on lymphocytes
- Clarified techniques for coping with stress

- Included data on the incidence of smoking and disease among whites versus African Americans
- Clarified the social causes of smoking
- Discussed the relationship between poverty and sadness
- Added information on buying time savers versus buying goods and the relationship to happiness
- Added a new figure on smoking incidence

Chapter 15–Psychological Disorders

- Added a new case study of a woman with anxiety disorder
- Added references to magic and spells as explanations for abnormal behavior
- Add a feature on increases in self-reported psychological disorders
- Removed the explication of historical change in the DSM
- Discussed epigenetic approaches to schizophrenia
- Discussed the relationship between homelessness and psychological disorders
- Added new statistics on the mentally ill homeless population
- Clarified deviation from the typical definition of abnormality
- Clarified deviation from an ideal definition of abnormality
- Clarified the discussion of insanity
- Explicitly defined abnormal behavior
- Clarified the importance of the neurological basis of psychological disorders
- Clarified criticisms of psychoanalytic theory
- Added a new example of rationality of negative emotions regarding cognitive perspectives
- Clarified the discussion of the humanistic perspective
- Added a new definition of the sociocultural perspective
- Clarified the atheoretical, descriptive approach of the DSM
- Clarified the lack of objective danger in phobic stimuli
- Redefined compulsion
- Clarified the definition of illness anxiety disorder
- Clarified the discussion of dissociative identity disorder
- Redefined mood disorder
- Clarified the causes of gender differences in depression in women

- Clarified the label and explanation of internal unconscious conflicts as a cause of depression
- Changed "inappropriate emotional displays" to "inappropriate emotions" in the discussion of schizophrenia
- Added an explanation of the action of glutamate in treating schizophrenia
- Added material on the genes responsible for schizophrenia
- Discussed gray matter differences in the brains of people with schizophrenia
- Clarified and qualified the psychoanalytic explanations of schizophrenia
- Clarified the predispositional model of schizophrenia
- Clarified the lack of distress for those with personality disorders
- Clarified the explanation of borderline personality disorder
- Redefined neurocognitive disorders
- Clarified the statistics on the prevalence of psychological disorders
- Condensed and clarified the discussion of cross-cultural influences on definitions of abnormal behavior

Chapter 16–Treatment of Psychological Disorders
- Redefined psychotherapy
- Redefined biomedical therapy
- Reframed the discussion of psychodynamic therapies (versus psychoanalysis)
- Redefined psychoanalysis
- Clarified free association
- Redefined the behavioral approaches to therapy
- Clarified aversive therapy
- Revised the discussion of aversion therapy

- Clarified the definition of systematic desensitization
- Revised the discussion of contingency contracting
- Added a new definition of observational learning
- Reframed the discussion of behavioral techniques
- Expanded the definition of unconditional positive regard
- Clarified the discussion of contemporary versions of client-centered therapy
- Revised the discussion of interpersonal therapy effectiveness
- Revised the discussion of the goals of family therapy
- Clarified the definition of self-help therapy
- Clarified the discussion of the effectiveness of therapy in general versus specific kinds of therapy
- Added a new case study on use of deep brain stimulation
- Discussed the use of online therapy
- Reframed the distinction between biomedical approaches and other treatments
- Updated the definition of drug therapy
- Clarified the inhibition of neurotransmitter transmission
- Discussed virtual reality exposure therapy
- Added psychotherapy to the biomedical treatments for schizophrenia
- Added a discussion of brain scan neurofeedback for treatment
- Clarified the prefrontal lobotomy discussion
- Clarified the drawbacks to biomedical therapies

- Revised the definition of deinstitutionalization
- Added material on drug treatments that is more explicitly linked to the neuroscience chapter
- Discussed cognitive appraisal retraining on academic tasks
- Added information on memory deficits as side effect of antidepressant drugs
- Referenced Satir's family therapy work

Chapter 17–Social Psychology
- Added a new prologue on Dylann Roof in South Carolina
- Discussed mentoring approaches to reducing self-stereotyping
- Clarified the description of the warm-cold person perception experiment
- Clarified the example of fundamental attribution error
- Redefined norms
- Clarified the description of the foot-in-the-door technique
- Clarified the door-in-the-face technique
- Clarified the effect of proximity on liking
- Clarified the mere exposure effect
- Clarified the effect of similarity on liking
- Clarified the relationship between physical attractiveness and a general attraction
- Clarified frustration-aggression approaches
- Clarified diffusion of responsibility explanations of helping
- Added information on global warming and aggression
- Added research on microaggressions

Acknowledgments

One of the central features of *Understanding Psychology* is the involvement of professionals as well as students in the review process. The 14th edition of *Understanding Psychology* has relied heavily—and benefited substantially—from the advice of instructors and students from a wide range of backgrounds.

Many teachers along my educational path have shaped my thinking. I was introduced to psychology at Wesleyan University, where several committed and inspiring teachers—and in particular, Karl Scheibe—conveyed their sense of excitement about the field and made its relevance clear to me. Karl epitomizes the teacher-scholar combination to which I aspire, and I continue to marvel at my good fortune in having such a role model.

By the time I left Wesleyan, I could envision no other career but that of psychologist. Although the nature of the University of Wisconsin, where I did my graduate work, could not have been more different from the much smaller Wesleyan, the excitement and inspiration were similar. Again, a cadre of excellent teachers–led, especially, by the late Vernon Allen–molded my thinking and taught me to appreciate the beauty and science of the discipline of psychology.

My colleagues and students at the University of Massachusetts Amherst provide ongoing intellectual stimulation, and I thank them for making the university a fine place to work. Several people also provided extraordinary research and editorial help. In particular, I am especially grateful to my superb students, past and present, including Erik Coats, Ben Happ, Sara Levine, Chris Poirier, Jim Tyler, and Matt Zimbler. John Bickford, in particular, provided invaluable editorial input that has enhanced the content considerably. Finally, I am grateful to John Graiff and Michelle Goncalves, whose hard work and dedication helped immeasurably on just about everything involving this material.

I am also grateful to Erika Nyhus of Bowdoin College, who provided exceptional support in helping identify appropriate neuroscientific research to include in the *Neuroscience in Your Life* features. I thank her for her fine work.

I offer great thanks to the McGraw-Hill Education editorial and marketing teams that participated in this new AP edition. Vice President and General Manager Mike Ryan and Senior Portfolio Manager Nancy Welcher foster a creative, energetic, and environment. I am in awe of their enthusiasm, commitment, and never-ending good ideas. I also thank my award-winning Marketing Managers AJ Laferrera and Ann Helgerson for their enthusiasm and commitment to this project and for being so great to work with. I'm also happy that the indefatigable, inventive Cory Reeves provided input about all sorts of things, and I especially thank him for his mentorship in the realm of all things musical. I thank these folks not only for their superb professionalism, but also for their friendship.

I am very grateful to Susan Messer, product developer on this edition. Susan did a superb job of managing a myriad of details (as well as me), bringing motivation, intelligence, and a fine literary sense to the project. Finally, every reader of this book owes a debt to Rhona Robbin and Judith Kromm, developmental editors on earlier editions of *Understanding Psychology*. Their relentless pursuit of excellence helped form the essence of this book, and they taught me a great deal about the craft and art of writing. Central to the design, production, and marketing process were Program Manager Debra Hash, Text Content Licensing Specialist Melisa Seegmiller, Image Content Licensing Specialist Shawntel Schmitt, and Designer David Hash, as well as Marilynn Taylor and Mary Powers, key members of the production group. I am proud to be a part of this world-class McGraw-Hill team.

Finally, I remain completely indebted to my family. My parents, Leah Brochstein and Saul Feldman, provided a lifetime foundation of love and support, and I continue to see their influence in every corner of my life. My extended family also plays a central role in my life. They include, more or less in order of age, my nieces and nephews, my terrific brother, my brothers- and sisters-in-law, and the late Ethel Radler. My mother-in-law, the late Mary Evans Vorwerk, had an important influence on this book, and I remain ever grateful to her.

Ultimately, my children, Jonathan, Joshua, and Sarah; my daughters-in-law Leigh and Julie; my son-in-law Jeffrey; my grandsons Alex and Miles; my granddaughters Naomi, Lilia, Marina, and Rose; and my wife, Katherine, remain the focal points of my life. I thank them, with immense love, and thank my lucky stars that they are in my life.

Robert S. Feldman
Amherst, Massachusetts

Personalized, Adaptive, and Dynamic
Digital Resources

Understanding Psychology is enriched with resources including videos with assessments, interactivities, case studies, and adaptive learning tools that enhance the teaching and learning experience both inside and outside of the classroom.

Authored by one of the world's leading subject matter experts and organized by chapter and module level, the resources provide students with multiple opportunities to contextualize and apply their understanding. Teachers can save time, customize lessons, monitor student progress, and make data-driven decisions in the classroom with the flexible, easy-to-navigate instructional tools.

Intuitive Design

Resources are organized at the chapter and module levels. To enhance the core content, teachers can add assignments, activities, and instructional aides to any lesson.

The chapter and module landing pages give students access to:

- assigned activities,
- resources and assessments,
- interactive eBook,
- adaptive **SmartBook**® assignments.

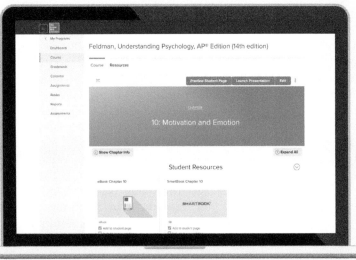

Chapter and module landing pages link students to resources that support success.

Mobile Ready
Access to course content on-the-go is easier and more effective than ever before with the ReadAnywhere mobile app.

Adaptive Study Tools

SMARTBOOK® is the assignable, online, adaptive study tool. Teachers can assign content down to the sub-topic level and deliver a personalized learning experience tailored to each student's needs that

- assesses a student's proficiency and knowledge,

- tracks which topics have been mastered,

- identifies areas that need more study,

- provides targeted remediation at the chapter, topic, or concept level,

- creates meaningful practice opportunities with instant feedback and guidance

Highlighted content continuously adapts as students work through exercises.

Practice sets measure depth of understanding and present a personalized learning path based on student responses.

Teacher Resources

Teachers have access to the interactive eBook, adaptive *SmartBook®*, plus a wealth of customizable module resources and powerful gradebook tools.

Resources include:

- Online *Teacher Manual* with module summaries, teaching suggestions, additional activities, and pacing guides

- Student performance reports to help teachers identify gaps, make data-driven decisions, and adjust instruction

- Customizable PowerPoint presentations

- Labeled visual aids and additional ideas for lecture enrichment

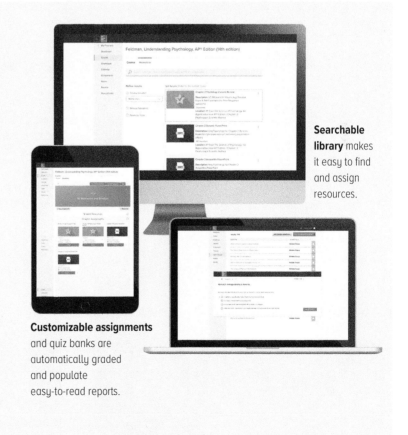

Searchable library makes it easy to find and assign resources.

Customizable assignments and quiz banks are automatically graded and populate easy-to-read reports.

Harness technology, unlock success with the digital resources for this text
Visit My.MHEducation.com

Making the Grade: A Practical Guide to Smarter Studying

Regardless of why you are taking AP Psychology, it's a safe bet you're interested in maximizing your understanding of the material and getting a good grade. And you want to accomplish these goals as quickly and efficiently as possible.

Good news: Several subfields of psychology have identified different ways to help you learn and remember material you will study throughout high school and beyond. Here's my guarantee to you: If you learn and follow the guidelines in each of these areas, you'll become a better student and get better grades. Always remember that *good students are made, not born.*

Adopt a General Study Strategy: Using the Power Framework

Psychologists have devised several excellent techniques to improve study skills. One of the best, based on a substantial body of research, is "P.O.W.E.R." or *P*repare, *O*rganize, *W*ork, *E*valuate, and *R*ethink

P.O.W.E.R. system entails the following steps:

- **Prepare.** In *Understanding Psychology*, 14th Edition, read the broad questions called *Learning Targets* to *Prepare* yourself for the material that follows. *Learning Targets* are at the start of each chapter and each module.

- **Organize.** The *Organize* stage involves developing a mental roadmap of where you are headed. *Understanding Psychology* includes an outline at the beginning of each chapter. Read it to get an idea of what topics are covered and how they are organized.

- **Work.** Because of your effort in the *Power* and *Organize* stages, the *Work* stage will be easier. You know what questions the material will answer based on the *Learning Targets*, and you know how it is organized based on the outline. Read everything in the content, including the material in boxes and the margins, to fully understand the material.

- **Evaluate.** *Evaluate* provides the opportunity to determine how effectively you have mastered the material. In *Understanding Psychology*, questions at the end of each module offer a rapid check of your understanding of the material. *Evaluate* your progress to assess your degree of mastery.

- **Rethink.** This final stage, *Rethink*, entails reanalyzing, reviewing, questioning, and challenging assumptions. Rethinking allows you to consider how the material fits with other information you have already learned. Every major section of *Understanding Psychology* ends with an *AP* summary and test practice section that allows you to think about the material at a deeper level.

Using the P.O.W.E.R. framework will help you maximize the efficiency and effectiveness of your study. In addition, the P.O.W.E.R. framework can be applied beyond the classroom, helping you to achieve success in your career and life.

Manage Your Time

Managing your time as you study is a central aspect of academic success. But remember: The goal of time management is to permit us to make informed choices about how we use our time. Use these time management procedures to harness time for your own advantage.

SET YOUR PRIORITIES. First, determine your priorities. *Priorities* are the tasks and activities you need and want to do, rank-ordered from most important to least important.

The best procedure is to start off by identifying priorities for an entire term. What do you need to accomplish? Rather than making these goals too general, make them specific, such as, "studying 10 hours before each chemistry exam."

IDENTIFY YOUR PRIME TIME. Are you a morning person or do you prefer studying later at night? Being aware of the time or times of day when you can do your best work will help you plan and schedule your time most effectively.

MASTER THE MOMENT. Here's what you'll need to organize your time:

- A *master calendar* that shows all the weeks of the term on one page. It should include every week of the term and seven days per week. On the master calendar, note the due date of every assignment and test you will have. Also include important activities from your personal life, drawn from your list of priorities. Add some free time for yourself.

- A *weekly timetable* that shows the days of the week across the top and the hours, from 6:00 a.m. to midnight, along the side. Fill in the times of all your fixed, prescheduled activities, for example the times that your classes meet and any other recurring appointments. Add assignment due dates, tests, and any other activities on the appropriate days of the week. Then add blocks of time necessary to prepare for those events.

- A *daily to-do list* using a small calendar or your smartphone. List all the things that you intend to do during the day and their priority. Start with the things you *must* do and that have fixed times, such as classes and work schedules. Then add in the other things that you *should* accomplish, such as researching an upcoming paper or finishing a lab report. Finally, list things that are a low priority, such as taking in a new movie.

CONTROL YOUR TIME. If you follow the schedules that you've prepared, you've taken the most important steps in time management. Things, however, always seem to take longer than planned.

©Michele Constantini

When inevitable surprises occur, there are several ways to take control of your days to follow your intended schedule:

- **Say no.** You don't have to agree to every favor that others ask of you.

- **Get away from it all.** Adopt a specific spot to call your own, such as a corner desk in a secluded nook in the library. If you use it enough, your body and mind will automatically get into study mode as soon as you get there.

- **Enjoy the sounds of silence.** Studies suggest that we are able to concentrate most when our environment is silent. Experiment and work in silence for a few days. You may find that you get more done in less time than you would in a more distracting environment.

- **Take an e-break.** Take an e-break and shut down your communication sources for some period of time. Phone calls, text messages, IMs, and e-mail can be saved on a phone or computer. They'll wait.

- **Expect the unexpected.** You'll never be able to escape from unexpected interruptions and surprises that require your attention. But by trying to anticipate them and thinking about how you'll react to them, you can position yourself to react effectively when they do occur.

Take Good Notes in Class

Let's consider some of the basic principles of notetaking:

- **Identify the teacher's–and your–goals for the course.** The information you get during the first day of class is critical. In addition to the teacher's goals, you should have your own. How will the information from the course help you to enhance your knowledge, improve yourself as a person, achieve your goals?

- **Complete assignments before coming to class.**

- **Listen for the key ideas.** Listen for such phrases as "you need to know . . . ," "the most important thing to consider . . . ," "there are four problems with this approach . . . ," and–a big one–"this will be on the test . . . "; phrases like these should cause you to sit up and take notice. Also, if teacher says the same thing in several ways, the material being discussed is important.

- **Use short, abbreviated phrases–not full sentences–when taking notes.**

- **Pay attention to PowerPoint slides or what is displayed in class on overhead projectors, whiteboards, or chalkboards. Remember these tips:**
  - Listening is more important than seeing.
  - Don't copy everything that is on every slide.
  - Remember that key points on slides are . . . key points.
  - Check to see if the presentation slides are available online.
  - Remember that presentation slides are not the same as good notes for a class.

Memorize Efficiently

Here's a key principle of effective memorization: Memorize what you need to memorize. *Forget about the rest.*

You have your choice of dozens of techniques of memorization. Also, feel free to devise your own strategies or add those that have worked for you in the past.

REHEARSAL. Say it aloud: rehearsal. Think of this word in terms of its three syllables: re–hear–sal. If you're scratching your head about why you should do this, it's to illustrate the point of *rehearsal:* to transfer material that you encounter into long-term memory.

MNEMONICS. This odd word (pronounced "neh MON ix"–the "m" is silent) describes formal techniques used to make material more readily remembered.

Among the most common mnemonics are the following:

- **Acronyms.** *Acronyms* are words or phrases formed by the first letters of a series of terms.

  For example, Roy G. Biv helps people to remember the colors of the spectrum (red, orange, yellow, green, blue, indigo, and violet).

- **Acrostics.** *Acrostics* are sentences in which the first letters spell out something that needs to be recalled. The benefits of acrostics are similar to those of acronyms.

- **Rhymes and jingles.** "Thirty days hath September, April, June, and November." If you know the rest of the rhyme, you're familiar with one of the most commonly used mnemonic jingles in the English language.

USE OF MULTIPLE SENSES. Every time we encounter new information, all of our senses are potentially at work. Each piece of sensory information is stored in a separate location in the brain, and yet all the pieces are linked in extraordinarily intricate ways.

- **When you learn something, use your body.** Move around. Stand up; sit down. Touch the page. Trace figures with your fingers. Talk to yourself. Think out loud. By involving every part of your body, you've increased the number of potential ways to trigger a relevant memory later, when you need to recall it.

- **Draw and diagram the material.** Structuring written material by graphically grouping and connecting key ideas and themes is a powerful technique. Creating drawings, sketches, and even cartoons can help us remember better.

- **Visualize.** Visualization is effective because it helps make abstract ideas concrete; it engages multiple senses; it permits us to link different bits of information together; and it provides us with a context for storing information.

- **Overlearning.** *Overlearning* consists of studying and rehearsing material past the point of initial mastery. Through overlearning, you can recall the information without even thinking about it.

Study for Tests Strategically

Here are some guidelines that can help you do your best on tests:

KNOW WHAT YOU ARE PREPARING FOR. To find out about an upcoming test, ask if it is a "test," an "exam," a "quiz," or something else. These names imply different things. In addition, each kind of test question requires a somewhat different style of preparation.

- **Free Response questions.** The best approach to studying for a free response (essay) test involves four steps:

  1. Reread your class notes and any notes you've made on assigned readings that will be covered on the upcoming exam. Also go through the readings themselves, reviewing underlined or highlighted material and marginal notes.

  2. Think of likely exam questions. Some teachers give lists of possible essay topics; if yours does, focus on this list and think of other possibilities.

  3. Answer each potential essay question–aloud. You can also write down the main points that any answer should cover.

  4. After you've answered the questions, look at the notes and readings again. If you feel confident that you've answered specific questions adequately, check them off. If you had trouble with some questions, review that material immediately. Then repeat step 3, answering the questions again.

- **Multiple-choice, true–false, and matching questions.** Studying for multiple-choice, true-false, and matching questions requires attention to the details. Write down important facts on index cards: They're portable and available all the time, and the act of creating them helps drive the material into your memory.

- **Short-answer and fill-in questions.** Short-answer and fill-in questions are similar to essays in that they require you to recall key pieces of information, but they don't demand that you integrate or compare different types of information. Consequently, the focus of your study should be on the recall of specific, detailed information.

TEST YOURSELF. When you believe you've mastered the material, test yourself on it. You can create a test for yourself, in writing, making its form as close as possible to what you expect the actual test to be.

DEAL WITH TEST ANXIETY. What does the anticipation of a test do to you? *Test anxiety* is a temporary condition characterized by fears and concerns about test-taking. You'll never eliminate test anxiety completely, nor do you want to. A little bit of nervousness can energize us, making us more attentive and vigilant.

On the other hand, for some students, anxiety can spiral into the kind of paralyzing fear that makes their minds go blank. There are several ways to keep this from happening to you:

- *Prepare thoroughly.*

- *Take a realistic view of the test.*

- *Learn relaxation techniques.*

- *Visualize success.*

FORM A STUDY GROUP. *Study groups* can be extremely powerful tools because they help accomplish several things by:

- helping you organize and structure the material to approach studying in a systematic and logical way.
- allowing you to share different perspectives on the material, making it more likely that you will not overlook any potentially important information.
- forcing you to rethink the course material to help with both the understanding and recall needed for the test.
- helping motivate you to do your best. As part of a study group, you're no longer working just for yourself; your studying also benefits other study group members. A study group may encourage you to put in your best effort.

About the AP Psychology Course

Are you ready to open the door? The AP Psychology course introduces you to the study of human behavior and mental processes. It may give you some insight into yourself and your thought processes, as well as give you some insight into why we, as humans, do some of the things we do. And some of the most fascinating things you'll learn are about how the brain and body function together and, sometimes, independently–the magnificence of our physical and psychological selves.

©ESB Professional/Shutterstock

As you know, the course is designed to be equivalent to introduction to psychology courses typically taken during the first college year. You'll explore and apply psychological theories, key concepts, and phenomena associated with such topics as the biological bases of behavior, sensation and perception, learning and cognition, motivation, developmental psychology, testing and individual differences, treatments of psychological disorders, and social psychology. Freud, one of the most recognizable names associated with psychology, Skinner, James, and Pavlov, among others, made great impacts on and contributions to the field of psychology. You'll learn about these psychologists and the different fields of study within the realm of psychology. Throughout the course, you'll learn about research methods, consider the ethics of some of the early research, and you'll evaluate evidence.

The AP Psychology course comprises the two essential components from the College Board Course and Exam Description course framework, Skills and Content, that you will need to know to better navigate the path toward the exam. Skills are the foundation in the study and practice of psychology, and you'll develop and apply these skills on a regular basis throughout the course. The course content is organized in such a way that there is a logical and methodical sequence for topics and concepts. The chapters and modules in **AP** *Understanding Psychology* are designed to give you multiple ways to integrate skills with your course content in preparation for the AP Psychology Exam.

AP Psychology Skills

The following table presents the skills that you will need to develop during the AP Psychology course. These skills also form the basis of tasks on the AP Exam.

Skill Category 1	Skill Category 2	Skill Category 3
Concept Understanding	*Data Analysis*	*Scientific Investigation*
Define, explain, and apply concepts, behavior, theories, and perspectives	Analyze and interpret quantitative data.	Analyze psychological research studies.
Skills 1.A Define and/or apply concepts. 1.B Explain behavior in authentic context. 1C. Apply theories and perspectives in authentic contexts.		

AP Psychology Course Content

Your success is the goal, and the AP edition of *Understanding Psychology* presents a defined and detailed progression that will help you to succeed. Chapters and Modules comprise the structure of the course. At the chapter level, you are given the overall, broad topic and then chapters are broken down into modules which delve deeper into specific aspects of the topic. For example, Chapter 8, Cognition and Language, includes modules about thinking and reasoning, problem solving, and language. Presenting information in this way, allows you to see the interrelationship between modules and topics, and, most importantly, concepts.

The AP course framework is divided into units, which are covered in the following the Chapters and Modules.

Units	Exam Weighting	Chapters/Modules in *Understanding Psychology*
Unit 1: Scientific Foundations of Psychology	10–14%	Chapters: 1, 2 Modules: 1, 2, 5, 6
Unit 2: Biological Bases of Behavior	8–10%	Chapters: 3, 5 Modules: 7, 8, 9, 14. 15, 16
Unit 3: Sensation and Perception	6–8%	Chapters: 4 Modules: 10, 11, 12, 13
Unit 4: Learning	7–9%	Chapters: 6, 14 Modules: 17, 18, 19, 43
Unit 5: Cognitive Psychology	13–17%	Chapters: 7, 8, 9 Modules: 20, 21, 22, 23, 24, 25, 26, 28
Unit 6: Developmental Psychology	7–9%	Chapters: 11, 12 Modules: 32, 36, 37, 38, 39
Unit 7: Motivation, Emotion, and Personality	11–15%	Chapters: 2, 10, 11, 13, 14 Modules: 5, 29, 31, 33, 40, 41, 42, 43, 44, 45
Unit 8: Clinical Psychology	12–16%	Chapters: 15, 16 Modules: 46, 47, 49, 50, 51
Unit 9: Social Psychology	8–10%	Chapters: 17 Modules: 52, 53, 54, 55

About the AP Psychology Exam

Okay. You've opened that door and discovered more than you imagined you would about yourself and others. Now it's time to take the exam.

This will assess your understanding of the learning targets, skills, and concepts in the course with 100 multiple-choice questions and 2 free-response questions. The AP Psychology Exam is 2 hours long and will give you an opportunity to practice some of the techniques–deep breathing, relaxation, how your body responds to stress–you learned in the course to keep any nervousness at bay.

Section	Question Type	Number of Questions	Exam Weighting	Timing
I	Multiple-choice questions	100	66.7%	70 minutes
II	Free-response questions	2	33.3%	50 minutes
	Question 1: Concept Application (7 points)			
	Question 2: Research Design (7 points)			

HOW STUDENT LEARNING IS ASSESSED ON THE AP EXAM

Section I: Multiple Choice

All three skill categories are assessed in the multiple-choice section of the AP Exam with the following exam weighting:

Skill Category	Exam Weighting
Skill Category 1: Concept Understanding	75–80%
Skill Category 2: Data Analysis	8–12%
Skill Category 3: Scientific Investigation	12–16%

Section II: Free-Response

Question 1: Concept Application assesses students' ability to explain behavior and apply theories and perspectives in authentic contexts. Skill Category 1 is assessed.

Question 2: Research Design assesses students' ability to analyze psychological research studies, including analyzing and interpreting quantitative data. All three skill categories are assessed with an emphasis on Skill Category 3.

TASK VERBS USED IN THE FREE RESPONSE QUESTIONS

The following task verbs are commonly used in the free-response questions:

Construct/Draw: Create a graph that illustrates or explains relationships or phenomena. Labels may or may not be required.

Define: Provide a specific meaning for a word or concept.

Describe: Provide the relevant characteristics of a specified topic.

Draw a conclusion: Use available information to formulate an accurate statement that demonstrates understanding based on evidence. Sometimes phrased as, "What is the most appropriate conclusion?"

Explain: Provide information about how or why a relationship, process, pattern, position, situation, or outcome occurs, using evidence and/or reasoning to support or qualify a claim. Explain "how" typically requires analyzing the relationship, process, pattern, position, situation, or outcome; whereas, explain "why" typically requires analysis of motivations or reasons for the relationship, process, pattern, position, situation, or outcome.

Identify/State: Indicate or provide information about a specified topic, without elaboration or explanation.

CHAPTER 1
Introduction to Psychology

AP'I ESSENTIAL QUESTIONS

- Why don't psychologists agree?

AP'I LEARNING TARGETS FOR CHAPTER 1

MODULE 1

- Describe and compare different theoretical approaches in explaining behavior.
- Distinguish the different domains of psychology.

PSYCHOLOGISTS AT WORK
The Subfields of Psychology: Psychology's Family Tree
Working at Psychology

MODULE 2

- Recognize how philosophical and physiological perspectives shaped the development of psychological thought.
- Identify the research contributions of major historical figures in psychology.
- Describe and compare different theoretical approaches in explaining behavior.

A SCIENCE EVOLVES: THE PAST, THE PRESENT, AND THE FUTURE
The Roots of Psychology
Today's Five Major Perspectives
AP'I Applying Psychology in the 21st Century: Psychology Matters

MODULE 3

- Recognize how philosophical and physiological perspectives shaped the development of psycho-logical thought.
- Describe and compare different theoretical ap-proaches in explaining behavior.
- Recognize the strengths and limitations of applying theories to explain behavior.

PSYCHOLOGY'S KEY ISSUES AND CONTROVERSIES
Exploring Diversity: Understanding How Culture, Ethnicity, and Race Influence Behavior
Psychology's Future
AP'I Neuroscience in Your Life: Enhancing Your Mind
Becoming an Informed Consumer of Psychology: Thinking Critically About Psychology: Distinguishing Legitimate Psychology from Pseudo-Psychology

PROLOGUE *HIGH SCHOOL MASSACRE*

It started like any other school day on a balmy Wednesday at the Marjory Stoneman Douglas High School campus in Parkland, Florida. But it ended with one of the most horrific school shootings in U.S. history. By the time the shooter, 19-year-old Nikolas Cruz, finished walking the halls with a blazing AR-15 rifle, 17 students and teachers lay dead, and many others were wounded.

But in the midst of this carnage, the best of humanity was also on display. Teachers and staff put their own lives at risk in an effort to shield and protect their students, in some cases dying as a result. And despite the danger, first responders rushed to help the wounded, and many students sought to comfort and aid their wounded classmates. As people all around the world expressed their grief, many joined together to work toward legal change that would make such shootings less likely.

Mourning the deaths of 17 individuals following the shooting at Marjory Stoneman Douglas High School in Florida.
©Matt McClain/The Washington Post via Getty Images

LOOKING *Ahead*

The Florida school massacre gives rise to a host of important psychological issues. For example, consider these questions asked by psychologists following the catastrophe:

- What motivated the shooter's rampage? Was he driven by political, social, or religious beliefs, or was he psychologically disturbed?

- What internal, biologically based changes occurred in those fleeing for their lives from the shooter?

- What memories did people have of the massacre afterward? How accurate were they?

- What will be the long-term effects of the massacre on the psychological and physical health of the survivors and witnesses?

- What are the most effective ways to help people cope with the sudden and unexpected loss of friends and loved ones?

- Could this tragedy have been prevented if the shooter had received psychological treatment?

As you'll soon see, the field of psychology addresses questions like these—and many, many more. In this chapter, we begin our examination of psychology, the different types of psychologists, and the various roles that psychologists play.

Module 1
Psychologists at Work

Psychology is the scientific study of behavior and mental processes. The simplicity of this definition is in some ways deceiving, concealing ongoing debates about how broad the scope of psychology should be. Should psychologists limit themselves to the study of outward, observable behavior? Is it possible to scientifically study thinking? Should the field encompass the study of such diverse topics as physical and mental health, perception, dreaming, and motivation? Is it appropriate to focus solely on human behavior, or should the behavior of other species be included?

Most psychologists would argue that the field should be receptive to a variety of viewpoints and approaches. Consequently, the phrase *behavior and mental processes* in the definition of psychology must be understood to mean many things: It encompasses not just what people do but also their thoughts, emotions, perceptions, reasoning processes, memories, and even the biological activities that maintain bodily functioning.

Psychologists try to describe, predict, and explain human behavior and mental processes, as well as help to change and improve the lives of people and the world in which they live. They use scientific methods to find answers that are far more valid and legitimate than those resulting from intuition and speculation, which are often inaccurate (see Figure 1; Ferguson, 2015).

AP® | LEARNING TARGETS

- Describe and compare different theoretical approaches in explaining behavior.
- Distinguish the different domains of psychology.

psychology The scientific study of behavior and mental processes. (Module 1)

FIGURE 1 The scientific method is the basis of all psychological research and is used to find valid answers. Test your knowledge of psychology by answering these questions.
Source: Adapted from Lamal, P. A. (1979). College students' common beliefs about psychology. Teaching of Psychology, 6, 155–158.

Psychological Truths?

To test your knowledge of psychology, try answering the following questions:

1. Infants love their mothers primarily because their mothers fulfill their basic biological needs, such as providing food. True or false?

2. Geniuses generally have poor social adjustment. True or false?

3. The best way to ensure that a desired behavior will continue after training is completed is to reward that behavior every single time it occurs during training rather than rewarding it only periodically. True or false?

4. People with schizophrenia have at least two distinct personalities. True or false?

5. Parents should do everything they can to ensure their children have high self-esteem and a strong sense that they are highly competent. True or false?

6. Children's IQ scores have little to do with how well they do in school. True or false?

7. Frequent masturbation can lead to mental illness. True or false?

8. Once people reach old age, their leisure activities change radically. True or false?

9. Most people would refuse to give painful electric shocks to other people. True or false?

10. People who talk about suicide are unlikely to actually try to kill themselves. True or false?

Scoring: The truth about each of these items: They are all false. Based on psychological research, each of these "facts" has been proven untrue. You will learn the reasons why as we explore what psychologists have discovered about human behavior.

The Subfields of Psychology: Psychology's Family Tree

As the study of psychology has grown, it has given rise to a number of subfields (described in Figure 2). The subfields of psychology can be likened to an extended family, with assorted nieces and nephews, aunts and uncles, and cousins who, although they may not interact on a day-to-day basis, are related to one another because they share a common goal: understanding behavior. One way to identify the key subfields is to look at some of the basic questions about behavior that they address.

WHAT ARE THE BIOLOGICAL FOUNDATIONS OF BEHAVIOR?

Study Alert

The different subfields of psychology allow psychologists to explain the same behavior in multiple ways. Review Figure 2 for a summary of the subfields.

In the most fundamental sense, people are biological organisms. *Behavioral neuroscience* is the subfield of psychology that focuses on the ways in which the brain, the nervous system, and the other biological aspects of the body determine behavior.

Thus, neuroscientists consider how our body influences our behavior. For example, they may examine the link between specific sites in the brain and the muscular tremors of people affected by Parkinson's disease or attempt to determine how our emotions are related to physical sensations.

HOW DO PEOPLE SENSE, PERCEIVE, LEARN, AND THINK ABOUT THE WORLD?

PsychTech

It's now common knowledge that we cannot safely text and drive at the same time. This awareness came from the work of cognitive psychologists, who demonstrated that it is impossible to do both without a serious and potentially deadly decline in driving ability.

If you have ever wondered why you are susceptible to optical illusions, how your body registers pain, or how to make the most of your study time, an experimental psychologist can answer your questions. *Experimental psychology* is the branch of psychology that studies the processes of sensing, perceiving, learning, and thinking about the world. (The term *experimental psychologist* is somewhat misleading: Psychologists in every specialty area use experimental techniques.)

Several subspecialties of experimental psychology have become specialties in their own right. One is *cognitive psychology*, which focuses on higher mental processes, including thinking, memory, reasoning, problem solving, judging, decision making, and language.

WHAT ARE THE SOURCES OF CHANGE AND STABILITY IN BEHAVIOR ACROSS THE LIFE SPAN?

A baby producing her first smile . . . taking his first step . . . saying her first word. These universal milestones in development are also singularly special and unique for each person. *Developmental psychology* studies how people grow and change from the moment of conception through death. *Personality psychology* focuses on the consistency in people's behavior over time and the traits that differentiate one person from another.

HOW DO PSYCHOLOGICAL FACTORS AFFECT PHYSICAL AND MENTAL HEALTH?

Frequent depression, stress, and fears that prevent people from carrying out their normal activities are topics that interest a health psychologist, a clinical psychologist, and a counseling psychologist. *Health psychology* explores the relationship between psychological factors and physical ailments or disease. For example, health psychologists are interested in assessing how long-term stress (a psychological factor) can affect physical health and in identifying ways to promote behavior that brings about good health (Yardley & Moss-Morris, 2009; Proyer et al., 2013; Sauter & Hurrell, 2017).

Subfield	Description
Behavioral genetics	*Behavioral genetics* studies the inheritance of traits related to behavior.
Behavioral neuroscience	*Behavioral neuroscience* examines the biological basis of behavior.
Clinical psychology	*Clinical psychology* deals with the study, diagnosis, and treatment of psychological disorders.
Clinical neuropsychology	*Clinical neuropsychology* unites the areas of biopsychology and clinical psychology, focusing on the relationship between biological factors and psychological disorders.
Cognitive psychology	*Cognitive psychology* focuses on the study of higher mental processes.
Counseling psychology	*Counseling psychology* focuses primarily on educational, social, and career adjustment problems.
Cross-cultural psychology	*Cross-cultural psychology* investigates the similarities and differences in psychological functioning in and across various cultures and ethnic groups.
Developmental psychology	*Developmental psychology* examines how people grow and change from the moment of conception through death.
Educational psychology	*Educational psychology* is concerned with teaching and learning processes, such as the relationship between motivation and school performance.
Environmental psychology	*Environmental psychology* considers the relationship between people and their physical environment.
Evolutionary psychology	*Evolutionary psychology* considers how behavior is influenced by our genetic inheritance from our ancestors.
Experimental psychology	*Experimental psychology* studies the processes of sensing, perceiving, learning, and thinking about the world.
Forensic psychology	*Forensic psychology* focuses on legal issues, such as determining the accuracy of witness memories.
Health psychology	*Health psychology* explores the relationship between psychological factors and physical ailments or disease.
Industrial/organizational psychology	*Industrial/organizational* psychology is concerned with the psychology of the workplace.
Personality psychology	*Personality psychology* focuses on the consistency in people's behavior over time and the traits that differentiate one person from another.
Program evaluation	*Program evaluation* focuses on assessing large-scale programs, such as the Head Start preschool program, to determine whether they are effective in meeting their goals.
Psychology of women	*Psychology* of women focuses on issues such as discrimination against women and the causes of violence against women.
School psychology	*School psychology* is devoted to counseling children in elementary and secondary schools who have academic or emotional problems.
Social psychology	*Social psychology* is the study of how people's thoughts, feelings, and actions are affected by others.
Sport psychology	*Sport psychology* applies psychology to athletic activity and exercise.

FIGURE 2 The major subfields of psychology.
(Top): ©Spencer Grant/Science Source; (Middle): ©Monkey Business Images/Shutterstock; (Bottom): ©Don Hammond/DesignPics

Clinical psychology deals with the study, diagnosis, and treatment of psychological disorders. Clinical psychologists are trained to diagnose and treat problems that range from the crises of everyday life, such as unhappiness over the breakup of a relationship, to more extreme conditions, such as profound, lingering depression. Some clinical psychologists also research and investigate issues that vary from identifying the early signs of psychological disturbance to studying the relationship between family communication patterns and psychological disorders.

Like clinical psychologists, counseling psychologists deal with people's psychological problems, but the problems they deal with are more specific. *Counseling psychology* focuses primarily on educational, social, and career adjustment problems. Almost every college has a center staffed with counseling psychologists. This is where students can get advice on the kinds of jobs they might be best suited for, on methods of studying effectively, and on strategies for resolving everyday difficulties, such as problems with roommates and concerns about a specific professor's grading practices. Many large business organizations also employ counseling psychologists to help employees with work-related problems.

HOW DO OUR SOCIAL NETWORKS AFFECT BEHAVIOR?

Our complex networks of social interrelationships are the focus for many subfields of psychology. For example, *social psychology* is the study of how people's thoughts, feelings, and actions are affected by others. Social psychologists concentrate on such diverse topics as human aggression, liking and loving, persuasion, and conformity.

Cross-cultural psychology investigates the similarities and differences in psychological functioning in and across various cultures and ethnic groups. For example, cross-cultural psychologists examine how cultures differ in their use of punishment during child-rearing.

EXPANDING PSYCHOLOGY'S FRONTIERS

The boundaries of the science of psychology are constantly growing. Three newer members of the field's family tree–evolutionary psychology, behavioral genetics, and clinical neuropsychology–have sparked particular excitement, and debate, within psychology.

Evolutionary Psychology *Evolutionary psychology* considers how behavior is influenced by our genetic inheritance from our ancestors. The evolutionary approach suggests that the chemical coding of information in our cells not only determines traits such as hair color and race but also holds the key to understanding a broad variety of behaviors that helped our ancestors survive and reproduce.

Evolutionary psychology stems from Charles Darwin's arguments in his groundbreaking 1859 book, *On the Origin of Species*. Darwin suggested that a process of natural selection leads to the survival of the fittest and the development of traits that enable a species to adapt to its environment.

Evolutionary psychologists take Darwin's arguments a step further. They argue that our genetic inheritance determines not only physical traits such as skin and eye color but certain personality traits and social behaviors as well. For example, evolutionary psychologists suggest that behavior such as shyness, jealousy, and cross-cultural similarities in qualities desired in potential mates are at least partially determined by genetics, presumably because such behavior helped increase the survival rate of humans' ancient relatives (Sefcek, Brumbach, & Vasquez, 2007; Fost, 2015; Lewis et al., 2017).

Although they are increasingly popular, evolutionary explanations of behavior have stirred controversy. By suggesting that many significant behaviors unfold automatically because they are wired into the human species, evolutionary approaches minimize the role of environmental and social forces. Still, the evolutionary approach has stimulated a significant amount of research on how our biological inheritance influences our traits and behaviors (Buss, 2004; Mesoudi, 2011; Flannelly, 2017).

Behavioral Genetics Another rapidly growing area in psychology focuses on the biological mechanisms, such as genes and chromosomes, that enable inherited behavior to unfold. *Behavioral genetics* seeks to understand how we might inherit certain behavioral traits and how the environment influences whether we actually display such traits (Vukasović & Bratko, 2015; Krüger, Korsten, & Hoffman, 2017).

Clinical Neuropsychology *Clinical neuropsychology* unites the areas of neuroscience and clinical psychology: It focuses on the origin of psychological disorders in biological factors. Building on advances in our understanding of the structure and chemistry of the brain, this specialty has already led to promising new treatments for psychological disorders as well as debates over the use of medication to control behavior (Boake, 2008; Holtz, 2011; Craig, 2017).

Working at Psychology

Help Wanted: Assistant professor at a small liberal arts college. Teach undergraduate courses in introductory psychology and courses in specialty areas of cognitive psychology, perception, and learning. Strong commitment to quality teaching as well as evidence of scholarship and research productivity necessary.

Help Wanted: Industrial-organizational consulting psychologist. International firm seeks psychologists for full-time career positions as consultants to management. Candidates must have the ability to establish a rapport with senior business executives and help them find innovative and practical solutions to problems concerning people and organizations.

Help Wanted: Clinical psychologist. PhD, internship experience, and license required. Comprehensive clinic seeks psychologist to work with children and adults providing individual and group therapy, psychological evaluations, crisis intervention, and development of behavior treatment plans on multidisciplinary team.

As these job ads suggest, psychologists are employed in a variety of settings. Many doctoral-level psychologists are employed by institutions of higher learning (universities and colleges) or are self-employed, usually working as private practitioners treating clients (see Figure 3). Other work sites include hospitals, clinics, mental health centers,

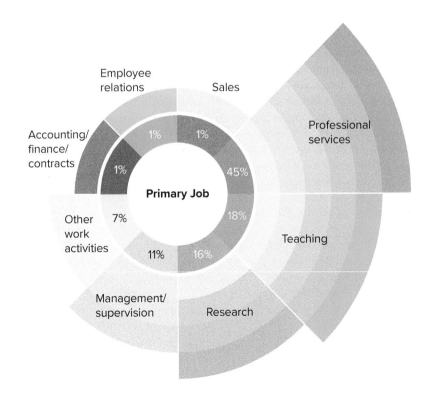

FIGURE 3 The breakdown of where U.S. psychologists (who have a PhD or PsyD) work.

Source: Stamm, K., Lin, Luona, and Cristidis, P. (2016, June). Datapoint. *Monitor on Psychology,* 12.

counseling centers, government human-services organizations, businesses, schools, and even prisons. Psychologists are employed in the military, working with soldiers, veterans, and their families, and they work for the federal government Department of Homeland Security, fighting terrorism. Psychologists who specialize in program evaluation are increasingly employed by foundations that want to assess the value of programs they fund (American Psychological Association, 2016; DeAngelis & Monahan, 2008; Moscoso et al., 2013).

Most psychologists, though, work in academic settings, allowing them to combine the three major roles played by psychologists in society: teacher, scientist, and clinical practitioner. Many psychology professors are also actively involved in research or in serving clients. Whatever the particular job site, however, psychologists share a commitment to improving individual lives as well as society in general.

Keep in mind that professionals from a variety of occupations use the findings of psychologists. To understand how nonpsychologists use psychology, you will find a feature titled "From the perspective of . . ." throughout the text.

From the perspective of...

An Educator Imagine that a classroom teacher wants to improve the performance of a 10-year-old boy who is not doing well in math. What branches of psychology might she draw on to get ideas about how to help him?

©Andersen Ross/Blend Images/Getty Images

PSYCHOLOGISTS: A PORTRAIT

Although there is no "average" psychologist in terms of personal characteristics, we can draw a statistical portrait of the field. Nearly 200,000 active psychologists are working today in the United States, but they are outnumbered by psychologists in other countries. In fact, psychologists in the United States now make up only between 20% to 24% of the world's psychologists. Although most research is conducted in the United States, psychologists in other countries are increasingly influential in adding to the knowledge base and practices of psychology (Rees & Seaton, 2011; American Psychological Association, 2015; Takooshian et al., 2016).

In the United States, women outnumber men in the field, a big change from earlier years, when women faced bias and were actively discouraged from becoming psychologists. Today, for every male psychologist, there are 2.1 female psychologists. Those in the field are actively debating whether and how to seek balance in the proportion of men and women in the field (Cynkar, 2007; Willyard, 2011; American Psychological Association, 2015).

Furthermore, despite the higher proportion of women in the field, women still lag behind when it comes to salaries and high-status positions within the field. For example, female psychologists working in four-year colleges and medical schools earn, on average, 82.7% of what males make (Clay, 2017).

The majority of psychologists in the United States are white, limiting the diversity of the field. Only around 16% of all professionally active psychologists are members of racial minority groups. Although the numbers of minority individuals entering the field are far greater than a decade ago and continue to grow, the numbers have not kept up with the dramatic growth of the minority population at large (Maton et al., 2006; Chandler, 2011; American Psychological Association, 2015).

The underrepresentation of racial and ethnic minorities among psychologists is significant for several reasons. First, the field of psychology is diminished by a lack of the diverse perspectives and talents that minority-group members can provide. Furthermore, minority-group psychologists serve as role models for members of minority communities, and their underrepresentation in the profession might deter other minority-group members from entering the field. Finally, because members of minority groups often prefer to receive psychological therapy from treatment providers of their own race or ethnic group, the rarity of minority psychologists can discourage some members of minority groups from seeking treatment (Bryant et al., 2005; Stevens, 2015; Stewart et al., 2017).

Study Alert

Be sure you can differentiate between a PhD (doctor of philosophy) and a PsyD (doctor of psychology), as well as between psychologists and psychiatrists.

THE EDUCATION OF A PSYCHOLOGIST

How do people become psychologists? The most common route is a long one. Most psychologists have a doctorate, either a *PhD* (doctor of philosophy) or, less frequently, a *PsyD* (doctor of psychology). The PhD is a research degree that requires a dissertation based on an original investigation. The PsyD is obtained by psychologists who want to focus on the treatment of psychological disorders. Note that psychologists are distinct from psychiatrists, who have a medical degree and specialize in the diagnosis and treatment of psychological disorders, often using treatments that involve the prescription of drugs.

Both the PhD and the PsyD typically take 4 or 5 years of work past the bachelor's level. Some fields of psychology involve education beyond the doctorate. For instance, doctoral-level clinical psychologists, who deal with people with psychological disorders, typically spend an additional year doing an internship.

About a third of people working in the field of psychology have a master's degree as their highest degree, which they earn after 2 or 3 years of graduate work. These psychologists teach, provide therapy, conduct research, or work in specialized programs dealing with drug abuse or crisis intervention. Some work in universities, government, and business, collecting and analyzing data.

CAREERS FOR PSYCHOLOGY MAJORS

Although some psychology majors head for graduate school in psychology or an unrelated field, the majority join the workforce immediately after graduation. Most report that the jobs they take after graduation are related to their psychology background.

An undergraduate major in psychology provides excellent preparation for a variety of occupations. Because undergraduates who specialize in psychology develop good analytical skills, are trained to think critically, and are able to synthesize and evaluate information well, employers in business, industry, and the government value their preparation (Kuther, 2003).

The most common areas of employment for psychology majors are in the social services, including working as administrators, serving as a counselors, and providing direct care. Some 20% of recipients of bachelor's degrees in psychology work in the social services or in some other form of public affairs. In addition, psychology majors often enter the fields of education or business or work for federal, state, and local governments (see Figure 4; Murray, 2002; Rajecki & Borden, 2011; Sternberg, 2017).

FIGURE 4 Although many psychology majors pursue employment in social services, a background in psychology can prepare one for many professions outside the social services field. What is it about the science and art of psychology that make it such a versatile field?

Source: Adapted from Kuther, T. L. (2003). *Your career in psychology: Psychology and the law.* New York: Wadsworth.

Positions Obtained by Psychology Majors		
Business Field	**Education/ Academic Field**	**Social Field**
Administrative assistant	Administration	Activities coordinator
Advertising trainee	Child-care provider	Behavioral specialist
Affirmative action officer	Child-care worker/	Career counselor
Benefits manager	supervisor	Case worker
Claims specialist	Data management	Child protection worker
Community relations officer	Laboratory assistant	Clinical coordinator
Customer relations	Parent/family education	Community outreach worker
Data management	Preschool teacher	Corrections officer
Employee counselor	Public opinion surveyor	Counselor assistant
Employee recruitment	Research assistant	Crisis intervention counselor
Human resources	Teaching assistant	Employment counselor
coordinator/manager/		Group home attendant
specialist		Mental health assistant
Labor relations manager/		Occupational therapist
specialist		Probation officer
Loan officer		Program manager
Management trainee		Rehabilitation counselor
Marketing		Residence counselor
Personnel manager/officer		Social service assistant
Product and services		Social worker
research		Substance abuse counselor
Programs/events		Youth counselor
coordination		
Public relations		
Retail sales management		
Sales representative		
Special features writing/		
reporting		
Staff training and		
development		
Trainer/training office		

AP⏐ MODULE 1: PSYCHOLOGISTS AT WORK

AP SUMMARY

- Distinguish the different domains of psychology.
- Behavioral neuroscientists focus on the biological basis of behavior.
- Clinical psychologists focus on the study, diagnosis, and treatment of psychological disorders.
- Cognitive psychologists focus on higher mental processes.
- Counseling psychologists focus on educational, social, and career adjustment problems.
- Developmental psychologists study how people grow and change throughout the life span.

- Educational psychologists focus on teaching and learning processes.
- Experimental psychologists study the process of sensing, perceiving, learning, and thinking about the world.
- Industrial-organizational psychologists focus on the psychology of the workplace.
- Personality psychologists consider the consistency and change in an individual's behavior, as well as the individual's differences that distinguish one person's behavior from another's.

- Social psychologists study how people's thoughts, feelings, and actions are affected by others.
- Cross-cultural psychologists examine the similarities and differences in psychological functioning among various cultures.
- Psychologists are employed in a variety of settings. Although the primary sites of employment are private practice and colleges, many psychologists are found in hospitals, clinics, community mental health centers, and counseling centers.

AP KEY TERMS

psychology

AP TEST PRACTICE

Section I: Multiple Choice

1. An industrial-organizational psychologist would be most likely to study
   A. coping techniques of students with failing grades.
   B. chemicals released in the body during times of stress.
   C. management strategies to encourage safe work practices.
   D. the fear of leaving one's home.
   E. how to motivate adolescents to complete their homework.

2. Reasoning, problem solving, judging, and decision making are probably studied within which psychological domain?
   A. Biological
   B. Cognitive
   C. Developmental
   D. Industrial-organizational
   E. Psychometric

3. Dr. Rosa studies the age when children normally form an attachment to their caregiver. In what field of psychology is Dr. Rosa most likely employed?
   A. Educational domain
   B. Biological domain
   C. Experimental domain
   D. Developmental domain
   E. Social domain

Section II: Free Response

Jona is studying to be a psychologist but is unsure which domain to declare as her major. For each of the following domains provide a short description and a specific job Jona might do in the future.
- Clinical domain
- Cognitive domain
- Counseling domain
- Developmental domain
- Educational domain
- Industrial-organizational domain
- Social domain

Module 2
A Science Evolves: The Past, the Present, and the Future

Seven thousand years ago, people assumed that psychological problems were caused by evil spirits. To allow those spirits to escape from a person's body, ancient healers chipped a hole in a patient's skull with crude instruments–a procedure called *trephining*.

According to the 17th-century French philosopher René Descartes, nerves were hollow tubes through which "animal spirits" conducted impulses in the same way that water is transmitted through a pipe. When a person put a finger too close to a fire, heat was transmitted to the brain through the tubes.

Franz Josef Gall, an 18th-century physician, argued that a trained observer could discern intelligence, moral character, and other basic personality characteristics from the shape and number of bumps on a person's skull. His theory gave rise to the field of phrenology, employed by hundreds of practitioners in the 19th century.

Although these explanations might sound far-fetched, in their own times they represented the most advanced thinking about what might be called the psychology of the era. Our understanding of behavior has progressed tremendously since the 18th century, but most of the advances have been recent. As sciences go, psychology is one of the new kids on the block. (For highlights in the development of the field, see Figure 1.)

5,000 BCE Trephining used to allow the escape of evil spirits

430 BCE Hippocrates argues for four temperaments of personality

1690 John Locke introduces idea of *tabula rasa*

1879 Wilhelm Wundt inaugurates first psychology laboratory in Leipzig, Germany

1895 Functionalist model formulated

1900 Sigmund Freud develops the psychodynamic perspective

1905 Mary Calkins works on memory

1915 Strong emphasis on intelligence testing

Forerunners of Psychology

1800

1900

First Psychologists

1637 Descartes describes animal spirits

1807 Franz Josef Gall proposes phrenology

1890 *Principles of Psychology* published by William James

1904 Ivan Pavlov wins Nobel Prize for work on digestion that led to fundamental principles of learning

1920 Gestalt psychology becomes influential

FIGURE 1 This time line illustrates major milestones in the development of psychology.

The Roots of Psychology

We can trace psychology's roots back to the ancient Greeks, who considered the mind to be a suitable topic for scholarly contemplation. Later philosophers argued for hundreds of years about some of the questions psychologists grapple with today. For example, the 17th-century British philosopher John Locke believed that children were born into the world with minds like "blank slates" (*tabula rasa* in Latin) and that their experiences determined what kind of adults they would become. His views contrasted with those of Plato and Descartes, who argued that some knowledge was inborn in humans.

However, the formal beginning of psychology as a scientific discipline is generally considered to be in the late 19th century, when Wilhelm Wundt established the first experimental laboratory devoted to psychological phenomena in Leipzig, Germany. At about the same time, William James was setting up his laboratory in Cambridge, Massachusetts.

When Wundt set up his laboratory in 1879, his goal was to study the structures of the mind and their relationship to conscious experience—an approach he called structuralism. **Structuralism** focused on uncovering the fundamental mental components of perception, consciousness, thinking, emotions, and other kinds of mental states and activities.

To determine how basic sensory processes shape our understanding of the world, Wundt and other structuralists used a method called introspection. **Introspection** is a procedure in which people are presented with a stimulus—such as an image or a sentence—and asked to describe, in their own words and in as much detail as they can, what they were experiencing. Wundt argued that by analyzing people's reports, psychologists could come to a better understanding of the structure of the mind.

Over time, psychologists challenged Wundt's approach. They became increasingly dissatisfied with the assumption that introspection could reveal the structure of the mind. Introspection was not a truly scientific technique because there were few ways an outside observer could confirm the accuracy of others' introspections. Moreover, people had difficulty describing some kinds of inner experiences, such as emotional

Wilhelm Wundt
©Bettmann/Getty Images

structuralism Wundt's approach, which focuses on understanding the fundamental mental components of consciousness, thinking, and other kinds of mental states and activities. (Module 2)

introspection A procedure used to study the structure of the mind in which a person is asked to describe in detail what they are experiencing when they are exposed to a stimulus. (Module 2)

1924
John B. Watson, an early behaviorist, publishes *Behaviorism*

1951
Carl Rogers publishes *Client-Centered Therapy,* helping to establish the humanistic perspective

1957
Leon Festinger publishes *A Theory of Cognitive Dissonance,* producing a major impact on social psychology

1980
Jean Piaget, an influential developmental psychologist, dies

1985
Increasing emphasis on cognitive perspective

2010
New subfields develop such as clinical neuropsychology and evolutionary psychology

Modern Psychology

2000

1928
Leta Stetter Hollingworth publishes work on adolescence

1953
B. F. Skinner publishes *Science and Human Behavior,* advocating the behavioral perspective

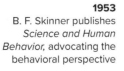

1954
Abraham Maslow publishes *Motivation and Personality,* developing the concept of self-actualization

1969
Arguments regarding the genetic basis of IQ fuel lingering controversies

1981 David Hubel and Torsten Wiesel win Nobel Prize for work on vision cells in the brain

2000
Elizabeth Loftus does pioneering work on false memory and eyewitness testimony

William James
©Paul Thompson/FPG/Getty Images

functionalism An early approach to psychology that concentrated on what the mind does–the functions of mental activity–and the role of behavior in allowing people to adapt to their environments. (Module 2)

Gestalt psychology An approach to psychology that focuses on the organization of perception and thinking in a "whole" sense rather than on the individual elements of perception. (Module 2)

Study Alert
Knowing the basic outlines of the history of the field will help you understand how today's major perspectives have evolved.

Study Alert
Use Figure 2 to differentiate the five perspectives, which are important, because they provide a foundation for every topic covered throughout the text.

responses. Those drawbacks led to the development of new approaches, which largely replaced structuralism.

The perspective that replaced structuralism is known as functionalism. Rather than focusing on the mind's structure, **functionalism** concentrated on what the mind *does* and how behavior *functions*. Functionalists, whose perspective became prominent in the early 1900s, asked what role behavior plays in allowing people to adapt to their environments. For example, a functionalist might examine the function of the emotion of fear in preparing us to deal with emergency situations.

William James, an American psychologist, led the functionalist movement. Functionalists examined how people satisfy their needs through their behavior and focused on the purpose of thinking, unlike the structuralists, who were more interested in the structure of the brain. The functionalists also considered how the flexibility of the mind allowed people to continually change their thinking as they interacted with a complex world, something the functionalists discussed as the "stream of consciousness" of the mind. The American educator John Dewey drew on functionalism to develop the field of school psychology, proposing ways to best meet students' educational needs.

Another important reaction to structuralism was the development of gestalt psychology in the early 1900s. **Gestalt psychology** emphasizes how perception is organized. Instead of considering the individual parts that make up thinking, gestalt psychologists took the opposite tack, studying how people consider individual elements together as units or wholes. Led by German scientists such as Hermann Ebbinghaus and Max Wertheimer, gestalt psychologists proposed that "The whole is different from the sum of its parts," meaning that our perception, or understanding, of objects is greater and more meaningful than the individual elements that make up our perceptions. Gestalt psychologists have made substantial contributions to our understanding of perception.

WOMEN IN PSYCHOLOGY: FOUNDING MOTHERS

As in many scientific fields, social prejudices hindered women's participation in the early development of psychology. For example, many universities would not admit women to their graduate psychology programs in the early 1900s.

Despite the hurdles they faced, women made notable contributions to psychology, although their impact on the field was largely overlooked until recently. For example, Margaret Floy Washburn (1871-1939) was the first woman to receive a doctorate in psychology, and she did important work on animal behavior. Leta Stetter Hollingworth (1886-1939) was one of the first psychologists to focus on child development and on women's issues. She collected data to refute the view, popular in the early 1900s, that women's abilities periodically declined during parts of the menstrual cycle (Hollingworth, 1943/1990; Denmark & Fernandez, 1993; Furumoto & Scarborough, 2002).

Mary Calkins (1863-1930), who studied memory in the early part of the 20th century, became the first female president of the American Psychological Association. Karen Horney (pronounced "HORN-eye") (1885-1952) focused on the social and cultural factors behind personality; she also was the founder of the American Journal of Psychoanalysis. June Etta Downey (1875-1932) spearheaded the study of personality traits and became the first woman to head a psychology department at a state university. Anna Freud (1895-1982), the daughter of Sigmund Freud, also made notable contributions to the treatment of abnormal behavior, and Mamie Phipps Clark (1917-1983) carried out pioneering work on how children of color grew to recognize racial differences (Lal, 2002; Galdi, 2015).

Today's Five Major Perspectives

The men and women who laid the foundations of psychology shared a common goal: to explain and understand behavior using scientific methods. Seeking to achieve the same goal, the tens of thousands of psychologists who followed those early pioneers embraced–and often rejected–a variety of broad perspectives.

Neuroscience
Views behavior from the perspective of biological functioning

Behavioral
Focuses on observable behavior

Psychodynamic
Believes behavior is motivated by inner, unconscious forces over which a person has little control

Cognitive
Examines how people understand and think about the world

Humanistic
Contends that people can control their behavior and that they naturally try to reach their full potential

FIGURE 2 The major perspectives of psychology.
(Neuroscience): ©Science Photo Library/Alamy Stock Photo; (Cognitive): ©David Sanger/The Image Bank/Getty Images; (Behavioral): ©Ariel Skelley/Blend Images; (Humanistic): ©White Packert/The Image Bank/Getty Images; (Psychodynamic): ©Athanasia Nomikou/Shutterstock

The perspectives of psychology offer distinct outlooks and emphasize different factors. Just as we can use more than one map to find our way around a particular region–for instance, a map that shows roads and highways and another map that shows major landmarks–psychologists developed a variety of approaches to understanding behavior. When considered jointly, the different perspectives provide the means to explain behavior in its amazing variety.

Today, the field of psychology includes five major perspectives (summarized in Figure 2). These broad perspectives emphasize different aspects of behavior and mental processes, and each takes our understanding of behavior in a somewhat different direction.

THE NEUROSCIENCE PERSPECTIVE: BLOOD, SWEAT, AND FEARS

When we get down to the basics, humans are animals made of skin and bones. The **neuroscience perspective** considers how people and nonhumans function biologically: how individual nerve cells are joined together, how the inheritance of certain characteristics from parents and other ancestors influences behavior, how the functioning of the body affects hopes and fears, which behaviors are instinctual, and so forth. Even more complex kinds of behaviors, such as a baby's response to strangers, are viewed as having critical biological components by psychologists who embrace the neuroscience perspective. This perspective includes the study of heredity and evolution, which considers how heredity may influence behavior; and behavioral neuroscience, which examines how the brain and the nervous system affect behavior.

Because every behavior ultimately can be broken down into its biological components, the neuroscience perspective has broad appeal. Psychologists who subscribe to this perspective have made major contributions to the understanding and betterment of human life, ranging from cures for certain types of deafness to drug treatments for people with severe mental disorders. Furthermore, advances in methods for examining the anatomy and functioning of the brain have permitted the neuroscientific perspective to extend its influence across a broad range of

neuroscience perspective The approach that views behavior from the perspective of the brain, the nervous system, and other biological functions. (Module 2)

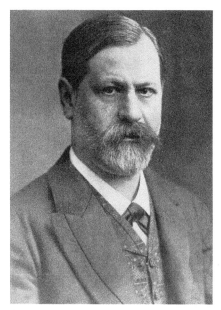

Sigmund Freud
©Ingram Publishing

psychodynamic perspective The approach based on the view that behavior is motivated by unconscious inner forces over which the individual has little control. (Module 2)

behavioral perspective The approach that suggests that observable, external behavior, which can be objectively measured, should be the focus of study. (Module 2)

cognitive perspective The approach that focuses on how people think, understand, and know about the world. (Module 2)

subfields in psychology. (We'll see examples of these methods throughout this book in *Neuroscience in Your Life*.)

THE PSYCHODYNAMIC PERSPECTIVE: UNDERSTANDING THE INNER PERSON

To many people who have never taken a psychology course, psychology begins and ends with the psychodynamic perspective. Proponents of the **psychodynamic perspective** argue that behavior is motivated by inner forces and conflicts about which we have little awareness or control. They view dreams and slips of the tongue as indications of what a person is truly feeling within a seething cauldron of unconscious psychic activity.

The origins of the psychodynamic view are linked to one person: Sigmund Freud. Freud was an Austrian physician in the early 1900s whose ideas about unconscious determinants of behavior had a revolutionary effect on 20th-century thinking, not just in psychology but in related fields as well. Although some of the original Freudian principles have been roundly criticized, the contemporary psychodynamic perspective has provided a means not only to understand and treat some kinds of psychological disorders but also to understand everyday phenomena such as prejudice and aggression.

THE BEHAVIORAL PERSPECTIVE: OBSERVING THE OUTER PERSON

Whereas the neuroscience and psychodynamic approaches look inside the organism to determine the causes of its behavior, the behavioral perspective takes a different approach. Proponents of the behavioral perspective rejected psychology's early emphasis on the internal workings of the mind. Instead, the **behavioral perspective** suggests that the focus should be on external behavior that can be observed and measured objectively.

John B. Watson was the first major American psychologist to use a behavioral approach. Working in the 1920s, Watson believed that one could gain a complete understanding of behavior by studying the environment in which a person operated.

In fact, Watson believed rather optimistically that it was possible to bring about any desired type of behavior by controlling a person's environment. This philosophy is clear in his own words: "Give me a dozen healthy infants, well-formed, and my own specified world to bring them up in and I'll guarantee to take any one at random and train him to become any type of specialist I might select—doctor, lawyer, artist, merchant-chief, and yes, even beggar-man and thief, regardless of his talents, penchants, tendencies, abilities, vocations and race of his ancestors" (Watson, 1924).

The behavioral perspective was championed by B. F. Skinner, a pioneer in the field. Much of our understanding of how people learn new behaviors is based on the behavioral perspective. As we will see, the behavioral perspective crops up along every byway of psychology. Along with its influence in the area of learning processes, this perspective has made contributions in such diverse areas as treating mental disorders, curbing aggression, resolving sexual problems, and ending drug addiction (Schlinger, 2011; Ruiz, 2015; Fryling, 2017).

THE COGNITIVE PERSPECTIVE: IDENTIFYING THE ROOTS OF UNDERSTANDING

Efforts to understand behavior lead some psychologists straight into the mind. Evolving in part from structuralism and in part as a reaction to behaviorism, which focused so heavily on observable behavior and the environment, the **cognitive perspective** focuses on how people think, understand, and know about the world. The emphasis is on learning how people comprehend and represent the outside world within themselves and how our ways of thinking about the world influence our behavior.

Many psychologists who adhere to the cognitive perspective compare human thinking to the workings of a computer, which takes in information and transforms, stores, and retrieves it. In their view, thinking is *information processing*.

Psychologists who rely on the cognitive perspective ask questions on subjects ranging from how people make decisions to whether a person can watch television and study at the same time. The common elements that link cognitive approaches are an emphasis on how people understand and think about the world and an interest in describing the patterns and irregularities in the operation of our minds.

From the perspective of...

A Health-Care Provider How can a basic understanding of psychology improve your job performance in the health-care industry?

©Tetra Images/Getty Images

THE HUMANISTIC PERSPECTIVE: THE UNIQUE QUALITIES OF THE HUMAN SPECIES

The humanistic perspective rejects the view that behavior is determined largely by automatically unfolding biological forces, unconscious processes, or the environment. Instead, the **humanistic perspective** suggests that all individuals naturally strive to grow, develop, and be in control of their lives and behavior. Humanistic psychologists maintain that each of us has the capacity to seek and reach fulfillment.

According to Carl Rogers and Abraham Maslow, who were central figures in the development of the humanistic perspective, people strive to reach their full potential if they are given the opportunity. The emphasis of the humanistic perspective is on *free will*, the ability to freely make decisions about one's own behavior and life. The notion of free will stands in contrast to *determinism*, which sees behavior as caused, or determined, by things beyond a person's control.

The humanistic perspective assumes that people have the ability to make their own choices about their behavior rather than relying on societal standards. More than any other approach, it stresses the role of psychology in enriching people's lives and helping them achieve self-fulfillment. By reminding psychologists of their commitment to the individual person in society, the humanistic perspective has been an important influence (Nichols, 2011; Linley, 2013; Hayes, 2015).

Don't let the abstract qualities of the broad approaches we have discussed lull you into thinking that they are purely theoretical: These perspectives underlie ongoing work of a practical nature, as we discuss throughout this book. To start seeing how psychology can improve everyday life, read *Applying Psychology in the 21st Century*.

humanistic perspective The approach that suggests that all individuals naturally strive to grow, develop, and be in control of their lives and behavior. (Module 2)

AP APPLYING PSYCHOLOGY IN THE 21ST CENTURY

PSYCHOLOGY MATTERS

"Investigators search for clues at site of suicide bombing."

"Good jobs for college graduates remain hard to find."

"Eyewitness to killing proves unable to provide reliable clues."

"Social media like Facebook, Twitter, Snapchat, and Instagram change how people interact with others."

"Childhood obesity rates surge."

"Black suspect in robbery dies after scuffle with police."

A quick review of any day's news headlines reminds us that the world is beset by a variety of stubborn problems that resist easy solutions. At the same time, a considerable number of psychologists are devoting their energies and expertise to addressing these problems and improving the human condition. Let's consider some of the ways in which psychology has addressed and helped work toward solutions of major societal problems:

- *What are the causes of terrorism?* What motivates suicide bombers? Are they psychologically disordered, or can their behavior be seen as a rational response to a particular system of beliefs? As we'll see when we discuss psychological disorders, psychologists are gaining an understanding of the factors that lead people to embrace suicide and to engage in terrorism to further a cause in which they deeply believe (Post, 2015; Theriault, Krause, & Young, 2017; Choma et al., 2018)

- *How are social media changing the way we live?* Social networking media such as Facebook and Twitter have changed the way people communicate and the way news spreads around the world. How do social media affect the way people relate to each other? How do they affect our perceptions of world events? Psychologists are examining the motivations behind social networking, its

©Rena Schild/Shutterstock

influence on individuals and social institutions, and possible beneficial applications of the technology (Kosinski et al., 2015; Young et al., 2017; Zyoud et al., 2018).

- *What are the roots of autism spectrum disorder, and why is it on the rise?* Autism spectrum disorder is a severe developmental disability that impairs one's ability to communicate and relate to others. It exists on a continuum from mild symptoms, such as social awkwardness, to profound dysfunction, such as a complete inability to communicate or care for oneself. Psychologists are rapidly gaining insights into the hereditary and environmental factors that influence autism; the need for this understanding is urgent because the incidence of autism has been growing sharply in recent years and it's unclear why (Pelphrey & Shultz, 2013; Gillespie-Lynch et al., 2015: Commons et al., 2017).

- *Why do eyewitnesses to crimes often remember the events inaccurately, and how can we increase the precision of eyewitness accounts?* Psychologists' research has come to an important conclusion: Eyewitness testimony in criminal cases is often inaccurate and biased. Memories

of crimes are often clouded by emotion, and the questions asked by police investigators often elicit inaccurate responses. Work by psychologists has been used to provide national guidelines for obtaining more accurate memories during criminal investigations (Beaudry et al., 2015; Wixted et al., 2015; Kassin et al., 2018).

- *What are the roots of racism in the United States?* Psychologists have discovered that even subtle forms of prejudice and discrimination can cause significant harm in recipients. Furthermore, they have learned that people who sincerely believe themselves to not be racist still harbor unconscious racist thoughts that can translate into discriminatory behavior. On the positive side, they are developing strategies that break down racial barriers and heal the hurt and stigma of decades of racism (Fisher et al., 2017; Mason et al., 2017; David & Derthick, 2018).

- *What gives people satisfaction with life and a sense of well being?* Research has found that during difficult economic times, it's important to understand that wealth and possessions don't make people happy. Instead, happiness comes from enjoying life's little moments and finding purpose and meaning in what you do (Pavot & Diener, 2013; Crespo & Mesurado, 2015; Jin & Kim, 2017).

These topics represent just a few of the issues that psychologists address daily. To further explore the many ways that psychology has an impact on everyday life, check out the American Psychological Association (APA) website, which features psychological applications in everyday life, at www.apa.org.

AP SKILL: EXPLAIN BEHAVIOR IN AUTHENTIC CONTEXT/APPLY THEORIES AND PERSPECTIVES IN AUTHENTIC CONTEXTS

1. Describe a behavior that is affecting society today.
2. Explain the behavior listed above from the five major perspectives.

AP MODULE 2: A SCIENCE EVOLVES: THE PAST, THE PRESENT, AND THE FUTURE

AP SUMMARY

- Recognize how philosophical and physiological perspectives shaped the development of psychological thought.
- Psychological problems were once explained with physiological explanations and psychology's roots can be traced back to ancient Greek philosophers.
- Identify the research contributions of major historical figures in psychology, including Mary Whiton Calkins, Sigmund Freud, Ivan Pavlov, Jean Piaget, B.F. Skinner, Margaret Floy Washburn, and John B. Watson.
- Describe and compare different theoretical approaches in explaining behavior.
- Early approaches that guided the work of psychologists were structuralism (led by Wilhelm Wundt), functionalism (led by William James), and Gestalt theory.
- Today, the field of psychology includes five major perspectives that emphasize different aspects of behavior and mental processes.
- The behavioral perspective deemphasizes internal processes and concentrates instead on observable, measurable behavior, suggesting that understanding and control of a person's environment are sufficient to fully explain and modify behavior. This perspective influences our understanding of learning processes and has contributed to the treatment of mental disorders, curbing aggression, resolving sexual problems, and ending drug addiction.
- The psychodynamic perspective suggests that powerful, unconscious inner forces and conflicts about which people have little or no awareness are the primary determinants of behavior. This perspective has been criticized, but the contemporary approach has helped explain and treat psychological disorders and everyday phenomena.
- The humanistic perspective emphasizes that people are uniquely inclined toward psychological growth and higher levels of functioning and will strive to reach their full potential. It maintains that each of us has the capacity to seek and reach fulfillment. The emphasis of this perspective is on free will and it stresses the role of psychology in enriching people's lives and achieving self-fulfillment.
- The neuroscience approach focuses on the biological components of behavior and has influenced a broad range of subfields in psychology. This perspective has broad appeal because every behavior can be broken down into biological components. Psychologists from this perspective have made major contributions to the understanding and betterment of human life.
- The cognitive approach to behavior considers how people know, understand, and think about the world. Psychologists from this perspective are interested in describing the patterns and irregularities in the operation of our minds.
- Recognize the strengths and limitations of applying theories to explain behavior.

AP KEY TERMS

structuralism
introspection
functionalism
Gestalt (geh-SHTALLT) psychology
neuroscience perspective

psychodynamic perspective
behavioral perspective
cognitive perspective
humanistic perspective

AP TEST PRACTICE

Section I: Multiple Choice

1. William was presented with an apple and asked to describe in as much as detail as possible what he was experiencing. This early procedure used to study the structure of the mind is known as
   - **A.** Trephination
   - **B.** phrenology
   - **C.** functionalism
   - **D.** introspection
   - **E.** Gestalt

2. Who studied memory in the early 20th century and was the first female president of the American Psychological Association?
   - **A.** Mary Whiton Calkins
   - **B.** Margaret Floy Washburn
   - **C.** Mamie Phipps Clark
   - **D.** Karen Horney
   - **E.** Anna Freud

3. The statement "In order to study human behavior, we must consider the whole perception rather than its component parts" might be made by a person subscribing to which perspective of psychology?
   - **A.** Behaviorism
   - **B.** Structuralism
   - **C.** Gestalt
   - **D.** Cognitive
   - **E.** Psychodynamic

Section II: Free Response

Each perspective of psychology offers a distinct outlook and emphasizes different factors. Identify each perspective below and how the approach might explain depression.

- Neuroscience
- Behavioral
- Cognitive
- Humanistic
- Psychodynamic
- Evolutionary

Module 3
Psychology's Key Issues and Controversies

AP® LEARNING TARGETS

- Recognize how philosophical and physiological perspectives shaped the development of psychological thought.

- Describe and compare different theoretical approaches in explaining behavior.

- Recognize the strengths and limitations of applying theories to explain behavior.

Study Alert

Use Figure 1 to learn the key issues that underlie every subfield of psychology.

As you consider the many topics and perspectives that make up psychology, ranging from a narrow focus on minute biochemical influences on behavior to a broad focus on social behaviors, you might find yourself thinking that the discipline lacks cohesion. However, the field is more unified than a first glimpse might suggest. For one thing, no matter what topical area a psychologist specializes in, he or she will rely primarily on one of the five major perspectives. For example, a developmental psychologist who specializes in the study of children could make use of the cognitive perspective or the psychodynamic perspective or any of the other major perspectives.

Psychologists also agree on what the key issues of the field are (see Figure 1). Although there are major arguments regarding how best to address and resolve the key issues, psychology is a unified science because psychologists of all perspectives agree that the issues must be addressed if the field is going to advance. As you contemplate these key issues, try not to think of them in "either/or" terms. Instead, consider the opposing viewpoints on each issue as the opposite ends of a continuum, with the positions of individual psychologists typically falling somewhere between the two ends.

Issue 1: *Nature (heredity) versus nurture (environment)* is one of the major issues that psychologists address in trying to determine the causes of behavior. How much of people's behavior is due to their genetically determined nature (heredity), and how much is due to nurture, the influences of the physical and social environment in which a child is raised? Furthermore, what is the interplay between heredity and environment?

Issue	Neuroscience	Cognitive	Behavioral	Humanistic	Psychodynamic
Nature (heredity) vs. nurture (environment)	Nature (heredity)	Both	Nurture (environment)	Nurture (environment)	Nature (heredity)
Conscious vs. unconscious determinants of behavior	Unconscious	Both	Conscious	Conscious	Unconscious
Observable behavior vs internal mental processes	Internal emphasis	Internal emphasis	Observable emphasis	Internal emphasis	Internal emphasis
Free will vs. determinism	Determinism	Free will	Determinism	Free will	Determinism
Individual differences vs. universal principles	Universal emphasis	Individual emphasis	Both	Individual emphasis	Universal emphasis

FIGURE 1 Key issues in psychology and the positions taken by psychologists subscribing to the five major perspectives of psychology.

(Neuroscience): ©Science Photo Library/Alamy Stock Photo; (Cognitive): ©David Sanger/The Image Bank/Getty Images; (Behavioral): ©Ariel Skelley/Blend Images; (Humanistic): ©White Packert/The Image Bank/Getty Images; (Psychodynamic): ©Athanasia Nomikou/Shutterstock

These questions have deep philosophical and historical roots, and they are involved in many topics in psychology.

A psychologist's take on this issue depends partly on which major perspective he or she subscribes to. For example, developmental psychologists whose focus is on how people grow and change throughout the course of their lives may be most interested in learning more about hereditary influences if they follow a neuroscience perspective. In contrast, developmental psychologists who are proponents of the behavioral perspective are more likely to focus on environment (Rutter, 2002; Moffitt, Caspi, & Rutter, 2006; Barrett, 2011).

However, every psychologist would agree that neither nature nor nurture alone is the sole determinant of behavior; rather, it is a combination of the two. In a sense, then, the real controversy involves how much of our behavior is caused by heredity and how much is caused by environmental influences.

Issue 2: Conscious versus unconscious causes of behavior. How much of our behavior is produced by forces of which we are fully aware, and how much is due to unconscious activity–mental processes that are not accessible to the conscious mind? This question represents one of the great controversies in the field of psychology. For example, clinical psychologists adopting a psychodynamic perspective argue that psychological disorders are brought about by unconscious factors, whereas psychologists employing the cognitive perspective suggest that psychological disorders largely are the result of faulty thinking processes.

Issue 3: Observable behavior versus internal mental processes. Should psychology concentrate solely on behavior that can be seen by outside observers, or should it focus on unseen thinking processes? Some psychologists, particularly those relying on the behavioral perspective, contend that the only legitimate source of information for psychologists is behavior that can be observed directly. Other psychologists, building on the cognitive perspective, argue that what goes on inside a person's mind is critical to understanding behavior, and so we must concern ourselves with mental processes.

Issue 4: Free will versus determinism. How much of our behavior is a matter of **free will** (choices made freely by an individual), and how much is subject to **determinism**, the notion that behavior is largely produced by factors beyond people's willful control? An issue long debated by philosophers, the free-will/determinism argument is also central to the field of psychology (Goto et al., 2015; Moynihan, Igou, & van Tilburg, 2017).

For example, some psychologists who specialize in psychological disorders argue that people make intentional choices and that those who display so-called abnormal behavior should be considered responsible for their actions. Other psychologists disagree and contend that such individuals are the victims of forces beyond their control. The position psychologists take on this issue has important implications for the way they treat psychological disorders, especially in deciding whether treatment should be forced on people who don't want it.

Issue 5: Individual differences versus universal principles. Specifically, how much of behavior is due to the unique and special qualities of each person, and how do those individual differences differentiate one person from others? Conversely, how much of our behavior stems from the culture and society in which we live, reflecting universal principles that underlie the behavior of all humans?

Psychologists who rely on the neuroscience perspective tend to look for universal principles of behavior, such as how the nervous system operates or the way certain hormones automatically prime us for sexual activity. Such psychologists concentrate on the similarities in our behavioral destinies despite vast differences in our upbringing. In contrast, psychologists who employ the humanistic perspective focus more on the uniqueness of every individual. They consider every person's behavior a reflection of distinct and special individual qualities.

The question of the degree to which psychologists can identify universal principles that apply to all people has taken on new significance in light of the tremendous demographic changes now occurring in the United States and around the world. As we discuss next, these changes raise new and critical issues for the discipline of psychology in the 21st century.

free will The idea that behavior is caused primarily by choices that are made freely by the individual. (Module 3)

determinism The idea that people's behavior is produced primarily by factors outside of their willful control. (Module 3)

Exploring Diversity

Understanding How Culture, Ethnicity, and Race Influence Behavior

A mother in Burr Ridge, Illinois, helps her son with his math assignment. After he complains that he is "terrible at math," she tries to cheer him up by saying, "Don't feel bad; some people are born to do well in math, and others have a lot of trouble with it. It's just the way things are."

At the same time, on the other side of the world in Taipei, Taiwan, a mother is helping her daughter with her math homework. When the daughter complains that she's no good at math, the mother tells her to keep at it because everyone has pretty much the same ability in math, and it is hard work that guarantees success.

These two apparently simple parent-child exchanges reveal a deep difference in perspectives on the world. People in North America and Europe are far more likely to attribute success to what they see as stable, unchanging causes, such as a person's intelligence. In contrast, people in Asia are more likely to attribute school performance to temporary, situational factors, such as the amount of expended effort.

These different perspectives may help explain the fact that Asian students often outperform U.S. students in international comparisons of student achievement. Asian students are taught that hard work and increased effort lead to academic success, and so they may be more willing to put in more effort to achieve success. In contrast, North American students tend to believe that their ability is fixed at birth and largely determines their success, and so they may be less willing to work hard (Chen & Stevenson, 1995; Pearce & Lin, 2007; Yoo & Castro, 2011).

Our knowledge that people in different cultures can have very different views of the world underlines the importance of moving beyond North America and studying other cultural groups to identify universal principles of behavior. Furthermore, broad cultural differences are not the only ones taken into account by psychologists in their attempts to identify general principles of behavior. Subcultural, ethnic, racial, and socioeconomic differences are increasingly important targets of study by psychologists (Tucker & Herman, 2002; Cardemil, Pinedo, & Miller, 2005; Hunt, 2017).

Although the discipline is growing more aware of the importance of taking cultural and subcultural factors into account, progress has not been rapid in actual practice. For example, the amount of research conducted in the United States on groups other than white middle-class college students is woefully small.

Furthermore, there's a lack of clarity on the use of terms such as *race* and *ethnic group*. Race, for instance, originated as a biological concept that, technically, should be used only to refer to classifications based on the physical characteristics of an organism or species. But such a definition has little validity for humans, given that we are all 99.9 percent identical in our genetic makeup. Consequently, today race is generally thought

Members of different cultures attribute academic success to different factors. How might differing cultural perspectives affect the performance of Asian students and American students?

(Left): ©Tanya Constantine/Blend Images; (Right): ©Ingram Publishing/SuperStock of as a social construct—that is, something defined by people and their beliefs. In contrast, *ethnic group* and *ethnicity* are broader terms that refer to cultural background, nationality, religion, and language (Bonham, Warshauer-Baker, & Collins, 2005; Freeman, 2006; French, Coleman, & DiLorenzo, 2013).

To compound the difficulty, there are no universally acceptable names for races and ethnic groups. Psychologists—like other members of U.S. society—are divided on whether they should use the label *African American* (which focuses on geographical origins) or *black* (which focuses on skin color), just as they disagree about whether to use *Caucasian* or *white, Hispanic* or *Latino,* and *Native American* or *American Indian* (Council of National Psychological Associations for the Advancement of Ethnic Minority Interests, 2000; Phinney, 2003; Wang & Sue, 2005).

Psychologists also know that the consequences of race cannot be understood without taking into account environmental and cultural factors. People's behavior is a joint product of their race and of the treatment they receive from others because of it. In sum, only by examining behavior across ethnic, cultural, and racial lines can psychologists differentiate principles that are universal from those that are culture-bound.

Psychology's Future

We have examined psychology's foundations, but what does the future hold for the discipline? Although the course of scientific development is notoriously difficult to predict, several trends seem likely:

- As its knowledge base grows, psychology will become increasingly specialized, and new perspectives will evolve. For example, our growing understanding of the brain and the nervous system, combined with scientific advances in genetics and gene therapy, will allow psychologists to focus on *prevention* of psychological disorders rather than only on their treatment (Cuijpers et al., 2008).

- The evolving sophistication of neuroscientific approaches is likely to have an increasing influence over other branches of psychology. For instance, social psychologists already are increasing their understanding of social behaviors such as persuasion by using brain scans as part of an evolving field known as *social neuroscience.* Furthermore, as neuroscientific techniques become more sophisticated, there will be new ways of applying that knowledge, as we discuss in *Neuroscience in Your Life* (Cacioppo & Decety, 2009; Di Ieva et al., 2015; Mattan, Kubota, & Cloutier, 2017).

- Psychology's influence on issues of public interest also will grow. The major problems of our time–such as violence, terrorism, racial and ethnic prejudice, poverty, environmental changes, and technological disasters–have important psychological components Already, psychology has had significant influences on social policy, informing lawmakers' decision-making, a trend that is likely to increase (Dweck, 2017; Fiske, 2017).

- Psychologists will follow increasingly strict ethical and moral guidelines. When it was revealed in 2015 that several psychologists participated in the interrogation and torture of military prisoners in the aftermath of the 9/11 terrorist attacks and that some of the leadership of the American Psychological Association (APA) were aware of these activities, a national scandal ensued. As a consequence, the APA adopted strict new guidelines that prohibit psychologists from participating in national security interrogations, and the psychologists who devised the interrogation techniques are being put on trial. In addition, psychologists are barred from working at the Guantánamo base in Cuba and at CIA black sites (Risen, 2015; Fink, 2017).

- The public's view of psychology will become more informed. Surveys show that the public at large does not fully understand the scientific underpinnings of the field. However, as the field itself embraces such practices as using scientific evidence to choose the best treatments for psychological disorders, psychology's reputation will grow (Lilienfeld, 2012; Ferguson, 2015).

- Finally, as the population becomes more diverse, issues of diversity–embodied in the study of racial, ethnic, linguistic, and cultural factors–will become more important to psychologists providing services and doing research. The result will be a field that can provide an understanding of *human* behavior in its broadest sense (Quintana. Aboud, & Chao, 2006; Richmond et al., 2015).

From the perspective of...

A Social Worker Imagine that you have a caseload of clients who come from diverse cultures, ethnicities, and races. How might you consider their diverse backgrounds when assisting them?

©Sam Edwards/age fotostock

AP NEUROSCIENCE IN YOUR LIFE: ENHANCING YOUR MIND

AP SKILL: CONCEPT UNDERSTANDING/ SCIENTIFIC INVESTIGATION

1. Why might an individual receive repetitive transcranial stimulation (TMS) to enhance their cognitive abilities?

2. Before receiving repetitive transcranial stimulation (TMS) what types of research studies regarding the procedure would you like to know about?

Neuroscientists have strived to understand how the normal brain works, as well as what happens to it following injury or disease. Recently, they have begun to use technologies to enhance people's typical existing abilities. For example, researchers are exploring how repetitive transcranial magnetic stimulation (TMS), a form of noninvasive brain stimulation, can enhance cognitive abilities. In one study, researchers used repetitive TMS to stimulate the hippocampus, a brain region involved in memory (see the image below of the area targeted for stimulation). Stimulation over the course of a week led to increased brain connectivity and improved memory (Wang et al., 2014).

MRI-guided stimulation delivery

Source: Adapted from Wang, J. X., Rogers, L. M., Gross, E. Z., Ryals, A. J., Dokucu, M. E., Brandstatt, K. L., . . . Voss, J. L. (2014). Targeted enhancement of cortical-hippocampal brain networks and associative memory. Science, *345*(6200), 1054–1057.

BECOMING AN INFORMED CONSUMER
of Psychology

Thinking Critically About Psychology: Distinguishing Legitimate Psychology from Pseudo-Psychology

"Expand Your Mind Beyond Virtual Reality . . . & Learn at the Speed of Light!" declares the sales pitch that arrives in the day's spam. "I have an astounding technology I'm going to share with you. Something so profound it will . . . transform your mind and soul forever."

From advertisements to television and radio talk shows to the Internet, we are subjected to a barrage of information about psychology. We are told that we can become better adjusted, smarter, more insightful, and happier individuals by learning the secrets that psychologists have revealed.

However, such promises are usually empty. So how can we separate accurate information, which is backed by science and objective research, from pseudo-psychology based on anecdotes, opinions, and even outright fraud? The best approach is to employ critical thinking techniques. Developed by psychologists who specialize in learning, memory, cognition, intelligence, and education, critical thinking procedures provide the tools to scrutinize assumptions, evaluate assertions, and think with greater precision (Roediger & McCabe, 2007; Meltzoff & Harris, 2018).

We'll be considering ways to boost critical thinking skills in *Becoming an Informed Consumer of Psychology* sections throughout the book. To get started, let's consider what you need in order to evaluate information of a psychological nature, whether the source is an advertisement, a television show, a magazine article, or even a book as seemingly reliable as a college textbook.

- For starters, know who is offering the information and advice. Are the providers of the information trained psychologists? What kinds of degrees do they have? Are they licensed? Are they affiliated with a particular institution? Before seriously relying on experts' advice, check out their credentials.
- Keep in mind that there is no free ride. If it is possible to solve major psychological ills by buying a $29.95 book, why do many people who suffer from such problems typically expend a considerable amount of time and money to obtain help? If you could buy a computer program that would really "unlock the hidden truths" about others, wouldn't it be in widespread use? Be wary of simple, glib responses to major difficulties.
- Be aware that few universal cures exist for humankind's ills. No method or technique works for everyone. The range of difficulties attached to the human condition is so broad that any procedure that purports to resolve all problems is certain to disappoint.
- Finally, remember that no source of information or advice is definitive. The notion of infallibility is best left to the realm of religion; you should approach psychological information and advice from a critical and thoughtful perspective.

AP▌ MODULE 3: PSYCHOLOGY'S KEY ISSUES AND CONTROVERSIES

AP SUMMARY

- Recognize how philosophical and physiological perspectives shaped the development of psychological thought.
- Psychology's key issues and controversies center on how much of human behavior is a product of nature or nurture, conscious or unconscious thoughts, observable actions or internal mental processes, free will or determinism, and individual differences or universal principles.
- Describe and compare different theoretical approaches in explaining behavior.

- Psychologists subscribing to the five major perspectives of psychology agree on the key issues of the field, but argue on how best to address and resolve the key issues.
- Recognize the strengths and limitations of applying theories to explain behavior.
- Psychology will become increasingly specialized and new perspectives will evolve. More attention will shift to prevention rather than just treatment and neuroscience will continue to impact other branches of psychology. Psychology will influence issues of public interest, address growing diversity, and follow increasingly strict ethical and moral guidelines. The public will become more informed of the field of psychology and its scientific underpinnings.

AP KEY TERMS

free will   **determinism**

AP TEST PRACTICE

Section I: Multiple Choice

1. In the debate known as nature versus nurture, advocates for nature support which of the following?
   A. Environment
   B. Heredity
   C. Unconscious
   D. Experience
   E. Free will

2. Some psychologists believe that people make intentional choices and should be considered responsible for their actions. This belief would most likely be made by someone that subscribes to which perspective?
   A. Neuroscience or biological
   B. Psychodynamic
   C. Behavioral
   D. Evolutionary
   E. Humanistic

3. Carl's therapist asked him to recount an upsetting dream he recently experienced in order to gain insight into the unconscious forces affecting his behavior. Carl's therapist is working from a ___ perspective.
   A. Behavioral
   B. Humanistic
   C. Evolutionary
   D. Cognitive
   E. Psychodynamic

Section II: Free Response

Since the beginning of the discipline, psychology has had several key issues and controversies. Identify the following issues and connect them to the five major perspectives.

- Nature versus nurture
- Conscious versus unconscious
- Observable versus internal mental processes
- Free will versus determinism
- Individual differences versus universal principles

LOOKING *Back*

EPILOGUE

The field of psychology, as you have seen, is broad and diverse. It encompasses many different subfields and specialties practiced in a variety of settings, with new subfields continually arising. You have also seen that even within the various subfields of the field, it is possible to adopt several different approaches, including the neuroscience, psychodynamic, behavioral, cognitive, and humanistic perspectives.

For all its diversity, though, psychology focuses on certain key issues that serve to unify the field along common lines and shared findings. These issues will reappear as themes throughout this text as you learn about the work and accomplishments of psychologists in the many subfields of the discipline.

VISUAL SUMMARY 1 Introduction to Psychology

MODULE 1 Psychologists at Work

Subfields of Psychology

- Biological foundations
  - Behavioral neuroscience
- Sensing, perceiving, learning, and thinking
  - Experimental and cognitive psychology
- Sources of change and stability
  - Development and personality psychology
- Physical and mental health
  - Health, clinical, and counseling psychology
- Social networks
  - Social and cross-cultural psychology
- Expanding frontiers
  - Evolutionary psychology
  - Behavioral genetics
  - Clinical neuropsychology

Working at Psychology

Where U.S. psychologists work

Employee relations 1%
Sales 1%
Accounting/finance/contracts 1%
Primary Job
Professional services 45%
Teaching 18%
Research 16%
Management/supervision 11%
Other work activities 7%

MODULE 2 A Science Evolves

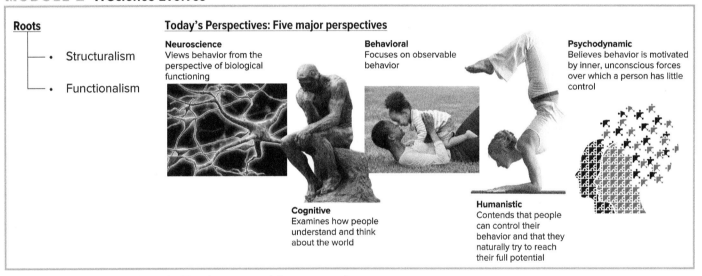

Roots

- Structuralism
- Functionalism

Today's Perspectives: Five major perspectives

Neuroscience
Views behavior from the perspective of biological functioning

Behavioral
Focuses on observable behavior

Psychodynamic
Believes behavior is motivated by inner, unconscious forces over which a person has little control

Cognitive
Examines how people understand and think about the world

Humanistic
Contends that people can control their behavior and that they naturally try to reach their full potential

MODULE 3 Psychology's Key Issues and Controversies

Issues in psychology and positions psychologists take on them

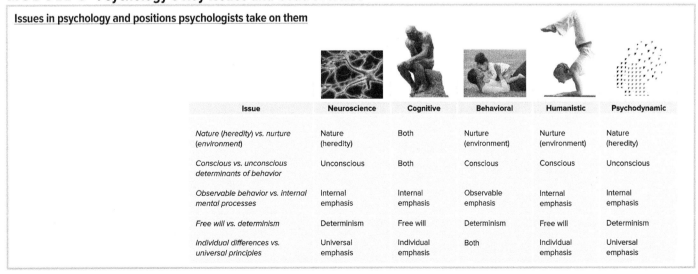

Issue	Neuroscience	Cognitive	Behavioral	Humanistic	Psychodynamic
Nature (heredity) vs. nurture (environment)	Nature (heredity)	Both	Nurture (environment)	Nurture (environment)	Nature (heredity)
Conscious vs. unconscious determinants of behavior	Unconscious	Both	Conscious	Conscious	Unconscious
Observable behavior vs. internal mental processes	Internal emphasis	Internal emphasis	Observable emphasis	Internal emphasis	Internal emphasis
Free will vs. determinism	Determinism	Free will	Determinism	Free will	Determinism
Individual differences vs. universal principles	Universal emphasis	Individual emphasis	Both	Individual emphasis	Universal emphasis

Source: (MODULE 1) Stamm, K., Lin, Luona, and Cristidis, P. (2016, June). Datapoint. *Monitor on Psychology,* 12. (MODULE 2 and MODULE 3) (Neuroscience): ©Science Photo Library/Alamy Stock Photo; (Cognitive): ©David Sanger/The Image Bank/Getty Images; (Behavioral): ©Ariel Skelley/Blend Images; (Humanistic): ©White Packert/The Image Bank/Getty Images; (Psychodynamic): ©Athanasia Nomikou/Shutterstock

©Philippe Psaila/Science Source

CHAPTER 2
Psychological Research

AP'I ESSENTIAL QUESTIONS

- How does the methodology of the research affect the outcome of a study?
- How do ethical guidelines impact psychological research?
- How does the bias of a researcher affect their conclusions?

AP'I LEARNING TARGETS FOR CHAPTER 2

	MODULE 4
• Discuss the value of reliance on operational definitions and measurement in behavioral research.	**THE SCIENTIFIC METHOD** Theories: Specifying Broad Explanations Hypotheses: Crafting Testable Predictions

	MODULE 5
• Differentiate types of research with regard to purpose, strengths, and weaknesses. • Identify independent, dependent, confounding, and control variables in experimental designs. • Distinguish between random assignment of participants to conditions in experiments and random selection of participants, primarily in correlational studies and surveys. • Predict the validity of behavioral expectations based on the quality of research design. • Apply basic descriptive statistical concepts, including interpreting and constructing graphs and calculating simple descriptive statistics. • Distinguish the purposes of descriptive statistics and inferential statistics.	**CONDUCTING PSYCHOLOGICAL RESEARCH** Archival Research Naturalistic Observation Survey Research The Case Study Correlational Research Experimental Research

- Describe how research design drives the reasonable conclusions that can be drawn.

- Identify how ethical issues inform and constrain research practices.

- Describe how ethical and legal guidelines protect research participants and promote sound ethical practice.

PROLOGUE *A CRY FOR HELP*

On a Saturday afternoon in April 2017, a disturbing sight greeted riders entering the Second Avenue subway station in Manhattan. A man, dirty and bent over, with his pants bunched around his feet, was leaning against a pillar near the edge of the platform. He was incoherent, nearly asleep, and reeling dangerously. Dozens of people saw him and, other than avoiding him, did nothing.

Minutes later, the man lost his balance and fell to the tracks. For seconds, nothing happened, and then someone screamed. One observer, a man named David Capuzzo, ran to the edge, jumped down, and hoisted the man to the platform, where others pulled him to safety. Then the rescuer himself scrambled from the tracks (Wilson, 2017).

LOOKING *Ahead*

Why didn't the bystanders act more promptly to help a man who was clearly in trouble? Did they not care? Did they just not want to be bothered? Whatever the reason, it wasn't until his need for assistance became urgent that a few of them were stirred to help.

David Capuzzo, the man who jumped onto the tracks, offers some insight into the thought processes of the people on the platform. He says, "I pictured myself helping him, but I didn't. I just kept looking back at him and looking at everyone else look at him." Because no one else rushed to help him, Capuzzo at first felt no urgency either. He returned to looking at his phone. In other words, Capuzzo took his cue from the other bystanders rather than from the situation itself.

If this were an isolated incident, we might be able to attribute the inaction to something particular about the situation or to the specific people involved. However, events such as this one are all too common.

In one infamous case in the United States in 1964, a woman named Kitty Genovese was attacked by a man near an apartment building in Queens, New York. At one point during the assault, which lasted 30 minutes, she managed to free herself and screamed, "Oh, my God, he stabbed me. Please help me!"

According to most accounts—although there were significant discrepancies in witness recollections—no fewer than 38 neighbors heard her screams. Windows opened, and lights went on. One couple pulled chairs up to the window and turned off the lights so that they could see better. Someone called out, "Let that girl alone." But shouts were not enough to scare off the killer. He chased Genovese, stabbing her eight more times, and sexually molested her before leaving her to die. And how many of those 38 witnesses came to her aid? Not one person helped (Gallo, 2015; Griggs, 2015; Kassan, 2017).

Such incidents remain dismaying—and perplexing. Why don't bystanders intervene, particularly when there are so many who could potentially offer help? At the time of the Kitty Genovese murder, editorial writers suggested that the incidents could be attributed to the basic shortcomings of "human nature," but such an explanation is woefully inadequate. Many people have risked their own lives to help others in dangerous situations, and so "human nature" encompasses a wide range of both negative and positive responses.

Psychologists puzzled over the problem for many years. After much research, they reached an unexpected conclusion: Kitty Genovese probably would have been better off if only a few people, rather than many, had heard her cries for help. In fact, if only a single, lone bystander had been present, the chances that this person would have intervened might have been fairly high. It turns out that the fewer the witnesses to an assault, the better the victim's chances of getting help.

How did psychologists come to such a curious conclusion? After all, logic and common sense clearly suggest that more bystanders would produce a greater likelihood that someone would help a person in need. This seeming contradiction—and the way psychologists resolved it—illustrates a central challenge for the field of psychology: asking useful questions about the unknown and getting valid answers.

Like professionals in any science, psychologists are vitally concerned with refining and expanding knowledge within their field. In the following modules, we'll see how psychologists pose questions of interest and answer them through scientific research. We will find that the answers psychologists obtain from their research not only advance our understanding of behavior but also offer the potential to improve the human condition.

Module 4
The Scientific Method

- Discuss the value of reliance on operational definitions and measurement in behavioral research.

scientific method The approach through which psychologists systematically acquire knowledge and understanding about behavior and other phenomena of interest. (Module 4)

"Birds of a feather flock together" . . . or "Opposites attract"? "Two heads are better than one" . . . or "If you want a thing done well, do it yourself"? "The more the merrier" . . . or "Two's company, three's a crowd"?

If we were to rely on common sense to understand behavior, we'd have considerable difficulty–especially because commonsense views are often contradictory. In fact, one of the major undertakings for the field of psychology is to develop suppositions about behavior and to determine which of those suppositions are accurate (Ferguson, 2015).

Psychologists–as well as scientists in other disciplines–meet the challenge of posing appropriate questions and properly answering them by relying on the scientific method. The **scientific method** is the approach used by psychologists to systematically acquire knowledge and understanding about behavior and other phenomena of interest. As illustrated in Figure 1, it consists of four main steps: (1) identifying questions of interest, (2) formulating an explanation, (3) carrying out research designed to support or refute the explanation, and (4) communicating the findings.

Theories: Specifying Broad Explanations

In using the scientific method, psychologists start by identifying questions of interest. We have all been curious at some time about our observations of everyday behavior. If you have ever asked yourself why a particular teacher is so easily annoyed, why a friend is always late for appointments, or how your dog understands your commands, you have been formulating questions about behavior.

FIGURE 1 The scientific method, which encompasses the process of identifying, asking, and answering questions, is used by psychologists and researchers from every other scientific discipline to come to an understanding about the world. What do you think are the advantages of this method?

 Study Alert
Use Figure 1 to remember the four steps of the scientific method (identifying questions, formulating an explanation, carrying out research, and communicating the findings).

Psychologists, too, ask questions about the nature and causes of behavior. They may want to explore explanations for everyday behaviors or for various phenomena. They may also pose questions that build on findings from their previous research or from research carried out by other psychologists. Or they may produce new questions that are based on curiosity, creativity, or insight.

After a question has been identified, the next step in the scientific method is to develop a theory to explain the observed phenomenon. **Theories** are broad explanations and predictions concerning observations of interest. They provide a framework for understanding the relationships among a set of otherwise unorganized facts or principles.

All of us have developed our own informal theories of human behavior, such as "People are basically good" or "People's behavior is usually motivated by self-interest." However, psychologists' theories are more formal and focused. They are established on the basis of a careful study of the psychological literature to identify earlier relevant research and previously formulated theories, as well as psychologists' general knowledge of the field.

Growing out of the diverse approaches employed by psychologists, theories vary both in their breadth and in their level of detail. For example, one theory might seek to explain and predict a phenomenon as broad as emotional experience. A narrower theory might attempt to explain why people display the emotion of fear nonverbally after receiving a threat (Anker & Feeley, 2011; Croom, 2015; Smith et al., 2017).

Psychologists Bibb Latané and John Darley, responding to the failure of bystanders to intervene when Kitty Genovese was murdered in New York, developed what they called a theory of *diffusion of responsibility* (Latané & Darley, 1970). According to their theory, the greater the number of bystanders or witnesses to an event that calls for helping behavior, the more the responsibility for helping is perceived to be shared by all the bystanders. Thus, the greater the number of bystanders in an emergency situation, the smaller the share of the responsibility each person feels–and the less likely that any single person will come forward to help.

theories Broad explanations and predictions concerning phenomena of interest. (Module 4)

Hypotheses: Crafting Testable Predictions

Although the diffusion of responsibility theory seems to make sense, it represented only the beginning phase of Latané and Darley's investigative process. Their next step was to devise a way to test their theory. To do this, they needed to create a hypothesis. A **hypothesis** is a prediction stated in a way that allows it to be tested. Hypotheses stem from theories; they help test the underlying soundness of theories.

In the same way that we develop our own broad theories about the world, we also construct hypotheses about events and behavior. Those hypotheses can range from trivialities (such as why our English instructor wears those weird shirts) to more meaningful matters (such as what is the best way to study for a test). Although we rarely test these hypotheses systematically, we do try to determine whether they are right. Perhaps we try comparing two strategies: cramming the night before an exam versus spreading out our study over several nights. By assessing which approach yields better test performance, we have created a way to compare the two strategies.

A hypothesis must be stated in a way that will allow it to be tested, which involves creating an operational definition. An **operational definition** is the translation of a hypothesis into specific, testable procedures that can be measured and observed in an experiment.

There is no single way to go about devising an operational definition for a hypothesis; it depends on logic, the equipment and facilities available, the psychological perspective being employed, and ultimately the creativity of the researcher. For example, one researcher might develop a hypothesis that uses as an operational definition

hypothesis A prediction, stemming from a theory, stated in a way that allows it to be tested. (Module 4)

operational definition The translation of a hypothesis into specific, testable procedures that can be measured and observed in an experiment. (Module 4)

Study Alert
Remember that a theory is a broad explanation, whereas a hypothesis is a more narrow prediction.

of "fear" an increase in heart rate. In contrast, another psychologist might use as an operational definition of "fear" a written response to the question "How much fear are you experiencing at this moment?"

Latané and Darley's hypothesis was a straightforward prediction from their more general theory of diffusion of responsibility: The more people who witness an emergency situation, the less likely it is that help will be given to a victim. They could, of course, have chosen another hypothesis (try to think of one!), but their initial formulation seemed to offer the most direct test of the theory.

Psychologists rely on formal theories and hypotheses for many reasons. For one thing, theories and hypotheses allow them to make sense of unorganized, separate observations and bits of data. They permit them to place observations and data within a coherent framework. In addition, theories and hypotheses allow psychologists to move beyond known facts and make deductions about unexplained phenomena and develop ideas for future investigation (van Wesel, Boeije, & Hoijtink, 2013; Barrett & Russell, 2015).

In short, the scientific method, with its emphasis on theories and hypotheses, helps psychologists pose appropriate questions. With properly stated questions in hand, psychologists then can choose from a variety of research methods to find answers.

AP¹ MODULE 4: THE SCIENTIFIC METHOD

AP SUMMARY

- The scientific method is the approach psychologists use to understand behavior. It consists of four steps: identifying questions of interest, formulating an explanation, carrying out research that is designed to support or refute the explanation, and communicating the findings.
- Research in psychology is guided by theories (broad explanations and predictions regarding phenomena of interest) and hypotheses (theory-based predictions stated in a way that allows them to be tested).
- To test a hypothesis, researchers must formulate an operational definition, which translates the abstract concepts of the hypothesis into the actual procedures used in the study.

AP KEY TERMS

scientific method	**hypothesis**
theories	**operational definition**

AP TEST PRACTICE

Section I: Multiple Choice

1. What is the procedure for translating a hypothesis into a specific, testable procedure?
   A. Theory
   B. Operational definition
   C. Introspection
   D. Determinism
   E. Structuralism

2. An experimenter wants to investigate the effect of social media on happiness. She decides to measure happiness by the number of smiles per hour while on social media. Clarifying the variable of happiness is called a(n)
   A. theory
   B. hypothesis
   C. scientific method
   D. operational definition
   E. statistical procedure

3. Latané and Darley predicted that the more people who witness an emergency situation, the less likely it is that help will be given to a victim. This statement is known as a(n)
   A. hypothesis
   B. operational definition
   C. theory
   D. universal principle
   E. introspective statement

Section II: Free Response

Design a study on whether color impacts mood. Address how each of the following would apply to your study.
- Hypothesis
- Operationally define the independent variable
- Operationally define the dependent variable

Module 5
Conducting Psychological Research

Research–systematic inquiry aimed at the discovery of new knowledge–is a central ingredient of the scientific method in psychology. It provides the key to understanding the degree to which hypotheses (and the theories behind them) are accurate.

Just as we can apply different theories and hypotheses to explain the same phenomena, we can use a number of alternative methods to conduct research. As we consider the major tools that psychologists use to conduct research, keep in mind that their relevance extends beyond testing and evaluating hypotheses in psychology. All of us carry out elementary forms of research on our own. For instance, a supervisor might evaluate an employee's performance; a physician might systematically test the effects of different doses of a drug on a patient; a salesperson might compare different persuasive strategies. Each of these situations draws on the research practices we are about to discuss.

Let's begin by considering several types of *descriptive research* designed to systematically investigate a person, group, or patterns of behavior. These methods include archival research, naturalistic observation, survey research, and case studies.

Archival Research

Suppose that, like the psychologists Latané and Darley (1970), you were interested in finding out more about emergency situations in which bystanders did not provide help. One of the first places you might turn to would be historical accounts. By searching newspaper records, for example, you might find support for the notion that a decrease in helping behavior historically has accompanied an increase in the number of bystanders.

Using newspaper articles is an example of archival research. In **archival research**, existing data, such as census documents, college records, online databases, and newspaper articles, are examined to test a hypothesis. For example, college transcripts may be used to determine if there are gender differences in academic performance. Similarly, Facebook provides a huge pool of data from millions of users that can be used to collect data (Sullivan, Riccio, & Reynolds, 2008; Fisher & Barnes-Farrell, 2013; Kosinski et al., 2015).

Archival research is a relatively inexpensive means of testing a hypothesis because someone else has already collected the basic data. Of course, the use of existing data has several drawbacks. For one thing, the data may not be in a form that allows the researcher to test a hypothesis fully. The information could be incomplete, or it could have been collected haphazardly (Riniolo et al., 2003; Vega, 2006; Zickar, 2015).

Most attempts at archival research are hampered by the simple fact that records with the necessary information often do not exist. In these instances, researchers often turn to another research method: naturalistic observation.

Naturalistic Observation

In **naturalistic observation**, the investigator observes some naturally occurring behavior and does not make a change in the situation. For example, a researcher investigating helping behavior might observe the kind of help given to victims in a high-crime area of a city. The important point to remember about naturalistic observation is that the researcher simply records what occurs, making no modification in the situation that is being observed (Kennison & Bowers, 2011; Haas et al., 2015; Wilson & Joye, 2017).

AP® LEARNING TARGETS

- Differentiate types of research with regard to purpose, strengths, and weaknesses.
- Identify independent, dependent, confounding, and control variables in experimental designs.
- Distinguish between random assignment of participants to conditions in experiments and random selection of participants, primarily in correlational studies and surveys.
- Predict the validity of behavioral expectations based on the quality of research design.
- Apply basic descriptive statistical concepts, including interpreting and constructing graphs and calculating simple descriptive statistics.
- Distinguish the purposes of descriptive statistics and inferential statistics.

archival research Research in which existing data, such as census documents, college records, and newspaper clippings, are examined to test a hypothesis. (Module 5)

naturalistic observation Research in which an investigator simply observes some naturally occurring behavior and does not make a change in the situation. (Module 5)

Observing behavior in its natural habitat, without making any changes in the setting, is characteristic of naturalistic observation.
©Suzanne Long/Alamy Stock Photo

Although the advantage of naturalistic observation is obvious–we get a sample of what people do in their "natural habitat"–there is also an important drawback: the inability to control any of the factors of interest. For example, we might find so few naturally occurring instances of helping behavior that we would be unable to draw any conclusions. Because naturalistic observation prevents researchers from making changes in a situation, they must wait until the appropriate conditions occur. Furthermore, if people know they are being watched, they may alter their reactions and produce behavior that is not truly representative.

Survey Research

survey research Research in which people chosen to represent a larger population are asked a series of questions about their behavior, thoughts, or attitudes. (Module 5)

There is no more straightforward way of finding out what people think, feel, and do than asking them directly. For this reason, surveys are an important research method. In **survey research**, a *sample* of people chosen to represent a larger group of interest (a *population*) is asked a series of questions about their behavior, thoughts, or attitudes. Survey methods have become so sophisticated that even with a very small sample, researchers are able to infer with great accuracy how a larger group would respond. For instance, a sample of just a few thousand voters is sufficient to predict within one or two percentage points who will win a presidential election–if the representative sample is chosen with care (Groves et al., 2004; Igo, 2006; Rea & Parker, 2014).

Researchers investigating helping behavior might conduct a survey by asking people to complete a questionnaire in which they indicate their reluctance for giving aid to someone. Similarly, researchers interested in learning about sexual practices have carried out surveys to learn which practices are common and which are not and to chart changing notions of sexual morality over the last several decades (Reece et al., 2009; Santelli et al., 2009).

However, survey research has several potential pitfalls. For one thing, if the sample of people who are surveyed is not representative of the broader population of interest, the results of the survey will have little meaning. For instance, if a sample of voters in a town only includes Republicans, it would hardly be useful for predicting the results of an election in which both Republicans and Democrats are voting. Consequently, researchers using surveys strive to obtain a *random sample* of the population in question, in which every voter in the town has an equal chance of being included in the sample receiving the survey (Davern, 2013; Engel et al., 2015; Nedelec, 2017).

In addition, survey respondents may not want to admit to holding socially undesirable attitudes. (Most racists know they are racists and might not want to admit it.)

PsychTech

One of the most efficient ways to conduct surveys is via the web. But web surveys may have sampling problems, given that not everyone has easy access to the web, such as people living in poverty. Consequently, web surveys may not be representative of the broader population.

Furthermore, people may not want to admit they engage in behaviors that they feel are somehow abnormal–a problem that plagues surveys of sexual behavior because people are often reluctant to admit what they really do in private. Finally, in some cases, people may not even be consciously aware of what their true attitudes are or why they hold them.

From the perspective of . . .

A Marketing Manager How would you design a survey that targets the customers in which you are most interested?

©Jack Hollingsworth/Getty Images

The Case Study

When they read of a suicide bomber in the Middle East, many people wonder what it is about the terrorist's personality or background that leads to such behavior. To answer this question, psychologists might conduct a case study. In contrast to a survey, in which many people are studied, a **case study** is an in-depth, intensive investigation of a single individual or a small group. Case studies often include *psychological testing*, a procedure in which a carefully designed set of questions is used to gain some insight into the personality of the individual or group.

> **case study** An in-depth, intensive investigation of an individual or small group of people. (Module 5)

When case studies are used as a research technique, the goal is to use the insights gained from the study of a few individuals to improve our understanding of people in general. Sigmund Freud developed his theories through case studies of individual patients. Similarly, case studies of terrorists might help identify others who are prone to violence.

The drawback to case studies? If the individuals examined are unique in certain ways, it is impossible to make valid generalizations to a larger population. Still, case studies sometimes lead the way to new theories and treatments for psychological disorders.

Correlational Research

In using the descriptive research methods we have discussed, researchers often wish to determine the relationship between two variables. **Variables** are behaviors, events, or other characteristics that can change, or vary, in some way. For example, in a study to determine whether the amount of studying makes a difference in test scores, the variables would be study time and test scores.

> **variables** Behaviors, events, or other characteristics that can change, or vary, in some way. (Module 5)

In **correlational research**, two sets of variables are examined to determine whether they are associated, or "correlated." The strength and direction of the relationship between the two variables are represented by a mathematical statistic known as a *correlation* (or, more formally, a *correlation coefficient*), which can range from +1.0 to −1.0.

> **correlational research** Research in which the relationship between two sets of variables is examined to determine whether they are associated, or "correlated." (Module 5)

A *positive correlation* indicates that as the value of one variable increases, we can predict that the value of the other variable will also increase. For example, if we predict that the more time students spend studying for a test, the higher their grades on the test will be, and that the less they study, the lower their test scores will be, we are expecting to find a positive correlation. (Higher values of the variable "amount of study time" would be associated with higher values of the variable "test score," and lower values of "amount of study time" would be associated with lower values of "test score.") The correlation, then, would be indicated by a positive number, and the stronger the association was between studying and test scores, the closer the number would be to +1.0. For example, we might find a correlation of +.85 between test scores and amount of study time, indicating a strong positive association.

In contrast, a *negative correlation* tells us that as the value of one variable increases, the value of the other decreases. For instance, we might predict that as the number of hours spent studying increases, the number of hours spent partying decreases. Here we are expecting a negative correlation, ranging between 0 and −1.0. More studying is associated with less partying, and less studying is associated with more partying. The stronger the association between studying and partying is, the closer the correlation will be to −1.0. For instance, a correlation of −.85 would indicate a strong negative association between partying and studying.

Of course, it's quite possible that little or no relationship exists between two variables. For instance, we would probably not expect to find a relationship between number of study hours and height. Lack of a relationship would be indicated by a correlation close to 0. For example, if we found a correlation of −.02 or +.03, it would indicate that there is virtually no association between the two variables; knowing how much someone studies does not tell us anything about how tall he or she is.

When two variables are strongly correlated with each other, we are tempted to assume that one variable causes the other. For example, if we find that more study time is associated with higher grades, we might guess that more studying *causes* higher grades. Although this is not a bad guess, it remains just a guess—because finding that two variables are correlated does not mean that there is a causal relationship between them. The strong correlation suggests that knowing how much a person studies can help us predict how that person will do on a test, but it does not mean that the studying *causes* the test performance. Instead, for instance, people who are more interested in the subject matter might study more than do those who are less interested, and so the amount of interest, not the number of hours spent studying, would predict test performance. The mere fact that two variables occur together does not mean that one causes the other.

Similarly, suppose you learned that the number of houses of worship in a large sample of cities was positively correlated with the number of people arrested, meaning that the more houses of worship, the more arrests there were in a city. Does this mean that the presence of more houses of worship caused the greater number of arrests? Almost surely not, of course. In this case, the underlying cause is probably the size of the city: in bigger cities, there are both more houses of worship *and* more arrests.

One more example illustrates the critical point that correlations tell us nothing about cause and effect but only provide a measure of the strength of a relationship between two variables. We might find that children who watch a lot of television programs featuring high levels of aggression are likely to demonstrate a relatively high degree of aggressive behavior and that those who watch few television shows that portray aggression are apt to exhibit a relatively low degree of such behavior (see Figure 1). But we cannot say that the aggression is *caused* by the TV viewing because many other explanations are possible.

For instance, it could be that children who have an unusually high level of energy seek out programs with aggressive content *and* are more aggressive. The children's energy level, then, could be the true cause of the children's higher incidence of aggression. Also, people who are already highly aggressive might choose to watch shows with a high aggressive content *because* they are aggressive. Clearly, then, any number of causal sequences are possible—none of which can be ruled out by correlational research.

Study Alert
The concept that "correlation does not imply causation" is a key principle.

Many studies show that the observation of violence in the media is associated with aggression in viewers. Can we conclude that the observations of violence cause aggression?
©Andrey_Popov/Shutterstock

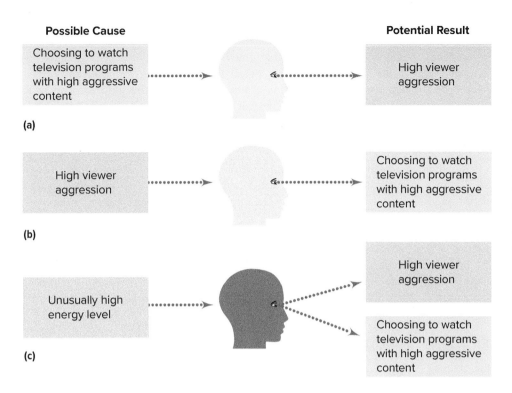

Possible Cause

Potential Result

(a) Choosing to watch television programs with high aggressive content → High viewer aggression

(b) High viewer aggression → Choosing to watch television programs with high aggressive content

(c) Unusually high energy level → High viewer aggression / Choosing to watch television programs with high aggressive content

FIGURE 1 If we find that frequent viewing of television programs with aggressive content is associated with high levels of aggressive behavior, we might cite several plausible causes, as suggested in this figure. For example, (a) choosing to watch shows with aggressive content could produce aggression; or (b) being a highly aggressive person might cause one to choose to watch televised aggression; or (c) having a high energy level might cause a person to choose both to watch aggressive shows and to act aggressively. Correlational findings, then, do not permit us to determine causality. Can you think of a way to study the effects of televised aggression on aggressive behavior that is not correlational?

The fact that correlational research is unable to demonstrate cause-and-effect relationships is a crucial drawback to its use. There is, however, an alternative technique that does establish causality: the experiment.

Experimental Research

Carrying out experiments is the *only* way psychologists can establish cause-and-effect relationships. In a formal **experiment**, a researcher investigates the relationship between two (or more) variables by deliberately changing one variable in a controlled situation and observing the effects of that change on other aspects of the situation. In an experiment then, the conditions are created and controlled by the researcher, who deliberately makes a change in those conditions in order to observe the effects of that change.

The **experimental manipulation** is the change that a researcher deliberately makes in an experiment. Experimental manipulations are used to detect relationships between different variables (Salazar, Crosby, & DiClemente, 2015).

Several steps are involved in carrying out an experiment, but the process typically begins with the development of one or more hypotheses for the experiment to test. For example, Latané and Darley, in testing their theory of the diffusion of responsibility in bystander behavior, developed this hypothesis: The higher the number of people who witness an emergency situation is, the less likely it is that any of them will help the victim. They then designed an experiment to test this hypothesis.

Their first step was to formulate an operational definition of the hypothesis by conceptualizing it in a way that could be tested. Latané and Darley had to take into account the fundamental principle of experimental research mentioned earlier: Experimenters must manipulate at least one variable in order to observe the effects of the manipulation on another variable while keeping other factors in the situation constant. However, the manipulation cannot be viewed by itself, in isolation; if a cause-and-effect relationship is to be established, the effects of the manipulation must be compared with the effects of no manipulation or a different kind of manipulation.

experiment The investigation of the relationship between two (or more) variables by deliberately producing a change in one variable in a situation and observing the effects of that change on other aspects of the situation. (Module 5)

experimental manipulation The change that an experimenter deliberately produces in a situation. (Module 5)

EXPERIMENTAL GROUPS AND CONTROL GROUPS

treatment The manipulation implemented by the experimenter. (Module 5)

experimental group Any group participating in an experiment that receives a treatment. (Module 5)

control group A group participating in an experiment that receives no treatment. (Module 5)

Experimental research requires, then, that the responses of at least two groups be compared. One group will receive some special **treatment**–the manipulation implemented by the experimenter–and another group will receive either no treatment or a different treatment. Any group that receives a treatment is called an **experimental group**; a group that receives no treatment is called a **control group**. (In some experiments, there are multiple experimental and control groups, each of which is compared with another group.)

By employing both experimental and control groups in an experiment, researchers are able to rule out the possibility that something other than the experimental manipulation produced the results observed in the experiment. Without a control group, we couldn't be sure that some other variable, such as the temperature at the time we were running the experiment, the color of the experimenter's hair, or even the mere passage of time, wasn't causing the changes observed.

For example, consider a medical researcher who thinks he has invented a medicine that cures the common cold. To test his claim, he gives the medicine one day to a group of 20 people who have colds and finds that 10 days later all of them are cured.

Eureka? Not so fast. An observer viewing this flawed study might reasonably argue that the people would have gotten better even without the medicine. What the researcher obviously needed was a control group consisting of people with colds who *don't* get the medicine and whose health is also checked 10 days later. Only if there is a significant difference between experimental and control groups can the effectiveness of the medicine be assessed. Through the use of control groups, then, researchers can isolate specific causes for their findings–and draw cause-and-effect inferences.

Returning to Latané and Darley's experiment, we see that the researchers needed to translate their hypothesis into something testable. To do this, they decided to create a false emergency situation that would appear to require the aid of a bystander. As their experimental manipulation, they decided to vary the number of bystanders present. They could have had just one experimental group with, say, two people present and a control group for comparison purposes with just one person present. Instead, they settled on a more complex procedure involving the creation of groups of three sizes–consisting of two, three, and six people–that could be compared with one another.

In this experiment, preschoolers' reactions to the puppet are monitored. Can you think of a hypothesis that might be tested in this way?
©Thierry Berrod, Mona Lisa Production/Science Source

INDEPENDENT AND DEPENDENT VARIABLES

independent variable The variable that is manipulated by an experimenter. (Module 5)

dependent variable The variable that is measured in an experiment. It is expected to change as a result of the experimenter's manipulation of the independent variable. (Module 5)

Latané and Darley's experimental design now included an operational definition of what is called the **independent variable**. The independent variable is the condition that is manipulated by an experimenter. (You can think of the independent variable as being independent of the actions of those taking part in an experiment; it is controlled by the experimenter.) In the case of the Latané and Darley experiment, the independent variable was the number of people present, which was manipulated by the experimenters.

The next step was to decide how they were going to determine the effect that varying the number of bystanders had on behavior of those in the experiment. Crucial to every experiment is the **dependent variable**. The dependent variable is the variable that is measured in a study. The dependent variable is expected to change as a result of the experimenter's manipulation of the independent variable. The dependent variable is dependent on the actions of the *participants* or *subjects*–the people taking part in the experiment.

Latané and Darley had several possible choices for their dependent measure. One might have been a simple yes/no measure of the participants' helping behavior. But the investigators also wanted a more precise analysis of helping behavior. Consequently, they also measured the amount of time it took for a participant to provide help.

Latané and Darley now had all the necessary components of an experiment. The independent variable, manipulated by them, was the number of bystanders present in an emergency situation. The dependent variable was the measure of whether bystanders in each of the groups provided help and the amount of time it took them to do so. Consequently, like all experiments, this one had both an independent variable and a dependent variable. *All* true experiments in psychology fit this straightforward model.

RANDOM ASSIGNMENT OF PARTICIPANTS

To make the experiment a valid test of the hypothesis, Latané and Darley needed to add a final step to the design: properly assigning participants to a particular experimental group.

The significance of this step becomes clear when we examine various alternative procedures. For example, the experimenters might have assigned just males to the group with two bystanders, just females to the group with three bystanders, and both males and females to the group with six bystanders. If they had done this, however, any differences they found in helping behavior could not be attributed with any certainty solely to group size, because the differences might just as well have been due to the composition of the group. A more reasonable procedure would be to ensure that each group had the same composition in terms of gender; then the researchers would be able to make comparisons across groups with considerably more accuracy.

Participants in each of the experimental groups ought to be comparable, and it is easy enough to create groups that are similar in terms of gender. The problem becomes a bit more tricky, though, when we consider other participant characteristics. How can we ensure that participants in each experimental group will be equally intelligent, extroverted, cooperative, and so forth, when the list of characteristics–any one of which could be important–is potentially endless?

The solution is a simple but elegant procedure called **random assignment to condition**: Participants are assigned to different experimental groups, or *conditions*, on the basis of chance and chance alone. The experimenter might, for instance, flip a coin for each participant and assign a participant to one group when "heads" came up and to the other group when "tails" came up. The advantage of this technique is that there is an equal chance that participant characteristics will be distributed across the various groups. When a researcher uses random assignment–which in practice is usually carried out using computer-generated random numbers–chances are that each of the groups will have approximately the same proportion of intelligent people, cooperative people, extroverted people, males and females, and so on.

Figure 2 provides another example of an experiment. Like all experiments, it includes the following set of key elements, which you should keep in mind as you consider whether a research study is truly an experiment:

- An independent variable, the variable that is manipulated by the experimenter
- A dependent variable, the variable that is measured by the experimenter and that is expected to change as a result of the manipulation of the independent variable
- A procedure that randomly assigns participants to different experimental groups (called *conditions*) of the independent variable
- A hypothesis that predicts the effect the independent variable will have on the dependent variable

Only if each of these elements is present can a research study be considered a true experiment in which cause-and-effect relationships can be determined. (For a summary of the different types of research that we've discussed, see Figure 3.)

Study Alert
To remember the difference between dependent and independent variables, recall that a hypothesis predicts how a dependent variable *depends* on the manipulation of the independent variable.

random assignment to condition A procedure in which participants are assigned to different experimental groups or "conditions" on the basis of chance and chance alone. (Module 5)

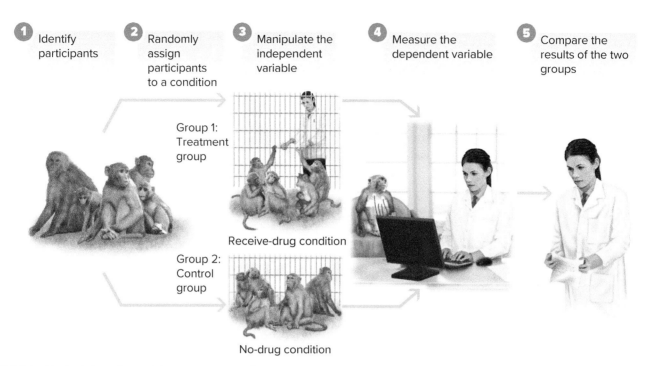

1 Identify participants

2 Randomly assign participants to a condition

3 Manipulate the independent variable

4 Measure the dependent variable

5 Compare the results of the two groups

Group 1: Treatment group

Receive-drug condition

Group 2: Control group

No-drug condition

FIGURE 2 In this depiction of a study investigating the effects of the drug propranolol on heart disease, we can see the basic elements of all true experiments. The participants in the experiment were monkeys that were randomly assigned to one of two groups. Monkeys assigned to the treatment group were given propranolol, hypothesized to prevent heart disease, whereas those in the control group were not given the drug. Administration of the drugs, then, was the independent variable.

All the monkeys were given a high-fat diet that was the human equivalent of two eggs with bacon every morning, and they occasionally were reassigned to different cages to increase their stress. To determine the effects of the drug, the monkeys' heart rates and other measures of heart disease were assessed after 26 months. These measures constituted the dependent variable. The results? As hypothesized, monkeys that received the drug showed lower heart rates and fewer symptoms of heart disease than those that did not.

Source: Based on a study by Kaplan, J. R., & Manuck, S. B. (1989). The effect of propranolol on behavioral interactions among adult male cynomolgus monkeys (Macacafascicularis) housed in disrupted social groupings. *Psychosomatic Medicine, 51,* 449–462.

WERE LATANÉ AND DARLEY RIGHT?

To test their hypothesis that increasing the number of bystanders in an emergency situation would lower the degree of helping behavior, Latané and Darley placed the participants in a room and told them that the purpose of the experiment was to talk about personal problems associated with college. The discussion was to be held over an intercom, supposedly to avoid the potential embarrassment of face-to-face contact. Chatting about personal problems was not, of course, the true purpose of the experiment, but telling the participants that it was provided a way of keeping their expectations from biasing their behavior. (Consider how they would have been affected if they had been told that their helping behavior in emergencies was being tested. The experimenters could never have gotten an accurate assessment of what the participants would actually do in an emergency. By definition, emergencies are rarely announced in advance.)

The sizes of the discussion groups were two, three, and six people, which constituted the manipulation of the independent variable of group size. Participants were randomly assigned to these groups upon their arrival at the laboratory. Each group included one trained confederate of the experimenters. A *confederate* is an actor employed by a researcher who participates in a psychological experiment, pretending to be a participant. The researcher trains the confederate to act in a particular way during the experiment.

As the participants in each group were holding their discussion, they suddenly heard through the intercom one of the other participants—but who in reality was the confederate—having what sounded like an epileptic seizure. The confederate then called for help.

The actual participants' behavior was now what counted. The dependent variable was the time that elapsed from the start of the "seizure" to the time a participant began

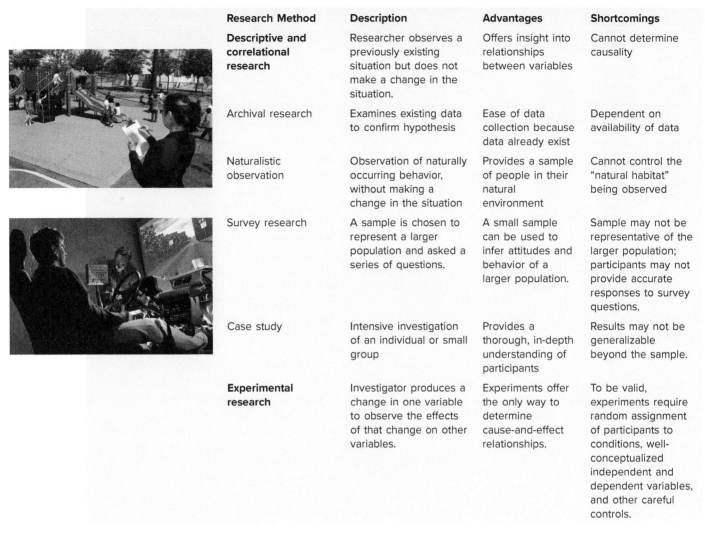

Research Method	Description	Advantages	Shortcomings
Descriptive and correlational research	Researcher observes a previously existing situation but does not make a change in the situation.	Offers insight into relationships between variables	Cannot determine causality
Archival research	Examines existing data to confirm hypothesis	Ease of data collection because data already exist	Dependent on availability of data
Naturalistic observation	Observation of naturally occurring behavior, without making a change in the situation	Provides a sample of people in their natural environment	Cannot control the "natural habitat" being observed
Survey research	A sample is chosen to represent a larger population and asked a series of questions.	A small sample can be used to infer attitudes and behavior of a larger population.	Sample may not be representative of the larger population; participants may not provide accurate responses to survey questions.
Case study	Intensive investigation of an individual or small group	Provides a thorough, in-depth understanding of participants	Results may not be generalizable beyond the sample.
Experimental research	Investigator produces a change in one variable to observe the effects of that change on other variables.	Experiments offer the only way to determine cause-and-effect relationships.	To be valid, experiments require random assignment of participants to conditions, well-conceptualized independent and dependent variables, and other careful controls.

FIGURE 3 Research strategies.
(Top): ©Bill Aron/PhotoEdit; (Bottom): ©Marc Steinmetz/Visum/The Image Works

trying to help the "victim." If 6 minutes went by without a participant offering help, the experiment was ended.

As predicted by the hypothesis, the size of the group had a significant effect on whether a participant provided help. The more people who were present, the less likely it was that someone would supply help, as you can see in Figure 4 (Latané & Darley, 1970).

Because these results are straightforward, it seems clear that the experiment confirmed the original hypothesis. However, Latané and Darley could not be sure that the results were truly meaningful until they determined whether the results represented what statisticians call a significant outcome.

A **significant outcome** indicates that the findings are statistically meaningful, showing that the differences between conditions are large enough for researchers to feel confident that they have confirmed their hypotheses. Using statistical analysis, researchers can determine whether a numeric difference is a real difference or is due merely to chance. Only when differences between groups are large enough that statistical tests show them to be significant is it possible for researchers to confirm a hypothesis.

significant outcome Meaningful results that make it possible for researchers to feel confident that they have confirmed their hypotheses. (Module 5)

MOVING BEYOND THE STUDY

The Latané and Darley study contains all the elements of an experiment: an independent variable, a dependent variable, random assignment to conditions, and multiple experimental groups. Consequently, we can say with some confidence that group size *caused* changes in the degree of helping behavior.

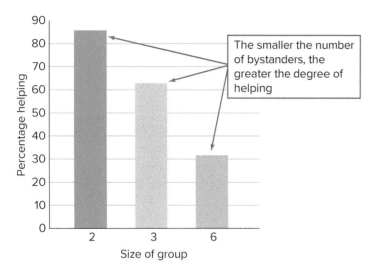

FIGURE 4 The Latané and Darley experiment showed that as the size of the group witnessing an emergency increased, helping behavior decreased.

Source: Adapted from Darley, J. M., & Latané, B. (1968). Bystanders' intervention in emergencies: Diffusion of responsibility. *Journal of Personality and Social Psychology, 8,* 377–383.

replicated research Research that is repeated, sometimes using other procedures, settings, and groups of participants, to increase confidence in prior findings. (Module 5)

Of course, one experiment alone does not forever resolve the question of bystander intervention in emergencies. Psychologists–like other scientists–require that findings be **replicated**, or repeated, sometimes using other procedures, in other settings, with other groups of participants, before full confidence can be placed in the results of any single experiment.

For example, follow-up research shows that college students aren't the only ones who show the bystander effect; for instance, young children do as well. Furthermore, a procedure called *meta-analysis* permits psychologists to combine the results of many separate studies into one overall conclusion (Kisely et al., 2015; Plotner et al., 2015; Stone & Rosopa, 2017).

Replication is a critical activity, and many researchers believe that psychologists need to increase the number of studies that are replications of earlier research in order to have greater confidence in their findings. They point to an influential study that attempted to replicate 100 previous findings but that found that only 36% of the replications yielded similarly significant findings as in the original studies. The takeaway message: in order to be fully confident about the meaning of research studies, they need to be replicated (Maxwell, Lau, & Howard, 2015; Open Science Collaboration, 2015; Card, 2017).

In addition to replicating experimental results, psychologists need to test the limitations of their theories and hypotheses to determine under which specific circumstances they do and do not apply. It seems unlikely, for instance, that increasing the number of bystanders *always* results in less helping.

In fact, follow-up research shows that bystander intervention is more likely to occur in situations viewed as clear-cut and dangerous because bystanders are more likely to perceive that the presence of others will provide resources for helping. In short, it is critical to continue carrying out experiments to understand the conditions in which exceptions to this general rule occur and other circumstances in which the rule holds (Garcia et al., 2002; Fischer et al., 2011).

Before leaving the Latané and Darley study, note that it represents a good illustration of the basic principles of the scientific method. The two psychologists began with a *question of interest,* in this case stemming from a real-world incident in which bystanders in an emergency did not offer help. They then *formulated an explanation* by specifying a theory of diffusion of responsibility and from that formulated the specific hypothesis that increasing the number of bystanders in an emergency situation would lower the degree of helping behavior. Finally, they *carried out research* to confirm their hypothesis, and they eventually *communicated their findings* by publishing their results. This four-step process embodied in the scientific method underlies all scientific inquiry, allowing us to develop a valid understanding of others'–and our own–behavior.

AP MODULE 5: CONDUCTING PSYCHOLOGICAL RESEARCH

AP SUMMARY

- Descriptive research methods rely on correlation techniques that describe associations between variables but cannot determine cause-and-effect relationships.
- In correlational research, two sets of variables are examined to see a relationship. This method can only provide a measure of the strength and offers insight of a relationship between two variables.

- In naturalistic observation, the investigator acts mainly as an observer, making no change in a naturally occurring situation.
- In survey research, people are asked questions about their behavior, thoughts, and attitudes. Researchers can infer how a larger group would respond from a small sample, but results will not be meaningful if the sample is not representative.

- The case study is an in-depth interview and examination of one person or a group. The goal is to gain an in-depth understanding of participants and generalize results of a few to the larger group.
- In a formal experiment, the relationship between variables is investigated by deliberately producing a change—called the experimental manipulation—in one variable and observing changes in the other.
- Experiments are the only method to establish causality. To design an experiment first formulate an operational definition of the hypothesis by conceptualizing it in a way that could be tested. Valid experiments require random assignment, operationally defined independent and dependent variables, and other controls. Results must be replicated for full confidence in the results of any single experiment.
- Researchers must test the limitations of their theories and hypotheses to determine under which specific circumstances they do and do not apply.
- Experimenters manipulate the independent variable. The variable they measure and expect to change as a result of the independent variable manipulation is the dependent variable. Experimenters must manipulate at least one variable in order to observe effects of the manipulation on another variable while keeping other factors constant.
- Experiments with at least two groups in which effects of the manipulation must be compared with effects of no manipulation or a different kind of manipulation are the are the only way to establish cause-and-effect relationships.
- By using experimental and control groups, researchers can rule out that something other than the experimental manipulation produced the results. Researchers use surveys to obtain a random sample of the population in order to correctly infer the results.
- The correlation coefficient is a mathematical statistic that represents the strength and direction of the relationship between two variables and can range from +1.0 to -1.0.
- Positive correlations have two variables with values that move in the same direction, while negative correlations have variables with values that move in opposite directions.
- Psychologists use statistical tests to determine whether research findings are significant.

AP KEY TERMS

archival research
naturalistic observation
survey research
case study
variables
correlational research

experiment
experimental
   manipulation
treatment
experimental group
control group

independent variable
dependent variable
random assignment to
   condition

significant outcome
replicated research

AP TEST PRACTICE

Section I: Multiple Choice

1. Which of the following is a strength of the case study?
   A. It makes data collection easy because data already exists.
   B. It provides a thorough, in-depth understanding of participants.
   C. It allows researchers to manipulate a variable.
   D. It allows researchers to draw conclusions about cause-and-effect.
   E. It minimizes artificial behaviors that could be a problem in laboratory settings.

2. A researcher designed a study to test the effect of caffeine consumption on test performance. Participants were randomly assigned to receive one cup of coffee or no coffee before their assessment. In the study, coffee consumption would be described as the
   A. independent variable
   B. dependent variable
   C. confounding variable
   D. control group
   E. operational definition

3. Which of the following describes the strongest correlation?
   A. .20
   B. .89
   C. −.45
   D. .01
   E. −.92

Section II: Free Response

Researchers are interested in how children play when in small groups with other children.

- Describe how the researchers would make this a naturalistic observation study.
- Provide an advantage of using a naturalistic observation study.
- Provide a disadvantage of using a naturalistic observation study.
- Describe how researchers would make this an experimental study.
- Provide an advantage of using an experimental study.
- Operationally define the dependent variable.
- Explain how a precise operational definition of the dependent variable is important to the experimental study.

Module 6
Critical Research Issues

Study Alert

Because the protection of experiment participants is essential, remember the key ethical guideline of informed consent.

informed consent A document signed by participants affirming that they have been told the basic outlines of the study and are aware of what their participation will involve. (Module 6)

You probably realize by now that there are few simple formulas for psychological research. Psychologists must make choices about the type of study to conduct, the measures to take, and the most effective way to analyze the results. Even after they have made these essential decisions, they must still consider several critical issues. We turn first to the most fundamental of these issues: ethics.

The Ethics of Research

Put yourself in the place of one of the participants in the experiment conducted by Latané and Darley to examine the helping behavior of bystanders in which another "bystander" simulating a seizure turned out to be a confederate of the experimenters (Latané & Darley, 1970). How would you feel when you learned that the supposed victim was in reality a paid accomplice?

Although you might at first experience relief that there had been no real emergency, you might also feel some resentment that you had been deceived by the experimenter. You might also experience concern that you had been placed in an embarrassing or compromising situation—one that might have dealt a blow to your self-esteem, depending on how you had behaved.

Most psychologists argue that deception is sometimes necessary to prevent participants from being influenced by what they think a study's true purpose is. (If you knew that Latané and Darley were actually studying your helping behavior, wouldn't you automatically have been tempted to intervene in the emergency?) To avoid such outcomes, a small proportion of research involves deception.

Nonetheless, because research has the potential to violate the rights of participants, psychologists are expected to adhere to a strict set of ethical guidelines aimed at protecting participants (American Psychological Association, 2002; Tien et al., 2012; Young, 2017). Those guidelines involve the following safeguards:

- Protection of participants from physical and mental harm

- The right of participants to privacy regarding their behavior

- The assurance that participation in research is completely voluntary

- The necessity of informing participants about the nature of procedures before their participation in the experiment

- All experiments must be reviewed by an independent panel before being conducted (Fisher, 2003; Coventry et al., 2003; Crano, Brewer, & Lac, 2015)

One of psychologists' key ethical principles is **informed consent**. Before participating in an experiment, the participants must sign a document affirming that they have been told the basic outlines of the study and are aware of what their participation will involve, what risks the experiment may hold, and the fact that their participation is purely voluntary, and they may terminate it at any time.

Furthermore, after participation in a study, participants must be given a debriefing in which they receive an explanation of the study and the procedures that were involved. The only time informed consent and a debriefing can be eliminated is in experiments in which the risks are minimal, as in a purely observational study in a public place (Barnett, Wise, & Johnson-Greene, 2007; Nagy, 2011; Hetzel-Riggin, 2017).

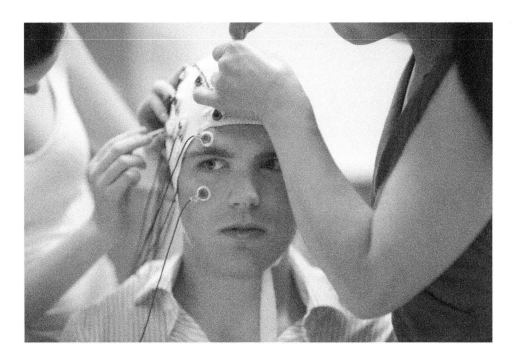

Although readily available and widely used as research subjects, college students may not represent the population at large. What are some advantages and drawbacks of using college students as subjects?
©annedde/Getty Images

 # Exploring Diversity

Choosing Participants Who Represent the Scope of Human Behavior

When Latané and Darley, both college professors, decided who would participate in their experiment, they turned to the people most easily available: college students. Using college students as participants has both advantages and drawbacks. The big benefit is that because most research occurs in university settings, college students are readily available. Typically, they cost the researcher very little: They participate for either extra course credit or a relatively small payment.

The problem is that college students may not represent the general population adequately. In fact, undergraduate research participants are typically a special group of people: relative to the general population, college students tend to be from **W**estern, **e**ducated, **i**ndustrialized, **r**ich, and **d**emocratic cultures. That description forms the acronym WEIRD, which led one researcher to apply the nickname to research participants (Jones, 2010; Lancy, 2015).

It's not that there's anything particularly wrong with WEIRD participants. It's just that they may be different from most other people—those who don't go to college or who didn't grow up in a democratic Western culture, who are less affluent, and so forth. All these characteristics could be psychologically relevant. Yet one review found that most research participants do come from the United States, and about the same proportion of those are psychology majors (Arnett, 2008; Henrich, Heine, & Norenzayan, 2010; Kaiser, Thomas, & Bowers, 2017).

Because psychology is a science whose goal is to explain *all* human behavior generally, its studies must use participants who are fully representative of the general population in terms of gender, age, race, ethnicity, socioeconomic status, and educational level (see *Neuroscience in Your Life* and *Applying Psychology in the 21st Century* features).

To encourage a wider range of participants, the National Institute of Mental Health and the National Science Foundation—the primary U.S. funding sources for psychological research—now require that experiments address issues of diverse populations (Carpenter, 2002; Lindley, 2006).

AP| NEUROSCIENCE IN YOUR LIFE: THE IMPORTANCE OF USING REPRESENTATIVE PARTICIPANTS

AP SKILL: DATA ANALYSIS/ SCIENTIFIC INVESTIGATION

1. What other explanations might account for the differences in Easterner's and Westerner's brains?

2. In order to represent the rich diversity of humanity, what type of factors might be controlled for a representative sample?

Most neuroscience research is conducted to understand the brains of all individuals. But people differ significantly in the way they process information. For example, culture and experiences shape the way our brains process information. A recent review of seven studies showed that individuals raised in Eastern countries, such as Japan, and individuals raised in Western countries, such as the United States, process information differently during cognitive tasks.

In the images below, each brain indicates a different area in which differences were seen. The key indicates within a brain whether Easterners showed greater activation (green) or whether Westerners did (yellow). Overall, Easterners show more activity in the left hemisphere (green), whereas Westerners show more activity in the right hemisphere (yellow).

Might these differences mean that there are clear genetic differences in Easterner's and Westerner's brains? Not at all. It is equally plausible that cultural factors (exposure to certain kinds of experiences) cause the brains to develop after birth in different ways. In any case, it is clear that researchers must include participants who represent the rich diversity of the humanity (Han & Ma, 2014).

■ East > West
West > East

Source: Adapted from Han, S., & Ma, Y. (2014). Cultural differences in human brain activity: A quantitative meta-analysis. *Neuroimage, 99,* 293-300.

Should Animals Be Used in Research?

Like those who work with humans, researchers who use nonhuman animals in experiments have their own set of exacting guidelines to ensure that the animals do not suffer. Specifically, researchers must make every effort to minimize discomfort, illness, and pain. Procedures that subject animals to distress are permitted only when an alternative procedure is unavailable and when the research is justified by its prospective value. Moreover, researchers strive to avoid causing physical discomfort, but they are also required to promote the *psychological* well-being of some species of research animals, such as primates (Lutz & Novak, 2005; Miller & Williams, 2011; Herzog, 2017).

But why should animals be used for research in the first place? Is it really possible to learn about human behavior from the results of research employing rats, gerbils, and pigeons?

The answer is that psychological research that employs nonhumans is designed to answer questions different from those posed in research with humans. For example, the shorter life span of animals (rats live an average of 2 years) allows researchers to learn about the effects of aging in a relatively short time frame. It is also possible to provide greater experimental control over nonhumans and to carry out procedures that might not be possible with people. For example, some studies require large numbers of participants that share similar backgrounds or have been exposed to particular environments—conditions that could not practically be met with human beings.

Research involving animals is controversial but, when conducted within ethical guidelines, yields significant benefits for humans.
©Douglas Faulkner/Science Source

AP APPLYING PSYCHOLOGY IN THE 21ST CENTURY

FINDING RESEARCH PARTICIPANTS ON FACEBOOK

We've already noted that the most common source of research participants, college undergraduates, is problematic for a variety of reasons. College students are overwhelmingly young and tend strongly to be Western, industrialized, educated, and relatively well off–hardly representative of the whole population.

This is where the social media giant Facebook can come to the rescue: the sheer size of its user base–some 2 billion people–virtually guarantees a broad diversity of potential research participants. The base even includes groups that are small or otherwise typically hard to reach, such as people living in other countries or shut-ins who would never agree to venture out to a research lab (Kosinski et al., 2015, 2016).

Another strong advantage to Facebook as a source of research participants is the enormous amount of rich demographic data that Facebook already collects. Users disclose such common information as age, gender, and location but also highly specific information such as political beliefs, sexual orientation, hobbies and interests, preferred activities, favorite movies, and much more. Researchers can take advantage of this existing data to selectively tar-

©Charnsit Ramyarupa/123RF

get specific groups for study, such as coal miners, or early risers, or unmarried retired military veterans living in California. Facebook's targeted advertising helps researchers reach out selectively to the exact potential participants they need, making it a very cost-effective recruitment method.

Even researchers who aren't particular about who participates in their study benefit enormously by using Facebook as a recruiting tool. A procedure called *snowball sampling*, whereby initial participants are tapped to recruit their own friends and

acquaintances as additional participants (who then in turn recruit their friends and acquaintances, and so on) works especially well in the Facebook environment, yielding a potentially very large sample size in a relatively short time. If a study is compelling enough because it's fun or interesting or provides useful feedback to the participant, it can even go viral.

Of course, Facebook recruitment has special concerns of its own. Some researchers fear the quality of data may be poor due to users who lie or exaggerate or even create fake profiles. Although studies show that this fear is largely unfounded, it remains a concern. Another concern is the lack of clear ethical guidelines for the collection of Facebook users' personal data. If users make their information public, is it acceptable for researchers to take that information without the users' permission or even knowledge? Ethical questions such as these will be better sorted out as more and more researchers turn to Facebook (Kosinski et al., 2015, 2016).

AP SKILL: SCIENTIFIC INVESTIGATION

1. Describe ethical and/or research design flaws of using Facebook for research.
2. Explain how ethical and/or research design flaws of using Facebook for research can be corrected.

Research with animals has provided psychologists with information that has profoundly benefited humans. For instance, it furnished the keys to detecting eye disorders in children early enough to prevent permanent damage, to communicating more effectively with children with severe intellectual disability, and to reducing chronic pain in people. Still, the use of research using nonhumans is controversial, involving complex moral and philosophical concerns. Consequently, all research involving nonhumans must be carefully reviewed beforehand to ensure that it is conducted ethically (Grundy, 2015; Guidelines for the Treatment of Animals, 2017).

Threats to Experimental Validity: Avoiding Experimental Bias

Even the best-laid experimental plans are susceptible to **experimental bias**–factors that distort the way the independent variable affects the dependent variable in an experiment.

experimental bias Factors that distort how the independent variable affects the dependent variable in an experiment. (Module 6)

One of the most common forms of experimenter bias relates to the unintentional transmission of expectations to participants by the experimenter, thereby affecting the results. When *experimenter expectations* occur, an experimenter unintentionally transmits cues to participants about the way the experimenter expects them to behave. The danger is that those expectations actually cause the expected result to happen—results that otherwise might not have occurred (Rosenthal, 2003).

A related problem is *participant expectations* about appropriate behavior. If you have ever been a participant in an experiment, you probably developed guesses about what was expected of you. In fact, participants often develop their own hypotheses about what the experimenter hopes to learn from the study. If participants form their own hypotheses and then act on their hunches, it may be their expectations, rather than the experimental manipulation, that produce the results (Rutherford et al., 2009).

To guard against participant expectations biasing the results of an experiment, the experimenter may try to disguise the true purpose of the experiment. Participants who do not know that helping behavior is being studied, for example, are more apt to act in a "natural" way than they would if they knew.

Sometimes it is impossible to hide the actual purpose of research; when that is the case, other techniques are available to prevent bias. Suppose you were interested in testing the ability of a new drug to alleviate the symptoms of severe depression. If you simply gave the drug to half your participants and not to the other half, the participants who were given the drug might report feeling less depressed merely because they knew they were getting a drug. Similarly, the participants who got nothing might report feeling no better because they knew that they were in a no-treatment control group.

To solve this problem, psychologists typically use a procedure in which all the participants receive a treatment but those in the control group receive only a **placebo**—a false treatment, such as a pill, "drug," or other substance that has no significant chemical properties or active ingredient. Because members of both groups are kept in the dark about whether they are getting a real or a false treatment, any differences in outcome can be attributed to the quality of the drug and not to the possible psychological effects of being administered a pill or other substance (Justman, 2011; Keränen et al., 2015).

However, there is one more safeguard that a careful researcher must apply in an experiment such as this one. To overcome the possibility that *experimenter* expectations will affect the participant, the person who administers the drug shouldn't know whether it is actually the true drug or the placebo. By keeping both the participant and the experimenter who interacts with the participant "blind" to the nature of the drug that is being administered, researchers can more accurately assess the effects of the drug. This method is known as the *double-blind procedure.*

placebo A false treatment, such as a pill, "drug," or other substance, without any significant chemical properties or active ingredient. (Module 6)

BECOMING AN INFORMED CONSUMER
of Psychology

Thinking Critically About Research

If you were about to purchase an automobile, you would not likely stop at the nearest car dealership and drive off with the first car a salesperson recommended. Instead, you would probably mull over the purchase, read about automobiles, consider the alternatives, talk to others about their experiences, and ultimately put in a fair amount of thought before you made such a major purchase.

In contrast, many of us are considerably less conscientious when we hear about research findings. People often jump to conclusions on the basis of incomplete and inaccurate information, and only rarely do they take the time to critically evaluate research and data.

Because the field of psychology is based on an accumulated body of research, we must scrutinize thoroughly the methods, results, and claims of researchers. Three questions can help us sort through what is valid and what is not:

- *What was the purpose of the research?* Research studies should evolve from a clearly specified theory. Furthermore, we must take into account the specific hypothesis that is being tested. Unless we know what hypothesis is being examined, we cannot judge how successful a study has been.
- *How was the study conducted?* Consider who the participants were, how many were involved, what methods were employed, and what problems the researcher encountered in collecting the data. There are important differences, for example, between a case study that reports the comments of a handful of respondents and a survey that collects data from several thousand people.
- *Are the results presented fairly?* The research findings must be assessed in terms of how closely they relate to the way in which a study was carried out and how they reflect what was found. For instance, suppose a drug producer claims that "no other sleeping pill has been shown to be more effective in helping people get a good night's sleep." This does not mean that theirs is the *best* sleeping pill on the market. It just means that no other sleeping pill has been proved *more* effective; other pills may be just as effective. Expressed in the latter fashion, the finding doesn't seem worth bragging about.

These three basic questions can help you assess the validity of research findings you come across—both within and outside the field of psychology. The more you know how to evaluate research, the better you will be able to assess what the field of psychology has to offer.

AP⃞ MODULE 6: CRITICAL RESEARCH ISSUES

AP SUMMARY

- We must scrutinize thoroughly the methods, results, and claims of researchers. Three questions can help assess the validity of research findings: What was the purpose of the research? How was the study conducted? Are the results presented fairly?
- Experiments are subject to biases that threaten experimental validity. Experimenter expectations can produce bias when an experimenter unintentionally transmits cues to participants about her or his expectations regarding their behavior in a given experimental condition. Participant expectations can also bias an experiment. Among the tools experimenters use to help eliminate bias are placebos and double-blind procedures.
- Using college students as participants has the advantage of easy availability; however, there are drawbacks, i.e., students do not necessarily represent the population as a whole.
- The use of nonhuman animals as participants may have costs in terms of the ability to generalize to humans, although the benefits of using animals in research have been profound.

- Researchers must adhere to a strict set of ethical guidelines that include: participant protection from physical and mental harm, privacy regarding participant behavior, assurance of voluntary participation, informed consent for participants, and debriefing.
- One of the key ethical principles followed by psychologists is that of informed consent. Participants must be informed, before participation, about the basic outline of the experiment and the risks and potential benefits of their participation.
- After the experiment participants should be given a debriefing in which they can receive an explanation of the study and procedures used in the experiment.
- All experiments must be reviewed by an independent panel before being conducted.
- Researchers who use nonhuman animals in experiments have their own set of guidelines that include: minimize discomfort, illness, and pain; distress is only permitted when there is no alternative procedure available and the research is justified by its value; avoid causing physical discomfort; and promote psychological well-being of some species.

informed consent   **placebo**
experimental bias

Section I: Multiple Choice

1. A key ethical principle for research includes getting participant permission before an experiment. This ethical guideline is called
   A. debriefing
   B. confidentiality
   C. deception
   D. informed consent
   E. right to withdraw

2. Psychologists are expected to adhere to strict ethical guidelines that include all of the following EXCEPT
   A. explanation of the study after participation
   B. protection of privacy
   C. assurance of voluntary participation
   D. approval from an IRB before the study is conducted
   E. protection from all types of deception

3. Researchers were conducting an experiment involving a new drug on the progression of Alzheimer's disease. Patient A was provided a fake pill that did not have an active ingredient. Both the researcher and Patient A not knowing if the real or false treatment was provided is an example of what type of research procedure?
   A. Double-blind
   B. Representative sample
   C. Informed consent
   D. Debriefing
   E. Experimental control

Section II: Free Response

Dr. Cory would like to investigate the ability of a new medication to alleviate symptoms of anxiety. She will randomly assign participants to one of two groups. The first group will receive the new medication. The second group will receive a placebo. Neither the experimenter or the participants will know who is in the control or experimental group.

A. Explain how each of the following might help Dr. Cory get the study passed by the IRB.
   - Informed consent
   - Debriefing
   - Confidentiality

B. Explain how each of the following need to be accounted for before the study can be passed by the IRB.
   - Participant bias
   - Experimenter bias

C. Discuss the cause of anxiety from each of the following perspectives.
   - Biological
   - Cognitive

LOOKING Back

EPILOGUE

We have been discussing the ways in which psychologists seek to understand phenomena and answer questions of interest. We examined the scientific method and its reliance on posing good questions, creating productive theories, and crafting testable hypotheses. We also looked at the basic methods psychologists use to conduct research studies and compared correlational methods and experimental methods. Finally, we explored some of the major challenges that psychologists have to deal with when conducting research, including ethical considerations, the use of animals in research, and potential bias.

VISUAL SUMMARY 2 Psychological Research

MODULE 4 The Scientific Method

Scientific Method

Identify questions of interest stemming from
- Behavior and phenomenon requiring explanation
- Prior research findings
- Curiosity, creativity, insight

Formulate an explanation
Specify a theory

Develop a hypothesis

Carry out research
Devise an operational definition of the hypothesis

Select a research method

Collect the data

Analyze the data

Communicate the findings

Theories: Broad explanations

Hypotheses: Testable predictions

MODULE 5 Conducting Psychological Research

Descriptive Research: Describes associations among variables
- Archival research
- Naturalistic observation
- Survey research
- Case study
- Correlational research
  - Does not explain causality

Possible Cause — Potential Result

(a) Choosing to watch television programs with high aggressive content → High viewer aggression

(b) High viewer aggression → Choosing to watch television programs with high aggressive content

(c) Unusually high energy level → High viewer aggression / Choosing to watch television programs with high aggressive content

Experimental Research: Assesses cause-and-effect relationships between variables
- Experimental manipulation
- Experimental and control groups
- Independent and dependent variables
- Random assignment of participants

1 Identify participants
2 Randomly assign participants to a condition
3 Manipulate the independent variable
4 Measure the dependent variable
5 Compare the results of the two groups

Group 1: Treatment group — Receive-drug condition

Group 2: Control group — No-drug condition

MODULE 6 Critical Research Issues

Ethics of Research
Informed consent

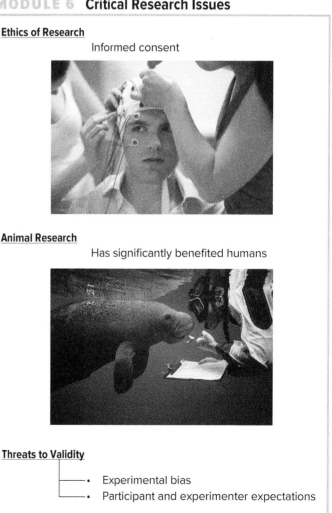

Animal Research
Has significantly benefited humans

Threats to Validity
- Experimental bias
- Participant and experimenter expectations

Source: (MODULE 5) Based on a study by Kaplan, J. R., & Manuck, S. B. (1989). The effect of propranolol on behavioral interactions among adult male cynomolgus monkeys (Macacafas-cicularis) housed in disrupted social groupings. *Psychosomatic Medicine, 51,* 449–462.
(MODULE 6) (Top): ©annedde/Getty Images; (Bottom): ©Douglas Faulkner/Science Source

CHAPTER 3
Neuroscience and Behavior

AP'I ESSENTIAL QUESTIONS

- What happens when a particular neurotransmitter is absent from the body?

- How can biology influence our behavior and mental processes?

- How do biological and environmental factors interact to influence our behaviors and mental processes?

AP'I LEARNING TARGETS FOR CHAPTER 3

	MODULE 7

- Describe the nervous system and its subdivisions and functions.

- Identify basic processes and systems in the biological bases of behavior, including parts of the neuron.

- Identify basic process of transmission of a signal between neurons.

- Discuss the influence of drugs on neurotransmitters.

NEURONS: THE BASIC ELEMENTS OF BEHAVIOR

The Structure of the Neuron

How Neurons Fire

Where Neurons Meet: Bridging the Gap

Neurotransmitters: Multitalented Chemical Couriers

	MODULE 8

- Discuss psychology's abiding interest in how heredity, environment, and evolution work together to shape behavior.

- Discuss the effect of the endocrine system on behavior.

- Describe the nervous system and its subdivisions and functions.

- Identify basic processes and systems in the biological bases of behavior, including parts of the neuron.

THE NERVOUS SYSTEM AND THE ENDOCRINE SYSTEM: COMMUNICATING WITHIN THE BODY

The Nervous System: Linking Neurons

The Evolutionary Foundations of the Nervous System

The Endocrine System: Of Chemicals and Glands

- Describe the nervous system and its subdivisions and functions in the brain.

- Identify the contributions of key researchers to the study of the brain.

- Recount historic and contemporary research strategies and technologies that support research.

- Identify the contributions of key researchers to the development of tools for examining the brain.

- Discuss the role of neuroplasticity in traumatic brain injury.

- Identify the contributions of key researchers to the study of neuroplasticity.

PROLOGUE *THE POWER OF THOUGHT*

Dennis Degray was taking out the trash when he slipped on a patch of wet grass and landed chin first. The fall severely injured his spinal cord, leaving Degray a quadriplegic, all communication severed between his brain and the musculature below his head.

But thanks to recent advances in brain-computer interface (BCI) research, Degray, 64, can now type about eight words a minute. That's almost as fast as you can type a text on your cellphone. By merely visualizing his own arm, hand, and finger movements, he can control a computer cursor to spell out words.

One of three test subjects used in the pilot experiment at Stanford University, Degray had two silicon chips, each measuring 1/6-inch square, implanted in his brain. These chips record signals from the motor cortex and send them through a cable to a computer where algorithms translate them into point-and click commands (Goldman, 2017).

LOOKING *Ahead*

It's hard to believe that someone can write words on a computer just by imagining the motions of their hand pressing the keys of an online keyboard. But that's just one way neuroscience is harnessing the remarkable capacity of the brain to improve life for people who suffer severe motor impairment due to disease or injury.

An organ roughly half the size of a loaf of bread, the brain controls our physical, emotional, and intellectual behavior through every waking and sleeping moment. Our movements, thoughts, hopes, aspirations, dreams—our very awareness that we are human—all depend on the brain and the nerves that extend throughout the body, constituting the nervous system.

Because of the importance of the nervous system in controlling behavior and because humans at their most basic level are biological beings, many researchers in psychology and other fields as diverse as computer science, zoology, and medicine have made the biological underpinnings of behavior their specialty. These experts collectively are called *neuroscientists* (Gazzaniga, Ivry, & Mangun, 2002; Cartwright, 2006; Kasemsap, 2017).

Psychologists who specialize in considering the ways in which the biological structures and functions of the body affect behavior are known as **behavioral neuroscientists** (or *biopsychologists*). They seek to answer several key questions: How does the brain control the voluntary and involuntary functioning of the body? How does the brain communicate with other parts of the body? What is the physical structure of the brain, and how does this structure affect behavior? Are psychological disorders caused by biological factors, and how can such disorders be treated?

As you consider the biological processes that we discuss in this chapter, keep in mind the reason why behavioral neuroscience is an essential part of psychology: Our understanding of human behavior requires knowledge of the brain and other parts of the nervous system. Biological factors are central to our sensory experiences, states of consciousness, motivation and emotion, development throughout the life span, and physical and psychological health. Furthermore, advances in behavioral neuroscience have led to the creation of drugs and other treatments for psychological and physical disorders. In short, we cannot understand behavior without understanding our biological makeup (Plomin, 2003; Compagni & Manderscheid, 2006; Schlinger, 2015).

behavioral neuroscientists (or biopsychologists) Psychologists who specialize in considering the ways in which the biological structures and functions of the body affect behavior. (Module 7)

Module 7

Neurons: The Basic Elements of Behavior

AP® LEARNING TARGETS

- Describe the nervous system and its subdivisions and functions.
- Identify basic processes and systems in the biological bases of behavior, including parts of the neuron.
- Identify basic process of transmission of a signal between neurons.
- Discuss the influence of drugs on neurotransmitters.

neurons Nerve cells, the basic elements of the nervous system. (Module 7)

Watching Serena Williams hit a stinging backhand, Dario Vaccaro dance a complex ballet routine, or Derek Jeter swing at a baseball, you may have marveled at the complexity—and wondrous abilities—of the human body. But even the most everyday tasks, such as pouring a cup of coffee or humming a tune, depend on a sophisticated sequence of events in the body that is itself truly impressive.

The nervous system is the pathway for the instructions that permit our bodies to carry out such precise activities. Here, we look at the structure and function of neurons, the cells that make up the nervous system, including the brain.

The Structure of the Neuron

Playing the piano, driving a car, or hitting a tennis ball depends, at one level, on exact muscle coordination. But if we consider *how* the muscles can be activated so precisely, we see that more fundamental processes are involved. For the muscles to produce the complex movements that make up any meaningful physical activity, the brain has to provide the right messages to them and coordinate those messages.

Such messages—as well as those that enable us to think, remember, and experience emotion—are passed through specialized cells called neurons. **Neurons,** or nerve cells, are the basic elements of the nervous system. Their quantity is staggering—perhaps as many as 1 *trillion* neurons throughout the body are involved in the control of behavior (Boahen, 2005).

Although there are several types of neurons, they all have a similar structure, as illustrated in Figure 1. Like most cells in the body, neurons have a cell body that contains a nucleus. The nucleus incorporates the hereditary material that determines

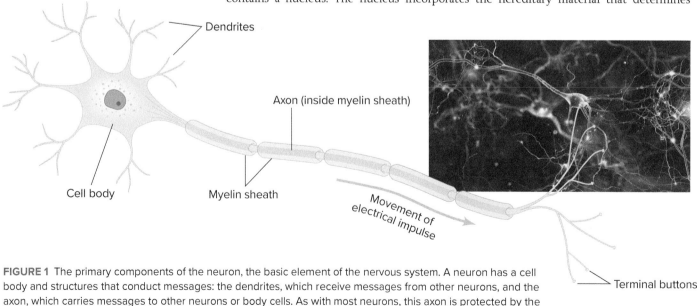

FIGURE 1 The primary components of the neuron, the basic element of the nervous system. A neuron has a cell body and structures that conduct messages: the dendrites, which receive messages from other neurons, and the axon, which carries messages to other neurons or body cells. As with most neurons, this axon is protected by the sausagelike myelin sheath. What advantages does the treelike structure of the neuron provide?
©McGraw-Hill Global Education Holdings LLC, 2000; (Photo): ©whitehoune/Shutterstock

how a cell will function. Neurons are physically held in place by *glial cells*. Glial cells provide nourishment to neurons, insulate them, help repair damage, and generally support neural functioning (Bassotti & Villanacci, 2011; Toft et al., 2013; Keshavarz, 2017).

In contrast to most other cells, however, neurons have a distinctive feature: the ability to communicate with other cells and transmit information across relatively long distances. Many of the body's neurons receive signals from the environment or relay the nervous system's messages to muscles and other target cells, but the vast majority of neurons communicate only with other neurons in the elaborate information system that regulates behavior.

As shown in Figure 1, there's a cluster of fibers at the end of every neuron that are called dendrites. **Dendrites** are the part of the neuron that receives messages from other neurons. They look like the twisted branches of a tree.

On the opposite side of every neuron is a long, slim, tube-like extension called an axon. The **axon** carries messages received by the dendrites to other neurons. The axon is considerably longer than the rest of the neuron. Although most axons are several millimeters in length, some are as long as 3 feet. Axons end in small bulges called terminal buttons. **Terminal buttons** send messages to other neurons. They look like a small bulge at the end of the axon.

The messages that travel through a neuron are electrical in nature. Although there are exceptions, those electrical messages, or *impulses,* generally move across neurons in one direction only, as if they were traveling on a one-way street. Impulses follow a route that begins with the dendrites, continues into the cell body, and leads ultimately along the tube-like extension, the axon, to adjacent neurons.

To prevent messages from short-circuiting one another, axons must be insulated in some fashion (just as electrical wires must be insulated). Most axons are insulated by a **myelin sheath,** a protective coating of fat and protein that wraps around the axon like the casing on links of sausage.

The myelin sheath also serves to increase the velocity with which electrical impulses travel through axons. Those axons that carry the most important and most urgently required information have the greatest concentrations of myelin. If your hand touches a painfully hot stove, for example, the information regarding the pain is passed through axons in the hand and arm that have a relatively thick coating of myelin, speeding the message of pain to the brain so that you can react instantly.

dendrite A cluster of fibers at one end of a neuron that receives messages from other neurons. (Module 7)

axon The part of the neuron that carries messages to other neurons. (Module 7)

terminal buttons The part of the axon that sends messages to other neurons. They look like a small bulge at the end of the axon. (Module 7)

Study Alert
Remember that *dendrites* *d*etect messages from other neurons; *a*xons carry signals *a*way from the neuron.

myelin sheath A protective coat of fat and protein that wraps around the axon. (Module 7)

How Neurons Fire

Like a gun, neurons either fire–that is, transmit an electrical impulse along the axon–or don't fire. There is no in-between stage, just as pulling harder on a gun trigger doesn't make the bullet travel faster. Similarly, neurons follow an **all-or-none law:** They are either on or off, with nothing in between the on state and the off state. When there is enough force to pull the trigger, a neuron fires.

Before a neuron is triggered–that is, when it is in a **resting state**–it has a negative electrical charge of about −70 millivolts (a millivolt is one $\frac{1}{1,000}$ of a volt). This charge is caused by the presence of more negatively charged ions within the neuron than outside it. (An ion is an atom that is electrically charged.) You might think of the neuron as a miniature battery in which the inside of the neuron represents the negative pole and the outside represents the positive pole.

When a message arrives at a neuron, gates along the cell membrane open briefly to allow positively charged ions to rush in at rates as high as 100 million ions per second. The sudden arrival of these positive ions causes the charge within the nearby part of the cell to change momentarily from negative to positive. When the positive charge reaches a critical level, the "trigger" is pulled, and an electrical impulse, known as an *action potential,* travels along the axon of the neuron (see Figure 2).

The **action potential** moves from one end of the axon to the other like a flame moving along a fuse. As the impulse travels along the axon, the movement of ions

all-or-none law The rule that neurons are either on or off. (Module 7)

resting state The state in which there is a negative electrical charge of about −70 millivolts within a neuron. (Module 7)

action potential An electric nerve impulse that travels through a neuron's axon when it is set off by a "trigger," changing the neuron's charge from negative to positive. (Module 7)

FIGURE 2 Movement of an action potential along an axon. Just before Time 1,
positively charged ions enter the cell
membrane, changing the charge in the
nearby part of the axon from negative to
positive and triggering an action potential. The action potential travels along the
axon, as illustrated in the changes occurring from Time 1 to Time 3 (from top to
bottom in this drawing). Immediately after
the action potential has passed through a
section of the axon, positive ions are
pumped out, restoring the charge in that
section to negative. The change in voltage illustrated by the blue line above the
axon can be seen in greater detail in
Figure 3.

causes a change in charge from negative to positive in successive sections of the axon
(see Figure 3). After the impulse has passed through a particular section of the axon,
positive ions are pumped out of that section, and its charge returns to negative while
the action potential continues to move along the axon.

Just after an action potential has passed through a section of the axon, the cell
membrane in that region cannot admit positive ions again for a few milliseconds, and
so a neuron cannot fire again immediately no matter how much stimulation it receives.

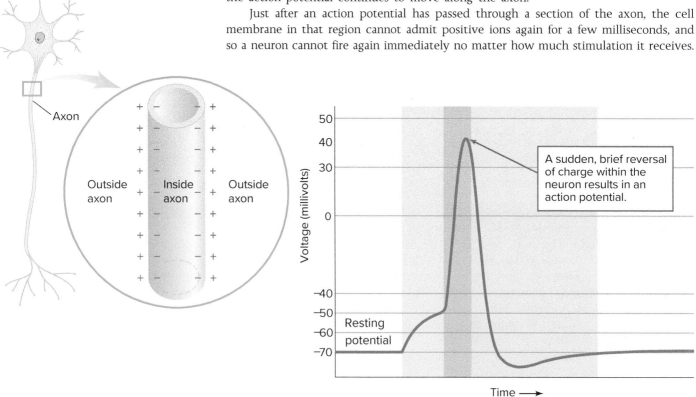

FIGURE 3 Changes in the voltage in a neuron during the passage of an action potential. In its normal resting state, a neuron has a negative
charge of about −70 millivolts. When an action potential is triggered, however, the charge becomes positive, increasing from about
−70 millivolts to about +40 millivolts. Immediately following the passage of the action potential, the charge becomes even more negative than
it is in its typical resting state. After the charge returns to its normal resting state, the neuron will be fully ready to be triggered once again.

Module 7 Neurons: The Basic Elements of Behavior

It is as if the gun has to be reloaded after each shot. There then follows a period in which, though it is possible for the neuron to fire, a stronger stimulus is needed than would be if the neuron had reached its normal resting state. Eventually, though, the neuron is ready to fire again.

SPEED OF TRANSMISSION

These complex events can occur at dizzying speeds, although there is great variation among different neurons. The particular speed at which an action potential travels along an axon is determined by the axon's size and the thickness of its myelin sheath. Axons with small diameters carry impulses at about 2 miles per hour; longer and thicker ones can average speeds of more than 225 miles per hour.

Neurons differ not only in terms of how quickly an impulse moves along the axon but also in their potential rate of firing. Some neurons are capable of firing as many as 1,000 times per second; others fire at much slower rates. The intensity of a stimulus determines how much of a neuron's potential firing rate is reached. A strong stimulus, such as a bright light or a loud sound, leads to a higher rate of firing than a less intense stimulus does. Thus, even though all impulses move at the same strength or speed through a particular axon–because of the all-or-none law–there is variation in the frequency of impulses, providing a mechanism by which we can distinguish the tickle of a feather from the weight of someone standing on our toes.

MIRROR NEURONS

Although all neurons operate through the firing of action potentials, there is significant specialization among different types of neurons. For example, neuroscientists have discovered the existence of **mirror neurons,** neurons that fire not only when a person enacts a particular behavior but also when a person simply observes *another* individual carrying out the same behavior (Spaulding, 2013; Brucker et al., 2015; Bonini, 2017).

mirror neurons Specialized neurons that fire not only when a person enacts a particular behavior but also when a person simply observes *another* individual carrying out the same behavior. (Module 7)

Mirror neurons may help explain how (and why) humans have the capacity to understand others' intentions. Specifically, mirror neurons may fire when we view someone doing something, helping us to predict what their goals are and what they may do next.

The discovery of mirror neurons suggests that the capacity of even young children to imitate others may be an inborn behavior. Furthermore, mirror neurons may be at the root of empathy–those feelings of concern, compassion, and sympathy for others–and even the development of language in humans (Ramachandra, 2009; Rogalsky et al., 2011; Lim & Okuno, 2015).

Some researchers suggest an even broader role for mirror neurons. For example, mirror neurons, which respond to sound, appear to be related to speech perception and language comprehension. Furthermore, stimulating the mirror neuron system can help stroke victims as well and may prove to be helpful for those with emotional problems by helping them to develop greater empathy (Gallese et al., 2011; Hoenen, Lübke, & Pause, 2017).

Where Neurons Meet: Bridging the Gap

If you have looked inside a computer, you've seen that each part is physically connected to another part. In contrast, evolution has produced a neural transmission system that at some points has no need for a structural connection between its components. Instead, a chemical connection bridges the gap, known as a synapse, between two neurons (see Figure 4). The **synapse** is the space between two neurons where the axon of a sending neuron communicates with the dendrites of a receiving neuron by using chemical messages.

synapse The space between two neurons where the axon of a sending neuron communicates with the dendrites of a receiving neuron by using chemical messages. (Module 7)

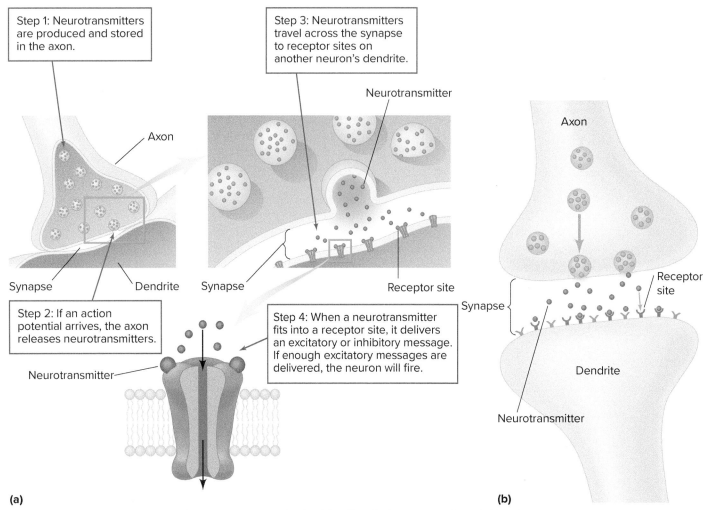

Step 1: Neurotransmitters are produced and stored in the axon.

Step 3: Neurotransmitters travel across the synapse to receptor sites on another neuron's dendrite.

Neurotransmitter

Axon

Synapse   Dendrite   Synapse   Receptor site

Step 2: If an action potential arrives, the axon releases neurotransmitters.

Step 4: When a neurotransmitter fits into a receptor site, it delivers an excitatory or inhibitory message. If enough excitatory messages are delivered, the neuron will fire.

Neurotransmitter

Axon

Synapse

Receptor site

Dendrite

Neurotransmitter

(a)   **(b)**

FIGURE 4 A synapse is the junction between an axon and a dendrite. Chemical neurotransmitters bridge the synaptic gap between the axon and the dendrite (Mader, 2000). (a) Read Step 1 through Step 4 to follow this chemical process. (b) Just as the pieces of a jigsaw puzzle can fit in only one specific location in a puzzle, each kind of neurotransmitter has a distinctive configuration that allows it to fit into a specific type of receptor cell (Johnson, 2000). Why is it advantageous for axons and dendrites to be linked by temporary chemical bridges rather than by the hard wiring typical of a radio connection or telephone hookup?

(a and b): ©McGraw-Hill Global Education Holdings LLC, 2000.

neurotransmitters Chemicals that communicate messages from one neuron to another neuron across the synapse. (Module 7)

Study Alert

Remember this key fact: Messages inside neurons are transmitted in electrical form, whereas messages traveling between neurons travel via chemical means.

When a nerve impulse comes to the end of the axon and reaches a terminal button, the terminal button releases a chemical messenger called a neurotransmitter. **Neurotransmitters** carry messages from one neuron to another neuron. Like a boat that ferries passengers across a river, these chemical messengers move from the axon of one neuron to the dendrite of a receiving neurons.

Keep in mind that the chemical mode of message transmission that occurs between neurons differs strikingly from the means by which communication occurs inside neurons: Although messages travel in electrical form *within* a neuron, they move *between* neurons through a chemical transmission system.

There are several types of neurotransmitters, and not all neurons are capable of receiving the chemical message carried by a particular neurotransmitter. In the same way that a jigsaw puzzle piece can fit in only one specific location in a puzzle, each kind of neurotransmitter has a distinctive configuration that allows it to fit into a specific type of receptor site on the receiving neuron (see Figure 4b). It is only when a neurotransmitter fits precisely into a receptor site that successful chemical communication is possible.

If a neurotransmitter does fit into a site on the receiving neuron, the chemical message it delivers is basically one of two types: excitatory or inhibitory.

Excitatory messages are chemical messages that make it more likely that a receiving neuron will fire and an action potential will travel down its axon. In contrast, inhibitory messages do just the opposite: **inhibitory messages** provide chemical information that prevents or decreases the likelihood that the receiving neuron will fire.

Because the dendrites of a neuron receive both excitatory and inhibitory messages simultaneously, the neuron must integrate the messages by using a kind of chemical calculator. Put simply, if the excitatory messages ("Fire!") outnumber the inhibitory ones ("Don't fire!"), the neuron fires. In contrast, if the inhibitory messages outnumber the excitatory ones, nothing happens, and the neuron remains in its resting state.

If neurotransmitters remained at the site of the synapse, receiving neurons would be awash in a continual chemical bath, producing constant stimulation or constant inhibition of the receiving neurons. This would make effective communication across the synapse impossible. To avoid this problem, enzymes deactivate the neurotransmitters, or–more commonly–the terminal button sucks them back up in an example of chemical recycling called reuptake.

Reuptake is the process in which a neurotransmitter produced by a terminal button is reabsorbed by the terminal button. Like a vacuum cleaner sucking up dust, neurons reabsorb the neurotransmitters that are now clogging the synapse. All this activity occurs at lightning speed, with the process taking just several milliseconds (Gingrich et al., 2017).

Our understanding of the process of reuptake has permitted the development of a number of drugs used in the treatment of psychological disorders. Some antidepressant drugs, called *SSRIs*, or *selective serotonin reuptake inhibitors*, permit certain neurotransmitters to remain active for a longer period at certain synapses in the brain, thereby reducing the symptoms of depression (Guiard et al., 2011; Hilton et al., 2013; Leong et al., 2017).

Neurotransmitters: Multitalented Chemical Couriers

Neurotransmitters are a particularly important link between the nervous system and behavior. Not only are they important for maintaining vital brain and body functions, but a deficiency or an excess of a neurotransmitter can produce severe behavior disorders. More than a hundred chemicals have been found to act as neurotransmitters, and neuroscientists believe that more may ultimately be identified. The major neurotransmitters and their effects are described in Figure 5 (Schmidt, 2006).

One of the most common neurotransmitters is *acetylcholine* (or *ACh*, its chemical symbol), which is found throughout the nervous system. ACh is involved in our every physical move because–among other things–it transmits messages relating to our skeletal muscles. ACh also aids in memory capabilities. In fact, diminished production of ACh may be related to Alzheimer's disease (Bazalakova et al., 2007; Van der Zee, Platt, & Riedel, 2011; Betterton et al., 2017).

Another common excitatory neurotransmitter, *glutamate*, plays a role in memory. Memories appear to be produced by specific biochemical changes at particular synapses, and glutamate, along with other neurotransmitters, plays an important role in this process (Winters & Bussey, 2005; Micheau & Marighetto, 2011; Solomonia & McCabe, 2015).

Gamma-amino butyric acid (GABA), which is found in both the brain and the spinal cord, appears to be the nervous system's primary inhibitory neurotransmitter. It moderates a variety of behaviors, ranging from eating to aggression. Several common substances, such as the tranquilizer Valium and alcohol, are effective because they permit GABA to operate more efficiently (Ball, 2004; Criswell et al., 2008; Lobo & Harris, 2008).

Another major neurotransmitter is *dopamine (DA)*, which is involved in movement, attention, and learning. The discovery that certain drugs can have a significant effect on dopamine release has led to the development of effective treatments for a wide variety of physical and mental ailments. For instance, Parkinson's disease, from which actor Michael J. Fox suffers, is caused by a deficiency of dopamine in the brain. Techniques for increasing the production of dopamine in Parkinson's patients are proving effective (Iversen & Iversen, 2007; Antonini & Barone, 2008; Hanna-Pladdy, Pahwa, & Lyons, 2015).

excitatory message A chemical message that makes it more likely that a receiving neuron will fire and an action potential will travel down its axon. (Module 7)

inhibitory message A chemical message that prevents or decreases the likelihood that a receiving neuron will fire. (Module 7)

reuptake The reabsorption of neurotransmitters by a terminal button. (Module 7)

Michael J. Fox suffers from Parkinson's disease, and he has become a strong advocate for research into the disorder.
©Theo Wargo/Getty Images

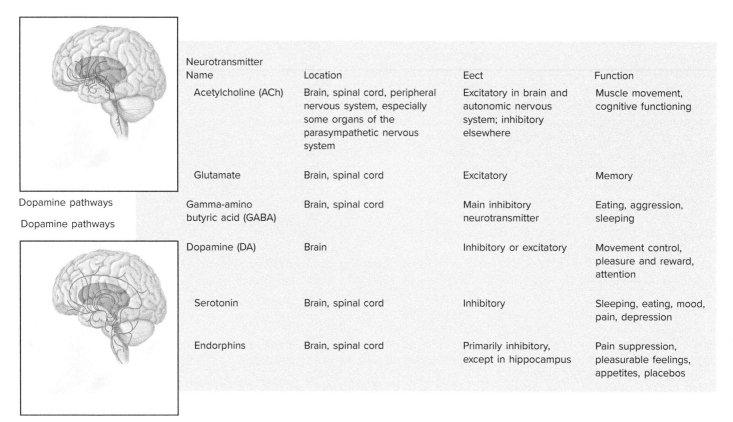

Dopamine pathways

Dopamine pathways

Neurotransmitter Name	Location	Eect	Function
Acetylcholine (ACh)	Brain, spinal cord, peripheral nervous system, especially some organs of the parasympathetic nervous system	Excitatory in brain and autonomic nervous system; inhibitory elsewhere	Muscle movement, cognitive functioning
Glutamate	Brain, spinal cord	Excitatory	Memory
Gamma-amino butyric acid (GABA)	Brain, spinal cord	Main inhibitory neurotransmitter	Eating, aggression, sleeping
Dopamine (DA)	Brain	Inhibitory or excitatory	Movement control, pleasure and reward, attention
Serotonin	Brain, spinal cord	Inhibitory	Sleeping, eating, mood, pain, depression
Endorphins	Brain, spinal cord	Primarily inhibitory, except in hippocampus	Pain suppression, pleasurable feelings, appetites, placebos

FIGURE 5 Major neurotransmitters.

PsychTech

A team of Swedish researchers has discovered a way to stimulate specific neurons via chemical neurotransmitters, rather than using earlier technologies involving electrical signals to stimulate them. This discovery opens a novel path to treat those who suffer from severe psychological disorders produced by brain dysfunction.

In other instances, overproduction of dopamine produces negative consequences. For example, researchers have hypothesized that schizophrenia and some other severe mental disturbances are affected or perhaps even caused by the presence of unusually high levels of dopamine. Drugs that block the reception of dopamine reduce the symptoms displayed by some people diagnosed with schizophrenia (Howes & Kapur, 2009; Seeman, 2011; Howes et al., 2017).

From the perspective of...

A Health-Care Provider How might your understanding of the nervous system help you explain the symptoms of Parkinson's disease to a patient with the disorder?

©Tetra Images/Getty Images

Another neurotransmitter, *serotonin,* is associated with the regulation of sleep, eating, mood, and pain. A growing body of research points toward a broader role for serotonin, suggesting its involvement in such diverse behaviors as alcoholism, depression, suicide, impulsivity, aggression, and coping with stress (Murray et al., 2008; Popa et al., 2008; Carrillo et al., 2009).

Endorphins, another class of neurotransmitters, are a family of chemicals produced by the brain that are similar in structure to painkilling drugs such as morphine. The production of endorphins reflects the brain's effort to deal with pain as well as to elevate mood.

Endorphins also may produce the euphoric feelings that runners sometimes experience after long runs. The exertion and perhaps the pain involved in a long run may stimulate the production of endorphins, ultimately resulting in what has been called "runner's high" (Kolata, 2002; Pert, 2002; Stanojevic, Mitic, & Vujic, 2007).

Endorphin release might also explain other phenomena that have long puzzled psychologists. For example, the act of taking placebos (pills or other substances that contain no actual drugs but that patients *believe* will make them better) may induce the release of endorphins, leading to the reduction of pain (Rajagopal, 2006; Crum & Langer, 2007; Bruehl et al., 2017).

AP MODULE 7: NEURONS: THE BASIC ELEMENTS OF BEHAVIOR

AP SUMMARY

- Full understanding of human behavior requires knowledge of the biological influences underlying that behavior, especially those originating in the nervous system.
- Neurons carry nerve impulses from one part of the body to another. Information in neurons usually follows a route that begins with dendrites, continues into the cell body, and down the axon. Most axons are insulated by the myelin sheath. Neurons differ in their potential rate of firing and how quickly an impulse moves along the axon. Neurons operate through the firing of action potentials. Speed of an action potential is determined by the size and thickness of the myelin sheath.
- Neurons operate on an all-or-none law: either they are at rest or an action potential is moving through them. Mirror neurons may be involved in imitation, language, and empathy.
- Messages travel in electrical form within a neuron and move between them through a chemical transmission system. When a neuron fires, impulses reach other neurons via neurotransmitters that bridge the gaps–known as synapses–between neurons.
- Neurotransmitters are reabsorbed in reuptake. Drugs affecting reuptake have been developed to treat psychological disorders.
- Neurotransmitters may be either excitatory or inhibitory.
- Neurotransmitters include: ACh, physical movement and memory; GABA, made in brain cells from glutamate, appears to be the primary inhibitory neurotransmitter and is involved in a variety of behaviors, it also plays a role in memory; dopamine is involved in movement, pleasure and reward, attention, and learning; diminished levels cause Parkinson's, while an overproduction is related to schizophrenia.

AP KEY TERMS

behavioral neuroscientists (or biopsychologists)	**axon**
neurons	**terminal buttons**
dendrite	**myelin sheath**
	all-or-none law

resting state	**neurotransmitters**
action potential	**excitatory message**
mirror neurons	**inhibitory message**
synapse	**reuptake**

AP TEST PRACTICE

Section I: Multiple Choice

1. Michael J. Fox suffers from Parkinson's disease, which is caused by a deficiency in what neurotransmitter?
- **A.** Acetylcholine
- **B.** Glutamate
- **C.** Dopamine
- **D.** Serotonin
- **E.** Endorphins

2. What determines the speed of an action potential?
- **A.** Length of dendrites
- **B.** Thickness of myelin sheath
- **C.** Number of neurotransmitters received
- **D.** Electrical charge inside the neuron
- **E.** Size of synapse

3. Which of the following correctly identifies the first step of an action potential?
- **A.** Neurotransmitters are released from the dendrites.
- **B.** Positively charged ions are pumped out of a section of the axon.
- **C.** The cell membrane cannot admit positive ions for a few milliseconds.
- **D.** Positively charged ions enter the cell membrane.
- **E.** The charge of the neuron becomes more negative than typical resting state.

Section II: Free Response

Psychologists are using drugs that mimic the effects of neurotransmitters to treat disorders.

A. Explain the disorders associated with diminished levels of the neurotransmitters listed below.
- Acetylcholine
- Dopamine

B. How could the following terms relate to pain?
- Endorphins
- Placebo effect

Module 8

The Nervous System and the Endocrine System: Communicating Within the Body

In light of the complexity of individual neurons and the neurotransmission process, it should come as no surprise that the connections and structures formed by the neurons are complicated. Because each neuron can be connected to 80,000 other neurons, the total number of possible connections is astonishing. For instance, estimates of the number of neural connections within the brain fall in the neighborhood of 10 quadrillion–a 1 followed by 16 zeros–and some experts put the number even higher. However, connections among neurons are not the only means of communication within the body; as we'll see, the endocrine system, which secretes chemical messages that circulate through the blood, also communicates messages that influence behavior and many aspects of biological functioning (Boahen, 2005; Heintz, Brander, & White, 2015).

The Nervous System: Linking Neurons

Whatever the actual number of neural connections, the human nervous system has both logic and elegance. We turn now to a discussion of its basic structures.

CENTRAL AND PERIPHERAL NERVOUS SYSTEMS

As you can see from the schematic representation in Figure 1, the nervous system is divided into two main parts: the central nervous system and the peripheral nervous system. The **central nervous system (CNS)** is composed of the brain and spinal cord. The **spinal cord,** which is about the thickness of a pencil, contains a bundle of neurons that leaves the brain and runs down the length of the back (see Figure 2). As you can see in Figure 2, the spinal cord is the primary means for transmitting messages between the brain and the rest of the body.

However, the spinal cord is not just a communication channel. It also controls some simple behaviors on its own, without any help from the brain. An example is the way the knee jerks forward when it is tapped with a rubber hammer. This behavior is a type of **reflex,** an automatic, involuntary response to an incoming stimulus. A reflex is also at work when you touch a hot stove and immediately withdraw your hand. Although the brain eventually analyzes and reacts to the situation ("Ouch–hot stove–pull away!"), the initial withdrawal is directed only by neurons in the spinal cord.

Several kinds of neurons are involved in reflexes. **Sensory (afferent) neurons** transmit information from the perimeter of the body to the central nervous system and the brain. For example, touching a hot stove sends a message to the brain (hot!) via sensory neurons. **Motor (efferent) neurons** communicate information in the opposite direction, sending messages from the brain and nervous system to the muscles

central nervous system (CNS) The part of the nervous system that includes the brain and spinal cord. (Module 8)

spinal cord A bundle of neurons that leaves the brain and runs down the length of the back and is the main means for transmitting messages between the brain and the body. (Module 8)

reflex An automatic, involuntary response to an incoming stimulus. (Module 8)

sensory (afferent) neurons Neurons that transmit information from the perimeter of the body to the nervous system and brain. (Module 8)

motor (efferent) neurons Neurons that communicate information from the brain and nervous system to muscles and glands. (Module 8)

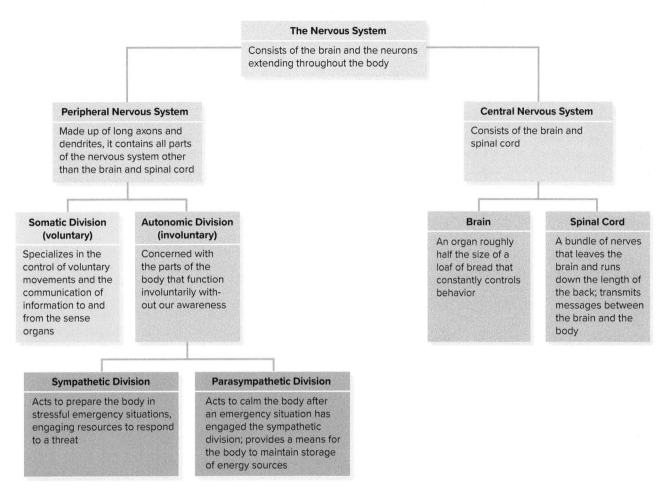

The Nervous System

Consists of the brain and the neurons extending throughout the body

Peripheral Nervous System

Made up of long axons and dendrites, it contains all parts of the nervous system other than the brain and spinal cord

Central Nervous System

Consists of the brain and spinal cord

Somatic Division (voluntary)

Specializes in the control of voluntary movements and the communication of information to and from the sense organs

Autonomic Division (involuntary)

Concerned with the parts of the body that function involuntarily without our awareness

Brain

An organ roughly half the size of a loaf of bread that constantly controls behavior

Spinal Cord

A bundle of nerves that leaves the brain and runs down the length of the back; transmits messages between the brain and the body

Sympathetic Division

Acts to prepare the body in stressful emergency situations, engaging resources to respond to a threat

Parasympathetic Division

Acts to calm the body after an emergency situation has engaged the sympathetic division; provides a means for the body to maintain storage of energy sources

FIGURE 1 A schematic diagram of the relationship of the parts of the nervous system.

Central Nervous System

Brain

Spinal cord

Peripheral Nervous System

Spinal nerves

FIGURE 2 The central nervous system consists of the brain and spinal cord, and the peripheral nervous system encompasses the network of nerves connecting the brain and spinal cord to other parts of the body.

©Larry Williams/Blend Images/Corbis

Study Alert

Use Figures 1 and 2 to learn the components of the central and peripheral nervous systems.

and glands. When the brain sends a message to the muscles of the hand (hot–move away!), the message travels via motor neurons.

The importance of the spinal cord and reflexes is illustrated by the outcome of accidents in which the cord is injured or severed. In some cases, injury results in *quadriplegia*, a condition in which people lose voluntary muscle movement below the neck. In a less severe but still disabling condition, *paraplegia*, people are unable to voluntarily move any muscles in the lower half of the body.

peripheral nervous system The part of the nervous system that includes the autonomic and somatic subdivisions; made up of neurons with long axons and dendrites, it branches out from the spinal cord and brain and reaches the extremities of the body. (Module 8)

As suggested by its name, the **peripheral nervous system** branches out from the spinal cord and brain and reaches the extremities of the body. Made up of neurons with long axons and dendrites, the peripheral nervous system encompasses all the parts of the nervous system other than the brain and spinal cord. There are two major divisions of the peripheral nervous system—the somatic division and the autonomic division—both of which connect the central nervous system with the sense organs, muscles, glands, and other organs.

somatic division The part of the peripheral nervous system that specializes in the control of voluntary movements and the communication of information to and from the sense organs. (Module 8)

The **somatic division** of the peripheral nervous system specializes in the control of voluntary movements, such as the motion of the eyes to read this sentence or those of the hand to scroll down a page. The somatic division also communicates information to and from the sense organs.

autonomic division The part of the peripheral nervous system that controls involuntary movement of the heart, glands, lungs, and other organs. (Module 8)

The **autonomic division** of the peripheral nervous system controls the parts of the body that keep us alive—the heart, blood vessels, glands, lungs, and other organs that function involuntarily without our awareness. As you are reading at this moment, the autonomic division of the peripheral nervous system is pumping blood through your body, pushing your lungs in and out, and overseeing the digestion of your last meal.

ACTIVATING THE DIVISIONS OF THE AUTONOMIC NERVOUS SYSTEM

The autonomic division plays a particularly crucial role during emergencies. Suppose that as you are reading, you suddenly sense that a stranger is watching you through the window. As you look up, you see the glint of something that might be a knife. As confusion clouds your mind and fear overcomes your attempts to think rationally, what happens to your body? If you are like most people, you react immediately on a physiological level. Your heart rate increases, you begin to sweat, and you develop goose bumps all over your body.

sympathetic division The part of the autonomic division of the nervous system that acts to prepare the body for action in stressful situations, engaging all the organism's resources to respond to a threat. (Module 8)

The physiological changes that occur during a crisis result from the activation of one of the two parts of the autonomic nervous system: the **sympathetic division.** The sympathetic division acts to prepare the body for action in stressful situations by engaging all of the organism's resources to run away or to confront the threat. This is often called the "fight-or-flight" response.

parasympathetic division The part of the autonomic division of the nervous system that acts to calm the body after an emergency has ended. (Module 8)

In contrast, the **parasympathetic division** acts to calm the body after the emergency has ended. When you find, for instance, that the stranger at the window is actually your roommate, who has lost his keys and is climbing in the window to avoid waking you, your parasympathetic division begins to take over, lowering your heart rate, stopping your sweating, and returning your body to the state it was in before you became alarmed. The parasympathetic division also directs the body to store energy for use in emergencies.

The sympathetic and parasympathetic divisions work together to regulate many functions of the body (see Figure 3). For instance, sexual arousal is controlled by the parasympathetic division, but sexual orgasm is a function of the sympathetic division. The sympathetic and parasympathetic divisions also are involved in a number of disorders. For example, one explanation of documented examples of "voodoo death"—in which a person is literally scared to death resulting from a voodoo curse—may be produced by overstimulation of the sympathetic division due to extreme fear.

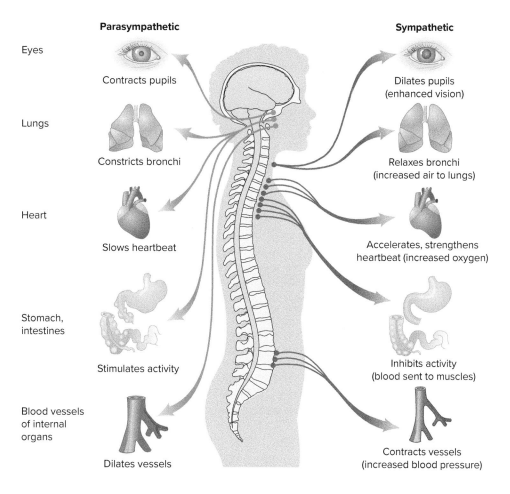

Parasympathetic

Eyes — Contracts pupils

Lungs — Constricts bronchi

Heart — Slows heartbeat

Stomach, intestines — Stimulates activity

Blood vessels of internal organs — Dilates vessels

Sympathetic

Dilates pupils (enhanced vision)

Relaxes bronchi (increased air to lungs)

Accelerates, strengthens heartbeat (increased oxygen)

Inhibits activity (blood sent to muscles)

Contracts vessels (increased blood pressure)

FIGURE 3 The major functions of the autonomic nervous system. The sympathetic division acts to prepare certain organs of the body for stressful situations, and the parasympathetic division acts to calm the body after the emergency has passed. Can you explain why each response of the sympathetic division might be useful in an emergency? ©McGraw-Hill Global Education Holdings LLC, 2001.

PsychTech
Rob Summers, who was paralyzed when hit by a car at age 20, took his first steps 5 years later after he received an experimental treatment in which electrodes were implanted into his back to stimulate his spinal cord.

From the perspective of...

A Health-Care Provider How would an understanding of the nervous system be valuable in your job as a medical care provider?

©Rubberball Productions/Getty Images

The Evolutionary Foundations of the Nervous System

The complexities of the nervous system can be better understood if we take the course of evolution into consideration. The forerunner of the human nervous system is found in the earliest simple organisms to have a spinal cord. Basically, those organisms were simple input-output devices: When the upper side of the spinal cord was stimulated by, for instance, being touched, the organism reacted with a simple response, such as jerking away. Such responses were completely a consequence of the organism's genetic makeup.

Over millions of years, the spinal cord became more specialized, and organisms became capable of distinguishing between different kinds of stimuli and responding appropriately to them. Ultimately, a portion of the spinal cord evolved into what we would consider a primitive brain.

Today, the nervous system is *hierarchically organized*, meaning that relatively newer (from an evolutionary point of view) and more sophisticated regions of the brain regulate the older, and more primitive, parts of the nervous system. As we move up along the spinal cord and continue upward into the brain then, the functions controlled by the various regions become progressively more advanced.

Why should we care about the evolutionary background of the human nervous system? The answer comes from researchers working in the area of **evolutionary psychology,** the branch of psychology that seeks to identify how behavior is influenced and produced by our genetic inheritance from our ancestors.

evolutionary psychology The branch of psychology that seeks to identify behavior patterns that are a result of our genetic inheritance from our ancestors. (Module 8)

Evolutionary psychologists argue that the course of evolution is reflected in the structure and functioning of the nervous system and that evolutionary factors consequently have a significant influence on our everyday behavior. Their work, in conjunction with the research of scientists studying genetics, biochemistry, and medicine, has led to an understanding of how our behavior is affected by heredity, our genetically determined heritage.

Evolutionary psychologists have spawned a new and increasingly influential field: behavioral genetics. As we will discuss further in the chapter on development, **behavioral genetics** is the study of the effects of heredity on behavior. Consistent with the evolutionary perspective, behavioral genetics researchers are finding increasing evidence that cognitive abilities, personality traits, sexual orientation, and psychological disorders are determined to some extent by genetic factors (Maxson, 2013; Appelbaum, Scurich, & Raad, 2015; Barbaro et al., 2017).

behavioral genetics The study of the effects of heredity on behavior. (Module 8)

The Endocrine System: Of Chemicals and Glands

Another of the body's communication systems, the **endocrine system** is a chemical communication network that sends messages throughout the body via the bloodstream. Its job is to secrete **hormones,** chemicals that circulate through the blood and regulate the functioning or growth of the body. It also influences–and is influenced by–the functioning of the nervous system. Although the endocrine system is not part of the brain, it is closely linked to the hypothalamus.

endocrine system A chemical communication network that sends messages throughout the body via the bloodstream. (Module 8)

hormones Chemicals that circulate through the blood and regulate the functioning or growth of the body. (Module 8)

As chemical messengers, hormones are like neurotransmitters, although their speed and mode of transmission are quite different. Whereas neural messages are measured in thousandths of a second, hormonal communications may take minutes to reach their destination. Furthermore, neural messages move through neurons in specific lines (like a signal carried by wires strung along telephone poles), whereas hormones travel throughout the body, similar to the way radio waves are transmitted across the entire landscape. Just as radio waves evoke a response only when a radio is tuned to the correct station, hormones flowing through the bloodstream activate only those cells that are receptive and "tuned" to the appropriate hormonal message.

pituitary gland The major component of the endocrine system, or "master gland," that secretes hormones that control growth and other parts of the endocrine system. (Module 8)

A key component of the endocrine system is the tiny **pituitary gland,** which is found near–and regulated by–the hypothalamus in the brain. The pituitary gland has sometimes been called the "master gland" because it controls the functioning of the rest of the endocrine system. But the pituitary gland is more than just the taskmaster of other glands; it has important functions in its own right. For instance, hormones secreted by the pituitary gland control growth. Extremely short people and unusually tall ones usually have pituitary gland abnormalities. Other endocrine glands, shown in Figure 4, affect emotional reactions, sexual urges, and energy levels.

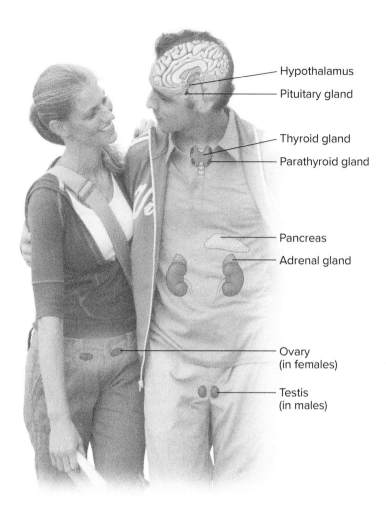

Hypothalamus

Pituitary gland

Thyroid gland

Parathyroid gland

Pancreas

Adrenal gland

Ovary
(in females)

Testis
(in males)

FIGURE 4 Location and function of the major endocrine glands. The pituitary gland controls the functioning of the other endocrine glands and, in turn, is regulated by the hypothalamus.
©Laurence Mouton/Getty Images

Despite its designation as the "master gland," the pituitary is actually a servant of the brain because the brain is ultimately responsible for the endocrine system's functioning. The brain maintains the internal balance of the body through the hypothalamus.

Individual hormones can wear many hats, depending on circumstances. For example, the hormone oxytocin is at the root of many of life's satisfactions and pleasures. In new mothers, oxytocin produces an urge to nurse newborn offspring. The same hormone also seems to stimulate cuddling between species members. And–at least in rats–it encourages sexually active males to seek out females more passionately and females to be more receptive to males' sexual advances. There's even evidence that oxytocin is related to the development of trust in others, helping to grease the wheels of effective social interaction (Guastella, Mitchell, & Dadds, 2008; De Dreu et al., 2011; de Visser et al., 2017).

Although hormones are produced naturally by the endocrine system, the ingestion of artificial hormones has proved to be both beneficial and potentially dangerous. For example, before the early 2000s, physicians frequently prescribed hormone replacement therapy to treat symptoms of menopause in older women. However, because recent research suggests that the treatment has potentially dangerous side effects, health experts now warn that in many cases, the dangers outweigh the benefits (Alexandersen, Karsdal, & Christiansen, 2009; Jacobs et al., 2013; Doty et al., 2015).

The use of testosterone, a male hormone, and drugs known as *steroids*, which act like testosterone, is increasingly common. For athletes and others who want to bulk up their appearance, steroids provide a way to add muscle weight and increase strength.

Study Alert

The endocrine system produces hormones, chemicals that circulate through the body via the bloodstream.

Steroids can provide added muscle and strength, but they have dangerous side effects. A number of well-known athletes in a variety of sports, such as baseball player Alex Rodriguez, pictured here, have been accused of using the drugs illegally. In fact, a number of them have publicly said they have used them.
©Corey Sipkin/NY Daily News Archive/Getty Images

However, these drugs can lead to stunted growth, shrinking of the testicles, heart attacks, strokes, and cancer, making them extremely dangerous. Furthermore, they can even produce violent behavior. For example, in one tragic case, professional wrestler Chris Benoit strangled his wife, suffocated his son, and later hanged himself–acts that were attributed to his use of steroids (Pagonis, Angelopoulos, & Koukoulis, 2006; Sandomir, 2007; Zahnow et al., 2017).

AP MODULE 8: THE NERVOUS SYSTEM AND THE ENDOCRINE SYSTEM: COMMUNICATING WITHIN THE BODY

AP SUMMARY

- Psychology has an abiding interest in how heredity, environment, and evolution work together to shape behavior.
- Evolutionary psychology, the branch of psychology that seeks to identify behavior patterns that are a result of our genetic inheritance, has led to increased understanding of the evolutionary basis of the structure and organization of the human nervous system.
- Behavioral genetics, a newer field in psychology, studies the effects of heredity on behavior.
- The endocrine system affects behavior.
- The endocrine system secretes hormones, chemicals that regulate the functioning of the body, via the

bloodstream. Hormones are similar to neurotransmitters but differ in speed and mode of transportation.
- Endocrine glands affect emotion reactions, sexual urges, and energy levels.
- The pituitary gland, also known as the "master gland," secretes growth hormones and influences the release of hormones by other endocrine glands and in turn is regulated by the hypothalamus.
- The nervous system is made up of two main parts: the central nervous system (the brain and spinal cord) and the peripheral nervous system.
- The peripheral nervous system is made up of the somatic division, which controls voluntary movements and the communication of information to and from the

sense organs, and the autonomic division, which controls involuntary functions such as those of the heart, blood vessels, and lungs.

- The autonomic division of the peripheral nervous system is further divided into the sympathetic and parasympathetic divisions. The sympathetic division prepares the body in emergency situations, and the parasympathetic division helps the body return to its typical resting state.
- Several kinds of neurons are involved in a reflex, an automatic, involuntary response to an incoming stimulus. Sensory (afferent) neurons transmit information into the central nervous system, while motor (efferent) neurons send messages out from the brain and nervous system to the muscles and glands.

AP KEY TERMS

central nervous system
  (CNS)
spinal cord
reflex
sensory (afferent) neurons
motor (efferent) neurons
peripheral nervous system
somatic division

autonomic division
sympathetic division
parasympathetic division
evolutionary psychology
behavioral genetics
endocrine system
hormones
pituitary gland

AP TEST PRACTICE

Section I: Multiple Choice

1. Casey was startled by a large moving object in the middle of the night. She was sweating and her heart was beating. Her biological state resulted from the activation of what nervous system?
   A. Sympathetic
   B. Parasympathetic
   C. Central
   D. Cerebral
   E. Somatic

2. Which of the following correctly identifies the divisions of the nervous system from broadest to specific?
   A. Autonomic; Parasympathetic
   B. Somatic; Central
   C. Sympathetic; Parasympathetic
   D. Autonomic; Peripheral
   E. Sympathetic; Central

3. The endocrine system is linked to the nervous system because it is controlled by what brain part?
   A. Hippocampus
   B. Hypothalamus
   C. Thalamus
   D. Pineal
   E. Thyroid

Section II: Free Response

Linda is a new mother and spends lots of time cuddling with her daughter. Explain how the following terms are involved in their relationship.

- Parasympathetic nervous system
- Motor neurons
- Hormones
- Mirror neurons
- Glutamate

Module 9
The Brain

It is not much to look at. Soft, spongy, mottled, and pinkish-gray in color, it hardly can be said to possess much in the way of physical beauty. Despite its physical appearance, however, it ranks as the greatest natural marvel that we know and has a beauty and sophistication all its own.

The object to which this description applies: the brain. The brain is responsible for our loftiest thoughts–and our most primitive urges. It is the overseer of the intricate workings of the human body. If one were to attempt to design a computer to mimic the range of capabilities of the brain, the task would be nearly impossible; in fact, it has proved difficult even to come close. The sheer quantity of nerve cells in the brain is enough to daunt even the most ambitious computer engineer. Many billions of neurons make up a structure weighing just 3 pounds in the average adult. However, it is not the number of cells that is the most astounding thing about the brain but its ability to allow the human intellect to flourish by guiding our behavior and thoughts.

We turn now to a consideration of the particular structures of the brain and the primary functions to which they are related. However, a caution is in order. Although we'll discuss specific areas of the brain in relation to specific behaviors, this approach is an oversimplification. No straightforward one-to-one correspondence exists between a distinct part of the brain and a particular behavior. Instead, behavior is produced by complex interconnections among sets of neurons in many areas of the brain: Our behavior, emotions, thoughts, hopes, and dreams are produced by a variety of neurons throughout the nervous system working in concert.

Studying the Brain's Structure and Functions: Spying on the Brain

The brain has posed a continual challenge to those who would study it. For most of history, its examination was possible only after an individual had died. Only then could the skull be opened and the brain cut into without serious injury. Although informative, this procedure could hardly tell us much about the functioning of the healthy brain.

Today, however, brain-scanning techniques provide a window into the living brain. Using these techniques, investigators can take a "snapshot" of the internal workings of the brain without having to cut open a person's skull. The most important scanning techniques, illustrated in Figure 1, are the electroencephalogram (EEG), positron emission tomography (PET), functional magnetic resonance imaging (fMRI), and transcranial magnetic stimulation imaging (TMS).

The *electroencephalogram (EEG)* records electrical activity in the brain through electrodes placed on the outside of the skull. Although traditionally the EEG could produce only a graph of electrical wave patterns, new techniques are now used to transform the brain's electrical activity into a pictorial representation of the brain that allows more precise diagnosis of disorders such as epilepsy and learning disabilities.

The brain (shown here in cross-section) may not be much to look at, but it represents one of the great marvels of human development. Why do most scientists believe that it will be difficult, if not impossible, to duplicate the brain's abilities?

©Martin M. Rotker/Science Source

(a) EEG

(b) fMRI

(c) PET scan

(d) TMS Apparatus

FIGURE 1 Brain scans produced by different techniques. (a) A computer-produced EEG image. (b) The fMRI scan uses a magnetic field to provide a detailed view of brain activity on a moment-by-moment basis. (c) The PET scan displays the functioning of the brain at a given moment. (d) Transcranial magnetic stimulation (TMS), the newest type of scan, produces a momentary disruption in an area of the brain, allowing researchers to see what activities are controlled by that area. TMS also has the potential to treat some psychological disorders.
(a) ©SPL/Science Source; (b) ©Steger Photo/Photolibrary/Getty Images; (c) ©Science History Images/Alamy Stock Photo; (d) ©Garo/Phanie/Science Source

Functional magnetic resonance imaging (fMRI) scans provide a detailed, three-dimensional computer-generated image of brain structures and activity by aiming a powerful magnetic field at the body. With fMRI scanning, it is possible to produce vivid, detailed images of the functioning of the brain.

Using fMRI scans, researchers are able to view features of less than a millimeter in size and view changes occurring in intervals of $1/10$ of a second. For example, fMRI scans can show the operation of individual bundles of nerves by tracing the flow of blood, opening the way for improved diagnosis of ailments ranging from chronic back pain to nervous system disorders such as strokes, multiple sclerosis, and Alzheimer's. Scans using fMRI are routinely used in planning brain surgery because they can help surgeons distinguish areas of the brain involved in normal and disturbed functioning (Loitfelder et al., 2011; Hurschler et al., 2015).

Positron emission tomography (PET) scans show biochemical activity within the brain at a given moment. PET scans begin with the injection of a radioactive (but safe) liquid into the bloodstream, which makes its way to the brain. By locating radiation within the brain, a computer can determine which are the more active regions, providing a striking picture of the brain at work. For example, PET scans may be used in cases of memory problems, seeking to identify the presence of brain tumors (Gronholm et al., 2005; McMurtray et al., 2007).

Transcranial magnetic stimulation (TMS) uses magnetic fields to produce an understanding of the functioning of the brain. In TMS, a tiny region of the brain is bombarded by a strong magnetic field that causes a momentary interruption of electrical activity. Researchers then are able to note the effects of this interruption on normal brain functioning.

One of the newest procedures used to study the brain, TMS is sometimes called a "virtual lesion" because it produces effects similar to what would occur if areas of the brain were physically cut. The enormous advantage of TMS, of course, is that the virtual cut is only temporary. In addition to identifying areas of the brain that are

Study Alert
Remember how EEG, fMRI, PET, and TMS scans differ in the ways that they produce an image of the brain.

responsible for particular functions, TMS has the potential to treat certain kinds of psychological disorders, such as depression and schizophrenia, by shooting brief magnetic pulses through the brain (Pallanti & Bernardi, 2009; Prasser et al., 2015).

Future discoveries may yield even more sophisticated methods of examining the brain. For example, the emerging field of *optogenetics* involves genetic engineering and the use of special types of light to view individual circuits of neurons. In addition, researchers are developing *hydrogel-embedding* methods. which allow observation of individual brain cells and the wiring of brain circuitry (Deisseroth, 2016; Shirai & Hayashi-Takagi, 2017; Yang, Song, & Qing, 2017).

Advances in our understanding of the brain also are paving the way for the development of new methods for harnessing the brain's neural signals. We consider some of these intriguing findings in *Applying Psychology in the 21st Century*.

AP | APPLYING PSYCHOLOGY IN THE 21ST CENTURY

BYPASSING BROKEN NEURAL PATHWAYS WITH A CHIP IN THE BRAIN

Ian Burkhart was a typical college freshman who was just enjoying a fun, leisurely day with his family at a beach in North Carolina when his whole life changed forever. Ian jumped headfirst into an approaching wave and struck his head on the soft sand of the ocean floor, breaking his neck. From that moment on, Ian permanently lost the feeling and movement in his hands, legs, and feet. He would never walk again or be able to complete even the simplest task with his hands, such as buttoning his shirt or stirring his coffee (Carey, 2016).

But advancements in neural engineering gave Ian a seemingly miraculous opportunity to use his hands again, albeit only for a limited time. To begin, in a delicate brain surgery, doctors implanted a chip in Ian's skull that comprises many tiny electrodes. Each electrode can detect the firing of an individual neuron within a very specific region of Ian's motor cortex–the region responsible for hand movements. Doctors identified this region with brain imaging before the surgery and then further refined their placement of the electrodes during the surgery to isolate nearly 100 specific neurons. The chip sends signals to a port in Ian's skull, which can be connected to computer equipment in the researchers' lab (Bouton et al., 2016).

After Ian healed from the surgery, the next step was to train both Ian and the computer software. Ian spent many hours watching video simulations of specific

©Lee Powell/The Washington Post via Getty Images

hand and finger movements. As Ian watched, he was instructed to imagine himself making those movements. The neurons in his motor cortex responsible for hand movement would fire, attempting to send a signal to Ian's paralyzed hand to move in the way Ian was imagining. Computer software read and analyzed the specific pattern of firing in the neurons monitored by the chip in Ian's skull, learning what patterns corresponded to specific movements. The computer then sent instructions to a device attached to Ian's forearm that could stimulate specific muscles controlling Ian's hand and fingers. So instead of the signal being sent directly from Ian's brain to his hand via motor pathways in the spinal cord, as would happen in a nonparalyzed person, the signal was instead being relayed from the brain to the muscles by an external computer. In this

way, the technology bypassed the blockage caused by Ian's damaged spinal cord.

It took a great deal of effort and months of training, but Ian first regained the ability to close and open his hand just by thinking about it. Eventually, he became able to grasp and lift items with his whole hand and with his fingers, allowing him to lift and pour from a bottle and then pick up a small stirrer and use it. He even learned to manipulate a video game controller. Such reanimation, as it's called, of a paralyzed limb was until recently the stuff of science fiction only. It became a reality for Ian, who is the first person to successfully control his muscles using his own neural signals relayed by computer.

Sadly, the success Ian experienced in the lab will not reverse his paralysis or help him function better in real life. The neural bypass only works when connected to bulky computers and other devices in the researchers' lab, which are not portable at all. At the conclusion of the research, Ian returned to his new normal life of dependence on others for care. Still, the research represented a major advancement toward a day when such technology could be put to more practical use, and Ian is gratified to have played a part in bringing a successful treatment for paralysis one step closer to fruition (Bouton et al., 2016).

AP SKILL: SCIENTIFIC INVESTIGATION

1. Summarize the research on limb reanimation.
2. Describe implications or limitations of the research.

The Central Core: Our "Old Brain"

Although the capabilities of the human brain far exceed those of the brain of any other species, humans share some basic functions, such as breathing, eating, and sleeping, with more primitive animals. Not surprisingly, those activities are directed by a relatively primitive part of the brain. A portion of the brain known as the **central core** (see Figure 2) is quite similar in all vertebrates (species with backbones). The central core is sometimes referred to as the "old brain" because its evolution can be traced back some 500 million years to primitive structures found in nonhuman species.

If we were to move up the spinal cord from the base of the skull to locate the structures of the central core of the brain, the first part we would come to would be the *hindbrain*, which contains the medulla, pons, and cerebellum (see Figure 3). The *medulla* controls a number of critical body functions, the most important of which are breathing and heartbeat. The *pons* is a bridge in the hindbrain. Containing large bundles of nerves, the pons acts as a transmitter of motor information, coordinating muscles and integrating movement between the right and left halves of the body. It is also involved in regulating sleep.

The **cerebellum** extends from the rear of the hindbrain. Without the help of the cerebellum, we would be unable to walk a straight line without staggering and lurching forward, for it is the job of the cerebellum to control bodily balance. It constantly monitors feedback from the muscles to coordinate their placement, movement, and tension. In fact, drinking too much alcohol seems to depress the activity of the cerebellum, leading to the unsteady gait and movement characteristic of drunkenness. The cerebellum is also involved in several intellectual functions, ranging from the analysis and coordination of sensory information to problem solving (Vandervert, Schimpf, & Liu, 2007; Swain, Kerr, & Thompson, 2011; Ronconi et al., 2017).

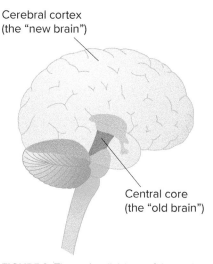

FIGURE 2 The major divisions of the brain: the cerebral cortex and the central core.
©McGraw-Hill Global Education Holdings LLC, 2000.

central core The "old brain," which controls basic functions such as eating and sleeping and is common to all vertebrates. (Module 9)

cerebellum (ser-uh-BELL-um) The part of the brain that controls bodily balance. (Module 9)

Hypothalamus
Responsible for regulating basic biological needs: hunger, thirst, temperature control

Pituitary Gland
"Master" gland that regulates other endocrine glands

Pons
Involved in sleep and arousal

Reticular Formation
A network of neurons related to sleep, arousal, and attention

Spinal Cord
Responsible for communication between brain and rest of body; involved with simple reflexes

Cerebral Cortex
The "new brain" responsible for the most sophisticated processing

Corpus Callosum
Bridge of fibers passing information between the two cerebral hemispheres

Thalamus
Relay center for cortex; handles incoming and outgoing signals

Cerebellum
Controls bodily balance

Medulla
Responsible for regulating largely unconscious functions such as breathing and circulation

FIGURE 3 The major structures in the brain.
Source: Adapted from Bloom, F. (1975). *Brain, mind, and behavior,* New York: Educational Broadcasting Corp.; (Photo): ©Dana Neely/Taxi/Getty Images

reticular formation The part of the brain extending from the medulla through the pons; it is related to changes in the level of arousal of the body. (Module 9)

thalamus The part of the brain located in the middle of the central core that acts primarily to relay information about the senses. (Module 9)

hypothalamus A tiny part of the brain, located below the thalamus, that maintains homeostasis and produces and regulates vital behavior, such as eating, drinking, and sexual behavior. (Module 9)

The **reticular formation** is a nerve network in the brain that extends from the medulla through the pons, passing through the middle section of the brain, called the *midbrain,* and into the front-most part of the brain, called the *forebrain.* Like an ever-vigilant guard, the reticular formation produces general arousal of our body. If, for example, we are startled by a loud noise, the reticular formation can prompt a heightened state of awareness to determine whether a response is necessary. The reticular formation also helps regulate our sleep-wake cycle by filtering out background stimuli to allow us to sleep undisturbed.

The **thalamus,** which is hidden within the forebrain, acts primarily as a relay station for information about the senses. Messages from the eyes, ears, and skin travel to the thalamus to be communicated upward to higher parts of the brain. The thalamus also integrates information from higher parts of the brain, sorting it out so that it can be sent to the cerebellum and medulla.

The **hypothalamus** is located just below the thalamus. Although tiny–about the size of a fingertip–the hypothalamus plays an extremely important role. One of its major functions is to maintain *homeostasis,* a steady internal environment for the body. The hypothalamus helps provide a constant body temperature and monitors the amount of nutrients stored in the cells. A second major function is equally important: the hypothalamus produces and regulates behavior that is critical to the basic survival of the species, such as eating, self-protection, and sex.

The Limbic System: Beyond the Central Core

In an eerie view of the future, science fiction writers have suggested that people someday will routinely have electrodes implanted in their brains. Those electrodes will permit them to receive tiny shocks that will produce the sensation of pleasure by stimulating certain centers of the brain. When they feel upset, people will simply activate their electrodes to achieve an immediate high.

limbic system The part of the brain that controls eating, aggression, and reproduction. (Module 9)

Although far-fetched–and ultimately improbable–such a futuristic fantasy is based on fact. The brain does have pleasure centers in several areas, including some in the **limbic system.** Consisting of a series of doughnut-shaped structures that include the *amygdala* and *hippocampus,* the limbic system borders the top of the central core and has connections with the cerebral cortex (see Figure 4).

The structures of the limbic system jointly control a variety of basic functions relating to emotions and self-preservation, such as eating, aggression, and reproduction. Injury to the limbic system can produce striking changes in behavior. For example, injury to the amygdala, which is involved in fear and aggression, can turn animals that are usually docile and tame into belligerent savages. Conversely, animals that are usually wild and uncontrollable may become meek and obedient following injury to the amygdala (Gontkovsky, 2005; Smith et al., 2013; Reznikova et al., 2015).

Research examining the effects of mild electric shocks to parts of the limbic system and other parts of the brain has produced some thought-provoking findings. In one classic experiment, rats that pressed a bar received mild electric stimulation through an electrode implanted in their brains, which produced pleasurable feelings. Even starving rats on their way to food would stop to press the bar as many times as they could. Some rats would actually stimulate themselves literally thousands of times an hour–until they collapsed with fatigue (Routtenberg & Lindy, 1965; Fountas & Smith, 2007).

Some humans have also experienced the extraordinarily pleasurable quality of certain kinds of stimulation: As part of the treatment for certain

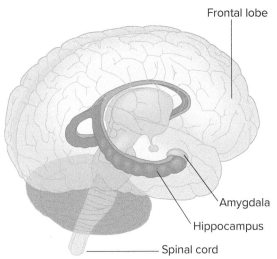

Frontal lobe

Amygdala

Hippocampus

Spinal cord

FIGURE 4 The limbic system is involved in self-preservation, learning, memory, and the experience of pleasure.

kinds of brain disorders, some people have received electrical stimulation to certain areas of the limbic system. Although at a loss to describe just what it feels like, these people report the experience to be intensely pleasurable, similar in some respects to sexual orgasm.

The limbic system and hippocampus, in particular, play an important role in learning and memory. Their importance is demonstrated in certain patients with epilepsy, who, in an effort to stop their seizures, have had portions of the limbic system removed. One unintended consequence of the surgery is that individuals sometimes have difficulty learning and remembering new information. In one case, a patient who had undergone surgery was unable to remember where he lived, although he had resided at the same address for 8 years. Further, even though the patient was able to carry on animated conversations, he was unable, a few minutes later, to recall what had been discussed (Milner, 1966; Grimm, 2011; de Voogd et al., 2017).

The limbic system, then, is involved in several important functions, including self-preservation, learning, memory, and the experience of pleasure. These functions are hardly unique to humans; in fact, the limbic system is sometimes referred to as the "animal brain" because its structures and functions are so similar to those of other mammals. To identify the part of the brain that provides the complex and subtle capabilities that are uniquely human, we need to turn to another structure—the cerebral cortex.

The Cerebral Cortex: Our "New Brain"

As we have proceeded up the spinal cord and into the brain, our discussion has centered on areas of the brain that control functions similar to those found in less sophisticated organisms. But where, you may be asking, are the portions of the brain that enable humans to do what they do best and that distinguish humans from all other animals? Those unique features of the human brain—indeed, the very capabilities that allow you to come up with such a question in the first place—are embodied in the ability to think, evaluate, and make complex judgments. The principal location of these abilities, along with many others, is the **cerebral cortex.**

The cerebral cortex is referred to as the "new brain" because of its relatively recent evolution. It consists of a mass of deeply folded, rippled, convoluted tissue. Although only about $\frac{1}{12}$ of an inch thick, it would, if flattened out, cover an area more than 2 feet square. This configuration allows the surface area of the cortex to be considerably greater than it would be if it were smoother and more uniformly packed into the skull. The uneven shape also permits a high level of integration of neurons, allowing sophisticated information processing.

The cerebral cortex consists of four major sections called **lobes.** Each lobe has specialized areas that relate to particular functions. If we take a side view of the brain, the *frontal lobes* lie at the front center of the cortex and the *parietal lobes* lie behind them. The *temporal lobes* are found in the lower-center portion of the cortex, with the *occipital lobes* lying behind them. These four sets of lobes are physically separated by deep grooves called *sulci.* Figure 5 shows the four areas.

Another way to describe the brain is in terms of the functions associated with a particular area. Figure 5 also shows the specialized regions within the lobes related to specific functions and areas of the body. Three major areas are known: the motor areas, the sensory areas, and the association areas. Although we will discuss these areas as though they were separate and independent, keep in mind that this is an oversimplification. In most instances, behavior is influenced simultaneously by several structures and areas within the brain, operating interdependently. To give one example, people use different areas of the brain when they create sentences (a verbal task) compared with when they improvise musical tunes. Furthermore, when people suffer brain injury, uninjured portions of the brain can sometimes take over the functions that were previously handled by the damaged area. In short, the brain is extraordinarily adaptable (Sacks, 2003; Boller, 2004; Brown, Martinez, & Parsons, 2006).

cerebral cortex The "new brain," responsible for the most sophisticated information processing in the brain; contains four lobes. (Module 9)

lobes The four major sections of the cerebral cortex: frontal, parietal, temporal, and occipital. (Module 9)

FIGURE 5 The cerebral cortex of the brain. The major physical structures of the cerebral cortex are called lobes. This figure also illustrates the functions associated with particular areas of the cerebral cortex. Are any areas of the cerebral cortex present in nonhuman animals?
©Ron Krisel/Getty Images

THE MOTOR AREA OF THE CORTEX

motor area The part of the cortex that is largely responsible for the body's voluntary movement. (Module 9)

If you look at the frontal lobe in Figure 5, you will see a shaded portion labeled **motor area.** This part of the cortex is largely responsible for the body's voluntary movement. Every portion of the motor area corresponds to a specific locale within the body. If we were to insert an electrode into a particular part of the motor area of the cortex and apply mild electrical stimulation, there would be involuntary movement in the corresponding part of the body. If we moved to another part of the motor area and stimulated it, a different part of the body would move.

The motor area is so well mapped that researchers have identified the amount and relative location of cortical tissue used to produce movement in specific parts of the human body. For example, the control of movements that are relatively large scale and require little precision, such as the movement of a knee or a hip, is centered in a very small space in the motor area. In contrast, movements that must be precise and delicate, such as facial expressions and finger movements, are controlled by a considerably larger portion of the motor area (Schwenkreis et al., 2007).

In short, the motor area of the cortex provides a guide to the degree of complexity and the importance of the motor capabilities of specific parts of the body. In fact, it may do even more: Increasing evidence shows that not only does the motor cortex control different parts of the body, but it may also direct body parts into complex postures, such as the stance of a football center just before the ball is snapped to the quarterback or a swimmer standing at the edge of a diving board (Pool et al., 2013; Massé-Alarie et al., 2017).

Ultimately, movement, like other behavior, is produced through the coordinated firing of a complex variety of neurons in the nervous system. The neurons that produce movement are linked in elaborate ways and work closely together.

THE SENSORY AREA OF THE CORTEX

Given the one-to-one correspondence between the motor area and body location, it is not surprising to find a similar relationship between specific portions of the cortex and specific senses. The **sensory area** of the cortex includes three regions: one that corresponds primarily to body sensations (including touch and pressure), one relating to sight, and a third relating to sound.

For instance, the *somatosensory area* in the parietal lobe encompasses specific locations associated with the ability to perceive touch and pressure in a particular area of the body. As with the motor area, the amount of brain tissue related to a particular location on the body determines the degree of sensitivity of that location. Specifically, the greater the area devoted to a specific area of the body within the cortex, the more sensitive is that area of the body.

For example, our fingers are related to a larger portion of the somatosensory area in the brain and are the most sensitive to touch. The weird-looking individual in Figure 6 shows what we would look like if the size of every external part of our body corresponded to the amount of brain tissue related to touch sensitivity.

The senses of sound and sight are also represented in specific areas of the cerebral cortex. An *auditory area* located in the temporal lobe is responsible for the sense of hearing. If the auditory area is stimulated electrically, a person will hear sounds such as clicks or hums. It also appears that particular locations within the auditory area respond to specific pitches (Tsuchida, Ueno, & Shimada, 2015; Anderson, Lazard, & Hartley, 2017).

The visual area in the cortex, located in the occipital lobe, responds in the same way to electrical stimulation. Stimulation by electrodes produces the experience of flashes of light or colors, suggesting that the raw sensory input of images from the eyes is received in this area of the brain and transformed into meaningful stimuli. The visual area provides another example of how areas of the brain are intimately related to specific areas of the body: Specific structures in the eye are related to a particular part of the cortex—with, as you might guess, more area of the brain given to the most sensitive portions of the retina (Stenbacka & Vanni, 2007; Libedinsky & Livingstone, 2011).

sensory area The site in the brain of the tissue that corresponds to each of the senses, with the degree of sensitivity related to the amount of tissue. (Module 9)

THE ASSOCIATION AREAS OF THE CORTEX

In a freak accident in 1848, an explosion drove a 3-foot-long iron bar completely through the skull of railroad worker Phineas Gage, where it remained after the accident. Amazingly, Gage survived and, despite the rod lodged through his head, a few minutes later seemed to be fine.

But he wasn't. Before the accident, Gage was hardworking and cautious. Afterward, he became irresponsible, drank heavily, and drifted from one wild scheme to another. In the words of one of his physicians, "He was 'no longer Gage'" (Harlow, 1869).

What had happened to the old Gage? Although there is no way of knowing for sure, we can speculate that the accident injured the region of Gage's cerebral cortex known as the association areas. The **association areas** are the site of higher mental processes such as thinking, language, memory, and speech.

association areas One of the major regions of the cerebral cortex; the site of the higher mental processes, such as thought, language, memory, and speech. (Module 9)

The association areas make up a large portion of the cerebral cortex. The association areas control *executive functions*, which are abilities that are related to planning, goal setting, judgment, and impulse control.

Much of our understanding of the association areas comes from patients who, like Phineas Gage, have suffered some type of brain injury. For example, when parts of the association areas are damaged, people undergo personality changes that affect their ability to make moral judgments and process emotions. At the same time, people with damage in those areas can still be capable of reasoning logically, performing calculations, and recalling information (Bechara et al., 1994).

Injuries to the association areas of the brain can produce *aphasia*, problems with language. In *Broca's aphasia*, speech becomes halting, laborious, and often ungrammatical, and a

FIGURE 6 The greater the amount of tissue in the somatosensory area of the brain that is related to a specific body part, the more sensitive is that body part. If the size of our body parts reflected the corresponding amount of brain tissue, we would look like this strange creature.
©Natural History Museum, London/Science Source

speaker is unable to find the right words. In contrast, *Wernicke's aphasia* produces difficulties both in understanding others' speech and in the production of language. The disorder is characterized by speech that sounds fluent but makes no sense, as in this example from a Wernicke's patient: "Boy, I'm sweating, I'm awful nervous, you know, once in a while I get caught up, I can't mention the tarripoi, a month ago, quite a little . . ." (Caplan, Waters, & Dede, 2007; Robson et al., 2013; Ardila, 2015).

Neuroplasticity and the Brain

Shortly after he was born, Jacob Stark's arms and legs started jerking every 20 minutes. Weeks later he could not focus his eyes on his mother's face. The diagnosis: uncontrollable epileptic seizures involving his entire brain.

His mother, Sally Stark, recalled: "When Jacob was 2½ months old, they said he would never learn to sit up, would never be able to feed himself. . . . They told us to take him home, love him, and find an institution." (Blakeslee, 1992)

Instead, Jacob had brain surgery when he was 5 months old in which physicians removed 20% of his brain. The operation was a complete success. Three years later, Jacob seemed normal in every way, with no sign of seizures.

The surgery that helped Jacob was based on the premise that the diseased part of his brain was producing seizures throughout the brain. Surgeons reasoned that if they removed the misfiring portion, the remaining parts of the brain, which appeared intact in PET scans, would take over. They correctly bet that Jacob could still lead a normal life after surgery, particularly because the surgery was being done at so young an age.

The success of Jacob's surgery illustrates that the brain has the ability to shift functions to different locations after injury to a specific area or in cases of surgery. But equally encouraging are some new findings about the *regenerative* powers of the brain and nervous system.

Scientists have learned in recent years that the brain continually changes, reorganizes itself, and is far more resilient than they once thought. **Neuroplasticity** refers to the brain's ability to change throughout the life span through the addition of new neurons, new interconnections between neurons, and the reorganization of information-processing areas.

Advances in our understanding of neuroplasticity have changed the earlier view that no new brain cells are created after childhood. The reality is very different: Not only do the interconnections between neurons become more complex throughout life, but it now appears that new neurons are also created in certain areas of the brain during adulthood—a process called *neurogenesis*. Each day, thousands of new neurons are created, especially in areas of the brain related to learning and memory (Shors, 2009; Kempermann, 2011; Apple, Fonseca, & Kokovay, 2017).

The ability of neurons to renew themselves during adulthood has significant implications for the potential treatment of disorders of the nervous system (see *Neuroscience in Your Life*). For example, drugs that trigger the development of new neurons might be used to counter such diseases as Alzheimer's, which are produced when neurons die (Waddell & Shors, 2008; Hamilton et al., 2013; Ekonomou et al., 2015).

Furthermore, specific experiences can modify the way in which information is processed. For example, if you learn to read Braille, the amount of tissue in your cortex related to sensation in the fingertips will expand. Similarly, if you take up the violin, the area of the brain that receives messages from your fingers will grow—but only relating to the fingers that actually move across the violin's strings (Schwartz & Begley, 2002; Kolb, Gibb, & Robinson, 2003).

The future also holds promise for people who suffer from the tremors and loss of motor control produced by Parkinson's disease, although the research is mired in controversy. Because Parkinson's disease is caused by a gradual loss of cells that stimulate the production of dopamine in the brain, many investigators have reasoned that a procedure that would increase the supply of dopamine might be effective. They seem to be on the right track. When *stem cells*—immature cells from human fetuses that have the potential to develop into a variety of specialized cell types, depending on where they are implanted—are

neuroplasticity The brain's ability to change throughout the life span through the addition of new neurons, new interconnections between neurons, and the reorganization of information-processing areas. (Module 9)

AP NEUROSCIENCE IN YOUR LIFE: THE PLASTIC BRAIN

The brain is highly plastic, meaning that it can change in significant ways over the course of the life span. For example, brain plasticity is apparent in patients who lose a limb due to injury. Many such patients experience pain in their missing limb, called phantom limb pain. In a recent study, brain scans of participants with phantom hand pain showed changes in activity within sensory and motor brain regions. For example, regions involved in processing elbow information migrated into regions that previously processed missing hand information.

The images below show brain activity when participants moved their elbows (left) and hands (right; imagined for amputees). In the column labeled elbows, we see differences between activity during movement and rest (yellow indicates the greatest differences) in the same areas as in the column labeled hands, indicating that activity for elbow movements has migrated into regions for hand movements (Raffin et al., 2016).

AMPUTEES

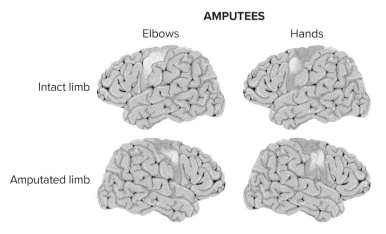

Source: Adapted from Raffin, E., Richard, N., Giraux, P., & Reilly, K. T. (2016). Primary motor cortex changes after amputation correlate with phantom limb pain and the ability to move the phantom limb. *Neuroimage, 130,* 134–144.

AP SKILL: EXPLAIN BEHAVIOR IN AUTHENTIC CONTEXT / DEFINE AND/ OR APPLY CONCEPTS

1. How is phantom limb explained with neuroplasticity?

2. With a better understanding of neuroplasticity, how could researchers use this process to improve human functioning?

3. Dr. Michael Gazzaniga, a cognitive neuroscientist and expert on split brain research, believes in neuroplasticity. Why would a patient have split-brain surgery and how could the results of the procedure apply to neuroplasticity?

injected directly into the brains of Parkinson's sufferers, they take root and stimulate dopamine production. Preliminary results have been promising, with some patients showing great improvement (Parish & Arenas, 2007; Newman & Bakay, 2008; Wang et al., 2011).

Stem cells thus hold great promise. When a stem cell divides, each newly created cell has the potential to be transformed into more specialized cells that have the potential to repair damaged cells. Because many of the most disabling diseases, ranging from cancer to stroke, result from cell damage, the potential of stem cells to revolutionize medicine is significant.

However, because the source of implanted stem cells typically is aborted fetuses, their use is controversial. Some critics have argued that the use of stem cells in research and treatment should be prohibited, while supporters argue that the potential benefits of the research are so great that stem cell research should be unrestricted. The issue has been politicized, and the question of whether and how stem cell research should be regulated is not clear (Giacomini, Baylis, & Robert, 2007; Holden, 2007; Towns, 2017).

The Specialization of the Hemispheres: Two Brains or One?

The most recent development, at least in evolutionary terms, in the organization and operation of the human brain probably occurred in the last several million years: a specialization of the functions controlled by the left and right sides of the brain (Hopkins & Cantalupo, 2008; MacNeilage, Rogers, & Vallortigara, 2009; Tommasi, 2009).

The brain is divided into two roughly mirror-image halves. Just as we have two arms, two legs, and two lungs, we have a left brain and a right brain. Because of the

hemispheres Symmetrical left and right halves of the brain that control the side of the body opposite to their location. (Module 9)

lateralization The dominance of one hemisphere of the brain in specific functions, such as language. (Module 9)

Study Alert

Although the hemispheres of the brain specialize in particular kinds of functions, the degree of specialization is not great, and the two hemispheres work interdependently.

PsychTech

Using a procedure called *hemispherectomy,* in which an entire hemisphere of the brain is removed, surgeons ended Christina Santhouse's seizures, which occurred at the rate of hundreds a day. Despite the removal of the right side of her brain, Christina recently completed a master's degree in speech pathology.

way nerves in the brain are connected to the rest of the body, these symmetrical left and right halves, called **hemispheres,** control motion in–and receive sensation from– the side of the body opposite their location. The left hemisphere of the brain, then, generally controls the right side of the body, and the right hemisphere controls the left side of the body. Thus, damage to the right side of the brain is typically indicated by functional difficulties in the left side of the body.

Despite the appearance of similarity between the two hemispheres of the brain, they are somewhat different in the functions they control and in the ways they control them. Certain behaviors are more likely to reflect activity in one hemisphere than in the other, or are **lateralized.**

For example, for most people, language processing occurs more in the left side of the brain. In general, the left hemisphere concentrates more on tasks that require verbal competence, such as speaking, reading, thinking, and reasoning. In addition, the left hemisphere tends to process information sequentially, one bit at a time (Hines, 2004).

The right hemisphere has its own strengths, particularly in nonverbal areas such as the understanding of spatial relationships, recognition of patterns and drawings, music, and emotional expression. The right hemisphere tends to process information globally, considering it as a whole (Holowka & Petitto, 2002; Gotts et al., 2013; Longo et al., 2015).

The degree and nature of lateralization vary from one person to another. If, like most people, you are right-handed, the control of language is probably concentrated more in your left hemisphere. By contrast, if you are among the 10% of people who are left-handed or are ambidextrous (you use both hands interchangeably), it is much more likely that the language centers of your brain are located more in the right hemisphere or are divided equally between the left and right hemispheres.

Keep in mind that despite the different strengths of the two hemispheres, the differences in specialization between the hemispheres are not great. Furthermore, the two hemispheres of the brain function in tandem. It is a mistake to think of particular kinds of information as being processed solely in the right or the left hemisphere. The hemispheres work interdependently in deciphering, interpreting, and reacting to the world.

In addition, people who suffer injury to the left side of the brain and lose linguistic capabilities often recover the ability to speak: The right side of the brain often takes over some of the functions of the left side, especially in young children; the extent of recovery increases the earlier the injury occurs (Johnston, 2004).

Furthermore, not every researcher believes that the differences between the two hemispheres of the brain are terribly significant. According to neuroscientist Stephen Kosslyn, a more critical difference occurs in processing between the upper and lower halves of the brain. In his theory, the top-brain system of the brain specializes in planning and goal-setting. In contrast, the bottom-brain system helps classify information coming from our senses, allowing us to understand and classify information. It is still too early to know the accuracy of Kosslyn's theory, but it provides an intriguing alternative to the notion that left-right brain differences are of primary importance (Kosslyn & Miller, 2013).

In any case, evidence continues to grow that the difference between processing in the left and right hemispheres are meaningful. For example, researchers have unearthed evidence that there may be subtle differences in brain lateralization patterns between males and females and members of different cultures, as we see in *Exploring Diversity.*

From the perspective of...

An Office Worker Could personal differences in people's specialization of right and left hemispheres be related to occupational success? For example, might a designer who relies on spatial skills have a different pattern of hemispheric specialization than does a lawyer?

©Caia Images/Glow Images

Exploring Diversity

Human Diversity and the Brain

The interplay of biology and environment in behavior is especially clear when we consider evidence suggesting that even in brain structure and function, there are both sex and cultural differences. Let's consider sex differences first. Accumulating evidence seems to show intriguing differences in males' and females' brain lateralization and weight (Boles, 2005; Clements, Rimrodt, & Abel, 2006; Joel & McCarthy, 2017).

For instance, the two sexes show differences in the speed at which their brains develop. Young girls show earlier development in the frontal lobes, which control aggressiveness and language development. On the other hand, boys' brains develop faster in the visual region that facilitates visual and spatial tasks such as geometry (Giedd et al., 2010; Raznahan et al., 2010).

Furthermore, most males tend to show greater lateralization of language in the left hemisphere. For them, language is clearly relegated largely to the left side of the brain. In contrast, women display less lateralization, with language abilities apt to be more evenly divided between the two hemispheres. Such differences in brain lateralization may account, in part, for the superiority often displayed by females on certain measures of verbal skills, such as the onset and fluency of speech (Petersson et al., 2007; Mercadillo et al., 2011).

Other research suggests that men's brains are somewhat bigger than women's brains, even after taking differences in body size into account. In contrast, part of the *corpus callosum,* a bundle of fibers that connects the hemispheres of the brain, is proportionally larger in women than in men (Smith et al., 2007; Taki et al., 2013).

The meaning of such sex differences is far from clear. Consider one possibility related to differences in the proportional size of the corpus callosum: Its greater size in women may permit stronger connections to develop between the parts of the brain that control speech. In turn, this would explain why speech tends to emerge slightly earlier in girls than in boys.

Before we rush to such a conclusion, though, we must consider an alternative hypothesis: The reason verbal abilities emerge earlier in girls may be that infant girls receive greater encouragement to talk than do infant boys. In turn, this greater early experience may foster the growth of certain parts of the brain. Hence, physical brain differences may be a *reflection* of social and environmental influences rather than a *cause* of the differences in men's and women's behavior. At this point, it is impossible to know which of these alternative hypotheses is correct.

Furthermore, newer research suggests that most brains contain elements of male *and* female characteristics. Such findings contradict the notion that a brain is essentially either male or female (Denworth, 2017).

Culture also gives rise to differences in brain size and lateralization. For example, the volume of gray-matter material in the cortex is greater in higher-income adolescents than in low-income adolescents. Furthermore, brain development is related to differences in academic achievement between students of different income levels. Specifically, the brain's cortex is thicker in higher-income students than in lower-income students, and cortex configuration is related to their academic achievement (Mackey et al., 2015).

Clearly, our brains reflect a combination of genetically determined structure and functioning. But they also reflect the impact of the social and cultural experiences to which we are exposed.

The Split Brain: Exploring the Two Hemispheres

When Vicki visited her neurologist, she was desperate: Her frequent and severe epileptic seizures weren't just interfering with her day-to-day life—they were putting her in danger. She never knew when she might just collapse suddenly, making many mundane situations such as climbing stairs potentially life-threatening for her.

Vicki's neurologist had a solution, but a radical and potentially dangerous one: surgically severing the bundle of fibers connecting the two hemispheres of her brain. This procedure would stop the firestorms of electrical impulses that were causing Vicki's seizures, but it would also have its own curious effects on her day-to-day functioning.

In the months after the surgery, Vicki was relieved to be free of the seizures that had taken over her life. But she had new challenges to overcome. Simple tasks such as food shopping or even dressing herself became lengthy ordeals—not because she had difficulty moving or thinking but because the two sides of her brain no longer worked in a coordinated way. Each side directed its half of the body to work independently of the other (Wolman, 2012).

People like Vicki, whose corpus collosums have been cut or injured, are called *split-brain patients*. They offer a rare opportunity for researchers investigating the independent functioning of the two hemispheres of the brain. For example, psychologist Roger Sperry—who won the Nobel Prize for his work—developed a number of ingenious techniques for studying how each hemisphere operates (Sperry, 1982; Savazzi et al., 2007; Bagattini et al., 2015).

In one experimental procedure, patients who were prevented from seeing an object by a screen touched the object with their right hand and were asked to name it (see Figure 7). Because the right side of the body corresponds to the language-oriented left side of the brain, split-brain patients were able to name it. However, if patients touched the object with their left hand, they were unable to name it aloud, even though the information had registered in their brains. When the screen was removed, patients could identify the object they had touched. Information can be learned and remembered, then, using only the right side of the brain. (By the way, unless you've had split-brain surgery, this experiment won't work with you because the bundle of fibers connecting the two hemispheres of a normal brain immediately transfers the information from one hemisphere to the other.)

FIGURE 7 Hemispheres of the brain. (a) The corpus callosum connects the cerebral hemispheres of the brain, as shown in this cross section. (b) A split-brain patient is tested by touching objects behind a screen. Patients could name the objects they touched with their right hand but couldn't name them when they touched them with their left hand. If a split-brain patient with her eyes closed was given a pencil to hold and called it a pencil, what hand was the pencil in?

(a and b): ©McGraw-Hill Global Education Holdings LLC, 2008.

Site where corpus collosum is severed

Corpus collosum

Right cerebral hemisphere

Left cerebral hemisphere

A

Screen prevents participant from seeing objects

B

It is clear from experiments like this one that the right and left hemispheres of the brain specialize in handling different sorts of information. At the same time, it is important to realize that both hemispheres are capable of understanding, knowing, and being aware of the world, in somewhat different ways. The two hemispheres, then, should be regarded as different in terms of the efficiency with which they process certain kinds of information, rather than as two entirely separate brains. The hemispheres work interdependently to allow the full range and richness of thought of which humans are capable.

BECOMING AN INFORMED CONSUMER
of Psychology

Learning to Control Your Heart—and Mind—Through Biofeedback

When Tammy DeMichael was involved in a horrific car accident that broke her neck and crushed her spinal cord, experts told her that she was doomed to be a quadriplegic for the rest of her life, unable to move from the neck down. But they were wrong. Not only did she regain the use of her arms, but she also was able to walk 60 feet with a cane (Hess, Houg, & Tammaro, 2007).

The key to DeMichael's astounding recovery: biofeedback. **Biofeedback** is a procedure in which a person learns to control through conscious thought internal physiological processes such as blood pressure, heart and respiration rate, skin temperature, sweating, and the constriction of particular muscles. Although it traditionally had been thought that heart rate, respiration rate, blood pressure, and other bodily functions are under the control of parts of the brain over which we have no influence, psychologists have discovered that these responses are actually susceptible to voluntary control (Cho, Holyoak, & Cannon, 2007; Badke et al., 2011).

In biofeedback, a person is hooked up to electronic devices that provide continuous feedback relating to the physiological response in question. For instance, someone trying to control headaches through biofeedback might have electronic sensors placed on certain muscles on her head and learn to control the constriction and relaxation of those muscles. Later, when she felt a headache starting, she could relax the relevant muscles and abort the pain (Andrasik, 2007; Nestoriuc et al., 2008; Magis & Schoenen, 2011).

DeMichael's treatment was related to a form of biofeedback called *neurofeedback*, in which brain activity is displayed for a patient. Because not all of her nervous system's connections between the brain and her legs were severed, she was able to learn how to send messages to specific muscles, "ordering" them to move. Although it took more than a year, DeMichael was successful in restoring a large degree of her mobility.

Although the control of physiological processes through the use of biofeedback is not easy to learn, it has been employed with success in a variety of ailments, including emotional problems (such as anxiety, depression, phobias, tension headaches, insomnia, and hyperactivity), physical illnesses with a psychological component (such as asthma, high blood pressure, ulcers, muscle spasms, and migraine headaches), and physical problems (such as DeMichael's injuries, strokes, cerebral palsy, and curvature of the spine) (Morone & Greco, 2007; Reiner, 2008; Dias & van Deusen, 2011).

biofeedback A procedure in which a person learns to control through conscious thought internal physiological processes such as blood pressure, heart and respiration rate, skin temperature, sweating, and the constriction of particular muscles. (Module 9)

AP MODULE 9: THE BRAIN

AP SUMMARY

- The central core of the brain is sometimes referred to as the "old brain." The functions of the central core structures are similar to those found in other

vertebrates. The hindbrain consists of the medulla (regulates breathing, heartbeat, circulation), the pons (coordinates the muscles and the two sides of the body, regulates sleep and arousal), and the cerebellum (controls bodily balance, intellectual functions). The reticular formation extends from the medulla through the pons, passing through the midbrain and into the forebrain. This brain part is related to changes in arousal and regulates the sleep-wake cycle. The forebrain consists of the thalamus (relays sensory messages except smell) and the hypothalamus (maintains homeostasis and regulates behavior related to basic survival).

- The limbic system, found on the border of the "old" and "new" brains, is associated with eating, aggression, reproduction, and the experiences of pleasure and pain. It consists of the amygdala (fear and aggression) and hippocampus (learning and memory).

- The cerebral cortex–the "new brain"–consists of four main lobes: frontal, parietal, occipital, and temporal. It has areas that control voluntary movement (the motor area); the senses (the sensory area); and thinking, reasoning, speech, and memory (the association areas).

- Researchers have mapped the motor area and sensory area of the cortex to identify the amount and relative location of cortical tissue used for specific body parts. The greater the amount of tissue related to that specific body part, the more sensitive the body part.

- The brain is divided into left and right halves, or hemispheres, each of which generally controls the opposite side of the body. Each hemisphere can be thought of as being specialized in the functions it carries out: The left specializes in verbal tasks, such as logical reasoning, speaking, and reading; the right specializes in nonverbal tasks, such as spatial perception, pattern recognition, and emotional expression. The degree and nature of lateralization vary from one person to another and the difference between hemisphere specializations is not great.

- Injuries to the association areas can produce problems with language known as aphasia. Broca's aphasia is where speech production becomes laborious and the speaker is unable to find the right words. Wernicke's aphasia produces difficulties both in understanding and producing language.

- For most of history the brain could only be studied through an autopsy after the individual died. Although informative, this method could tell us little about the functioning of a healthy brain.

- Today, imaging techniques provide a window into the internal workings of the brain without having to cut surgically into a person's skull. Major brain-scanning techniques include the electroencephalogram (EEG), positron emission tomography (PET), functional magnetic resonance imaging (fMRI), and transcranial magnetic stimulation imaging (TMS).

- Case studies and lesioning are also research tools for understanding the brain. Some patients with epilepsy, in an effort to stop their seizures, have had portions of the limbic system removed and been unable to learn and remember information. These case studies have tied the limbic system, and specifically the hippocampus, to the functions of learning and memory. Some humans experience pleasure when the limbic system is stimulated. Much of our understanding of the association areas comes from patients who, like Phineas Gage, have suffered a brain injury.

- In cases of severe epilepsy, researchers have surgically severed the corpus callosum to stop the electrical impulses traveling across the hemispheres. Split-brain patients offer a rare opportunity to investigate the functioning of the two hemispheres of the brain, which are different in their efficiency of processing certain kinds of information.

- Roger Sperry won the Nobel Prize for studying split-brain patients and how each hemisphere operates.

AP KEY TERMS

central core	lobes
cerebellum	motor area
(ser-uh-BELL-um)	sensory area
reticular formation	association areas
thalamus	neuroplasticity
hypothalamus	hemispheres
limbic system	lateralization
cerebral cortex	biofeedback

AP TEST PRACTICE

Section I: Multiple Choice

1. A surgeon places an electrode on a portion of your brain and stimulates it. Immediately, your right arm involuntarily twitches. The doctor has most likely stimulated a portion of what brain part?
   A. Sensory cortex
   B. Association area
   C. Corpus callosum
   D. Auditory cortex
   E. Motor cortex

2. What psychologist won the Nobel Prize for their research involving split-brain patients?
   A. Paul Broca
   B. Roger Sperry
   C. Carl Wernicke
   D. Charles Darwin
   E. Sigmund Freud

3. If a split-brain patient was tested by staring at a dot in the middle of the screen, while the word HE·ART flashed around the dot, what would the patient verbally report seeing?
A. HE
B. ART
C. HEART
D. Blank screen
E. Heart shape

Section II: Free Response

Jamal is playing the saxophone in a large musical concert with several other musicians.
A. Explain how the brain parts below can help his performance.

- Cerebellum
- Motor cortex
- Occipital lobe

Jamal accidentally trips on the stage and bumps his head.

B. Explain the following brain imaging techniques and how they might help identify if Jamal has brain damage.

- PET scan
- fMRI scan

After bumping his head, Jamal is having problems with his speech.

C. Explain how the following brain parts might have been impacted.

- Left frontal lobe
- Left temporal lobe

LOOKING *Back*

EPILOGUE

In our examination of neuroscience, we've traced the ways in which biological structures and functions of the body affect behavior. Starting with neurons, we considered each of the components of the nervous system, culminating in an examination of how the brain permits us to think, reason, speak, recall, and experience emotions—the hallmarks of being human.

MODULE 7 Neurons: The Basic Element

Neuron Structure

Neuron Function

Synapse

Neurotransmitters

- Acetylcholine
- Serotonin
- Dopamine
- Endorphins

MODULE 8 Nervous System

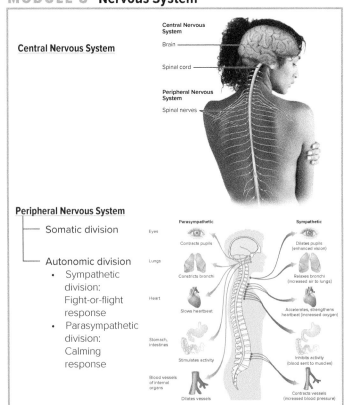

Central Nervous System

Peripheral Nervous System

- Somatic division
- Autonomic division
  - Sympathetic division: Fight-or-flight response
  - Parasympathetic division: Calming response

Endocrine System

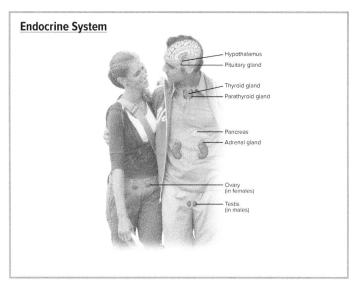

MODULE 9 The Brain

Areas of the Brain

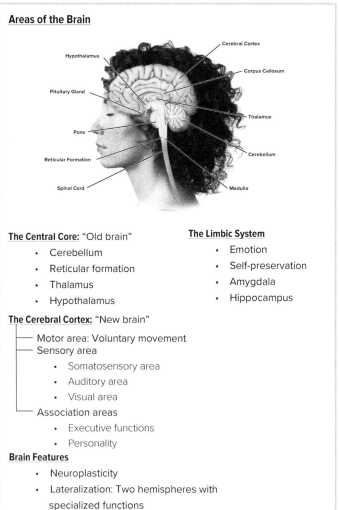

The Central Core: "Old brain"

- Cerebellum
- Reticular formation
- Thalamus
- Hypothalamus

The Cerebral Cortex: "New brain"

- Motor area: Voluntary movement
- Sensory area
  - Somatosensory area
  - Auditory area
  - Visual area
- Association areas
  - Executive functions
  - Personality

The Limbic System

- Emotion
- Self-preservation
- Amygdala
- Hippocampus

Brain Features

- Neuroplasticity
- Lateralization: Two hemispheres with specialized functions
- The Split Brain: Corpus callosum with independent hemispheric functions

©Uppercut/SuperStock

CHAPTER 4
Sensation and Perception

AP| ESSENTIAL QUESTIONS

- How do we process the information we receive from our environments?
- How does our interpretation of the information we receive from the environment influence our behaviors and mental processes?

AP| LEARNING TARGETS FOR CHAPTER 4

MODULE 10

- Discuss basic principles of sensory transduction, including absolute threshold, difference threshold, signal detection, and sensory adaptation.
- Explain common sensory conditions.

SENSING THE WORLD AROUND US
Absolute Thresholds: Detecting What's Out There
Difference Thresholds: Noticing Distinctions Between Stimuli
Sensory Adaptation: Turning Down Our Responses

MODULE 11

- Describe the vision process, including the specific nature of energy transduction, relevant anatomical structures, and specialized pathways in the brain for each of the senses.
- Identify the research contributions of major historical figures in sensation and perception.

VISION: SHEDDING LIGHT ON THE EYE
Illuminating the Structure of the Eye
AP| **Neuroscience in Your Life:** Recognizing Faces
Color Vision and Color Blindness: The 7-Million-Color Spectrum

MODULE 12

- Describe the hearing process, taste and smell processes, and sensory processes, including the specific nature of energy transduction, relevant anatomical structures, and specialized pathways in the brain for each of the body senses.

HEARING AND THE OTHER SENSES
Sensing Sound
Smell and Taste
AP| **Applying Psychology in the 21st Century:** Sniffing Out Flash Drives
The Skin Senses: Touch, Pressure, Temperature, and Pain
Becoming an Informed Consumer of Psychology: Managing Pain
How Our Senses Interact

87

- Describe general principles of organizing and integrating sensation to promote stable awareness of the external world.

- Discuss how experience and culture can influence perceptual processes.

- Explain the role of top-down processing in producing vulnerability to illusion.

PROLOGUE *I FEEL YOUR PAIN, I TASTE YOUR WORDS*

For Sean Day, a college instructor in Charleston, South Carolina, the smell of fresh-cut grass is a dark purple color, and a sip of diet cola produces an unpleasant, sweat-stained yellow. Carol Steen, a New York City-based artist, sees touch, sound, and smell as ranges of colors, an experience that caused her to give up painting and turn to sculpture until she learned to let her color sensations inspire her instead of distract her (Reddy, 2017).

Day and Steen have *synesthesia,* a trait found in about 4.5% of the population in which sensations that are usually experienced separately merge into an amalgam of sensation. Some synesthetes feel pain as colors or feel touch when another person is being touched. Others experience spoken or read words as particular tastes.

LOOKING *Ahead*

Neurologists aren't certain what causes synesthesia, but some research suggests it may result from surviving connections between adjacent sensory brain regions that are normally pruned away as children age. Other studies suggest that synesthetes lack neural controls that usually inhibit connections between sensory areas. In any case, synesthesia isn't considered a condition that needs to be cured, and most of those who experience it consider it a gift rather than a disadvantage.

Phenomena such as synesthesia illustrate how complex and mysterious our senses are and how central they are to normal functioning. Our senses offer a window to the world, not only providing us with an awareness, understanding, and appreciation of the world's beauty but also alerting us to its dangers. Our senses enable us to feel the gentlest of breezes, see flickering lights miles away, and hear the soft murmuring of distant songbirds.

In the upcoming modules, we focus on the field of psychology that is concerned with the ways our bodies take in information through the senses and the ways we interpret that information. We explore both sensation and perception. *Sensation* encompasses the processes by which our sense organs receive information from the environment. *Perception* is the brain's and the sense organs' sorting out, interpretation, analysis, and integration of stimuli.

Although perception clearly represents a step beyond sensation, in practice it is sometimes difficult to find the precise boundary between the two. Indeed, psychologists—and philosophers as well—have argued for years over the distinction. The primary difference is that sensation can be thought of as an organism's first encounter with a raw sensory stimulus, whereas perception is the process by which it interprets, analyzes, and integrates that stimulus with other sensory information.

For example, if we were considering sensation, we might ask about the loudness of a ringing fire alarm. If we were considering perception, we might ask whether someone recognizes the ringing sound as an alarm and identifies its meaning.

To a psychologist interested in understanding the causes of behavior, sensation and perception are fundamental topics because so much of our behavior is a reflection of how we react to and interpret stimuli from the world around us. The areas of sensation and perception deal with a wide range of questions—among them, how we respond to the characteristics of physical stimuli; what processes enable us to see, hear, and experience pain; why visual illusions fool us; and how we distinguish one person from another. As we explore these issues, we'll see how the senses work together to provide us with an integrated view and understanding of the world.

Module 10
Sensing the World Around Us

As Isabel sat down to Thanksgiving dinner, her father carried the turkey in on a tray and placed it squarely in the center of the table. The noise level, already high from the talking and laughter of family members, grew louder still. As Isabel picked up her fork, the smell of the turkey reached her, and she felt her stomach growl hungrily. The sight and sound of her family around the table, along with the smells and tastes of the holiday meal, made Isabel feel more relaxed than she had since starting school in the fall.

Put yourself in this setting and consider how different it might be if any one of your senses were not functioning. What if you were blind and unable to see the faces of your family members or the welcome shape of the golden-brown turkey? What if you had no sense of hearing and could not listen to the conversations of family members or were unable to feel your stomach growl, smell the dinner, or taste the food? Clearly, you would experience the dinner very differently than someone whose sensory apparatus was intact.

Moreover, the sensations mentioned above barely scratch the surface of sensory experience. Although perhaps you were taught, as I was, that there are just five senses—sight, sound, taste, smell, and touch—that enumeration is too modest. Human sensory capabilities go well beyond the basic five senses. For example, we are sensitive not merely to touch but to a considerably wider set of stimuli—pain, pressure, temperature, and vibration, to name a few. In addition, vision has two subsystems—relating to day and night vision—and the ear is responsive to information that allows us not only to hear but also to keep our balance.

To consider how psychologists understand the senses and, more broadly, sensation and perception, we first need a basic working vocabulary. In formal terms, **sensation** is the activation of the sense organs by a source of physical energy. **Perception** is the sorting out, interpretation, analysis, and integration of stimuli carried out by the sense organs and brain. A **stimulus** is any passing source of physical energy that produces a response in a sense organ.

Stimuli vary in both type and intensity. Different types of stimuli activate different sense organs. For instance, we can differentiate light stimuli (which activate the sense of sight and allow us to see the colors of a tree in autumn) from sound stimuli (which, through the sense of hearing, permit us to hear the sounds of an orchestra). In addition, stimuli differ in intensity, relating to how strong a stimulus needs to be before it can be detected.

Questions of stimulus type and intensity are considered in a branch of psychology known as psychophysics. **Psychophysics** is the study of the relationship between the physical aspects of stimuli and our psychological experience of them. Psychophysics played a central role in the development of the field of psychology. Many of the first psychologists studied issues related to psychophysics, and there is still an active group of psychophysics researchers (Bonezzi, Brendl, & De Angelis, 2011; Acuna et al., 2015; Jack & Schyns, 2017).

Absolute Thresholds: Detecting What's Out There

Just when does a stimulus become strong enough to be detected by our sense organs? The answer to this question requires an understanding of the concept of absolute threshold. An **absolute threshold** is the smallest intensity of a stimulus that must be present for it to be detected (Aazh & Moore, 2007).

 AP® LEARNING TARGETS

- Discuss basic principles of sensory transduction, including absolute threshold, difference threshold, signal detection, and sensory adaptation.
- Explain common sensory conditions.

Study Alert
Remember that *sensation* refers to the activation of the sense organs (a physical response), whereas *perception* refers to how stimuli are interpreted (a psychological response).

sensation The activation of the sense organs by a source of physical energy. (Module 10)

perception The sorting out, interpretation, analysis, and integration of stimuli by the sense organs and brain. (Module 10)

stimulus Energy that produces a response in a sense organ. (Module 10)

psychophysics The study of the relationship between the physical aspects of stimuli and our psychological experience of them. (Module 10)

absolute threshold The smallest intensity of a stimulus that must be present for the stimulus to be detected. (Module 10)

FIGURE 1 This test can shed some light on how sensitive the human senses are.

Source: Galanter, E. (1962). Contemporary psychophysics. In R. Brown, E. Galanter, E. Hess, & G. Maroler (Eds.), *New directions in psychology.* New York: Holt.

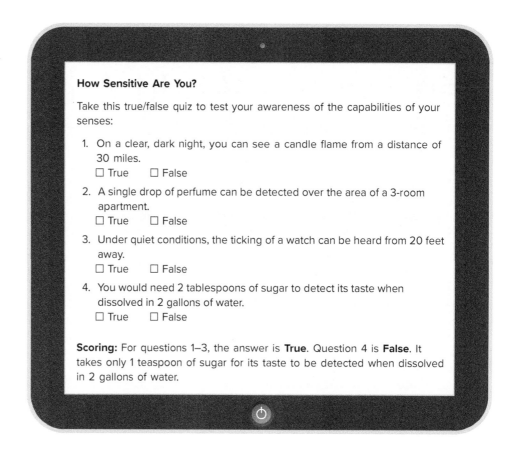

How Sensitive Are You?

Take this true/false quiz to test your awareness of the capabilities of your senses:

1. On a clear, dark night, you can see a candle flame from a distance of 30 miles.
   ☐ True   ☐ False

2. A single drop of perfume can be detected over the area of a 3-room apartment.
   ☐ True   ☐ False

3. Under quiet conditions, the ticking of a watch can be heard from 20 feet away.
   ☐ True   ☐ False

4. You would need 2 tablespoons of sugar to detect its taste when dissolved in 2 gallons of water.
   ☐ True   ☐ False

Scoring: For questions 1–3, the answer is **True**. Question 4 is **False**. It takes only 1 teaspoon of sugar for its taste to be detected when dissolved in 2 gallons of water.

PsychTech

Our inability to focus on multiple stimuli simultaneously is the reason why texting while driving is so dangerous. One study mounted video cameras inside trucks and found that truckers were 23 times more likely to be in a collision while texting than while not texting.

Despite the "absolute" in absolute threshold, things are not so cut and dried. As the strength of a stimulus increases, the likelihood that it will be detected increases gradually. Technically, then, an absolute threshold is the stimulus intensity that is detected 50% of the time.

It often takes a very small stimulus to produce a response in our senses. For example, the sense of touch is so sensitive that we can feel a bee's wing falling on our cheeks when it is dropped from a distance of 1 centimeter. Test your knowledge of the absolute thresholds of other senses by completing the questionnaire in Figure 1.

In fact, our senses are so fine-tuned that we might have problems if they were any more sensitive. For instance, if our ears were slightly more acute, we would be able to hear the sound of air molecules in our ears knocking into the eardrum—a phenomenon that would surely prove distracting and might even prevent us from hearing sounds outside our bodies.

Of course, the absolute thresholds we have been discussing are measured under ideal conditions. Normally our senses cannot detect stimulation quite as well because of the presence of noise. *Noise,* as defined by psychophysicists, is background stimulation that interferes with the perception of other stimuli. Hence, noise refers not just to auditory stimuli, as the word suggests, but also to unwanted stimuli that interfere with other senses.

For example, picture a talkative group of people crammed into a small, crowded room at a party. The din of the crowd makes it hard to hear individual voices. In this case, the crowded conditions would be considered "noise," because they are preventing sensation at more discriminating levels. Similarly, we have limited ability to concentrate on several stimuli simultaneously.

Crowded conditions, sounds, and sights can all be considered as noise that interferes with sensation. Can you think of other examples of noise that is not auditory in nature?
©Adam Lubroth/Getty Images

Difference Thresholds: Noticing Distinctions Between Stimuli

Suppose you wanted to choose the six best apples from a supermarket display–the biggest, reddest, and sweetest apples. One approach would be to compare one apple with another systematically until you were left with a few so similar that you could not tell the difference between them. At that point, it wouldn't matter which ones you choose.

Psychologists have discussed this comparison problem in terms of the **difference threshold,** the smallest level of added or reduced stimulation required to sense that a *change* in stimulation has occurred. Thus, the difference threshold is the minimum change in stimulation required to detect the difference between two stimuli, and so it also is called a **just noticeable difference** (Nittrouer & Lowenstein, 2007; Heath & Manzone, 2017).

The size of a stimulus that constitutes a just noticeable difference depends on the initial intensity of the stimulus. The relationship between changes in the original size of a stimulus and the degree to which a change will be noticed forms one of the basic laws of psychophysics: Weber's law. **Weber's law** (*Weber* is pronounced "VAY-ber") states that a just noticeable difference is a *constant proportion* of the intensity of an initial stimulus (rather than a constant amount).

For example, Weber found that the just noticeable difference for weight is 1:50. Consequently, it takes a 1-ounce increase in a 50-ounce weight to produce a noticeable difference, and it would take a 10-ounce increase to produce a noticeable difference if the initial weight were 500 ounces. In both cases, the same proportional increase is necessary to produce a just noticeable difference (1:50 = 10:500). Similarly, the just noticeable difference distinguishing changes in loudness between sounds is larger for sounds that are initially loud than it is for sounds that are initially soft, but the *proportional* increase remains the same.

Weber's law helps explain why a person in a quiet room is more startled by the ringing of a cellphone than is a person in an already noisy room. To produce the same amount of reaction in a noisy room, a cellphone ring would have to be set to a much higher level. Similarly, when the moon is visible during the late afternoon, it appears relatively dim. On the other hand, the moon appears much brighter when it is in the dark night sky.

difference threshold (just noticeable difference) The smallest level of added or reduced stimulation required to sense that a change in stimulation has occurred. (Module 10)

Weber's law A basic law of psychophysics stating that a just noticeable difference is a constant proportion to the intensity of an initial stimulus (rather than a constant amount). (Module 10)

Study Alert
Remember that Weber's law holds for every type of sensory stimuli: vision, sound, taste, and so on.

From the perspective of...

A Software Designer How might you use principles of psychophysics to direct the attention of a software user to a particular part of the computer screen?

©Rubberball/Punchstock

Sensory Adaptation: Turning Down Our Responses

adaptation An adjustment in sensory capacity after prolonged exposure to unchanging stimuli. (Module 10)

You enter a movie theater, and the smell of popcorn is everywhere. A few minutes later, though, you barely notice the smell. The reason you become accustomed to the odor is sensory adaptation. **Adaptation** is an adjustment in sensory capacity after prolonged exposure to unchanging stimuli. Adaptation occurs as people become accustomed to a stimulus and change their frame of reference. In a sense, our brain mentally turns down the volume of the stimulation that it's experiencing (Carbon & Ditye, 2011; Erb et al., 2013; Nourouzpour et al., 2015).

One example of adaptation is the decrease in sensitivity that occurs after repeated exposure to a strong stimulus. If you were to hear a loud tone over and over, eventually it would begin to sound softer. Similarly, although jumping into a cold lake may be temporarily unpleasant, eventually you probably will get used to the temperature.

This apparent decline in sensitivity to sensory stimuli is due to the inability of the sensory nerve receptors to fire off messages to the brain indefinitely. Because these receptor cells are most responsive to *changes* in stimulation, constant stimulation is not effective in producing a sustained reaction (Wark, Lundstrom, & Fairhall, 2007; Summers et al., 2017).

Although initially difficult to tolerate, exposure to cold temperatures eventually becomes less unpleasant due to the phenomenon of adaptation.
©Pashkov Andrey/123RF

Judgments of sensory stimuli are also affected by the context in which the judgments are made. This is the case because judgments are made not in isolation from other stimuli but in terms of preceding sensory experience. You can demonstrate this for yourself by trying a simple experiment:

Take two envelopes, one large and one small, and put 15 nickels in each one. Now lift the large envelope, put it down, and lift the small one. Which seems to weigh more? Most people report that the small one is heavier, although, as you know, the weights are nearly identical. The reason for this misconception is that the visual context of the envelope interferes with the sensory experience of weight. Adaptation to the context of one stimulus (the size of the envelope) alters responses to another stimulus (the weight of the envelope) (Coren, 2004).

AP MODULE 10: SENSING THE WORLD AROUND US

AP SUMMARY

- Sensation is the activation of the sense organs by any source of physical energy. In contrast, perception is the process by which we sort out, interpret, analyze, and integrate stimuli to which our senses are exposed.
- Psychophysics studies the relationship between the physical nature of stimuli and the sensory responses they evoke.
- The absolute threshold is the smallest amount of physical intensity at which a stimulus can be detected. Under ideal conditions, absolute thresholds are extraordinarily sensitive, but the presence of noise (background stimuli that interfere with other stimuli) reduces detection capabilities.
- The difference threshold, or just noticeable difference, is the smallest change in the level of stimulation required to sense that a change has occurred. According to Weber's law, a just noticeable difference is a constant proportion of the intensity of an initial stimulus.
- Sensory adaptation occurs when we become accustomed to a constant stimulus and change our evaluation of it. Repeated exposure to a stimulus results in an apparent decline in sensitivity to it.
- Ernst Weber created one of the main laws of psychophysics. Weber's law states that a just noticeable difference is a constant proportion of the intensity of an initial stimulus.

AP KEY TERMS

sensation	difference threshold
perception	(just noticeable
stimulus	difference)
psychophysics	Weber's law
absolute threshold	adaptation

AP TEST PRACTICE

Section I: Multiple Choice

1. Gustav Fechner studied the difference threshold and the relationship between physical aspects of stimuli and our psychological experience of them. He was a key figure in the founding of what psychology domain?
   A. Cognitive neuroscience
   B. Synesthesia
   C. Sensory adaptation
   D. Psychophysics
   E. Psychometrics

2. Trisha spent all day preparing food for a holiday celebration. When her guests arrived she could no longer smell the food, but her guests could. This could be best explained by which of the following?
   A. Just difference threshold
   B. Sensory adaptation
   C. Difference threshold
   D. Weber's law
   E. Synesthesia

3. The smallest intensity of a stimulus that must be present for it to be detected is known as the individual's
   A. absolute threshold
   B. all-or-none principle
   C. biofeedback
   D. difference threshold
   E. sensory adaptation

Section II: Free Response

Beau loves to cook and try new recipes.
A. Explain how the following terms will <u>help</u> him in the kitchen.
   - Absolute threshold
   - Difference threshold
B. Explain how the following term will <u>hinder</u> him in the kitchen.
   - Sensory adaptation

Module 11
Vision: Shedding Light on the Eye

If, as poets say, the eyes provide a window to the soul, they also provide us with a window to the world. Our visual capabilities permit us to admire and to react to scenes ranging from the beauty of a sunset, to the configuration of a lover's face, to the words written on the pages of a book.

Vision starts with *light*, the physical energy that stimulates the eye. Light is a form of electromagnetic radiation waves. Like ocean waves, light is measured in *wavelengths*, the distance between peaks of the lightwaves.

The *visual spectrum* is the range of wavelengths that the human eye can detect. As shown in Figure 1, the visible spectrum that humans can see includes the wavelengths that make up the colors of a rainbow, from the shortest wavelength of violet blue to the longest wavelength of red. Compared to that of nonhumans, the visual spectrum in humans is relatively restricted. For instance, some reptiles and fish sense energies of longer wavelengths than humans do, and certain insects sense energies of shorter wavelengths than humans do.

Light waves coming from some object outside the body (such as the tree in Figure 2) are sensed by the only organ that is capable of responding to the visible spectrum: the eye. Our eyes convert light to a form that can be used by the neurons that serve as messengers to the brain. The neurons themselves take up a relatively small percentage of the total eye. Most of the eye is a mechanical device that is similar in many respects to a nonelectronic camera that uses film, as you can see in Figure 2.

Despite the similarities between the eye and a camera, vision involves processes that are far more complex and sophisticated than those of any camera. Furthermore, once an image reaches the neuronal receptors of the eye, the eye/camera analogy ends, for the processing of the visual image in the brain is more reflective of a computer than it is of a camera.

Illuminating the Structure of the Eye

The ray of light being reflected off the tree in Figure 2 first travels through the *cornea*, a transparent, protective window. The cornea, because of its curvature, bends (or *refracts*) light as it passes through, playing a primary role in focusing the light more sharply. After moving through the cornea, the light traverses the pupil. The *pupil* is a

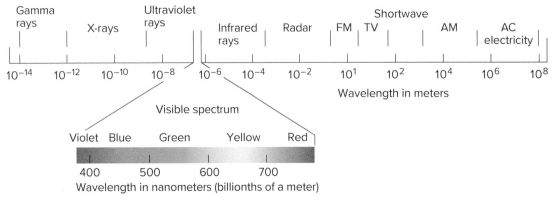

FIGURE 1 The visible spectrum—the range of wavelengths to which people are sensitive—is only a small part of the kinds of wavelengths present in our environment. Is it a benefit or disadvantage to our everyday lives that we aren't more sensitive to a broader range of visual stimuli? Why?

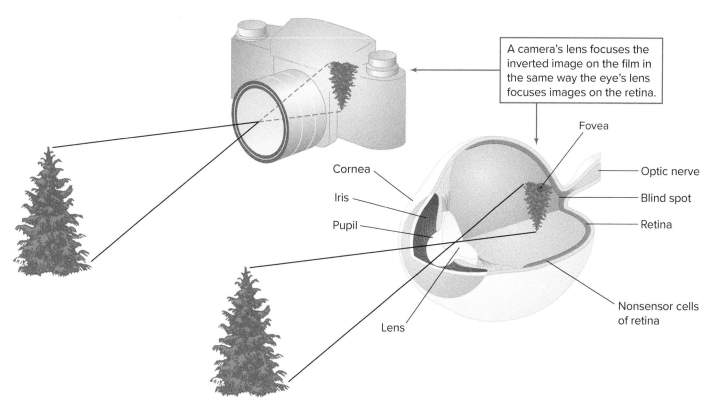

A camera's lens focuses the inverted image on the film in the same way the eye's lens focuses images on the retina.

Fovea

Cornea

Iris

Pupil

Optic nerve

Blind spot

Retina

Nonsensor cells of retina

Lens

FIGURE 2 Although human vision is far more complicated than the most sophisticated camera, in some ways basic visual processes are analogous to those used in photography. Like the automatic lighting system of a traditional, nondigital camera, the human eye dilates to let in more light and contracts to block out light.

dark hole in the center of the *iris,* the colored part of the eye, which in humans ranges from a light blue to a dark brown. The size of the pupil opening depends on the amount of light in the environment. The dimmer the surroundings are, the more the pupil opens to allow more light to enter.

Why shouldn't the pupil be open completely all the time, allowing the greatest amount of light into the eye? The answer relates to the basic physics of light. A small pupil greatly increases the range of distances at which objects are in focus. With a wide-open pupil, the range is relatively small, and details are harder to discern. The eye takes advantage of bright light by decreasing the size of the pupil and thereby becoming more discriminating. In dim light, the pupil expands to enable us to view the situation better—but at the expense of visual detail. (Perhaps one reason candlelight dinners are thought of as romantic is that the dim light prevents one from seeing a partner's physical flaws.)

Once light passes through the pupil, it enters the *lens,* which is directly behind the pupil. The lens acts to bend the rays of light so that they are properly focused on

Like the automatic lighting system on a camera, the pupil in the human eye expands to let in more light (left) and contracts to block out light (right). Can humans adjust their ears to let in more or less sound in a similar manner?
(Both): ©Biophoto Associates/Science Source

the rear of the eye. The lens focuses light by changing its own thickness, a process called *accommodation:* It becomes flatter when viewing distant objects and rounder when looking at closer objects.

REACHING THE RETINA

Having traveled through the pupil and lens, the image of the tree finally reaches its ultimate destination in the eye: the retina. The **retina** is the part of the eye that converts the electromagnetic energy of light to electrical impulses for transmission to the brain.

Interestingly, as the image travels through the lens, it has reversed itself. Consequently, the image reaches the retina upside down (relative to its original position). Although it might seem that this reversal would cause difficulties in understanding and moving about the world, this is not the case. The brain automatically interprets the image in terms of its original position.

The retina consists of a thin layer of nerve cells at the back of the eyeball (see Figure 3). There are two kinds of light-sensitive receptor cells in the retina. The names they have been given describe their shapes: rods and cones. **Rods** are thin, cylindrical

retina The part of the eye that converts the electromagnetic energy of light to electrical impulses for transmission to the brain. (Module 11)

rods Thin, cylindrical receptor cells in the retina that are highly sensitive to light. (Module 11)

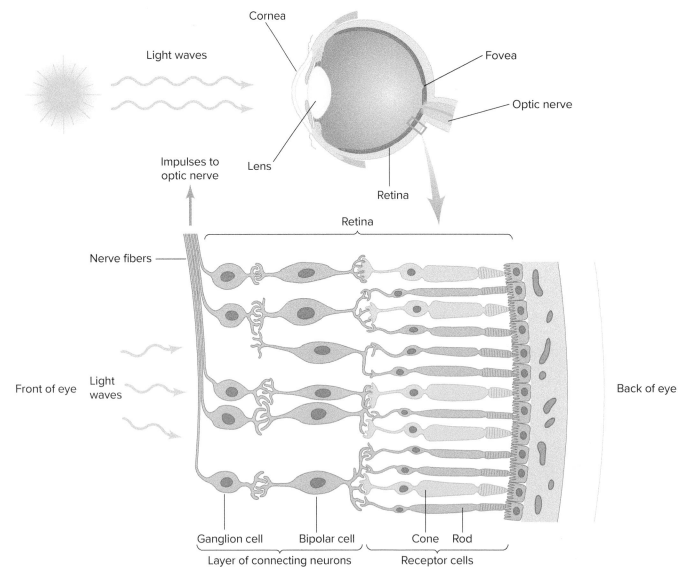

FIGURE 3 The basic cells of the eye. Light entering the eye travels through the ganglion and bipolar cells and strikes the light-sensitive rods and cones located at the back of the eye. The rods and cones then transmit nerve impulses to the brain via the bipolar and ganglion cells.
©McGraw-Hill Global Education Holdings LLC, 2000.

receptor cells that are highly sensitive to light. **Cones** are typically cone-shaped, light-sensitive receptor cells that are responsible for sharp focus and color perception, particularly in bright light. The rods and cones are distributed unevenly throughout the retina. Cones are concentrated on the part of the retina called the *fovea*. The fovea is a particularly sensitive region of the retina. If you want to focus on something of particular interest, you will automatically try to center the image on the fovea to see it more sharply.

The rods and cones not only are structurally dissimilar, but they also play distinctly different roles in vision. Cones are primarily responsible for the sharply focused perception of color, particularly in brightly lit situations; rods are related to vision in dimly lit situations and are largely insensitive to color and to details as sharp as those the cones are capable of recognizing. The rods play a key role in *peripheral vision*–seeing objects that are outside the main center of focus–and in night vision.

Rods and cones also are involved in *dark adaptation*, the phenomenon of adjusting to dim light after being in brighter light. (Think of the experience of walking into a dark movie theater and groping your way to a seat but a few minutes later seeing the seats quite clearly.) The speed at which dark adaptation occurs is a result of the rate of change in the chemical composition of the rods and cones. Although the cones reach their greatest level of adaptation in just a few minutes, the rods take 20 to 30 minutes to reach the maximum level. The opposite phenomenon–*light adaptation*, or the process of adjusting to bright light after exposure to dim light–occurs much faster, taking only a minute or so.

SENDING THE MESSAGE FROM THE EYE TO THE BRAIN

When light energy strikes the rods and cones, it starts a chain of events that transforms light into neural impulses that can be communicated to the brain. Even before the neural message reaches the brain, however, some initial coding of the visual information takes place.

What happens when light energy strikes the retina depends in part on whether it encounters a rod or a cone. Rods contain *rhodopsin*, a complex reddish-purple protein whose composition changes chemically when energized by light. The substance in cone receptors is different, but the principles are similar. Stimulation of the nerve cells in the eye triggers a neural response that is transmitted to other nerve cells in the retina called *bipolar cells* and *ganglion cells.*

Bipolar cells receive information directly from the rods and cones and communicate that information to the ganglion cells. The ganglion cells collect and summarize visual information, which is then moved out the back of the eyeball and sent to the brain through a bundle of ganglion axons called the **optic nerve.**

Because the opening for the optic nerve passes through the retina, there are no rods or cones in the area, and that creates a blind spot. Normally, however, this absence of nerve cells does not interfere with vision because you automatically compensate for the missing part of your field of vision. (To find your blind spot, see Figure 4.)

cones Cone-shaped, light-sensitive receptor cells in the retina that are responsible for sharp focus and color perception, particularly in bright light. (Module 11)

Study Alert
Remember that cones relate to color vision.

optic nerve A bundle of ganglion axons that carry visual information to the brain. (Module 11)

 —————————————————————————————— ———

FIGURE 4 To find your blind spot, close your right eye and look at the haunted house with your left eye. You will see the ghost on the periphery of your vision. Now, while staring at the house, move the page toward you. When the page is about a foot from your eye, the ghost will disappear. At this moment, the image of the ghost is falling on your blind spot.

But also notice how, when the page is at that distance, not only does the ghost seem to disappear, but the line also seems to run continuously through the area where the ghost used to be. This simple experiment shows how we automatically compensate for missing information by using nearby material to complete what is unseen. That's the reason you never notice the blind spot. What is missing is replaced by what is seen next to the blind spot. Can you think of any advantages that this tendency to provide missing information gives humans as a species?

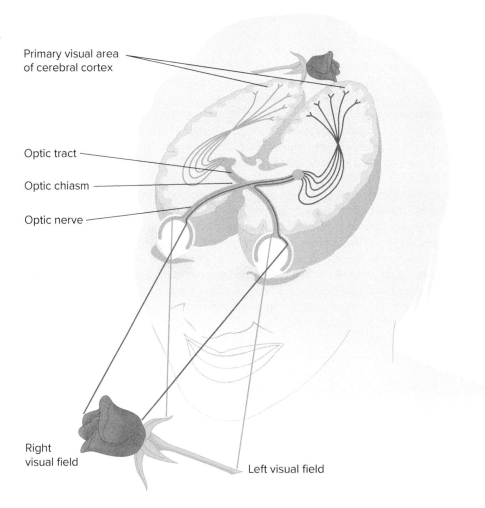

Primary visual area
of cerebral cortex

Optic tract

Optic chiasm

Optic nerve

Right
visual field

Left visual field

PsychTech

New technologies are helping the blind to see. For example, by surgically implanting electrodes into the eyes and using a nose-mounted camera and a video processor strapped to the waist, previously totally blind individuals can differentiate plates from cups and can identify large letters.

Once beyond the eye itself, the neural impulses relating to the image move through the optic nerve. As the optic nerve leaves the eyeball, its path does not take the most direct route to the part of the brain right behind the eye. Instead, the optic nerves from each eye meet at a point roughly between the two eyes–called the *optic chiasm* (pronounced KI-asm)–where each optic nerve then splits.

When the optic nerves split, the nerve impulses coming from the right half of each retina are sent to the right side of the brain, and the impulses arriving from the left half of each retina are sent to the left side of the brain. Because the image on the retinas is reversed and upside down, however, those images coming from the right half of each retina actually originated in the field of vision to the person's left, and the images coming from the left half of each retina originated in the field of vision to the person's right (see Figure 5).

PROCESSING THE VISUAL MESSAGE

By the time a visual message reaches the brain, it has passed through several stages of processing. One of the initial sites is the ganglion cells. Each ganglion cell gathers information from a group of rods and cones in a particular area of the eye and compares the amount of light entering the center of that area with the amount of light in the area around it. Some ganglion cells are activated by light in the center (and darkness in the surrounding area). Other ganglion cells are activated when there is darkness in the center and light in the surrounding areas. The outcome of this process is to maximize the detection of variations in light and darkness. The image that is passed on to the brain, then, is an enhanced version of the actual visual stimulus outside the body (Lascaratos, Ji, & Wood, 2007; Grünert et al., 2011; Sanes & Masland, 2015).

The ultimate processing of visual images takes place in the visual cortex of the brain, and it is here that the most complex kinds of processing occur. Psychologists David Hubel and Torsten Wiesel won the Nobel Prize in 1981 for their discovery of feature detectors. **Feature detectors** are specialized neurons that are activated only by visual stimuli having certain features, such as a particular shape or pattern. For instance, some feature detectors are activated only by lines of a particular width, shape, or orientation. Other feature detectors are activated only by moving, as opposed to stationary, stimuli (Hubel & Wiesel, 2004; Sebastiani, Castellani, & D'Alessandro, 2011; Jacoby & Schwartz, 2017).

Visual information coming from individual neurons is combined and processed in extraordinarily specialized ways, and different parts of the brain jointly process nerve impulses according to the attributes of an image. For instance, one brain system processes shapes, one processes colors, and others process movement, location, and depth. The specialization goes further: specific parts of the brain are involved in the perception of certain *kinds* of stimuli, such as reacting to human faces, nonhuman animal faces, and inanimate stimuli (Zvyagintsev et al., 2013; Stevens, 2015).

If separate neural systems exist for processing information about specific aspects of the visual world, how are all these data integrated by the brain? The brain makes use of information regarding the frequency, rhythm, and timing of the firing of particular sets of neural cells. Furthermore, the brain's integration of visual information does not occur in any single step or location in the brain but rather is a process that occurs on several levels simultaneously. The ultimate outcome, though, is indisputable: a vision of the world around us (Macaluso, Frith, & Driver, 2000; Werner, Pinna, & Spillmann, 2007).

feature detector Specialized neurons that are activated only by visual stimuli having specific features, such as a particular shape or pattern. (Module 11)

AP NEUROSCIENCE IN YOUR LIFE: RECOGNIZING FACES

The ability to recognize faces is important for social bonding in humans as well as other animals. Although it has long been believed that face processing in the brain is genetically determined, recent evidence shows that experience plays an important role as well. To examine whether innate face-processing regions of the brain exist, researchers kept one group of monkeys from seeing faces during development. When the monkeys were approximately 200 days old, the researchers measured their brain activity while they viewed faces and other common objects. Compared to normal monkeys (labeled the controls), those that were face-deprived show less activity for faces (red/yellow areas) compared to objects (purple areas) in visual regions of the brain (the circled regions in the images below). These results show that early sensory experience is important for the development of face recognition and has important implications for those who suffer from prosopagnosia, an inability to recognize faces (Arcaro et al., 2017).

AP SKILL: SCIENTIFIC INVESTIGATION / DATA ANALYSIS

1. Identify the independent and dependent variable.

2. How do the results of this study have important implications for those who suffer from prosopagnosia?

Control | Face-deprived

Right   Left   Object   Faces   Right   Left

% signal
4.0   0.1   4.0

Source: Adapted from Arcaro, M. J., Schade, P. F., Vincent, J. L., Ponce, C. R., & Livingstone, M. S. (2017). Seeing faces is necessary for face-domain formation. *Nature Neuroscience, 20*(10), 1404–1412.

Color Vision and Color Blindness: The 7-Million-Color Spectrum

Although the range of wavelengths to which humans are sensitive is relatively narrow, at least in comparison with the entire electromagnetic spectrum, the portion to which we are capable of responding allows us great flexibility in sensing the world. Nowhere is this clearer than in terms of the number of colors we can discern. A person with normal color vision is capable of distinguishing no less than 7 million different colors (Rabin, 2004).

Although the variety of colors that people are generally able to distinguish is vast, there are certain individuals whose ability to perceive color is quite limited–the color blind. Interestingly, the condition of these individuals has provided some of the most important clues to understanding how color vision operates (Nijboer, te Pas, & van der Smagt, 2011; Alfaro et al., 2015).

From the perspective of...

A Graphic Designer How might you market your products to those who are color blind versus those who have normal color vision?

©Zoonar GmbH/Alamy Stock Photo

Approximately 7% of men and 0.4% of women are color blind. For most people with color-blindness, the world looks dull and lacks contrast (see Figure 6). Red fire engines appear yellow, green grass seems yellow, and the three colors of a traffic light all look yellow. In fact, in the most common form of color-blindness, all red and green objects are seen as yellow. In other forms of color-blindness, people are unable to tell the difference between yellow and blue. In the most extreme cases of color-blindness, which are quite rare, people perceive no color at all. To such individuals, the world looks something like the picture on an old black-and-white TV.

trichromatic theory of color vision The theory that there are three kinds of cones in the retina, each of which responds primarily to a specific range of wavelengths. (Module 11)

EXPLAINING COLOR VISION

To understand why some people are color blind, we need to consider the basics of color vision. Two processes are involved. The first process is explained by the **trichromatic theory of color vision,** which was first proposed by Thomas Young and extended by

FIGURE 6 Those with color blindness see a very different view of the world (left) compared to those who have normal vision (right).
(Both): ©Ralph C. Eagle Jr./Science Source

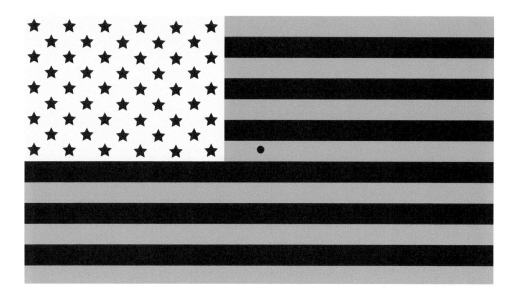

FIGURE 7 Stare at the dot in this flag for about a minute and then look at a piece of plain white paper. What do you see? Most people see an afterimage that converts the colors in the figure into the traditional red, white, and blue U.S. flag. If you have trouble seeing it the first time, blink once and try again.

Hermann von Helmholtz in the first half of the 1800s. This theory suggests that there are three kinds of cones in the retina, each of which responds primarily to a specific range of wavelengths. One is most responsive to blue-violet colors, one to green, and the third to yellow-red (Brown & Wald, 1964). According to trichromatic theory, perception of color is influenced by the relative strength with which each of the three kinds of cones is activated. If we see a blue sky, the blue-violet cones are primarily triggered, and the others show less activity.

However, there are aspects of color vision that the trichromatic theory is less successful at explaining. For example, the theory does not explain what happens after you stare at something like the flag shown in Figure 7 for about a minute. Try this yourself and then look at a blank white page: You'll see an image of the traditional red, white, and blue U.S. flag. Where there was yellow, you'll see blue, and where there were green and black, you'll see red and white.

The phenomenon you have just experienced is called an *afterimage*. It occurs because activity in the retina continues even when you are no longer staring at the original picture.

However, the fact that the colors perceived in the afterimage differ from those in the original image calls into question the validity of the trichromatic theory. To explain this failure of the trichromatic theory, alternative explanations for color vision have been developed. One alternative is the opponent-process theory.

According to the **opponent-process theory of color vision,** first proposed by German physiologist Ewald Hering in the 19th century, receptor cells are linked in pairs, working in opposition to each other. Specifically, there are a blue-yellow pairing, a red-green pairing, and a black-white pairing. If an object reflects light that contains more blue than yellow, it will stimulate the firing of the cells sensitive to blue, simultaneously discouraging or inhibiting the firing of receptor cells sensitive to yellow—and the object will appear blue. If, in contrast, a light contains more yellow than blue, the cells that respond to yellow will be stimulated to fire while the blue ones are inhibited, and the object will appear yellow (Robinson, 2007).

The opponent-process theory provides a good explanation for afterimages. When we stare at the yellow in the figure, for instance, our receptor cells for the yellow component of the yellow-blue pairing become fatigued and are less able to respond to yellow stimuli. In contrast, the receptor cells for the blue part of the pair are not tired because they are not being stimulated. When we look at a white surface, the light reflected off it would normally stimulate both the yellow and the blue receptors equally. But the fatigue of the yellow receptors prevents this from happening. They temporarily do not respond to the yellow, which makes the white light appear to be blue. Because the other colors in the figure do the same thing relative to their specific

opponent-process theory of color vision The theory that receptor cells for color are linked in pairs, working in opposition to each other. (Module 11)

Study Alert
Keep in mind that there are two explanations for color vision: trichromatic and opponent-process theories.

opponents, the afterimage produces the opponent colors–for a while. The afterimage lasts only a short time because the fatigue of the yellow receptors is soon overcome, and the white light begins to be perceived more accurately.

We now know that both opponent processes and trichromatic mechanisms are at work in producing the perception of color vision but in different parts of the visual sensing system. Trichromatic processes work within the retina itself, whereas opponent mechanisms operate both in the retina and at later stages of neuronal processing (Horiguchi et al., 2013; Bunce, 2015).

AP MODULE 11: VISION: SHEDDING LIGHT ON THE EYE

AP SUMMARY

- Vision depends on sensitivity to light, electromagnetic waves in the visible part of the spectrum that are either reflected off objects or produced by an energy source. Light is measured in wavelengths. Short wavelengths make up blue-violet; long wavelengths make up red.
- The eye shapes light into an image that is transformed into nerve impulses and interpreted by the brain. The ultimate processing of visual images is by feature detectors activated by certain shapes or patterns of visual stimuli, located in the visual cortex of the occipital lobe in the brain.
- Light enters the eye, passes through the cornea, pupil, and lens and reaches the retina, where the electromagnetic energy of light converts to nerve impulses for transmission to the brain. These impulses leave the eye via the optic nerve.
- Rods (receptor cells sensitive to dim light and used for peripheral vision) and cones (receptor cells sensitive to bright light, color, and clarity) are involved in light and dark adaptation.
- Visual information gathered by the rods and cones is transferred via bipolar and ganglion cells through the optic nerve to the optic chiasm–the point where the optic nerve splits. There are no rods and cones where the optic nerve leaves the eye, creating a blind spot. This does not interfere with vision because of an automatic compensation for the missing part of the visual field.
- There are two theories for color vision: trichromatic - suggests three kinds of cones (blue, green, red) in the retina, each responding to a range of wavelengths; opponent-process - presumes pairs of different types of cells (blue-yellow, black-white, red-green) work in opposition. This second theory explains negative afterimages.
- Color-blind individuals experience dull images that lack contrast, most common is that all red and green objects look yellow. Approximately 7% of men and 0.4% of women are color blind.

AP KEY TERMS

retina
rods
cones
optic nerve
feature detector

trichromatic theory of
    color vision
opponent-process theory of
    color vision

AP TEST PRACTICE

Section I: Multiple Choice

1. Psychologists David Hubel and Torsten Wiesel discovered that specific parts of the brain are involved in perception of certain kinds of stimuli, such as reacting to human faces, nonhuman animal faces, and inanimate stimuli. The results of this research relate to the specialization of
   A. mirror neurons
   B. rods and cones
   C. feature detectors
   D. the hypothalamus
   E. the optic chiasm

2. After staring at a blue wall and then looking at a white wall, the color yellow is visible. What theory does this negative afterimage support?
   A. Accommodation
   B. Light adaptation
   C. Sensory adaptation
   D. Opponent-process
   E. Trichromatic

3. The three colors of a traffic light all appear yellow to Trevor. Most likely Trevor has problems with his
   A. cornea
   B. rods
   C. optic chiasm
   D. lens
   E. cones

Section II: Free Response

Connie is having problems with her vision so she went to see an optometrist.

A. Describe how each of the following could relate to her vision problems.
   - Color vision
   - Foveal vision
   - Peripheral vision

The optometrist suggested that it might be cataracts and told her about a research study involving a new drug for cataracts. One group was given an eye drop medication to reduce the clouding of the lens. The second group was provided a saline solution.

B. Identify the following terms for the research study
   - Independent variable
   - Dependent variable

C. Describe how each of the following might relate to the research findings
   - Random assignment
   - Placebo effect

Module 12
Hearing and the Other Senses

The blast-off was easy compared with what the astronaut was experiencing now: space sickness. The constant nausea and vomiting were enough to make him wonder why he had worked so hard to become an astronaut. Even though he had been warned that there was a two-thirds chance that his first experience in space would cause these symptoms, he wasn't prepared for how terribly sick he really felt.

Whether or not the astronaut wishes he could head right back to Earth, his experience, a major problem for space travelers, is related to a basic sensory process: the sense of motion and balance. This sense allows people to navigate their bodies through the world and keep themselves upright without falling. Along with hearing–the process by which sound waves are translated into understandable and meaningful forms–the sense of motion and balance resides in the ear.

Sensing Sound

Although many of us think primarily of the outer ear when we speak of the ear, that structure is only one simple part of the whole. The outer ear acts as a reverse megaphone, designed to collect and bring sounds into the internal portions of the ear (see Figure 1). The location of the outer ears on different sides of the head helps with *sound localization*, the process by which we identify the direction from which a sound is coming. Wave patterns in the air enter each ear at a slightly different time, and the brain uses the discrepancy as a clue to the sound's point of origin. In addition, the two outer ears delay or amplify sounds of particular frequencies to different degrees (Schnupp, Nelken, & King, 2011; Tolnai, Beutelmann & Klump, 2017).

Sound is the movement of air molecules brought about by a source of vibration. Sounds travel through the air in wave patterns similar in shape to those made in water when a stone is thrown into a still pond. Sounds, arriving at the outer ear in the form of wavelike vibrations, are funneled into the *auditory canal*, a tube-like passage that leads to the eardrum. The **eardrum** is the part of the ear that vibrates when sound waves hit it. The more intense the sound, the more the eardrum vibrates. These vibrations are then transferred into the *middle ear*, a tiny chamber containing three bones (the *hammer*, the *anvil*, and the *stirrup*) that transmit vibrations to the oval window, a thin membrane leading to the inner ear. Because the hammer, anvil, and stirrup act as a set of levers, they not only transmit vibrations but also increase their strength. Moreover, because the opening into the middle ear (the eardrum) is considerably larger than the opening out of it (the *oval window*), the force of sound waves on the oval window becomes amplified. The middle ear, then, acts as a tiny mechanical amplifier.

The *inner ear* is the portion of the ear that changes the sound vibrations into a form in which they can be transmitted to the brain. (As you will see, it also contains the organs that allow us to locate our position and determine how we are moving through space.) When sound enters the inner ear through the oval window, it moves into the **cochlea,** a coiled tube that looks something like a snail and is filled with fluid that vibrates in response to sound. Inside the cochlea is the **basilar membrane,** a structure that runs through the center of the cochlea, dividing it into an upper chamber and a lower chamber. The basilar membrane is covered with **hair cells.** When the hair cells are bent by the vibrations entering the cochlea, the cells send a neural message to the brain (Zhou, Liu, & Davis, 2005; Møller, 2011; Curthoys, 2017).

AP® LEARNING TARGETS

- Describe the hearing process, including the specific nature of energy transduction, relevant anatomical structures, and specialized pathways in the brain for each of the senses.

- Describe taste and smell processes, including the specific nature of energy transduction, relevant anatomical structures, and specialized pathways in the brain for each of the senses.

- Describe sensory processes, including the specific nature of energy transduction, relevant anatomical structures, and specialized pathways in the brain for each of the body senses.

sound The movement of air molecules brought about by a source of vibration. (Module 12)

eardrum The part of the ear that vibrates when sound waves hit it. (Module 12)

cochlea (KOKE-lee-uh) A coiled tube in the ear filled with fluid that vibrates in response to sound. (Module 12)

basilar membrane A vibrating structure that runs through the center of the cochlea, dividing it into an upper chamber and a lower chamber and containing sense receptors for sound. (Module 12)

hair cells Tiny cells covering the basilar membrane that, when bent by vibrations entering the cochlea, transmit neural messages to the brain. (Module 12)

103

FIGURE 1 The major parts of the ear.
©McGraw-Hill Global Education Holdings LLC, 2008.

THE PHYSICAL ASPECTS OF SOUND

As we mentioned earlier, what we refer to as sound is actually the physical movement of air molecules in regular, wavelike patterns caused by a vibrating source. Sometimes it is even possible to see these vibrations: If you have ever seen an audio speaker that has no enclosure, you know that, at least when the lowest notes are playing, you can see the speaker moving in and out. Less obvious is what happens next: The speaker pushes air molecules into waves with the same pattern as its movement. Those wave patterns soon reach your ear, although their strength has been weakened considerably during their travels. All other sources that produce sound work in essentially the same fashion, setting off wave patterns that move through the air to the ear. Air–or some other medium, such as water–is necessary to make the vibrations of objects reach us. This explains why there can be no sound in a vacuum.

We are able to see the audio speaker moving when low notes are played because of a primary characteristic of sound called frequency. *Frequency* is the number of wave cycles that occur in a second. At very low frequencies, there are relatively few wave cycles per second (see Figure 2). These cycles are visible to the naked eye as vibrations in the speaker. Low frequencies are translated into a sound that is very low in pitch. (*Pitch* is the characteristic that makes sound seem "high" or "low.") For example, the lowest frequency that humans are capable of hearing is 20 cycles per second. Higher frequencies are heard as sounds of higher pitch. At the upper end of the sound spectrum, people can detect sounds with frequencies as high as 20,000 cycles per second.

Amplitude is a feature of wave patterns that allows us to distinguish between loud and soft sounds. Amplitude is the spread between the up-and-down peaks and valleys of air pressure in a sound wave as it travels through the air. Waves with small peaks and valleys produce soft sounds; those with relatively large peaks and valleys produce loud sounds.

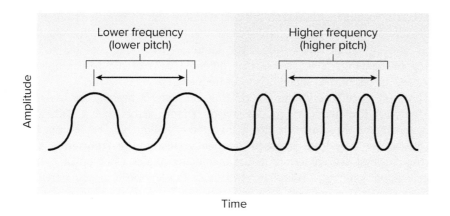

FIGURE 2 The sound waves produced by different stimuli are transmitted—usually through the air—in different patterns, with lower frequencies indicated by fewer peaks and valleys per second.
©McGraw-Hill Global Education Holdings LLC, 2000.

We are sensitive to broad variations in sound amplitudes. The strongest sounds we are capable of hearing are over a trillion times as intense as the very weakest sound we can hear. This range is measured in *decibels*. When sounds get higher than 120 decibels, they become painful to the human ear.

Our sensitivity to different frequencies changes as we age. For instance, as we get older, the range of frequencies we can detect declines, particularly for high-pitched sounds. This is why high school students sometimes choose high-pitched ring tones for their cell phones in settings where cell phone use is forbidden: the ringing sound goes undetected by their aging teachers (Vitello, 2006; Moreno-Gómez et al., 2017) (see Figure 3).

Explaining Hearing: Listen to the Theories of Sound How are our brains able to sort out wavelengths of different frequencies and intensities? One important clue comes from studies of the basilar membrane, the area in the cochlea that translates physical vibrations into nerve impulses. It turns out that sounds affect different areas of the basilar membrane according to the frequency of the sound wave reaching it. The part

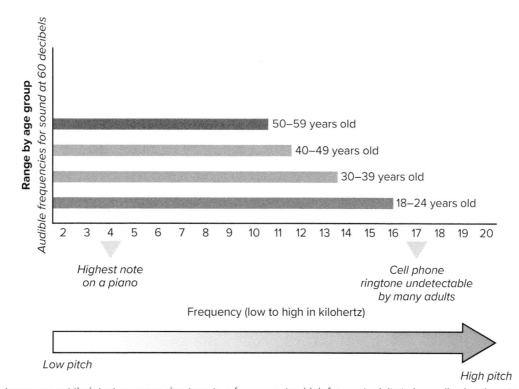

FIGURE 3 Some teenagers set their text-message ring tone to a frequency too high for most adults to hear, allowing them to use cell phones where they are prohibited.
Source: Adapted from Vitello, P. (2006, June 12). A ring tone meant to fall on deaf ears. The New York Times, A1.

place theory of hearing The theory that different areas of the basilar membrane respond to different frequencies.

frequency theory of hearing The theory that the entire basilar membrane acts like a microphone, vibrating as a whole in response to a sound. (Module 12)

Study Alert
Be sure to understand the differences between the place and frequency theories of hearing.

of the basilar membrane nearest to the oval window is most sensitive to high-frequency sounds. In contrast, the part of the basilar membrane nearest to the cochlea's inner end is most sensitive to low-frequency sounds. This finding has led to the **place theory of hearing,** which states that different areas of the basilar membrane are specialized to respond to different sound frequencies.

However, place theory does not tell the full story of hearing because of a significant fact: very low frequency sounds trigger neurons across such a wide area of the basilar membrane that no single site is involved. Consequently, an additional explanation for hearing has been proposed: frequency theory. The **frequency theory of hearing** suggests that the entire basilar membrane acts as a microphone, vibrating as a whole in response to a sound. According to this explanation, the nerve receptors send out signals that are tied directly to the frequency (the number of wave crests per second) of the sounds to which we are exposed, with the number of nerve impulses being a direct function of a sound's frequency. Thus, the higher the pitch of a sound (and therefore the greater the frequency of its wave crests), the greater the number of nerve impulses that are transmitted up the auditory nerve to the brain.

Ultimately, it seems that we need both place theory and frequency theory to understand the process of hearing. Specifically, place theory provides a better explanation for the sensing of high-frequency sounds, whereas frequency theory explains what happens when low-frequency sounds are encountered. Medium-frequency sounds incorporate both processes (Hirsh & Watson, 1996; Hudspeth, 2000).

Regardless of whether we employ place theory or frequency theory, we know that after an auditory message leaves the ear, it is transmitted to the auditory cortex of the brain through a complex series of nerve interconnections. And similar to visual nerve cells in the brain that respond to specific kinds of stimuli, auditory neurons respond to specific types of sounds. For example, certain neurons respond selectively to clicks and whistles. Other neurons respond only to a specific sound pattern, such as a steady tone but not an intermittent one. Furthermore, specific neurons transfer information about a sound's location through their particular pattern of firing (Wang et al., 2005; Alho et al., 2006; Romero-Guevara et al., 2015).

If we were to analyze the configuration of the cells in the auditory cortex, we would find that neighboring cells are responsive to similar frequencies. The auditory cortex, then, provides us with a "map" of sound frequencies, just as the visual cortex furnishes a representation of the visual field. In addition, because of the asymmetry in the two hemispheres of the brain, the left and right ears process sound differently. The right ear reacts more to speech, whereas the left ear responds more to music (Sininger & Cone-Wesson, 2004, 2006; McCulloch et al., 2017).

Speech perception requires that we make fine discriminations among sounds that are quite similar in terms of their physical properties. Furthermore, not only are we able to understand *what* is being said from speech, we also can use vocal cues to determine who is speaking, whether they have an accent and where they may be from, and even their emotional state. Such capabilities illustrate the sophistication of our sense of hearing (Pell et al., 2009; Ross et al., 2011; Mattys et al., 2013).

Scientists are also beginning to investigate how we use sound to navigate through our environment. *Echolocation* is the use of sound waves and echoes to determine where objects are. It is the navigational technique that bats use, and some people with impaired vision have learned to use echolocation by generating sounds (such as snapping their fingers or making clicking noises) and using the echoes that bounce off objects to navigate. Although psychologists are early in their research on the phenomenon, it may provide a window into sensory processes and ultimately improve the lives of those with sensory impairments (Thaler, 2015).

Balance: The Ups and Downs of Life Several structures of the ear are related more to our sense of balance than to our hearing. Collectively, these structures are known as the *vestibular system*, which responds to the pull of gravity and allows us to maintain our balance, even when standing in a bus in stop-and-go traffic.

Zero gravity presents numerous challenges, some of which were depicted in the film *The Martian* with Matt Damon. For example, the weightlessness of the ear's otoliths produces space sickness in most astronauts.
©GENRE FILMS/INTERNATIONAL TRADERS/MID ATLACTIC FILD/20TH CEN/Album/Newscom

The main structure of the vestibular system is formed by the **semicircular canals** of the inner ear (refer to Figure 1), which consist of three tubes containing fluid that sloshes through them when the head moves, signaling rotational or angular movement to the brain. The pull on our bodies caused by the acceleration of forward, backward, or up-and-down motion, as well as the constant pull of gravity, is sensed by the *otoliths*, tiny, motion-sensitive crystals in the semicircular canals. When we move, these crystals shift as sands do on a windy beach, contacting the specialized receptor *hair cells* in the semicircular canals. The brain's inexperience in interpreting messages from the weightless otoliths is the cause of the space sickness commonly experienced by two-thirds of all space travelers, mentioned at the start of this module (Yoder et al., 2015).

semicircular canals Three tube-like structures of the inner ear containing fluid that sloshes through them when the head moves, signaling rotational or angular movement to the brain. (Module 12)

Smell and Taste

Until he bit into a piece of raw cabbage on that February evening . . ., Raymond Fowler had not thought much about the sense of taste. The cabbage, part of a pasta dish he was preparing for his family's dinner, had an odd, burning taste, but he did not pay it much attention. Then a few minutes later, his daughter handed him a glass of cola, and he took a swallow. "It was like sulfuric acid," he said. "It was like the hottest thing you could imagine boring into your mouth." (Goode, 1999)

It was evident that something was very wrong with Fowler's sense of taste. After extensive testing, it became clear that the nerves involved in his sense of taste had been damaged, probably because of a viral infection or a medicine he was taking. (Luckily for him, a few months later, his sense of taste returned to normal.)

Even without disruptions in our ability to perceive the world such as those experienced by Fowler, we all know the important roles that taste and smell play. We'll consider these two senses next.

SMELL

Although many animals have keener abilities to detect odors than we do, the human sense of smell (*olfaction*) permits us to detect more than 10,000 separate smells. We also have a good memory for smells, and long-forgotten events and memories–good

More than 1,000 olfactory receptor cells, like this one in the center of the scan, are spread across the nasal cavity. The cells are specialized to react to particular odors. Do you think it is possible to "train" the nose to pick up a greater number of odors?
©Prof. P. Motta/Dept. of Anatomy/University "La Sapienza", Rome/SPL/Science Source

and bad—can be brought back with the mere whiff of an odor associated with a memory (Willander & Larsson, 2006; Schroers, Prigot, & Fagen, 2007; Arshamian et al., 2013).

Results of "sniff tests" have shown that women generally have a better sense of smell than men do (Engen, 1987). People also have the ability to distinguish males from females on the basis of smell alone. In one experiment, blindfolded students who were asked to sniff the breath of a female or male volunteer who was hidden from view were able to distinguish the sex of the donor at better-than-chance levels. People can also distinguish happy from sad emotions by sniffing underarm smells, and women are able to identify their babies solely on the basis of smell just a few hours after birth (Doty et al., 1982; Fusari & Ballesteros, 2008; Flohr et al., 2017).

The sense of smell is sparked when the molecules of a substance enter the nasal passages and meet *olfactory cells*, the receptor neurons of the nose, which are spread across the nasal cavity. More than 1,000 separate types of receptors have been identified on those cells so far. Each of these receptors is so specialized that it responds only to a small band of different odors. The responses of the separate olfactory cells are then transmitted to the brain, where they are combined into recognition of a particular smell (Marshall, Laing, & Jinks, 2006; Zhou & Buck, 2006; Jia & Hegg, 2015).

Smell may also act as a hidden means of communication for humans. It has long been known that nonhumans release *pheromones*, chemicals they secrete into the environment that produce a social response in other members of the same species. Pheromones transmit messages such as alarm ("danger—predators are close by!") or sexual availability ("I'm interested in sex"). For instance, the vaginal secretions of female monkeys contain pheromones that stimulate the sexual interest of male monkeys (Touhara, 2007; Brennan, 2011; Zizzari et al., 2017).

The degree to which pheromones are part of the human experience remains an open question. Some psychologists believe that human pheromones affect emotional responses, although the evidence is inconclusive. For one thing, it is not clear what specific sense organ is receptive to pheromones. In nonhumans, it is the *vomeronasal organ* in the nose, but in humans, the organ appears to recede during fetal development (Haviland-Jones & Wilson, 2008; Hummer & McClintock, 2009; Gelstein et al., 2011); also see *Applying Psychology in the 21st Century*.

PsychTech

When male participants in a study sniffed women's tears, fMRI brain scans showed reduced activity in the parts of the brain associated with sexual arousal. Apparently, tears contain a chemical signal.

TASTE

The sense of taste (*gustation*) involves receptor cells that respond to four basic stimulus qualities: sweet, sour, salty, and bitter. A fifth category also exists, a flavor called *umami*, although there is controversy about whether it qualifies as a fundamental taste. *Umami* is a hard-to-translate Japanese word, although the English "meaty" or "savory" comes close. Chemically, umami involves food stimuli that contain amino acids (the substances that make up proteins) (McCabe & Rolls, 2007; Erickson, 2008; Nakamura et al., 2011).

Although the specialization of the receptor cells leads them to respond most strongly to a particular type of taste, they are capable of responding to other tastes as well. Ultimately, every taste is simply a combination of the basic flavor qualities, in the same way that the primary colors blend into a vast variety of shades and hues (Yeomans, Tepper, & Ritezschel, 2007; Spence, Auvray, & Smith, 2015).

The receptor cells for taste are located in roughly 10,000 *taste buds*, which are distributed across the tongue and other parts of the mouth and throat. The taste buds wear out and are replaced every 10 days or so. That's a good thing because if our taste buds weren't constantly reproducing, we'd lose the ability to taste after we'd accidentally burned our tongues.

There are 10,000 taste buds on the tongue and on other parts of the mouth. Taste buds wear out and are replaced every 10 days. What would happen if taste buds were not regenerated?
©Science Source

SNIFFING OUT FLASH DRIVES

Sensation and perception tell us everything we know about the world around us. But as amazing as these processes are, they do have their limits. We can't see microbes or ultraviolet light, for example, nor can we detect radiation at all. Our ability to apprehend and respond to our environment diminishes greatly beyond the limits of our senses. Indeed, our very understanding of reality is largely bound by our limited sensory and perceptual abilities.

Many nonhuman animals have different or greater sensory abilities than we do. Some insects can see ultraviolet light. Bats can hear sounds at much higher frequencies than we can. And dogs can detect much fainter scents. We have a long history of using our canine companions' remarkable sense of smell to help us navigate the world, from hunting foxes to detecting illicit drugs. Enter Iris, an 18-month-old Labrador retriever with an amazingly skillful nose (Polgár et al., 2016).

Iris is a police dog trained by the U.S. Federal Bureau of Investigation with a unique ability: she can sniff out electronics. Iris is one of only four dogs in the United States that have been successfully trained to

The sense of smell in dogs is much better than that of humans, and their skill can even help detect illegal electronic equipment. ©Tengku Bahar/AFP/Getty Images

detect a chemical commonly used on memory chips and present in most electronic storage devices such as flash drives, hard drives, or SD cards. Certain kinds of serious criminal activity such as data theft, espionage, or child pornography typically entail the use of such storage devices, and investigators often need to find these devices to stop the criminal activity or to use them as evidence in court. The problem, though, is that these devices are now small enough to

easily conceal in what would seem to be unlikely places–inside jewelry, in hollowed-out hiding spaces within walls or furnishings, or even inside more innocuous kinds of electronic devices. Finding these devices has become all but impossible for human investigators (Dienst, Schreiber, & Valiquette, 2016).

But not for Iris. Deception doesn't work on a dog. Not even the cleverest hiding spaces escape her outstanding canine senses. Her nose leads her right to them. A person would be hard pressed to detect the unique scent of a memory chip right under her own nose, but Iris can detect it at a distance–and quickly, too. She follows the scent trail to the hiding spot and then sits passively as officers retrieve the evidence and reward Iris for a job well done (Merrill, 2016).

We may be just scratching the surface of the capabilities of dogs such as Iris. So if you are passing through airport security, consider that you may be safer because of the extraordinary sensory capabilities of nonhumans.

AP SKILL: DEFINE AND/OR APPLY CONCEPT / EXPLAIN BEHAVIOR IN AUTHENTIC CONTEXT

1. Dogs detect smells that humans are not able to detect. What type of threshold is lower for dogs than humans?
2. How would your life change if you had an increased sense of smell like dogs?

The sense of taste differs significantly from one person to another, largely as a result of genetic factors. Some people, dubbed "supertasters," are highly sensitive to taste; they have twice as many taste receptors as "nontasters," who are relatively insensitive to taste. Supertasters (who, for unknown reasons, are more likely to be female than male) find sweets sweeter, cream creamier, and spicy dishes spicier, and weaker concentrations of flavor are enough to satisfy any cravings they may have (Pickering & Gordon, 2006; Cornelis et al., 2017).

Supertasters–who make up about 15% of the U.S. population–may even be healthier than nontasters. Because supertasters find fatty foods distasteful, they are thinner than the general population. In contrast, because they aren't so sensitive to taste, nontasters may seek out relatively sweeter and fattier foods in order to maximize the taste. As a consequence, they may be prone to obesity (Reddy, 2013).

Are you a supertaster? To find out, complete the questionnaire in Figure 4.

Take a Taste Test

1. Taste Bud Count
   Punch a hole with a standard hole punch in a square of wax paper. Paint the front of your tongue with a cotton swab dipped in blue food coloring. Put wax paper on the tip of your tongue, just to the right of center. With a flashlight and magnifying glass, count the number of pink, unstained circles. They contain taste buds.

2. Sweet Taste
   Rinse your mouth with water before tasting each sample. Put a ½ cup of sugar in a measuring cup, and then add enough water to make I cup. Mix. Coat the front half of your tongue, including the tip, with a cotton swab dipped in the solution. Wait a few moments. Rate the sweetness according to the scale shown below.

3. Salt Taste
   Put 2 teaspoons of salt in a measuring cup and add enough water to make I cup. Repeat the steps listed above, rating how salty the solution is.

4. Spicy Taste
   Add I teaspoon of Tabasco sauce to I cup of water. Apply with a cotton swab to the first ½ inch of the tongue, including the tip. Keep your tongue out of your mouth until the burn reaches a peak, then rate the burn according to the scale.

TASTE SCALE

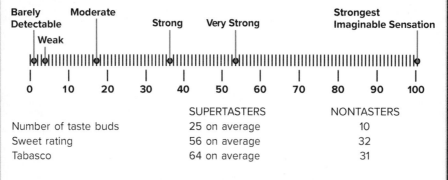

	SUPERTASTERS	NONTASTERS
Number of taste buds	25 on average	10
Sweet rating	56 on average	32
Tabasco	64 on average	31

Average tasters lie in between supertasters and nontasters. Bartoshuk and Lucchina lack the data at this time to rate salt reliably, but you can compare your results with others taking the test.

FIGURE 4 All tongues are not created equal, according to taste researchers Linda Bartoshuk and Laurie Lucchina. Instead, they suggest that the intensity of a flavor experienced by a given person is determined by that person's genetic background. This taste test can help determine if you are a nontaster, average taster, or supertaster.
Source: Bartoshuk, L., & Lucchina, L. (1997, January 13). Are you a supertaster? *U.S. News & World Report,* 58–59.

The Skin Senses: Touch, Pressure, Temperature, and Pain

It started innocently when Jennifer Darling hurt her right wrist during gym class. At first, it seemed like a simple sprain. But even though the initial injury healed, the excruciating, burning pain accompanying it did not go away. Instead, it spread to her other arm and then to her legs. The pain, which Jennifer described as similar to "a hot iron on your arm," was unbearable—and never stopped.

The source of Darling's pain turned out to be a rare condition known as *reflex sympathetic dystrophy syndrome*, or RSDS. RSDS is a disease characterized by constant, intense pain that is out of proportion to any injury. For a victim of RSDS, a stimulus as mild as a gentle breeze or the touch of a feather can produce agony. Even bright sunlight or a loud noise can trigger intense pain (Coderre, 2011; Harden et al., 2013).

Pain such as Darling's can be devastating, yet a lack of pain can be equally bad. If you never experience pain, for instance, you might not notice that your arm had brushed against a hot pan, and you would suffer a severe burn. Similarly, without the warning sign of abdominal pain that typically accompanies an inflamed appendix, your appendix might eventually rupture, spreading a fatal infection throughout your body.

Pain has other benefits, as well. Pain helps us better appreciate pleasurable experiences. It also may lead us to affiliate more closely with others, by arousing their empathy. And pain may lead us to be more vigilant about our surroundings as we seek to avoid or moderate pain we are experiencing (Bastian et al., 2014; Cameron, Spring, & Todd, 2017).

In fact, all our **skin senses**–touch, pressure, temperature, and pain–play a critical role in survival, making us aware of potential danger to our bodies. Most of these senses operate through nerve receptor cells located at various depths throughout the skin, distributed unevenly throughout the body. For example, some areas, such as the fingertips, have many more receptor cells sensitive to touch and as a consequence are notably more sensitive than other areas of the body (Gardner & Kandel, 2000) (see Figure 5).

Probably the most extensively researched skin sense is pain, and with good reason: People consult physicians and take medication for pain more than for any other symptom or condition. Chronic pain afflicts more than 116 million American adults and costs around $600 billion a year in the United States alone (Park, 2011; Jensen & Turk, 2014; Robinson-Papp et al., 2015).

Pain is a response to a great variety of different kinds of stimuli. A light that is too bright can produce pain, and sound that is too loud can be painful. There are also

skin senses The senses of touch, pressure, temperature, and pain. (Module 12)

Study Alert
Remember that there are multiple skin senses, including touch, pressure, temperature, and pain.

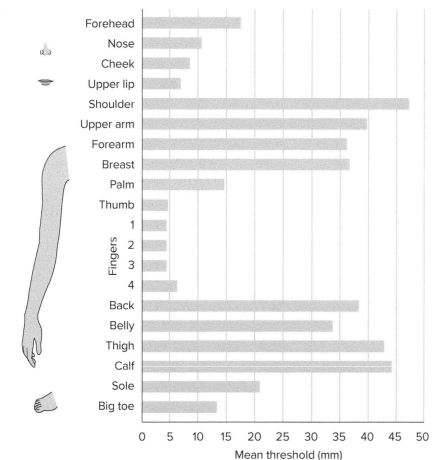

FIGURE 5 Skin sensitivity in various areas of the body. The lower the average threshold is, the more sensitive a body part is. The fingers and thumb, lips, nose, cheeks, and big toe are the most sensitive. Why do you think certain areas are more sensitive than others?

multiple forms of pain; even itching can be considered a form of pain (Papoiu et al., 2013; Bautista, Wilson, & Hoon, 2014; Sutherland, 2016.)

One explanation for pain is that it is an outcome of cell injury; when a cell is damaged, regardless of the source of damage, it releases a chemical called *substance P* that transmits pain messages to the brain.

Some people are more susceptible to pain than others. For example, women experience painful stimuli more intensely than men do. These gender differences are associated with the production of hormones related to menstrual cycles. In addition, certain genes are linked to the experience of pain, so that we may inherit our sensitivity to pain (Kim, Clark, & Dionne, 2009; Park, 2011; Berke et al., 2017).

But the experience of pain is not determined by biological factors alone. For example, women report that the pain experienced in childbirth is moderated to some degree by the joyful nature of the situation. In contrast, even a minor stimulus can produce the perception of strong pain if it is accompanied by anxiety (for example, during a visit to the dentist). Clearly, then, pain is a perceptual response that depends heavily on our emotions and thoughts (Lang, Sorrell, & Rodgers, 2006; Kennedy et al., 2011; Jensen & Turk, 2014).

From the perspective of...

A Medical or Dental Services Provider How would you handle a patient who is anxiously awaiting treatment and complaining that her pain is getting worse?

©Robert Daly/age fotostock

gate-control theory of pain The theory that particular nerve receptors in the spinal cord lead to specific areas of the brain related to pain. (Module 12)

According to the **gate-control theory of pain,** particular nerve receptors in the spinal cord lead to specific areas of the brain related to pain. When these receptors are activated because of an injury or problem with a part of the body, a "gate" to the brain is opened, causing us to experience the sensation of pain (Melzack & Katz, 2004; Vasudeva et al., 2015).

But the gate that produces pain does not necessarily remain open. Specifically, another set of neural receptors can, when stimulated, close the "gate" to the brain, thereby reducing the experience of pain.

The gate can be shut in two different ways. First, other impulses can overwhelm the nerve pathways relating to pain, which are spread throughout the brain. In this case, non-painful stimuli compete with and sometimes displace the neural message of pain, thereby shutting off the painful stimulus. This explains why rubbing the skin around an injury (or even listening to distracting music) helps reduce pain. The competing stimuli can overpower the painful ones (Villemure, Slotnick, & Bushnell, 2003; Somers et al., 2011).

PsychTech

Researcher Sean Mackey exposed participants in a study to a painful stimulus while watching an fMRI scan of their brain. Mackey found that the participants could be trained to exert control over the region of the brain activated by the pain, thereby reducing their experience of pain.

Second, the neural gate producing pain can be shut by psychological factors relating to an individual's current emotions, interpretation of events, and previous experience. Specifically, the brain can close a gate by sending a message down the spinal cord to an injured area, producing a reduction in or relief from pain. Thus, soldiers who are injured in battle may experience no pain–the surprising situation in more than half of all combat injuries. The lack of pain probably occurs because a soldier experiences such relief at still being alive that the brain sends a signal to the injury site to shut down the pain gate (Gatchel & Weisberg, 2000; Pincus & Morley, 2001).

Gate-control theory also may explain cultural differences in the experience of pain. Some of these variations are astounding. For example, in India, people who participate in the "hook-swinging" ritual to celebrate the power of the gods have steel hooks embedded under the skin and muscles of their backs. During the ritual, they swing from a pole, suspended by the hooks. What would seem likely to induce excruciating pain instead produces a state of celebration and near euphoria. In fact, when the hooks are later removed, the wounds heal quickly, and after 2 weeks almost no visible marks remain (Kosambi, 1967; Melzack & Katz, 2001).

Gate-control theory suggests that the lack of pain is due to a message from the participant's brain that shuts down the pain pathways. Gate-control theory also may explain the effectiveness of *acupuncture*, an ancient Chinese technique in which sharp needles are inserted into various parts of the body. The sensation from the needles may close the gateway to the brain, reducing the experience of pain. It is also possible that the body's own painkillers–called *endorphins*–as well as positive and negative emotions, play a role in opening and closing the gate (Witt, Jena, & Brinkhaus, 2006; Cabioglu, Ergene, & Tan, 2007; Khedr et al., 2017).

The ancient practice of acupuncture is still used in the 21st century. How does the gate-control theory of pain explain how acupuncture works?
©Fuse/Corbis/Getty Images

Although the basic ideas behind gate-control theory have been supported by research, other processes are involved in the perception of pain. For instance, it appears that there are multiple neural pathways involved in the experience of pain. Furthermore, the suppression of pain can occur through the natural release of endorphins and other compounds that produce a reduction of discomfort and a sense of well-being. Finally, cognitive factors–such as people's expectations and their prior learning about pain–play a significant role in the perception of pain (Grahek, 2007; Wiech, 2016).

BECOMING AN INFORMED CONSUMER
of Psychology

Managing Pain

Are you one of the more than 116 million people in the United States who suffers from chronic pain? Psychologists and medical specialists have devised several strategies to fight pain. Among the most important approaches are these:

- *Medication.* Painkilling drugs are the most popular treatment in fighting pain. Drugs range from those that directly treat the source of the pain—such as reducing swelling in painful joints—to those that work on the symptoms. Medication can be in the form of pills, patches, injections, or liquids. In a recent innovation, drugs are pumped directly into the spinal cord (Kalb, 2003; Pesmen, 2006; Bagnall, 2010).
- *Nerve and brain stimulation.* Pain can sometimes be relieved when a low-voltage electric current is passed through the specific part of the body that is in pain. For example, in *peripheral-nerve stimulation,* a tiny battery-operated generator is implanted in the lower back. In even more severe cases, electrodes can be implanted surgically directly into the brain, or a handheld battery pack can stimulate nerve cells to provide direct relief (Tugay et al., 2007; Landro, 2010; Tan et al., 2011).
- *Light therapy.* One of the newest forms of pain reduction involves exposure to specific wavelengths of red or infrared light. Certain kinds of light increase the production of enzymes that may promote healing (Underwood, 2005; Evcik et al., 2007).
- *Hypnosis.* For people who can be hypnotized—and not everyone is susceptible—hypnosis can greatly relieve pain. In fact, it can affect the brain and spinal-cord functioning in injured people, actually improving their physical functioning (Accardi & Milling, 2009; Lee & Raja, 2011; Jensen & Patterson, 2014).

- *Biofeedback and relaxation techniques.* Using *biofeedback,* people learn to control what are usually involuntary functions such as heartbeat, respiration, blood pressure, and muscle tension. Through biofeedback, a person can learn to control the stimulus that is causing the pain. For instance, people with tension headaches or back pain can be trained to relax their bodies to bring themselves relief (Vitiello, Bonello, & Pollard, 2007; Sielski, Rief, & Glombiewski, 2017).

- *Surgery.* In one of the most extreme methods, specific nerve fibers that carry pain messages to the brain can be cut surgically. Still, because of the danger that other bodily functions will be affected, surgery is a treatment of last resort, used most frequently with dying patients (Cullinane, Chu, & Mamelak, 2002; Amid & Chen, 2011).

- *Cognitive restructuring.* Cognitive treatments are effective for people who continually say to themselves, "This pain will never stop," "The pain is ruining my life," or "I can't take it anymore," and are thereby likely to make their pain even worse. By substituting more positive ways of thinking, people can increase their sense of control—and actually reduce the pain they experience (Bogart et al., 2007; Liedl et al., 2011; Ehde, Dillworth, & Turner, 2014).

- *Mirror pain therapy.* One surprising treatment for people who suffer from phantom-limb pain (in which a person with an amputated limb experiences pain where the missing limb used to be) employs mirrors. By using a mirror to make it appear that both limbs are intact, the brain of the amputee stops sending messages perceived as pain (Foell et al., 2014).

How Our Senses Interact

When Matthew Blakeslee shapes hamburger patties with his hands, he experiences a vivid bitter taste in his mouth. Esmerelda Jones (a pseudonym) sees blue when she listens to the note C sharp played on the piano; other notes evoke different hues–so much so that the piano keys are actually color-coded, making it easier for her to remember and play musical scales. (Ramachandran & Hubbard, 2006)

The explanation? Both of these people have an unusual condition known as synesthesia. *Synesthesia* is a perceptual phenomenon in which the stimulation of one sensory system (such as hearing) involuntarily leads a person to experience an additional sensory response in a different sensory system (such as vision).

The origins of synesthesia are a mystery. It is possible that people with synesthesia have unusually dense neural linkages between the different sensory areas of the brain. Another hypothesis is that they lack neural controls that usually inhibit connections between sensory areas (Kadosh, Henik, & Walsh, 2009; Deroy & Spence, 2013; Meier & Rothen, 2015).

Whatever the reason for synesthesia, it is a rare condition. (If you'd like to check out this phenomenon, see Figure 6.) Even so, the senses of all of us do interact and integrate in a variety of ways. For example, the taste of food is influenced by its texture and temperature. We perceive food that is warmer as sweeter (think of the

FIGURE 6 (a) Try to pick out the 0s in the display. (Note: each 0 appears as a rectangular "ø" with a slash through it.) Most people take several seconds to find them buried among the 8s and to see that the øs form a triangle. For people with certain forms of synesthesia, however, it's easy because they perceive the different numbers in contrasting colors as in (b).

(a and b): Source: Adapted from Ramachandran, V. S., & Hubbard, E. M. (2006). Hearing colors, tasting shapes. *Scientific American, 16,* 76–83.

(a)

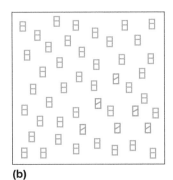
(b)

sweetness of steamy hot chocolate compared with cold chocolate milk). Spicy foods stimulate some of the same pain receptors that are also stimulated by heat—making the use of *hot* as a synonym for *spicy* quite accurate (Balaban, McBurney, & Affeltranger, 2005; Brang et al., 2011; Alfaro et al., 2015).

It's important, then, to think of our senses as interacting with one another. For instance, brain imaging studies show that the senses work in tandem to build our understanding of the world around us. We engage in *multimodal perception,* in which the brain collects the information from the individual sensory systems and integrates and coordinates it (Macaluso & Driver, 2005; Paulmann, Jessen, & Kotz, 2009; Gruber & Block, 2017).

Moreover, despite the fact that very different sorts of stimuli activate our individual senses, they all react according to the same basic principles that we discussed at the start of this chapter. For example, our responses to visual, auditory, and taste stimuli all follow Weber's law involving our sensitivity to changes in the strength of stimuli.

In short, in some ways our senses are more similar to one another than different. Each of them is designed to pick up information from the environment and translate it into useable information. Furthermore, individually and collectively, our senses help us to understand the complexities of the world around us, allowing us to navigate through the world effectively and intelligently.

AP MODULE 12: HEARING AND THE OTHER SENSES

AP SUMMARY

- Synesthesia is a rare perceptual phenomenon in which the stimulation of one sense involuntarily leads to a sensory experience in a different sensory system.
- Describe the hearing process, including the specific nature of energy transduction, relevant anatomical structures, and specialized pathways in the brain for each of the senses.
- Describe sensory processes, including the specific nature of energy transduction, relevant anatomical structures, and specialized pathways in the brain for each of the body senses.
- The location of the outer ears helps with sound localization, the process to identify where a sound is coming from. Sounds, in the form of vibrating air waves, enter through the outer ear and travel through the auditory canal until they reach the eardrum. The vibrations of the eardrum are transmitted into the middle ear, which consists of three bones: the hammer, the anvil, and the stirrup. These bones transmit vibrations to the oval window. Sound, motion, and balance are centered in the ear.
- In the inner ear, vibrations move into the cochlea, which encloses the basilar membrane. Hair cells on the basilar membrane change the mechanical energy of sound waves into nerve impulses that are transmitted to the auditory cortex in the temporal lobe of the brain. The vestibular system, our sense of balance, is located in the inner ear. The main structure responsible is the semicircular canals, which are filled with fluid and hair cells that signal movement to the brain.
- Sound has several physical characteristics, including frequency (determines pitch) and amplitude (wave patterns that allow us to distinguish between loud and soft sound). The process of hearing pitch is based on two theories. The place theory states that different locations on the basilar membrane are specialized for hearing different pitches. The frequency theory suggests the entire basilar membrane vibrates to a sound. The higher the pitch, the greater the number of nerve impulses transmitted to the brain. As we get older our sensitivity to high-pitched sounds decreases.
- Scientists are exploring echolocation—the use of sound waves and echoes to determine where objects are located—to improve the lives of those with sensory impairments.
- Describe taste and smell processes, including the specific nature of energy transduction, relevant anatomical structures, and specialized pathways in the brain for each of the senses.
- Taste (gustation) is centered on taste receptors located in the taste buds on the tongue and mouth. Taste buds regenerate approximately every 10 days. Receptor cells respond to basic tastes, such as sweet, sour, salty, bitter, and umami (meaty or savory).
- Genetic factors contribute to one's sense of taste. There are supertasters and non-tasters.

- Smell (olfaction) depends on olfactory cells (the receptor cells of the nose). Over 1,000 separate types of receptors have been identified so far. The responses of the separate olfactory cells are sent to the brain to be combined into recognition of a certain smell. Humans are able to detect over 10,000 separate smells and have a good memory for smells. Women have a better sense of smell than men.
- Nonhumans are able to communicate through pheromones, chemicals secreted for alarm or sexual availability. The possibility of human pheromones is still being investigated.
- Skin senses–touch, pressure, temperature, and pain–are critical to survival. Most of these senses operate through nerve receptor cells located in the skin, distributed unevenly throughout the body. The fingertips and thumb, lips, nose, cheeks, and big toe are the most sensitive.
- Pain is the most researched skin sense. One explanation for pain is that when a cell is damaged, it releases a chemical that transmits pain messages to the brain. Other explanations explore gender, genes, and perceptual interpretations that rely on emotions and thoughts. Pain is devastating but can provide helpful benefits. It can provide important warning signals, help us appreciate pleasurable experiences, and invoke empathy.
- Gate-control theory suggests that certain nerve receptors in the spinal cord open a "gate" to specific areas of the brain related to pain. This "gate" can be shut by competing stimuli (such as rubbing the skin around an injury), or psychological factors (emotions, interpretation of events, experience) by sending a message down the spinal cord to the injured area. This theory may explain cultural differences in the experience of pain.
- It appears multiple processes are involved in the perception of pain, including neural pathways, endorphins, and cognitive factors (e.g., expectations and prior learning).
- Among techniques to alleviate pain are medication, hypnosis, biofeedback, relaxation techniques, surgery, nerve and brain stimulation, and cognitive therapy.

AP KEY TERMS

sound
eardrum
cochlea (KOKE-lee-uh)
basilar membrane
hair cells
place theory of hearing

frequency theory of hearing
semicircular canals
skin senses
gate-control theory of pain

AP TEST PRACTICE

Section I: Multiple Choice

1. Which theory helps an individual determine the frequency of a sound wave?
   A. Place theory
   B. Trichromatic theory
   C. Opponent-process theory
   D. Feature detection
   E. Sound localization

2. Which of the following statements is true?
   A. Pain is controlled by only genetic factors.
   B. Women generally have a better olfactory sense.
   C. Supertasters tend to seek out sweeter and fattier foods.
   D. Gustation consists of five main receptor cells: sweet, salty, spicy, sour, and bitter.
   E. Men are more likely to be supertasters.

3. The main structure for the vestibular system is located in the
   A. nose
   B. skin
   C. inner ear
   D. retina
   E. olfactory bulb

Section II: Free Response

Describe how each of following terms are associated to an anatomical structure and particular sensory process.
- Place theory
- Sound localization
- Semicircular canals
- Gate-control theory
- Receptor cells for umami

Module 13
Perceptual Organization: Constructing Our View of the World

Consider the vase shown in Figure 1a for a moment. Or is it a vase? Take another look, and instead you may see the profiles of two people.

Now that an alternative interpretation has been pointed out, you will probably shift back and forth between the two interpretations. Similarly, if you examine the shapes in Figure 1b long enough, you will probably experience a shift in what you're seeing. The reason for these reversals is this: Because each figure is two-dimensional, the usual means we employ for distinguishing the figure (the object being perceived) from the *ground* (the background or spaces within the object) do not work.

The fact that we can look at the same figure in more than one way illustrates an important point. We do not just passively respond to visual stimuli that happen to fall on our retinas. Rather, we actively try to organize and make sense of what we see.

We turn now from a focus on the initial response to a stimulus (sensation) to what our minds make of that stimulus (perception). Perception is a constructive process by which we go beyond the stimuli that are presented to us and attempt to construct a meaningful situation.

The Gestalt Laws of Organization

Some of the most basic perceptual processes can be described by a series of principles that focus on the ways we organize bits and pieces of information into meaningful wholes. Known as **Gestalt laws of organization,** these principles were set forth in the early 1900s by a group of German psychologists who studied patterns, or *gestalts* (Wertheimer, 1923). Those psychologists discovered a number of important principles that are valid for visual (as well as auditory) stimuli, illustrated in Figure 2: closure, proximity, similarity, and simplicity.

Figure 2a illustrates *closure*: We usually group elements to form enclosed or complete figures rather than open ones. We tend to ignore the breaks in Figure 2a and concentrate on the overall form. Figure 2b demonstrates the principle of *proximity*: We

Gestalt (geh-SHTALLT) laws of organization A series of principles that describe how we organize bits and pieces of information into meaningful wholes. (Module 13)

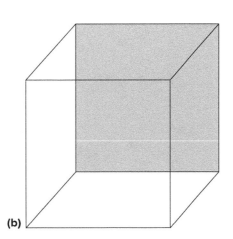

(a)   (b)

FIGURE 1 When the usual cues we use to distinguish figure from ground are absent, we may shift back and forth between different views of the same figure. In (a), you can see either a vase or the profiles of two people. In (b), the shaded portion of the figure, called a Necker cube, can appear to be either the front or the back of the cube.

(a) Closure   **(b)** Proximity   **(c)** Similarity   **(d)** Simplicity

FIGURE 2 Organizing these various bits and pieces of information into meaningful wholes constitutes some of the most basic processes of perception, which are summed up in the gestalt laws of organization. How might we determine if any other species share this organizational tendency?

perceive elements that are closer together as grouped together. As a result, we tend to see pairs of dots rather than a row of single dots in Figure 2b.

Elements that are *similar* in appearance we perceive as grouped together. We see, then, horizontal rows of circles and squares in Figure 2c, rather than vertical mixed columns. Finally, in a general sense, the overriding gestalt principle is *simplicity*: When we observe a pattern, we perceive it in the most basic, straightforward manner that we can. For example, most of us see Figure 2d as a square with lines on two sides, rather than as the block letter *W* on top of the letter *M*. If we have a choice of interpretations, we generally opt for the simpler one.

Although Gestalt psychology no longer plays a prominent role in contemporary psychology, its legacy endures. One fundamental Gestalt principle that remains influential is that two objects considered together form a whole that is different from the simple combination of the objects. Gestalt psychologists argued that the perception of stimuli in our environment goes well beyond the individual elements that we sense. Instead, it represents an active, constructive process carried out within the brain (Wagemans et al., 2012; Chiu, Lo, & Hsieh, 2017) (see Figure 3).

Top-Down and Bottom-Up Processing

Ca- yo- re-d t-is -en-en-e, w-ic- ha- ev-ry -hi-d l-tt-r m-ss-ng? It probably won't take you too long to figure out that it says: "Can you read this sentence, which has every third letter missing?"

If perception were based primarily on breaking down a stimulus into its most basic elements, understanding the sentence, as well as other ambiguous stimuli, would not

Study Alert

The Gestalt laws of organization are classic principles in the field of psychology. Figure 2 can help you remember them.

FIGURE 3 Although at first it is difficult to distinguish anything in this drawing, keep looking, and eventually you may see the figure of a dog. The dog represents a Gestalt, or perceptual, whole, which is something greater than the sum of the individual elements.

Republished with permission of the Royal Society, from "The Medawar Lecture 2001 Knowledge for vision: vision for knowledge," Richard L. Gregory, Volume 360, Issue 1458, 2005. Permission conveyed through Copyright Clearance Center, Inc.

ABCDEF
9 10 11 12 13 14

FIGURE 4 The power of context is shown in this figure. Note how the B and the 13 are identical.

Source: Adapted from Coren, S., & Ward, L. M. (1989). *Sensation and perception* (3rd ed.). San Diego, CA: Harcourt Brace Jovanovich.

be possible. The fact that you were probably able to recognize such an imprecise stimulus illustrates that perception proceeds along two different avenues, called top-down processing and bottom-up processing.

In **top-down processing,** perception is guided by higher-level knowledge, experience, expectations, and motivations. You were able to figure out the meaning of the sentence with the missing letters because of your prior reading experience and because written English contains redundancies. Not every letter of each word is necessary to decode its meaning. Moreover, your expectations played a role in your being able to read the sentence. You were probably expecting a statement that had *something* to do with psychology, not the lyrics to a Lady Gaga song.

Top-down processing is illustrated by the importance of context in determining how we perceive objects. Look, for example, at Figure 4. Most of us perceive that the first row consists of the letters *A* through *F*, while the second contains the numbers 9 through 14. But take a more careful look, and you'll see that the B and the 13 are identical. Clearly, our perception is affected by our expectations about the two sequences–even though the two stimuli are exactly the same.

However, top-down processing cannot occur on its own. Even though top-down processing allows us to fill in the gaps in ambiguous and out-of-context stimuli, we would be unable to perceive the meaning of such stimuli without bottom-up processing. **Bottom-up processing** consists of the progression of recognizing and processing information from individual components of a stimuli and moving to the perception of the whole. We would make no headway in our recognition of the sentence without being able to perceive the individual shapes that make up the letters. Some perception, then, occurs at the level of the patterns and features of each of the separate letters.

Top-down and bottom-up processing occur simultaneously and interact with each other in our perception of the world around us. Bottom-up processing permits us to process the fundamental characteristics of stimuli, whereas top-down processing allows us to bring our experience to bear on perception. As we learn more about the complex processes involved in perception, we are developing a better understanding of how the brain continually interprets information from the senses and permits us to make responses appropriate to the environment (Folk & Remington, 2008; Westerhausen et al., 2009; Falasca et al., 2015).

top-down processing Perception that is guided by higher-level knowledge, experience, expectations, and motivations. (Module 13)

bottom-up processing Perception that consists of the progression of recognizing and processing information from individual components of a stimuli and moving to the perception of the whole. (Module 13)

Depth Perception: Translating 2-D to 3-D

As sophisticated as the retina is, the images projected onto it are flat and two-dimensional. Yet the world around us is three-dimensional, and we perceive it that way. How do we make the transformation from 2-D to 3-D?

The ability to view the world in three dimensions and to perceive distance–a skill known as **depth perception**–is due largely to the fact that we have two eyes. Because there is a certain distance between the eyes, a slightly different image reaches each retina. The brain integrates the two images into one view, but it also recognizes the difference in images and uses this difference to estimate the distance of an object from us. The difference in the images seen by the left eye and the right eye is known as *binocular disparity* (Gillam, Palmisano, & Govan, 2011; Valsecchi et al., 2013; Gao, Schneider, & Li, 2017).

depth perception The ability to view the world in three dimensions and to perceive distance. (Module 13)

Railroad tracks that seem to join together in the distance are an example of linear perspective.

©Fuse/Getty Images

To get a sense of binocular disparity, hold a pencil at arm's length and look at it first with one eye and then with the other. There is little difference between the two views relative to the background. Now bring the pencil just 6 inches away from your face, and try the same thing. This time you will perceive a greater difference between the two views.

The difference between the images in the two eyes provides us with a way of determining distance. If we view two objects and one is considerably closer to us than the other is, the retinal disparity will be relatively large. That disparity leads us to have a greater sense of depth between the two. However, if two objects are a similar distance from us, the retinal disparity will be minor. Therefore, we will perceive them as being a similar distance from us.

In some cases, certain cues permit us to obtain a sense of depth and distance with just one eye. These cues are known as *monocular cues*.

For example, *motion parallax* is the monocular cue in which a change in position of an object on the retina allows the perception of movement. For example, suppose you are a passenger in a moving car, and you focus your eye on a stable object such as a tree. Objects that are closer than the tree will appear to move backward, and the nearer the object is, the more quickly it will appear to move. In contrast, objects beyond the tree will seem to move at a slower speed but in the same direction as you are. Your brain is able to use these cues to calculate the relative distances of the tree and other objects.

Similarly, the monocular cue of *relative size* reflects the assumption that if two objects are the same size, the object that makes a smaller image on the retina is farther away than the one that makes a larger image. But it's not just size of an object that provides information about distance; the quality of the image on the retina helps us judge distance. The monocular cue of *texture gradient* provides information about distance because the details of things that are far away are less distinct (Proffitt, 2006).

Finally, anyone who has ever seen railroad tracks that seem to come together in the distance knows that distant objects appear to be closer together than are nearer ones, a phenomenon called linear perspective. *Linear perspective* is a type of perspective in which objects in the distance appear to converge. We use linear perspective as a monocular cue in estimating distance, allowing the two-dimensional image on the retina to record the three-dimensional world (Shimono & Wade, 2002; Bruggeman, Yonas, & Konczak, 2007).

From the perspective of...

A Computer Game Designer What are some techniques you might use to produce the appearance of three-dimensional terrain on a two-dimensional computer screen? What are some techniques you might use to suggest motion?

©Sam Edwards/age fotostock

Perceptual Constancy

Consider what happens as you finish a conversation with a friend and she begins to walk away from you. As you watch her walk down the street, the image on your retina becomes smaller and smaller. Do you wonder why she is shrinking?

Of course not. Despite the very real change in the size of the retinal image, because of perceptual constancy you factor into your thinking the knowledge that your friend is moving farther away from you. **Perceptual constancy** is the recognition that physical objects are consistent and do not vary, even though our sensory input about them changes.

Perceptual constancy allows us to view objects as having an unchanging size, shape, color, and brightness, even if the image on our retina changes. For example, despite the varying size or shape of the images on the retina as an airplane approaches, flies overhead, and then disappears, we do not perceive the airplane as changing shape or size. Experience has taught us that the plane's size remains constant (Wickelgren, 2004; Garrigan & Kellman, 2008; Sachse et al., 2017).

In some cases, though, our application of perceptual constancy can mislead us. One good example of this involves the rising moon. When the moon first appears at night, close to the horizon, it seems to be huge–much larger than when it is high in the sky later in the evening. You may have thought that the apparent change in the size of the moon was caused by the moon's being physically closer to the earth when

perceptual constancy Our understanding that physical objects are consistent and do not vary, even though sensory input about them may vary. (Module 13)

Despite the moon appearing very large when it is close to the horizon, perceptual constancy helps us to know that the moon's size has not changed and remains the same.

©Paul Souders/The Image Bank/Getty Images

it first appears. In fact, though, this is not the case at all: the actual image of the moon on our retina is the same, whether it is low or high in the sky.

There are several explanations for the moon illusion. One suggests that the moon appears to be larger when it is close to the horizon primarily because of perceptual constancy. When the moon is near the horizon, the perceptual cues of intervening terrain and objects such as trees on the horizon produce a misleading sense of distance, leading us to misperceive the moon as relatively large.

In contrast, when the moon is high in the sky, we see it by itself, and we don't try to compensate for its distance from us. In this case, then, perceptual constancy leads us to perceive it as relatively small. To experience perceptual constancy, try looking at the moon when it is relatively low on the horizon through a paper-towel tube; the moon suddenly will appear to "shrink" back to normal size (Imamura & Nakamizo, 2006; Kaufman, Johnson, & Liu, 2008; Rogers & Naumenko, 2015).

Perceptual constancy is not the only explanation for the moon illusion, and it remains a puzzle to psychologists. It may be that several different perceptual processes are involved in the illusion (Gregory, 2008; Kim, 2008).

Motion Perception: As the World Turns

When a batter tries to hit a pitched ball, the most important factor is the motion of the ball. How is a batter able to judge the speed and location of a target that is moving at some 90 miles per hour?

The answer rests in part on several cues that provide us with relevant information about the perception of motion. For one thing, the movement of an object across the retina is typically perceived relative to some stable, unmoving background. Moreover, if the stimulus is heading toward us, the image on the retina expands in size, filling more and more of the visual field. In such cases, we assume that the stimulus is approaching—not that it is an expanding stimulus viewed at a constant distance.

It is not, however, just the movement of images across the retina that brings about the perception of motion. If it were, we would perceive the world as moving every time we moved our heads. Instead, one of the critical things we learn about perception is to factor information about our own head and eye movements along with information about changes in the retinal image.

Sometimes we perceive motion when it doesn't occur. Have you ever been on a stationary train that feels as if it is moving because a train on an adjacent track begins to slowly move past? Or have you been in an IMAX movie theater in which you feel as if you were falling as a huge image of a plane moves across the screen? In both cases, the experience of motion is convincing. *Apparent movement* is the perception that a stationary object is moving. It occurs when different areas of the retina are quickly stimulated, leading us to interpret motion (Ekroll & Scherzer, 2009; Lindemann & Bekkering, 2009; Brandon & Saffran, 2011).

Perceptual Illusions: The Deceptions of Perceptions

If you look carefully at the Parthenon, one of the most famous buildings of ancient Greece, still standing at the top of an Athens hill, you'll see that it was built with a bulge on one side. If it didn't have that bulge—and quite a few other architectural "tricks" like it, such as columns that incline inward—it would look as if it were crooked and about to fall down. Instead, it appears to stand completely straight, at right angles to the ground.

visual illusions Physical stimuli that consistently produce errors in perception. (Module 13)

The fact that the Parthenon appears to be completely upright is the result of a series of visual illusions. **Visual illusions** are physical stimuli that consistently produce errors in perception. In the case of the Parthenon, the building appears to be completely

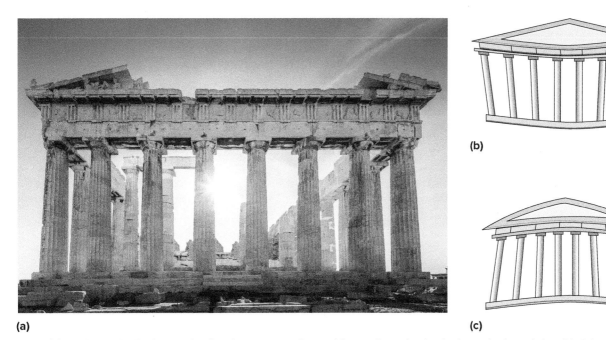

(a)

(b)

(c)

FIGURE 5 (a) In building the Parthenon, the Greeks constructed an architectural wonder that looks perfectly straight, with right angles at every corner. (b) However, if it had been built with completely true right angles, it would have looked as it does here. (c) To compensate for this illusion, the Parthenon was designed to have a slight upward curvature, as shown here.

(Photo): ©Mlenny Photography/E+/Getty Images; (b): Source: Adapted from Luckiesh, M. (1921). *Scientific American Monthly,* 3, 497-501.

square, as illustrated in Figure 5a. However, if it had been built that way, it would look to us as it does in Figure 5b. The reason for this is an illusion that makes right angles placed above a line appear as if they were bent. To offset the illusion, the Parthenon was constructed as in Figure 5c, with a slight upward curvature.

The *Müller-Lyer illusion* (illustrated in Figure 6) has fascinated psychologists for decades. Although the two lines are the same length, the one with the arrow tips pointing outward, away from the vertical line (Figure 6a, left) appears to be shorter than the one with the arrow tips pointing inward (Figure 6a, right).

Although all kinds of explanations for visual illusions have been suggested, most concentrate either on the physical operation of the eye or on our misinterpretation of the visual stimulus. For example, one explanation for the Müller-Lyer illusion is that eye movements are greater when the arrow tips point inward, making us perceive the line as longer than it is when the arrow tips face outward. In contrast, a different explanation for the illusion suggests that we unconsciously attribute particular significance to each of the lines (Gregory, 1978). When we see the left line in Figure 6a, we tend to perceive it as if it were the relatively close outside corner of a rectangular object, such as the outside corner of the room illustrated in Figure 6b. In contrast,

Study Alert
The explanation for the Müller-Lyer illusion is complicated. Figure 6 will help you master it.

(a)   **(b)**   **(c)**

FIGURE 6 In the Müller-Lyer illusion (a), the vertical line on the left appears shorter than the one on the right, even though they are identical in length. One explanation for the Müller-Lyer illusion suggests that the line on the left (with arrow points directed outward) is perceived as the relatively close corner of a rectangular object, such as the building corner in (b), and the line on the right (with the arrow points directed inward) is interpreted as the inside corner of a rectangular object, such as the room extending away from us (c). Our previous experience with distance cues leads us to assume that the outside corner is closer than the inside corner, and, consequently, the inside corner must be longer.

Optical illusions have been used to slow traffic, as these virtual speed bumps in Iceland illustrate. Although they appear to be hovering above-ground, in fact they are flush to the ground.
©Thorir Ingvarsson/Shutterstock

when we view the line on the right in Figure 6a, we perceive it as the relatively more distant inside corner of a rectangular object, such as the inside room corner in Figure 6c. Because previous experience leads us to assume that the outside corner is closer than the inside corner, we make the further assumption that the inside corner must therefore be longer.

Despite the complexity of the latter explanation, a good deal of evidence supports it. For instance, cross-cultural studies show that people raised in areas where there are few right angles—such as the Zulu in Africa—are much less susceptible to the illusion than are people who grow up where most structures are built using right angles and rectangles (Segall, Campbell, & Herskovits, 1966; Fujita et al., 2017).

Exploring DIVERSITY

Culture and Perception

As the example of the Zulu indicates, the culture in which we are raised has clear consequences for how we perceive the world. Consider the drawing in Figure 7. Sometimes called the "devil's tuning fork," it is likely to produce a mind-boggling effect, as the center tine of the fork alternates between appearing and disappearing.

Now try to reproduce the drawing on a piece of paper. Chances are that the task is nearly impossible for you—unless you are a member of an African tribe with little exposure to Western cultures. For such individuals, the task is simple; they have no trouble reproducing the figure. The reason is that Westerners automatically interpret the drawing as something that cannot exist in three dimensions, and they therefore are inhibited from reproducing it. The African tribal members, in contrast, do not make the assumption that the figure is "impossible" and instead view it in two dimensions, a perception that enables them to copy the figure with ease (Deregowski, 1973).

Cultural differences are also reflected in depth perception. A Western viewer of Figure 8 would interpret the hunter in the drawing as aiming for the antelope in the foreground, while an elephant stands under the tree in the background. A member of an isolated African tribe, however, interprets the scene very differently by assuming that the hunter is aiming at the elephant. Westerners use the difference in sizes between the two animals as a cue that the elephant is farther away than the antelope (Hudson, 1960).

FIGURE 7 The "devil's tuning fork" has three prongs...or does it have two?

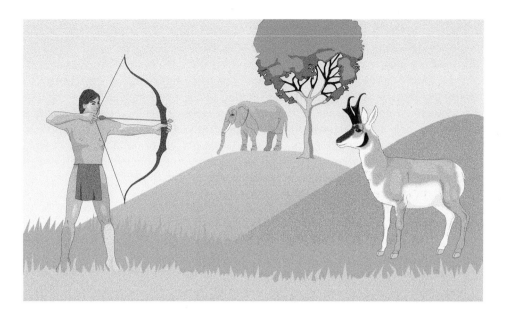

FIGURE 8 Is the man aiming for the elephant or the antelope? Westerners assume that the difference in size between the two animals indicates that the elephant is farther away, and therefore, the man is aiming for the antelope. In contrast, members of some African tribes, not used to depth cues in two-dimensional drawings, assume that the man is aiming for the elephant. Do you think people who view the picture in three dimensions could explain what they see to someone who views the scene in two dimensions and eventually get that person to view it in three dimensions? Source: Adapted from Hudson, W. (1960). Pictorial depth perception in subcultural groups in Africa. *Journal of Social Psychology, 52,* 183–208.

Does this mean that basic perceptual processes differ among people of different cultures? No. Variations in learning and experience produce cross-cultural differences in perception, and the underlying psychological processes involved in perception are similar (McCauley & Henrich, 2006).

Although visual illusions may seem like mere psychological curiosities, they actually illustrate something fundamental about perception. There is a basic connection between our prior knowledge, needs, motivations, and expectations about how the world is put together and the way we perceive it. Our view of the world is very much an outcome, then, of fundamental psychological factors. Furthermore, each person perceives the environment in a way that is unique and special (Knoblich & Sebanz, 2006; Repp & Knoblich, 2007).

SUBLIMINAL PERCEPTION

Can stimuli that we're not consciously aware of change our behavior? In some ways, yes.

Subliminal perception refers to the perception of messages about which we have no awareness. The stimulus could be a written word, a sound, or even a smell that activates the sensory system but that is not intense enough for a person to report having experienced it. For example, in some studies, people are exposed to a descriptive label–called a *prime*–about a person (such as the word *smart* or *happy*) so briefly that they cannot report seeing the label. Later, however, they form impressions that are influenced by the content of the prime. Somehow, they have been influenced by the prime that they say they couldn't see, providing some evidence for subliminal perception (Key, 2003; Kawakami & Miura, 2015).

Although subliminal messages (which social psychologists refer to as *priming*) can influence behavior in subtle ways, there's little evidence that they can lead to *major* changes in attitudes or behavior. Most research suggests that they cannot. For example, people who are subliminally exposed to an image of a Coke can and the word *thirst* do later rate themselves as thirstier, and they actually do drink more when given the opportunity. However, they don't particularly care if they drink Coke or some other liquid to quench their thirst (Dijksterhuis, Chartrand, & Aarts, 2007; Parkinson et al., 2017).

In short, although we are able to perceive at least some kinds of information of which we are unaware, there's little evidence that subliminal messages can change our attitudes or behavior in substantial ways. At the same time, subliminal perception does have at least some consequences. If our motivation to carry out a behavior is already high and the appropriate stimuli are presented subliminally, subliminal perception may have at least some effect on our behavior (Pratkanis, Epley, & Savitsky, 2007; Randolph-Seng & Nielsen, 2009; Gafner, 2013).

EXTRASENSORY PERCEPTION (ESP)

Psychologists are highly skeptical of reports of *extrasensory perception*, or ESP–perception that does not involve our known senses. Although almost half of the general population of the United States believes it exists, most psychologists reject the existence of ESP, asserting that there is no sound documentation of the phenomenon (Moore, 2005).

However, a debate in one of the most prestigious psychology journals, *Psychological Bulletin*, heightened interest in ESP in the early 2000s. According to proponents of ESP, reliable evidence existed for an "anomalous process of information transfer," or *psi*. These researchers, who painstakingly reviewed considerable evidence, argued that a cumulative body of research shows reliable support for the existence of psi (Storm & Ertel, 2001; Parra & Argibay, 2007; Storm & Rock, 2015).

Ultimately, their conclusion was challenged and largely discredited for several reasons. For example, critics suggested that the research methodology was inadequate and that the experiments supporting psi are flawed (Kennedy, 2004; Rouder, Morey, & Province, 2013).

Because of questions about the quality of the research, as well as a lack of any credible theoretical explanation for how extrasensory perception might take place, almost no psychologists would claim that there is reliable scientific support for ESP. Still, the topic continues to inspire research, which is the only way the issue will be fully settled (Rose & Blackmore, 2002; Wiseman & Greening, 2002; Bem, 2012).

AP MODULE 13: PERCEPTUAL ORGANIZATION: CONSTRUCTING OUR VIEW OF THE WORLD

AP SUMMARY

- The Gestalt laws of organization are used to describe the way in which we organize bits and pieces of information into meaningful wholes, known as Gestalts, through closure, proximity, similarity, and simplicity. Figure-ground is also a perceptual grouping cue for vision.
- In top-down processing, perception is guided by higher-level knowledge, experience, expectations, and motivations. In bottom-up processing, perception consists of the progression of recognizing and processing information from individual components of a stimuli and moving to the perception of the whole. Both processes occur simultaneously and interact with each other in our perception of the world.
- Depth perception is the ability to perceive distance and view the world in three dimensions, even though the images projected on our retinas are two-dimensional. We are able to judge depth and distance as a result of binocular disparity and monocular cues, such as motion parallax, relative size, texture gradient, and linear perspective.
- One of the best-known illusions is the Müller Lyer illusion is based on the principles of convergence and divergence: the lines seem to lead the eye either inward or outward to create a false impression of

length. One explanation for this illusion is that previous experience perceives it as an outside corner of a rectangle, such as the outside corner of a room. Our previous experience leads us to believe that the outside corner is closer than the inside corner, and we make the assumption that that the inside corner must, therefore, be closer. Visual illusions are usually the result of errors in the brain's interpretation of visual stimuli. Furthermore, culture clearly affects how we perceive the world.

- Cultural differences are also reflective in depth perception. Westerners use the difference in size to interpret depth, while members of some African tribes, who are not familiar with viewing two-dimensional drawings, may not.
- Subliminal perception refers to the perception of messages about which we have no awareness. The reality of the phenomenon, as well as ESP, is open to question and debate.
- Visual illusions are physical stimuli that consistently produce errors in perception, causing judgments that do not accurately reflect the physical reality of a stimulus. Visual illusions illustrate how our prior knowledge, needs, motivations, and expectations about the world help influence what we perceive.

- Perceptual constancy permits us to perceive stimuli as unvarying in size, shape, and color despite changes in the environment or the appearance of the objects being perceived.
- Motion perception depends on cues, such as the perceived movement of an object across the retina and information about how the head and eyes are moving. Apparent movement is the perception that a stationary object is moving, and it occurs when different areas of the retina are quickly stimulated.

AP KEY TERMS

Gestalt (geh-SHTALLT) laws of organization
top-down processing
bottom-up processing
depth perception
perceptual constancy
visual illusions

AP TEST PRACTICE

Section I: Multiple Choice

1. Often when proofreading their own papers students miss typos because their brain is guided by expectations. This can be explained by
   A. place theory
   B. binocular disparity
   C. perceptual constancy
   D. subliminal perception
   E. top-down processing

2. One explanation for a popular visual illusion is that an individual's previous experience with distance cues leads them to assume the outside corner is closer than the inside corner, making the inside corner longer. What visual illusion is being described?
   A. Moon illusion
   B. Ames room illusion
   C. Ponzo illusion
   D. Müller-Lyer illusion
   E. Parthenon illusion

3. Which of the following explains how sensory input varies, but we know that physical objects do not?
   A. Motion parallax
   B. Size constancy
   C. Bottom-up processing
   D. Gestalt laws of organization
   E. Binocular disparity

Section II: Free Response

Various perceptual cues help to construct our view of the world. Ariana boards a train and looks out over a beautiful field of flowers. As the train starts to move she can see mountain peaks and the path she hiked in the morning converging in the distance. Three animals near each other are drinking from the river close to the train. Farther back another group of similar animals is walking near the hiking trail.

A. Explain how the following Gestalt principles determine her perception.
   - figure-ground
   - proximity
B. Explain how the following depth perception cues determine her perception.
   - binocular disparity
   - relative size
   - texture gradient
   - linear perspective
   - motion parallax

LOOKING *Back*

EPILOGUE

We have noted the important distinction between sensation and perception, and we have examined the processes that underlie both of them. We've seen how external stimuli evoke sensory responses and how our different senses process the information contained in those responses. We also have focused on the physical structure and internal workings of the individual senses, including vision, hearing, balance, smell, taste, and the skin senses, and we've explored how our brains organize and process sensory information to construct a consistent, integrated picture of the world around us.

VISUAL SUMMARY 4 Sensation and Perception

MODULE 10 Sensing the World

Absolute thresholds

Difference thresholds
- Just noticeable difference
- Weber's law

Sensory Adaptation

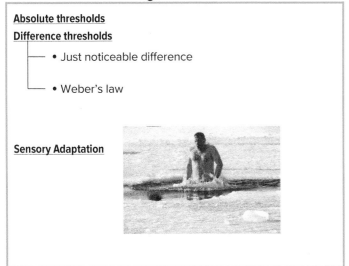

MODULE 11 Vision

Eye Structure

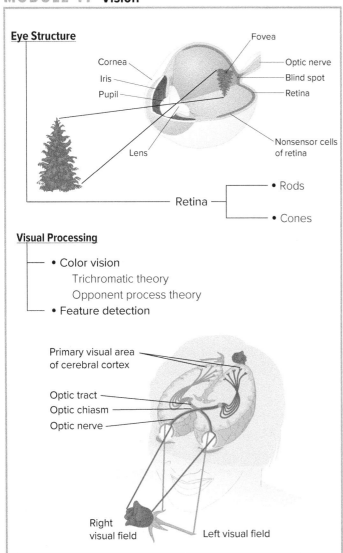

Cornea
Iris
Pupil
Fovea
Optic nerve
Blind spot
Retina
Nonsensor cells of retina
Lens

Retina
- Rods
- Cones

Visual Processing
- Color vision
  Trichromatic theory
  Opponent process theory
- Feature detection

Primary visual area of cerebral cortex
Optic tract
Optic chiasm
Optic nerve
Right visual field
Left visual field

MODULE 12 Hearing and Other Senses

Ear Structure

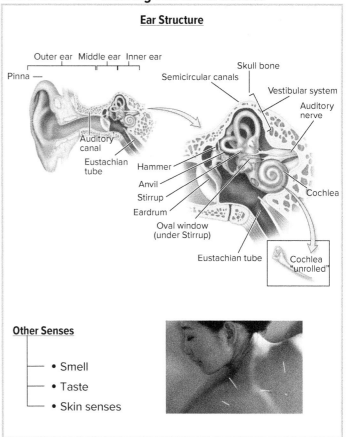

Outer ear Middle ear Inner ear
Pinna
Skull bone
Semicircular canals
Vestibular system
Auditory nerve
Auditory canal
Eustachian tube
Hammer
Anvil
Stirrup
Eardrum
Oval window (under Stirrup)
Eustachian tube
Cochlea
Cochlea "unrolled"

Other Senses
- Smell
- Taste
- Skin senses

MODULE 13 Perception

Gestalt Laws of Organization

(a) Closure   (b) Proximity   (c) Similarity   (d) Simplicity

Top-down and Bottom-up Processing

A B C D E F
9 10 11 12 13 14

Perceptual Constancy

Perceptual Illusions

Depth Perception

Motion Perception

CHAPTER 5
States of Consciousness

AP'I ESSENTIAL QUESTIONS
- How do we perceive and understand ourselves?

AP'I LEARNING TARGETS FOR CHAPTER 5

MODULE 14

- Describe various states of consciousness and their impact on behavior.
- Identify the contributions of major figures in consciousness research.
- Discuss aspects of sleep and dreaming.

SLEEP AND DREAMS

The Stages of Sleep

REM Sleep: The Paradox of Sleep

Why Do We Sleep, and How Much Sleep Is Necessary?

AP'I Applying Psychology in the 21st Century: Sleeping to Forget

AP'I Neuroscience in Your Life: Why Are We So Emotional When We Don't Get Enough Sleep?

The Function and Meaning of Dreaming

Sleep Disturbances: Slumbering Problems

Circadian Rhythms: Life Cycles

Daydreams: Dreams Without Sleep

Becoming an Informed Consumer of Psychology: Sleeping Better

MODULE 15

- Describe various states of consciousness and their impact on behavior.

HYPNOSIS AND MEDITATION

Hypnosis: A Trance-Forming Experience?

Meditation: Regulating Our Own State of Consciousness

Exploring Diversity: Cross-Cultural Routes to Altered States of Consciousness

- Discuss the influence of drugs on neurotransmitters.
- Identify the major psychoactive drug categories and classify specific drugs.
- Discuss drug dependence, addiction, tolerance, and withdrawal.

DRUG USE: THE HIGHS AND LOWS OF CONSCIOUSNESS

Stimulants: Drug Highs

Depressants: Drug Lows

Narcotics, Opiates, and Opioids: Relieving Pain and Anxiety

Hallucinogens: Psychedelic Drugs

Becoming an Informed Consumer of Psychology: Identifying Drug and Alcohol Problems

PROLOGUE *AN EPIDEMIC HITS CLOSE TO HOME*

Eric Morin's sister described him as a person with a big heart, someone who was cheerful and energetic. His family remembers him as being happy and healthy at their last Thanksgiving celebration. But Eric Morin, father of two children, died a few weeks later, on Christmas Eve of that year, from acute fentanyl poisoning, killed by an overdose of opioids.

Morin had struggled with substance abuse since high school, when he began using marijuana and alcohol. Later, he turned to pills and heroin. It was heroin laced with fentanyl—an opioid so potent that most overdose cases never make it to the emergency room—that killed him.

Morin sought treatment on several occasions. His mother remembers his struggles to get clean—the sweats, the vomiting, the shakes. But despite his best efforts, Morin became one more statistic in the growing list of opioid-related deaths (Hewitt, 2017).

LOOKING *Ahead*

Eric Morin's experience is far from unique. The United States is experiencing a full-blown opiate epidemic, with over 50,000 deaths from drug overdoses in 2016 alone. Drug overdoses are now the most frequent cause of death of those under the age of 50 (Katz, 2017).

Opiates such as heroin and fentanyl promise relief from anxiety and stress. While we don't know exactly what drove Eric Morin to use narcotics, his early experiments with alcohol and marijuana indicate a continual desire for an altered state of consciousness. Why people seek to alter their consciousness, what conscious experience is, and how and why we can alter it are some of the questions we address as we turn our attention to the study of consciousness.

Consciousness is the awareness of the sensations, thoughts, and feelings we experience at a given moment. Consciousness is our subjective understanding of both the environment around us and our private internal world, unobservable to outsiders.

In *waking consciousness*, we are awake and aware of our thoughts, emotions, and perceptions. All other states of consciousness are considered *altered states of consciousness*. Among these, sleeping and dreaming occur naturally; drug use and hypnosis, in contrast, are methods of deliberately altering one's state of consciousness.

In the past, because consciousness is so personal a phenomenon, psychologists were sometimes reluctant to study it. After all, who can say that your consciousness is similar to or, for that matter,

different from anyone else's? Although the earliest psychologists, including William James (1890), saw the study of consciousness as central to the field, later psychologists suggested that it was out of bounds for the discipline. They argued that consciousness could be understood only by relying "unscientifically" on what experimental participants said they were experiencing. In this view, it was philosophers—not psychologists—who should speculate on such knotty issues as whether consciousness is separate from the physical body, how people know they exist, and how the body and mind are related to each other (Gennaro, 2004; Barresi, 2007; James, 2015).

Contemporary psychologists reject the view that the study of consciousness is unsuitable for the field of psychology. Instead, they argue that several approaches permit the scientific study of consciousness. For example, behavioral neuroscientists can measure brain-wave patterns under conditions of consciousness ranging from sleep to waking to hypnotic trances. And new understanding of the chemistry of drugs such as marijuana and alcohol has provided insights into the way they produce their pleasurable—as well as adverse—effects (Wells, Phillips, & McCarthy, 2011; Malouff & Rooke, 2013; Liechti, Dolder & Schmid, 2017).

Yet how humans experience consciousness remains an open question. Some psychologists believe that the experience of consciousness is produced by a quantitative increase in neuronal activity that occurs throughout the brain. For example, an alarm clock moves us from sleep to waking consciousness by its loud ringing, which stimulates neurons throughout the brain as a whole (Greenfield, 2002; Koch & Greenfield, 2007; Ward, 2011).

In contrast, others believe that states of consciousness are produced by particular sets of neurons and neuronal pathways that are activated in specific ways. In this view, an alarm clock wakes us from sleep into consciousness because specific neurons related to the auditory nerve are activated; the auditory nerve then sends a message to other neurons to release particular neurotransmitters that produce awareness of the alarm (Tononi & Koch, 2008; Saper, 2013; Schurger et al., 2015).

Although we don't know yet which of these views is correct, it is clear that whatever state of consciousness we are in—be it waking, sleeping, hypnotic, or drug-induced—the complexities of consciousness are profound.

consciousness The awareness of the sensations, thoughts, and feelings being experienced at a given moment. (Module 14)

Module 14
Sleep and Dreams

During a 9-day cross-country bike race, 29-year-old Mike Trevino averaged 1 hour of sleep per day. The first 3 days he didn't sleep at all, and over the next 6, he took completely dream-free naps of at most 90 minutes. His waking thoughts became fuzzy, depicting movielike plots starring himself and his crew. The whole experience was like a serial dream in which he remained conscious, if only barely. He finished in second place.

Trevino's case is unusual–in part because he was able to function with so little sleep for so long–and it raises a host of questions about sleep and dreams. Can we live without sleep? What is the meaning of dreams? More generally, what is sleep?

Although sleeping is a state that we all experience, there are still many unanswered questions about sleep that remain, along with a considerable number of myths. Test your knowledge of sleep and dreams by answering the questionnaire in Figure 1.

AP® | LEARNING TARGETS

- Describe various states of consciousness and their impact on behavior.
- Identify the contributions of major figures in consciousness research.
- Discuss aspects of sleep and dreaming.

Sleep Quiz

Although sleeping is something we all do for a significant part of our lives, myths and misconceptions about the topic abound. Check your knowledge by reading each statement below and check True or False.

1. It is a proven fact that 8 hours of sleep are needed to remain mentally healthy. ☐ True ☐ False	6. The best long-term cure for sleeplessness is regular use of insomnia medications. ☐ True ☐ False
2. Sleep "turns off" most brain activity to promote brain rest and recovery. ☐ True ☐ False	7. Dreams are most often the result of stomach distress caused by what and when we eat. ☐ True ☐ False
3. Sleep deprivation always causes mental imbalance. ☐ True ☐ False	8. When we are asleep and dreaming, our muscles are the most relaxed they can get. ☐ True ☐ False
4. It is impossible to go more than 48 hours without sleep. ☐ True ☐ False	9. If you can't remember your dreams, it's because you want to forget them. ☐ True ☐ False
5. If we lose sleep we can always make it up another night or on the weekend. ☐ True ☐ False	10. Many people never dream. ☐ True ☐ False

Scoring: It is easy to score this quiz because every statement is false. But don't lose any sleep if you missed a few; these are among the most widely held misconceptions about sleeping and dreaming.

FIGURE 1 There are many unanswered questions about sleep. Taking this quiz can help you clear up some of the myths.
Source: Palladino, J. J., & Carducci, B. J., (1984). Students' knowledge of sleep and dreams. *Teaching of Psychology, 11*(3), 189–191.

The Stages of Sleep

Most of us consider sleep a time of tranquility when we set aside the tensions of the day and spend the night in uneventful slumber. However, a closer look at sleep shows that a good deal of activity occurs throughout the night.

Measures of electrical activity in the brain show that the brain is quite active during sleep. It produces electrical discharges with systematic, wavelike patterns that change in height (or amplitude) and speed (or frequency) in regular sequences. There is also significant physical activity in muscle and eye movements.

People progress through a series of distinct stages of sleep during a night's rest–known as *stage 1* through *stage 3* and *REM sleep*–moving through the stages in cycles lasting about 90 minutes. Each of these sleep stages is associated with a unique pattern of brain waves, which you can see in Figure 2.

When people first go to sleep, they move from a waking state in which they are relaxed with their eyes closed into **stage 1 sleep,** which is characterized by relatively rapid, low-amplitude brain waves. This is actually a stage of transition between wakefulness and sleep and lasts only a few minutes. During stage 1, images sometimes appear, as if we were viewing still photos, although this is not true dreaming, which occurs later in the night.

As sleep becomes deeper, people enter **stage 2 sleep,** which makes up about half of the total sleep of those in their early 20s and is characterized by a slower, more regular wave pattern. However, there are also momentary interruptions of sharply pointed, spiky waves that are called, because of their configuration, *sleep spindles*. It becomes increasingly difficult to awaken a person from sleep as stage 2 progresses.

As people drift into **stage 3 sleep,** the deepest stage, the brain waves become slower, with higher peaks and lower valleys in the wave pattern. During stage 3, people are least responsive to outside stimulation.

As you can see in Figure 3, stage 3 sleep is most likely to occur during the early part of the night. In the first half of the night, sleep is dominated by stage 3. The second half is characterized by stages 1 and 2–as well as a fourth stage, REM sleep, during which dreams occur.

stage 1 sleep The state of transition between wakefulness and sleep, characterized by relatively rapid, low-amplitude brain waves. (Module 14)

stage 2 sleep A sleep deeper than that of stage 1, characterized by a slower, more regular wave pattern, along with momentary interruptions of "sleep spindles." (Module 14)

stage 3 sleep The deepest stage of sleep, during which we are least responsive to outside stimulation. (Module 14)

FIGURE 2 Brain-wave patterns (measured by an EEG apparatus) vary significantly during the different stages of sleep (adapted from Hobson, [1989]). As sleep moves from stage 1 through stage 3, brain waves become slower. During REM sleep, however, the fast wave patterns are similar to relaxed wakefulness.

Source: Adapted from Hobson, J. A. (1989). *Sleep.* New York: W. H. Freeman.

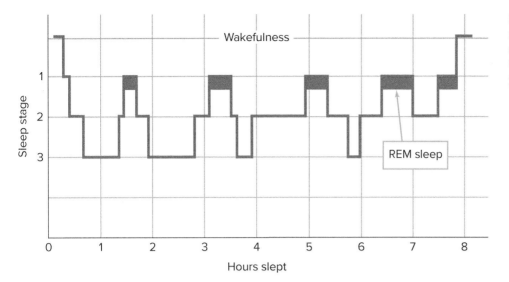

FIGURE 3 During the night, the typical sleeper passes through all three stages of sleep and several REM periods.
Source: Adapted from Hartmann, E. (1967). *The biology of dreaming*. Springfield, IL: Charles C. Thomas Publisher.

REM Sleep: The Paradox of Sleep

Several times a night, when sleepers have cycled back to a shallower state of sleep, something curious happens. Their heart rate increases and becomes irregular, their blood pressure rises, and their breathing rate increases. Most characteristic of this period is the back-and-forth movement of their eyes, as if they were watching an action-filled movie. This period of sleep is called **rapid eye movement, or REM, sleep,** and it contrasts with stages 1 through 3, which are collectively labeled *non-REM* (or *NREM*) sleep. REM sleep occupies a little more than 20% of adults' total sleeping time.

Paradoxically, while heart rate, blood pressure, and breathing increase during REM sleep, the major muscles of the body appear to be paralyzed. In addition, and most important, REM sleep is usually accompanied by dreams, which—whether or not people remember them—are experienced by *everyone* during some part of their night's sleep. Although some dreaming occurs in non-REM stages of sleep, dreams

rapid eye movement (REM) sleep Sleep occupying 20% of an adult's sleeping time, characterized by increased heart rate, blood pressure, and breathing rate; erections; eye movements; and the experience of dreaming. (Module 14)

People progress through three distinct stages of sleep during a night's rest spread over cycles lasting about 90 minutes. REM sleep occupies only 20% of adults' sleeping time. These photos, taken at different times of night, show the synchronized patterns of a couple accustomed to sleeping in the same bed.
©Ted Spagna/Science Source

are most likely to occur in the REM period, where they are the most vivid and easily remembered (Leclair-Visonneau et al., 2011; Manni & Terzaghi, 2013; Sikka et al., 2017).

There is good reason to believe that REM sleep plays a critical role in everyday human functioning. People deprived of REM sleep–by being awakened every time they begin to display the physiological signs of that stage–show a *rebound effect* when allowed to rest undisturbed. With this rebound effect, REM-deprived sleepers spend significantly more time in REM sleep than they normally would. In addition, REM sleep may play a role in learning and memory, allowing us to rethink and restore information and emotional experiences that we've had during the day (Nishida et al., 2009; Walker & van der Helm, 2009; Nielsen et al., 2015).

From the perspective of...

An Educator How might you use the findings in sleep research to maximize student learning?

©Andersen Ross/Blend Images/Getty Images

Why Do We Sleep, and How Much Sleep Is Necessary?

Sleep is a requirement for normal human functioning, although, surprisingly, the reason why has long baffled scientists. It certainly is reasonable to expect that our bodies would require a tranquil "rest and relaxation" period to revitalize themselves, and experiments with rats show that total sleep deprivation results in death. But why?

One explanation, based on an evolutionary perspective, suggests that sleep permitted our ancestors to conserve energy at night, a time when food was relatively hard to come by. Consequently, they were better able to forage for food when the sun was up.

A second explanation for why we sleep is that sleep restores and replenishes our brains and bodies. For instance, the reduced activity of the brain during non-REM sleep may give neurons in the brain a chance to repair themselves. That reduced activity may also weaken connections among particular nerve cells to conserve energy, which has the effect of aiding memory. Furthermore, the onset of REM sleep stops the release of neurotransmitters called *monoamines* and so permits receptor cells to get some necessary rest and to increase their sensitivity during periods of wakefulness (Steiger, 2007; Bub, Buckhalt, & El-Sheikh, 2011; Tononi & Cirelli, 2013). (Also see *Applying Psychology in the 21st Century*).

Finally, sleep may be essential because it assists physical growth and brain development in children. For example, the release of growth hormones is associated with deep sleep (Peterfi et al., 2010; Grigg-Damberger, 2017).

Still, these explanations remain speculative, and there is no definitive answer as to why sleep is essential. What is increasingly clear is that sleep serves multiple functions and that without sleep, we will eventually die (Stickgold, 2015).

AP| APPLYING PSYCHOLOGY IN THE 21ST CENTURY

SLEEPING TO FORGET

Do we sleep to forget?

An increasing amount of evidence suggests that one primary purpose of sleep may be to help us forget. In this view, sleep allows the brain to eliminate unnecessary information that accumulates throughout the day so that it doesn't become burdensome or confusing, a process called *reverse learning* (Heller et al., 2014).

In support of the reverse-learning view, one study hypothesized that the day's activities trigger increased synaptic growth, which can drown out the strong signal of neural impulses with excessive noise. Our brains must therefore prune back these new connections, the hypothesis goes, which it does while we sleep.

Evidence for this hypothesis comes from research in which investigators examined thin slices of brain tissue taken from mice, some of which had been asleep and some of which had been awake and alert. Looking closely at the size and shape of the synapses, the researchers found an 18% reduction in the size of the synapses in the sleeping mice's brain tissue relative to those of the awake mice (de Vivo et al., 2017).

Another study examined the brains of live mice. The researchers monitored the presence of surface proteins on the mice's

©Stockbyte/Getty Images

brains while they were awake and after they fell asleep and noted a drop in these proteins during sleep, which was consistent with a reduction in synapses (Diering et al., 2017).

To see how synaptic pruning affects what mice remember, the researchers put mice in a cage that delivered a mild but unpleasant electric shock to their feet if they walked on a particular section of the floor. Some of those mice were then given a chemical known to inhibit synaptic pruning, and then all of the mice were allowed to sleep.

When they were put back in the same cage the next day, all of the mice unsurprisingly acted fearful, refusing to walk across the floor that had previously shocked them. But a difference emerged when the mice were placed in a different cage. The mice that had not been given the chemical explored this new environment curiously, but the mice whose synaptic pruning had been inhibited reacted with fear again, as if they were in the original cage. The researchers concluded that the inhibited mice were unable to focus on the specific attributes of the cage in which they had received shocks. In short, the lack of pruning left them with excessive synapses that produced confused memories (Diering et al., 2017).

While more research needs to be done to fully understand the association of sleep with synaptic pruning, these early findings lend some tentative weight to the process of reverse learning and its role in sleep.

AP SKILL: SCIENTIFIC INVESTIGATION/DATA ANALYSIS

1. Identify the hypothesis for reverse learning.
2. Summarize the three pieces of evidence for this hypothesis.

Furthermore, scientists have been unable to establish just how much sleep is absolutely required. Most people today sleep between 7 and 8 hours each night, which is 3 hours a night *less* than people slept a hundred years ago (see Figure 4).

In addition, individuals vary widely, with some people needing as little as 3 hours of sleep. Still, survey data shows that for most people, the more sleep they get, the greater their sense of well-being (McCarthy & Brown, 2015).

Men and women sleep differently. Women typically fall asleep more quickly, they sleep for longer periods and more deeply than men do, and they get up fewer times in the night. On the other hand, men have fewer concerns about the amount of sleep they get than women do, even though they get less sleep. Furthermore, sleep requirements vary over the course of a lifetime: As they age, people generally need less and less sleep (Monk et al., 2011; Petersen, 2011).

People who participate in sleep deprivation experiments, in which they are kept awake for stretches as long as 200 hours, show no lasting effects. It's no fun–they feel weary and irritable, can't concentrate, and show a loss of creativity, even after only minor deprivation. They also show a decline in logical reasoning ability. However, after being allowed to sleep normally, they bounce back quickly and are able to perform at

FIGURE 4 Although most people sleep between 7 and 8 hours each night, the amount that individuals need varies a great deal. Where would you place yourself on this graph, and why do you think you need more or less sleep than others?

Source: Adapted from National Sleep Foundation. (2017). How Much Sleep Do We Really Need?

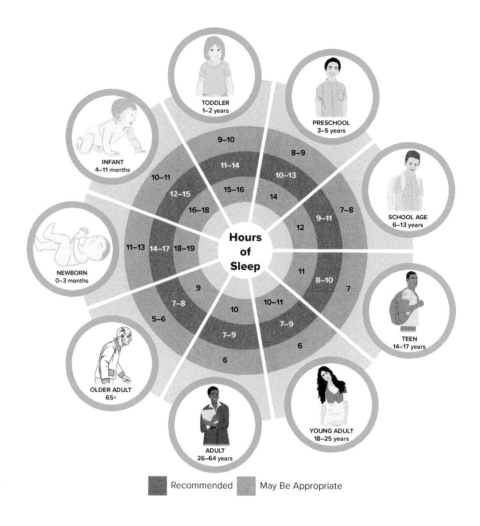

Recommended   May Be Appropriate

AP NEUROSCIENCE IN YOUR LIFE: WHY ARE WE SO EMOTIONAL WHEN WE DON'T GET ENOUGH SLEEP?

AP SKILL: DEFINE AND/OR APPLY CONCEPTS / SCIENTIFIC INVESTIGATION

1. What are some additional effects of sleep deprivation?

2. Describe the independent and dependent variables found in the experiment.

After a restless night, many people feel increased stress and overreact to events in their lives the next day. Recent research has now identified the neural basis for these reactions. For example, in one study, participants were kept awake all night and then asked to perform an experiment involving exposure to emotional and neutral images. Participants who were sleep deprived reacted to the neutral images as if they were emotional, and they had less connectivity between the amygdala (a region of the brain that processes emotion) and the anterior cingulate cortex (a region of frontal cortex important for emotional regulation). The green in the scan below shows the area of anterior cingulate that has greater connectivity to the amygdala for sleep-rested than sleep-deprived participants. These findings suggest that sleep loss increases emotional reactivity by interfering with our ability to control our emotions (Simon et al., 2015).

Left

Source: Adapted from Simon, E. B., Oren, N., Sharon, H., Kirschner, A., Goldway, N., Okon-Singer, H., . . . Hendler, T. (2016). Losing neutrality: The neural basis of impaired emotional control without sleep. *Journal of Neuroscience*, *35*(38), 13194-13205.

predeprivation levels after just a few days (Mograss et al., 2009; Jackson et al., 2013; Maturana et al., 2015).

In short, as far as we know, most people suffer no permanent consequences of such temporary sleep deprivation. But–and this is an important but–a lack of sleep can make us feel edgy, slow our reaction time, and lower our performance on academic and physical tasks. In addition, we put ourselves and others at risk when we carry out routine activities, such as driving, when we're very sleepy (Anderson & Home, 2006; Morad et al., 2009; Simon et al., 2017). (Also see *Neuroscience in Your Life*.)

The Function and Meaning of Dreaming

> I was being chased, and I couldn't get away. My attacker, wearing a mask, was carrying a long knife. He was gaining ground on me. I felt it was hopeless; I knew I was about to be killed.

If you have had a similar dream, you know how utterly convincing are the panic and fear that the events in the dream can bring about. *Nightmares* are unusually frightening dreams. Perhaps surprisingly, they occur fairly often. In one survey, almost half of a group of college students who kept records of their dreams over a 2-week period reported having at least one nightmare. Furthermore, nightmares are associated with negative experiences during the day, including worry and anxiety (Schredl & Reinhard, 2011; Cranston et al., 2017; Reks, Sheaves, & Freeman, 2017).

However, most of the 150,000 dreams the average person experiences by the age of 70 are much less dramatic. They typically encompass everyday events such as going to the supermarket, working at the office, and preparing a meal. Students dream about going to class; professors dream about lecturing. Dental patients dream of getting their teeth drilled; dentists dream of drilling the wrong tooth. The English have tea with the queen in their dreams; in the United States, people go to a bar with the president (Schredl & Piel, 2005; Taylor & Bryant, 2007; Nosek et al., 2015). Figure 5 shows the most common themes found in people's dreams.

But what, if anything, do all these dreams mean? Whether dreams have a specific significance and function is a question that scientists have considered for many years, and they have developed the three alternative theories we discuss below (and summarize in Figure 6).

PSYCHOANALYTIC EXPLANATIONS OF DREAMS: DO DREAMS REPRESENT UNCONSCIOUS WISH FULFILLMENT?

Using psychoanalytic theory, Sigmund Freud viewed dreams as a guide to the unconscious (Freud, 1900). In his **unconscious wish fulfillment theory,** he proposed that dreams represent unconscious wishes that dreamers desire to see fulfilled. To Freud,

Study Alert
Use Figure 6 to learn the differences between the three main explanations of dreaming.

unconscious wish fulfillment theory Sigmund Freud's theory that dreams represent unconscious wishes that dreamers desire to see fulfilled. (Module 14)

Thematic Event	Percentage of Dreams Reporting at Least One Event	
	Males	**Females**
Aggression	47%	44%
Friendliness	38	42
Sexuality	12	4
Misfortune	36	33
Success	15	8
Failure	15	10

FIGURE 5 Although dreams tend to be subjective to the person having them, common elements frequently occur in everyone's dreams. Why do you think so many common dreams are unpleasant and so few are pleasant? Do you think this tells us anything about the function of dreams?

Source: Adapted from Schneider, A., & Domhoff, G. W. (2015). The quantitative study of dreams.

Theory	Basic Explanation	Meaning of Dreams	Is Meaning of Dream Disguised?
Unconscious wish fulfillment theory (Freud)	Psychoanalytical explanation in which dreams represent unconscious wishes the dreamer wants to fulfill	Latent content reveals unconscious wishes.	Yes, by manifest content of dreams
Dreams-for-survival theory	Evolutionary explanation in which information relevant to daily survival is reconsidered and reprocessed	Clues to everyday concerns about survival	Not necessarily
Activation-synthesis theory	Neuroscience explanation in which dreams are the result of random activation of various memories, which are tied together in a logical story line	Dream scenario that is constructed is related to dreamer's concerns	Not necessarily

FIGURE 6 Three theories of dreams. As researchers have yet to agree on the fundamental meaning of dreams, several theories about dreaming have emerged.

the *manifest content* of the dream is what we remember and report about the dream—its story line. The manifest content, however, disguises the *latent content,* which includes the actual, underlying wishes that the dream represents. Because the underlying wishes (the latent content) are threatening to the dreamer, they are hidden in the dream's story line (the manifest content).

To Freud, it was important to pierce the armor of a dream's manifest content to understand its true meaning. To do this, Freud tried to get people to discuss their dreams, associating symbols in the dreams with events in the past. He also suggested that certain common symbols with universal meanings appear in dreams. For example, to Freud, dreams in which a person is flying symbolize a wish for sexual intercourse. (See Figure 7 for other common symbols.)

Many psychologists reject Freud's view that dreams typically represent unconscious wishes and that particular objects and events in a dream are symbolic. Rather, they believe that the direct, overt action of a dream is the focal point of its meaning. For example, a dream in which we are walking down a long hallway to take an exam for which we haven't studied does not relate to unconscious, unacceptable wishes. Instead, it simply may mean that we are concerned about an impending test. Even more complex dreams can often be interpreted in terms of everyday concerns and stress (Cartwright, Agargum, & Kirkby, 2006; Boag, 2017).

Moreover, some dreams reflect events occurring in the dreamer's environment as he or she is sleeping. For example, sleeping participants in one experiment were

Symbol (Manifest Content of Dream)	Interpretation (Latent Content)
Climbing up a stairway, crossing a bridge, riding an elevator, flying in an airplane, walking down a long hallway, entering a room, train traveling through a tunnel	Sexual intercourse
Apples, peaches, grapefruits	Breasts
Bullets, fire, snakes, sticks, umbrellas, guns, hoses, knives	Male sex organs
Ovens, boxes, tunnels, closets, caves, bottles, ships	Female sex organs

FIGURE 7 According to Freud, dreams contain common symbols with universal meanings.
©Digital Vision

sprayed with water while they were dreaming. Those unlucky volunteers reported more dreams involving water than did a comparison group of participants who were left to sleep undisturbed (Dement & Wolpert, 1958). Similarly, it is not unusual to wake up to find that the doorbell that was heard ringing in a dream is actually an alarm clock telling us it is time to get up.

However, PET brain scan research does lend a degree of support for the wish fulfillment view. For instance, the limbic and paralimbic regions of the brain, which are associated with emotion and motivation, are particularly active during REM sleep. At the same time, the association areas of the prefrontal cortex, which control logical analysis and attention, are inactive during REM sleep. The high activation of emotional and motivational centers of the brain during dreaming makes it more plausible that dreams may reflect unconscious wishes and instinctual needs, as Freud suggested (Occhionero, 2004; Wehrle et al., 2007; Perogamvros & Schwartz, 2015).

EVOLUTIONARY EXPLANATIONS OF DREAMS: DREAMS-FOR-SURVIVAL THEORY

According to the **dreams-for-survival theory,** which is based in the evolutionary perspective, dreams permit us to reconsider and reprocess during sleep information that is critical for our daily survival. Dreaming is considered an inheritance from our animal ancestors, whose small brains were unable to sift sufficient information during waking hours. Consequently, dreaming provided a mechanism that permitted the processing of information 24 hours a day.

dreams-for-survival theory The theory suggesting that dreams permit information that is critical for our daily survival to be reconsidered and reprocessed during sleep. (Module 14)

In the dreams-for-survival theory, dreams represent concerns about our daily lives, illustrating our uncertainties, indecisions, ideas, and desires. Dreams are seen, then, as consistent with everyday living. Rather than being disguised wishes, as Freud suggested, they represent key concerns growing out of our daily experiences (Ross, 2006; Horton, 2011).

Research supports the dreams-for-survival theory, suggesting that certain dreams permit people to focus on and to consolidate memories, particularly dreams that pertain to "how-to-do-it" memories related to motor skills. For example, rats seem to dream about mazes that they learned to run through during the day, at least according to the patterns of brain activity that appear while they are sleeping (Stickgold et al., 2001; Kuriyama, Stickgold, & Walker, 2004; Smith, 2006).

A similar phenomenon appears to work in humans. For instance, in one experiment, participants learned a visual memory task late in the day. They were then sent to bed but awakened at certain times during the night. When they were awakened at times that did not interrupt dreaming, their performance on the memory task typically improved the next day. But when they were awakened during rapid eye movement (REM) sleep–the stage of sleep when people dream–their performance declined. The implication is that dreaming, at least when it is uninterrupted, can play a role in helping us remember material to which we have been previously exposed (Marshall & Born, 2007; Nishida et al., 2009; Blechner, 2013).

NEUROSCIENCE EXPLANATIONS OF DREAMS: ACTIVATION-SYNTHESIS THEORY

Using the neuroscience perspective, psychiatrist J. Allan Hobson has proposed the activation-synthesis theory of dreams. The **activation-synthesis theory** focuses on the random electrical energy that the brain produces during REM sleep, possibly as a result of changes in the production of particular neurotransmitters. This electrical energy randomly stimulates memories stored in the brain. Because we have a need to make sense of our world even while asleep, the brain takes these chaotic memories and weaves them into a logical story line, filling in the gaps to produce a rational scenario (Hobson, 2005; Hangya et al., 2011).

activation-synthesis theory Hobson's theory that the brain produces random electrical energy during REM sleep that stimulates memories stored in the brain. (Module 14)

Activation-synthesis theory has been refined by the *activation information modulation (AIM) theory*. According to AIM, dreams are initiated in the brain's pons, which sends random signals to the cortex. Areas of the cortex that are involved in particular waking behaviors are related to the content of dreams. For example, areas of the brain related to vision are involved in the visual aspects of the dream, whereas areas of the brain related to movement are involved in aspects of the dream related to motion (Hobson, 2007).

Activation-synthesis and AIM theories do not entirely reject the view that dreams reflect unconscious wishes. They suggest that the particular scenario a dreamer produces is not random but instead is a clue to the dreamer's fears, emotions, and concerns. Hence, what starts out as a random process culminates in something meaningful.

Sleep Disturbances: Slumbering Problems

PsychTech

Surveys show that use of laptops, tablets, texting, or other technologies in the hour prior to going to bed is associated with sleeping problems.

At one time or another, almost all of us have difficulty sleeping–a condition known as insomnia. It could be due to a particular situation, such as the breakup of a relationship, concern about a test score, or the loss of a job. Some cases of insomnia, however, have no obvious cause. Some people are simply unable to fall asleep easily, or they go to sleep readily but wake up frequently during the night. Insomnia is a problem that afflicts as many as one-third of all people. Women and older adults are more likely to suffer from insomnia, as well as people who are unusually thin or are depressed (Henry et al., 2008; Karlson et al., 2013; Ong, 2017).

Some people who *think* they have sleeping problems actually are mistaken. For example, researchers in sleep laboratories have found that some people who report being up all night actually fall asleep in 30 minutes and stay asleep all night. Furthermore, some people with insomnia accurately recall sounds that they heard while they were asleep, which gives them the impression that they were awake during the night (Semler & Harvey, 2005; Yapko, 2006).

Other sleep problems are less common than insomnia, although they are still widespread. For instance, some 20 million people suffer from sleep apnea. *Sleep apnea* is a condition in which a person has difficulty breathing while sleeping. The result is disturbed, fitful sleep and a significant loss of REM sleep, as the person is constantly reawakened when the lack of oxygen becomes great enough to trigger a waking response. Some people with apnea wake as many as 500 times during the course of a night, although they may not even be aware that they have wakened. Not surprisingly, such disturbed sleep results in extreme fatigue the next day. Sleep apnea also may play a role in *sudden infant death syndrome (SIDS)*, a mysterious killer of seemingly normal infants who die while sleeping (Tippin, Sparks, & Rizzo, 2009; Arimoto et al., 2011; Bjornsdottir et al., 2015).

Night terrors are sudden awakenings from non-REM sleep that are accompanied by extreme fear, panic, and strong physiological arousal. Usually occurring in stage 3 sleep, night terrors may be so frightening that a sleeper awakens with a shriek. Although night terrors initially produce great agitation, victims usually can get back to sleep fairly quickly. They are far less frequent than nightmares, and, unlike nightmares, they typically occur during slow-wave, non-REM sleep. They occur most frequently in children between the ages of 3 and 8 (Lowe, Humphreys, & Williams, 2007).

Narcolepsy is uncontrollable sleeping that occurs for short periods while a person is awake. No matter what the activity–holding a heated conversation, exercising, or driving–a narcoleptic will suddenly fall asleep. People with narcolepsy go directly from wakefulness to REM sleep, skipping the other stages. The causes of narcolepsy are not known, although there could be a genetic component, because narcolepsy runs in families (Ervik, Abdelnoor, & Heier, 2006; Nishino, 2007; Billiard, 2008; Zamarian et al., 2015).

Sleepwalking and sleeptalking are more common in children than adults, and they both occur during stage 3 of sleep.
©Don Smith/Alamy

We know relatively little about sleeptalking and sleepwalking, two sleep disturbances that are usually harmless. Both occur during stage 3 sleep and are more common in children than in adults. Sleeptalkers and sleepwalkers usually have a vague consciousness of the world around them, and a sleepwalker may be able to walk with agility around obstructions in a crowded room. Unless a sleepwalker wanders into a dangerous environment, sleepwalking typically poses little risk. And the common idea that it's dangerous to wake a sleepwalker? It's just superstition (Lee-Chiong, 2006; Licis et al., 2011; Haridi et al., 2017).

Circadian Rhythms: Life Cycles

The fact that we cycle back and forth between wakefulness and sleep is one example of the body's circadian rhythms. **Circadian rhythms** (from the Latin *circa diem*, or "about a day") are biological processes that occur regularly on approximately a 24-hour cycle. Sleeping and waking, for instance, occur naturally to the beat of an internal pacemaker that works on a cycle of about 24 hours. Several other bodily functions, such as body temperature, hormone production, and blood pressure, also follow circadian rhythms (Beersma & Gordijn, 2007; Blatter & Cajochen, 2007; Labrecque & Cermakian, 2015).

Circadian cycles are complex, and they involve a variety of behaviors. For instance, sleepiness occurs not just in the evening but throughout the day in regular patterns, with most of us getting drowsy in mid-afternoon–regardless of whether or not we have eaten a heavy lunch. By making an afternoon siesta part of their everyday habit, people in several cultures take advantage of the body's natural inclination to sleep at this time (Takahashi et al., 2004; Reilly & Waterhouse, 2007; Egan et al., 2017).

The brain's *suprachiasmatic nucleus (SCN)* controls our circadian rhythms, but there are a number of circadian "clocks" associated with specific parts of the body. For instance, circadian rhythms speed up the heart before dawn to prepare us for the day's challenges. Similarly, the release and retention of various substances in the kidneys are affected by circadian rhythms. Even the processing of information in various areas of the brain may be affected by circadian rhythms and help shape how we perceive the world (Hickok, 2015; Summa & Turek, 2015).

circadian rhythms Biological processes that occur regularly on approximately a 24-hour cycle. (Module 14)

Bright lights may counter some of the symptoms of seasonal affective disorder, which occur during the winter.
©Image Point Fr/Shutterstock

FIGURE 8 A year of tweets shows that Fridays (orange dots), Saturdays (red dots), and Sundays (dark blue dots) are happier than weekdays. The happiest days are holidays, and the unhappiest days are associated with bad news.

Source: Adapted from Dodds, P. & Danforth, C. (2011). in Miller, G. Social scientists wade into the Tweet stream. *Science, 333,* 1814–1815.

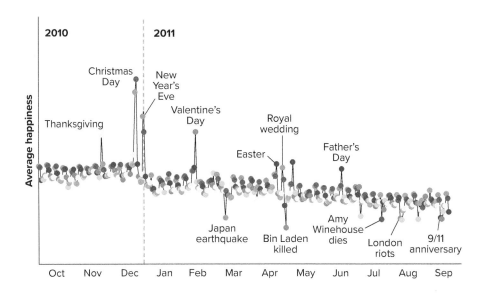

Furthermore, the relative amount of light and darkness, which varies with the seasons of the year, also plays a role in regulating circadian rhythms. In fact, some people experience *seasonal affective disorder,* a form of severe depression in which feelings of despair and hopelessness increase during the winter and lift during the rest of the year. The disorder appears to be a result of the brevity and gloom of winter days. Daily exposure to bright lights is sometimes sufficient to improve the mood of those with this disorder (Kasof, 2009; Monteleone, Martiadis, & Maj, 2011; Patten et al., 2017).

People's moods also follow regular patterns. By examining more than 500 million tweets using publicly available Twitter records, a team of psychologists found that words with positive associations (fantastic, super) and negative associations (afraid, mad) followed regular patterns. Across the globe and among different cultures, people were happier in the morning, less so during the day, with a rebound in the evening. Moods are also happier on certain days of the week: we're happier on weekends and holidays. Finally, positive emotions increase from late December to late June as the days get longer, and negative emotions increase as days get shorter (see Figure 8; Golder & Macy, 2011).

Furthermore, there seem to be optimal times for carrying out various tasks. Most adults are at their peak for carrying out cognitive tasks in the late morning. In contrast, focus and concentration on academic tasks declines throughout the afternoon. On the other hand, some research findings show that creativity increases in the evening when people are tired. It may be that fatigue decreases inhibitions, allowing for more creative thought (Matchock & Mordkoff, 2009; Wieth & Zacks, 2011; Shellenbarger, 2012).

Finally, health issues are more apt to appear at certain times of the day. For instance, heart attacks and strokes occur most frequently and are most severe between 6:00 A.M. and noon. Asthma attacks and heartburn are more common during the evening hours (Beck, 2015).

Daydreams: Dreams Without Sleep

It is the stuff of magic: Our past mistakes can be wiped out and the future filled with noteworthy accomplishments. Fame, happiness, and wealth can be ours. In the next moment, though, the most horrible tragedies can occur, leaving us devastated, alone, and penniless.

daydreams Fantasies that people construct while awake. (Module 14)

The source of these scenarios is **daydreams,** fantasies people construct while awake. Unlike dreaming that occurs during sleep, daydreams are more under people's control. Therefore, their content is often related to immediate events in the environment than is the content of the dreams that occur during sleep. Although they may include sexual content, daydreams also pertain to the full gamut of activities or events that are

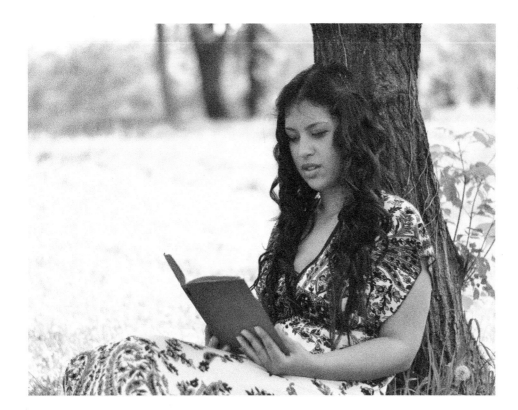

Daydreams are fantasies that people construct while they are awake. What are the similarities and differences between daydreams and night dreams?
©Aleksandar Mijatovic/Shutterstock

relevant to a person's life. While we are daydreaming, we are still experiencing waking consciousness. However, our awareness of the environment around us declines.

People vary considerably in the amount of daydreaming they do. For example, around 2% to 4% of the population spend at least half their free time fantasizing. Although most people daydream much less frequently, almost everyone fantasizes to some degree. In fact, a study in which experimenters sent texts at random times found that the participants were thinking about something other than what they were doing about half the time (Singer, 2006; Pisarik, Rowell, & Currie, 2013; Reddy, 2016).

The brain is surprisingly active during daydreaming. For example, several areas of the brain that are associated with complex problem solving become activated during daydreaming. In fact, daydreaming may be the only time these areas are activated simultaneously, suggesting that daydreaming may lead to insights about problems that we are grappling with (Fleck et al., 2008; Kounios et al., 2008; Carciofo et al., 2017).

Furthermore, daydreaming may contain elements of *inner speech*, in which people talk to themselves in their heads. Inner speech may help us to plan, be creative, and regulate our emotions (Ren, Wang, & Jarrold, 2016; Alderson-Day et al., 2017; Fernyhough, 2017).

Some scientists see a link between daydreaming and dreams during sleep. The content of daydreams and dreams show many parallels, and the brain areas and processes involved in daydreaming and dreams during sleep are related (Domhoff, 2011).

BECOMING AN INFORMED CONSUMER
of Psychology

Sleeping Better

Do you have trouble sleeping? You're not alone—70 million people in the United States have sleep problems. Half of Americans aged 19 to 29 report they rarely or never get a good night's sleep on weekdays, and nearly a third of working adults get less than 6 hours of sleep a night (Randall, 2012).

For those of us who spend hours tossing and turning in bed, psychologists studying sleep disturbances have a number of suggestions for overcoming insomnia. Here are some ideas (Finley & Cowley, 2005; Buysse et al., 2011; Reddy, 2013):

- *Exercise during the day (at least 6 hours before bedtime).* Not surprisingly, it helps to be tired before going to sleep! Moreover, learning systematic relaxation techniques and biofeedback can help you unwind from the day's stresses and tensions.
- *Avoid long naps—but consider taking short ones.* If you have trouble sleeping at night, it's best to avoid long naps. On the other hand, a short nap lasting 10 to 20 minutes may be ideal to boost energy and increase alertness. In fact, research shows that, at least in preschool children, midday naps improve recall of material learned earlier in the day—although we don't yet know if that applies to older individuals (Kurdziel, Duclos, & Spencer, 2013; Weir, 2016).
- *Choose a regular bedtime and stick to it.* Adhering to a habitual schedule helps your internal timing mechanisms regulate your body more effectively.
- *Avoid drinks with caffeine after lunch.* The effects of beverages such as coffee, tea, and some soft drinks can linger for as long as 8 to 12 hours after they are consumed.
- *Drink a glass of warm milk at bedtime.* Your grandparents were right when they dispensed this advice: Milk contains the chemical tryptophan, which helps people fall asleep.
- *Avoid sleeping pills.* Even though 25% of U.S. adults report having taken medication for sleep in the previous year and some 60 *million* sleeping aid prescriptions are filled annually, in the long run sleep medications can do more harm than good because they disrupt the normal sleep cycle. Rather than sleeping pills, try therapy; it's been proven to work better than drugs (DeAngelis, 2016).
- *Try* not *to sleep.* This approach works because people often have difficulty falling asleep because they are trying so hard. A better strategy is to go to bed only when you feel tired. If you don't get to sleep within 10 minutes, leave the bedroom and do something else, returning to bed only when you feel sleepy. Continue this process all night if necessary. But get up at your usual hour in the morning, and don't take any naps during the day. After 3 or 4 weeks, most people become conditioned to associate their beds with sleep—and fall asleep rapidly at night (Smith & Lazarus, 2001).

For long-term problems with sleep, you might consider visiting a sleep disorders center. For information on accredited clinics, consult the American Academy of Sleep Medicine at www.aasmnet.org.

AP MODULE 14: SLEEP AND DREAMS

AP SUMMARY

- Consciousness is a person's awareness of the sensations, thoughts, and feelings at a given moment. Waking consciousness can vary from more active to more passive states. Altered states of consciousness include naturally occurring sleep and dreaming, as well as deliberately altered hypnotic and drug-induced states.
- William James saw the study of consciousness as central to the field of psychology.
- Sigmund Freud viewed dreams as a guide to the unconscious.
- The brain is active throughout the night, and sleep proceeds through stages 1 through 3, collectively labeled as non-REM, which are identified by unique patterns of brain waves.

- REM (rapid eye movement) sleep is characterized by an increase in heart rate, a rise in blood pressure, an increase in the rate of breathing, and, in males, erections. It is called paradoxical because while this internal stimulation is occurring, the major muscles of the body appear to be paralyzed. Dreams most often occur during this stage.
- Psychologists have developed multiple theories for why we sleep. The evolutionary perspective suggests sleep allowed our ancestors to conserve energy. The biological perspective suggests sleep restores and replenishes our brains and bodies. Another explanation is that sleep is necessary for physical growth and development in children.
- The amount of sleep necessary varies for each individual, but most people sleep between 7

and 8 hours per night. Most people do not suffer permanent consequences of temporary sleep deprivation, but a lack of sleep can impact mood, reaction time, and performance.

- Psychologists have developed multiple theories for why we dream. According to Sigmund Freud's psychoanalytic approach, dreams have both a manifest content (an apparent story line) and a latent content (a true meaning). He suggested that latent content provides a guide to a dreamer's unconscious, revealing unfulfilled wishes or desires (wish fulfillment theory). The dreams-for-survival theory, grounded in an evolutionary perspective, suggests that information relevant to daily survival is reconsidered and reprocessed in dreams. Taking a neuroscience approach, the activation-synthesis theory proposes that dreams are a result of random electrical energy that stimulates different memories, which then are woven into a coherent story line.

- There are a variety of sleep disturbances. Insomnia is a sleep disorder characterized by difficulty sleeping. Sleep apnea is a condition in which people have difficulty sleeping and breathing at the same time. Nightmares happen during REM sleep, whereas night terrors are sudden awakenings during stage 3 sleep that are accompanied by extreme fear or panic. People with narcolepsy have an uncontrollable urge to sleep. Sleepwalking and sleep talking occur during stage 3 sleep and are relatively harmless.

- The circadian rhythm follows a 24-hour cycle that controls biological functions, such as sleep-wake, body temperature, hormone production, and blood pressure. This biological clock is controlled by the brain's suprachiasmatic nucleus. Other biological patterns include mood, cognitive functioning, and health issues.

- Wide individual differences exist in the amount of time devoted to daydreaming. Almost everyone daydreams or fantasizes to some degree.

AP KEY TERMS

consciousness
stage 1 sleep
stage 2 sleep
stage 3 sleep
rapid eye movement (REM) sleep
unconscious wish fulfillment theory
dreams-for-survival theory
activation-synthesis theory

circadian rhythms
daydreams

AP TEST PRACTICE

Section I: Multiple Choice

1. Which of the following statements follows Freud's psychoanalytic perspective?
   - **A.** Dreams are the result of random activation of various memories tied into a logical storyline.
   - **B.** Dreams allow information necessary for survival to be reconsidered and reprocessed.
   - **C.** Dreams reveal unconscious wishes.
   - **D.** Sleep assists physical growth and brain development in children.
   - **E.** Sleep consolidates memories.

2. Tia is asleep and in the stage of sleep that is least responsive to outside stimulation. This stage also dominates the beginning part of the night. What stage of sleep is Tia experiencing?
   - **A.** REM
   - **B.** Paradoxical
   - **C.** Stage 1
   - **D.** Stage 2
   - **E.** Stage 3

3. Which of the following sleep disorders is associated with the cessation of breathing?
   - **A.** Narcolepsy
   - **B.** Night terrors
   - **C.** Insomnia
   - **D.** Nightmares
   - **E.** Sleep apnea

Section II: Free Response

John returned from an overseas trip and his sleep schedule was all messed up. He tossed and turned in bed for hours.

A. Explain how the following terms affected his sleep.
   - Circadian rhythm
   - Rebound effect
   - Insomnia

B. When he finally fell asleep, John had some crazy dreams. Explain the research associated with the following theories for why we dream.
   - PET scan research and wish fulfillment theory
   - Research and dreams for survival theory

Module 15
Hypnosis and Meditation

You are feeling relaxed and drowsy. You are getting sleepier. Your body is becoming limp. Your eyelids are feeling heavier. Your eyes are closing; you can't keep them open anymore. You are totally relaxed. Now, place your hands above your head. But you will find they are getting heavier and heavier–so heavy you can barely keep them up. In fact, although you are straining as hard as you can, you will be unable to hold them up any longer.

An observer watching this scene would notice a curious phenomenon. Many of the people listening to the voice are dropping their arms to their sides. The reason for this strange behavior? Those people have been hypnotized.

Hypnosis: A Trance-Forming Experience?

hypnosis A trancelike state of heightened susceptibility to the suggestions of others. (Module 15)

People under **hypnosis** are in a trancelike state of heightened susceptibility to the suggestions of others. In some respects, it appears that they are asleep. Yet other aspects of their behavior contradict this notion, for people are attentive to the hypnotist's suggestions and may carry out bizarre or silly suggestions.

How is someone hypnotized? Typically, the process follows a series of four steps. First, a person is made comfortable in a quiet environment. Second, the hypnotist explains what is going to happen, such as telling the person that he or she will experience a pleasant, relaxed state. Third, the hypnotist tells the person to concentrate on a specific object or image, such as the hypnotist's moving finger or an image of a calm lake. The hypnotist may have the person concentrate on relaxing different parts of the body, such as the arms, legs, and chest. Fourth, once the subject is in a highly relaxed state, the hypnotist may make suggestions that the person interprets as being produced by hypnosis, such as "Your arms are getting heavy" and "Your eyelids are more difficult to open." Because the person begins to experience these sensations, he or she believes they are caused by the hypnotist and becomes susceptible to the suggestions of the hypnotist.

Despite their compliance when hypnotized, people do not lose all will of their own. They will not perform antisocial behaviors, and they will not carry out self-destructive acts. People will not reveal hidden truths about themselves, and they are capable of lying. Moreover, people cannot be hypnotized against their will–despite popular misconceptions (Raz, 2007; Lynn, Laurence, & Kirsch, 2015).

There are wide variations in people's susceptibility to hypnosis. About 5% to 20% of the population cannot be hypnotized at all, and some 15% are very easily hypnotized. Most people fall somewhere in between. Moreover, the ease with which a person is hypnotized is related to a number of other characteristics. People who are readily hypnotized are also easily absorbed while reading books or listening to music, becoming unaware of what is happening around them, and they often spend an unusual amount of time daydreaming. In sum, then, they show a high ability to concentrate and to become completely absorbed in what they are doing (Rubichi et al., 2005; Benham, Woody, & Wilson, 2006; Parris, 2017).

Despite common misconceptions, people cannot be hypnotized against their will, nor do they lose all will of their own when they are hypnotized. Why, then, do people sometimes behave so unusually when asked to by a hypnotist?
©Erin Painter/Midland Daily News/AP Images

A DIFFERENT STATE OF CONSCIOUSNESS?

The question of whether hypnosis is a state of consciousness that differs qualitatively from normal waking consciousness is controversial. Some psychologists believe hypnosis represents a state of consciousness that differs significantly from other states. In this view, high suggestibility, increased ability to recall and construct images, and acceptance of suggestions that clearly contradict reality characterize it as a different state. Moreover, people who are hypnotized show certain kinds of changes in electrical activity in the brain. Such electrical changes support the position that hypnosis is a state of consciousness different from normal waking (Fingelkurts, Fingelkurts, & Kallio, 2007; Hinterberger, Schöner, & Halsband, 2011; Keppler, 2017).

In this view, hypnosis represents a state of *divided consciousness*. According to famed hypnosis researcher Ernest Hilgard, hypnosis brings about a *dissociation*, or division, of consciousness into two simultaneous components. In one stream of consciousness, hypnotized people are following the commands of the hypnotist. Yet on another level of consciousness, they are acting as "hidden observers," aware of what is happening to them. For instance, hypnotic subjects may appear to be following the hypnotist's suggestion about feeling no pain, yet in another stream of consciousness, they may be actually aware of the pain.

On the other side of the controversy are psychologists who reject the notion that hypnosis is a state significantly different from normal waking consciousness. They argue that altered brain-wave patterns are not sufficient to demonstrate a qualitative difference because no other specific physiological changes occur when people are in trances. Furthermore, little support exists for the contention that adults can recall memories of childhood events accurately while hypnotized. That lack of evidence suggests that there is nothing qualitatively special about the hypnotic trance (Hongchun & Ming, 2006; Wagstaff, 2009; Wagstaff, Wheatcroft, & Jones, 2011).

The controversy over the nature of hypnosis has led to extreme positions on both sides of the issue. In contrast, more recent approaches suggest that the hypnotic state may best be viewed as lying along a continuum. In this view, hypnosis is neither a totally different state of consciousness nor totally similar to normal waking consciousness (Lynn et al., 2000; Kihlstrom, 2005b; Jamieson, 2007).

Study Alert
The question of whether hypnosis represents a different state of consciousness or is similar to normal waking consciousness is a key issue.

THE VALUE OF HYPNOSIS

As arguments about the true nature of hypnosis continue, though, one thing is clear: Hypnosis has been used successfully to solve practical human problems. In fact, psychologists working in many different areas have found hypnosis to be a reliable, effective tool. It has been applied to a number of areas, including the following:

- *Controlling pain.* Patients have had chronic pain reduced through hypnotic suggestion. In addition, people can be taught to hypnotize themselves to relieve pain or gain a sense of control over their symptoms. Hypnosis has proved to be particularly useful during childbirth and dental procedures (Hammond, 2007; Accardi & Milling, 2009; Spiegel, 2015).

- *Reducing smoking.* Although it hasn't been successful in stopping drug and alcohol abuse, hypnosis more frequently helps people stop smoking through hypnotic suggestions that the taste and smell of cigarettes are unpleasant (Elkins et al., 2006; Fuller, 2006; Green, Lynn, & Montgomery, 2008).

- *Treating psychological disorders.* Hypnosis sometimes is used during treatment for psychological disorders. For example, it may be employed to heighten relaxation, reduce anxiety, increase expectations of success, or modify self-defeating thoughts (Iglesias, 2005; Golden, 2006; Etzrodt, 2013).

- *Assisting in law enforcement.* Witnesses and victims are sometimes better able to recall the details of a crime when hypnotized. In one case, a witness to the kidnapping of a group of California schoolchildren was placed under hypnosis and was able to recall all but one digit of the license number on the kidnapper's vehicle. On the other hand, hypnotic recollections may also be inaccurate. Consequently, the legal status of hypnosis is unresolved (Whitehouse et al., 2005; Kazar, 2006; Knight & Meyer, 2007).

- *Improving athletic performance.* Athletes sometimes turn to hypnosis to improve their performance. For example, some baseball players have used hypnotism to increase their concentration when batting, with considerable success (Barker & Jones, 2008; Tramontana, 2011; Carlstedt, 2017).

Meditation: Regulating Our Own State of Consciousness

When traditional practitioners of the ancient Eastern religion of Zen Buddhism want to achieve greater spiritual insight, they turn to a technique that has been used for centuries to alter their state of consciousness. This technique is called meditation.

meditation A learned technique for refocusing attention that brings about an altered state of consciousness. (Module 15)

Meditation is a learned technique for refocusing attention that brings about an altered state of consciousness. Meditation typically consists of the repetition of a *mantra*—a sound, word, or syllable—over and over. In some forms of meditation, the focus is on a picture, flame, or specific part of the body. Regardless of the nature of the particular initial stimulus, the key to the procedure is concentrating on it so thoroughly that the meditator becomes unaware of any outside stimulation and reaches a different state of consciousness.

After meditation, people report feeling thoroughly relaxed. They sometimes relate that they have gained new insights into themselves and the problems they are facing. The long-term practice of meditation may even improve health because of the biological changes it produces. For example, during meditation, oxygen usage decreases, heart rate and blood pressure decline, and brain-wave patterns change (Lee, Kleinman, & Kleinman, 2007; Travis et al., 2009; Steinhubl et al., 2015).

Anyone can meditate by following a few simple procedures. The fundamentals include sitting in a quiet room with the eyes closed, breathing deeply and rhythmically, and repeating a word or sound—such as the word *one*—over and over.

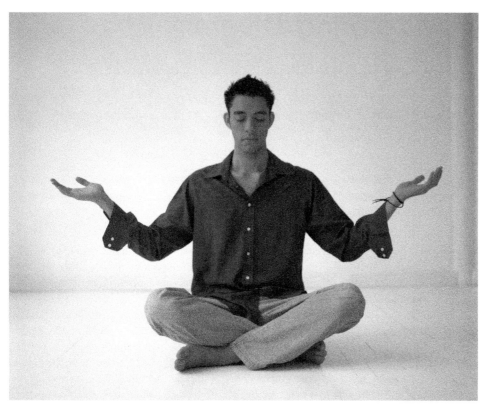

Meditation leads to short-term changes in a person's physiological state, as well as longer-term health benefits.
©Liquidlibrary/Getty Images

Practiced twice a day for 20 minutes, the technique is effective in bringing about greater relaxation not only during meditation but afterward. Evidence even supports long-term positive effects of some kinds of meditation, such as in the reduction of heart disease (Mohan, Sharma, & Bijlani, 2011; Shaner et al., 2017; Yadav et al., 2017).

From the perspective of...

A Human Resources Specialist Would you allow (or even encourage) employees to engage in meditation during the workday? Why or why not?

©Dex Image/Getty Images

Many cultures use meditation to alter consciousness, though it can take different forms and serve different purposes, depending on the culture. In fact, one reason psychologists study consciousness is the realization that people in many cultures routinely seek ways to alter their states of consciousness (Walsh & Shapiro, 2006).

Exploring Diversity

Cross-Cultural Routes to Altered States of Consciousness

A group of Native-American Sioux men sit naked in a steaming sweat lodge as a medicine man throws water on sizzling rocks to send billows of scalding steam into the air.

Aztec priests smear themselves with a mixture of crushed poisonous herbs, hairy black worms, scorpions, and lizards. Sometimes they drink the potion.

During the 16th century, a devout Hasidic Jew lies across the tombstone of a celebrated scholar. As he murmurs the name of God repeatedly, he seeks to be possessed by the soul of the dead wise man's spirit. If successful, he will attain a mystical state, and the deceased's words will flow out of his mouth.

Each of these rituals has a common goal: suspension from the bonds of everyday awareness and access to an altered state of consciousness. Although they may seem exotic from the vantage point of many Western cultures, these rituals represent an apparently universal effort to alter consciousness (Bartocci, 2004; Irwin, 2006).

Some scholars suggest that the quest to alter consciousness represents a basic human desire. Whether or not we accept such an extreme view, variations in states of consciousness clearly share some basic characteristics across a variety of cultures. One is an alteration in thinking, which may become shallow, illogical, or otherwise different from normal. In addition, people's sense of time can become disturbed, and their perceptions of the physical world and of themselves may change. They may lose self-control, doing things that they would never otherwise do. Finally, they may feel a sense of *ineffability*—the inability to understand an experience rationally or describe it in words (Finkler, 2004; Travis, 2006).

Of course, realizing that efforts to produce altered states of consciousness are widespread throughout the world's societies does not answer a fundamental question: Is the experience of unaltered states of consciousness similar across different cultures?

Because humans share basic biological commonalities in the ways their brains and bodies are wired, we might assume that the fundamental experience of consciousness is similar across cultures. As a result, we could suppose that consciousness shows some basic similarities across cultures. However, the ways in which certain aspects of consciousness are interpreted and viewed show substantial differences from culture to culture. For example, people in disparate cultures view the experience of the passage of time in varying ways. For instance, Arabs appear to perceive the passage of time more slowly than North Americans do (Alon & Brett, 2007).

Study Alert

Remember that although there are alternate techniques used in meditation, they are all designed to bring about an altered state of consciousness in which attention is refocused.

AP MODULE 15: HYPNOSIS AND MEDITATION

AP SUMMARY

- Describe various states of consciousness and their impact on behavior.
- Hypnosis produces a state of heightened susceptibility to the suggestions of the hypnotist. Under hypnosis, significant behavioral changes occur, including increased concentration and suggestibility, heightened ability to recall and construct images, lack of initiative, and acceptance of suggestions that clearly contradict reality.

- Meditation is a learned technique for refocusing attention that brings about an altered state of consciousness.
- Different cultures have developed their own unique ways to alter states of consciousness.

AP KEY TERMS

hypnosis
meditation

Section I: Multiple Choice

1. Hypnosis researcher Ernest Hilgard proposed that hypnotic subjects appeared to be following the hypnotist's suggestion about feeling no pain, but in another stream of consciousness, they were actually aware of the pain. Being hypnotized divided consciousness into two simultaneous components known as
   A. dissociation
   B. meditation
   C. night terrors
   D. social influence
   E. susceptibility

2. Carl repeats a mantra, his favorite phrase, in order to refocus his attention and bring about an altered state of consciousness. This is an example of
   A. hypnosis
   B. meditation
   C. drug-induced state
   D. sleeping
   E. dreaming

3. Some research suggests that certain types of meditation have led to what long-term positive effect?
   A. REM rebound
   B. Reduced heart disease
   C. Increased daydreaming
   D. Consolidation of memories
   E. Wish fulfillment

Section II: Free Response

Meditation is an altered state of consciousness that has been found to improve health. Identify and explain how meditation may be helpful according to the following perspectives from Modules 1 and 2.
- Evolutionary
- Neuroscience
- Behavioral
- Cognitive
- Humanistic
- Psychodynamic

Module 16
Drug Use: The Highs and Lows of Consciousness

psychoactive drugs Drugs that influence a person's emotions, perceptions, and behavior. (Module 16)

addictive drugs Drugs that produce a biological or psychological dependence in the user so that withdrawal from them leads to a craving for the drug that, in some cases, may be nearly irresistible. (Module 16)

Brittany was desperate. As the rest of her family were grieving over the loss of her grandmother, whose funeral they had just attended, she was searching for cash. She finally found a $5 bill in the purse belonging to her 6-year-old cousin. How low was it to steal from a 6-year-old to buy drugs? she wondered. But it didn't matter. Her head was aching, and her mouth was dry, and she would do anything to buy the drugs she needed to get high.

Like many others caught up in the opioid crisis facing the United States, Brittany's descent into addiction started with a legal drug, Percocet, that she was prescribed to deal with pain following the removal of her wisdom teeth. She didn't know that it was highly addictive, and even after the pain was gone, Brittany kept on craving the drug. It turned her from an honors student to an addict desperate for drugs. (Larsen, 2014)

Drugs of one sort or another are a part of almost everyone's life. From infancy on, most people take vitamins, aspirin, cold-relief medicine. However, these drugs rarely produce an altered state of consciousness.

In contrast, some substances, known as psychoactive drugs, lead to an altered state of consciousness. **Psychoactive drugs** influence a person's emotions, perceptions, and behavior. Yet even this category of drugs is common in most of our lives. If you have ever had a cup of coffee or sipped a beer, you have taken a psychoactive drug. A large number of individuals have used more potent—and more dangerous—psychoactive drugs than coffee and beer (see Figure 1); for instance, surveys find that 41% of high school seniors have used an illegal drug in the last year. In addition, 30% report having been drunk on alcohol. The figures for the adult population are even higher (Johnston et al., 2016).

Of course, drugs vary widely in the effects they have on users, in part because they affect the nervous system in very different ways. Some drugs alter the limbic system, and others affect the operation of specific neurotransmitters across the synapses of neurons. For example, some drugs block or enhance the release of neurotransmitters, others block the receipt or the removal of a neurotransmitter, and still others mimic the effects of a particular neurotransmitter (see Figure 2).

Addictive drugs produce a physiological or psychological dependence (or both) on a drug in the user. When a drug is addictive, withdrawal from the drug leads to a craving for it that may be overpowering and nearly irresistible. In *physiological drug dependence*, the body becomes so accustomed to functioning in the presence of a drug that it cannot function without it. In *psychological drug dependence*, people believe that they need the drug to respond to the stresses of daily living. Although we generally associate addiction with drugs such as heroin, everyday sorts of drugs, such as caffeine (found in coffee) and nicotine (found in cigarettes), have addictive aspects as well (Li, Volkow, & Baler, 2007).

We know surprisingly little about the underlying causes of addiction. One of the problems in identifying those causes is that different drugs (such as alcohol and cocaine) affect the brain in very different ways—yet they may be equally addicting. Furthermore, it takes longer to become addicted to some drugs than to others, even though the ultimate consequences of addiction may be equally grave (Nestler & Malenka, 2004; Smart, 2007; Holmes, 2017).

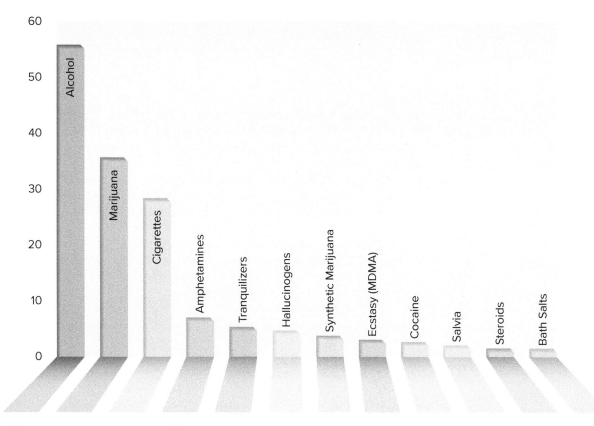

FIGURE 1 How many teenagers use drugs? The results of the most recent comprehensive survey of 14,000 high school seniors across the United States show the percentage of respondents who have used various substances for nonmedical purposes at least once. Can you think of any reasons why teenagers—as opposed to older people—might be particularly likely to use drugs?

Source: Adapted from Johnston, L. D., Miech, R. A., O'Malley, P. M., Bachman, J. G., & Schulenberg, J. E. (2016, December 13). Teen use of any illicit drug other than marijuana at new low, same true for alcohol. University of Michigan News Service: Ann Arbor, MI.

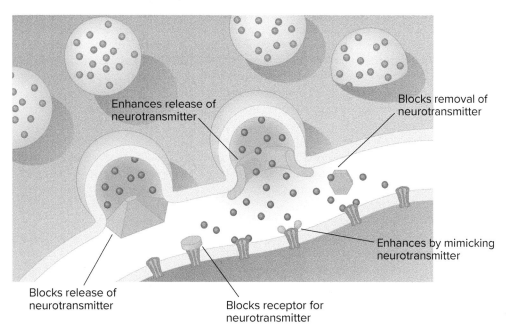

FIGURE 2 Different drugs affect different parts of the nervous system and brain, and each drug functions in one of these specific ways.

Study Alert

Use Figure 2 to learn the different ways that drugs produce their effects on a neurological level.

stimulants Drugs that have an arousal effect on the central nervous system, causing a rise in heart rate, blood pressure, and muscular tension. (Module 16)

Why do people take drugs in the first place? They do so for many reasons, including the perceived pleasure of the experience. In other words, it simply feels good.

In addition, though, a drug-induced high allows people to escape, at least temporarily, from the everyday pressures of life. And in some cases, people use drugs to attempt to achieve a religious or spiritual state (Korcha et al., 2011; Chapman & Wu, 2015).

In addition, people may be influenced to use drugs by the highly publicized drug use of role models such as movie stars and professional athletes, the easy availability of some illegal drugs, or peer pressure. In some cases, the motive is simply the thrill of trying something new.

Finally, genetic factors may predispose some people to be more susceptible to drugs and to become addicted to them. Regardless of the forces that lead a person to begin using drugs, drug addiction is among the most difficult of all behaviors to modify, even with extensive treatment (Ray & Hutchison, 2007; Vrieze et al., 2013; Reilly et al., 2017).

Because of the difficulty in treating drug problems, most experts believe that the best hope for dealing with the overall societal problem of substance abuse is to prevent people from becoming involved with addictive drugs in the first place. However, there is little accord on how to accomplish this goal.

Even widely employed drug reduction programs—such as D.A.R.E. (Drug Abuse Resistance Education)—are of questionable effectiveness. Used in more than 80% of school districts in the United States, D.A.R.E. consists of a 10-week series of lessons on the dangers of drugs, alcohol, and gangs taught to 5th- and 6th-graders by a police officer. The program is highly popular with school officials, parents, and politicians.

The problem with D.A.R.E.? Repeated careful evaluations have been unable to demonstrate that the D.A.R.E. program is effective in reducing drug use over the long term. In fact, one study even showed that D.A.R.E. graduates were more likely to use marijuana than was a comparison group of nongraduates. On the other hand, D.A.R.E. has updated its curriculum, and some preliminary evidence suggests it may be more successful than the previous version. But the jury is still out on its effectiveness (Lucas, 2008; Vincus et al., 2010; Singh et al., 2011).

Stimulants: Drug Highs

It's 1:00 A.M., and you still haven't finished reading the last chapter of the text on which you will be tested later in the morning. Feeling exhausted, you turn to the one thing that may help you stay awake for the next 2 hours: a cup of strong black coffee.

If you have ever found yourself in such a position, you have resorted to a major *stimulant*, caffeine, to stay awake. *Caffeine* is one of a number of **stimulants,** drugs whose effect on the central nervous system causes a rise in heart rate, blood pressure, and muscular tension. Caffeine is present not only in coffee; it is an important ingredient in tea, soft drinks, and chocolate as well (see Figure 3).

Caffeine produces several reactions. The major behavioral effects are an increase in attentiveness and a decrease in reaction time. Caffeine can also bring about an improvement in mood, most likely by mimicking the effects of a natural brain chemical, adenosine. Too much caffeine, however, can result in nervousness and insomnia. People can build up a biological dependence on the drug. Regular users who suddenly stop drinking coffee may experience headaches or depression. Many people who drink large amounts of coffee on weekdays have headaches on weekends because of the sudden drop in the amount of caffeine they are consuming (Kennedy & Haskell, 2011; Kamimori et al., 2015).

Nicotine, found in cigarettes, is another common stimulant. The soothing effects of nicotine help explain why cigarette smoking is addictive. Smokers develop a dependence on nicotine, and those who suddenly stop smoking develop a strong craving for the drug. This is not surprising: Nicotine activates neural mechanisms similar to those activated by cocaine, which, as we see in the section on cocaine, is also highly addictive (Haberstick et al., 2005; Ray et al., 2008; Wilcox et al., 2017).

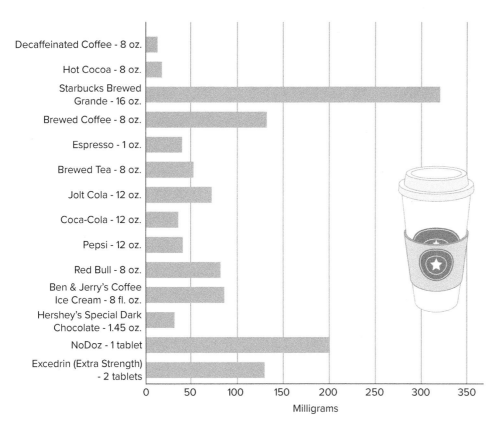

FIGURE 3 How much caffeine do you consume? This chart shows the range of caffeine found in common foods, drinks, and legal drugs.

Source: Adapted from Center for Science in the Public Interest. (2007). *Caffeine content of food & drugs.* Washington, DC: Center for Science in the Public Interest.

AMPHETAMINES

Amphetamines such as dexedrine and benzedrine, popularly known as speed, are strong stimulants. In small quantities, amphetamines–which stimulate the central nervous system–bring about a sense of energy and alertness, talkativeness, heightened confidence, and a mood "high." They increase concentration and reduce fatigue.

But not all the effects of amphetamines are positive: They also cause a loss of appetite, increased anxiety, and irritability. When taken over long periods of time, amphetamines can cause feelings of being persecuted by others, as well as a general sense of suspiciousness. People taking amphetamines may lose interest in sex. If taken in too large a quantity, amphetamines overstimulate the central nervous system to such an extent that convulsions and death can occur (Carhart-Harris, 2007).

Methamphetamine is a white, crystalline drug that U.S. police now say is the most dangerous street drug. "Meth" is highly addictive and relatively cheap, and it produces a strong, lingering high. It has made addicts of people across the social spectrum, ranging from soccer moms to urban professionals to poverty-stricken inner-city residents. After becoming addicted, users take it more and more frequently and in increasing doses. Long-term use of the drug can lead to brain damage (Halkitis, 2009; Kish et al., 2009; Rindone, 2015).

More than 1.5 million people in the United States are regular methamphetamine users. Because it can be made from nonprescription cold pills, retailers such as Walmart and Target have removed these medications from the shelves and keep them behind the pharmacy counter. Illicit labs devoted to the manufacture of methamphetamine have sprung up in many locations around the United States.

Adderall is an amphetamine college students often abuse. It was developed to help those who suffer from ADHD, or attention-deficit hyperactivity disorder. However, many college students use the drug illegally, believing that it increases their focus and the ability to study for long hours. Unfortunately, Adderall is addictive, and users need higher and higher doses to achieve the drug's supposed benefits (Diller, 2017).

Figure 4 provides a summary of the effects of amphetamines and other illegal drugs.

Drugs	Street Name	Effects	Withdrawal Symptoms	Adverse/Overdose Reactions
Stimulants				
Amphetamines		Increased confidence, mood elevation, sense of energy and alertness, decreased appetite, anxiety, irritability, insomnia, transient drowsiness, delayed orgasm	Apathy, general fatigue, prolonged sleep, depression, disorientation, suicidal thoughts, agitated motor activity, irritability, bizarre dreams	Elevated blood pressure, increase in body temperature, face picking, suspiciousness, bizarre and repetitious behavior, vivid hallucinations, convulsions, possible death
Benzedrine	Speed			
Dexedrine	Speed			
Cocaine	Coke, blow, snow, lady, crack			
Cathinone	Bath salts			
Depressants				
Alcohol	Booze	Anxiety reduction, impulsiveness, dramatic mood swings, bizarre thoughts, suicidal behavior, slurred speech, disorientation, slowed mental and physical functioning, limited attention span	Weakness, restlessness, nausea and vomiting, headaches, nightmares, irritability, depression, acute anxiety, hallucinations, seizures, possible death	Confusion, decreased response to pain, shallow respiration, dilated pupils, weak and rapid pulse, coma, possible death
Barbiturates				
Nembutal	Yellowjackets			
Seconal	Reds			
Phenobarbital				
Rohypnol	Roofies, rope, "date-rape drug"	Muscle relaxation, amnesia, sleep	Seizures	Seizures, coma, incapacitation, inability to resist sexual assault
Narcotics				
Heroin	H, Hombre, junk, smack	Reduction of anxiety and pain, difficulty in concentration, slowed speech, decreased physical activity, euphoria	Anxiety, vomiting, sneezing, diarrhea, lower back pain, watery eyes, runny nose, yawning, irritability, tremors, panic, chills and sweating, cramps	Depressed levels of consciousness, low blood pressure, rapid heart rate, shallow breathing, convulsions, coma, possible death
Morphine	Drugstore dope, cube, first line, mud			
Opioids (synthetic drugs such as Vicodin, Percocet, fentanyl, OxyContin)	Oxy, OC, Percs	Pain reduction, shallow breathing, slow heartbeat, seizure (convulsions); cold, clammy skin; confusion	Sweating, chills, abdominal cramps, insomnia, vomiting, diarrhea	Extreme drowsiness, muscle weakness, confusion, cold and clammy skin, pinpoint pupils, shallow breathing, slow heart rate, fainting, or coma
Hallucinogens				
Cannabis	Bhang, kif, ganja, dope, grass, pot, hemp, joint, weed, bone, Mary Jane, reefer	Euphoria, relaxed inhibitions, increased appetite, disoriented behavior	Hyperactivity, insomnia, decreased appetite, anxiety	Severe reactions rare but include panic, paranoia, fatigue, bizarre and dangerous behavior, decreased testosterone over long-term; immune-system effects
Marijuana				
Hashish				
Hash oil				
MDMA	Ecstasy, Molly	Heightened sense of oneself and insight, feelings of peace, empathy, energy	Depression, anxiety, sleeplessness	Increase in body temperature, memory difficulties
LSD	Acid, quasey, microdot, white lightning	Heightened aesthetic responses; vision and depth distortion; heightened sensitivity to faces and gestures; magnified feelings; paranoia, panic, euphoria	Not reported	Nausea and chills; increased pulse, temperature, and blood pressure; slow, deep breathing; loss of appetite; insomnia; bizarre, dangerous behavior
Steroids				
	Rhoids, juice	Aggression, depression, acne, mood swings, masculine traits in women and feminine traits in men	Symptoms can mimic other medical problems and include weakness, fatigue, decreased appetite, weight loss; women may note menstrual changes	Long-term, high-dose effects of steroid use are largely unknown but can lead to swelling and weight gain

FIGURE 4 Drugs and their effects. A comprehensive breakdown of effects of the most commonly used drugs.

Bath salts are an amphetamine-like stimulant containing chemicals related to cathinone. They can produce euphoria and a rise in sociability and sex drive, but the side effects can be severe, including paranoia and agitation (Cottencin, Rolland, & Karila, 2013; Airuehia, Walker, & Nittler, 2015).

COCAINE

The stimulant *cocaine*, and its derivative *crack*, represent a serious concern, although the scope of the problem has declined in recent years. Cocaine is inhaled or "snorted" through the nose, smoked, or injected directly into the bloodstream. It is rapidly absorbed into the body and takes effect almost immediately.

When used in relatively small quantities, cocaine produces feelings of profound psychological well-being, increased confidence, and alertness. Cocaine produces this "high" through the neurotransmitter dopamine. Dopamine is one of the chemicals that transmit between neurons messages that are related to ordinary feelings of pleasure. Normally, when dopamine is released, excess amounts of the neurotransmitter are reabsorbed by the releasing neuron. However, when cocaine enters the brain, it blocks reabsorption of leftover dopamine. As a result, the brain is flooded with dopamine-produced pleasurable sensations (Redish, 2004; Jarlais, Arasteh, & Perlis, 2007; Singer et al., 2017).

However, there is a steep price to be paid for the pleasurable effects of cocaine. The brain may become permanently rewired, triggering a psychological and physical addiction in which users grow obsessed with obtaining the drug. Over time, users deteriorate mentally and physically. In extreme cases, cocaine can cause hallucinations–a common one is of insects crawling over one's body. Ultimately, an overdose of cocaine can lead to death (Little et al., 2009; Roncero et al., 2013; Li et al., 2015).

Almost 2.5 million people in the United States are occasional cocaine users, and as many as 1.5 million people use the drug regularly. Given the strength of cocaine, withdrawal from the drug is difficult. Although the use of cocaine among high school students has declined in recent years, the drug still represents a major problem (Johnston et al., 2009; National Institute on Drug Abuse, 2018).

Study Alert
Figure 4, which summarizes the different categories of drugs (stimulants, depressants, narcotics, and hallucinogens), will help you learn the effects of particular drugs.

Depressants: Drug Lows

In contrast to the initial effect of stimulants, which is an increase in arousal of the central nervous system, the effect of **depressants** is to impede the nervous system by causing neurons to fire more slowly. Small doses result in at least temporary feelings of *intoxication*–drunkenness–along with a sense of euphoria and joy. When large amounts are taken, however, speech becomes slurred and muscle control becomes disjointed, making motion difficult. Ultimately, heavy users may lose consciousness entirely.

depressants Drugs that slow down the nervous system. (Module 16)

ALCOHOL

The most common depressant is alcohol, which is used by more people than is any other drug. Based on liquor sales, the average person over the age of 14 drinks 2½ gallons of pure alcohol over the course of a year. This works out to more than 200 drinks per person. Although alcohol consumption has declined steadily over the last decade, surveys show that more than three-fourths of college students indicate that they have had a drink within the last 30 days (Jung, 2002; Midanik, Tam, & Weisner, 2007).

One of the more disturbing trends is the high frequency of binge drinking among college students. For men, *binge drinking* is defined as having five or more drinks in one sitting; for women, who generally weigh less than men and whose bodies absorb alcohol less efficiently, binge drinking is defined as having four or more drinks at one sitting (Mokdad, Brewer, & Naimi, 2007; Rooke & Hine, 2011).

In Figure 5, people of different ages reported binge drinking in the last 30 days. Note that the highest percentage is that of college-age people. Furthermore, even light

FIGURE 5 Self-reported binge drinking at different ages. For men, binge drinking was defined as consuming five or more drinks in one sitting; for women, the total was four or more.

Note: High school students are defined as those in grades 9-12.
Source: Adapted from Centers for Disease Control and Prevention. (2013). *Youth risk behavior surveillance system—2013. Surveillance Summaries.* WR 2010; 59.

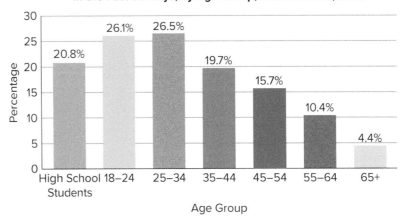

Percentage of People Who Reported Binge Drinking in the Past 30 Days, by Age Group, United States, 2013

drinkers were affected by the high rate of alcohol use: Two-thirds of lighter drinkers said that they had had their studying or sleep disturbed by drunk students, and a quarter of the women said they had been targets of unwanted sexual advances by drunk classmates (Wechsler et al., 2002; CDC Vitalsigns, 2010; Greene & Maggs, 2017).

Women are typically somewhat lighter drinkers than men—although the gap between the sexes is narrowing for older women and has closed completely for teenagers. Women are more susceptible to the effects of alcohol, and alcohol abuse may harm the brains of women more than it harms the brains of men (Mancinelli, Binetti, & Ceccanti, 2007; Chavez et al., 2011; Holzhauer, Wemm & Wulfert, 2017).

There are also cultural and ethnic differences in alcohol consumption. For example, teenagers in Europe drink more than teenagers in the United States do. Furthermore, people of East Asian backgrounds who live in the United States tend to drink significantly less than do Caucasians and African Americans, and their incidence of alcohol-related problems is lower. It may be that physical reactions to drinking, which may include sweating, a quickened heartbeat, and flushing, are more unpleasant for East Asians than for other groups (Garlow, Purselle, & Heninger, 2007; Kantrowitz & Underwood, 2007).

Although alcohol is a depressant, most people believe that it increases their sense of sociability and well-being. This belief is caused because initially alcohol may lead to a reduction in tension and stress, feelings of happiness, and loss of inhibitions.

The effects of alcohol vary significantly, depending on who is drinking it and the setting in which people drink. If alcohol were a newly discovered drug, do you think its sale would be legal?

(Left): ©Exactostock/SuperStock; (Right): ©Jim Arbogast/Getty Images

Number of drinks consumed in 2 hours		Alcohol in blood (percentage)	Typical effects
	2	0.05	Judgment, thought, and restraint weakened; tension released, giving carefree sensation
	3	0.08	Tensions and inhibitions of everyday life lessened; cheerfulness
	4	0.10	Voluntary motor action affected, making hand and arm movements, walk, and speech clumsy
	7	0.20	Severe impairment—staggering, loud, incoherent, emotionally unstable, 100 times greater traffic risk; exuberance and aggressive inclinations magnified
	9	0.30	Deeper areas of brain affected, with stimulus-response and understanding confused; stuporous; blurred vision
	12	0.40	Incapable of voluntary action; sleepy, difficult to arouse; equivalent of surgical anesthesia
	15	0.50	Comatose; centers controlling breathing and heartbeat anesthetized; death increasingly probable

FIGURE 6 The effects of alcohol. The quantities represent only rough benchmarks; the effects vary significantly depending on an individual's weight, height, recent food intake, genetic factors, and even psychological state. *Note:* A drink refers to a typical 12-ounce bottle of beer, a 1.5-ounce shot of hard liquor, or a 5-ounce glass of wine.

However, as the dose of alcohol increases, the depressive effects become more pronounced (see Figure 6). People may feel emotionally and physically unstable. They also show poor judgment and may act aggressively. Moreover, memory is impaired, brain processing of spatial information is diminished, and speech becomes slurred and incoherent. Eventually, they may fall into a stupor and pass out. If they drink enough alcohol in a short time, they may die of alcohol poisoning (Zeigler et al., 2005; Thatcher & Clark, 2006).

Although most people fall into the category of casual users, 14 million people in the United States—1 in every 13 adults—have a drinking problem. *Alcoholics,* people with alcohol-abuse problems, come to rely on alcohol and continue to drink even though it causes serious difficulties. In addition, they become increasingly immune to the effects of alcohol. Consequently, alcoholics must drink progressively more to experience the initial positive feelings that alcohol produces.

In some cases of alcoholism, people must drink constantly in order to feel well enough to function in their daily lives. In other cases, though, people drink inconsistently but occasionally go on binges in which they consume large quantities of alcohol.

Even legal drugs, when used improperly, lead to addiction.
©David Smart/Shutterstock

It is not clear why certain people become alcoholics and develop a tolerance for alcohol, whereas others do not. There may be a genetic cause, although the question of whether there is a specific inherited gene that produces alcoholism is controversial. What is clear is that the chances of becoming an alcoholic are considerably higher if alcoholics are present in earlier generations of a person's family. However, not all alcoholics have close relatives who are alcoholics. In these cases, environmental stressors are suspected of playing a larger role (Nurnberger & Bierut, 2007; Gizer et al., 2011; Buckner & Shah, 2015).

BARBITURATES

Barbiturates are another form of depressant. They include drugs such as Nembutal, Seconal, and phenobarbital. Barbiturates produce a sense of relaxation and are frequently prescribed by physicians to induce sleep or reduce stress. At larger doses, they produce altered thinking, faulty judgment, and sluggishness.

Barbiturates are psychologically and physically addictive. When combined with alcohol, they can be deadly because such a combination relaxes the muscles of the diaphragm to such an extent that the user stops breathing.

ROHYPNOL

Rohypnol is sometimes called the "date rape drug" because when it is mixed with alcohol, it can prevent victims from resisting sexual assault. Sometimes people who are unknowingly given the drug are so incapacitated that they have no memory of the assault.

Narcotics, Opiates, and Opioids: Relieving Pain and Anxiety

narcotics Drugs that increase relaxation and relieve pain and anxiety. (Module 16)

Narcotics are drugs that increase relaxation and relieve pain and anxiety. Two of the most powerful narcotics, *morphine* and *heroin*, are derived from the poppy seed pod. Although morphine is used medically to control severe pain, heroin is illegal in the United States. This status has not prevented its widespread abuse.

Heroin users usually inject the drug directly into their veins with a hypodermic needle. The immediate effect has been described as a "rush" of positive feeling, similar in some respects to a sexual orgasm–and just as difficult to describe. After the rush, a heroin user experiences a sense of well-being and peacefulness that lasts 3 to 5 hours.

However, when the effects of heroin wear off, users feel extreme anxiety and a desperate desire to repeat the experience. Moreover, larger amounts of heroin are needed each time to produce the same pleasurable effect. These last two properties are all the ingredients necessary for physiological and psychological dependence: The user is constantly either shooting up or attempting to obtain ever-increasing amounts of the drug. Eventually, the life of the addict revolves around heroin.

Heroin is part of a class of drugs called opiates. *Opiates* are narcotics that are derived from natural substances, and they include such drugs as morphine and codeine in addition to heroin. In contrast, *opioids* are synthetic narcotics such as Vicodin, Percocet, fentanyl, and OxyContin, all of which are created in laboratories and are often prescribed to alleviate pain. (The terms *opiates* and *opioids* are often used interchangeably, and when people speak of the "opioid crisis," it typically refers to both categories.)

Opiate and opioid use has reached epidemic proportions. For example, heroin use has more than doubled among young adults 18 to 25 years old from 2002–2004 to 2011–2013. Furthermore, the rate of overdose deaths related to heroin increased 500% between 2000 and 2016 (Cook, 2015; Katz, 2017).

Although it's not totally clear why use of opioids has increased so rapidly, one reason is that the cost of the drugs has plummeted at the same time the supply has increased substantially Furthermore, some of the newest opioids are 100 times as potent as natural heroin. And that means drugs bought on the street, which could contain virtually anything, are particularly dangerous and can easily lead to overdoses.

Because of the powerful positive feelings opioids produce, addiction to them is particularly difficult to cure. In one treatment that has shown some success, users are given alternative drugs that reduce dependence on heroin and other addictive opiates. For example, *methadone* is a synthetic chemical that satisfies a heroin user's physiological cravings for the drug without providing the "high" that accompanies heroin. Similarly, *Suboxone* is a painkiller that reduces the withdrawal symptoms from heroin. Suboxone comes in tablet form as well as small film strips, both of which are put under the tongue to dissolve quickly. Another treatment is *Vivitrol*, an injection that lasts about a month. It prevents withdrawal symptoms, and it also prevents heroin from producing the positive effects that users crave if heroin is used (Shah, Young, & Vieira, 2014).

Methadone, Suboxone, and Vivitrol allow heroin users to function relatively normally and without the drug cravings. However, although such drugs remove the psychological dependence on heroin, they replace the physiological dependence on heroin with a physiological dependence on the alternative drugs. Consequently, researchers are attempting to identify nonaddictive chemical substitutes that do not produce a physiological craving (Verdejo, Toribio, & Orozco, 2005; Joe, Flynn, & Broome, 2007; Oviedo-Joekes et al., 2009).

Hallucinogens: Psychedelic Drugs

Hallucinogens are drugs that alter perceptions, thoughts, and feelings. They can even produce *hallucinations*, the experience of sensing things such as sights, sounds, or smells that seem real but are not.

hallucinogens Drugs that are capable of producing alterations in perception, thoughts, and feelings. (Module 16)

MARIJUANA

The most common hallucinogen in widespread use today is *marijuana*, whose active ingredient–tetrahydrocannabinol (THC)–is found in a common weed, cannabis. Marijuana is typically smoked in cigarettes or pipes, although it can be cooked and eaten. Close to 40% of high school seniors and around 15% of 8th-graders report having used marijuana in the last year (Johnston et al., 2016; see Figure 7).

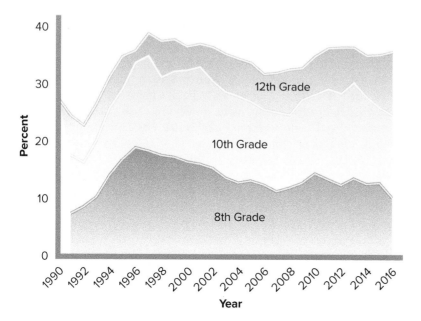

FIGURE 7 Although the level of marijuana use has declined slightly in recent years, overall the absolute number of teenagers who have used the drug in the past year remains relatively high.

Source: Adapted from Johnston, L. D., Miech, R. A., O'Malley, P. M., Bachman, J. G., & Schulenberg, J. E. (2016, December 13). Teen use of any illicit drug other than marijuana at new low, same true for alcohol. University of Michigan News Service: Ann Arbor, MI.

The effects of marijuana vary from person to person, but they typically consist of feelings of euphoria and general well-being. Sensory experiences seem more vivid and intense, and a person's sense of self-importance seems to grow. Memory may be impaired, causing users to feel pleasantly "spaced out."

Marijuana does not seem to produce addiction except for a small number of heavy users. Furthermore, there is little scientific evidence for the popular belief that users "graduate" from marijuana to more dangerous drugs. Overall, most research suggests its use is less harmful than the use of tobacco and alcohol (Barcott & Scherer, 2015).

On the other hand, some research suggests that there are similarities in the way marijuana and drugs such as cocaine and heroin affect the brain, as well as evidence that heavy use may impact negatively on cognitive ability in the long run. Furthermore, heavy use may at least temporarily decrease the production of the male sex hormone testosterone, potentially affecting sexual activity and sperm count (Lane, Cherek, & Tcheremissine, 2007; Rossato, Pagano, & Vettor, 2008; Pardini et al., 2015).

In addition, marijuana smoked during pregnancy may have lasting effects on children who are exposed prenatally, although the research results are inconsistent. Heavy use also affects the ability of the immune system to fight off germs and increases stress on the heart, although it is unclear how strong these effects are. Finally, there is one unquestionably negative consequence of smoking marijuana: The smoke damages the lungs much the way cigarette smoke does, producing an increased likelihood of developing cancer and other lung diseases (Julien, 2001; Reid, MacLeod, & Robertson, 2010).

Despite the possible dangers of marijuana, its use is increasingly accepted. It clearly has several medical uses: it can prevent nausea from chemotherapy, treat some AIDS symptoms, and relieve muscle spasms for people with spinal cord injuries. Furthermore, it may be helpful in the treatment of Alzheimer's disease (Barcott & Scherer, 2015; Finn, 2015).

Many states have made the use of the drug legal if it is prescribed by a health care provider–although it remains illegal under U.S. federal law. And a handful of states, including Alaska, California, Colorado, Massachusetts, Nevada, Oregon, and Washington, have made its use and sale legal, even for recreational use, with no prescription required (Baumrucker et al., 2011; Roffman, 2013; Bradford & Bradford, 2017).

MDMA (ECSTASY OR MOLLY) AND LSD

MDMA (*Ecstasy* or *Molly*) and *lysergic acid diethylamide* (*LSD* or *acid*) fall into the category of hallucinogens. Both drugs affect the operation of the neurotransmitter serotonin in the brain, causing an alteration in brain-cell activity and perception (Buchert et al., 2004; Aleksander, 2013).

MDMA produces feelings of increased energy and euphoria, and users report feeling increased empathy and connection with others. A form of MDMA known as *Molly* is often used at raves and music festivals, and it has led to a rising number of overdoses and even deaths. Furthermore, those who use MDMA may experience declines in memory and performance on intellectual tasks. Such findings suggest that MDMA use may lead to long-term changes in serotonin receptors in the brain (McKinley, 2013; Ebrahimian et al., 2017; Parrott et al., 2017).

LSD, which is structurally similar to serotonin, produces vivid hallucinations. Perceptions of colors, sounds, and shapes are altered so much that even the most mundane experience–such as looking at the knots in a wooden table–can seem moving and exciting. Time perception is distorted, and objects and people may be viewed in a new way, with some users reporting that LSD increases their understanding of the world. For others, however, the experience brought on by LSD can be terrifying, particularly if users have had emotional difficulties in the past. Furthermore, people occasionally experience flashbacks, in which they hallucinate long after they initially used the drug (Baruss, 2003; Wu, Schlenger, & Galvin, 2006).

This drawing, made by someone taking LSD, suggests the effects of hallucinogens on thinking.

©Omikron/Science Source/Getty Images

BECOMING AN INFORMED CONSUMER
of Psychology

Identifying Drug and Alcohol Problems

In a society bombarded with commercials for drugs that are guaranteed to cure everything from restless leg syndrome to erectile dysfunction, it is no wonder that drug-related problems are a major social issue. Yet many people with drug and alcohol problems deny that they have them, and even close friends and family members may fail to realize when occasional social use of drugs or alcohol has turned into abuse.

Certain signs, however, indicate when use becomes abuse (National Institute on Drug Abuse, 2000). Among them are the following:

- Always getting high to have a good time
- Being high more often than not
- Getting high to get oneself going
- Going to work or class while high
- Missing or being unprepared for class or work because you were high
- Feeling bad later about something you said or did while high
- Driving a car while high
- Coming in conflict with the law because of drugs
- Doing something while high that you wouldn't do otherwise
- Being high in nonsocial, solitary situations
- Being unable to stop getting high
- Feeling a need for a drink or a drug to get through the day
- Becoming physically unhealthy
- Failing at school or on the job
- Thinking about liquor or drugs all the time
- Avoiding family or friends while using liquor or drugs

Any combination of these symptoms should be sufficient to alert you to the potential of a serious drug problem. Because drug and alcohol dependence are almost impossible to cure on one's own, people who suspect that they have a problem should seek immediate attention from a psychologist, physician, or counselor.

You can also get help from national hotlines. For alcohol difficulties, call the National Council on Alcoholism at (800) 622-2255. For drug problems, call the National Institute on Drug Abuse at (800) 662-4357. You can also check the Web for a local listing of Alcoholics Anonymous or Narcotics Anonymous. In addition, you can check out the websites of the National Institute on Alcohol Abuse and Alcoholism (www.niaaa.nih.gov) and the National Institute on Drug Abuse (www.nida.nih.gov).

From the perspective of...

A Substance Abuse Counselor How would you explain why people start using drugs to the family members of someone who was addicted? What types of drug prevention programs would you advocate?

©Uppercut/Getty Images

AP MODULE 16: DRUG USE: THE HIGHS AND LOWS OF CONSCIOUSNESS

AP SUMMARY

- Some drugs affect the operation of specific neurotransmitters across the synapses of neurons.
- Psychoactive drugs can produce an altered state of consciousness. However, they vary in how dangerous they are and whether they are addictive.
- Stimulants cause arousal in the central nervous system. Two common stimulants are caffeine and nicotine. More dangerous are cocaine and amphetamines, which in large quantities can lead to death.
- Depressants decrease arousal in the central nervous system. They can cause intoxication along with feelings of euphoria. Alcohol is the most frequently used depressant. Its initial effects of released tension and positive feelings yield to depressive effects as the dose of alcohol increases. Both hereditary and environmental stressors can lead to alcoholism. Barbiturates, another type of depressant, produce relaxation and are used to induce sleep or reduce stress.
- Narcotics are drugs that produce relaxation and relieve pain and anxiety. Because of their addictive qualities, morphine and heroin are particularly dangerous. Opiates are narcotics derived from natural substances, while opioids are synthetic narcotics. Use of both types have reached epidemic proportions and addiction to them is difficult to break. Synthetic chemicals have been used to remove the psychological dependence on heroin, but they just replace the physiological dependence from heroin onto the alternative drug.
- Hallucinogens are drugs that produce hallucinations or other changes in perception. The most frequently used hallucinogen is marijuana, which has several long-term risks. It has several medical uses and its use is increasingly accepted. Two other hallucinogens are MDMA (Ecstasy) and LSD.
- Addictive drugs produce a physiological or psychological dependence on a drug in the user. Little is known about the underlying causes of addiction, but there are nature and nurture explanations for addiction. Treating drug problems is difficult, but most experts agree on the necessity of prevention.
- Withdrawal from an addictive drug can lead to an irresistible craving. Withdrawal symptoms are listed for the most commonly used drugs. Some individuals take progressively more of a drug to feel the initial positive feelings. It is not clear why some individuals develop a tolerance, whereas others do not.
- A number of signals indicate when drug use becomes drug abuse. A person who suspects that he or she has a drug problem should get professional help. People are almost never capable of solving drug problems on their own.

AP KEY TERMS

psychoactive drugs	**depressants**
addictive drugs	**narcotics**
stimulants	**hallucinogens**

AP TEST PRACTICE

Section I: Multiple Choice

1. Cocaine is classified as what category of psychoactive drug?
   - **A.** Depressant
   - **B.** Opiate
   - **C.** Stimulant
   - **D.** Narcotic
   - **E.** Hallucinogen

2. Which drug can be used to treat people with heroin addiction?
   - **A.** LSD
   - **B.** MDMA
   - **C.** Barbiturates
   - **D.** Methadone
   - **E.** Rohypnol

3. Alcoholics can become increasingly immune to the effects of alcohol and need higher doses in order to feel the initial positive feelings that alcohol produces. This is an example of
   - **A.** euphoria
   - **B.** relaxed inhibition
   - **C.** paranoia
   - **D.** withdrawal
   - **E.** tolerance

Section II: Free Response

Psychoactive drugs lead to an altered state of mind. Drugs vary widely in the effects they have on users. Some drugs are commonly used and some are highly addictive.
A. Identify each drug's category and some common symptoms associated with their use.
  - Caffeine
  - Alcohol
  - Amphetamines

Some drugs affect the operation of specific neurotransmitters across the synapses of neurons.
B. Explain the impact of the following drugs on their respective neurotransmitter.
  - Cocaine and dopamine
  - MDMA and serotonin

Many addictive drugs produce a dependence on the drug.
C. Explain the following terms related to addiction
  - Tolerance and Methamphetamine
  - Withdrawal and Opioids

LOOKING *Back*

EPILOGUE

Our examination of states of consciousness has ranged widely. It focuses both on natural factors, such as sleep, dreaming, and daydreaming, and on more intentional modes of altering consciousness, including hypnosis, meditation, and drugs. As we consider why people seek to alter their consciousness, we need to reflect on the uses and abuses of the various consciousness-altering strategies in which people engage.

VISUAL SUMMARY 5 States of Consciousness

MODULE 14 Sleep and Dreams

Stages of Sleep: Three stages of sleep, plus REM sleep

As sleep becomes deeper, brain waves take on a slower wave pattern.

Awake

Stage 1 (non-REM)

Sleep spindle

Stage 2 (non-REM)

Stage 3 (non-REM)

REM

- Stage 1
  - Transition from wakefulness to sleep
  - Rapid brain waves
- Stage 2
  - Slower, more regular brain waves
  - Sleep spindles
- Stages 3
  - Slow, high-peaked waves
  - Least responsive to stimulation
- REM sleep
  - Rebound effect
  - Dreaming

Function and Meaning of Dreams: Dreams typically encompass everyday events

- Unconscious wish fulfillment theory
- Dreams-for-survival theory
- Activation-synthesis theory

Sleep Disturbances

- Insomnia
- Sleep apnea
- SIDS
- Night terrors
- Narcolepsy

Circadian Rhythms: 24-hour cycle

MODULE 15 Hypnosis and Meditation

Hypnosis: A trancelike state of heightened suggestibility

Meditation: Learned technique for refocusing attention

MODULE 16 Drug Use

Stimulants: Increase arousal in the nervous system

- Caffeine
- Cocaine
- Amphetamines

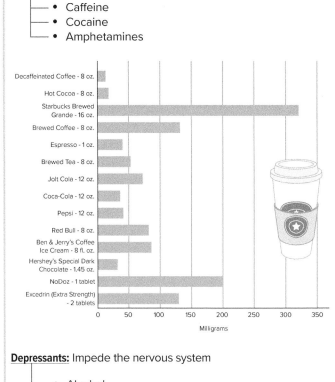

Decaffeinated Coffee - 8 oz.
Hot Cocoa - 8 oz.
Starbucks Brewed Grande - 16 oz.
Brewed Coffee - 8 oz.
Espresso - 1 oz.
Brewed Tea - 8 oz.
Jolt Cola - 12 oz.
Coca-Cola - 12 oz.
Pepsi - 12 oz.
Red Bull - 8 oz.
Ben & Jerry's Coffee Ice Cream - 8 fl. oz.
Hershey's Special Dark Chocolate - 1.45 oz.
NoDoz - 1 tablet
Excedrin (Extra Strength) - 2 tablets

0   50   100   150   200   250   300   350
Milligrams

Depressants: Impede the nervous system

- Alcohol
- Barbiturates
- Rohypnol: "Date-rape" drug

Percentage of People Who Reported Binge Drinking in the Past 30 Days

Percentage

Students* 24.2%
18–24 25.6%
25–34 22.5%
35–44 17.8%
45–64 12.1%
≥65 3.8%

Age Groups (years)

* High school students
Sources: CDC, Youth Risk Behavior Surveillance System and Behavioral Risk Factor Surveillance System, 2009.

Narcotics: Reduce pain and anxiety

- Heroin
- Morphine

Hallucinogens: Produce changes in perceptual processes

- Marijuana
- MDMA
- LSD

(MODULE 14) (Photo): ©Don Smith/Alamy Stock Photo; Source: Adapted from Hobson, J. A. (1989). *Sleep.* New York: W. H. Freeman. (MODULE 15) (Hypnosis): ©Erin Painter/ Midland Daily News/AP Images; (Meditation): ©Liquidlibrary/Getty Images (MODULE 16) Source: Adapted from Center for Science in the Public Interest. (2007). *Caffeine content of food & drugs.* Washington, DC: Center for Science in the Public Interest; Adapted from Centers for Disease Control and Prevention. (2013). *Youth risk behavior surveillance system—2013. Surveillance Summaries.* WR 2010; 59.

©MJTH/Shutterstock

CHAPTER 6
Learning

AP ESSENTIAL QUESTIONS

- How do we learn?
- How do our experiences influence our behaviors and mental processes?

AP LEARNING TARGETS FOR CHAPTER 6

MODULE 17

- Identify the contributions of key researchers in the psychology of learning.
- Interpret graphs that exhibit the results of learning experiments.
- Apply learning principles to explain emotional learning, taste aversion, superstitious behavior, and learned helplessness.
- Provide examples of how biological constraints create learning predispositions.
- Describe basic classical conditioning phenomena.

CLASSICAL CONDITIONING
The Basics of Classical Conditioning
Applying Conditioning Principles to Human Behavior
Extinction
Generalization and Discrimination
Beyond Traditional Classical Conditioning: Challenging Basic Assumptions

MODULE 18

- Provide examples of how biological constraints create learning predispositions.
- Predict the effects of operant conditioning.
- Predict how practice, schedules of reinforcement, other aspects of reinforcement, and motivation will influence quality of learning.

OPERANT CONDITIONING
Thorndike's Law of Effect
The Basics of Operant Conditioning
AP Applying Psychology in the 21st Century: How Uber and Lyft Put Themselves in the Driver's Seat
Becoming an Informed Consumer of Psychology: Using Behavior Analysis and Behavior Modification

- Suggest how behavior modification, biofeedback, coping strategies, and self-control can be used to address behavioral problems.

- Identify the contributions of key researchers in the psychology of learning.

- Interpret graphs that exhibit the results of learning experiments.

- Describe the essential characteristics of insight learning, latent learning, and social learning.

- Distinguish general differences between principles of classical conditioning, operant conditioning, and observational learning.

PROLOGUE *NOSING OUT DISEASE*

Seven-year-old Luke Nuttall has Type 1 diabetes. One night his blood sugar levels dropped suddenly while he was sleeping, but his glucose monitor—that is, his *mechanical* glucose monitor—didn't detect the drop. However, his *canine* monitor, a black Labrador named Jedi, picked up the change and immediately woke Luke's mother, as he was trained to do.

Jedi is a diabetes alert dog—a DAD—carefully trained, through procedures developed by psychologists specializing in learning, to detect changes in the bodies of diabetics. Because of their supersensitive noses, dogs are famous for sniffing out bombs and drugs, but they can also learn to detect cancers, urinary tract infections, and diabetic glucose levels.

So add another job title to the services dogs routinely provide to humans in exchange for room and board and a little cuddling (Langley, 2016).

LOOKING *Ahead*

Luke Nuttall may well owe his life to the fact that dogs can learn so effectively. Not only did Jedi learn to detect changes in glucose levels in a diabetic, he also learned what to do when he discovered a change. He didn't try to wake Luke; he ran to Luke's mother, who could provide further help.

Learning is a fundamental topic for psychologists and plays a central role in almost every specialty area of psychology. For example, a psychologist studying perception might ask, "How do we learn that people who look small from a distance are far away and not simply tiny?" A developmental psychologist might inquire, "How do babies learn to distinguish their mothers from other people?" A clinical psychologist might wonder, "Why do some people learn to be afraid when they see a spider?" A social psychologist might ask, "How do we learn to believe that we've fallen in love?"

Each of these questions, although drawn from very different branches of psychology, can be answered only through an understanding of basic learning processes. In each case, a skill or a behavior is acquired, altered, or refined through experience.

In this chapter, we will explore several ways in which learning occurs, including through classical and operant conditioning approaches, which focus on outward, behavioral processes, as well as through cognitive approaches, which focus on mental processes. We will discuss cultural differences in learning and individual differences in learning styles that influence learning effectiveness, and we will examine practical learning programs, such as behavior modification, which are based on these learning approaches.

Module 17
Classical Conditioning

Does the mere sight of the golden arches in front of McDonald's make you feel pangs of hunger and think about hamburgers? If it does, you are displaying an elementary form of learning called classical conditioning. *Classical conditioning* helps explain such diverse phenomena as crying at the sight of a bride walking down the aisle, fearing the dark, and falling in love.

Classical conditioning is one of a number of different types of learning that psychologists have identified, but a general definition encompasses them all: **Learning** is a relatively permanent change in behavior that is brought about by experience.

How do we know when a behavior has been influenced by learning–or even is a result of learning? Part of the answer relates to the nature-nurture question, one of the fundamental issues underlying the field of psychology. In the acquisition of behaviors, experience–which is essential to the definition of learning–is the "nurture" part of the nature-nurture question.

However, it's not always easy to identify whether a change in behavior is due to nature or nurture because some changes in behavior or performance come about through maturation alone and don't involve experience. For instance, children become better tennis players as they grow older partly because their strength increases with their size–a maturational phenomenon. To understand when learning has occurred, we must differentiate maturational changes from improvements resulting from practice, which indicate that learning actually has occurred.

Similarly, short-term changes in behavior that are due to factors other than learning, such as declines in performance resulting from fatigue or lack of effort, are different from performance changes that are due to actual learning. If Serena Williams has a bad day on the tennis court because of tension or fatigue, this does not mean that she has not learned to play correctly or has "unlearned" how to play well. Because there is not always a one-to-one correspondence between learning and performance, understanding when true learning has occurred is difficult.

It is clear that we are primed for learning from the beginning of life. Infants exhibit a simple type of learning called habituation. *Habituation* is the decrease in response to a stimulus that occurs after repeated presentations of the same stimulus. For example, young infants may initially show interest in a novel stimulus, such as a brightly colored toy, but they will soon lose interest if they see the same toy over and over. (Adults exhibit habituation, too: Newlyweds soon stop noticing that they are wearing a wedding ring.) Habituation permits us to ignore things that have stopped providing new information.

Most learning is considerably more complex than habituation, and the study of learning has been at the core of the field of psychology. Although philosophers since the time of Aristotle have speculated on the foundations of learning, the first systematic research on learning was done at the beginning of the 20th century, when Ivan Pavlov (does the name ring a bell?) developed the framework for learning called classical conditioning.

The Basics of Classical Conditioning

Ivan Pavlov, a Russian physiologist, never intended to do psychological research. In 1904 he won the Nobel Prize for his work on digestion, testimony to his contribution to that field. Yet Pavlov is remembered not for his physiological research but for his

AP® LEARNING TARGETS

- Identify the contributions of key researchers in the psychology of learning.

- Interpret graphs that exhibit the results of learning experiments.

- Apply learning principles to explain emotional learning, taste aversion, superstitious behavior, and learned helplessness.

- Provide examples of how biological constraints create learning predispositions.

- Describe basic classical conditioning phenomena.

learning A relatively permanent change in behavior brought about by experience. (Module 17)

Ivan Pavlov (center) developed the principles of classical conditioning.
©Sovfoto/UIG/Getty Images

classical conditioning A type of learning in which a neutral stimulus comes to bring about a response after it is paired with a stimulus that naturally brings about that response. (Module 17)

neutral stimulus A stimulus that, before conditioning, does not naturally bring about the response of interest. (Module 17)

unconditioned stimulus (UCS) A stimulus that naturally brings about a particular response without having been learned. (Module 17)

unconditioned response (UCR) A response that is natural and needs no training (e.g., salivation at the smell of food). (Module 17)

conditioned stimulus (CS) A once-neutral stimulus that has been paired with an unconditioned stimulus to bring about a response formerly caused only by the unconditioned stimulus. (Module 17)

conditioned response (CR) A response that, after conditioning, follows a previously neutral stimulus (e.g., salivation at the ringing of a bell). (Module 17)

experiments on basic learning processes—work that he began quite accidentally (Marks, 2004; Samoilov & Zayas, 2007; Grant & Wingate, 2011).

Pavlov had been studying the secretion of stomach acids and salivation in dogs in response to eating varying amounts and kinds of food. While doing his research, he observed a curious phenomenon: Sometimes salivation would begin in the dogs when they had not yet eaten any food. Just the sight of the experimenter who normally brought the food or even the sound of the experimenter's footsteps was enough to produce salivation in the dogs.

Pavlov's genius lay in his ability to recognize the implications of this discovery. He saw that the dogs were responding not only on the basis of a biological need (hunger) but also as a result of learning—or, as it came to be called, classical conditioning. **Classical conditioning** is a type of learning in which a neutral stimulus (such as the experimenter's footsteps) comes to elicit a response after being paired with a stimulus (such as food) that naturally brings about that response.

To demonstrate classical conditioning, Pavlov (1927) attached a tube to the salivary gland of a dog, allowing him to measure precisely the dog's salivation. He then rang a bell and, just a few seconds later, presented the dog with meat. This pairing occurred repeatedly and was carefully planned so that, each time, exactly the same amount of time elapsed between the presentation of the bell and the meat. At first the dog would salivate only when the meat was presented, but soon it began to salivate at the sound of the bell. In fact, even when Pavlov stopped presenting the meat, the dog still salivated after hearing the sound. The dog had been classically conditioned to salivate to the bell.

As you can see in Figure 1, the basic processes of classical conditioning that underlie Pavlov's discovery are straightforward. However, the terminology he chose is not simple.

First, consider the diagram in Figure 1a. Before conditioning, there are two unrelated stimuli: the ringing of a bell and meat. We know that normally the sound of a bell does not lead to salivation but instead to some irrelevant response, such as pricking up the ears or perhaps a startle reaction. The bell is therefore called the neutral stimulus. A **neutral stimulus** is a stimulus that, before conditioning, does not naturally bring about the response in which we are interested.

Prior to conditioning, we also know that meat naturally causes a dog to salivate. Because food placed in a dog's mouth automatically causes salivation to occur, it is known as an unconditioned stimulus. An **unconditioned stimulus (UCS)** is a stimulus that naturally brings about a particular response without having been learned.

The response that the meat elicits (salivation) is called an unconditioned response. An **unconditioned response (UCR)** is a natural, innate response that occurs automatically and needs no training. Unconditioned responses are always brought about by the presence of unconditioned stimuli.

Figure 1b illustrates what happens during conditioning. The bell is rung just before each presentation of the meat. The goal of conditioning is for the dog to associate the bell with the unconditioned stimulus (meat) and therefore to bring about the same sort of response as the unconditioned stimulus.

After a number of pairings of the bell and meat, the bell alone causes the dog to salivate (as in Figure 1c). When conditioning is complete, the bell has changed from a neutral stimulus to what is called a conditioned stimulus. A **conditioned stimulus (CS)** is a once-neutral stimulus that has been paired with an unconditioned stimulus to bring about a response formerly caused only by the unconditioned stimulus. This time, salivation that occurs as a response to the conditioned stimulus (bell) is called a **conditioned response (CR).** After conditioning, then, the conditioned stimulus brings about the conditioned response.

The sequence and timing of the presentation of the unconditioned stimulus and the conditioned stimulus are particularly important. Like a malfunctioning warning

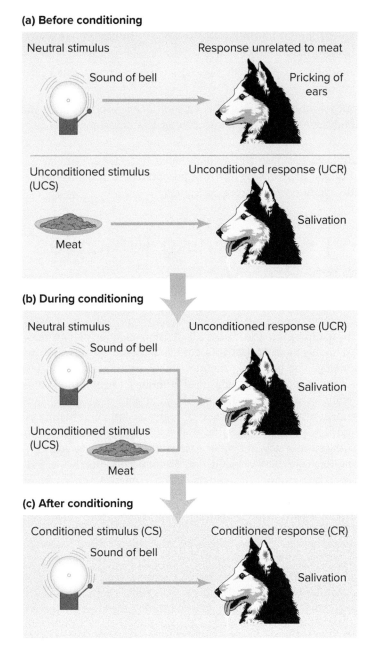

(a) Before conditioning

Neutral stimulus

Sound of bell

Response unrelated to meat

Pricking of ears

Unconditioned stimulus (UCS)

Meat

Unconditioned response (UCR)

Salivation

(b) During conditioning

Neutral stimulus

Sound of bell

Unconditioned stimulus (UCS)

Meat

Unconditioned response (UCR)

Salivation

(c) After conditioning

Conditioned stimulus (CS)

Sound of bell

Conditioned response (CR)

Salivation

FIGURE 1 The basic process of classical conditioning. (a) *Before conditioning:* The sound of a bell does *not* produce salivation, meaning that the bell is a neutral stimulus. In contrast, meat naturally brings about salivation, making the meat an unconditioned stimulus (UCS) and salivation an unconditioned response (UCR). (b) *During conditioning:* The bell rings just before the presentation of the meat. (c) *After conditioning:* Eventually, the sound of the bell alone produces salivation. We now can say that conditioning has been accomplished: The previously neutral stimulus of the bell is now considered a conditioned stimulus (CS) that brings about the conditioned response of salivation (CR).

light at a railroad crossing that goes on after the train has passed by, a neutral stimulus that *follows* an unconditioned stimulus has little chance of becoming a conditioned stimulus. However, just as a warning light works best if it goes on right before a train passes, a neutral stimulus that is presented *just before* the unconditioned stimulus is most apt to result in successful conditioning. More specifically, conditioning is most effective if the neutral stimulus (which will become a conditioned stimulus) precedes the unconditioned stimulus by between a half second and several seconds, depending on what kind of response is being conditioned (Bitterman, 2006; Jennings et al., 2013; Harvie, Moseley, & Hillier, 2017).

Although the terminology Pavlov used to describe classical conditioning may seem confusing, the following summary can help make the relationships between stimuli and responses easier to understand and remember:

- Conditioned = learned
- Unconditioned = not learned

Study Alert

Figure 1 can help you to learn and understand the process (and terminology) of classical conditioning, which can be confusing.

- An *un*conditioned stimulus (UCS) leads to an *un*conditioned response (UCR).
- *Un*conditioned stimulus-*un*conditioned response pairings are *not* learned and *not* trained: They are naturally occurring.
- During conditioning, a previously neutral stimulus is transformed into the conditioned stimulus.
- A conditioned stimulus (CS) leads to a conditioned response (CR), and a conditioned stimulus-conditioned response pairing is a consequence of learning and training.
- An *un*conditioned response and a conditioned response are similar (such as salivation in Pavlov's experiment). But the *un*conditioned response occurs naturally, whereas the conditioned response is learned.

Applying Conditioning Principles to Human Behavior

Although the initial conditioning experiments were carried out with animals, classical conditioning principles were soon found to explain many aspects of everyday human behavior. Recall, for instance, the earlier illustration of how people may experience hunger pangs at the sight of McDonald's golden arches. The cause of this reaction is classical conditioning: The previously neutral arches have become associated with the food inside the restaurant (the unconditioned stimulus), causing the arches to become a conditioned stimulus that brings about the conditioned response of hunger.

Many emotional responses are learned through classical conditioning processes. For instance, how do some of us develop fears of mice, spiders, and other creatures that are typically harmless? In a now infamous case study, psychologist John B. Watson and colleague Rosalie Rayner (1920) showed that classical conditioning was at the root of such fears by conditioning an 11-month-old infant named Albert to be afraid of rats. "Little Albert," like most infants, initially was frightened by loud noises but had no fear of rats.

In the study, the experimenters sounded a loud noise whenever Little Albert touched a white, furry rat. The noise (the unconditioned stimulus) evoked fear (the unconditioned response). After just a few pairings of noise and rat, Albert began to show fear of the rat by itself, bursting into tears when he saw it. The rat, then, had become a CS that brought about the CR, fear. Furthermore, the effects of the conditioning lingered: five days later, Albert reacted with some degree of fear not only when shown a rat but also when shown objects that looked similar to the white, furry rat, including a white rabbit, a white sealskin coat, and even a white Santa Claus mask. (By the way, we don't know for certain what happened to Little Albert, and his fate remains a source of considerable speculation. In any case, Watson, the experimenter, has been condemned for using ethically questionable procedures that could never be conducted today [Powell et al., 2014; Griggs, 2015; Digdon, 2017].)

Learning by means of classical conditioning also occurs during adulthood. For example, you may not go to a dentist as often as you should because of previous associations of dentists with pain. In more extreme cases, classical conditioning can lead to the development of *phobias*, which are intense, irrational fears. For example, an insect phobia might develop in someone who is stung by a bee. The insect phobia might be so severe that the person refrains from leaving home.

Posttraumatic stress disorder (PTSD), suffered by some war veterans and others who have had traumatic experiences, can also be produced by classical conditioning. Even years after their battlefield experiences, veterans may feel a rush of fear and anxiety at a stimulus such as a loud noise (Roberts, Moore, & Beckham, 2007; Schreurs, Smith-Bell, & Burhans, 2011; Rosellini et al., 2015).

On the other hand, classical conditioning also relates to pleasant experiences. For instance, you may have a particular fondness for the smell of a certain perfume or aftershave lotion because thoughts of an early love come rushing back whenever you encounter it. Or hearing a certain song can bring back happy or bittersweet emotions due to associations that you have developed in the past.

Classical conditioning also explains why drug addictions are so difficult to treat. Drug addicts learn to associate certain stimuli–such as drug paraphernalia such as a syringe or a room where they use drugs–with the pleasant feelings produced by the drugs. So simply seeing a syringe or entering a certain room can produce reactions associated with the drug and continued cravings for it (Saunders, Yager, & Robinson, 2013; Valyear, Villaruel, & Chaudhri, 2017).

From the perspective of...

An Advertising Executive How might knowledge of classical conditioning be useful in creating an advertising campaign? What, if any, ethical issues arise from this use?

©Image Source/Getty Images

Extinction

What do you think would happen if a dog that had become classically conditioned to salivate at the ringing of a bell never again received food when the bell was rung? The answer lies in one of the basic phenomena of learning: extinction. **Extinction** occurs when a previously conditioned response decreases in frequency and eventually disappears.

To produce extinction, one needs to end the association between conditioned stimuli and unconditioned stimuli. For instance, if we had trained a dog to salivate (the conditioned response) at the ringing of a bell (the conditioned stimulus), we could produce extinction by repeatedly ringing the bell but *not* providing meat (the unconditioned stimulus; see Figure 2). At first the dog would continue to salivate when it

extinction A basic phenomenon of learning that occurs when a previously conditioned response decreases in frequency and eventually disappears. (Module 17)

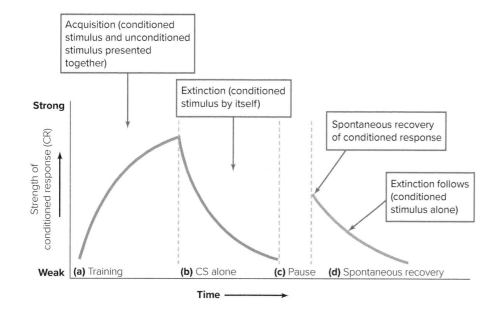

FIGURE 2 Acquisition, extinction, and spontaneous recovery of a classically conditioned response. (a) A conditioned response (CR) gradually increases in strength during training. (b) However, if the conditioned stimulus (CS) is presented by itself enough times, the conditioned response gradually fades, and extinction occurs. (c) After a pause (d) in which the conditioned stimulus is not presented, spontaneous recovery can occur. However, extinction typically reoccurs soon after.

Because of a previous unpleasant experience, a person may expect a similar occurrence when faced with a comparable situation in the future, a process known as stimulus generalization. Can you think of ways that this process occurs in everyday life?
©Scott T. Baxter/Stockbyte/Getty Images

spontaneous recovery The reemergence of an extinguished conditioned response after a period of rest and with no further conditioning. (Module 17)

Study Alert
Remember that stimulus generalization relates to stimuli that are similar to one another, whereas stimulus discrimination relates to stimuli that are different from one another.

stimulus generalization A process in which after a stimulus has been conditioned to produce a particular response, stimuli that are similar to the original stimulus produce the same response. (Module 17)

stimulus discrimination The process that occurs if two stimuli are sufficiently distinct from one another such that one evokes a conditioned response but the other does not; the ability to differentiate between stimuli. (Module 17)

heard the bell, but after a few such instances, the amount of salivation would probably decline, and the dog would eventually stop responding to the bell altogether. At that point, we could say that the response had been extinguished. In sum, extinction occurs when the conditioned stimulus is presented repeatedly without the unconditioned stimulus.

We should keep in mind that extinction can be a helpful phenomenon. Consider, for instance, what it would be like if the fear you experienced while watching the shower murder scene in the classic movie *Psycho* never was extinguished. You might well tremble with fright every time you took a shower.

Once a conditioned response has been extinguished, has it vanished forever? Not necessarily. Pavlov discovered this phenomenon when he returned to his dog a few days after the conditioned behavior had seemingly been extinguished. If he rang a bell, the dog once again salivated–an effect known as **spontaneous recovery,** or the reemergence of an extinguished conditioned response after a period of time and with no further conditioning.

Spontaneous recovery also helps explain why it is so hard to overcome drug addictions. For example, cocaine addicts who are thought to be "cured" can experience an irresistible impulse to use the drug again if they are subsequently confronted by a stimulus with strong connections to the drug, such as a white powder (Diaz & De la Casa, 2011; Tunstall, Verendeev, & Kearns, 2013; Santos, Carey, & Carrera, 2017).

Generalization and Discrimination

Despite differences in color and shape, to most of us a rose is a rose is a rose. The pleasure we experience at the beauty, smell, and grace of the flower is similar for different types of roses. Pavlov noticed a similar phenomenon. His dogs often salivated not only at the ringing of the bell that was used during their original conditioning but at the sound of a buzzer as well.

Such behavior is the result of stimulus generalization. **Stimulus generalization** is a process in which after a stimulus has been conditioned to produce a particular response, other stimuli that are similar to the original stimulus produce the same response. The greater the similarity between two stimuli, the greater the likelihood of stimulus generalization. Little Albert, who, as we mentioned earlier, was conditioned to be fearful of white rats, grew afraid of other furry white things as well. However, according to the principle of stimulus generalization, it is unlikely that he would have been afraid of a black dog because its color would have differentiated it sufficiently from the original fear-evoking stimulus.

The conditioned response elicited by the new stimulus is usually not as intense as the original conditioned response, although the more similar the new stimulus is to the old one, the more similar the new response will be. It is unlikely, then, that Little Albert's fear of the Santa Claus mask was as great as his learned fear of a rat. Still, stimulus generalization permits us to know, for example, that we ought to brake at all red lights, even if there are minor variations in size, shape, and shade.

In contrast, **stimulus discrimination** occurs if two stimuli are sufficiently distinct from each other such that one evokes a conditioned response but the other does not. Stimulus discrimination provides the ability to differentiate between stimuli. For example, my dog Cleo comes running into the kitchen when she hears the sound of the electric can opener, which she has learned is used to open her dog food when her dinner is about to be served. She does not bound into the kitchen at the sound of the food processor, although it sounds similar. In other words, she discriminates between the stimuli of can opener and food processor. Similarly, our ability to discriminate between the behavior of a growling dog and that of one whose tail is wagging can lead to adaptive behavior–avoiding the growling dog and petting the friendly one.

Beyond Traditional Classical Conditioning: Challenging Basic Assumptions

Although Pavlov hypothesized that all learning is nothing more than long strings of conditioned responses, this notion has not been supported by subsequent research. It turns out that classical conditioning provides us with only a partial explanation of how people and animals learn; indeed, Pavlov was wrong in some of his basic assumptions.

For example, according to Pavlov, the process of linking stimuli and responses occurs in a mechanistic, unthinking way. In contrast to this perspective, learning theorists influenced by cognitive psychology have argued that learners actively develop an understanding and expectancy about which particular unconditioned stimuli are matched with specific conditioned stimuli. A ringing bell, for instance, gives a dog something to think about: the impending arrival of food (Kirsch et al., 2004).

Traditional explanations of how classical conditioning operates have also been challenged by John Garcia, a learning psychologist. He found that some organisms—including humans—were *biologically prepared* to quickly learn to avoid foods that smelled or tasted like something that made them sick. For instance, a dog quickly learns to avoid rotting food that in the past made it sick. Similarly, if every time you ate peanuts you had an upset stomach several hours later, eventually you would learn to avoid peanuts. In fact, you might develop a learned *taste aversion,* when the taste of a particular food is associated with unpleasant symptoms such as nausea or vomiting. If you developed a taste aversion to peanuts, merely tasting (or even smelling or in more extreme cases seeing a peanut) could produce such disagreeable symptoms (Garcia, 2003; Masi et al., 2013; Lin, Arthurs, & Reilly, 2017).

The surprising part of Garcia's discovery was his demonstration that conditioning could occur even when the interval between exposure to the conditioned stimulus of tainted food and the response of sickness was as long as 8 hours. Furthermore, the conditioning persisted over very long periods and sometimes occurred after just one exposure.

These findings have had important practical implications. For example, to keep crows from stealing eggs, dairy farmers may lace an egg with a chemical and leave it in a place where crows will find it. The drug temporarily makes the crows ill, but it does not harm them permanently. After exposure to a chemical-laden egg, crows no longer find the eggs appetizing (Cox et al., 2004; Baker, Johnson, & Slater, 2007; Bouton et al., 2011).

AP MODULE 17: CLASSICAL CONDITIONING

AP SUMMARY

- Identify the contributions of key researchers in the psychology of learning, including: Ivan Pavlov, John B. Watson, Robert Rescorla, and John Garcia.
- The basic process of classical conditioning includes three main stages: before, during, and after conditioning. Before conditioning the neutral stimulus (sound of bell) causes an unrelated response (pricking of ears). The unconditioned stimulus (meat) causes an unconditioned response (salivation). During conditioning the neutral stimulus (sound of bell) and unconditioned stimulus (meat) are paired together to create an unconditioned response (salivation). After

conditioning the conditioned stimulus (sound of bell) causes a conditioned response (salivation).
- Acquisition, extinction, and spontaneous recovery of a classically conditioned response can be represented on a graph. First, the conditioned response will strengthen during acquisition or training. If the conditioned stimulus is presented alone a few times, extinction will occur, and the conditioned response will decline. After a pause in which the conditioned stimulus is not presented, spontaneous recovery can occur, and the conditioned response will be strengthened; however, extinction typically reoccurs soon after.
- Many emotional responses are learned through classical conditioning, e.g., phobias, posttraumatic stress

disorder, or drug addictions. Pleasant experiences, such as a smell or song, can also be learned through classical conditioning.

- John Garcia discovered learned taste aversions, when the taste of a particular food is associated with unpleasant symptoms such as nausea or vomiting. Surprisingly, taste aversions can be learned over long periods of time and sometimes occur after just one exposure.

- Learning is a relatively permanent change in behavior resulting from experience. Infants exhibit a simple type of learning known as habituation, which is the decrease in response to a stimulus that occurs after repeated presentations of the same stimulus.

- Some organisms—including humans—are biologically prepared to learn quickly to avoid foods that smell or taste like something that made them sick. Taste is paired with nausea.

- One major form of learning is classical conditioning in which a neutral stimulus comes to bring about a response after it is repeatedly paired with an unconditioned stimulus that naturally brings about that response.

- Conditioning occurs when the neutral stimulus—one that normally brings about no relevant response—is repeatedly presented just before the unconditioned stimulus. After repeated pairings, the neutral stimulus elicits the same response that the unconditioned stimulus brings about. When this occurs, the neutral stimulus has become a conditioned stimulus, and the response is a conditioned response.

- During acquisition, the sequence and timing of the unconditioned stimulus and conditioned stimulus are important. Conditioning is most effective if the neutral stimulus precedes the unconditioned stimulus by between a half second and several seconds.

- Learning is not always permanent. Extinction occurs when a conditioned response decreases in frequency and eventually disappears because the conditioned stimulus and the unconditioned stimulus were no longer paired. The conditioned response may not vanish forever. Spontaneous recovery is the reemergence of the extinguished conditioned response after a period of time and with no further conditioning.

- Stimulus generalization is the tendency for a conditioned response to follow a stimulus that is similar to, but not the same as, the original conditioned stimulus. The opposite phenomenon, stimulus discrimination, occurs when an organism learns to distinguish between stimuli.

AP KEY TERMS

learning	unconditioned stimulus (UCS)
classical conditioning	
neutral stimulus	unconditioned response (UCR)
conditioned stimulus (CS)	spontaneous recovery
conditioned response (CR)	stimulus generalization
extinction	stimulus discrimination

AP TEST PRACTICE

Section I: Multiple Choice

1. The experiment involving Pavlov's dogs demonstrated
   A. consequences can strengthen behavior
   B. many emotional responses are learned through classical conditioning
   C. learning by means of classical conditioning also occurs during adulthood
   D. some organisms are biologically prepared to quickly learn to avoid foods that make them sick
   E. a neutral stimulus can elicit a response after being paired with a stimulus that brings about that response

2. Lily will no longer eat blueberries because she got sick on them once. What is unique about her taste aversion compared to other behaviors that are classically conditioned?
   A. Only occurs with humans
   B. Learned through observation
   C. Emotions can be conditioned in humans
   D. Extended time during acquisition
   E. Repeated presentations of the same stimulus result in learning

3. During acquisition, what sequence is best for learning to occur?
   A. Neutral stimulus just before unconditioned stimulus
   B. Unconditioned stimulus before conditioned stimulus
   C. Unconditioned response after conditioned stimulus
   D. Neutral stimulus after unconditioned stimulus
   E. Neutral stimulus and unconditioned stimulus at the same time

Section II: Free Response

Little Albert was conditioned to fear rats. When exposed to a white, furry rat an experimenter made a loud noise. After a few pairings, Little Albert started to cry when he saw the rat alone. Soon he reacted the same way to objects that looked similar to the white, furry rat.

A. Explain how each of the following psychological concepts relate to Little Albert.
   - Conditioned response
   - Unconditioned stimulus
   - Acquisition
   - Stimulus generalization
   - Extinction

B. The procedures used in the 1920 experiment with Little Albert are ethically questionable by today's standards.
   - Describe an ethical and/or research design flaw.
   - Describe implications of the research.

Module 18
Operant Conditioning

Very good . . . What a clever idea . . . Fantastic . . . I agree . . . Thank you . . . Excellent . . . Super . . . Right on . . . This is the best paper you've ever written; you get an A . . . You are really getting the hang of it . . . I'm impressed . . . You're getting a raise . . . Have a cookie . . . You look great . . . I love you . . . .

Few of us mind being the recipient of any of these comments. But what is especially noteworthy about them is that each of these simple statements can be used, through a process known as operant conditioning, to bring about powerful changes in behavior and to teach the most complex tasks. Operant conditioning is the basis for many of the most important kinds of human and animal learning.

Operant conditioning is learning in which a voluntary response is strengthened or weakened, depending on the response's favorable or unfavorable consequences. When we say that a response has been strengthened or weakened, we mean that it has been made more or less likely to recur regularly.

Unlike classical conditioning, in which the original behaviors are the natural, biological responses to the presence of a stimulus such as food, water, or pain, operant conditioning applies to voluntary responses that an organism performs deliberately to produce a desirable outcome. The term *operant* emphasizes this point: The organism *operates* on its environment to produce a desirable result. Operant conditioning is at work when we learn that toiling industriously can bring about a raise or that studying hard results in good grades.

As with classical conditioning, the basis for understanding operant conditioning was laid by work with animals. We turn now to some of that early research, which began with a simple inquiry into the behavior of cats.

Thorndike's Law of Effect

If you placed a hungry cat in a cage and then put a small piece of food outside the cage, just beyond the cat's reach, chances are that the cat would eagerly search for a way out of the cage. The cat might first claw at the sides or push against an opening. Suppose, though, you had rigged things so that the cat could escape by stepping on a small paddle that released the latch to the door of the cage (see Figure 1). Eventually,

AP® LEARNING TARGETS

- Provide examples of how biological constraints create learning predispositions.

- Distinguish general differences between principles of classical conditioning, operant conditioning, and observational learning.

- Predict the effects of operant conditioning.

- Predict how practice, schedules of reinforcement, other aspects of reinforcement, and motivation will influence quality of learning.

- Suggest how behavior modification, biofeedback, coping strategies, and self-control can be used to address behavioral problems.

operant conditioning Learning in which a voluntary response is strengthened or weakened, depending on the response's favorable or unfavorable consequences. (Module 18)

FIGURE 1 Edward L. Thorndike devised this puzzle box to study the process by which a cat learns to press a paddle to escape from the box and receive food. Do you think Thorndike's work has relevance to the question of why people voluntarily work on puzzles and play games, such as sudoku, Angry Birds, and jigsaw puzzles? Do they receive any rewards?

as it moved around the cage, the cat would happen to step on the paddle, the door would open, and the cat would eat the food.

What would happen if you then returned the cat to the box? The next time, it would probably take a little less time for the cat to step on the paddle and escape. After a few trials, the cat would deliberately step on the paddle as soon as it was placed in the cage. What would have occurred, according to Edward L. Thorndike (1932), who studied this situation extensively, was that the cat would have learned that pressing the paddle was associated with the desirable consequence of getting food. To summarize that relationship, Thorndike formulated the *law of effect*, which states that *r*esponses that lead to satisfying consequences are more likely to be repeated.

Thorndike believed that the law of effect operates as automatically as leaves fall off a tree in autumn. It was not necessary for an organism to understand that there was a link between a response and a reward. Instead, Thorndike believed, over time and through experience, the organism would make a direct connection between the stimulus and the response without any awareness that the connection existed.

The Basics of Operant Conditioning

Thorndike's early research served as the foundation for the work of one of the 20th century's most influential psychologists, B. F. Skinner (1904–1990). You may have heard of the Skinner box (shown in Figure 2), a chamber with a highly controlled environment that was used to study operant conditioning processes with laboratory animals. Whereas Thorndike's goal was to get his cats to learn to obtain food by leaving the box, animals in a Skinner box learn to obtain food by operating on their environment within the box. Skinner became interested in specifying how behavior varies as a result of alterations in the environment.

Skinner, whose work went far beyond perfecting Thorndike's earlier apparatus, is considered the inspiration for a whole generation of psychologists studying operant conditioning. To illustrate Skinner's contribution, let's consider what happens to a rat in the typical Skinner box (Soorya, Carpenter, & Romanczyk, 2011; Huston et al., 2013).

Suppose you want to teach a hungry rat to press a lever that is in its box. At first, the rat will wander around the box, exploring the environment in a relatively

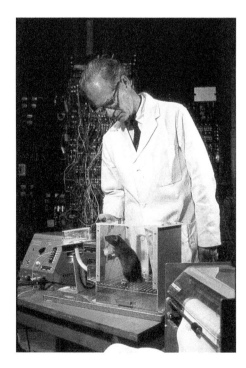

FIGURE 2 B. F. Skinner with a Skinner box used to study operant conditioning. Laboratory rats learn to press the lever in order to obtain food, which is delivered in the tray.

(Right): ©Nina Leen/Time Life Pictures/Getty Images

random fashion. At some point, however, it will probably press the lever by chance, and when it does, it will receive a food pellet. The first time this happens, the rat will not learn the connection between pressing a lever and receiving food and will continue to explore the box. Sooner or later, the rat will press the lever again and receive a pellet, and in time the frequency of the pressing response will increase. Eventually, the rat will press the lever continually until it satisfies its hunger, thereby demonstrating that it has learned that the receipt of food is contingent on pressing the lever.

REINFORCEMENT: THE CENTRAL CONCEPT OF OPERANT CONDITIONING

Skinner called the process that leads the rat to continue pressing the key "reinforcement." **Reinforcement** is the process by which a stimulus increases the probability that a preceding behavior will be repeated. In other words, pressing the lever is more likely to occur again because of the stimulus of food.

In a situation such as this one, the food is called a reinforcer. A **reinforcer** is any stimulus that increases the probability that a preceding behavior will occur again. Hence, food is a reinforcer because it increases the probability that the behavior of pressing (formally referred to as the *response* of pressing) will take place.

What kind of stimuli can act as reinforcers? Bonuses, toys, and good grades can serve as reinforcers–if they strengthen the probability of the response that occurred before their introduction. What makes something a reinforcer depends on individual preferences. Although a Hershey's bar can act as a reinforcer for one person, an individual who dislikes chocolate may find one dollar more desirable. The only way we can know if a stimulus is a reinforcer for a particular organism is to observe whether the frequency of a previously occurring behavior increases after the presentation of the stimulus.

Of course, we are not born knowing that one dollar can buy us a candy bar. Rather, through experience we learn that money is a valuable commodity because of its association with stimuli, such as food and drink, that are naturally reinforcing. This fact suggests a distinction between primary reinforcers and secondary reinforcers. A *primary reinforcer* satisfies some biological need and works naturally, regardless of a person's previous experience. Food for a hungry person, warmth for a cold person, and relief for a person in pain all would be classified as primary reinforcers.

In contrast, a *secondary reinforcer* is a stimulus that becomes reinforcing because of its association with a primary reinforcer. For instance, we know that money is valuable because we have learned that it allows us to obtain other desirable objects, including primary reinforcers such as food and shelter. Money thus becomes a secondary reinforcer (Moher et al., 2008; Qu, Zhang, & Chen, 2013; Thrailkill & Bouton, 2017).

Secondary reinforcers make up the heart of *token systems* sometimes used in the treatment of some psychological disorders for those who are in institutions. In a token system, a patient is rewarded for showing desired behavior with a token such as a poker chip. The token–an example of a secondary reinforcer–can then be redeemed for something desirable, such as snacks, games, or money.

Neuroscientists are beginning to explore the biological underpinnings of reinforcers. For example, we now know that the neurotransmitter *dopamine* plays a key role in the reinforcement of behavior. When we are exposed to certain kinds of stimuli, a flood of dopamine cascades through parts of the brain, leading to feelings of pleasure that are reinforcing (Trujillo-Pisanty et al., 2011; Thompson & Wolpaw, 2015).

POSITIVE REINFORCERS, NEGATIVE REINFORCERS, AND PUNISHMENT

In many respects, reinforcers can be thought of in terms of rewards; both a reinforcer and a reward increase the probability that a preceding response will occur again. But the term *reward* is limited to *positive* occurrences, and this is where it differs from a reinforcer–for it turns out that reinforcers can be positive or negative.

reinforcement The process by which a stimulus increases the probability that a preceding behavior will be repeated. (Module 18)

reinforcer Any stimulus that increases the probability that a preceding behavior will occur again. (Module 18)

Study Alert
Remember that primary reinforcers satisfy a biological need; secondary reinforcers are effective due to previous association with a primary reinforcer.

positive reinforcer A stimulus added to the environment that brings about an increase in a preceding response. (Module 18)

negative reinforcer An unpleasant stimulus whose removal leads to an increase in the probability that a preceding response will be repeated in the future. (Module 18)

punishment A stimulus that decreases the probability that a previous behavior will occur again. (Module 18)

A **positive reinforcer** is a stimulus *added* to the environment that brings about an increase in a preceding response. If food, water, money, or praise is provided after a response, it is more likely that that response will occur again in the future. The paychecks that workers get at the end of the week, for example, increase the likelihood that they will return to their jobs the following week.

In contrast, a **negative reinforcer** refers to an unpleasant stimulus whose removal leads to an increase in the probability that a preceding response will be repeated in the future. For example, if you have an itchy rash (an unpleasant stimulus) that is relieved when you apply a certain brand of ointment, you are more likely to use that ointment the next time you have an itchy rash. Using the ointment, then, is negatively reinforcing because it removes the unpleasant itch. Similarly, if your iPod volume is so loud that it hurts your ears when you first turn it on, you are likely to reduce the volume level. Lowering the volume is negatively reinforcing, and you are more apt to repeat the action in the future when you first turn it on. Negative reinforcement, then, teaches the individual that taking an action removes a negative condition that exists in the environment. Like positive reinforcers, negative reinforcers increase the likelihood that preceding behaviors will be repeated (Magoon & Critchfield, 2008).

Note that negative reinforcement is not the same as punishment. **Punishment** refers to a stimulus that *decreases* the probability that a prior behavior will occur again. Unlike negative reinforcement, which produces an *increase* in behavior, punishment reduces the likelihood of a prior response. If we receive a shock that is meant to decrease a certain behavior, then we are receiving punishment, but if we are already receiving a shock and do something to stop that shock, the behavior that stops the shock is considered to be negatively reinforced. In the first case, the specific behavior is apt to decrease because of the punishment; in the second, it is likely to increase because of the negative reinforcement.

There are two types of punishment: positive punishment and negative punishment, just as there are positive reinforcement and negative reinforcement. In both cases, "positive" means adding something, and "negative" means removing something. *Positive punishment* weakens a response by applying an unpleasant stimulus. For instance, spanking a child for misbehaving or sending someone to jail for 10 years for committing a crime are examples of positive punishment. (In both cases, an unpleasant stimulus has been applied.)

In contrast, *negative punishment* consists of the removal of something pleasant. For instance, when a teenager is told she can no longer use her cell phone because she stayed out past her curfew or when an employee is informed that he will have a cut in pay because of a poor job evaluation, negative punishment is being administered. (In both cases, something pleasant–cell phone use or more pay–is being removed.)

Both positive and negative punishment result in a decrease in the likelihood that a prior behavior will be repeated. So a jail term is meant to lead to a reduction in criminal behavior, and loss of a teenager's cell phone is meant to reduce the likelihood of staying out past curfew.

The following rules (and the summary in Figure 3) can help you distinguish these concepts from one another:

- Reinforcement *increases* the frequency of the behavior preceding it; punishment *decreases* the frequency of the behavior preceding it.

- The *application* of a *positive* stimulus brings about an increase in the frequency of behavior and is referred to as positive reinforcement; the *application* of a *negative* stimulus decreases or reduces the frequency of behavior and is called positive punishment.

- The *removal* of a *negative* stimulus that results in an increase in the frequency of behavior is negative reinforcement; the *removal* of a *positive* stimulus that decreases the frequency of behavior is negative punishment.

Study Alert

The differences between positive reinforcement, negative reinforcement, positive punishment, and negative punishment are tricky, so pay special attention to Figure 3 and the definitions in the text.

Intended Result	When stimulus is added, the result is . . .	When stimulus is removed or terminated, the result is . . .
Increase in behavior (reinforcement)	**Positive reinforcement** Example: Giving a raise for good performance Result: *Increase* in response of good performance	**Negative reinforcement** Example: Applying ointment to relieve an itchy rash leads to a higher future likelihood of applying the ointment Result: *Increase* in response of using ointment
Decrease in behavior (punishment)	**Positive punishment** Example: Yelling at a teenager when she steals a bracelet Result: *Decrease* in frequency of response of stealing	**Negative punishment** Example: Restricting teenager's access to car due to breaking curfew Result: *Decrease* in response of breaking curfew

FIGURE 3 Types of reinforcement and punishment.
(Top, Left): ©Andrey_Popov/Shutterstock; (Top, Right): ©Stockbyte/Getty Images; (Bottom, Left): ©Agnieszka Marcinska/Shutterstock; (Bottom, Right): ©Amy Etra/PhotoEdit

THE PROS AND CONS OF PUNISHMENT: WHY REINFORCEMENT BEATS PUNISHMENT

Is punishment an effective way to modify behavior? Punishment often presents the quickest route to changing behavior that, if allowed to continue, might be dangerous to an individual. For instance, a parent may not have a second chance to warn a child not to run into a busy street, and so punishing the first incidence of this behavior may prove to be wise. Moreover, the use of punishment to suppress behavior, even temporarily, provides an opportunity to reinforce a person for subsequently behaving in a more desirable way (Bruno, 2016).

However, punishment has several disadvantages that make its routine use questionable. For one thing, punishment is frequently ineffective, particularly if it is not delivered shortly after the undesired behavior or if the individual is able to leave the setting in which the punishment is being given. An employee who is reprimanded by the boss may quit; a teenager who loses the use of the family car may borrow a friend's car instead. In such instances, the initial behavior that is being punished may be replaced by one that is even less desirable.

Even worse, physical punishment can convey to the recipient the idea that physical aggression is permissible and perhaps even desirable. A father who yells at and hits his son for misbehaving teaches the son that aggression is an appropriate, adult response. The son soon may copy his father's behavior by acting aggressively toward others. In addition, physical punishment is often administered by people who are themselves angry or enraged. It is unlikely that individuals in such an emotional state will be able to think through what they are doing or control carefully the degree of punishment they are inflicting. Ultimately, those who resort to physical punishment run the risk that they will grow to be feared. Punishment can also reduce the self-esteem of recipients unless they can understand the reasons for it (Miller-Perrin, Perrin, & Kocur, 2009; Smith, Springer, & Barrett, 2011; Alampay et al., 2017).

Finally, punishment does not convey any information about what an alternative, more appropriate behavior might be. To be useful in bringing about more desirable behavior in the future, punishment must be accompanied by specific information about the behavior that is being punished, along with specific suggestions concerning a more desirable behavior. Punishing a child for staring out the window in school could merely lead her to stare at the floor instead. Unless we teach her appropriate ways to respond, we have merely managed to substitute one undesirable behavior for another. If punishment is not followed up with reinforcement for subsequent behavior that is more appropriate, little will be accomplished. That's why the scientific research is clear: spanking is both ineffective and ultimately harmful to children. Even punishment in the form of yelling is damaging (Wang & Kenny, 2013; Kubanek, Snyder, & Abrams, 2015).

In short, reinforcing desired behavior is a more appropriate technique for modifying behavior than is using punishment. Both in and out of the scientific arena, then, reinforcement usually beats punishment (Sidman, 2006; Hall et al., 2011; Bruno, 2016).

SCHEDULES OF REINFORCEMENT: TIMING LIFE'S REWARDS

The world would be a different place if poker players never played cards again after the first losing hand, fishermen returned to shore as soon as they missed a catch, or telemarketers never made another phone call after their first hang-up. The fact that such unreinforced behaviors continue, often with great frequency and persistence, illustrates that reinforcement need not be received continually for behavior to be learned and maintained. In fact, behavior that is reinforced only occasionally can ultimately be learned better than can behavior that is always reinforced.

schedule of reinforcement The pattern of frequency and timing of reinforcement following desired behavior. (Module 18)

continuous reinforcement schedule A schedule in which behavior is reinforced every time the behavior occurs. (Module 18)

partial (or intermittent) reinforcement schedule Reinforcing of a behavior some but not all of the time. (Module 18)

The pattern of the frequency and timing of reinforcement that follow desired behavior is known as the **schedule of reinforcement.** Behavior that is reinforced every time it occurs is on a **continuous reinforcement schedule.** In contrast, behavior that is reinforced some but not all of the time is on a **partial** (or **intermittent**) **reinforcement schedule.** Although learning occurs more rapidly under a continuous reinforcement schedule, behavior lasts longer after reinforcement stops when it was learned under a partial reinforcement schedule (Reed, 2007; Holtyn & Lattal, 2013; Mullane et al., 2017).

Why should intermittent reinforcement result in stronger, longer-lasting learning than with continuous reinforcement? We can answer the question by examining how we might behave when using a candy vending machine compared with a Las Vegas slot machine. When we use a vending machine, previous experience has taught us that every time we put in the appropriate amount of money, the reinforcement, a candy bar, ought to be delivered. In other words, the schedule of reinforcement is continuous. In comparison, a slot machine offers intermittent reinforcement. We have learned that after putting in our cash, most of the time we will not receive anything in return. At the same time, though, we know that we will occasionally win something.

Now suppose that, unknown to us, both the candy vending machine and the slot machine are broken, and so neither one is able to dispense anything. It would not be very long before we stopped depositing coins into the broken candy machine. Probably at most we would try only two or three times before leaving the machine in disgust. But the story would be quite different with the broken slot machine. Here, we would drop in money for a considerably longer time, even though there would be no payoff.

In formal terms, we can see the difference between the two reinforcement schedules: Partial reinforcement schedules (such as those provided by slot machines) maintain performance longer than do continuous reinforcement schedules (such as those established in candy vending machines) before *extinction*—the disappearance of the conditioned response—occurs.

Fixed- and Variable-Ratio Schedules Certain kinds of partial reinforcement schedules produce stronger and lengthier responding before extinction than do others. Some schedules are related to the *number of responses* made before reinforcement is given, and others are related to the *amount of time* that elapses before reinforcement is provided (Reed & Morgan, 2008; Miguez, Witnauer, & Miller, 2011; Manzo et al., 2015).

In a **fixed-ratio schedule,** reinforcement is given only after a specific number of responses. For instance, a rat might receive a food pellet every 10th time it pressed a lever; here, the ratio would be 1:10. Similarly, garment workers are generally paid on fixed-ratio schedules: They receive a specific number of dollars for every blouse they sew. Because a greater rate of production means more reinforcement, people on fixed-ratio schedules are apt to work as quickly as possible (see Figure 4).

In a **variable-ratio schedule,** behaviors are reinforced after an average number of responses, but exactly when reinforcement will occur is unpredictable. A good example of a variable-ratio schedule is a telephone salesperson's job. He might make a sale during the 3rd, 8th, 9th, and 20th calls without being successful during any call in between. Although the number of responses he must make before closing a sale varies, it averages out to a 20% success rate. Under these circumstances, you might expect that the salesperson would try to make as many calls as possible in as short a time as possible. This is the case with all variable-ratio schedules, which lead to a high rate of response and resistance to extinction.

Fixed- and Variable-Interval Schedules: The Passage of Time In contrast to fixed and variable-ratio schedules, in which the crucial factor is the number of responses,

fixed-ratio schedule A schedule in which reinforcement is given only after a specific number of responses are made. (Module 18)

variable-ratio schedule A schedule in which reinforcement occurs after an average number of responses, but the reinforcement schedule is unpredictable. (Module 18)

Study Alert
Remember that the different schedules of reinforcement affect the rapidity with which a response is learned and how long it lasts after reinforcement is no longer provided.

(a) Fixed-ratio schedule

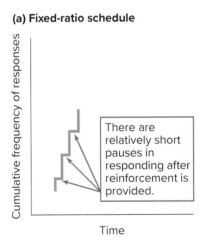

There are relatively short pauses in responding after reinforcement is provided.

Time

(b) Variable-ratio schedule

Responding occurs at a high, steady rate.

Time

(c) Fixed-interval schedule

There are typically long pauses in responding after reinforcement is provided.

Time

(d) Variable-interval schedule

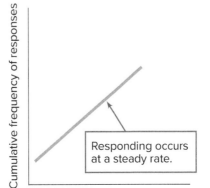

Responding occurs at a steady rate.

Time

FIGURE 4 Typical outcomes of different reinforcement schedules. (a) In a fixed-ratio schedule, reinforcement is provided after a specific number of responses are made. Because the more responses lead to more reinforcement, fixed-ratio schedules produce a high rate of responding. (b) In a variable-ratio schedule, responding also occurs at a high rate. (c) A fixed-interval schedule produces lower rates of responding, especially just after reinforcement has been presented, because the organism learns that a specified time period must elapse between reinforcements. (d) A variable-interval schedule produces a fairly steady stream of responses.

fixed-interval schedule A schedule in which reinforcement is provided for a response only after a fixed time period has elapsed. (Module 18)

variable-interval schedule A schedule by which the time between reinforcements varies around some average rather than being fixed. (Module 18)

fixed-*interval* and variable-*interval* schedules focus on the amount of time that has elapsed since a person or animal was rewarded. One example of a fixed-interval schedule is a weekly paycheck. For people who receive regular, weekly paychecks, it typically makes relatively little difference exactly how much they produce in a given week.

Because a **fixed-interval schedule** provides reinforcement for a response only if a fixed time period has elapsed, overall rates of response are relatively low. This is especially true in the period just after reinforcement, when the time before another reinforcement is relatively great. Students' study habits often exemplify this reality. If the periods between exams are relatively long (meaning that the opportunity for reinforcement for good performance is given fairly infrequently), students often study minimally or not at all until the day of the exam draws near. Just before the exam, however, students begin to cram for it, signaling a rapid increase in the rate of their studying response. As you might expect, immediately after the exam there is a rapid decline in the rate of responding, with few people opening a book the day after a test. Fixed-interval schedules produce the kind of "scalloping effect" shown in Figure 4 (Saville, 2009; Daniels & Sanabria, 2017).

One way to decrease the delay in responding that occurs just after reinforcement and to maintain the desired behavior more consistently throughout an interval is to use a variable-interval schedule. In a **variable-interval schedule,** the time between reinforcements varies around some average rather than being fixed. For example, a professor who gives surprise quizzes that vary from one every 3 days to one every 3 weeks, averaging one every 2 weeks, is using a variable-interval schedule. Compared to the study habits we observed with a fixed-interval schedule, students' study habits under such a variable-interval schedule would most likely be very different. Students would be apt to study more regularly because they would never know when the next surprise quiz was coming. Variable-interval schedules, in general, are more likely to produce relatively steady rates of responding than are fixed-interval schedules, with responses that take longer to extinguish after reinforcement ends.

From the perspective of...

An Educator How would you use your knowledge of operant conditioning to set up a program to increase the likelihood that students will complete their homework more frequently?

©Andersen Ross/Blend Images/Getty Images

DISCRIMINATION AND GENERALIZATION IN OPERANT CONDITIONING

It does not take a child long to learn that a red light at an intersection means stop and a green light indicates that it is permissible to continue, in the same way that a pigeon can learn to peck a key when a green light goes on but not when a red light appears. Just as in classical conditioning, then, operant learning involves the phenomena of discrimination and generalization.

The process by which people learn to discriminate stimuli is known as stimulus control training. In *stimulus control training,* a behavior is reinforced in the presence of a specific stimulus but not in its absence. For example, one of the most difficult discriminations many people face is determining when someone's friendliness is not mere friendliness but a signal of romantic interest. People learn to make the discrimination by observing the presence of certain nonverbal cues—such as increased eye contact and touching—that indicate romantic interest. When such cues are absent, people learn that no romantic interest is indicated. In this case, the nonverbal cue acts as a discriminative stimulus, one to which an organism learns to respond during stimulus control training. A *discriminative stimulus* signals the likelihood that reinforcement will follow a response. For example, if you wait until your roommate is in a good mood before you ask to borrow her favorite CD, your behavior can be said to be under stimulus control because you can discriminate between her moods.

Just as in classical conditioning, the phenomenon of stimulus generalization, in which an organism learns a response to one stimulus and then exhibits the same response to slightly different stimuli, occurs in operant conditioning. If you have learned that being polite helps you to get your way in a certain situation (reinforcing your politeness), you are likely to generalize your response to other situations. Sometimes, though, generalization can have unfortunate consequences, as when people behave negatively toward all members of a racial group because they have had an unpleasant experience with one member of that group.

SHAPING: REINFORCING WHAT DOESN'T COME NATURALLY

Consider the difficulty of using operant conditioning to teach people to repair an automobile transmission. If you had to wait until they chanced to fix a transmission perfectly before you provided them with reinforcement, the Model T Ford might be back in style long before they mastered the repair process.

There are many complex behaviors, ranging from auto repair to zoo management, that we would not expect to occur naturally as part of anyone's spontaneous behavior. For such behaviors, for which there might otherwise be no opportunity to provide reinforcement (because the behavior would never occur in the first place), a procedure known as shaping is used. **Shaping** is the process of teaching a complex behavior by rewarding closer and closer approximations of the desired behavior. In shaping, you start by reinforcing any behavior that is at all similar to the behavior you want the person to learn. Later, you reinforce only responses that are closer to the behavior you ultimately want to teach. Finally, you reinforce only the desired response. Each step in shaping, then, moves only slightly beyond the previously learned behavior, permitting the person to link the new step to the behavior learned earlier (Krueger & Dayan, 2009; Egervari et al., 2017).

Shaping allows even lower animals to learn complex responses that would never occur naturally, ranging from lions jumping through hoops, dolphins rescuing divers lost at sea, or rodents finding hidden land mines. Shaping also underlies the learning of many complex human skills. For instance, the organization of most textbooks is based on the principles of shaping. Typically, information is presented so that new material builds on previously learned concepts or skills. Thus, the concept of shaping could not be presented until we had discussed the more basic principles of operant learning; also see *Applying Psychology in the 21st Century.*

BIOLOGICAL CONSTRAINTS ON LEARNING: YOU CAN'T TEACH AN OLD DOG JUST ANY TRICK

Not all behaviors can be trained in all species equally well. Instead, there are *biological constraints,* built-in limitations in the ability of animals to learn particular behaviors. In some cases, an organism has a special predisposition that will aid in its learning a behavior (such as pecking behaviors in pigeons). In other cases, biological constraints act to prevent or inhibit an organism from learning a behavior.

For example, it's impossible to train pigs to pick up a disk because they are biologically programmed to push objects like it along the ground. Similarly, although a raccoon can be conditioned to drop a single coin into a piggy bank, it will do so only after rubbing the coin against the outside of the bank. The reason? After catching a fish, raccoons instinctively rub them against the ground to remove their outer covering (Breland & Breland, 1966; Stevens & Pashler, 2002; Thurman & Lu, 2013).

PsychTech
Computer-based *adaptive learning* techniques—based on the principles of shaping—present students with new material and then quiz them on it online. Presentation of subsequent material is based on students' previous performance on the quiz, so that the level and difficulty of new material are personalized, leading to great student success.

shaping The process of teaching a complex behavior by rewarding closer and closer approximations of the desired behavior. (Module 18)

HOW UBER AND LYFT PUT THEMSELVES IN THE DRIVER'S SEAT

Uber and Lyft, the transportation companies that use smartphone apps to connect users with drivers, don't actually employ drivers. Instead they operate on an independent-contractor model. That is, drivers work whenever and wherever they like, for as long as they like, and share their profits with the company. Although drivers have challenged the position that they are independent contractors, the arrangement gives Uber and Lyft certain important tax advantages, but one big disadvantage: they can't manage the availability of their drivers. So both companies have turned to the principles of learning to gain better control over when, where, and how long drivers work.

One such tactic is simply telling drivers how close they are to an earnings goal, even alerting them to their next earning opportunity before their current ride is over. For example, a driver who has earned $180 for the night and is trying to sign off might get a message saying "You're $20 away from $200. Are you sure you want to go offline?" The option to "go offline" would be presented, but the button to "keep driving" would be the highlighted one. It's a subtle but effective way to push drivers to go just a little longer than they otherwise would.

Another tactic uses deceptively simple messages to encourage drivers to adopt corporate goals. For example, company research showed that new drivers are much less likely to abandon Uber after

©MikeDotta/Shutterstock

they reach the 25-ride threshold. So Uber gives drivers a signing bonus when they achieve that threshold and sends them encouraging messages along the way, such as "Congratulations, you're halfway there!"

These strategies work by giving people concrete behavioral goals, whether it's to reach a particular earning level for the night, to match that of their previous night, or to exceed their maximum from the week before. People will push themselves to obtain specific targets, much like a video-game player who wants to exceed her prior high score or a runner who wants to get his mile time under 6 minutes. The goal doesn't have to be a defined one, though; the feeling of making progress toward a

goal that is always just out of reach can be powerful reinforcement. Uber is happy to exploit this motivation by showing drivers an array of performance statistics such as trips completed, dollars earned, and time spent online, making driving feel a bit like playing a video game and triggering a compulsion to level up. Drivers can even earn achievement badges (Camerer et al., 1997; Alter, 2017).

One of the most successful tactics Uber uses to keep drivers on the road is showing them the next potential fare while the current passenger is still in the driver's car, much as Netflix cues up the next episode in a series at the end of the current episode. In both cases, control is taken away from the user, as the potential next fare acts as a powerful potential reinforcer.

By applying these simple behavioral principles, Uber and Lyft teach their drivers to choose work schedules that are consistent with the companies' own goals. And drivers learn that lesson well (Rosenblat & Stark, 2016; Ahrens, Pirschel, & Snower, 2017).

AP SKILL: SCIENTIFIC INVESTIGATION/ EXPLAIN BEHAVIOR IN AUTHENTIC CONTEXT

1. Do you believe it is ethical for companies such as Uber and Lyft to use principles of learning to manipulate when, where, and how long their drivers work? Why or why not?
2. What are the best schedules of reinforcement to use with the Uber and Lyft drivers? Why?

The existence of biological constraints is consistent with evolutionary explanations of behavior. Clearly, there are adaptive benefits that promote survival for organisms that quickly learn–or avoid–certain behaviors. For example, our ability to rapidly learn to avoid touching hot surfaces increases our chances of survival. Additional support for the evolutionary interpretation of biological constraints lies in the fact the associations that animals learn most readily involve stimuli that are most relevant to the specific environment in which they live (Cosmides & Tooby, 2004; Davis, 2007; Behrendt, 2011).

Furthermore, psychologists taking an evolutionary perspective have suggested that we may be genetically predisposed to be fearful of certain stimuli, such as snakes or even threatening faces. For example, people in experiments learn associations relatively quickly between photos of faces with threatening expressions and neutral stimuli (such as an umbrella). In contrast, they are slower to learn associations between faces that have pleasant expressions and neutral stimuli. Stimuli that pose potential threats, like snakes or people with hostile facial expressions, posed a potential danger to early humans, and there may be an evolved "fear module" in the brain that is sensitized to such threats (DeLoache & LoBue, 2009; Gerdes, Uhl, & Alpers, 2009; Lester et al., 2017).

COMPARING CLASSICAL AND OPERANT CONDITIONING

We've considered classical conditioning and operant conditioning as two completely different processes. And, as summarized in Figure 5, there are a number of key distinctions between the two forms of learning. For example, the key concept in classical conditioning is the association between stimuli, whereas in operant conditioning it is reinforcement. Furthermore, classical conditioning involves an involuntary, natural, innate behavior, but operant conditioning is based on voluntary responses made by an organism.

Biological constraints make it nearly impossible for animals to learn certain behaviors. Here, psychologist Marian Breland Bailey attempts to overcome the natural limitations that inhibit the success of conditioning this rooster.
©Dr. Marian Breland Bailey

Concept	Classical Conditioning	Operant Conditioning
Basic principle	Building associations between a conditioned stimulus and conditioned response.	Reinforcement *increases* the frequency of the behavior preceding it; punishment *decreases* the frequency of the behavior preceding it.
Nature of behavior	Based on involuntary, natural, innate behavior. Behavior is elicited by the unconditioned or conditioned stimulus.	Organism voluntarily operates on its environment to produce a desirable result. After behavior occurs, the likelihood of the behavior occurring again is increased or decreased by the behavior's consequences.
Order of events	Before conditioning, an unconditioned stimulus leads to an unconditioned response. After conditioning, a conditioned stimulus leads to a conditioned response.	Reinforcement leads to an increase in behavior; punishment leads to a decrease in behavior.
Example	After a physician gives a child a series of painful injections (an unconditioned stimulus) that produce an emotional reaction (an unconditioned response), the child develops an emotional reaction (a conditioned response) whenever he sees the physician (the conditioned stimulus).	A student who, after studying hard for a test, earns an A (the positive reinforcer), is more likely to study hard in the future. A student who, after going out drinking the night before a test, fails the test (punishment) is less likely to go out drinking the night before the next test.

FIGURE 5 Comparing key concepts in classical conditioning and operant conditioning.
(Left): ©McGraw-Hill Education/Jill Braaten, photographer; (Right): ©Robin Nelson/PhotoEdit

Some researchers are asking if, in fact, the two types of learning are so different after all. Some learning psychologists have suggested that classical and operant conditioning might share some underlying processes. Arguing from an evolutionary viewpoint, they contend that it is unlikely that two completely separate basic processes would evolve. Instead, one process—albeit with considerable complexity in the way it operates—might better explain behavior. Although it's too early to know if this point of view will be supported, it is clear that there are a number of processes that operate both in classical and operant conditioning, including extinction, stimulus generalization, and stimulus discrimination (Donahoe & Vegas, 2004; Silva, Gonçalves, & Garcia-Mijares, 2007; Lattal et al., 2017).

BECOMING AN INFORMED CONSUMER
of Psychology

Using Behavior Analysis and Behavior Modification

A couple who had been living together for 3 years began to fight frequently. The issues of disagreement ranged from who was going to do the dishes to the quality of their love life.

Disturbed, the couple went to a *behavior analyst,* a psychologist who specialized in behavior-modification techniques. He asked them to keep a detailed written record of their interactions over the next 2 weeks.

When they returned with the data, he carefully reviewed the records with them. In doing so, he noticed a pattern: Each of their arguments had occurred just after one or the other had left a household chore undone, such as leaving dirty dishes in the sink or draping clothes on the only chair in the bedroom.

Using the data the couple had collected, the behavior analyst asked them to list all the chores that could possibly arise and assign each one a point value depending on how long it took to complete. Then he had them divide the chores equally and agree in a written contract to fulfill the ones assigned to them. If either failed to carry out one of the assigned chores, he or she would have to place $1 per point in a fund for the other to spend. They also agreed to a program of verbal praise, promising to reward each other verbally for completing a chore.

The couple agreed to try it for a month and to keep careful records of the number of arguments they had during that period. To their surprise, the number declined rapidly.

behavior modification A technique whose goal is to increase the frequency of desirable behaviors and decrease the incidence of unwanted ones. (Module 18)

The case just presented provides an illustration of behavior modification. **Behavior modification** is a technique for increasing the frequency of desirable behaviors and decreasing the incidence of unwanted ones.

Using the basic principles of learning theory, behavior-modification techniques have proved to be helpful in a variety of situations. People with severe intellectual disability have been taught to dress and feed themselves for the first time in their lives. Behavior modification has also helped people lose weight, give up smoking, behave more safely, and study more effectively (Carels et al., 2011; Geller, 2011; Etienne, 2013; Warmbold-Brann et al., 2017).

The techniques used by behavior analysts are as varied as the list of processes that modify behavior. They include reinforcement scheduling, shaping, generalization training, discrimination training, and extinction. Participants in a behavior-change program do, however, typically follow a series of similar basic steps that include the following:

- *Identifying goals and target behaviors.* The first step is to define desired behavior. Is it an increase in time spent studying? A decrease in weight? An increase in the use of language? A reduction in the amount of aggression displayed by a child? The goals must be stated in observable terms and must lead to specific targets. For instance, a goal might be "to increase study time," whereas the target behavior would be "to study at least 2 hours per day on weekdays and an hour on Saturdays."

- *Designing a data-recording system and recording preliminary data.* To determine whether behavior has changed, it is necessary to collect data before any changes are made in the situation. This information provides a baseline against which future changes can be measured.
- *Selecting a behavior-change strategy.* The crucial step is to choose an appropriate strategy. Typically, a variety of treatments is used. This might include the systematic use of positive reinforcement for desired behavior (verbal praise or something more tangible, such as food), as well as a program of extinction for undesirable behavior (ignoring a child who throws a tantrum). Selecting the right reinforcers is critical, and it may be necessary to experiment a bit to find out what is important to a particular individual.
- *Implementing the program.* Probably the most important aspect of program implementation is consistency. It is also important to reinforce the intended behavior. For example, suppose a mother wants her son to spend more time on his homework, but as soon as he sits down to study, he asks for a snack. If the mother gets a snack for him, she is likely to be reinforcing her son's delaying tactic, not his studying.
- *Keeping careful records after the program is implemented.* Another crucial task is record keeping. If the target behaviors are not monitored, there is no way of knowing whether the program has actually been successful.
- *Evaluating and altering the ongoing program.* Finally, the results of the program should be compared with baseline, preimplementation data to determine its effectiveness. If the program has been successful, the procedures employed can be phased out gradually. For instance, if the program called for reinforcing every instance of picking up one's clothes from the bedroom floor, the reinforcement schedule could be modified to a fixed-ratio schedule in which every third instance was reinforced. However, if the program has not been successful in bringing about the desired behavior change, consideration of other approaches might be advisable.

Behavior-change techniques based on these general principles have enjoyed wide success and have proved to be one of the most powerful means of modifying behavior. Clearly, it is possible to employ the basic notions of learning theory to improve our lives.

AP MODULE 18: OPERANT CONDITIONING

AP SUMMARY

- Identify the contributions of key researchers in the psychology of learning, including Edward Thorndike: the law of effect states responses that lead to satisfying consequences are more likely to be repeated; B.F. Skinner, operant conditioning. Skinner believed the major mechanism underlying learning is reinforcement, the process by which a stimulus increases the probability that a preceding behavior will be repeated.

- Types of reinforcements and punishments can be determined by the desired behavior and if the stimulus is added or removed. When a pleasant stimulus is added to increase behavior, it is a positive reinforcement. When an unpleasant stimulus is added to decrease behavior, it is a positive punishment. When an unpleasant stimulus is removed to increase behavior, it is a negative reinforcement. When a pleasant stimulus is removed to decrease behavior, it is a negative punishment.

- Among the major categories of reinforcement schedules are fixed- and variable-ratio schedules, which are based on the number of responses made. Reinforcement with a fixed-ratio schedule is more likely to work quickly. Variable-ratio schedules lead to a high rate of response and resistance to extinction. Fixed- and variable-interval schedules are based on the amount of time that elapses before reinforcement is provided. Variable-interval schedules are more likely to produce a steady rate of response than fixed-interval schedules and take longer to extinguish after reinforcement ends.

- There are biological constraints/built-in limitations on the ability of an organism to learn: Certain behaviors will be relatively easy for individuals of a species to learn, whereas other behaviors will be either difficult or impossible to learn. These constraints are consistent with evolutionary explanations of behavior. There are adaptive benefits that promote survival for organisms who quickly learn or avoid certain behaviors. Evolutionary psychologists suggest we may be genetically predisposed to be fearful of certain stimuli, such as snakes or threatening faces.

- Classical conditioning consists of original behaviors that are natural, biological responses to a stimulus. Operant conditioning applies to voluntary responses that are used deliberately to produce a desirable outcome. It is a form of learning in which a voluntary behavior is strengthened or weakened, depending on consequences.

- Classical conditioning and operant conditioning are two separate learning processes with several key distinctions, including a basic principle, nature of behavior, and order of events. There are also several similar underlying processes, including extinction, stimulus generalization, and stimulus discrimination.

- Punishment decreases the probability that a prior behavior will occur. Positive punishment weakens a response through the application of an unpleasant stimulus, whereas negative punishment weakens a response by the removal of something pleasant. punishment is meant to decrease or suppress behavior. Punishment has pros and cons, but the scientific research supports reinforcement over punishment.

- Primary reinforcers are rewards that are naturally effective without previous experience because they satisfy a biological need. Secondary reinforcers begin to act as if they were primary reinforcers through association with a primary reinforcer. Secondary reinforcers make up token systems, where a token can be redeemed for something desirable.

- Stimulus control training is reinforcement of a behavior in the presence of a specific stimulus but not in its absence. In stimulus generalization, an organism learns a response to slightly different stimuli.

- Shaping is a process for teaching complex behaviors by rewarding closer and closer approximations of the desired final behavior.

- Behavior modification is a method for formally using the principles of learning theory to promote the frequency of desired behaviors and to decrease or eliminate unwanted ones. There are a variety of behavior-change techniques that follow a general pattern of principles and have been successful in modifying behavior.

AP KEY TERMS

operant conditioning
reinforcement
reinforcer
positive reinforcer

negative reinforcer
punishment
schedule of
    reinforcement

continuous
    reinforcement
    schedule
partial (or intermittent)
    reinforcement
    schedule
fixed-ratio schedule

variable-ratio schedule
fixed-interval schedule
variable-interval schedule
shaping
behavior modification

AP TEST PRACTICE

Section I: Multiple Choice

1. Using earplugs to get rid of extraneous noise in the environment so one can concentrate is an example of what type of consequence?
   A. Negative reinforcement   **D.** Positive punishment
   B. Positive reinforcement   **E.** Partial reinforcement
   C. Negative punishment

2. Checking when your favorite weekly program is scheduled to start is an example of what type of intermittent reinforcement schedule?
   A. Fixed-ratio   **D.** Variable-interval
   B. Fixed-interval   **E.** Continuous
   C. Variable-ratio

3. How was B.F. Skinner able to teach his rat to press the lever for food? It was not a spontaneous behavior so he had to provide rewards for behaviors close to the goal. This can best be explained by
   A. extinction   **D.** latent learning
   B. spontaneous recovery   **E.** shaping
   C. stimulus discrimination

Section II: Free Response

The Smith family likes a clean home. Nancy checks the kids' bedrooms every Sunday evening, so Bella picks up her bedroom every Sunday morning to avoid her mom's nagging. Johnny helps with the yard work. One time he was wearing his favorite striped socks and found money in the yard. Now he wears those socks every time he does yard work. Kurt doesn't take out the garbage and recycling anymore because his older brother always told him that he was doing it wrong. Now Cory, the youngest brother, does the garbage and recycling because he gets paid $2 each time.

Explain how the following terms relate to the Smith family.
- Negative reinforcement
- Fixed-interval schedule of reinforcement
- Secondary reinforcer
- Operant conditioning of a superstitious behavior
- Positive punishment

Module 19

Cognitive Approaches to Learning

Consider what happens when people learn to drive a car. They don't just get behind the wheel and stumble around until they randomly put the key into the ignition and, later, after many false starts, accidentally manage to get the car to move forward, thereby receiving positive reinforcement. Rather, they already know the basic elements of driving from previous experience as passengers, when they more than likely noticed how the key was inserted into the ignition, the car was put in drive, and the gas pedal was pressed to make the car go forward.

Clearly, not all learning is due to operant and classical conditioning. In fact, such activities as learning to drive a car imply that some kinds of learning must involve higher-order processes in which people's thoughts and memories and the way they process information account for their responses. Such situations argue against regarding learning as the unthinking, mechanical, and automatic acquisition of associations between stimuli and responses, as in classical conditioning, or the presentation of reinforcement, as in operant conditioning.

Some psychologists view learning in terms of the thought processes, or cognitions, that underlie it–an approach known as **cognitive learning theory.** Although psychologists working from the cognitive learning perspective do not deny the importance of classical and operant conditioning, they have developed approaches that focus on the unseen mental processes that occur during learning, rather than concentrating solely on external stimuli, responses, and reinforcements.

In its most basic formulation, cognitive learning theory suggests that it is not enough to say that people make responses because there is an assumed link between a stimulus and a response–a link that is the result of a past history of reinforcement for a response. Instead, according to this point of view, people and even lower animals develop an *expectation* that they will receive a reinforcer after making a response. Two types of learning in which no obvious prior reinforcement is present are latent learning and observational learning.

Latent Learning

Evidence for the importance of cognitive processes comes from a series of animal experiments that revealed a type of cognitive learning called latent learning. In **latent learning,** a new behavior is learned but not demonstrated until some incentive is provided for displaying it (Tolman & Honzik, 1930). In short, latent learning occurs without reinforcement.

In the studies demonstrating latent learning, psychologists examined the behavior of rats in a maze such as the one shown in Figure 1a. In one experiment, a group of rats was allowed to wander around the maze once a day for 17 days without ever receiving a reward (called the unrewarded group). Understandably, those rats made many errors and spent a relatively long time reaching the end of the maze. A second group, however, was always given food at the end of the maze (the rewarded group). Not surprisingly, those rats learned to run quickly and directly to the food box, making few errors.

A third group of rats (the experimental group) started out in the same situation as the unrewarded rats but only for the first 10 days. On the 11th day, a critical experimental manipulation was introduced: From that point on, the rats in this group were given food for completing the maze. The results of this manipulation were

- Identify the contributions of key researchers in the psychology of learning.

- Interpret graphs that exhibit the results of learning experiments.

- Describe the essential characteristics of insight learning, latent learning, and social learning.

- Distinguish general differences between principles of classical conditioning, operant conditioning, and observational learning.

cognitive learning theory An approach to the study of learning that focuses on the thought processes that underlie learning. (Module 19)

Study Alert

Remember that the cognitive learning approach focuses on the *internal* thoughts and expectations of learners, whereas classical and operant conditioning approaches focus on *external* stimuli, responses, and reinforcement.

latent learning Learning in which a new behavior is acquired but is not demonstrated until some incentive is provided for displaying it. (Module 19)

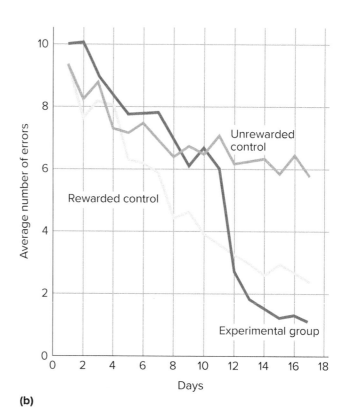

(a)   **(b)**

FIGURE 1 Latent learning. (a) Rats were allowed to roam through a maze of this sort once a day for 17 days. (b) The rats that were never rewarded (the unrewarded control condition) consistently made the most errors, whereas those that received food at the finish every day (the rewarded control condition) consistently made far fewer errors. But the results also showed latent learning: Rats that were rewarded only after the 10th day (the experimental group) showed an immediate reduction in errors and soon became similar in error rate to the rats that had been rewarded consistently. According to cognitive learning theorists, the reduction in errors indicates that the rats had developed a cognitive map—a mental representation—of the maze. Can you think of other examples of latent learning?

(a and b): Source: Adapted from Tolman, E. C., & Honzik, C. H. (1930). Introduction and removal of reward and maze performance in rats. *University of California Publications in Psychology, 4,* 257–275.

dramatic, as you can see from the graph in Figure 1b. The previously unrewarded rats, which had earlier seemed to wander about aimlessly, showed such reductions in running time and declines in error rates that their performance almost immediately matched that of the group that had received rewards from the start.

To cognitive theorists, it seemed clear that the unrewarded rats had learned the layout of the maze early in their explorations; they just never displayed their latent learning until the reinforcement was offered. Instead, those rats seemed to develop a *cognitive map* of the maze—a mental representation of spatial locations and directions.

People, too, develop cognitive maps of their surroundings. For example, latent learning may permit you to know the location of a kitchenware store at a local mall you've frequently visited, even though you've never entered the store and don't even like to cook.

The possibility that we develop our cognitive maps through latent learning presents something of a problem for strict operant conditioning theorists. If we consider the results of the maze-learning experiment, for instance, it is unclear what reinforcement permitted the rats that initially received no reward to learn the layout of the maze because there was no obvious reinforcer present. Instead,

Albert Bandura examined the principles of observational learning.
©Jon Brenneis/Life Magazine/The LIFE Images Collection/Getty Images

the results support a cognitive view of learning, in which changes occurred in unobservable mental processes (Lin et al., 2011; Malin et al., 2015; Forbus, Liang, & Rabkina, 2017).

Observational Learning: Learning Through Imitation

Let's return for a moment to the case of a person learning to drive. How can we account for instances in which an individual with no direct experience in carrying out a particular behavior learns the behavior and then performs it? To answer this question, psychologists have focused on another aspect of cognitive learning: observational learning.

According to psychologist Albert Bandura and colleagues, a major part of human learning consists of **observational learning,** which is learning by watching the behavior of another person, or *model*. Because of its reliance on observation of others–a social phenomenon–the perspective taken by Bandura is often referred to as a *social cognitive* approach to learning (Bandura, 2004, 2009; Waismeyer & Meltzoff, 2017).

Bandura dramatically demonstrated the ability of models to stimulate learning in a classic experiment. In the study, young children saw a film of an adult wildly hitting a 5-foot-tall inflatable punching toy called a Bobo doll (Bandura, Ross, & Ross, 1963a, 1963b). Later the children were given the opportunity to play with the Bobo doll themselves, and, sure enough, most displayed the same kind of behavior, in some cases mimicking the aggressive behavior almost identically.

Not only negative behaviors are acquired through observational learning. In one experiment, for example, children who were afraid of dogs were exposed to a model–dubbed the Fearless Peer–playing with a dog (Bandura, Grusec, & Menlove, 1967). After exposure, observers were considerably more likely to approach a strange dog than were children who had not viewed the Fearless Peer.

Observational learning is particularly important in acquiring skills in which the operant conditioning technique of shaping is inappropriate. Piloting an airplane and performing brain surgery, for example, are behaviors that could hardly be learned by using trial-and-error methods without grave cost–literally–to those involved in the learning process.

Observational learning may have a genetic basis. For example, we find observational learning at work with mother animals teaching their young such activities as hunting. In addition, the discovery of *mirror neurons* that fire when we observe another person carrying out a behavior suggests that the capacity to imitate others may be innate (Huesmann, Dubow, & Boxer, 2011; McElreath, Wallin, & Fasolo, 2013; Fernald, 2015); also see *Neuroscience in Your Life*.

Not all behavior that we witness is learned or carried out, of course. One crucial factor that determines whether we later imitate a model is whether the model is rewarded for his or her behavior. If we observe a friend being rewarded for putting more time into his studies by receiving higher grades, we are more likely to imitate his behavior than we would if his behavior resulted only in being stressed and tired. Models who are rewarded for behaving in a particular way are more apt to be mimicked than are models who receive punishment. Observing the punishment of a model, however, does not necessarily stop observers from learning the behavior. Observers can still describe the model's behavior–they are just less apt to perform it (Bandura, 1994).

Observational learning is central to a number of important issues relating to the extent to which people learn simply by watching the behavior of others. For instance, the degree to which observation of media aggression produces subsequent aggression on the part of viewers is a crucial–and controversial–question, as we discuss next.

observational learning Learning by observing the behavior of another person, or model. (Module 19)

Study Alert

A key point of observational learning approaches: Behavior of models who are rewarded for a given behavior is more likely to be imitated than that of models who are punished for the behavior.

This boy is displaying observational learning based on previous observation of his father. How does observational learning contribute to learning gender roles?
©Ty Milford/Getty Images

AP| NEUROSCIENCE IN YOUR LIFE: LEARNING THROUGH IMITATION

1. What perspective supports a neural mechanism for the ability to imitate a behavior? Besides mu activity, what other neural explanation has been offered for observational learning?

2. Identify the independent and dependent variable.

Infants often learn by imitating adults. But what is the neural mechanism for this ability to imitate? Previous research with adults has focused on decreases in *mu activity*, a neural indicator of motor activity in the brain, when subjects are watching and producing actions. But until now this neural marker of imitative behavior has not been tested in infants. A recent study showed that imitation by 7-month-old infants was also related to decreases in mu activity. Specifically, trials in which the infants imitated the experimenter showed a greater decrease in mu activity (shown in green; left image) compared with mu activity on trials in which the infants did not imitate the experimenter (shown in green; image on the right) (Filippi et al., 2016).

Source: Adapted from Filippi, C. A., Cannon, E. N., Fox, N. A., Thorpe, S. G., Ferrari, P. F., & Woodward, A. L. (2016).Motor system activation predicts goal imitation in 7-month-old infants. *Psychological Science* 27(5), 675–684.

VIOLENCE IN TELEVISION AND VIDEO GAMES: DO THE MEDIA'S MESSAGES MATTER?

In an episode of *The Sopranos*, the famous television series, fictional mobster Tony Soprano murdered one of his associates. To make identification of the victim's body difficult, Soprano and one of his henchmen dismembered the body and dumped the body parts.

A few months later, in real life, two half brothers in Riverside, California, strangled their mother and then cut her head and hands from her body. Victor Bautista, 20, and Matthew Montejo, 15, were caught by police after a security guard noticed that the bundle they were attempting to throw in a Dumpster had a foot sticking out of it. They told police that the plan to dismember their mother was inspired by the *Sopranos* episode (Martelle, Hanley, & Yoshino, 2003).

Like other "media copycat" killings, the brothers' cold-blooded brutality raises a critical issue: Does observing violent, antisocial acts in the media lead viewers to behave in similar ways? Because research on modeling shows that people frequently learn and imitate the aggression that they observe, this question is among the most important issues being addressed by psychologists.

Certainly, the amount of violence in the mass media is enormous. By the time of elementary school graduation, the average child in the United States will have viewed more than 8,000 murders and more than 800,000 violent acts on network television (Mifflin, 1998).

Most psychologists agree that watching high levels of media violence makes viewers more susceptible to acting aggressively. For example, one survey showed that one-fourth of violent young male offenders incarcerated in Florida had attempted to commit a media-inspired copycat crime. A significant proportion of those teenage offenders noted that they paid close attention to the media (Savage & Yancey, 2008; Boxer et al., 2009; Ferguson, 2015).

Violent video games have also been linked with actual aggression. In one of a series of studies by psychologist Craig Anderson and his colleagues, college students who frequently played violent video games, such as *Postal* or *Doom,* were more likely

PsychTech

Video gaming can also have positive consequences: Playing video games with positive, prosocial themes increases empathy and thoughts about helping others.

to have been involved in delinquent behavior and aggression. Frequent players also had lower academic achievement.

On the other hand, there are a few contrary research findings. For example, one meta-analysis of video game influences finds minimal effects on aggression. Furthermore, some researchers argue that violent video games may produce certain positive results—such as a rise in social networking among players (Ferguson, 2011, 2015b; Ferguson & Beresin, 2017).

However, most experts agree that the clear preponderance of evidence points to negative outcomes from violent video games. In fact, a recent task force of the American Psychological Association found substantial evidence that violent video game exposure was associated with higher levels of aggressive behavior, increased thoughts about aggression, higher levels of desensitization to violence, and decreased empathy relating to exposure to violence. Furthermore, the American Pediatric Association has urged parents to minimize their children's exposure to violent media of any sort (Anderson et al., 2015; Groves & Anderson, 2015; American Academy of Pediatrics Council on Communications and Media, 2016; Calvert et al., 2017).

From the perspective of...

A Social Worker What advice would you give to families about children's exposure to violent media and video games?

©Sam Edwards/age fotostock

Several aspects of media violence may contribute to real-life aggressive behavior. First, viewing violent media may lower inhibitions against behaving aggressively. In other words, watching television portrayals of violence or using violence to win a video game makes aggression seem a legitimate response to particular situations.

Second, exposure to media violence may distort our understanding of the meaning of others' behavior, predisposing us to view even nonaggressive acts by others as aggressive. For example, a teenager who watches considerable media violence may be predisposed to think that a person who accidentally bumps into him as he walks down the street is being purposely aggressive, even if the reality is that it is truly an accident.

Third, a continuous diet of media aggression may leave us desensitized to violence, and what previously would have repelled us now produces little emotional response. Our sense of the pain and suffering brought about by aggression consequently may be diminished (Carnagey, Anderson, & Bushman, 2007; Ramos et al., 2013).

What about real-life exposure to *actual* violence? Does it also lead to increases in aggression? The answer is yes. Exposure to actual firearm violence (being shot or being shot at) doubles the probability that an adolescent will commit serious violence over the next 2 years. In short, whether the violence is real or fictionalized, observing violent behavior leads to increases in aggressive behavior (Bingenheimer, Brennan, & Earls, 2005; Allwood, 2007; Quinn et al., 2017).

Illustrating observational learning, this infant observes an adult on television and then is able to imitate his behavior. Learning has obviously occurred through the mere observation of the television model.

From: A.N. Meltzoff, Imitation of televised models by infants. (1988). *Child Development, 59,* 1221–1229. Copyright © 1988 Andrew Meltzoff and M. Hanak.

Exploring Diversity

Does Culture Influence How We Learn?

> When a member of the Chilcotin Indian tribe teaches her daughter to prepare salmon, at first she allows the daughter only to observe the entire process. A little later, she permits her child to try out some basic parts of the task. Her response to questions is noteworthy. For example, when the daughter asks about how to do "the backbone part," the mother's response is to repeat the entire process with another salmon. The reason? The mother feels that one cannot learn the individual parts of the task apart from the context of preparing the whole fish. (Tharp, 1989)

It should not be surprising that children raised in the Chilcotin tradition, which stresses instruction that starts by communicating the entire task, may have difficulty with traditional Western schooling. In the approach to teaching most characteristic of Western culture, tasks are broken down into their component parts. Only after each small step is learned is it thought possible to master the complete task.

Do the differences in teaching approaches between cultures affect how people learn? Some psychologists, taking a cognitive perspective on learning, suggest that people develop particular *learning styles,* characteristic ways of approaching material, based on their cultural background and unique pattern of abilities (Barmeyer, 2004; Wilkinson & Olliver-Gray, 2006; Sternberg, 2011).

Learning styles differ along several dimensions. For example, one central dimension is relational versus analytical approaches to learning. As illustrated in Figure 2, people with a *relational learning style* master material best through understanding the "big picture" about something. They need to understand the complete picture of what they're studying before they understand its component parts. For example, students with a relational learning style might learn about the brain by first focusing on the brain as a whole and how it

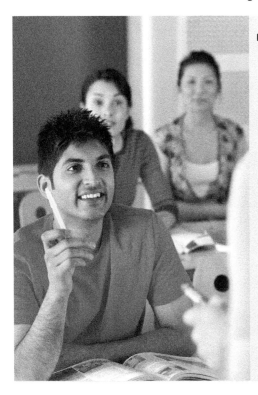

Relational Style	Analytical Style
• Perceive information as part of total picture	• Focus on detail
• Show intuitive thinking	• Show sequential and structured thinking
• More easily learn materials that have a human, social content	• More easily learn materials that are impersonal
• Have a good memory for verbally presented ideas and information	• Have a good memory for abstract ideas
• Are influenced by others' opinions	• Are not greatly affected by the opinions of others
• Style conflicts with the traditional school environment	• Style matches traditional school environments

FIGURE 2 A comparison of relational versus analytical approaches to learning offers one example of how learning styles differ along several dimensions.

(Photo): ©Fuse/Corbis/Getty Images; Source: Adams et al. *Teaching for diversity and social justice* (2nd ed.). New York: Routledge/Taylor & Francis Group, 2017.

functions. Only after doing that would they then focus on the specific functions of separate areas of the brain.

In contrast, those with an *analytical learning style* do best when they first analyze the the various components underlying an object, phenomenon, or situation. By developing an understanding of the individual parts, they are best able to grasp the full picture. So students with an analytic learning style might learn about the brain most easily by first considering its component parts (neurons, specific areas, lobes) and then by focusing on how they fit together to form the brain.

According to educator Maurianne Adams, certain minority groups in Western societies display characteristic learning styles. For instance, she argues that Caucasian females and African-American, Native-American, and Hispanic-American males and females are more apt to use a relational style of learning than are Caucasian and Asian-American males, who are more likely to employ an analytical style (Adams, Bell, & Griffin, 2007; Chin, 2013).

The conclusion that members of particular ethnic and gender groups have similar learning styles is controversial. Because there is so much diversity within each particular racial and ethnic group, critics argue that generalizations about learning styles cannot be used to predict the style of any single individual, regardless of group membership.

Still, it is clear that values about learning, which are communicated through a person's family and cultural background, have an impact on how successful students are in school. One theory suggests that members of minority groups who were voluntary immigrants are more apt to be successful in school than those who were brought into a majority culture against their will. For example, Korean children in the United States—the sons and daughters of voluntary immigrants—perform quite well, as a group, in school. In contrast, Korean children in Japan, who were often the sons and daughters of people who were forced to immigrate during World War II, essentially as forced laborers, do less well in school. The theory suggests that the motivation to succeed is lower for children in forced immigration groups (Ogbu, 2003; Foster, 2005).

AP MODULE 19: COGNITIVE APPROACHES TO LEARNING

AP SUMMARY

- Albert Bandura studied observational learning and his perspective is often referred to as the social cognitive approach to learning. He demonstrated the ability of models to stimulate learning in his Bobo doll experiment.
- Edward Tolman demonstrated latent learning by examining rats in a maze and recording the average number of errors made over 17 days. He found that the group of rats that received a food reward on the eleventh day of the experiment suddenly reduced their total number of errors. The unrewarded rats learned the maze early but did not display their learning until the reinforcement was offered. The reduction in the number of errors surpassed the rewarded control group.
- Cognitive approaches to learning consider learning in terms of thought processes, or cognition. Organisms develop an expectation that they will receive a reinforcer after making a response. Latent learning—in which a new behavior is learned but not performed until some incentive is provided for its performance—and the apparent development of cognitive maps support cognitive approaches.
- Observational learning is learning by watching the behavior of another person, or a model. It is often

referred to as the social cognitive approach to learning because of its reliance on observation of others—a social phenomenon. Not all behavior we observe is learned or carried out. The major factor that determines whether an observed behavior will be performed is the nature of the reinforcement or punishment a model receives.
- Observation of violence is linked to a greater likelihood of subsequently acting aggressively.
- Cognitive psychologists suggest that people develop learning styles, which are characteristic ways of approaching learning, based on a person's cultural background and unique pattern of abilities. Whether an individual has an analytical or a relational style of learning, for example, may reflect family background or culture.
- Observational learning is important in acquiring skills in which the operant conditioning technique of shaping is inappropriate, such as piloting a plane or performing brain surgery.

AP KEY TERMS

cognitive learning theory
latent learning
observational learning

Section I: Multiple Choice

1. The graph at right depicts the results of an experiment in which three groups of rats roamed a maze once a day for 17 days. What do the results of the experimental group reveal?
   A. Observational learning
   B. Stimulus discrimination
   C. Cognitive mapping
   D. Classical conditioning
   E. Stimulus generalization

2. What perspective believes organisms develop an expectation that they will receive a reinforcer after making a response?
   A. Cognitive
   B. Neuroscience
   C. Psychoanalytic
   D. Humanistic
   E. Observational

3. A major part of learning is observation of others–a social phenomenon. This is most closely associated with what researcher?
   A. Ivan Pavlov
   B. B.F. Skinner
   C. John Garcia
   D. Albert Bandura
   E. Edward Thorndike

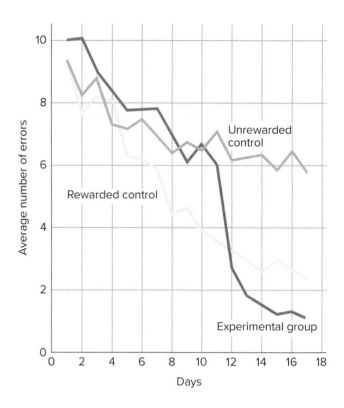

Section II: Free Response

Samantha recently moved and now she attends Behaviorism High School. She has met lots of new friends and is doing well in all of her classes. If she follows the school rules she earns Skinner Bucks that can be exchanged for various prizes.

Describe how the following might <u>help</u> her at the new school.

- Latent learning
- Cognitive map
- Observational learning
- Secondary reinforcer
- Hippocampus

LOOKING *Back*

EPILOGUE

In this chapter, we discussed several kinds of learning, ranging from classical conditioning, which depends on the existence of natural stimulus–response pairings, to operant conditioning, in which reinforcement is used to increase desired behavior. These approaches to learning focus on outward, behavioral learning processes. Cognitive approaches to learning focus on mental processes that enable learning.

We have also noted that learning is affected by culture and individual differences, with individual learning styles potentially affecting the ways in which people learn most effectively. And we saw some ways in which our learning about learning can be put to practical use through such means as behavior-modification programs designed to decrease negative behaviors and increase positive ones.

VISUAL SUMMARY 6 Learning

MODULE 17 Classical Conditioning

Ivan Pavlov: Basic principles of classical conditioning

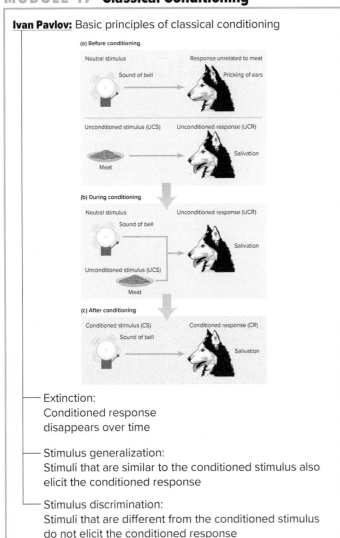

Extinction:
Conditioned response
disappears over time

Stimulus generalization:
Stimuli that are similar to the conditioned stimulus also
elicit the conditioned response

Stimulus discrimination:
Stimuli that are different from the conditioned stimulus
do not elicit the conditioned response

MODULE 18 Operant Conditioning

Basic Principle: Behavior changes in frequency according
to its consequences

Reinforcement: A stimulus that increases the
probability that a preceding behavior will be repeated

Positive reinforcement:
A pleasant stimulus is presented

Negative reinforcement:
An unpleasant stimulus is withdrawn

Basic Principle: Behavior changes in frequency according
to its consequences *(continued)*

Punishment : A stimulus that decreases the probability
that a preceding behavior will be repeated

Positive punishment:
An unpleasant stimulus is presented

Negative punishment:
A pleasant stimulus
is withdrawn

Schedules of reinforcement

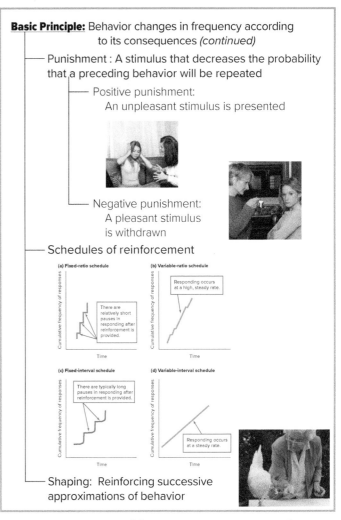

Shaping: Reinforcing successive
approximations of behavior

MODULE 19 Cognitive Approaches to Learning

Cognitive Learning Theory: Focuses on the internal
thoughts and expectations

Latent learning: A new behavior is learned but is not
demonstrated until it is reinforced

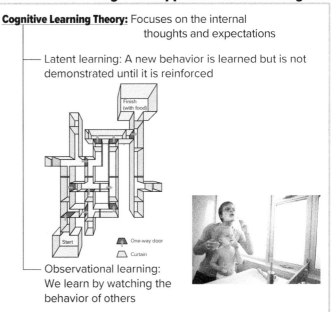

Observational learning:
We learn by watching the
behavior of others

(MODULE 17) Source: Adapted from Tolman, E. C., & Honzik, C. H. (1930). Introduction and removal of reward and maze performance in rats. *University of California Publications in Psychology, 4,* 257–275; (MODULE 18) (Interview): ©Andrey_Popov/Shutterstock; (Ointment): ©Stockbyte/Getty Images; (Yelling): ©Agnieszka Marcinska/Shutterstock; (Restricting) ©Amy Etra/PhotoEdit; (Dr. Marian Breland Bailey): ©Dr. Marian Breland Bailey; (MODULE 19) (Photo): ©Ty Milford/Getty Images

©Eugenio Marongiu/Shutterstock

CHAPTER 7
Memory

AP'I LEARNING TARGETS FOR CHAPTER 7

- Identify the contributions of key researchers in cognitive psychology.
- Outline the principles that underlie construction and encoding of memories.
- Describe strategies for memory improvement and typical memory errors.

PROLOGUE *SHE CAN NEVER FORGET*

Jill Price, 51, is a walking diary of everything that has happened in her life since adolescence. Although she has kept a daily journal since 1980, Price doesn't need to check it to recall the events of any given day. Ask her when she first heard the Rick Springfield song "Jessie's Girl," and she'll tell you it was March 7, 1981. She was 16 years and 2 months old. She was in the car with her mom, who was yelling at her. Jill Price *never* forgets.

A New York City native, Price moved twice in her childhood, first to New Jersey, then California. The second move was difficult for her. So in an attempt to memorize all she was leaving, she made lists, took photos, and collected artifacts. After the move, she recalls that she suddenly felt something change dramatically in her brain, and her recall improved drastically. The date was July 1, 1974. Jill was 8 years old.

Intriguingly, Price's perfect recall works only with details that relate to her personally. She remembers lots of '60s and '70s television trivia but finds it more difficult to recall facts and figures from her studies.

Having total recall may seem like a wonderful ability, but Price often finds it maddening and likens it to living with a split-screen view: On one side is the present and on the other, a continually rolling reel of memories of the past (McRobbie, 2017).

LOOKING *Ahead*

Jill Price was the first person to be diagnosed with what scientists now term *highly superior autobiographical memory (HSAM)*, a condition affecting the part of memory that stores experiences related to life events. Researchers have discovered that people with HSAM process short-term memories the same way most of us do. The difference is the accuracy and detail of their memories actually *improve* over time. (By the way, if you are wondering if people with HSAM have accurate recall, it appears so: every time they say something that can be corroborated by evidence, they have been proven to be accurate; McGaugh & LePort, 2014; Morris, 2017; Wolk et al., 2017.)

Price's extraordinary memory illustrates the complexity and the mystery of the phenomenon we call memory. Memory allows us to retrieve a vast amount of information. We are able to remember the name of a friend we haven't talked with for years and recall the details of a picture that hung in our childhood bedroom. At the same time, though, memory failures are common. We forget where we left the keys to the car and fail to answer an exam question about material we studied only a few hours earlier. Why?

We turn now to the nature of memory, considering the ways in which information is stored and retrieved. We examine the problems of retrieving information from memory, the accuracy of memories, and the reasons information is sometimes forgotten. We also consider the biological foundations of memory and discuss some practical means of increasing memory capacity.

Module 20
The Foundations of Memory

memory The process by which we encode, store, and retrieve information. (Module 20)

You are playing a game of Trivial Pursuit, and winning the game comes down to one question: On what body of water is Mumbai located? As you rack your brain for the answer, several fundamental processes relating to memory come into play. You may never, for instance, have been exposed to information regarding Mumbai's location. Or if you have been exposed to it, it may simply not have registered in a meaningful way. In other words, the information might not have been recorded properly in your memory. The initial process of recording information in a form usable to memory, a process called *encoding*, is the first stage in remembering something.

Even if you had been exposed to the information and originally knew the name of the body of water, you may still be unable to recall it during the game because of a failure to retain it. Memory specialists speak of *storage*, the maintenance of material saved in memory. If the material is not stored adequately, it cannot be recalled later.

Memory also depends on one last process—*retrieval*: Material in memory storage has to be located and brought into awareness to be useful. Your failure to recall Mumbai's location, then, may rest on your inability to retrieve information that you learned earlier.

In sum, psychologists consider **memory** to be the process by which we encode, store, and retrieve information (see Figure 1). Each of the three parts of this definition—encoding, storage, and retrieval—represents a different process. You can think of these processes as being analogous to a computer's keyboard (encoding), hard drive (storage), and software that accesses the information for display on the screen (retrieval). Only if all three processes have operated will you experience success and be able to recall the body of water on which Mumbai is located: the Arabian Sea.

Recognizing that memory involves encoding, storage, and retrieval gives us a start in understanding the concept. But how does memory actually function? How do we explain what information is initially encoded, what gets stored, and how it is retrieved?

According to the *three-system approach to memory* that dominated memory research for several decades, there are different memory storage systems or stages through which information must travel if it is to be remembered (Atkinson & Shiffrin, 1968). Historically, the approach has been extremely influential in the development of our understanding of memory, and—although new theories have augmented it—it still provides a useful framework for understanding how information is recalled.

FIGURE 1 Memory is built on three basic processes—encoding, storage, and retrieval—that are analogous to a computer's keyboard, hard drive, and software to access the information for display on the screen. The analogy is not perfect, however, because human memory is less precise than a computer. How might you modify the analogy to make it more accurate?

Encoding
(Initial recording of information)

Storage
(Information saved for future use)

Retrieval
(Recovery of stored information)

FIGURE 2 In this three-stage model of memory, information initially recorded by the person's sensory system enters sensory memory, which momentarily holds the information. The information then moves to short-term memory, which stores it for 15 to 25 seconds. Finally, the information can move into long-term memory, which is relatively permanent. Whether the information moves from short-term to long-term memory depends on the kind and amount of rehearsal of the material that is performed.

Source: Adapted from Baddeley, A., Chincotta, D., & Adlam, A. (2001). Working memory and the control of action: Evidence from task switching. *Journal of Experimental Psychology: General, 130,* 641–657.; (Photo): ©C Squared Studios/Getty Images.

The three-system memory theory proposes the existence of the three separate memory stores shown in Figure 2. **Sensory memory** refers to the initial, momentary storage of information that lasts only an instant. Here, an exact replica of the stimulus recorded by a person's sensory system is stored very briefly. In a second stage, **short-term memory** holds information for 15 to 25 seconds and stores it according to its meaning, rather than as mere sensory stimulation. The third type of storage system is **long-term memory.** Information is stored in long-term memory on a relatively permanent basis, although it may be difficult to retrieve.

sensory memory The initial, momentary storage of information, lasting only an instant. (Module 20)

short-term memory Memory that holds information for 15 to 25 seconds. (Module 20)

long-term memory Memory that stores information on a relatively permanent basis, although it may be difficult to retrieve. (Module 20)

Sensory Memory

A momentary flash of lightning, the sound of a twig snapping, and the sting of a pinprick all represent stimulation of exceedingly brief duration, but they may nonetheless provide important information that can require a response. Such stimuli are initially—and fleetingly—stored in sensory memory.

Sensory memory is the first storehouse of the information the world presents to us. Actually, we have several types of sensory memories, each related to a different source of sensory information. For instance, *iconic memory* reflects information from the visual system. *Echoic memory* stores auditory information coming from the ears. In addition, there are corresponding memories for each of the other senses.

Sensory memory can store information for only a very short time. If information does not pass into short-term memory, it is lost for good. For instance, iconic memory seems to last less than a second, and echoic memory typically fades within 2 or 3 seconds. However, despite the brief duration of sensory memory, its precision is high: Sensory memory can store an almost exact replica of each stimulus to which it is exposed (Vlassova & Pearson, 2013; Rimmele, Sussman, & Poeppel, 2015).

Psychologist George Sperling (1960) demonstrated the existence of sensory memory in a series of clever and now-classic studies. He briefly exposed people to a series of 12 letters arranged in the following pattern:

Study Alert
Although the three types of memory are discussed as separate memory stores, these are not mini-warehouses located in specific areas of the brain. Instead, they represent three different types of memory systems with different characteristics.

A momentary flash of lightning leaves a sensory visual memory, a fleeting but exact replica of the stimulus, which then fades away.
©Brand X Pictures

```
F    T    Y    C
K    D    N    L
Y    W    B    M
```

When exposed to this pattern of letters for just one twentieth of a second, most people could recall only four or five of the letters accurately. Although they knew that they had seen more, the memory of those letters had faded by the time they reported the first few letters. It was possible, then, that the information had initially been accurately stored in sensory memory. But during the time it took to verbalize the first four or five letters, the memory of the other letters faded.

To test that possibility, Sperling conducted an experiment in which a high, medium, or low tone sounded just after a person had been exposed to the full pattern of letters. People were told to report the letters in the highest line if a high tone was sounded, the middle line if the medium tone occurred, or the lowest line at the sound of the low tone. Because the tone occurred after the exposure, people had to rely on their memories to report the correct row.

The results of the study clearly showed that people had been storing the complete pattern in memory. They accurately recalled the letters in the line that had been indicated by the tone regardless of whether it was the top, middle, or bottom line. Obviously, *all* the lines they had seen had been stored in sensory memory. Despite its rapid loss, then, the information in sensory memory was an accurate representation of what people had seen.

By gradually lengthening the time between the presentation of the visual pattern and the tone, Sperling was able to determine with some accuracy the length of time that information was stored in sensory memory. The ability to recall a particular row of the pattern when a tone was sounded declined progressively as the period between the visual exposure and the tone increased. This decline continued until the period reached about 1 second in duration, at which point the row could not be recalled accurately at all. Sperling concluded that the entire visual image was stored in sensory memory for less than a second.

In sum, sensory memory operates as a kind of snapshot that stores information–which may be of a visual, auditory, or other sensory nature–for a brief moment in time. But it is as if each snapshot, immediately after being taken, is destroyed and replaced with a new one. Unless the information in the snapshot is transferred to some other type of memory, it is lost.

Short-Term Memory

Because the information that is stored briefly in sensory memory consists of representations of raw sensory stimuli, it is not meaningful to us. If we are to make sense of it and possibly retain it, the information must be transferred to the next stage of memory: short-term memory. Short-term memory is the memory store in which information first has meaning, although the maximum length of retention there is relatively short (Hamilton & Martin, 2007; Cao, Nosofsky, & Shiffrin, 2017).

The specific process by which sensory memories are transformed into short-term memories is not clear. Some theorists suggest that the information is first translated into graphical representations or images, and others hypothesize that the transfer occurs when the sensory stimuli are changed to words (Baddeley & Wilson, 1985). What is clear, however, is that unlike sensory memory, which holds a relatively full and detailed–if short-lived–representation of the world, short-term memory has incomplete representational capabilities.

chunk A group of separate pieces of information stored as a single unit in short-term memory. (Module 20)

In fact, researchers have identified the specific amount of information we can hold in short-term memory: 7 items, or "chunks," of information, with variations up to plus or minus 2 chunks (remember it this way: 7 ± 2). A **chunk** is a group of separate pieces of information stored as a single unit in short-term memory. For example, telephone numbers are typically depicted in three chunks of information in order to make them easier to remember: (201) 226-4610, rather than a string of the separate numbers 2012264610.

Chunks also may consist of categories as words or other meaningful units. For example, consider the following list of 21 letters:

P B S F O X C N N A B C C B S M T V N B C

Because the list of individual letters exceeds seven items, it is difficult to recall the letters after one exposure. But suppose they were presented as follows:

PBS FOX CNN ABC CBS MTV NBC

In this case, even though there are still 21 letters, you'd be able to store them in short-term memory since they represent only seven chunks.

Chunks can vary in size from single letters or numbers to categories that are far more complicated. The specific nature of what constitutes a chunk varies according to one's past experience. You can see this for yourself by trying an experiment that was first carried out as a comparison between expert and inexperienced chess players and is illustrated in Figure 3 (deGroot, 1978; Grossberg, 2013; Schneider & Logan, 2015).

The chunks of information in short-term memory do not last very long. Just how brief is short-term memory? If you've ever looked up a telephone number, repeated the number to yourself, and then forgotten the number after you've tapped the first three numbers into your phone, you know that information does not remain in short-term memory very long. Most psychologists believe that information in short-term memory is lost after 15 to 25 seconds—unless it is transferred to long-term memory.

REHEARSAL

The transfer of material from short- to long-term memory proceeds largely on the basis of **rehearsal,** the repetition of information that has entered short-term memory. Rehearsal accomplishes two things. First, as long as the information is repeated, it is maintained in short-term memory. More important, however, rehearsal allows us to

rehearsal The repetition of information that has entered short-term memory. (Module 20)

 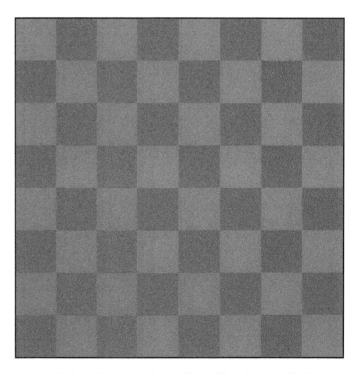

FIGURE 3 Examine the chessboard on the left for about 5 seconds. Then cover up the board and draw the position of the pieces on the blank chessboard. (You could also use your own chessboard and place the pieces in the same positions.) Unless you are an experienced chess player, you are likely to have great difficulty carrying out such a task. Yet chess masters—those who win tournaments—do this quite well (deGroot, 1966). They are able to reproduce correctly 90% of the pieces on the board. In comparison, inexperienced chess players are typically able to reproduce only 40% of the board properly. The chess masters do not have superior memories in other respects; they generally test normally on other measures of memory. What they can do better than others is see the board in terms of chunks or meaningful units and reproduce the position of the chess pieces by using those units.

transfer the information into long-term memory (Jarrold & Tam, 2011; Grenfell-Essam, Ward, & Tan, 2013; Festini & Reuter-Lorenz, 2017).

Whether the transfer is made from short- to long-term memory seems to depend largely on the kind of rehearsal that is carried out. If the information is simply repeated over and over again–as we might do with a telephone number someone tells us as we rush to store it in our phone–it is kept current in short-term memory, but it will not necessarily be placed in long-term memory. Instead, as soon as we stop punching in the phone numbers, the number is likely to be replaced by other information and will be completely forgotten.

In contrast, if the information in short-term memory is rehearsed using a process called elaborative rehearsal, it is much more likely to be transferred into long-term memory. *Elaborative rehearsal* occurs when the information is considered and organized in some fashion. The organization might include expanding the information to make it fit into a logical framework, linking it to another memory, turning it into an image, or transforming it in some other way. For example, a list of vegetables to be purchased at a store could be woven together in memory as items being used to prepare an elaborate salad, could be linked to the items bought on an earlier shopping trip, or could be thought of in terms of the image of a farm with rows of each item.

We can vastly improve our retention of information using such organizational strategies, which are known as mnemonics. *Mnemonics* (pronounced "neh MON ix") are strategies for organizing information in a way that makes the information more likely to be remembered. For instance, when a beginning musician learns that the spaces on the music staff spell the word *FACE*, or when we learn the rhyme "Thirty days hath September, April, June, and November . . . ," we are using mnemonics (Stålhammar, Nordlund, & Wallin, 2015; Choi, Kensinger, & Rajaram, 2017).

Working Memory

Rather than seeing short-term memory as an independent way station into which memories arrive, either to fade or to be passed on to long-term memory, most contemporary memory theorists conceive of short-term memory as far more active. In this view, short-term memory is like an information-processing system that manages both new material gathered from sensory memory and older material that has been pulled from long-term storage. In this increasingly influential view, short-term memory is referred to as working memory.

working memory A memory system that holds information temporarily while actively manipulating and rehearsing that information. (Module 20)

Working memory is the memory system that holds information temporarily while actively manipulating and rehearsing that information. If you use the analogy of a computer, working memory is the processing that occurs in an open window on your desktop, as compared with the long-term storage of information in the computer's hard drive (Unsworth & Engle, 2005; Vandierendonck & Szmalec, 2011).

Researchers now assume that working memory is made up of several parts. First, it contains a *central executive* processor that is involved in reasoning, decision making, and planning. The central executive integrates and coordinates information from three distinct subsystems, and it determines what we pay attention to and what we ignore.

The three subsystems of working memory serve as storage-and-rehearsal systems: the visual store, the verbal store, and the episodic buffer. The *visual store* specializes in visual and spatial information. In contrast, the *verbal store* holds and manipulates material relating to language, including speech, words, and numbers. Finally, the *episodic buffer* contains information that represents events and occurrences–things that happen to us (see Figure 4; Baddeley, Allen, & Hitch, 2011; Kuncel & Beatty, 2013; Hilbert et al., 2017).

Working memory permits us to keep information in an active state briefly so that we can do something with the information. For instance, we use working memory when we're doing a multistep arithmetic problem in our heads, storing the result of

FIGURE 4 Working memory is an active "workspace" in which information is retrieved and manipulated and in which information is held through rehearsal.

Source: Adapted from Baddeley, A., Chincotta, D., & Adlam, A. (2001). Working memory and the control of action: Evidence from task switching. *Journal of Experimental Psychology: General, 130,* 641–657.

one calculation while getting ready to move to the next stage. (I make use of my working memory when I figure a 20% tip in a restaurant by first calculating 10% of the total bill and then doubling it.)

As working memory processes information, it uses a significant amount of cognitive resources during its operation. Furthermore, the amount of information that can be held and processed in working memory seems to be just three to four chunks, depending on the nature of the chunks (Cowan, 2001; Beam, 2014; Heathcoate et al., 2015).

The cognitive effort in the processing of information in working memory also can make us less aware of our surroundings–something that has implications for why it's unsafe to use cell phones while driving. If a phone conversation requires thinking, it will burden working memory and leave drivers less aware of their surroundings, an obviously dangerous state of affairs (Sifrit, 2006; Strayer & Drews, 2007).

Furthermore, stress can reduce the effectiveness of working memory by reducing its capacity. In fact, one study found that students with the highest working memory capacity and greatest math ability were the ones who were most vulnerable to pressure to perform well. Those who should have performed best, then, were the ones most apt to choke on the test because their working memory capacities were reduced by the stress (Schoofs et al., 2013; Edwards et al., 2015; Banks & Boals, 2017).

Long-Term Memory

Material that makes its way from short-term memory to long-term memory enters a storehouse of almost unlimited capacity. Like a new file we save on a hard drive, the information in long-term memory is filed and coded so that we can retrieve it when we need it.

Evidence of the existence of long-term memory, as distinct from short-term memory, comes from a number of sources. For example, people with certain kinds of brain damage have no lasting recall of new information received after the damage occurred, although people and events stored in memory before the injury remain intact (Milner, 1966). Because information that was encoded and stored before the injury can be

PsychTech
Research shows that when we are faced with complicated questions and material, we are primed to think of computers and search engines such as Google. In what is called the *Google effect,* we are then less likely to store the information in short-term memory and less likely to recall it—but have a better memory for where we can find it on the web (Sparrow, Liu, & Wegner, 2011).

recalled and because short-term memory after the injury appears to be operational–new material can be recalled for a very brief period–we can infer that there are two distinct types of memory: one for short-term and one for long-term storage.

Results from laboratory experiments are also consistent with the notion of separate short-term and long-term memory. For example, in one set of studies, people were asked to recall a relatively small amount of information (such as a set of three letters). Then, to prevent practice of the initial information, participants were required to recite some extraneous material aloud, such as counting backward by threes (Brown, 1958; Peterson & Peterson, 1959). By varying the amount of time between the presentation of the initial material and the need for its recall, investigators found that recall was quite good when the interval was very short, but recall declined rapidly thereafter. After 15 seconds had gone by, recall hovered at around 10% of the material initially presented.

Apparently, the distraction of counting backward prevented almost all the initial material from reaching long-term memory. Initial recall was good because it was coming from short-term memory, but those memories were lost at a rapid rate. Eventually, all that could be recalled was the small amount of material that had made its way into long-term storage despite the distraction of counting backward.

The distinction between short- and long-term memory is also demonstrated by the fact that ability to recall information in a list depends on where in the list an item appears. For instance, in some cases, a *primacy effect* occurs, in which items presented early in a list are remembered better. In other cases, a *recency effect* is seen, in which items presented late in a list are remembered best (Tydgat & Grainger, 2009; Jacoby & Wahlheim, 2013; Tam, Bonardi, & Robinson, 2015).

LONG-TERM MEMORY MODULES

Just as short-term memory is often conceptualized in terms of working memory, many contemporary researchers now regard long-term memory as having several components, or *memory modules*. Each of these modules represents a separate memory system in the brain.

One major distinction within long-term memory is that between declarative and procedural memory. **Declarative memory** is memory for factual information: names, faces, dates, and facts, such as "a bike has two wheels." The information stored in declarative memory can be verbally communicated to others and is sometimes called "explicit memory."

In contrast, **procedural memory** (sometimes called *nondeclarative memory* or *implicit memory*) refers to memory for skills and habits, such as how to ride a bike or hit a baseball. For example, procedural memory allows us to ice skate, even if we haven't done it for a long time. (Try to explain how you know how to balance on a bike or catch a ball; it's nearly impossible. Yet you're able to do so because the information is stored in procedural memory.)

You can remember the difference between declarative and procedural memory this way: Information about *things* is stored in declarative memory; information about *how to do things* (procedures) is stored in procedural memory (Bauer, 2008; Freedberg, 2011; Gade et al., 2017).

Declarative memory can be subdivided into semantic memory and episodic memory. **Semantic memory** is memory for general knowledge and facts about the world, as well as memory for the rules of logic that are used to deduce other facts. Because of semantic memory, we remember that the ZIP code for Beverly Hills is 90210, that Mumbai is on the Arabian Sea, and that *memoree* is the incorrect spelling of *memory*. Thus, semantic memory is somewhat like a mental almanac of facts (Tulving, 2002; McNamara, 2013; Grady, St-Laurent, & Burianová, 2015).

In contrast, **episodic memory** is memory for events that occur in a particular time, place, or context. For example, recall of learning to hit a baseball, our first kiss, or arranging a surprise 21st birthday party for our brother is based on episodic memories. Episodic memories relate to particular contexts. For example, remembering *when* and *how* we learned that 2 × 2 = 4 would be an episodic memory; the fact itself (that 2 × 2 = 4) is a semantic memory. (Also see Figure 5.)

declarative memory Memory for factual information: names, faces, dates, and the like. (Module 20)

procedural memory Memory for skills and habits, such as riding a bike or hitting a baseball; sometimes referred to as *nondeclarative memory* or *implicit memory*. (Module 20)

semantic memory Memory for general knowledge and facts about the world, as well as memory for the rules of logic that are used to deduce other facts. (Module 20)

episodic memory Memory for events that occur in a particular time, place, or context. (Module 20)

FIGURE 5 Long-term memory can be subdivided into several different types. What type of long-term memory is involved in your recollection of the moment you first arrived on your campus at the start of college? What type of long-term memory is involved in remembering the lyrics to a song, compared with the tune of a song?

Study Alert
Use Figure 5 to help clarify the distinctions between the different types of long-term memory.

Episodic memories can be surprisingly detailed. Consider, for instance, how you'd respond if you were asked to identify what you were doing on a specific day 2 years ago. Impossible? You may think otherwise as you read the following exchange between a researcher and a participant in a study who was asked, in a memory experiment, what he was doing "on Monday afternoon in the third week of September two years ago."

PARTICIPANT: Come on. How should I know?

EXPERIMENTER: Just try it anyhow.

PARTICIPANT: OK. Let's see: Two years ago . . . I would be in high school in Pittsburgh. . . . That would be my senior year. Third week in September–that's just after summer–that would be the fall term. . . . Let me see. I think I had chemistry lab on Mondays. I don't know. I was probably in chemistry lab. Wait a minute–that would be the second week of school. I remember he started off with the atomic table–a big fancy chart. I thought he was crazy trying to make us memorize that thing. You know, I think I can remember sitting . . . . (Lindsay & Norman, 1977)

Episodic memory, then, can provide information about events that happened long in the past. But semantic memory is no less impressive, permitting us to dredge up tens of thousands of facts ranging from the date of our birthday to the knowledge that $1 is less than $5.

SEMANTIC NETWORKS

Try to recall, for a moment, as many things as you can think of that are the color red. Now pull from your memory the names of as many fruits as you can recall.

Did the same item appear when you did both tasks? For many people, an apple comes to mind in both cases since it fits equally well in each category. And the fact that you might have thought of an apple when doing the first task makes it even more likely that you'll think of it when doing the second task.

It's actually quite amazing that we're able to retrieve specific material from the vast store of information in our long-term memories. According to some memory researchers, one key organizational tool that allows us to recall detailed information from long-term memory is the associations that we build between different pieces of information. In this view, knowledge is stored in **semantic networks,** mental representations of clusters of interconnected information (Cummings, Ceponiene, & Koyama, 2006; Poirier et al., 2015).

semantic networks Mental representations of clusters of interconnected information. (Module 20)

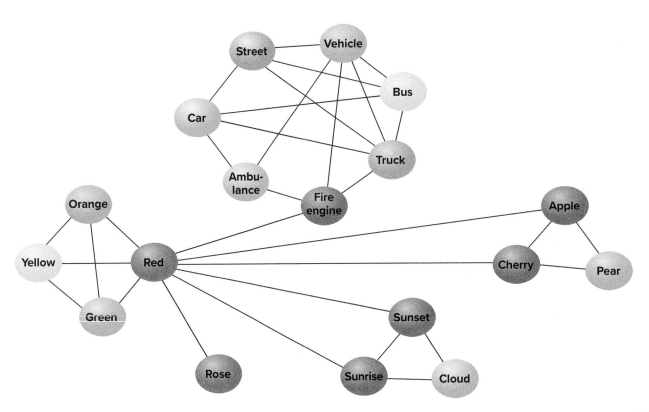

FIGURE 6 Semantic networks in memory consist of relationships between pieces of information, such as those relating to the concept of a fire engine. The lines suggest the connections that indicate how the information is organized within memory. The closer together two concepts are, the greater the strength of the association.

Source: Baddeley, A., Chincotta, D., & Adlam, A. (2001). Working memory and the control of action: Evidence from task switching. *Journal of Experimental Psychology: General,* *130,* 641–657.

Consider, for example, Figure 6, which shows some of the relationships in memory relating to fire engines, the color red, and a variety of other semantic concepts. Thinking about a particular concept leads to recall of related concepts. For example, seeing a fire engine may activate our recollections of other kinds of emergency vehicles, such as an ambulance, which in turn may activate recall of the related concept of a vehicle. And thinking of a vehicle may lead us to think about a bus that we've seen in the past. Activating one memory triggers the activation of related memories in a process known as *spreading activation* (Kreher et al., 2008; Nelson et al., 2013; Kenett et al., 2017).

From the perspective of...

A Marketing Specialist How might advertisers use ways of enhancing memory to promote their products? What ethical principles are involved?

©McGraw-Hill Education

THE NEUROSCIENCE OF MEMORY

Can we pinpoint a location in the brain where long-term memories reside? Is there a single site that corresponds to a particular memory, or is memory distributed in different regions across the brain? Do memories leave an actual physical trace that scientists can view?

The *engram* is the term for the physical memory trace in the brain that corresponds to a memory. Locating the engram has proved to be a major challenge to psychologists and neuroscientists interested in memory. But by using advanced brain scanning procedures, investigators have learned that certain brain areas and structures specialize in different types of memory-related activities.

The *hippocampus,* a part of the brain's limbic system (see Figure 7), helps to consolidate memories, stabilizing them after they are initially acquired. The hippocampus acts as a kind of neurological e-mail system. That information is subsequently passed along to the cerebral cortex of the brain, where it is actually stored (Peters et al., 2007; Lavenex & Lavenex, 2009; Dudai, 2011).

The significance of the hippocampus is exemplified by studies of individuals who have particularly good, yet specialized, types of memories. For instance, taxi drivers in London, England, must have accurate, complete recall of the location of the maze of streets and alleys within a 6-mile radius of the center of the city. It takes years of study to memorize the material.

It turns out that MRI brain scans of taxi drivers show differences in the shape of the hippocampus compared to non–taxi drivers. The differences are consistent with the idea that particular areas of the hippocampus are involved in the consolidation of spatial memories (Woollett & Maguire, 2009; Jiang, Miao, & Chen, 2017).

The *amygdala,* another part of the limbic system, also plays an important role in memory. The amygdala is especially involved with memories involving emotion. For example, if you are frightened by a large, growling pit bull dog, you're likely to remember the event vividly–an outcome related to the functioning of the amygdala. Encountering the pit bull or any large dog in the future is likely to reactivate the amygdala and bring back the unpleasant memory (Talmi et al., 2008; Pendyam et al., 2013; Kochli et al., 2015).

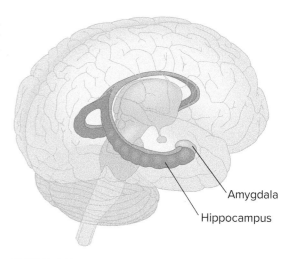

FIGURE 7 The hippocampus and amygdala, parts of the brain's limbic system, play a central role in the consolidation of memories.

Source: Adapted from Van De Graaff, K. (2000). *Human anatomy* (5th ed.). Boston: McGraw-Hill.

Memory at the Level of Neurons   Although it is clear that the hippocampus and amygdala play a central role in memory formation, how is the transformation of information into a memory reflected at the level of neurons?

One answer is *long-term potentiation,* which shows that certain neural pathways become easily excited while a new response is being learned. At the same time, the number of synapses between neurons increases as the dendrites branch out to receive messages. These changes reflect a process called *consolidation,* in which memories become fixed and stable in long-term memory. Long-term memories take some time to stabilize; this explains why events and other stimuli are not suddenly fixed in memory. Instead, consolidation may continue for days and even years (Meeter & Murre, 2004; Kawashima, Izaki, & Grace, 2006; Hwang et al., 2017).

Because a stimulus may contain different sensory aspects, visual, auditory, and other areas of the brain may be simultaneously processing information about that stimulus. Information storage appears to be linked to the sites where this processing occurs, and it is therefore located in the particular areas that initially processed the information in terms of its visual, auditory, and other sensory stimuli. For this reason, memory traces are distributed throughout the brain. For example, when you recall a beautiful beach sunset, your recollection draws on memory stores located in visual areas of the brain (the view of the sunset), auditory areas (the sounds of the ocean), and tactile areas (the feel of the wind) (Squire, Clark, & Bayley, 2004; Murayama & Kitagami, 2013).

In short, the physical stuff of memory–the engram–is produced by a complex of biochemical and neural processes. Scientists are just beginning to understand how the brain compiles the individual neural components into a single, coherent memory. It may be that the same neurons that fire when we are initially exposed to material are reactivated during efforts to recall that information.

In addition to increasingly understanding the biological basis of how memories are formed and recalled, memory specialists are also beginning to understand how to help people *forget* information through biological treatment. Specifically, they are seeking to understand how to help people forget traumatic events, persistent fears, or even annoying habits. And they are making advances in that direction, learning how to reliably alter memories in mice through a combination of a drug called HDAC inhibitor and training. In humans, such drugs might be used to disrupt the initial encoding of memories, such as treating rape victims soon after the rape to reduce the long-term trauma of the event (Johnson, 2014; Lu, 2015).

Still, although memory researchers have made considerable strides in understanding the neuroscience behind memory, more remains to be learned—and remembered (Gelbard-Sagiv et al., 2008; Brown & Banks, 2015). (For more on the biological basis of memory, see *Neuroscience in Your Life*.)

AP NEUROSCIENCE IN YOUR LIFE: SUPERIOR MEMORY

AP SKILL: SCIENTIFIC
INVESTIGATION/ DATA
ANALYSIS

1. Identify the independent and dependent variable.
2. Memory athletes often use mnemonics. What type of mnemonics could be used to enhance memory?

Some people have astounding memory and can memorize as many as 100 words in just 5 minutes. But can anyone have superior memory with the appropriate training? Apparently, the answer is yes, for recent research has shown that people's memory can be trained to show significant changes in capacity, and these changes are reflected in changes in the brain. For example, participants in one study spent 30 minutes a day for 6 weeks practicing to improve their memory. Following training, participants were given 10 minutes to remember as many words as they could, and their memory capacity increased from 26 words to 62 words. This improvement was paralleled by increased connectivity between areas of the *medial temporal lobe,* including the hippocampus, and the frontal cortex, similar to what is found in those with strongly superior memories (memory athletes).

In the view of the brain below, the lines show the difference between nonathletes and athletes, with the blue lines showing more connectivity for nonathletes and the red lines showing more connectivity for athletes. The balls indicate major hubs for these connections, with the largest hubs in the frontal cortex. This research demonstrates that even after our ability to remember information is established, practice can enhance it, and that practice results in lasting effects on the way our brains are wired (Dresler et al., 2017).

Source: Adapted from Dresler, M., Shirer, W. R., Konrad, B. N., Muller, N. C., Wagner, I. C., Fernandez, G., . . . Greicius, M. D. (2017). Mnemonic training reshapes brain networks to support superior memory. *Neuron, 93*(5), 1227–1235 e1226. doi: 10.1016/j.neuron.2017.02.003.

AP MODULE 20: THE FOUNDATIONS OF MEMORY

AP SUMMARY

- Memory is the process by which we encode (in), store (maintain), and retrieve (out) information. Sensory memory is the first place where information is saved. Sensory memories are very brief, but they are precise.

- Short-term memory is the memory store in which information first has meaning and it can hold roughly seven chunks of information. The information is held from 15 to 25 seconds and, if not transferred to long-term memory, is lost.

- Some theorists view short-term memory as a working memory in which information is retrieved, manipulated, and held through rehearsal. In this view, it is a central executive processor involved in reasoning and decision making; it coordinates a visual store, a verbal store, and an episodic buffer. Working memory uses significant cognitive resources and may hold only three to four chunks of information.

- Long-term memory is a storehouse of almost unlimited capacity. It can be viewed in terms of memory modules, each of which is related to separate memory systems in the brain. For instance, we can distinguish between declarative memory (explicit) and procedural (implicit) memory.

- Declarative memory (explicit) is memory for factual information. It can be further divided into episodic memory (personal knowledge) and semantic memory (general knowledge).

- Procedural memory (nondeclarative or implicit) is memory for skills and habits.

- If information is simply repeated (shallow processing) it will remain in short-term memory but may not transfer to long-term memory. If information is processed with elaborative rehearsal (deep processing) it is more likely to transfer to long-term memory and become permanent.

AP KEY TERMS

memory
sensory memory
short-term memory
long-term memory
chunk
rehearsal
working memory

declarative memory
procedural memory
semantic memory
episodic memory
semantic networks

AP TEST PRACTICE

Section I: Multiple Choice

1. George Miller investigated short-term memory and found its capacity consists of approximately how many items?
   A. Three or four
   B. Seven plus or minus two
   C. Ten to twelve
   D. Fifteen
   E. Unlimited

2. Participants were exposed to a matrix of three rows of three letters for a brief period of time and then asked to recall as many letters as possible. Next, researchers presented a high, medium, or low tone that corresponded with the row the participant was supposed to recall. By lengthening the time between the presentation of the visual pattern and the tone, researchers were able to determine the duration of what memory storehouse?
   A. Short-term
   B. Long-term
   C. Sensory
   D. Working
   E. Episodic

3. Gavin needs to remember, in order, a list of words for his English class. He is most likely to forget words
   A. in the middle of the list
   B. at the end of the list
   C. that are hard to pronounce
   D. that have meaning to him
   E. at the beginning of the list

Section II: Free Response

Kurt would like to participate in the World Memory Championships next year. In order to be competitive, he is practicing by memorizing a list of 72 words.
Describe how the following psychological concepts relate to his memory training.
- Mnemonics
- Elaborative rehearsal
- Chunking
- Long-term potentiation
- Primacy effect

Module 21
Recalling Long-Term Memories

AP® LEARNING TARGETS

- Describe strategies for retrieving memories.
- Describe strategies for memory improvement and typical memory errors.

tip-of-the-tongue phenomenon The inability to recall information that one realizes one knows–a result of the difficulty of retrieving information from long-term memory. (Module 21)

recall Memory task in which specific information must be retrieved. (Module 21)

recognition Memory task in which individuals are presented with a stimulus and asked whether they have been exposed to it in the past or to identify it from a list of alternatives. (Module 21)

Study Alert

Remember the distinction between recall (in which specific information must be retrieved) and recognition (in which information is presented and must be identified or distinguished from other material).

FIGURE 1 Try to recall the names of these characters. Because this is a recall task, it is relatively difficult.
©WALT DISNEY PRODUCTIONS/Album/Newscom

An hour after his job interview, Ricardo was sitting in a coffee shop, telling his friend Laura how well it had gone, when the woman who had interviewed him walked in. "Well, hello, Ricardo. How are you doing?" Trying to make a good impression, Ricardo began to make introductions but suddenly realized he could not remember the interviewer's name. Stammering, he desperately searched his memory but to no avail. "I *know* her name," he thought to himself, "but here I am, looking like a fool. I can kiss this job good-bye."

Have you ever tried to remember someone's name, convinced that you knew it but unable to recall it no matter how hard you tried? This common occurrence–known as the **tip-of-the-tongue phenomenon**–exemplifies how difficult it can be to retrieve information stored in long-term memory (Brennen, Vikan, & Dybdahl, 2007; Schwartz, 2008; Schwartz & Metcalfe, 2011).

Retrieval Cues

Perhaps recall of names and other memories is not perfect because there is so much information stored in long-term memory. Because the material that makes its way to long-term memory is relatively permanent, the capacity of long-term memory is vast. For instance, if you are like the average college student, your vocabulary includes some 50,000 words, you know hundreds of mathematical "facts," and you are able to conjure up images–such as the way your childhood home looked–with no trouble at all. In fact, simply cataloging all your memories would probably take years of work.

How do we sort through this vast array of material and retrieve specific information at the appropriate time? One way is through retrieval cues. A *retrieval cue* is a stimulus that allows us to recall more easily information that is in long-term memory. It may be a word, an emotion, or a sound; whatever the specific cue, a memory will suddenly come to mind when the retrieval cue is present. For example, the smell of roasting turkey may evoke memories of Thanksgiving or family gatherings.

Retrieval cues guide people through the information stored in long-term memory in much the same way that a search engine such as Google guides people through the Internet. They are particularly important when we are making an effort to *recall* information, as opposed to being asked to *recognize* material stored in memory. In **recall,** a specific piece of information must be retrieved–such as that needed to answer a fill-in-the-blank question or to write an essay on a test. In contrast, **recognition** occurs when people are presented with a stimulus and asked whether they have been exposed to it previously or are asked to identify it from a list of alternatives.

As you might guess, recognition is generally a much easier task than recall (see Figures 1 and 2). Recall is more difficult because it consists of a series of processes: a search through memory, retrieval of potentially relevant information, and then a decision regarding whether the information you have found is accurate. If the information appears to be correct, the search is over, but if it is not, the search must continue. In contrast, recognition is simpler because it involves fewer steps (Leigh, Zinkhan, & Swaminathan, 2006; Moen, Miller, & Lloyd, 2017).

Answer this recognition question:
Which of the following are the names of the seven dwarfs in the Disney movie
Snow White and the Seven Dwarfs?

Goofy	Bashful
Sleepy	Meanie
Smarty	Doc
Scaredy	Happy
Dopey	Angry
Grumpy	Sneezy
Wheezy	Crazy

(The correct answers are Bashful, Doc, Dopey, Grumpy, Happy, Sleepy, and Sneezy.)

FIGURE 2 Naming the characters in Figure 1 (a recall task) is more difficult than solving the recognition problem posed in this list.

Levels of Processing

One determinant of how well memories are recalled is the way in which material is first perceived, processed, and understood. The **levels-of-processing theory** emphasizes the degree to which new material is mentally analyzed. It suggests that the amount of information processing that occurs when material is initially encountered is central in determining how much of the information is ultimately remembered. According to this approach, the depth of information processing during exposure to material–meaning the degree to which it is analyzed and considered–is critical; the greater the intensity of its initial processing, the more likely we are to remember it (Craik & Lockhart, 2008; Mungan, Peynircioğlu, & Halpern, 2011).

Because we do not pay close attention to much of the information to which we are exposed, very little mental processing typically takes place, and we forget new material almost immediately. However, information to which we pay greater attention is processed more thoroughly. Therefore, it enters memory at a deeper level–and is less apt to be forgotten than is information processed at shallower levels.

The theory goes on to suggest that there are considerable differences in the ways in which information is processed at various levels of memory. At shallow levels, information is processed merely in terms of its physical and sensory aspects. For example, we may pay attention only to the shapes that make up the letters in the word *dog*. At an intermediate level of processing, the shapes are translated into meaningful units–in this case, letters of the alphabet. Those letters are considered in the context of words, and specific phonetic sounds may be attached to the letters.

At the deepest level of processing, information is analyzed in terms of its meaning. We may see it in a wider context and draw associations between the meaning of the information and broader networks of knowledge. For instance, we may think of dogs not merely as animals with four legs and a tail but also in terms of their relationship to cats and other mammals. We may form an image of our own dog, thereby relating the concept to our own lives. According to the levels-of-processing approach, the deeper the initial level of processing of specific information, the longer the information will be retained.

There are considerable practical implications to the notion that recall depends on the degree to which information is initially processed. For example, the depth of information processing is critical when learning and studying course material. Rote memorization of a list of key terms for a test is unlikely to produce long-term recollection of information because processing occurs at a shallow level. In contrast, thinking about the meaning of the terms and reflecting on how they relate to information that one currently knows results in far more effective long-term retention (Conway, 2002; Wenzel, Zetocha, & Ferraro, 2007; Albanese & Case, 2015).

levels-of-processing theory The theory of memory that emphasizes the degree to which new material is mentally analyzed. (Module 21)

Explicit and Implicit Memory

If you've ever had surgery, you probably hoped that the surgeons were focused completely on the surgery and gave you their undivided attention while slicing into your body. The reality in most operating rooms is quite different, though. Surgeons may be chatting with nurses about a new restaurant as soon as they sew you up.

If you are like most patients, you are left with no recollection of the conversation that occurred while you were under anesthesia. However, it is very possible that although you had no conscious memories of the discussions on the merits of the restaurant, on some level you probably did recall at least some information. In fact, careful studies have found that people who are anesthetized during surgery can sometimes recall snippets of conversations they heard during surgery–even though they have no conscious recollection of the information (Sebel, Bonke, & Winograd, 1993).

The discovery that people have memories about which they are unaware has been an important one. It has led to speculation that two forms of memory, explicit and implicit, may exist side by side. **Explicit memory** refers to intentional or conscious recollection of information. When we try to remember a name or date we have encountered or learned about previously, we are searching our explicit memory.

In contrast, **implicit memory** refers to memories of which people are not consciously aware but that can affect subsequent performance and behavior. Skills that operate automatically and without thinking, such as jumping out of the path of an automobile coming toward us as we walk down the side of a road, are stored in implicit memory. Similarly, a feeling of vague dislike for an acquaintance, without knowing why we have that feeling, may be a reflection of implicit memories. Perhaps the person reminds us of someone else in our past that we didn't like, even though we are not aware of the memory of that other individual (Gopie, Craik, & Hasher, 2011; Wu, 2013; Vöhringer et al., 2017).

Implicit memory is closely related to the prejudice and discrimination people exhibit toward members of minority groups. Although people may say and even believe they harbor no prejudice, assessment of their implicit memories may reveal that they have negative associations about members of minority groups. Such associations can influence people's behavior without their being aware of their underlying beliefs (Greenwald, Nosek, & Sriram, 2006; Hofmann et al., 2008; Enge, Lupo, & Zárate, 2015).

One way that memory specialists study implicit memory is through experiments that use priming. **Priming** occurs when exposure to a word or concept (called a *prime*) later makes it easier to recall information related to the prime. Priming allows us to remember new information better and faster because of material we already have stored in memory. Priming effects occur even when people have no conscious memory of the original word or concept (Toth & Daniels, 2002; Schacter, Dobbins, & Schnyer, 2004; Geyer, Gokce, & Müller, 2011).

The typical experiment designed to illustrate priming helps clarify the phenomenon. In priming experiments, participants are rapidly exposed to a stimulus such as a word, an object, or perhaps a drawing of a face. The second phase of the experiment is done after an interval ranging from several seconds to several months. At that point, participants are exposed to incomplete perceptual information that is related to the first stimulus, and they are asked whether they recognize it. For example, the new material may consist of the first letter of a word that had been presented earlier or a part of a face that had been shown earlier. If participants are able to identify the stimulus more readily than they identify stimuli that have not been presented earlier, priming has taken place. Clearly, the earlier stimulus has been remembered–although the material resides in implicit memory, not explicit memory.

The same thing happens to us in our everyday lives. Suppose several months ago you watched a documentary on the planets, and the narrator described the moons of Mars, focusing on its moon named Phobos. You promptly forget the name of the moon, at least consciously. Then, several months later, you're completing a crossword puzzle

explicit memory Intentional or conscious recollection of information. (Module 21)

implicit memory Memories of which people are not consciously aware but that can affect subsequent performance and behavior. (Module 21)

priming A phenomenon that occurs when exposure to a word or concept (called a *prime*) later makes it easier to recall information related to the prime. (Module 21) that you have partially filled in, and it includes the letters *obos*. As soon as you look at the set of letters, you think of Phobos, and suddenly you recall for the first time since your initial exposure to the information that it is one of the moons of Mars. The sudden recollection occurred because your memory was primed by the letters *obos*.

In short, when information that we are unable to consciously recall affects our behavior, implicit memory is at work. Our behavior may be influenced by experiences of which we are unaware–an example of what has been called "retention without remembering" (Horton et al., 2005; White, 2013; Rossi-Arnaud et al, 2017).

Flashbulb Memories

Ask anyone old enough to recall the day terrorist attacks brought down the Twin Towers in New York City on September 11, 2001. They will likely recall exactly where they were when they heard the news, even though the incident happened years ago.

Their ability to remember details about this fatal event illustrates a phenomenon known as flashbulb memory. **Flashbulb memories** are memories related to a specific, important, or surprising event that are so vivid they represent a virtual snapshot of the event. Several types of flashbulb memories are common among college students. For example, involvement in a car accident, meeting one's roommate for the first time, and the night of high school graduation are all typical flashbulb memories (see Figure 3; Bohn & Berntsen, 2007; Talarico, 2009; Lanciano et al., 2013).

flashbulb memories Memories of a specific, important, or surprising emotionally significant event that are recalled easily and with vivid imagery. (Module 21)

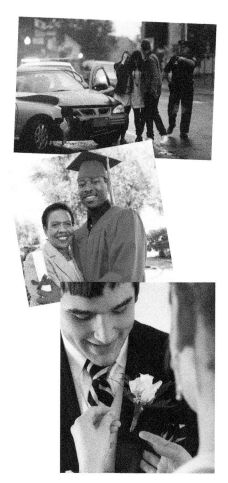

FIGURE 3 These are the most common flashbulb memory events, based on a survey of college students. What are some of your flashbulb memories?

(Right, top): ©Image Source/Getty Images; (Right, middle): ©Digital Vision/SuperStock; (Right, bottom): ©DreamPictures/VStock/Getty Images; (Graph): Source: Adapted from Rubin, D. C. (1986, September). The subtle deceiver: Recalling our past. *Psychology Today,* pp. 39–46.

Of course, flashbulb memories do not contain every detail of an original scene. I remember vividly that decades ago I was sitting in Mr. Sharp's 10th-grade geometry class when I heard that President John Kennedy had been shot. However, although I recall where I was sitting and how my classmates reacted to the news, I do not recollect what I was wearing or what I had for lunch that day.

Furthermore, the details recalled in flashbulb memories are often inaccurate, particularly when they involve highly emotional events. For example, those old enough to remember the day when the World Trade Center in New York was attacked by terrorists typically remember watching television that morning and seeing images of the first plane and then the second plane striking the towers. However, that recollection is wrong: In fact, television broadcasts showed images only of the second plane on September 11. No video of the first plane was available until early the following morning, September 12, when it was shown on television (Schaefer, Halldorson, & Dizon-Reynante, 2011; Hirst et al., 2015).

Flashbulb memories illustrate a more general phenomenon about memory: Memories that are exceptional are more easily retrieved (although not necessarily accurately) than are those relating to events that are commonplace. The more distinctive a stimulus is and the more personal relevance the event has, the more likely we are to recall it later (Talarico & Rubin, 2007; Schaefer, Halldorson, & Dizon-Reynante, 2011; Gandolphe & El Haj, 2017).

Even with a distinctive stimulus, however, we may not remember where the information came from. *Source amnesia* occurs when an individual has a memory for some material but cannot recall where he or she encountered it. For example, source amnesia can explain situations in which you meet someone you know but can't remember where you met that person initially.

Similarly, our motivation to remember material when we are exposed to it initially affects how well we can later recall it. If we know we are going to need to recall material later, we are going to be more attentive to it. In contrast, if we don't expect to need to recall material later, then we are less likely to remember it (Naveh-Benjamin, Guez, & Sorek, 2007; Kassam et al., 2009).

Constructive Processes in Memory: Rebuilding the Past

As we have seen, although it is clear that we can have detailed recollections of significant and distinctive events, it is difficult to gauge the accuracy of such memories. In fact, it is apparent that our memories reflect, at least in part, **constructive processes,** processes in which memories are influenced by the meaning we give to events. When we retrieve information, then, the memory that is produced is affected not just by the direct prior experience we have had with the stimulus but also by our guesses and inferences about its meaning.

The notion that memory is based on constructive processes was first put forward by Frederic Bartlett, a British psychologist. He suggested that people tend to remember information in terms of **schemas,** organized bodies of information stored in memory that bias the way new information is interpreted, stored, and recalled (Bartlett, 1932). Because we use schemas to organize information, our memories often consist of a reconstruction of previous experience. Consequently, schemas are based not only on the actual material to which people are exposed but also on their understanding of the situation, their expectations about the situation, and their awareness of the motivations underlying the behavior of others.

One of the earliest demonstrations of schemas came from a classic study that involved a procedure similar to the children's game of "telephone," in which information from memory is passed sequentially from one person to another. In the study, a participant viewed a drawing in which there were a variety of people of differing racial and ethnic backgrounds on a subway car, one of whom—a white person—was shown

constructive processes Processes in which memories are influenced by the meaning we give to events. (Module 21)

schemas Organized bodies of information stored in memory that bias the way new information is interpreted, stored, and recalled. (Modules 21, 52)

Study Alert

A key fact about memory is that it is a constructive process in which memories are influenced by the meaning given to what is being recalled.

with a razor in his hand (Allport & Postman, 1958). The first participant was asked to describe the drawing to someone else without looking back at it. Then that person was asked to describe it to another person (without looking at the drawing), and then the process was repeated with still one more participant.

The report of the last person differed in significant, yet systematic, ways from the initial drawing. Specifically, many people described the drawing as depicting an African American with a knife—an incorrect recollection, given that the drawing showed a razor in the hand of a Caucasian person. The transformation of the Caucasian's razor into an African American's knife clearly indicates that the participants held a schema that included the unwarranted prejudice that African Americans are more violent than Caucasians and thus more apt to be holding a knife. In short, our expectations and knowledge—and prejudices—affect the reliability of our memories (McDonald & Hirt, 1997; Newby-Clark & Ross, 2003; De Brigard et al., 2017).

Although the constructive nature of memory can result in memories that are partially or completely false, they also may be beneficial in some ways. For example, false memories may allow us to keep hold of positive self-images. In addition, they may help us maintain positive relationships with others as we construct overly positive views of them (Howe, 2011).

Similarly, memory is affected by the emotional meaning of experiences. For example, in one experiment, researchers asked devoted Yankee or Red Sox fans about details of two decisive baseball championship games between the teams, one won by the Yankees and the other won by the Red Sox. Fans recalled details of the game their team won significantly more accurately than the game their team lost (see Figure 4; Breslin & Safer, 2011; Guida et al., 2013).

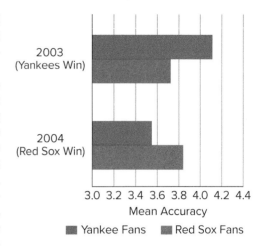

FIGURE 4 Yankee and Red Sox fans were more accurate recalling details of a championship game their team won than they were of a championship game that their team lost.

Source: Adapted from Breslin, C. W., & Safer, M. A. (2011). Effects of event valence on long-term memory for two baseball championship games. *Psychological Science, 20,* 1–5.

MEMORY IN THE COURTROOM: THE EYEWITNESS ON TRIAL

For Calvin Willis, the inadequate memories of two people cost him more than two decades of his life. Willis was the victim of mistaken identity when a young rape victim picked out his photo as the perpetrator of the rape. On that basis, he was tried, convicted, and sentenced to life in prison. Twenty-one years later, DNA testing showed that Willis was innocent and the victim's identification wrong. (Corsello, 2005)

Unfortunately, Willis is not the only victim to whom apologies have had to be made; many cases of mistaken identity have led to unjustified legal actions. Research on eyewitness identification of suspects, as well as on memory for other details of crimes, has shown that eyewitnesses are apt to make significant errors when they try to recall details of criminal activity—even if they are highly confident about their recollections. Because more than 75,000 prosecutions a year are totally based on eyewitness recollections, the problem is significant (Paterson, Kemp, & Ng, 2011; Lehrer, 2012; McCann et al., 2015).

One reason eyewitnesses tend to make significant errors is the impact of the weapons used in crimes. When a criminal perpetrator displays a gun or knife, it acts like a perceptual magnet, attracting the eyes of the witnesses. As a consequence, witnesses pay less attention to other details of the crime and are less able to recall what actually occurred (Zaitsu, 2007; Pickel, 2009; Sheahan et al., 2017).

The specific wording of questions posed to eyewitnesses by police officers or attorneys also can lead to memory errors. For example, in one experiment, the participants were shown a film of two cars crashing into each other. Some were then asked the question, "About how fast were the cars going when they *smashed* into each other?" On average, they estimated the speed to be 40.8 miles per hour. In contrast, when another group of participants was asked, "About how fast were the cars going when they *contacted* each other?" the average estimated speed was only 31.8 miles per hour (see Figure 5; Loftus & Palmer, 1974).

Although eyewitnesses are often confident in their recollections, in many cases, their confidence is misplaced. In fact, the relationship between confidence and accuracy

FIGURE 5 After viewing an accident involving two cars, the participants in a study were asked to estimate the speed of the two cars involved in the collision. Estimates varied substantially, depending on the way the question was worded.

Source: Adapted from Loftus, E. F., & Palmer, J. C. (1974). Reconstruction of automobile destruction: An example of the interface between language and memory. *Journal of Verbal Learning and Verbal Behavior, 13,* 585–589.

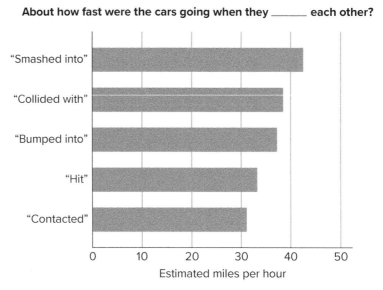

About how fast were the cars going when they _____ each other?

is often small and sometimes even negative; in some cases, the more confident a witness, the less accurate are their recollections. On the other hand, several conditions affect the relationship between eyewitness confidence and better accuracy. Specifically, accuracy improves when witnesses see only one suspect at a time; when the suspects don't look conspicuous in the lineup due to their clothing or ethnicity or race; and when the witness is told the offender is not necessarily in the lineup (Wixted & Wells, 2017).

Children's Reliability The problem of memory reliability becomes even more acute when children are witnesses because increasing evidence suggests that children's memories are highly vulnerable to the influence of others. For instance, in one experiment, 5- to 7-year-old girls who had just had routine physical examinations were shown an anatomically explicit doll. The girls were shown the doll's genital area and asked, "Did the doctor touch you here?" Three of the girls who did not have a vaginal or anal exam said that the doctor had in fact touched them in the genital area, and one of those three made up the detail "The doctor did it with a stick" (Brown, Goldstein, & Bjorklund, 2000).

Children's memories are especially susceptible to influence when the situation is highly emotional or stressful. For example, in trials in which there is significant pretrial publicity or in which alleged victims are questioned repeatedly, often by untrained interviewers, the memories of the alleged victims may be influenced by the types of questions they are asked (Goodman & Quas, 2008; Wright, Nash, & Wade, 2015).

Repressed and False Memories: Separating Truth from Fiction Consider the case of Paul Shanley, a Catholic priest. He was convicted and jailed for 12 years for sexual abuse of a victim who claimed he had no memory until adulthood of being abused as a child over a 6-year period. It was not until adulthood that he claimed his repressed memories gradually moved into consciousness. At that point, he reported clearly recalling his years of abuse, and on the basis of those previously repressed memories, the priest was convicted (Wolf, Guyer, & Sharpe, 2010; Otgaar, Howe, & Muris, 2017).

Repressed memories are apparent recollections of events that are initially so shocking that the mind responds by pushing them into the unconscious. Supporters of the notion of repressed memory (based on Freud's psychoanalytic theory) suggest that traumatic memories may remain hidden, possibly throughout a person's lifetime, unless they are triggered by some current circumstance, such as the probing that occurs during psychological therapy.

However, memory researcher Elizabeth Loftus, and many others, maintain that there is little evidence for the phenomenon of repressed memories. They believe that so-called repressed memories may well be inaccurate or even wholly false–representing *false memory.* For example, false memories develop when people are unable to recall

Paul Shanley, a Catholic priest, spent 12 years in jail for the purported sexual abuse of a child over a 6-year period. The victim only recalled the abuse years later when he was an adult.
©Charles Krupa-Pool/Getty Images

MEMORIES ARE MADE TO BE MEANINGFUL

One of Giacomo Regaldi's earliest memories is the day his dad took a day off from work to attend his third-grade clarinet recital and then took the whole family out for dinner to celebrate. Now a professional musician, Giacomo has long cherished this memory as evidence not only of his father's love but also of his approval of Giacomo's musical talents and aspirations.

The problem, though, is that it never happened–Giacomo had no clarinet recital in the third grade. He didn't even take up clarinet until 2 years after that. His father did attend a number of Giacomo's concerts and recitals, and he also did take the family out for dinner many times, but those events never happened together on the same day. Giacomo has taken fragmented memories of different events at different times and woven them together to form a single, cherished memory–although a false one.

This sort of memory error happens to people all the time. The reconstructive nature of memory means that we piece together facts and details of an event with our own interpretations, inferences, and assumptions about it. That memory can then become further contaminated with bits of information we learned later on, with fragments of memories of similar events or even with details that we merely imagined. Indeed, we may even sometimes

©Nicholas Burningham/Alamy Stock Photo

confuse entirely imaginary events with real memories (Pickrell et al., 2017).

These kinds of memory errors would seem to be problematic, and they can be in certain circumstances, such as when the memory of an eyewitness is a key piece of evidence in a criminal trial. But most of the time, they are harmless, and researchers are now learning that in fact, they may serve a useful purpose by reinforcing important parts of our identities. Certain memories take on a special importance because we incorporate them into a narrative; they become part of "the story of my life" and reveal something we value about ourselves,

such as a formative experience we believe shaped us into the person we are today.

In these cases, the accuracy of the memory matters less than what the memory means to us. We might, in our reimagining of the event, exaggerate its drama, minimize details that contradict our interpretation, and in other similar ways unintentionally mold the memory into a form that best fits our favored narrative. In the telling and retelling of a meaningful memory, we may embellish for effect, shift the emphasis to appeal to different listeners, add newly learned details, or incorporate reactions of people we told it to previously. Such alterations and embellishments often endear the memory to us even more strongly (Schacter, Guerin, & St. Jacques, 2011; Dunlop, Guo, & McAdams, 2016).

In one study illustrating false memories, students who opposed a tuition increase at their school were asked to write an essay in support of the tuition increase. Having taken that position and defended it, these students later tended to misremember their initial attitudes and recall that they were more in favor of an increase than they actually had been (Rodriguez & Strange, 2015).

At least sometimes, the value of memory may not lie in its accuracy as much as in the meaning it gives our lives.

> ### AP SKILL: SCIENTIFIC INVESTIGATION / DEFINE AND/OR APPLY CONCEPTS
>
> **1.** How might researchers test the accuracy of flashbulb memories?
> **2.** What age group is particularly vulnerable to constructive processes?

the source of a memory of a particular event about which they have only vague recollections. When the source of the memory becomes unclear or ambiguous, people may become confused about whether they actually experienced the event or whether it was imagined. Ultimately, people come to believe that the event actually occurred (Bernstein & Loftus, 2009a; Choi, Kensinger, & Rajaram, 2013; Lynn et al., 2015).

There is great controversy regarding the legitimacy of repressed memories. Many therapists give great weight to authenticity of repressed memories, and their views are supported by research showing that there are specific regions of the brain that help keep unwanted memories out of awareness. On the other side of the issue are researchers who maintain that there is insufficient scientific support for the existence of such memories. There is also a middle ground: memory researchers who suggest that false memories are a result of normal information processing. The challenge for those on all sides of the issue is to distinguish truth from fiction (Strange, Clifasefi, & Garry, 2007; Bernstein & Loftus, 2009b; also see *Applying Psychology in the 21st Century*).

autobiographical memory Our recollections of our own life experiences. (Module 21)

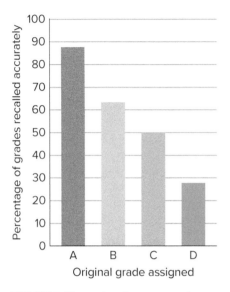

FIGURE 6 We tend to distort memories of unpleasant events. For example, college students are much more likely to accurately recall their good grades while inaccurately recalling their poor ones. Now that you know this, how well do you think you can recall your high school grades?

Source: Adapted from Bahrick, H. P., Hall, L. K., & Berger, S. A. (1996). Accuracy and distortion in memory for high school grades. *Psychological Science, 7,* 265–269.

AUTOBIOGRAPHICAL MEMORY: WHERE PAST MEETS PRESENT

Your memory of experiences in your own past may well be a fiction–or at least a distortion of what actually occurred. The same constructive processes that make us inaccurately recall the behavior of others also reduce the accuracy of autobiographical memories. **Autobiographical memory** is our recollections of our own life experiences. Autobiographical memories encompass the episodic memories we hold about ourselves (Sutin & Robins, 2007; Nalbantian, 2011).

For example, we tend to forget information about our past that is incompatible with the way in which we currently see ourselves. One study found that adults who were well adjusted but who had been treated for emotional problems during the early years of their lives tended to forget important but troubling childhood events, such as being in foster care. College students misremember their bad grades–but remember their good ones (see Figure 6; Walker, Skowronski, & Thompson, 2003; Kemps & Tiggemann, 2007; Stanley et al., 2017).

Similarly, when a group of 48-year-olds was asked to recall how they had responded on a questionnaire they had completed when they were high school freshmen, their accuracy was no better than chance. For example, although 61% of the questionnaire respondents said that playing sports and other physical activities was their favorite pastime, only 23% of the adults recalled it accurately (Offer et al., 2000).

It is not just certain kinds of events that are distorted; particular periods of life are remembered more easily than others. For example, when people reach late adulthood, they remember periods of life in which they experienced major transitions, such as attending college and working at their first jobs, better than they remember their middle-age years. Similarly, although most adults' earliest memories of their own lives are of events that occurred when they were toddlers, toddlers show evidence of recall of events that occurred when they were as young as 6 months old (Cordnoldi, De Beni, & Helstrup, 2007; Mace, Bernas, & Clevinger, 2015).

 # Exploring Diversity

Are There Cross-Cultural Differences in Memory?

Explorers who have visited parts of the world in which there is no written language sometimes return with tales of individuals with phenomenal memories. For instance, storytellers in some preliterate cultures recount long chronicles that include the names and activities of people over multiple generations.

Such feats of memory initially led experts to believe that people in preliterate societies develop a different, and perhaps better, type of memory than do those in cultures that employ a written language. They suggested that in a society that lacks writing, people are motivated to recall information with accuracy, especially information relating to tribal histories and traditions that would be lost if they were not passed down orally from one generation to another (Daftary & Meri, 2002; Berntsen & Rubin, 2004).

Today, however, memory researchers dismiss that view. For one thing, preliterate peoples don't have an exclusive claim to amazing memory feats. Some Hebrew scholars memorize thousands of pages of text and can recall the locations of particular words on the page. Similarly, poetry singers in the Balkans can recall thousands of lines of poetry. Even in cultures in which written language exists, then, astounding feats of memory are possible (Strathern & Stewart, 2003; Rubin et al., 2007).

Memory researchers now believe that there are both similarities and differences in memory across cultures. Basic memory processes seem to be similar. For example, short-term memory capacity, working memory, and the structure of long-term memory—the "hardware"—are universal and operate similarly in people in all cultures.

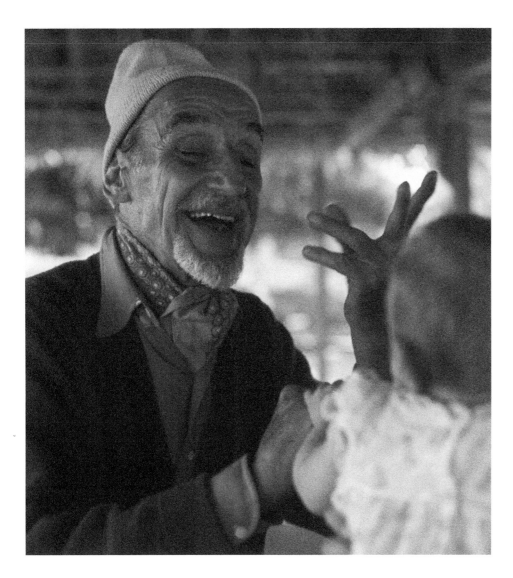

Storytellers in many cultures can recount hundreds of years of history in vivid detail. Research has found that this amazing ability is due less to basic memory processes than to the ways in which they acquire and retain information.
©Albert Moldvay/National Geographic/ Getty Images

In contrast, the way information is acquired and the degree to which it is rehearsed—the "software" of memory—do differ from culture to culture. Culture determines how people frame information initially, how much they practice learning it, and which strategies they use to recall it (Mack, 2003; Wang & Conway, 2006; Rubin et al., 2007).

AP | MODULE 21: RECALLING LONG-TERM MEMORIES

AP SUMMARY

- The levels-of-processing approach to memory suggests that the way in which information is initially perceived and analyzed determines the success with which it is recalled. At shallow levels, information is processed for physical and sensory aspects. At deeper levels, information is analyzed for meaning. The deeper the initial processing, the greater the recall.
- Explicit memory refers to intentional or conscious recollection of information. In contrast, implicit memory refers to memories of which people are not

consciously aware but that can affect subsequent performance and behavior.
- One way implicit memory (procedural) is studied is through experiments that use priming.
- Elizabeth Loftus is a memory researcher who investigates memory construction and eyewitness testimony. Her famous experiment involved participants viewing a car crash then being asked how fast the cars were going when they "smashed" vs. "contacted." The average estimated speed was impacted by the way the question was worded. In addition, Loftus has found little evidence for the validity of repressed memories.

- The tip-of-the-tongue phenomenon shows the difficulty of retrieving from long-term memory.
- Recall is more difficult than recognition. Retrieval cues are a major strategy for recalling information successfully.
- Flashbulb memories are memories centered on a specific, emotionally significant event. The memory is vivid, but the details can be inaccurate.
- The more distinctive and personally relevant a memory is, the more easily it can be retrieved.
- Source amnesia suggests we may not remember the source of our information. In addition, our level of attention and motivation during exposure to the material affects our ability to recall it.
- Memory is a constructive process: We relate memories to the meaning, guesses, and expectations we give to events. Specific information is recalled in terms of schemas, organized bodies of information stored in memory that bias the way new information is interpreted, stored, and recalled.
- Eyewitnesses are apt to make substantial errors when they try to recall the details of crimes. The problem of memory reliability becomes even more acute when the witnesses are children.
- There is great controversy regarding the legitimacy of repressed memories.
- Autobiographical memory is influenced by constructive processes.

AP KEY TERMS

tip-of-the-tongue phenomenon	implicit memory
recall	priming
recognition	flashbulb memories
levels-of-processing theory	constructive processes
explicit memory	schemas
	autobiographical memory

AP TEST PRACTICE

Section I: Multiple Choice

1. While studying for their psychology test Sasha looks over her notes multiple times, while Madison connects the material to her personal life. Madison will probably do better on the test due to
   A. priming
   B. levels of processing
   C. selective attention
   D. procedural memory
   E. proactive interference

2. Elizabeth Loftus' car crash experiment demonstrated that
   A. wording of questions influences memory
   B. forgetting declines sharply at first, then levels off
   C. seven plus or minus two items can be stored in short-term memory
   D. sensory memory operates as a kind of snapshot that stores information
   E. working memory uses a significant amount of cognitive resources

3. The results of the experiment, summarized in the graph above, best illustrate which psychological concept?
   A. Schemas
   B. Flashbulb memory
   C. Forgetting curve
   D. Levels-of-processing theory
   E. Constructive processes of memory

Section II: Free Response

Maria witnessed a burglary and now has to give her report to the police.
A. Describe how the following concepts can help her memory.
   • Recognition
   • Deep processing

B. Describe how the following concepts can hinder her memory.
   • Schema
   • Source amnesia
   • Tip-of-the-tongue
   • Flashbulb memory

Module 22
Forgetting: When Memory Fails

He could not remember his childhood friends, the house he grew up in, or what he had eaten for breakfast that morning. H. M., as he is referred to in the scientific literature, had lost his ability to remember anything beyond a few minutes, the result of experimental surgery intended to minimize his epileptic seizures. But the removal of his brain's hippocampus and the loss of his temporal lobes quite literally erased H. M.'s past. He had enjoyed a normal memory until he underwent the operation at age 27. After that, H. M. said, every moment felt like waking from a dream. He never knew where he was or the identities of the people around him (Milner, 2005).

As the case of H. M. illustrates, a person without a normal memory faces severe difficulties. All of us who have experienced even routine instances of forgetting—such as not remembering an acquaintance's name or a fact on a test—understand the very real consequences of memory failure.

Of course, memory failure is also essential to remembering important information. The ability to forget inconsequential details about experiences, people, and objects helps us avoid being burdened and distracted by trivial stores of meaningless data. Forgetting helps keep unwanted and unnecessary information from interfering with retrieving information that is wanted and necessary (Schooler & Hertwig, 2012).

Forgetting also permits us to form general impressions and recollections. For example, the reason our friends consistently look familiar to us is because we're able to forget their clothing, facial blemishes, and other transient features that change from one occasion to the next. Instead, our memories are based on a summary of various critical features—a far more economical use of our memory capabilities.

Finally, forgetting provides a practical educational benefit: When we have forgotten something and then are forced to relearn it, we're more likely to remember it better in the future (Bjork, 2015; Boser, 2017).

The first attempts to study forgetting were made by German psychologist Hermann Ebbinghaus about 100 years ago. Using himself as the only participant in his study, Ebbinghaus memorized lists of three-letter nonsense syllables—meaningless sets of two consonants with a vowel in between, such as FIW and BOZ. By measuring how easy it was to relearn a given list of words after varying periods of time had passed since the initial learning, he found that forgetting occurred systematically, as shown in Figure 1. As the figure indicates, the most rapid forgetting occurs in the first 9 hours, particularly in the first hour. After 9 hours, the rate of forgetting slows and declines little, even after the passage of many days.

Despite his primitive methods, Ebbinghaus's study had an important influence on subsequent research, and his basic conclusions have been upheld. There is almost always a strong initial decline in memory, followed by a more gradual drop over time. Furthermore, relearning of previously mastered material is almost always faster than starting from scratch, whether the material is academic information or a motor skill such as serving a tennis ball (Wixted & Carpenter, 2007; Radvansky, Pettijohn, & Kim, 2015).

AP® LEARNING TARGETS

- Identify the contributions of key researchers in cognitive psychology.

- Outline the principles that underlie construction and encoding of memories.

- Describe strategies for memory improvement and typical memory errors.

FIGURE 1 In his classic work, Ebbinghaus found that the most rapid forgetting occurs in the first 9 hours after exposure to new material. However, the rate of forgetting then slows down and declines very little even after many days have passed. Check your own memory: What were you doing exactly 2 hours ago? What were you doing last Tuesday at 5 P.M.? Which information is easier to retrieve?

Source: Adapted from Ebbinghaus, H. (1885/1913). *Memory: A contribution to experimental psychology* (H. A. Roger & C. E. Bussenius, Trans.). New York: Columbia University Press.

Why We Forget

Why do we forget? One reason is that we may not have paid attention to the material in the first place—a failure of *encoding*. For example, if you live in the United States, you probably have been exposed to thousands of pennies during your life. Despite this experience, you probably don't have a clear sense of the details of the coin. (See this for yourself by looking at Figure 2.) Consequently, the reason for your memory failure is that you probably never encoded the information into long-term memory initially. Obviously, if information was not placed in memory to start with, there is no way the information can be recalled.

But what about material that has been encoded into memory and that can't later be remembered? Several processes account for memory failures, including decay, interference, and cue-dependent forgetting.

FIGURE 2 One of these pennies is the real thing. Can you find it? Why is this task harder than it seems at first?

Source: Adapted from Nickerson, R. S., & Adams, M. J. (1979). Long-term memory for a common object. *Cognitive Psychology, 11,* 297.

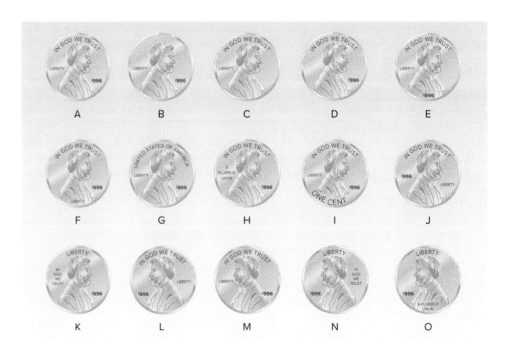

Decay is the loss of information in memory through nonuse. This explanation for forgetting assumes that *memory traces,* the physical changes that take place in the brain when new material is learned, simply fade away or disintegrate over time (Grann, 2007).

Although there is evidence that decay does occur, this does not seem to be the complete explanation for forgetting. Often there is no relationship between how long ago a person was exposed to information and how well that information is recalled. If decay explained all forgetting, we would expect that the more time that has elapsed between the initial learning of information and our attempt to recall it, the harder it would be to remember it because there would be more time for the memory trace to decay. Yet people who take several consecutive tests on the same material often recall more of the initial information when taking later tests than they did on earlier tests. If decay were operating, we would expect the opposite to occur (Hardt, Nader, & Nadel, 2013; Sachser et al., 2017).

Because decay does not fully account for forgetting, memory specialists have proposed an additional mechanism: interference. In **interference,** information stored in memory disrupts the recall of other information stored in memory. For example, if I'm trying to recall my college classmate Jake's name and all I can remember is the name of another classmate, James, interference may be at work (Solesio-Jofre et al., 2011; Ecker, Tay, & Brown, 2015).

To distinguish between decay and interference, think of the two processes in terms of a row of books on a library shelf. In decay, the old books are constantly crumbling and rotting away, leaving room for new arrivals. Interference processes suggest that new books knock the old ones off the shelf, where they become hard to find or even totally inaccessible.

Finally, forgetting may occur because of **cue-dependent forgetting,** forgetting that occurs when there are insufficient retrieval cues to rekindle information that is in memory. For example, you may not be able to remember where you lost a set of keys until you mentally walk through your day, thinking of each place you visited. When you think of the place where you lost the keys–say, the library–the retrieval cue of the library may be sufficient to help you recall that you left them on the desk in the library. Without that retrieval cue, you may be unable to recall the location of the keys (Weller et al., 2013).

Most research suggests that interference and cue-dependent forgetting are key processes in forgetting. We forget things mainly because new memories interfere with the retrieval of old ones or because appropriate retrieval cues are unavailable, not because the memory trace has decayed (Radvansky, 2010).

Proactive and Retroactive Interference: The Before and After of Forgetting

There are actually two sorts of interference that influence forgetting. One is proactive interference, and the other is retroactive interference (Bunting, 2006; Jacoby et al., 2007; Oberauer, Awh, & Sutterer, 2017).

In **proactive interference,** information learned earlier disrupts the recall of newer material. Suppose, as a student of foreign languages, you first learned French in the 10th grade, and then in the 11th grade you took Spanish. When in the 12th grade you take a college subject achievement test in Spanish, you may find you have difficulty recalling the Spanish translation of a word because all you can think of is its French equivalent.

In contrast, **retroactive interference** occurs when material that was learned later disrupts the retrieval of information that was learned earlier. If, for example, you have difficulty on a French subject achievement test because of your more recent exposure to Spanish, retroactive interference is the culprit (see Figure 3). Similarly, retroactive interference can account for the lack of accuracy of eyewitness memories, as newer

decay The loss of information in memory through its nonuse. (Module 22)

interference The phenomenon by which information in memory disrupts the recall of other information. (Module 22)

cue-dependent forgetting Forgetting that occurs when there are insufficient retrieval cues to rekindle information that is in memory. (Module 22)

 Study Alert
Memory loss through decay comes from nonuse of the memory; memory loss through interference is due to the presence of other information in memory.

proactive interference Interference in which information learned earlier disrupts the recall of material learned later. (Module 22)

retroactive interference Interference in which material that was learned later disrupts the retrieval of information that was learned earlier. (Module 22)

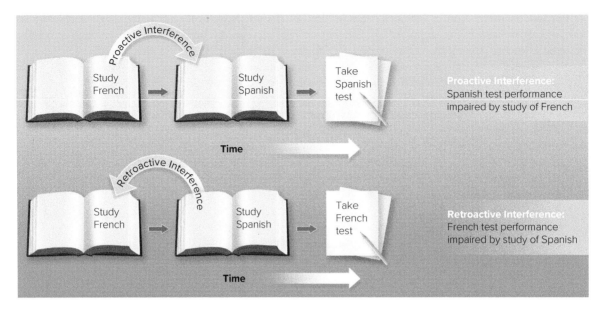

FIGURE 3 Proactive interference occurs when material learned earlier interferes with the recall of newer material. In this example, studying French before studying Spanish interferes with performance on a Spanish test. In contrast, retroactive interference exists when material learned after initial exposure to other material interferes with the recall of the first material. In this case, retroactive interference occurs when recall of French is impaired because of later exposure to Spanish.

PsychTech

Having trouble remembering something on your computer screen? According to research by Connor Diemand-Yauman (2010) and colleagues, changing the font into something *harder* to read may make it easier to remember. The explanation is that the unusual font forces us to concentrate more intently on the information, making it more memorable.

information about a crime obtained from newspaper accounts may disrupt the initial memory of the observation of the crime.

One way to remember the difference between proactive and retroactive interference is to keep in mind that *pro*active interference progresses in time—the past interferes with the present. In contrast, *retro*active interference retrogresses in time, working backward as the present interferes with the past.

Although the concepts of proactive and retroactive interference illustrate how material may be forgotten, they still do not explain whether forgetting is caused by the actual loss or modification of information or by problems in the retrieval of information. Most research suggests that material that has apparently been lost because of interference can eventually be recalled if appropriate stimuli are presented, but the question has not been fully answered (Radvansky, 2010).

Memory Dysfunctions: Afflictions of Forgetting

Memory loss creeps up on its victims. It starts with little things such as misplacing keys or glasses. Then, you forget the names of common household items, and you miss appointments. Next, you can't drive in traffic without becoming confused and anxious. You try to hide what's happening, but everybody knows. Finally, your lapses become more consequential: You nearly get run over; you have a traffic accident. When you can no longer do the things you rely on for everyday living, such as getting dressed or making coffee, you know what's going on, though you're helpless to change it.

Alzheimer's disease A progressive brain disorder that leads to a gradual and irreversible decline in cognitive abilities. (Modules 22, 39)

These memory problems are symptomatic of **Alzheimer's disease,** a progressive brain disorder that leads to a gradual and irreversible decline in cognitive abilities. Alzheimer's is the fourth-leading cause of death among adults in the United States, affecting an estimated 5 million people.

In the beginning, Alzheimer's symptoms appear as simple forgetfulness of things such as appointments and birthdays. As the disease progresses, memory loss becomes more profound, and even the simplest tasks—such as using a telephone—are forgotten.

Ultimately, victims may lose their ability to speak or comprehend language, and physical deterioration sets in, leading to death.

The causes of Alzheimer's disease are not fully understood. Increasing evidence suggests that Alzheimer's results from an inherited susceptibility to a defect in the production of the protein beta amyloid, which is necessary for the maintenance of nerve cell connections. When the synthesis of beta amyloid goes awry, large clumps of cells form, triggering inflammation and the deterioration of nerve cells in the brain (Hyman, 2011; Tan, Yu, & Tan, 2015).

From the perspective of...

A Health-Care Provider What sorts of activities might health-care providers offer their patients to help them combat the memory loss of Alzheimer's disease?

©Rubberball/Getty Images

Alzheimer's disease is one of a number of memory dysfunctions. Another is **amnesia,** memory loss that occurs without other mental difficulties. The type of amnesia immortalized in countless Hollywood films involves a victim who receives a blow to the head and is unable to remember anything from his or her past. In reality, amnesia of this type, known as retrograde amnesia, is quite rare. In **retrograde amnesia,** memory is lost for occurrences prior to a certain event but not for new events. Usually, lost memories gradually reappear, although full restoration may take as long as several years. In certain cases, some memories are lost forever. But even in cases of severe memory loss, the loss is generally selective. For example, although people suffering from retrograde amnesia may be unable to recall friends and family members, they still may be able to play complicated card games or knit a sweater quite well (Verfaellie & Keane, 2002; Bright, Buckman, & Fradera, 2006).

A second type of amnesia is exemplified by people who remember nothing of their current activities. In **anterograde amnesia,** loss of memory occurs for events that follow an injury. Information cannot be transferred from short-term to long-term memory, resulting in the inability to remember anything other than what was in long-term storage before the injury (Gilboa, Winocur, & Rosenbaum, 2006).

Amnesia is also a result of **Korsakoff's syndrome,** a disease that afflicts long-term alcoholics. Although many of their intellectual abilities may be intact, Korsakoff's sufferers display a strange array of symptoms, including hallucinations and a tendency to repeat the same story over and over (Wester et al., 2013; Scalzo, Bowden, & Hillborn, 2015).

Fortunately, most of us have intact memory, and the occasional failures we suffer may actually be preferable to having a perfect memory. Consider, for instance, the case of a man who had total recall. After reading passages of Dante's *The Divine Comedy* in Italian—a language he did not speak—he was able to repeat them from memory some 15 years later. He could memorize lists of 50 unrelated words and recall them at will more than a decade later. He could even repeat the same list of words backward, if asked (Luria, 1968).

Such a skill at first may seem to be enviable, but it actually presented quite a problem. The man's memory became a jumble of lists of words, numbers, and names; when he tried to relax, his mind was filled with images. Even reading was difficult because every word evoked a flood of thoughts from the past that interfered with his ability to understand the meaning of what he was reading. Partially as a consequence of the man's unusual memory, psychologist A. R. Luria, who studied his case, found him to be a "disorganized and rather dull-witted person" (Luria, 1968). We might be grateful, then, that forgetfulness plays a role in our lives.

amnesia Memory loss that occurs without other mental difficulties. (Module 22)

retrograde amnesia Amnesia in which memory is lost for occurrences prior to a certain event but not for new events. (Module 22)

anterograde amnesia Amnesia in which memory is lost for events that follow an injury. (Module 22)

Korsakoff's syndrome A disease that afflicts long-term alcoholics, leaving some abilities intact but including hallucinations and a tendency to repeat the same story. (Module 22)

Study Alert
Except for Alzheimer's disease, memory disorders are relatively rare.

BECOMING AN INFORMED CONSUMER
of Psychology

Improving Your Memory

Apart from the advantages of forgetting, say, a bad date, most of us would like to find ways to improve our memories. Among the effective strategies for studying and remembering course material are:

- *Rely on organization cues.* Recall material you read in textbooks or online by organizing the material in memory the first time you read it. For example, use cues such as chapter outlines or learning objectives. If you take advantage of these "advance organizers," you can make connections, see relationships among the various facts, and process the material at a deeper level, which in turn will later aid recall (Korur, Toker, & Eryilmaz, 2016).

- *Take effective notes.* "Less is more" is perhaps the best advice for taking lecture notes that facilitate recall. Rather than trying to jot down every detail of a lecture, it is better to listen and think about the material, and take down the main points. In effective note taking, thinking about the material when you first hear it is more important than writing it down. This is one reason that borrowing someone else's notes is a bad idea; you will have no framework in memory that you can use to understand them (Feldman, 2017).

- *Practice, practice, practice.* Although practice does not necessarily make perfect, it helps. Use *overlearning,* the process of studying and rehearsing material well beyond your initial mastery of it. Lots of research shows that people demonstrate better long-term recall when they overlearn rather than when they stop practicing just after they initially learn the material (Shibata et al., 2017).

- *Use the keyword technique.* If you are studying a foreign language, try pairing a foreign word with a common English word that has a similar sound. This English word is known as the *keyword*. For example, to learn the Spanish word for duck (*pato,* pronounced *pot-o*), you might choose the keyword *pot*. Once you have thought of a keyword, think of an image in which the the Spanish word *pato* is interacting with the English keyword. For example, you might envision a duck being cooked in a pot to remember the word *pato* (Wyra, Lawson, & Hungi, 2007).

- *Talk to yourself.* If you have trouble remembering names of people who you have recently met, one way to help yourself is to say their names out loud when you are first introduced. It will make it easier to retrieve the information later because the information is stored in additional ways in your brain.

- *Be skeptical about claims that certain drugs improve memory.* Advertisements for vitamins with ginkgo biloba or a "Mental Sharpness Product" would have you believe that taking a drug or supplement can improve your memory. Not so, according to the results of numerous studies. No research has shown that commercial memory enhancers are effective (McDaniel, Maier, & Einstein, 2002; Burns, Bryan, & Nettelbeck, 2006).

AP MODULE 22: FORGETTING: WHEN MEMORY FAILS

AP SUMMARY

- Ebbinghaus studied forgetting. To do this he memorized lists of three-letter nonsense syllables. After varying time periods, he measured how easy it was to relearn the list of words. He found a forgetting curve: A strong initial decline in memory, followed by a more gradual drop.

- A lack of attention results in encoding failure.

- Several processes account for memory failure, including decay, interference, and cue-dependent forgetting.

- There are two main types of interference that lead to forgetting. Proactive interference in which old information disrupts retrieval of new information and retroactive interference in which new information disrupts retrieval of old information.
- Among the memory dysfunctions are Alzheimer's disease and amnesia. Korsakoff's syndrome is a disease that afflicts long-term alcoholics, resulting in memory impairment.
- Techniques for improving memory include the keyword technique to memorize foreign language vocabulary; organizing text material and lecture notes; talking to yourself; and practice and rehearsal, leading to overlearning.

AP KEY TERMS

decay	Alzheimer's disease
interference	amnesia
cue-dependent forgetting	retrograde amnesia
proactive interference	anterograde amnesia
retroactive interference	Korsakoff's syndrome

AP TEST PRACTICE

Section I: Multiple Choice

1. José just started a new school year, but his old locker combination keeps getting in the way of him remembering his new locker combination. This is an example of
   - **A.** source amnesia
   - **B.** retrograde amnesia
   - **C.** anterograde amnesia
   - **D.** proactive interference
   - **E.** retroactive interference

2. During class, Cody was thinking about the upcoming dance rather than paying attention to his teacher. When it came time to take the test his mind was blank. This problem in recall was most likely due to
   - **A.** retrieval failure
   - **B.** priming
   - **C.** amnesia
   - **D.** repression
   - **E.** encoding failure

3. Hermann Ebbinghaus discovered that the most rapid forgetting occurs in the first
   - **A.** 9 hours
   - **B.** 48 hours
   - **C.** 4 days
   - **D** 7 days
   - **E.** 2 weeks

Section II: Free Response

Henry Gustav Molaison, commonly known as H.M., was a patient who had his medial temporal lobes, including most of his hippocampi, removed to minimize his epileptic seizures. After the surgery his seizures ceased, but his memory was forever impacted. He was unable to form new memories or recall memories up to an eleven year period before his surgery. He could not learn new words, songs, or faces. Also, he could not remember personal events, such as his birthday, or general knowledge, such as the current president. Surprisingly, he was able to learn new motor skills, such as completing a maze or mirror-drawing.

A. Explain how the following relate to H.M.
   - Hippocampus
   - Explicit memory
   - Procedural memory
   - Anterograde amnesia

B. Describe how the following research terms relate to H.M.
   - Advantage of case study
   - Confidentiality
   - Magnetic resonance imaging (MRI scan)

LOOKING *Back*

EPILOGUE

Our examination of memory has highlighted the processes of encoding, storage, and retrieval, and theories about how these processes occur. We also encountered several phenomena relating to memory, including the tip-of-the-tongue phenomenon and flashbulb memories. Above all, we observed that memory is a constructive process by which interpretations, expectations, and guesses contribute to the nature of our memories.

VISUAL SUMMARY 7 Memory

MODULE 20 The Foundations of Memory

Memory: Encoding, storing, and retrieving information

Chunks

Groupings of stimuli stored as a unit

Capacity is seven chunks, plus or minus two

Long-term memory

Declarative memory
(factual information)
Example: George Washington was the first president of the United States

Procedural memory
(skills and habits)
Example: Riding a bicycle

Semantic memory
(general memory)
Example: George Washington wore a wig

Episodic memory
(personal knowledge)
Example: Remembering your visit to Washington's home, Mount Vernon

MODULE 21 Recalling Long-Term Memories

Retrieval Cues: Stimuli that allow recall of information stored in long-term memory
- Recall: Remembering specific information
- Recognition: Knowing whether one has been previously exposed to given information

Levels of Processing Theory: Recall depends on how much the information was processed when it was first encountered

Explicit Memories: Conscious recall of information

Implicit Memories: Memories of which people are not consciously aware

Flashbulb Memories: Memories of a specific, important, or surprising emotionally significant event that are recalled easily and with vivid imagery

Constructive Processes: Processes in which memories are influenced by the meaning we give to events

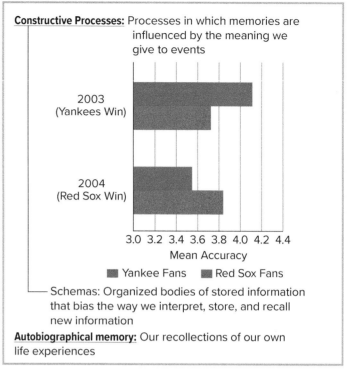

Schemas: Organized bodies of stored information that bias the way we interpret, store, and recall new information

Autobiographical memory: Our recollections of our own life experiences

MODULE 22 Forgetting: When Memory Fails

Decay: Loss of information through nonuse

Cue-dependent forgetting: Forgetting that occurs when insufficient retrieval cues are available

Interference: Information in memory disrupts the recall of other information

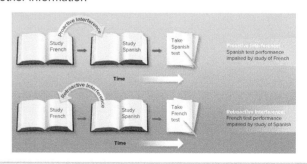

(MODULE 20) (Photo): ©C Squared Studios/Getty Images; Source: Adapted from Baddeley, A., Chincotta, D., & Adlam, A. (2001). Working memory and the control of action: Evidence from task switching. *Journal of Experimental Psychology: General, 130,* 641–657. (MODULE 21) (Photo): ©Digital Vision/SuperStock; Source: Adapted from Breslin, C. W., & Safer, M. A. (2011). Effects of event valence on long-term memory for two baseball championship games. *Psychological Science, 20,* 1–5. (MODULE 22) Source: Adapted from Ebbinghaus, H. (1885/1913). *Memory: A contribution to experimental psychology* (H. A. Roger & C. E. Bussenius, Trans.). New York: Columbia University Press.

©Chris Robbins/Moodboard/Glow Images

CHAPTER 8
Cognition and Language

AP' ESSENTIAL QUESTIONS
- How do our experiences influence our behaviors and mental processes?

AP' LEARNING TARGETS FOR CHAPTER 8

- Identify the contributions of key researchers in cognitive psychology.

- Synthesize how biological, cognitive, and cultural factors converge to facilitate acquisition, development, and use of language.

PROLOGUE *MIND GAMES*

Shawn Green, a research assistant in a psychology lab at the University of Rochester, was designing a computerized test to study neuroplasticity—the brain's ability to rewire itself in response to new experiences. The test would measure the ability to find particular shapes in a busy visual scene. To try out the test, he took it himself. He discovered what he felt must be an error in the test: he consistently achieved perfect scores, a result not at all in keeping with the results from similar tests at other labs.

Green decided to administer the test to other people. He recruited some of his friends, and astonishingly, they too achieved perfect scores. He tried the test one more time, this time on his supervisor. In contrast to Green and his friends, her performance wasn't exceptional; she had an average score.

What was going on? Eventually, Green and his supervisor realized that he and his friends shared one key trait that enabled them to overachieve on the neuroplasticity test: they were all avid video-game players, spending hours each week online subduing zombies and other villains (Bavelier & Green, 2016).

LOOKING *Ahead*

It turns out that video games, often criticized for producing such negative traits as aggression and mindless addiction, can, under the right circumstances, positively affect some kinds of cognitive abilities. Certain types of games can improve reaction times, decision making under pressure, fine-motor control, task switching, spatial sense, and, especially, attention focusing and distribution.

Results such these have led researchers to consider developing games for therapeutic uses to address targeted types of cognitive deficits induced by aging or trauma (Granic, Lobel, & Engels, 2014; Gabbiandini & Greitemeyer, 2017).

Adapting to new experiences and honing new or existing cognitive skills are just two of the many tasks that our own amazing human computer—the brain—can accomplish in the course of our daily lives, even though we may have little or no idea how it does so. The mystery of how the brain processes language and all its nuances—as well as how it uses information to solve problems and make decisions—is the subject to which we now turn.

Cognitive psychology is the branch of psychology that focuses on the study of higher mental processes, including thinking, language, memory, problem solving, knowing, reasoning, judging, and decision making. Although the realm of cognitive psychology is broad, we will focus on three major topics. The first topic we consider in this chapter is thinking and reasoning. Then we examine different strategies for approaching problems, means of generating solutions, and ways of making judgments about the usefulness and accuracy of solutions. Finally, we discuss how language is developed and acquired, its basic characteristics, and the relationship between language and thought.

cognitive psychology The branch of psychology that focuses on the study of higher mental processes, including thinking, language, memory, problem solving, knowing, reasoning, judging, and decision making. (Module 23)

Module 23
Thinking and Reasoning

What are you thinking about at this moment?

The mere ability to pose such a question underscores the distinctive nature of the human ability to think. No other species contemplates, analyzes, recollects, or plans the way humans do. Understanding what thinking is, however, goes beyond knowing that we think. Philosophers, for example, have argued for generations about the meaning of thinking, with some placing it at the core of human beings' understanding of their own existence.

Psychologists define **thinking** as brain activity in which we mentally manipulate information, including words, visual images, sounds, or other data. Thinking transforms information into new and different forms, allowing us to answer questions, make decisions, solve problems, or make plans.

Although a clear sense of what specifically occurs when we think remains elusive, our understanding of the nature of the fundamental elements involved in thinking is growing. We begin by considering our use of mental images and concepts, the building blocks of thought.

Mental Images: Examining the Mind's Eye

Think of your best friend.

Chances are that you "see" some kind of visual image when asked to think of her or him, or any other person or object, for that matter. To some cognitive psychologists, such mental images constitute a major part of thinking.

Mental images are representations in the mind of an object or event. They are not just visual representations; our ability to "hear" a tune in our heads also relies on a mental image. In fact, every sensory modality may produce corresponding mental images (De Bini, Pazzaglia, & Gardini, 2007; Gardini et al., 2009; Koçak et al., 2011).

Research has found that our mental images have many of the properties of the actual stimuli they represent. For example, it takes the mind longer to scan mental images of large objects than small ones, just as the eye takes longer to scan an actual large object than to scan an actual small one. Similarly, we are able to manipulate and rotate mental images of objects, just as we are able to manipulate and rotate them in the real world (Mast & Kosslyn, 2002; Zacks, 2008; Reisberg, 2013; see Figure 1).

Some experts see the production of mental images as a way to improve various skills. For instance, many athletes use mental imagery in their training. Basketball players may try to produce vivid and detailed images of the court, the basket, the ball, and the noisy crowd. They may visualize themselves taking a foul shot, watching the ball, and hearing the swish as it goes through the net. And it works: The use of mental imagery can lead to improved performance in sports (Moran, 2009; Velentzas, Heinen, & Schack, 2011; Wimmer et al., 2017).

Mental imagery may improve other types of skills as well. For example, piano players who simply mentally rehearse an exercise show brain activity that is virtually identical to that of the people who actually practice the exercise manually. Apparently, carrying out the task involved the same network of brain cells as the network used in mentally rehearsing it (Sanders et al., 2008; Davidson-Kelly et al., 2015).

AP® LEARNING TARGETS

- Identify problem-solving strategies as well as factors that influence their effectiveness.

thinking Brain activity in which people mentally manipulate information, including words, visual images, sounds, or other data. (Module 23)

mental images Representations in the mind of an object or event. (Module 23)

PsychTech

Researcher Adam Wilson has developed a method of tweeting by thinking. The process involves being outfitted with electrodes that react to changes in brain activity. It's slow going, though: the fastest tweeters by thinking are able to create tweets at only 8 characters per minute.

FIGURE 1 Try to mentally rotate one of each pair of patterns to see if it is the same as the other member of that pair. It's likely that the farther you have to mentally rotate a pattern, the longer it will take to decide if the patterns match one another. Does this mean that it will take you longer to visualize a map of the world than a map of the United States? Why or why not?

Source: Adapted from Shepard, R. N., & Metzler, J. (1971). Mental rotation of three-dimensional objects. *Science, 171*(3972), 701–703.

(a)

(b)

(c)

From the perspective of...

A Human Resources Specialist How might you use the research on mental imagery to improve employees' performance?

©Dex Image/Getty Images

Many athletes use mental imagery to focus on a task, a process they call "getting in the zone." What are some other occupations that require the use of strong mental imagery?

©Echo/Getty Images

Concepts: Categorizing the World

If someone asks you what is in your kitchen cabinet, you might answer with a detailed list of items (a jar of peanut butter, three boxes of macaroni and cheese, six unmatched dinner plates, and so forth). More likely, though, you would respond by naming some broader categories, such as "food" and "dishes."

Using such categories reflects the operation of concepts. **Concepts** are mental groupings of similar objects, events, or people. Concepts enable us to organize complex phenomena into cognitive categories that are easier to understand and remember (Connolly, 2007; Kreppner et al., 2011; Mack, Love, & Preston, 2016).

Concepts help us classify newly encountered objects on the basis of our past experience. For example, we can surmise that someone tapping a handheld screen is probably using some kind of computer or tablet, even if we have never encountered that specific model before. Ultimately, concepts influence behavior. We would assume, for instance, that it might be appropriate to pet an animal after determining that it is a dog, whereas we would behave differently after classifying the animal as a wolf.

When cognitive psychologists first studied concepts, they focused on those that were clearly defined by a unique set of properties or features. For example, an equilateral triangle is a closed shape that has three sides of equal length. If an object has these characteristics, it is an equilateral triangle; if it does not, it is not an equilateral triangle.

Other concepts–often those with the most relevance to our everyday lives–are more ambiguous and difficult to define. For instance, broader concepts such as "table" and "bird" have a set of general, relatively loose characteristic features, rather than unique, clearly defined properties that distinguish an example of the concept from a nonexample.

When we consider these more ambiguous concepts, we usually think in terms of examples called prototypes. **Prototypes** are typical, highly representative examples of a concept that correspond to our mental image or best example of the concept. For instance, for most people, the prototype of a dog is something like the common beagle, rather than the relatively rare shih tzu, Finnish spitz, otterhound, or mudi (breeds you've probably never heard of). Similarly, although a robin and an ostrich are both examples of birds, the robin is an example that comes to most people's minds far more readily. Consequently, robin is a prototype of the concept "bird."

Relatively high agreement exists among people in particular cultures about which examples of a concept are prototypes as well as which examples are not. For instance, most people in Western cultures consider cars and trucks good examples of vehicles, whereas elevators and wheelbarrows are not considered very good examples. Consequently, cars and trucks are prototypes of the concept of a vehicle (see Figure 2).

Concepts enable us to think about and understand more readily the complex world in which we live. For example, the suppositions we make about the reasons for other

concepts Mental groupings of similar objects, events, or people. (Module 23)

prototypes Typical, highly representative examples of a concept. (Module 23)

 Study Alert
Figure 2 will help you remember that prototypes represent "best" or most common examples of a particular concept. For example, a Prius might be a prototype of the concept of "hybrid car."

How do you view these dogs? Whether you categorize them as guard dogs (left and middle), as service dogs (middle and right), or simply as three dogs, you are using concepts.
(all): ©Purestock/SuperStock

FIGURE 2 Prototypes are typical, highly representative examples of a concept. For instance, a highly typical prototype of the concept "furniture" is a chair, whereas a stove is not a good prototype. High agreement exists within a culture about which examples of a concept are prototypes.

(chair): ©Stockbyte/Getty Images; (car): ©McGraw-Hill Education/Gary He, photographer; (gun): ©suradin/123RF; (peas): ©Isabelle Rozenbaum & Frederic Cirou/PhotoAlto/Getty Images; Source: Adapted from Rosch, E., & Mervis, C. B. (1975). Family resemblances: Studies in the internal structure of categories. *Cognitive Psychology, 7,* 573–605

Concept Category

Ranking of Prototype	Furniture	Vehicle	Weapon	Vegetable
1—Most Typical	Chair	Car	Gun	Peas
2	Sofa	Truck	Knife	Carrots
3	Table	Bus	Sword	String beans
4	Dresser	Motorcycle	Bomb	Spinach
5	Desk	Train	Hand grenade	Broccoli
6	Bed	Trolley car	Spear	Asparagus
7	Bookcase	Bicycle	Cannon	Corn
8	Footstool	Airplane	Bow and arrow	Cauliflower
9	Lamp	Boat	Club	Brussels sprouts
10	Piano	Tractor	Tank	Lettuce
11	Cushion	Cart	Tear gas	Beets
12	Mirror	Wheelchair	Whip	Tomato
13	Rug	Tank	Ice pick	Lima beans
14	Radio	Raft	Fists	Eggplant
15—Least Typical	Stove	Sled	Rocket	Onion

people's behavior are based on the ways in which we classify behavior. Hence, our conclusion about a person who washes her hands 20 times a day could vary, depending on whether we place her behavior within the conceptual framework of a health-care worker or a mental patient. Similarly, physicians make diagnoses by drawing on concepts and prototypes of symptoms that they learned about in medical school. Finally, concepts and prototypes facilitate our efforts to draw suitable conclusions through the cognitive process we turn to next: reasoning.

Reasoning: Making Up Your Mind

Professors deciding when students' assignments are due.

An employer determining who to hire out of a pool of job applicants.

The president concluding that it is necessary to send troops to a foreign nation.

What do these three situations have in common? Each requires *reasoning,* the process by which information is used to draw conclusions and make decisions.

Although philosophers and logicians have considered the foundations of reasoning for centuries, it is only relatively recently that cognitive psychologists have begun to investigate how people reason and make decisions. Their efforts have contributed to our understanding of formal reasoning processes as well as the cognitive shortcuts we routinely use–shortcuts that sometimes may lead our reasoning capabilities astray (Johnson-Laird, 2006).

FORMAL REASONING

When (the fictitious) Sherlock Holmes sought to solve a crime, he carefully observed the scene of the crime and then made informed guesses about what those observations meant. For example, in one story, the ever-observant Holmes noted that cuts on the side of a shoe suggested that a potential criminal must have had mud on his shoes that needed to be scraped off.

The type of reasoning that Holmes used is known as deductive reasoning. **Deductive reasoning** is reasoning from the general to the specific. Psychologists, like all scientists, use deductive reasoning when they start with a general, broad theory, then derive a hypothesis from the theory, and ultimately test the hypothesis by collecting data to arrive at a conclusion.

The other major class of reasoning is inductive reasoning. **Inductive reasoning** is reasoning from the specific to the general. Inductive reasoning is data driven, in that we accumulate pieces of information and put them together to form a conclusion. That's what psychologists do when they study a sample of participants (for instance, 20 color-blind college students), and then they use the information they observe to form a conclusion about the broader population from which the sample is drawn (all color-blind college students).

If we consistently used deductive and inductive reasoning, we would make decisions and solve problems quite logically. However, as we'll see next, that often doesn't happen, leading to less-than-optimal results.

deductive reasoning Reasoning from the general to the specific. (Module 23)

inductive reasoning Reasoning from the specific to the general. (Module 23)

ALGORITHMS AND HEURISTICS

When faced with making a decision, we often turn to various kinds of cognitive short-cuts, known as algorithms and heuristics, to help us. An **algorithm** is a rule that, if applied appropriately, guarantees a solution to a problem. We can use an algorithm even if we cannot understand why it works. For example, you may know that you can find the length of the third side of a right triangle by using the formula $a^2 + b^2 = c^2$, although you may not have the foggiest notion of the mathematical principles behind the formula.

For many problems and decisions, however, no algorithm is available. In those instances, we may be able to use heuristics to help us. A **heuristic** is a thinking strategy that may lead us to a solution to a problem or decision but–unlike algorithms–may sometimes lead to errors. Heuristics increase the likelihood of success in coming to a solution, but, unlike algorithms, they cannot ensure it. For example, when I play tic-tac-toe, I follow the heuristic of placing an X in the center square when I start the game. This tactic doesn't guarantee that I will win, but experience has taught me that it will increase my chances of success. Similarly, some students follow the heuristic of preparing for a test by ignoring the assigned textbook reading and only studying their lecture notes–a strategy that may or may not pay off.

Although heuristics often help people solve problems and make decisions, certain kinds of heuristics may lead to inaccurate conclusions. For example, the *availability heuristic* involves judging the likelihood of an event occurring on the basis of how easy it is to think of examples. According to this heuristic, we assume that events we remember easily are likely to have occurred more frequently in the past–and are more likely to occur in the future–than events that are harder to remember.

For instance, the availability heuristic makes us more afraid of dying in a plane crash than in an auto accident, despite statistics clearly showing that airplane travel is much safer than auto travel. Similarly, although 10 times as many people die from falling out of bed than from lightning strikes, we're more afraid of being hit by lightning. The reason is that plane crashes and lightning strikes receive far more publicity, and they are therefore more easily remembered (Kluger, 2006; Caruso, 2008; Geurten et al., 2015).

We also make use of a familiarity heuristic. The *familiarity heuristic* leads us to prefer familiar objects, people, and things to those that that are unfamiliar or strange to us. For example, we might purchase a book written by a familiar author rather than one written by an author we never heard of, even if the topic of the book by the unfamiliar author sounds more appealing.

The familiarity heuristic typically saves us a great deal of time when we are making decisions, since we often just go with what seems most familiar. On the other hand, it's not so good if you are an emergency room physician susceptible to the familiarity heuristic. If you simply settle on the first, most obvious diagnosis for a

algorithm A rule that, if applied appropriately, guarantees a solution to a problem. (Module 23)

heuristic A thinking strategy that may lead us to a solution to a problem or decision but–unlike algorithms–may sometimes lead to errors. (Module 23)

Study Alert
Remember that algorithms are rules that *always* provide a solution, whereas heuristics are shortcuts that *may* provide a solution.

patient presenting particular symptoms (the ones that are most familiar to you), you may miss making a more accurate diagnosis (Herbert, 2011).

Are algorithms and heuristics confined to human thinking, or can we program computers to mimic human thinking and problem solving? As we discuss next, scientists are certainly trying.

Computers and Problem Solving: Searching for Artificial Intelligence

A computer using artificial intelligence software was able to mimic compositions by Johann Sebastian Bach so successfully it fooled expert musicologists.
©Photos.com/Getty Images

To the music experts, there was no mistaking who had written the piano piece: Johann Sebastian Bach, the prolific German composer who was born in the 17th century.

But the experts were wrong. The piece they all thought was a Bach composition was actually created by a computer named "EMI" by David Cope of the University of California. After a variety of Bach pieces had been scanned into its memory, EMI was able to produce music that was so similar to Bach's actual music that it fooled knowledgeable listeners (Johnson, 1997; Cope, 2001).

Such computer mimicry is possible because composers have a particular "signature" that reflects patterns, sequences, and combinations of notes. By employing those "signatures," computers can create compositions that have the full scope and emotional appeal of actual works–and show just as much creativity as those written by the actual composer (Cope, 2001, 2003).

Computers are making significant inroads in terms of the ability to solve problems and carry out some forms of intellectual activities. According to experts who study *artificial intelligence*, the field that examines how to use technology to imitate the outcome of human thinking, problem solving, and creative activities, computers can show rudiments of humanlike thinking because of their knowledge of where to look–and where not to look–for answers to problems. They suggest that the capacity of computer programs such as those that play chess to evaluate potential moves and to ignore unimportant possibilities gives them thinking ability (Megill, 2013; Ghahramani, 2015; Hernández-Orallo, 2017).

Computers using artificial intelligence are particularly good at tasks that require speed, persistence, and a huge memory, as you might realize if you've used Apple's Siri or Amazon's Alexa. For example, artificial intelligence is used today to inform decisions about whether a bank should loan money to a customer, which involve synthesizing vast amounts of information (including loan-repayment history) to determine how likely the customer is to repay the loan. And this is just the start; thousands of job categories, ranging from radiology to truck driving, will likely use artificial intelligence in the future. Still, it remains to be seen whether the quality of thinking produced by artificial intelligence will match that of humans (Luxton, 2016; Gopnik, 2017; Lee, 2017).

Does Playing Video Games Improve Your Thinking?

People who love video games spend a great many hours engaged in their pastime. Some rationalize the time spent by claiming that video games sharpen their cognitive skills–that is, they help them become better at solving challenges and problems, or they improve their memory, or they sharpen their attention. And a large number of studies back up those claims, studies showing that gamers perform better than nongamers on a number of tests of cognitive and perceptual abilities, ranging from hand-eye coordination to working memory to control of attention (Powers et al., 2013; Granic, Lobel, & Engels, 2014).

AP APPLYING PSYCHOLOGY IN THE 21ST CENTURY

ARE OUR ATTENTION SPANS BECOMING SHORTER?

Do you have a low tolerance for down time? When you find you have a few minutes to spare, such as while waiting in line at a store checkout or riding in an elevator, do you feel a compulsion to pull out your smartphone and check your e-mail or social media?

If you answered yes, you're not alone; many people report they multitask more than ever. This increase in multitasking has led researchers to ask if the vast and ever-increasing amount of media vying for our attention has had an impact on our attention spans.

To address the issue, software giant Microsoft conducted research involving surveys and brain scans of 2,000 Canadians. The findings showed that attention span, which was defined as the duration of concentrated effort on a task without becoming distracted, had fallen from an average of 12 seconds in 2000 (around the time when mobile devices were taking off) to 8 seconds 15 years later. Attention was worst for participants who were heavier consumers of media, particularly social media, and who were early adopters of new technology or frequently used multiple media devices, such as using a tablet or smartphone while watching television (McSpadden, 2015).

©Jetta Productions/Blend Images

The researchers suggested that digital media enthusiasts might have simply become very good at quickly determining whether a new task is interesting enough to merit their continued attention. When they become bored, they quickly look elsewhere. However, they also show bursts of high attention, suggesting they are capable of focusing intently when they want to do so.

But this research is not without its critics, who rightly point out that attention span likely varies according to the task we are carrying out. Some tasks are simply more interesting to us than others, and our attention span will likely be lengthier for more engaging activities than for less interesting ones.

Furthermore, attention span reflects the fact that the brain is simply good at adapting to its environment and picking out the stimuli that are the most useful. For example, other research shows that people who play a lot of video games have an enhanced ability to track moving objects, mentally rotate objects, and notice changes–that is, in many ways, their attention to detail is actually better than that of nongamers. Perhaps it's not all that surprising that given the choice between staring at the walls in a waiting room or reading something engaging on a screen in your hand, most people would choose the latter (Basak et al., 2008).

AP SKILL: SCIENTIFIC INVESTIGATION / DEFINE AND/OR APPLY CONCEPTS

1. Describe the correlation between social media and attention span.
2. Do you think there is an advantage to being bored or do you always need to have focused attention?

But this research has its critics, who suggest the benefits of gaming may be overstated. A recent study addressed some of these criticisms, and it found surprising results. Instead of categorizing participants into just two groups, as most studies do (frequent players versus nonplayers), the new study considered the full range of playing frequency, from nonplayers to low-frequency, moderate-frequency, and high-frequency players. When looked at this way, the previous findings that gamers outperformed nongamers on cognitive abilities simply vanished. The researchers concluded that previous studies used methods that had the unintended effect of inflating the apparent influence of video-game play on cognitive measures (Unsworth et al., 2015).

It thus seems that it's still too early to know the actual effects of video game play on cognitive abilities. But the conflicting sets of results suggest caution is necessary when drawing conclusions. (Also see *Applying Psychology in the 21st Century*.)

AP᾿ MODULE 23: THINKING AND REASONING

AP SUMMARY

- Cognitive psychology encompasses the higher mental processes, including the way people know and understand the world, process information, make decisions and judgments, and describe their knowledge and understanding to others.
- Mental images are representations in the mind of an object or event. The production of mental images can be used to improve various skills.
- Concepts are categorizations of objects, events, or people that share common properties. Prototypes are representative examples of concepts.
- Deductive reasoning is reasoning from the general to the specific, whereas inductive reasoning is reasoning from the specific to the general.
- Decisions may be improved through the use of algorithms and heuristics. An algorithm is a rule that guarantees a solution; a heuristic is a cognitive shortcut that may lead to a solution but is not guaranteed to do so. Types of heuristics include the availability heuristic and familiarity heuristic.

AP KEY TERMS

cognitive psychology
thinking
mental images
concepts
prototypes

deductive reasoning
inductive reasoning
algorithm
heuristic

AP TEST PRACTICE

Section I: Multiple Choice

1. In order to find condensed milk at the grocery store, Jessica started in aisle one and systematically went through each aisle until she found the product she was looking for. What problem-solving technique did Jessica use?
   A. Algorithm
   B. Concept
   C. Deductive reasoning
   D. Heuristic
   E. Inductive reasoning

2. What problem-solving technique saves time but is prone to errors?
   A. Echoic
   B. Syllogism
   C. Heuristic
   D. Iconic
   E. Algorithm

3. Savannah took one foreign language class and struggled to succeed. Now she thinks all foreign language classes are too challenging for her. What type of reasoning was used to come to this conclusion?
   A. Inductive
   B. Deductive
   C. Convergent
   D. Divergent
   E. Implicit

Section II: Free Response

Brian needs to buy a new car. Describe how the following terms can help him problem solve when selecting a new car.
- Concept
- Prototype
- Inductive reasoning
- Deductive reasoning
- Availability heuristic

Module 24
Problem Solving

According to an old legend, a group of Vietnamese monks guard three towers on which sit 64 golden rings. The monks believe that if they succeed in moving the rings from the first tower to the third according to a series of rigid rules, the world as we know it will come to an end. (Should you prefer that the world remain in its present state, there's no need for immediate concern: The puzzle is so complex that it will take the monks about a trillion years to solve it.)

In the Tower of Hanoi puzzle, a simpler version of the task facing the monks, three disks are placed on three posts in the order shown in Figure 1. The goal of the puzzle is to move all three disks to the third post, arranged in the same order, by using as few moves as possible. There are two restrictions: Only one disk can be moved at a time, and no disk can ever cover a smaller one during a move.

Why are cognitive psychologists interested in the Tower of Hanoi problem? Because the way people go about solving such puzzles helps illuminate how people solve complex, real-life problems. Psychologists have found that problem solving typically involves the three steps illustrated in Figure 2: preparing to create solutions, producing solutions, and evaluating the solutions that have been generated.

Preparation: Understanding and Diagnosing Problems

When approaching a problem like the Tower of Hanoi, most people begin by trying to understand the problem thoroughly. If the problem is a novel one, they probably will pay particular attention to any restrictions placed on coming up with a solution—such as the rule for moving only one disk at a time in the Tower of Hanoi problem. If, by contrast, the problem is a familiar one, they are apt to spend considerably less time in this preparation stage.

Problems vary from well defined to ill defined. In a *well-defined problem*—such as a mathematical equation or the solution to a jigsaw puzzle—both the nature of the problem itself and the information needed to solve it are available and clear. Thus, we can make straightforward judgments about whether a potential solution is appropriate. With an *ill-defined problem*, such as how to increase morale on an assembly line or to bring peace to the Middle East, not only may the specific nature of the problem be

Study Alert
Use the three steps of problem solving to organize your studying: Preparation, Production, and Judgment (PPJ).

Start   Finish

FIGURE 1 The goal of the Tower of Hanoi puzzle is to move all three disks from the first post to the third and still preserve the original order of the disks, using the fewest number of moves possible while following the rules that only one disk at a time can be moved and no disk can cover a smaller one during a move. Try it yourself before you look at the solution, which is given according to the sequence of moves.

Solution: Move C to 3, B to 2, C to 2, A to 3, C to 1, B to 3, and C to 3.

Preparation
Understanding
and diagnosing
problems

Production
Generating
solutions

Judgment
Evaluating
solutions

FIGURE 2 Steps in problem solving.

unclear, the information required to solve the problem may be even less obvious (Newman, Willoughby, & Pruce, 2011; Mayer, 2013; Tschentscher & Hauk, 2017).

KINDS OF PROBLEMS

Typically, a problem falls into one of the three categories shown in Figure 3: arrangement, inducing structure, and transformation. Solving each type requires somewhat different kinds of psychological skills and knowledge. (See Figure 4 for solutions to these problems.)

Arrangement problems require the problem solver to rearrange or recombine elements of the problem in a way that will satisfy specific criteria. Usually, several different arrangements can be made, but only one or a few of the arrangements will produce a solution. Anagram problems and jigsaw puzzles are examples of arrangement problems (Coventry et al., 2003; Reed, 2017).

In *problems of inducing structure*, a person must identify the existing relationships among the elements presented in the problem and then construct a new relationship among them. In such a problem, the problem solver must determine not only the relationships among the elements but also the structure and size of the elements involved. In the example shown in Figure 3b, a person must first determine that the solution requires the numbers to be considered in pairs (14-24-34-44-54-64). Only after identifying that part of the problem can a person determine the solution rule (the first number of each pair increases by one, while the second number remains the same).

The Tower of Hanoi puzzle represents the third kind of problem–*transformation problems*–that consist of an initial state, a goal state, and a method for changing the initial state into the goal state. In the Tower of Hanoi problem, the initial state is the original configuration, the goal state is to have the three disks on the third peg, and the method is the rules for moving the disks (Majeres, 2007; Van Belle et al., 2011; Schiff & Vakil, 2015).

Whether the problem is one of arrangement, inducing structure, or transformation, the preparation stage of understanding and diagnosing is critical in problem solving because it allows us to develop our own cognitive representation of the problem and to place it within a personal framework. We may divide the problem into subparts or ignore some information as we try to simplify the task. Winnowing out nonessential information is often a critical step in the preparation stage of problem solving.

REPRESENTING AND ORGANIZING THE PROBLEM

A crucial aspect of the initial encounter with a problem is the way in which we represent, characterize, and organize the information presented to us. Consider the following problem:

> A man climbs a mountain on Saturday, leaving at daybreak and arriving at the top near sundown. He spends the night at the top. The next day, Sunday, he leaves at daybreak and heads down the mountain, following the same path that he climbed the day before. The question is this: Will there be any time during the 2nd day when he will be at exactly the same point on the mountain as he was at exactly that time on the 1st day?

If you try to solve this problem by using algebraic or verbal representations, you will have a good deal of trouble. However, if you represent the problem with the kind of simple diagram shown in Figure 5, the solution will become apparent.

The way in which we represent a problem–and the solution we eventually come to–depends on the way a problem is initially framed for us. Imagine that you were a cancer patient having to choose between either the option of surgery or of radiation, as shown in Figure 6, and you were given some statistical information about the options. What would you choose?

It turns out that participants in a study made very different choices depending on how the problem was framed. When their choices were framed in terms of the likelihood of *survival,* only 18% of participants chose radiation over surgery. However, when the choice was framed in terms of the likelihood of *dying,* 44% chose radiation over surgery–even though the outcomes are similar with either treatment option (Tversky & Kahneman, 1987; Chandran & Menon, 2004).

a. Arrangement problems

1. Anagrams: Rearrange the letters in each set to make an English word:

2. Two strings hang from a ceiling but are too far apart to allow a person to hold one and walk to the other. On the floor are a book of matches, a screwdriver, and a few pieces of cotton. How could the strings be tied together?

b. Problems of inducing structure

1. What number comes next in the series?
   1 4 2 4 3 4 4 4 5 4 6 4

2. Complete these analogies:
   baseball is to bat as tennis is to _____

   merchant is to sell as customer is to _____

c. Transformation problems

1. Water jars: A person has three jars with the following capacities:

Jar A:
28 ounces

Jar B:
7 ounces

Jar C:
5 ounces

How can the person measure exactly 11 ounces of water?

2. Ten coins are arranged in the following way. By moving only *two* of the coins make two rows that each contains six coins.

FIGURE 3 The three major categories of problems: (a) arrangement, (b) inducing structure, and (c) transformation. Solutions appear in Figure 4.

Source: Adapted from Bourne, L. E., Dominowski, R. L., Loftus, E. F., & Healy, A. F. (1986). *Cognitive processes* (2nd ed.). Englewood Cliffs, NJ: Prentice Hall.

a. Arrangement problems

1. FACET, DOUBT, THICK, NAIVE, ANVIL

2. The screwdriver is tied to one of the strings. This makes a pendulum that can be swung to reach the other string.

b. Problems of inducing structure

1. 7

2. racket; buy

c. Transformation problems

1. Fill jar A; empty into jar B once and into jar C twice. What remains in jar A is 11 ounces.

2.

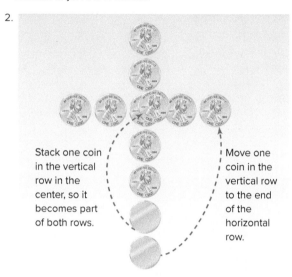

Stack one coin in the vertical row in the center, so it becomes part of both rows.

Move one coin in the vertical row to the end of the horizontal row.

FIGURE 4 Solutions to the problems in Figure 3.

Source: Adapted from Bourne, L. E., Dominowski, R. L., Loftus, E. F., & Healy, A. F. (1986). *Cognitive processes* (2nd ed.). Englewood Cliffs, NJ: Prentice Hall.

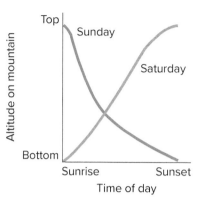

FIGURE 5 You can solve the mountain-climbing problem by using a graph. Keep in mind that the goal is not to determine the time but just to indicate whether an exact time exists. Consequently, the speed at which the traveler is moving is unimportant. Can you think of other approaches that might lead to a solution?

Source: Anderson, B. F. (1980). *The complete thinker: A handbook of techniques for creative and critical problem solving*. Englewood Cliffs, NJ: Prentice Hall.

Problem: Surgery or radiation?

Survival Frame

Surgery: Of 100 people having surgery, 90 live through the post-operative period, 68 are alive at the end of the 1st year, and 34 are alive at the end of 5 years.

Radiation: Of 100 people having radiation therapy, all live through the treatment, 77 are alive at the end of 1 year, and 22 are alive at the end of 5 years.

Far more patients choose surgery

Mortality Frame

Surgery: Of 100 people having surgery, 10 die during surgery, 32 die by the end of the 1st year, and 66 die by the end of 5 years.

Radiation: Of 100 people having radiation therapy, none die during the treatment, 23 die by the end of 1 year, and 78 die by the end of 5 years.

Far more patients choose radiation

FIGURE 6 A decision often is affected by the way a problem is framed. In this case, most would choose radiation over surgery, despite similar results.

(left): ©Hoby Finn/Photodisc/Getty Images; (right): ©Stockbyte/Getty Images

Production: Generating Solutions

After preparation, the next stage in problem solving is the production of possible solutions. If a problem is relatively simple, we may already have a direct solution stored in long-term memory, and all we need to do is retrieve the appropriate information. If we cannot retrieve or do not know the solution, we must generate possible solutions and compare them with information in long- and short-term memory.

At the most basic level, we can solve problems through trial and error. Thomas Edison invented the lightbulb only because he tried thousands of different kinds of materials for a filament before he found one that worked (carbon). The difficulty with trial and error, of course, is that some problems are so complicated that it would take a lifetime to try out every possibility. For example, according to some estimates, there are some 10^{120} possible sequences of chess moves (Fine & Fine, 2003).

In place of trial and error, complex problem solving often involves the use of heuristics, cognitive shortcuts that can generate solutions, as we have discussed. One of the most frequently applied heuristics in problem solving is a means-ends analysis. In a **means-ends analysis,** a problem solver starts by considering the ultimate goal (the end) and determining the best strategy (the means) for attaining the goal. Using a means-end analysis, problem solvers repeatedly test for differences between a desired outcome and the situation that currently exists, trying to get closer and closer to the goal (Bosse, Gerritsen, & Treur, 2011; Bieberstein & Roosen, 2015).

Consider this simple example of a means-ends analysis:

> I want to take my son to preschool. What's the difference between what I have and what I want? One of distance. What changes distance? My automobile. My automobile won't work. What is needed to make it work? A new battery. What has new batteries? An auto repair shop. . . .

In a means-end analysis, each step brings the problem solver closer to a resolution. Although this approach is often effective, if the problem requires indirect steps that temporarily *increase* the discrepancy between a current state and the solution, means-ends analysis can be counterproductive. For example, sometimes the fastest route to the summit of a mountain requires a mountain climber to backtrack temporarily; a means-end approach–which implies that the mountain climber should always forge ahead and upward–will be ineffective in such instances.

For other problems, the best approach is to work backward by focusing on the goal, rather than the starting point, of the problem. Consider, for example, the water lily problem:

> Water lilies are growing on Blue Lake. The water lilies grow rapidly, so that the amount of water surface covered by lilies doubles every 24 hours. On the first day of summer, there was just one water lily. On the 90th day of the summer, the lake was entirely covered. On what day was the lake half covered? (Reisberg, 1997)

If you start searching for a solution to the problem by thinking about the initial state on day 1 (one water lily) and move forward from there, you're facing a daunting task of trial-and-error estimation. But try taking a different approach: Start with day 90, when the entire lake was covered with lilies. Given that the lilies double their coverage daily, on the prior day only half the lake was covered. The answer, then, is day 89, a solution found by working backward (Bourne et al., 1986; Hunt, 1994; Shogren & Wehrmeyer, 2017).

FORMING SUBGOALS: DIVIDING PROBLEMS INTO THEIR PARTS

Another heuristic commonly used to generate solutions is to divide a problem into intermediate steps, or *subgoals*, and solve each of those steps. For instance, in our modified Tower of Hanoi problem, we could choose several obvious subgoals, such as moving the largest disk to the third post.

means-ends analysis A strategy in which a problem-solver considers the ultimate goal (the end) and determines the best strategy for attaining the goal. (Module 24)

If solving a subgoal is a step toward the ultimate solution to a problem, identifying subgoals is an appropriate strategy. In some cases, however, forming subgoals is not all that helpful and may actually increase the time needed to find a solution. For example, some problems cannot be subdivided. Others–like some complicated mathematical problems–are so complex that it takes longer to identify the appropriate subdivisions than to solve the problem by other means (Kaller et al., 2004; Fishbach, Dhar, & Zhang, 2006).

INSIGHT: SUDDEN AWARENESS

Have you ever had this experience? You're working on a difficult problem, mulling over possible answers, but you can't seem to come up with a viable solution. And then, seemingly out of nowhere, a solution comes to you.

insight A sudden awareness of the relationships among various elements that had previously appeared to be independent of one another. (Module 24)

If this has happened to you, you experienced a process known as insight. **Insight** is a sudden awareness of the relationships among various elements that had previously appeared to be unrelated. The phenomenon of insight was demonstrated in a classic study by German psychologist Wolfgang Köhler, who examined learning and problem-solving processes in chimpanzees (Köhler, 1927). In his studies, Köhler exposed chimps to challenging situations in which the elements of the solution were all present; all the chimps needed to do was put them together.

In one of Köhler's studies, chimps were kept in a cage in which boxes and sticks were strewn about, and a bunch of tantalizing bananas was hung from the ceiling, out of reach. Initially, the chimps made trial-and-error attempts to get to the bananas: They would throw the sticks at the bananas, jump from one of the boxes, or leap wildly from the ground. Frequently, they would seem to give up in frustration, leaving the bananas dangling temptingly overhead. But then, in what seemed like a sudden revelation, they would stop whatever they were doing and stand on a box to reach the bananas with a stick (Figure 7). Köhler used the term *insight* to label the cognitive process underlying the chimps' new behavior.

Although Köhler emphasized the apparent suddenness of insightful solutions, subsequent research has shown that prior experience and trial-and-error practice in problem solving must precede "insight." Consequently, the chimps' behavior may simply

PsychTech

Research comparing people working together to solve problems face-to-face versus communicating via e-mail finds that those using e-mail are more satisfied with the process and believe they find better solutions.

(a)

(b)

(c)

FIGURE 7 (a) In an impressive display of insight, Sultan, one of the chimpanzees in Köhler's experiments in problem solving, sees a bunch of bananas that is out of reach. (b) He then carries over several crates, stacks them, and (c) stands on them to reach the bananas.
(all): ©Superstock

represent the chaining together of previously learned responses, no different from the way a pigeon learns, by trial and error, to peck a key (Kizilirmak et al., 2015).

Can we help people achieve insight when they are seeking to solve problems? The answer is yes. One way is to directly train them, giving them practice in generating solutions that require out-of-the-box thinking. Another way is to provide cross-cultural experiences that show people that their traditional ways of thinking may be inadequate when applied to the problems faced by those living in other cultures (Leung & Chiu, 2010; Wen, Butler, & Koutstaal, 2013).

Judgment: Evaluating Solutions

The final stage in problem solving is judging the adequacy of a solution. Often this is a simple matter: If the solution is clear—as in the Tower of Hanoi problem—we will know immediately whether we have been successful (Varma, 2007).

If the solution is less concrete or if there is no single correct solution, evaluating solutions becomes more difficult. In such instances, we must decide which alternative solution is best. Unfortunately, we often quite inaccurately estimate the quality of our own ideas. For instance, a team of drug researchers working for a particular company may consider their remedy for an illness to be superior to all others, overestimating the likelihood of their success and downplaying the approaches of competing drug companies (Eizenberg & Zaslavsky, 2004; Mihalca, Mengelkamp, & Schnotz, 2017).

Theoretically, if we rely on appropriate heuristics and valid information, we can make accurate choices among alternative solutions. However, several kinds of obstacles to problem solving act to bias the decisions and judgments we make. In fact, a wide range of behaviors are affected by these biases, ranging from the judgments we form of others to the choices we make about financial investments. Examining biases in decision making has influenced the development of an influential new field known as *behavioral economics*, which examines how psychological factors can explain economic decision making (Cox, Green, & Hennig-Schmidt, 2016; Peters et al., 2017).

Impediments to Solutions: Why Is Problem Solving Such a Problem?

Consider the following problem-solving test illustrated in Figure 8 (Duncker, 1945):

> You are given a set of tacks, candles, and matches, each in a small box, and told your goal is to place three candles at eye level on a nearby door so that wax will not drip on the floor as the candles burn. How would you approach this challenge?

If you have difficulty solving the problem, you are not alone. Most people cannot solve it when it is presented in the manner illustrated in the figure, in which the objects are *inside* the boxes. However, if the objects were presented *beside* the boxes, just resting on the table, chances are that you would solve the problem much more readily—which, in case you are wondering, requires tacking the boxes to the door and then placing the candles inside them (see Figure 9).

FIGURE 8 The problem here is to place three candles at eye level on a nearby door so that the wax will not drip on the floor as the candles burn—using only material in the figure. For a solution, see Figure 9.

Source: Adapted from Duncker, K. (1945). On problem solving. *Psychological Monographs, 58* (5, whole no. 270).

FIGURE 9 A solution to the problem in Figure 8 involves tacking the boxes to the door and placing the candles in the boxes.

Source: Adapted from Duncker, K. (1945). On problem solving. *Psychological Monographs, 58* (5, whole no. 270).

functional fixedness The tendency to think of an object only in terms of the way it is most frequently or typically used. (Module 24)

The difficulty you probably encountered in solving this problem stems from its presentation, which misled you at the initial preparation stage. Actually, significant obstacles to problem solving can exist at each of the three major stages. Although cognitive approaches to problem solving suggest that thinking proceeds along fairly rational, logical lines as a person confronts a problem and considers various solutions, several factors can hinder the development of creative, appropriate, and accurate solutions.

FUNCTIONAL FIXEDNESS

The impediment to solving the candle problem is functional fixedness. **Functional fixedness** is the tendency to think of an object only in terms of the way it is most frequently or typically used. For instance, functional fixedness probably leads you to think of a book as something to read instead of its potential use as a doorstop or as kindling for a fire. In the candle problem, because the objects are first presented inside the boxes, functional fixedness leads most people to see the boxes simply as containers for the objects they hold rather than as a potential part of the solution. They cannot envision another function for the boxes.

A classic experiment (Luchins, 1946) demonstrates functional fixedness. As you can see in Figure 10, the object of the task is to use the jars in each row to measure out the designated amount of liquid. (Try it yourself to get a sense of the power of functional fixedness before moving on.)

If you have tried to solve the problem, you know that the first five rows are all solved in the same way: First fill the largest jar (B) and then from it fill the middle-size jar (A) once and the smallest jar (C) two times. What is left in B is the designated amount. (Stated as a formula, the designated amount is B–A–2C.) The demonstration of functional fixedness comes in the sixth row of the problem, a point at which you probably encountered some difficulty. If you are like most people, you tried the formula and were perplexed when it failed. Chances are, in fact, that you missed the simple (but different) solution to the problem, which involves merely subtracting C from A. Interestingly, people who were given the problem in row 6 *first* had no difficulty with it at all.

Functional fixedness can affect perceptions as well as patterns of problem solving. It can prevent you from seeing beyond the apparent constraints of a problem. For example, try to draw four straight lines so that they pass through all nine dots in the grid below–without lifting your pencil from the page.

● ● ●

● ● ●

● ● ●

FIGURE 10 Try this classic demonstration, which illustrates the importance of functional fixedness in problem solving. The object is to use the jars in each row to obtain the designated amount of liquid.

	Given jars with these capacities (in ounces):			
	A	B	C	Obtain:
1.	21	127	3	100
2.	14	163	25	99
3.	18	43	10	5
4.	9	42	6	21
5.	20	59	4	31
6.	28	76	3	25

If you had difficulty with the problem, it was probably because you felt compelled to keep your lines within the grid. If you had gone outside the boundaries, however, you would have succeeded by using the solution shown in Figure 11. (The phrase "thinking outside the box"–a commonly used term to encourage creativity–stems from research on overcoming the constraining effects of functional fixedness.)

INACCURATE EVALUATION OF SOLUTIONS

When the United States invaded Iraq in 2003, it did so because governmental leaders believed that the country secretly had weapons of mass destruction that posed a danger to the United States. But later evidence showed that the belief was false. Still, government leaders had made up their minds early on that there were such weapons, and they ignored contradictory evidence and focused more on information that supported their view (U.S. Senate Select Committee on Intelligence, 2004).

The mistake made by governmental leaders exemplifies **confirmation bias** in which problem solvers prefer their first hypothesis and ignore contradictory information that supports alternative hypotheses or solutions. Even when we find evidence that contradicts a solution we have chosen, we are apt to stick with our original hypothesis.

Confirmation bias occurs for several reasons. For one thing, because rethinking a problem that appears to be solved already takes extra cognitive effort, we are apt to stick with our first solution. For another, we give greater weight to subsequent information that supports our initial position than to information that is not supportive of it (Koslowski, 2013; Rajsic, Wilson, & Pratt, 2015; Mercier, 2017).

FIGURE 11 A solution to the nine-dot problem requires the use of lines drawn beyond the boundaries of the figure— something that our functional fixedness may prevent us from seeing easily.

confirmation bias The tendency to seek out and weight more heavily information that supports one's initial hypothesis and to ignore contradictory information that supports alternative hypotheses or solutions. (Module 24)

Creativity and Problem Solving

Despite obstacles to problem solving, many people adeptly discover creative solutions to problems. One enduring question that cognitive psychologists have sought to answer is what factors underlie **creativity,** the ability to generate original ideas or solve problems in novel ways.

Understanding the stages people go through as they approach and solve problems still leaves us with the question: Why are some people better at finding good solutions than other people are? Even the simplest situations reveal a wide range of abilities in problem solving. To explore this for yourself, make a list of all the uses you can think of for a glass jar. When you feel you have run out of possibilities, compare your list to this one compiled by a 12-year-old girl:

creativity The ability to generate original ideas or solve problems in novel ways. (Module 24)

> You can keep seashells from your vacation in it to decorate your room. You can put sand on the bottom of it and pour melted wax over the sand and stick a wick in it to make a candle. You can use it as a drinking glass. You can keep rubber bands or paper clips or colored marbles in it. You can make a granola mix and store it for months if the jar has a tight lid. You can put water in the bottom and start an avocado tree from a pit. You can store bacon grease in a jar or fill it with hand soaps and place it by the bathroom sink. You can use it as a flower vase or a "candy dish" for wrapped candies. If you punch holes in the lid, a jar can be a salt or sugar shaker. You can layer pudding and berries and whipped cream in it for a fancy dessert. You can keep your loose change in a jar or use it as a cocktail shaker. You can keep your goldfish in it while you clean the tank. You can organize shelves in the garage or basement by putting small things like nails and screws and bolts with others of the same size, each in their own jar. You can organize your pantry, too: a jar for white rice, one for wild rice, another for black beans, and so on. You can measure rainfall for a month with a jar. Or place it beneath a leaky sink pipe.

Singer, songwriter, and activist Lady Gaga is considered a trailblazer in both music and fashion. Do you think she relies more on convergent or divergent thinking in her work?

©vipflash/Shutterstock

divergent thinking Thinking that generates multiple and unusual, although appropriate, responses to problems or questions. (Module 24)

convergent thinking Thinking in which a problem is viewed as having a single answer and which produces a solution that is based primarily on knowledge and logic. (Module 24)

Study Alert

Remember *d*ivergent thinking produces *d*ifferent and *d*iverse kinds of responses, whereas convergent thinking produces more commonsense kinds of responses.

This list shows extraordinary creativity. Unfortunately, it is much easier to identify *examples* of creativity than to determine its causes. Similarly, it's not clear that the kind of creativity shown by highly creative people in the arts, such as singer Lady Gaga, is the same kind of creativity shown by highly creative people in the sciences, such as Steven Hawking (Simonton, 2009; Lavazza & Manzotti, 2013; Yi, Plucker, & Guo, 2015).

However, we do know that several characteristics are associated with creativity. For one thing, highly creative individuals show divergent thinking. **Divergent thinking** is thinking that generates multiple and unusual, although appropriate, responses to problems or questions. When we use "out-of-the-box" thinking, we're showing divergent thinking.

Divergent thinking contrasts with convergent thinking. **Convergent thinking** is thinking in which a problem is viewed as having a single answer and which produces a solution that is based primarily on knowledge and logic. For instance, someone relying on convergent thinking would answer "You read it" to the query "What can you do with a newspaper?" In contrast, "You can use it as a dustpan" is a more divergent–and creative–response (Schepers & van den Berg, 2007; Zeng, Proctor, & Salvendy, 2011; Haas, 2017).

Creative people also show cognitive complexity in their thinking. *Cognitive complexity* is the preference for elaborate, intricate, and complex thoughts and solutions to problems. For instance, creative people often have a wider range of interests and are more independent and more interested in philosophical or abstract problems than are less creative individuals (Barron, 1990; Richards, 2006; Kaufman & Plucker, 2011).

From the perspective of...

A Manufacturer How might you encourage your employees to develop creative ways to improve the products you produce?

©Kali Nine LLC/Getty Images

One factor that is *not* closely related to creativity is intelligence. Traditional intelligence tests, which ask focused questions that have only one acceptable answer, tap convergent thinking skills. Highly creative people may therefore find that such tests penalize their divergent thinking. This may explain why researchers consistently find that creativity is only slightly related to school grades and intelligence when intelligence is measured using traditional intelligence tests (Heilman, 2005; Norton, Heath, & Ventura, 2013; Jung & Chang, 2017).

Does creativity change as we age? Research suggests that we actually become *less* creative the older we get. One reason may be that as we get older, we know more. Although this increased knowledge is generally advantageous, it may hinder creativity because we are more apt to ignore evidence that contradicts what we believe to be true. In a sense, we get stuck in our ways. Furthermore, when we get older, we already have developed a set of solutions to common problems, and we are more likely to turn to them and avoid exploring more creative ideas. In short, getting older is not helpful in finding creative solutions to problems (Gopnik, Griffiths, & Lucas, 2015; Gopnik & Griffiths, 2017).

Thinking Critically and Creatively

Can we learn to be better and more creative thinkers?

Cognitive researchers have found that people can learn the abstract rules of logic and reasoning and that such knowledge can improve our reasoning about the underlying causes of everyday events in our lives. Research suggests that critical and creative thinkers are made, not born. Consider, for instance, the following suggestions for increasing critical thinking and creativity (Burbach, Matkin, & Fritz, 2004; Kaufman & Baer, 2006).

- *Redefine problems.* We can modify boundaries and assumptions by rephrasing a problem at either a more abstract or a more concrete level.
- *Use subgoals.* By developing subgoals, we can divide a problem into intermediate steps. This process, known as *fractionation*, allows us to examine each part for new possibilities and approaches, leading to a novel solution for the problem as a whole.
- *Adopt a critical perspective.* Rather than passively accepting assumptions or arguments, we can evaluate material critically, consider its implications, and think about possible exceptions and contradictions.
- *Consider the opposite.* By considering the opposite of a concept we're seeking to understand, we can sometimes make progress. For example, to define "good mental health," it may be useful to consider what "bad mental health" means.
- *Use analogies.* Analogies provide alternative frameworks for the interpretation of facts and help us uncover new understanding. One particularly effective means of coming up with analogies is to look for examples in the animal world. For instance, architects discovered how to construct the earliest skyscrapers by noting how lily pads on a pond could support the weight of a person (Getner & Holyoak, 1997; Bearman, Ball, & Ormerod, 2007; Cho, Holyoak, & Cannon, 2007).

The Disney Concert Hall in Los Angeles, designed by legendary architect Frank Gehry, is known as a masterpiece of visionary architecture. What processes might account for Gehry's creativity?
©tupungato/123RF

- *Think divergently.* Instead of the most logical or common use for an object, consider how you might use the object if you were forbidden to use it in the usual way.
- *Think convergently.* Although it sounds counterintuitive, researchers have found that a combination of divergent *and* convergent thinking can lead to greater creativity. Programs that attempt to teach children to be more creative train participants to alternate periods of divergent thinking with intense convergent thinking (Beghetto & Kaufman, 2010).
- *Use heuristics.* Heuristics are cognitive shortcuts that can help bring about a solution to a problem. If the problem has a single correct answer and you can use or construct a heuristic, you can often find the solution more rapidly and effectively.
- *Experiment with various solutions.* Don't be afraid to use different routes to find solutions for problems (verbal, mathematical, graphic, even dramatic). For instance, try to come up with every conceivable idea you can, no matter how wild or bizarre it may seem at first. After you've come up with a list of solutions, review each one and try to think of ways to make what at first appeared impractical seem more feasible.
- *Walk away.* Sometimes just taking a step back from a problem you're trying to solve and doing something routine and even thoughtless can help bring about creativity. Watching TV, taking a shower, or having a snack may free our minds to come up with innovative solutions (Wiley & Jarosz, 2012; Shellenbarger, 2013).

AP MODULE 24: PROBLEM SOLVING

AP SUMMARY

- Wolfgang Köhler's research with chimpanzees illustrated insight, a sudden awareness of the relationships among elements that had previously seemed unrelated.
- Creativity is the ability to generate original ideas or solve problems in novel and useful ways. Creativity is related to divergent thinking (the ability to generate multiple unusual, but still appropriate, responses to problems) and cognitive complexity. In contrast, convergent thinking is seen as thinking in which a problem is viewed as having a single answer and produces a solution based primarily on knowledge and logic.
- Intelligence is not closely related to creativity and research suggests we become less creative the older we get.
- Suggestions to increase critical thinking and creativity include redefining a problem; adopting a critical perspective and considering the opposite; using an analogy, divergent and convergent thinking, and a heuristic; experimenting with solutions; and sometimes just walking away from the problem.
- Problem solving typically involves three major stages: preparation, production of solutions, and evaluation of solutions that have been generated.
- Preparation involves placing the problem in one of

three categories. In arrangements problems, a group of elements must be rearranged in a way that will satisfy a certain criterion. In problems of inducing structure, a person first must identify the existing relationship among the elements presented and then construct a new relationship among them. Finally, transformation problems consist of an initial state, a goal state, and a method for changing the initial state into the goal state.

- A crucial aspect of the preparation stage is the representation and organization of the problem.
- In the production stage, people try to generate solutions. They may find solutions to some problems in long-term memory. Alternatively, they may solve some problems through simple trial and error and use algorithms and heuristics to solve more complex problems. Common heuristics include a means-end analysis or dividing a problem into subgoals and solving each of those steps.
- Obstacles to problem solving act to bias the decisions and judgments we make. Behavioral economics examines how psychological factors and biases can explain economic decision making.
- Several factors hinder effective problem solving. Functional fixedness is the cognitive bias in which we think of an object only in terms of the way it is most frequently or typically used. Confirmation bias, in which initial hypotheses are favored, can hinder the accurate evaluation of solutions to problems.

means-ends analysis
insight
functional fixedness
confirmation bias
creativity
divergent thinking
convergent thinking

AP TEST PRACTICE

Section I: Multiple Choice

1. In a famous problem-solving experiment, chimpanzees were provided bananas just out of their reach. Suddenly, a chimp carries over several crates, stacks them, and stands on them to reach the bananas. What problem solving strategy was used in this experiment?
   A. Insight
   B. Deductive reasoning
   C. Convergent thinking
   D. Functional fixedness
   E. Means-ends analysis

2. Why type of thinking is associated with creativity?
   A. Convergent
   B. Deductive
   C. Divergent
   D. Inductive
   E. Explicit

3. Serena can think of over 30 things to do with a paper clip. She has overcome which obstacle to problem solving?
   A. Framing
   B. Hindsight bias
   C. Confirmation bias
   D. Convergent thinking
   E. Functional fixedness

Section II: Free Response

Mrs. Karlin is having problems with her third hour class. There are multiple students that are talking out of turn, so she seats those students at the front of the room. She has found several education articles that support that strategy. In addition, each time they talk out of turn she firmly scolds them. However, these methods do not appear to be working because the students continue to talk and even more students are now misbehaving.

A. Explain how the following concepts could relate to Mrs. Karlin and her problem solving.
   - Confirmation bias
   - Convergent thinking
   - Insight

B. Describe how the following concepts could help explain what is happening in Mrs. Karlin's classroom.
   - Positive reinforcement
   - Observational learning

Module 25
Language

AP® LEARNING TARGETS

- Identify the contributions of key researchers in cognitive psychology.
- Synthesize how biological, cognitive, and cultural factors converge to facilitate acquisition, development, and use of language.

language The communication of information through symbols arranged according to systematic rules. (Module 25)

grammar The system of rules that determine how our thoughts can be expressed. (Module 25)

phonology The study of the smallest units of speech, called phonemes. (Module 25)

phonemes The smallest units of speech. (Module 25)

syntax Ways in which words and phrases can be combined to form sentences. (Module 25)

semantics The aspect of language referring to the meaning of words and sentences. (Module 25)

'Twas brillig, and the slithy toves
Did gyre and gimble in the wabe:
All mimsy were the borogoves,
And the mome raths outgrabe.

Although few of us have ever come face to face with a tove, we have little difficulty in discerning that in Lewis Carroll's (1872) poem "Jabberwocky," the expression *slithy toves* contains an adjective, *slithy,* and the noun it modifies, *toves.*

Our ability to make sense out of nonsense, if the nonsense follows typical rules of language, illustrates the complexity of both human language and the cognitive processes that underlie its development and use. The use of **language**–the communication of information through symbols arranged according to systematic rules–is a central cognitive ability, one that is indispensable for us to communicate with one another. Not only is language central to communication, but it is also closely tied to the very way in which we think about and understand the world. Without language, our ability to transmit information, acquire knowledge, and cooperate with others would be tremendously hindered. No wonder psychologists have devoted considerable attention to studying language (Reisberg, 2009; LaPointe, 2013; Carnevale, Luna, & Lerman, 2017).

Grammar: Language's Language

To understand how language develops and relates to thought, we first need to review some of the formal elements of language. The basic structure of language rests on **grammar,** the system of rules that determine how our thoughts can be expressed.

Grammar deals with three major components of language: phonology, syntax, and semantics. **Phonology** is the study of **phonemes,** the smallest basic units of speech that affect meaning, and of the way we use those sounds to form words and produce meaning. For instance, the *a* sound in *fat* and the *a* sound in *fate* represent two different phonemes in English (Hardison, 2006; Creel & Bregman, 2011).

Linguists have identified 869 different phonemes among all the world's languages. Although English speakers use just 52 phonemes to produce words, other languages use as few as 15 to as many as 141. Differences in phonemes are one reason people have difficulty learning other languages. For example, for a Japanese speaker, whose native language does not have an *r* phoneme, pronouncing such English words as *roar* presents some difficulty (Gibbs, 2002; Iverson et al., 2003; Redford, 2017).

Syntax refers to the rules that indicate how words and phrases can be combined to form sentences. Every language has intricate rules that guide the order in which words may be strung together to communicate meaning. English speakers have no difficulty recognizing that "TV down the turn" is not a meaningful sequence, whereas "Turn down the TV" is. To understand the effect of syntax in English, consider the changes in meaning caused by the different word orders in the following three utterances: "John kidnapped the boy," "John, the kidnapped boy," and "The boy kidnapped John" (Robert, 2006; Frank, Goldwater, & Keller, 2013).

Semantics is the third major component of language. **Semantics** refers to the meaning of words and sentences. Every word has particular semantic features. For example, *boy* and *man* share certain semantic features (both refer to males), but they also differ semantically (in terms of age).

Semantic rules allow us to use words to convey the subtle nuances in meaning. For instance, we can use slightly different wording–semantics–about an event to convey subtle differences in meaning. If we had just seen a girl named Laura get hit by a truck, we might say, "A truck hit Laura." But if we were answering a question about why Laura was not at a party the night before, we might say, "Laura was hit by a truck" (Pietarinen, 2006; Paciorek & Williams, 2015; Srinivasan et al., 2017).

Despite the complexities of language, most of us acquire the basics of grammar without even being aware that we have learned its rules. Moreover, even though we may have difficulty explicitly stating the rules of grammar, our linguistic abilities are so sophisticated that we can utter an infinite number of different statements. How do we acquire such abilities?

Language Development: Developing a Way with Words

To parents, the sounds of their infant babbling and cooing are music to their ears (except, perhaps, at 3 o'clock in the morning). These sounds also serve an important function. They mark the first step on the road to the development of language.

BABBLING

Children **babble**–make speechlike but meaningless sounds–from around the age of 3 months through 1 year. While babbling, they may produce, at one time or another, any of the sounds found in all languages, not just the language to which they are exposed. Even deaf children display their own form of babbling because infants who are unable to hear yet who are exposed to sign language from birth "babble" with their hands (Pettito, 1993; Majorano & D'Odorico, 2011; Shehata-Dieler et al., 2013).

babble Meaningless, speechlike sounds made by children from around the age of 3 months through 1 year. (Module 25)

An infant's babbling increasingly reflects the specific language being spoken in the infant's environment, initially in terms of pitch and tone and eventually in terms of specific sounds. Young infants can distinguish among all 869 phonemes that have been identified across the world's languages. However, after the age of 6 to 8 months, that ability begins to decline. Infants begin to "specialize" in the language to which they are exposed as neurons in their brains reorganize to respond to the particular phonemes infants routinely hear.

Some theorists argue that a *critical period* exists for language development early in life in which a child is particularly sensitive to language cues and most easily acquires language. In fact, if children are not exposed to language during this critical period, later they will have great difficulty overcoming this deficit (Bates, 2005; Shafer & Garrido-Nag, 2007; Choubsaz & Gheitury, 2017).

Cases in which abused children have been isolated from contact with others support the theory of such critical periods. In one case, for example, a girl named Genie was exposed to virtually no language from the age of 20 months until she was rescued at age 13. She was unable to speak at all. Despite intensive instruction, she learned only some words and was never able to master the complexities of language (Rymer, 1994; Veltman & Browne, 2001).

PRODUCTION OF LANGUAGE

By the time children are approximately 1 year old, they stop producing sounds that are not in the language to which they have been exposed. It is then a short step to the production of actual words. In English, these are typically short words that start with a consonant sound such as b, d, m, p, and t–this helps explain why *mama* and *dada* are so often among babies' first words. Of course, even before they produce their first words, children can understand a fair amount of the language they hear. Language comprehension precedes language production.

A syllable in signed language, similar to the ones seen in the manual babbling of deaf infants and in the spoken babbling of hearing infants. The similarities in language structure suggest that language has biological roots.

Courtesy of Dr. Laura Ann Petitto. Photo by Robert LaMarche

After the age of 1 year, children begin to learn more complicated forms of language. They produce two-word combinations, the building blocks of sentences, and sharply increase the number of different words they are able to use.

By age 2, the average child has a vocabulary of more than 50 words. Just 6 months later, at $2\frac{1}{2}$ years of age, that vocabulary has grown to several hundred words.

Also around the age of 2, children begin to produce short, two-word sentences. However, the sentences children first produce are characterized as telegraphic speech. **Telegraphic speech** consists of sentences in which only essential words are used, usually nouns and verbs only. Rather than saying, "I showed you the book," a child using telegraphic speech may say, "I show book," and "I am drawing a dog" may become "Drawing dog." As children get older, of course, they use less telegraphic speech and produce increasingly complex sentences (Volterra et al., 2003; Pérez-Leroux, Pirvulescu, & Roberge, 2011).

By age 3, children learn to make plurals by adding *-s* to nouns and to form the past tense by adding *-ed* to verbs. However, these skills also lead to speech errors, since children tend to apply rules inflexibly, a process known as overgeneralization. In **overgeneralization,** children employ rules even when doing so results in an error. Thus, although it is correct to say "he walked" for the past tense of *walk*, the *-ed* rule doesn't work quite so well when children say "he runned" for the past tense of *run* (Gershkoff-Stowe, Connell, & Smith, 2006; Kidd & Lum, 2008; Pozzan & Valian, 2017).

By age 5, children have acquired the basic rules of language. However, they do not attain a full vocabulary and the ability to comprehend and use subtle grammatical rules until later. For example, a 5-year-old boy who sees a blindfolded doll and is asked, "Is the doll easy or hard to see?" would have great trouble answering the question. In fact, if he were asked to make the doll easier to see, he would probably try to remove the doll's blindfold. By the time they are 8 years old, however, children have little difficulty understanding this question because they realize that the doll's blindfold has nothing to do with an observer's ability to see the doll (Hoff, 2003; Dockrell & Marshall, 2015).

UNDERSTANDING LANGUAGE ACQUISITION: IDENTIFYING THE ROOTS OF LANGUAGE

Anyone who spends even a little time with children will notice the enormous strides that they make in language development throughout childhood. However, the reasons for this rapid growth are far from obvious. Psychologists have offered three major explanations: one based on learning theory, one based on innate processes, and one that involves something of a combination of the two.

Learning-Theory Approaches: Language as a Learned Skill The **learning-theory approach** suggests that language acquisition follows the principles of reinforcement and conditioning discovered by psychologists who study learning. For example, a child who says "mama" receives hugs and praise from her mother, which reinforce the behavior of saying "mama" and make its repetition more likely. This view suggests that children first learn to speak by being rewarded for making sounds that approximate speech. Ultimately, through a process of shaping, language becomes more and more like adult speech (Skinner, 1957; Ornat & Gallo, 2004).

In support of the learning-theory approach to language acquisition, the more that parents speak to their young children, the more proficient the children become in language use. In addition, by the time they are 3 years old, children who hear higher levels of linguistic sophistication in their parents' speech show a greater rate of vocabulary growth, vocabulary use, and even general intellectual achievement than do children whose parents' speech is simpler (Hart & Risley, 1997).

The learning-theory approach is less successful in explaining how children acquire language rules. Children are reinforced not only when they use language correctly but also when they use it incorrectly. For example, parents answer a child's query of "Why the dog won't eat?" as readily as they do the correctly phrased question, "Why won't

telegraphic speech Sentences in which only essential words are used, typically including only nouns and verbs. (Module 25)

overgeneralization The phenomenon by which children over-apply a language rule, thereby making a linguistic error. (Module 25)

learning-theory approach (to language development) The theory that language acquisition follows the principles of reinforcement and conditioning. (Module 25) the dog eat?" Listeners understand both sentences equally well. Learning theory, then, has difficulty fully explaining language acquisition.

Nativist Approaches: Language as an Innate Skill Pointing to such problems with learning-theory approaches to language acquisition, linguist Noam Chomsky (1978, 1991) provided a groundbreaking alternative. He argued that humans are born with an innate linguistic capability that emerges primarily as a function of maturation.

According to Chomsky's **nativist approach,** humans are genetically prewired to learn language at certain periods in their lives and in a particular way. Furthermore, he suggests that all the world's languages share a common underlying structure that is prewired, genetically determined, and universal across all people.

The nativist approach argues that the human brain contains an inherited neural system, which Chomsky calls *universal grammar,* that lets us understand the structure language provides. These inborn capabilities give us strategies and techniques for learning the unique characteristics of our own native language (McGilvray, 2004; White, 2007; Yang et al., 2017).

Evidence collected by neuroscientists supports Chomsky's view. This research suggests that the ability to use language, which was a significant evolutionary advance in human beings, is tied to specific neurological developments. For example, scientists have discovered a gene related to the development of language abilities that may have emerged as recently–in evolutionary terms–as 100,000 years ago.

Furthermore, it is clear that there are specific sites within the brain that are closely tied to language and that the shape of the human mouth and throat are tailored to the production of speech. And there is evidence that features of specific types of languages are tied to particular genes, such as in "tonal" languages in which pitch is used to convey meaning (Grigorenko, 2009; Perovic & Radenovic, 2011; Lieberman, 2015).

However, Chomsky's nativist view is contradicted by some researchers. For instance, learning theorists contend that the apparent ability of certain animals, such as chimpanzees, to learn the fundamentals of human language (as we discuss later in this module) contradicts the innate linguistic capability view. Furthermore, some cognitive psychologists believe that what underlies children's language learning is their use of

nativist approach (to language development) The theory that humans are genetically prewired to learn language at certain times and in particular ways. (Module 25)

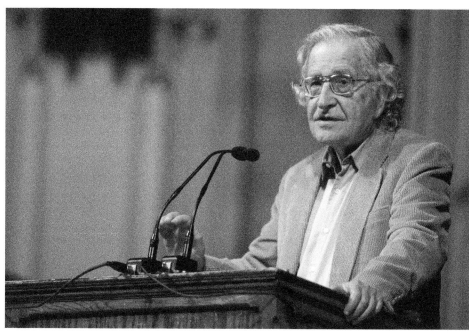
Noam Chomsky argues that all languages share a universal grammar.
©Dennis Van Tine/ABACAUSA.COM/Newscom

general cognitive abilities, as well as skills attained through social interaction with others (Ibbotson & Tomasello, 2016).

Interactionist Approaches   To reconcile the differing views of the learning-theory and nativist approaches, many theorists hold a compromise view, known as the interactionist approach to language development. The **interactionist approach** suggests that language development is determined by both genetic and social factors, produced through a combination of genetically determined predispositions *and* the social world in which one is raised.

Specifically, proponents of the interactionist approach suggest that the brain is hardwired for our acquisition of language, in essence providing the "hardware" that allows us to develop language. However, it is the exposure to language from social interactions with others that allows us to develop the appropriate "software" to understand and produce language.

The interactionist approach has many proponents. Still, the issue of how language is acquired remains hotly contested (Pinker & Jackendoff, 2005; Hoff, 2008; Waxman, 2009).

interactionist approach (to language development) The view that language development is determined by genetic and social factors, produced through a combination of genetically determined predispositions and the social world in which one is raised. (Module 25)

Study Alert

It's important to be able to compare and contrast the major approaches to language development: learning-theory, nativist, and interactionist approaches.

From the perspective of . . .

A Child-Care Provider How would you encourage children's language abilities at the different stages of development?

©Rubberball/Getty Images

The Influence of Language on Thinking: Do Eskimos Have More Words for Snow Than Texans Do?

Do Eskimos living in the frigid Arctic have a more expansive vocabulary for discussing snow than people living in warmer climates do?

It makes sense, and arguments that the Eskimo language has many more words than English does for snow have been made since the early 1900s. At that time, linguist Benjamin Lee Whorf contended that because snow is so relevant to Eskimos' lives, their language provides a particularly rich vocabulary to describe it–considerably larger than what we find in other languages, such as English (Martin & Pullum, 1991; Pinker, 1994).

The contention that the Eskimo language is especially abundant in snow-related terms led to the linguistic-relativity hypothesis. According to the **linguistic-relativity hypothesis,** language shapes and helps determine the way people perceive and understand the world. That is, language provides us with categories we use to construct our view of others and events in the world around us. In this way, language shapes and produces thought (Whorf, 1956; Tan et al., 2008; Bylund & Athanasopoulos, 2017).

Let's consider another possibility, however. Suppose that instead of language being the *cause* of certain ways of thinking, thought *produces* language. The only reason to expect that Eskimo language might have more words for snow than English does is that snow is considerably more relevant to Eskimos than it is to people in other cultures.

Which view is correct? Most recent research refutes the linguistic-relativity hypothesis and suggests, instead, that thinking produces language. In fact, new analyses of the

linguistic-relativity hypothesis The hypothesis that language shapes and may determine the way people perceive and understand the world. (Module 25)

Eskimo language suggest that Eskimos have no more words for snow than English speakers do. If one examines the English language closely, one sees that it is hardly impoverished when it comes to describing snow (consider, for example, *sleet, slush, blizzard, dusting,* and *avalanche*).

Still, the linguistic-relativity hypothesis has not been entirely discarded. A newer version of the hypothesis suggests that speech patterns may influence certain aspects of thinking. For example, in some languages, such as English, speakers distinguish between nouns that can be counted (such as "five chairs") and nouns that require a measurement unit to be quantified (such as "a liter of water"). In some other languages, such as the Mayan language called Yucatec, however, all nouns require a measurement unit. In such cultures, people appear to think more closely about what things are made of than do people in cultures in which languages such as English are spoken (Gentner, Goldin, & Goldin-Meadow, 2003; Tsukasaki & Ishii, 2004; Stam, 2015).

Similarly, Russian speakers have more words for light and dark blues and are better able to discriminate shades of blue visually than English speakers. The Icelandic language contains 24 words for types of waves. Furthermore, some tribes say north, south, east, and west instead of left and right, and they have better spatial orientation. And the Piraha language uses terms such as *few* and *many*, rather than specific numbers, and speakers are unable to keep track of exact quantities (Boroditsky, 2010; Fuhrman et al., 2011).

Finally, language seems to foster and support certain kinds of reasoning. In essence, language makes us better able to think in more sophisticated ways, helping us to understand such concepts as cause and effect (Gentner, 2016).

In short, although research does not support the linguistic-relativity hypothesis that language *causes* thought, it is clear that language influences how we think. And, of course, it certainly is the case that thought influences language, suggesting that language and thinking interact in complex ways (Ross, 2004; Thorkildsen, 2006; Proudfoot, 2009).

> **Study Alert**
> The linguistic-relativity hypothesis suggests language leads to thought.

Do Animals Use Language?

One question that has long puzzled psychologists is whether language is uniquely human or if other animals are able to acquire it as well. Many animals communicate with one another in rudimentary forms. For instance, fiddler crabs wave their claws to signal, bees dance to indicate the direction in which food will be found, and certain birds call "*zick, zick*" during courtship and "*kia*" when they are about to fly away. However, researchers have yet to demonstrate conclusively that these animals use true language, which is characterized in part by the ability to produce and communicate new and unique meanings by following a formal grammar.

Psychologists, however, have been able to teach chimps to communicate at surprisingly high levels. For instance, after 4 years of training, a chimp named Washoe learned to make signs for 132 words and combine those signs into simple sentences. Even more impressively, Kanzi, a bonobo (a kind of small chimpanzee), has linguistic skills that some psychologists claim are close to those of a 2-year-old human being. Kanzi's trainers suggest that he can create grammatically sophisticated sentences and can even invent new rules of syntax (Savage-Rumbaugh, Toth, & Schick, 2007; Slocombe, Waller, & Liebal, 2011).

More generally, researchers have found evidence that nonhuman primates use several basic components of human language. For example, they use vocalizations that they modify based on social and other environmental influences, and they take turns communicating about food resources. Furthermore, they have physical structures that allow them to produce vowel sounds similar to human language (Snowdon, 2017).

Despite the languagelike capabilities of primates such as Kanzi, critics contend that the language such animals use still lacks the grammar and the complex and novel constructions of human language. Instead, they maintain that the chimps are displaying a skill no different from that of a dog that learns to lie down on command to get a reward. Furthermore, we lack firm evidence that animals can recognize and

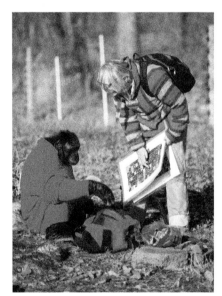

Psychologist and primatologist Sue Savage-Rumbaugh with a primate friend, Kanzi. Does the use of sign language by primates indicate true mastery of language?

©Laurentiu Garofeanu/Barcroft USA/Barcoft Media via Getty Images respond to the mental states of others of their species, an important aspect of human communication. Consequently, the issue of whether other animals can use language in a way that humans do remains controversial (Beran, Smith, & Perdue, 2013; Crockford, Wittig, & Zuberbühler, 2015; ten Cate, 2017).

Exploring Diversity

Teaching with Linguistic Variety: Bilingual Education

In New York City, nearly half of the students speak a language other than English in their homes, with more than 180 languages represented. Furthermore, 1 in 6 of the city's 1.1 million students is enrolled in some form of bilingual or English as a Second Language instruction.

And New York City is far from the only school district with a significant population of nonnative English speakers. From the biggest cities to the most rural areas, the face—and voice—of education in the United States is changing. More and more schoolchildren today have last names like Kim, Valdez, and Karachnicoff. In seven states, including Texas and Colorado, more than one-quarter of the students are not native English speakers. For some 55 million Americans, English is their second language (see Figure 1; Holloway, 2000; Shin & Kominski, 2010).

How to appropriately and effectively teach the increasing number of children who do not speak English is not always clear. Many educators maintain that *bilingual education* is best. With a bilingual approach, students learn some subjects in their native language while simultaneously learning English. Proponents of bilingualism believe that students must develop a sound footing in basic subject areas and that, initially at least, teaching those subjects in their native language is the only way to provide them with that foundation. During the same period, they learn English, with the eventual goal of shifting all instruction into English.

In contrast, other educators insist that all instruction ought to be in English from the moment students, including those who speak no English at all, enroll in school. In *immersion programs,* students are immediately plunged into English instruction in all subjects. The reasoning—endorsed by voters in California in a referendum designed to end bilingual education—is that teaching students in a language other than English simply hinders nonnative English speakers' integration into society and ultimately does them a disservice. Proponents of English immersion programs point as evidence to improvements in standardized test scores that followed the end of bilingual education programs (Wildavsky, 2000).

FIGURE 1 The language of diversity. One-fifth of the people in the United States speak a language other than English at home. Spanish is most prevalent; the rest of non-English speakers use an astounding variety of different languages.

Source: Adapted from MLA. (2010). MLA Language Map; all languages other than English combined. Retrieved from http://www.mla.org/census_map&source=county (based on 2000 U.S. Census Bureau figures).

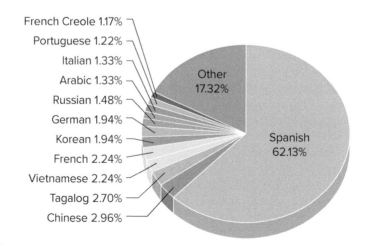

French Creole 1.17%
Portuguese 1.22%
Italian 1.33%
Arabic 1.33%
Russian 1.48%
German 1.94%
Korean 1.94%
French 2.24%
Vietnamese 2.24%
Tagalog 2.70%
Chinese 2.96%
Other 17.32%
Spanish 62.13%

Although the controversial issue of bilingual education versus immersion has strong political undercurrents, evidence shows that the ability to speak two languages provides significant cognitive benefits over speaking only one language. For example, bilingual speakers show more cognitive flexibility and may understand concepts more easily than do those who speak only one language. They have more linguistic tools for thinking because of their multiple-language abilities. In turn, this makes them more creative and flexible in solving problems (Kuo, 2007; Yim & Rudoy, 2013; Christoffels et al., 2015).

In addition, the advantages of bilingualism start early: by the time bilingual children are 3 or 4 years old, their cognitive development is superior to that of children who speak only one language. It's an advantage that lasts into old age. In fact, bilingualism provides protection from the cognitive declines that are typical in late adulthood (Bialystok et al., 2010; Bialystok & Craik, 2011; Bialystok, 2011).

Furthermore, speaking several languages changes the organization of the brain. For example, bilingual speakers who learn their second language as adults show different areas of brain activation compared with those who learn their second language in childhood. And those who are immersed in intensive language instruction show growth in the hippocampus. In addition, brain scans show that people who speak multiple languages have distinct patterns of brain activity according to the language that they are using, and bilingualism produces more efficient processing on some cognitive tasks (Kovacs & Mehler, 2009; Bialystok et al., 2010; Kluger, 2013). (Also see *Neuroscience in Your Life.*)

Related to questions about bilingual education is the matter of *biculturalism*—that is, being a member of two cultures and its psychological impact. Some psychologists argue that society should promote an *alternation model* of bicultural competence. Such a model supports members of a culture in their efforts to maintain their original cultural identity as well as in their integration into the adopted culture. In this view, a person can belong to two cultures and have two cultural identities without having to choose between them. Whether society will adopt the alternation model remains to be seen (Carter, 2003; Benet-Martínez, Lee, & Leu, 2006; Tadmor, 2007).

AP NEUROSCIENCE IN YOUR LIFE: BEING BILINGUAL AFFECTS THE BRAIN

Because it appears increasingly clear that people who are bilingual have certain cognitive advantages, such as greater cognitive flexibility, researchers are now exploring whether being bilingual affects the structure and functioning of the brain. And they have found, for example, that Spanish-English bilingual adults have more grey matter volume in frontal and parietal brain regions than English monolinguals. This can be seen in the two images of the brain below, where the red indicates the areas that have more grey matter volume for bilinguals. The findings suggest that managing the use of two separate languages affects the structure of the brain, potentially affecting its functioning (Olulade et al., 2016).

AP SKILL: SCIENTIFIC INVESTIGATION / EXPLAIN BEHAVIOR IN AUTHENTIC CONTEXT

1. Provide a hypothesis for the experiment described.

2. Why might bilinguals have more grey matter volume in the frontal and parietal lobes?

Left side of brain   **Right side of brain**

Source: Adapted from Olulade, O. A., Jamal, N. I., Koo, D. S., Perfetti, C. A., LaSasso, C., & Eden, G. F. (2016). Neuroanatomical evidence in support of the bilingual advantage theory. *Cerebral Cortex, 26*(7), 3196-3204. doi: 10.1093/cercor/bhv152

AP MODULE 25: LANGUAGE

AP SUMMARY

- Noam Chomsky's nativist approach to language development argues that humans are genetically prewired to learn language at certain periods of their lives and in a specific way. The human brain contains an inherited neural system, called universal grammar, that lets us understand the structure language provides.

- Language is the communication of information through symbols arranged according to systematic rules. All languages have a grammar–a system or structure of rules that determines how thoughts can be expressed–that encompasses the three major components of language: phonology, syntax, and semantics.

- Language production, which follows language comprehension, develops out of babbling, which then leads to the production of actual words. By age 1, children stop producing sounds that are not from the language to which they have been exposed and begin speaking single words. After 1 year of age, children use two-word combinations, increase their vocabulary, and use telegraphic speech, which drops words not critical to the message. By age 3, children being to apply rules inflexibly that result in errors, a process known as overgeneralization. By age 5, acquisition of basic language rules is relatively complete.

- Some theorists argue that a critical period exists for language development early in life in which a child is sensitive to language cues and easily acquires language. Cases involving isolation from contact, such as Genie, support this theory.

- Learning theorists, such as B.F. Skinner, suggest that language is acquired through reinforcement and conditioning. In contrast, the nativist approach suggests that an innate linguistic ability guides the development of language. The interactionist approach argues that language development is produced through a combination of genetically determined predispositions and environmental circumstances that help teach language.

- The linguistic-relativity hypothesis, proposed by Benjamin Lee Whorf, suggests that language shapes and may determine the way people think about the world. Most evidence suggests that although language does not determine thoughts, it does influence it.

- The degree to which language is a uniquely human skill remains an open question. Some psychologists argue that even though certain primates communicate at a high level, those animals do not use language. Other psychologists suggest that those primates truly understand and produce language in much the same way as humans.

- People who speak more than one language may have a cognitive advantage over those who speak only one.

AP KEY TERMS

language
grammar
phonology
phonemes
syntax
semantics
babble
telegraphic speech
overgeneralization
learning-theory approach (to language development)
nativist approach (to language development)
interactionist approach (to language development)
linguistic-relativity hypothesis

AP TEST PRACTICE

Section I: Multiple Choice

1. Who supports the nativist approach to language development?
   A. B.F. Skinner
   B. Wolfgang Köhler
   C. Benjamin Lee Whorf
   D. Noam Chomsky
   E. George Miller

2. As you age it is more challenging to pronounce sounds from a foreign language. Basic units of sound are known as
   A. grammar
   B. morphemes
   C. phonemes
   D. semantics
   E. syntax

3. According to Benjamin Lee Whorf's linguistic-relativity hypothesis, what is the relationship between language and cognition?
   A. Language acquisition follows the principles of reinforcement and conditioning
   B. Language influences how we think
   C. Language is genetically prewired in humans
   D. Language is uniquely human
   E. Language must be learned during a critical period

Section II: Free Response

Researchers conducted an experiment involving a new learning method for a foreign language. Each participant was randomly assigned to one of two conditions. One group of participants was provided an electronic translator to help learn a new language. Another group was provided traditional methods for learning a new language. After six months, both groups were given an oral assessment and received a score from 0–100.

- Provide the independent variable
- Operationally define the dependent variable

- What makes the study experimental rather than correlational?
- What is the control group?

Describe how each of the following relates to language acquisition and age.

- Phonemes
- Universal grammar
- Critical period

LOOKING *Back*

EPILOGUE

The study of cognition occupies a central place in the field of psychology and encompasses a variety of areas—including thinking, problem solving, decision making, creativity, language, memory, and intelligence. Specialists in cognitive psychology have made significant advances in the last decade that have influenced the entire field of psychology.

VISUAL SUMMARY 8 Cognition and Language

MODULES 23 and 24 Thinking, Reasoning, and Problem Solving

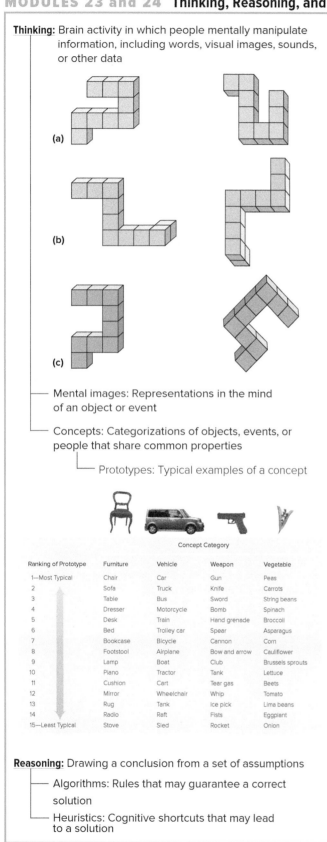

Thinking: Brain activity in which people mentally manipulate information, including words, visual images, sounds, or other data

(a)

(b)

(c)

— Mental images: Representations in the mind of an object or event

— Concepts: Categorizations of objects, events, or people that share common properties

    └ Prototypes: Typical examples of a concept

Concept Category

Ranking of Prototype	Furniture	Vehicle	Weapon	Vegetable
1—Most Typical	Chair	Car	Gun	Peas
2	Sofa	Truck	Knife	Carrots
3	Table	Bus	Sword	String beans
4	Dresser	Motorcycle	Bomb	Spinach
5	Desk	Train	Hand grenade	Broccoli
6	Bed	Trolley car	Spear	Asparagus
7	Bookcase	Bicycle	Cannon	Corn
8	Footstool	Airplane	Bow and arrow	Cauliflower
9	Lamp	Boat	Club	Brussels sprouts
10	Piano	Tractor	Tank	Lettuce
11	Cushion	Cart	Tear gas	Beets
12	Mirror	Wheelchair	Whip	Tomato
13	Rug	Tank	Ice pick	Lima beans
14	Radio	Raft	Fists	Eggplant
15—Least Typical	Stove	Sled	Rocket	Onion

Reasoning: Drawing a conclusion from a set of assumptions

— Algorithms: Rules that may guarantee a correct solution

— Heuristics: Cognitive shortcuts that may lead to a solution

Problem Solving: Well-defined and ill-defined problems

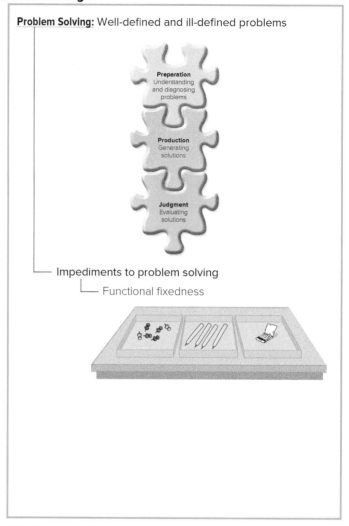

Preparation
Understanding and diagnosing problems

Production
Generating solutions

Judgment
Evaluating solutions

— Impediments to problem solving

    └ Functional fixedness

MODULE 25 Language

Language Development: Acquiring language

— Babbling: Speechlike sounds that are meaningless

— Telegraphic speech: Sentences in which only essential words are used

— Overgeneralization: The phenomenon in which children over-apply a language rule, thereby making a linguistic error

— Approaches to learning language

    — Learning-theory approach

    — Nativist approach

    — Interactionist approach

Linguistic-Relativity Hypothesis: The hypothesis that language shapes and may determine the way people perceive and understand the world

(MODULES 23 and 24): Source: Adapted from Shepard, R. N., & Metzler, J. (1971). Mental rotation of three-dimensional objects. *Science, 171*(3972), 701–703; Source: Adapted from Rosch, E., & Mervis, C. B. (1975). Family resemblances: Studies in the internal structure of categories. *Cognitive Psychology, 7*, 573–605; (MODULE 25): Source: Adapted from Duncker, K. (1945). On problem solving. *Psychological Monographs, 58* (5, whole no. 270). (MODULES 23 and 24, Photo), (chair): ©Stockbyte/Getty Images; (car): ©McGraw-Hill Education/Gary He, photographer; (gun): ©suradin/123RF; (peas): ©Isabelle Rozenbaum & Frederic Cirou/PhotoAlto/Getty Images; (MODULE 25, photo): ©Laurentiu Garofeanu/Barcroft USA/Barcroft Media via Getty Images

©Digital Vision

CHAPTER 9
Intelligence

AP'I ESSENTIAL QUESTIONS

- What is intelligence and how can we study it to understand it?

AP'I LEARNING TARGETS FOR CHAPTER 9

MODULE 26

- Define intelligence and list characteristics of how psychologists measure intelligence.

- Discuss how culture influences the definition of intelligence.

- Compare and contrast historic and contemporary theories of intelligence.

- Identify the contributions of key researchers in intelligence research and testing.

- Explain how psychologists design tests, including standardization strategies and other techniques to establish reliability and validity.

- Interpret the meaning of scores in terms of the normal curve.

WHAT IS INTELLIGENCE?

Theories of Intelligence: Are There Different Kinds of Intelligence?

The Biological Basis of Intelligence

AP'I Neuroscience in Your Life: What Makes Someone Intelligent?

Practical and Emotional Intelligence: Toward a More Intelligent View of Intelligence

Assessing Intelligence

Contemporary IQ Tests: Gauging Intelligence

Becoming an Informed Consumer of Psychology: Scoring Better on Standardized Tests

MODULE 27

- Define intelligence and list characteristics of how psychologists measure intelligence.

- Identify the contributions of key researchers in intelligence research and testing.

- Describe relevant labels related to intelligence testing.

VARIATIONS IN INTELLECTUAL ABILITY

Intellectual Disabilities

AP'I Applying Psychology in the 21st Century: Does a Hidden Genius Lie Within Us?

The Intellectually Gifted

- Define intelligence and list characteristics of how psychologists measure intelligence.

- Debate the appropriate testing practices, particularly in relation to culture-fair test uses.

PROLOGUE *THE WHIZ KID FROM TAIWAN*

Chiang Ching-liang read *Harry Potter* and began learning piano at age 6. The next year, he took up violin, and he passed the Cambridge English exams for university level at age 9. His mother says he reads more than a dozen books every week.

Now 13, Chiang has become the youngest student ever to be admitted to New York University. The Taiwanese high school student was also accepted by the University of California, Santa Cruz, but chose NYU because it has both a medical school and a music department. Chiang wants to study rare diseases because one of his relatives suffers from a progressive, degenerative genetic disease. (Kai-hsiang and Wu, 2017).

LOOKING *Ahead*

By most people's standards, Chiang is a genius. But what is genius exactly, and how might it be measured? In the following modules, we consider questions such as these as we look at intelligence in all its many varieties. We begin by considering the challenges involved in defining and measuring intelligence. If you are like most people, you have probably wondered how smart you are compared with others. Psychologists, too, have pondered the nature of intelligence. We examine some of their conceptions of intelligence as well as efforts to develop and use standardized tests as a means of measuring intelligence.

We also consider the two extremes of individual differences in intelligence: intellectual disability and giftedness. Finally, we explore what are probably the two most controversial issues surrounding intelligence: the degree to which intelligence is influenced by heredity and by the environment, and whether traditional tests of intelligence are biased toward the dominant cultural groups in society—difficult issues that have both psychological and social significance.

Module 26
What Is Intelligence?

Native sailors in the Marshall Islands in the South Pacific are capable of traveling 100 miles in open ocean waters. Although their destination may be just a small dot of land less than a mile wide, the sailors are able to navigate precisely toward it without the aid of a compass, chronometer, sextant, or any of the other sailing tools that are used by Western navigators. They are able to sail accurately even when the winds do not allow a direct approach to the island and they must take a zigzag course. (Tingley, 2016)

How are the Marshall Islands sailors able to navigate so effectively? If you asked them, they could not explain it. They might tell you that they use a process that takes into account the rising and setting of the stars and the appearance, sound, and feel of the waves against the side of the boat. But at any given moment as they are sailing along, they could not identify their position or say why they are doing what they are doing. Nor could they explain the navigational theory underlying their sailing technique.

Some people might say that the inability of the Marshall Islands sailors to explain in Western terms how their sailing technique works is a sign of primitive or even unintelligent behavior. In fact, if we gave these sailors a Western standardized test of navigational knowledge and theory or, for that matter, a traditional test of intelligence, they might do poorly on it. Yet, as a practical matter, it is not possible to accuse the sailors of being unintelligent: Despite their inability to explain how they do it, they are able to navigate successfully through the open ocean waters.

The navigation used by Marshall Island natives points out the difficulty in coming to grips with what is meant by intelligence. To a Westerner, traveling in a straight line along the most direct and quickest route by using a sextant and other navigational tools is likely to represent the most "intelligent" kind of behavior; in contrast, a zigzag course, based on the "feel" of the waves, would not seem very reasonable. To the Marshall Island sailors, who are used to their own system of navigation, however, the use of complicated navigational tools might seem so overly complex and unnecessary that they might think of Western navigators as lacking in intelligence.

It is clear from this example that the term *intelligence* can take on many different meanings. If, for instance, you lived in a remote part of the Australian outback, the way you would differentiate between more intelligent and less intelligent people might have to do with successfully mastering hunting skills, whereas to someone living in the heart of urban Miami, intelligence might be exemplified by being "streetwise" or by achieving success in business.

Each of these conceptions of intelligence is reasonable. Each represents an instance in which more intelligent people are better able to use the resources of their environment than are less-intelligent people, a distinction that is presumably basic to any definition of intelligence. Yet it is also clear that these conceptions represent very different views of intelligence.

That two such different sets of behavior can exemplify the same psychological concept has long posed a challenge to psychologists. For years they have grappled with the issue of

- Define intelligence and list characteristics of how psychologists measure intelligence.

- Discuss how culture influences the definition of intelligence.

- Compare and contrast historic and contemporary theories of intelligence.

- Identify the contributions of key researchers in intelligence research and testing.

- Explain how psychologists design tests, including standardization strategies and other techniques to establish reliability and validity.

- Interpret the meaning of scores in terms of the normal curve.

Some South Pacific islanders are able to navigate with great accuracy across open seas without the standard navigation tools used by sailors in Western cultures. Their abilities illustrate that there are multiple ways to attain our goals and that there is no single route to success.
©Danita Delimont/Galo Images/Getty Images

devising a general definition of intelligence. Ironically, laypersons have fairly clear ideas of what intelligence is, although the nature of their ideas is related to their culture. Westerners view intelligence as the ability to establish categories and debate rationally. In contrast, people in Eastern cultures and some African communities view intelligence more in terms of understanding and relating to one another (Crowne, 2013; Blackwell, Rodriguez, & Guerra-Carrillo, 2015; Chao, Takeuchi, & Farh, 2017).

The definition of intelligence that psychologists employ contains some of the same elements found in the layperson's conception. To psychologists, **intelligence** is the capacity to understand the world, think rationally, and use resources effectively when faced with challenges.

This definition does not lay to rest a key question asked by psychologists: Is intelligence a unitary attribute, or are there different kinds of intelligence? We turn now to various theories of intelligence that address the issue.

Theories of Intelligence: Are There Different Kinds of Intelligence?

Perhaps you see yourself as a good writer but as someone who lacks ability in math. Or maybe you view yourself as a "science" person who easily masters physics but has few strengths in interpreting literature. Perhaps you view yourself as generally fairly smart with intelligence that permits you to excel across domains.

The different ways in which people view their own talents mirror a question that psychologists have grappled with. Is intelligence a single, general ability, or is it multifaceted and related to specific abilities? Early psychologists interested in intelligence assumed that there was a single, general factor for mental ability, which they called **g, or the g-factor.** This assumption was based on the fact that different types of measures of intelligence, whether they focused on, say, mathematical expertise, verbal competency, or spatial visualization skills, all ranked test-takers in roughly the same order. People who were good on one test generally were good on others; those who did poorly on one test tended to do poorly on others.

Given that there was a correlation between performance on the different types of tests, the assumption was that there was a general, global intellectual ability underlying performance on the various measures—the *g-factor*. This general intelligence factor was thought to underlie performance in every aspect of intelligence, and it was the *g*-factor that was presumably being measured on tests of intelligence (Haier et al., 2009; Major, Johnson, & Bouchard, 2011; Das, 2015).

More recent theories explain intelligence in a different light. Rather than viewing intelligence as a unitary entity, some psychologists consider it to be a multidimensional concept that includes different types of intelligence (Stankov, 2003; Sternberg & Pretz, 2005; Tutwiler, Lin, & Chang, 2013).

FLUID AND CRYSTALLIZED INTELLIGENCE

Some psychologists suggest that there are two kinds of intelligence: fluid intelligence and crystallized intelligence. **Fluid intelligence** is the ability to think logically, reason abstractly, solve problems, and find patterns. We use fluid intelligence when we are applying a strategy to resolve an issue (Di Fabio & Palazzeschi, 2009; Euler et al., 2015; Kyllonen & Kell, 2017).

In contrast, **crystallized intelligence** is the accumulation of information, knowledge, and skills that people have learned through experience and education. It reflects the facts that we have learned and information that resides in our long-term memory. When we learn a new language, we use crystallized intelligence as we acquire new vocabulary words.

intelligence The capacity to understand the world, think rationally, and use resources effectively when faced with challenges. (Module 26)

g or g-factor The single, general factor for mental ability assumed to underlie intelligence in some early theories of intelligence. (Module 26)

fluid intelligence Intelligence that reflects the ability to think logically, reason abstractly, solve problems, and find patterns. (Module 26)

crystallized intelligence The accumulation of information, knowledge, and skills that people have learned through experience and education, reflecting the facts that we have learned. (Module 26)

The differences between fluid intelligence and crystallized intelligence become especially evident in late adulthood. At that point in the life span, people show declines in fluid, but not crystallized, intelligence (Tranter & Koutstaal, 2008; Ackerman, 2011; Pezoulas et al., 2017).

GARDNER'S MULTIPLE INTELLIGENCES: THE MANY WAYS OF SHOWING INTELLIGENCE

Psychologist Howard Gardner has taken an approach very different from traditional thinking about intelligence. Gardner argues that rather than asking "How smart are you?" we should be asking a different question: "How are you smart?" In answering the latter question, Gardner has developed a **theory of multiple intelligences** that has become quite influential (Gardner, 2000; Kaufman, Kaufman, & Plucker, 2013; Jung & Chang, 2017).

Piloting a helicopter requires the use of both fluid intelligence and crystallized intelligence. Which of the two kinds of intelligence do you believe is more important for such a task?
©bennymarty/123RF

Gardner argues that we have a minimum of eight different forms of intelligence, each relatively independent of the others: musical, bodily kinesthetic, logical-mathematical, linguistic, spatial, interpersonal, intrapersonal, and naturalist. (Figure 1 describes the eight types of intelligence, with some of Gardner's examples of people who excel in each type.) In Gardner's view, each of the multiple intelligences is linked to an independent system in the brain. Furthermore, he suggests that there may be even more types of intelligence, such as *existential intelligence*, which involves identifying and thinking about the fundamental questions of human existence. For example, the Dalai Lama might exemplify this type of intelligence (Gardner, 1999, 2000).

Although Gardner illustrates his conception of the specific types of intelligence with descriptions of well-known people, each person has the same eight kinds of intelligence–in different degrees. Moreover, although the eight basic types of intelligence are presented individually, Gardner suggests that these separate intelligences do not operate in isolation. Normally, any activity encompasses several kinds of intelligence working together.

The concept of multiple intelligences has led to the development of intelligence tests that include questions in which more than one answer can be correct; these provide an opportunity for test-takers to demonstrate creative thinking. In addition, many educators, embracing the concept of multiple intelligences, have designed classroom curricula that are meant to draw on different aspects of intelligence (Tirri & Nokelainen, 2008; Davis et al., 2011; Sternberg, 2015).

theory of multiple intelligences
Gardner's intelligence theory that proposes that there are eight distinct spheres of intelligence. (Module 26)

Study Alert
Remember, Gardner's theory suggests that each individual has every kind of intelligence but in different degrees.

The Biological Basis of Intelligence

Using brain-scanning methods, researchers have identified several areas of the brain that relate to intelligence. For example, the brains of people completing intelligence test questions in both verbal and spatial domains show activation in a similar location: the lateral prefrontal cortex. That area is above the outer edge of the eyebrow about where people rest their heads in the palms of their hands if they are thinking hard about a problem. This area of the brain is critical to juggling many pieces of information simultaneously and solving new problems. In addition, higher intelligence is related to the thickness of the cerebral cortex (Karama et al., 2009; Luders et al., 2009; Brant et al., 2013; MacLennan, 2017).

Similarly, tasks requiring different types of intelligence involve different areas of the brain. For instance, when tasks require more general global intelligence, more areas of the brain are involved than in tasks requiring more specific sorts of intelligence (such as fluid and crystallized intelligence) (Colom et al., 2009; Haier, 2011).

1. Musical intelligence (skills in tasks involving music). Example:

When he was 3, Yehudi Menuhin was smuggled into San Francisco Orchestra concerts by his parents. By the time he was 10 years old, Menuhin was an international performer.

2. Bodily kinesthetic intelligence (skills in using the whole body or various portions of it in the solution of problems or in the construction of products or displays, exemplified by dancers, athletes, actors, and surgeons). Example:

Known for his athleticism, New York Yankees baseball captain Derek Jeter played baseball and basketball, and he also ran track in high school.

3. Logical-mathematical intelligence (skills in problem solving and scientific thinking). Example:

Barbara McClintock, who won the Nobel Prize in medicine, describes one of her breakthroughs, which came after thinking about a problem for half an hour . . . : "Suddenly I jumped and ran back to the (corn) field. At the top of the field (the others were still at the bottom) I shouted, 'Eureka, I have it!'"

4. Linguistic intelligence (skills involved in the production and use of language). Example:

At the age of 10, poet T. S. Eliot created a magazine called *Fireside*, to which he was the sole contributor.

5. Spatial intelligence (skills involving spatial configurations, such as those used by artists and architects). Example:

Natives of the Truk Islands navigate at sea without instruments. During the actual trip, the navigator must envision mentally a reference island as it passes under a particular star, and from that he computes the number of segments completed, the proportion of the trip remaining, and any corrections in heading.

6. Interpersonal intelligence (skills in interacting with others, such as sensitivity to the moods, temperaments, motivations, and intentions of others). Example:

When Anne Sullivan began instructing the deaf and blind Helen Keller, her task was one that had eluded others for years. Yet, just 2 weeks after beginning her work with Keller, Sullivan achieved great success.

7. Intrapersonal intelligence (knowledge of the internal aspects of oneself; access to one's own feelings and emotions). Example:

Writer Toni Morrison, who won Pulitzer and Nobel Prizes, began writing as a college student at Howard University. She wrote her first novel while working at a full-time job and raising two children as a single mother, getting up at 4 A.M. each morning to work on the book.

8. Naturalist intelligence (ability to identify and classify patterns in nature). Example:

During prehistoric times, hunter-gatherers would rely on naturalist intelligence to identify what flora and fauna were edible. People who are adept at distinguishing nuances between large numbers of similar objects may be expressing naturalist intelligence abilities.

FIGURE 1 Howard Gardner describes eight major kinds of intelligences, corresponding to abilities in different domains. In what area does your greatest intelligence reside, and why do you think you have particular strengths in that area?

These findings suggest that there is a global "workspace" in the brain that organizes and coordinates information, helping to transfer material to other parts of the brain. In this view, the activity in the workspace represents general intelligence (Gray, Chabris, & Braver, 2003).

Research using nonhumans has also begun to help us better understand the biological underpinnings of intelligence. For example, rats raised in enriched environments (meaning an environment containing more toys, tunnels, and so on) develop more complex connections between neurons along with more rapid learning and better memory. Other studies show differences in metabolism (the rate at which food is converted to energy and expended by the body) that seem to be related to intelligence (Haier, 2003; Yang et al., 2007; Santarnecchi, Rossi, & Rossi, 2015).

Ultimately, the search for the biological underpinnings of intelligence will not lead in a single direction. Rather, the most plausible scenario is that multiple areas of the brain, as well as multiple kinds of functioning, are related to intelligent behavior (also see *Neuroscience in Your Life* feature).

AP NEUROSCIENCE IN YOUR LIFE: WHAT MAKES SOMEONE INTELLIGENT?

In their efforts to understand the neural basis of intelligence, neuroscientists have recently found that individual differences in general intelligence are associated with differences in both structure and function of the brain. For example, a review of 16 studies showed that general intelligence, as measured by standard intelligence tests, was related to brain activity in eight clusters in the frontal, parietal, and temporal cortices. The images below show five views of the brain and indicate regions related to intelligence that were active across experiments in the review, with red indicating more studies showing effects in this region. These results suggest that a network of frontal and parietal brain regions may be the main neural basis of intelligence (Basten, Hilger, & Fiebach, 2015).

AP SKILL: SCIENTIFIC INVESTIGATION / DATA ANALYSIS

1. What research procedure involves a review of 16 different studies?

2. It was found that a network of frontal and parietal brain regions may be the neural basis of intelligence. What brain scanning technique could be used to measure brain structure and function to support this theory?

Left   Right

Source: Adapted from Basten, U., Hilger, K., & Fiebach, C. J. (2015). Where smart brains are different: A quantitative meta-analysis of functional and structural brain imaging studies on intelligence. *Intelligence, 51,* 10–17.

Practical and Emotional Intelligence: Toward a More Intelligent View of Intelligence

Consider the following situation:

> An employee who reports to one of your subordinates has asked to talk with you about waste, poor management practices, and possible violations of both company policy and the law on the part of your subordinate. You have been in your present position only a year, but in that time, you have had no indications of trouble about the subordinate in question. Neither you nor your company has an "open door" policy, so it is expected that employees should take their concerns to their immediate supervisors before bringing a matter to the attention of anyone else. The employee who wishes to meet with you has not discussed this matter with her supervisors because of its delicate nature. (Sternberg, 1998)

Your response to this situation has a lot to do with your future success in a business career, according to psychologist Robert Sternberg. The question is one of a series designed to help give an indication of your intelligence. However, it is not traditional intelligence that the question is designed to tap but rather intelligence of a specific kind: practical intelligence. **Practical intelligence** is intelligence related to overall success in living (Muammar, 2007; Wagner, 2011; Baczyńska & Thornton, 2017).

Noting that traditional tests were designed to relate to academic success, Sternberg points to evidence showing that most traditional measures of intelligence do not relate especially well to *career* success. Specifically, although successful business executives usually score at least moderately well on intelligence tests, the rate at which they advance and their ultimate business achievements are only minimally associated with traditional measures of their intelligence.

Sternberg argues that career success requires a very different type of intelligence from that required for academic success. Whereas academic success is based on knowledge of a specific information base obtained from reading and listening, practical intelligence is learned mainly through observation of others' behavior. People who are high in practical intelligence are able to learn general norms and principles and apply them appropriately. Consequently, practical intelligence tests, such as the one shown in Figure 2, measure the ability to employ broad principles in solving everyday problems (Stemler & Sternberg, 2006; Stemler et al., 2009; Sternberg, 2013).

In addition to practical intelligence, Sternberg argues there are two other basic, interrelated types of intelligence related to life success: analytical and creative. *Analytical intelligence* focuses on abstract but traditional types of problems measured on IQ tests, whereas *creative intelligence* involves the generation of novel ideas and products (Benderly, 2004; Sternberg, Kaufman, & Pretz, 2004; Sternberg, Grigorenko, & Kidd, 2005).

Some psychologists broaden the concept of intelligence even further beyond the intellectual realm to include emotions. **Emotional intelligence** is the set of skills that underlie the accurate assessment, evaluation, expression, and regulation of emotions (Mayer, Salovey, & Caruso, 2008; Humphrey, Curran, & Morris, 2007; Anderson, Paul, & Brown, 2017).

Emotional intelligence is the basis of empathy for others, self-awareness, and social skills. It encompasses the ability to get along well with others. It provides us with an understanding of what other people are feeling and experiencing, which permits us to respond appropriately to others' needs. These abilities may help explain why people with only modest scores on traditional intelligence tests can be quite successful: the basis of their success may be a high emotional intelligence, which allows them to respond appropriately and quickly to others' feelings.

Although the notion of emotional intelligence makes sense, it has yet to be quantified in a rigorous manner. Furthermore, the view that emotional intelligence is so important that skills related to it should be taught in school has raised concerns among

practical intelligence According to Sternberg, intelligence related to overall success in living. (Module 26)

emotional intelligence The set of skills that underlie the accurate assessment, evaluation, expression, and regulation of emotions. (Module 26)

Study Alert

Traditional intelligence relates to academic performance; practical intelligence relates to success in life; emotional intelligence relates to emotional skills.

You are given a map of an entertainment park.
You walk from the lemonade stand to the computer games arcade.
Your friend walks from the shooting gallery to the roller coaster.
Which of these are you BOTH most likely to pass?

Ⓐ the merry-go-round Ⓑ the music hall

Ⓒ the pizza stand Ⓓ the dog show

FIGURE 2 Most standard tests of intelligence primarily measure analytical skills; more comprehensive tests measure creative and practical abilities as well.

Source: Adapted from Sternberg, R. J. (2000). Intelligence and wisdom. In R. J. Sternberg (Ed.), *Handbook of intelligence*. New York: Cambridge University Press.

some educators. They suggest that the nurturance of emotional intelligence is best left to students' families, especially because there is no well-specified set of criteria for what constitutes emotional intelligence (Becker, 2003; Vesely, Saklofske, & Leschied, 2013).

Still, the notion of emotional intelligence reminds us that there are many ways to demonstrate intelligent behavior—just as there are multiple views of the nature of intelligence (Fox & Spector, 2000; Barrett & Salovey, 2002; Parke, Seo, & Sherf, 2015). Figure 3 presents a summary of the different approaches used by psychologists.

Major Approaches to Intelligence	
Approach	**Characteristics**
Fluid and crystallized intelligence	Fluid intelligence relates to the ability to think logically, reason abstractly, and solve problems; crystallized intelligence relates to information, skills, and strategies learned through experience
Gardner's multiple intelligences	Eight independent forms of intelligence
Practical intelligence	Intelligence in terms of nonacademic, career, and personal success
Emotional intelligence	Intelligence that provides an understanding of what other people are feeling and experiencing and permits us to respond appropriately to others' needs

FIGURE 3 Just as there are many views of the nature of intelligence, there are also numerous ways to demonstrate intelligent behavior. This summary provides an overview of the various approaches used by psychologists.

Assessing Intelligence

intelligence tests Tests devised to quantify a person's level of intelligence. (Module 26)

Given the variety of approaches to the components of intelligence, it is not surprising that measuring intelligence has proved challenging. Psychologists who study intelligence have focused much of their attention on the development of **intelligence tests** that quantify a person's level of intelligence. These tests have proved to be of great benefit in identifying students in need of special attention in school, diagnosing specific learning difficulties, and helping people make the best educational and vocational choices. At the same time, their use has proved controversial, raising important social and educational issues.

Historically, the first effort at intelligence testing was based on an uncomplicated but completely wrong assumption: that the size and shape of a person's head could be used as an objective measure of intelligence. The idea was put forward by Sir Francis Galton (1822-1911), an eminent English scientist whose ideas in other domains proved to be considerably better than his notions about intelligence.

Galton's motivation to identify people of high intelligence stemmed from personal prejudices. He sought to demonstrate the natural superiority of people of high social class (including himself) by showing that intelligence is inherited. He hypothesized that head configuration, which is genetically determined, is related to brain size and therefore is related to intelligence.

Galton's theories were proved wrong on virtually every count. Head size and shape are not related to intellectual performance, and subsequent research has found little relationship between brain size and intelligence. However, Galton's work did have at least one desirable result: He was the first person to suggest that intelligence could be quantified and measured in an objective manner (Jensen, 2002).

BINET AND THE DEVELOPMENT OF IQ TESTS

French psychologist Alfred Binet (1857-1911) developed the first real intelligence test. His tests followed from a simple premise: If performance on certain tasks or test items improved with *chronological*, or physical, age, performance could be used to distinguish more intelligent people from less intelligent ones within a particular age group. On the basis of this principle, Binet devised the first formal intelligence test, which was designed to identify the "dullest" students in the Paris school system in order to provide them with remedial aid.

Alfred Binet
©Albert Harlingue/Roger Viollet/The Image Works

mental age The age for which a given level of performance is average or typical. (Module 26)

Binet began by presenting tasks to same-age students who had been labeled "bright" or "dull" by their teachers. If a task could be completed by the bright students but not by the dull ones, he retained that task as a proper test item; otherwise, it was discarded. In the end, he came up with a test that distinguished between the bright and dull groups, and—with further work—one that distinguished among children in different age groups (Binet & Simon, 1916; Sternberg & Jarvin, 2003).

On the basis of the Binet test, children were assigned a score relating to their **mental age,** the age for which a given level of performance is average or typical. For example, if the average 8-year-old answered, say, 45 items correctly on a test, anyone who answered 45 items correctly would be assigned a mental age of 8 years. Consequently, whether the person taking the test was 20 years old or 5 years old, he or she would have the same mental age of 8 years (Cornell, 2006).

Assigning a mental age to students provided an indication of their general level of performance. However, it did not allow for adequate comparisons among people of different chronological ages. By using mental age alone, for instance, we might assume that an 18-year-old responding at a 20-year-old's level would be demonstrating the same degree of intelligence as a 5-year-old answering at a 7-year-old's level, when actually the 5-year-old would be displaying a much greater *relative* degree of intelligence.

intelligence quotient (IQ) A score that takes into account an individual's mental and chronological ages. (Module 26)

A solution to the problem came in the form of the intelligence quotient, or IQ. The **intelligence quotient (IQ)** is a measure of intelligence that takes into account an individual's mental *and* chronological (physical) age. Historically, the first IQ scores

The average IQ score is 100, and 68% of people score between 85 and 115.

68%

95%

0.1% 2% 14% 34% 34% 14% 2% 0.1%

0 55 70 85 100 115 130 145 160

Intelligence test score

Number of scores →

FIGURE 4 The average and most common IQ score is 100, and 68% of all people are within a 30-point range centered on 100. Some 95% of the population have scores that are within 30 points above or below 100, and 99.8% have scores that are between 55 and 145.

employed the following formula in which *MA* stands for mental age and *CA* for chronological age:

$$\text{IQ score} = \frac{\text{MA}}{\text{CA}} \times 100$$

Using this formula, we can return to the earlier example of an 18-year-old performing at a mental age of 20 and calculate an IQ score of $(20/18) \times 100 = 111$. In contrast, the 5-year-old performing at a mental age of 7 comes out with a considerably higher IQ score: $(7/5) \times 100 = 140$.

As a bit of trial and error with the formula will show you, anyone who has a mental age equal to his or her chronological age will have an IQ equal to 100. Moreover, people with a mental age that is lower than their chronological age will have IQs that are lower than 100.

Although the basic principles behind the calculation of an IQ score still hold, today IQ scores are determined in a different manner and are known as *deviation IQ scores*. First, the average test score for everyone of the same age who takes the test is determined, and that average score is assigned an IQ of 100. Then, with the aid of statistical techniques that calculate the differences (or "deviations") between each score and the average, IQ scores are assigned.

As you can see in Figure 4, when IQ scores from large numbers of people are plotted on a graph, they form a *bell-shaped distribution* (called "bell-shaped" because it looks like a bell when plotted). Approximately two-thirds of all individuals fall within 15 IQ points of the average score of 100. As scores increase or fall beyond that range, the percentage of people in a category falls considerably.

 Study Alert

It's important to know the traditional formula for IQ scores in which IQ is the ratio of mental age divided by chronological age, multiplied by 100. Remember, though, that today, the actual calculator of IQ scores is done in a more sophisticated manner.

Contemporary IQ Tests: Gauging Intelligence

Remnants of Binet's original intelligence test are still with us, although the test has been revised in significant ways. Now in its fifth edition and called the *Stanford-Binet Intelligence Scale*, the test consists of a series of items that vary according to the age of the person being tested (Roid, Nellis, & McLellan, 2003). For example, young children are asked to copy figures or answer questions about everyday activities. Older people are asked to solve analogies, explain proverbs, and describe similarities that underlie sets of words.

The test is administered orally and includes both verbal and nonverbal assessments. An examiner begins by finding a mental age level at which a person is able to answer all the questions correctly and then moves on to successively more difficult problems.

Now in its fifth edition, the Stanford-Binet test consists of a series of items that vary in nature according to the age of the person being tested. What can we learn about a person from a test of this type?
©Lewis J. Merrim/Science Source

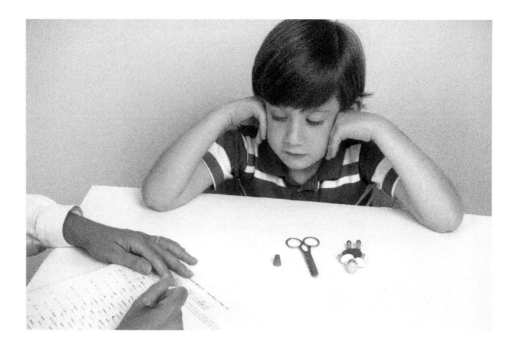

When a mental age level is reached at which no items can be answered, the test is over. By studying the pattern of correct and incorrect responses, the examiner is able to compute an IQ score for the person being tested. In addition, the Stanford-Binet test yields separate subscores that provide clues to a test-taker's particular strengths and weaknesses.

The IQ tests most frequently used in the United States were devised by psychologist David Wechsler and are known as the *Wechsler Adult Intelligence Scale-IV*, or, more commonly, the *WAIS-IV* (for adults) and a children's version, the *Wechsler Intelligence Scale for Children-V*, or *WISC-V*. Both the WAIS-IV and the WISC-V measure verbal comprehension, perceptual reasoning, working memory, and processing speed (see sample WAIS-IV items in Figure 5).

Because the Stanford-Binet, WAIS-IV, and WISC-V all require individualized, one-on-one administration, they are relatively difficult to administer and score on a large-scale basis. Consequently, there are now a number of IQ tests that allow group administration. Rather than having one examiner ask one person at a time to respond to individual items, group IQ tests are strictly paper-and-pencil tests. The primary advantage of group tests is their ease of administration (Anastasi & Urbina, 1997; Danner et al., 2011).

However, sacrifices are made in group testing that, in some cases, may outweigh the benefits. For instance, group tests generally offer fewer kinds of questions than do tests administered individually. Furthermore, people may be more motivated to perform at their highest ability level when working on a one-to-one basis with a test administrator than they are in a group. Finally, in some cases, it is simply impossible to employ group tests, particularly with young children or people with unusually low IQs (Brown-Chidsey & Andren, 2015).

RELIABILITY AND VALIDITY: TAKING THE MEASURE OF TESTS

When we use a ruler, we expect to find that it measures an inch in the same way it did the last time we used it. When we weigh ourselves on the bathroom scale, we hope that the variations we see on the scale are due to changes in our weight and not to errors on the part of the scale (unless the change in weight is in an unwanted direction!).

reliability The consistency of a test in measuring what it is trying to measure. (Module 26)

In the same way, we hope that psychological tests have reliability. **Reliability** refers to the consistency of a test in measuring what it is trying to measure. We need to be sure that each time we administer a test, a test-taker will achieve the same or nearly similar results, assuming that nothing about the person has changed relevant to what is being measured.

Types of Items on WAIS-IV		
Name	**Goal of Item**	**Example**
Information	Assess general information	Who wrote *Tom Sawyer?*
Comprehension	Assess understanding and evaluation of social norms and past experience	Why is copper often used for electrical wires?
Arithmetic	Assess math reasoning through verbal problems	Three women divided 18 golf balls equally among themselves. How many golf balls did each person receive?
Similarities	Test understanding of how objects or concepts are alike, tapping abstract reasoning	In what way are a circle and a triangle alike?
Figure weights	Test perceptual reasoning	Problems require test-taker to determine which possibility balances the final scale.
Matrix reasoning	Test spatial reasoning	Test-taker must decide which of the five possibilities replaces the question mark and completes the sequence.
Block design item	Test understanding of relationship of parts to whole	Problems require test-takers to reproduce a design in fixed amount of time.

FIGURE 5 Typical kinds of items similar to those found on the Wechsler Adult Intelligence Scales (WAIS-IV). (Simulated items similar to those in the *Wechsler Adult Intelligence Scale, Fourth Edition [WAIS-IV]*)

Source: Adapted from *Wechsler Adult Intelligence Scale-Fourth Edition* (WAIS-IV). (2008). Pearson Education, Inc.

Suppose, for instance, that when you first took the SAT exams, you scored 400 on the verbal section of the test. Then, after taking the test again a few months later, you scored 700. On receiving your new score, you might well stop celebrating for a moment to question whether the test is reliable because the score is so different. Your abilities could not likely have changed enough to raise your score by 300 points.

But suppose your score changed hardly at all, and both times you received a score of about 400. You couldn't complain about a lack of reliability. However, if you knew your verbal skills were above average, you might be concerned that the test did not adequately measure what it was supposed to measure. In sum, the question has now

validity The degree to which a test actually measures what it is supposed to measure. (Module 26)

become one of validity rather than reliability. A test has **validity** when it actually measures what it is supposed to measure.

Knowing that a test is reliable is no guarantee that it is also valid. For instance, in the 19th century, Sir Francis Galton believed that skull size is related to intelligence, and he was able to measure skull size with great reliability. However, the measure of skull size was not valid–it had nothing to do with intelligence. In this case, then, we have reliability without validity.

However, if a test is unreliable, it cannot be valid. Assuming that all other factors–motivation to score well, knowledge of the material, health, and so forth–are similar, if a person scores high the first time he or she takes a specific test and low the second time, the test cannot be measuring what it is supposed to measure. Therefore, the test is both unreliable and not valid.

Test validity and reliability are prerequisites for accurate assessment of intelligence, as well as for any other measurement task psychologists carry out. Consequently, the measures of personality carried out by personality psychologists, clinical psychologists' assessments of psychological disorders, and social psychologists' measures of attitudes must meet the tests of validity and reliability for the results to be meaningful (Markus & Borsboom, 2013; Deng & Georgiou, 2015).

Assuming that a test is both valid and reliable, one further step is necessary in order to interpret the meaning of a particular test-taker's score: the establishment of norms. **Norms** are standards of test performance that permit the comparison of one person's score on a test to the scores of others who have taken the same test. For example, a norm permits test-takers to know that they have scored, say, in the top 15% of those who have taken the test previously. Tests for which norms have been developed are known as *standardized tests*.

norms Standards of test performance that permit the comparison of one person's score on a test with the scores of other individuals who have taken the same test. (Module 26)

Test designers develop norms by calculating the average score achieved by a specific group of people for whom the test has been designed. Then the test designers can determine the extent to which each person's score differs from the scores of the other individuals who have taken the test in the past and provide future test-takers with a qualitative sense of their performance.

Obviously, the samples of test-takers who are employed in the establishment of norms are critical to the norming process. The people used to determine norms must be representative of the individuals to whom the test is directed.

From the perspective of...

A Human Resource Specialist Job interviews are really a kind of test, but they rely on interviewers' judgments and have no formal validity or reliability. Do you think job interviews can be made to have greater validity and reliability?

©Dex Image/Getty Images

ADAPTIVE TESTING: USING COMPUTERS TO ASSESS PERFORMANCE

Ensuring that tests are reliable, valid, and based on appropriate norms has become more critical with computer-administered testing. In computerized versions of tests such as the Graduate Record Exam, a test used to determine entrance to graduate school, not only are test questions viewed and answered on a computer, but the test itself is individualized. With adaptive testing, every test-taker receives a different set of test questions. With *adaptive testing*, not every test-taker receives identical sets of questions. Or every test-taker receives different sets of test questions. Instead, the computer first presents a randomly selected question of moderate difficulty. If the test-taker answers it correctly, the computer then presents a randomly chosen item of slightly greater difficulty. If the test-taker answers it incorrectly, the computer presents a slightly easier item. Each question becomes slightly harder or easier than the question preceding it, depending on whether the previous response is correct. Ultimately, the greater the number of difficult questions answered correctly, the higher the score (see Figure 6) (Barrada, Abad, & Olea, 2011; Liu, Ying, & Zhang, 2015; Cheng, Diao, & Behrens, 2017).

Because computerized adaptive testing pinpoints a test-taker's level of proficiency fairly quickly, the total time spent taking the exam is shorter than it is with a traditional exam. Test-takers are not forced to spend a great deal of time answering questions that are either much easier or much harder than they can handle.

On the other hand, adaptive testing has its drawbacks. For example, a large number of test items must be created and carefully calibrated in terms of their difficulty. Moreover, high-ability test-takers who make an early mistake and find the items getting easier may begin to feel anxious, leading to a downward spiral in their performance. Still, most research suggests that adaptive testing provides scores equivalent to those of traditional paper-and-pencil measures for most types of testing (Tonidandel, Quinones, & Adams, 2002; Passos, Berger, & Tan, 2007; Rulison & Loken, 2009).

PsychTech
Critics of adaptive testing suggest that it may discriminate against lower socioeconomic test-takers who have less access to computers and thus may have less practice with them, thereby increasing the "digital divide."

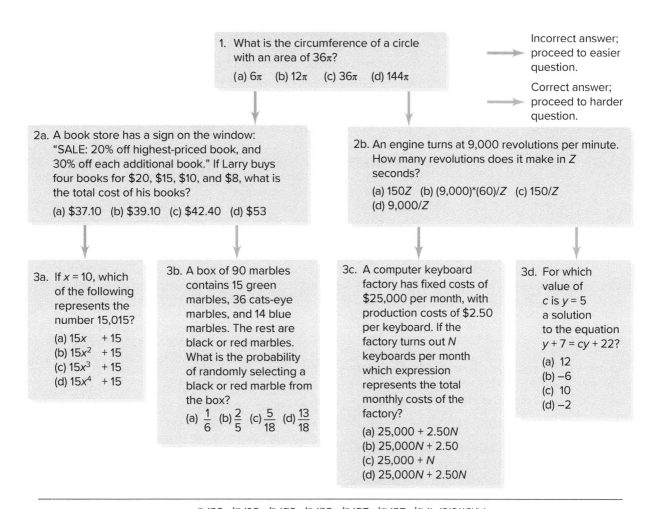

FIGURE 6 **Adaptive testing.** In computer adaptive testing, a computer randomly selects a first question of medium difficulty. When the test-taker answers correctly, the computer selects a harder question. When the test-taker answers incorrectly, the computer "backs off," selecting a question at the next-lower level of difficulty, as shown in the example. Scores are based on the difficulty level of the questions that have been answered correctly, meaning that test-takers who answer the same number of questions correctly may end up with very different scores. What do you think are the drawbacks of adaptive testing of this sort? Do you think such tests may discriminate against test-takers who have less access to computers compared with those who have greater access to them?
Source: Adapted from Winerip, M. (1993, November 15). A new approach in testing. *The New York Times*, B9.

BECOMING AN INFORMED CONSUMER
of Psychology

Scoring Better on Standardized Tests

Even though psychologists disagree about the nature of intelligence, intelligence tests—as well as many other kinds of tests—are widely used in a variety of situations. For example, if you are thinking about becoming a physician, a lawyer, or almost any other kind of professional in a field that requires advanced training, you will have to take a formal exam in order to be accepted for postgraduate training.

If you do have to take such an exam, you can do several things to maximize your score, including the following (Lurie, Robinson, & Pecsenye, 2005; Feldman, 2013):

- *Learn as much as you can about the test before you take it.* Know what sections will be on the test and how much each section is worth.
- *Practice, practice, practice.* Try as many practice tests as you can find. The more practice you have, the easier it will be when you actually take the test.
- *If the test is administered on a computer, as it probably will be, take practice tests on a computer.* The more familiar you are with computers, the more at ease you will feel when you sit down to take the test.
- *Time yourself carefully.* Don't spend too much time on early items at the expense of later ones. Your goal should be not perfection but maximization of the number of correct responses you get.
- *Be aware of the scoring policy.* If you are not penalized for wrong answers, guess. If there are penalties, be more conservative about guessing.
- *If it is a paper-and-pencil test, complete answer sheets accurately.* Check and check again. If the test is on a computer, check your answer thoroughly before going on to the next question because you won't be able to go back and change your answer once you've submitted it.
- *Reduce text anxiety by eating right and getting enough sleep.* You also should take a realistic view of the test, remembering that your future does not hinge on your performance on a single test.

AP‖ MODULE 26: WHAT IS INTELLIGENCE?

AP SUMMARY

- Because intelligence can take many forms, defining it is challenging. One commonly accepted view is that intelligence is the capacity to understand the world, think rationally, and use resources effectively when faced with challenges.
- Some researchers suggest that intelligence can be broken down into fluid intelligence and crystallized intelligence. The difference becomes apparent in late adulthood when fluid intelligence, but not crystallized intelligence, declines.
- The *Stanford-Binet* (*SB-5*) is administered orally and includes both verbal and nonverbal assessments. Both the *Wechsler Scales* (*WAIS-IV* and *WISC-V*) measure verbal comprehension, perceptual reasoning, working memory, and processing speed. All three of these

intelligence tests require individualized, one-on-one administration. There are a number of IQ tests that allow group administration, but they bring their own disadvantages.

- One's definition of intelligence is related to their culture. Westerners view intelligence as the ability to establish categories and debate rationally. Eastern cultures and some African communities view intelligence in terms of understanding and relating to one another.
- The earliest psychologists, including Charles Spearman, assumed that there was a general intelligence for mental ability called g factor. However, later psychologists disputed the view that intelligence is unidimensional.
- Howard Gardner's theory of multiple intelligences proposed that there are eight spheres of intelligence.

- Robert Sternberg argued that there are three types of intelligence: practical intelligence (related to overall success in living), analytical intelligence (abstract but traditional types of problem solving), and creative intelligence (the generation of novel ideas and products).
- Some psychologists broaden intelligence even further to include emotions. Emotional intelligence is the set of skills that underlie the accurate assessment, evaluation, expression, and regulation of emotions.
- Francis Galton first measured intelligence by the size and shape of a person's head. His theory was proven wrong and further research has found little relationship between head size and intelligence.
- Alfred Binet developed the first formal intelligence test used in the Paris school system to distinguish dull students for remedial aid. Intelligence tests have traditionally compared a person's mental age and chronological age to yield an IQ, or intelligence quotient, score.
- Binet's test was revised by Lewis Terman to the *Stanford-Binet Intelligence Scale*. The test is currently in its fifth edition and yields subscores to provide the test-taker's strengths and weaknesses.
- David Wechsler created the IQ test most frequently used in the United States known as the *Wechsler Adult Intelligence Scale (WAIS-IV)* and *the Wechsler Intelligence Scale for Children (WISC-V)*.
- Intelligence tests are expected to be both reliable and valid. Reliability refers to the consistency in which a test measures what it is trying to measure, whereas validity refers to whether a test measures what it is supposed to measure. Just because a test is reliable there is no guarantee it is also valid.
- The establishment of norms is necessary for accurate assessment of intelligence. Norms are standards of test performance that permit the comparison of one person's score on a test to the scores of others who have taken the same test. Tests for which norms have been developed are known as standardized tests.
- Ensuring that tests are reliable, valid, and based on appropriate norms has become more critical with computer-administered testing that uses adaptive testing.
- Today intelligence is determined by deviation IQ scores. Previously, an IQ score was determined by mental age divided by chronological age and then multiplied by 100.
- IQ scores from large numbers of people form a bell-shaped distribution. The average IQ score is 100, and 68% of all individuals score between 85 and 115, 95% score 30 points above or below 100, and 99.8% score between 55 and 145.

AP KEY TERMS

intelligence	emotional intelligence
g or *g*-factor	intelligence tests
fluid intelligence	mental age
crystallized intelligence	intelligence quotient (IQ)
theory of multiple intelligences	reliability
	validity
practical intelligence	norms

AP TEST PRACTICE

Section I: Multiple Choice

1. All of the following are characteristics of fluid intelligence EXCEPT
   A. solving a problem D. increases with age
   B. abstract reasoning E. finding patterns
   C. thinking logically

2. Corbin took a test and earned a B and then took the test again the next day and received the exact same score. Which psychometric property describes this test?
   A. Valid D. Achievement
   B. Reliable E. Aptitude
   C. Standardized

3. Approximately what percent of the population has an IQ score between 85 and 115?
   A. 95 D. 50
   B. 99 E. 34
   C. 68

Section II: Free Response

Psychologists have struggled to operationally define intelligence. There are various theories for what makes up intelligence. Explain each of the following types of intelligence.

- General intelligence
- Interpersonal intelligence
- Practical intelligence
- Emotional intelligence
- Crystallized intelligence

Module 27
Variations in Intellectual Ability

- Define intelligence and list characteristics of how psychologists measure intelligence.

- Identify the contributions of key researchers in intelligence research and testing.

- Describe relevant labels related to intelligence testing.

"Hey, hey, hey, Fact Track!" The 11-year-old speaker chose one of his favorite programs. . . .

"What is your name?" appeared on the monitor.

"Daniel Skandera," he typed. A menu scrolled up listing the program's possibilities. Daniel chose multiplication facts, Level 1. . . .

Randomly generated multiplication facts flashed on the screen: "4 × 6," "2 × 9," "3 × 3," "7 × 6." Daniel responded, deftly punching in his answers on the computer's numeric keypad. . . .

The computer tallied the results. "You completed 20 problems in 66 seconds. You beat your goal. Problems correct = 20. Congratulations Daniel!" And with that the 11-year-old retreated hastily to the TV room. The Lakers and 76ers were about to tip off for an NBA championship game. (Heward & Orlansky, 1988)

If you consider people with intellectual disabilities as inept and dull, it is time to revise your view. As in the case of Daniel Skandera, individuals with deficits of intellectual abilities can lead full, rounded lives and in some cases perform well in certain kinds of academic endeavors.

More than 7 million people in the United States, including around 11 per 1,000 children, have been identified as far enough below average in intelligence that they can be regarded as having serious deficits (they don't all have the same deficit). Individuals with low IQs (people with intellectual disabilities) as well as those with unusually high IQs (the intellectually gifted) require special attention if they are to reach their full potential.

Intellectual Disabilities

intellectual disability A disability characterized by significant limitations in both intellectual functioning and in adaptive behavior, which covers many everyday social and practical skills. (Module 27)

Although sometimes thought of as a rare phenomenon, intellectual disabilities occur in 1% to 3% of the population. There is wide variation among those labeled intellectually disabled (formerly known as *mentally retarded*), in large part because of the inclusiveness of the definition developed by the American Association on Intellectual and Developmental Disabilities. The association suggests that **intellectual disability** is a disability characterized by significant limitations in both intellectual functioning and in adaptive behavior, which covers many everyday social and practical skills, and originates before the age of 18 (American Association of Intellectual and Developmental Disabilities, 2015).

Although below-average intellectual functioning can be measured in a relatively straightforward manner–using standard IQ tests–it is more difficult to determine how to gauge limitations in adaptive behavior. Consequently, there is a lack of uniformity in how experts apply the term *intellectual disabilities*. People labeled intellectually disabled vary from those who can be taught to work and function with little special attention to those who cannot be trained and are institutionalized throughout their lives (Greenspan, 2006; American Association of Intellectual and Developmental Disabilities, 2015).

Most people with intellectual disabilities have relatively minor deficits and are classified as having *mild intellectual disability*. These individuals, who have IQ scores ranging from 55 to 69, constitute some 90% of all people with intellectual disabilities. Although their development is typically slower than that of their peers, they can function quite independently by adulthood and are able to hold jobs and have families of their own (Smith, 2006; van Nieuwenhuijzen et al., 2011; Nouwens et al., 2017).

With greater degrees of intellectual deficit, the difficulties are more pronounced. For people with *moderate intellectual disability* (IQs of 40 to 54), deficits are obvious early, with language and motor skills lagging behind those of peers. Although these individuals can hold simple jobs, they need to have a some degree of supervision throughout their lives. Individuals with *severe intellectual disability* (IQs of 25 to 39) and *profound intellectual disability* (IQs below 25) are generally unable to function independently and typically require care for their entire lives (Garwick, 2007*)*.

IDENTIFYING THE ROOTS OF INTELLECTUAL DISABILITIES

What produces intellectual disabilities? In nearly one-third of the cases, there is an identifiable cause related to biological or environmental factors. The most common preventable cause of intellectual disabilities is **fetal alcohol syndrome,** produced by a mother's use of alcohol while pregnant. Increasing evidence shows that even small amounts of alcohol intake can produce intellectual deficits. One in every 750 infants is born with fetal alcohol syndrome in the United States (Murthy et al., 2009; Jacobson et al., 2011; Lewis et al., 2015).

Down syndrome represents another major cause of intellectual disabilities. *Down syndrome* results when a person is born with 47 chromosomes instead of the usual 46. In most cases, there is an extra copy of the 21st chromosome, which leads to problems in how the brain and body develop (Sherman et al., 2007; Vicari, Pontillo, & Armando, 2013).

In other cases of intellectual disabilities, an abnormality occurs in the structure of particular chromosomes. Birth complications, such as a temporary lack of oxygen, may also cause intellectual disability. In some cases, intellectual disabilities begin after birth following a head injury, a stroke, or infections such as meningitis (Plomin, 2005; Bittles, Bower, & Hussain, 2007; Fevang et al., 2017).

However, the majority of cases of intellectual disabilities are classified as familial intellectual disability. **Familial intellectual disability** is intellectual disability in which no apparent biological or genetic problems exist, but there is a history of intellectual disability among family members. Whether the family background of intellectual disabilities is caused by environmental factors, such as extreme continuous poverty leading to malnutrition, or by some underlying genetic factor is usually impossible to determine (Zigler et al., 2002; Franklin & Mansuy, 2011); also see *Applying Psychology in the 21st Century.*

INTEGRATING INDIVIDUALS WITH INTELLECTUAL DISABILITIES

Important advances in the care and treatment of those with intellectual disabilities have been made since the Education for All Handicapped Children Act (Public Law 94-142) was passed by Congress in the mid-1970s. In this federal law, Congress stipulated that people with intellectual disabilities are entitled to a full education and that they must be educated and trained in the least restrictive environment–a process known as mainstreaming. *Mainstreaming* is the practice of educating students with intellectual deficits and other special needs in regular classes during specific time periods (Katsiyannis, Zhang, & Woodruff, 2005; Aussilloux & Bagdadli, 2006; Gibb et al., 2007).

The philosophy behind mainstreaming suggests that the interaction of students with and without intellectual disabilities in regular classrooms will improve educational opportunities for those with intellectual disabilities, increase their social acceptance, and facilitate their integration into society as a whole. In mainstreaming, special education classes still exist; some individuals with intellectual disabilities function at too low of a level to benefit from placement in regular classrooms. Moreover, children with intellectual disabilities who are mainstreamed into regular classes typically attend special classes for at least part of the day (Hastings & Oakford, 2003; Williamson, McLeskey, & Hoppey, 2006; Benitez et al., 2017).

fetal alcohol syndrome The most common cause of intellectual disability in newborns, occurring when the mother uses alcohol during pregnancy. (Module 27)

familial intellectual disability Intellectual disability in which no apparent biological or genetic problems exist, but there is a history of intellectual disability among family members. (Module 27)

AP APPLYING PSYCHOLOGY IN THE 21ST CENTURY

DOES A HIDDEN GENIUS LIE WITHIN US?

If you've seen the movie *Rain Man*, you're familiar with the phenomenon known as *savant syndrome*. In that movie, actor Dustin Hoffman's character was a man with autism spectrum disorder who displayed extraordinary mathematical, memory, and date-calculating skills despite his other cognitive and behavioral impairments. This is how savant syndrome has classically been understood—as an inborn island of extraordinary but narrowly focused mathematical, mechanical, musical, or artistic ability in developmentally disabled people who are otherwise intellectually impaired (Treffert, 2014).

But a small number of savants acquired their incredible skills only after a brain injury. For example, after 10-year-old Orlando Serrell woke up from being knocked unconscious by a baseball, he was suddenly able to deduce the day of the week for any date and showed remarkable memory for events since the accident. *Acquired savant syndrome*, as this phenomenon is known, suggests a fascinating possibility: we all may have some incredible intellectual or artistic talent lying latent in our brains, needing only the right trigger to emerge.

Savant syndrome is quite rare and the acquired variety rarer still—only a few dozen cases have been documented. Many of the cases involve a disease of old age known as *fronto-temporal dementia*

©ESB Professional/Shutterstock

that attacks the frontal lobes of the brain. Tellingly, the parts of the brain that are affected are normally involved in inhibiting certain sensory processing pathways, suggesting a mechanism that gives rise to acquired savant syndrome: Perhaps taking the brakes off sensory processing allows the brain to engage with sensory information in new and creative ways. Researchers think the key lies in the process of a damaged brain trying to heal itself, creating new neural pathways between regions that were not previously connected and thereby releasing abilities that had been lying dormant (Treffert, 2014; Cerami et al., 2016).

To test this hypothesis, researchers tried to induce savantlike ability in typical people by using a device that passes an electrical current through the skull, temporarily altering the functioning of certain brain regions. Before applying the pulse of electricity, the researchers asked a group of participants to work on a problem-solving task that required a creative and nonintuitive solution. None could figure it out. Then the researchers used the device to inhibit a brain region in the left hemisphere involved in sensory input, while simultaneously stimulating regions in the right hemisphere. Following this procedure, 40% of the participants were able to solve the problem. A control group that was fitted with the device but for whom it was never switched on remained unable to solve the problem (Chi, Fregni, & Snyder, 2010).

So we have evidence that many of us may have unknown abilities, waiting for the right circumstances to be released. Researchers are hopeful that one day we will find a more precise and practical way to enable people to release this untapped potential in the brain.

AP SKILLS: EXPLAIN BEHAVIOR IN AUTHENTIC CONTEXT / SCIENTIFIC INVESTIGATION

1. Researchers believe acquired savant syndrome may be caused by the damaged brain trying to heal itself, by creating new neural pathways between regions that were not previously connected. What is this ability for the brain to modify itself known as?
2. What is the purpose of randomly assigning participants to a control or experimental group?

Study Alert

Remember that in most cases of intellectual disability, there is no apparent biological deficiency, but a history of intellectual disability exists in the family.

Some educators argue that an alternative to mainstreaming, called full inclusion, is a better strategy for educating students with intellectual disabilities. *Full inclusion* is the total integration of all students, even those with the most severe intellectual disabilities, into regular classes.

Schools with full inclusion programs have no separate special education classes. Instead, teacher aides are assigned to help children with special needs progress in the classrooms they share with non-special-needs students (Hassouneh, Alcala-Moss, & McNeff, 2011; Stainton & Clare, 2012; Nepi et al., 2015).

Full inclusion is a controversial practice. Although proponents of full inclusion—who essentially want to abolish special-needs classes—argue that it is the legal and moral right of all students to be educated together, parents of students without special needs sometimes assert that the presence of special-needs students will be disruptive. Furthermore, the use of classroom aides is expensive. Consequently, full inclusion is not widely used (Praisner, 2003; Spence-Cochran & Pearl, 2006; Begeny & Martens, 2007).

From the perspective of...

An Educator What advantages and disadvantages do you think full inclusion programs would present for students with intellectual disability? For students without it?

©Andersen Ross/Blend Images/Getty Images

The Intellectually Gifted

Another group of people–the intellectually gifted–differ from those with average intelligence as much as individuals with intellectual disability do, although in a different manner. Accounting for 2% to 4% of the population, the **intellectually gifted** have IQ scores greater than 130.

Although stereotypes about the gifted suggests that they are awkward, shy social misfits who don't get along well with peers, most research indicates just the opposite: The intellectually gifted do well across almost every domain. They are most often outgoing, well-adjusted, healthy, popular people who are able to do most things better than the average person can (Mueller, 2009; Sternberg, Jarvin, & Grigorenko, 2011; Strenze, 2015).

For example, in a famous study by psychologist Lewis Terman that started in the early 1920s and continued for decades, 1,500 children who had IQ scores above 140 were followed for the rest of their lives. From the start, the members of this group were more physically, academically, and socially capable than their nongifted peers. In addition to doing better in school, they also showed better social adjustment than average. All these advantages paid off in terms of career success: As a group, the gifted received more awards and distinctions, earned higher incomes, and made more contributions in art and literature than typical individuals. Perhaps most important, they reported greater satisfaction in life than did the nongifted (Hegarty, 2007; Warne & Liu, 2017).

Of course, not every member of the group Terman studied was successful. Furthermore, high intelligence is not a homogeneous quality; a person with a high overall IQ is not necessarily gifted in every academic subject but may excel in just one or two. A high IQ is not a universal guarantee of success (Shurkin, 1992; Winner, 2003; Clemons, 2006).

Although special programs attempting to overcome the deficits of people with intellectual disability are common, programs targeted at the intellectually gifted are rarer. One reason for this lack of attention is that although there are as many gifted individuals as there are those with intellectual disability, the definition of *gifted* is vague, especially compared with definitions of intellectual disability. Furthermore, there is a persistent view that the gifted ought to be able to "make it on their own"; if they can't, they really weren't gifted in the first place (Parke, 2003; Robinson, 2003; Sparks, 2007).

More enlightened approaches, however, have acknowledged that without some form of special attention, the gifted become bored and frustrated with the pace of their schooling and may never reach their potential. Consequently, programs for the gifted are designed to provide enrichment that allows participants' talents to flourish (Adams-Byers, Squilkr, & Moon, 2004; Delcourt, Cornell, & Goldberg, 2007; Freeman, 2013).

intellectually gifted The 2%-4% segment of the population who have IQ scores greater than 130. (Module 27)

AP | MODULE 27: VARIATIONS IN INTELLECTUAL ABILITY

AP SUMMARY

- Savant syndrome is an island of extraordinary but narrowly focused ability amidst a developmental disorder or intellectual disability. Acquired savant syndrome suggests we may all have some incredible talent hiding in our brains, needing only the right trigger to emerge.
- Lewis Terman conducted a longitudinal study on intellectually gifted children in the 1920s. He found they were more physically, academically, and socially capable than their nongifted peers. They also reported greater satisfaction in life than their peers.
- Intellectual disability is characterized by significant limitations in both intellectual functioning and in adaptive behavior and originates before age 18. The levels of intellectual disability include mild, moderate, severe, and profound intellectual disability.
- About one-third of the cases of intellectual disability have a known biological cause; fetal alcohol syndrome is the most common. Down syndrome is another major cause of intellectual disabilities. Most cases, however, are classified as familial intellectual disability, for which there is no known biological or genetic cause but there is a family history of intellectual disability.
- The intellectually gifted are people with IQ scores greater than 130. Intellectually gifted people tend to be healthier and more successful than the average person.

AP KEY TERMS

intellectual disability
fetal alcohol syndrome
familial intellectual disability
intellectually gifted

AP TEST PRACTICE

Section I: Multiple Choice

1. Leslie Lemke was born premature, and complications led to brain damage and loss of eye sight. Despite his impairments, he is considered a musical genius. He played Tchaikovsky's Piano Concerto No. 1 at age 14 after hearing it only once. Which of the following best describes Leslie's characteristics?
   A. Giftedness
   B. Down syndrome
   C. Intellectual disability
   D. Savant syndrome
   E. Standardization

2. Who conducted a longitudinal study on gifted children to prove they were socially adjusted?
   A. Lewis Terman
   B. Alfred Binet
   C. Howard Gardner
   D. Robert Sternberg
   E. Charles Spearman

3. What cause of intellectual disability is the result of an extra copy of the 21st chromosome?
   A. Fetal alcohol syndrome
   B. Down syndrome
   C. Familial intellectual disability
   D. Savant syndrome
   E. Phenylketonuria (PKU)

Section II: Free Response

Stephen has an IQ score of 52 and a language deficit. He can hold a simple job but needs regular supervision. He also has an island of brilliance in calendar calculating and can tell you with accuracy what day of the week a given date falls on. Matt, his brother, is a 14-year-old boy with an IQ score of 140. Explain how the following concepts could relate to the brothers' intelligence.

- Intellectual disability
- Savant syndrome
- Giftedness
- Longitudinal study results for giftedness
- *WISC-V*

Module 28

Group Differences in Intelligence: Genetic and Environmental Determinants

Kwang is often washed with a pleck tied to a:
(a) rundel
(b) flink
(c) pove
(d) quirj

AP® | LEARNING TARGETS

- Define intelligence and list characteristics of how psychologists measure intelligence.

- Debate the appropriate testing practices, particularly in relation to culture-fair test uses.

If you found this kind of item on an intelligence test, you would probably complain that the test was totally absurd and had nothing to do with your intelligence or anyone else's–and rightly so. How could anyone be expected to respond to items presented in a language that was so unfamiliar?

Yet to some people, even more reasonable questions may appear just as nonsensical. Consider the example of a child raised in a city who is asked about procedures for milking cows or someone raised in a rural area who is asked about subway ticketing procedures. Obviously, the previous experience of the test-takers would affect their ability to answer correctly. And if such types of questions were included on an IQ test, a critic could rightly contend that the test had more to do with prior experience than with intelligence.

Although IQ tests do not include questions that are so clearly dependent on prior knowledge as questions about cows and subways, the background and experiences of test-takers do have the potential to affect results. In fact, the issue of devising fair intelligence tests that measure knowledge unrelated to culture and family background and experience is central to explaining an important and persistent finding: Members of certain racial and cultural groups consistently score lower on traditional intelligence tests than do members of other groups.

For example, as a group, blacks tend to average 10 to 15 IQ points lower than whites. Does this variation reflect a true difference in intelligence, or are the questions biased with regard to the kinds of knowledge they test? Clearly, if whites perform better because of their greater familiarity with the kind of information that is being tested, their higher IQ scores are not an indication that they are more intelligent than members of other groups (Morgan, Marsiske, & Whitfield, 2008; Suzuki, Short, & Lee, 2011; Loehlin et al., 2015).

There is good reason to believe that some standardized IQ tests contain elements that discriminate against minority-group members whose experiences differ from those of the white majority. As we discuss in *Exploring Diversity*, these issues have led to the development of what are known as *culture-fair IQ tests*.

Exploring Diversity

Can We Develop Culture-Fair IQ Tests?

Consider this question: "What should you do if another child grabs your hat and runs off with it?" Most white middle-class children answer that they would tell an adult, and this response is scored as correct on a common IQ test. However, a reasonable response might

culture-fair IQ test A test that does not discriminate against the members of any minority group. (Module 28)

be to chase the person and fight to get the hat back, the answer that many urban black children choose—but one that is scored as incorrect (Reynolds & Ramsay, 2003).

In an attempt to produce a **culture-fair IQ test,** one that does not discriminate against the members of any minority group, psychologists have tried to devise test items that assess experiences common to all cultures or emphasize questions that do not require language usage. However, test makers have found this difficult to do because past experiences, attitudes, and values almost always have an impact on respondents' answers (Fagan & Holland, 2009; Rizzi & Posthuma, 2013).

For example, children raised in Western cultures group things on the basis of what they are (such as putting *dog* and *fish* into the category of *animal*). In contrast, members of the Kpelle tribe in Africa group things according to what they *do* (grouping *fish* with *swim*). Similarly, when asked to memorize the positions on a chessboard of objects typical to a U.S. household, children in the United States performed better than did children living in remote African villages. But if rocks are used instead of household objects, the African children do better (Serpell, 2000; Valencia & Suzuki, 2003; Barnett et al., 2011).

Finally, tests may include even subtler forms of bias against minority groups. For example, assessments of cognitive ability developed in the United States may favor responses that implicitly reflect North American or European values, customs, or traditions, such as the "rugged individualism" of Western cultures. At the same time, such tests may be biased against African and other cultural value systems in which there is a greater emphasis on the importance of social groups and a more communal worldview. In short, it is difficult to produce a truly culture-fair test (Byrne & Watkins, 2003; Teovanović, Knežević, & Stankov, 2015).

IQ and Heritability: The Relative Influence of Genetics and Environment

The efforts of psychologists to produce culture-fair measures of intelligence relate to a lingering controversy over whether members of different racial and ethnic groups differ in intelligence. In attempting to identify whether such differences do indeed exist, psychologists have had to confront a broader issue: what is the relative contribution to intelligence of genetic factors (heredity) versus experience (environment)–the nature-nurture issue that is so basic in psychology.

Richard Herrnstein, a psychologist, and Charles Murray, a sociologist, fanned the flames of the debate with the publication of their book *The Bell Curve* in the mid-1990s (Herrnstein & Murray, 1994). They argued that an analysis of IQ differences between whites and blacks demonstrated that although environmental factors played a role, basic genetic differences also existed between the two races.

They based their argument on a number of findings. For instance, on average, whites score 15 points higher than blacks on traditional IQ tests even when socioeconomic status (SES) is taken into account. According to Herrnstein and Murray, middle- and upper-SES blacks score lower than middle- and upper-SES whites, just as lower-SES blacks score lower on average than lower-SES whites. Intelligence differences between blacks and whites, they concluded, could not be attributed to environmental differences alone.

heritability The degree to which a characteristic is related to inherited genetic factors. (Module 28)

Intelligence undoubtedly shows high heritability. **Heritability** is the degree to which a characteristic is related to inherited genetic factors. That is, a trait with high heritability is strongly related to genetic factors. In contrast, low-heritability traits are weakly related to genetic factors and thus more influenced by the environment in which a person is raised (e.g., Plomin, 2009; van Soelen et al., 2011; Tosto et al., 2017).

As can be seen in Figure 1, the closer the genetic link between two related people, the greater the correspondence of IQ scores. Using data such as these, Herrnstein and Murray argued that differences between races in IQ scores were largely caused by genetically based differences in intelligence.

Relationship	Genetic overlap	Rearing	Correlation
Monozygotic (identical) twins	100%	Together	.86
Dizygotic (fraternal) twins	50%	Together	.62
Siblings	50%	Together	.41
Siblings	50%	Apart	.24
Parent-child	50%	Together	.35
Parent-child	50%	Apart	.31
Adoptive parent-child	0%	Together	.16
Unrelated children	0%	Together	.25
Spouses	0%	Apart	.29

> The difference between these two correlations shows the impact of the environment

> The relatively low correlation for unrelated children raised together shows the importance of genetic factors

FIGURE 1 The relationship between IQ and closeness of genetic relationship. In general, the more similar the genetic and environmental background of two people, the greater the correlation is. Note, for example, that the correlation for spouses, who are genetically unrelated and have been reared apart, is relatively low, whereas the correlation for identical twins reared together is substantial.
Source: Adapted from Henderson, N. D. (1982). Correlations in IQ for pairs of people with varying degrees of genetic relatedness and shared environment. *Annual Review of Psychology, 33,* 219–243.

However, many psychologists reacted strongly against the arguments laid out in *The Bell Curve,* refuting several of the book's basic conclusions. One criticism is that even within similar socioeconomic groups, wide variations in IQ remain among individual households. Furthermore, the living conditions of blacks and whites are likely different even when their socioeconomic status is similar. In addition, as we discussed earlier, there is reason to believe that traditional IQ tests may discriminate against lower-SES urban blacks by asking for information pertaining to experiences they are unlikely to have had (Nisbett, 2007; Levine, 2011).

Moreover, blacks who are raised in economically enriched environments have IQ scores similar to whites in comparable environments. For example, in a study of black children who had been adopted at an early age by white middle-class families of above-average intelligence, the IQ scores of those children averaged 106–about 15 points above the average IQ scores of unadopted black children in the study. Other research shows that the racial gap in IQ narrows considerably after a college education, and cross-cultural data demonstrate that when racial gaps exist in other cultures, the economically disadvantaged groups typically have lower scores. In short, the evidence that genetic factors play the major role in determining racial differences in IQ is not compelling (Scarr & Weinberg, 1976; Fagan & Holland, 2007; Nisbett, 2009; Thaler et al., 2015).

Furthermore, drawing comparisons between races on any dimension, including IQ scores, is an imprecise, potentially misleading, and often fruitless venture. By far, the greatest discrepancies in IQ scores occur when comparing *individuals,* not when comparing mean IQ scores of different *groups.* Some blacks score high on IQ tests and some whites score low, just as some whites score high and some blacks score low. For the concept of intelligence to aid in the betterment of society, we must examine how *individuals* perform and not the groups to which they belong (Fagan & Holland, 2002, 2007).

Study Alert
Remember that the differences in IQ scores are much greater when comparing individuals than when comparing groups.

ARE WE GETTING SMARTER?: WHY IQ SCORES ARE RISING

IQ tests are normed, which means that individual scores indicate performance on the test relative to the average score, which is set to 100. However, over the course of the roughly 100-year history of IQ tests, the test designers have noticed something peculiar: They have had to repeatedly renorm the test as the average score kept creeping up, gradually making it more and more challenging. The

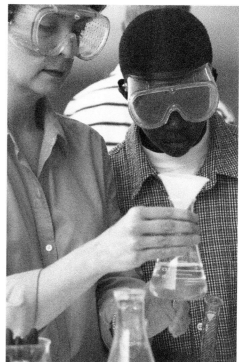

Social and economic inequality are associated with differences in performance on IQ tests. Those who have greater educational opportunities and who suffer fewer economic constraints score higher on measures of intelligence.
©Creatas/Getty Images

phenomenon has become known as the *Flynn effect*, named for a researcher who brought early attention to it (Flynn, 2009; Rindermann, Becker, & Coyle, 2017).

The change in IQ scores amounts to roughly a 3-point increase every decade. That may not sound like much, but it means that test-takers today score a staggering 30 points higher on average than test-takers did a century ago. It's unclear why this change is happening, but many theories have been offered, including improvements in education, nutrition, technology, and even in test-taking behavior.

A recent meta-analysis, combining the results of 271 studies going back to the start of intelligence testing, helps us to make better sense of the Flynn effect. The study confirmed the existence and the extent of the growth of IQ scores. The gains were strong between the two world wars but weakened during World War II. Scores grew steadily after the war until about 1970, when the gains slowed down again, although they have continued to increase to the present (Williams, 2013; Pietschnig & Voracek, 2015).

Why is this happening? Some of the study's findings are informative. The gains are stronger for adults than for children, which points to improvements in education as a possible cause (although the gains were in fluid intelligence rather than crystallized intelligence, and children showed gains too, so education cannot be the entire cause). Gains in IQ were associated with increases in gross domestic product, an indicator of economic prosperity, suggesting that perhaps better nutrition or access to technology are contributing factors.

But the answer may not be something direct and simple. One complex explanation is that even small initial environmental changes, such as improved health, become magnified by a feedback loop wherein cognitive function improves, which produces even better health, which produces even more improvement in cognitive function, and so on. Another complex explanation is that better living conditions favor a longer childhood, whereas stressful living conditions favor a short childhood (given that delaying the responsibilities of adulthood is in many ways a luxury). Longer childhood in turn leads to better learning.

Finally, researchers caution against reading too much into the changes over time. For example, rather than all of us being geniuses compared to the early 20th-century population, it's more likely that we are simply smarter in different ways–the ways that the test happens to measure most accurately (Pietschnig & Voracek, 2015).

From the perspective of...

A College Admissions Officer Imagine you notice that students who are members of minority groups systematically receive lower scores on standardized college entrance exams. What suggestions do you have for helping these students improve their scores?

©Flying Colours Ltd/Getty Images

PLACING THE HEREDITY–ENVIRONMENT QUESTION IN PERSPECTIVE

Ultimately, we have no final answer to the question of how much intelligence is influenced by heredity as compared with the environment. No definitive experiments can be devised to unambiguously determine cause and effect. And given that we can't come to a precise answer, the more critical question to ask may be this: *What can we do to maximize the intellectual development of every individual?*

By focusing on how to improve each person's intellectual performance, we can focus on how to make changes in the environment, which may take the form of enriched home environments and better schooling. Such changes may lead each person to reach his or her potential.

AP MODULE 28: GROUP DIFFERENCES IN INTELLIGENCE: GENETIC AND ENVIRONMENTAL DETERMINANTS

AP SUMMARY

- Test designers have had to repeatedly renormalize their assessments because IQ scores have increased by approximately 3-points every decade. This rise in IQ scores is known as the Flynn effect. There are various explanations for this increase, but researchers caution against reading too much into the changes over time.
- Traditional intelligence tests have been frequently criticized for being biased in favor of the white middle-class population. This controversy has led to attempts to devise culture-fair tests and IQ measures that avoid questions dependent on a particular cultural background.
- Intelligence undoubtedly shows high heritability, the degree to which a characteristic is related to inherited genetic factors.
- Issues of racial differences in intelligence are very controversial in part due to disagreement over what constitutes unbiased measures of racial differences and also because there are confounding factors, such as socio-economic status differences related to race. Evidence that genetic factors play the major role in determining racial differences in IQ is not compelling.
- Attempting to distinguish environmental from hereditary factors in intelligence is probably futile and misguided. Because individual IQ scores vary far more than group IQ scores do, it is more critical to ask what can be done to maximize the intellectual development of each individual.

AP KEY TERMS

culture-fair IQ test
heritability

AP TEST PRACTICE

Section I: Multiple Choice

1. Which statement best describes the Flynn effect?
   A. There are multiple types of intelligence
   B. Crystallized intelligence decreases with age
   C. Intelligence shows high heritability
   D. IQ scores increase every decade
   E. Functional fixedness decreases with age

2. What type of test tries to ask questions that do not require language usage?
   A. Achievement
   B. Aptitude
   C. Culture-fair
   D. Culture-relevant
   E. Reliable

3. If a trait is strongly related to genetic factors, it is said to have high
   A. heritability
   B. reliability
   C. validity
   D. insight
   E. standardization

Section II: Free Response

Test designers would like to create a new intelligence test. Describe how the following will need to be considered by the test designers when creating an accurate assessment of intelligence.
- Cultural bias
- Flynn effect
- Reliability
- Validity
- Norms

LOOKING *Back*

EPILOGUE

We've just examined one of the most controversial areas of psychology—intelligence. Some of the most heated discussions in all of psychology focus on this topic, engaging educators, policymakers, politicians, and psychologists. The issues include the very meaning of intelligence, its measurement, individual extremes of intelligence, and, finally, the heredity–environment question. We saw that the quest to partition intelligence into hereditary factors versus environmental factors is generally pointless. In the area of intelligence, the focus of our efforts should be on making sure that every individual has the opportunity to achieve his or her potential.

VISUAL SUMMARY 9 Intelligence

MODULE 26 What Is Intelligence?

Theories of Intelligence

Major Approaches to Intelligence	
Approach	**Characteristics**
Fluid and crystallized intelligence	Fluid intelligence relates to the ability to think logically, reason abstractly, and solve problems; crystallized intelligence relates to information, skills, and strategies learned through experience
Gardner's multiple intelligences	Eight independent forms of intelligence
Practical intelligence	Intelligence in terms of nonacademic, career, and personal success
Emotional intelligence	Intelligence that provides an understanding of what other people are feeling and experiencing and permits us to respond appropriately to others' needs

- *g*-factor: Single factor underlying mental ability
- Fluid intelligence: ability to think logically, reason abstractly, and solve problems
- Crystallized intelligence: accumulation of information, knowledge, and skills learned through experience and education

- Gardner's multiple intelligences

- Practical intelligence: Intelligence related to overall success in living
- Emotional intelligence: Skills that underlie the accurate assessment, evaluation, expression, and regulation of emotions

Assessing Intelligence: Intelligence tests

- Binet developed IQ tests
  - Mental age: the average age of individuals who achieve a particular level of performance on a test
  - IQ: a score based on an individual's mental and chronological ages

$$\text{IQ score} = \frac{MA}{CA} \times 100$$

The average IQ score is 100, and 68% of people score between 85 and 115.

- Contemporary IQ tests
  - Wechsler Adult Intelligence Scale–III
  - Wechsler Intelligence Scale for Children–V

MODULE 27 Variations in Intellectual Ability

Intellectual Disability

- A disability characterized by significant limitations both in intellectual functioning and in conceptual, social, and practical adaptive skills
- Fetal alcohol syndrome and familial intellectual disability

Intellectually Gifted

- IQ scores greater than 130
- Most often outgoing, well adjusted, healthy, popular

MODULE 28 Group Differences in Intelligence: Genetic and Environmental Determinants

Culture-fair IQ Test

- IQ and Heritability

Relationship	Genetic overlap	Rearing	Correlation	
Monozygotic (identical) twins	100%	Together	.86	
Dizygotic (fraternal) twins	50%	Together	.62	The difference between these two correlations shows the impact of the environment
Siblings	50%	Together	.41	
Siblings	50%	Apart	.24	
Parent-child	50%	Together	.35	
Parent-child	50%	Apart	.31	
Adoptive parent-child	0%	Together	.16	
Unrelated children	0%	Together	.25	The relatively low correlation for unrelated children raised together shows the importance of genetic factors
Spouses	0%	Apart	.29	

(MODULE 26, photo), top: ©bennymarty/123RF; (bottom): ©Rena Schild/Shutterstock; Source: Adapted from Henderson, N. D. (1982). Correlations in IQ for pairs of people with varying degrees of genetic relatedness and shared environment. *Annual Review of Psychology, 33,* 219–243.

©Yasuyoshi Chiba/AFP/Getty Images

CHAPTER 10
Motivation and Emotion

AP¹ ESSENTIAL QUESTIONS

- What motivates us to think and act the way we do?
- Why don't psychologists agree?

AP¹ LEARNING TARGETS FOR CHAPTER 10

- Compare and contrast major theories of emotion.

- Describe how cultural influences shape emotional expression, including variations in body language.

PROLOGUE *THE (FALSE) PICTURE OF HEALTH*

Daniella Isaacs, already on a gluten-free diet because of her celiac disease, became fixated on "clean living" and "healthy eating" and entirely cut sugar, dairy, and even gluten-free bread and pasta out of her diet. She liked the results so much that she began posting pictures of her food and her thinning body on Instagram.

Then it got intense. Feeding off the "likes" on Instagram, she restricted her diet even more and added gym work and running to her routine. She avoided eating out because she wanted to control the food on her plate. If she went to a friend's house, she volunteered to cook so she could choose the food.

Daniella's periods stopped, her hair began to fall out, and she felt more and more unwell, but her Instagram following kept growing. "People were giving me compliments about how thin I was," she says, "despite looking borderline anorexic. I got sucked up by Instagram and got sick. Being thinner didn't make me any happier" (Nagesh, 2017).

LOOKING *Ahead*

What explains Daniella Isaacs's obsession with "healthy eating"—an obsession that led to excessive weight loss and dietary deficiencies? Was she driven mainly by concern for her health? Was she motivated by the desire to become more attractive? And considering her craving for approval from her Instagram followers, were her emotional needs and attitude the primary factors driving her behavior?

These questions and many others are addressed by psychologists who study the topics of motivation and emotion. Psychologists who study motivation seek to discover the particular desired goals—the motives—that underlie behavior. Behaviors as basic as drinking to satisfy thirst and as inconsequential as taking a stroll to get exercise exemplify motives. Psychologists specializing in the study of motivation assume that such underlying motives steer our choices of activities.

While motivation concerns the forces that direct future behavior, emotion pertains to the feelings we experience throughout our lives. The study of emotions focuses on our internal experiences at any given moment. All of us feel a variety of emotions: happiness at succeeding at a difficult task, sadness over the death of a loved one, anger at being treated unfairly. Because emotions not only play a role in motivating our behavior but also act as a reflection of our underlying motivation, they play an important role in our lives.

We begin this set of modules by focusing on the major conceptions of motivation, discussing how different motives and needs jointly affect behavior. We consider motives that are biologically based and universal in the animal kingdom, such as hunger, as well as motives that are unique to humans, such as the need for achievement.

We then turn to emotions. We consider the roles and functions that emotions play in people's lives and discuss several approaches that explain how people understand their emotions. Finally, we look at how nonverbal behavior communicates emotions.

Module 29
Explaining Motivation

- Identify and apply basic motivational concepts to understand the behavior of humans and other animals.

- Compare and contrast motivational theories, including the strengths and weaknesses of each.

- Identify contributions of key researchers in the psychological field of motivation and emotion.

- Discuss the biological underpinnings of motivation, including needs, drives, and homeostasis.

motivation The factors that direct and energize the behavior of humans and other organisms. (Module 29)

In just a moment, 27-year-old Aron Ralston's life changed. An 800-pound boulder dislodged where Ralston was hiking in a narrow, isolated Utah canyon, pinning his lower arm to the ground.

For the next 5 days, Ralston lay trapped, unable to escape. An experienced climber who had search-and-rescue training, he had ample time to consider his options. He tried unsuccessfully to chip away at the rock, and he rigged up ropes and pulleys around the boulder in a vain effort to move it.

Finally, out of water and nearly dehydrated, Ralston reasoned there was only one option left short of dying. In acts of incredible bravery, Ralston broke two bones in his wrist, applied a tourniquet, and used a dull pen knife to amputate his arm beneath the elbow.

Freed from his entrapment, Ralston climbed out from where he had been pinned and then hiked 5 miles to safety. (Cox, 2003; Lofholm, 2003)

What factors lay behind Ralston's resolve?

To answer this question, psychologists employ the concept of **motivation,** the factors that direct and energize the behavior of humans and other organisms. Motivation has biological, cognitive, and social aspects, and the complexity of the concept has led psychologists to develop a variety of approaches. All seek to explain the energy that guides people's behavior in specific directions.

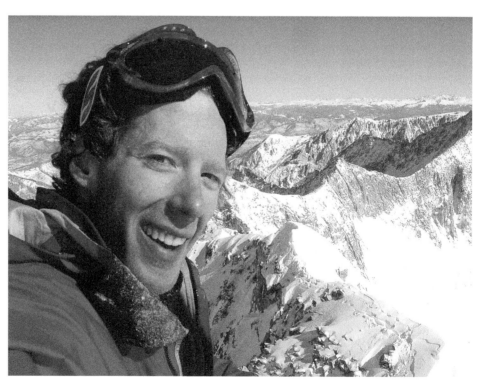

What was the motivation behind Aron Ralston's heroic efforts to free himself from the rock that had pinned his arm to the ground?
©Aron Ralston/ZUMA Press/Newscom

Instinct Approaches: Born to Be Motivated

When psychologists first tried to explain motivation, they turned to **instincts,** inborn patterns of behavior that are biologically determined rather than learned. According to **instinct approaches to motivation,** people and animals are born preprogrammed with sets of behaviors essential to their survival. Those instincts provide the energy that channels behavior in appropriate directions. Hence, sexual behavior may be a response to an instinct to reproduce, and exploratory behavior may be motivated by an instinct to examine one's territory.

This instinct approach presents several difficulties, however. For one thing, psychologists do not agree on what, or even how many, primary instincts exist. One early psychologist, William McDougall (1908), suggested that there are 18 instincts. Other theorists came up with even more—with one sociologist (Bernard, 1924) claiming that there are exactly 5,759 distinct instincts!

Furthermore, instinct approaches are unable to explain why certain patterns of behavior and not others have evolved in a given species. In addition, although it is clear that a great deal of animal behavior is based on instincts, much of the variety and complexity of human behavior is learned and thus cannot be seen as instinctual.

As a result of these shortcomings, newer explanations have replaced conceptions of motivation based on instincts. However, instinct approaches still play a role in certain theories, especially those based on evolutionary approaches that focus on our genetic inheritance. Furthermore, Freud's work suggests that instinctual drives of sex and aggression motivate behavior (Katz, 2001).

instincts Inborn patterns of behavior that are biologically determined rather than learned. (Module 29)

instinct approaches to motivation The explanation of motivation that suggests people and animals are born preprogrammed with sets of behaviors essential to their survival. (Module 29)

Drive-Reduction Approaches: Satisfying Our Needs

After rejecting instinct theory, psychologists first proposed simple drive-reduction theories of motivation to take its place (Hull, 1943). **Drive-reduction approaches to motivation** suggest that a lack of some basic biological need (such as a lack of water) produces a drive to push an organism to satisfy that need (in this case, seeking water).

To understand this approach, we begin with the concept of drive. A **drive** is motivational tension, or arousal, that energizes behavior to fulfill a need. Many basic drives, such as hunger, thirst, sleep, and sex, are related to biological needs of the body or of the species as a whole. These are called *primary drives*. Primary drives contrast with secondary drives in which behavior fulfills no obvious biological need. In *secondary drives*, prior experience and learning bring about needs. For instance, some people have strong needs to achieve academically and professionally. We can say that their achievement need is reflected in a secondary drive that motivates their behavior (Johnson, Stewart, & Bachman, 2015; Huang, Etkin, & Jin, 2017).

We usually try to satisfy a primary drive by reducing the need underlying it. For example, we become hungry after not eating for a few hours and may raid the refrigerator, especially if the next scheduled meal is not imminent. If the weather turns cold, we put on extra clothing or raise the setting on the thermostat to keep warm. If our bodies need liquids to function properly, we experience thirst and seek out water.

drive-reduction approaches to motivation Theories suggesting that a lack of some basic biological need produces a drive to push an organism to satisfy that need. (Module 29)

drive Motivational tension, or arousal, that energizes behavior to fulfill a need. (Module 29)

HOMEOSTASIS

Homeostasis, the body's tendency to maintain a steady internal state, underlies primary drives. Using feedback loops, homeostasis brings deviations in body functioning back to an optimal state, similar to the way a thermostat and a furnace work in a home heating system to maintain a steady temperature (see Figure 1). Receptor cells

homeostasis The body's tendency to maintain a steady internal state. (Module 29)

FIGURE 1 With homeostasis, a series of feedback loops is used to regulate body functions, similar to the way a thermostat turns on the furnace when a room's air temperature becomes too cool and turns it off when the air temperature becomes too warm. Similarly, when body temperature becomes too low, the blood vessels constrict, and we shiver and seek warmth. When body temperature becomes too high, the blood vessels expand, and we sweat as our bodies try to lower the temperature. Can you think of other internal systems that operate via homeostasis?

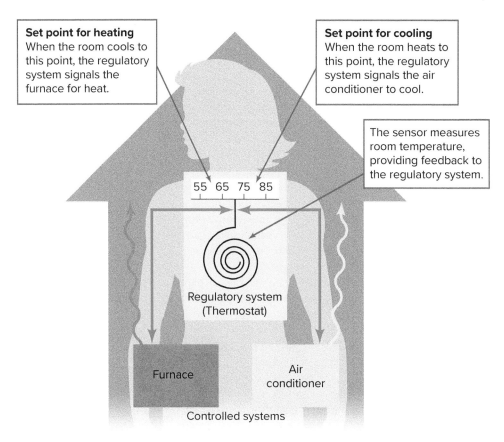

Set point for heating
When the room cools to this point, the regulatory system signals the furnace for heat.

Set point for cooling
When the room heats to this point, the regulatory system signals the air conditioner to cool.

The sensor measures room temperature, providing feedback to the regulatory system.

55 65 75 85

Regulatory system
(Thermostat)

Furnace

Air conditioner

Controlled systems

throughout the body constantly monitor such factors as temperature and nutrient levels. When deviations from the ideal state occur, the body adjusts in an effort to return to an optimal state. Many fundamental needs, including the needs for food, water, stable body temperature, and sleep, operate via homeostasis (Porkka-Heiskanen & Kalinchuk, 2011; Porkka-Heiskanen, 2013; Betley et al., 2015).

Although drive-reduction theories provide a good explanation of how primary drives motivate behavior, they cannot fully explain a behavior in which the goal is not to reduce a drive but rather to maintain or even increase the level of excitement or arousal. For instance, some behaviors seem to be motivated by nothing more than curiosity, such as rushing to check e-mail messages. Similarly, many people pursue thrilling activities such as riding a roller coaster or steering a raft down the rapids of a river. Such behaviors certainly don't suggest that people seek to reduce all drives as drive-reduction approaches would indicate (Begg & Langley, 2001; Rosenbloom & Wolf, 2002; Wishart, Somoray, & Rowland, 2017).

Both curiosity and thrill-seeking behavior, then, shed doubt on drive-reduction approaches as a complete explanation for motivation. In both cases, rather than seeking to reduce an underlying drive, people and animals appear to be motivated to increase their overall level of stimulation and activity. To explain this phenomenon, psychologists have devised an alternative: arousal approaches to motivation.

Study Alert
To remember the concept of homeostasis, keep in mind the analogy of a thermostat that regulates the temperature in a house.

Arousal Approaches: Beyond Drive Reduction

arousal approaches to motivation
The belief that people try to maintain a steady level of stimulation and activity. (Module 29)

Arousal approaches seek to explain behavior in which the goal is to maintain or increase excitement. According to **arousal approaches to motivation,** people try to maintain a steady level of stimulation and activity. As with the drive-reduction model, this approach suggests that if our stimulation and activity levels become too high, we try to reduce them. But, in contrast to the drive-reduction perspective, the arousal approach

Are You a Sensation Seeker?

How much do you crave stimulation in your everyday life? Complete the following questionnaire to find out. Circle either A or B in each pair or statements.

1. A My definition of the good life is to be at peace and comfortable in my skin.
   B My definition of the good life is to grab every experience possible.
2. A When I see an unfamiliar ride at an amusement park, I get right in line.
   B When I see a new ride, I need to watch how it works a few times before trying it.
3. A My ideal job would involve travel and a wealth of new experiences.
   B My ideal job would be to do something I like and keep getting better at it.
4. A I am a big fan of a lazy summer day, a beach or backyard, and a good book.
   B I love winter with its brisk days and outdoor activities such as skiing and snowboarding.
5. A I look forward to meeting new people and trying new things.
   B I like hanging out with my friends and doing things we know we enjoy.
6. A I think it's foolish to take unnecessary risks just for a sense of adventure.
   B I am attracted to challenges, even if they're a bit dangerous.
7. A I like movies that are funny or where I know the good guys are going to win.
   B I like edgy movies that are unpredictable or explore new ideas.
8. A The best art makes you think or shakes up your old ideas and preconceptions.
   B Good art is beautiful and makes you feel serene.
9. A For vacations, I prefer to go places I like and eat at restaurants I know.
   B My ideal vacation is to go somewhere new where I can try different things.
10. A If I lived in frontier days, I would head West to pursue potential opportunities.
    B If I lived in frontier days, I would stay in the East and make a good life there.
11. A The people I'm drawn to are unusual and have kind of wild ideas.
    B I like people who are like me and know who they are.
12. A I would never allow myself to be hypnotized, especially in public.
    B I would probably volunteer to be hypnotized, just to give it a try.
13. A I would love to try things like parachuting, bungee jumping, and hang gliding.
    B It makes no sense to jump out of a perfectly good airplane or off a bridge.

Scoring: Give yourself a point for each of these responses: 1B, 2A, 3A, 4B, 5A, 6B, 7B, 8A, 9B, 10A, 11A, 12B, 13A. Add up the points, and then use the following key to find your sensation-seeking score.

12–13 Very high sensation seeking
10–11 High sensation seeking
6–9 Average sensation seeking
4–5 Low sensation seeking
1–3 Very low sensation seeking

Your results can give you a rough idea of your sensation-seeking tendencies. Understand that this is a short questionnaire based on the responses of a small sample of college students, giving at best an imprecise picture. Understand, too, that as people age, their sensation scores tend to become lower.

FIGURE 2 Some people seek high levels of arousal, while others are more easygoing. You can get a sense of your own preferred level of stimulation by completing this questionnaire.

Source: Adapted from Zuckerman, M. (1978, February). The search for high sensation. *Psychology Today,* pp. 30–46.

also suggests that if levels of stimulation and activity are too low, we will try to increase them by seeking stimulation.

People vary widely in the optimal level of arousal they seek out, with some people looking for especially high levels of arousal. For example, people who participate in daredevil sports, high-stakes gamblers, and criminals who pull off high-risk robberies may be exhibiting a particularly high need for arousal (see Figure 2; Roets & Van Hiel, 2011; Lang & Bradley, 2013; Stevens et al., 2015).

Incentive Approaches: Motivation's Pull

When a luscious dessert appears on the table after a filling meal, its appeal has little or nothing to do with internal drives or the maintenance of arousal. Rather, if we choose to eat the dessert, such behavior is motivated by the external stimulus of the dessert itself, which acts as an anticipated reward. This reward, in motivational terms, is an *incentive*.

incentive approaches to motivation
Theories suggesting that motivation stems from the desire to attain external rewards, known as incentives. (Module 29)

Incentive approaches to motivation suggest that motivation stems from the desire to attain external rewards, known as incentives. In this view, the desirable properties of external stimuli–whether grades, money, affection, food, or sex–account for a person's motivation (Festinger et al., 2009).

Although the theory explains why we may succumb to an incentive (such as a mouth-watering dessert) even though we lack internal cues (such as hunger), it does not provide a complete explanation of motivation because organisms sometimes seek to fulfill needs even when incentives are not apparent. Consequently, many psychologists believe that the internal drives proposed by drive-reduction theory work in tandem with the external incentives of incentive theory to "push" and "pull" behavior, respectively. Thus, at the same time that we seek to satisfy our underlying hunger needs (the push of drive-reduction theory), we are drawn to food that appears very appetizing (the pull of incentive theory). Rather than contradicting each other, then, drives and incentives may work together in motivating behavior (Berridge, 2004; Belasen & Fortunato, 2013; Goswami & Urminsky, 2017).

Cognitive Approaches: The Thoughts Behind Motivation

cognitive approaches to motivation
Theories suggesting that motivation is the outcomes of people's thoughts, beliefs, expectations, and goals. (Module 29)

Cognitive approaches to motivation suggest that motivation is the outcome of people's thoughts, beliefs, expectations, and goals. For instance, the degree to which people are motivated to study for a test is based on their expectation of how well studying will pay off in terms of a good grade.

Cognitive theories of motivation draw a key distinction between intrinsic and extrinsic motivation. *Intrinsic motivation* causes us to participate in an activity for our own enjoyment rather than for any actual or concrete reward that it will bring us. In contrast, *extrinsic motivation* causes us to do something for money, a grade, or some other actual, concrete reward (Shaikholeslami & Khayyer, 2006; Finkelstein, 2009; Hofeditz et al., 2017).

For example, when a physician works long hours because she loves medicine, intrinsic motivation is prompting her; if she works hard to make a lot of money, extrinsic motivation underlies her efforts. Similarly, if we study a lot because we love the subject matter, we are being guided by intrinsic motivation. On the other hand,

From the perspective of...

An Educator Do you think that giving students grades serves as an external reward that may decrease intrinsic motivation for learning about the subject matter? Why or why not?

©Andersen Ross/Blend Images/Getty Images

if all we care about is the grade we get in the course, that studying is due to extrinsic motivation (Emmett & McGee, 2013).

We are more apt to persevere, work harder, and produce work of higher quality when motivation for a task is intrinsic rather than extrinsic. In fact, in some cases, providing rewards for desirable behavior (thereby increasing extrinsic motivation) actually may decrease intrinsic motivation (Grant, 2008; Nishimura, Kawamura, & Sakurai, 2011; Bolkan, 2015).

Maslow's Hierarchy: Ordering Motivational Needs

What do Eleanor Roosevelt, Abraham Lincoln, and Albert Einstein have in common? The common thread, according to a model of motivation devised by psychologist Abraham Maslow, is that each of them fulfilled the highest levels of motivational needs underlying human behavior.

Maslow's model places motivational needs in a hierarchy and suggests that before more sophisticated, higher-order needs can be met, certain primary needs must be satisfied (Maslow, 1970, 1987). A pyramid can represent the model with the more basic needs at the bottom and the higher-level needs at the top (see Figure 3). To activate a specific higher-order need, thereby guiding behavior, a person must first fulfill the more basic needs in the hierarchy.

The basic needs are primary drives: needs for water, food, sleep, sex, and the like. To move up the hierarchy, a person must first meet these basic physiological needs. Safety needs come next in the hierarchy; Maslow suggests that people need a safe, secure environment in order to function effectively. Physiological and safety needs compose the lower-order needs.

Only after meeting the basic lower-order needs can a person consider fulfilling higher-order needs, such as the needs for love and a sense of belonging, esteem, and

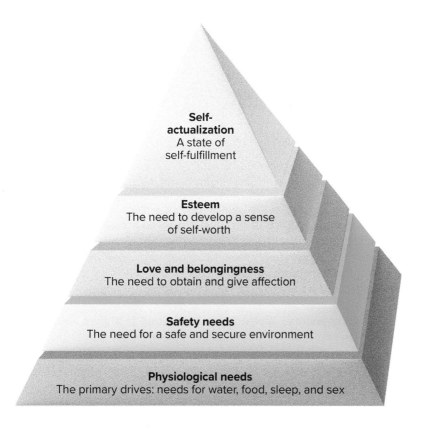

FIGURE 3 Maslow's hierarchy shows how our motivation progresses up the pyramid from the broadest, most fundamental biological needs to higher-order ones. Do you agree that lower-order needs must be satisfied before higher-order needs? Do hermits and monks who attempt to fulfill spiritual needs while denying basic physical needs contradict Maslow's hierarchy?

Source: Maslow, A. H. (1970). *Motivation and personality.* New York: Harper & Row.

Self-actualization
A state of self-fulfillment

Esteem
The need to develop a sense of self-worth

Love and belongingness
The need to obtain and give affection

Safety needs
The need for a safe and secure environment

Physiological needs
The primary drives: needs for water, food, sleep, and sex

self-actualization. Love and belongingness needs include the needs to obtain and give affection and to be a contributing member of some group or society. After fulfilling these needs, a person strives for esteem. Esteem is the recognition that others value your competence and worth, and that they admire you for your qualities.

After these four sets of needs (physiological needs, safety needs, love and belongingness, and esteem) are fulfilled—no easy task—a person is able to strive for the highest-level need, self-actualization. **Self-actualization** is a state of self-fulfillment in which people realize their highest potentials in their own unique way. Although Maslow first suggested that self-actualization occurred in only a few famous individuals, he later expanded the concept to encompass everyday people. For example, a parent with excellent nurturing skills who raises a family, a teacher who year after year creates an environment that maximizes students' opportunities for success, and an artist who realizes his creative potential all may be self-actualized. The important thing is that people feel at ease with themselves and satisfied that they are using their talents to the fullest. In a sense, achieving self-actualization reduces the striving and yearning for greater fulfillment that mark most people's lives and instead provides a sense of satisfaction with their current state of affairs (Bauer, Schwab, & McAdams, 2011; Ivtzan et al., 2013; Winston, Maher, & Easvaradoss, 2017).

Although research has been unable to validate the specific ordering of Maslow's stages and it is difficult to measure self-actualization objectively, Maslow's hierarchy of needs is important for two reasons: It highlights the complexity of human needs, and it emphasizes the idea that until more basic biological needs are met, people will be relatively unconcerned with higher-order needs. For example, if people are hungry, their first interest will be in obtaining food; they will not be concerned with needs such as love and self-esteem (Ojha & Pramanick, 2009; LaLumiere & Kalivas, 2013; Beitel et al., 2015).

Maslow's hierarchy of needs has also spawned other approaches to motivation. For example, Richard Ryan and Edward Deci have considered human needs in terms of psychological well-being. They suggest in their *self-determination theory* that people have the need for these three basics: (1) competence, (2) autonomy, and (3) relatedness. Competence is the need to produce desirable outcomes, whereas autonomy is the need to feel control over our own lives. Finally, relatedness is the need to be involved in close, warm relationships with others. In the view of self-determination theory, these three psychological needs are genetically determined and universal across cultures, and they are as essential as basic biological needs (Jang et al., 2009; Ryan & Deci, 2011; Ryan & Deci, 2017).

Applying the Different Approaches to Motivation

The various theories of motivation (summarized in Figure 4) give several perspectives on it. Which provides the fullest account of motivation? Actually, many of the approaches are complementary rather than contradictory. In fact, employing more than one approach can help us understand motivation in a particular instance.

Consider, for example, Aron Ralston's accident while hiking (described earlier). His interest in climbing in an isolated and potentially dangerous area may be explained by arousal approaches to motivation. From the perspective of instinct approaches, we realize that Aron had an overwhelming instinct to preserve his life at all costs. From a cognitive perspective, we see his careful consideration of various strategies to extricate himself from the boulder.

In short, applying multiple approaches to motivation in a given situation provides a broader understanding than we might obtain by employing only a single approach. We'll see this again when we consider specific motives—such as the needs for food, achievement, affiliation, and power—and draw on several of the theories for the fullest account of what motivates our behavior.

self-actualization A state of self-fulfillment in which people realize their highest potential in their own unique way. (Modules 29, 41)

Study Alert

Use Figure 4 to learn the distinctions among the different explanations for motivation (instinct, drive reduction, arousal, incentive, cognitive, and Maslow's hierarchy of needs).

Instinct

People and animals are born with preprogrammed sets of behaviors essential to their survival.

Drive reduction

When some basic biological requirement is lacking, a drive is produced.

Arousal

People seek an optimal level of stimulation. If the level of stimulation is too high, they act to reduce it; if it is too low, they act to increase it.

Incentive

External rewards direct and energize behavior.

Cognitive

Thoughts, beliefs, expectations, and goals direct motivation.

Hierarchy of needs

Needs form a hierarchy; before higher-order needs are met, lower-order needs must be fulfilled.

FIGURE 4 The major approaches to motivation.

(top, left): ©Blend Images/Getty Images; (top, middle): ©Digital Vision/Getty Images; (top, right): ©wavebreakmedia/Shutterstock; (bottom, left): Source: LCPL Casey N. Thurston, USMC/DoD Media; (bottom, right): ©Corbis/VCG/Getty Images

AP⁞ MODULE 29: EXPLAINING MOTIVATION

AP SUMMARY

- Psychologists first used instinct approaches to explain motivation, but new explanations have been provided.
- Incentive approaches focus on the positive aspects of the environment that direct and energize behavior.
- Cognitive approaches focus on the role of thoughts and expectations in producing motivation. Cognitive theories distinguish between intrinsic and extrinsic motivation.
- Drive reduction theory suggests that a biological need produces a drive to push an organism to satisfy that need.
- Arousal approaches suggest that we try to maintain a certain level of stimulation.
- Evolutionary theory focuses on our genetic inheritance and builds on basic instinct theory.
- Abraham Maslow's hierarchy of needs suggests that there are five basic needs: physiological, safety, love and belongingness, esteem, and self-actualization. Only after the basic needs are fulfilled can a person move toward meeting higher-order needs.
- A drive is the motivational tension that energizes behavior to fulfill a need. There are primary and secondary drives.
- Homeostasis, the maintenance of a steady internal state, often underlies motivational drives.

AP KEY TERMS

motivation
instincts
instinct approaches to motivation
drive-reduction approaches to motivation
drive

homeostasis
arousal approaches to motivation
incentive approaches to motivation
cognitive approaches to motivation
self-actualization

AP TEST PRACTICE

Section I: Multiple Choices

1. Tori is full from dinner, but she still wants to try the apple pie because it looks good. What theory best describes her motivation to eat dessert?
   A. Homeostasis
   B. Instinct
   C. Set point
   D. Incentive
   E. Intrinsic

2. Seth enjoys bungee jumping, while Trisha has no desire to plunge 300 feet into a canyon. What theory best explains the difference in their motivations?
   A. Affiliation
   B. Achievement
   C. Incentive
   D. Drive-reduction
   E. Optimal arousal

3. Homeostasis supports which theory of motivation?
   A. Achievement
   B. Drive-reduction
   C. Incentive
   D. Instinct
   E. Evolutionary

Section II: Free Response

Explain how the following motivation theories could relate to employment.
- Instinct
- Arousal
- Incentive
- Intrinsic

Module 30
Human Needs and Motivation: Eat, Drink, and Be Daring

As a sophomore at the University of California, Santa Cruz, Lisa Arndt followed a menu of her own making: For breakfast, she ate cereal or fruit with 10 diet pills and 50 chocolate-flavored laxatives. Lunch was a salad or sandwich; dinner, chicken and rice. But it was the feast that followed that Arndt relished most. Almost every night at about 9 p.m., she would retreat to her room and eat an entire small pizza and a whole batch of cookies. Then she'd wait for the day's laxatives to take effect. "It was extremely painful," says Arndt of those days. . . . "But I was that desperate to make up for my bingeing. I was terrified of fat the way other people are afraid of lions or guns." (Hubbard, O'Neill, & Cheakalos, 1999)

Lisa was one of the estimated 10 million women and 1 million men who suffer from eating disorders. These disorders, which usually appear during adolescence, can bring about extraordinary weight loss and other forms of physical deterioration. Extremely dangerous, they sometimes result in death.

Why are Lisa and others like her subject to such disordered eating, which revolves around the motivation to avoid weight gain at all costs? And why do so many other people engage in overeating, which leads to obesity?

To answer these questions, we must consider some of the specific needs that underlie behavior. In this module, we examine several of the most important human needs. We begin with hunger, the primary drive that has received the most attention from researchers, and then we turn to secondary drives–those uniquely human endeavors based on learned needs and past experience that help explain why people strive to achieve, to affiliate with others, and to seek power over others.

AP® LEARNING TARGETS

- Identify and apply basic motivational concepts to understand the behavior of humans and other animals.

- Describe classic research findings in specific motivations.

The Motivation Behind Hunger and Eating

Two hundred million people in the United States–some two-thirds of the population– are overweight. More than one-third of the U.S. population is so heavy that they have **obesity,** body weight that is more than 20% above the average weight for a person of a particular height (Sharpe, 2013; Ogden et al., 2014).

And the rest of the world is not far behind: A billion people around the globe are overweight or obese. With average weight rising in most countries, the World Health Organization has said that worldwide obesity has reached epidemic proportions, producing increases in heart disease, diabetes, cancer, and premature deaths. Obesity rates have doubled in 73 countries, and that has led to 4 million premature deaths (Fischetti, 2016; Datar, 2017; Jacobs & Richtel, 2017).

The most widely used measure of obesity is *body mass index (BMI),* which is based on a ratio of weight to height. People with a BMI greater than 30 are considered obese, whereas those with a BMI between 25 and 30 are overweight. (Use the formulas in Figure 1 to determine your own BMI.)

Although the definition of obesity is clear from a scientific point of view, people's perceptions of what an ideal body looks like vary significantly across different cultures and, within Western cultures, from one time period to another. For instance, many

obesity Body weight that is more than 20% above the average weight for a person of a particular height. (Module 30)

FIGURE 1 Use this procedure to find your body mass index.

To calculate your body mass index, follow these steps:

1. Indicate your weight in pounds: _____ pounds
2. Indicate your height in inches: _____ inches
3. Divide your weight (item 1) by your height (item 2), and write the outcome here: _____.
4. Divide the result above (item 3) by your height (item 2), and write the outcome here: _____.
5. Multiply the number above by 703, and write the product here: _____. This is your body mass index.

Example:
For a person who weights 210 pounds and who is 6 feet tall, divide 210 pounds by 72 inches, which equals 2.917. Then divide 2.917 by 72 inches (item 3), which yields .041. Multiplying .041 (from item 4) by 703 yields a BMI of 28.5.

Interpretation:
- Underweight = less than 18.5
- Normal weight = 18.5–24.9
- Overweight = 25–29.9
- Obesity = BMI of 30 or greater

Keep in mind that a BMI greater than 25 may or may not be due to excess body fat. For example, professional athletes may have little fat but weigh more than the average person because they have greater muscle mass.

contemporary Western cultures stress the importance of slimness in women–a relatively recent view. In 19th-century Hawaii, the most attractive women were those who were the heaviest. Furthermore, for most of the 20th century–except for periods in the 1920s and the most recent decades–the ideal female figure was relatively full. Even today, weight standards differ among different cultural groups. For instance, in some traditional Arab cultures, obese women are so prized as wives that parents force-feed their female children to make them more desirable (Marsh, Hau, & Sung, 2007; Franko & Roehrig, 2011; Lin et al., 2015).

Regardless of cultural standards for appearance and weight, no one doubts that being overweight represents a major health risk. However, controlling weight is complicated because eating behavior involves a variety of mechanisms. In our discussion of what motivates people to eat, we'll start with the biological aspects of eating.

BIOLOGICAL FACTORS IN THE REGULATION OF HUNGER

In contrast to human beings, other species are unlikely to become obese. Internal mechanisms regulate not only the quantity of food they take in but also the kind of food they desire. For example, rats that have been deprived of particular foods seek out alternatives that contain the specific nutrients their diet is lacking, and many species, given the choice of a wide variety of foods, select a well-balanced diet (Woods et al., 2000; Jones & Corp, 2003; Adler, 2013).

Complex biological mechanisms tell organisms whether they require food or should stop eating. It's not just a matter of an empty stomach causing hunger pangs and a full one alleviating those pangs. (Even individuals who have had their stomachs removed still experience the sensation of hunger.) One important factor is changes in the chemical composition of the blood. For instance, changes in levels of *glucose*, a kind of sugar, regulate feelings of hunger. In addition, the hormone *insulin* leads the body to store excess sugar in the blood as fats and carbohydrates. Finally, the hormone *ghrelin*

FIGURE 2 The hypothalamus acts as the brain's "feeding center" and is primarily responsible for monitoring food intake.
©McGraw-Hill Global Education Holdings LLC, 2000; (photo) ©Ryan McVay/Photodisc/Getty Images

communicates to the brain feelings of hunger. The production of ghrelin increases according to meal schedules as well as the sight or smell of food, producing the feeling that tells us we're hungry and should eat (Kojima & Kangawa, 2008; Langlois et al., 2011; Massadi et al., 2017).

The brain's *hypothalamus* monitors glucose levels (see Figure 2). Increasing evidence suggests that the hypothalamus carries the primary responsibility for monitoring food intake. Injury to the hypothalamus has radical consequences for eating behavior, depending on the site of the injury. For example, rats whose *lateral hypothalamus* is damaged may literally starve to death. They refuse food when it is offered; unless they are force-fed, they eventually die. Rats with an injury to the *ventromedial hypothalamus* display the opposite problem: extreme overeating. Rats with this injury can increase in weight by as much as 400%. Similar phenomena occur in humans who have tumors of the hypothalamus (Seymour, 2006; Fedeli et al., 2009; Barson, Morganstern, & Leibowitz, 2011).

Although the important role the hypothalamus plays in regulating food intake is clear, the exact way this organ operates is still unclear. One hypothesis suggests that injury to the hypothalamus affects the **weight set point,** or the particular level of weight that the body strives to maintain, which in turn regulates food intake. Acting as a kind of internal weight thermostat, the hypothalamus calls for either greater or less food intake (Berthoud, 2002; Cornier, 2011; Alboni et al., 2017).

In most cases, the hypothalamus does a good job. Even people who are not deliberately monitoring their weight show only minor weight fluctuations in spite of substantial day-to-day variations in how much they eat and exercise. However, injury to the hypothalamus can alter the weight set point, and a person then struggles to meet the internal goal by increasing or decreasing food consumption. Even temporary exposure to certain drugs can alter the weight set point (Khazaal et al., 2008; Sternson, Betley, & Cao, 2013; Palmiter, 2015).

Genetic factors determine the weight set point, at least in part. People seem destined, through heredity, to have a particular **metabolism,** the rate at which food is converted to energy and expended by the body. People with a high metabolic rate can eat virtually as much as they want without gaining weight, whereas others with low metabolism may eat literally half as much yet gain weight readily (Jequier, 2002; Westerterp, 2006).

SOCIAL FACTORS IN EATING

You've just finished a full meal and feel completely stuffed. Suddenly your host announces with great fanfare that he will be serving his "house specialty" dessert, bananas flambé, and that he has spent the better part of the afternoon preparing it. Even though you are full and don't even like bananas, you accept a serving of his dessert and eat it all.

weight set point The particular level of weight that the body strives to maintain. (Module 30)

metabolism The rate at which food is converted to energy and expended by the body. (Module 30)

Study Alert

A key point: Eating and hunger are influenced both by biological and social factors.

Clearly, internal biological factors do not fully explain our eating behavior. External social factors, based on societal rules and on what we have learned about appropriate eating behavior, also play an important role. Take, for example, the simple fact that people customarily eat breakfast, lunch, and dinner at approximately the same times every day. Because we tend to eat on schedule every day, we feel hungry as the usual hour approaches, sometimes quite independently of what our internal cues are telling us.

Similarly, we put roughly the same amount of food on our plates every day, even though the amount of exercise we may have had (and consequently our need for energy replenishment) varies from day to day. We also tend to prefer particular foods over others. Rats and dogs may be a delicacy in certain Asian cultures, but few people in Western cultures find them appealing, despite their potentially high nutritional value. Even the amount of food we eat varies according to cultural norms. For instance, people in the United States eat bigger portions than do people in France. In sum, cultural influences and our individual habits play important roles in determining when, what, and how much we eat (Rozin et al., 2003; Leeman, Fischler, & Rozin, 2011; Gu et al., 2017).

Other social factors relate to our eating behavior as well. Some of us head toward the refrigerator after a difficult day, seeking solace in a pint of Heath Bar Crunch ice cream. Why? Perhaps when we were children, our parents gave us food when we were upset. Eventually, we may have learned through the basic mechanisms of classical and operant conditioning to associate food with comfort and consolation. Similarly, we may learn that eating, which focuses our attention on immediate pleasures, provides an escape from unpleasant thoughts. Consequently, we may eat when we feel distressed (Elfhag, Tynelius, & Rasmussen, 2007; Tsenkova, Boylan, & Ryff, 2013; Higgs, 2015).

THE ROOTS OF OBESITY

Given that both biological and social factors influence eating behavior, determining the causes of obesity has proved to be a challenging task. Researchers have followed several paths.

Some psychologists suggest that oversensitivity to external eating cues based on social factors, coupled with insensitivity to internal hunger cues, produces obesity.

Although obesity is reaching epidemic proportions in the United States, its exact causes remain unclear.
©Roberto Michel/Shutterstock

Others argue that overweight people have higher weight set points than other people do. Because their set points are unusually high, their attempts to lose weight by eating less may make them especially sensitive to external, food-related cues and therefore more apt to overeat and perpetuate their obesity (Tremblay, 2004; West, Harvey-Berino, & Raczynski, 2004; Kanoski et al., 2011).

But why might some people's weight set points be higher than those of others? One biological explanation is that obese individuals have higher levels of the hormone *leptin,* which appears to be designed, from an evolutionary standpoint, to "protect" the body against weight loss. The body's weight-regulation system thus appears to be designed more to protect against losing weight than to protect against gaining it. Therefore, it's easier to gain weight than to lose it (Thanos et al., 2013; Wabitsch et al., 2015; Pontzer, 2017).

Another biologically based explanation for obesity relates to fat cells in the body. Starting at birth, the body stores fat either by increasing the number of fat cells or by increasing the size of existing fat cells. Furthermore, any loss of weight past infancy does not decrease the number of fat cells; it only affects their size. Consequently, people are stuck with the number of fat cells they inherit from an early age, and the rate of weight gain during the first 4 months of life is related to being overweight during later childhood (Stettler et al., 2005; Moore, Wilkie, & Desrochers, 2017).

According to the *weight-set-point hypothesis,* the presence of too many fat cells from earlier weight gain may result in the set point's becoming "stuck" at a higher level than desirable. In such circumstances, losing weight becomes a difficult proposition because one is constantly at odds with one's own internal set point when dieting (Müller, Bosy-Wesphal, & Heymsfield, 2010).

Not everyone agrees with the set-point explanation for obesity. For example, it's hard to see how the set-point explanation could explain the rapid rise in obesity that has occurred over the past several decades in the United States. Why would so many people's weight set points simultaneously increase?

Consequently, some researchers argue that the body does not try to maintain a fixed weight set point. Instead, they suggest, the body has a *settling point,* determined by a combination of our genetic heritage and the nature of the environment in which we live. If high-fat foods are prevalent in our environment and we are genetically predisposed to obesity, we settle into an equilibrium that maintains relatively high weight. In contrast, if our environment is nutritionally healthier, a genetic predisposition to obesity will not be triggered, and we will settle into an equilibrium in which our weight is lower (Pi-Sunyer, 2003; Sullivan, Smith, & Grove, 2011; also see *Applying Psychology in the 21st Century).*

Eating Disorders

Eating disorders are among the 10 most frequent causes of disability in young women. One devastating weight-related disorder is **anorexia nervosa.** In this severe eating disorder, people may refuse to eat while denying that their behavior and appearance—which can become skeleton-like—are unusual. Some 10% of people with anorexia literally starve themselves to death (Striegel-Moore & Bulik, 2007; Arcelus et al., 2011).

Anorexia nervosa mainly afflicts females between the ages of 12 and 40, although both men and women of any age may develop it. People with the disorder are often successful, attractive, and relatively affluent. The disorder often begins after serious dieting, which somehow gets out of control. Life begins to revolve around food: Although people with the disorder eat little, they may cook for others, go shopping for food frequently, or collect cookbooks (Polivy, Herman, & Boivin, 2005; Myers, 2007; Jacobs et al., 2009).

A related problem, **bulimia,** from which Lisa Arndt (described at the start of this module) suffered, is a disorder in which people binge on large quantities of food. For instance, they may consume an entire gallon of ice cream and a whole pie in a single

anorexia nervosa A severe eating disorder in which people may refuse to eat while denying that their behavior and appearance—which can become skeleton-like —are unusual. (Module 30)

bulimia A disorder in which a person binges on large quantities of food, followed by efforts to purge the food through vomiting or other means. (Module 30)

AP APPLYING PSYCHOLOGY IN THE 21ST CENTURY

A LOSING BATTLE FOR THE BIGGEST LOSERS

Losing weight is challenging, but keeping the weight off over the long term may be even a greater challenge. Many successful dieters struggle to maintain their new weight, and many end up gaining much of their original weight back. To find out why, a recent study looked at what happened to some of the most successful dieters: contestants on the eighth season of the reality television show *The Biggest Loser* in the 6 years after they finished their remarkable weight loss. The news wasn't good. Of the 14 contestants studied, all of whom had lost substantial weight during the show, all but one regained much of that weight in the subsequent 6 years. Four of them not only regained all the weight they had lost but gained more (Fothergill et al., 2016).

The researchers discovered that the dieters were locked in a chronic battle against their own biology: their bodies were fighting hard to resume their original weight, and their bodies had powerful biological tools for doing so. One of these is called *resting metabolism*, the rate at which food is converted to energy and expended by the body while one is not physically active. When the dieters began their weight-loss journey, they showed normal metabolic rates for their size (burning 2,600 calories per day, on average). By the

©Stockbyte/Getty Images

end of the season, the contestants had all lost substantial weight, but their metabolisms also slowed markedly. The rate was too slow for them to burn enough calories each day (2,000 on average) to stay at their new weights.

That wasn't the surprise, though– researchers already knew that decreased metabolism accompanies weight loss. What was new and surprising about this research was the finding that the depressed metabolism didn't rise over time. Even at

the 6-year follow up, the average metabolic rate had gone even further down, to 1,900 calories burned per day. This is despite the fact that the physical activity level of the former contestants, which nearly doubled from the start to the end of the competition, remained at its new heightened level at the 6-year follow-up. In essence, the contestants' bodies were playing a cruel trick on them: even though they stayed physically active, they were burning far fewer calories than before. Maintaining their new weight was impossible without continuing their restrictive diet. Essentially, they were doomed to either gain the weight back or stay perpetually hungry and feel deprived.

The news isn't entirely hopeless, though. What about that one contestant who maintained her weight loss for 6 years after the season ended? She wasn't immune to the effect, as she now burns nearly 600 fewer calories per day than before. But she maintained her weight loss by constantly watching her diet and staying active. So losing weight remains a constant battle, one that entails a state of constant dieting (Fothergill et al., 2016; Hao et al., 2016).

AP SKILLS: APPLY THEORIES AND PERSPECTIVES IN AUTHENTIC CONTEXTS / DATA ANALYSIS

1. How do these findings support a biological explanation for obesity?
2. Based on the findings of this research, what advice would you give a friend who is struggling to lose weight?

---

sitting. After such a binge, sufferers feel guilt and depression and often induce vomiting or take laxatives to rid themselves of the food–behavior known as purging. Constant bingeing-and-purging cycles and the use of drugs to induce vomiting or diarrhea can lead to heart failure. Often, though, the weight of a person with bulimia remains normal (Mora-Giral et al., 2004; Couturier & Lock, 2006; Lampard et al., 2011).

Eating disorders represent a significant problem: Estimates show that between 1% and 4% of high school-age and college-age women have either anorexia nervosa or bulimia. As many as 10% of women suffer from bulimia at some point in their lives. Furthermore, an increasing amount of research shows that almost as many men suffer from binge eating as do women (Swain, 2006; Park, 2007; Striegel et al., 2011).

What are the causes of anorexia nervosa and bulimia? Some researchers suspect a biological cause, such as a chemical imbalance in the hypothalamus or pituitary gland. Furthermore, the *orbitofrontal cortex*, which is involved in signaling when we should stop eating, functions differently in those with eating disorders. Furthermore, brain scans of people with eating disorders show that they process information about food differently from healthy individuals. Eating disorders also may have genetic roots; both are highly heritable (see *Neuroscience in Your Life;* Mohr & Messina, 2015; Weir, 2016; deAbreu & Filho, 2017).

Others believe that the cause has roots in society's valuation of slenderness and the parallel notion that obesity is undesirable. These researchers maintain that people with anorexia nervosa and bulimia become preoccupied with their weight and take to heart the cliché that one can never be too thin. This may explain why eating disorders increase as countries become more developed and Westernized, and dieting becomes more popular. Finally, some psychologists suggest that the disorders result from overly demanding parents or other family problems (Kluck, 2008; Cook-Cottone & Smith, 2013; Milos et al., 2017).

The complete explanations for anorexia nervosa and bulimia remain elusive. These disorders most likely stem from both biological and social causes, and successful treatment probably encompasses several strategies, including therapy and dietary changes (O'Brien & LeBow, 2007; Wilson, Grilo, & Vitousek, 2007; Cooper & Shafran, 2008).

If you or a family member needs advice or help with an eating problem, contact the American Anorexia Bulimia Association at www.aabainc.org or call (212) 575-6200. You can get more information at www.nlm.nih.gov/medlineplus/eatingdisorders.html.

Despite looking skeleton-like to others, people with the eating disorder anorexia nervosa see themselves as overweight.
©Denis Putilov/Alamy Stock Photo

BECOMING AN INFORMED CONSUMER
of Psychology

Dieting and Losing Weight Successfully

Although 60% of the people in the United States say they want to lose weight, it's a losing battle for most of them. Most people who diet eventually regain the weight they lost, so they try again and get caught in a seemingly endless cycle of weight loss and gain (Parker-Pope, 2003; Cachelin & Regan, 2006).

You should keep several things in mind when trying to lose weight (Heshka et al., 2003; Freedman & Waldrop, 2011):

- *There is no easy route to weight control.* You will have to make permanent changes in your life to lose weight without gaining it back. The most obvious strategy—cutting down on the amount of food you eat—is just the first step toward a lifetime commitment to changing your eating habits.
- *Keep track of what you eat and what you weigh.* Unless you keep careful records, you won't really know how much you are eating and whether any diet is working.
- *Eat "big" foods.* Eat fiber and foods that are bulky and heavy but low in calories, such as grapes and soup. Such foods trick your body into thinking you've eaten more and thus decrease hunger.
- *Cut out television.* One reason for the epidemic of obesity is the number of hours people in the United States spend viewing television. Not only does watching television preclude other activities that burn calories (even walking around the house is helpful), people often gorge on junk food while watching TV (Hu et al., 2003).

PsychTech
Wireless monitoring systems that track what dieters eat and how much they exercise help them to increase self-monitoring, one of the keys to effective weight loss.

	Activity	Duration
Less Vigorous, More Time	Washing and waxing a car	45–60 minutes
	Washing windows or floors	45–60 minutes
	Playing volleyball	45 minutes
	Playing touch football	30–45 minutes
	Gardening	30–45 minutes
	Wheeling self in wheelchair	30–40 minutes
	Walking 1¾ miles	35 minutes (20 min/mile)
	Basketball (shooting baskets)	30 minutes
	Bicycling 5 miles	30 minutes
	Dancing fast (social)	30 minutes
	Pushing a stroller 1½ miles	30 minutes
	Raking leaves	30 minutes
	Walking 2 miles	30 minutes (15 min/mile)
	Water aerobics	30 minutes
	Swimming laps	20 minutes
	Wheelchair basketball	20 minutes
	Basketball (playing a game)	15–20 minutes
	Bicycling 4 miles	15 minutes
	Jumping rope	15 minutes
	Running 1½ miles	15 minutes (10 min/mile)
More Vigorous, Less Time	Shoveling snow	15 minutes
	Stairwalking	15 minutes

FIGURE 3 Ways to burn 150 calories: People can expend 150 calories by spending more time at a less vigorous activity or spending less time at a more vigorous activity.

Source: U.S. Department of Health and Human Services. (1996). *Physical Activity and Health: A Report of the Surgeon General.* Atlanta, GA: U.S. Department of Health and Human Services, Centers for Disease Control and Prevention, National Center for Chronic Disease Prevention and Health Promotion; (photos) ©Image Source/Getty Images (top); ©oleg66/Getty Images (bottom)

- *Exercise.* Exercise at least 30 consecutive minutes three times each week. When you exercise, you use up fat stored in your body as fuel for muscles, which is measured in calories. As you use up this fat, you will probably lose weight. Almost any activity helps burn calories (see Figure 3).
- *Decrease the influence of external social stimuli on your eating behavior.* Serve yourself smaller portions of food, and leave the table before you see what is being served for dessert. Don't even buy snack foods such as nachos and potato chips; if they're not readily available in the kitchen cupboard, you're not apt to eat them. Wrap refrigerated foods in aluminum foil so that you cannot see the contents and be tempted every time you open the refrigerator.
- *Avoid fad diets.* No matter how popular they are at a particular time, extreme diets, including liquid diets, usually don't work in the long run and can be dangerous to your health.
- *Avoid taking any of the numerous diet pills advertised on television that promise quick and easy results.* They don't work.
- *Lose weight with others by joining a support group.* Being part of a group that is working to lose weight will encourage you to keep to your diet.
- *Maintain good eating habits.* When you have reached your desired weight, maintain the new habits you learned while dieting to avoid gaining back the weight you have lost.
- *Set reasonable goals.* Know how much weight you want to lose before you start to diet. Don't try to lose too much weight too quickly, or you may doom yourself to failure. Even small changes in behavior—such as walking 15 minutes a day or eating a few less bites at each meal—can prevent weight gain (Kirk et al., 2003; Freedman & Waldrop , 2011).

The Need for Achievement: Striving for Success

Although hunger may be one of the more potent primary drives in our day-to-day lives, powerful secondary drives that have no clear biological basis also motivate us. Among the more prominent of these is the need for achievement.

The **need for achievement** refers to a person's desire to strive for and achieve challenging accomplishments (McClelland et al., 1953). People with a high need for achievement seek out situations in which they can compete against some objective standard–such as grades, money, or winning a game–and prove themselves successful.

But people who have a high need for achievement are selective when it comes to picking their challenges: They tend to avoid situations in which success will come too easily (which would be unchallenging) or situations in which success is highly unlikely. Instead, people high in achievement motivation generally choose tasks that are of intermediate difficulty (Speirs-Neumeister & Finch, 2006; Mills, 2011).

In contrast, people with low achievement motivation tend to be motivated primarily by a desire to avoid failure. As a result, they seek out easy tasks so they are sure to avoid failure, or they seek out very difficult tasks for which failure has no negative implications because almost anyone would fail at them. People with a high fear of failure will stay away from tasks of intermediate difficulty because they may fail where others have been successful (Puca, 2005; Morrone & Pintrich, 2006; Pekrun, 2017).

A high need for achievement generally produces positive outcomes, at least in a success-oriented culture such as Western society. For instance, people motivated by a high need for achievement are more likely to attend college than are their low-achievement counterparts; once they are in college, they tend to receive higher grades in classes that are related to their future careers. Furthermore, high achievement motivation indicates future economic and occupational success (McClelland, 1985; Thrash & Elliot, 2002; Liem, 2015).

MEASURING ACHIEVEMENT MOTIVATION

How can we measure a person's need for achievement? The measuring instrument used most frequently is the *Thematic Apperception Test (TAT)* (Spangler, 1992). In the TAT, an examiner shows a series of ambiguous pictures, such as the one in Figure 4. The examiner tells participants to write a story that describes what is happening, who the people are, what led to the situation, what the people are thinking or wanting, and what will happen next. Researchers then use a standard scoring system to determine the amount of achievement imagery in people's stories. For example, someone who writes a story in which the main character strives to beat an opponent, studies in order to do well at some task, or works hard in order to get a promotion shows clear signs of an achievement orientation. The inclusion of such achievement-related imagery in the participants' stories is assumed to indicate an unusually high degree of concern with–and therefore a relatively strong need for–achievement (Tuerlinckx, DeBoeck, & Lens, 2002; Verdon, 2011).

need for achievement A person's desire to strive for and achieve challenging accomplishments. (Module 30)

Study Alert
A key feature of people with a high need for achievement is that they prefer tasks of *moderate* difficulty.

FIGURE 4 This ambiguous picture is similar to those used in the Thematic Apperception Test to determine people's underlying motivation. What do you see? Do you think your response is related to your motivation?
©Science Source

The Need for Affiliation: Striving for Friendship

Few of us choose to lead our lives as hermits. Why?

One main reason is that most people have a **need for affiliation,** an interest in establishing and maintaining relationships with other people. Individuals with a high need for affiliation write TAT stories that emphasize the desire to maintain or reinstate friendships and show concern over being rejected by friends.

need for affiliation An interest in establishing and maintaining relationships with other people. (Module 30)

People who have higher affiliation needs are particularly sensitive to relationships with others. They desire to be with their friends more of the time and alone less often, compared with people who are lower in the need for affiliation. However, gender is a greater determinant of how much time is actually spent with friends: Regardless of their affiliative orientation, female students spend significantly more time with their friends and less time alone than male students do (Johnson, 2004; Semykina & Linz, 2007; Hofer et al., 2017).

The Need for Power: Striving for Impact on Others

need for power A tendency to seek impact, control, or influence over others and to be seen as a powerful individual. (Module 30)

If your fantasies include becoming president of the United States or running Microsoft, your dreams may reflect a high need for power. The **need for power,** a tendency to seek impact, control, or influence over others and to be seen as a powerful individual, is an additional type of motivation (Winter, 2007; Pratto et al., 2011; Winter, 2016).

As you might expect, people with strong needs for power are more apt to belong to organizations and seek office than are those low in the need for power. They also tend to work in professions in which their power needs may be fulfilled, such as business management and—you may or may not be surprised—teaching (Jenkins, 1994). In addition, they seek to display the trappings of power. Even in college, they are more likely to collect prestigious possessions, such as electronic equipment and sports cars.

Some significant gender differences exist in the display of need for power. Men with high power needs tend to show unusually high levels of aggression, drink heavily, act in a sexually exploitative manner, and participate more frequently in competitive sports—behaviors that collectively represent somewhat extravagant, flamboyant behavior. In contrast, women display their power needs with more restraint; this is congruent with traditional societal constraints on women's behavior. Women with high power needs are more apt than men to channel those needs in a socially responsible manner, such as by showing concern for others or displaying highly nurturing behavior (Schubert & Koole, 2009; Schultheiss & Schiepe-Tiska, 2013; Sibunruang, Capezio, & Restubog, 2015).

From the perspective of...

A Human Resources Specialist How might you use characteristics such as need for achievement, need for affiliation, and need for power to select workers for jobs?

©Dex Image/Getty Images

AP MODULE 30: HUMAN NEEDS AND MOTIVATION: EAT, DRINK, AND BE DARING

AP SUMMARY

- Achievement motivation refers to the desire to strive for and achieve challenging accomplishments. It is usually measured through the Thematic Apperception Test (TAT).
- Hunger is regulated by biological factors, such as hormones and the hypothalamus. Genetic factors also play a role in weight set point and metabolism.
- Hunger is regulated by social factors, such as mealtimes, cultural food preferences, and other learned habits.
- Eating disorders, such as anorexia nervosa and bulimia, represent a significant problem, especially for young women. The causes for these eating disorders and obesity appear to be both biological and social.
- The need for affiliation is a concern with establishing and maintaining relationships with others, whereas the need for power is a tendency to seek to exert an impact on others.

AP KEY TERMS

obesity
weight set point
metabolism
anorexia nervosa
bulimia
need for achievement
need for affiliation
need for power

AP TEST PRACTICE

Section I: Multiple Choice

1. Individuals with high achievement tend to select what type of challenge?
   A. Hard tasks
   B. Easy tasks
   C. Power tasks
   D. Speed tasks
   E. Intermediate tasks

2. Serena's Thematic Apperception Test (TAT) story depicts a young girl who is rejected by her peers and seeks to regain friendship. What major type of motivation is Serena displaying in her story?
   A. Need for affiliation
   B. Need for achievement
   C. Need for power
   D. Need for self-actualization
   E. Need for intrinsic motivation

3. Rats who display overeating may have damage to what brain part?
   A. Amygdala
   B. Cerebellum
   C. Corpus callosum
   D. Hippocampus
   E. Hypothalamus

Section II: Free Response

Explain how the following concepts relate to hunger.
- Drive-reduction
- Arousal Theory
- Maslow's Hierarchy of Needs

Provide an explanation for hunger from each of the following approaches.
- Biological
- Social

Module 31
Understanding Emotional Experiences

AP® LEARNING TARGETS

- Compare and contrast major theories of emotion.
- Describe how cultural influences shape emotional expression, including variations in body language.

emotions Feelings that generally have both physiological and cognitive elements and that influence behavior. (Module 31)

Karl Andrews held in his hands the envelope he had been waiting for. It could be the ticket to his future: an offer of admission to his first-choice college. But what was it going to say? He knew it could go either way. His grades were pretty good, and he had been involved in some extracurricular activities, but his SAT scores had not been terrific. He felt so nervous that his hands shook as he opened the thin envelope (not a good sign, he thought). Here it comes. "Dear Mr. Andrews," it read. "The Trustees of the University are pleased to admit you. . . ." That was all he needed to see. With a whoop of excitement, Karl found himself jumping up and down gleefully. A rush of emotion overcame him as it sank in that he had, in fact, been accepted. He was on his way.

At one time or another, all of us have experienced the strong feelings that accompany both very pleasant and very negative experiences. Perhaps we have felt the thrill of getting a sought-after job, the joy of being in love, the sorrow over someone's death, or the anguish of inadvertently hurting someone. Moreover, we experience such reactions on a less intense level throughout our daily lives with such things as the pleasure of a friendship, the enjoyment of a movie, and the embarrassment of breaking a borrowed item.

Despite the varied nature of these feelings, they all represent emotions. Although everyone has an idea of what an emotion is, formally defining the concept has proved to be an elusive task. Here, we'll use a general definition: **Emotions** are feelings that generally have both physiological and cognitive elements and that influence behavior.

Think, for example, about how it feels to be happy. First, we obviously experience a feeling that we can differentiate from other emotions. It is likely that we also experience some identifiable physical changes in our bodies: Perhaps the heart rate increases, or–as in the example of Karl Andrews–we find ourselves "jumping for joy." Finally, the emotion probably encompasses cognitive elements: Our understanding and evaluation of the meaning of what is happening prompt our feelings of happiness.

It is also possible, however, to experience an emotion without the presence of cognitive elements. For instance, we may react with fear to an unusual or novel situation (such as coming into contact with an erratic, unpredictable individual), or we may experience pleasure over sexual excitation without having cognitive awareness or understanding of just what makes the situation exciting.

Some psychologists argue that one system governs emotional responses to a given situation and another governs cognitive reactions to it. Assuming there are two systems, does one predominate over the other? Some theorists suggest that we first respond to a situation with an emotional reaction and later try to make sense of it cognitively. For example, we may enjoy a complex modern symphony without at first understanding it or knowing why we like it. In contrast, other theorists propose that people first develop cognitions about a situation and then react emotionally. This school of thought suggests that we must think about and understand a stimulus or situation, relating it to what we already know, before we can react on an emotional level (Lazarus, 1995; Martin & Kerns, 2011).

Because proponents of both sides of this debate can cite research to support their viewpoints, the question is far from resolved. Perhaps the sequence varies from situation to situation, with emotions predominating in some instances and cognitive processes occurring first in others. Both sides agree that we can experience emotions that involve little or no conscious thought. We may not know why we're afraid of mice because we understand objectively that they represent no danger, but we may still be frightened when we see them. Neuroimaging studies of the brain may help resolve this debate as well as others about the nature of emotions (Niedenthal, 2007; Karaszewski, 2008; López-Pérez, 2015).

The Functions of Emotions

Imagine what it would be like if we didn't experience emotion. We would have no depths of despair, no depression, and no remorse, but at the same time, we would also have no happiness, joy, or love. Obviously, life would be considerably less satisfying and even dull if we lacked the capacity to sense and express emotion.

But do emotions serve any purpose beyond making life interesting? Indeed they do. Psychologists have identified several important functions that emotions play in our daily lives (Gross, 2006; Siemer, Mauss, & Gross, 2007; Rolls, 2011). Among the most important of those functions are the following:

- *Preparing us for action.* Emotions act as a link between events in our environment and our responses to them. For example, if you saw an angry dog charging toward you, your emotional reaction (fear) would be associated with physiological arousal of the sympathetic division of the autonomic nervous system, the activation of the "fight-or-flight" response.

- *Shaping our future behavior.* Emotions promote learning that will help us make appropriate responses in the future. For instance, your emotional response to unpleasant events teaches you to avoid similar circumstances in the future.

- *Helping us interact more effectively with others.* We often communicate the emotions we experience through our verbal and nonverbal behaviors, making our emotions obvious to observers. These behaviors can act as signals to observers, allowing them to understand better what we are experiencing and to help them predict our future behavior.

Determining the Range of Emotions: Labeling Our Feelings

If we were to list the words in the English language that have been used to describe emotions, we would end up with at least 500 examples (Averill, 1975). The list would range from such obvious emotions as *happiness* and *fear* to less common ones, such as *adventurousness* and *pensiveness*.

One challenge for psychologists has been to sort through this list to identify the most important, fundamental emotions. Theorists have hotly contested the issue of cataloging emotions and have come up with different lists, depending on how they define the concept of emotion. In fact, some reject the question entirely, saying that *no* set of emotions should be singled out as most basic and that emotions are best understood by breaking them down into their component parts. Other researchers argue for looking at emotions in terms of a hierarchy, dividing them into positive and negative categories and then organizing them into increasingly narrower subcategories (see Figure 1; Manstead, Frijda, & Fischer, 2003; Dillard & Shen, 2007; Livingstone et al., 2011).

Still, most researchers suggest that a list of basic emotions would include, at a minimum, happiness, anger, fear, sadness, and disgust. Other lists are broader, including emotions such as surprise, contempt, guilt, and joy (Shweder, 1994; Tracy & Robins, 2004; Greenberg, 2015).

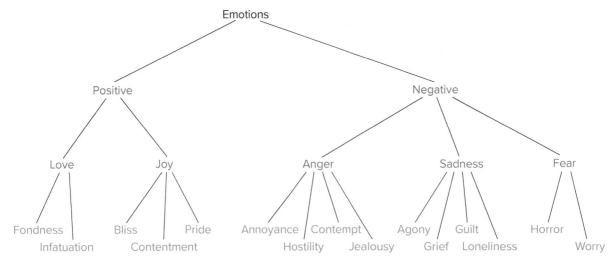

FIGURE 1 One approach to organizing emotions is to use a hierarchy, which divides emotions into increasingly narrow subcategories.
Source: Adapted from Fischer, K. W., Shaver, P. R., & Carnochan, P. (1990). How emotions develop and how they organize development. *Cognition and Emotion, 4,* 81–127.

One difficulty in defining a basic set of emotions is that substantial differences exist in descriptions of emotions among various cultures. For instance, Germans report experiencing *schadenfreude*, a feeling of pleasure over another person's difficulties, and the Japanese experience *hagaii*, a mood of vulnerable heartache colored by frustration. In Tahiti, people experience *musu*, a feeling of reluctance to yield to unreasonable demands made by one's parents.

Finding *schadenfreude, hagaii,* or *musu* in a particular culture doesn't mean that the members of other cultures are incapable of experiencing such emotions, of course. It suggests, though, that fitting a particular emotion into a linguistic category to describe that emotion may make it easier to discuss, contemplate, and perhaps experience (Kuppens et al., 2006; van Dijk et al., 2011; Dasborough & Harvey, 2017).

The Roots of Emotions

I've never been so angry before; I feel my heart pounding, and I'm trembling all over. . . . I don't know how I'll get through the performance. I feel like my stomach is filled with butterflies. . . . That was quite a mistake I made! My face must be incredibly red. . . . When I heard the footsteps in the night, I was so frightened that I couldn't catch my breath.

If you examine our language, you will find that there are literally dozens of ways to describe how we feel when we experience an emotion and that the language we use to describe emotions is, for the most part, based on the physical symptoms that are associated with a particular emotional experience (Kobayashi, Schallert, & Ogren, 2003; Manstead & Wagner, 2004; Spackman, Fujiki, & Brinton, 2006).

Consider, for instance, the experience of fear. Pretend that it is late on New Year's Eve. You are walking down a dark road, and you hear a stranger approaching behind you. It is clear that he is not trying to hurry by but is coming directly toward you. You think about what you will do if the stranger attempts to rob you or, worse, hurt you in some way.

While these thoughts are running through your head, something dramatic will be happening to your body. The most likely reactions, which are associated with activation of the autonomic nervous system, include an increase in your rate of breathing, an acceleration of your heart rate, a widening of your pupils (to increase visual sensitivity), and a dryness in your mouth as the functioning of your salivary glands and in fact of your entire digestive system ceases. At the same time, though, your sweat glands probably will increase their activity because increased sweating will help you rid yourself of the excess heat developed by any emergency activity in which you engage.

Of course, all these physiological changes are likely to occur without your awareness. At the same time, though, the emotional experience accompanying them will be obvious to you: You most surely would report being fearful.

Although it is easy to describe the general physical reactions that accompany emotions, defining the specific role that those physiological responses play in the experience of emotions has proved to be a major puzzle for psychologists. As we shall see, some theorists suggest that specific physiological reactions *cause* us to experience a particular emotion. For example, when the heart is pounding and we are breathing deeply, we then experience fear. In contrast, other theorists suggest the opposite sequence–that is, we experience an emotion, and that causes us to have a physiological reaction. In this view, then, as a result of experiencing the emotion of fear, our heart pounds and our breathing deepens.

THE JAMES-LANGE THEORY: DO GUT REACTIONS EQUAL EMOTIONS?

William James and Carl Lange were among the first researchers to explore the nature of emotions. To them, emotional experience is, very simply, our body's reactions that instinctively occur as a result of some situation or event in the environment. This view is summarized in James's statement, "We feel sorry because we cry, angry because we strike, afraid because we tremble" (James, 1890).

James and Lange took the view that the instinctive response of crying at a loss leads us to feel sorrow, that striking out at someone who frustrates us results in our feeling anger, that trembling at a menacing threat causes us to feel fear. They suggested that for every major emotion there is an accompanying physiological or "gut" reaction of internal organs–called a *visceral experience*. It is this specific pattern of visceral response that leads us to label the emotional experience.

In sum, James and Lange proposed that we experience emotions as a result of physiological changes that produce specific sensations. The brain interprets these sensations as specific kinds of emotional experiences (see the first part of Figure 2). This view has come to be called the **James-Lange theory of emotion** (Cobos et al., 2002; Stolorow & Stolorow, 2013; Šolcová & Lačev, 2017).

James-Lange theory of emotion The belief that emotional experience is a reaction to bodily events occurring as a result of an external situation ("I feel sad because I am crying"). (Module 31)

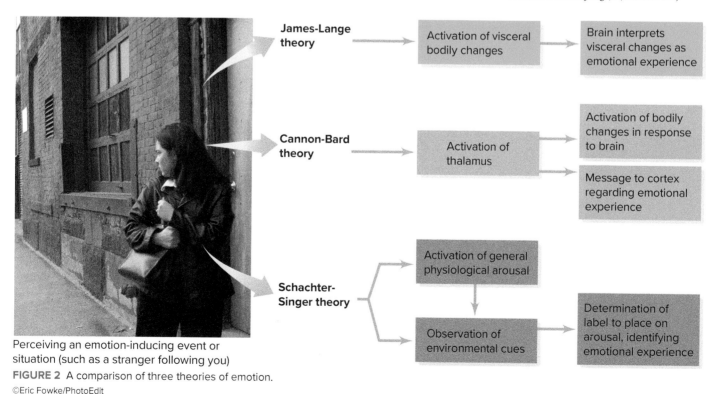

Perceiving an emotion-inducing event or situation (such as a stranger following you)

FIGURE 2 A comparison of three theories of emotion.
©Eric Fowke/PhotoEdit

However, the James-Lange theory has some serious shortcomings. For the theory to be valid, visceral changes would have to occur rapidly because we experience some emotions–such as fear upon hearing a stranger rapidly approaching on a dark night–almost instantaneously. Yet certain kinds of visceral changes occur slowly. Therefore, it's hard to see how they could be the source of an immediate emotional experience.

The James-Lange theory poses another difficulty: Physiological arousal does not invariably produce emotional experience. For example, a person who is jogging has an increased heartbeat and respiration rate, as well as many of the other physiological changes associated with certain emotions. Yet joggers typically do not think of such changes in terms of emotion. Thus, visceral changes by themselves are not always sufficient to produce emotion.

Finally, our internal organs produce a relatively limited range of sensations. Although some types of physiological changes are associated with specific emotional experiences, it is difficult to imagine how each of the many emotions that people are capable of experiencing could be the result of a unique visceral change. Many emotions actually are associated with relatively similar sorts of visceral changes, a fact that contradicts the James-Lange theory (Cameron, 2002; Rinaman, Banihashemi, & Koehnle, 2011).

THE CANNON-BARD THEORY: PHYSIOLOGICAL REACTIONS AS THE RESULT OF EMOTIONS

In response to the difficulties inherent in the James-Lange theory, Walter Cannon and later Philip Bard suggested an alternative view. In what has come to be known as the **Cannon-Bard theory of emotion,** they proposed the model illustrated in the second part of Figure 2 (Cannon, 1929). This theory rejects the view that physiological arousal alone leads to the perception of emotion. Instead, the theory assumes that both physiological arousal *and* the emotional experience are produced simultaneously by the same nerve stimulus, which Cannon and Bard suggested emanates from the *thalamus* in the brain.

The theory states that after we perceive an emotion-producing stimulus, the thalamus is the initial site of the emotional response. Next, the thalamus sends a signal to the autonomic nervous system, thereby producing a visceral response. At the same time, the thalamus also communicates a message to the cerebral cortex regarding the nature of the emotion being experienced. Hence, it is not necessary for different emotions to have unique physiological patterns associated with them–as long as the message sent to the cerebral cortex differs according to the specific emotion.

The Cannon-Bard theory seems to have been accurate in rejecting the view that physiological arousal alone accounts for emotions. However, more recent research has led to some important modifications of the theory. For one thing, we now understand that the hypothalamus and the limbic system, not the thalamus, play a major role in emotional experience. In addition, the simultaneous occurrence of the physiological and emotional responses, which is a fundamental assumption of the Cannon-Bard theory, has yet to be demonstrated conclusively. This ambiguity has allowed room for yet another theory of emotions: the Schachter-Singer theory.

THE SCHACHTER-SINGER THEORY: EMOTIONS AS LABELS

Suppose that as you are being followed down that dark street on New Year's Eve, you notice a man being followed by another shady figure on the other side of the street. Now assume that instead of reacting with fear, the man begins to laugh and act gleeful. Would the reactions of this other individual be sufficient to lay your fears to rest? Might you, in fact, decide there is nothing to fear and get into the spirit of the evening by beginning to feel happiness and glee yourself?

According to an explanation that focuses on the role of cognition, the **Schachter-Singer theory of emotion,** this might very well happen. This approach to explaining emotions emphasizes that we identify the emotion we are experiencing by observing

Cannon-Bard theory of emotion
The belief that both physiological arousal and emotional experience are produced simultaneously by the same nerve stimulus. (Module 31)

Study Alert
Use Figure 2 to distinguish the three classic theories of emotion (James-Lange, Cannon-Bard, and Schachter-Singer).

Schachter-Singer theory of emotion
The belief that emotions are determined jointly by a nonspecific kind of physiological arousal and its interpretation, based on environmental cues. (Module 31)

our environment and comparing ourselves with others (Schachter & Singer, 1962; Schachter & Singer, 2001; Shaked & Clore, 2017).

Schachter and Singer's classic experiment found evidence for this hypothesis. In the study, participants were told that they would receive an injection of a vitamin. In reality, they were given epinephrine, a drug that causes responses that typically occur during strong emotional reactions, such as an increase in physiological arousal, including higher heart and respiration rates and a reddening of the face. The members of both groups were then placed individually in a situation in which a confederate of the experimenter acted in one of two ways. In one condition, he acted angry and hostile; in the other condition, he behaved as if he were exuberantly happy.

The purpose of the experiment was to determine whether participants' emotions would be influenced by the confederate's behavior. And they were: When participants were asked to describe their own emotional state at the end of the experiment, those participants exposed to the angry confederate reported that they felt angry, whereas those participants exposed to the happy confederate reported feeling happy. In sum, the results suggest that participants used the behavior of the confederate to explain the physiological arousal they were experiencing.

The results of the Schachter-Singer experiment, then, supported a cognitive view of emotions in which emotions are determined jointly by a relatively nonspecific kind of physiological arousal *and* the labeling of that arousal on the basis of cues from the environment (refer to the third part of Figure 2). Although later research has found that arousal is more specific than Schachter and Singer believed, they were right in assuming that when the source of physiological arousal is unclear, we may look to our surroundings to determine what we are experiencing.

From the perspective of...

An Advertising Executive How might you use Schachter and Singer's findings on the labeling of arousal to create interest in a product?

©Image Source/Getty Images

CONTEMPORARY PERSPECTIVES ON THE NEUROSCIENCE OF EMOTIONS

When Schachter and Singer carried out their groundbreaking experiment on the cognitive influences of emotions in the early 1960s, the ways in which they could evaluate the physiological changes that accompany emotion were limited. However, advances in the measurement of the nervous system and other parts of the body have allowed researchers to examine more closely the biological responses involved in individual emotions. As a result, evidence is growing that specific patterns of biological arousal are associated with specific emotions (Woodson, 2006; Stifter, Dollar, & Cipriano, 2011; Christensen et al., 2017).

For instance, researchers have found that different emotions produce activation of different portions of the brain. In one study, participants undergoing positron emission tomography (PET) brain scans were asked to recall events that made them sad, such as deaths and funerals, or events that made them feel happy, such as weddings and births. They also looked at photos of faces that appeared to be happy or sad. The results of the PET scans were clear: Happiness was related to a decrease in activity in certain areas of the cerebral cortex, whereas sadness was associated with increases in activity in particular portions of the cortex (Hamann et al., 2002; Prohovnik et al., 2004; Johnston & Olson, 2015).

FIGURE 3 Connections from the amygdala allow it to mediate many of the autonomic expressions of emotional states through the hippocampus and visual cortex.

(photo): ©Image Source/Getty Images; Source: Adapted from Dolan, R. J. (2002). Emotion, cognition, and behavior. *Science, 298,* 1191–1194.

Hippocampus

Visual cortex

Amygdala

Study Alert

It is important to understand the basic neuroscience of emotional experience.

In addition, new research shows that the *amygdala,* in the brain's temporal lobe, plays an important role in the experience of emotions. The amygdala provides a link between the perception of an emotion-producing stimulus and the recall of that stimulus later. For example, if we've once been attacked by a vicious pit bull, the amygdala processes that information and leads us to react with fear when we see a pit bull at future times (LaBar, 2007; Pessoa, 2011; Christensen et al., 2017).

Because neural pathways connect the amygdala, the visual cortex, and the *hippocampus* (which plays an important role in the consolidation of memories), some scientists speculate that emotion-related stimuli can be processed and responded to almost instantaneously (see Figure 3). This immediate response occurs so rapidly that higher-order, more rational thinking, which takes more time, seems not to be involved initially. In a slower but more thoughtful response to emotion-evoking stimuli, emotion-related sensory information is first evaluated and then sent on to the amygdala. It appears that the quicker system offers an immediate response to emotion-evoking stimuli, whereas the slower system helps confirm a threat and prepare a more thoughtful response (Dolan, 2002).

AP｜ NEUROSCIENCE IN YOUR LIFE: EMOTION AND THE BRAIN

AP SKILL: APPLY THEORIES AND PERSPECTIVES IN AUTHENTIC CONTEXTS / SCIENTIFIC INVESTIGATION

1. Would universal emotions be explained with nature or nurture?

2. What is an advantage of the research to accurately predict which emotion someone is experiencing?

Our emotions may seem very personal, but neuroscientists are now discovering that they have a distinct neurological basis that is similar across individuals. In an innovative approach to studying the brain, researchers measured brain activity while participants watched movies or imagined six basic emotions (disgust, fear, happiness, sadness, anger, and surprise). The researchers then identified a distributed pattern of activity across the brain for each basic emotion (see images below). Based on the activity pattern for each emotion, the researchers accurately predicted which emotion the participants were experiencing (Saarimaki et al., 2016).

Movies   **Imagery**

■ Anger
  Disgust
■ Fear
■ Happiness
■ Sadness
  Surprise
■ Neutral

Source: Adapted from Saarimaki, H., Gotsopoulos, A., Jaaskelainen, I. P., Lampinen, J., Vuilleumier, P., Hari, R., . . . Nummenmaa, L. (2016). Discrete neural signatures of basic emotions. *Cerebral Cortex, 26*(6), 2563–2573.
doi: 10.1093/cercor/bhv086

MAKING SENSE OF THE MULTIPLE PERSPECTIVES ON EMOTION

As new approaches to emotion continue to develop, it is reasonable to ask why so many theories of emotion exist and, perhaps more important, which one provides the most complete explanation. Actually, we have only scratched the surface. There are almost as many explanatory theories of emotion as there are individual emotions (e.g., Manstead, Frijda, & Fischer, 2003; Frijda, 2005; Prinz, 2007; Herzberg, 2009).

Why are theories of emotion so plentiful? For one thing, emotions are not a simple phenomenon but are intertwined closely with motivation, cognition, neuroscience, and a host of related branches of psychology. For example, evidence from brain imaging studies shows that even when people come to supposedly rational, nonemotional decisions—such as making moral, philosophical judgments—emotions come into play.

In short, emotions are such complex phenomena, encompassing both biological and cognitive aspects, that no single theory has been able to explain fully all the facets of emotional experience. Furthermore, contradictory evidence of one sort or another challenges each approach, and therefore, no theory has proved invariably accurate in its predictions.

This abundance of perspectives on emotion is not a cause for despair—or unhappiness, fear, or any other negative emotion. It simply reflects the fact that psychology is an evolving, developing science. As we gather more evidence, the specific answers to questions about the nature of emotions will become clearer.

PsychTech
Because human facial expressions of emotions involve using dozens of muscles, it is only recently that researchers, such as Rana el-Kaliouby at MIT Media Lab, have been able to develop software to read them reasonably accurately.

Exploring Diversity

Do People in All Cultures Express Emotion Similarly?

Consider, for a moment, the six photos displayed in Figure 4. Can you identify the emotions being expressed by the person in each of the photos?

If you are a good judge of facial expressions, you will conclude that these expressions display six of the basic emotions: happiness, anger, sadness, surprise, disgust, and fear. Hundreds of studies of nonverbal behavior show that these emotions are consistently distinct and identifiable even by untrained observers (Ekman, 2007).

Interestingly, these six emotions are not unique to members of Western cultures; rather, they constitute the basic emotions expressed universally by members of the human race, regardless of where individuals have been raised and what learning experiences they have had. Psychologist Paul Ekman convincingly demonstrated this point when he studied members of an isolated New Guinea jungle tribe who had had almost no contact with Westerners (Ekman, 1972). The people of the tribe did not speak or understand English, had never seen a movie, and had very limited experience with Caucasians before Ekman's arrival. Yet their nonverbal responses to emotion-evoking stories, as well as their ability to identify basic emotions, were quite similar to those of Westerners.

Being so isolated, the New Guineans could not have learned from Westerners to recognize or produce similar facial expressions. Instead, their similar abilities and manner of responding emotionally appear to have been present innately. Although one could argue that similar experiences in both cultures led the members of each one to learn similar types of nonverbal behavior, this appears unlikely because the two cultures are so very different. The expression of basic emotions, thus, seems to be universal (Ekman, 1994b; Izard, 1994; Matsumoto, 2002).

Why do people across cultures express emotions similarly? A hypothesis known as the **facial-affect program** offers one explanation. The facial-affect program—which is assumed to be universally present at birth—is analogous to a computer software program that is activated when a particular emotion is experienced. When set in motion, the "program" produces a set of nerve impulses that make the face display an appropriate expression. Each primary emotion is related to a unique set of muscular movements, forming the kinds of expressions shown in Figure 4. For example, the emotion of happiness is universally displayed by movement of the zygomatic major, a muscle that raises the corners of the mouth and forms what we would call a smile (Ekman, 2003; Kendler et al., 2008; Krumhuber & Scherer, 2011).

facial-affect program The theory that a set of nerve impulses produce a facial display reflecting an emotion that is universal across cultures. (Module 31)

FIGURE 4 These photos demonstrate six of the primary emotions: happiness, anger, sadness, surprise, disgust, and fear.

(all, photos): ©Matsumoto Photos 1988

facial-feedback hypothesis The hypothesis that facial expressions not only reflect emotional experience but also help determine how people experience and label emotions. (Module 31)

The importance of facial expressions is illustrated by an intriguing notion known as the **facial-feedback hypothesis.** According to this hypothesis, facial expressions not only *reflect* emotional experience, but they also help *determine* how people experience and label emotions. Basically, "wearing" an emotional expression provides muscular feedback to the brain that helps produce an emotion congruent with that expression (Balconi, Bortolotti, & Crivelli, 2013; Damjanovic, Meyer, & Sepulveda, 2017).

For instance, the muscles activated when we smile may send a message to the brain indicating the experience of happiness—even if there is nothing in the environment that would produce that particular emotion. Some theoreticians have gone further by suggesting that facial expressions are *necessary* for an emotion to be experienced (Rinn, 1991). In this view, if no facial expression is present, the emotion cannot be felt.

Support for this facial-feedback hypothesis comes from a classic experiment carried out by psychologist Paul Ekman and colleagues (Ekman, Levenson, & Friesen, 1983). In the study, professional actors were asked to follow very explicit instructions regarding the movements of muscles in their faces. You might try this example yourself:

- Raise your brows and pull them together.
- Raise your upper eyelids.
- Now stretch your lips horizontally back toward your ears.

After carrying out these directions—which, as you may have guessed, are meant to produce an expression of fear—the actors' heart rates rose and their body temperatures declined, physiological reactions that characterize fear. Overall, facial expressions representing the primary emotions produced physiological effects similar to those accompanying the genuine emotions in other circumstances (Keillor et al., 2002; Soussignan, 2002).

AP SUMMARY

- James-Lange theory suggests that an environmental event activates a body change that is then interpreted by the brain as an emotional response.
- The Cannon-Bard theory contends that both physiological arousal and an emotional experience are produced simultaneously and that the visceral experience does not necessarily differ among differing emotions.
- The Schachter-Singer theory suggests that emotions are determined jointly by a physiological arousal and the subsequent labeling of that arousal, using cues from the environment.
- Researchers suggest there are primary emotions: happiness, anger, fear, sadness, and disgust. Others might include: surprise, contempt, guilt, and joy. However, substantial differences exist in descriptions of emotions among various cultures.
- Lazarus and other cognitive theorists say that we must first think about a stimulus before we can react on an emotional level.
- The facial-feedback hypothesis suggests that facial expressions not only reflect, but also produce emotional experiences.
- Newer research has found emotional responses are associated with fast and slow routes to the amygdala.
- Ekman found the expression of basic emotions to be universal. One explanation for universal emotions is the facial-affect program.

AP KEY TERMS

emotions
James-Lange theory of emotion
Cannon-Bard theory of emotion
Schachter-Singer theory of emotion
facial-affect program
facial-feedback hypothesis

AP TEST PRACTICE

Section I: Multiple Choice

1. Paul Ekman instructed participants to follow specific instructions, such as "Raise your brows and pull them together, then raise your upper eyelids." After carrying out these instructions, participants expressed feeling fearful. This experiment supports what theory of emotion?
   A. Cannon-Bard Theory
   B. Joseph LeDoux's Dual Road Theory
   C. Facial Feedback Hypothesis
   D. Schachter-Singer Two Factor Theory
   E. Lazarus's Appraisal Theory

2. Susie was crossing a shaky bridge and was stopped by a man. When she reached the other side of the bridge her heart was pounding, so she assumed she was attracted to the man. What theory of emotion would best explain Susie's emotional experience?
   A. Schachter-Singer
   B. James-Lange
   C. Cannon-Bard
   D. Universal emotions
   E. Display rules

3. All of the following are considered primary emotions EXCEPT
   A. sadness
   B. happiness
   C. adventurous
   D. anger
   E. disgust

Section II: Free Response

Researchers wanted to test if participants' emotions would be influenced by a confederate's behavior. Participants were told that they would be given an injection of a vitamin. In reality, they were given epinephrine to increase their arousal. Members of both groups were then placed individually in a situation with a confederate who acted one of two ways. In one condition, the confederate was happy and in the second condition the confederate was hostile. When participants were asked how they felt at the end of the experiment, those with the happy confederate reported feeling happy. Participants exposed to the hostile confederate reported feeling angry.

A. Explain how the following terms relate to this experiment.
   - Schachter-Singer theory of emotion
   - Independent variable
   - Confederate
   - Deception
   - Debriefing

B. Describe how rival theories of emotion would explain an emotional experience and provide a disadvantage for each theory.
   - James-Lange theory of emotion
   - Cannon-Bard theory of emotion

LOOKING *Back*

EPILOGUE

Motivation and emotions are two interrelated aspects of psychology. In these modules, we first considered the topic of motivation, which has spawned a great deal of theory and research examining primary and secondary drives. We then turned to a discussion of emotions, beginning with their functions and proceeding to a review of three major theories that seek to explain what emotions are and how they, and their associated physiological symptoms, emerge in the individual. Finally, we looked at cultural differences in the expression and display of emotions, and discussed the facial-affect program, which seems to be innate and to regulate the nonverbal expression of the basic emotions.

VISUAL SUMMARY 10 Motivation and Emotion

MODULE 29 Explaining Motivation

__Motivation:__ The factors that direct and energize the behavior of humans and other organisms

— The major approaches to motivation

Instinct
People and animals are born with preprogrammed sets of behaviors essential to their survival.

Drive reduction
When some basic biological requirement is lacking, a drive is produced.

Arousal
People seek an optimal level of stimulation. If the level of stimulation is too high, they act to reduce it; if it is too low, they act to increase it.

Incentive
External rewards direct and energize behavior.

Cognitive
Thoughts, beliefs, expectations, and goals direct motivation.

Hierarchy of needs
Needs form a hierarchy; before higher-order needs are met, lower-order needs must be fulfilled.

MODULE 30 Human Needs and Motivation

__Motivation Behind Hunger and Eating:__ Obesity has reached epidemic proportions

Factors that affect eating
- Biological factors
- Social factors and learned eating behaviors

Eating disorders
- Anorexia nervosa
- Bulimia

__Need for Achievement:__ Striving for and attaining a level of excellence

__Need for Affiliation:__ Establishing and maintaining relationships with other people

__Need for Power:__ Impacting, controlling, or influencing others

MODULE 31 Understanding Emotional Experiences

Functions of Emotions

— Prepare us for action

— Shape our future behavior

— Help us to interact more effectively with others

Theories of Emotions

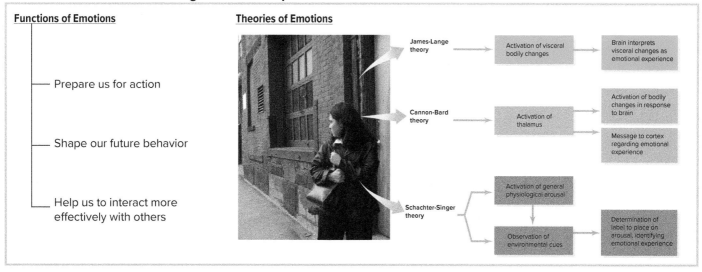

James-Lange theory → Activation of visceral bodily changes → Brain interprets visceral changes as emotional experience

Cannon-Bard theory → Activation of thalamus → Activation of bodily changes in response to brain / Message to cortex regarding emotional experience

Schachter-Singer theory → Activation of general physiological arousal / Observation of environmental cues → Determination of label to place on arousal, identifying emotional experience

©Jade/Getty Images

CHAPTER 11
Sexuality and Gender

AP'| LEARNING TARGETS FOR CHAPTER 11

- Describe how sex and gender influence socialization and other aspects of development.

PROLOGUE *BEYOND GENDER*

Tyler Ford, 26, has spent much of the past decade dealing with gender identity issues. "I was like, I don't know who I am," Ford recalls. Ultimately rejecting the notion that one is either male or female as too narrow and restrictive, Ford has adopted an agender identity—that is, not identifying as either male or female.

But achieving an identity that felt right and true didn't happen overnight. Assigned the gender of female at birth, Ford came out as a transgender man at age 20. Several years of hormone therapy gave Ford a more comfortable body, one that people couldn't pinpoint so easily as male or female.

"I really like being neutral," Ford says. "I don't like having to identify with either binary gender. I like being beyond" (Steinmetz, 2017).

LOOKING *Ahead*

Tyler Ford represents a small but growing number of young people who are looking beyond the conventional binary gender and sexuality labels of male/female and straight/gay in their search for an identity they believe accurately describes who they are. Lesbian, gay, pansexual, transgender, gender fluid, asexual, aromantic, bisexual, agender, and genderqueer are just a few of the identity labels millennials are adopting—and inventing in some cases—to express what they view as the wide spectrum of possibilities within the human experience (DeBord et al., 2017).

Tyler Ford's story illustrates the emotion and confusion that often characterize one of the most universal behaviors: sexuality. Exemplifying major personal as well as societal concerns, sex and the interrelated topic of gender are also key subjects for psychologists in a variety of specialties.

For instance, psychologists interested in motivation view sexuality in terms of sexual needs, drives, and gratification. Neuroscientists consider sexuality from the perspective of the relationship of the brain and nervous system to the functioning of the sexual organs. Social psychologists and psychologists who specialize in the study of women focus on society's rules of sexual conduct and the role sexual behavior plays in interpersonal behavior.

In this set of modules, we consider human sexuality from several of these vantage points. We begin by examining gender and discussing differences in societal expectations about how men and women should behave and the impact of those expectations on behavior and attitudes. Next, we turn to sexual behavior. We describe the biological aspects of sexual excitement and arousal, and then examine the variety of sexual activities in which people engage. We conclude with a discussion of nonconsenting sex, sexually transmitted infections, and the psychological aspects of sexual difficulties.

Module 32
Gender and Sex

gender The perception of being male or female. (Module 32)

Study Alert
The distinction between gender and sex is subtle. Keep in mind that *sex* relates to anatomy and *gender* relates to perception.

"It's a girl!" "It's a boy!"

A variant of one of these exclamations is typically the first sentence uttered upon the birth of a child. However, the consequences of whether we are born with male or female sex organs extend well beyond the moment of birth. Throughout our lives, the ways that others think of us, and even the ways we view ourselves are based to a large extent on whether society labels us as a male or a female—our gender.

Gender is the perception of being male or female. Although there is a good deal of overlap (and sometimes confusion) between the concepts of sex and gender, they are not the same: *Sex* typically refers to sexual anatomy and sexual behavior, whereas *gender* refers to one's sense of being a male or a female. Sex is biological; gender is psychological.

Although most people think of their own gender identity in terms of the two categories of female or male, a minority of individuals reject those designations as inappropriate or too rigid (as we first discussed in the chapter prologue). The range of gender labels now includes lesbian, gay, bisexual, transgender, cisgender, pansexual, asexual, queer, genderqueer, and more. This broader view of gender has moved toward mainstream acceptance: Facebook, for example, offers its 1 billion users 60 options for identifying their gender, and more than 200 recurring characters with nontraditional gender identities now appear on cable television and streaming media. Furthermore, Canada now allows "X" as a third sex category on its passports (Steinmetz, 2017).

Gender Roles: Society's Expectations for Women and Men

gender roles The set of expectations, defined by a particular society, that indicate what is appropriate behavior for men and women. (Module 32)

Gender roles are the set of expectations, defined by a particular society, that indicate what is appropriate behavior for men and women. Our beliefs about what is or is not "appropriate" behavior for others and ourselves are based on gender roles.

Beliefs about gender roles may result in favoritism toward members of one of the sexes. Gender roles also may produce *stereotyping*, judgments about individual members of a group on the basis of their membership in that group. Stereotypes about gender roles can result in sexism. **Sexism** refers to negative attitudes and behavior toward a person that are based on that person's gender.

sexism Negative attitudes and behavior toward a person based on that person's gender. (Module 32)

Regardless of their age, economic status, and social and educational background, people in Western societies often hold stereotypes about men and women. Specifically, men are more apt to be viewed as having personality traits involving competence, such as independence, objectivity, and competitiveness. In contrast, women tend to be seen as having personality traits involving warmth and expressiveness, such as gentleness and awareness of others' feelings. However, Western society traditionally values competence (attributed more to men than women) more than it values warmth and expressiveness (attributed more to women than men), which means that the perceived differences between men and women are biased in favor of men (Eagly, Beall, & Sternberg, 2004; González-Torres & Fernandez-Rivas, 2015; Bian, Leslie, & Cimpian, 2017).

In addition, cross-cultural research finds remarkable similarity in the content of gender stereotypes in different societies. For example, a 25-nation study identified a core set of descriptors that were consistently used to describe men and women. Women

Words Used to Describe Males		Words Used to Describe Females
Active	Initiative	Affected
Adventurous	Inventive	Affectionate
Aggressive	Lazy	Attractive
Ambitious	Logical	Charming
Arrogant	Loud	Curious
Assertive	Masculine	Dependent
Autocratic	Opportunistic	Dreamy
Clear-thinking	Progressive	Emotional
Coarse	Rational	Fearful
Courageous	Realistic	Feminine
Cruel	Reckless	Gentle
Daring	Robust	Mild
Determined	Rude	Sensitive
Disorderly	Self-confident	Sentimental
Dominant	Serious	Sexy
Egotistical	Severe	Softhearted
Energetic	Stern	Submissive
Enterprising	Stolid	Superstitious
Forceful	Strong	Talkative
Hardheaded	Unemotional	Weak
Hardhearted	Wise	
Independent		

FIGURE 1 In spite of numerous differences among cultures, research has found strong similarities in the content of gender stereotypes.

Source: Williams, J. E., & Best, D. L (1990). *Measuring sex stereotypes: A multinational study.* Newbury Park, CA: Sage.

were seen as sentimental, submissive, and superstitious, whereas men were seen as adventurous, forceful, and independent. These stereotypical similarities across cultures may be due to similarities in status between men and women across the cultures; in most, men typically attain higher status than women do (see Figure 1; (Williams & Best, 1990; Ghavami & Peplau, 2013; Safdar & Kosakowska-Berezecka, 2015).

Such stereotypes matter. By shaping beliefs about how men and women should behave, these stereotypes potentially keep inequalities between the genders alive. Stereotypes put pressure on people to fulfill the stereotypes, and they may lead people to perform in accordance with the stereotypes rather than in accordance with their own abilities. Attaining gender equality remains a significant challenge throughout the world (see Figure 2; Lips, 2003; Verhaeghen, Aikman, & Van Gulick, 2011; Li, Bagger, & Cropanzano, 2017).

Sexism on the Job

Differences still exist regarding which occupations are deemed appropriate for men and which for women. Women continue to be viewed as best suited for traditionally female jobs–that is, pink-collar jobs such as secretary, nurse, cashier, and jobs in other female-dominated professions that often feature low pay and low status. Men and women alike still report that they expect greater success when they enter a profession viewed as appropriate for their gender. Furthermore, women hold lower expectations than men do about the size of their starting salaries and how high their peak salaries will be (Casad, 2007; Ragins & Winkel, 2011; Heilman & Kusev, 2017).

Consistent with these expectations, women, on average, earn less than men do. Although the gap has been decreasing, women overall earn an average of 82¢ for every dollar that men earn. Women who are members of minority groups fare worse: Black women earn 63¢ for every dollar white, non-Hispanic men make, and Hispanic and Latino women earn just 59¢ for every dollar white men earn. Furthermore, even when they are in the same professions as men, women generally earn less than men in similar jobs (see Figure 3; Bureau of Labor Statistics, 2017).

FIGURE 2 Gender discrepancies throughout the world. The World Economic Forum ranks countries on the basis of gender equality, considering educational attainment, economic participation and opportunity, political empowerment, and health and survival. Out of 134 countries, the United States ranks 45th worldwide.

Source: Samans, R. & Zahidi, S. (2016). *The global gender gap report 2016.* Geneva: World Economic Forum.

Country	Rank	Country	Rank
Iceland	1	Moldova	26
Finland	2	Cuba	27
Norway	3	Barbados	28
Sweden	4	Spain	29
Rwanda	5	Belarus	30
Ireland	6	Portugal	31
Philippines	7	Costa Rica	32
Slovenia	8	Argentina	33
New Zealand	9	Luxembourg	34
Nicaragua	10	Canada	35
Switzerland	11	Cape Verde	36
Burundi	12	Bahamas	37
Germany	13	Poland	38
Namibia	14	Colombia	39
South Africa	15	Ecuador	40
Netherlands	16	Bulgaria	41
France	17	Jamaica	42
Latvia	18	Lao PDR	43
Denmark	19	Trinidad and Tobago	44
United Kingdom	20	United States	45
Mozambique	21	Australia	46
Estonia	22	Panama	47
Bolivia	23	Serbia	48
Belgium	24	Israel	49
Lithuania	25	Italy	50

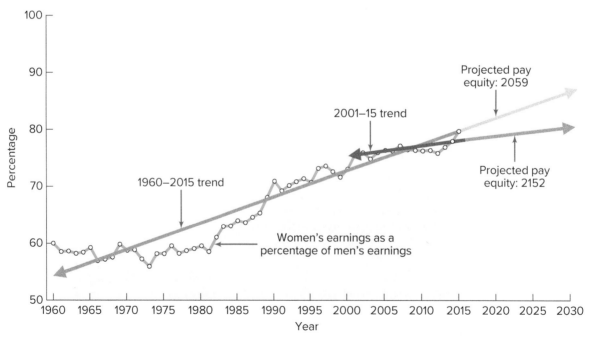

FIGURE 3 Although the disparity between women's and men's wages has improved in the United States since the 1960s, projections show that some sort of disparity will remain for many years. What factors account for the continuing gap between men's and women's wages?

Source: American Association of University Women. (2016). *The simple truth about the gender pay gap,* Washington, DC: AAUW.

On the other hand, most people believe that there should be gender equality in the workplace. Furthermore, they believe that women should be given the same opportunities as men.

For example, just about as many men as women endorse the idea that jobs should offer flexible work schedules in order to be family friendly. In addition, polls today find that most men no longer believe that a woman's most appropriate role is to care for her home and children while men should be earning money—a shift from the 1970s, when the majority of men endorsed that traditional view (Barnett, 2004; Stam, Verbakel, & Graaf, 2013; Sørensen, 2017).

Still, even when women are successful on the job and are promoted into upper-level, high-status positions, they may face significant hurdles in their efforts to move up the corporate ladder. Such obstacles are especially true for professional women who become mothers; they tend to be newly perceived as warm but less competent than they were prior to motherhood. The same thing doesn't happen to men who become fathers; they are most likely to be viewed as warm *and* competent (Cuddy, Fiske, & Glick, 2004; Hagelskamp et al., 2011; Moen, 2015).

Because of such stereotypical views, many women eventually hit what has come to be called the glass ceiling. The *glass ceiling* is the term for unstated but real barriers within an organization that prevent women from being promoted beyond a certain level because of gender discrimination. The glass ceiling is even found in colleges and universities. For example, although women hold 29% of science and engineering jobs at U.S. educational institutions, they occupy only 15% of those positions at the top 50 research universities (Sampson & Moore, 2008; Hoobler, Lemmon, & Wayne, 2011; Faniko et al., 2017).

As phenomena such as the glass ceiling make clear, gender stereotypes about males are typically more positive than are stereotypes about females. And such stereotypes matter because people often act as if they were real and modify their behavior to conform to the stereotypes. As a result, gender stereotypes determine both women's and men's behavior and ultimately lead to the unfortunate consequence of preferential treatment of men.

SEXUAL HARASSMENT

In addition to pay inequity and limited job advancement, women—even those in high-status professions—may face workplace sexism in the form of sexual harassment. *Sexual harassment* is unwanted sexual attention, the creation of a hostile or abusive environment, or explicit coercion to engage in unwanted sexual activity.

Sexual harassment is not a minor problem. Twenty percent of women say they have been sexually harassed at work, and some surveys find that one-third of women report being sexually harassed at some point in their career. And it is not just women who encounter harassment: Some 10% of men report experiencing sexual harassment on the job (Pina, Gannon, & Saunders, 2009; Stockdale & Sagrestano, 2011; Vagianos, 2015).

Sexual harassment is not only a workplace issue. Thirty percent of the female graduates of one large California university reported receiving some form of harassment. Such harassment begins early in life. In one survey, 81% of middle and high school students reported receiving some form of sexual harassment in school; 6 in 10 experienced physical sexual harassment at some point in their school lives (see Figure 4). One-third of students are afraid of being sexually harassed; girls are more than twice as likely as boys to report concern. Overall, estimates suggest that one of every two women will be harassed at some point during her academic or working life (Klein, Apple, & Kahn, 2011; AAUW, 2012; Gialopsos, 2017).

Sexual harassment often has more to do with men's desire to demonstrate power over females than with sexual motivations. In this view, higher-status persons who engage in harassment seek to exert power over their victims (Huerta, Cortina, & Pang, 2006).

Hollywood producer Harvey Weinstein was accused of having sexually harassed or assaulted dozens of women over the course of many years, bringing the issue of sexual harassment to the center of a nation-wide debate.

©Kathy Hutchins/Shutterstock

FIGURE 4 Sexual harassment in school. The number of students who report experiencing unwelcomed sexual attention often or occasionally at school is significant.

Source: Adapted from American Association of University Women. (2012). *Hostile hallways: Bullying, teasing, and sexual harassment in school.* Washington, DC: AAUW.

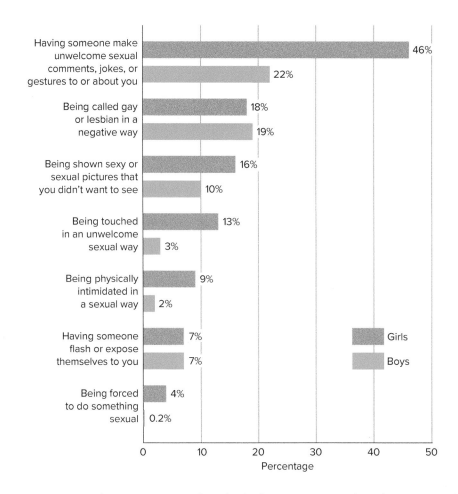

In some cases, harassment stems from *benevolent sexism,* attitudes relating to gender that appear on the surface to be beneficial to women but are, in reality, harmful. For example, a male employer may compliment a woman on her physical attractiveness or offer her an easy job so that she'll have more time with her children. The reality, however, is that such comments may undermine the employee's sense of competence, and she may feel that she is not being taken seriously (Glick et al., 2004; Delacollette et al., 2013; Reilly, Rackley, & Awad, 2017).

From the perspective of...

A Business Executive If you wanted to end sexism in business settings, how might you narrow the gap between men and women in terms of occupations and salary?

©Stuart Pearce/Pixtal/age fotostock

Regardless of the motivation that lies behind sexual harassment, the consequences for the victim are clear. Feelings of shame and embarrassment are typical and may be compounded by a sense of helplessness and powerlessness because targets of harassment are typically in lower-status positions. People who experience harassment often suffer emotional and physical consequences, and the quality of their work may decline. Furthermore, they have lower aspirations, believing they are unlikely to attain better positions (Magley, 2002; Miner-Rubino & Cortina, 2007; Chiodo et al., 2009).

Gender Differences: More Similar Than Dissimilar

Not surprisingly, gender stereotyping, combined with other factors, results in actual behavior differences between men and women. Before we consider the nature of gender differences, however, it is important to keep in mind men and women are more similar to one another in most respects than they are different. Furthermore, the differences that have been found reflect *average* male and female differences; this finding tells us little or nothing about any *individual* male or female.

For example, even if we find that males are generally more talkative than females—as research shows they are despite the stereotype that women talk more—an individual man can be less talkative than most women. Similarly, an individual woman may be more talkative than most men. When we consider any single person, our focus should be on the individual rather than on his or her gender group. It is important to take this into account as we examine the findings on gender differences (Mehl et al., 2007; Halpern, 2010).

PERSONALITY FACTORS

One of the most pronounced differences between men and women lies in their degree of aggressive behavior. By the time they are 2 years old, boys tend to display more aggression than girls do, and this higher level of aggression persists throughout the life span. Furthermore, compared with men, women experience greater anxiety and guilt about their aggressiveness and are more concerned about its effects on their victims (Hyde, Mezulis, & Abramson, 2008; Cross & Campbell, 2011; Helgeson, 2015).

Men generally have higher self-esteem than women do, although the difference is not large. Furthermore, women's self-esteem is influenced primarily by their perception of their sense of interdependence and connection with others. In contrast, men's self-esteem stems more from their assessment of their unique characteristics and abilities, traits that help them distinguish themselves from other people (Gentile et al., 2009; Hasnain, Ansari, & Sethi, 2011; Stapleton et al., 2017).

Men and women also view their relationships in terms of self-esteem, although they view them differently. Men tend to view relationships in terms of the social status they provide, and women tend to view them in terms of the companionship they provide (Kwang et al., 2013).

Men and women differ in how positively they view their own abilities and how they estimate the probability of their future success. In general, women evaluate themselves more harshly than men do. For example, a survey of first-year college students compared men's and women's views of whether they were above or below average. As you can see in Figure 5, more men than women considered themselves above average in overall academic and mathematical ability, competitiveness, and emotional health. Such self-perceptions matter because they influence motivation as well as academic and career choices, and even may affect performance (Steele, Spencer, & Aronson, 2002; Keller, 2007; Carr & Steele, 2009).

The content of men's and women's speech also differs. For example, women's speech patterns lead others to view them as more tentative and less assertive. Women more often raise their pitch at the end of a sentence and add qualifiers at the end of an opinion rather than stating the opinion outright. For example, instead of saying, "It's awfully warm today," a female speaker might say, "It's awfully warm today, *isn't it?*"—which makes her appear less certain of her opinion. When women use such tentative language, they are judged to be less competent and knowledgeable than they are when they speak assertively (Matlin, 1996; Popp, Donovan, & Crawford, 2003; Leaper & Ayres, 2007).

Women's and men's nonverbal behavior differs as well in several significant respects. In conversations with people of the other sex, women look at their partners significantly more while listening than while speaking (thereby communicating cooperation). In contrast, men look at their partners about the same length of time while listening

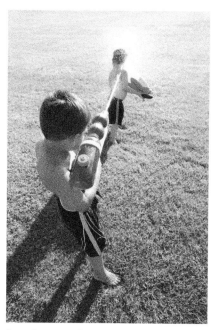

Boys from age 2 tend to be more aggressive than girls, a pattern that continues throughout the life span.
©Don Hammond/DesignPics

PsychTech

According to a survey by the Pew Research Center, men engage in Internet activities more intensively than women, and men are more likely to try new technologies earlier than women—although these differences may be diminishing.

FIGURE 5 Male first-year college students are much more likely than female first-year college students to rate themselves as above average in academic ability, mathematical ability, and emotional health.

Source: Sax, L. J., Hurtado, S., Lindholm, J. A., Astin, A. W., Korn, W. S., & Mahoney, K. M. (2004). *The American Freshman: National norms for fall 2004.* Los Angeles: Higher Education Research Institute, UCLA.

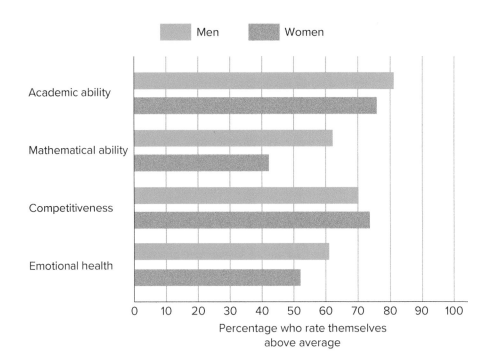

and speaking, which is typically interpreted as a sign of power. Furthermore, women are generally better than men at reading the meaning of others' facial expressions, allowing them greater sensitivity, compared with men, regarding the communications of others (Coats & Feldman, 1996; Burgoon & Bacue, 2003; LaFrance & Harris, 2004).

COGNITIVE ABILITIES

Research is clear in showing that no general differences exist between men and women in average IQ scores, learning, memory, problem solving, and concept-formation tasks. Although a few differences in more specific cognitive subareas have been identified in some studies, other research has called into question the true nature of those differences—and even their existence (Halpern, 2011).

This was not always the accepted wisdom about sex differences. When Eleanor Maccoby and Carol Jacklin carried out a pioneering study of sex differences almost 50 years ago (Maccoby & Jacklin, 1974), they concluded that girls outperformed boys in verbal abilities and that boys had superior quantitative and spatial abilities. Psychologists—and the public—widely accepted that conclusion as true, and it was widely believed for decades.

However, more sophisticated analyses have questioned these earlier findings. In a ground-breaking study, psychologist Janet Hyde and colleagues examined the mathematical performance of 7 million U.S. students in grades 2 through 11—a huge sample of students. Contrary to traditional wisdom, the average mathematical performance of males and females did not differ. Even when they looked at only the most gifted students, they found no gender difference (Hyde et al., 2008).

Similarly, cross-cultural data also show no difference between genders in math performance. For example, Japanese boys and girls perform quite similarly on math tests except for the single math area of probability; Japanese girls routinely outperform both boys and girls in the United States on comparable tests of mathematical ability. In addition, cross-cultural data show that on international science test results, girls often outperform boys—except in the United States. In short, no consistent nor meaningful differences appear to exist between males and females in math performance (Hyde & Mertz, 2009; Fairfield, 2012; Bench et al., 2015).

Psychologists have drawn a similar conclusion about the extent of gender differences in verbal skills. Despite the earlier view that women show superior verbal abilities compared with men, a more careful analysis of 165 studies of gender differences in verbal ability, which represents the testing of close to 1.5 million subjects, has led to the conclusion that verbal gender differences are insignificant. Furthermore, verbal SAT scores are quite similar for boys and girls (Hyde, 2005; Pahlke, Hyde, & Mertz, 2013).

In short, current evidence suggests that gender differences in cognitive skills are minimal. On the other hand, particular tests of mathematical and verbal skills do elicit differences in performance, as in the example of the mathematics part of the SAT in which most of the very high scorers are male (Hyde, 2005; Ripley, 2005; Zell, Krizan, & Teeter, 2015).

Furthermore, even when no differences are found in men's and women's performance on specific tasks, there may be underlying differences in how the brain processes information. For example, one study found that when men and women named particular objects, such as tools and plants, their brains were activated in different ways, depending on their experience with the objects (see *Neuroscience in Your Life*). In short, gender differences are complex, and we still do not have the full story on differences between men and women when it comes to their cognitive abilities (Hugdahl, Thomsen, & Ersland, 2006).

AP **NEUROSCIENCE IN YOUR LIFE:** DO WOMEN'S BRAINS DIFFER FROM MEN'S?

A continuing controversy in neuroscience research is the role of the brain's structure and function in determining differences in behavior between men and women. Because research has found that nonhuman males show a larger amygdala than nonhuman females, investigators recently examined the structure in humans. However, in a review of 46 studies comparing the volume of the amygdala in men and women, researchers found no difference when correcting for overall brain size. These findings suggest that the neurobiology of men and women may be more similar than different (Marwha, Halari, & Eliot, 2017).

AP SKILL: DATA ANALYSIS/ SCIENTIFIC INVESTIGATION

1. What were the implications of the findings involving nonhuman males and females?

2. What is the procedure for combining 46 studies called, and why is this procedure used?

The amygdala is highlighted in red.
©CLIPAREA | Custom media/Shutterstock

Sources of Gender Differences: Where Biology and Society Meet

If the identification of gender differences has presented a difficult challenge for researchers, the search for their causes has proved even more daunting. Given the indisputable fact that sex is a biological variable, it would seem reasonable to look at factors involving biological differences between men and women. It is also true that people are treated differently on the basis of their sex from the time they are born. Consequently, we must take into account both biological and social factors when we try to understand the source of gender differences.

Although we'll consider biological and environmental variables separately, neither alone can provide a full explanation for gender differences. Some combination of the two, interacting with each other, will ultimately provide us with an understanding of why men and women may behave differently.

BIOLOGICAL AND EVOLUTIONARY FACTORS

Do differences between male and female brains cause sex and gender differences? This intriguing hypothesis has been put forward by psychologists studying brain structure and functioning. For instance, in one study, scientists studied a group of girls whose mothers had accidentally taken drugs containing high levels of *androgen,* a male hormone, prior to their birth. Girls exposed to androgens were more likely to play with toys that boys stereotypically prefer (such as cars) and less likely to play with toys that girls stereotypically prefer (such as dolls). Perhaps exposure to particular hormones prior to birth affected the children's brain development, making children favor toys that involve certain kinds of skills, such as those related to spatial abilities (Fink, Manning, & Williams, 2007; Hines & Alexander, 2008; Moskowitz et al., 2015).

Similarly, research studies have found that women perform better on tasks involving verbal skill and muscular coordination during periods when their production of the female sex hormone *estrogen* is relatively high. In contrast, they perform better on tasks involving spatial relationships when their estrogen level is relatively low (Rosenberg & Park, 2002; Abraham et al., 2013).

Some psychologists argue that evolutionary forces lead to certain differences between men's and women's behavior. For example, David Buss and colleagues point to differences in the nature of jealousy between men and women. Men are more jealous in cases of sexual infidelity than in cases of emotional infidelity; women are more jealous in cases of emotional infidelity than in cases of sexual infidelity (Buss, 2003; Salmon, 2017).

According to Buss's controversial explanation, the root cause for the differences in jealousy lies in the evolutionary implications of sexual infidelity versus emotional infidelity for men and women. (*Sexual infidelity* occurs when a partner has sex with another individual outside of a relationship. *Emotional infidelity* occurs when a partner develops an emotional attachment to someone outside of a relationship.)

Buss argues that for males, sexual infidelity represents a threat to their ability to ensure that their children are actually their own (and are the ones who have inherited their genes). In contrast, females have no doubt that a child they carry through pregnancy is their own. However, their major concern is ensuring the male's protection and support during child rearing. Thus, to females, maintaining males' emotional attachment is crucial.

Psychologists using the evolutionary approach also argue that similarities in the division of labor between men and women

From the moment of birth, gender differences are defined by outside influences. Is it possible for a family to block these influences completely? Would it be desirable to do so?
©Stockbyte/Getty Images

across different cultures suggest that sex differences are due to evolutionary factors. In a controversial argument, they point to evidence that even in very different types of cultures, men tend to be more aggressive, competitive, and prone to taking risks than women. Such traits are assumed to hold an evolutionary advantage (Buss, 2003; Chang & Geary, 2007; Frank & Hou, 2015).

However, many critics question the assumptions of the evolutionary approach. Rather than assuming that the differences are due to evolutionary forces, some psychologists suggest that differences in males' and females' beliefs about the meaning of infidelity are the actual cause of their jealousy differences. For instance, men may believe that women have sex only when they are in love. Consequently, sexual infidelity may be seen as a sign that a woman is in love with another man and may produce more jealousy than emotional infidelity alone would. In contrast, women may believe that men are capable of having sex without being in love; consequently, they may find a man's sexual infidelity less bothersome because it does not necessarily mean that he is in love with someone else (Fine, 2010; Jordan-Young, 2010; Lalasz & Weigel, 2011).

Psychologists Alice Eagly and Wendy Wood criticize evolutionary explanations for gender differences on different grounds. In their *biosocial explanation of gender differences*, they argue that one important source of gender differences lies in the differing physical capabilities of men and women. Consistently across cultures, men carry out tasks that are based on their greater size, strength, and speed. In contrast, women carry out tasks that are related to their capacity for pregnancy and caring for children.

For example, women may be more caring and sensitive not because they are genetically so. Instead, it is their physical attributes (the ability to give birth to children) that lead them to be more caring and sensitive during child rearing. Hence, a combination of biological and social factors leads to their behavior (Wood & Eagly, 2002, 2015; Eagly & Wood, 2013; Eagly, 2016).

The extent to which biological and evolutionary factors may underlie gender differences is an unanswered and highly controversial question. One thing is clear, however: Biological factors and evolutionary factors alone do not explain the complete range of differences between male and female behavior. To fully understand the source of gender differences, we also must consider the social environment, which we do next.

Study Alert

Remember that gender differences are caused by a combination of biological, evolutionary, and social factors.

THE SOCIAL ENVIRONMENT

From the moment of birth, with blue blankets for boys and pink ones for girls, most parents and other adults provide environments that differ in important respects according to gender. For example, boys and girls are given different kinds of toys, and–until protests brought the practice to an end–items in the largest toy store chain in the United States were laid out according to the gender appropriateness of particular toys (Wood, Desmarais, & Gugula, 2002; Dender & Stagnitti, 2011; Endendijk et al., 2017).

Parents interact with their children differently, depending on their sex. Fathers play more roughly with their infant sons than they do with their infant daughters. Middle-class mothers tend to talk more to their daughters than to their sons. It is clear that adults in general frequently treat children differently on the basis of gender (Tenenbaum & Leaper, 2002; Kwon et al., 2013).

Such differences in behavior (and there are many more) produce different socialization experiences for men and women. *Socialization* is the process by which individuals learn the rules and norms of appropriate behavior in a given society or culture. In this case, socialization refers to learning the different rules about behavior for men versus women. According to social learning theory, boys are taught and rewarded for performing the socially perceived appropriate behaviors for men, while girls are taught what society says is appropriate for women (Liben & Bigler, 2002; Leaper & Friedman, 2007; Lee & Troop-Gordon, 2011).

It is not just parents, of course, who provide socialization experiences for children. Society as a whole communicates clear messages to children as they are growing up.

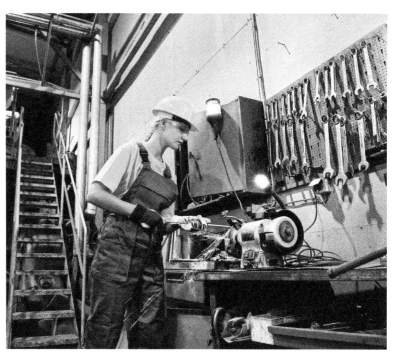

Androgynous people tend to defy stereotypes by combining the psychological and behavioral characteristics thought to be typical of both sexes.
(left): ©Purestock/Getty Images; (right): ©Nejron Photo/Shutterstock

gender schema A mental framework that organizes and guides a child's understanding of information relevant to gender. (Module 32)

Children's story books traditionally have portrayed girls in stereotypically nurturing roles, whereas boys have been given more physical and action-oriented roles. The media, too, act as a particularly influential source of socialization. For example, men outnumber women on television, and women are often cast in such stereotypical roles as housewife, secretary, and mother. The potency of television as an agent of socialization is underscored by data indicating that the more television children watch, the more sexist they become (Ogletree, Martinez, & Turner, 2004; Abelman, 2007; Dill & Thill, 2007).

Our educational system also treats boys and girls differently. For example, in elementary school, boys are five times more likely than girls to receive attention from classroom teachers. Boys receive significantly more praise, criticism, and remedial help than girls do. They are also more likely to be praised for the intelligence shown in their work, whereas girls are more apt to be commended for their neatness. Even in college classes, male students receive more eye contact from their professors than female students do, men are called upon more frequently in class, and men are more apt to receive extra help from their professors (Einarsson & Granstroem, 2002; Koch, 2003).

Socialization produces a **gender schema,** a mental framework that organizes and guides a child's understanding of information relevant to gender. On the basis of their schemas for appropriate and inappropriate behavior for males and females, children begin to behave in ways that reflect society's gender roles. Hence, children who are offered the opportunity to sew a costume for a school play may evaluate the activity not in terms of the intrinsic components of the process (such as the mechanics of using a needle and thread) but in terms of whether the activity is compatible with their gender schema. Such evaluation may potentially limit the range of experiences to which children are exposed (Le Maner-Idrissi & Renault, 2006; Frawley, 2008; Clément-Guillotin & Fontayne, 2011).

AP MODULE 32: GENDER AND SEX

AP SUMMARY

- Gender is the perception of being male or female. Gender roles are the expectations, defined by society, of what is appropriate behavior for men and women. When gender roles reflect favoritism toward one sex, they lead to stereotyping and produce sexism.
- The gender-role stereotypes for men suggest that they are endowed with competence-related traits, whereas women are seen in terms of their capacity for warmth and expressiveness. Actual sex differences are much less clear and of a smaller magnitude than suggested. The differences that do exist are produced by a combination of biological and environmental factors.
- Biological causes of sex difference are reflected by evidence suggesting a possible differences in brain structure and functioning and may be associated with differential exposure to hormones before birth.
- An evolutionary approach explains gender differences in terms of different male-female concerns regarding the inheritance of genes and the need for child rearing, but this approach is highly controversial.
- Socialization experiences produce gender schemas, mental frameworks that organize and guide a child's understanding of information relevant to gender.

AP KEY TERMS

gender
gender roles

sexism
gender schema

AP TEST PRACTICE

Section I: Multiple Choice

1. Women are viewed around the world as being best suited for pink-collar jobs, such as in the beauty industry, nursing, teaching, secretarial work, or child care. This expectation is known as (a)
   A. gender role
   B. transgender
   C. primary sex characteristic
   D. secondary sex characteristic
   E. double standard

2. Austin tried on nail polish, but his father quickly scolded him and told him boys do not wear nail polish. What theory explains how Austin will understand gender?
   A. Evolutionary
   B. Biological
   C. Cognitive
   D. Psychoanalytic
   E. Social learning

3. What are the mental frameworks that organize and guide a child's understanding of gender?
   A. Gender role
   B. Transgender
   C. Sexual orientation
   D. Gender schema
   E. Androgyny

Section II: Free Response

Gender differences are caused by a combination of factors. Explain the cause of gender differences from the following approaches.
- Biological
- Evolutionary
- Social
- Cognitive

Module 33

Understanding Human Sexual Response: The Facts of Life

When I started "tuning out," teachers thought I was sick—physically sick, that is. They kept sending me to the school nurse to have my temperature taken. If I'd told them I was carrying on with Jennifer Lopez in their classes while supposedly learning my Caesar and my Latin vocabulary, they'd have thought I was—well, delirious. I was! (based on Coles & Stokes, 1985)

Not everyone's sexual fantasies are as consuming as those reported by this teenage boy. Yet sex is an important consideration in most people's lives; although the physical aspects of human sex are not all that different from those of other species, the meaning, values, and feelings that humans place on sexual behavior elevate it to a special plane. To fully appreciate this difference, however, it is necessary to understand the basic biology underlying sexual responses.

The Basic Biology of Sexual Behavior

Anyone who has seen two dogs mating knows that sexual behavior has a biological basis. Their sexual behavior appears to occur naturally without much prompting on the part of others. A number of genetically controlled factors influence the sexual behavior of nonhuman animals. For instance, animal behavior is affected by the presence of certain hormones in the blood. Moreover, female animals are receptive to sexual advances only during certain relatively limited periods of the year.

Human sexual behavior, by comparison, is more complicated, although the underlying biology is not all that different from that of related species. In males, for example, the *testes* begin to secrete **androgens,** male sex hormones, at puberty. (See Figure 1 for the basic anatomy of the male and female **genitals,** or sex organs.) Not only do androgens produce secondary sex characteristics, such as the growth of body hair and a deepening of the voice, they also increase the sex drive. Because the level of androgen production by the testes is fairly constant, men are capable of (and interested in) sexual activities without any regard to biological cycles. Given the proper stimuli leading to arousal, male sexual behavior can occur at any time (Goldstein, 2000).

Women show a different pattern. When they reach maturity at puberty, the two *ovaries* begin to produce **estrogens,** female sex hormones. However, those hormones are not produced consistently; instead, their production follows a cyclical pattern. The greatest output occurs during **ovulation,** when an egg is released from the ovaries, making the chances of fertilization by a sperm cell highest. While in nonhumans the period around ovulation is the only time the female is receptive to sex, people are different. Although there are variations in reported sex drive, women are receptive to sex throughout their cycles (Leiblum & Chivers, 2007).

In addition, some evidence suggests that males have a stronger sex drive than females do or at least spend more time than women do thinking about it. For instance, while 54% of men report thinking about sex every day, only 19% of women report thinking about it on a daily basis (Gangestad et al., 2004; Baumeister & Stillman, 2006; Carvalho & Nobre, 2011).

Though biological factors "prime" people for sex, it takes more than hormones to motivate and produce sexual behavior. In animals, the presence of a partner who provides

androgens Male sex hormones secreted by the testes. (Module 33)

genitals The male and female sex organs. (Module 33)

estrogens Class of female sex hormones. (Module 33)

ovulation The point at which an egg is released from the ovaries. (Module 33)

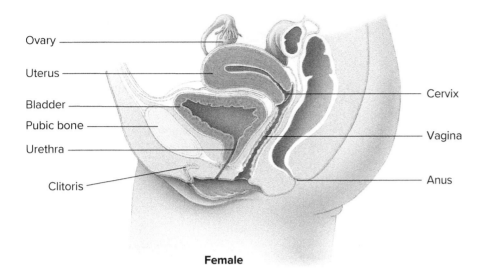

Ovary
Uterus
Bladder
Pubic bone
Urethra
Clitoris
Cervix
Vagina
Anus

Female

Bladder
Pubic bone
Vas deferens
Urethra
Penis
Glans
Large intestine
Seminal vesicle
Ejaculatory duct
Prostate
Anus
Testis
Scrotum

Male

FIGURE 1 Cutaway side views of the female and male sex organs.

arousing stimuli leads to sexual activity. Humans are considerably more versatile; not only other people but nearly any object, sight, smell, sound, or other stimulus can lead to sexual excitement. Because of prior associations, then, people may be turned on sexually by the smell of perfume or the sound of a favorite song hummed softly in their ears. The reaction to a specific, potentially arousing stimulus, as we shall see, is highly individual—what turns one person on may do just the opposite for another (Benson, 2003).

Physiological Aspects of Sexual Excitement: What Turns People On?

If you were to argue that the major human sex organ is the brain, in a sense you would be right. Much of what is considered sexually arousing in our society has little or nothing to do with our genitals; instead, it is related to external stimuli that, through a process of learning, have come to be labeled as erotic, or sexually stimulating.

For example, there are no areas of the body that *automatically* produce sexual arousal when touched. Areas of the body, called **erogenous zones,** that have an unusually rich array of nerve receptors are particularly sensitive not just to sexual

erogenous zones Areas of the body that are particularly sensitive because of the presence of an unusually rich array of nerve receptors. (Module 33) touch but to any kind of touch. When a physician touches a breast or a penis, the information sent to the brain by the nerve cells is essentially the same as that sent when a sexual partner touches that spot. What differs is the interpretation given to the touch. Sexual arousal is likely only when a certain part of the body is touched in what people define as a sexual manner and when a person is receptive to sexual activity (Goldstein, 2000; Wiederman, 2011).

Although people can learn to respond sexually to almost any stimulus, there is a good deal of agreement within a society or culture about what usually represents an erotic stimulus. In many Western societies, breast size is often the standard by which female appeal is measured, but in many other cultures, breast size is irrelevant (Furnham & Swami, 2007; Dawson, Fretz, & Chivers, 2017).

Sexual fantasies also play an important role in people's lives. People often have fantasies of a sexual nature during their everyday, nonsexual activities. Furthermore, most people fantasize about sex during sexual intercourse–and they often fantasize about people other than their current partner (Critelli & Bivona, 2008; Goldey & van Anders, 2011; Bogaert, Visser, & Pozzebon, 2015).

Men's and women's fantasies differ little from each other in terms of content or quantity, although men seem to fantasize about sex more than women do. But both men and women wish they kissed more, engaged in more oral sex, and had vaginal intercourse more frequently than they actually do (Shulman & Horne, 2006; Santtila et al., 2008; Wehrum et al., 2013).

The Phases of Sexual Response: The Ups and Downs of Sex

Although the kinds of stimuli that produce sexual arousal are to some degree unique to each individual, we all share some basic aspects of sexual responsiveness. According to pioneering work done by William Masters and Virginia Johnson (1966), who studied sexual behavior in carefully controlled laboratory settings, sexual responses follow a regular pattern consisting of four phases: excitement, plateau, orgasm, and resolution. Although other researchers argue that sexual responses proceed somewhat differently (e.g., Zilbergeld & Ellison, 1980), Masters and Johnson's research is the most widely accepted account of what happens when people become sexually excited.

In the **excitement phase,** which can last from just a few minutes to more than an hour, an arousing stimulus begins a sequence that prepares the genitals for sexual intercourse. In the male, the *penis* becomes erect when blood flows into it. In the female, the *clitoris* swells because of an increase in the blood supply to that area, and the *vagina* becomes lubricated. Women may also experience a "sex flush," a red rash that typically spreads over the chest and throat.

Next comes the **plateau phase,** the body's preparation for orgasm. During this stage, the maximum level of sexual arousal is attained as the penis and clitoris swell with blood. Women's breasts and vaginas expand, heartbeat and blood pressure rise, and breathing rate increases. Muscle tension becomes greater as the body prepares itself for the next stage, orgasm. Although it is difficult to explain the sensation of **orgasm** beyond saying that it is an intense, highly pleasurable experience, the biological events that accompany the feeling are fairly straightforward. When the orgasm stage is reached, rhythmic muscular contractions occur in the genitals every eight-tenths of a second. In the male, the contractions expel *semen,* a fluid containing sperm, from the penis–a process known as *ejaculation.* For women and men, breathing and heart rates reach their maximum.

After orgasm, people move into the last stage of sexual arousal, the **resolution stage.** The body returns to its resting state, reversing the changes brought about by

excitement phase The period in which an arousing stimulus begins a sequence that prepares the genitals for sexual intercourse. (Module 33)

plateau phase The period in which the maximum level of arousal is attained, the penis and clitoris swell with blood, and the body prepares for orgasm. (Module 33)

orgasm The peak of sexual excitement, during which rhythmic muscular contractions occur in the genitals. (Module 33)

resolution stage The interval after orgasm in which the body returns to its unaroused state, reversing the changes brought about by arousal. (Module 33)

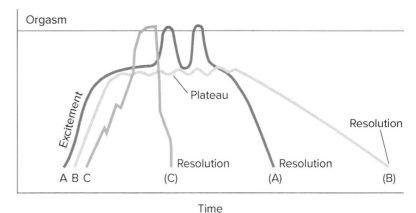

(a) Male pattern   **(b) Female patterns**

FIGURE 2 A four-stage model of the sexual response cycle for males and females based on the findings of Masters and Johnson (1966). Note how the male pattern (a) includes a refractory period. Part (b) shows three possible female patterns. In A, the pattern is closest to the male cycle except that the woman has two orgasms in a row. In B, there is no orgasm, whereas in C, orgasm is reached quickly and the woman rapidly returns to an unaroused state.

Source: Adapted from Masters, W. H., & Johnson, V. E. (1966). *Human sexual response*. Boston: Little, Brown.

arousal. The genitals resume their unaroused size and shape; blood pressure, breathing, and heart rate return to normal.

Male and female responses differ significantly during the resolution stage; these differences are depicted in Figure 2. Women are able to cycle back to the orgasm phase and experience repeated orgasms. Ultimately, of course, females enter the final resolution stage, and then they return to their prestimulation state. In contrast, it generally is thought that men enter a refractory period during the resolution stage. During the **refractory period,** men are unable to develop an erection. Therefore, men are unable to have another orgasm and ejaculate. The refractory period may last from a few minutes to several hours; in the elderly, it may continue for several days (Goldstein, 2000).

refractory period A temporary period that follows the resolution stage and during which the male cannot develop an erection again. (Module 33)

 # Exploring Diversity

Female Circumcision: A Celebration of Culture—or Genital Mutilation?

> Waris Dirie was only 5 when her mother agreed to the operation that would cleanse her of her inborn "filth" and make her worthy of marriage. Waris, a normal Somali girl who just wanted a husband some day, was innocently eager to be circumcised.
>
> A few months later, her mother blindfolded her and held her down while a woman performed the operation with a dull, dirty razor and no anesthetic, using a thorn and thread to sew up the incision. "It's not a pain you forget," Waris recalls. Neither can she escape intense pain every time she urinates or menstruates—pain to the point of fainting. (Dirie, 2011; London, 2013)

The operation in question—female circumcision—represents one of the most controversial procedures relating to sex throughout the world. In such an operation, the clitoris is removed, resulting in permanent inability to experience sexual pleasure.

Some 125 million women have undergone female circumcision. Most of them live in Africa and Asia, but this number includes around 500,000 women and girls in the United States who underwent the procedure or are at risk for it in the future. More than 90% of women in countries such as Somalia, Guinea, and Egypt have been circumcised during childhood, with most cutting occurring between the ages of 5 and 14 years. Furthermore, in some cases, more extensive surgery is carried out in which additional parts of the female genitals are removed or are sewn together with catgut or thorns (Djamba, 2013; United Nations Children's Fund, 2013; Davidson, 2016).

Those who practice female circumcision say it upholds an ancient societal tradition and is no different from other cultural customs. Its purpose, they say, is to preserve virginity before marriage, keep women faithful to their husbands after marriage, and enhance a woman's beauty. Furthermore, proponents believe that it differs little from the common Western practice of male circumcision in which the foreskin of the penis is surgically removed soon after birth.

In contrast, critics argue that female circumcision is nothing less than female mutilation. Not only does the practice permanently eliminate sexual pleasure, but it can also lead to constant pain, infection, and, in some cases, death. Furthermore, because the procedure is traditionally conducted in a ritualistic fashion using a razor blade, sawtooth knife, or glass and without an anesthetic, the circumcision itself can be physically traumatic (Renshaw, 2006).

The procedure raises some difficult issues that have been brought to light in various court cases. For instance, a Nigerian immigrant, living temporarily in the United States, went to court to argue that she should be allowed to remain permanently. Her plea: If she and her young daughters were sent back to Nigeria, her daughters would face circumcision upon their return. The court agreed and permitted her to stay indefinitely (Gregory, 1994; Dugger, 1996).

In reaction to the controversy about female circumcision, Congress made the practice illegal in the United States. Still, some critics argue that female circumcision is a valued cultural custom and that no one, particularly someone judging from the perspective of another culture, should prevent people from carrying out the customs they think are important. In addition, they point out that the practice of male circumcision is an accepted practice in the United States, based largely on religious, social, and cultural traditions (Boyle et al., 2002; Johnsdotter & Essén, 2005; Renshaw, 2006).

In any case, the practice of female circumcision is showing a gradual, although significant, decline in Africa and the Middle East. In Egypt, for example, 81% of 15- to 19-year-old girls have been circumcised, compared to 96% of women in their late 40s. Moreover, attitudes are changing: just one-third of teenage girls in Egypt thought the practice should continue, whereas two-thirds of older women approved of it (Dugger, 2013).

AP❚ MODULE 33: UNDERSTANDING HUMAN SEXUAL RESPONSE: THE FACTS OF LIFE

AP SUMMARY

- Biological factors, such as the presence of androgens and estrogens, prime people for sex. Almost any kind of stimulus can produce sexual arousal, depending on a person's prior experience.
- People's sexual responses follow a regular pattern consisting of four phases: excitement, plateau, orgasm, and resolution.

AP KEY TERMS

androgens	excitement phase
genitals	plateau phase
estrogens	orgasm
ovulation	resolution stage
erogenous zones	refractory period

AP TEST PRACTICE

Section I: Multiple Choice

1. The male sex hormones are known as
  A. testis
  B. androgens
  C. scrotums
  D. gonads
  E. estrogens

2. The following statements about sexual behavior are true EXCEPT
  A. Males have a stronger sex drive than females.
  B. Men are capable of sexual activities without regard to biological cycles.
  C. Females are receptive to sex throughout their cycles.
  D. People often have sexual fantasies of a sexual nature during their everyday, nonsexual activities.
  E. Men and women have significant differences in the content and quality of their sexual fantasies.

3. What is the correct sequence of the sexual response cycle?
  A. Excitement, plateau, orgasm, resolution
  B. Excitement, plateau, refractory, orgasm
  C. Plateau, orgasm, excitement, resolution
  D. Refractory, orgasm, excitement, plateau
  E. Orgasm, plateau, excitement, refractory

Section II: Free Response

Explain how the following terms relate to human sexual behavior.
  • Androgens
  • Estrogens
  • Secondary sex characteristics
  • Sexual response cycle
  • Refractory period

Module 34
The Diversity of Sexual Behavior

AP® | LEARNING TARGETS

- Describe how sex and gender influence socialization and other aspects of development.

A boy who practices this habit can never be the best that Nature intended him to be. His wits are not so sharp. His memory is not so good. His power of fixing his attention on whatever he is doing is lessened. . . . A boy like this is a poor thing to look at. . . . [He is] untrustworthy, unreliable, untruthful, and probably even dishonest. (Schofield & Vaughan-Jackson, 1913)

The cause of this condition: masturbation—at least according to the authors of the early 1900s sex manual *What Every Boy Should Know*. The consequences of masturbation for women were considered no less severe. In the words of one 19th-century physician, "There is hardly an end to the diseases caused by masturbation: dyspepsia, spinal disease, headache, epilepsy, various kinds of fits . . . impaired eyesight, palpitation of the heart, pain in the side and bleeding at the lungs, spasm of the heart, and sometimes sudden death" (Gregory, 1856).

Such views may seem as bizarre and far-fetched to you as they do to contemporary experts on human sexual behavior. However, at one time they were considered perfectly sound by quite reasonable people. Indeed, trivia buffs might be interested to learn that corn flakes owe their invention to a 19th-century physician, J. W. Kellogg, who believed that the enjoyment of tasty food provoked sexual excitation so an alternative of "unstimulating" grains was needed.

Clearly, sex and sex-related behavior are influenced by expectations, attitudes, beliefs, and the state of medical and biological knowledge in a given period. Today we know that sexual behavior may take diverse forms, and much of what was once seen as "unnatural" and "lewd" is often more likely to be accepted in contemporary society. Similarly, sexual behavior that is commonplace in one culture is seen as appalling in others. For instance, seven societies are known in which kissing never occurs (Mason, 1995).

Times change: The veiled sexuality of Victorian-era paintings has given way to a more frank acknowledgment of sexual behavior.
©SuperStock/Getty Images

Approaches to Sexual Normality

One approach to sexual normality is to behavior in terms of deviation from the average, or typical, behavior. To determine abnormality, we simply observe what behaviors are rare and uncommon in a society and label those deviations from the norm as abnormal.

The difficulty with such an approach, however, is that some behaviors that are statistically unusual hardly seem worthy of concern. Even though most people have sexual intercourse in the bedroom, does the fact that someone prefers sex in the dining room imply abnormality? If some people prefer portly sexual partners, are they abnormal in a society that holds slimness in high regard? Since the answer to both of these questions is clearly no, an approach that defines sexual abnormality in terms of deviation from the average is inappropriate. (The same difficulties are encountered in considering definitions of psychological abnormality.)

An alternative approach would be to compare sexual behavior against some standard or ideal. But here, again, there is a problem: What standard should we use? Some of us might suggest philosophy, some might turn to the Bible, and some might even consider psychology the ultimate determinant. The trouble is that none of these potential sources of standards is universally acceptable. Furthermore, since standards change radically with shifts in societal attitudes and new knowledge, such an approach is undesirable. For instance, at one point, the American Psychiatric Association labeled homosexuality a mental illness. However, as evidence to the contrary accumulated, in 1973 the organization determined that homosexuality should no longer be considered a mental disorder. Obviously, the behavior had not changed. Only the label the psychiatric profession gave it had been modified.

In light of the difficulties with other approaches, probably the most reasonable definition of sexual normality is one that considers the psychological consequences of the behavior. In this approach, sexual behavior is considered abnormal if it produces a sense of distress, anxiety, or guilt—or if it is harmful to some other person. According to this view, then, sexual behaviors can be seen as abnormal only when they have a negative impact on a person's sense of well-being or if they hurt someone else.

Study Alert

Remember the different approaches to sexual normality (deviation from the average, comparison against a standard, and psychological consequences).

Same-sex marriage, now legal throughout the United States, still is a social issue dividing people. It is also becoming an increasingly accepted part of American society, representing a major change in attitudes.
©Rawpixel.com/Shutterstock

It is important to recognize that what is seen as normal and what is seen as abnormal sexual behavior are dictated primarily by societal values; there have been dramatic shifts from one generation to another in definitions of what constitutes appropriate sexual behavior. People can and should make their own personal value judgments about what is appropriate in their own sex lives, but there are few universally accepted absolute rights and wrongs.

Surveying Sexual Behavior: What's Happening Behind Closed Doors?

For most of recorded history, the vast variety of sexual practices remained shrouded in ignorance. However, in the late 1930s, biologist Alfred Kinsey launched a series of surveys on the sexual behavior of people in the United States. The result was the first comprehensive attempt to see what people were actually doing sexually and was highlighted by the publication of Kinsey's landmark volumes, *Sexual Behavior in the Human Male* (Kinsey, Pomeroy, & Martin, 1948) and *Sexual Behavior in the Human Female* (Kinsey et al., 1953).

Kinsey's research was the first major systematic effort in learning about human sexual behavior. Kinsey and his colleagues interviewed tens of thousands of people. The interview techniques they devised are still regarded as a model for other sex researchers because of their ability to prompt sensitive information without causing embarrassment.

On the other hand, Kinsey's samples reflected an overrepresentation of college students, young people, well-educated individuals, urban dwellers, and people living in Indiana and the Northeast. Furthermore, as with all surveys involving volunteer participants, it is unclear how representative his data are of people who refused to participate in the study. Similarly, because no survey observes behavior directly, it is difficult to assess how accurately people's descriptions of what they do in private match their actual sexual practices.

Kinsey's work set the stage for later surveys. But due to political reasons (the use of government funding for sex surveys is controversial), surprisingly few comprehensive, large-scale, representative surveys–either in the United States or in other countries– have been carried out since Kinsey did his initial work. However, by examining the common results gleaned from different samples of subjects, we now have a reasonably complete picture of contemporary sexual practices–to which we turn next.

MASTURBATION

masturbation Sexual self-stimulation. (Module 34)

If you listened to physicians 100 years ago, you would have been told that **masturbation,** sexual self-stimulation often using the hand to rub the genitals, would lead to a wide variety of physical and mental disorders, ranging from hairy palms to insanity. If those physicians had been correct, however, most of us would be wearing gloves to hide the sight of our hair-covered palms because masturbation is one of the most frequently practiced sexual activities. Some 94% of all males and 63% of all females have masturbated at least once; among college students, the frequency ranges from "never" to "several times a day" (Hunt, 1974; Michael et al., 1994; Polonsky, 2006; Buerkle, 2011).

Men and women typically begin to masturbate for the first time at different ages, as you can see in Figure 1. Furthermore, men masturbate considerably more often than women do, although there are differences in frequency according to age. Male masturbation is most common in the early teens and then declines; females both begin and reach a maximum frequency later. There are also some racial differences: African American men and women masturbate less than whites do (Oliver & Hyde, 1993; Pinkerton et al., 2002; Das, Parish, & Laumann, 2009).

Although masturbation is often considered an activity to engage in only if no other sexual outlets are available, this view bears little relationship to reality. Close to three-fourths of married men ages 20 to 40 report masturbating an average of 24 times a

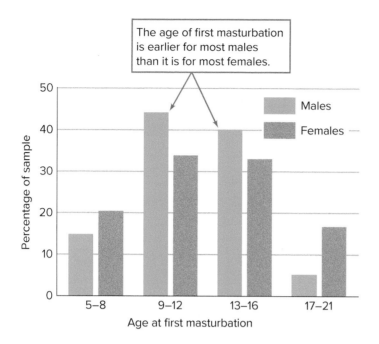

The age of first masturbation is earlier for most males than it is for most females.

FIGURE 1 The age at which a sample of college students first masturbated. The percentages are based on only those people who had experience with masturbation.

Source: Adapted from Arafat, I., & Cotton, W. L. (1974). Masturbation practices of males and females. *Journal of Sex Research, 10,* 293–307.

year, and 68% of the married women in the same age group masturbate an average of 10 times a year (Michael et al., 1994; Das, 2007; Regnerus, Price, & Gordon, 2017).

Despite the high incidence of masturbation, attitudes toward it still reflect some of the negative views of yesteryear. For instance, one survey found that around 10% of people who masturbated experienced feelings of guilt; 5% of the males and 1% of the females considered their behavior perverted. Despite these negative attitudes, however, most experts on sex view masturbation as a healthy and legitimate—and harmless—sexual activity. In addition, masturbation is seen as providing a means of learning about one's own sexuality and a way of discovering changes in one's body, such as the emergence of precancerous lumps (Arafat & Cotton, 1974; Levin, 2007; Herbenick et al., 2009).

Heterosexuality

For heterosexuals, engaging in sexual intercourse often is perceived as achieving one of life's major milestones. However, **heterosexuality,** sexual attraction and behavior directed to the other sex, consists of far more than male-female intercourse. Kissing, petting, caressing, massaging, and other forms of sex play are all components of heterosexual behavior. Still, sex researchers' focus has been on the act of intercourse, especially in terms of its first occurrence and its frequency.

heterosexuality Sexual attraction and behavior directed to the other sex. (Module 34)

PREMARITAL SEX

Until fairly recently, premarital sexual intercourse, at least for women, was considered one of the major taboos in our society. Traditionally, women have been warned by society that "nice girls don't do it"; men have been told that premarital sex is okay for them, but they should marry virgins. This view that premarital sex is permissible for males but not for females is called the **double standard** (Liang, 2007; Lyons et al., 2011; Penhollow, Young, & Nnaka, 2017).

As recently as the 1970s, the majority of adult Americans believed that premarital sex was always wrong. But there has been a dramatic change in public opinion since then. For example, as you can see in Figure 2, the percentage of people who believe that premarital sex is "not wrong at all" has increased from just over 25% in the early 1970s to more than 55% in 2012. More than half say that living together before marriage is morally acceptable (Thornton & Young-DeMarco, 2001; Harding & Jencks, 2003; Smith & Son, 2013).

double standard The view that premarital sex is permissible for males but not for females. (Module 34)

FIGURE 2 Percentage of people who believe premarital sex is "not wrong at all." Attitudes toward premarital sex have become considerably more positive over the past decades.
Source: Adapted from Smith, T. W., & Son, J. (2013). *Trends in public attitudes about sexual morality.* Chicago: NORC at the University of Chicago.

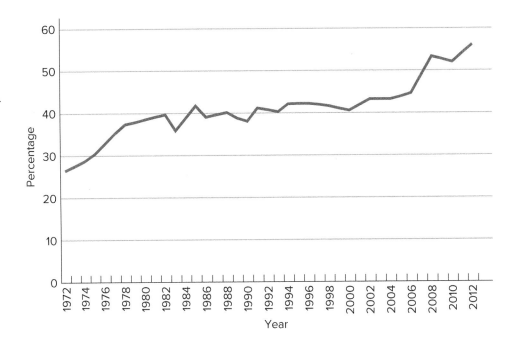

Actual rates of premarital sexual activity have matched changes in attitude. For instance, more than one-half of women between the ages of 15 and 19 have had premarital sexual intercourse. These figures are close to double the number of women in the same age range who reported having intercourse in 1970. Clearly, the trend over the last 50 years has been toward more women engaging in premarital sexual activity (Jones, Darroch, & Singh, 2005; Sprecher, Treger, & Sakaluk, 2013; Elias, Fullerton, & Simpson, 2015).

Males, too, have shown an increase in the incidence of premarital sexual intercourse, although the increase has not been as dramatic as it has been for females–probably because the rates for males were higher to begin with. For instance, the first surveys of premarital intercourse carried out in the 1940s showed an incidence of 84% across males of all ages; recent figures are closer to 95%. Moreover, the average age of males' first sexual experience has been declining steadily. Almost half of males have had sexual intercourse by the age of 18; by the time they reach age 20, 88% have had intercourse. Overall, 70% of all teens have had intercourse by their 19th birthday (Hyde, Mezulis, & Abramson, 2008; Guttmacher Institute, 2012).

What may be most interesting about the patterns of premarital sex is that they show a convergence of male and female attitudes and behavior. But is the change sufficient to signal an end to the double standard?

Probably. For many people, particularly younger individuals, the double standard has been succeeded by a new view: *permissiveness with affection.* According to those holding this view, premarital intercourse is permissible for both men and women if it occurs within a long-term, committed, or loving relationship (DeGaton, Weed, & Jensen, 1996; Hyde, Mezulis, & Abramson, 2008).

Still, the double standard has not disappeared completely. Where differing standards remain, the attitudes are almost always more lenient toward the male than toward the female (Sprecher & Hatfield, 1996).

Furthermore, there are substantial cultural differences regarding the incidence and acceptability of premarital intercourse. For instance, the proportions of male teenagers who have intercourse before their 17th birthday in Jamaica, the United States, and Brazil are about 10 times the level reported in the Philippines. And in some cultures, such as those in sub-Saharan Africa, women become sexually active at an earlier age than men–although this may be due to the fact that they marry at a younger age than men (Singh et al., 2000). (Also see *Applying Psychology in the 21st Century.)*

AP APPLYING PSYCHOLOGY IN THE 21ST CENTURY

TEEN SEXTING

Sexting by teenagers, in which a person sends sexually explicit photos or messages in a text message, has received a lot of media coverage in recent years, including some high-profile cases of teens getting themselves into considerable legal trouble with their sexting exploits. But how prevalent–and how problematic–is teen sexting really?

Research findings vary widely, with some studies suggesting that half or more of all teens engage in this practice. But high estimates such as these come from studies that use a broad definition of sexting that may include receiving a sext as well as sending one or even sending sexually explicit text-only messages (the revelation that teens talk to other teens about sex is neither new nor surprising). A stricter definition of sexting as sending sexual photos of oneself nude or nearly nude via digital communication produces estimates of roughly 3–7% of all teens–far less than what some media reports suggest (Strohmaier, Murphy, & DeMatteo, 2014; Ybarra & Mitchell, 2014; Strassberg, Cann, & Velarde, 2017).

Whether common or not, how much of a problem is sexting for teens who do participate in it? Some argue that sexting represents little more than a new technological twist on an old game of youthful sexual

©DGLimages/Shutterstock

exploration, and indeed, one study reports that negative fallout from sexting is fairly rare: 8% reported experiencing humiliation or damage to one's reputation, 5% reported getting in trouble with parents, and 1% reported getting in trouble with school. Other research associates sexting with other kinds of troublesome behavior such as alcohol use (girls who sext are about three times as likely and boys who sext about four times as likely as other teens to use alcohol), marijuana use (girls three times as likely, boys six times as likely), and

risky sexual behavior (girls 30% less likely to use condoms, boys 40% less likely). Of course, these data are correlational; one obvious explanation is that teens who are already taking risks are more likely to engage in all of these behaviors (Strohmaier, Murphy, & DeMatteo, 2014; Ybarra & Mitchell, 2014).

Why do teens sext? Sometimes it's because they feel pressure to do so. For example, they may be cajoled to reciprocate a sext that was sent to them by someone else first. But one study found that teens who initiate a sext are more likely to be sexually active 1 year later, suggesting that sexting may function as a way to initiate sexual activity or at least to signal sexual receptivity (Temple & Choi, 2014; Choi, Van Ouytsel, & Temple, 2016).

What teens should understand is that sexting, unlike in-person sexual banter, has the potential to cause them real and lasting reputational or legal harm and that it's far less common among their peers than they probably think it is.

AP SKILL: SCIENTIFIC INVESTIGATION

1. What are the specific and testable explanations of the variables and procedures of an experiment called and why are they necessary?
2. Research has associated sexting with various kinds of troublesome behavior. What type of research is this and what is its major limitation?

MARITAL SEX

To judge by the number of articles about sex in heterosexual marriages, one would think that sexual behavior was the number one standard by which marital bliss is measured. Married couples are often concerned that they are having too little sex, too much sex, or the wrong kind of sex (Harvey, Wenzel, & Sprecher, 2004).

Although there are many different dimensions along which sex in marriage is measured, one is certainly the frequency of sexual intercourse. What is typical? As with most other types of sexual activities, there is no easy answer to the question because there are such wide variations in patterns between individuals. We do know that 43% of married couples have sexual intercourse a few times a month and 36% of couples have it two or three times a week. With increasing age and length of marriage, the frequency of intercourse declines. Still, sex continues into late adulthood, with almost half of people reporting that they engage in high-quality sexual activity at least once a month (see Figure 3; Michael et al., 1994; Powell, 2006).

Furthermore, sexual activity provides benefits beyond the immediate pleasure. Sexual activity generates a kind of sexual afterglow that cements relationships and

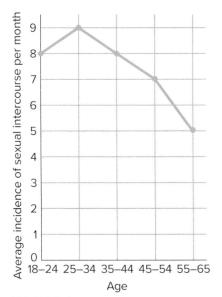

FIGURE 3 Once a couple is past their mid-30s, the average number of times per month they have sexual intercourse declines. Why do older couples have intercourse less frequently than younger ones do?

Source: Adapted from Clements, M. (1994, August 7). Making love, how old, how often. *Parade*, p. 18.

extramarital sex Sexual activity between a married person and someone who is not his or her spouse. (Module 34)

homosexuals Persons who are sexually attracted to members of their own sex. (Module 34)

bisexuals Persons who are sexually attracted to people of the same sex and the other sex. (Module 34)

increases marital satisfaction. Moreover, the frequency of sexual intercourse may be related to relationship satisfaction (Brody & Costa, 2017; Meltzer et al., 2017).

Although early research found **extramarital sex** to be widespread, the current reality appears to be otherwise. According to surveys, 85% of married women and more than 75% of married men report having no sexual partners other than their spouses. Furthermore, the median number of sex partners inside and outside of marriage since the age of 18 was six for men and two for women. Accompanying these numbers is a high, consistent degree of disapproval of extramarital sex, with 9 of 10 people saying that it is "always" or "almost always" wrong (Whisman & Snyder, 2007; DeMaris, 2013; Labrecque & Whisman, 2017).

Homosexuality and Bisexuality

Homosexuals are sexually attracted to members of their own sex, whereas **bisexuals** are sexually attracted to people of the same sex and the other sex. Most people now use the terms *gay* and *lesbian* to refer to male and female homosexuals, respectively, in part because the terms *gay* and *lesbian* refer to a broader array of attitudes and lifestyles than the term *homosexual*, which focuses on the sexual act.

The number of people who have had same-sex sexual partners at one point in their lives is considerable. Estimates suggest that around 20-25% of males and about 15% of females have had at least one gay or lesbian experience during adulthood. The exact number of people who identify themselves as exclusively homosexual has proved difficult to gauge; some estimates are as low as 1.1% and some as high as 10%. Most experts suggest that 5-10% of both men and women are exclusively gay or lesbian during extended periods of their lives (Hunt, 1974; Sells, 1994; Firestein, 1996).

Although people often view homosexuality and heterosexuality as two completely distinct sexual orientations, the issue is not that simple. Pioneering sex researcher Alfred Kinsey acknowledged this when he considered sexual orientation along a scale or continuum with "exclusively homosexual" at one end and "exclusively heterosexual" at the other. In the middle were people who showed both homosexual and heterosexual behavior (see Figure 4). Kinsey's approach suggests that sexual orientation is dependent on a person's sexual feelings and behaviors and romantic feelings (Weinberg, Williams, & Pryor, 1991; Jeffery, 2015).

DETERMINING THE CAUSES OF SEXUAL ORIENTATION

What determines people's sexual orientation? Although there are a number of theories, none has proved completely satisfactory.

Considerable research suggests that biological and genetic factors underlie sexual orientation. For example, studies of identical twins provide evidence for a genetic cause of sexual orientation. Studies find that when one twin identified himself or herself as homosexual, the occurrence of homosexuality in the other twin was higher than it

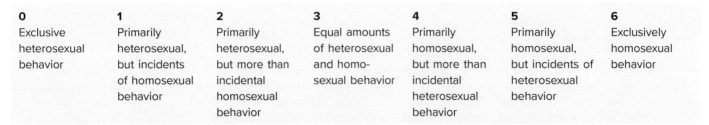

0	1	2	3	4	5	6
Exclusive heterosexual behavior	Primarily heterosexual, but incidents of homosexual behavior	Primarily heterosexual, but more than incidental homosexual behavior	Equal amounts of heterosexual and homo-sexual behavior	Primarily homosexual, but more than incidental heterosexual behavior	Primarily homosexual, but incidents of heterosexual behavior	Exclusively homosexual behavior

FIGURE 4 The Kinsey scale is designed to define the degree to which sexual orientation is heterosexual, homosexual, or bisexual. Although Kinsey saw people as falling along a continuum, most people believe that they belonged to a specific category.

Source: Kinsey, A. C., Pomeroy, W. B., & Martin, C. E. (1948). *Sexual behavior in the human male.* Philadelphia: Saunders.

was in the general population. Such results occur even for twins who have been separated early in life and who therefore are not necessarily raised in similar social environments. Furthermore, some research suggests there is an area on the X chromosome associated with homosexuality (Gooren, 2006; LeVay, 2011; Servick, 2014).

Hormones also may play a role in determining sexual orientation. For example, research shows that women exposed before birth to DES (diethylstilbestrol), a drug their mothers took to avoid miscarriage, were more likely to be gay or bisexual (Meyer-Bahlburg, 1997; Reinisch, Mortensen, & Sanders, 2017).

Further evidence suggests that differences in brain structures may be related to sexual orientation. For instance, the structure of the anterior hypothalamus, an area of the brain that governs sexual behavior, differs in male homosexuals and heterosexuals. Similarly, other research shows that, compared with heterosexual men or women, gay men have a larger anterior commissure, which is a bundle of neurons connecting the right and left hemispheres of the brain (LeVay, 1993; Byne, 1996; Witelson et al., 2008; Rahman & Yusuf, 2015).

In short, considerable research suggests the importance of biological and genetic factors at the roots of homosexuality, but the research is not conclusive in pinpointing the specific cause. Nevertheless, it seems likely that some inherited or biological factor predisposes people toward homosexuality (Teodorov et al., 2002; Rahman, Kumari, & Wilson, 2003; Burri, Spector, & Qazi, 2015).

In contrast, little evidence suggests that sexual orientation is brought about by child-rearing practices or family dynamics. Although proponents of psychoanalytic theories once argued that the nature of the parent-child relationship can produce homosexuality (e.g., Freud, 1922/1959), research evidence does not support such explanations (Isay, 1994; Roughton, 2002).

Another explanation for sexual orientation rests on learning theory (Masters & Johnson, 1979). According to this view, sexual orientation is learned through rewards and punishments in much the same way that we may learn to prefer swimming over tennis. For example, a young adolescent who had an unpleasant heterosexual experience might develop disagreeable associations with the other sex. If the same person had a rewarding, pleasant gay or lesbian experience, homosexuality might be incorporated into his or her sexual fantasies. If such fantasies are used during later sexual activities–such as masturbation–they may be positively reinforced through orgasm, and the association of homosexual behavior and sexual pleasure eventually may cause homosexuality to become the preferred form of sexual behavior.

Although the learning-theory explanation is plausible, several difficulties rule it out as a definitive explanation. Because our society has traditionally held homosexuality in low esteem, one ought to expect that the negative treatment of homosexual behavior would outweigh the rewards attached to it. Furthermore, children growing up with a gay or lesbian parent are statistically unlikely to become homosexual, which contradicts the notion that homosexual behavior may be learned from others (Tasker, 2005).

Because of the difficulty in finding a consistent explanation for sexual orientation, we can't definitively answer the question of what determines it. It seems unlikely that any single factor orients a person toward homosexuality or heterosexuality. Instead, it seems reasonable to assume that a combination of biological and environmental factors is involved (Hyde, Mezulis, & Abramson, 2008; Bailey et al, 2016).

Although we don't know exactly why people develop a certain sexual orientation, one thing is clear: Despite increasingly positive attitudes toward homosexuality, many gays and lesbians face antigay attitudes and discrimination, and it can take a toll. Lesbians and gays have higher rates of depression and suicide than do their straight counterparts. There are even physical health disparities due to prejudice that gays and lesbians may experience. Because of this, the American Psychological Association and other major mental health organizations have endorsed efforts to eliminate discrimination against gays and lesbians (Kwon, 2013; Lick, Durso, & Johnson, 2013; Moody et al., 2017).

Transgender Individuals

transgender A general term for persons whose gender identity, gender expression, or behavior is not consistent with that typically associated with the sex to which they were assigned at birth. (Module 34)

An increasing number of individuals consider themselves transgender. **Transgender** is a general term encompassing people whose gender identity, gender expression, or behavior is not consistent with the sex to which they were assigned at birth.

Transgender people may have male bodies but view their gender identity as female or may have female bodies and have a male gender identity. In other cases, transgender individuals may view themselves as a third gender (neither male nor female). They also may wish to be referred to not as "she" or "he" but rather some other, more neutral pronoun, such as "ze" or "they" (Prince, 2005; Hyde, Mezulis, & Abramson, 2008; Scelfo, 2015).

In some cases, transgender individuals may seek sex-change operations in which their existing genitals are surgically removed and the genitals of the desired sex are fashioned. Several steps, including intensive counseling, hormone injections, and living as a member of the desired sex for several years, precede surgery, which is, not surprisingly, highly complicated. The outcome, though, can be quite positive (Lobato, Koff, & Manenti, 2006; Richards, 2011; Gorton & Erickson-Schroth, 2017).

Transgender issues have become increasingly prominent in recent years. For instance, college campuses have struggled with how to best provide restrooms that address the needs of the transgender community. Do individuals who have the genitals of a male but identify as females use traditional men's rooms or women's rooms? One solution has been the establishment of unisex or all-gender restrooms (Steinmetz, 2015).

Whereas the term transgender centers on gender identity concerns, the term *intersex* refers to the small number of people born with genitals that make their sexual identity ambiguous. An *intersex person* has an atypical combination of sexual organs or chromosomal or gene patterns. In some cases, they are born with both male and female sexual organs, or the organs are ambiguous. It is an extremely rare condition, found in 1 in 4,500 births. Intersexism involves a complex mix of physiological and psychological issues (Lehrman, 2007; Diamond, 2009).

©TheChoperPilot/Shutterstock

Sexual Difficulties and Issues

When sex—an activity that should be pleasurable, joyful, and intimate—is forced on someone, it becomes one of the ultimate acts of aggression and brutality, and few crimes produce such profound and long-lasting consequences. But sexual crimes are not the only category of serious problems related to sex. Few personal difficulties produce as much anxiety, embarrassment, and even shame as sexually transmitted infections and sexual dysfunctions. We now turn to the major types of problems related to sex.

RAPE

rape The act by which one person forces another person to submit to sexual activity. (Module 34)

Rape occurs when one person forces another person to submit to sexual activity such as intercourse or oral-genital sex. Although it usually applies to a male forcing a female, rape can occur when members of either sex are forced into sexual activities without their consent.

Most people think of rape as a rare crime committed by strangers. Unfortunately, they are wrong on both counts. In fact, rape occurs far more frequently than is commonly thought, and rapists are typically acquaintances of their victims. A 2011 survey by the Centers for Disease Control and Prevention found that 20% of women report that they have been the victim of a rape or attempted rape during their lifetimes. Furthermore, more than 200,000 sexual assaults directed against women are reported to police in the United States each year. Because only about one-third of rapes and sexual assaults are reported to police, the actual figure is probably much higher (Catalano, 2006; CDC, 2011).

In fact, a national survey of college students found that 25% of women and 7% of men say they suffered unwanted sexual incidents. Another survey conducted at 35 universities revealed that 1 out of 8 female college students reported having been raped. Among the women who had been raped, about half said the rapists were first dates, casual dates, or romantic acquaintances–a phenomenon called **date rape** (Koss, 2011; DiJulio et al., 2015).

Girls in high school also suffer both sexual and physical abuse: In one survey, 9% of 14- to 18-year-old girls said they had been forced into sexual activity by a date, and in more than half of those cases, the incident had been accompanied by hitting, slapping, or shoving (Koss, 1993; Ackard & Neumark-Sztainer, 2002; Aiello, 2006; Koss, 2011).

Women in some segments of society are more at risk for rape than are others. Although the likelihood of sexual assault is considerably lower among Latino women in comparison to non-Latino white women, the rate for black women is slightly higher in comparison to white women. Such racial differences may stem from differing cultural views of women and male dominance (Koss, 1993; Black & Weisz, 2004).

Although on the surface it might appear that rape is primarily a sex crime, other types of motivation also underlie the behavior. In many cases, the rapist uses sex as a means of demonstrating power and control over the victim. In such cases, little is sexually satisfying about rape to the rapist; instead, the pleasure comes from forcing someone else to be submissive (Gowaty, 2003; Yamawaki, Darby, & Queiroz, 2007; Hipp et al., 2017).

In other cases of rape, anger is the primary motivation. Sexual behavior is used to show the rapist's rage at women in general, usually because of some perceived rejection or hurt that he has suffered in the past. Such rapes are likely to include physical violence and degrading acts against the victim.

Still, some rapes are based primarily on a desire for sexual gratification. Some men hold the attitude that it is appropriate and desirable for them to actively seek out sex. To them, sexual encounters represent a form of "war" between the sexes–with winners and losers–and violence is sometimes considered an appropriate way to obtain what they want. According to their reasoning, using force to obtain sexual gratification is permissible (Malamuth et al., 1995; Hall, 1996; Mann & Hollin, 2007).

Finally, there is a common, although unfounded, societal belief that many women offer token resistance to sex, saying no to sex when they mean yes. If a man holds such a view, he feels he may ignore a woman's protestations that she doesn't want sex (Anderson, Cooper, & Okamura, 1997; Yost & Zurbriggen, 2006; Sarmiento, 2011).

The repercussions of rape are devastating for the victims. During a rape, women experience fear, terror, and physical pain. The prefrontal cortex shuts down due to a surge of chemicals that significantly impairs thinking. Later, victims report shock, disbelief, panic, extreme anxiety, and suspiciousness–reactions that are sometimes intensified by implications that somehow the victim was to blame because of her style of dress, her presence in the wrong neighborhood, or because she did not fight back (Hopper & Lisak, 2014).

It doesn't matter whether a rape involves a date or a stranger; the psychological reactions are just as bad. The negative feelings may continue for years, even though the victim outwardly appears to have recovered. However, immediate psychological intervention, such as that provided by rape crisis centers, may help diminish the long-term reactions to rape (Ullman & Townsend, 2007; Campbell, 2008; Westmarland & Alderson, 2013).

CHILDHOOD SEXUAL ABUSE

One form of sexual behavior that is surprisingly common yet little understood is the sexual abuse of children. Although it is difficult to make accurate estimates of the true incidence of child sexual abuse because most cases go unreported, experts estimate that each year a half million children are sexually abused. Between 5% and 10% of boys and 20% of girls will be abused at some point (see Figure 5; Villarosa, 2002; Finkelhor & Jones, 2004).

Who commits child sexual abuse? In most cases, it is a relative or acquaintance; in only about one-quarter of the cases is the abuse carried out by a stranger. The most vulnerable age for being molested is between the ages of 7 and 13; the abusers tend to

date rape Rape in which the rapist is either a date or a romantic acquaintance. (Module 34)

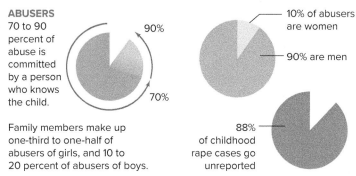

VICTIMS
Every year, 500,000 children in the United States are sexually abused. The peak age of vulnerability is 7 to 13.

1 or 2 of every 20 boys will be abused during childhood.

4 of every 20 girls will be abused.

ABUSERS
70 to 90 percent of abuse is committed by a person who knows the child.

90%

70%

Family members make up one-third to one-half of abusers of girls, and 10 to 20 percent of abusers of boys.

10% of abusers are women

90% are men

88% of childhood rape cases go unreported

FIGURE 5 Studies have found that the sexual abuse of children often is committed by a person who knows the child, with almost a third of the abusers being family members.
Source: Adapted from Finkelhor, D. (2002). *Sexual abuse in the United States.* Durham, NH: University of New Hampshire.

be about 20 years older than their victims. In most instances, the abuser is a male heterosexual. Furthermore, there are increasing cases of child predators using the web to make contact with potential victims (Wolfe, 1999; Finkelhor, Ormrod, & Turner, 2005).

The short- and long-term consequences of childhood sexual abuse can be extremely damaging. In terms of initial effects, victims report fear, anxiety, depression, anger, and hostility. Long-term effects may include depression, self-destructive behavior, feelings of isolation, poor self-esteem, and substance abuse. Although they may experience sexual difficulties later in life, the victims are not more likely to become sexual abusers themselves. Ultimately, the consequences of childhood sexual abuse are related to the specific nature of the abuse. Experiences involving fathers, genital contact, and the use of force are the most damaging (Buzi, Weinman, & Smith, 2007; Malloy, Brubacher, & Lamb, 2011; Turner et al., 2017).

Sexual Difficulties and Issues

Few personal difficulties produce as much anxiety, embarrassment, and even shame as sexually transmitted infections and sexual dysfunctions. We now turn to the major types of problems related to sex.

SEXUALLY TRANSMITTED INFECTIONS

sexually transmitted infection (STI)
A disease acquired through sexual contact. (Module 34)

Millions of people suffer the discomfort–not to mention the psychological distress–of a **sexually transmitted infection (STI)**, a disease acquired through sexual contact. Estimates suggest that in the United States, 1 person in 5 is infected with some form of STI, and at least 1 person in 4 will probably contract an STI during his or her lifetime. Some 19 million new infections occur every year, nearly half in people ages 15 to 24 (National Prevention Information Network, 2011).

The United States has the highest rate of sexually transmitted infections of all the economically developed countries in the world, in part because people in the United States don't talk about sex as frankly or receive as much sex education as people in other developed nations (see Figure 6; CDC, 2013).

These are the major STIs:

- *Human papilloma virus (HPV).* HPV is the most common sexually transmitted infection, with more than 14 million new cases each year. Spread through vaginal, anal, or oral sex, it is usually not harmful, although it can lead to serious health problems such as genital warts and cervical cancer. HPV vaccines are now available that protect against some of the most harmful types of HPV.

- *Chlamydia.* Another widespread STI is *chlamydia,* a disease that in women initially produces no symptoms and in men causes a burning sensation during urination and a discharge from the penis. If it is left untreated, chlamydia can lead to pelvic inflammation, urethral damage, arthritis, and even sterility. There are almost 3 million new cases each year in the United States. Because it usually produces no symptoms in females, the Centers for Disease Control and Prevention recommends that sexually active women under age 26 should be tested for the disease every year. Once diagnosed, chlamydia can be cured with antibiotics, most often azithromycin or doxycycline.

- *Genital herpes. Genital herpes* is a virus related to the cold sores that sometimes appear around the mouth. Herpes first appears as small blisters or sores around the genitals that later break open, causing severe pain. These sores heal after a few weeks, but the disease usually reappears typically four or five times in the year following infection. Later outbreaks are less frequent, but the infection, which cannot be cured, often causes psychological distress for those who know they are infected. During the active phases of the disease, it can be transmitted to sexual partners. Genital herpes is common among college-age students: About 17% of 20- to 29-year-olds have the infection.

- *Trichomoniasis. Trichomoniasis* is an infection in the vagina or penis. Caused by a parasite, it is often without symptoms, especially in men. Eventually, it can cause painful urination and intercourse, a discharge from the vagina, itching, and an unpleasant odor. The 5 million cases reported each year can be treated with antibiotics.

- *Gonorrhea. Gonorrhea* often has no symptoms but can produce a burning sensation during urination or a discharge from the penis or vagina. The infection can lead to fertility problems and, in women, pelvic inflammatory disease. Although antibiotics usually can cure gonorrhea, the number of drug-resistant strains of the disease is growing, making treatment more difficult.

- *Syphilis.* If untreated, *syphilis* may affect the brain, the heart, and a developing fetus. It can even be fatal. Syphilis first reveals itself through a small sore at the point of sexual contact. In its secondary stage, it may include a rash. Syphilis can be treated successfully with antibiotics if it is diagnosed early enough.

- *AIDS.* In the near past, no sexually transmitted infection has had a greater impact on sexual behavior—and society as a whole—than **acquired immune deficiency syndrome (AIDS).** Although in the United States, AIDS at first was found primarily in gay men, it soon spread to other populations, such as intravenous drug users and heterosexuals. In the United States, AIDS is the seventh leading cause of death among men 25-44 years of age, and 1.8 million people are living with the disease. The worldwide figures are even more daunting: Already, 39 million people have died from AIDS, and people living with the disease number 35 million worldwide (UNAIDS, 2013; Kaiser Family Foundation, 2014).

The spread of AIDS is particularly pronounced among women, who now make up almost half the cases worldwide. Younger women and women of color are particularly vulnerable. For instance, the rate of AIDS diagnosis is around 25 times higher for African American women than for white women and four times higher for Hispanic women. In the United States, young African American men who have sex with men are most seriously affected by AIDS (Quinn & Overbaugh, 2005; CDC, 2013).

The AIDS epidemic led to significant changes in sexual behavior. People are less likely to engage in casual sex with new acquaintances, and the use of condoms during sexual intercourse has increased. Nonetheless, the only foolproof method of avoiding

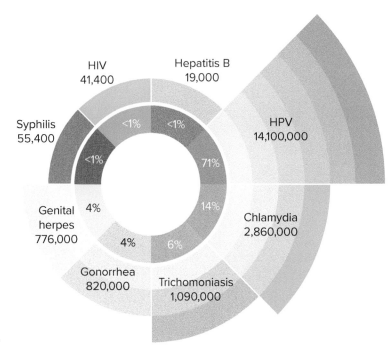

FIGURE 6 Estimates of the numbers of new cases annually of sexually transmitted infections in the United States. Each year, new cases of HPV greatly outnumber any other sexually transmitted infection.

Source: Adapted from Centers for Disease Control and Prevention. (2013). *STD surveillance tables.* Atlanta: Centers for Disease Control and Prevention.

acquired immune deficiency syndrome (AIDS) A sexually transmitted infection caused by a virus that destroys the body's immune system. (Module 34)

Study Alert
Use Figure 6 to learn the major types of sexually transmitted infections and their prevalence.

AIDS is total abstinence–an alternative that many people find unrealistic. However, there are several ways to reduce the risk of contracting AIDS as well as other sexually transmitted infections; these methods are "safer sex" practices:

- *Knowing a sexual partner's history.* Before having sex with someone, learn about his or her sexual history.

- *Use of condoms.* For those in sexual relationships, condoms are the most reliable means of preventing transmission of the AIDS virus.

- *Avoiding the exchange of bodily fluids, particularly semen.* Avoiding anal intercourse is especially important. The AIDS virus can spread through small tears in the rectum, making anal intercourse without condoms particularly dangerous. Oral sex, once thought relatively safe, is now viewed as potentially dangerous.

- *Staying sober.* Using alcohol and drugs impairs judgment and can lead to poor decisions–and it makes using a condom correctly more difficult.

- *Benefiting from monogamy.* People in long-term, monogamous relationships in which both partners have been faithful are at a lower risk of contracting AIDS and other sexually transmitted infections.

From the perspective of...

A Politician What responsibilities do people who learn they have a sexually transmitted infection have to their sexual partners, and what responsibilities do public health officials have? Should legislation be designed to restrict sexual behavior for those who have sexually transmitted infections?

©Exactostock/SuperStock

SEXUAL PROBLEMS

Few people would feel embarrassed by a sprained ankle or broken arm. In contrast, sexual difficulties are often a source of concern and self-consciousness because of the importance that society places on "desirable" sexual conduct. And such difficulties are surprisingly common, with more than 40% of women and about one-third of men experiencing problems associated with sexual performance. Among the most widespread are the disorders we discuss here (Goldstein, 2000; Rosner, 2001).

erectile disorder A male's inability to achieve or maintain an erection. (Module 34)

Erectile disorder is a male's inability to achieve or maintain an erection. The rare case is a male who has never been able to have an erection, and the more common case is a male who, though now unable to have an erection, has had one at least once in the past. Erectile dysfunction is not an uncommon problem, even among younger men–about 5% to 10% of men under 50 have erection problems. It is the rare man who has never experienced it at least once during his lifetime. This is hardly surprising because the ability to achieve and hold an erection is sensitive to alcohol, drugs, performance fears, anxiety, and a host of other factors. Erectile dysfunction becomes a more serious problem when it occurs more than occasionally (Jacob, 2011; Brody & Weiss, 2015; Balon, 2017).

Drugs such as Viagra have brought about significant advances in the treatment of erectile dysfunction and have brought the disorder into the open through a constant barrage of commercials on television and in magazines. Viagra treats erectile dysfunction by increasing the flow of blood through a man's penis and producing an erection relatively quickly.

premature (early) ejaculation A male's inability to delay orgasm as long as he wishes. (Module 34)

In **premature (early) ejaculation,** a male is unable to delay orgasm as long as he wishes. Because "as long as he wishes" is dependent on a man's–and his partner's–attitudes and opinions about how long is appropriate, this is a difficult disorder to diagnose. Sometimes the problem can be resolved simply by having a male redefine how long he wants to delay ejaculation. Premature ejaculation is most often a psychological problem since there are rarely physical reasons for it. One cause may be early sexual learning: Because sexual experiences during adolescence are often accompanied by a fear of being caught, some men learn early in their lives to reach orgasm as quickly as possible (Barnes & Eardley, 2007; Sadeghi-Nejad & Watson, 2008; Jannini, McMahon, & Waldinger, 2013).

Delayed ejaculation disorder occurs when it takes an extended period of sexual stimulation for a male to ejaculate. Delayed ejaculation disorder is only a problem if it causes stress for the male or his partner. Sometimes, learning general relaxation techniques allows men to overcome this difficulty.

In **female orgasmic disorder**, women do not experience orgasm, or the orgasm is delayed or of reduced intensity. In *primary orgasmic dysfunction*, a woman has never experienced orgasm during her lifetime. In *secondary orgasmic dysfunction*, a woman has had an orgasm at some point in her life but no longer does, or she is able to have orgasms only under certain conditions–such as during masturbation–but not during sexual intercourse.

In fact, the lack of orgasm during sexual intercourse is common (despite Hollywood film depictions to the contrary). By far the majority of women report they do not receive sufficient stimulation to reach orgasm during sexual intercourse. Consequently, most scientists today believe that the lack of orgasm during sexual intercourse is not dysfunctional at all but is merely a normal variation of female sexuality (McCabe, 2009; Wallen & Lloyd, 2011).

Finally, **sexual interest/arousal disorder** occurs when the motivation for sexual activity is restrained or lacking entirely. When people with inhibited sexual desire find themselves in circumstances that typically would evoke sexual feelings, they begin to turn off sexually and may even experience a kind of "sexual anesthesia." Ultimately, they may begin to avoid situations of a sexual nature, thereby forgoing intimacy with others (Meston, 2003; Hertlein, Weeks, & Gambescia, 2007).

It is important to realize that many of the problems we have discussed turn up at one time or another in most people's sex lives. It is only when these problems persist, cause undue anxiety, and turn sex from play into work that they are cause for concern. Furthermore, treatments for common sexual problems have a good rate of success (Rosner, 2001).

delayed ejaculation disorder A disorder in which it takes an extended period of sexual stimulation for a male to be able to ejaculate (Module 34)

female orgasmic disorder A female's lack of orgasm. (Module 34)

sexual interest/arousal disorder A sexual dysfunction in which the motivation for sexual activity is restrained or lacking entirely. (Module 34)

AP SUMMARY

- The frequency of masturbation is high, particularly for males. Although attitudes toward masturbation are increasingly liberal, they traditionally have been negative.
- Heterosexuality, or sexual attraction to members of the other sex, is the most common sexual orientation.
- The double standards by which premarital sex is thought to be more permissible for men than for women has declined, particularly among young people. For many people, the double standard has been replaced by endorsement of "permissiveness with affection."
- The frequency of marital sex varies widely. However, younger couples tend to have sexual intercourse more frequently than older couples. In addition, most married men and women do not engage in extramarital sex.
- Homosexuals are sexually attracted to members of their own sex; bisexuals are sexually attracted to people of the same sex and the other sex. No explanation for why people are homosexual has been confirmed; considerable research suggests genetic or biological factors, and little evidence suggests child-rearing and family dynamics. Learning theory is plausible, but problematic. It may be that a combination of biological and environmental factors are involved.
- Transgender is a broad term encompassing people whose gender identity, gender expression, or behavior does not conform to the sex they were assigned at birth.
- Rape occurs when one person forces another person to submit to sexual activity. Often the victim is acquainted with the rapist.
- Childhood sexual abuse is surprisingly widespread. Most often the perpetrator is an acquaintance or family member.
- AIDS has brought profound changes in people's sexual practices. Other sexually transmitted infections include chlamydia, genital herpes, trichomoniasis, gonorrhea, syphilis, and genital warts.
- Among the major sexual problems are erectile disorder, premature (early) ejaculation, delayed ejaculation disorder, female orgasmic disorder, and sexual interest/arousal disorder.
- Alfred Kinsey conducted surveys on the sexual behavior of Americans in the late 1930s.

AP KEY TERMS

masturbation
heterosexuality
double standard

extramarital sex
homosexuals
bisexuals

transgender
rape
date rape
sexually transmitted
  infection (STI)
acquired immune
  deficiency syndrome
  (AIDS)

erectile disorder
premature (early)
  ejaculation
delayed ejaculation
  disorder
female orgasmic disorder
sexual interest/arousal
  disorder

AP TEST PRACTICE

Section I: Multiple Choice

1. Which theory for sexual orientation has the least amount of evidence?
   A. Genetic inheritance
   B. Hormones during prenatal development
   C. Size of hypothalamus
   D. Child-rearing
   E. Size of corpus callosum

2. What is the general term encompassing people whose gender identity, gender expression, or behavior is not consistent with the sex they were assigned at birth?
   A. Homosexuality
   B. Transgender
   C. Bisexual
   D. Intersex
   E. Sexual orientation

3. Who carried out the first systematic study of sexual behavior in the late 1930s?
   A. William James
   B. Masters and Johnson
   C. Hans Selye
   D. Alfred Kinsey
   E. Abraham Maslow

Section II: Free Response

A lot of research has been conducted on human sexuality. Summarize the findings, then describe the research method and problems with the research method for these two main research studies.
- Kinsey research
- Sexual response cycle

LOOKING *Back*

EPILOGUE

We have seen how psychologists are dealing with the topics of gender and sex, first with regard to gender roles, gender stereotyping, gender schemas, and sexism. Society's expectations regarding male and female characteristics and behaviors lead to inequities in the treatment of men and women in school, the workplace, and the rest of society—inequities that largely favor men.

With regard to sexuality, we discussed the nature of the physical processes that surround sexuality and addressed the controversial issue of "normality" in sexual behavior. We saw the broad diversity of sexual behavior, and we discussed premarital sex and marital sex, as well as heterosexuality, homosexuality, and bisexuality. We also examined rape and other forms of nonconsensual sex, including childhood sexual abuse.

Finally, we looked at the sexual problems that people may have, including STIs and sexual dysfunctions. We explored the nature of these problems and discussed ways to deal with and treat them.

VISUAL SUMMARY 11 Sexuality and Gender

MODULE 32 Gender and Sex

Distinction between gender and sex

Gender: The perception of being male or female

Sex: Refers to sexual anatomy and sexual behavior

Gender Differences: More similar than different

- Large difference in aggressive behavior
- Men view their own abilities and estimates of future success more positively than women do
- No general differences in cognitive abilities

Sources of Gender Differences

- Biological causes suggest a difference in brain structure and functioning
- Socialization experiences produce gender schemas

MODULE 33 Understanding Human Sexual Response: The Facts of Life

Basic Biology of Sexual Behavior

- Puberty
  - Boys: Testes begin to secrete androgens
  - Girls: Ovaries begin to produce estrogen and progesterone

- Men and women differ in hormone production and perhaps differ in sex drive
- Sexual responsiveness includes excitement, plateau, orgasm, resolution, refractory period

MODULE 34 The Diversity of Sexual Behavior

Approaches to Sexual Normality

- Sexual behaviors may be abnormal when they negatively impact a person's well-being or hurt someone else

Sexual Behavior

- Masturbation: widely viewed as healthy, legitimate, and harmless
- Heterosexuality: sexual attraction to the other sex
- Premarital sex: permissible for men but not for women, which is a double standard
- Homosexuality: sexual attraction to one's own sex

0	1	2	3	4	5	6
Exclusive heterosexual behavior	Primarily heterosexual, but incidents of homosexual behavior	Primarily heterosexual, but more than incidental homosexual behavior	Equal amounts of heterosexual and homosexual behavior	Primarily homosexual, but more than incidental heterosexual behavior	Primarily homosexual, but incidents of heterosexual behavior	Exclusively homosexual behavior

- Bisexuality: sexual attraction to one's own sex and to the other sex
- Transgender: refers to persons whose gender identity, gender expression, or behavior does not conform to that associated with the sex to which they were assigned at birth

Sexual Difficulties

- Rape: forced sexual activities without consent
- Childhood sexual abuse: often committed by relative or acquaintance
- One in five people in the United States: infected with an STI

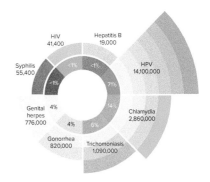

Sexual disorders

- Erectile dysfunction
- Premature ejaculation
- Delayed ejaculation disorder
- Female orgasmic disorder
- Inhibited sexual desire

(MODULE 32) (photo), (right, top): ©Don Hammond/DesignPics; (right, bottom): ©Stockbyte/Getty Images; (MODULE 33) (male and female patterns): Source: Adapted from Masters, W. H., & Johnson, V. E. (1966). *Human sexual response*. Boston: Little, Brown; (MODULE 34) (Kinsey scale) Source: Kinsey, A. C., Pomeroy, W. B., & Martin, C. E. (1948). *Sexual behavior in the human male*. Philadelphia: Saunders; (STIs) Source: Adapted from Centers for Disease Control and Prevention. (2013). STD surveillance tables. Atlanta: CDC.

©Nancy Mao Smith/Shutterstock

CHAPTER 12

Development

AP'I ESSENTIAL QUESTIONS

- How can biology influence our behavior and mental processes?
- How do we perceive and understand ourselves?

AP'I LEARNING TARGETS FOR CHAPTER 12

MODULE 35

- Differentiate types of research with regard to purpose, strengths, and weaknesses.
- Discuss the interaction of nature and nurture.

NATURE AND NURTURE: THE ENDURING DEVELOPMENTAL ISSUE
Determining the Relative Influence of Nature and Nurture
Developmental Research Techniques

MODULE 36

- Explain the process of conception and gestation.
- Discuss the interaction of nature and nurture specifically physical development.

PRENATAL DEVELOPMENT: CONCEPTION TO BIRTH
The Basics of Genetics
The Earliest Development

MODULE 37

- Compare and contrast various cognitive processes.
- Discuss maturation of motor skills.
- Describe the influence of temperament.
- Identify the contributions of major researchers in the area of social development.
- Explain how parenting styles influence development.
- Explain the maturation of cognitive abilities.
- Identify the contributions of major researchers in cognitive development.

INFANCY AND CHILDHOOD
The Extraordinary Newborn
AP'I **Neuroscience in Your Life:** Emotional Responses in Infancy
Infancy Through Childhood

- Discuss maturational challenges in adolescence, including related family conflicts.
- Identify the contributions of key researchers in the area of adulthood and aging.
- Identify the contributions of major researchers in the area of moral development.
- Compare and contrast models of moral development.

- Characterize the development of decisions related to intimacy as people mature.
- Predict the physical and cognitive changes that emerge through the lifespan, including steps that can be taken to maximize function.

PROLOGUE *THE LITTLEST PIONEER*

He doesn't know it yet, but Zain Rajani is a pioneer. Zain's parents tried to conceive for 4 years before his birth—at first naturally, next with hormones, and then through *in vitro fertilization* (IVF), in which his mother's eggs were gathered, fertilized outside the body, and returned to her uterus to develop.

When these methods failed, the family moved on to a new technique. Instead of removing eggs from Zain's mother's body, the doctors removed mitochondria—essentially the powerhouse of a cell—from her egg stem cells. Then, they added the mitochondria to her eggs—on the theory that this would "rejuvenate" her existing eggs and stimulate fertilization.

It worked. Zain became one of the first success stories using this technique, and his parents couldn't be happier (Park, 2015).

LOOKING *Ahead*

It used to be simpler. People came into the world in one basic way: a man's sperm fertilized a woman's egg, and the resulting embryo developed over the course of 9 months into an infant. Today, scientists, motivated by the desire to help people for whom the basics aren't working, have developed a range of techniques to give the fertilization and birth process a helping hand.

Developmental psychology is the branch of psychology that studies the patterns of growth and change that occur throughout life. It deals with issues ranging from new ways of conceiving children, to learning how to raise children most sensibly, to understanding the milestones of life that we all face.

Developmental psychologists study the interaction between the unfolding of biologically predetermined patterns of behavior and a constantly changing, dynamic environment. They ask how our genetic background affects our behavior throughout our lives and whether heredity limits our potential. Similarly, they seek to understand the ways in which the environment works with—or against—our genetic capabilities, how the world we live in affects our development, and how we can be encouraged to reach our full potential.

We begin by examining the approaches psychologists use to study development change across the life span. Then we consider the very start of development, beginning with conception and the 9 months of life before birth. We look at both genetic and environmental influences on the unborn individual and the way they can affect behavior throughout the remainder of the life cycle.

Next, we examine development that occurs after birth: the enormous and rapid growth that takes place during the early stages of life and the physical, social, and cognitive change throughout infancy, toddlerhood, and middle childhood. We then move on to development from adolescence through adulthood and end with a discussion of the ways in which people prepare themselves for death.

Module 35

Nature and Nurture: The Enduring Developmental Issue

How many bald, 6-foot-6, 250-pound volunteer firefighters in New Jersey wear droopy mustaches, aviator-style eyeglasses, and a key ring on the right side of the belt? The answer is two: Gerald Levey and Mark Newman. They are twins who were separated at birth. Neither twin even knew the other existed until they were reunited—in a fire station—by a fellow firefighter who knew Newman and was startled to see his double, Levey, at a firefighters' convention.

The lives of the twins, although separate, took remarkably similar paths. Levey went to college and studied forestry; Newman planned to study forestry in college but instead took a job trimming trees. Both had jobs in supermarkets. One had a job installing sprinkler systems; the other installed fire alarms.

Both men are unmarried and find the same kind of woman—"tall, slender, long hair"—attractive. They share similar hobbies and enjoy hunting, fishing, going to the beach, and watching old John Wayne movies and professional wrestling. Both like Chinese food and drink the same brand of beer. Their mannerisms are also similar—for example, each one throws his head back when he laughs. And, of course, there is one more thing: They share a passion for fighting fires.

The similarities we see in twins Gerald Levey and Mark Newman vividly raise one of the fundamental questions posed by **developmental psychology,** the study of the patterns of growth and change that occur throughout life. The question is this: How can we distinguish between the *environmental* causes of behavior (the influence of parents, siblings, family, friends, schooling, nutrition, and all the other experiences to which a child is exposed) and *hereditary* causes (those based on an individual's genetic makeup that influence growth and development throughout life)? This question embodies the **nature–nurture issue.** In this context, nature refers to hereditary factors, and nurture refers to environmental influences.

AP® LEARNING TARGETS

- Differentiate types of research with regard to purpose, strengths, and weaknesses.

- Discuss the interaction of nature and nurture (including cultural variations), specifically physical development, in the determination of behavior.

developmental psychology The branch of psychology that studies the patterns of growth and change that occur throughout life. (Module 35)

nature–nurture issue The issue of the degree to which environment and heredity influence behavior. (Module 35)

Gerald Levey and Mark Newman.
©Thomas Wanstall/The Image Works

Although the question was first posed as a nature-*versus*-nurture issue, developmental psychologists today agree that *both* nature and nurture interact to produce specific developmental patterns and outcomes. Consequently, the question has evolved into this: *How and to what degree* do environment and heredity both produce their effects? No one develops free of environmental influences or without being affected by his or her inherited *genetic makeup*. However, the debate over the comparative influence of the two factors remains active; different approaches and different theories of development emphasize the environment or heredity to a greater or lesser degree (Perovic & Radenovic, 2011; Gruber, 2013; Limberg, 2015).

For example, some developmental theories rely on basic psychological principles of learning and stress the role learning plays in producing changes in a developing child's behavior. Such theories emphasize the role of the environment in development. In contrast, other developmental theories emphasize the influence of one's physiological makeup and functioning on development. Such theories stress the role of heredity and *maturation*–the unfolding of biologically predetermined patterns of behavior–in producing developmental change. Maturation can be seen, for instance, in the development of sex characteristics (such as breasts and body hair) that occurs at the start of adolescence.

Furthermore, the work of *behavioral geneticists*, who study the effects of heredity on behavior, and the theories of evolutionary psychologists, who identify behavior patterns that result from our genetic inheritance, have influenced developmental psychologists. Behavioral geneticists are finding increasing evidence that cognitive abilities, personality traits, sexual orientation, and psychological disorders are determined to some extent by genetic factors (Schermer et al., 2011; Krüger, Korsten, & Hoffman, 2017).

Behavioral genetics lies at the heart of the nature-nurture question. Although no one would argue that our behavior is determined *solely* by inherited factors, evidence collected by behavioral geneticists does suggest that our genetic inheritance predisposes us to respond in particular ways to our environment and even to seek out particular kinds of environments (Davis, Haworth, & Plomin, 2009; Bienvenu, Davydow, & Kendler, 2011; Barnes & Jacobs, 2013).

Despite their differences over theory, developmental psychologists concur on some points. They agree that genetic factors not only provide the potential for specific behaviors or traits to emerge but also place limitations on the emergence of such behavior or traits. For instance, heredity defines people's general level of intelligence and sets an upper limit that–regardless of the quality of the environment–people cannot exceed. Heredity also places limits on physical abilities; humans simply cannot run at a speed of 60 miles an hour or grow as tall as 10 feet, no matter the quality of their environment (Dodge, 2004; Pinker, 2004; Loehlin et al., 2015).

Figure 1 lists some of the characteristics most affected by heredity. As you consider these items, keep in mind that these characteristics are not *entirely* determined by heredity because environmental factors also play a role.

Developmental psychologists also agree that in most instances, environmental factors play a critical role in enabling people to reach the potential capabilities that their genetic background makes possible. If Albert Einstein had received no intellectual stimulation as a child and had not been sent to school, it is unlikely that he would have reached his genetic potential. Similarly, a great athlete such as baseball star Derek Jeter would have been unlikely to display much physical skill if he had not been raised in an environment that nurtured his innate talent and gave him the opportunity to train and perfect his natural abilities.

Clearly, the relationship between heredity and environment is complex. Therefore, developmental psychologists typically take an *interactionist* position on the nature-nurture issue by suggesting that a combination of hereditary and environmental factors influences development. Developmental psychologists face the challenge of identifying the relative strength of each of these influences on the individual as well as that of identifying the specific changes that occur over the course of development (McGregor & Capone, 2004; Moffitt, Caspi, & Rutter, 2006; Steinbeis et al., 2017).

Study Alert

The nature–nurture issue is a key question that is pervasive throughout the field of psychology. It explores how and to what degree environment and heredity produce their joint effects.

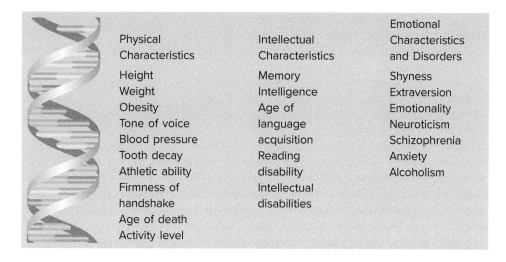

Physical Characteristics	Intellectual Characteristics	Emotional Characteristics and Disorders
Height	Memory	Shyness
Weight	Intelligence	Extraversion
Obesity	Age of	Emotionality
Tone of voice	language	Neuroticism
Blood pressure	acquisition	Schizophrenia
Tooth decay	Reading	Anxiety
Athletic ability	disability	Alcoholism
Firmness of	Intellectual	
handshake	disabilities	
Age of death		
Activity level		

FIGURE 1 Characteristics influenced significantly by genetic factors. Although these characteristics have strong genetic components, they are also affected by environmental factors.

Determining the Relative Influence of Nature and Nurture

Developmental psychologists use several approaches to determine the relative influence of genetic and environmental factors on behavior. In one approach, researchers can experimentally control the genetic makeup of laboratory animals by carefully breeding them for specific traits. For instance, by observing animals with identical genetic backgrounds placed in varied environments, researchers can learn the effects of specific kinds of environmental stimulation. Although researchers must be careful when generalizing the findings of nonhuman research to a human population, findings from animal research provide important information that cannot be obtained for ethical reasons by using human participants.

Human twins serve as another important source of information about the relative effects of genetic and environmental factors. If **identical twins** (those who are genetically identical) display different patterns of development, those differences have to be attributed to variations in the environment in which the twins were raised. The most useful data come from identical twins (such as Gerald Levey and Mark Newman) who are adopted at birth by different sets of adoptive parents and raised apart in differing environments. Studies of nontwin siblings who are raised in totally different environments also shed some light on the issue. Because they have relatively similar genetic backgrounds, siblings who show similarities as adults provide strong evidence for the importance of heredity (Vitaro, Brendgen, & Arseneault, 2009; Sternberg, 2011; Farnsworth, 2015).

Researchers can also take the opposite tack. Instead of concentrating on people with similar genetic backgrounds who are raised in different environments, they may consider people raised in similar environments who have totally dissimilar genetic backgrounds. For example, if they find similar courses of development in two adopted children who have different genetic backgrounds and have been raised in the same family, they have evidence for the importance of environmental influences on development. Moreover, psychologists can carry out research involving animals with dissimilar genetic backgrounds; by experimentally varying the environment in which the animals are raised, they can determine the influence of environmental factors (independent of heredity) on development (Petrill & Deater-Deckard, 2004; Beam & Turkheimer, 2013; Tosto et al., 2017).

identical twins Twins who are genetically identical. (Module 35)

Developmental Research Techniques

Because of the demands of measuring behavioral change across different ages, developmental researchers use several unique methods. The most frequently used, **cross-sectional research,** compares people of different ages at the same point in time.

cross-sectional research A research method that compares people of different ages at the same point in time. (Module 35)

Cross-sectional studies provide information about differences in development between different age groups (Creasey, 2005; Card, 2017).

Suppose, for instance, we were interested in the development of intellectual ability in adulthood. To carry out a cross-sectional study, we might compare a sample of 25-, 45-, and 65-year-olds who all take the same IQ test. We then can determine whether average IQ test scores differ in each age group.

Cross-sectional research has limitations, however. For instance, we cannot be sure that the differences in IQ scores we might find in our example are due to age differences alone. Instead, the scores may reflect differences in the educational attainment of the cohorts represented. A *cohort* is a group of people who grow up at similar times, in similar places, and in similar conditions. In the case of IQ differences, any age differences we find in a cross-sectional study may reflect educational differences among the cohorts studied: People in the older age group may belong to a cohort that was less likely to attend college than were the people in the younger groups.

longitudinal research A research method that investigates behavior as participants get older. (Module 35)

A longitudinal study, the second major research strategy developmental psychologists use, provides one way around this problem. **Longitudinal research** assesses the behavior of one or more participants as the participants get older. Longitudinal studies assess *change* in behavior over time, whereas cross-sectional studies assess *differences* among groups of people.

For instance, consider how we might investigate intellectual development during adulthood by using a longitudinal research strategy. First, we might give an IQ test to a group of 25-year-olds. We'd then come back to the same people 20 years later and retest them at age 45. Finally, we'd return to them once more when they were 65 years old and test them again.

Study Alert

Be sure to be able to distinguish the two different types of developmental research: cross-sectional (comparing people of different ages at the same time) and longitudinal (studying participants as they age).

By examining changes at several points in time, we can see how individuals develop. Clearly, though, longitudinal research requires a significant expenditure of time as the researcher waits for the participants to get older. In addition, participants who begin a study at an early age may drop out, move away, or even die as the research continues. Moreover, participants who take the same test at several points in time may become "test-wise" and perform better each time they take it because they have become more familiar with the test. Still, longitudinal research is an important technique of developmental researchers.

AP| MODULE 35: NATURE AND NURTURE: THE ENDURING DEVELOPMENTAL ISSUE

AP SUMMARY

- Cross-sectional research compares people of different ages with one another at the same point in time. In contrast, longitudinal research traces the behavior of participants as the participants become older.
- Developmental psychology studies how much developmental change is due to heredity and how much is due to environment—the nature-nurture issue.
- To study the relative influence of nature and nurture, researchers use human twin studies and children who have been adopted.

AP KEY TERMS

developmental psychology   cross-sectional research
nature–nurture issue   longitudinal research
identical twins

AP TEST PRACTICE

Section I: Multiple Choice

1. What type of research strategy do developmental psychologists use to get around the cohort effect?
   A. Cross-sectional
   B. Survey
   C. Longitudinal
   D. Meta-analysis
   E. Correlation

2. What type of study provides the most important information regarding the effects of nature and nurture?
   A. Identical twins raised in different environments
   B. Identical twins raised in the same environment
   C. Fraternal twins raised in different environments
   D. Fraternal twins raised in the same environment
   E. Adopted children in different environments

3. All of the following words are associated with nature EXCEPT
A. Maturation
B. Genetic inheritance
C. Innate
D. Predisposed
E. Learning

Section II: Free Response

Consider the factors that might determine when a child begins to walk. Provide an explanation for each of the following approaches.
- Nature
- Nurture

Describe how the following research strategies could be used to study when a child will begin to walk.
- Cross-sectional
- Longitudinal

Module 36
Prenatal Development: Conception to Birth

- Explain the process of conception and gestation, including factors that influence successful prenatal development.

- Discuss the interaction of nature and nurture (including cultural variations), specifically physical development, in the determination of behavior.

Leah and John Howard's joy at learning Leah was pregnant turned to anxiety when Leah's doctor discovered that her brother had died from Duchenne muscular dystrophy (DMD) at age 12. The disease, the doctor explained, was an X-linked inherited disorder. If Leah turned out to be a carrier, there was a 50% chance that the baby would inherit the disease if it were male. The doctor advised them to have an ultrasound to determine the baby's sex. It turned out to be a boy.

The Howards faced two options. The doctor could take a chorion villus sampling now or wait a month and perform an amniocentesis. Both carried a very low risk for miscarriage. Leah chose amniocentesis, but the results were inconclusive. The doctor then suggested a fetal muscle biopsy to confirm the presence or lack of the muscle protein dystrophin. The absence of dystrophin would signal DMD. The risk of miscarriage, however, was not inconsiderable.

Four months pregnant at this point and tired of the worries and tears, Leah and John decided to take their chances and look forward to their baby's birth.

The Howards' case shows the difficult choices that parents may encounter due to our increasing understanding of life spent inside a mother's womb.

Yet, our knowledge of the biology of *conception*–when a male's sperm cell penetrates a female's egg cell–and its aftermath makes the start of life no less of a miracle. Let's consider how an individual is created by looking first at the genetic endowment that a child receives at the moment of conception.

The Basics of Genetics

chromosomes Rod-shaped structures that contain all basic hereditary information. (Module 36)

genes The parts of the chromosomes through which genetic information is transmitted. (Module 36)

Study Alert
It's important to understand the basic building-blocks of genetics: chromosomes, which contain genes, which in turn are composed of sequences of DNA.

The one-cell entity established at conception contains 23 pairs of **chromosomes,** rod-shaped structures that contain all basic hereditary information. One member of each pair is from the mother, and the other is from the father.

Each chromosome contains thousands of **genes**–smaller units through which genetic information is transmitted. Either individually or in combination, genes produce each person's particular characteristics. Composed of sequences of *DNA (deoxyribonucleic acid)* molecules, genes are the biological equivalent of "software" that programs the future development of all parts of the body's hardware. Humans have some 25,000 different genes (see Figure 1).

Some genes control the development of systems common to all members of the human species–the heart, circulatory system, brain, lungs, and so forth; others shape the characteristics that make each human unique, such as facial configuration, height, and eye color. The child's sex is also determined by a particular combination of genes. Specifically, a child inherits an X chromosome from its mother and either an X or a Y chromosome from its father. When it receives an XX combination, it is a female; with an XY combination, it develops as a male. Male development is triggered by a single gene on the Y chromosome; without the presence of that specific gene, the individual will develop as a female (see Figure 2).

| (a) Conception | (b) 23 pairs of chromosomes | (c) DNA sequence | (d) Genes |

FIGURE 1 One's characteristics are determined by specific genetic information. (a) At the moment of conception, (b) humans receive 23 pairs of chromosomes, half from the mother and half from the father. (c) These chromosomes are made up of sequences of DNA. (d) Each chromosome contains thousands of genes that "program" the future development of the body.

(a): ©D. W. Fawcett/Science Source; (b): ©Willatt, East Anglian Regional Genetics Service/SPL/Science Source; (c): ©Double Brain/Shutterstock; (d): ©Biophoto Associates/Science Source

As behavioral geneticists have discovered, genes are also at least partially responsible for a wide variety of personal characteristics, including cognitive abilities, personality traits, and psychological disorders. Of course, few of these characteristics are determined by a single gene. Instead, most traits result from a combination of multiple genes that operate together with environmental influences (Ramus, 2006; Armbruster et al., 2011; Kazantseva et al., 2015).

THE HUMAN GENOME PROJECT

Our understanding of genetics took a giant leap forward in 2001, when scientists were able to map the specific location and sequence of every human gene as part of the

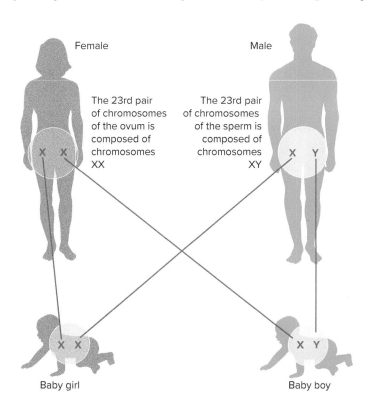

Female

Male

The 23rd pair of chromosomes of the ovum is composed of chromosomes XX

The 23rd pair of chromosomes of the sperm is composed of chromosomes XY

X X

X Y

X X

X Y

Baby girl

Baby boy

FIGURE 2 When an egg and a sperm meet at the moment of fertilization, the egg provides an X chromosome, and the sperm provides either an X or a Y chromosome. If the sperm contributes an X chromosome, the child will have an XX pairing on the 23rd chromosome and will be a girl. If the sperm contributes a Y chromosome, the result will be an XY pairing—a boy.

massive *Human Genome Project.* The accomplishment was one of the most important in the history of biology (International Human Genome Sequencing Consortium, 2003; Grigorenko & Dozier, 2013; Özdemir et al., 2017).

The success of the Human Genome Project started a revolution in health care because scientists can identify the particular genes responsible for genetically caused disorders. It is already leading not only to the identification of risk factors in children but also to the development of new treatments for physical and psychological disorders.

The Earliest Development

zygote The new cell formed by the union of an egg and sperm. (Module 36)

When an egg becomes fertilized by the sperm, the resulting one-celled entity, called a **zygote,** immediately begins to develop. The zygote starts out as a microscopic speck. Three days after fertilization, though, the zygote increases to around 32 cells; within a week, it has grown to 100–150 cells. These first 2 weeks are known as the *germinal period.*

embryo A developed zygote that has a heart, a brain, and other organs. (Module 36)

Two weeks after conception, the developing individual enters the *embryonic period,* which lasts from week 2 through week 8; he or she is now called an **embryo.** As an embryo develops through an intricate, preprogrammed process of cell division, it grows 10,000 times larger by 4 weeks of age and attains a length of about one-fifth of an inch. At this point, it has developed a rudimentary beating heart, a brain, an intestinal tract, and a number of other organs. Although all these organs are at a primitive stage of development, they are clearly recognizable. Moreover, by week 8, the embryo is about an inch long and has discernible arms, legs, and a face.

fetus A developing individual from 8 weeks after conception until birth. (Module 36)

From week 8 and continuing until birth, the developing individual enters the *fetal period* and is called a **fetus.** At the start of this period, it begins to respond to touch; it bends its fingers when touched on the hand. At 16 to 18 weeks, its movements become strong enough for the mother to sense them. At the same time, hair may begin to grow on its head, and the facial features become similar to those the child will display at birth. The major organs begin functioning, although the fetus could not be kept alive outside the mother. In addition, a lifetime's worth of brain neurons are produced–although it is unclear whether the brain is capable of thinking at this early stage.

age of viability The point at which a fetus can survive if born prematurely. (Module 36)

Within the womb, the fetus continues to develop before birth. It begins to grow fatty deposits under the skin, and it gains weight. The fetus reaches the **age of viability,** the point at which it can survive if born prematurely, at about prenatal age 22 weeks. By week 24, a fetus has many of the characteristics it will display as a newborn. In fact, when an infant is born prematurely at this age, it can open and close its eyes; suck; cry; look up, down, and around; and even grasp objects placed in its hands.

These remarkable photos of live fetuses display the degree of physical development at prenatal ages 5 and 15 weeks.
(left): ©SPL/Science Source; (right): ©Petit Format/Science Source

At prenatal age 28 weeks, the fetus weighs less than 3 pounds and is about 16 inches long. It may be capable of learning: One study found that the infants of mothers who had repeatedly read aloud *The Cat in the Hat* by Dr. Seuss before the infants' birth preferred the sound of that particular story to other stories after they were born (Spence & DeCasper, 1982; Del Giudice, 2011; Moon, Lagercrantz, & Kuhl, 2013).

Before birth, a fetus passes through several *sensitive periods*. A sensitive period is the time when organisms are particularly susceptible to certain kinds of stimuli. For example, fetuses are especially affected by their mothers' use of drugs during certain sensitive periods before birth. If they are exposed to a particular drug before or after the sensitive period, it may have relatively little impact; if exposure comes during a sensitive period, the impact will be significant (Werker & Tees, 2005; Uylings, 2006; Sandman, 2015).

Sensitive periods can also occur after birth. Some language specialists suggest, for instance, that there is a period in which children are particularly receptive to developing language. If children are not exposed to appropriate linguistic stimuli, their language development may be impaired (Innocenti, 2007; Sohr-Preston & Scaramella, 2006; Opendak, Gould, & Sullivan, 2017).

Study Alert
Sensitive (or critical) periods, which can occur before or after birth, are important because they indicate the time when organisms are particularly susceptible to damage that may affect them for the rest of their lives.

From the perspective of...

An Educator How would you use your knowledge of sensitive periods in language development to improve students' learning? Would you want to teach children more than one language during this time?

©Andersen Ross/Blend Images/Getty Images

In the final weeks of pregnancy, the fetus continues to gain weight and grow. At the end of the normal 38 weeks of pregnancy, the fetus typically weighs 7 pounds and is about 20 inches in length. However, the story is different for *preterm infants*, who are born before week 38. Because they have not been able to develop fully, they are at higher risk for illness, future problems, and even death. For infants who have been in the womb for more than 30 weeks, the prospects are relatively good. However, for those born before week 30, the story is often less positive. Such newborns, who may weigh as little as 2 pounds at birth, are in grave danger because they have immature organs; they have less than a 50-50 chance of survival. If they do survive—and it takes extraordinarily heroic (and expensive) medical intervention to ensure this—they may later experience significant developmental delays.

GENETIC INFLUENCES ON THE FETUS

The process of fetal growth that we have just described reflects normal development, which occurs in 95-98% of all pregnancies. Some individuals are less fortunate; in the remaining 2-5% of cases, children are born with serious birth defects. A major cause of such defects is faulty genes or chromosomes. Here are some of the more common genetic and chromosomal difficulties.

- *Phenylketonuria (PKU).* A child born with the inherited disease phenylketonuria cannot produce an enzyme that is required for normal development. This deficiency results in an accumulation of poisons that eventually cause profound intellectual disability. The disease is treatable, however, if it is caught early. Most infants today are routinely tested for PKU, and children with the disorder can be placed on a special diet that allows them to develop normally (Widaman, 2009; Romani et al., 2017).

- *Sickle-cell anemia.* About 10% of the African American population has the possibility of passing on sickle-cell anemia, a disease that gets its name from the abnormally shaped red blood cells it causes. Children with the disease may have episodes of pain, yellowish eyes, stunted growth, and vision problems (Selove, 2007; Wills, 2013).

- *Tay-Sachs disease.* Children born with Tay-Sachs disease, a disorder most often found in Jews of Eastern European ancestry, usually die by age 3 or 4 because of the body's inability to break down fat. If both parents carry the genetic defect that produces the fatal illness, their child has a 1 in 4 chance of being born with the disease (Leib et al., 2005; Weinstein, 2007).

- *Down syndrome.* Down syndrome, one of the causes of intellectual disability, occurs when the zygote receives an extra chromosome at the moment of conception. Down syndrome is often related to the mother's age; mothers over 35 stand a higher risk than do other women of having a child with the syndrome (Sherman et al., 2007; Nærland et al., 2017).

PRENATAL ENVIRONMENTAL INFLUENCES

teratogens Environmental agents such as a drug, chemical, virus, or other factor that produce a birth defect. (Module 36)

Genetic factors are not the only causes of difficulties in fetal development. Environmental influences–the *nurture* part of the nature–nurture equation–also affect the fetus. Some of the more profound consequences are brought about by **teratogens,** environmental agents such as a drug, chemical, virus, or other factor that produce a birth defect. Among the major prenatal environmental influences on the fetus are the following:

- *Mother's nutrition.* What a mother eats during her pregnancy can have important implications for the health of her baby. Seriously undernourished mothers cannot provide adequate nutrition to a growing fetus, and they are likely to give birth to underweight babies. Poorly nourished babies are also more susceptible to disease, and a lack of nourishment may have an adverse impact on their mental development (Najman et al., 2004; Everette, 2008; Nyaradi et al., 2013).

- *Mother's illness.* Even minor illnesses that a mother catches during the early months of pregnancy can have devastating consequences for a developing fetus. For example, contracting rubella (German measles), syphilis, diabetes, and high blood pressure may produce permanent, lifelong effects on the fetus (Nesheim et al., 2004; Magoni et al., 2005).

- *Mother's emotional state.* A mother's emotional state affects her baby. Mothers who are anxious and tense during the last months of their pregnancies are more apt to have irritable infants who sleep and eat poorly. The reason? The autonomic nervous system of the fetus becomes especially sensitive as a result of chemical changes produced by the mother's emotional state (Hollins, 2007; Kumari & Joshi, 2013).

- *Mother's use of drugs.* Mothers who take illegal, physically addictive drugs such as cocaine run the risk of giving birth to babies who are similarly addicted. Their newborns suffer painful withdrawal symptoms and sometimes show permanent physical and mental impairment. Even legal drugs taken by a pregnant woman (who may not know that she has become pregnant) can have a tragic effect (Singer & Richardson, 2011; Nygaard et al., 2017).

- *Alcohol.* Alcohol is extremely dangerous to fetal development. For example, as many as 1.5 out of every 1,000 infants are born with *fetal alcohol syndrome disorder (FASD),* a condition resulting in below-average intelligence, growth delays, and facial deformities. FASD is now the primary preventable cause of intellectual disability. Even mothers who use small amounts of alcohol during pregnancy place their child at risk (Niccols, 2007; Murthy et al., 2009; Lewis et al., 2015).

Environmental Factor	Possible Effect on Prenatal Development
Rubella (German measles)	Blindness, deafness, heart abnormalities, stillbirth
Syphilis	Intellectual disability, physical deformities, maternal miscarriage
Addictive drugs	Low birth weight, addiction of infant to drug, with possible death after birth from withdrawal
Nicotine	Premature birth, low birth weight and length
Alcohol	Intellectual disability, lower-than-average birth weight, small head, limb deformities
Radiation from X-rays	Physical deformities, intellectual disability
Inadequate diet	Reduction in growth of brain, smaller-than-average weight and length at birth
Mother's age—younger than 18 at birth of child	Premature birth, increased incidence of Down syndrome
Mother's age—older than 35 at birth of child	Increased incidence of Down syndrome
DES (diethylstilbestrol)	Reproductive difficulties and increased incidence of genital cancer in children of mothers who were given DES during pregnancy to prevent miscarriage
AIDS	Possible spread of AIDS virus to infant; facial deformities; growth failure
Accutane	Intellectual disability and physical deformities

FIGURE 3 A variety of environmental factors can play a role in prenatal development.

- *Nicotine use.* Pregnant mothers who smoke put their children at considerable risk. Smoking while pregnant can lead to miscarriage and infant death. For children who do survive, the negative consequences of mother's tobacco use can last a lifetime (Shea & Steiner, 2008; Rogers, 2009; Magee et al., 2013).

Several other environmental factors have an impact on the child before and during birth (see Figure 3). Keep in mind, however, that although we have been discussing the influences of genetics and environment separately, neither factor works alone. Furthermore, despite the emphasis here on some of the ways in which development can go wrong, the vast majority of births occur without difficulty. And in most instances, subsequent development also proceeds normally.

ALTERNATIVE PATHS TO CONCEPTION

For most couples, conception is routine, and pregnancy unfolds without incident. In other cases, though, conception represents a major challenge. Sometimes infertility, the inability to become pregnant, results because the male produces too few sperm. In other cases, it is due to the advanced age of the parents, use of drugs, or previous cases of sexually transmitted infection.

Scientists have devised several remedies to overcome infertility. One option is *in vitro fertilization (IVF)*. IVF is a procedure in which a woman's eggs are removed from her ovaries, and a man's sperm is used to fertilize the eggs in a laboratory. A fertilized egg is then implanted in a woman's uterus. Similarly, *gamete intrafallopian transfer (GIFT)* and *zygote intrafallopian transfer (ZIFT)* are procedures in which an egg and sperm or fertilized egg are implanted in a woman's fallopian tubes. In IVF, GIFT, and ZIFT, the fertilized egg typically is implanted in the woman who provided the eggs. In some cases, eggs are implanted in a *surrogate mother,* a woman who agrees to carry the child to term.

AP | MODULE 36: PRENATAL DEVELOPMENT: CONCEPTION TO BIRTH

AP SUMMARY

- At the moment of conception, a male's sperm cell and a female's egg cell unite. The union of sperm and egg produces a zygote, which contains 23 pairs of chromosomes; one member of each pair comes from the father, and the other comes from the mother.
- After 2 weeks, the zygote becomes an embryo. By week 8, the embryo is called a fetus. At about week 22, it reaches the age of viability. A fetus is normally born after 38 weeks.
- Before birth the fetus passes through sensitive periods. These can also occur after birth.
- Genetic abnormalities produce birth defects, such as PKU, sickle-cell anemia, Tay-Sachs disease, and Down syndrome.
- Teratogens are environmental agents that produce a birth defect. Among the environmental influences on fetal growth are the mother's nutrition, illnesses, emotional state, and drug intake.
- Each chromosome contains genes through which genetic information is transmitted. Genes, which are composed of DNA sequences, are the "software" that programs the future development of the body's hardware.
- Genes affect not only physical attributes but also a wide array of personal characteristics, such as cognitive abilities, personality traits, and psychological disorders.
- The Human Genome Project led to a better understanding of our genetics.

AP KEY TERMS

chromosomes   fetus
genes   age of viability
zygote   teratogens
embryo

AP TEST PRACTICE

Section I: Multiple Choice

1. What is the correct order of prenatal development?
   A. Fetus, embryo, zygote
   B. Zygote, fetus, embryo
   C. Embryo, zygote, fetus
   D. Zygote, embryo, fetus
   E. Embryo, fetus, zygote

2. All of the following are examples of teratogens EXCEPT
   A. Alcohol
   B. Diabetes
   C. Nicotine
   D. Accutane
   E. PKU

3. Humans have approximately how many different genes?
   A. 23
   B. 46
   C. 1,000
   D. 10,000
   E. 25,000

Section II: Free Response

A couple is pregnant with their first child. Explain how the following concepts relate to their pregnancy.
- Sensitive period
- Embryo
- Age of viability
- PKU
- Chromosomes

Module 37
Infancy and Childhood

His head was molded into a long melon shape and came to a point at the back. . . . He was covered with a thick greasy white material known as "vernix," which made him slippery to hold and also allowed him to slip easily through the birth canal. In addition to a shock of black hair on his head, his body was covered with dark, fine hair known as "lanugo." His ears, his back, his shoulders, and even his cheeks were furry. . . . His skin was wrinkled and quite loose, ready to scale in creased places such as his feet and hands. . . . His ears were pressed to his head in unusual positions—one ear was matted firmly forward on his cheek. His nose was flattened and pushed to one side by the squeeze as he came through the pelvis. (Brazelton, 1969)

What kind of creature is this? Although the description hardly fits that of the adorable babies seen in advertisements for baby food, we are in fact talking about a normal, completely developed child just after the moment of birth. Called a **neonate,** a new-born arrives in the world in a form that hardly meets the standards of beauty against which we typically measure babies. Yet ask any parents: Nothing is more beautiful or exciting than the first glimpse of their newborn.

The Extraordinary Newborn

Several factors cause a neonate's strange appearance. The trip through the mother's birth canal may have squeezed the incompletely formed bones of the skull together and squashed the nose into the head. The skin secretes *vernix*, a white greasy covering, for protection before birth, and the baby may have *lanugo*, a soft fuzz, over the entire body for a similar purpose. The infant's eyelids may be puffy with an accumulation of fluids because of the upside-down position during birth.

All these features change during the first 2 weeks of life as the neonate takes on a more familiar appearance. Even more impressive are the capabilities a neonate begins to display from the moment of birth—capabilities that grow at an astounding rate over the ensuing months.

AP® | LEARNING TARGETS

- Compare and contrast various cognitive processes.
- Discuss maturation of motor skills.
- Describe the influence of temperament and other social factors on attachment and appropriate socialization.
- Identify contributions of major researchers in developmental psychology in social development in childhood.
- Explain how parenting styles influence development.
- Explain the maturation of cognitive abilities.
- Identify the contributions of major researchers in the area of cognitive development in childhood.

neonate A newborn child. (Module 37)

reflexes Unlearned, involuntary responses that occur automatically in the presence of certain stimuli. (Module 37)

REFLEXES

A neonate is born with a number of **reflexes**—unlearned, involuntary responses that occur automatically in the presence of certain stimuli. Critical for survival, many of those reflexes unfold naturally as part of an infant's ongoing maturation. The *rooting reflex*, for instance, causes neonates to turn their heads toward things that touch their cheeks—such as the mother's nipple or a bottle. Similarly, a *sucking reflex* prompts infants to suck at things that touch their lips. Among other reflexes are a *gag reflex* (to clear the throat), the *startle reflex* (a series of movements in which an infant flings out the arms, fans the fingers, and arches the back in response to a sudden noise), and the *Babinski reflex* (a baby's toes fan out when the outer edge of the sole of the foot is stroked).

Infants lose these primitive reflexes after the first few months of life and replace them with more complex and

Many of the reflexes that a neonate is born with are critical for survival and unfold naturally as a part of the infant's ongoing maturation.
©Emma Kim/Cultura/Getty Images

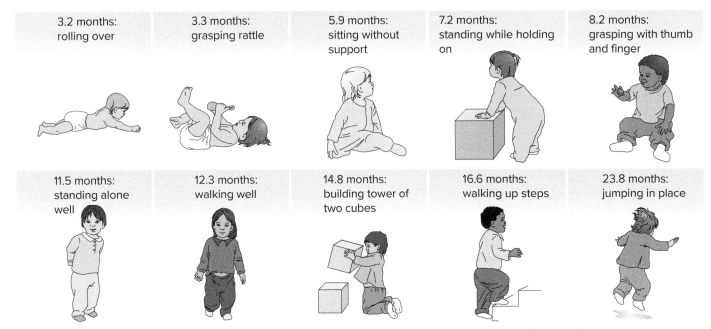

FIGURE 1 Although at birth a neonate can make only jerky, limited voluntary movements, during the first year of life, the ability to move independently grows enormously. The ages indicate the time when 50% of children are able to perform each skill. Remember, however, that the time when each skill appears can vary considerably. For example, 25% of children are able to walk well at age 11 months; by 15 months, 90% of children are walking well.
Source: Adapted from Frankenburg, W. K., Dodds, J. Archer, P., Shapiro, H. & Bresnick, B. (1992). The Denver II: A major revision and restandardization of the Denver developmental screening test. *Pediatrics, 89,* 91–97.

Study Alert
The basic reflexes—unlearned, involuntary responses—include the rooting reflex, the sucking reflex, the gag reflex, the startle reflex, and the Babinski reflex.

habituation The decrease in the response to a stimulus that occurs after repeated presentations of the same stimulus. (Module 37)

organized behaviors. Although at birth a neonate is capable of only jerky, limited voluntary movements, the ability to move independently grows enormously during the first year of life. The typical baby rolls over by the age of about 3 months, sits without support at about 6 months, stands alone at about 11 months, and walks at just over a year old. Not only does the ability to make large-scale movements improve during this time but fine-muscle movements also become increasingly sophisticated (see Figure 1).

DEVELOPMENT OF THE SENSES: TAKING IN THE WORLD

When proud parents peer into the eyes of their neonate, is the child able to return their gaze? Although it was thought for some time that newborns can only see a hazy blur, most current findings indicate that neonates' capabilities are far more impressive. Newborns can see objects reasonably well that are within 7- to 8-inches of their eyes, although they have a limited capacity to see beyond that distance, and can follow moving objects within their field of vision. They also show the beginnings of depth perception as they react by raising their hands when an object appears to be moving rapidly toward the face (Maurer et al., 1999; Craighero et al., 2011).

You might think that it would be hard to figure out just how well neonates can see because their lack of both language and reading ability clearly prevents them from saying what direction the E on a vision chart is facing. However, researchers have devised a number of ingenious methods that rely on the newborn's biological responses and innate reflexes to test perceptual skills.

For instance, infants who see a novel stimulus typically pay close attention to it; as a consequence, their heart rates increase. But if they repeatedly see the same stimulus, their attention to it decreases, as indicated by a return to a slower heart rate. This phenomenon is known as **habituation,** the decrease in the response to a stimulus that occurs after repeated presentations of the same stimulus. By studying habituation, developmental psychologists can tell when a child who is too young to speak can detect and discriminate a stimulus (del Rosal, Alonso, & Moreno, 2006; Molina et al., 2015).

Researchers have developed many other methods for measuring neonate and infant perception. One technique, for instance, involves babies sucking on a nipple attached to a computer. A change in the rate and vigor with which the babies suck helps researchers infer that babies can perceive variations in stimuli. Other approaches include examining babies' eye movements and observing which way babies move their heads in response to a visual stimulus (Franklin, Pilling, & Davies, 2005; Bulf, Johnson, & Valenza, 2011).

Through the use of such research techniques, we now know that infants' visual perception is remarkably sophisticated from the start of life. At birth, babies prefer patterns with contours and edges over less distinct patterns, indicating that they can respond to the configuration of stimuli. Furthermore, even newborns are aware of size constancy because they are apparently sensitive to the phenomenon by which objects stay the same size even though the image on the retina may change size as the distance between the object and the retina varies (Norcia et al., 2005; Moore, Goodwin, & George, 2007; Hadad, Maurer, & Lewis, 2017).

In fact, neonates can discriminate facial expressions—and even imitate them. As you can see in Figure 2, newborns can produce a good imitation of an adult's expressions. Even very young infants, then, can respond to the emotions and moods that their caregivers' facial expressions reveal. This capability provides the foundation for social interaction skills in children (Meltzoff, 1996; Grossmann, Striano, & Friederici, 2007; Bahrick, Lickliter, & Castellanos, 2013).

Other visual abilities grow rapidly after birth. By the end of their first month, babies can distinguish some colors from others; after 4 months, they can focus on near or far objects. By the age of 4 or 5 months, they are able to recognize two- and three-dimensional objects, and they can perceive the Gestalt organizing principles discovered by psychologists who study perception. By the age of 7 months, neural systems

FIGURE 2 This newborn infant is clearly imitating the expressions of the adult model in these amazing photos. How does this ability contribute to social development?

(all photos): Meltzoff, A. N., & Moore, M. K. (1977). Imitation of facial and manual gestures by human neonates. *Science, 198*, 75-78. Copyright ©1977 Andrew Meltzoff

AP| NEUROSCIENCE IN YOUR LIFE: EMOTIONAL RESPONSES IN INFANCY

AP SKILL: APPLY THEORIES AND PERSPECTIVES IN AUTHENTIC CONTEXTS / DATA ANALYSIS

1. Is temperament better explained by nature or nurture?

2. Use the statistics to summarize the results of this study.

Particular emotions elicit particular neural responses, even in early infancy. Furthermore, infants differ significantly in their neural responses to different emotions. Are these differences in brain response related to temperament? To answer this question, researchers measured neural activity while 7-month-old infants looked at pictures of happy faces. Compared with those who scored high on negative emotionality, the infants who scored low on negative emotionality—that is, those who had a propensity toward more positive thinking—had a greater neural response to happy faces in the left frontal cortex. The results suggest that neural responses to emotional stimuli are related to an infant's temperament (Ravicz et al, 2015).

In the image, you can see when brain activity occurred (*x*-axis) and how much hemoglobin levels changed (*y*-axis) as blood went to active brain areas.

Source: Adapted from Ravicz, M. M., Perdue, K. L., Westerlund, A., Vanderwert, R. E., & Nelson, C. A. (2016). Infants' neural responses to facial emotion in the prefrontal cortex are correlated with temperament: a functional near-infrared spectroscopy study. *Frontiers in Psychology, 6,* 922.

related to the processing of information about facial expressions are highly sophisticated and cause babies to respond differently to specific facial expressions (see *Neuroscience in Your Life*). Overall, their perceptual abilities rapidly improve: Sensitivity to visual stimuli, for instance, becomes three to four times greater at 1 year of age than it was at birth (Striano & Vaish, 2006; Leppänen et al., 2007; Xiao et al., 2015).

In addition to vision, infants display other impressive sensory capabilities. Newborns can distinguish different sounds to the point of being able to recognize their own mothers' voices at the age of 3 days. They can also make the subtle perceptual distinctions that underlie language abilities. For example, at 2 days of age, infants can distinguish between their native tongue and foreign languages, and they can discriminate between such closely related sounds as *ba* and *pa* when they are 4 days old. By 6 months of age, they can discriminate virtually any difference in sound that is relevant to the production of language. Moreover, they can recognize different tastes and smells at a very early age. There even seems to be something of a built-in sweet tooth: Neonates prefer liquids that have been sweetened with sugar over their unsweetened counterparts (Cohen & Cashon, 2003; Rivera-Gaxiola et al., 2005; Purdy et al., 2013; Smith et al., 2017).

Infancy Through Childhood

Three-year-old Lisa Palermo always had Cheerios on her breath. Mindy Crowell, Lisa's day care teacher, thought little of it until she noticed that the classroom Cheerios stash was steadily dwindling.

The Cheerios were stored in a plastic bin in the clothes closet. Keeping an eye on the closet, Mindy soon saw Lisa enter it, manipulate the fastener of the bin, reach in, withdraw a hand laden with Cheerios, and let the bin refasten itself, as it was designed to do. Mindy was amazed: Somehow, Lisa, barely able to navigate a crayon, had learned how to undo the supposedly child-proof fastener–a task that Mindy herself found difficult.

Mindy waited to see what would happen next. What she found was that Lisa was an excellent teacher. In the next few days, Paul, Olivia, and Kelly began to frequent the bin and do exactly what Lisa had done.

At 3 years old, Lisa asserted her personality, illustrating the tremendous growth that occurs in a variety of domains during the first year of life. Throughout the remainder of childhood, moving from infancy into middle childhood and the start of adolescence around age 11 or 12, children develop physically, socially, and cognitively in extraordinary ways. In the remainder of this module, we'll consider this development.

PHYSICAL DEVELOPMENT

Children's physical growth provides the most obvious sign of development. During the first year of life, children typically triple their birthweight, and their height increases by about half. This rapid growth slows down as the child gets older–think how gigantic adults would be if that rate of growth was constant. From age 3 to the beginning of adolescence at around age 13, growth averages a gain of about 5 pounds and 3 inches a year (see Figure 3).

The physical changes that occur as children develop are not just a matter of increasing growth; the relationship of the size of the various body parts to one another

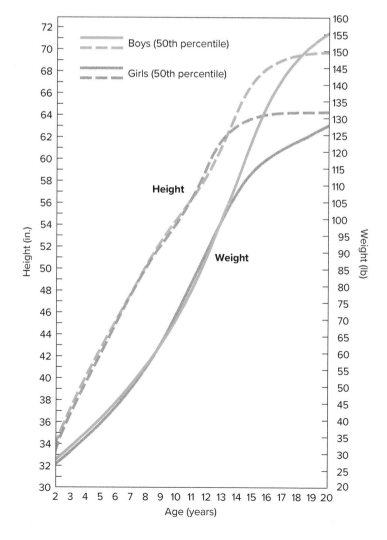

FIGURE 3 The average heights and weights of males and females in the United States from age 2 through age 20. At what ages are girls typically heavier and taller than boys?

Source: Adapted from National Center for Health Statistics. (2000). *Health United States, 2000 with adolescent health chartbook.* National Center for Health Statistics, Hyattsville, MD.

FIGURE 4 As development progresses, the size of the head relative to the rest of the body decreases until the individual reaches adulthood. Why do you think the head starts out so large?

Source: Adapted from Robbins, W. J. (1929). *Growth.* New Haven, CT: Yale University Press.

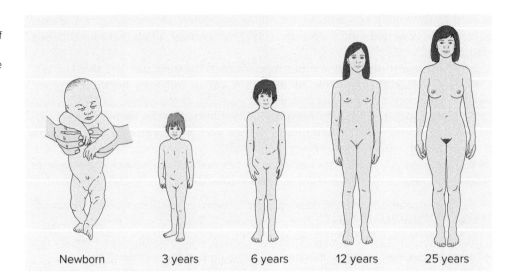

Newborn   3 years   6 years   12 years   25 years

changes dramatically as children age. As you can see in Figure 4, the head of a fetus (and a newborn) is disproportionately large. However, the head soon becomes more proportional in size to the rest of the body as growth occurs mainly in the trunk and legs (Adolph & Berger, 2011).

DEVELOPMENT OF SOCIAL BEHAVIOR: TAKING ON THE WORLD

As anyone who has seen infants smiling at the sight of their mothers can guess, at the same time that infants grow physically and hone their perceptual abilities, they also develop socially. The nature of a child's early social development provides the foundation for social relationships that will last a lifetime.

Attachment, the positive emotional bond that develops between a child and a particular individual, is the most important form of social development that occurs during infancy. The earliest studies of attachment were carried out by animal ethologist Konrad Lorenz (1966). Lorenz focused on newborn goslings, which under normal circumstances instinctively follow their mother, the first moving object they perceive after birth. Lorenz found that goslings whose eggs were raised in an incubator and which viewed him immediately after hatching would follow his every movement as if he were their mother. He labeled this process *imprinting,* behavior that takes place during a critical period and involves attachment to the first moving object that is observed.

Our understanding of attachment progressed when psychologist Harry Harlow, in a classic study, gave infant monkeys the choice of cuddling a wire "monkey" that provided milk or a soft, terry-cloth "monkey" that was warm but did not provide milk. Their choice was clear: They spent most of their time clinging to the warm cloth "monkey," although they made occasional forays to the wire monkey to nurse. Obviously, the cloth monkey provided greater comfort to the infants; milk alone was insufficient to create attachment (see Figure 5; Harlow & Zimmerman, 1959; Blum, 2002; Levine & Munsch, 2011).

Building on this pioneering work, developmental psychologists have suggested that human attachment grows through the responsiveness of infants' caregivers to signals, such as crying, smiling, reaching, and clinging. The more that caregivers respond to signals that children give off regarding their emotions, the more likely it is that the child will become securely attached to the caregiver.

Full attachment eventually develops as a result of the complex series of interactions between caregiver and child. In the course of these interactions, the infant plays as critical and active of a role as the caregiver in the formation of the bond between them. Infants who respond positively to a caregiver produce more positive behavior on the caregiver's part, which, in turn, produces an even stronger degree of attachment in the child.

attachment The positive emotional bond that develops between a child and a particular individual. (Module 37)

FIGURE 5 Although the wire "mother" dispensed milk to the hungry infant monkey, the infant preferred the soft, terry-cloth "mother." Do you think human babies would react the same way? What does this experiment tell us about attachment?
©Nina Leen/Time Life Pictures/Getty Images

Assessing Attachment Developmental psychologists have devised a quick and direct way to measure attachment. Developed by Mary Ainsworth, the *Ainsworth strange situation* consists of a sequence of events involving a child and (typically) his or her mother. Initially, the mother and baby enter an unfamiliar room, and the mother permits the baby to explore while she sits down. An adult stranger then enters the room; after this, the mother leaves. The mother returns, and the stranger leaves. The mother once again leaves the baby alone, and the stranger returns. Finally, the stranger leaves, and the mother returns (Ainsworth et al., 1978; Van Rosmalen, Van der Veer, & Van der Horst, 2015; Posada & Trumbell, 2017).

Babies' reactions to the experimental situation vary drastically, depending, according to Ainsworth, on their degree of attachment to the mother:

- *Securely attached children.* Children who are *securely attached* employ the mother as a kind of home base; they explore independently but return to her occasionally. When she leaves, they exhibit distress, and they go to her when she returns.

- *Avoidant children. Avoidant* children do not cry when the mother leaves, and they seem to avoid her when she returns as if they were indifferent to her.

- *Ambivalent children. Ambivalent* children display anxiety before they are separated and are upset when the mother leaves, but they may show ambivalent reactions to her return, such as seeking close contact but simultaneously hitting and kicking her.

- *Disorganized-disoriented children.* A fourth reaction is *disorganized-disoriented;* these children show inconsistent and often contradictory behavior. For example, they may approach their mother but do so avoiding eye contact or otherwise acting in an inappropriate way.

The nature of attachment between children and their mothers has far-reaching consequences for later development. For example, children who are securely attached to their mothers tend to be more socially and emotionally competent than are their less securely attached peers, and others find them more cooperative, capable, and playful. Furthermore, children who are securely attached at age 1 show fewer psychological difficulties when they grow older compared with avoidant and ambivalent youngsters. Children who are securely attached tend, as adults, to have more successful romantic relationships. On the other hand, being securely attached at an early age does not guarantee good adjustment later; conversely, children who lack secure attachment do not always have difficulties later in life (Hardy, 2007; Redshaw & Martin, 2013; Hennessy & Shair, 2017).

The Father's Role Although early developmental research focused largely on the mother-child relationship, more recent research has highlighted the father's role in parenting—and with good reason: The number of fathers who are primary caregivers for their children has grown significantly, and fathers play an increasingly important role in their children's lives. For example, in almost 13% of families with children, the father is the parent who stays at home to care for preschoolers (Day & Lamb, 2004; Halford, 2006; Kulik & Sadeh, 2015).

When fathers interact with their children, their play often differs from mothers' play. Fathers engage in more physical, rough-and-tumble sorts of activities, whereas mothers play more verbal and traditional games, such as peekaboo. Despite such behavioral differences, the nature of attachment between fathers and children compared with that between mothers and children can be similar. In fact, children can form multiple attachments simultaneously (Pellis & Pellis, 2007; Diener et al., 2008; Bureau et al., 2017).

Social Relationships with Peers By the time they are 2 years old, children become less dependent on their parents, more self-reliant, and increasingly prefer to play with friends. Initially, play is relatively independent: Even though they may be sitting side by side, 2-year-olds pay more attention to toys than to one another when playing. Later, however, children actively interact, modify one another's behavior, and exchange roles during play (Lindsey & Colwell, 2003; Colwell & Lindsey, 2005; Whitney & Green, 2011).

Study Alert

Attachment—the positive emotional bond that develops between a child and a particular individual—is a key concept in understanding the social development of children.

Cultural factors also affect children's styles of play. For example, Korean American children engage in less pretend play than do their Anglo American counterparts (Bai, 2005; Drewes, 2005; Suizzo & Bornstein, 2006).

As children reach school age, their social interactions become more frequent, and they begin to follow set patterns of behavior. For example, they may engage in elaborate games involving teams and rigid rules. In addition to providing enjoyment, such play allows children to become increasingly competent in their interactions with others. For instance, during play, they learn to take the perspective of other people. Children also learn to infer others' thoughts and feelings, even when those thoughts and feelings are not directly expressed (Royzman, Cassidy, & Baron, 2003; Yang et al., 2013).

In short, social interaction helps children interpret the meaning of others' behavior and develop the capacity to respond appropriately. Furthermore, children learn physical and emotional self-control: They learn to avoid hitting a playmate who beats them at a game. They learn to be polite and to control their emotional displays and facial expressions (e.g., smiling even when receiving a disappointing gift). Situations that provide children with opportunities for social interaction, then, may enhance their social development (Talukdar & Shastri, 2006; Whitebread et al., 2009).

The Consequences of Child Care Outside the Home Research on the importance of social interaction is corroborated by work that examines the benefits of child care out of the home, which is an important part of an increasing number of children's lives. For instance, almost 30% of preschool children whose mothers work outside the home spend their days in child-care centers. By the age of 6 months, almost two-thirds of infants are cared for by people other than their mothers for part of the day. Most of these infants begin child care before the age of 4 months and are cared for by people other than their mothers almost 30 hours per week (see Figure 6; National Research Council, 2001; NICHD Early Child Care Research Network, 2006).

Do child-care arrangements outside the home benefit children's development? If the programs are of high quality, they can. According to the results of a large study supported by the U.S. National Institute of Child Health and Development, children who attend high-quality child-care centers may not only do as well as children who stay at home with their parents but in some respects they may actually do better. Children in child care are generally more considerate and sociable than other children, and they interact more positively with teachers. They may also be more compliant and regulate their own behavior more effectively (NICHD Early Child Care Research Network, 1999, 2001).

FIGURE 6 According to a study by the National Institute of Child Health and Human Development, children were more likely to spend time in some kind of child care outside the home or family as they got older.

Source: Adapted from National Institute of Child Health and Human Development (NICHD) Early Child Care Research Network. (2006). Child-care effect sizes for the NICHD study of early child care and youth development. *American Psychologist, 61,* 99–116.

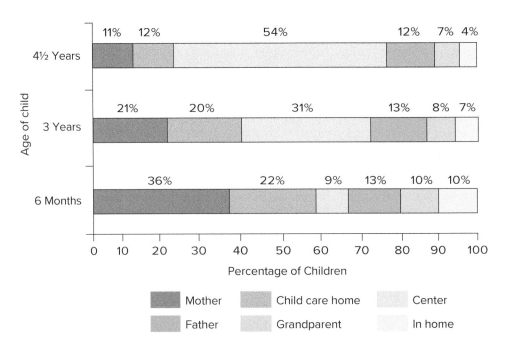

In addition, especially for children from poor or disadvantaged homes, child care in specially enriched environments–those with many toys, books, a variety of children, and high-quality providers–may be more intellectually stimulating than the home environment. Such child care can lead to increased intellectual achievement, demonstrated in higher IQ scores, and better language development. In fact, children in care centers sometimes are found to score higher on tests of cognitive abilities than those who are cared for by their mothers or by sitters or home day-care providers–effects that last into adulthood (Burchinal, Roberts, & Riggins, 2000; Dearing, McCartney, & Taylor, 2009; Reid, Martin, & Brooks-Gunn, 2017).

However, child care outside the home does not have universally positive outcomes. Children may feel insecure after placement in low-quality child care or in multiple child-care settings. Furthermore, some research suggests that infants who are involved in outside care more than 20 hours a week in the first year show less secure attachment to their mothers than do those who have not been in child care outside the home. Finally, children who spent long hours in child care as infants and preschoolers may have a reduced ability to work independently and to manage their time effectively when they reach elementary school (NICHD Early Child Care Research Network, 2001; Vandell et al., 2005; Pluess & Belsky, 2009).

The key to the success of nonparental child care is its quality. High-quality child care produces benefits; low-quality child care provides little or no gain and may even hinder children's development. In short, significant benefits result from the social interaction and intellectual stimulation provided by high-quality child-care centers–especially for children from impoverished environments (NICHD Early Child Care Research Network, 2002; National Association for the Education of Young Children, 2005; Landry et al., 2013).

Parenting Styles and Social Development Parents' child-rearing practices are critical in shaping their children's social competence. According to classic research by developmental psychologist Diana Baumrind, four main categories describe different parenting styles (see Figure 7).

- **Authoritarian parents** are rigid and punitive, and they value unquestioning obedience from their children. They have strict standards and discourage expressions of disagreement.

- **Permissive parents** give their children relaxed or inconsistent direction and, although they are warm, require little of them.

- **Authoritative parents** are firm and set limits for their children. As the children get older, these parents try to reason and explain things to them. They also set clear goals and encourage their children's independence.

- **Uninvolved parents** show little interest in their children. Emotionally detached, they view parenting as nothing more than providing food, clothing, and shelter for children. At their most extreme, uninvolved parents are guilty of neglect, a form of child abuse (Baumrind, 2005; Lagacé-Séguin & d'Entremont, 2006; Lewis & Lamb, 2011).

As you might expect, the four kinds of child-rearing styles seem to produce very different kinds of behavior in children (with many exceptions, of course). Children of authoritarian parents tend to be unsociable, unfriendly, and relatively withdrawn. In contrast, permissive parents' children show immaturity, moodiness, dependence, and low self-control. The children of authoritative parents fare best: With high social skills, they are likable, self-reliant, independent, and cooperative. Worst off are the children of uninvolved parents; they feel unloved and emotionally detached, and their physical and cognitive development are impeded (Berk, 2005; Snyder, Cramer, & Afrank, 2005; Llorca-Mestre et al., 2017).

Before we rush to congratulate authoritative parents and condemn authoritarian, permissive, and uninvolved ones, it is important to note that in many cases, nonauthoritative

authoritarian parents Parents who are rigid and punitive and value unquestioning obedience from their children. (Module 37)

permissive parents Parents who give their children relaxed or inconsistent direction and, although they are warm, require little of them. (Module 37)

authoritative parents Parents who are firm, set clear limits, reason with their children, and explain things to them. (Module 37)

uninvolved parents Parents who show little interest in their children and are emotionally detached. (Module 37)

Study Alert

Know the four major types of child-rearing practices—authoritarian, permissive, authoritative, and uninvolved—and their effects.

Parenting Style	Parent Behavior	Type of Behavior Produced in Child
Authoritarian	Rigid, punitive, strict standards (example: "If you don't clean your room, I'm going to take away your iPhone for good and ground you.")	Unsociable, unfriendly, withdrawn
Permissive	Lax, inconsistent, undemanding (example: "It might be good to clean your room, but I guess it can wait.")	Immature, moody, dependent, low self-control
Authoritative	Firm, sets limits and goals, uses reasoning, encourages independence (example: "You'll need to clean your room before we can go out to the restaurant. As soon as you finish, we'll leave.")	Good social skills, likable, self-reliant, independent
Uninvolved	Detached emotionally, sees role only as providing food, clothing, and shelter (example: "I couldn't care less if your room is a pigsty.")	Indifferent, rejecting behavior

FIGURE 7 According to developmental psychologist Diana Baumrind (1971), four main parenting styles characterize child rearing.

Source: National Institute of Child Health and Human Development (NICHD) Early Child Care Research Network. (2006). Child-care effect sizes for the NICHD study of early child care and youth development. *American Psychologist, 61,* 99–116; (photo):©Gary John Norman/Getty Images.

temperament A basic, inborn characteristic way of responding and behavioral style. (Module 37)

parents also produce perfectly well-adjusted children. Moreover, children are born with a particular **temperament**—a basic, inborn characteristic way of responding and behavioral style. Some children are naturally easygoing and cheerful, whereas others are irritable and fussy or pensive and quiet. The kind of temperament a baby is born with may in part bring about specific kinds of parental child-rearing styles (Miner & Clarke-Stewart, 2008; Coplan, Reichel, & Rowan, 2009; Costa & Figueiredo, 2011).

In addition, children vary considerably in their degree of *resilience*, the ability to overcome circumstances that place them at high risk for psychological or even physical harm. Highly resilient children have temperaments that evoke positive responses from caregivers. Such children display unusual social skills: outgoingness, intelligence, and a feeling that they have control over their lives. In a sense, resilient children try to shape their own environment rather than being victimized by it (Deater-Deckard, Ivy, & Smith, 2005; Vellacott, 2007; Naglieri, LeBuffe, & Ross, 2013).

We also need to keep in mind that these findings regarding child-rearing styles apply primarily to U.S. society, which highly values children's growing independence and diminishing reliance on their parents. In contrast, Japanese parents encourage dependence to promote the values of cooperation and community life. These differences in cultural values result in very different philosophies of child rearing. For example, Japanese mothers believe it is a punishment to make a young child sleep alone; thus, many children sleep next to their mothers throughout infancy and toddlerhood (Kawasaki et al., 1994; Jones, 2007; Pinquart & Kauser, 2017).

In sum, a child's upbringing results from the child-rearing philosophy parents hold, the specific practices they use, and the nature of their own and their child's personalities. As is the case with other aspects of development, then, behavior is a function of a complex interaction of environmental and genetic factors.

Erikson's Theory of Psychosocial Development In tracing the course of social development, some theorists have considered how the challenges of society and culture change as an individual matures. Following this path, psychoanalyst Erik Erikson developed one of the more comprehensive theories of social development. Erikson (1963) viewed the developmental changes that occur throughout life as a series of eight stages of psychosocial development; of these, four occur during childhood. **Psychosocial development** involves changes in our interactions and understanding of one another as well as in our knowledge and understanding of ourselves as members of society.

Erikson suggests that passage through each of the stages necessitates the resolution of a crisis or conflict. Accordingly, Erikson represents each stage as a pairing of the most positive and most negative aspects of the crisis of that period. Although each crisis is never resolved entirely–life becomes increasingly complicated as we grow older–it has to be resolved sufficiently to equip us to deal with demands made during the following stage of development.

The first stage of psychosocial development is the **trust-versus-mistrust stage** (ages birth to 1½ years). During this period, infants develop feelings of trust or mistrust, primarily depending on how well their caregivers meet their needs. If their physical requirements and psychological needs for attachment are consistently met and their interactions with the world are generally positive, they will develop a sense of trust. In contrast, inconsistent care and unpleasant interactions with others can lead to mistrust and a view of the world as a harsh and unfriendly place.

In the second stage, the **autonomy-versus-shame-and-doubt stage** (ages 1½-3 years), toddlers develop independence and autonomy if caregivers encourage exploration and freedom. On the other hand, they experience shame, self-doubt, and unhappiness if they are overly restricted and protected. According to Erikson, the key to the development of a sense of independence during this period is for the child's caregivers to provide a reasonable amount of control. If parents are overly controlling, children cannot assert themselves nor develop their own sense of control over their world.

Next, children face the crises of the **initiative-versus-guilt stage** (ages 3-6 years). In this stage, children's desire to act independently conflicts with the guilt that comes from the unintended and unexpected consequences of such behavior. Children in this period come to understand that they are persons in their own right, and they begin to make decisions about their behavior. If parents react positively to children's attempts at independence, their children will develop skills in accomplishing tasks and overcoming challenges.

The fourth and last stage of childhood is the **industry-versus-inferiority stage** (ages 6-12 years), which is focused on efforts to meet the challenges presented by parents, peers, school, and other societal institutions. During this period, increasing competency in all areas, whether social interactions or academic skills, characterizes successful psychosocial development. In contrast, difficulties in this stage lead to feelings of failure and inadequacy.

Erikson's theory suggests that psychosocial development continues throughout life, and he proposes four more crises that are faced after childhood (described in module 38). Although his theory has been criticized on several grounds–such as the imprecision of the concepts he employs and his greater emphasis on male development than female development–it remains influential and is one of the few theories that encompass the entire life span.

COGNITIVE DEVELOPMENT: CHILDREN'S THINKING ABOUT THE WORLD

Suppose you had two drinking glasses of different shapes–one short and broad, and one tall and thin. Now imagine that you filled the short, broad one with soda about halfway and then poured the liquid from that glass into the tall one. The soda would appear to fill about three-quarters of the second glass. If someone asked you whether there was more soda in the second glass than there had been in the first, what would you say?

You might think that such a simple question hardly deserves an answer; of course, there is no difference in the amount of soda in the two glasses. However, most 4-year-olds would be likely to say that there is more soda in the second glass. If you then poured the soda back into the short glass, they would say there is now less soda than there was in the taller glass.

Why are young children confused by this problem? The reason is not immediately obvious. Anyone who has observed preschoolers must be impressed by how far they have

psychosocial development Development of individuals' interactions and understanding of each other and of their knowledge and understanding of themselves as members of society. (Module 37)

trust-versus-mistrust stage According to Erikson, the first stage of psychosocial development, occurring from birth to age 1½ years, during which time infants develop feelings of trust or lack of trust. (Module 37)

autonomy-versus-shame-and-doubt stage The period during which, according to Erikson, toddlers (ages 1½ to 3 years) develop independence and autonomy if exploration and freedom are encouraged or shame and self-doubt if they are restricted and overprotected. (Module 37)

initiative-versus-guilt stage According to Erikson, the period during which children ages 3 to 6 years experience conflict between independence of action and the sometimes negative results of that action. (Module 37)

industry-versus-inferiority stage According to Erikson, the last stage of childhood, during which children ages 6 to 12 years may develop positive social interactions with others or may feel inadequate and become less sociable. (Module 37)

Study Alert
Four of Erikson's stages of psychosocial development occur during childhood: trust-versus-mistrust, autonomy-versus-shame-and-doubt, initiative-versus-guilt, and industry-versus-inferiority.

progressed from the early stages of development. They speak with ease, know the alphabet, count, play complex games, use computers, tell stories, and communicate ably. Yet despite this seeming sophistication, there are deep gaps in children's understanding of the world. The gaps in children's understanding relate to their level of cognitive development.

cognitive development The process by which a child's understanding of the world changes due to the child's age and experience. (Module 37)

Cognitive development is the process by which a child's understanding of the world changes due to their age and experience. In contrast to the theories of physical and social development discussed earlier (such as those of Erikson), theories of cognitive development seek to explain the quantitative and qualitative intellectual advances that occur during development.

Study Alert

Use Figure 8 to help remember Piaget's stages of cognitive development.

Piaget's Theory of Cognitive Development No theory of cognitive development has had more impact than that of Swiss psychologist Jean Piaget. Piaget (1970) suggested that children around the world proceed through a series of four stages in a fixed order. He maintained that these stages differ not only in the *quantity* of information acquired at each stage but in the *quality* of knowledge and understanding as well. Taking an interactionist point of view, he suggested that movement from one stage to the next occurs when a child reaches an appropriate level of maturation *and* is exposed to relevant types of experiences. Piaget assumed that, without having such experiences, children cannot reach their highest level of cognitive growth.

Piaget proposed four stages: the sensorimotor, preoperational, concrete operational, and formal operational (see Figure 8). Let's examine each of them and the approximate ages that they span.

sensorimotor stage According to Piaget, the stage from birth to 2 years, during which a child has little competence in representing the environment by using images, language, or other symbols. (Module 37)

Sensorimotor Stage: Birth to 2 Years. During the **sensorimotor stage,** children base their understanding of the world primarily on touching, sucking, chewing, shaking, and manipulating objects. In the initial part of the stage, children have relatively little competence in representing the environment by using images, language, or other kinds of symbols. Consequently, infants lack what Piaget calls **object permanence,** the awareness that objects–and people–continue to exist even if they are out of sight.

object permanence The awareness that objects–and people–continue to exist even if they are out of sight. (Module 37)

How can we know that children lack object permanence? Although we cannot ask infants, we can observe their reactions when a toy they are playing with is hidden under a blanket. Until the age of about 9 months, children will make no attempt to locate the hidden toy. However, soon after that age, they will begin an active search for the missing object, indicating that they have developed a mental representation of the toy. Object permanence, then, is a critical development during the sensorimotor stage.

preoperational stage According to Piaget, the period from 2 to 7 years of age that is characterized by language development. (Module 37)

Preoperational Stage: 2-7 Years. During the the **preoperational stage,** children develop the use of language. The internal representational systems they develop allows them to describe people, events, and feelings. They even use symbols in play, pretending, for example, that a book pushed across the floor is a car.

Cognitive Stage	Approximate Age Range	Major Characteristics
Sensorimotor	Birth–2 years	Development of object permanence, development of motor skills, little or no capacity for symbolic representation
Preoperational	2–7 years	Development of language and symbolic thinking, egocentric thinking
Concrete operational	7–12 years	Development of conservation, mastery of the concept of reversibility
Formal operational	12 years–adulthood	Development of logical and abstract thinking

FIGURE 8 According to Piaget, all children pass through four stages of cognitive development.

(photo): ©Farrell Grehan/Corbis via Getty Images

Although children use more advanced thinking in this stage than they did in the earlier sensorimotor stage, their thinking is still qualitatively inferior to that of adults. We see this when we observe a preoperational child using **egocentric thought,** a way of thinking in which the child views the world entirely from his or her own perspective. Preoperational children think that everyone shares their perspective and knowledge. Thus, children's stories and explanations to adults can be maddeningly uninformative because they are delivered without any context. For example, a preoperational child may start a story with, "He wouldn't let me go," neglecting to mention who "he" is or where the storyteller wanted to go. We also see egocentric thinking when children at the preoperational stage play hiding games. For instance, 3-year-olds frequently hide with their faces against a wall and covering their eyes–although they are still in plain view. It seems to them that if *they* cannot see, then no one else will be able to see them because they assume that others share their view.

In addition, preoperational children have not yet developed the ability to comprehend the **principle of conservation,** which is the understanding that quantity is unrelated to the arrangement and physical appearance of objects. Children who can use the principle of conservation have awareness that important attributes of objects (such as amount or volume) do not change despite superficial changes. In contrast, children who have not mastered conservation do not understand that the overall amount or volume of an object does not change when its shape or configuration changes.

The question about the two glasses–one short and broad, and the other tall and thin–with which we began our discussion of cognitive development illustrates this point clearly. Children who do not understand the principle of conservation believe that the amount of liquid changes as it is poured back and forth between glasses of different sizes. They simply are unable to comprehend that a change in appearance does not mean there is a change in amount. Instead, they truly believe that quantity changes as appearance changes (see Figure 9).

Concrete Operational Stage: 7-12 Years. Mastery of the principle of conservation marks the beginning of the **concrete operational stage.** However, children do not fully understand some aspects of conservation–such as conservation of weight and volume–for a number of years.

During the concrete operational stage, children develop the ability to think in a more logical manner and begin to overcome some of the egocentrism characteristic of the preoperational period. One of the major principles children learn during this stage is reversibility, the idea that some changes can be undone by reversing an earlier action. For example, they can understand that when someone rolls a ball of clay into a long sausage shape, that person can recreate the original ball by reversing the action. Children can even conceptualize this principle in their heads without having to see the action performed before them.

Although children make important advances in their logical capabilities during the concrete operational stage, their thinking still displays one major limitation: They are largely bound to the concrete, physical reality of the world. For the most part, they have difficulty understanding questions of an abstract or hypothetical nature.

Formal Operational Stage: 12 Years to Adulthood. The **formal operational stage** produces a new kind of thinking that is abstract, formal, and logical. Thinking is no longer tied to events that individuals observe in the environment but makes use of logical techniques to resolve problems.

The way in which children approach the "pendulum problem" devised by Piaget (Piaget & Inhelder, 1958) illustrates the emergence of formal operational thinking. The problem solver is asked to figure out what determines how fast a pendulum swings. Is it the length of the string, the weight of the pendulum, or the force with which the pendulum is pushed? (For the record, the answer is the length of the string.)

Children in the concrete operational stage approach the problem haphazardly without a logical or rational plan of action. For example, they may simultaneously change the length of the string, the weight on the string, and the force with which they push the pendulum. Because they are varying all the factors at once, they cannot

Children who have not mastered the principle of conservation assume that the volume of liquid increases when it is poured from a short, wide container to a tall, thin one. What other tasks might a child under age 7 have difficulty comprehending?
©Tony Freeman/PhotoEdit

egocentric thought A way of thinking in which a child views the world entirely from his or her own perspective. (Module 37)

principle of conservation The understanding that quantity is unrelated to the arrangement and physical appearance of objects. (Module 37)

concrete operational stage According to Piaget, the period from 7 to 12 years of age that is characterized by logical thought and a loss of egocentrism. (Module 37)

formal operational stage According to Piaget, the period from age 12 to adulthood that is characterized by abstract thought. (Module 37)

FIGURE 9 These tests are frequently used to assess whether children have learned the principle of conservation across a variety of dimensions. Do you think children in the preoperational stage can be taught to avoid conservation mistakes before the typical age of mastery?

Source: Adapted from Schickedanz, J. A., Schickedanz, D. I., Forsyth, P. D., & Forsyth, G. A. (2001). *Understanding Children and Adolescents* (4th ed.). Upper Saddle River, NJ: Pearson Education.

Conservation of …	Modality	Change in physical appearance	Average age at full mastery
Number	Number of elements in a collection	Rearranging or dislocating elements	6–7 years
Substance (mass)	Amount of a malleable substance (e.g., clay or liquid)	Altering shape	7–8 years
Length	Length of a line or object	Altering shape or configuration	7–8 years
Area	Amount of surface covered by a set of plane figures	Rearranging the figures	8–9 years
Weight	Weight of an object	Altering shape	9–10 years
Volume	Volume of an object (in terms of water displacement)	Altering shape	14–15 years

tell which factor is the critical one. In contrast, people in the formal operational stage approach the problem systematically. Acting as if they were scientists conducting an experiment, they examine the effects of changes in one variable at a time. This ability to rule out competing possibilities characterizes formal operational thought.

Although formal operational thought emerges during the teenage years, some individuals use this type of thinking only infrequently. Moreover, it appears that many individuals never reach this stage at all; most studies show that only 40-60% of college students and adults fully reach it, with some estimates running as low as 25% of the general population. In addition, in certain cultures–particularly those that are less technically oriented than Western societies–almost no one reaches the formal operational stage (Keating & Clark, 1980; Super, 1980; Genovese, 2006).

Stages Versus Continuous Development: Is Piaget Right? No other theorist has given us as comprehensive of a theory of cognitive development as Piaget has. Still, many contemporary theorists suggest that a better explanation of how children develop cognitively can be provided by theories that do not involve a stage approach. For instance, children are not always consistent in their performance of tasks that–if Piaget's theory is accurate–ought to be performed equally well at a particular stage (Feldman, 2003, 2004).

Furthermore, some developmental psychologists suggest that cognitive development proceeds in a more continuous fashion than Piaget's stage theory implies. They propose that cognitive development is primarily quantitative rather than qualitative. They argue that although there are differences in when, how, and to what extent a child can use specific cognitive abilities–reflecting quantitative changes–the underlying cognitive processes change relatively little with age (Gelman & Baillargeon, 1983; Case & Okamoto, 1996).

Piaget also underestimated the age at which infants and children can understand specific concepts and principles; in fact, they seem to be more sophisticated in their cognitive abilities than Piaget believed. For instance, some evidence suggests that infants as young as 5 months have rudimentary mathematical skills (Wynn, Bloom, & Chiang, 2002; McCrink & Wynn, 2007; van Marle & Wynn, 2009).

Despite such criticisms, most developmental psychologists agree that although the processes that underlie changes in cognitive abilities may not unfold in the manner Piaget's theory suggests, he has generally provided us with an accurate account of age-related changes in cognitive development. Moreover, his theory has had an enormous influence in education. For example, Piaget suggests that individuals cannot increase their cognitive performance unless both cognitive readiness brought about by maturation and appropriate environmental stimulation are present. This view has inspired the nature and structure of educational curricula and teaching methods. Researchers have also used Piaget's theory and methods to investigate issues surrounding animal cognition, such as whether primates show object permanence (they seem to) (Egan, 2005; Cunningham, 2006; Jablonka, 2017).

INFORMATION-PROCESSING APPROACHES: CHARTING CHILDREN'S MENTAL PROGRAMS

If cognitive development does not proceed as a series of stages as Piaget suggested, what does underlie the enormous growth in children's cognitive abilities that even the most untutored eye can observe? To many developmental psychologists, changes in information-processing capabilities account for cognitive development. **Information processing** refers to the way in which people take in, use, and store information (Casasola, 2011; Lillard & Woolley, 2015).

According to the information-processing approach, quantitative changes occur in children's ability to organize and manipulate information. From this perspective, children become increasingly adept at information processing, much as a computer program may become more sophisticated as a programmer modifies it on the basis of experience. Information-processing approaches consider the kinds of "mental programs" that children invoke when approaching problems.

Several significant changes occur in children's information-processing capabilities. For one thing, speed of processing increases with age as some abilities become more automatic. The speed at which children can scan, recognize, and compare stimuli increases with age. As they grow older, children can pay attention to stimuli longer and discriminate between different stimuli more readily, and they are less easily distracted (Van den Wildenberg & Van der Molen, 2004; Diaz & Bell, 2011).

Memory also improves dramatically with age. Preschoolers can hold only two or three chunks of information in short-term memory, 5-year-olds can hold four, and 7-year-olds can hold five. (Adults are able to keep seven, plus or minus two, chunks in short-term memory.) The size of the chunks also grows with age, as does the sophistication and organization of knowledge stored in memory (see Figure 10). Still, memory capabilities are impressive at a very early age: Even before they can speak, infants can remember for months events in which they actively participated (Bayliss et al., 2005; Slusarczyk & Niedzwienska, 2013).

Finally, improvement in information processing relates to advances in **metacognition,** an awareness and understanding of one's own cognitive processes. Metacognition involves the planning, monitoring, and revising of cognitive strategies. Younger children, who lack an awareness of their own cognitive

information processing The way in which people take in, use, and store information. (Module 37)

metacognition An awareness and understanding of one's own cognitive processes. (Module 37)

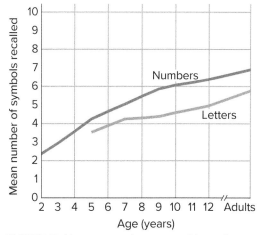

FIGURE 10 Memory span increases with age for both numbers and letters.

Source: Adapted from Dempster, F. N. (1981). Memory span: Sources for individual and developmental differences. *Psychological Bulletin, 89*, 63–100.

processes, often do not realize their incapabilities. Thus, when they misunderstand others, they may fail to recognize their own errors. It is only later, when metacognitive abilities become more sophisticated, that children are able to know when they *don't* understand. Such increasing sophistication reflects a change in children's *theory of mind,* their knowledge and beliefs about the way the mind operates (Lockl & Schneider, 2007; Sodian, 2011; O'Leary & Sloutsky, 2017).

PsychTech

A quarter of parents with children between the ages of 0–5 report that their children use the Internet.

zone of proximal development (ZPD) According to Vygotsky, the gap between what children already are able to accomplish on their own and what they are not quite ready to do by themselves. (Module 37)

Vygotsky's View of Cognitive Development: Considering Culture According to Russian developmental psychologist Lev Vygotsky, the culture in which we are raised significantly affects the nature of our cognitive development. In an increasingly influential view, Vygotsky suggests that the focus on individual performance of both Piagetian and information-processing approaches is misplaced. Instead, he holds that we cannot understand cognitive development without taking into account the social and cultural aspects of learning (Vygotsky, 1926/1997; Maynard & Martini, 2005; Rieber & Robinson, 2006).

Vygotsky argues that cognitive development occurs as a consequence of social interactions in which children work with others to jointly solve problems. Through such interactions, children's cognitive skills increase, and they gain the ability to function intellectually on their own. More specifically, he suggests that children's cognitive abilities increase when they encounter information that falls within their zone of proximal development. The **zone of proximal development (ZPD)** is the gap between what children already are able to accomplish on their own and what they are not quite ready to do by themselves. When children receive information that falls within the ZPD, they can increase their understanding or master a new task. In contrast, if the information lies outside children's ZPD, they will not be able to master it.

In short, cognitive development occurs when parents, teachers, or skilled peers assist a child by presenting new information that resides within the child's ZPD, a process Vygotsky calls scaffolding. *Scaffolding* is support for learning and problem solving that encourages independence and growth. Vygotsky claims that scaffolding not only helps children to solve specific problems but also aids in the development of overall cognitive abilities (Schaller & Crandall, 2004; Coulson & Harvey, 2013).

More than other approaches to cognitive development, Vygotsky's theory considers how an individual's specific cultural and social context affects intellectual growth. The way in which children understand the world grows out of interactions with parents, peers, and other members of a specific culture (John-Steiner & Mahn, 2003; Kozulin et al., 2003).

AP MODULE 37: INFANCY AND CHILDHOOD

AP SUMMARY

- Newborns have reflexes, such as rooting, sucking, gag, startle, and Babinski.
- Sensory abilities develop rapidly; infants can distinguish color, depth, sound, tastes, and smells relatively soon after birth.
- After birth, physical development is rapid and motor skills follow a genetically predetermined timeline.
- Children are born with a temperament, which may influence how others react to them.
- According to Erikson, there are eight stages of psychosocial development. During childhood, the four stages are trust vs. mistrust, autonomy vs. shame-and-doubt, initiative vs. guilt, and industry vs. inferiority.
- Harlow revealed that baby monkeys preferred physical comfort over milk alone to create an attachment.

- Measured in the laboratory by means of the Ainsworth strange situation, attachment relates to later social and emotional adjustment. Ainsworth found four types of attachment: secure, avoidant, ambivalent, and disorganized-disoriented.
- Lorenz discovered goslings imprint to the first moving object that is observed.
- Human attachment grows through the responsiveness of infants' caregivers to signals.
- As children become older, the nature of their social interactions with peers changes. Initially play occurs relatively independently, but it becomes increasingly cooperative. Cultural factors also influence children's styles of play.
- Baumrind researched different child-rearing styles and social competence. The styles include: authoritarian, permissive, authoritative, and uninvolved.

- Parenting styles are also influenced by temperament, resilience, and cultural factors.
- Habituation is when an infant's attention decreases if they repeatedly see the same stimulus.
- Piaget's theory suggests that cognitive development proceeds through four stages: sensorimotor, preoperational, concrete operational, and formal operational.
- Information-processing approaches suggest that quantitative changes occur in children's ability to organize and manipulate information about the world.
- Children advance in metacognition and develop theory of mind.
- Piaget offers a theory for stage vs. continuous development. His theory has been criticized but has had an enormous influence on education.
- Vygotsky argued that children's cognitive development occurs as a consequence of social interactions in which children and others work together to solve problems.
- Metacognition is the awareness and understanding of one's own cognitive processes. It improves with age.

AP KEY TERMS

neonate	industry-versus-inferiority
reflexes	stage
habituation	cognitive development
attachment	sensorimotor stage
authoritarian parents	object permanence
permissive parents	preoperational stage
authoritative parents	egocentric thought
uninvolved parents	principle of conservation
temperament	concrete operational stage
psychosocial development	formal operational stage
trust-versus-mistrust stage	information processing
autonomy-versus-shame-	metacognition
and-doubt stage	zone of proximal
initiative-versus-guilt stage	development (ZPD)

Section I: Multiple Choice

1. Touching a baby's cheek triggers them to open their mouth and turn to the source of the touch. This is known as the
   A. Babinski reflex
   B. Moro reflex
   C. rooting reflex
   D. gag reflex
   E. startle reflex

2. Learning to walk follows a biologically predetermined pattern of behavior. This is an example of
   A. conservation
   B. egocentrism
   C. habituation
   D. maturation
   E. object permanence

3. Who discovered that some animals create an attachment to the first moving object they see after birth?
   A. Erik Erikson
   B. Harry Harlow
   C. Konrad Lorenz
   D. Jean Piaget
   E. Lev Vygotsky

Section II: Free Response

Use your knowledge of psychology research to explain how the following terms may help development.
- Authoritative parenting
- Secure attachment
- Contact comfort
- Zone of proximal development

Explain how the following terms may hinder the relationship between the parent and child.
- Temperament
- Egocentrism
- Autonomy-versus-shame-and-doubt

Module 38
Adolescence: Becoming an Adult

adolescence The developmental stage between childhood and adulthood. (Module 38)

Joseph Charles, age 13: "Being 13 is very hard at school. I have to be bad in order to be considered cool. I sometimes do things that aren't good. I have talked back to my teachers and been disrespectful to them. I do want to be good, but it's just too hard." (Gibbs, 2005)

Marco Colson, age 15: "Trevor Kelson" says the sign on Marco's door. Inside, the floor is cluttered with dirty clothes, candy wrappers, and other debris. What color is the carpet on the floor? "I don't think I remember," says Marco with a smile.

Alissa Cruz, age 17: "I was invited to join the National Honor Society because of my grades. But at the induction, the parents just stared at me. It was like they couldn't believe that someone with a nose stud and pink streaks in her hair could be smart enough to be in the National Honor Society. I'm hoping to be a teacher in the public schools, but do you think they'd hire someone who looks like me?"

Although Joseph, Marco, and Alissa have never met, they share anxieties that are common to adolescence—concerns about friends, parents, appearance, independence, and their futures. **Adolescence,** the developmental stage between childhood and adulthood, is a crucial period. It is a time of profound changes and, occasionally, turmoil. Considerable biological change occurs as adolescents attain sexual and physical maturity. At the same time and rivaling these physiological changes, important social, emotional, and cognitive changes occur as adolescents strive for independence and move toward adulthood.

Because many years of schooling precede most people's entry into the workforce in Western societies, the stage of adolescence is fairly long; it begins just before the teenage years and ends just after them. Adolescents are no longer children, yet society doesn't quite consider them adults. They face a period of rapid physical, cognitive, and social change that affects them for the rest of their lives.

Dramatic changes in society also affect adolescents' development. More than half of all children in the United States will spend all or some of their childhood and adolescence in single-parent families. Furthermore, adolescents spend considerably less time with their parents and more with their peers than they did several decades ago. Finally, the ethnic and cultural diversity of adolescents as a group is increasing dramatically. A third of all adolescents today are of non-European descent; by the year 2050, the number of adolescents of Hispanic, African American, Native American, and Asian origin collectively will surpass that of whites (National Adolescent Health Information Center, 2003).

Physical Development: The Changing Adolescent

If you think back to the start of your own adolescence, the most dramatic changes you probably remember are physical. A spurt in height, the growth of breasts in girls, deepening voices in boys, the development of body hair, and intense sexual feelings cause curiosity, interest, and sometimes embarrassment for individuals entering adolescence.

Not since infancy has development been so dramatic. Beginning around age 10 for girls and age 12 for boys, a growth spurt leads to rapid increases in weight and height. Adolescents may grow as much as 5 inches in 1 year. The physical changes that occur at the start of adolescence result largely from a surge in levels of growth hormone, and they affect virtually every aspect of an adolescent's life.

Average male

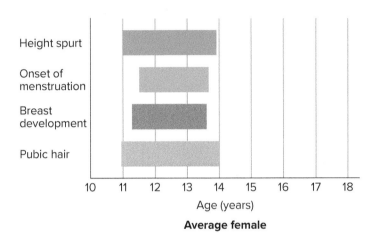

Average female

FIGURE 1 The range of ages during which major sexual changes occur during adolescence is shown by the colored bars.

Source: Adapted from Tanner, J. M. (1978). *Education and physical growth* (2nd ed.). New York: International Universities Press.

Puberty is the period at which maturation of the sexual organs occurs. Over the past century in Western cultures, the average age at which adolescents reach sexual maturity has been steadily decreasing, most likely as a result of improved nutrition and medical care.

For girls, puberty typically begins at about age 11 or 12, when menstruation starts. However, there are wide variations (see Figure 1). For example, some girls begin to menstruate as early as age 8 or 9 or as late as age 16. Furthermore, sexual attraction to others begins even before the maturation of the sexual organs at around age 10 (Finlay, Jones, & Coleman, 2002; Shanahan et al., 2013; Herting & Sowell, 2017).

For boys, their first ejaculation, formally known as *spermarche*, typically happens at the beginning of puberty. Spermarche usually occurs around the age of 13 (see Figure 1). At first, relatively few sperm are produced during an ejaculation, but the amount increases significantly within a few years.

The age at which puberty begins has significant implications for the way adolescents feel about themselves—as well as the way others treat them. Preadolescents who start puberty considerably earlier than their peers may feel isolated and different, and they are at risk for mental health issues (Mendle et al., 2016; Weir, 2016; Park, Yun, & Walsh, 2017).

In some cases, early maturation is favorable for boys. For example, early-maturing boys do better in athletics, are generally more popular with peers, and have more positive self-concepts. However, the picture differs for girls. Although early-maturing girls are more sought after as dates and have better self-esteem than later-maturing girls do, some consequences of early physical

puberty The period at which maturation of the sexual organs occurs, beginning at about age 11 or 12 for girls and 13 or 14 for boys. (Module 38)

Although puberty begins around 11 or 12 for girls and 13 or 14 for boys, there are wide variations. What are some of the advantages and disadvantages of early puberty?
©Purestock/SuperStock

maturation may be less positive. For example, early breast development may set them apart from their peers and be a source of ridicule (Blumenthal et al., 2011; Mensah et al., 2013; Natsuaki, Samuels, & Leve, 2015).

Late physical maturation may produce certain psychological difficulties for both boys and girls. Boys who are smaller and less coordinated than their more mature peers tend to feel ridiculed and less attractive. Similarly, late-maturing girls are at a disadvantage in middle school and early high school. They hold relatively low social status and may be overlooked in dating (Lanza & Collins, 2002).

Clearly, the rate at which physical changes occur during adolescence can affect the way in which people are viewed by others and the way they view themselves. Just as important as physical changes, however, are the psychological and social changes that unfold during adolescence.

Moral and Cognitive Development: Distinguishing Right from Wrong

In a European country, a woman is near death from a special kind of cancer. The one drug that the doctors think might save her is a medicine that a medical researcher has recently discovered. The drug is expensive to make, and the researcher is charging 10 times the cost, or $5,000, for a small dose. The sick woman's husband, Henry, approaches everyone he knows in hope of borrowing money, but he can get together only about $2,500. He tells the researcher that his wife is dying and asks him to lower the price of the drug or let him pay later. The researcher says, "No, I discovered the drug, and I'm going to make money from it." Henry is desperate and considers stealing the drug for his wife.

What would you tell Henry to do?

KOHLBERG'S THEORY OF MORAL DEVELOPMENT

In the view of psychologist Lawrence Kohlberg, the advice you give Henry reflects your level of moral development. According to Kohlberg, people pass through a series of stages in the evolution of their sense of justice and in the kind of reasoning they use to make moral judgments (Kohlberg, 1984).

Specifically, Kohlberg suggests that changes in moral reasoning can be understood best as the three-level sequence described in Figure 2. Because of their cognitive limitations, preadolescent children who reason at Level 1 morality tend to think in terms of concrete, unvarying rules ("It is always wrong to steal" or "I'll be punished if I steal"). At Level 2 morality, older children tend to focus on the broad rules of society ("Good people don't steal" or "What if everyone stole?"). Those at Level 2 consider moral questions in terms of their own position as good and responsible members of society.

Adolescents, however, however, can reason on a higher plane and potentially have the ability to reason at Level 3. At Level 3, adolescents consider moral issues in terms of principles that are broader than the rules of individual societies. Because they can comprehend broad, universal moral principles, they understand that morality is not always black and white and that conflict can exist between two sets of socially accepted standards.

Kohlberg's theory assumes that people move through the levels in a fixed order and that they cannot reach the highest level until about age 13–primarily because of limitations in cognitive development before that age. However, many people never reach the highest level of moral reasoning. In fact, Kohlberg found that only a relatively small percentage of adults rise above the second level of his model (Kohlberg & Ryncarz, 1990; Moshman, 2011; Vera-Estay, Dooley, & Beauchamp, 2015).

Although Kohlberg's theory has had a substantial influence on our understanding of moral development, the research support is mixed. One difficulty with the theory

Level	Sample Moral Reasoning	
	In Favor of Stealing the Drug	**Against Stealing the Drug**
Level 1 Preconventional morality: The main considerations at this level are the avoidance of punishment and the desire for rewards.	"You shouldn't just let your wife die. People will blame you for not doing enough, and they'll blame the scientist for not selling you the drug for less money."	"You can't steal the drug because you'll be arrested and go to jail. Even if you aren't caught, you'll feel guilty, and you'll always worry that the police may figure out what you did."
Level 2 Conventional morality: Membership in society becomes important at this level. People behave in ways that will win the approval of others.	"Who will blame you if you steal a life-saving drug? But if you just let your wife die, you won't be able to hold your head up in front of your family or neighbors."	"If you steal the drug, everyone will treat you like a criminal. They will wonder why you couldn't have found some other way to save your wife."
Level 3 Postconventional morality: People accept that there are certain broad principles of morality that should govern our actions. These principles are more critical than the particular laws in a society.	"If you simply follow the law, you will violate the underlying principle of saving your wife's life. If you do steal the drug, society will understand your actions and respect them. You can't let an inadequate, outdated law prevent you from doing the right thing."	"You can't change your standards of honesty whenever it suits your needs. Others may not blame you for stealing the drug, but your conscience will blame you for betraying your own moral code."

FIGURE 2 Developmental psychologist Lawrence Kohlberg theorized that people move through a three-level sequence of moral reasoning in a fixed order. However, he contended that few people ever reach the highest level of moral reasoning.
Source: Adapted from Kohlberg, L. (1969). Stage and sequence: The cognitive-developmental approach to socialization. In D. Goslin (Ed.), *Handbook of socialization theory and research* (381–382). Chicago: Rand McNally; (photo): ©Steven Puetzer/Photograher's Choice/Getty Images

is that it pertains to moral *judgments*, not moral *behavior*. Knowing right from wrong does not mean that we will always act in accordance with our judgments. In addition, the theory applies primarily to Western society and its moral code; cross-cultural research conducted in cultures with different moral systems suggests that Kohlberg's theory is not necessarily applicable (Barandiaran, Pascual, & Samaniego, 2006; Stey, Lapsley, & McKeever, 2013; Buon, Habib, & Frey, 2017).

MORAL DEVELOPMENT IN WOMEN

One glaring shortcoming of Kohlberg's research is that he primarily used male participants. Furthermore, psychologist Carol Gilligan (1996) argues that because of men's and women's distinctive socialization experiences, a fundamental difference exists in the way each gender views moral behavior. According to Gilligan, men view morality primarily in terms of broad principles, such as justice and fairness. In contrast, women see it in terms of responsibility toward individuals and willingness to make sacrifices to help a specific individual within the context of a particular relationship. Compassion for individuals is a more salient factor in moral behavior for women than it is for men.

Because Kohlberg's model defines moral behavior largely in terms of abstract principles such as justice, Gilligan finds that it inadequately describes females' moral development. She suggests that women's morality centers on individual well-being and social relationships–a morality of *caring*. In her view, compassionate concern for the welfare of others represents the highest level of morality.

The fact that Gilligan's conception of morality differs greatly from Kohlberg's suggests that gender plays an important role in determining what a person sees as moral. Although the research evidence is not definitive, it seems plausible that their differing conceptions of what constitutes moral behavior may lead men and women to regard the morality of a specific behavior in different ways (Sherblom, 2008; Walker & Frimer, 2009; Capraro & Sippel, 2017).

Study Alert
The difference between the Kohlberg and Gilligan approaches to moral development is significant. Kohlberg's theory focuses on stages, and Gilligan's rests on gender differences.

Social Development: Finding One's Self in a Social World

"Who am I?" "How do I fit into the world?" "What is life all about?"

Questions such as these assume special significance during the teenage years as adolescents seek to find their place in the broader social world. As we will see, this quest takes adolescents along several routes.

ERIKSON'S THEORY OF PSYCHOSOCIAL DEVELOPMENT: THE SEARCH FOR IDENTITY

Erikson's theory of psychosocial development emphasizes the search for identity during the adolescent years. As noted earlier, psychosocial development encompasses the way people's understanding of themselves, one another, and the world around them changes during the course of development (Erikson, 1963).

The fifth stage of Erikson's theory (summarized, with the other stages, in Figure 3), the **identity-versus-role-confusion stage,** encompasses adolescence. During this stage, a time of major testing, people try to determine what is unique about themselves. They attempt to discover who they are, what their strengths are, and what kinds of roles they are best suited to play for the rest of their lives–in short, their **identity.** A person confused about the most appropriate role to play in life may lack a stable identity, adopt an unacceptable role such as that of a social deviant, or have difficulty maintaining close personal relationships later in life (Updegraff et al., 2004; Vleioras & Bosma, 2005; Goldstein, 2006).

During the identity-versus-role-confusion period, an adolescent feels pressure to identify what to do with his or her life. Because these pressures come at a time of major physical changes as well as important changes in what society expects of them, adolescents can find the period an especially difficult one. The identity-versus-role-confusion stage has another important characteristic: declining reliance on adults for information with a shift toward using the peer group as a source of social judgments. The peer group becomes increasingly important, enabling adolescents to form close, adultlike

identity-versus-role-confusion stage According to Erikson, a time in adolescence of major testing to determine one's unique qualities. (Module 38)

identity The distinguishing character of the individual: who each of us is, what our roles are, and what we are capable of. (Module 38)

Stage	Approximate Age	Positive Outcomes	Negative Outcomes
1. Trust-vs.-mistrust	Birth–1½ years	Feelings of trust from environmental support	Fear and concern regarding others
2. Autonomy-vs.-shame-and-doubt	1½–3 years	Self-suffciency if exploration is encouraged	Doubts about self, lack of independence
3. Initiative-vs.-guilt	3–6 years	Discovery of ways to initiate actions	Guilt from actions and thoughts
4. Industry-vs.-inferiority	6–12 years	Development of sense of competence	Feelings of inferiority, no sense of mastery
5. Identity-vs.-role-confusion	Adolescence	Awareness of uniqueness of self, knowledge of role to be followed	Inability to identify appropriate roles in life
6. Intimacy-vs.-isolation	Early adulthood	Development of loving, sexual relationships and close friendships	Fear of relationships with others
7. Generativity-vs.-stagnation	Middle adulthood	Sense of contribution to continuity of life	Trivialization of one's activities
8. Ego-integrity-vs.-despair	Late adulthood	Sense of unity in life's accomplishments	Regret over lost opportunities of life

FIGURE 3 Erikson's stages of psychosocial development. According to Erikson, people proceed through eight stages of psychosocial development across their lives. He suggested that each stage requires the resolution of a crisis or conflict and may produce both positive and negative outcomes. (photo): ©Jon Erikson/Science Source

relationships and helping them clarify their personal identities. According to Erikson, the identity-versus-role-confusion stage marks a pivotal point in psychosocial development, paving the way for continued growth and the future development of personal relationships.

During early adulthood, people enter the **intimacy-versus-isolation stage.** Spanning the period of early adulthood (from postadolescence to the early 30s), this stage focuses on developing close relationships with others. Difficulties during this stage result in feelings of loneliness and a fear of such relationships; successful resolution of the crises of this stage results in the possibility of forming relationships that are intimate on a physical, intellectual, and emotional level.

Development continues during middle adulthood as people enter the **generativity-versus-stagnation stage.** Generativity is the ability to contribute to one's family, community, work, and society, and to assist the development of the younger generation. Success in this stage results in a people feeling positive and optimistic about the continuity of life and their contribution to humanity. On the other hand, difficulties in this stage lead people to feel that their activities are trivial and unimportant and that their lives are stagnant. They may feel they have made poor choices.

Finally, the last stage of psychosocial development, the **ego-integrity-versus-despair stage,** spans later adulthood and continues until death. People in this stage ask themselves if they have lived a meaningful life. If they see their lives positively, they feel a sense of accomplishment; if not, they feel regret over a misspent life.

Notably, Erikson's theory suggests that development does not stop at adolescence but continues throughout adulthood. A substantial amount of research now confirms this view. For instance, a 22-year study by psychologist Susan Whitbourne found considerable support for the fundamentals of Erikson's theory; the study determined that psychosocial development continues through adolescence and adulthood. In sum, adolescence is not an end point but rather a way station on the path of psychosocial development (Whitbourne et al., 1992; McAdams et al., 1997).

Although Erikson's theory provides a broad outline of identity development, critics have pointed out that his approach is anchored in male-oriented concepts of individuality and competitiveness. In an alternative conception, psychologist Carol Gilligan suggests that women may develop identity through the establishment of relationships. In her view, a primary component of women's identity is the construction of caring networks among themselves and others (Gilligan, 2004).

STORMY ADOLESCENCE: MYTH OR REALITY?

Does puberty invariably foreshadow a stormy, rebellious period of adolescence?

At one time, psychologists thought that adolescence was a period filled with stress and unhappiness. Today, however, research shows that this characterization is largely a myth. The reality is that most young people pass through adolescence without great turmoil in their lives and that they get along with their parents reasonably well (Granic, Hollenstein, & Dishion, 2003; Steinberg, 2016).

Not that adolescence is completely calm! In most families with adolescents, the amount of arguing and bickering clearly rises. Most young teenagers, as part of their search for identity, experience tension between their attempts to become independent from their parents and their actual dependence on them. They may experiment with a range of behaviors and flirt with a variety of activities that their parents, and even society as a whole, find objectionable. Happily, though, for most families such tensions stabilize during middle adolescence—around age 15 or 16—and eventually decline around age 18 (Smetana, Daddis, & Chuang, 2003; Smetana, 2005; Hadiwijaya et al., 2017).

One reason for the increase in discord during adolescence appears to be the protracted period in which children stay at home with their parents. In prior historical periods—and in some non-Western cultures today—children leave home immediately after puberty and are considered adults. Today, however, sexually mature adolescents may spend as many as 7 or 8 years with their parents. Current social trends even

intimacy-versus-isolation stage
According to Erikson, a period during early adulthood that focuses on developing close relationships. (Module 38)

generativity-versus-stagnation stage
According to Erikson, a period in middle adulthood during which we take stock of our contributions to family and society. (Module 38)

ego-integrity-versus-despair stage
According to Erikson, a period from late adulthood until death during which we review life's accomplishments and failures. (Module 38)

Study Alert
The characterization of a stormy adolescence is a myth for most adolescents.

PsychTech
Adolescent use of social media such as Facebook is growing rapidly: 94% of teenagers use Facebook, and a quarter of them access their Facebook pages continuously throughout the day.

hint at an extension of the conflicts of adolescence beyond the teenage years because a significant number of young adults–known as *boomerang children*–return to live with their parents, typically for economic reasons, after leaving home for some period. Although some parents welcome the return of their children, others are less sympathetic, which opens the way to conflict (Bianchi & Casper, 2000; Lewin, 2003; Otters & Hollander, 2015).

Another source of strife with parents lies in the way adolescents think. Adolescence fosters *adolescent egocentrism,* a state of self-absorption in which a teenager views the world from his or her own point of view. Egocentrism leads adolescents to be highly critical of authority figures, unwilling to accept criticism, and quick to fault others. It also makes them believe that they are the center of everyone else's attention, which leads to self-consciousness.

Furthermore, adolescents develop *personal fables*–the belief that one's experience and beliefs are unique, exceptional, and shared by no one else. Such personal fables may make adolescents feel invulnerable to the risks that threaten others (Alberts, Elkind, & Ginsberg, 2007; Schwartz, Maynard, & Uzelac, 2008; Boeve-de Pauw, Donche, & Van Petegem, 2011).

Finally, parent-adolescent discord occurs because adolescents are much more apt to engage in risky behavior than they are later in life. In part, their riskiness is due to the immaturity of brain systems that regulate impulse control, some of which do not fully develop until people are in their mid-20s. Furthermore, adolescents have a greater tolerance for ambiguity and uncertainty, leading them to tolerate risks that adults would be less likely to accept (Steinberg, 2007; Steinberg, 2016).

ADOLESCENT SUICIDE

Although the vast majority of teenagers pass through adolescence without major psychological difficulties, some experience unusually severe psychological problems. Sometimes those problems become so extreme that adolescents take their own lives. Suicide is the third leading cause of death for adolescents (after accidents and homicide) in the United States. More teenagers and young adults die from suicide than from cancer, heart disease, AIDS, birth defects, stroke, pneumonia and influenza, and chronic lung disease combined (CDC, 2004b).

A teenager commits suicide every 90 minutes. Furthermore, the reported rate of suicide may actually be understated because medical personnel hesitate to report suicide as a cause of death. Instead, they frequently label a death as an accident in an effort to protect the survivors. Overall, as many as 200 adolescents may attempt suicide for every one who actually takes his or her own life (CDC, 2000; Brausch & Gutierrez, 2009).

Male adolescents are five times more likely to commit suicide than females are, although females *attempt* suicide more often than males do. The rate of adolescent suicide is significantly greater among whites than among nonwhites. On the other hand, Native Americans have the highest suicide rate of any ethnic group in the United States, and Asian Americans have the lowest rate (CDC, 2004b; Boden, Fergusson, & Horwood, 2007; Bossarte & Swahn, 2011).

Although the rate of suicide has slowly declined for adolescents, it is still higher than for any other age group except for the elderly. Some psychologists suggest that the sharp rise in stress that teenagers experience–in terms of academic and social pressure, alcoholism, drug abuse, and family difficulties–provokes the most troubled adolescents to take their own lives. However, that is not the whole story because the suicide rate for other age groups has remained fairly stable in the past few decades. It is unlikely that stress has increased only for adolescents and not for the rest of the population (Lubell et al., 2004; Valois, Zullig, & Hunter, 2013; Sood & Linker, 2017).

Although the question of why adolescent suicide rates are so high remains unanswered, several factors put adolescents at risk. One factor is depression, characterized by unhappiness, extreme fatigue, and–a variable that seems especially important–a

These young people are mourning the death of a peer who committed suicide. Why do you think the suicide rate among teenagers has risen significantly over the past few decades?

©RichLegg/E+/Getty Images

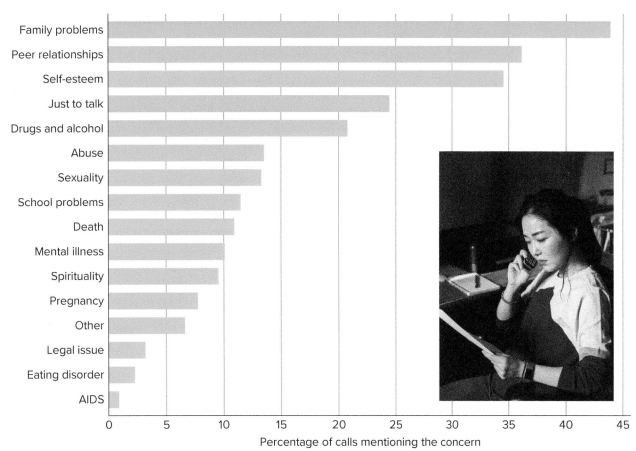

FIGURE 4 According to a review of phone calls to one telephone help line, adolescents who were considering suicide most often mentioned family, peer relationships, and self-esteem problems.

Source: Adapted from Boehm, K. E., & Campbell, N. B. (1995). Suicide: A review of calls to an adolescent peer listening phone service. *Child Psychiatry and Human Development, 26,* 61–66; (photo): ©10'000 Hours/DigitalVision/Getty Images

profound sense of hopelessness. In other cases, adolescents who commit suicide are perfectionists who are inhibited socially and prone to extreme anxiety when they face any social or academic challenge. Furthermore, in some cases, bullying, both in person and cyberbullying, may result in suicide (see Figure 4; Caelian, 2006; Barzilay et al., 2015; Young et al., 2017).

Family background and adjustment difficulties are also related to suicide. A long-standing history of conflicts between parents and children may lead to adolescent behavior problems, such as delinquency, dropping out of school, and aggressive tendencies. In addition, teenage alcoholics and abusers of other drugs have a relatively high rate of suicide (Winstead & Sanchez, 2005; Bagge & Sher, 2008; Hardt et al., 2008).

Several warning signs indicate when a teenager's problems may be severe enough to warrant concern about the possibility of a suicide attempt. They include the following:

- School problems, such as missing classes, truancy, and a sudden change in grades
- Frequent incidents of self-destructive behavior, such as careless accidents
- Loss of appetite or excessive eating
- Withdrawal from friends and peers
- Sleeping problems
- Signs of depression, tearfulness, or overt indications of psychological difficulties, such as hallucinations
- A preoccupation with death, an afterlife, or what would happen "if I died"

- Putting affairs in order, such as giving away prized possessions or making arrangements for the care of a pet
- An explicit announcement of thoughts of suicide

If you know someone who shows signs that he or she is suicidal, urge that person to seek professional help. You may need to take assertive action, such as enlisting the assistance of family members or friends. Talk of suicide is a serious signal for help and not a confidence to be kept.

For immediate help with a suicide-related problem, call (800) 273-8255, a national hotline staffed with trained counselors, or access www.suicidepreventionlifeline.org. You can also text 741741 to reach help.

From the perspective of...

A Social Worker How might you determine if an adolescent is at risk for suicide? What strategies would you use to prevent the teen from committing suicide? Would you use different strategies depending on the teenager's gender?

©Sam Edwards/age fotostock

 # Exploring Diversity

Rites of Passage: Coming of Age Around the World

It is not easy for male members of the Awa tribe in New Guinea to make the transition from childhood to adulthood. First come whippings with sticks and prickly branches both for the boys' own past misdeeds and in honor of those tribesmen who were killed in warfare. In the next phase of the ritual, adults jab sharpened sticks into the boys' nostrils. Then they force a 5-foot length of vine into the boys' throats until they gag and vomit. Finally, tribesmen cut the boys' genitals, causing severe bleeding.

Although the rites that mark the coming of age of boys in the Awa tribe sound horrifying to Westerners, they are comparable to those in other cultures. In some, youths must kneel on hot coals without displaying pain. In others, girls must toss wads of burning cotton from hand to hand and allow themselves to be bitten by hundreds of ants (Selsky, 1997).

Other cultures have less fearsome although equally important ceremonies that mark the passage from childhood to adulthood. For instance, when a girl first menstruates in traditional Apache tribes, the event is marked by dawn-to-dusk chanting. Western religions, too, have several types of celebrations, including bar mitzvahs and bat mitzvahs at age 13 for Jewish boys and girls, respectively, and confirmation ceremonies for children in many Christian denominations (Magida, 2006).

In most societies, males are the focus of coming-of-age ceremonies. The reason for this gender distinction may be that in most cultures, men traditionally have higher status than women, and therefore, those cultures regard boys' transition into adulthood as more important to celebrate.

However, another fact may explain why most cultures place greater emphasis on male rather than female rites: For females, the transition from childhood is marked by a definite biological event: menstruation. For males, in contrast, no single event can be used to pinpoint entry into adulthood. Thus, men are forced to rely on culturally determined rituals to acknowledge their arrival into adulthood.

AP MODULE 38: ADOLESCENCE: BECOMING AN ADULT

AP SUMMARY

- Adolescence is marked by the onset of puberty, the point at which sexual maturation occurs. The age at which puberty begins has implications for the way people view themselves and the way others see them.
- Most teenagers experience tension as they search for their identity and attempt independence from their parents. A rise in family conflict might be due to increased time living at home, adolescent egocentrism, personal fables, or the willingness to engage in risky behaviors.
- During early adulthood, individuals focus on developing close relationships with others on a physical, intellectual, and emotional level. Difficulties in this stage can lead to feelings of loneliness and fear of relationships.
- According to Erikson's model of psychosocial development, adolescence may be accompanied by an identity crisis. Adolescence is followed by three more stages: intimacy vs. isolation, generativity vs. stagnation, and ego-integrity vs. despair.
- Kohlberg theorized a three-level sequence of morals: preconventional, conventional, and postconventional.
- Gilligan suggested that women view morality in terms of caring for individuals rather than in terms of broad general principles of justice.
- Criticisms of Kohlberg's theory is that it pertains to moral judgments, not moral behaviors and the research pertains to males and Western cultures.

AP KEY TERMS

adolescence
puberty
identity-versus-role-
  confusion stage
identity

intimacy-versus-isolation
  stage
generativity-versus-
  stagnation stage
ego-integrity-versus-
  despair stage

AP TEST PRACTICE

Section I: Multiple Choice

1. Maturation of the sex organs occurs at what approximate age for girls?
   A. 7
   B. 9
   C. 11
   D. 13
   E. 14

2. What psychosocial stage is associated with contributing to family and work?
   A. Ego-integrity-versus-despair
   B. Generativity-versus-stagnation
   C. Intimacy-versus-isolation
   D. Industry-versus-inferiority
   E. Identity-versus-role-confusion

3. Carol Gilligan criticized Kohlberg's research for which of the following reasons?
   A. As children grow older, they can pay attention to stimuli longer than originally thought.
   B. Child-rearing is not the only determinant for well-adjusted children.
   C. Distinctive socialization processes determine each gender's moral behavior.
   D. Psychosocial development occurs during the entire lifespan, not just childhood.
   E. The age children can understand specific concepts and principles was underestimated.

Section II: Free Response

It was once believed that adolescence was universally a time of storm and stress. Describe how the following terms relate to the challenges faced in adolescence.
- Identity-versus-role-confusion
- Postconventional stage of moral development
- Adolescent egocentrism
- Personal fable

Module 39
Adulthood

- Characterize the development of decisions related to intimacy as people mature.

- Predict the physical and cognitive changes that emerge through the lifespan, including steps that can be taken to maximize function.

emerging adulthood The period beginning in the late teenage years and extending into the mid-20s. (Module 39)

I thought I got better as I got older. I found out that wasn't the case in a real hurry last year. After going 12 years in professional football and 12 years before that in amateur football without ever having surgery performed on me, the last two seasons of my career I went under the knife three times. It happened very quickly and without warning, and I began to ask myself, "Is this age? Is this what's happening?" Because up until that moment, I'd never realized that I was getting older. (Kotre & Hall, 1990)

As a former professional football player, Brian Sipe intensely felt the changes in his body brought about by aging. But the challenges he experienced are part of a normal process that affects all people as they move through adulthood.

Psychologists generally agree that early adulthood begins around age 20 and lasts until about age 40 to 45, when middle adulthood begins and continues until around age 65. Despite the enormous importance of these periods of life in terms of both the accomplishments that occur in them and their overall length (together they span some 44 years), they have been studied less than has any other stage. For one reason, the physical changes that occur during these periods are less apparent and more gradual than those at other times during the life span. In addition, the diverse social changes that arise during this period defy simple categorization.

The variety of changes that occur in early adulthood have led many developmental psychologists to view the start of the period as a transitional phase called emerging adulthood. **Emerging adulthood** is the period beginning in the late teenage years and extending into the mid-20s.

During emerging adulthood, people are no longer adolescents, although the brain is still growing and modifying its neural pathways. It is typically a period of uncertainty in which postadolescents haven't fully taken on the responsibilities of adulthood. Instead, they are still engaged in determining who they are and what their life and career paths should be. It is a time of uncertainty and instability, as well as self-discovery (Bukobza, 2009; Lamborn & Groh, 2009; Schwartz et al., 2013).

The view that adulthood is preceded by an extended period of emerging adulthood reflects the reality of the economies of industrialized countries. These economies have shifted away from manufacturing to a focus on technology and information, thus requiring increasing time spent in educational training. Furthermore, the age at which most people marry and have children has risen significantly (Arnett, 2007, 2011).

There's also an increasing ambivalence about reaching adulthood. When people in their late teens and early 20s are asked if they feel they have reached adulthood, most say "yes and no" (see Figure 1). In short, emerging adulthood is an age of identity exploration in which individuals are more self-focused and uncertain than they will be later in early adulthood (Arnett, 2000, 2006; Verschueren et al., 2017).

As we discuss the changes that occur through emerging adulthood, early adulthood, middle adulthood, and ultimately late adulthood, keep in mind the demarcations between the periods are fuzzy. However, the changes are certainly no less profound than they were in earlier periods of development.

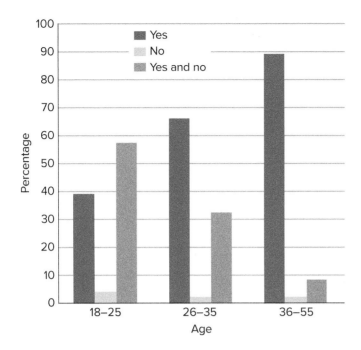

FIGURE 1 Evidence of a period of emerging adulthood is provided by the responses to a questionnaire asking, "Do you feel that you have reached adulthood?" Most people between the ages of 18 and 25 were ambivalent, responding "yes and no." Later, this ambivalence disappeared, with most people 26–35 saying "yes."

Source: Adapted from Arnett, J. J. (2006). *Emerging adulthood: The winding road from the late teens through the twenties.* New York: Oxford University Press.

Physical Development: The Peak of Health

For most people, early adulthood marks the peak of physical health. From about 18 to 25 years of age, people's strength is greatest, their reflexes are quickest, and their chances of dying from disease are quite slim. Moreover, reproductive capabilities are at their highest level.

Around age 25, the body becomes slightly less efficient and more susceptible to disease. Overall, however, ill health remains the exception; most people stay remarkably healthy during early adulthood. (Can you think of any machine other than the body that can operate without pause for so long a period?)

During middle adulthood, people gradually become aware of changes in their bodies. They often experience weight gain (although they can avoid such increases through diet and exercise). Furthermore, the sense organs gradually become less sensitive, and reactions to stimuli are slower. But generally, the physical declines that occur during middle adulthood are minor and often unnoticeable (DiGiovanna, 1994). The major biological change that does occur during middle adulthood pertains to reproductive capabilities. On average, during their late 40s or early 50s, women begin **menopause,** during which they stop menstruating and are no longer fertile. Because menopause is accompanied by a significant reduction in the production of estrogen, a female hormone, women sometimes experience symptoms such as hot flashes, sudden sensations of heat. Many symptoms can be treated through *hormone therapy (HT)* in which menopausal women take the hormones estrogen and progesterone.

However, hormone therapy poses several dangers, such as an increase in the risk of breast cancer, blood clots, and coronary heart disease. These uncertainties make the routine use of HT controversial. Currently, the medical consensus seems to be that younger women with severe menopausal symptoms ought to consider HT on a short-term basis. On the other hand, HT is less appropriate for older women after menopause (MacLennan, 2009; McCarrey & Resnick, 2015).

Menopause was once blamed for a variety of psychological symptoms, including depression and memory loss. However, if such difficulties occur, they may be caused

menopause The period during which women stop menstruating and are no longer fertile. (Module 39)

Women's reactions to menopause vary significantly across cultures. According to one study, the more a society values old age, the less difficulty its women have during menopause. Why do you think this would be the case?

©BananaStock/Alamy Stock Photo

by women's expectations about reaching an "old" age in a society that highly values youth. For example, women's reactions to menopause vary significantly across cultures. The more a society values old age, the less difficulty its women have during menopause (Elliott, Berman, & Kim, 2002; Beyene, Gilliss, & Lee, 2007; Espinola, DeVinney & Steinberg, 2017).

For men, the aging process during middle adulthood is somewhat subtler. There are no physiological signals of increasing age equivalent to the end of menstruation in women; that is, no male menopause exists. In fact, men remain fertile and capable of fathering children until well into late adulthood. However, some gradual physical decline occurs. Sperm production decreases, and the frequency of orgasm tends to decline. Once again, though, any psychological difficulties associated with these changes are usually brought about by an aging individual's inability to meet the exaggerated standards of youthfulness and not by the person's physical deterioration.

Social Development: Working at Life

Whereas physical changes during adulthood reflect development of a quantitative nature, social developmental transitions are qualitative and more profound. During this period, people typically launch themselves into careers, marriage, and families.

The entry into early adulthood is usually marked by leaving one's childhood home and entering the world of work. People envision life goals and make career choices. Their lives often center on their careers, which form an important part of their identity (Vaillant & Vaillant, 1990; Levinson, 1990, 1992).

In their early 40s, however, people may begin to question their lives as they enter a period called the *midlife transition*. The idea that life will end at some point can become more influential in their thinking, which leads them to question their past accomplishments (Gould, 1978; Boylan & Ryff, 2015).

Although some psychologists–and popular opinion–suggest that physical aging and dissatisfaction with one's life mark a so-called "midlife crisis," there is little evidence for such a "crisis." In fact, the passage into middle age is relatively calm for most people. Most 40-year-olds view their lives and accomplishments positively enough to proceed relatively smoothly through midlife, and the 40s and 50s are often a particularly rewarding period. Rather than looking to the future, people concentrate on the present; their involvement with their families, friends, and other social groups takes on new importance. A major developmental thrust of this period is coming to terms with one's circumstances (Whitbourne, 2010; Dare, 2011; Wojciechowska, 2017).

Finally, during the last stages of adulthood, people become more accepting of others and of their own lives and are less concerned about issues or problems that once bothered them. They come to accept the fact that death is inevitable, and they try to understand their accomplishments in terms of the broader meaning of life. Although people may begin for the first time to label themselves as "old," many also develop a sense of wisdom and feel freer to enjoy life (Miner-Rubino, Winter, & Stewart, 2004; Ward-Baker, 2007; Galambos et al., 2015).

Marriage, Children, and Divorce: Family Ties

In the typical fairy tale, a dashing young man and a beautiful young woman marry, have children, and live happily ever after. However, that scenario does not match the realities of love and marriage in the 21st century. Today, it is just as likely that the man and woman would first live together, then get married and have children, but ultimately get divorced.

The percentage of U.S. households made up of unmarried couples has increased dramatically over the last two decades. At the same time, the average age at which marriage takes place is higher than at any time since the turn of the last century. These changes have been dramatic, and they suggest that the institution of marriage has changed considerably from earlier historical periods.

When people do marry, the probability of divorce is high, especially for younger couples. Even though divorce rates have been declining since they peaked in 1981, about half of all first marriages end in divorce. Before they are 18 years old, two-fifths of children will experience the breakup of their parents' marriages. Moreover, the rise in divorce is not just a U.S. phenomenon: The divorce rate has accelerated over the past several decades in most industrialized countries. In some countries, the increase has been enormous. In South Korea, for example, the divorce rate quadrupled from 11% to 47% in the 12-year period ending in 2002 (Lankov, 2004; Olson & DeFrain, 2005; Park & Raymo, 2013).

Changes in marriage and divorce trends have doubled the number of single-parent households in the United States over the last two decades. Almost 25% of all family households are now headed by one parent, compared with 13% in 1970. If present trends continue, almost three-fourths of American children will spend some portion of their lives in a single-parent family before they turn 18. For children in minority households, the numbers are even higher. Almost 60% of all African American children and more than a third of all Hispanic children live in homes with only one parent. Furthermore, in most single-parent families, the children live with the mother rather than the father—a phenomenon that is consistent across racial and ethnic groups throughout the industrialized world (U.S. Bureau of the Census, 2000; Sarsour et al., 2011).

What are the economic and emotional consequences for children living in homes with only one parent? Single-parent families are often economically less well off, and this economic disadvantage has an impact on children's opportunities. More than a third of single-mother families with children have incomes below the poverty line. In addition, good child care at an affordable price is often hard to find. Furthermore, for children of divorce, the parents' separation is often a painful experience that may result in obstacles to establishing close relationships later in life. Children may blame themselves for the breakup or feel pressure to take sides (U.S. Bureau of the Census, 2000; Wallerstein et al., 2000; Liu, He, & Wu, 2007).

Most evidence suggests, however, that children from single-parent families are no less well adjusted than are those from two-parent families. In fact, children may be more successful growing up in a harmonious single-parent family than in a two-parent family that engages in continuous conflict (Kelly, 2000; Olson & DeFrain, 2005; Koh et al., 2017).

Changing Roles of Men and Women

One of the major changes in family life in the last two decades has been the evolution of men's and women's roles. More women than ever before act simultaneously as wives, mothers, and wage earners—in contrast to women in traditional marriages in which the husband is the sole wage earner and the wife assumes primary responsibility for care of the home and children.

Almost three-fourths of all women with children under the age of 18 are employed outside the home, and 65% of mothers with children under age 6 are working. In the mid-1960s, only 17% of mothers of 1-year-olds worked full-time; now, more than half are in the labor force (Bureau of Labor Statistics, 2013).

Most married working women are not free of household responsibilities. Even in marriages in which the spouses hold jobs that have similar status and require similar hours, the distribution of household tasks between husbands and wives has not changed substantially. Working wives are still more likely than husbands to feel responsible for traditional homemaking tasks such as cooking and cleaning. In contrast, husbands still view themselves as responsible primarily for household tasks such as repairing broken appliances and doing yardwork (Juster, Ono, & Stafford, 2002; Damaske, 2011).

WOMEN'S "SECOND SHIFT"

Working mothers can put in a staggering number of hours. One survey, for instance, found that if we add the number of hours worked on the job and in the home, employed mothers of children under 3 years of age put in an average of 90 hours per week! The additional work women perform is sometimes called the "second shift." National surveys show women who are both employed and mothers put in an extra month of 24-hour days during the course of a year. Researchers see similar patterns in many developing societies throughout the world, with women working at full-time jobs and also having primary responsibilities for child care (Hochschild, 2001; Jacobs & Gerson, 2004; U.S. Bureau of Labor Statistics, 2007).

Consequently, rather than careers being a substitute for what women do at home, they are often an addition to the role of homemaker. It is not surprising that some wives feel resentment toward husbands who spend less time on child care and housework than the wives had expected before the birth of their children (Kiecolt, 2003; Gerstel, 2005; Fagan & Press, 2008).

Later Years of Life: Growing Old

I've always enjoyed doing things in the mountains–hiking or, more recently, active cliff-climbing. The more difficult the climb, the more absorbing it is. The climbs I really remember are the ones I had to work on. Maybe a particular section where it took two or three tries before I found the right combination of moves that got me up easily–and, preferably, elegantly. It's a wonderful exhilaration to get to the top and sit down and perhaps have lunch and look out over the landscape and be so grateful that it's still possible for me to do that sort of thing. (Lyman Spitzer, age 74, quoted in Kotre & Hall, 1990)

If you can't quite picture a 74-year-old rock-climbing, some rethinking of your view of late adulthood may be in order. In spite of the societal stereotype of "old age" as a time of inactivity and physical and mental decline, gerontologists, specialists who study aging, are beginning to paint a very different portrait of late adulthood.

By focusing on the period of life that starts at around age 65, gerontologists are making important contributions to clarifying the capabilities of older adults. Their work is demonstrating that significant developmental processes continue even during old age. And as people live longer, the absolute numbers of people within older adulthood will continue to increase (see Figure 2). Consequently, developing an understanding of late adulthood has become a critical priority for psychologists (Schaie, 2005b; Jia, Zack, & Thompson, 2011).

Physical Changes in Late Adulthood: The Aging Body

Napping, eating, walking, conversing. It probably doesn't surprise you that these relatively nonstrenuous activities represent the typical pastimes of late adulthood. But it is striking that these activities are identical to the most common leisure activities

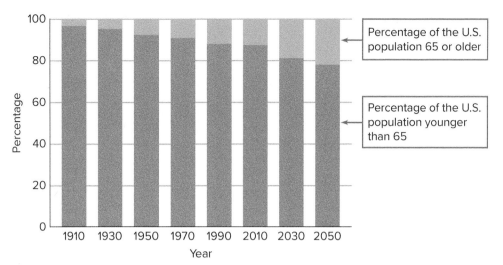

FIGURE 2 Projections suggest that by the year 2050, more than 20% of the U.S. population will be over age 65. What implications does this statistic have for U.S. society?

reported in a survey of college students (Harper, 1978). Although the students cited more active pursuits–such as sailing and playing basketball–as their favorite activities, in actuality they engaged in such sports relatively infrequently and spent most of their free time napping, eating, walking, and conversing.

Although the leisure activities in which older adults engage may not differ all that much from the ones that younger people pursue, many physical changes are, of course, brought about by the aging process. The most obvious are those of appearance–hair thinning and turning gray, skin wrinkling and folding, and sometimes a slight loss of height as the thickness of the disks between vertebrae in the spine decreases. But subtler changes also occur in the body's biological functioning. For example, sensory capabilities decrease as a result of aging: Vision, hearing, smell, and taste become less sensitive. Reaction time slows, and physical stamina changes (Schieber, 2006; Madden, 2007; Schilling & Diehl, 2015).

What are the reasons for these physical declines? **Genetic programming theories of aging** suggest that the DNA genetic code includes a built-in time limit for the reproduction of human cells. These theories suggest that after a certain time cells stop dividing or become harmful to the body–as if a kind of automatic self-destruct button had been pushed. In contrast, **wear-and-tear theories of aging** suggest that the mechanical functions of the body simply work less efficiently as people age. Waste by-products of energy production eventually accumulate, and mistakes are made when cells divide. Eventually, the body in effect wears out like an old automobile (Miquel, 2006; Hayflick, 2007; Helgeson & Zajdel, 2017).

Evidence supports both the genetic programming and the wear-and-tear views, and it may be that both processes contribute to natural aging. It is clear, however, that physical aging is not a disease but a natural biological process. Many physical functions do not decline with age. For example, sex remains pleasurable well into old age (although the frequency of sexual activity decreases), and some people report that the pleasure they derive from sex increases during late adulthood (Gelfand, 2000; DeLamater & Sill, 2005; Wilkin & Haddock, 2011).

Cognitive Changes: Thinking About— and During—Late Adulthood

At one time, many gerontologists would have agreed with the popular view that older adults are forgetful and confused. Today, however, most research indicates that this assessment is far from an accurate one of older people's capabilities.

One reason for the change in view is that more sophisticated research techniques exist for studying the cognitive changes that occur in late adulthood. For

genetic programming theories of aging Theories that suggest that our DNA genetic code includes a built-in time limit to the reproduction of human cells and that they are no longer able to divide after a certain time. (Module 39)

wear-and-tear theories of aging Theories that suggest that the mechanical functions of the body simply stop working efficiently. (Module 39)

Study Alert

Two major theories of aging—the genetic programming and the wear-and-tear views—explain some of the physical changes that take place in older adults.

example, if we were to give a group of older adults an IQ test, we might find that the average score was lower than the score achieved by a group of younger people. We might conclude that this signifies a decline in intelligence. Yet, if we looked a little more closely at the specific test, we might find that the conclusion was unwarranted. For instance, many IQ tests include portions based on physical performance (such as arranging a group of blocks) or on speed. In such cases, poorer performance on the IQ test may be due to gradual decreases in reaction time—a physical decline that accompanies late adulthood and has little or nothing to do with older adults' intellectual capabilities.

Other difficulties hamper research into cognitive functioning during late adulthood. For example, older people are often less healthy than younger ones; when only *healthy* older adults are compared to healthy younger adults, intellectual differences are far less evident. Furthermore, the average number of years in school is often lower in older adults (for historical reasons) than in younger ones, and older adults may be less motivated to perform well on intelligence tests than younger people are. Finally, traditional IQ tests may be inappropriate measures of intelligence in late adulthood. Older adults sometimes perform better on tests of practical intelligence than younger individuals do (Dixon & Cohen, 2003; Johnson & Deary, 2011).

Still, some declines in intellectual functioning during late adulthood do occur, although the pattern of age differences is not uniform for different types of cognitive abilities (see Figure 3). In general, skills relating to *fluid intelligence* (which involves information-processing skills such as memory, calculations, and analogy solving) show declines in late adulthood. In contrast, skills relating to *crystallized intelligence* (intelligence based on the accumulation of information, skills, and strategies learned through experience) remain steady and in some cases actually improve (van Hooren, Valentijn, & Bosma, 2007; Kaufman, Johnson, & Liu, 2008; Dixon et al., 2013).

Even when changes in intellectual functioning occur during later adulthood, people often are able to compensate for any decline. They can still learn what they want to learn; it may just take more time. Furthermore, teaching older adults strategies for dealing with new problems can prevent declines in performance (Cavallini, Pagnin, & Vecchi, 2003; Peters et al., 2007; Finke, Howe, & Huston, 2017).

FIGURE 3 Age-related changes in intellectual skills vary according to the specific cognitive ability in question.

Source: Adapted from Schaie, K. W. (2005). Longitudinal studies. In Schaie, K. W., *Developmental influences on adult intelligence: The Seattle Longitudinal Study.* New York: Oxford University Press.

Although fluid intelligence declines in late adulthood, skills relating to crystallized intelligence remain steady and may actually improve.
©icsnaps/Shutterstock

MEMORY CHANGES IN LATE ADULTHOOD: ARE OLDER ADULTS FORGETFUL?

One of the characteristics most frequently attributed to late adulthood is forgetfulness. How accurate is this assumption?

Most evidence suggests that memory change is not an inevitable part of the aging process. For instance, older people in cultures in which older adults are held in high esteem, such as China, are less likely to show memory losses than are those living in cultures in which the expectation is that memory will decline. Similarly, when older people in Western societies are reminded of the advantages of age (for example, "age brings wisdom"), they tend to do better on tests of memory (Levy, 1996; Dixon, Rust, & Feltmate, 2007; Pinal, Zurrón, & Díaz, 2015).

Even when people show memory declines during late adulthood, their deficits are limited to certain types of memory. For instance, losses tend to be limited to episodic memories that relate to specific experiences in people's lives. Other types of memories, such as semantic memories (those that refer to general knowledge and facts) and implicit memories (memories of which we are not consciously aware), are largely unaffected by age (Mitchell & Schmitt, 2006; St. Jacques & Levine, 2007; Blumen, Rajaram, & Henkel, 2013).

Declines in episodic memories can often be traced to changes in older adults' lives. For instance, it is not surprising that a retired person, who may no longer face the same kind of consistent intellectual challenges encountered on the job, may have less practice in using memory or even be less motivated to remember things, which leads to an apparent decline in memory. Even in cases in which long-term memory declines, older adults can profit from training that targets memory skills (West, Bagwell, & Dark-Freudeman, 2007; Morcom & Friston, 2011; Després et al., 2017).

In the past, older adults with severe cases of memory decline accompanied by other cognitive difficulties were said to suffer from *senility*. Now, most gerontologists view senility as an imprecise label that has outlived its usefulness. Instead, gerontologists explain symptoms of mental deterioration using more precise factors.

For example, rather than use *senility* to describe memory loss in general, gerontologists now recognize **Alzheimer's disease** as a progressive brain disorder that leads to a gradual and irreversible decline in cognitive abilities. More than 5.5 million Americans have the disease, and 1 in 10 people age 65 and older are afflicted. Unless a cure

Alzheimer's disease A progressive brain disorder that leads to a gradual and irreversible decline in cognitive abilities. (Modules 22, 39)

is found, some 11 million people are expected to have Alzheimer's in 2050 (Rogers, 2007; Alzheimer's Association, 2017).

Alzheimer's occurs when production of the *beta amyloid precursor protein* goes awry, producing large clumps of cells that trigger inflammation and deterioration of nerve cells. The brain shrinks, neurons die, and several areas of the hippocampus and frontal and temporal lobes deteriorate. So far, there is no effective treatment, although preliminary research suggests that diet, exercise, and an active social life can slow the decline in cognitive capabilities brought on by Alzheimer's (Medeiros et al., 2007; Behrens, Lendon, & Roe, 2009; Kivipelto & Hakansson, 2017.)

In other cases, cognitive declines may be caused by temporary anxiety and depression, which can be treated successfully, or may even be due to overmedication. The danger is that people with such symptoms may be left untreated, thereby continuing their decline (Sachs-Ericsson et al., 2005; Diniz et al., 2013).

In sum, declines in cognitive functioning in late adulthood are, for the most part, not inevitable. The key to maintaining cognitive skills may lie in intellectual stimulation. Like the rest of us, older adults need a stimulating environment in order to hone and maintain their skills (Bosma et al., 2003; Glisky, 2007; Hertzog et al., 2008; also see *Applying Psychology in the 21st Century*).

Study Alert

It's important to be able to describe the nature of intellectual changes during late adulthood.

AP｜ APPLYING PSYCHOLOGY IN THE 21ST CENTURY

HOW DO COGNITIVE ABILITIES RISE AND FALL AS WE AGE?

Common wisdom holds that young adults are quick-witted and that cognitive faculties decline over the lifespan until old age brings slow-minded confusion. This, however, is largely a myth, as only a moment of thought would suggest. The mind doesn't simply start out strong and weaken with age. A longer lifetime of experience typically means that older adults have a wider and deeper body of knowledge, and indeed, older adults tend to perform better on tests of crystallized intelligence than do younger adults. Younger adults, on the other hand, tend to do better on tests of fluid intelligence. So "what you know" tends to improve with age, but "figuring things out" peaks early.

At least this was the picture until recently. Intriguing new research conducted on nearly 50,000 participants via a battery of online tests of cognitive functioning suggests a more complex and nuanced perspective on changes over the lifespan. Rather than lumping together multiple tests results into composite scores on fluid intelligence and crystallized intelligence, as is often done, the researchers

©cwa/Alamy Stock Photo

analyzed performance on individual tests and found that different cognitive abilities develop in different ways (Hartshorne & Germine, 2015).

For example, the researchers showed that mental manipulation–a measure of fluid intelligence–reaches its peak in the late teen years and then quickly declines, which is consistent with other research. But they found that performance on short-term

memory tasks, such as remembering people's names, peaks in the mid-20s and remains strong until the mid-30s. Working memory capacity, however–the size of the work space in memory–doesn't peak until the 30s. In one particularly novel test included by these researchers, subjects were asked to determine a person's mood from just a photograph of his or her eyes–a vague and difficult judgment to make. Performance on this test didn't peak until around midlife and remained strong thereafter. And one test of crystallized intelligence–a vocabulary test–didn't show that skill peaking until the late 60s.

"At any given age, you're getting better at some things, you're getting worse at some other things, and you're at a plateau at some other things. There's probably not one age at which you're peak on most things, much less all of them," said Joshua Hartshorne, one of the researchers (Trafton, 2015, p. 8).

AP SKILL: SCIENTIFIC INVESTIGATION / EXPLAIN BEHAVIOR IN AUTHENTIC CONTEXT

1. Historically, what type of research methods have been used to study crystallized and fluid intelligence?
2. Declines in cognitive functioning are not inevitable. What explains the differences in cognitive abilities and how can one maintain their cognitive abilities?

THE SOCIAL WORLD OF LATE ADULTHOOD: OLD BUT NOT ALONE

Just as the view that old age predictably means mental decline has proved to be wrong, so has the view that late adulthood inevitably brings loneliness. People in late adulthood most often see themselves as functioning members of society; only a small number of them report that loneliness is a serious problem (Berkman, Ertel, & Glymour, 2011; Luong, Rauers & Fingerman, 2015).

Certainly, late adulthood brings significant challenges. People who have spent their adult lives working and then enter retirement bring about a major shift in the roles they play. Moreover, many people must face the death of their spouse. Especially if the marriage has been a long and good one, the death of a partner means the loss of a companion, confidante, and lover. It can also bring about changes in economic well-being.

There is no single way to age successfully, and several theories have been developed to describe the process. According to the **disengagement theory of aging,** aging is characterized by a gradual withdrawal from the world. In this view, as people get older, they separate themselves from others on physical, psychological, and social levels. In this view, such disengagement is appropriate and even beneficial. The reason is that disengagement serves the purpose of providing an opportunity for increased reflectiveness and decreased emotional investment in others at a time of life when social relationships will inevitably be ended by death (Adams, 2004; Wrosch, Bauer, & Scheier, 2005).

However, only a little research supports the disengagement theory of aging, and alternative theories have been suggested. The major alternative is the activity theory of aging. According to the **activity theory of aging,** people who age most successfully are those who maintain the interests, activities, and level of social interaction they experienced during their earlier periods of adulthood. Activity theory argues that people who are aging effectively show a continuation of the activities in which they participated during the earlier part of their lives (Crosnoe & Elder, 2002; Nimrod & Kleiber, 2007; Roos & Zaaiman, 2017).

Most research supports the activity theory of aging. On the other hand, not all people in late adulthood need a life filled with activities and social interaction to be happy. As in every stage of life, some older adults are just as satisfied leading a relatively inactive, solitary existence. What may be more important is how people view the aging process: Evidence shows that positive self-perceptions of aging are associated with increased longevity (Levy et al., 2002; Levy & Myers, 2004).

Regardless of how people age, most engage in a process of **life review** in which they examine and evaluate their lives. Remembering and reconsidering what has occurred in the past, people in late adulthood often come to a better understanding of themselves. They sometimes resolve lingering problems and conflicts, and face their lives with greater wisdom and serenity.

Clearly, people in late adulthood are not just marking time until death. Rather, old age is a time of continued growth and development as important as any other period of life.

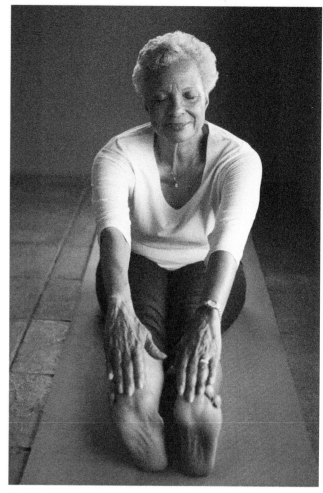

Maintaining interests and activities one had during middle age can contribute to a more successful late adulthood, according to the activity theory of aging.
©Jupiterimages/Getty Images

disengagement theory of aging The theory that suggests that successful aging is characterized by a gradual withdrawal from the world on physical, psychological, and social levels. (Module 39)

activity theory of aging The theory that suggests that successful aging is characterized by maintaining the interests and activities of earlier stages of life. (Module 39)

life review The process by which people examine and evaluate their lives. (Module 39)

From the perspective of...

A Health-Care Provider What sorts of recommendations would you make to your older patients about how to deal with aging? How would you handle someone who believed that getting older had only negative consequences?

©Tetra Images/Getty Images

BECOMING AN INFORMED CONSUMER

of Psychology

Adjusting to Death

At some time in our lives, we all face death—certainly our own as well as the deaths of friends, loved ones, and even strangers. Although there is nothing more inevitable in life, death remains a frightening, emotion-laden topic. Certainly, little is more stressful than the death of a loved one or the contemplation of our own imminent death, and preparing for death is one of our most crucial developmental tasks (Aiken, 2000).

A few generations ago, talk of death was taboo. The topic was never mentioned to dying people, and gerontologists had little to say about it. That changed, however, with the pioneering work of Elisabeth Kübler-Ross (1969), who brought the subject of death into the open with her observation that those facing impending death tend to move through five broad stages:

- *Denial.* In this stage, people resist the idea that they are dying. Even if told that their chances for survival are small, they refuse to admit that they are facing death.
- *Anger.* After moving beyond the denial stage, dying people become angry—angry at people around them who are in good health, angry at medical professionals for being ineffective, angry at God.
- *Bargaining.* Anger leads to bargaining in which the dying try to think of ways to postpone death. They may decide to dedicate their lives to religion if God saves them. They may say, "If only I can live to see my son married, I will accept death then."
- *Depression.* When dying people come to feel that bargaining is no use, they move to the next stage: depression. They realize that their lives really are coming to an end, which leads to what Kübler-Ross calls "preparatory grief" for their own deaths.
- *Acceptance.* In this stage, people accept impending death. Usually they are unemotional and uncommunicative; it is as if they have made peace with themselves and are expecting death with no bitterness.

It is important to keep in mind that not everyone experiences each of these stages in the same way. In fact, Kübler-Ross's stages pertain only to people who are fully aware that they are dying and have the time to evaluate their impending death. Furthermore, vast differences occur in the way individuals react to impending death. The specific cause and duration of dying, as well as the person's sex, age, personality, and the type of support received from family and friends, all have an impact on how people respond to death (Carver & Scheier, 2002; Coyle, 2006).

Few of us enjoy the contemplation of death. Yet awareness of its psychological aspects and consequences can make its inevitable arrival less anxiety producing and perhaps more understandable.

AP MODULE 39: ADULTHOOD

AP SUMMARY

- Among the important developmental milestones during adulthood are marriage, children, and divorce.
- Early adulthood marks the peak of physical health. Physical changes occur relatively gradually in men and women during middle adulthood. At the end of middle adulthood, women begin menopause.
- Early adulthood is associated with work. During middle adulthood, people typically experience a midlife transition. During late adulthood individuals become more accepting of others and of their own life.
- Old age may bring marked physical declines caused by genetic programming or physical wear and tear. Older adults experience declines in reaction time, sensory abilities, and physical stamina.
- Fluid intelligence declines with age, and long-term memory abilities are sometimes impaired. In contrast, crystallized intelligence shows slight increases, and short-term memory remains constant. Memory loss with age tends to be specific to episodic memory. Cognitive declines may be from temporary conditions, senility, or Alzheimer's disease.
- Although disengagement theory sees successful aging as a process of gradual withdrawal from the world, there is little research supporting this view. Instead, activity theory is a more accurate explanation.
- According to Kübler-Ross, dying people move through five stages as they face death: denial, anger, bargaining, depression, and acceptance.

AP KEY TERMS

emerging adulthood
menopause
genetic programming
  theories of aging
wear-and-tear theories
  of aging

Alzheimer's disease
disengagement theory
  of aging
activity theory of aging
life review

AP TEST PRACTICE

Section I: Multiple Choice

1. When individuals show memory decline in late adulthood, their deficits are limited to what type of memory?
   A. Implicit
   B. Semantic
   C. Episodic
   D. Working
   E. Crystallized

2. The period during which women are no longer fertile is known as
   A. midlife transition
   B. menopause
   C. menarche
   D. adolescence
   E. emerging adulthood

3. Rob recently turned 40 and surveyed his goals to date. He has accomplished a lot, but he realized that many of his goals will not be met in his lifetime. This stage is called
   A. bargaining
   B. denial
   C. intimacy
   D. emerging adulthood
   E. midlife transition

Section II: Free Response

Compare milestones in early adulthood, middle adulthood, and late adulthood for each type of development listed below.
- Physical
- Cognitive
- Social

LOOKING *Back*

EPILOGUE

We have traced major events in the development of physical, social, and cognitive growth throughout the life span. Clearly, people change throughout their lives.

As we explored each area of development, we encountered anew the nature–nurture issue, concluding in every significant instance that both nature and nurture contribute to a person's development of skills, personality, and interactions. Specifically, our genetic inheritance—nature—lays down general boundaries within which we can advance and grow; our environment—nurture—helps determine the extent to which we take advantage of our potential.

VISUAL SUMMARY 12 Development

MODULES 35 and 36

Nature and Nurture; Prenatal Development

Developmental Research Techniques
- Cross-sectional, longitudinal, sequential

Basics of Genetics: Chromosomes and genes

Earliest Development
- Zygote: a fertilized egg
- Embryo: between 2 and 8 weeks old after conception
- Fetus: between 8 weeks and birth
- Age of viability: about 22 weeks from conception

Nature and Nurture
- Nature: Refers to hereditary factors
- Nurture: Refers to environmental influences

MODULE 37 Infancy and Childhood

The Extraordinary Newborn
- Reflexes: Rooting, sucking, gag, Babinski
- Development of the senses

Infancy through Middle Childhood, about age 12
- Physical development: rapid growth
- Social development
  - Attachment: positive emotional bond between child and caregiver
  - Ainsworth strange situation
  - Social relationships with peers
  - Child care outside the home
  - Four parenting styles
  - Erikson's theory of psychosocial development
    - Trust-versus-mistrust stage: birth to age 1½
    - Autonomy-versus-shame-and-doubt stage: ages 1½ to 3
    - Initiative-versus-guilt stage: ages 3 to 6
    - Industry-versus-inferiority stage: ages 6 to 12
  - Cognitive development
    - Piaget's theory of cognitive development

Cognitive Stage	Approximate Age Range	Major Characteristics
Sensorimotor	Birth–2 years	Development of object permanence, development of motor skills, little or no capacity for symbolic representation
Preoperational thinking	2–7 years	Development of language and symbolic thinking, egocentric
Concrete operational mastery	7–12 years	Development of conservation, of concept of reversibility
Formal operational	12 years–adulthood	Development of logical and abstract thinking

  - Information processing approaches

MODULE 38 Adolescence: Becoming an Adult

Physical Development: Rapid weight and height gains; onset of puberty

Moral Development: Changes in moral reasoning

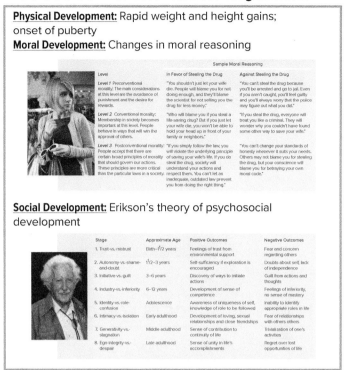

Sample Moral Reasoning		
Level	**In Favor of Stealing the Drug**	**Against Stealing the Drug**
Level 1 Preconventional morality: The main considerations at this level are the avoidance of punishment and the desire for rewards.	"You shouldn't just let your wife die. People will blame you for not doing enough, and they'll blame the scientist for not selling you the drug for less money."	"You can't steal the drug because you'll be arrested and go to jail. Even if you aren't caught, you'll feel guilty and you'll always worry that the police may figure out what you did."
Level 2 Conventional morality: Membership in society becomes important at this level. People behave in ways that will win the approval of others.	"Who will blame you if you steal a life-saving drug? But if you just let your wife die, you won't be able to hold your head up in front of your family or neighbors."	"If you steal the drug, everyone will treat you like a criminal. They will wonder why you couldn't have found some other way to save your wife."
Level 3 Postconventional morality: People accept that there are certain broad principles of morality that should govern our actions. These principles are more critical than the particular laws in a society.	"If you simply follow the law, you will violate the underlying principle of saving your wife's life. If you do steal the drug, society will understand your actions and respect them. You can't let an inadequate, outdated law prevent you from doing the right thing."	"You can't change your standards of honesty whenever it suits your needs. Others may not blame you for stealing the drug, but your conscience will blame you for betraying your own moral code."

Social Development: Erikson's theory of psychosocial development

Stage	Approximate Age	Positive Outcomes	Negative Outcomes
1. Trust-vs.-mistrust	Birth–1½ years	Feelings of trust from environmental support	Fear and concern regarding others
2. Autonomy-vs.-shame-and-doubt	1½–3 years	Self-sufficiency if exploration is encouraged	Doubts about self, lack of independence
3. Initiative-vs.-guilt	3–6 years	Discovery of ways to initiate actions	Guilt from actions and thoughts
4. Industry-vs.-inferiority	6–12 years	Development of sense of competence	Feelings of inferiority, no sense of mastery
5. Identity-vs.-role-confusion	Adolescence	Awareness of uniqueness of self, knowledge of role to be followed	Inability to identify appropriate roles in life
6. Intimacy-vs.-isolation	Early adulthood	Development of loving, sexual relationships and close friendships	Fear of relationships with others
7. Generativity-vs.-stagnation	Middle adulthood	Sense of contribution to continuity of life	Trivialization of one's activities
8. Ego-integrity-vs.-despair	Late adulthood	Sense of unity in life's accomplishments	Regret over lost opportunities of life

MODULE 39 Adulthood

Physical Development
- Early adulthood: peak of health
- Middle adulthood: menopause for women

Social Development
- Early adulthood: Focus on career, marriage, family
- Midlife transition: Relatively calm, come to terms with one's circumstances
- Late adulthood: Acceptance of others and one's circumstances

Marriage, Children, and Divorce
- People marry later in life than ever before; about half of all first marriages end in divorce
- Many single-parent households

Growing Old: Late adulthood
- Physical changes
  - Genetic preprogramming aging theory
  - Wear-and-tear aging theory
- Cognitive changes
  - Fluid intelligence declines; crystallized intelligence remains steady
  - Memory change not inevitable
    - Alzheimer's disease: Gradual, irreversible brain disorder that leads to a decline in cognitive abilities
- Social world
  - Disengagement theory of aging
  - Activity theory of aging

©santypan/Shutterstock

CHAPTER 13
Personality

AP ESSENTIAL QUESTIONS

- How can biology influence our behavior and mental processes?
- How do we perceive and understand ourselves?
- What motivates us to think and act the way we do?
- Why don't psychologists agree?

AP LEARNING TARGETS FOR CHAPTER 13

MODULE 40

- Identify the contributions of major researchers in personality theory.

- Compare and contrast the psychoanalytic theories of personality with other theories of personality.

PSYCHODYNAMIC APPROACHES TO PERSONALITY

Freud's Psychoanalytic Theory: Mapping the Unconscious Mind

The Neo-Freudian Psychoanalysts: Building on Freud

MODULE 41

- Identify the contributions of major researchers in personality theory.

- Compare and contrast the behaviorist and social cognitive theories of personality with other theories of personality.

- Compare and contrast humanistic theories of personality with other theories of personality.

- Speculate how cultural context can facilitate or constrain personality development, especially as it relates to self-concept.

- Compare and contrast trait theories of personality with other theories of personality.

TRAIT, LEARNING, BIOLOGICAL AND EVOLUTIONARY, AND HUMANISTIC APPROACHES TO PERSONALITY

Trait Approaches: Placing Labels on Personality

Learning Approaches: We Are What We've Learned

Biological and Evolutionary Approaches: Are We Born with Personality?

AP Applying Psychology in the 21st Century: Does Personality Shift from Generation to Generation?

AP Neuroscience in Your Life: The Neurological Underpinnings of Personality

Humanistic Approaches: The Uniqueness of You

Comparing Approaches to Personality

- Describe and compare research methods that psychologists use to investigate personality.

- Identify frequently used assessment strategies and evaluate relative test quality based on reliability and validity of the instruments.

PROLOGUE *GOOD GUY OR GOOD FELLA?*

Racing cyclist Lance Armstrong was an idol to many. He won the prestigious Tour de France road race seven consecutive times—a feat that had been unequaled in his sport. And remarkably, he did all this after having been diagnosed with stage-three testicular cancer that had spread to his lungs and brain. Despite his poor prognosis, Armstrong defeated the disease and made an amazing comeback as a professional athlete. Not only that but he also founded the Lance Armstrong Foundation to support cancer patients and helped to develop other charitable organizations.

But Armstrong had a side that most people never saw. His cycling comeback was haunted by allegations of doping—allegations that Armstrong repeatedly and strenuously denied for years. But in the end, the evidence caught up with him, and he publicly admitted that he had been doping. A federal prosecutor called him "a doper, dealer, and liar." He was stripped of his Tour de France titles, and he is the target of a $100 million suit for committing fraud (Schrotenboer, 2016; Macur, 2017).

LOOKING *Ahead*

Who is the real Lance Armstrong? Is he the disciplined, hardworking athlete-hero who overcame cancer to win the Tour de France seven times and started a foundation to aid cancer patients? Or is he the cheat who used drugs to enhance his athletic performance, lied about it when confronted, and now downplays the role doping played in his success?

Many people, like Armstong, have more than one side to their personalities, appearing one way to some people and quite differently to others. At the same time, you probably know people whose behavior is so consistent that you can easily predict how they are going to behave, no matter what the situation. Determining who a person truly is falls to a branch of psychology that seeks to understand the characteristic ways people behave—personality psychology.

Personality is the pattern of enduring characteristics that produce consistency and individuality in a given person. Personality encompasses the behaviors that make each of us unique and that differentiate us from others. Personality also leads us to act consistently in different situations and over extended periods of time.

We will consider a number of approaches to personality. For historical reasons, we begin with psychodynamic theories of personality, which emphasize the importance of the unconscious. Next, we consider approaches that concentrate on identifying the most fundamental personality traits; theories that view personality as a set of learned behaviors; biological and evolutionary perspectives on personality; and approaches, known as humanistic theories, that highlight the uniquely human aspects of personality. We end our discussion by focusing on how personality is measured and how personality tests can be used.

personality The pattern of enduring characteristics that produce consistency and individuality in a given person. (Module 40)

Module 40
Psychodynamic Approaches to Personality

AP® LEARNING TARGETS

- Identify the contributions of major researchers in personality theory.

- Compare and contrast the psychoanalytic theories of personality with other theories of personality.

psychodynamic approaches to personality Approaches that assume that personality is primarily unconscious and motivated by inner forces and conflicts about which people have little awareness. (Module 40)

psychoanalytic theory Freud's theory that unconscious forces act as determinants of personality. (Module 40)

unconscious A part of the personality that contains the memories, knowledge, beliefs, feelings, urges, drives, and instincts of which the individual is not aware. (Module 40)

The college student was intent on making a good first impression on an attractive woman he had spotted across a crowded room at a party. As he walked toward her, he mulled over a line he had heard in an old movie the night before: "I don't believe we've been properly introduced yet." To his horror, what came out was a bit different. After threading his way through the crowded room, he finally reached the woman and blurted out, "I don't believe we've been properly seduced yet."

Although this student's error may seem to be merely an embarrassing slip of the tongue, according to some personality theorists, such a mistake is not an error at all (Motley, 1987). Instead, *psychodynamic personality theorists* might argue that the error illustrates one way in which behavior is triggered by inner forces that are beyond our awareness. These hidden drives, shaped by childhood experiences, play an important role in energizing and directing everyday behavior.

Psychodynamic approaches to personality are based on the idea that personality is primarily unconscious and motivated by inner forces and conflicts about which people have little awareness. The most important pioneer of the psychodynamic approach was Sigmund Freud. A number of Freud's followers, including Carl Jung, Karen Horney, and Alfred Adler, refined Freud's theory and developed their own psychodynamic approaches.

Freud's Psychoanalytic Theory: Mapping the Unconscious Mind

Sigmund Freud, an Austrian physician, developed **psychoanalytic theory** in the early 1900s. According to Freud's theory, conscious experience is only a small part of our psychological makeup and experience. He argued that much of our behavior is motivated by the **unconscious**, a part of the personality that contains the memories, knowledge, beliefs, feelings, urges, drives, and instincts of which the individual is not aware.

Like the unseen mass of a floating iceberg, the contents of the unconscious far surpass in quantity the information in our conscious awareness. Freud maintained that to understand personality, it is necessary to expose what is in the unconscious. But because the unconscious disguises the meaning of the material it holds, the content of the unconscious cannot be observed directly. It is therefore necessary to interpret clues to the unconscious–slips of the tongue, fantasies, and dreams–to understand the unconscious processes that direct behavior. A slip of the tongue such as the one quoted earlier (sometimes termed a *Freudian slip*) may be interpreted as revealing the speaker's unconscious sexual desires.

To Freud, much of our personality is determined by our unconscious. Some of the unconscious is made up of the *preconscious*, which contains material that is not threatening and is easily brought to mind, such as the knowledge that $2 + 2 = 4$. But deeper in the unconscious are instinctual drives–the wishes, desires, demands, and needs that are hidden from conscious awareness because of the conflicts and pain they would cause if they were part of our everyday lives. The unconscious provides a "safe haven" for our recollections of threatening events.

STRUCTURING PERSONALITY: ID, EGO, AND SUPEREGO

To describe the structure of personality, Freud developed a comprehensive theory that held that personality consists of three separate but interacting components: the id, the ego, and the superego. Freud suggested that the three structures can be diagrammed to show how they relate to the conscious and the unconscious (see Figure 1).

Although the three components of personality Freud described may appear to be actual physical structures in the nervous system, they are not. Instead, they represent abstract conceptions of a general *model* of personality that describes the interaction of forces that motivate behavior.

If personality consisted only of primitive, instinctual cravings and longings, it would have just one component: the id. The **id** is the instinctual and unorganized part of personality. From the time of birth, the id attempts to reduce tension created by primitive drives related to hunger, sex, aggression, and irrational impulses. Those drives are fueled by "psychic energy," which we can think of as a limitless energy source constantly putting pressure on the various parts of the personality.

The id operates according to the *pleasure principle* in which the goal is the immediate reduction of tension and the maximization of satisfaction. However, in most cases, reality prevents the fulfillment of the demands of the pleasure principle: We cannot always eat when we are hungry, and we can discharge our sexual drives only when the time and place are appropriate. To account for this fact of life, Freud suggested a second component of personality, which he called the ego.

The **ego** is the rational and logical part of personality that attempts to balance the desires of the id and the realities of the objective, outside world. It starts to develop soon after birth.

In contrast to the pleasure-seeking id, the ego operates according to the *reality principle* in which instinctual energy is restrained to maintain the individual's safety and to help integrate the person into society. In a sense, then, the ego is the "executive" of personality: It makes decisions, controls actions, and allows thinking and problem solving of a higher order than the id's capabilities permit.

The superego is the final personality structure to develop in childhood. According to Freud, the **superego** is the part of personality that harshly judges the morality of

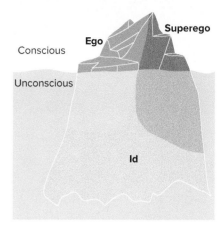

FIGURE 1 In Freud's personality model, there are three major components: the id, the ego, and the superego. As the iceberg analogy shows, only a small portion of personality is conscious. Why do you think that only the ego and superego have conscious components?

id The instinctual and unorganized part of personality whose sole purpose is to reduce tension created by primitive drives related to hunger, sex, aggression, and irrational impulses. (Module 40)

ego The rational, logical part of personality that attempts to balance the desires of the id and the realities of the objective, outside world. (Module 40)

superego The part of personality that harshly judges the morality of our behavior. (Module 40)

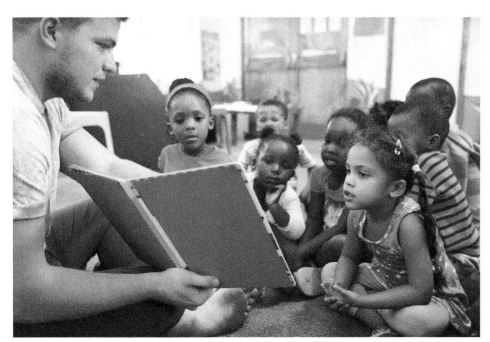

Freud suggests that the superego, the part of the personality that represents the rights and wrongs of society, develops from direct teaching from parents, teachers, and other significant individuals.
©Monkey Business Images/Shutterstock

Study Alert
Remember that the three parts of personality in Freud's theory—the id, the ego, and the superego—are abstract conceptions that don't exist as physical structures in the brain.

our behavior. It represents the rights and wrong of society as taught and modeled by a person's parents, teachers, and other significant individuals.

The superego includes the *conscience*, which prevents us from behaving in a morally improper way by making us feel guilty if we do wrong. The superego helps us control impulses coming from the id, making our behavior less selfish and more virtuous.

Neither the id nor superego parts of personality are realistic, practical, or logical in that they do not consider the realities society imposes. For example, the superego, if left to operate by itself and without restraint, would create perfectionists unable to make the moral compromises that life sometimes requires. On the other hand, an unrestrained id would produce a primitive, pleasure-seeking, thoughtless individual on a mission to fulfill every desire without delay. Consequently, the ego must constrain and negotiate between the conflicting demands of the superego and id.

DEVELOPING PERSONALITY: PSYCHOSEXUAL STAGES

Freud also provided us with a view of how personality develops. He suggests personality development proceeds through a series of five **psychosexual stages** during which children encounter conflicts between the demands of society and their own sexual urges (in which sexuality is more about experiencing pleasure and less about lust).

According to Freud, if we are not able to resolve the conflicts that occur at a particular psychosexual stage, we may become locked in that conflict throughout life–something he called fixation. **Fixations** are conflicts or concerns that persist beyond the developmental period in which they first occur. Such conflicts may be due to having needs ignored, such as ending breast feeding too early or being treated too strictly during toilet training. Alternatively, fixation may occur if children are overindulged during an earlier period, such as when parents are overly attentive to a child or provide lavish rewards during toilet training.

The sequence Freud proposed is noteworthy because it explains how experiences and difficulties during a particular childhood stage may predict specific characteristics in the adult personality. This theory is also unique in associating each stage with a major biological function, which Freud assumed to be the focus of pleasure in a given period. (See Figure 2 for a summary of the stages.)

In the first psychosexual stage of development, called the **oral stage,** the baby's mouth is the focal point of pleasure. During the first 12 to 18 months of life, children suck, eat, mouth, and bite anything they can put into their mouths. To Freud, this behavior suggested that the mouth is the primary site of a kind of sexual pleasure and that weaning (withdrawing the breast or bottle) represents the main conflict during the oral stage. If infants are either overindulged (perhaps by being fed every time they cry) or frustrated in their search for oral gratification, they may become fixated at this stage.

psychosexual stages Developmental periods that children pass through during which they encounter conflicts between the demands of society and their own sexual urges. (Module 40)

fixations Conflicts or concerns that persist beyond the developmental period in which they first occur. (Module 40)

oral stage According to Freud, a stage from birth to age 12-18 months in which an infant's center of pleasure is the mouth. (Module 40)

 Study Alert
The five psychosexual stages of personality development in Freud's theory—oral, anal, phallic, latency, and genital—indicate how personality develops as people age.

Stage	Age	Major Characteristics
Oral	Birth to 12–18 months	Interest in oral gratification from sucking, eating, mouthing, biting
Anal	12–18 months to 3 years	Gratification from expelling and withholding feces; coming to terms with society's controls relating to toilet training
Phallic	3 to 5–6 years	Interest in the genitals, coming to terms with Oedipal conflict leading to identification with same-sex parent
Latency	5–6 years to adolescence	Sexual concerns largely unimportant
Genital	Adolescence to adulthood	Reemergence of sexual interests and establishment of mature sexual relationships

FIGURE 2 Freud's theory of personality development suggests several distinct stages.
©Ingram Publishing

For example, fixation might occur if an infant's oral needs were constantly gratified immediately at the first sign of hunger rather than if the infant learned that feeding takes place on a schedule because eating whenever an infant wants to eat is not always realistic. Fixation at the oral stage might produce an adult who was unusually interested in oral activities–eating, talking, smoking–or who showed symbolic sorts of oral interests such as being "bitingly" sarcastic or very gullible ("swallowing" anything).

From around age 12-18 months until 3 years of age–a period in which the emphasis in Western cultures is on toilet training–a child enters the **anal stage.** At this point, the major source of pleasure changes from the mouth to the anal region, and children obtain considerable pleasure from both retention and expulsion of feces. If toilet training is particularly demanding, fixation might occur. Fixation during the anal stage might result in unusual rigidity, orderliness, punctuality–or extreme disorderliness or sloppiness–in adulthood.

At about age 3, the **phallic stage** begins. At this point, there is another major shift in the child's primary source of pleasure. Now interest focuses on the genitals and the pleasures derived from fondling them. During this stage, the child must also negotiate one of the most important hurdles of personality development: the Oedipal conflict.

The **Oedipal conflict** is a child's intense, sexual interest in his or her opposite-sex parent. According to Freudian theory, the Oedipal conflict plays out as children focus attention on their genitals, and the differences between male and female anatomy become more salient.

According to Freud, a male child unconsciously begins to develop a sexual interest in his mother, starts to see his father as a powerful rival, and harbors a wish to replace his father and enjoy the affections of his mother. (The situation mirrors a tragic Greek play in which the son Oedipus kills his father and marries his mother, hence the term "Oedipal conflict.") But because a son views his father as too powerful, he develops a fear that his father may retaliate drastically by removing the source of the threat: his penis.

Also according to Freud, the fear of losing his penis leads to *castration anxiety,* which ultimately becomes so powerful that the child represses his desires for his mother and identifies with his father. **Identification** is the process of wanting to be like another person as much as possible, imitating that person's behavior and adopting similar beliefs and values. By identifying with his father, a son seeks to obtain a woman like his unattainable mother.

Freud argued that the process is different for girls. He suggested that they experience sexual arousal related to their fathers and begin to have penis envy. They wish they had the anatomical part that seems most clearly "missing" from their bodies–that is, girls realize they lack a penis.

Blaming their mothers for this missing piece of anatomy, girls come to believe that their mothers are responsible for their "castration." Like males, though, they find that they can resolve such unacceptable feelings by identifying with the same-sex parent, behaving like her, and adopting her attitudes and values. In this way, a girl's identification with her mother is completed. (We should note that these ideas about the identification process in girls led to considerable criticism that Freud was sexist, favoring males over females.)

Through these complicated–and to many critics, far-fetched–sequences of events, Freud argued that the Oedipal conflict is resolved and that both males and females move on to the next stage of development. If difficulties arise during the resolution of the Oedipal conflict, however, all sorts of problems are thought to occur, including improper sex-role behavior and the failure to develop a conscience.

After the resolution of the Oedipal conflict, typically around age 5 or 6, children move into the **latency period,** which lasts until puberty. During this period, sexual interests become dormant, even in the unconscious. Then, during adolescence, sexual feelings re-emerge, which marks the start of the final period, the **genital stage,** which extends until death. The focus during the genital stage is on mature, adult sexuality, which Freud defined as sexual intercourse.

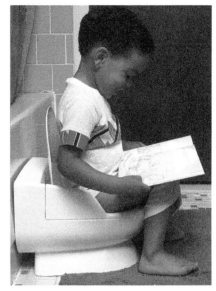

According to Freud, a child goes through the anal stage from age 12–18 months until 3 years of age. Toilet training is a crucial event at this stage—one that psychoanalytic theory claims directly influences the formation of an individual's personality.

©Miller Margaret/Science Source/Getty Images

anal stage According to Freud, a stage from age 12-18 months to 3 years of age in which a child's pleasure is centered on the anus. (Module 40)

phallic stage According to Freud, a period beginning around age 3 during which a child's pleasure focuses on the genitals. (Module 40)

Oedipal conflict A child's intense, sexual interest in his or her opposite-sex parent. (Module 40)

identification The process of wanting to be like another person as much as possible, imitating that person's behavior and adopting similar beliefs and values. (Module 40)

latency period According to Freud, the period between the phallic stage and puberty during which children's sexual concerns are temporarily put aside. (Module 40)

genital stage According to Freud, the period from puberty until death, marked by mature sexual behavior (that is, sexual intercourse). (Module 40)

DEFENSE MECHANISMS

Freud's efforts to describe and theorize about the underlying dynamics of personality and its development were motivated by very practical problems that his patients faced in dealing with *anxiety,* an intense, negative emotional experience. According to Freud, anxiety is a danger signal to the ego. Although anxiety can arise from realistic fears—such as seeing a poisonous snake about to strike—it can also occur in the form of *neurotic anxiety* in which irrational impulses emanating from the id threaten to burst through and become uncontrollable.

Because anxiety is obviously unpleasant, Freud believed that people develop a range of ways to deal with it, which he called defense mechanisms. **Defense mechanisms** are unconscious strategies that people use to reduce anxiety by distorting reality and concealing the source of the anxiety from themselves.

The primary defense mechanism is repression. **Repression** occurs when the ego pushes unacceptable or unpleasant thoughts and impulses out of consciousness but maintains them in the unconscious.

Repression is the most direct method of dealing with anxiety; instead of handling an anxiety-producing impulse on a conscious level, we simply ignore it. For example, a college student who feels hatred for his mother may repress those personally and socially unacceptable feelings. The feelings remain lodged within the unconscious because acknowledging them would provoke anxiety. Similarly, memories of childhood abuse may be repressed. Although such memories may not be consciously recalled, according to Freud they can affect later behavior, and they may be revealed through dreams or slips of the tongue or symbolically in some other fashion.

If repression is ineffective in keeping anxiety at bay, we might use other defense mechanisms. Freud and later his daughter, Anna Freud (who became a well-known psychoanalyst), formulated an extensive list of potential defense mechanisms. The major defense mechanisms are summarized in Figure 3 (Perry, Presniak, & Olson, 2013; Boag, 2015; Zhang & Guo, 2017).

defense mechanisms In Freudian theory, unconscious strategies that people use to reduce anxiety by distorting reality and concealing the source of the anxiety from themselves. (Module 40)

repression The defense mechanism in which the ego pushes unacceptable or unpleasant thoughts and impulses out of consciousness but maintains them in the unconscious. (Module 40)

Study Alert
Use Figure 3 to remember the most common defense mechanisms (unconscious strategies used to reduce anxiety by concealing its source from ourselves and others).

	Freud's Defense Mechanisms	
Defense Mechanism	**Explanation**	**Example**
Repression	Unacceptable or unpleasant impulses are pushed out of awareness and back into the unconscious.	A woman is unable to consciously recall that she was raped.
Regression	People behave as if they were at an earlier stage of development.	A boss has a temper tantrum when an employee makes a mistake.
Displacement	The expression of an unwanted feeling or thought is redirected from a more threatening powerful person to a weaker one.	A brother yells at his younger sister after a teacher gives him a bad grade.
Rationalization	People provide self-justifying explanations in place of the actual, but threatening, reason for their behavior.	A student who goes out drinking the night before a big test rationalizes his behavior by saying the test isn't all that important.
Denial	People refuse to accept or acknowledge an anxiety-producing piece of information.	A student refuses to believe that he has flunked a course.
Projection	People attribute unwanted impulses and feelings to someone else.	A man who is unfaithful to his wife and feels guilty suspects that his wife is unfaithful.
Sublimation	People divert unwanted impulses into socially approved thoughts, feelings, or behaviors.	A person with strong feelings of aggression becomes a soldier.
Reaction formation	Unconscious impulses are expressed as their opposite in consciousness.	A mother who unconsciously resents her child acts in an overly loving way toward the child.

FIGURE 3 According to Freud, people use a wide range of defense mechanisms to cope with anxieties.

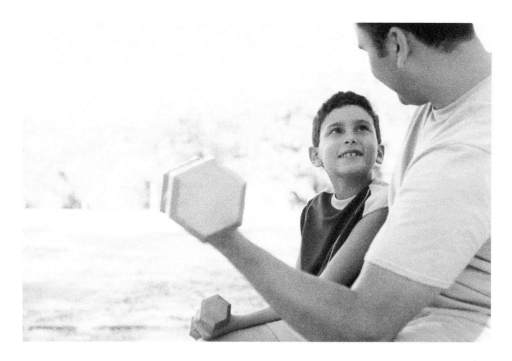

Imitating a person's behavior and adopting similar beliefs and values are part of Freud's concept of identification. How can this concept be applied to the definition of gender roles? Is identification similar in all cultures?
©Steve Hix/age fotostock

All of us employ defense mechanisms to some degree, according to Freudian theory, and they can serve a useful purpose by protecting us from unpleasant information. Yet some people fall prey to them to such an extent that they must constantly direct a large amount of psychic energy toward hiding and rechanneling unacceptable impulses. When this occurs, everyday living becomes difficult. In such cases, the result is a mental disorder produced by anxiety—what Freud called "neurosis." (Psychologists rarely use this term today, although it endures in everyday conversation.)

EVALUATING FREUD'S LEGACY

Freud's theory has had a significant impact on the field of psychology—and even more broadly on Western philosophy and literature. The general ideas that we have unconscious thoughts that influence behavior, that we employ defense mechanisms, and that some adult psychological problems have their roots in childhood difficulties are widely accepted (Boag, Brakel, & Tavitie, 2016; Zhang et al., 2016).

However, contemporary personality psychologists have leveled significant criticisms against many foundational explanations of personality development in psychoanalytic theory. Among the most important is the lack of compelling scientific data to support the process of personality development that Freud laid out. Although individual case studies *seem* supportive, we lack conclusive evidence that shows the personality is structured and operates along the lines Freud laid out (Tummala-Nara, 2016).

The lack of research evidence is due, in part, to the fact that Freud's conception of personality is built on unobservable abstract concepts. Moreover, it is not clear that the stages of personality Freud laid out provide an accurate description of personality development. We also know now that important changes in personality can occur in adolescence and adulthood—something that Freud did not believe happened. Instead, he argued that personality largely is set by the time we reach adolescence.

The vague nature of Freud's theory also makes it difficult to predict how an adult will display certain developmental difficulties. For instance, if a person is fixated at the anal stage, according to Freud, he or she may be unusually messy or unusually neat. Freud's theory offers no way to predict how the difficulty will be exhibited. Furthermore, Freud can be faulted for seeming to view women as inferior to men because he argued that women have weaker superegos than men do and in some ways unconsciously yearn to be men (the concept of penis envy).

Finally, Freud made his observations and derived his theory from a limited population. His theory was based almost entirely on upper-class Austrian women living in the strict, puritanical era of the early 1900s who had come to him seeking treatment for psychological and physical problems. How far one can generalize beyond this population is a matter of considerable debate. For instance, in some Pacific Island societies, the mother's oldest brother and not the father plays the role of disciplinarian. In such a culture, it is unreasonable to argue that the Oedipal conflict will progress in the same way that it did in Austrian society in which the father typically was the major disciplinarian. In short, a cross-cultural perspective raises questions about the universality of Freud's view of personality development (Doi, 1990; Grünbaum, 2015).

Still, Freud generated an important method of treating psychological disturbances called *psychoanalysis*. As we will see when we discuss treatment approaches to psychological disorders, psychoanalysis remains in use today (Frosch, 2011; Altman & Stile, 2015).

Moreover, Freud's emphasis on the unconscious has been partially supported by current research on dreams and implicit memory. As first noted when we discussed dreaming, advances in neuroscience are consistent with some of Freud's arguments. For example, the fact that some behavior is motivated by occurrences that apparently have been forgotten, as well as the discovery of neural pathways relating to emotional memories, supports the notion of repression.

Furthermore, cognitive and social psychologists have found increasing evidence that unconscious processes help us think about and evaluate our world, set goals, and choose a course of action. Unconscious processes also help determine how we form attitudes toward others (Teague, 2013; Bargh, 2014; Fayek, 2017).

The Neo-Freudian Psychoanalysts: Building on Freud

Freud laid the foundation for important work done by a series of successors who were trained in traditional Freudian theory but later rejected some of its major points. These theorists are known as **neo-Freudian psychoanalysts.**

The neo-Freudians placed greater emphasis than Freud did on the functions of the ego by suggesting that it has more control than the id does over day-to-day activities. They focused more on the social environment and minimized the importance of sex as a driving force in people's lives. They also paid greater attention to the effects of society and culture on personality development.

JUNG'S COLLECTIVE UNCONSCIOUS

Carl Jung (pronounced "yoong"), one of the most influential neo-Freudians, rejected Freud's view of the primary importance of unconscious sexual urges. Instead, he looked at the primitive urges of the unconscious more positively. He argued that they represented a more general and positive life force that goes back to the dawn of the existence of life, motivating creativity and positive conflict resolution (Cassells, 2007; Wilde, 2011; Addison, 2017).

Jung suggested that we have a universal **collective unconscious**—an inherited set of ideas, feelings, images, and symbols that are shared with all humans because of our common ancestral past. This collective unconscious, which is in the deepest layer of the unconscious, is similar in everyone and is displayed in behavior that is common across diverse cultures—such as love of mother, belief in a supreme being, and even behavior as specific as fear of snakes (Hauke, 2006; Finn, 2011).

Jung went on to propose that the collective unconscious contains **archetypes,** universal symbolic representations of particular types of people, objects, ideas, or experiences. For instance, a *mother archetype*, which contains reflections of our ancestors' relationships with mother figures, is suggested by the prevalence of mothers in art,

neo-Freudian psychoanalysts Psychoanalysts who were trained in traditional Freudian theory but who later rejected some of its major points. (Module 40)

collective unconscious According to Jung, an inherited set of ideas, feelings, images, and symbols that are shared with all humans because of our common ancestral past. (Module 40)

archetypes According to Jung, universal symbolic representations of particular types of people, objects, ideas, or experiences. (Module 40)

In terms of Jung's theory, Luke Skywalker and Kylo Ren from the *Star Wars* movies represent the archetypes, or universally recognizable symbols, of good and evil.
(left): ©AF archive/Alamy Stock Photo;
(right): ©Photo 12/Alamy Stock Photo

religion, literature, and mythology. (Think of the Virgin Mary, Earth Mother, wicked stepmothers in fairy tales, Mother's Day, and so forth!) Jung also suggested that men possess an unconscious *feminine archetype* that affects how they behave, and women have an unconscious *male archetype* that colors their behavior (Jung, 1961; Smetana, 2007; Potash, 2015).

To Jung, archetypes play an important role in determining our day-to-day reactions, attitudes, and values. For example, Jung might explain the popularity of the *Star Wars* movies as being due to their use of broad archetypes of good (Luke Skywalker) and evil (Kylo Ren).

Although no reliable research evidence confirms the existence of the collective unconscious—and even Jung acknowledged that such evidence would be difficult to produce—Jung's theory has had significant influence in areas beyond psychology. For example, personality types derived from Jung's personality approach form the basis for the Myers-Briggs personality test, which is widely used in business and industry to provide insights into how employees make decisions and perform on the job (Wilde, 2011; Mills, 2013; Wang et al., 2017).

From the perspective of...

An Advertising Executive How might you use Jung's concept of archetypes in designing your advertisements? Which of the archetypes would you use?

©Image Source/Getty Images

HORNEY'S NEO-FREUDIAN PERSPECTIVE

Karen Horney (pronounced "HORN-eye") was one of the earliest psychologists to champion women's issues and is sometimes called the first feminist psychologist. Horney suggested that personality develops in the context of social relationships and depends particularly on the relationship between parents and child and how well the child's needs are met. She rejected Freud's suggestion that women have penis envy; she asserted that what women envy most in men is not their anatomy but the independence, success, and freedom women often are denied (Horney, 1937; Smith, 2007; Coolidge et al., 2011).

Horney was also one of the first to stress the importance of cultural factors in the determination of personality. For example, she suggested that society's rigid gender

Karen Horney was one of the earliest proponents of women's issues.

©Bettmann/Getty Images

roles for women led them to experience ambivalence about success because they fear they will make enemies if they are too successful. Her conceptualizations, developed in the 1930s and 1940s, laid the groundwork for many of the central ideas of feminism that emerged decades later (Eckardt, 2005; Jones, 2006).

ADLER AND THE OTHER NEO-FREUDIANS

Alfred Adler, another important neo-Freudian psychoanalyst, also considered Freudian theory's emphasis on sexual needs misplaced. Instead, Adler proposed that the primary human motivation is a striving for superiority, not in terms of superiority over others but in a quest for self-improvement and perfection.

Adler used the term *inferiority complex* to describe adults who have not been able to overcome feelings of inadequacy they developed as children. An *inferiority complex* is a lack of self-worth, a feeling that one is not as good as others. Early social relationships with parents have an important effect on children's ability to outgrow feelings of personal inferiority. If children have positive experiences, they can orient themselves toward attaining socially useful goals.

Other neo-Freudians included Erik Erikson, whose theory of psychosocial development we discussed in other modules, and Freud's daughter, Anna Freud. Like Adler and Horney, they focused less than Freud did on inborn sexual and aggressive drives and more on the social and cultural factors behind personality.

AP SUMMARY

- Freud's psychoanalytic theory proposes that unconscious forces act as determinants for personality.
- Jung, a neo-Freudian, suggested that individuals have a collective unconscious that contains archetypes.
- Adler, a neo-Freudian, proposed that humans strive for superiority, while some individuals develop an inferiority complex.
- Psychodynamic approaches assume personality is primarily unconscious.
  Freud's personality structure consists of three parts: id, ego, and superego.
- Freud suggested that personality develops through five psychosexual stages: oral, anal, phallic, latency, and genital.
- Defense mechanisms are unconscious strategies used to reduce anxiety.
- The psychoanalytic theory has provoked several criticisms. However, recent neuroscience research has offered support for the unconscious.
- Neo-Freudians built on Freud's work, although they placed greater emphasis on the ego and paid more attention to social factors in determining behavior.

AP KEY TERMS

personality
psychodynamic approaches to personality
psychoanalytic theory
unconscious
id
ego
superego
psychosexual stages
fixations
oral stage
anal stage
phallic stage
Oedipal conflict
identification
latency period
genital stage
defense mechanisms
repression
neo-Freudian psychoanalysts
collective unconscious
archetypes

AP TEST PRACTICE

Section I: Multiple Choice

1. Jeremy skips in line and takes the last bag of candy. According to Freud, Jeremy is being controlled by his
   A. inferiority complex
   B. superego
   C. ego
   D. id
   E. amygdala

2. Psychoanalysts believe behavior is motived by
   A. the unconscious
   B. observable behavior
   C. the context of the situation
   D. cognitive appraisals
   E. inherent goodness

3. Holly doesn't want to admit she is selfish, so she accuses her friends of being selfish. What type of defense mechanism is Holly using?
   A. Sublimation
   B. Regression
   C. Reaction formation
   D. Displacement
   E. Projection

Section II: Free Response

Anna is having problems at work. She is disorganized and forgetting major deadlines. She often makes excuses for why her work is not done on time. Describe how a psychoanalyst would explain Anna's behavior using the following concepts.
- Fixation
- Repression
- Rationalization

In order to understand Anna's behavior a psychoanalyst will need to expose the unconscious.
- Provide a method to reveal the unconscious

Module 41

Trait, Learning, Biological and Evolutionary, and Humanistic Approaches to Personality

traits Consistent, habitual personality characteristics and behaviors that are displayed across different situations. (Module 41)

trait theory A model of personality that seeks to identify the basic traits necessary to describe personality. (Module 41)

Study Alert

All trait theories explain personality in terms of traits (consistent personality characteristics and behaviors), but they differ in terms of which and how many traits are seen as fundamental.

"Tell me about Nelson," said Johnetta.

"Oh, he's just terrific. He's the friendliest guy I know–goes out of his way to be nice to everyone. He hardly ever gets mad. He's just so even-tempered, no matter what's happening. And he's really smart, too. About the only thing I don't like is that he's always in such a hurry to get things done. He seems to have boundless energy, much more than I have."

"He sounds great to me, especially in comparison to Rico," replied Johnetta. "He is so self-centered and arrogant that it drives me crazy. I sometimes wonder why I ever started going out with him."

Friendly. Even-tempered. Smart. Energetic. Self-centered. Arrogant.

The above exchange is made up of a series of trait characterizations of the speakers' friends. In fact, much of our own understanding of others' behavior is based on the premise that people possess certain traits that are consistent across different situations. For example, we generally assume that if someone is outgoing and sociable in one situation, he or she is outgoing and sociable in other situations (Mischel, 2004; Leising et al., 2014).

Dissatisfaction with the emphasis in psychoanalytic theory on unconscious–and difficult-to-demonstrate–processes in explaining a person's behavior led to the development of alternative approaches to personality, including a number of trait-based approaches. Other theories reflect established psychological perspectives, such as learning theory, biological and evolutionary approaches, and the humanistic approach.

Trait Approaches: Placing Labels on Personality

If someone asked you to characterize another person, as Johnetta did of her friend, you probably would come up with a list of traits. **Traits** are consistent, habitual personality characteristics and behaviors that are displayed across different situations.

Trait theory is the personality approach that seeks to identify the basic traits necessary to describe personality. Trait theorists do not assume that some people have a particular trait while others do not. Instead, they propose that all people possess a set of traits, but the degree to which a particular trait applies to a specific person varies and can be quantified.

For instance, they might assume that all people have the trait of "friendliness" but in different degrees. You may be relatively friendly, whereas I may be relatively unfriendly. But we both have a "friendliness" trait, although your degree of "friendliness" is higher than mine.

The major challenge for trait theorists taking this approach has been to identify the specific basic traits necessary to describe personality. As we shall see, different theorists have come up with surprisingly different sets of traits.

ALLPORT'S TRAIT THEORY: IDENTIFYING BASIC CHARACTERISTICS

When personality psychologist Gordon Allport systematically pored over an unabridged dictionary in the 1930s, he came up with some 18,000 separate terms that could be used to describe personality. Although he was able to pare down the list to 4,500 descriptors after eliminating words with similar meanings, he was left with a problem crucial to all trait approaches: Which traits are the most important in characterizing personality?

Allport eventually answered this question by suggesting that there are three fundamental categories of traits: cardinal, central, and secondary (Allport, 1966):

- **Cardinal traits.** A *cardinal trait* is a single, overriding characteristic that directs most of a person's behavior. For example, a totally selfless woman may direct all her energy toward humanitarian activities; an intensely power-hungry person may be driven by an all-consuming need for control.

- **Central traits.** Few people have a single, comprehensive cardinal trait. Instead, they possess 5–10 central traits that make up the core of personality. *Central traits,* such as warmth or honesty, describe an individual's major characteristics. Each central trait is assumed to imply the presence of other traits. For example, people who have a central trait of warmth also are likely to be sociable and friendly.

- **Secondary traits.** Finally, *secondary traits* are characteristics that affect behavior in fewer situations and are less influential than central or cardinal traits. For instance, a reluctance to eat meat and a love of modern art would be considered secondary traits (Smrtnik-Vitulić & Zupančič, 2011; Kahn et al., 2013; Zhao & Smillie, 2015).

CATTELL AND EYSENCK: FACTORING OUT PERSONALITY

Later attempts to identify primary personality traits centered on a statistical technique known as factor analysis. *Factor analysis* is a statistical method of identifying patterns among a large number of variables and combining them into more fundamental groupings. For example, a personality researcher might ask a large group of people to rate themselves on a number of specific traits. By using factor analysis and statistically computing which traits are associated with one another, a researcher can identify the fundamental patterns of traits—called *factors*—that cluster together in the same person.

Using factor analysis, personality psychologist Raymond Cattell suggested that 16 pairs of *traits* represent the basic dimensions of personality. Using that set of traits, he developed the Sixteen Personality Factor Questionnaire, or 16 PF, a personality scale that is still in use today (Cattell, Cattell, & Cattell, 2000; Djapo et al., 2011; Wright, 2017).

Another trait theorist, psychologist Hans Eysenck (1995), also used factor analysis to identify patterns of traits, but he came to a very different conclusion about the nature of personality. He found that personality could best be described in terms of just three major dimensions: extraversion, neuroticism, and psychoticism. The *extraversion* dimension describes a person's level of sociability, whereas the *neuroticism* dimension encompasses an individual's emotional stability. Finally, *psychoticism* is the degree to which reality is distorted. By evaluating people along these three dimensions, Eysenck was able to predict behavior accurately in a variety of situations. Figure 1 lists specific traits associated with each of the dimensions.

THE BIG FIVE PERSONALITY TRAITS

For the last two decades, the most influential trait approach contends that five traits or factors—called the "Big Five"—lie at the core of personality. Using factor analytic statistical techniques, a consistent body of research has identified a similar set of five factors that underlie personality. The specific five factors are *openness to experience,*

Extraversion

- Sociable
- Lively
- Active
- Assertive
- Sensation-seeking

Neuroticism

- Anxious
- Depressed
- Guilt feelings
- Low self-esteem
- Tense

Psychoticism

- Aggressive
- Cold
- Egocentric
- Impersonal
- Impulsive

FIGURE 1 Eysenck described personality in terms of three major dimensions: extraversion, neuroticism, and psychoticism. Using these dimensions, he could predict people's behavior in many types of situations.

Source: Eysenck, H. J. (1991). Biological dimensions of personality. In L. A. Pervin (Ed.), *Handbook of personality: Theory and research.* New York: Guilford Press.

Study Alert

You can remember the "Big Five" set of personality traits by using the acronym OCEAN (openness to experience, conscientiousness, extraversion, *a*greeableness, and *n*euroticism).

FIGURE 2 Five broad trait factors, referred to as the "Big Five," are considered to be the core of personality.
Sources: Adapted from Pervin, 1990, and McCrae & Costa, 1986.

The Big Five Personality Factors and Dimensions of Sample Traits

Openness to experience
Independent—Conforming
Imaginative—Practical
Preference for variety—Preference for routine

Conscientiousness
Careful—Careless
Disciplined—Impulsive
Organized—Disorganized

Extraversion
Talkative—Quiet
Fun-loving—Sober
Sociable—Retiring

Agreeableness
Sympathetic—Fault-finding
Kind—Cold
Appreciative—Unfriendly

Neuroticism (Emotional stability)
Stable—Tense
Calm—Anxious
Secure—Insecure

conscientiousness, extraversion, agreeableness, and *neuroticism* (emotional stability). They are described in Figure 2.

The Big Five emerge consistently across a number of domains. For example, factor analyses of major personality inventories, self-report measures made by observers of others' personality traits, and checklists of self-descriptions yield similar factors. In addition, the Big Five emerge consistently in different populations of individuals, including children, college students, older adults, and speakers of different languages. Cross-cultural research conducted in areas ranging from Europe to the Middle East to Africa also has been supportive. Finally, studies of brain functioning show that Big Five personality traits are related to the way the brain processes information (Vecchione et al., 2011; Saucier & Srivastava, 2015; Bouvard & Roulin, 2017).

In short, a growing consensus exists that the Big Five represent the best description of personality traits we have today. Still, the debate over the specific number and kinds of traits–and even the usefulness of trait approaches in general–remains a lively one.

EVALUATING TRAIT APPROACHES TO PERSONALITY

Trait approaches have several virtues. They provide a clear, straightforward explanation of people's behavioral consistencies. Furthermore, traits allow us to readily compare one person with another. Because of these advantages, trait approaches to personality have had an important influence on the development of several useful personality measures (Wiggins, 2003; Larsen & Buss, 2006; Cook, 2013).

However, trait approaches also have some drawbacks. For example, we have seen that various trait theories describing personality come to different conclusions about which traits are the most fundamental and descriptive. The difficulty in determining which of the theories is the most accurate has led some personality psychologists to question the validity of trait conceptions of personality in general.

Trait approaches suffer from an even more fundamental difficulty: Even if we identify a set of primary traits, all we have done is provide a set of labels for personality. But labeling personality traits is not an *explanation* of how those traits developed in a person nor of how they function to determine behavior. For example, if we say that someone who donates money to charity has the trait of generosity, we still do not know *why* that person became generous in the first place or why the person displays generosity in a specific situation. In the view of some critics, then, traits do not provide explanations for behavior; they merely label it.

Learning Approaches: We Are What We've Learned

The psychodynamic and trait approaches we've been discussing concentrate on the "inner" person–the fury of a powerful id or a critical set of traits that describes the core of an individual. In contrast, learning approaches to personality focus on the external world in which a person lives and how external influences determine and affect personality.

SKINNER'S BEHAVIORIST APPROACH

According to the most influential learning theorist, B. F. Skinner (who carried out pioneering work on operant conditioning), personality is a collection of learned behavior patterns (Skinner, 1975). Similarities in responses across different situations are caused by similar patterns of reinforcement that have been received in such situations in the past. If I am sociable both at parties and at meetings, it is because I have been reinforced for displaying social behaviors–not because I am fulfilling an unconscious wish based on experiences during my childhood or because I have an internal trait of sociability.

Learning theorists such as Skinner are less interested in the consistencies in behavior across situations than in ways of modifying behavior. To a learning theorist who subscribes to Skinner's view, humans are infinitely changeable through the process of learning new behavior patterns. If we are able to control and modify the patterns of reinforcers in a situation, behavior that other theorists would view as stable and unyielding can be changed and ultimately improved. Learning theorists are optimistic in their attitudes about the potential for resolving personal and societal problems through treatment strategies based on learning theory.

SOCIAL COGNITIVE APPROACHES TO PERSONALITY

Not all learning theories of personality take such a rigid view in rejecting the importance of what is "inside" a person by focusing solely on the "outside." Unlike other learning approaches to personality, **social cognitive approaches to personality** emphasize the influence of cognition–thoughts, feelings, expectations, and values–as well as observation of others' behavior, on personality. According to Albert Bandura, one of the main proponents of this point of view, people can foresee the possible outcomes of certain behaviors in a specific setting without actually having to carry them out. This understanding comes primarily through *observational learning*–viewing the actions of others and observing the consequences (Bandura, 1999).

For instance, children who view a model behaving in, say, an aggressive manner tend to copy the behavior if the consequences of the model's behavior are seen as positive. If, in contrast, the model's aggressive behavior has resulted in no consequences or negative consequences, children are considerably less likely to act aggressively. According to social cognitive approaches, then, personality develops through repeated observation of others' behavior.

Bandura places particular emphasis on the role played by self-efficacy. **Self-efficacy** is the belief that we can master a situation and produce positive outcomes. Self-efficacy underlies people's faith in their ability to successfully carry out a particular task or to produce a desired outcome. People with high self-efficacy have higher aspirations and greater persistence in working to attain goals than those with lower self-efficacy. Furthermore, they ultimately achieve greater success (Bandura & Locke, 2003; Dunlop, Beatty, & Beauchamp, 2011; Sezgin & Erdogan, 2015).

social cognitive approaches to personality Theories that emphasize the influence of a person's cognitions–thoughts, feelings, expectations, and values–as well as observation of others' behavior, in determining personality. (Module 41)

self-efficacy The belief that we can master a situation and produce positive outcomes. (Module 41)

PsychTech

Researchers have been investigating differences in self-efficacy between people in their use of technology. One difference is age: younger adults appear to have more confidence in their technological expertise than older adults do.

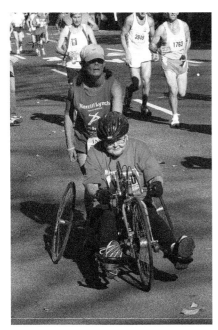

Self-efficacy, the belief in one's own capabilities, leads to higher aspirations and greater persistence.
©McGraw-Hill Education/Lars Niki, photographer

self-esteem The component of personality that encompasses our positive and negative self-evaluations. (Module 41)

How do we develop self-efficacy? One way is by paying close attention to our prior successes and failures. If we try snowboarding and experience little success, we'll be less likely to try it again. However, if our initial efforts appear promising, we'll be more likely to attempt it again. Direct reinforcement and encouragement from others also play a role in developing self-efficacy (Buchanan & Selmon, 2008; Artistico et al., 2013; Wright, 2017).

Compared with other learning theories of personality, social cognitive approaches are distinctive in their emphasis on the reciprocity between individuals and their environment. Not only is the environment assumed to affect personality, but people's behavior and personalities are also assumed to "feed back" and modify the environment (Bandura, 1999, 2000).

HOW MUCH CONSISTENCY EXISTS IN PERSONALITY?

Another social cognitive theorist, Walter Mischel, takes a different approach to personality from that of Albert Bandura. He rejects the view that personality consists of broad traits that lead to substantial consistencies in behavior across different situations. Instead, he sees personality as considerably more variable from one situation to another (Mischel, 2009).

In this view, particular situations give rise to particular kinds of behavior. Some situations are especially influential (think of a movie theater, where everyone displays pretty much the same behavior by sitting quietly and watching the film). Other situations permit much variability in behavior (think of a party, for example, where some people may be dancing, while others are eating and drinking).

From this perspective, personality cannot be considered without taking the particular context of the situation into account—a view known as *situationism*. In his *cognitive-affective processing system (CAPS)* theory, Mischel argues that people's thoughts and emotions about themselves and the world determine how they view, and then react, in particular situations. Personality is thus seen as a reflection of how people's prior experiences in different situations affect their behavior (Mischel & Shoda, 2008; McCrae et al., 2011; Huprich & Nelson, 2015).

SELF-ESTEEM

Our behavior also reflects the view we have of ourselves and the way we value the various parts of our personalities. **Self-esteem** is the component of personality that encompasses our positive and negative self-evaluations. Unlike self-efficacy, which focuses on our views of whether we are able to carry out a task, self-esteem relates to how we feel about ourselves.

Although people have a general level of self-esteem, it is not unidimensional. We may see ourselves positively in one domain but negatively in others. For example, a good student may have high self-esteem in academic domains but lower self-esteem in sports (Gentile et al., 2009; Gadbois & Sturgeon, 2011; Mirzairad et al., 2017).

The development of self-esteem is strongly affected by cultural factors. For example, consider the characteristic of *relationship harmony*, which is a sense of success in forming close bonds with others. For people living in Asian cultures, having high relationship harmony is a more important component of self-esteem than it is for those living in more individualistic Western societies (Lun & Bond, 2006; Cheng & Kwan, 2008; Chin, 2015).

Although almost all of us go through periods in which our self-esteem is challenged and temporarily reduced (for instance, after an undeniable failure), some people are chronically low in self-esteem. For them, failure seems to be an inevitable part of life. In fact, low self-esteem may lead to a cycle of failure in which past failure breeds future failure.

For example, consider students with low self-esteem who are studying for a test. Because of their low self-esteem, they expect to do poorly on the test. In turn, this

FIGURE 3 The cycle of low self-esteem begins with an individual already having low self-esteem. As a consequence, the person will have low performance expectations and expect to fail a test, thereby producing anxiety and reduced effort. As a result, the person will actually fail, and failure in turn reinforces low self-esteem.

belief raises their anxiety level, which makes it increasingly difficult to study and perhaps even leads them not to work as hard. Because of these attitudes, they do, in fact, perform badly on the test. Ultimately, the failure reinforces their low self-esteem, and the cycle is perpetuated, as illustrated in Figure 3. In short, low self-esteem can lead to a self-destructive cycle of failure.

On the other hand, high levels of self-esteem can also be troublesome if they are unwarranted. According to a growing body of data, an increasing number of college-age students have high levels of *narcissism*, in which people show self-absorption and hold inflated views of themselves. For example, over the past three decades, thousands of American college students participating in a variety of psychological research studies were asked to take the Narcissism Personality Inventory (NPI), a test of narcissistic tendencies. A summary of more than 100 such studies conducted over a 25-year period showed a significant increase in participants' narcissism scores (Dingfelder, 2011; Twenge & Kasser, 2013; Barry et al., 2017).

What might produce the increase in narcissism in young Americans? Research points to social networking media. In recent years, it has become typical for young people to self-promote in carefully edited online profiles. The most mundane aspects of their daily lives are viewed as worthy of broadcasting to the world, whether in Twitter tweets, Facebook postings, or YouTube videos. Another explanation is that parents may increasingly be inflating their children's sense of self-importance by shielding them from situations in which they might fail (Twenge, 2013; Twenge, Campbell, & Gentile, 2013; Kauten et al., 2015).

From the perspective of...

An Educator How might you encourage your students' development of self-esteem and self-efficacy? What steps would you take to ensure that their self-esteem did not become over-inflated?

©Andersen Ross/Blend Images/Getty Images

EVALUATING LEARNING APPROACHES TO PERSONALITY

Because they ignore the internal processes, such as thoughts and emotions, traditional learning theorists such as Skinner have been accused of oversimplifying personality far too much. Their critics think that reducing behavior to a series of stimuli and responses and excluding thoughts and feelings from the realm of personality leaves behaviorists practicing an unrealistic and inadequate form of science.

Of course, some of these criticisms are blunted by social cognitive approaches, which explicitly consider the role of cognitive processes in personality. Still, learning approaches tend to share a highly *deterministic* view of human behavior, which maintains that behavior is shaped primarily by forces beyond the individual's control. As in psychoanalytic theory (which suggests that personality is determined by the unconscious forces) and trait approaches (which view personality in part as a mixture of genetically determined traits), learning theory's reliance on deterministic principles de-emphasizes people's ability to pilot their own course through life.

Nonetheless, learning approaches have had a major impact on the study of personality. For one thing, they have helped make personality psychology an objective, scientific venture by focusing on observable behavior and the effects of the environments. In addition, they have produced important, successful means of treating a variety of psychological disorders. The degree of success of these treatments is a testimony to the merits of learning theory approaches to personality.

Biological and Evolutionary Approaches: Are We Born with Personality?

Approaching the question of what determines personality from a different direction, **biological and evolutionary approaches to personality** suggest that important components of personality are inherited. Building on the work of behavioral geneticists, researchers using biological and evolutionary approaches argue that personality is determined at least in part by our genes in much the same way that our height is largely a result of genetic contributions from our ancestors. The evolutionary perspective assumes that personality traits that led to our ancestors' survival and reproductive success are more likely to be preserved and passed on to subsequent generations (Buss, 2001, 2009, 2011; Yarkoni, 2015).

The results of research studies conducted on twins who are genetically identical but raised apart from one another by different caretakers illustrate the importance of genetic factors in personality. Personality tests indicate that in major respects, genetically identical twins raised apart are quite similar in personality, even if they were separated at an early age.

Moreover, certain traits are more heavily influenced by heredity than are others. For example, *social potency* (the degree to which a person assumes mastery and leadership roles in social situations) and *traditionalism* (the tendency to follow authority)

biological and evolutionary approaches to personality Theories that suggest that important components of personality are inherited. (Module 41)

Biological and evolutionary approaches to personality seek to explain the consistencies in personality that are found in some families.
©Image Source

Infants are born with particular temperaments—dispositions that are consistent throughout childhood.
©Image Source

had particularly strong genetic components, whereas achievement and social closeness had relatively weak genetic components (see Figure 4; Bouchard et al., 2004).

Furthermore, it is increasingly clear that the roots of adult personality emerge early in life. Infants are born with a specific **temperament,** an individual's behavioral style and characteristic way of responding. Temperament encompasses several dimensions, including general activity level and mood. For instance, some babies are quite active, whereas others are relatively calm. Similarly, some are relatively easygoing, whereas others are irritable, easily upset, and difficult to soothe. Temperament is quite consistent, with significant stability from infancy well into adolescence (Evans & Rothbart, 2009; Hori et al., 2011; Bates & Pettit, 2015; also see *Applying Psychology in the 21st Century*).

Some researchers contend that specific genes are related to personality. For example, people with a longer dopamine-4 receptor gene are more likely to be thrill-seekers than are those without such a gene. These thrill-seekers tend to be extroverted, impulsive, quick-tempered, and always in search of excitement and novel situations. Furthermore, the structure of their brains may reflect their thrill-seeking tendencies (Golimbet et al., 2007; Ray et al., 2009; Wishart, Somoray, & Rowland, 2017; also see *Neuroscience in Your Life*).

temperament An individual's behavioral style and characteristic way of responding that emerges early in life. (Module 41)

AP NEUROSCIENCE IN YOUR LIFE: THE NEUROLOGICAL UNDERPINNINGS OF PERSONALITY

A large part of what makes us who we are is personality. Although the five-factor model has been influential in describing personality traits, its neurobiological basis has been largely unknown. However, in a recent study with over 500 participants, neuroscientists looked at how the shape of the brain relates to the five basic personality traits of openness to experience, conscientiousness, extraversion, agreeableness, and neuroticism. They found that the shape of certain brain areas relates to each of the five personality traits. For example, high levels of conscientiousness related to thicker cortex in two brain areas (shown in blue in three views of the brain below) (Riccelli et al., 2017).

AP SKILL: APPLY THEORIES AND PERSPECTIVES IN AUTHENTIC CONTEXTS / SCIENTIFIC INVESTIGATION

1. The five-factor model is supported by which approach to personality?

2. What are possible implications of this study?

Caudal middle frontal   Precuneus

Source: Adapted from Riccelli, R., Toschi, N., Nigro, S., Terracciano, A., & Passamonti, L. (2017). Surface-based morphometry reveals the neuroanatomical basis of the five-factor model of personality. *Social Cognitive and Affective Neuroscience, 12*(4), 671-684. doi: 10.1093/scan/nsw175

AP APPLYING PSYCHOLOGY IN THE 21ST CENTURY

DOES PERSONALITY SHIFT FROM GENERATION TO GENERATION?

Research has long shown that personality is largely stable across the lifespan, and this is generally a good thing. It means that the person you hire (or befriend, or marry) today will, for the most part, continue to be that same person tomorrow and next year and 5 years from now. Our social world would be a lot harder to navigate if individual people's personalities drifted substantially over time (McCrae & Costa, 1994; Borghuis et al., 2017).

But are larger-scale changes in personality possible? That is, do average traits of a given population drift over time, from generation to generation? A moment's thought would suggest they do. After all, we might assume that people today are a lot different personality-wise from people in the Middle Ages. More important, compelling research out of Finland confirms this intuition.

Researchers took advantage of Finland's history of compulsory military conscription, which requires all Finnish men to spend time serving their country, mostly in military roles. For many years, those who choose military service–about 80% of all young Finnish men–have been given a standardized personality test at the start of their training. These tests provided an enormous data set for researchers to examine. They chose data from men born between 1962 and 1976, which allowed them to include tax data

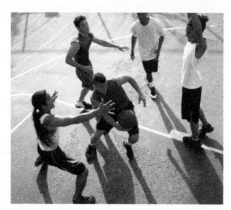
©Sam Edwards/Glow Images

showing these men's average earnings later in life (between ages 30 and 34). This data set included over 400,000 Finnish men and allowed researchers to look at personality trends over time and how those trends related to average income (Jokela et al., 2017).

What they found was remarkable: The personality traits of self-confidence, sociability, leadership motivation, activity-energy, achievement striving, dutifulness, and deliberation all increased year after year for each new cohort of soldiers between 1962 and

1978. (A *cohort* is a group of people sharing a characteristic in common–in this case, membership in a given year's military enrollees.) Of those traits, self-confidence, sociability, and leadership motivation increased the most, followed by activity-energy and achievement striving. Dutifulness and deliberation grew at a slower but still steady rate.

If it appears to you that these traits all seem to be related to career success, you're right. When they examined later income levels, they found that the relatively modest growth in these personality traits predicted substantially greater earnings, with the cohort born in 1976 earning about 12% more than the 1962 cohort. Why this should be the case was unclear. The researchers controlled for obvious factors such as inflation and educational attainment, but the underlying cause for the finding remains elusive.

Explaining why personality changes across generations will be the focus of further research, with likely candidates being changes in health, nutrition, and quality of education. But for the moment, it seems clear that personality can change in subtle yet important ways across generations (Jokela et al., 2017).

AP SKILL: SCIENTIFIC INVESTIGATION / DEFINE AND/OR APPLY CONCEPTS

1. What type of research method was used in the Finland study and what is an advantage of using this method?
2. Researchers have also studied changes in intelligence. What term, from Module 28, describes how intelligence has been increasing each decade?

Does the identification of specific genes linked to personality, coupled with the existence of temperaments from the time of birth, mean that we are destined to have certain types of personalities? Hardly. First, it is unlikely that any single gene is linked to a specific trait. For instance, the dopamine-4 receptor accounts for only around 10% of the variation in novelty seeking between different individuals. The rest of the variation is attributable to other genes and environmental factors (Keltikangas-Järvinen et al., 2004; Lahti et al., 2005; Kandler, Riemann, & Angleitner, 2013).

More important, genes interact with the environment. As we see in discussions of the heritability of intelligence and the nature–nurture issue, it is impossible to completely divorce genetic factors from environmental factors. Although studies of identical twins raised in different environments are helpful, they are not definitive because it is impossible to assess and control environmental factors fully. Furthermore, estimates of the influence of genetics are just that–estimates–and apply to groups, not individuals. Consequently, findings such as those shown in Figure 4 must be regarded as approximations.

Finally, even if more genes are found to be linked to specific personality characteristics, genes still cannot be viewed as the sole cause of personality. For one thing, genetically determined characteristics may not be expressed if they are not "turned on" by particular environmental experiences. Furthermore, behaviors produced by genes may help to create a specific environment. For instance, a cheerful, smiley baby may lead the parents to smile more and be more responsive, thereby creating a supportive, pleasant environment. In contrast, the parents of a cranky, fussy baby may be less inclined to smile at the child; in turn, the environment in which that child is raised will be less supportive and pleasant. In a sense, then, genes not only influence a person's behavior–they also help produce the environment in which a person develops (Kim-Cohen, Caspi, & Moffitt, 2003; Kim-Cohen et al., 2005; Kendler et al., 2017).

Although an increasing number of personality theorists are taking biological and evolutionary factors into account, no comprehensive, unified theory that considers biological and evolutionary factors is widely accepted. Still, it is clear that certain personality traits have substantial genetic components and that heredity and environment interact to determine personality (Bouchard, 2004; South & Krueger, 2008; South et al., 2013).

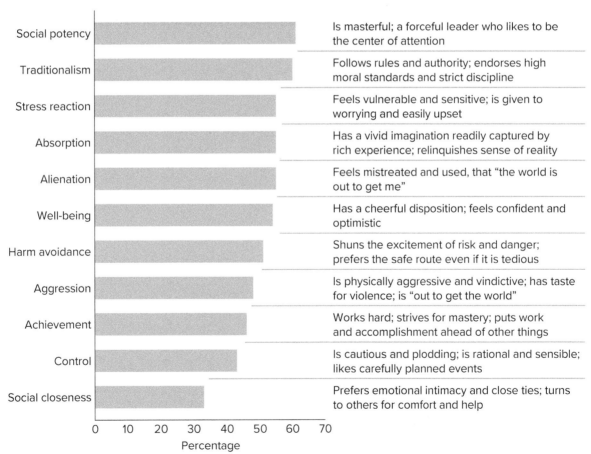

FIGURE 4 The inherited roots of personality. The percentages indicate the degree to which 11 personality characteristics reflect the influence of heredity.

Source: Adapted from Tellegen, A., Lykken, D. T., Bouchard, T. J., Jr., Wilcox, K. J., Segal, N. L., & Rich, S. (1998). Personality similarity in twins reared apart and together. *Journal of Personality and Social Psychology, 54,* 1031–1039.

Humanistic Approaches: The Uniqueness of You

In all the approaches to personality that we have discussed, where is an explanation for the saintliness of a Mother Teresa, the creativity of a Michelangelo, and the brilliance and perseverance of an Einstein? An understanding of such unique individuals—as well as more ordinary sorts of people who have some of the same attributes—comes from humanistic theory.

According to humanistic theorists, all the approaches to personality we have discussed share a fundamental misperception in their views of human nature. Instead of seeing people as controlled by unconscious, unseen forces (psychodynamic approaches), a set of stable traits (trait approaches), situational reinforcements and punishments (learning theory), or inherited factors (biological and evolutionary approaches), **humanistic approaches to personality** emphasize people's inherent goodness and their tendency to move toward higher levels of functioning. It is this conscious, self-motivated ability to change and improve, along with people's unique creative impulses, that humanistic theorists argue make up the core of personality.

humanistic approaches to personality Theories that emphasize people's innate goodness and desire to achieve higher levels of functioning. (Module 41)

ROGERS AND THE NEED FOR SELF-ACTUALIZATION

The major proponent of the humanistic point of view is Carl Rogers (1971). Along with other humanistic theorists, such as Abraham Maslow, Rogers maintains that all people have a fundamental need for **self-actualization,** a state of self-fulfillment in which people realize their highest potential, each in a unique way. He further suggests that people develop a need for positive regard that reflects the desire to be loved and respected. Because others provide this positive regard, we grow dependent on them. We begin to see and judge ourselves through the eyes of other people, relying on their values and being preoccupied with what they think of us.

self-actualization A state of self-fulfillment in which people realize their highest potential in their own unique way. (Modules 29, 41)

According to Rogers, one outgrowth of placing importance on others' opinions is that a conflict may grow between people's actual life experiences and their self-concept. *Self-concept* is the set of beliefs people hold about their own abilities, behavior, and personality. If the discrepancies between people's self-concepts and what they actually experience in their lives are minor, the consequences are minor. But if the discrepancies between one's experience and one's self-concept are great, they will lead to psychological disturbances in daily functioning. For instance, people with large discrepancies may experience frequent anxiety.

Rogers suggests that one way of overcoming the discrepancy between experience and self-concept is through the receipt of unconditional positive regard from another person—a parent, friend, spouse, or even a therapist. **Unconditional positive regard** refers to an attitude of acceptance and respect on the observer's part, no matter what a person says or does. This acceptance, says Rogers, gives people the opportunity to evolve and grow both cognitively and emotionally and to develop more realistic self-concepts. You may have experienced the power of unconditional positive regard when you confided in someone, revealing embarrassing secrets because you knew the listener would still love and respect you even after hearing the worst about you (Snyder, 2002; Marshall, 2007; Patterson & Joseph, 2013).

unconditional positive regard An attitude of acceptance and respect on the part of an observer, no matter what a person says or does. (Module 41)

In contrast, *conditional positive regard* depends on your behavior. In such cases, others withdraw their love and acceptance if you do something of which they don't approve. The result is a discrepancy between your true self and what others wish you would be, which leads to anxiety and frustration (see Figure 5).

EVALUATING HUMANISTIC APPROACHES

Although humanistic theories suggest the value of providing unconditional positive regard toward people, unconditional positive regard toward humanistic theories has

Others' behavior toward you → **Your response**

FIGURE 5 According to the humanistic view of Carl Rogers, people have a basic need to be loved and respected. If you receive unconditional positive regard from others, you will develop a more realistic self-concept, but if the response is conditional, it may lead to anxiety and frustration.

been less forthcoming. The criticisms have centered on the difficulty of verifying the basic assumptions of the approach as well as on the question of whether unconditional positive regard does, in fact, lead to greater personality adjustment.

Humanistic approaches have also been criticized for making the assumption that people are basically "good"–a notion that is unverifiable–and, equally important, for using nonscientific values to build supposedly scientific theories. Still, humanistic theories have been important in highlighting the uniqueness of human beings and guiding the development of a significant form of therapy designed to alleviate psychological difficulties (Elkins, 2009; Kogstad, Ekeland, & Hummelvoll, 2011; Hounkatin et al., 2015).

Comparing Approaches to Personality

In light of the multiple approaches we have discussed, you may be wondering which of the theories provides the most accurate description of personality. That question cannot be answered precisely. Each theory is built on different assumptions and focuses on somewhat different aspects of personality (see Figure 6).

Theoretical Approach and Major Theorists	Conscious Versus Unconscious Determinants of Personality	Nature (Hereditary Factors) Versus Nurture (Environmental Factors)	Free Will Versus Determinism	Stability Versus Modifiability
Psychodynamic (Freud, Jung, Horney, Adler)	Emphasizes the unconscious	Stresses innate, inherited structure of personality while emphasizing importance of childhood experience	Stresses determinism, the view that behavior is directed and caused by factors outside one's control	Emphasizes the stability of characteristics throughout a person's life
Trait (Allport, Cattell, Eysenck)	Disregards both conscious and unconscious	Approaches vary	Stresses determinism, the view that behavior is directed and caused by factors outside one's control	Emphasizes the stability of characteristics throughout a person's life
Learning (Skinner, Bandura)	Disregards both conscious and unconscious	Focuses on the environment	Stresses determinism, the view that behavior is directed and caused by factors outside one's control	Stresses that personality remains flexible and resilient throughout one's life
Biological and evolutionary (Tellegen)	Disregards both conscious and unconscious	Stresses the innate, inherited determinants of personality	Stresses determinism, the view that behavior is directed and caused by factors outside one's control	Emphasizes the stability of characteristics throughout a person's life
Humanistic (Rogers, Maslow)	Stresses the conscious more than the unconscious	Stresses the interaction between nature and nurture	Stresses the freedom of individuals to make their own choices	Stresses that personality remains flexible and resilient throughout one's life

FIGURE 6 The multiple perspectives on personality.

Furthermore, there is no clear way to scientifically test the various approaches and their assumptions against one another. Given the complexity of every individual, it seems reasonable that personality can be viewed from a number of perspectives simultaneously (Pervin, 2003).

AP MODULE 41: TRAIT, LEARNING, BIOLOGICAL AND EVOLUTIONARY, AND HUMANISTIC APPROACHES TO PERSONALITY

AP SUMMARY

- Bandura believes observational learning and cognition influence personality.
- Costa and McCrae used factor analysis to identify the Big Five personality traits: conscientiousness, agreeableness, neuroticism, openness, and extraversion.
- Maslow maintained that all people have a fundamental need for self-actualization in which they realize their highest potential.
- Rogers believed individuals can overcome the difference between their real and ideal self-concept by receiving unconditional positive regard.
- Learning approaches concentrate on observable behavior. To a strict learning theorist, such as Skinner, personality is the sum of learned responses to the external environment. This approach takes a deterministic view of behavior.
- Social cognitive approaches concentrate on the role of cognition in determining personality; they pay attention to self-efficacy and self-esteem in determining behavior.
- The context of a situation impacts personality. Mischel's CAPS theory argues people's thoughts about themselves determine their perception and reaction in situations.
- Humanistic approaches emphasize people's inherent goodness. They consider the core of personality in terms of a person's ability to change and improve.
- Cultural factors strongly affect the development of self-esteem. For collectivist cultures, having high relationship harmony is important to self-esteem.
- Trait approaches identify consistent, habitual personality characteristics. Theorists have struggled to identify the specific number of traits necessary to describe personality.
- Allport identified three categories of traits: cardinal, central, and secondary.
- Eysenck described three major dimensions of traits: extraversion, neuroticism, and psychoticism.

AP KEY TERMS

traits
trait theory
social cognitive approaches to personality
self-efficacy
self-esteem
biological and evolutionary approaches to personality
temperament
humanistic approaches to personality
self-actualization
unconditional positive regard

AP TEST PRACTICE

Section I: Multiple Choice

1. Morgan believes she will master playing the violin. Her belief in this task is an example of
   A. self-concept
   B. self-efficacy
   C. self-esteem
   D. positive regard
   E. conscientiousness

2. All of the following are Big Five personality traits EXCEPT
   A. Openness
   B. Neuroticism
   C. Extraversion
   D. Agreeableness
   E. Compassion

3. Though Ida has made some hurtful comments and canceled plans at the last minute, her friends still accept her as she is. According to Rogers, Ida's friends are displaying
   A. agreeableness
   B. reciprocal determinism
   C. relationship harmony
   D. situationism
   E. unconditional positive regard

Section II: Free Response

Tia must earn a high score on her college entrance standardized test to gain admission to her dream college.

A. Explain how each of the following will help her ability to complete this task.
   - Big Five trait of conscientiousness
   - Unconditional positive regard
   - Self-efficacy

B. Explain how the following will hinder her ability to complete this task.
   - Big Five trait of neuroticism
   - Defense mechanism of regression

Module 42

Assessing Personality: Determining What Makes Us Distinctive

You have a need for other people to like and admire you.

You have a tendency to be critical of yourself.

You have a great deal of unused potential that you have not turned to your advantage.

Although you have some personality weaknesses, you generally are able to compensate for them.

Relating to members of the opposite sex has presented problems for you.

Although you appear to be disciplined and self-controlled to others, you tend to be anxious and insecure inside.

At times you have serious doubts about whether you have made the right decision or done the right thing.

You prefer a certain amount of change and variety and become dissatisfied when hemmed in by restrictions and limitations.

You do not accept others' statements without satisfactory proof.

You have found it unwise to be too frank in revealing yourself to others.

If you think these statements provide a surprisingly accurate account of your personality, you are not alone: Most college students think that these descriptions are tailored just to them. In fact, the statements were designed intentionally to be so vague that they apply to just about anyone (Forer, 1949; Russo, 1981).

The ease with which we can agree with such imprecise statements underscores the difficulty in coming up with accurate and meaningful assessments of people's personalities. Psychologists interested in assessing personality must be able to define the most meaningful ways of discriminating between one person's personality and another's. To do this, they use **psychological tests,** standard measures devised to assess behavior objectively. With the results of such tests, psychologists can help people better understand themselves and make decisions about their lives. Researchers interested in the causes and consequences of personality also employ psychological tests (Hambleton, 2006; Miller, McIntire, & Lovler, 2011; Hambleton & Zenisky, 2013).

Like the assessments that seek to measure intelligence, all psychological tests must have reliability and validity. *Reliability* refers to a test's measurement consistency. If a test is reliable, it yields the same result each time it is administered to a specific person or group. In contrast, unreliable tests give different results each time they are administered.

For meaningful conclusions to be drawn, tests also must be valid. Tests have *validity* when they actually measure what they are designed to measure. If a test is constructed to measure sociability, for instance, we need to know that it actually measures sociability and not some other trait.

Finally, psychological tests are based on *test norms,* the distribution of test scores for a large sample of individuals who have taken a test. Test norms allow us to compare one person's score on a test with the scores of others who have taken the same test. For example, knowing the norms of a test permits test-takers who have received a certain score to know that they have scored in the top 10% of all those who have taken the test.

AP® LEARNING TARGETS

- Describe and compare research methods that psychologists use to investigate personality.

- Identify frequently used assessment strategies and evaluate relative test quality based on reliability and validity of the instruments.

psychological tests Standard measures devised to assess behavior objectively; used by psychologists to help people make decisions about their lives and understand more about themselves. (Module 42)

Study Alert
The distinction between reliability and validity is important. For instance, a test that measures trustfulness is reliable if it yields the same results each time it is administered, whereas it is valid if it measures trustfulness accurately.

Test norms are established by administering a specific test to a large number of people and determining the typical scores. It is then possible to compare a single person's score with the scores of the group, which provides a comparative measure of test performance against the performance of others who have taken the test.

The establishment of appropriate test norms is not a simple endeavor. For instance, the specific group that is employed to determine test norms has a profound effect on the way an individual's performance is evaluated. In fact, as we discuss next, the process of establishing test norms can take on political overtones.

 # Exploring Diversity

Should Race and Ethnicity Be Used to Establish Test Norms?

The passions of politics may confront the objectivity of science when test norms are established, at least in the realm of standardized tests that are meant to predict future job performance. In fact, a national controversy has developed around the question of whether different test norms should be established for members of various racial and ethnic groups (Manly, 2005; Manly & Echemendia, 2007; Pedraza & Mungas, 2008).

The test that sparked the controversy was the U.S. government's General Aptitude Test Battery, a test that measures a broad range of abilities from eye-hand coordination to reading proficiency. The problem was that African Americans and Hispanics tend to score lower on the test, on average, than do members of other groups. The lower scores often are due to a lack of prior relevant experience and job opportunities, which in turn has been due to prejudice and discrimination.

To promote the employment of minority racial groups, the government developed a separate set of test norms for African Americans and Hispanics. Rather than using the pool of all people who took the tests, the scores of African American and Hispanic applicants were compared only with the scores of other African Americans and Hispanics. Consequently, a Hispanic who scored in the top 20% of the Hispanics taking the test was considered to have performed equivalently to a white job applicant who scored in the top 20% of the whites who took the test, even though the absolute score of the Hispanic might be lower than that of the white.

Critics of the adjusted test norming system suggested that such a procedure discriminates in favor of certain racial and ethnic groups at the expense of others, thereby fanning the flames of racial bigotry. The practice was challenged legally; with the passage of the Civil Rights Act in 1991, race-based test norming on the General Aptitude Test Battery was discontinued (Galef, 2001).

However, proponents of race-based test norming continue to argue that test norming procedures that take race into account are an affirmative action tool that simply permits minority job-seekers to be placed on an equal footing with white job-seekers. Furthermore, a panel of the National Academy of Sciences supported the practice of adjusting test norms. It suggested that the unadjusted test norms are not very useful in predicting job performance and that they would tend to screen out otherwise qualified minority group members (Fleming, 2000).

Job testing is not the only area in which issues arise regarding test norms and the meaning of test scores. The issue of how to treat racial differences in IQ scores is also controversial and divisive. Clearly, race-based test norming raises profound and intense feelings that may come into conflict with scientific objectivity (Leiter & Leiter, 2003; Rushton & Jensen, 2006; Davis, 2009).

The issue of establishing test norms is further complicated by the existence of a wide array of personality measures and approaches to assessment. We next consider some of these measures.

From the perspective of...

A Politician Imagine that you had to vote on a law that would require institutions and organizations to perform race-based test norming procedures on standardized tests. Would you support such a law? Why or why not? In addition to race, should test norming procedures take other factors into account? Which ones and why?

©Exactostock/SuperStock

Self-Report Measures of Personality

If someone wanted to assess your personality, one possible approach would be to carry out an extensive interview with you to determine the most important events in your childhood, your social relationships, and your successes and failures. Obviously, though, such a technique would take extraordinary time and effort.

It is also unnecessary. Just as physicians draw only a small sample of your blood to test, psychologists can use self-report measures. In a **self-report measure,** people are asked questions about their own behavior and traits. This sampling of self-report data is then used to infer the presence of particular personality characteristics. For example, a researcher who was interested in assessing a person's orientation to life might administer the questionnaire shown in Figure 1. Although the questionnaire consists of only a few questions, the answers can be used to generalize about personality characteristics. (Try it yourself!)

One of the best examples of a self-report measure, and one of the most frequently used personality tests, is the **Minnesota Multiphasic Personality Inventory-2-Restructured Form (MMPI-2-RF).** Although the original purpose of this measure was to identify people with specific sorts of psychological difficulties, it has been found to predict a variety of other behaviors. For instance, MMPI-2-RF scores have been shown to be good predictors of whether college students will marry within 10 years of graduating and whether they will get advanced degrees. Police departments use the test to measure whether police officers are likely to use their weapons. Psychologists in Russia administer a modified form of the MMPI-2-RF to their astronauts and Olympic athletes (Sellbom, Fischler, & Ben-Porath, 2007; Butcher, 2011; Zahn et al., 2017).

The test consists of a series of 338 items to which a person responds "true," "false," or "cannot say." The questions cover a variety of issues ranging from mood ("I feel useless at times") to opinions ("People should try to understand their dreams") to physical and psychological health ("I am bothered by an upset stomach several times a week" and "I have strange and peculiar thoughts").

There are no right or wrong answers. Instead, interpretation of the results rests on the pattern of responses. The test yields scores on 51 separate scales, including several scales meant to measure the validity of the respondent's answers. For example, there is a "lie scale" that indicates when people are falsifying their responses in order to present themselves more favorably (through items such as, "I can't remember ever having a bad night's sleep") (Stein & Graham, 2005; Bacchiochi, 2006; Anderson et al., 2015).

self-report measures A method of gathering data about people by asking them questions about their own behavior and traits. (Module 42)

Minnesota Multiphasic Personality Inventory-2-Restructured Form (MMPI-2-RF) A widely used self-report test that identifies people with psychological difficulties and is employed to predict some everyday behaviors. (Module 42)

The Life Orientation Test

Use the following scale to answer the items below:

0	1	2	3	4
Strongly Disagree	Disagree	Neutral	Agree	Strongly agree

1. In uncertain times, I usually expect the best.
2. It's easy for me to relax.
3. If something can go wrong for me, it will.
4. I'm always optimistic about my future.
5. I enjoy my friends a lot.
6. It's important for me to keep busy.
7. I hardly ever expect things to go my way.
8. I don't get upset too easily.
9. I rarely count on good things happening to me.
10. Overall, I expect more good things to happen to me than bad.

Scoring: First, reverse your answers to questions 3, 7, and 9. Do this by changing a 0 to a 4, a 1 to a 3, a 3 to a 1, and a 4 to a 0 (answers of 2 stay as 2). Then sum the reversed scores, and add them to the scores you gave to questions 1, 4, and 10. (Ignore questions 2, 5, 6, and 8, which are filler items.)

The total score you get is a measure of a particular orientation to life: your degree of optimism. The higher your scores, the more positive and hopeful you generally are about life. For comparison purposes the average score for college students is 14.3, according to the results of a study by Scheier, Carver, and Bridges (1994). People with a higher degree of optimism generally deal with stress better than do those with lower scores.

FIGURE 1 The Life Orientation Test. Complete this test by indicating the degree to which you agree with each of the 10 statements, using the scale from 0 to 4 for each item. Try to be as accurate as possible. There are no right or wrong answers.

Source: Adapted from Scheier, M. F., Carver, C. S., & Bridges, M. W. (1994). Distinguishing optimism from neuroticism (and trait anxiety, self-mastery, and self-esteem): A reevaluation of the Life Orientation Test. *Journal of Personality and Social Psychology, 67,* 1063–1078.

test standardization A technique used to validate questions in personality tests by studying the responses of people with known diagnoses. (Module 42)

How did the authors of the MMPI-2-RF determine what specific patterns of responses indicate? The procedure they used is typical of personality test construction–a process known as **test standardization.** To create the test, the test authors asked groups of psychiatric patients with a specific diagnosis, such as depression or schizophrenia, to complete a large number of items. They then determined which items best differentiated members of those groups from a comparison group of normal participants and included those specific items in the final version of the test. By systematically carrying out this procedure on groups with different diagnoses, the test authors were able to devise a number of subscales that identified forms of abnormal behavior (see Figure 2).

When the MMPI-2-RF is used for the purpose for which it was devised–identification of personality disorders–it does a good job. However, like other personality tests, it presents an opportunity for abuse. For instance, employers who use it as a screening tool for job applicants may interpret the results improperly by relying too heavily on the results of individual scales instead of taking into account the overall patterns of results, which requires skilled interpretation. Furthermore, critics point out that the individual scales overlap, which makes their interpretation difficult. In sum, although the MMPI-2-RF remains the most widely used personality test and has been translated into more than 100 languages, it must be used with caution (Williams & Butcher, 2011; Ben-Porath, Corey, & Tarescavage, 2017).

Clinical scales

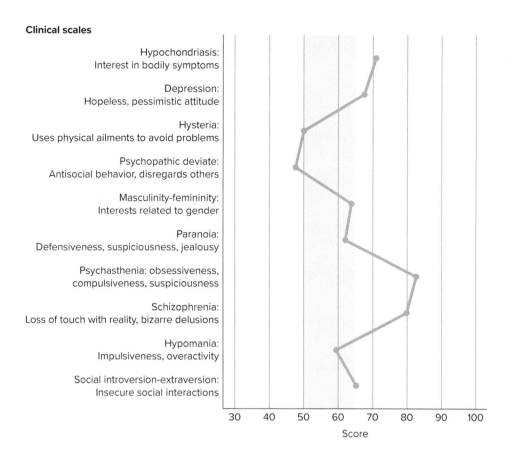

FIGURE 2 An MMPI-2-RF profile of a person who suffers from obsessional anxiety, social withdrawal, and delusional thinking.

Projective Methods

If you were shown the shape presented in Figure 3 and asked what it represented to you, you might not think that your impressions would mean very much. But to a psychodynamic theoretician, your responses to such an ambiguous figure would provide valuable clues to the state of your unconscious and ultimately to your general personality characteristics.

The shape in the figure is representative of inkblots used in projective personality tests. In **projective personality tests,** people are shown an ambiguous, vague stimulus and asked to describe it or to tell a story about it in order to infer information about their personality. Responses are considered to be "projections" of the test-taker's personality, and they are scored and interpreted using a standardized scoring method.

The best-known projective test is the **Rorschach test.** Devised by Swiss psychiatrist Hermann Rorschach (1924), the test involves showing a series of symmetrical stimuli similar to the one in Figure 3 to people who are then asked what the figures represent to them. Their responses are recorded, and people are classified into personality types requiring a complex set of judgments on the part of the examiner. For instance, individuals who see a bear in one particular Rorschach inkblot are thought to have a strong degree of emotional control, according to the scoring guidelines Rorschach developed (Silverstein, 2007; Searls, 2017).

The **Thematic Apperception Test (TAT)** is another well-known projective test. The TAT consists of a series of pictures about which a person is asked to write a story. The stories are then used to draw inferences about the writer's personality characteristics (Langan-Fox & Grant, 2006; Manjhi & Purty, 2017).

Tests with stimuli as ambiguous as those used in the Rorschach and TAT require a high degree of training, skill, and care in their interpretation—so much so that many psychologists question the validity of projective test results. The Rorschach in particular has been criticized for requiring examiners to make many broad inferences that

projective personality test A test in which a person is shown an ambiguous stimulus and asked to describe it or tell a story about it in order to infer information about their personality. (Module 42)

Rorschach test A test that involves showing a series of symmetrical visual stimuli to people who then are asked what the figures represent to them. (Module 42)

Thematic Apperception Test (TAT) A test consisting of a series of pictures about which a person is asked to write a story. (Module 42)

Study Alert

In projective tests such as the Rorschach, researchers present an ambiguous stimulus and ask a person to describe or tell a story about it. They then use the responses to make inferences about personality.

behavioral assessment Direct measures of an individual's behavior used to describe personality characteristics. (Module 42)

lack an objective basis, at least in the view of critics. Furthermore, attempts to standardize the scoring of the Rorschach have frequently failed.

Despite such problems, both the Rorschach and the TAT are widely used, especially in clinical settings, and their proponents suggest that their reliability and validity are great enough to provide useful inferences about personality (Society for Personality Assessment, 2005; Campos, 2011; Husain, 2015).

Behavioral Assessment

If you were a psychologist subscribing to a learning approach to personality, you would be likely to object to the indirect nature of projective tests. Instead, you would be more apt to use **behavioral assessment**–direct measures of an individual's behavior designed to describe characteristics indicative of personality. As with observational research, behavioral assessment may be carried out naturalistically by observing people in their own settings: in the workplace, at home, or in school. In other cases, behavioral assessment occurs in the laboratory under controlled conditions in which a psychologist sets up a situation and observes an individual's behavior (Miller & Leffard, 2007; O'Brien & Young, 2013; Wannez et al., 2017).

Regardless of the setting in which behavior is observed, an effort is made to ensure that behavioral assessment is carried out objectively and quantifies behavior as much as possible. For example, an observer may record the number of social contacts a person initiates, the number of questions asked, or the number of aggressive acts. Another method is to measure the duration of events: the duration of a child's temper tantrum, the length of a conversation, the amount of time spent working, or the time spent in cooperative behavior.

Behavioral assessment is particularly appropriate for observing–and eventually remedying–specific behavioral difficulties, such as shyness in children. It provides a means of assessing the specific nature and incidence of a problem and subsequently allows psychologists to determine whether intervention techniques have been successful.

Behavioral assessment techniques based on learning theories of personality have also made important contributions to the treatment of certain kinds of psychological difficulties. In addition, they are also used to make hiring and personnel decision in the workplace.

BECOMING AN INFORMED CONSUMER
of Psychology

Assessing Personality Assessments

Many companies, ranging from General Motors to Microsoft, employ personality tests to help determine who gets hired. In fact, workplace personality testing has become a big business, with companies spending $500 million a year to help identify the best employees (Weber & Dwoskin, 2014).

What kinds of questions are potential workers asked? In one example, potential Microsoft employees have been asked brainteasers such as "If you had to remove one of the 50 U.S. states, which would it be?" (Hint: First define *remove*. If you mean the death of everyone in the state, suggest a low-population state. If you mean quitting the country, then go for an outlying state such as Alaska or Hawaii.) Other employers ask questions that are even more vague ("Describe November"). With such questions, it's not always clear that the tests are reliable or valid (McGinn, 2003).

Before relying too heavily on the results of such personality testing as a potential employee, employer, or consumer of testing services, you should keep several points in mind:

- *Understand what the test claims to measure.* Standard personality measures are accompanied by information that discusses how the test was developed, to whom it is most applicable, and how the results should be interpreted. Read any explanations of the test; they will help you understand the results.
- *Do not base a decision only on the results of any one test.* Test results should be interpreted in the context of other information, such as academic records, social interests, and home and community activities.
- *Remember that test results are not always accurate.* The results may be in error; the test may be unreliable or invalid. For example, you may have had a "bad day" when you took the test, or the person scoring and interpreting the test may have made a mistake. You should not place too much significance on the results of a single administration of any test.

In sum, it is important to keep in mind the complexity of human behavior—particularly your own. No single test can provide an understanding of the intricacies of someone's personality without considering a good deal more information than can be provided in a single testing session (Gladwell, 2004; Paul, 2004; Hogan, Davies, & Hogan, 2007).

AP❚ MODULE 42: ASSESSING PERSONALITY: DETERMINING WHAT MAKES US DISTINCTIVE

AP SUMMARY

- Behavioral assessments directly measure an individual's behavior, naturalistically or in a lab, to determine characteristics related to personality.
- Self-report measures gather data by asking people about their own behavior and traits.
- Personality inventories, such as the MMPI-2-RF, are standard assessment tools that measure behavior objectively.
- Psychological tests for personality should be reliable, valid, and normed.

- The MMPI-2-RF was originally used to identify psychological disorders and has been standardized. It is now widely used to predict a variety of behaviors.
- Projective personality tests, such as the Rorschach and the TAT, are used to infer information about one's personality based on their response to ambiguous stimuli. The validity and reliability of these assessments have been criticized.

AP KEY TERMS

psychological tests
self-report measures
Minnesota Multiphasic Personality Inventory-2-
    Restructured Form (MMPI-2-RF)
test standardization
projective personality test
Rorschach test
Thematic Apperception Test (TAT)
behavioral assessment

AP TEST PRACTICE

Section I: Multiple Choice

1. What approach is most likely to use a projective test?
   A. Humanistic
   B. Behavioral
   C. Cognitive
   D. Trait
   E. Psychoanalytic

2. Brandon has been shown several symmetrical images and has been asked what the figures mean to him. What type of assessment has been administered to Brandon?
   A. Rorschach
   B. Thematic Apperception Test
   C. Draw-a-Person
   D. Sentence completion
   E. MMPI-2-RF

3. What type of assessment is the MMPI-2-RF?
   A. Cross-sectional
   B. Projective
   C. Achievement
   D. Personality inventory
   E. Longitudinal

Section II: Free Response

Sam has been asked to take a personality test for a future job.

A. Explain the purpose of these personality assessments related to Sam and his employment.
   • Projective
   • Personality inventory
   • Behavioral assessment

B. Describe how the following personality assessments would be administered to Sam.
   • MMPI-2-RF
   • Rorschach
   • Thematic Apperception Test

C. Sam should question these personality tests before he accepts the results.
   • Provide an example of a personality test construction consideration based on research.

LOOKING *Back*

EPILOGUE

We have discussed the different ways in which psychologists have interpreted the development and structure of personality. The perspectives we examined ranged from Freud's analysis of personality based primarily on internal, unconscious factors to the externally based view championed by learning theorists of personality as a learned set of traits and actions. We also noted that there are many ways to interpret personality; by no means does a consensus exist on what the key traits are that are central to personality.

VISUAL SUMMARY 13 Personality

MODULE 40 Psychodynamic Approaches

Freud's Psychoanalytic Theory

— Conscious experience: only part of our psychological experience

— Unconscious: part of the personality of which we are not aware

— Structure of personality

- Id: Represents the raw, unorganized, inborn part of personality
- Ego: Strives to balance desires of the id and realities of the outside world
- Superego: Harshly judges the morality of our behavior

— Psychosexual stages

Stage	Age	Major Characteristics
Oral	Birth to 12–18 months	Interest in oral gratification from sucking, eating, mouthing, biting
Anal	12–18 months to 3 years	Gratification from expelling and withholding feces; coming to terms with society's controls relating to toilet training
Phallic	3 to 5–6 years	Interest in the genitals, coming to terms with Oedipal conflict leading to identification with same-sex parent
Latency	5–6 years to adolescence	Sexual concerns largely unimportant
Genital	Adolescence to adulthood	Reemergence of sexual interests and establishment of mature sexual relationships

— Defense mechanisms: Unconscious strategies people use to reduce anxiety

Neo-Freudian Psychoanalysts: Emphasize the ego more than Freud: Carl Jung, Karen Horney, Alfred Adler

MODULE 41 Trait, Learning, Biological and Evolutionary, and Humanistic Approaches

Trait Approaches: Emphasize consistent personality characteristics and behaviors called traits

— Eysenck: Extraversion, neuroticism, and psychoticism

— The big five personality traits: Openness to experience, conscientiousness, extraversion, agreeableness, neuroticism

Learning Approaches: Emphasize that personality is the sum of learned responses to the external environment

— B. F. Skinner: Personality is a collection of learned behavior patterns that are a result of reinforcement

Learning Approaches (continued)

— Social cognitive approaches: Emphasize the influence of cognition as well as observation of others' behavior on personality

— Self-efficacy and self-esteem

Biological and Evolutionary Approaches:
Suggest that important components of personality are inherited, such as temperament

Humanistic Approaches: Emphasize people's inherent goodness and their tendency to move toward higher levels of functioning

— Carl Rogers

- Self-actualization

- Positive regard reflects the desire to be loved and respected

MODULE 42 Assessing Personality

Psychological Tests: Standard measures that assess behavior objectively

- Reliability
- Validity
- Norms

Self-report Measures: A method of gathering data by asking people questions about their own behavior and traits

Projective Methods: People are shown an ambiguous stimulus and asked to describe it or tell a story about it

— Rorschach test

— Thematic Apperception Test (TAT)

Behavioral Assessment: Measures of a person's behavior designed to describe characteristics indicative of personality

(MODULE 40) (photo): ©Ingram Publishing; (MODULE 41) (photo): ©Image Source; (MODULE 42) (photo): ©Spencer Grant/Science Source

©Fancy Collection/SuperStock

CHAPTER 14

Health Psychology: Stress, Coping, and Well-Being

AP'I ESSENTIAL QUESTIONS

- Why do some people respond to stress in a healthier way than others?

AP'I LEARNING TARGETS FOR CHAPTER 14

MODULE 43

- Apply learning principles to explain emotional learning, taste aversion, superstitious behavior, and learned helplessness.

- Identify contributions of key researchers in the psychological field of motivation and emotion.

- Discuss theories of stress and the effects of stress on psychological and physical well-being.

STRESS AND COPING

Stress: Reacting to Threat and Challenge

The High Cost of Stress

Coping with Stress

AP'I Applying Psychology in the 21st Century: Does Using Facebook Make You Feel Bad?

AP'I Neuroscience in Your Life: The Neuroscience of Resilience

Becoming an Informed Consumer of Psychology: Effective Coping Strategies

MODULE 44

- Discuss theories of stress and the effects of stress on psychological and physical well-being.

PSYCHOLOGICAL ASPECTS OF ILLNESS AND WELL-BEING

The As, Bs, and Ds of Coronary Heart Disease

Psychological Aspects of Cancer

Smoking

Exploring Diversity: Hucksters of Death: Promoting Smoking Throughout the World

MODULE 45

- Discuss theories of stress and the effects of stress on psychological and physical well-being.

PROMOTING HEALTH AND WELLNESS

Following Medical Advice

Well-Being and Happiness

PROLOGUE *BREAKING BAD NEWS*

The situation couldn't be more stressful: Dr. Morgan Wilber, an emergency medical resident at Orlando Health, must give a mom and dad the worst possible news: their child is brain-dead.

Thankfully, though, this is just for practice. The "parents" are professional actors in a program called "Breaking Bad News," which trains doctors in how to say these very difficult things to patients and families. According to Anthony Orsini, who developed the program, the only way to learn this skill is through experience. He therefore created scenarios in which a resident delivers bad news to actors while being videotaped and then receives feedback from doctors and real parents.

No communicative act in the doctor–patient relationship is more important. Says Noelle Moore, a mother who lost her baby and now works with the program, "When a child dies, that moment is like a snapshot in your mind. You never forget what the person says to you, how they say it, and the different sights and sounds in that moment" (Miller, 2016).

LOOKING *Ahead*

While the residents in Orsini's program don't look forward to their hour before the camera, they appreciate that their experience during the simulation can minimize the stress they will feel later, when they have to deliver actual bad news.

Stress and how we cope with it have long been central topics of interest for psychologists. However, in recent years, the focus has broadened as psychology has come to view stress in the broader context of one of psychology's newer subfields: health psychology.

Health psychology investigates the psychological factors related to wellness and illness, including the prevention, diagnosis, and treatment of medical problems. Health psychologists investigate the effects of psychological factors such as stress on illness. They examine the psychological principles underlying treatments for disease and illness. They also study prevention: how healthier behavior can help people avoid and reduce health problems such as stress and heart disease.

Health psychologists take a decisive stand on the enduring mind–body issue that philosophers and, later, psychologists have debated since the time of the ancient Greeks. In their view, the mind and the body are clearly linked rather than representing two distinct systems (Sternberg, 2000; Dalal & Misra, 2006; Grosso, 2015).

Health psychologists recognize that good health and the ability to cope with illness are affected by psychological factors such as thoughts, emotions, and the ability to manage stress. They have paid particular attention to the *immune system,* the complex system of organs, glands, and cells that constitutes our bodies' natural line of defense in fighting disease.

In fact, health psychologists are among the primary investigators in a growing field called **psychoneuroimmunology, or PNI,** the study of the relationship among psychological factors, the immune system, and the brain. PNI has led to discoveries such as the existence of an association between a person's emotional state and the success of the immune system in fighting disease (Mathews & Janusek, 2011; Sperner-Unterweger & Fuchs, 2015; Ayling et al., 2017).

In sum, health psychologists view the mind and the body as two parts of a whole human being that cannot be considered independently. This more recent view marks a sharp departure from earlier thinking. Previously, disease was seen as a purely biological phenomenon, and psychological factors were of little interest to most health-care workers. In the early 20th century, the primary causes of death were short-term infections from which one either rapidly recovered—or died. Now, however, the major causes of death, such as heart disease, cancer, and diabetes, are chronic illnesses that pose significant psychological issues because they often cannot be cured and may linger for years (Rotan & Ospina-Kammerer, 2007; Berecki-Gisolf et al., 2013; Chen et al., 2017).

Advances in health psychology have had an impact across a variety of disciplines and professions. For instance, health-care professionals such as physicians and nurses, social workers, dietitians, pharmacists, occupational therapists, and even clergy are increasingly likely to receive training in health psychology.

In modules 43 through 45, we discuss the ways in which psychological factors affect health. We first focus on the causes and consequences of stress as well as on the means of coping with it. Next, we explore the psychological aspects of several major health problems, including heart disease, cancer, and ailments resulting from smoking. Finally, we examine the ways in which patient–physician interactions influence our health and offer suggestions for increasing people's compliance with recommendations about behavior that will improve their well-being.

health psychology The branch of psychology that investigates the psychological factors related to wellness and illness, including the prevention, diagnosis, and treatment of medical problems. (Module 43)

psychoneuroimmunology (PNI) The study of the relationship among psychological factors, the immune system, and the brain. (Module 43)

Module 43
Stress and Coping

 LEARNING TARGETS

- Apply learning principles to explain emotional learning, taste aversion, superstitious behavior, and learned helplessness.

- Identify contributions of key researchers in the psychological field of motivation and emotion.

- Discuss theories of stress and the effects of stress on psychological and physical well-being.

stress A person's response to events that are threatening or challenging. (Module 43)

> **Study Alert**
> Remember the distinction between stressors and stress, which can be tricky: stressors (such as an exam) cause stress (the physiological and psychological reaction that comes from the exam).

Even positive events can produce significant stress.

©Beijing Eastphoto stockimages Co., Ltd/Alamy Stock Photo

Sheila Gray remembers the worst moment of her life: The day she heard about the mass shootings at Sandy Hook Elementary School in 2012 in Connecticut. Though Gray lives in Michigan, she immediately jumped in the car and drove to her 7-year-old daughter's school. She brought the girl home. "My heart was pounding. I started crying, and I just couldn't stop," Gray says. Then and there, she decided that her daughter, Merilee, would never return to her school. She began homeschooling the girl. Friends could come over, but Gray found she couldn't let Merilee out of her sight. "So much can happen when you walk away from your child," Gray says. "I was terrified by that loss of control."

Stress: Reacting to Threat and Challenge

Most of us need little introduction to the phenomenon of **stress,** people's response to events that threaten or challenge them. Whether they are a paper or an exam deadline, a family problem, or even the ongoing threat of a terrorist attack, life is full of circumstances and events known as *stressors* that produce threats to our well-being. Even pleasant events–such as planning a party or beginning a sought-after job–can produce stress, although negative events result in greater detrimental consequences than positive ones do.

All of us face stress in our lives. Some health psychologists believe that daily life actually involves a series of repeated sequences of perceiving a threat, considering ways to cope with it, and ultimately adapting to the threat with greater or lesser success. Although adaptation is often minor and occurs without our awareness, adaptation requires a major effort when stress is more severe or long lasting. Ultimately, our attempts to overcome stress may produce biological and psychological responses that result in health problems (Dolbier, Smith, & Steinhardt, 2007; Finan, Zautra, & Wershba, 2011; Dierolf et al., 2017).

THE NATURE OF STRESSORS: MY STRESS IS YOUR PLEASURE

Stress is a very personal thing. Although certain kinds of events, such as the death of a loved one or participation in military combat, are universally stressful, other situations may or may not be stressful to a specific person.

Consider, for instance, bungee jumping. Some people would find jumping off a bridge while attached to a slender rubber tether extremely stressful. However, there are individuals who see such an activity as challenging and fun-filled. Whether bungee jumping is stressful depends in part, then, on a person's perception of the activity.

For people to consider an event stressful, they must perceive it as threatening or challenging and must lack all the resources to deal with it effectively. Consequently, the same event may at some times be stressful and at other times provoke no stressful reaction at all. A young man experiences stress when he is turned down for a date–if he attributes the refusal to his unattractiveness or unworthiness. But if he attributes it to some factor unrelated to his self-esteem, such as a previous commitment of the woman he asked, the experience of being refused may create no stress at all. Hence, a person's interpretation of events plays an important role in the determination of what is stressful (Giacobbi et al., 2004; Friborg, Hjemdal, & Rosenvinge, 2006; Tuckey et al., 2015).

CATEGORIZING STRESSORS

What kinds of events tend to be seen as stressful? There are three general types of stressors: cataclysmic events, personal stressors, and background stressors.

Cataclysmic events are strong stressors that occur suddenly and typically affect many people simultaneously. Disasters such as tornadoes and plane crashes as well as terrorist attacks are examples of cataclysmic events that can affect hundreds or thousands of people simultaneously.

Although it might seem that cataclysmic events would produce potent, lingering stress, in many cases they do not. In fact, cataclysmic events involving natural disasters may produce less stress in the long run than events that initially are not as devastating. One reason is that natural disasters have a clear resolution. Once they are over, people can look to the future knowing that the worst is behind them. Moreover, others who also experienced the disaster share the stress induced by cataclysmic events. Such sharing permits people to offer one another social support and a firsthand understanding of the difficulties others are going through (Yesilyaprak, Kisac, & Sanlier, 2007; Schwarzer & Luszczynska, 2013).

In contrast, terrorist attacks such as the one on the World Trade Center in 2001 or the Boston Marathon bombings in 2013 are cataclysmic events that produce considerable stress. Terrorist attacks are deliberate, and victims (and observers) know that future attacks are likely. Government warnings in the form of heightened terror alerts may further increase the stress. Furthermore, exposure to repeated events, whether experienced directly or through the media, may lead to increased sensitivity to stress (Laugharne, Janca, & Widiger, 2007; Watson, Brymer, & Bonanno, 2011; Garfin, Holman, & Silver, 2015).

The second major category of stressor is the personal stressor. **Personal stressors** include major life events such as the death of a parent or spouse, the loss of one's job, a major personal failure, or even something positive such as getting married. Typically, personal stressors produce an immediate major reaction that soon tapers off. For example, stress arising from the death of a loved one tends to be greatest just after the time of death, but people begin to feel less stress and are better able to cope with the loss after the passage of time.

Some victims of major catastrophes and severe personal stressors experience **posttraumatic stress disorder,** or **PTSD,** in which a person has experienced a significantly stressful event that has long-lasting effects that may include re-experiencing the event in vivid flashbacks or dreams. An episode of PTSD may be triggered by an otherwise innocent stimulus, such as the sound of a honking horn, that leads a person to re-experience a past event that produced considerable stress.

Symptoms of posttraumatic stress disorder also include emotional numbing, sleep difficulties, interpersonal problems, alcohol and drug abuse, and in some cases suicide. For instance, the suicide rate for military veterans, many of whom participated in the Iraq and Afghanistan wars, is twice as high as for nonveterans (Pole, 2007; Magruder & Yeager, 2009; Munjiza et al., 2017).

Between 10-18% of soldiers returning from Iraq and Afghanistan show symptoms of PTSD, and the United States spends $3 billion a year on treating the disorder in military veterans. Furthermore, those who have experienced child abuse or rape, rescue workers facing overwhelming situations, and victims of sudden natural disasters or accidents that produce feelings of helplessness and shock may suffer from the same disorder (Horesh et al., 2011; Huang & Kashubeck-West, 2015; Thompson, 2015).

In addition to traditional forms of PTSD, soldiers who have faced multiple tours of duty and who may have actually thrived during years of combat face their own kind of PTSD. After they return home, they may have to unlearn the skills that helped them survive in combat, such as constant vigilance, an intolerance for carelessness, and extreme decisiveness (Carey, 2016).

Terrorist attacks produce high incidences of PTSD. For example, 11% of people in New York City had some form of PTSD in the months after the September 11 terrorist attacks. But the responses varied significantly with a resident's proximity to the attacks, as illustrated in Figure 1; the closer someone lived to the World Trade Center, the greater the likelihood of PTSD. Furthermore, for many people, the effects of PTSD were still evident a decade after the attacks (Lee, Isaac, & Janca, 2007; Marshall et al., 2007; Neria, DiGrande, & Adams, 2011).

Background stressors, or more informally, *daily hassles,* are the third major category of stressors. Exemplified by standing in a long line at a bank and getting

cataclysmic events Strong stressors that occur suddenly and typically affect many people at once (e.g., natural disasters). (Module 43)

personal stressors Major life events, such as the death of a family member, that have immediate negative consequences that generally fade with time. (Module 43)

posttraumatic stress disorder (PTSD) A phenomenon in which victims of major catastrophes or strong personal stressors feel long-lasting effects that may include re-experiencing the event in vivid flashbacks or dreams. (Module 43)

Study Alert
Remember the three categories of stressors—cataclysmic events, personal stressors, and background stressors—and that they produce different levels of stress.

background stressors ("daily hassles") Everyday annoyances, such as being stuck in traffic, that cause minor irritations and may have long-term ill effects if they continue or are compounded by other stressful events. (Module 43)

FIGURE 1 The closer people lived to the site of the World Trade Center terrorist attack, the greater the rate of post-traumatic stress disorder.

Source: Adapted from Susser, E. S., Herman, D. B., & Aaron, B. (2002). Combating the terror of terrorism. *Scientific American, 287,* 70–77.

Posttraumatic stress disorder (PTSD) in 20 percent of residents south of Canal Street, close to World Trade Center.

PTSD in 7.5 percent of residents north of Canal Street and south of 110th Street, the northernmost point surveyed.

stuck in a traffic jam, daily hassles are the minor irritations of life that we all face time and time again. Another type of background stressor is a long-term, chronic problem, such as experiencing dissatisfaction with school or a job, being in an unhappy relationship, or living in crowded quarters without privacy (Weinstein et al., 2004; McIntyre, Korn, & Matsuo, 2008; Barke, 2011).

By themselves, daily hassles do not require much coping or even a response on the individual's part, although they certainly produce unpleasant emotions and moods. Yet, daily hassles add up–and ultimately, they may take as great of a toll as a single, more stressful incident. In fact, the *number* of daily hassles people face is associated with psychological symptoms and health problems such as flu, sore throat, and backaches.

The flip side of hassles is *uplifts*, the minor positive events that make us feel good–even if only temporarily. As indicated in Figure 2, uplifts range from relating well to a companion to finding one's surroundings pleasing. What is especially intriguing about uplifts is that they are associated with people's psychological health in just the opposite way that hassles are: The greater the number of uplifts we experience, the fewer the psychological symptoms we report later (Chamberlain & Zika, 1990; Hurley & Kwon, 2013; Schmidt et al., 2017).

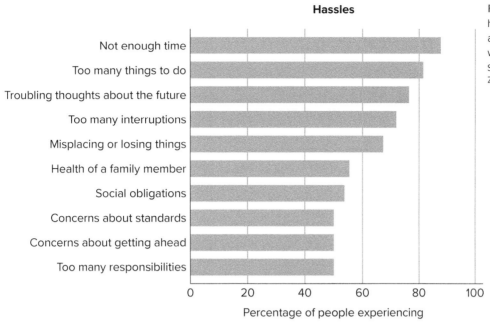

Hassles

Not enough time
Too many things to do
Troubling thoughts about the future
Too many interruptions
Misplacing or losing things
Health of a family member
Social obligations
Concerns about standards
Concerns about getting ahead
Too many responsibilities

Percentage of people experiencing

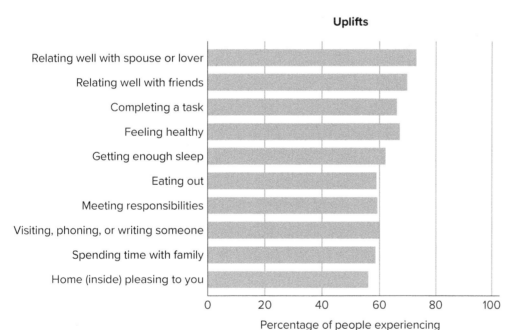

Uplifts

Relating well with spouse or lover
Relating well with friends
Completing a task
Feeling healthy
Getting enough sleep
Eating out
Meeting responsibilities
Visiting, phoning, or writing someone
Spending time with family
Home (inside) pleasing to you

Percentage of people experiencing

FIGURE 2 The most common everyday hassles and uplifts. How many of these are part of your life, and how do you cope with the hassles?
Sources: Adapted from (hassles) Chamberlain & Zika, 1990; (uplifts) Kanner et al., 1981.

The High Cost of Stress

Stress has both biological and psychological consequences. Some of those consequences begin almost instantaneously, whereas others unfold over time.

Often the most immediate reaction to stress is biological. Specifically, exposure to stressors generates a rise in hormone secretions by the adrenal glands, an increase in heart rate and blood pressure, and changes in how well the skin conducts electrical impulses. On a short-term basis, these responses may be adaptive because they produce an "emergency reaction" in which the body prepares to defend itself through activation of the sympathetic nervous system. Those responses may allow more effective coping with the stressful situation (Akil & Morano, 1996; McEwen, 1998).

However, continued exposure to stress results in a decline in the body's overall level of biological functioning because of the constant secretion of stress-related

PsychTech
An analysis of the emotional content of words sent in text messages during the hours following the 9/11 terrorist attack showed that over the course of the day, sadness and anxiety-related words remained steady but anger-related words increased steadily.

psychophysiological disorders
Medical problems influenced by an interaction of psychological, emotional, and physical difficulties. (Module 43)

hormones. Over time, stressful reactions can promote deterioration of body tissues such as blood vessels and the heart. Ultimately, we become more susceptible to disease as our ability to fight off infection is lowered (Ellins et al., 2008; Miller, Chen, & Parker, 2011; Farrell et al., 2017).

Furthermore, stress can produce or worsen physical problems. Specifically, **psychophysiological disorders** are medical problems that are influenced by an interaction of psychological, emotional, and physical difficulties. Common psychophysiological disorders include high blood pressure, headaches, backaches, skin rashes, indigestion, fatigue, and constipation. Stress has even been linked to the common cold (Andrasik, 2006; Gupta, 2013; Gianaros & Wager, 2015).

On a psychological level, high levels of stress prevent people from adequately coping with life. Their view of the environment can become clouded (for example, a minor criticism made by a friend is blown out of proportion). Moreover, at the highest levels of stress, emotional responses may be so extreme that people are unable to act at all. People under a lot of stress also become less able to deal with new stressors.

In short, stress affects us in multiple ways. It may increase the risk that we will become ill, it may directly cause illness, it may make us less able to recover from a disease, and it may reduce our ability to cope with future stress. (See Figure 3 to get a measure of your own level of stress.)

How Stressed Are You?

Find out how stressed you are by responding to the following statements in terms of the last month only. Add up the score from each box. The rough scoring guide below will help you get a sense of your stress level.

1. I was convinced that the big things in my life were beyond my control.
   ☐ 0=never, 1=infrequently, 2=sometimes, 3=fairly often, 4=very often

2. I felt that I could at least control the minor irritations in my life.
   ☐ 4=never, 3=infrequently, 2=sometimes, 1=fairly often, 0=very often

3. I became upset at something that I didn't expect to happen.
   ☐ 4=never, 3=infrequently, 2=sometimes, 1=fairly often, 0=very often

4. I felt confident that I could handle my personal problems.
   ☐ 4=never, 3=infrequently, 2=sometimes, 1=fairly often, 0=very often

5. I felt nervous, anxious, and under stress.
   ☐ 0=never, 1=infrequently, 2=sometimes, 3=fairly often, 4=very often

6. I felt myself to be the master of my life.
   ☐ 4=never, 3=infrequently, 2=sometimes, 1=fairly often, 0=very often

7. I realized that I simply couldn't manage or cope with everything I had to do.
   ☐ 0=never, 1=infrequently, 2=sometimes, 3=fairly often, 4=very often

8. I felt that troubles and worries were mounting so high I couldn't get past them.
   ☐ 0=never, 1=infrequently, 2=sometimes, 3=fairly often, 4=very often

9. I felt that, overall, things were heading in the right direction.
   ☐ 4=never, 3=infrequently, 2=sometimes, 1=fairly often, 0=very often

10. I lost my temper because of something that I couldn't control.
   ☐ 0=never, 1=infrequently, 2=sometimes, 3=fairly often, 4=very often

Here's a rough scoring guide:

0–10 low stress
11–20 moderately low stress
21–30 moderately high stress
31–40 high stress

FIGURE 3 To get a sense of the level of stress in your life, complete this questionnaire.

Source: Adapted from Cohen, S., Kamarck, T., & Mermelstein, R. (1983). A global measure of perceived stress. *Journal of Health and Social Behavior, 24,* 385–396.

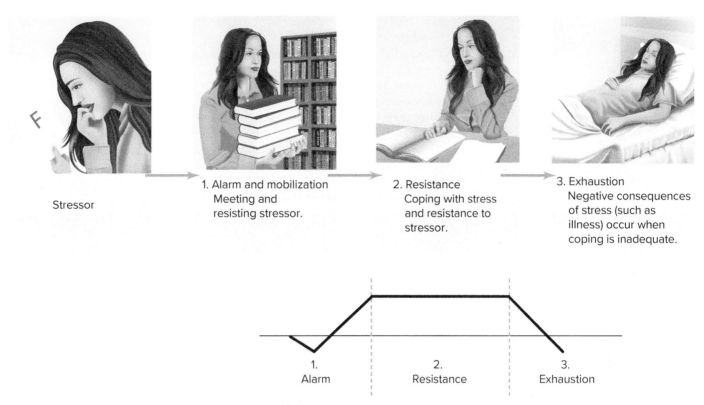

Stressor   1. Alarm and mobilization
Meeting and
resisting stressor.

2. Resistance
Coping with stress
and resistance to
stressor.

3. Exhaustion
Negative consequences
of stress (such as
illness) occur when
coping is inadequate.

1.
Alarm

2.
Resistance

3.
Exhaustion

FIGURE 4 According to the general adaptation syndrome (GAS) model, there are three major stages to stress responses: alarm and mobilization; resistance; and exhaustion. The graph below the illustration shows the degree of effort expended to cope with stressors at each of the three stages. ©McGraw-Hill Global Education Holdings LLC, 1978.

THE GENERAL ADAPTATION SYNDROME MODEL: THE COURSE OF STRESS

The effects of long-term stress are illustrated in a series of stages proposed by Hans Selye (pronounced "sell-yay"), a pioneering stress theorist (Selye, 1993). This model, the **general adaptation syndrome (GAS),** suggests that the physiological response to stress follows the same set pattern regardless of the cause of stress.

As shown in Figure 4, the GAS has three phases. The first stage—*alarm and mobilization*—occurs when people become aware of the presence of a stressor. On a biological level, the sympathetic nervous system becomes energized, which helps a person cope initially with the stressor.

However, if the stressor persists, people move into the second response stage: *resistance*. During this stage, the body is actively fighting the stressor on a biological level. During resistance, people use a variety of means to cope with the stressor—sometimes successfully but at a cost of some degree of physical or psychological well-being. For example, a student who faces the stress of failing several courses might spend long hours studying, seeking to cope with the stress.

If resistance is inadequate, people enter the last stage of the GAS: *exhaustion*. During the exhaustion stage, a person's ability to fight the stressor declines to the point where negative consequences of stress appear: physical illness and psychological symptoms in the form of an inability to concentrate, heightened irritability, or, in severe cases, disorientation and a loss of touch with reality. In a sense, people wear out, and their physiological resources to fight the stressor are used up.

How do people move out of the third stage after they have entered it? In some cases, exhaustion allows people to escape a stressor. For example, people who become ill from overwork may be excused from their duties for a time, which gives them a

general adaptation syndrome (GAS) A theory developed by Selye that suggests that a person's response to a stressor consists of three stages: alarm and mobilization, resistance, and exhaustion. (Module 43)

Study Alert

Remember the three stages of the general adaptation syndrome with the acronym *ARE* (*A*larm and mobilization; *R*esistance; and *E*xhaustion).

The ability to fight off disease is related to psychological factors. Here a cell from the body's immune system engulfs and destroys disease-producing bacteria.
©Science Source

psychoneuroimmunology (PNI)
The study of the relationship among psychological factors, the immune system, and the brain. (Module 43)

temporary respite from their responsibilities. At least for a time, then, the immediate stress is reduced.

Although the GAS has had a substantial impact on our understanding of stress, critics have challenged Selye's theory. Specifically, the theory suggests that one's biological reaction to stress is similar regardless of the stressor. However, some health psychologists disagree, asserting instead that people's biological responses are specific to the way they appraise a stressful event. Research supporting this perspective has led to an increased focus on psychoneuroimmunology, as we consider next (Gaab et al., 2005; Irwin, 2008; Taylor, 2015).

PSYCHONEUROIMMUNOLOGY AND STRESS

Contemporary health psychologists specializing in **psychoneuroimmunology (PNI)** have taken a broader approach to stress. Focusing on the outcomes of stress, they have identified three main consequences of it (see Figure 5).

First, stress has direct physiological results, including an increase in blood pressure, an increase in hormonal activity, and an overall decline in the functioning of the immune system. Second, stress leads people to engage in behaviors that are harmful to their health, including increased nicotine, drug, and alcohol use; poor eating habits; and decreased sleep. Third, stress produces some indirect consequences that ultimately result in declines in health. For example, high levels of stress reduce the likelihood a person will seek health care. In addition, stress may result in less compliance with medical advice when it is sought. Both the reductions in seeking medical care and decreased compliance can indirectly lead to declines in health (Lindblad, Lindahl, & Theorell, 2006; Stowell, Robles, & Kane, 2013; Douthit & Russotti, 2017).

Why is stress so damaging to the immune system? One reason is that stress likely decreases the ability of the immune system to respond to disease, permitting germs that produce colds to reproduce more easily or allowing cancer cells to spread more

FIGURE 5 Three major types of consequences result from stress: direct physiological effects, harmful behaviors, and indirect health-related behaviors.

Source: Adapted from Baum, A. (1994). Behavioral, biological, and environmental interactions in disease processes. In S. Blumenthal, K. Matthews, & S. Weiss (Eds.), *New research frontiers in behavioral medicine: Proceedings of the National Conference*. Washington, DC: NIH Publications.

rapidly. In normal circumstances, our bodies produce disease-fighting white blood cells called *lymphocytes*. Our bodies normally produce them at an extraordinary rate—some 10 million every few seconds. Stress may decrease this level of production (Zhou et al., 2017).

Another way that stress affects the immune system is by overstimulating it. Rather than fighting invading bacteria, viruses, and other foreign invaders, the immune system may begin to attack the body itself and damage healthy tissue. When that happens, it can lead to disorders such as arthritis and allergic reactions (Baum, Lorduy, & Jenkins, 2011; Marques et al., 2015).

Coping with Stress

Stress is a normal part of life—and not necessarily a completely bad part. For example, without stress, we might not be sufficiently motivated to complete the activities we need to accomplish.

However, it is also clear that too much stress can take a toll on physical and psychological health. How do people deal with stress? Is there a way to reduce its negative effects?

Efforts to control, reduce, or learn to tolerate the threats that lead to stress are known as **coping.** We habitually use certain coping responses to deal with stress. Most of the time, we're not aware of these responses—just as we may be unaware of the minor stressors of life until they build up to harmful levels (Wrzesniewski & Chylinska, 2007; Chao, 2011).

coping The efforts to control, reduce, or learn to tolerate the threats that lead to stress. (Module 43)

We also have other, more direct, and potentially more positive ways of coping with stress, which fall into two main categories (Folkman & Moskowitz, 2004; Baker & Berenbaum, 2007; Pow & Cashwell, 2017).

- **Emotion-focused coping.** In *emotion-focused coping,* people try to manage their emotions in the face of stress by seeking to change the way they feel about or perceive a problem. Examples of emotion-focused coping include strategies such as accepting sympathy from others and looking at the bright side of a situation.

- **Problem-focused coping.** *Problem-focused coping* attempts to modify the stressful problem or source of stress. Problem-focused strategies lead to changes in behavior or to the development of a plan of action to deal with stress. Starting a study group to improve poor classroom performance is an example of problem-focused coping. In addition, one might take a time-out from stress by creating positive events. For example, taking a day off from caring for a relative with a serious, chronic illness to go a health club or spa can bring significant relief from stress.

People often employ both emotion-focused and problem-solving coping strategies simultaneously to deal with stress. In other cases, the type of strategy differs according to the situation. For example, they tend to use emotion-focused strategies more frequently when they perceive circumstances as being unchangeable, and they use problem-focused strategies more often in situations they see as relatively modifiable (Stanton et al., 2000; Penley, Tomaka, & Wiebe, 2002).

Some forms of coping are less successful. One of the least effective forms of coping is avoidant coping. In *avoidant coping,* a person may use wishful thinking to reduce stress or use more direct escape routes, such as drug use, alcohol use, and overeating. An example of wishful thinking to avoid a test would be to say to oneself, "Maybe it will snow so hard tomorrow that the test will be canceled." Alternatively, a person might get drunk to avoid a problem. Either way, avoidant coping usually results in a postponement of dealing with a stressful situation, and this often makes the problem even worse (Glass et al., 2009; Sikkema et al., 2013; Dunkley et al., 2017).

Another way of dealing with stress occurs unconsciously through the use of defense mechanisms. *Defense mechanisms* are unconscious strategies that people use to reduce anxiety by concealing the source from themselves and others. Defense mechanisms permit people to avoid stress by acting as if the stress were not even there. For example, one study examined California college students who lived in dormitories close to a geological fault (Lehman & Taylor, 1988). Those who lived in dorms that were known to be unlikely to withstand an earthquake were significantly *more* likely to doubt experts' predictions of an impending earthquake than were those who lived in safer structures.

Another defense mechanism used to cope with stress is *emotional insulation* in which a person stops experiencing any emotions at all and thereby remains unaffected and unmoved by both positive and negative experiences. The problem with defense mechanisms, of course, is that they merely hide the problem and do not deal with reality.

LEARNED HELPLESSNESS

Have you ever faced an intolerable situation that you just couldn't resolve, and you finally simply gave up and accepted things the way they were? This example illustrates one of the possible consequences of being in an environment in which control over a situation is not possible—a state that produces learned helplessness. **Learned helplessness** occurs when people conclude that unpleasant or aversive stimuli cannot be controlled. They develop a view of the world that becomes so ingrained that they cease trying to remedy the aversive circumstances even if they actually can exert some influence on the situation. For example, students who decide they are simply "no good in math" may not work very hard in math classes because they believe that no matter how hard they try, they'll never succeed. Their learned helplessness virtually ensures that they won't do well in math classes (Aujoulat, Luminet, & Deccache, 2007; Seligman, 2007; Filippello et al., 2015).

Victims of learned helplessness have concluded that there is no link between the responses they make and the outcomes that occur. People experience more physical symptoms and depression when they perceive that they have little or no control than they do when they feel a sense of control over a situation (Chou, 2005; Bjornstad, 2006; Figen, 2011).

COPING STYLES: HARDINESS AND RESILIENCE

Most of us characteristically cope with stress by employing a *coping style* that represents our general tendency to deal with stress in a specific way. For example, you may know people who habitually react to even the smallest amount of stress with hysteria and others who calmly confront even the greatest stress in an unflappable manner. These kinds of people clearly have very different coping styles (Taylor, 2003; Kato & Pedersen, 2005).

Hardiness Among those who cope with stress most successfully are people who are equipped with **hardiness,** a personality trait characterized by a sense of commitment, the perception of problems as challenges, and a sense of control. People with the hardiness trait have a lower rate of stress-related illness (Baumgartner, 2002; Maddi, 2007; Maddi et al., 2011).

Specifically, the three components of hardiness operate in different ways:

- *Commitment.* People with a strong level of commitment tend to throw themselves into whatever they are doing. They have a sense that their activities are important and meaningful.

learned helplessness A state in which people conclude that unpleasant or aversive stimuli cannot be controlled—a view of the world that becomes so ingrained that they cease trying to remedy the aversive circumstances even if they actually can exert some influence on the situation. (Module 43)

hardiness A personality trait characterized by a sense of commitment, the perception of problems as challenges, and a sense of control. (Module 43)

- *Challenge.* Hardy people believe that change, rather than stability, is the standard condition of life. To them, the anticipation of change is something positive, rather than change being seen as a threat to their security.

- *Control.* Hardiness is marked by a sense of control–the perception that people can influence the events in their lives.

Hardy individuals approach stress optimistically and take direct action to learn about and deal with stressors; they thereby change stressful events into less threatening ones. As a consequence, hardiness acts as a defense against stress-related illness (Bartone et al., 2008; Vogt et al., 2008; Stoppelbein, McRae & Greening, 2017).

Resilience For those who confront the most profound difficulties, such as the death of a loved one or a permanent injury such as paralysis after an accident, a key ingredient in their psychological recovery is their degree of resilience. **Resilience** is the ability to withstand, overcome, and actually thrive after profound adversity (Bonanno, 2004; Norlander, Von Schedvin, & Archer, 2005; Jackson, 2006). (Also see *Neuroscience in Your Life.*)

Resilient people are generally optimistic, good-natured, and have good social skills. They are usually independent, and they have a sense of control over their own destiny–even if fate has dealt them a devastating blow. In short, they work with what they have and make the best of whatever situation they find themselves in (Friborg et al., 2005; Deshields et al., 2006; Sinclair et al., 2013).

Resilience may have its origins in a complex series of biological reactions that occur when people confront devastating situations. These reactions involve the

resilience The ability to withstand, overcome, and actually thrive after profound adversity. (Module 43)

Those who have experienced extreme stress, such as soldiers in combat, may develop psychological disorders such as posttraumatic stress disorder (PTSD). But not everyone who has lived through trauma develops these psychological disorders. What are the neurobiological differences between those who develop such disorders and those who are resilient to stress? Recent evidence suggests that resilience to stress is related to structural differences in certain parts of the brain involved in executive control and emotional arousal (shown in the images below). These brain differences may thus be important markers for understanding who is and is not predisposed to psychological disorders when exposed to high levels of stress (Gupta et al., 2017).

AP SKILL: SCIENTIFIC INVESTIGATION

1. Describe implications of this research.

2. What questions about research method or design should be investigated before accepting the conclusion that resilience to stress is related to structural brain differences?

Executive control network

Posterior pariental cortex

Dorsal-lateral prefrontal cortex

Hippocampus

Emotional arousal network

Amygdala

Anterior middle cingulate cortex

Anterior cingulate cortex

Subgenual cingulate cortex

Source: Adapted from Gupta, A., Love, A., Kilpatrick, L. A., Labus, J. S., Bhatt, R., Chang, L., . . . Mayer, E. A. (2017). Morphological brain measures of cortico-limbic inhibition related to resilience. *Journal of Neuroscience Research*, 95(9), 1760-1775. doi: 10.1002/jnr.24007 release of the hormone cortisol. Although cortisol is helpful in responding to challenges, too much can produce damage. Other chemicals, however, can moderate the effects of cortisol, and it may be that drugs or therapy can stimulate the production of these moderating chemicals. Furthermore, some people may be genetically predisposed to produce these chemicals, making them more resilient (Cole et al., 2010; Stix, 2011).

Resilience sometimes gives rise to *posttraumatic growth*, positive change that people experience as a result of a traumatic event. Rather than bouncing back to the psychological state they were in before the traumatic event, they actually see new opportunities emerge in their lives. Some people form closer connections with others who have also suffered. Finally, they may develop a sense of self-efficacy, the feeling that because they survived a highly stressful, life-altering event, they can live through anything life throws their way. In a sense, then, resilient people may find that a highly traumatic event leads to personal growth (Tedeschi et al., 2017; Wlodarczyk et al., 2017).

SOCIAL SUPPORT: TURNING TO OTHERS

social support A mutual network of caring, interested others. (Module 43)

Our relationships with others also help us cope with stress. Researchers have found that having **social support,** being part of a mutual network of caring, interested others, enables us to experience lower levels of stress, better cope with the stress we do undergo, and generally experience better health in general (Bolger & Amarel, 2007; García-Herrero et al., 2013; Pietromonaco & Collins, 2017).

The social and emotional support people provide each other helps in dealing with stress in several ways. For instance, such support demonstrates that a person is an important and valued member of a social network. Similarly, other people can provide information and advice about appropriate ways of dealing with stress (Day & Livingstone, 2003; Lindorff, 2005; Li et al., 2015; also see *Applying Psychology in the 21st Century).*

Finally, people who are part of a social support network can provide actual, physical aid to help others in stressful situations. For instance, they can supply temporary living quarters to a person whose house has burned down, or they can offer study help to a student who is experiencing stress because of poor academic performance (Takizawa, Kondo, & Sakihara, 2007).

Findings that attendance at religious services (as well as spirituality in general) provides health-related benefits also illustrate the importance of social support. For example, healthy people who regularly attend religious services live longer than those who do not attend regularly (Powell, Shahabi, & Thoresen, 2003; Gilbert, 2007; Hayward & Elliott, 2011).

Recent research is also beginning to identify how social support affects brain processing. For instance, one experiment found that activation of the areas of the brain reflecting stress was reduced when social support–simply being able to hold the hand of another person–was available (Coan, Schaefer, & Davidson, 2006).

From the perspective of...

A Social Worker How would you help people deal with and avoid stress in their everyday lives? How might you encourage people to create social support networks?

©Sam Edwards/age fotostock

AP APPLYING PSYCHOLOGY IN THE 21ST CENTURY

DOES USING FACEBOOK MAKE YOU FEEL BAD?

Research is clear: Social interaction is good for you. Having stronger social ties is associated with a host of beneficial outcomes, such as better health, reduced rates of mental illness, and reduced rates of harmful behaviors such as alcohol abuse. And you even live longer (Uchino, 2006; Pietromonaco & Collins, 2017).

However, the research literature that establishes these benefits is largely based on real-world, face-to-face interaction rather than interactions via online social networks. With the latter type growing in popularity, an important question emerges: Does online social networking provide the same health benefits as real-world social networking?

There are plenty of reasons to think that online social networking operates differently from face-to-face interaction. People often manage their social-networking profiles to display mostly positive events in their lives, which may create an illusion online that most other people are doing better that you are and in turn lead to reduced self-esteem and increased depression. Conversely, it's plausible that people use social media to reinforce existing real-world relationships and facilitate access to social support, producing positive benefits. Research literature has largely produced a confusing and difficult-to-interpret picture, with multiple studies supporting each of these hypotheses (Nabi, Prestin, & So, 2013; Appel, Gerlach, & Crusis, 2016).

One recent study sheds some light on this landscape. It used a large sample size of over 5,000 adults, monitored their Facebook use, and compared it to measures of their real-world social activity over a period of 2 years and self-reports of their mental health (Shakya & Christakis, 2017).

©Antonio Guillem/Shutterstock

The findings weren't very reassuring for Facebook users. The researchers looked at the frequency with which participants "liked" others' Facebook posts, clicked on posted links, and updated their own status message. Higher levels of these measures were associated with poorer life satisfaction and mental health. On the other hand, having more real-world friends, feeling closer to those real-world friends, and having more frequent interactions with real-world friends were all associated with greater life satisfaction and self-reported mental health.

One possible explanation for such findings is that people who are already feeling bad might be more inclined to take to Facebook, perhaps trying to gain social support or alleviate loneliness or boredom. But the research took into account how participants were feeling at the start, and it was still the case that the more they used Facebook, the worse they felt.

As for why Facebook usage had these ill effects, the researchers weren't sure. The drop in well-being associated with frequent liking of other people's posts seems consistent with the hypothesis that unfavorable comparison to other people's strategically edited lives is driving down self-esteem. But we need more research to fully understand the effects of Facebook use (Shakya & Christakis, 2017).

> **AP SKILL: EXPLAIN BEHAVIOR IN AUTHENTIC CONTEXT / SCIENTIFIC INVESTIGATION**
>
> **1.** What are possible pros and cons of using online social interactions?
> **2.** Summarize the research conclusion involving Facebook.

BECOMING AN INFORMED CONSUMER
of Psychology

Effective Coping Strategies

How can we deal with the stress in our lives? Although there is no universal solution because effective coping depends on the nature of the stressor and the degree to which it can be controlled, here are some general guidelines (AFolkman & Moskowitz, 2000):

- *Turn a threat into a challenge.* When a stressful situation might be controllable, the best coping strategy is to treat the situation as a challenge and focus on ways to control it. For instance, if you experience stress because your car is always breaking down, you might take a course in auto mechanics and learn to deal directly with the car's problems.

- *Make a threatening situation less threatening.* When a stressful situation seems to be uncontrollable, you need to take a different approach. It is possible to change your appraisal of the situation, view it in a different light, and modify your attitude toward it. Research supports the old truism, "Look for the silver lining in every cloud" (Smith & Lazarus, 2001; Cheng & Cheung, 2005).
- *Change your goals.* If you are faced with an uncontrollable situation, a reasonable strategy is to adopt new goals that are practical in view of the particular situation. For example, a dancer who has been in an automobile accident and has lost full use of her legs may no longer aspire to a career in dance but might modify her goals and try to become a choreographer.
- *Modify your physiological reactions to stress.* Many people don't know that they can directly change their physiological reactions to stress, which can help with coping. For example, biofeedback (in which a person learns to control internal physiological processes through conscious thought) can alter basic physiological reactions to stress and permit the person to reduce blood pressure, heart rate, and other consequences of heightened stress. Exercise can also be effective in reducing stress (Langreth, 2000; Spencer et al., 2003; Hamer, Taylor, & Steptoe, 2006).
- *Change the situations that are likely to cause stress.* In *proactive coping,* you anticipate and try to head off stress *before* you encounter it. For example, if you know your upcoming week is going to be grueling because you must take a number of major tests, rearrange your schedule so you have more time to study or take direct steps to improve your chances for success by attending test review sessions (Bode et al., 2007; Kalka, 2017).

AP MODULE 43: STRESS AND COPING

AP SUMMARY

- Stress can be reduced by developing a sense of control over one's circumstances. However, in some cases a lack of control leads to a state of learned helplessness causing individuals to give up.
- The consequences of stress can be explained in part by Selye's general adaptation syndrome (GAS), which suggests that there are three stages in stress responses: alarm, resistance, and exhaustion.
- Health psychology considers how psychology can be applied to the prevention, diagnosis, and treatment of medical problems.
- Stress is a response to threatening environmental conditions, both positive and negative. There are three general types of stressors: cataclysmic events, personal stressors, and background stressors.
- Stress produces immediate physiological reactions. In the short term, those reactions may be adaptive, but, in the long term, they may have negative consequences,

including the development of disorders and damage to the immune system.
- Coping with stress can take many different forms, including the use of defense mechanisms and emotion-focused or problem-focused coping strategies.
- Those who cope best with stress often possess hardiness, resilience, and social support.

AP KEY TERMS

health psychology
stress
cataclysmic events
personal stressors
posttraumatic stress
  disorder (PTSD)
background stressors
  ("daily hassles")
psychophysiological
  disorders

general adaptation
  syndrome (GAS)
psychoneuroimmunology
  (PNI)
coping
learned helplessness
hardiness
resilience
social support

AP TEST PRACTICE

Section I: Multiple Choice

1. High levels of stress can lead to all of the following EXCEPT
   A. deterioration of body tissues
   B. susceptibility to diseases
   C. lowered immune system
   D. worsened physical problems
   E. increased compliance in medical care

2. What stage of the general adaptation syndrome model is activated when the nervous system initially becomes energized to cope with the stressor?
   A. Alarm
   B. Resistance
   C. Exhaustion
   D. Cataclysmic
   E. Resilience

3. John recently lost his job. What type of stressor is John experiencing?
   A. Cataclysmic event
   B. Background stressor
   C. Daily hassles
   D. Personal stressor
   E. Major catastrophe

Section II: Free Response

Ali had been working on a large project for class but left it at home the morning it was due.

A. Describe how his body will react to this stressor.
   - Alarm stage of GAS
   - Resistance stage of GAS
   - Exhaustion stage of GAS
   - Immune system

B. Explain how Ali may deal with this stress.
   - Problem-focused coping
   - Defense mechanism
   - Learned helplessness

Module 44
Psychological Aspects of Illness and Well-Being

 LEARNING
TARGETS

- Discuss theories of stress and the effects of stress on psychological and physical well-being.

Can simply talking with others about your experiences as a patient fighting cancer extend your life?

As recently as three decades ago, most psychologists and health-care providers would have scoffed at the notion that participating in a discussion group could improve a cancer patient's chances of survival. Today, however, such methods have gained increasing acceptance.

Growing evidence suggests that psychological factors have a substantial impact both on major health problems that were once seen in purely physiological terms and on our everyday sense of health, well-being, and happiness. We'll consider the psychological components of three major health problems—heart disease, cancer, and smoking—and then consider the nature of people's well-being and happiness.

The As, Bs, and Ds of Coronary Heart Disease

Tim knew it wasn't going to be his day when he got stuck in traffic behind a slow-moving farm truck. How could the driver dawdle like that? Didn't he have anything of any importance to do? Things didn't get any better when Tim arrived on campus and discovered the library didn't have the books he needed. He could almost feel the tension rising.

"I need that material to finish my paper," he thought to himself.

He knew that meant he wouldn't be able to get his paper done early, and that meant he wouldn't have the time he wanted to revise the paper. He wanted it to be a first-class paper. This time, Tim wanted to get a better grade than his roommate, Luis. Although Luis didn't know it, Tim felt that they were in competition and that Luis was always trying to better him, whether academically or just playing cards.

"In fact," Tim mused to himself, "I feel like I'm in competition with everyone, no matter what I'm doing."

Have you, like Tim, ever seethed impatiently at being caught behind a slow-moving vehicle, felt anger and frustration at not finding material you needed at the library, or experienced a sense of competitiveness with your classmates?

Many of us experience these sorts of feelings at one time or another, but for some people, they represent a pervasive, characteristic set of personality traits known as the Type A behavior pattern. The **Type A behavior pattern** is a cluster of behaviors involving hostility, competitiveness, time urgency, and feeling driven. In contrast, the **Type B behavior pattern** is characterized by a patient, cooperative, noncompetitive, and nonaggressive manner. It's important to keep in mind that Type A and Type B represent the ends of a continuum, and most people fall somewhere in between the two endpoints. Few people are purely a Type A or a Type B.

The importance of the Type A behavior pattern lies in its links to coronary heart disease. Men who display the Type A pattern develop coronary heart disease twice as often and suffer significantly more fatal heart attacks than do those classified as having the Type B pattern. Moreover, the Type A pattern predicts who is going to develop

Type A behavior pattern A cluster of behaviors involving hostility, competitiveness, time urgency, and feeling driven. (Module 44)

Type B behavior pattern A cluster of behaviors characterized by a patient, cooperative, noncompetitive, and nonaggressive manner. (Module 44)

heart disease at least as well as—and independently of—any other single factor, including age, blood pressure, smoking habits, and cholesterol levels in the body (Beresnevaité, Taylor, & Bagby, 2007; Korotkov et al., 2011).

Hostility is the key component of the Type A behavior pattern that is related to heart disease. Although competition, time urgency, and feelings of being driven may produce stress and potentially other health and emotional problems, they aren't linked to coronary heart disease the way that hostility is (Williams et al., 2000; Boyle et al., 2005; Ohira et al., 2007).

Why is hostility so toxic? The key reason is that hostility produces excessive physiological arousal in stressful situations. That arousal, in turn, results in increased production of the hormones epinephrine and norepinephrine as well as increases in heart rate and blood pressure. Such an exaggerated physiological response ultimately produces an increased incidence of coronary heart disease (Demaree & Everhart, 2004; Eaker et al., 2004; Myrtek, 2007).

It's important to keep in mind that not everyone who displays Type A behaviors is destined to have coronary heart disease. For one thing, a firm association between Type A behaviors and coronary heart disease has not been established for women; most findings pertain to males partly because, until recently, most research was done on men. In addition, other types of negative emotions besides the hostility found in Type A behavior appear to be related to heart attacks. For example, psychologist Johan Denollet has found evidence that what he calls *Type D*—for "distressed"—behavior is linked to coronary heart disease. In this view, insecurity, anxiety, and the negative outlook Type Ds display put them at risk for repeated heart attacks (Denollet & Pedersen, 2011; Šmigelskas et al., 2015; Lin et al., 2017).

Study Alert

It's important to distinguish among Type A (hostility, competitiveness), Type B (patience, cooperativeness), and Type D (distressed) behaviors.

©Rubberball/Getty Images

From the perspective of...

A Health-Care Provider What type of advice would you give to your patients about the connections between personality and disease? For example, would you encourage Type A people to become "less Type A" to decrease their risk of heart disease?

Psychological Aspects of Cancer

Hardly any disease is feared more than cancer. Most people think of cancer in terms of lingering pain, and being diagnosed with the disease is typically viewed as receiving a death sentence.

Although a diagnosis of cancer is not as grim as it once was—several kinds of cancer have a high cure rate if detected early enough—cancer remains the second leading cause of death after coronary heart disease. The precise trigger for the disease is not well understood, but the process by which cancer spreads is straightforward. Certain cells in the body become altered and multiply rapidly in an uncontrolled fashion. As those cells grow, they form tumors; if left unchecked, the tumors suck nutrients from healthy cells and body tissue and ultimately destroy the body's ability to function properly.

Although the processes involved in the spread of cancer are basically physiological, some research suggests that the emotional responses of cancer patients to their disease may affect its course. For example, some findings show that a "fighting spirit" leads to better coping. On the other hand, there is little evidence that long-term survival rates are better than for patients with less-positive attitudes (Rom, Miller, & Peluso, 2009; Heitzmann et al., 2011; Brandao et al., 2015).

Despite conflicting evidence, health psychologists believe that patients' emotions may at least partially determine the course of their disease. In the case of cancer, it is possible that positive emotional responses may help generate specialized "killer" cells that help control the size and spread of cancerous tumors. Conversely, negative emotions may suppress the ability of those cells to fight tumors (Noy, 2006; Mosher et al., 2015; Lutgendorf & Andersen, 2015).

Is a particular personality type linked to cancer? Some researchers suggest that cancer patients are less emotionally reactive, suppress anger, and lack outlets for emotional release. However, the data are too tentative and inconsistent to suggest firm conclusions about a link between personality characteristics and cancer. Certainly no conclusive evidence suggests that people who develop cancer would not have done so if their personality had been of a different sort or if their attitudes had been more positive (Holland & Lewis, 2001; Porcerelli et al., 2015).

What is increasingly clear, however, is that certain types of psychological therapy have the potential for improving quality of life and even extending the lives of cancer patients by slowing the progression of the disease. For example, the results of one study showed that women with breast cancer who received psychological treatment lived at least a year and a half longer and experienced less anxiety and pain than did women who did not participate in therapy. Research on patients with other health problems, such as heart disease, also has found that therapy can be both psychologically and medically beneficial (Lemogne et al., 2013; Spiegel, 2014; Perrier & Ginis, 2017).

Smoking

Would you walk into a convenience store and buy an item with a label warning you that its use could kill you? Although most people would probably answer no, millions make such a purchase everyday: a pack of cigarettes. Furthermore, they do this despite clear, well-publicized evidence that smoking is linked to cancer, heart attacks, strokes, bronchitis, emphysema, and a host of other serious illnesses. Smoking is the leading preventable cause of death in the United States; worldwide, 7 million people die each year from the effects of smoking (World Health Organization, 2017).

WHY PEOPLE SMOKE

Why do people smoke despite all the evidence showing that it is bad for their health? It is not that they are somehow unaware of the link between smoking and disease; surveys show that most *smokers* agree with the statement "Cigarette smoking frequently causes disease and death." And almost three-quarters of the 45 million smokers in the United States say they would like to quit (Price, 2008; CDC, 2013).

Genetics seems to determine, in part, whether people will become smokers, how much they will smoke, and how easily they can quit. Genetics also influences how susceptible people are to the harmful effects of smoking. For instance, although African Americans smoke fewer cigarettes than whites, they are more likely to die from smoking-related illnesses than whites. This difference may be due to genetically produced variations in how efficiently enzymes can reduce the effects of the cancer-causing chemicals in tobacco smoke (Li et al., 2003; Li et al., 2008; Minică, 2017).

Although genetics plays a role in smoking, social factors are the primary cause of the habit. Smoking at first may be seen as "cool" or sophisticated, as a rebellious act, or as facilitating calm performance in stressful situations. Exposure to smoking in media such as film also leads to a higher risk of becoming an established smoker. In addition, smoking is sometimes viewed as a "rite of passage" for adolescents, undertaken at the urging of friends and seen as a sign of growing up (Wills et al., 2008; Heatherton & Sargent, 2009; Mayer et al., 2015).

Ultimately, smoking becomes a habit. And it's an easy habit to pick up: Smoking even a single cigarette can lead to a smoker finding that *not* smoking requires an

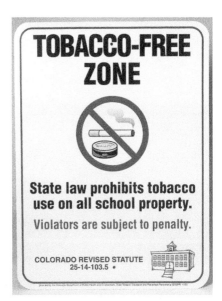

Although smoking is prohibited in an increasing number of places, it remains a substantial social problem.

©McGraw-Hill Education/Jack Holtel, photographer

effort or involves discomfort. Subsequently, people begin to label themselves smokers, and smoking becomes part of how they view themselves. Moreover, they become dependent physiologically because nicotine, a primary ingredient of tobacco, is highly addictive.

When people become addicted to smoking, a complex relationship develops among smoking, nicotine levels, and a smoker's emotions. When this happens, a certain nicotine level becomes associated with a positive emotional state brought about by smoking. As a result, people smoke in an effort to regulate *both* their emotional states and the nicotine levels in the blood (Kassel et al., 2007; Ursprung, Sanouri, & DiFranza, 2009; Dennis, 2011).

E-cigarettes The newest trend in smoking is the use of *electronic cigarettes*, or *e-cigarettes*, which are battery-powered, cigarette-shaped devices that deliver nicotine that is vaporized to form a mist. They simulate the experience of smoking tobacco.

E-cigarette use is growing: More than a third of high school students have tried e-cigarettes at least once, and the numbers continue to increase. Data from the Centers for Disease Control and Prevention show that e-cigarette use among middle- and high-school age youth rose 900% between 2011 and 2015, surpassing use of every other form of tobacco among those age groups. Some 16% of 12th-grade students report using e-cigarettes in the prior month (CDC, 2015; Tavernise, 2015; U.S. Department of Health & Human Services, 2016).

The trend is worrisome to health experts. Although e-cigarettes do not contain the tar and other toxic chemicals found in cigarette smoke, the nicotine itself is harmful to developing adolescent brains and is an addictive substance that can become a long-term habit. Ninety percent of all smokers began smoking as teenagers, and three-quarters of teen smokers continue the habit into adulthood (CDC, 2015).

Because they are so new, little is known about the long-term effects of using e-cigarettes. Teenagers who have a clear understanding of the risks of cigarette smoking are often unsure about the risks of using e-cigarettes, and instead, they point to benefits such as looking cool and being trendy, and the flavorings.

Not surprisingly, teens who perceive e-cigarettes as being less harmful than are other forms of tobacco are more likely to use them, even if they have never tried any form of tobacco before. Although some research finds that e-cigarette use may make it easier to give up smoking of regular cigarettes, the rise in e-cigarette use remains of concern (Giovenco & Delnevo, 2018).

QUITTING SMOKING

Because smoking has both psychological and biological components, few habits are as difficult to break. Long-term successful treatment typically occurs in just 15% of those who try to stop smoking; once smoking becomes a habit, it is as hard to stop as an addiction to cocaine or heroin. In fact, some of the biochemical reactions to nicotine are similar to those to cocaine, amphetamines, and morphine. Furthermore, changes in brain chemistry brought about by smoking may make smokers more resistant to anti-smoking messages (Vanasse, Niyonsenga, & Courteau, 2004; Foulds et al., 2006; Dani & Montague, 2007).

Many people try to quit smoking but fail. The average smoker tries to quit 8–10 times before being successful, and even then, many relapse. Even long-time quitters can fall off the wagon: About 10% relapse after more than a year of avoiding cigarettes (Grady & Altman, 2008).

Among the most effective tools for ending the smoking habit are drugs that replace the nicotine found in cigarettes. Whether in the form of gum, patches, nasal sprays, or inhalers, these products provide a dose of nicotine that reduces dependence on cigarettes. Another approach is exemplified by the drugs Zyban and Chantix; rather than replacing nicotine, they reduce the pleasure from smoking and suppress withdrawal symptoms that smokers experience when they try to stop (Shiffman, 2007; Brody, 2008; Dohnke, Weiss-Gerlach, & Spies, 2011).

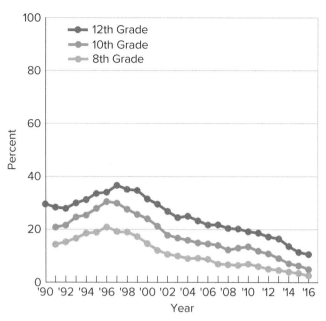

FIGURE 1 Although smoking among teenagers has declined considerably over the past several decades, a significant number still report smoking regularly. What factors might account for the continued high use of tobacco by teenagers despite the increase in antismoking advertising?

Source: Adapted from Johnston, L. D., O'Malley, P. M., Miech, R. A., Bachman, J. G., & Schulenberg, J. E. (2017). *Monitoring the Future national survey results on drug use, 1975–2016: Overview, key findings on adolescent drug use.* Ann Arbor, MI: Institute for Social Research.

Behavioral strategies, which view smoking as a learned habit and concentrate on changing the smoking response, can also be effective. Initial "cure" rates of 60% have been reported, and 1 year after treatment, more than half of those who quit have not resumed smoking. Individual or group counseling also increases the rate of success in breaking the habit. The best treatment seems to be a combination of nicotine replacement and counseling. What doesn't work? Going it alone: Only 5% of smokers who quit cold turkey on their own are successful (Rock, 1999; Woodruff, Conway, & Edwards, 2007).

In the long term, the most effective means of reducing smoking may be changes in societal norms and attitudes toward the habit. For instance, many cities and towns have made smoking in public places illegal; legislation based on strong popular sentiment that bans smoking in places such as college classrooms and buildings is being passed with increasing frequency. In addition, smokers are more likely to quit when their friends are quitting, so the social support of others quitting is helpful (Christakis & Fowler, 2008; McDermott et al., 2013; Mollen et al., 2017).

The long-term effect of the barrage of information regarding the negative consequences of smoking on people's health has been substantial; overall, smoking has declined over the last 2 decades, particularly among males. Still, more than one-fourth of students enrolled in high school are active smokers by the time they graduate, and there is evidence that the decline in smoking is leveling off. Among these students, around 10% become active smokers as early as the 8th grade (see Figure 1; Fichtenberg & Glantz, 2006; Johnston et al., 2017).

 # Exploring Diversity

Hucksters of Death: Promoting Smoking Throughout the World

A Jeep decorated with the Camel logo pulls up to a high school in Buenos Aires. A woman begins handing out free cigarettes to 15- and 16-year-olds during their lunch recess. At a video arcade in Taipei, free American cigarettes are strewn atop each game. At a disco filled with high school students, free packs of Salems are on each table. (Ecenbarger, 1993)

Because the number of smokers has steadily declined in the United States, cigarette manufacturers have turned their sights to other parts of the world, where they see a fertile market for their product. Although they must often sell cigarettes more cheaply than they do in the United States, the huge number of potential smokers still makes it financially worthwhile for the tobacco companies. The United States is now the world's largest exporter of cigarettes (Brown, 2001).

Clearly, the push into worldwide markets has been successful. In some Latin American cities, as many as 50% of teenagers smoke. Children as young as age 7 smoke in Hong Kong; 30% of children smoked their first whole cigarette before the age of 10 in India, Ghana, Jamaica, and Poland. The World Health Organization predicts that smoking will prematurely kill some 200 million of the world's children and that ultimately 10% of the world's population will die as a result of smoking. Of everyone alive today, 500 million will eventually die from tobacco use (Mackay & Eriksen, 2002).

One reason for the increase in smoking in developing countries is that their governments make little effort to discourage it. In fact, many governments are in the tobacco business themselves and rely on revenues from tobacco. For example, the world's largest manufacturer of cigarettes is the China National Tobacco Corporation, which is owned by the Chinese government (Marsh, 2008).

In some countries, children as young as age 6 smoke regularly.

©jan_ta_r/Shutterstock

AP MODULE 44: PSYCHOLOGICAL ASPECTS OF ILLNESS AND WELL-BEING

AP SUMMARY

- Psychologists have identified Type A and Type B behavior patterns. The Type A personality involves hostility, which is linked to coronary heart disease.
- People's attitudes and emotional responses may affect the course of cancer.
- Smoking has proved to be difficult to quit, even though most smokers are aware of the dangerous consequences of the behavior.

AP KEY TERMS

Type A behavior pattern   **Type B behavior pattern**

AP TEST PRACTICE

Section I: Multiple Choice

1. Luke has been described as easygoing. He likes to take long walks to clear his head and sometimes allows meeting times to slip right past him. What type of personality best describes Luke?
   A. Type A
   B. Type B
   C. Type D
   D. Type E
   E. Type T

2. What key component of Type A behavior patterns has been associated with heart disease?
   A. Urgency of time
   B. Feeling driven
   C. Hostility
   D. Competitiveness
   E. Insecurity

3. The following are the most likely reasons why someone smokes EXCEPT
   A. genetics
   B. exposure to smoking in media
   C. habit forming
   D. positive emotional state
   E. unaware of health risks

Section II: Free Response

Amy was recently diagnosed with cancer. She was informed that health psychologists believe there may be some links that determine the course of cancer.

A. Identify the connection of the following with cancer.
   - Positive emotions
   - Therapy

B. Explain how the following terms may relate to the diagnosis.
   - Psychoneuroimmunology
   - Emotion-focused coping
   - Social support

Module 45
Promoting Health and Wellness

- Discuss theories of stress and the effects of stress on psychological and physical well-being.

When Stuart Grinspoon first noticed the small lump in his arm, he assumed it was just a bruise from the touch football game he had played the previous week. But as he thought about it more, he considered more serious possibilities and decided that he'd better get it checked out at the university health service. But the visit was less than satisfactory. A shy person, Stuart felt embarrassed talking about his medical condition. Even worse, after answering a string of questions, he couldn't even understand the physician's diagnosis and was too embarrassed to ask for clarification.

Many of us share Stuart Grinspoon's attitudes toward health care. We approach physicians the same way we approach auto mechanics. When something goes wrong with the car, we want the mechanic to figure out the problem and then fix it. In the same way, when something isn't working right with our bodies, we want a diagnosis of the problem and then a (we hope, quick) repair.

Yet such an approach ignores the fact that—unlike auto repair—good health care requires taking psychological factors into account. Health psychologists have sought to determine the factors involved in the promotion of good health and, more broadly, a sense of well-being and happiness. Let's take a closer look at two areas they have tackled: increasing compliance with health-related advice and identifying the determinants of well-being and happiness.

Following Medical Advice

We're not very good at following medical advice. Consider these figures:

- As many as 85% of patients do not fully comply with their physician's recommendations.
- Some 10% of adolescent pregnancies result from noncompliance with birth control practices.
- Thirty-one percent of patients don't fill their drug prescriptions.
- Forty-nine percent of patients forget to take prescribed medications.
- Thirteen percent take someone else's medicine.
- Sixty percent of all patients cannot identify their own medicines.
- From 30–50% of all patients ignore instructions or make errors in taking medication

Some of these errors are deliberate: Patients sometimes practice *creative nonadherence*, in which they alter a treatment prescribed by a physician by substituting their own medical judgment. Not surprisingly, patients' lack of medical knowledge may be harmful (Taylor, 1995; Hamani et al., 2007).

Noncompliance also can be a result of misunderstanding medical directions. For example, patients with low literacy skills may find complex instructions difficult to understand. In one study, only 34% of patients were able to understand that the direction "take two tablets by mouth twice daily" meant that they should take a total of 4 pills a day (Landro, 2011).

Whatever their causes, medical errors committed by patients and health-care providers are the third-leading cause of death in the United States. Over 250,000 Americans die annually from medical mistakes (Colland et al., 2004; Hobson, 2011; DeAngelis, 2016).

COMMUNICATING EFFECTIVELY WITH HEALTH-CARE PROVIDERS

Teresa Logan lay in the surgical ward as a her doctor drew incision lines on her chest with a felt-tipped pen. The operation would be grueling: 6 hours of surgery to use muscle tissue from her back to reconstruct her breasts, which had been removed months earlier to combat her cancer.

Teresa knew the operation wasn't the worst part; the extended recovery time would be even more grueling. She dreaded the damper it would put on her life as the mother of three young children and a serious runner and swimmer. As the doctor decorated her chest with marker ink, her husband asked a question that no one had asked before. "Is this operation really necessary?"

The answer was mind-blowing: No, it wasn't. If she left her chest as it was, she would recover in half the time with less pain and no adverse effects. The doctor had simply assumed that Teresa would want the reconstructive surgery for cosmetic reasons. Teresa and her husband looked at each other and reached a silent decision. "Get me up off this gurney, please," said Teresa.

Lack of communication between medical care providers and patients can be a major obstacle to good medical care. Such communication failures occur for several reasons. One is that physicians make assumptions about what patients prefer, or they push a specific treatment that they prefer without consulting patients.

Furthermore, the relatively high prestige of physicians may intimidate patients. Patients may also be reluctant to volunteer information that might cast them in a bad light, and physicians may have difficulties encouraging their patients to provide information. In many cases, physicians dominate an interview with questions of a technical nature, whereas patients attempt to communicate a personal sense of their illness and the impact it is having on their lives (Wain, Grammer, & Stasinos, 2006; Wallace et al., 2013; Xiang & Stanley, 2017).

Furthermore, the view many patients hold that physicians are "all knowing" can result in serious communication problems. Many patients do not understand their treatments yet fail to ask their physicians for clear explanations of a prescribed course of action. About half of all patients are unable to report accurately how long they are to continue taking a medication prescribed for them, and about a quarter do not even know the purpose of the drug. In fact, some patients are not even sure, as they are about to be rolled into the operating room, why they are having surgery (Atkinson, 1997; Halpert, 2003)!

Sometimes patient–physician communication difficulties occur because the material that must be communicated is too technical for patients, who may lack fundamental knowledge about the body and basic medical practices. In an overreaction to this problem, some health-care providers use baby talk (calling patients "honey" or telling them to go "night-night") and assume that patients cannot understand even simple information. In other cases, physicians are uncomfortable breaking bad news to patients, so they use medical jargon to avoid being direct (Mika et al., 2007; Feng et al., 2011).

To address such problems, medical schools increasingly include training to improve the communication skills of health-care providers, as we discussed in the prologue to this chapter. For example, they teach physicians to allow patients to speak first and ask questions, and how to convey empathy and honesty through their speech (Reddy, 2015).

The amount and quality of physician–patient communication also are related to the gender of a physician and patient. Overall, female primary-care physicians provide more patient-centered communications than do male primary-care physicians. Furthermore, patients often prefer same-sex physicians (Bertakis, 2009; Bertakis, Franks, & Epstein, 2009; Shin et al., 2015).

Cultural values and expectations also contribute to communication barriers between patients and their physicians. Providing medical advice to a patient whose native language is not English may be problematic. Furthermore, medical practices differ between cultures, and medical practitioners need to be familiar with a patient's culture in order to produce compliance with medical recommendations (Ho et al., 2004; Culhane-Pera, Borkan, & Patten, 2007).

Finally, the newest approaches to improving communication between health-care providers and patients is *e-health communication,* which uses technology to convey information. For example, patients may be virtually reminded using smartphone technology to take their prescribed medicines. Similarly, some health-care providers offer virtual office hours in which patients can communicate with them via Skype or Facetime (Reynolds & Maughan, 2015; Celi et al., 2017).

What can patients do to improve communication with health-care providers? Here are some tips (National Institutes of Health, 2015):

- Make a list of your medical questions and concerns before your visit.
- To prepare for a visit, write down the names and dosages of every drug you currently take.
- Take notes during your visit so you can remember what your health-care provider tells you.
- Ask how to access your medical records online and whether you can communicate with your health-care provider via e-mail and phone.
- Consider bringing a friend or relative with you. They can ask questions and in general advocate for you.

INCREASING COMPLIANCE WITH MEDICAL ADVICE

Although compliance with medical advice does not guarantee that a patient's medical problems will go away, it does optimize the possibility that the patient's condition will improve. What, then, can health-care providers do to produce greater compliance on the part of their patients? One strategy is to provide clear instructions to patients regarding drug regimens. Maintaining good, warm relations with patients also leads to increased compliance (Arbuthnott & Sharpe, 2009).

In addition, honesty helps. Patients generally prefer to be well informed—even if the news is bad; their degree of satisfaction with their medical care is linked to how well and how accurately physicians are able to convey the nature of their medical problems and treatments (Zuger, 2005).

The way in which a message is framed also can result in more positive responses to health-related information. *Positively framed messages* suggest that a change in behavior will lead to a gain and thus emphasize the benefits of carrying out a health-related

Positively framed messages suggest that a change in behavior will lead to a health-related gain.
©UpperCut Images/SuperStock

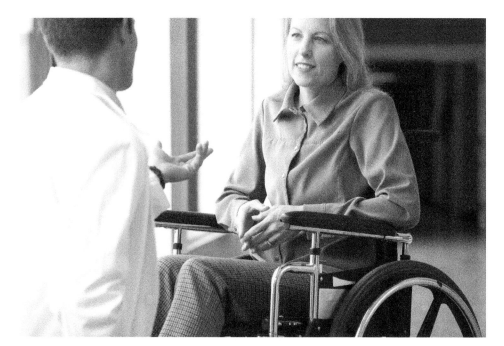

behavior. For instance, suggesting that skin cancer is curable if it is detected early and that you can reduce your chances of getting the disease by using a sunscreen places information in a positive frame. In contrast, *negatively framed messages* highlight what you can lose by not performing a behavior. For instance, a physician might say that if you don't use sunscreen, you're more likely to get skin cancer, which can kill you if it's not detected early.

What type of message is more effective? It depends on the type of health behavior the health-care provider is trying to bring about. Positively framed messages are best for motivating *preventive* behavior. However, negatively framed messages are most effective in producing behavior that will lead to the detection of a disease (McCaul, Johnson, & Rothman, 2002; Apanovich, McCarthy, & Salovey, 2003; Lee & Aaker, 2004).

From the perspective of...

A Health-Care Provider How would you try to better communicate with your patients? How might your techniques vary depending on the patient's background, gender, age, and culture?

©Tetra Images/Getty Images

Well-Being and Happiness

What makes for a good life?

This is a question that philosophers and theologians have pondered for centuries. Now health psychologists are turning their spotlight on the question by investigating **subjective well-being**, people's sense of their happiness and satisfaction with their lives (Tsaousis, Nikolaou, & Serdaris, 2007; Kesebir & Diener, 2008; Giannopoulos & Vella-Brodrick, 2011).

subjective well-being People's sense of their happiness and satisfaction with their lives. (Module 45)

WHAT ARE THE CHARACTERISTICS OF HAPPY PEOPLE?

Research on the subject of well-being shows that happy people share several characteristics (Otake, Shimai, & Tanaka-Matsumi, 2006; Nisbet, Zelenski, & Murphy, 2011; Burns, 2017):

- *Happy people have high self-esteem.* People who are happy like themselves. This is particularly true in Western cultures, which emphasize the importance of individuality. Furthermore, people who are happy see themselves as more intelligent and better able to get along with others than the average person is. In fact, they may hold *positive illusions* in which they hold moderately inflated views of themselves, believing that they are good, competent, and desirable (Taylor et al., 2000; Boyd-Wilson, McClure, & Walkey, 2004; McLeod, 2015).

- *Happy people have a firm sense of control.* They feel more in control of events in their lives, unlike those who feel they are the pawns of others and who experience learned helplessness.

- *Happy individuals are optimistic.* Their optimism permits them to persevere at tasks and ultimately to achieve more. In addition, their health is better (Peterson, 2000; Efklides & Moraitou, 2013).

- *Men and women generally are made happy by the same sorts of activities–but not always.* Most of the time, adult men and women achieve the same level of happiness from the same things, such as hanging out with friends. But there are some differences: For example, women get less pleasure from being with their parents than men do. The explanation? For women, time spent with their parents more closely resembles work, such as helping them cook or pay the bills. For men, it's more likely to involve recreational activities, such as watching a football game with their fathers. The result is that men report being slightly happier than women (Kreuger, 2007).

- *Happy people like to be around other people.* They tend to be extroverted and have a supportive network of close relationships.

Perhaps most important, most people living in a wide variety of circumstances report being at least moderately happy most of the time. Furthermore, life-altering events that one might expect would produce long-term spikes in happiness, such as winning the lottery, probably won't make you much happier than you already are, as we discuss next.

DOES MONEY BUY HAPPINESS?

If you were to win the lottery, would you be happier?

Probably not, at least in the long run. That's the implication of health psychologists' research on subjective well-being. That research shows that although winning the lottery brings an initial surge in happiness, a year later, winners' level of happiness returns to what it was before they won.

A similar pattern, although in reverse, occurs for people who have had extremely serious injuries in accidents, such as losing a limb or becoming paralyzed: Initially, they decline in happiness after the accident. But in the long run, most victims return to their prior levels of happiness after the passage of time (Priester & Petty, 2011; Weimann, Knabe, & Schöb, 2015; Wang et al., 2017).

Why is the level of subjective well-being so stable? One explanation is that people have a general *set point* for happiness, a marker that establishes the tone for one's life. Although specific events may temporarily elevate or depress one's mood (a surprise promotion or a job loss, for example), people ultimately return to their general level of happiness.

Although it is not certain how people's happiness set points are initially established, some evidence suggests that the set point is determined at least in part by genetic factors. Specifically, identical twins who grow up in widely different circumstances turn out to have very similar levels of happiness (Diener, Lucas, & Scollon, 2006; Weiss, Bates, & Luciano, 2008).

Most people's well-being set point is relatively high. For example, some 30% of people in the United States rate themselves as "very happy," and only 1 in 10 rate themselves "not too happy." Most people declare themselves to be "pretty happy." Such feelings are graphically confirmed by people who are asked to place themselves on the measure of happiness illustrated in Figure 1. The scale clearly illustrates that most people view their lives quite positively.

Study Alert

Remember the concept that individuals have a set point (a general, consistent level) relating to subjective well-being.

Faces Scale: "Which face comes closest to expressing how you feel about your life as a whole?"

| 20% | 46% | 27% | 4% | 2% | 1% | 0% |

FIGURE 1 Most people in the United States rate themselves as happy, while only a small minority indicate they are "not too happy."
Source: Adapted from Andrews, F. M., & Withey, S. B. (1976). *Social indicators of well-being: Americans' perceptions of life quality.* New York: Plenum.

Similar results are found when people are asked to compare themselves with others. For example, when asked "Who of the following people do you think is the happiest?" survey respondents answered "Oprah Winfrey" (23%), "Bill Gates" (7%), "the Pope" (12%), and "yourself" (49%), with 6% saying they didn't know (Black & McCafferty, 1998; Rosenthal, 2003).

Few differences exist between members of different demographic groups. Men and women report being equally happy, and African Americans are only slightly less likely than European Americans to rate themselves as "very happy." Furthermore, happiness is hardly unique to U.S. culture. Even countries that are not economically prosperous have, on the whole, happy residents (Diener & Clifton, 2002; Suh, 2002; Suhail & Chaudhry, 2004).

The bottom line: Money does *not* seem to buy happiness. Of course, one needs some minimal level of income; research shows that people living in extreme poverty are sadder than those with higher incomes. Furthermore, income used to purchase services that allow us more free time (someone to clean the house or bring us groceries) produces greater happiness than income spent on objects such as clothing (Kushlev, Dunn, & Lucas, 2015; Whillans et al., 2017).

Despite the ups and downs of life, then, most people tend to be reasonably happy, and they adapt to the trials and tribulations–and joys and delights–of life by returning to a steady-state level of happiness. That habitual level of happiness can have profound–and even life-prolonging–consequences (Diener & Seligman, 2004; Hecht, 2007).

AP MODULE 45: PROMOTING HEALTH AND WELLNESS

AP SUMMARY

- Communication between the physician and patient, as well as increased compliance with medical advice, is important for good health care.
- Subjective well-being is highest in people with high self-esteem, a sense of control, optimism, and a supportive network.
- Most people have a high set-point for happiness.
- Money, beyond the minimal levels needed, does not seem to increase happiness.

AP KEY TERMS

subjective well-being

AP TEST PRACTICE

Section I: Multiple Choice

1. Communication between medical care providers and patients consist of the following barriers EXCEPT
   A. high social prestige of physicians
   B. material is too technical for patients
   C. gender of physician and patient
   D. cultural values and expectations
   E. e-health communication

2. Health psychologists are most likely to focus on which of the following problems with health care?
   A. Incompetent health care providers
   B. Rising health care costs
   C. Ineffective communication between physician and patient
   D. Scarcity of medical research funding
   E. Lack of sufficient health care facilities

3. Winning the lottery is likely to lead to a(n)
   A. immediate and long-term increase in happiness
   B. immediate but not lingering increase in happiness
   C. increase in greed
   D. increase in guilt
   E. decline in happiness

Section II: Free Response

Jayden would like to promote health and well-being at his school. Explain how he could use the following concepts when offering advice to his classmates.
- Framing of messages
- Culture and communication
- Set point for subjective well-being

EPILOGUE

In this set of modules, we have explored the intersection of psychology and biology. We have seen how the emotional and psychological experience of stress can lead to physical symptoms of illness, how personality factors may be related to major health problems, and how psychological factors can interfere with effective communication between physician and patient. We have also looked at the other side of the coin, noting that some relatively simple strategies can help us control stress, affect illness, and improve our interactions with physicians.

MODULE 43 Stress and Coping

<u>Stress:</u> People's response to events that threaten or challenge them
- Interpretation of events is important in determining what is stressful
  - Cataclysmic events
  - Personal stressors
  - Background stressors (daily stressors)
- Posttraumatic Stress Disorder (PTSD)

The Cost of Stress

- Psychophysiological disorders: An interaction of psychological, emotional, and physical difficulties

Direct physiological effects
- Elevated blood pressure
- Decrease in immune system functioning
- Increased hormonal activity
- Psychophysiological conditions

Harmful behaviors
- Increased smoking, alcohol use
- Decreased nutrition
- Decreased sleep
- Increased drug use

Indirect health-related behaviors
- Decreased compliance with medical advice
- Increase in delays in seeking medical advice
- Decrease in likelihood of seeking medical advice

- General Adaptation Syndrome (GAS) Model: The physiological response to stress follows the same pattern regardless of the cause of stress

1. Alarm and mobilization Meeting and resisting stressor.
2. Resistance Coping with stress and resistance to stressor.
3. Exhaustion Negative consequences of stress (such as illness) occur when coping is inadequate.

- Psychoneuroimmunology: Relationship among psychological factors, the immune system, and the brain

<u>Coping with Stress:</u> Emotion-focused or problem-focused coping

MODULE 44 Psychological Aspects of Illness and Well-Being

Coronary Heart Disease

- Type A behavior: A cluster of behaviors involving hostility, competitiveness, time urgency, and feeling driven
- Type B behavior: Characterized by a patient, cooperative, noncompetitive and nonaggressive manner
- Type D behavior: Insecure, anxious, and negative outlook

<u>Cancer:</u> Psychological therapy may improve quality of life

Smoking

- Over 5 million people die each year from smoking
- Heredity, in part, determines whether people will become smokers and are susceptible to harmful effects of smoking
- Few habits are as difficult to break

MODULE 45 Promoting Health and Wellness

<u>Following Medical Advice:</u> Noncompliance with medical advice takes many forms
- Communicating with health-care providers
  - Lack of communication can be a major obstacle
- Increasing compliance with medical advice
  - Patients prefer to be well informed even if the news is bad
  - Positively framed messages: most likely to motivate preventive behavior

  - Negatively framed messages: most likely to lead to the detection of a disease

Well-Being and Happiness

- Subjective well-being: People's own evaluation of their lives in terms of their thoughts and their emotions
- Characteristics of happy people: high self-esteem, sense of control, optimism, enjoy being with others
- Most people are moderately happy most of the time

Faces Scale: "Which face comes closest to expressing how you feel about your life as a whole?"

| 20% | 46% | 27% | 4% | 2% | 1% | 0% |

(MODULE 43) Sources: (cost of stress) Adapted from Baum, A. (1994). Behavioral, biological, and environmental interactions in disease processes. In S. Blumenthal, K. Matthews, & S. Weiss Eds.), *New research frontiers in behavioral medicine: Proceedings of the National Conference*. Washington, DC: NIH Publications; (stressor) ©McGraw-Hill Global Education Holdings LLC, 1978; (MODULE 44) (photo): ©jan_ta_r/Shutterstock; (MODULE 45) (photo): ©UpperCut Images/SuperStock; (faces scale): Source: Adapted from Andrews, F. M., & Withey, S. B. (1976). *Social indicators of well-being: Americans' perceptions of life quality*. New York: Plenum.

©Andrey_Popov/Shutterstock

CHAPTER 15
Psychological Disorders

AP¹ ESSENTIAL QUESTIONS

- Why is psychological perspective necessary in the treatment of disorders?

AP¹ LEARNING TARGETS FOR CHAPTER 15

- Discuss the major diagnostic categories, including feeding and eating disorders, personality disorders, and their corresponding symptoms.

- Recognize the use of the most recent version of the *Diagnostic and Statistical Manual of Mental Disorders (DSM)* published by the American Psychiatric Association as the primary reference for making diagnostic judgments.

- Identify the positive and negative consequences of diagnostic labels.

- Describe contemporary and historical conceptions of what constitutes psychological disorders.

PSYCHOLOGICAL DISORDERS IN PERSPECTIVE

AP **Applying Psychology in the 21st Century:** Is the Newest Generation of College Students More Psychologically Disordered Than Their Predecessors?

The Social and Cultural Context of Psychological Disorders

Exploring Diversity: DSM and Culture—and the Culture of DSM

Becoming an Informed Consumer of Psychology: Deciding When You Need Help

PROLOGUE *RUNNING SCARED*

The first time it happened, Andrea Petersen was staring at a lengthy list of classes, trying to decide which ones to take in the coming semester. One moment the college sophomore felt fine, and the next moment her world exploded. Fear spiraled up her spine. Her stomach flipped. Her heart rate rocketed. Breathing became difficult, and her vision warped. The onset, Petersen recalls, was as sudden as a car crash. All she could think was: *I'm dying. I'm dying.*

Over the next few months, the list of Petersen's symptoms grew—tingling in her feet and face, chest pains, vertigo—and her list of fears lengthened: dentists, touching dirt, licking envelopes, driving on highways. And always, the fear of death.

Petersen saw numerous doctors, and she had EKGs, blood tests, echocardiograms, and an MRI. Doctors suspected many culprits, among them a brain tumor, multiple sclerosis, and Epstein-Barr virus. But no one really knew what was wrong with Petersen. It was at that point that she remembers peering over the banister of a rooftop parking garage and thinking: *Why not jump?* (Petersen, 2017).

LOOKING *Ahead*

Andrea Petersen was losing her grip on reality. It turned out that she was suffering from an anxiety disorder, a psychological disorder that affects millions of Americans, a growing number of them college students like herself. A combination of medication, cognitive behavioral therapy, and mindfulness techniques such as yoga and meditation have helped Petersen keep her anxiety in check, but her experience raises many questions. What caused her disorder? Were genetic factors involved, or were stressors in her life primarily responsible? Were there signs that family and friends should have noticed earlier? Could her anxiety disorder have been prevented? And, more generally, how do we distinguish normal from abnormal behavior, and how can Petersen's experiences be categorized and classified in such a way as to pinpoint the specific nature of her problem?

We address the issues raised by Andrea Petersen's case in this chapter. We begin by discussing the difference between normal and abnormal behavior, which can be surprisingly indistinct. We then turn to a consideration of the most significant kinds of psychological disorders. Finally, we'll consider ways of evaluating behavior—one's own and that of others—to determine whether seeking help from a mental health professional is warranted.

Module 46

Normal Versus Abnormal: Making the Distinction

AP® LEARNING TARGETS

- Recognize the use of the most recent version of the *Diagnostic and Statistical Manual of Mental Disorders (DSM)* published by the American Psychiatric Association as the primary reference for making diagnostic judgments.

- Describe contemporary and historical conceptions of what constitutes psychological disorders.

- Discuss the intersection between psychology and the legal system.

- Evaluate the strengths and limitations of various approaches to explaining psychological disorders.

- Identify the positive and negative consequences of diagnostic labels.

Study Alert

Remember the different definitions of abnormality (deviation from the average, deviation from the ideal, a sense of personal discomfort, inability to function effectively, and abnormality as a legal concept).

Universally that person's acumen is esteemed very little perceptive concerning whatsoever matters are being held as most profitable by mortals with sapience endowed to be studied who is ignorant of that which the most in doctrine erudite and certainly by reason of that in them high mind's ornament deserving of veneration constantly maintain when by general consent they affirm that other circumstances being equal by no exterior splendour is the prosperity of a nation....

It would be easy to conclude that these words are the musings of a madman. To most people, the passage does not seem to make any sense at all. But literary scholars would disagree. Actually, this passage is from James Joyce's classic *Ulysses*, hailed as one of the major works of 20th-century literature (Joyce, 1934).

As this example illustrates, casually examining a person's writing is insufficient to determine the degree to which that person is "normal." But even when we consider more extensive samples of a person's behavior, we will find that there may be only a fine line between behavior that is considered normal and behavior that is considered abnormal.

Defining Abnormality

Because of the difficulty in distinguishing normal from abnormal behavior, psychologists have struggled to devise a precise, scientific definition of "abnormal behavior." For instance, consider the following definitions, each of which has advantages and disadvantages:

- *Abnormality as a deviation from what is average behavior.* According to this definition, behaviors that are unusual or rare in a society or culture are considered abnormal. It is basically a statistical definition: If most people behave in a certain way, it is viewed as normal; if only a few people do it, it is considered abnormal.

    The difficulty with this definition is that some statistically unusual behaviors hardly seem abnormal. If most people eat meat, but you are a vegetarian, this deviation from the average hardly makes your behavior abnormal. Similarly, a concept of abnormality that depends on what is unusual would unreasonably label a person who has an unusually high IQ as abnormal simply because a high IQ is statistically rare. In short, a definition of abnormality that rests on deviation from the average is insufficient.

- *Abnormality as a deviation from an ideal.* An alternative definition of abnormality considers behavior in relation to some kind of ideal or morally appropriate standard toward which most people are striving.

    This sort of definition considers behavior abnormal if it is different from what society considers ideal behavior or from some moral standard. However, society has few ideals on which people universally agree. (For example, it would be hard to find agreement on whether the New Testament, the Koran, the Talmud, or the Book of Mormon provides the most appropriate ideal behavior.) Furthermore, standards that do arise change over time and vary across cultures. Thus, the deviation-from-the-ideal approach is also inadequate.

- *Abnormality as producing a sense of personal discomfort.* A more useful definition concentrates on the psychological consequences of behavior for the individual. In this approach, behavior is considered abnormal if it produces a sense of personal distress, anxiety, or guilt in an individual–or if it is harmful to others in some way.

However, even a definition that relies on personal discomfort has drawbacks. For example, in some especially severe forms of mental disturbance, people report feeling wonderful, even though their behavior seems bizarre to others. In such cases, a person feels fine, although most people would consider the behavior abnormal. Similarly, most of us would think that a woman who says she hears uplifting messages from Martians would be displaying abnormal behavior even though she may say that the messages bring her great satisfaction.

Andrea Yates, who initially was found sane by a jury despite having drowned her five children in a bathtub, was later found innocent due to insanity.
©Brett Coomer, Pool/AP Images

- *Abnormality as the inability to function effectively.* Most people are able to feed themselves, hold a job, get along with others, and in general live as productive members of society. Yet there are those who are unable to adjust to the demands of society or function effectively.

  According to this view of abnormality, people who are unable to function effectively and to adapt to the demands of society are considered abnormal. For example, an unemployed, homeless woman living on the street may be considered unable to function effectively. Therefore, her behavior can be viewed as abnormal even if she has chosen to live this way. Her inability to adapt to the requirements of society is what makes her "abnormal," according to this approach.

- *Abnormality as a legal concept.* According to the jury that first heard her case, Andrea Yates, a woman who drowned her five children in a bathtub, was sane. She was sentenced to life in prison for her act.

  Although you might question this view (and a later appeals jury overturned the conviction), the initial verdict reflected the way in which the law defines abnormal behavior. To the judicial system, the distinction between normal and abnormal behavior rests on the definition of *insanity*, which is a legal but not a psychological term. In fact, the definition of *insanity* varies from one jurisdiction to another. In some states, *insanity* simply means that defendants cannot understand the difference between right and wrong at the time they commit a criminal act. Other states consider whether defendants are substantially incapable of understanding the criminality of their behavior or unable to control themselves. And in some jurisdictions, pleas of insanity are not allowed at all (Ferguson & Ogloff, 2011; Reisner, Piel, & Makey, 2013; Yelderman & Miller, 2017).

Clearly, none of the previous definitions is broad enough to cover all instances of abnormal behavior, and the distinction between normal and abnormal behavior often remains ambiguous even to trained professionals. Furthermore, to a large extent, cultural expectations for "normal" behavior in a particular society influence the understanding of "abnormal behavior."

Given the difficulties in precisely defining the construct, psychologists typically use a broad definition of abnormal behavior. Specifically, **abnormal behavior** is generally defined as behavior that causes people to experience distress and hinders them from functioning in their daily lives (Nolen-Hoeksema, 2007; Bassett & Baker, 2015).

abnormal behavior Behavior that causes people to experience distress and prevents them from functioning in their daily lives. (Module 46)

From the perspective of...

An Employer Imagine that you learned that a well-paid employee was arrested for shoplifting a sweater that cost only $15. Would you fire the employee if you thought the behavior was caused by a psychological disorder?

©Sam Edwards/age fotostock

Because this definition is imprecise, it's best to view abnormal behavior and normal behavior as marking two ends of a continuum rather than as absolute, precise conditions. Behavior should be evaluated in terms of gradations that range from fully normal functioning to extremely abnormal behavior. Behavior typically falls somewhere between those extremes.

Perspectives on Abnormality: From Superstition to Science

Throughout much of human history, people linked abnormal behavior to superstition, magic, and spells. Individuals who displayed abnormal behavior were accused of being possessed by the devil or some sort of demonic god. Authorities felt justified in "treating" abnormal behavior by attempting to drive out the source of the problem. This often involved whipping, immersion in hot water, starvation, or other forms of torture in which the cure was worse than the affliction (Scull, 2016).

Contemporary approaches take a more enlightened view. Today, six major perspectives are used to understand psychological disorders. These perspectives, which are discussed next, suggest not only different causes of abnormal behavior but different treatment approaches as well. Furthermore, some perspectives are more applicable to specific disorders than are others.

MEDICAL PERSPECTIVE

medical perspective The perspective that suggests that when an individual displays symptoms of abnormal behavior, the root cause will be found in a physical examination of the individual, which may reveal a hormonal imbalance, a chemical deficiency, or a brain injury. (Module 46)

When people display the symptoms of tuberculosis, medical professionals can generally find tubercular bacteria in their body tissue. Similarly, the **medical perspective** suggests that when an individual displays symptoms of a psychological disorder, the fundamental cause will be found through a physical examination of the individual, which may reveal a hormonal imbalance, a chemical deficiency, or a brain injury. Indeed, when we speak of mental "illness," "symptoms" of psychological disorders, and mental "hospitals," we are using terminology associated with the medical perspective.

Because a growing body of research shows that many forms of abnormal behavior are linked to biological causes, the medical perspective provides at least part of the explanation for psychological disorders. Yet serious criticisms have been leveled against it. For one thing, some types of abnormal behavior have no apparent biological cause. In addition, some critics have argued that the use of the term *mental illness* implies that people who display abnormal behavior have no responsibility for or control over their actions (Yang et al., 2013; Prior & Bond, 2017).

Still, recent advances in our understanding of the neurological bases of behavior underscore the importance of considering physiological factors in abnormal behavior. For instance, some of the more severe forms of psychological disorders, such as major depression and schizophrenia, clearly are influenced in important ways by genetic factors and malfunctions in neurotransmitter signals (Howes & Kapur, 2009; Li et al., 2011; Hariri, 2015).

PSYCHOANALYTIC PERSPECTIVE

psychoanalytic perspective The perspective that suggests that abnormal behavior stems from childhood conflicts over opposing wishes regarding sex and aggression. (Module 46)

Whereas the medical perspective suggests that biological causes are at the root of abnormal behavior, the **psychoanalytic perspective** holds that abnormal behavior stems from childhood conflicts over opposing wishes regarding sex and aggression. According to Freud, children pass through a series of stages in which sexual and aggressive impulses take different forms and produce conflicts that require resolution. If these childhood conflicts are not dealt with successfully, they remain unresolved in the unconscious and eventually bring about abnormal behavior during adulthood.

To uncover the roots of people's disordered behavior, the psychoanalytic perspective scrutinizes their early life history. However, there is no sure way to link what happens to people during childhood to abnormal behavior that they display as adults. Consequently, we can never be sure that specific childhood experiences can be linked to specific adult abnormal behaviors.

In addition, psychoanalytic theory paints a picture of people as having relatively little control over their behavior. Instead, the theory assumes that behavior is largely guided by unconscious impulses over which people have neither control nor awareness. Consequently, in the eyes of some critics, this perspective suggests that people have little responsibility for their own behavior.

On the other hand, the contributions of psychoanalytic theory have been significant. More than any other approach to abnormal behavior, this perspective highlights the fact that people can have a rich, involved inner life. Furthermore, it underscores that experiences that occurred long in the past can have a profound effect on current psychological functioning (Bornstein, 2003; Rangell, 2007).

BEHAVIORAL PERSPECTIVE

Both the medical and psychoanalytic perspectives look at abnormal behaviors as *symptoms* of an underlying problem. In contrast, the **behavioral perspective** looks at the rewards and punishments in the environment that determine abnormal behavior. It views the disordered behavior itself as the problem. Using the basic principles of learning, behavioral theorists see both normal and abnormal behaviors as responses to various stimuli—responses that have been learned through past experience and are guided in the present by stimuli in the individual's environment. To explain why abnormal behavior occurs, we must analyze how an individual has learned it and observe the circumstances in which it is displayed.

behavioral perspective The perspective that looks at the rewards and punishments in the environment that determine abnormal behavior. (Module 46)

The emphasis on observable behavior represents both the greatest strength and the greatest weakness of the behavioral approach to abnormal behavior. This perspective provides the most precise and objective approach for examining behavioral symptoms of specific disorders, such as attention-deficit hyperactivity disorder (ADHD), which we discuss in module 47. At the same time, though, critics charge that the perspective ignores the rich inner world of thoughts, attitudes, and emotions that may contribute to abnormal behavior.

COGNITIVE PERSPECTIVE

The medical, psychoanalytic, and behavioral perspectives view people's behavior as the result of factors largely beyond their control. To many critics of these views, however, people's thoughts cannot be ignored.

In response to such concerns, some psychologists employ a **cognitive perspective**. Rather than considering only external behavior, as in traditional behavioral approaches, the cognitive approach assumes that *cognitions* (people's thoughts and beliefs) are central to a person's abnormal behavior. A primary goal of treatment using the cognitive perspective is to explicitly teach new, more adaptive ways of thinking.

cognitive perspective The perspective that suggests that people's thoughts and beliefs are central components of abnormal behavior. (Module 46)

For instance, suppose that you develop the erroneous belief that "doing well on this exam is crucial to my entire future" whenever you take an exam. Through therapy, you might learn to hold the more realistic and less anxiety-producing thought, "my entire future is not dependent on this one exam." By changing cognitions in this way, psychologists working within a cognitive framework help people free themselves from thoughts and behaviors that are potentially maladaptive (Everly & Lating, 2007; Ray et al., 2015).

The cognitive perspective also has its critics. For example, instead of maladaptive cognitions being the *cause* of a psychological disorder, they could be just another *symptom* of the disorder. Furthermore, under certain circumstances, negative beliefs may not be irrational at all but simply reflect accurately the realities of people's lives. (For example, feeling depressed because you've been found guilty of a crime may be entirely rational because you are, in fact, likely to go to jail.) Still, cognitive theorists would argue that there are adaptive ways of framing beliefs even in the most negative circumstances.

HUMANISTIC PERSPECTIVE

The **humanistic perspective** emphasizes the responsibility people have for their own behavior, even when such behavior is abnormal. The humanistic perspective–growing out of the work of Carl Rogers and Abraham Maslow–concentrates on what is uniquely human–that is, it views people as basically rational, oriented toward a social world, and motivated to seek self-actualization (Rogers, 1995).

Humanistic approaches focus on the relationship of the individual to society; they consider the ways in which people view themselves in relation to others and see their place in the world. The humanistic perspective views people as having an awareness of life and of themselves that leads them to search for meaning and self-worth. Rather than assuming that individuals require a "cure," the humanistic perspective suggests that they can, by and large, set their own limits of what is acceptable behavior. As long as they are not hurting others and do not feel personal distress, people should be free to choose the behaviors in which they engage.

Although the humanistic perspective has been criticized for its reliance on unscientific, unverifiable information and its vague, almost philosophical formulations, it offers a distinctive view of abnormal behavior. It stresses the unique aspects of being human and provides a number of important suggestions for helping those with psychological problems.

SOCIOCULTURAL PERSPECTIVE

The **sociocultural perspective** assumes that society and culture shape abnormal behavior. According to this view, societal and cultural factors such as poverty and prejudice may be at the root of abnormal behavior. Specifically, the kinds of stresses and conflicts people experience in their daily lives can promote and maintain abnormal behavior.

This perspective is supported by research showing that some kinds of psychological disorders are far more prevalent among particular social classes, races, and ethnicities than they are in others. For instance, diagnoses of schizophrenia tend to be higher among members of lower socioeconomic groups than among members of more affluent groups. Proportionally more African American individuals are hospitalized involuntarily for psychological disorders than are whites.

Furthermore, poor economic times seem to be linked to general declines in psychological functioning, and social problems such as homelessness are associated with psychological disorders. Homelessness, in particular, is linked with high levels of psychological disorder: between 20–25% of homeless people in the United States suffer

Perspectives on Psychological Disorders

Perspective	Description	Possible Application of Perspective to Andrea Petersen
Medical	Assumes that physiological causes are at the root of psychological disorders	Examine Petersen for medical problems, such as brain tumor, chemical imbalance in the brain, or disease.
Psychoanalytic	Argues that psychological disorders stem from childhood conflicts	Seek out information about Petersen's past, considering possible childhood conflicts.
Behavioral	Assumes that abnormal behaviors are learned responses	Concentrate on rewards and punishments for Petersen's behavior, and identify environmental stimuli that reinforce her behavior.
Cognitive	Assumes that cognitions (people's thoughts and beliefs) are central to psychological disorders	Focus on Petersen's perceptions of herself and her environment.
Humanistic	Emphasizes people's responsibility for their own behavior and the need to self-actualize	Consider Petersen's behavior in terms of her choices and efforts to reach her potential.
Sociocultural	Assumes that behavior is shaped by family, society, and culture	Focus on how societal demands contributed to Petersen's disorder.

FIGURE 1 In considering the case of Andrea Petersen, discussed in the prologue, we can employ each of the perspectives on abnormal behavior. Note that because of the nature of her psychological disorder, some of the perspectives are more applicable than others.

from serious psychological disorders (Greenberg & Rosenheck, 2008; Padgett, Stanhope, & Henwood, 2011; Brown et al., 2017).

On the other hand, there are many alternative explanations for the association between abnormal behavior and social factors. For example, people from lower socio-economic levels may be less likely than those from higher levels to seek help, gradually reaching a point where their symptoms become severe enough to warrant a serious diagnosis. Similarly, psychological disorders may cause people to become homeless, rather than homelessness producing psychological disorders.

Finally, sociocultural explanations provide relatively little specific guidance for the treatment of psychological disturbance. Because the focus is on broader societal factors, it is not obvious how to treat disorders in a specific individual (Paniagua, 2000; White et al., 2017).

Figure 1 summarizes the main perspectives on psychological disorders. In addition, it applies each of them to the case of Andrea Petersen, discussed in the chapter prologue.

Classifying Abnormal Behavior: The ABCs of DSM

Crazy. Nuts. Mental. Loony. Insane. Neurotic. Psycho. Strange. Demented. Odd. Possessed.

Society has long placed labels on people who display abnormal behavior. Unfortunately, most of the time, these labels have reflected intolerance and have been used with little thought as to what each signifies.

Providing appropriate and specific names and classifications for abnormal behavior has presented a major challenge to psychologists. It is not hard to understand why, given the difficulties discussed earlier in simply distinguishing normal from abnormal behavior. Yet psychologists and other careproviders need to classify abnormal behavior in order to diagnose it and ultimately treat it.

DSM-5: DETERMINING DIAGNOSTIC DISTINCTIONS

The ***Diagnostic and Statistical Manual of Mental Disorders,*** **Fifth Edition (DSM-5)** is the most widely used system to classify and define psychological disorders (American Psychiatric Association, 2013).

The DSM-5, most recently revised in 2013, provides comprehensive and relatively precise definitions for more than 200 disorders. By following the criteria presented in the DSM-5 classification system, diagnosticians use clients' reported symptoms to identify the specific problem the clients are experiencing. Figure 2 provides a brief outline of the major diagnostic categories (American Psychiatric Association, 2013).

The authors of the newest update of DSM suggest that the manual should be viewed as the "DSM-5.0." The "5.0" name emphasizes that the DSM-5 is a work in progress, subject to revision based on users' feedback. (The next revision will be called DSM-5.1; Kupfer, Kuhl, & Regier, 2013; Wakefield, 2013).

DSM-5 takes an *atheoretical* approach to identifying psychological disorders, meaning it does not rely on any particular theoretical perspective. Consequently, it is primarily descriptive and attempts to avoid suggesting an underlying cause for an individual's behavior and problems. Instead, it seeks to paint a picture of the behavior that is being displayed.

For example, DSM does not use the term *neurotic*—a label commonly used by people in their everyday descriptions of abnormal behavior—as a category. Because the term *neurosis* refers to problems associated with a specific cause based in Freud's theory of personality, it is not included in DSM-5.

Why is this atheoretical, descriptive approach be important? For one thing, it allows communication between mental health professionals of diverse backgrounds and theoretical approaches. In addition, precise classification enables researchers to explore the causes of a problem. Without reliable descriptions of abnormal behavior, researchers

Study Alert
Use Figure 1 to review the six major perspectives on abnormality and consider how they relate to the major perspectives on the field of psychology.

Diagnostic and Statistical Manual of Mental Disorders, Fifth Edition (DSM-5) A system, devised by the American Psychiatric Association, used by most professionals to classify and define psychological disorders. (Module 46)

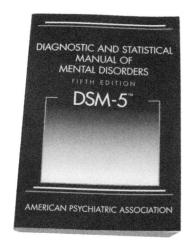

©H.S. Photos/Alamy Stock Photo

Categories of Disorders	Examples
Anxiety (problems in which anxiety impedes daily functioning)	Generalized anxiety disorder, panic disorder, phobic disorder
Somatic symptom and related disorders (psychological difficulties displayed through physical problems)	Illness anxiety disorder, conversion disorder
Dissociative (the splitting apart of crucial parts of personality that are usually integrated)	Dissociative identity disorder (multiple personality), dissociative amnesia, dissociative fugue
Mood (emotions of depression or euphoria that are so strong they intrude on everyday living)	Major depressive disorders, bipolar disorder
Schizophrenia spectrum and other psychotic disorders (declines in functioning, thought and language disturbances, perception disorders, emotional disturbances, and withdrawal from others)	Delusional disorder
Personality (problems that create little personal distress but that lead to an inability to function as a normal member of society)	Antisocial (sociopathic) personality disorder, narcissistic personality disorder
Sexual (problems related to sexual arousal from unusual objects or problems related to functioning)	Paraphilic disorders, sexual dysfunction
Substance-related (problems related to drug dependence and abuse)	Alcohol, cocaine, hallucinogens, marijuana
Neurocognitive disorders	Alzheimer's

FIGURE 2 This list of disorders represents the major categories from the DSM-5. It is only a partial list of the scores of disorders included in the diagnostic manual.

Source: Adapted from American Psychiatric Association. *Diagnostic and Statistical Manual of Mental Disorders, Fifth Edition* (DSM-5). Washington, DC: Author, 2013.

would be hard pressed to find ways to investigate the disorder. Finally, DSM-5 provides a kind of conceptual shorthand through which professionals can describe the behaviors that tend to occur together in an individual (Widiger, 2015; Busch, Morey & Hopwood, 2017).

CONNING THE CLASSIFIERS: THE SHORTCOMINGS OF DSM

When clinical psychologist David Rosenhan and eight colleagues sought admission to separate mental hospitals across the United States in the 1970s, each stated that he or she was hearing voices–"unclear voices" that said "empty," "hollow," and "thud"–and each was immediately admitted to the hospital. However, the truth was that they actually were conducting a study, and none of them was really hearing voices. Aside from these misrepresentations, *everything* else they did and said represented their true behavior, including the responses they gave during extensive admission interviews and their answers to the battery of tests they were asked to complete. In fact, as soon as they were admitted, they said they no longer heard any voices. In short, each of the pseudo-patients acted in a "normal" way (Rosenhan, 1973).

We might assume that Rosenhan and his colleagues would have been quickly discovered as the impostors they were, but this was not the case. Instead, each of them was diagnosed as severely abnormal on the basis of observed behavior. Mental health professionals labeled most as suffering from schizophrenia and kept them in the hospital 3 to 52 days, with the average stay of 19 days. Even when they were discharged, most of the "patients" left with the label *schizophrenia–in remission,* implying that the abnormal behavior had only temporarily subsided and could recur at any time. Most disturbing, no one on the hospital staff identified any of the pseudo-patients as impostors–although some of the actual patients figured out the ruse.

THE STIGMA OF LABELING

The results of Rosenhan's classic study illustrate that placing labels on individuals powerfully influences the way mental health workers perceive and interpret their actions. It also points out that determining who is psychologically disordered is not always a clear-cut or accurate process.

Gender dysphoria (in which one's gender identity is in conflict with one's biological sex) provides a modern illustration of the dilemma between the pros of a formal diagnosis and the cons of patient labeling. For example, most medical insurance providers require a formal, specific diagnosis in order to provide health-care coverage for procedures such as a sex change operation. Many individuals who experience a conflict between their gender identity and their biological sex object theoretically to the idea that their desire to be the other sex should be labeled a "disorder." Yet without a formal diagnosis, those same individuals may be forced to pay out of pocket for an expensive medical procedure.

This diagnosis-based system of insurance coverage often creates a Catch-22 for mental health-care professionals: They must decide between potentially stigmatizing their clients by providing a formal diagnosis, implying some type of disorder, or leaving patients undiagnosed and potentially without the financial support necessary to receive important procedures that will significantly improve the clients' quality of life (Kamens, 2011; Kleinplatz, Moser, & Lev, 2013).

Critics of the DSM argue that labeling an individual as abnormal provides a dehumanizing, lifelong stigma. (Think, for example, of political contenders whose candidacies have been terminated by the disclosure that they received treatment for severe psychological disorders.) Furthermore, after an initial diagnosis has been made, mental health professionals, who may concentrate on the initial diagnostic category, could overlook other diagnostic possibilities (Szasz, 2011; Frances, 2013; Kim et al., 2017).

Although the DSM-5 was developed to provide more accurate and consistent diagnoses of psychological disorders, it isn't always successful. For instance, critics charge that it relies too much on the medical perspective. Because it was drawn up by psychiatrists–who are physicians–some condemn it for viewing psychological disorders primarily in terms of the symptoms of an underlying physiological disorder. Moreover, critics suggest that DSM-5 compartmentalizes people into inflexible, all-or-none categories rather than considering the degree to which a person displays psychologically disordered behavior (Samuel & Widiger, 2006; Lasalvia, 2015).

Still, despite the drawbacks inherent in any labeling system, the DSM-5 has had an important influence on the way in which mental health professionals view psychological disorders. It has increased both the reliability and the validity of diagnostic categorization. In addition, it offers a logical way to organize examination of the major types of mental disturbances.

Study Alert

It is important to understand the advantages and weaknesses of the DSM classification system.

AP MODULE 46: NORMAL VERSUS ABNORMAL: MAKING THE DISTINCTION

AP SUMMARY

- The most widely used system for classifying psychological disorders is the *DSM-5.*
- Definitions of abnormality include deviation from the average or ideal, a sense of personal discomfort, and dysfunction.

- Historical views of abnormality consisted of superstition, magic, and spells. Six contemporary approaches take a more enlightened view.
- The medical perspective views abnormality as a symptom of an underlying disease.

- The psychoanalytic perspective suggests abnormal behavior stems from unconscious childhood conflicts.
- The behavioral perspective focuses on the rewards and punishments in the environment that determine abnormal behavior.
- The cognitive perspective suggests that abnormal behavior is the result of faulty thoughts.
- The humanistic perspective emphasizes people's responsibility for their own behavior even when it is seen as abnormal.
- The sociocultural perspective views abnormal behavior in terms of difficulties arising from family, society, and culture.
- Insanity is a legal term and often means that the defendant could not understand right and wrong at the time they committed the crime.
- The medical perspective is supported by growing research, but some abnormal behaviors appear to have no biological cause.
- Rosenhan and his colleagues investigated the danger of diagnostic labels after gaining admission to mental hospitals.
- A formal, specific diagnosis is often needed for insurance companies to provide coverage. The *DSM* has increased both the reliability and validity of diagnostic labels.
- Using diagnostic labels can lead to dehumanizing, lifelong stigma. The DSM labels may rely too much on categories rather than seeing abnormal behavior on a continuum.

AP KEY TERMS

abnormal behavior
medical perspective
psychoanalytic
  perspective
behavioral perspective
cognitive perspective
humanistic perspective

sociocultural perspective
Diagnostic and Statistical Manual of Mental Disorders, **Fifth Edition (DSM-5)**

AP TEST PRACTICE

Section I: Multiple Choice

1. To be considered abnormal, behavior should be characterized as all of the following EXCEPT
   A. deviant
   B. discomforting
   C. dysfunctional
   D. maladaptive
   E. deniable

2. Which perspective assumes people's thoughts are central to psychological disorders?
   A. Medical
   B. Behavioral
   C. Cognitive
   D. Humanistic
   E. Sociocultural

3. Which of the following is not one of the main *DSM-5* criticisms?
   A. Powerfully influencing mental health workers
   B. Relying too much on the medical perspective
   C. Compartmentalizing abnormal behavior into all-or-none categories
   D. Providing labels that are stigmatizing
   E. Increasing the reliability of diagnostic labels

Section II: Free Response

Cheryl is painfully shy and goes to a therapist for assistance.

A. Explain the criteria needed for her behavior to be considered abnormal.

B. Identify how the therapist would explain her behavior from each of the following perspectives.
   - Medical
   - Behavioral
   - Psychoanalytic
   - Sociocultural

C. The therapist used the *DSM* when diagnosing Cheryl's behavior.
   - Provide a benefit of using the *DSM*.
   - Provide a drawback of using the *DSM*.

Module 47
The Major Psychological Disorders

Sally's first panic attack was a surprise. Visiting her parents after college, she suddenly felt dizzy, broke into a cold sweat, and began hyperventilating. Her father clocked her pulse at 180 and rushed her to the hospital, where all symptoms vanished. She laughed it off and returned to her apartment.

But the panic attacks continued. At the gym, at work, in restaurants and movie theaters, Sally was never safe from them. Not just frightening, they were downright embarrassing. She quit her job to work at home. She avoided crowds and turned down dinners, parties, and movies. The only way to escape humiliation was to wall herself inside her apartment with a blanket and a pillow.

Sally suffered from panic disorder, one of the specific psychological disorders we'll consider in this module. Keep in mind that although we'll be discussing these disorders objectively, each represents a very human set of difficulties that influence and in some cases considerably disrupt people's lives.

Anxiety Disorders

All of us at one time or another experience *anxiety,* a feeling of apprehension or tension, in reaction to stressful situations. There is nothing "wrong" with such anxiety. It is a normal reaction to stress that often helps rather than hinders our daily functioning. Without some anxiety, for instance, most of us probably would not have much motivation to study hard, undergo physical exams, or spend long hours at our jobs.

But some people experience anxiety in situations in which there is no apparent reason or cause for such distress. **Anxiety disorders** occur when anxiety arises without external justification and begins to affect people's daily functioning. We'll discuss three major types of anxiety disorders: phobic disorder, panic disorder, and generalized anxiety disorder.

PHOBIC DISORDER

Forty-five-year-old Donna is terrified of electricity. She's unable to change a light bulb for fear of getting electrocuted. The thought of static electricity on clothing sends her into a panic. She can't even open a refrigerator door without being terrified a short circuit will send electricity through her body. And thunderstorms? Forget it: she is beside herself with fear of getting electrocuted by lightning (Kluger, 2001).

Donna suffers from a **specific phobia,** an intense, irrational fear of a specific object or situation. For example, claustrophobia is a fear of enclosed places, acrophobia is a fear of high places, xenophobia is a fear of strangers, social phobia is the fear of being judged or embarrassed by others, and–as in Donna's case–electrophobia is a fear of electricity.

The actual danger posed by an anxiety-producing stimulus (which can be just about anything, as you can see in Figure 1), is typically small or nonexistent. However, to someone suffering from the phobia, the danger is great, and a full-blown panic attack may follow exposure to the stimulus. Phobic disorders differ from generalized anxiety disorders and panic disorders in that there is a specific, identifiable stimulus that sets off the anxiety reaction.

- Describe contemporary and historical conceptions of what constitutes psychological disorders.

- Discuss the major diagnostic categories, including neurodevelopmental disorders, neurocognitive disorders, schizophrenia spectrum, and other psychotic disorders, and their corresponding symptoms.

- Discuss the major diagnostic categories, including anxiety disorders, bipolar and related disorders, depressive disorders, obsessive-compulsive and related disorders, and their corresponding symptoms.

- Discuss the major diagnostic categories, including dissociative disorders, somatic symptom and related disorders, and trauma- and stressor-related disorders and their corresponding symptoms.

- Discuss the major diagnostic categories, including feeding and eating disorders, personality disorders, and their corresponding symptoms.

anxiety disorder The occurrence of anxiety without an obvious external cause that affects daily functioning. (Module 47)

specific phobia Intense, irrational fear of specific objects or situations. (Module 47)

Phobic Disorder	Description	Example
Agoraphobia	Fear of places, such as unfamiliar or crowded spaces, where help might not be available in case of emergency	Person becomes housebound because any place other than the person's home arouses extreme anxiety symptoms.
Specific phobias	Fear of specific objects, places, or situations	
Animal type	Specific animals or insects	Person has extreme fear of dogs, cats, or spiders.
Natural environment type	Events or situations in the natural environment	Person has extreme fear of storms, heights, or water.
Situational type	Public transportation, tunnels, bridges, elevators, flying, driving	Person becomes extremely claustrophobic in elevators.
Blood injection injury type	Blood, injury, injections	Person panics when viewing a child's scraped knee.
Social phobia	Fear of being judged or embarrassed by others	Person avoids all social situations and becomes a recluse for fear of encountering others' judgment.

FIGURE 1 Phobic disorders differ from generalized anxiety and panic disorders because a specific stimulus can be identified. Listed here are a number of types of phobias and their triggers.
Source: Adapted from Nolen-Hoeksema, S. (2007). *Abnormal psychology* (4th ed.). New York: McGraw-Hill.

Phobias may have only a minor impact on people's lives if those who suffer from them can avoid the stimuli that trigger fear. For example, a fear of heights may have little impact on people's everyday lives (although it may prevent them from living in an apartment on a high floor)—unless they are firefighters or window washers. On the other hand, a *social phobia*, or a fear of strangers, presents a more serious problem. In one extreme case, a Washington woman left her home just three times in 30 years—once to visit her family, once for an operation, and once to purchase ice cream for a dying companion (Kimbrel, 2007; Wong, Sarver, & Beidel, 2011; Stopa et al., 2013).

PANIC DISORDER

panic disorder Anxiety disorder that takes the form of panic attacks lasting from a few seconds to several hours. (Module 47)

In another type of anxiety disorder, **panic disorder,** *panic attacks* occur that last from a few seconds to several hours. Panic disorders do not have any identifiable, specific triggers (unlike phobias, which are triggered by specific objects or situations). Instead, during an attack such as those Sally experienced in the case described earlier, anxiety suddenly—and often without warning—rises, and an individual feels a sense of impending, unavoidable doom.

Although the physical symptoms of a panic attack differ from person to person, they may include heart palpitations, shortness of breath, unusual amounts of sweating, faintness and dizziness, gastric sensations, and sometimes a sense of imminent death. After such an attack, it is no wonder that people tend to feel exhausted (Laederach-Hofmann & Messerli-Buergy, 2007; Montgomery, 2011; Carleton et al., 2014).

Panic attacks seemingly come out of nowhere and are unconnected to any specific stimulus. Because they don't know what triggers their feelings of panic, victims of panic attacks may become fearful of going places. In fact, some people with panic disorder develop a complication called *agoraphobia,* the fear of being in a situation in which escape is difficult and in which help for a possible panic attack would not be available. In extreme cases, people with agoraphobia never leave their homes (Wittchen et al., 2008; McTeague et al., 2011; Kim & Yoon, 2017).

In addition to the physical symptoms, panic disorder affects how the brain processes information. For instance, people with panic disorder have reduced reactions in the anterior cingulate cortex to stimuli (such as viewing a fearful face) that normally produce a strong reaction in those without the disorder. It may be that recurring high levels of emotional arousal that patients with panic disorder experience desensitize them to emotional stimuli (Pillay et al., 2007; Maddock et al., 2013).

GENERALIZED ANXIETY DISORDER

People with **generalized anxiety disorder** experience long-term, persistent anxiety and uncontrollable worry. Sometimes their concerns are about identifiable issues involving family, money, work, or health. In other cases, though, people with the disorder feel that something dreadful is about to happen but can't identify the reason and thus experience "free-floating" anxiety.

Because of persistent anxiety, people with generalized anxiety disorder cannot concentrate or set their worry and fears aside; their lives become centered on their worry. Furthermore, their anxiety is often accompanied by physiological symptoms, such as muscle tension, headaches, dizziness, heart palpitations, or insomnia (Starcevic et al., 2007). Figure 2 shows the most common symptoms of generalized anxiety disorder.

Acrophobia, the fear of heights, is not an uncommon phobia. What sort of behavior-modification approaches might be used to deal with acrophobia?
©Imaginechina/AP Images

generalized anxiety disorder The experience of long-term, persistent anxiety and worry. (Module 47)

Obsessive-Compulsive Disorder

In **obsessive-compulsive disorder (OCD),** people are plagued by unwanted thoughts, called *obsessions*, or feel that they must carry out behaviors, termed *compulsions*, that they feel driven to perform.

An **obsession** is a persistent, unwanted thought or idea that keeps recurring. For example, a student may be unable to stop thinking that she has neglected to put her name on a test and may think about it constantly for the 2 weeks it takes to get the paper back. A man may go on vacation and wonder the whole time whether he locked his house. A woman may hear the same tune running through her head over and over. In each case, the thought or idea is unwanted and difficult to put out of mind. Of course, many people suffer from mild obsessions from time to time, but usually such thoughts persist only for a short period. For people with serious obsessions, however, the thoughts persist for days or months and may consist of bizarre, troubling images (Rassin & Muris, 2007; Wenzel, 2011; Iliceto et al., 2017).

As the name suggests, as part of an obsessive-compulsive disorder, people may also experience compulsions. **Compulsions** are irresistible urges to repeatedly carry out some behavior that seems strange and unreasonable even to them. Whatever the compulsive behavior is, people experience extreme anxiety if they cannot do it, even if it is something they want to stop. The acts may be relatively trivial, such as repeatedly checking the stove to make sure all the burners are turned off, or more unusual, such as washing one's hands so much that they bleed (Clark, 2007; Moretz & McKay, 2009; Gillan & Sahakian, 2015).

For example, consider this passage from the autobiography of a person with obsessive-compulsive disorder:

> I thought my parents would die if I didn't do everything in exactly the right way. When I took my glasses off at night I'd have to place them on the dresser at a particular angle. Sometimes I'd turn on the light and get out of bed seven times until I felt comfortable with the angle. If the angle wasn't right, I felt that my parents would die. The feeling ate up my insides.

obsessive-compulsive disorder (OCD) A disorder characterized by obsessions or compulsions. (Module 47)

obsession A persistent, unwanted thought or idea that keeps recurring. (Module 47)

compulsion An irresistible urge to repeatedly carry out some behavior that seems strange and unreasonable. (Module 47)

FIGURE 2 Frequency of symptoms in cases of generalized anxiety disorder.
Source: Adapted from Beck, A. T., & Emery, G., with Greenberg, R. L. (1985). *Anxiety disorders and phobias: A cognitive perspective.* New York: Basic Books.

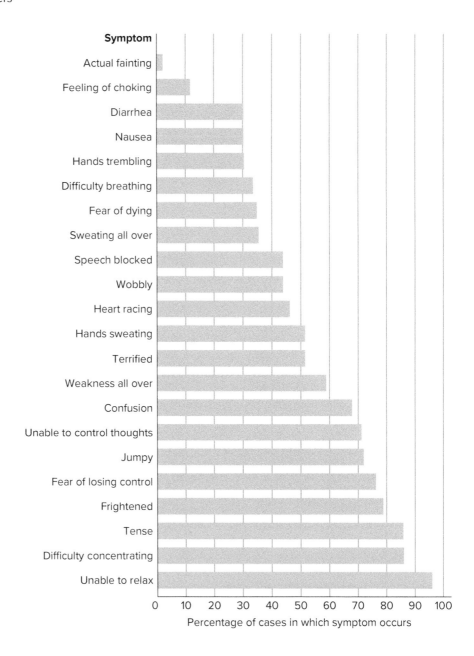

If I didn't grab the molding on the wall just the right way as I entered or exited my room; if I didn't hang a shirt in the closet perfectly; if I didn't read a paragraph a certain way; if my hands and nails weren't perfectly clean, I thought my incorrect behavior would kill my parents. (Summers, 2000)

Although carrying out compulsive rituals may lead to some immediate reduction of anxiety, in the long run the anxiety returns. In fact, people with severe cases lead lives filled with unrelenting tension (Dittrich, Johansen, & Fineberg, 2011; Kalanthroff et al., 2013).

PsychTech
Although some people seem to use the Internet compulsively, psychologists have yet to agree on whether it represents a true psychological disorder.

THE CAUSES OF ANXIETY DISORDERS AND OBSESSIVE-COMPULSIVE DISORDER

We've considered several of the major types of anxiety disorders and obsessive-compulsive disorder, but there are many other related disorders. The variety of anxiety disorders means that no single explanation fits all cases.

Genetic factors clearly are part of the picture. For example, if one member of a pair of identical twins has panic disorder, there is a 30% chance that the other twin will have it also. Furthermore, a person's characteristic level of anxiety is related to a specific gene involved in the production of the neurotransmitter serotonin. This is consistent with findings indicating that certain chemical deficiencies in the brain appear to produce some kinds of anxiety disorder (Beidel & Turner, 2007; Chamberlain et al., 2008; Yagi et al., 2017).

Some researchers believe that an overactive autonomic nervous system may be at the root of panic attacks. Specifically, they suggest that poor regulation of the brain's *locus ceruleus* may lead to panic attacks, which cause the limbic system to become overstimulated. In turn, the overstimulated limbic system produces chronic anxiety, which ultimately leads the locus ceruleus to generate still more panic attacks (Davies et al., 2008; Dresler et al., 2013).

There are also biological causes involved in obsessive-compulsive disorder. For example, researchers have found specific differences in the brains of those with the disorder compared to those without it (Christian et al., 2008; Okada et al., 2015).

Psychologists who employ the behavioral perspective have taken a different approach to explaining anxiety disorders that emphasize environmental factors. They consider anxiety to be a learned response to stress. For instance, suppose a dog bites a young girl. When the girl next sees a dog, she is frightened and runs away–a behavior that relieves her anxiety and thereby reinforces her avoidance behavior. After repeated encounters with dogs in which she is reinforced for her avoidance behavior, she may develop a full-fledged phobia regarding dogs.

Finally, the cognitive perspective suggests that anxiety disorders grow out of inappropriate and inaccurate thoughts and beliefs about circumstances in a person's world. For example, people with anxiety disorders may view a friendly puppy as a ferocious and savage pit bull, or they may see an air disaster looming every moment they are in the vicinity of an airplane. According to the cognitive perspective, people's maladaptive thoughts about the world are at the root of an anxiety disorder (Wang & Clark, 2002; Ouimet, Gawronski, & Dozois, 2009; Bouvard et al., 2017).

Somatic Symptom Disorders

Somatic symptom disorders are psychological difficulties that take on a physical (somatic) form for which there is no medical cause. Even though an individual with a somatic symptom disorder reports physical symptoms, no biological cause exists, or if there is a medical problem, the person's reaction is greatly exaggerated.

somatic symptom disorders Psychological difficulties that take on a physical (somatic) form for which there is no medical cause. (Module 47)

One relatively common type of somatic symptom disorder is illness anxiety disorder. Those with **illness anxiety disorder** have a constant fear of illness and a preoccupation with their health. These individuals believe that everyday aches and pains are symptoms of a dread disease. The "symptoms" are not faked; rather, they are misinterpreted as evidence of some serious illness–often in the face of inarguable medical evidence to the contrary (Abramowitz, Olatunji, & Deacon, 2007; Olatunji, 2008; Weck et al., 2011).

illness anxiety disorder A somatic symptom disorder in which people have a constant fear of illness and a preoccupation with their health. (Module 47)

Conversion disorder is another somatic symptom disorder. Unlike illness anxiety disorder, in which there is no physical problem, **conversion disorders** involve an apparent physical disturbance, such as the inability to see or hear or to move an arm or leg. However, *the cause* of the physical disturbance is purely psychological; there is no biological reason for the problem. Some of Freud's classic cases involved conversion disorders. For instance, one of Freud's patients suddenly became unable to use her arm without any apparent physiological cause. Later, just as abruptly, the problem disappeared.

conversion disorder A major somatic symptom disorder that involves an actual physical disturbance, such as the inability to use a sensory organ or the complete or partial inability to move an arm or leg. (Module 47)

Conversion disorders often begin suddenly. Previously normal people wake up one day blind or deaf, or they experience numbness that is restricted to a certain part of the body. A hand, for example, may become entirely numb, while an area above the wrist, controlled by the same nerves, remains sensitive to touch–something that is physiologically implausible. Mental health professionals refer to such a condition as

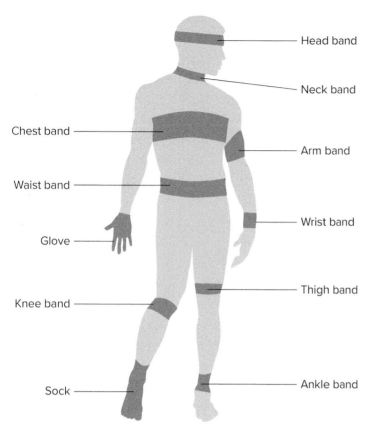

Head band

Neck band

Chest band

Arm band

Waist band

Wrist band

Glove

Thigh band

Knee band

Sock

Ankle band

FIGURE 3 Conversion disorders sometimes produce numbness in specific and isolated areas of the body (indicated by the shaded areas in the figure). For instance, in glove anesthesia, the area of the body covered by a glove feels numb. However, the condition is biologically implausible because of the nerves involved, which suggests that the problem results from a psychological disorder rather than from actual nerve damage.

dissociative disorders Psychological dysfunctions characterized by the separation of different facets of a person's personality that are normally integrated. (Module 47)

dissociative identity disorder (DID) A disorder in which a person displays characteristics of two or more distinct personalities. (Module 47)

dissociative amnesia A disorder in which a significant, selective memory loss occurs. (Module 47)

"glove anesthesia" because the numb area is the part of the hand covered by a glove and not a region related to pathways of the nervous system (see Figure 3).

Surprisingly, people who experience conversion disorders frequently remain unconcerned about symptoms that most of us would expect to be highly anxiety producing. For instance, a person in good health who wakes up blind may react in a bland, matter-of-fact way. Considering how most of us would feel if we woke up unable to see, this unemotional reaction hardly seems appropriate (Brasic, 2002; Loriedo & Leone, 2017).

Dissociative Disorders

The classic movie *The Three Faces of Eve* (about a woman with three wildly different personalities) and the book *Sybil* (about a girl who allegedly had 16 personalities) represent a highly dramatic, rare, and controversial class of disorders: dissociative disorders. **Dissociative disorders** are characterized by the separation (or dissociation) of different facets of a person's personality that are normally integrated and work together. By dissociating key parts of who they are, people are able to keep disturbing memories or perceptions from reaching conscious awareness and thereby reduce their anxiety (Houghtalen & Talbot, 2007; Laddis, Dell, & Korzekwa, 2017).

Several dissociative disorders exist, although all of them are rare. A person with a **dissociative identity disorder (DID)** (once called *multiple personality disorder*) displays characteristics of two or more distinct personalities, identities, or personality fragments. Individual personalities often have a unique set of likes and dislikes and their own reactions to situations. Some people with multiple personalities even carry several pairs of glasses because their vision changes with each personality. Moreover, each individual personality can be well adjusted when considered on its own (Stickley & Nickeas, 2006; Howell, 2011).

The diagnosis of dissociative identity disorder is controversial. It was rarely diagnosed before 1980, when it was added as a category in the third edition of DSM for the first time. At that point, the number of cases increased significantly. Some clinicians suggest the increase was due to more precise identification of the disorder. On the other hand, critics suggest that widespread publicity about cases of DID may have influenced patients to report symptoms of more common personality disorders in ways that made it more likely they would receive a diagnosis of DID (Kihlstrom, 2005a; Xiao et al., 2006; Ross, 2015).

Dissociative amnesia is another dissociative disorder in which a significant, selective memory loss occurs. Dissociative amnesia is unlike simple amnesia, which involves an actual loss of information from memory and typically results from a physiological cause. In contrast, in cases of dissociative amnesia, the "forgotten" material is still present in memory–it simply cannot be recalled. The term *repressed memories* is sometimes used to describe the lost memories of people with dissociative amnesia.

In the most severe form of dissociative amnesia, individuals cannot recall their names, are unable to recognize parents and other relatives, and do not know their addresses. In other respects, though, they may appear quite normal. Apart from an inability to remember certain facts about themselves, they may be able to recall skills and abilities that they developed earlier. For instance, even though a chef may not remember where he grew up and received training, he may still be able to prepare gourmet meals.

In some cases of dissociative amnesia, the memory loss is profound. For example, in one dramatic case, Raymond Power Jr., an attorney, husband, father of two, and Boy

Scout leader, left home to go to work one morning. Two days later, he was homeless, living a new life a thousand miles away, and had no memory of who he was or how he got there. He was found 6 months later but still had no recollection of his previous life, including any knowledge of his wife of 30 years or even that he had children (Foderaro, 2006; Dell, 2013).

Dissociative fugue is a form of amnesia in which a person leaves home suddenly and assumes a new identity. In this unusual and rare state, people take sudden, impulsive trips and adopt a new identity. After a period of time–days, months, or sometimes even years–they suddenly realize that they are in a strange place and completely forget the time they have spent wandering. Their last memories are those from the time just before they entered the fugue state (Hennig-Fast et al., 2008).

The common thread among dissociative disorders is that they allow people to escape from some anxiety-producing situation. Either the person produces a new personality to deal with stress, or the individual forgets or leaves behind the situation that caused the stress as he or she journeys to some new–and perhaps less anxiety-ridden–environment (Putnam, 2000; Brown, 2006).

dissociative fugue A form of amnesia in which a person leaves home and assumes a new identity. (Module 47)

Mood Disorders

From the time I woke up in the morning until the time I went to bed at night, I was unbearably miserable and seemingly incapable of any kind of joy or enthusiasm. Everything–every thought, word, movement–was an effort. Everything that once was sparkling now was flat. I seemed to myself to be dull, boring, inadequate, thick brained, unlit, unresponsive, chill skinned, bloodless, and sparrow drab. I doubted, completely, my ability to do anything well. It seemed as though my mind had slowed down and burned out to the point of being virtually useless. (Jamison, 1995)

We all experience mood swings. Sometimes we are happy, perhaps even euphoric; at other times, we feel upset, saddened, or depressed. Such changes in mood are a normal part of everyday life.

In some people, however, moods are so pronounced and lingering–like the feelings described above by writer (and psychiatrist) Kay Jamison–that they interfere with the ability to function effectively. **Mood disorders** are disturbances in emotional experience that are strong enough to interfere with everyday living. In extreme cases, a mood may become life threatening; in other cases, it may cause the person to lose touch with reality.

mood disorder A disturbance in emotional experience that is strong enough to interfere with everyday living. (Module 47)

MAJOR DEPRESSIVE DISORDER

President Abraham Lincoln. Queen Victoria. Newscaster Mike Wallace.

The common link among these people? Each suffered from periodic attacks of major depressive disorder. **Major depressive disorder** is a severe form of depression that interferes with concentration, decision making, and sociability.

Major depressive disorder is one of the more common forms of mood disorders. Some 15 million people in the United States suffer from major depression, and at any one time, 6–10% of the U.S. population is clinically depressed. Almost one in five people in the United States experiences major depression at some point in life, and 15% of college students have received a diagnosis of depression. The cost of depression is more than $34 billion a year in lost productivity (Scelfo, 2007; Simon et al., 2008; Edoka, Petrou, & Ramchandani, 2011).

major depressive disorder A severe form of depression that interferes with concentration, decision making, and sociability. (Module 47)

Women are twice as likely to experience major depression as men are, with one-fourth of all females apt to encounter it at some point during their lives. Furthermore, although no one is sure why, the rate of depression is going up throughout the world. Results of in-depth interviews conducted in the United States, Puerto Rico, Taiwan, Lebanon, Canada, Italy, Germany, and France indicate that the incidence of depression has increased significantly over previous rates in every area. In fact, in some countries, the likelihood that individuals will have major depression at some point in their lives is three times higher than it was for earlier generations. In addition, people are developing

Study Alert

Major depression differs from the normal depression that occasionally occurs during most people's lives; major depression is more intense, lasts longer, and may have no clear trigger.

mania An extended state of intense, wild elation. (Module 47)

major depression at increasingly younger ages (Staley, Sanacora, & Tamagnan, 2006; Sado et al., 2011; Sarubin et al., 2017).

When psychologists speak of major depressive disorder, they do not mean the sadness that accompanies one of life's disappointments, which we all have experienced. Some depression is normal after the breakup of a long-term relationship, the death of a loved one, or the loss of a job. It is normal even after less serious problems, such as doing badly on a test or having a romantic partner forget one's birthday.

People who suffer from major depressive disorder experience similar feelings, but the severity tends to be considerably greater. They may feel useless, worthless, and lonely, and they may think the future is hopeless and no one can help them. They may lose their appetite and have no energy. Moreover, they may experience such feelings for months or even years. They may cry uncontrollably, have sleep disturbances, and be at risk for suicide. The depth and duration of such behavior are the hallmarks of major depressive disorder. (Figure 4 provides a self-assessment of depression.)

MANIA AND BIPOLAR DISORDER

While depression leads to the depths of despair, mania leads to emotional heights. **Mania** is an extended state of intense, wild elation. People experiencing mania feel intense happiness, power, invulnerability, and energy. Believing they will succeed at anything they attempt, they may become involved in wild schemes. Consider, for example, the following description of an individual who experienced a manic episode:

> Mr. O'Reilly took a leave of absence from his civil service job. He purchased a large number of cuckoo clocks and then an expensive car, which he planned to use as a mobile showroom for his wares, anticipating that he would make a great deal of money. He proceeded to "tear around town" buying and selling clocks and other

FIGURE 4 This test is based on the list of signs and symptoms of depression found on the National Institute of Mental Health website at http://www.nimh.nih.gov/health/publications/depression/what-are-the-signs-and-symptoms-of-depression.shtml.
Source: National Institutes of Health, *Depression.*

A Test for Major Depression

To complete the questionnaire, count the number of statements with which you agree:

1. I feel sad, anxious, or empty.
2. I feel hopeless or pessimistic.
3. I feel guilty, worthless, or helpless.
4. I feel irritable or restless.
5. I have lost interest in activities or hobbies that were once pleasurable, including sex.
6. I feel tired and have decreased energy.
7. I have difficulty concentrating, remembering details, and making decisions.
8. I have insomnia, early-morning wakefulness, or sleep too much.
9. I overeat or have appetite loss.
10. I have thoughts of suicide or have attempted suicide.
11. I have aches or pains, headaches, cramps, or digestive problems that do not ease even with treatment.

Scoring: If you agree with at least five of the statements, including either 1 or 2, and if you have had these symptoms for at least 2 weeks, help from a professional is strongly recommended. If you answer yes to number 10, seek immediate help. And remember: These are only general guidelines. If you feel you may need help, seek it.

merchandise, and when he was not out, he was continuously on the phone making "deals." . . . He was $3,000 in debt and had driven his family to exhaustion with his excessive activity and talkativeness. He said, however, that he felt "on top of the world." (Spitzer et al., 1983)

Some people sequentially experience periods of mania and depression. This alternation of mania and depression is called **bipolar disorder** (a condition previously known as *manic-depressive disorder*). The swings between highs and lows may occur a few days apart or may alternate over a period of years. In addition, in bipolar disorder, periods of depression are usually longer than periods of mania.

Ironically, some of society's most creative individuals may have suffered from bipolar disorder. The imagination, drive, excitement, and energy that they display during manic stages allow them to make unusually creative contributions. For instance, historical analysis of the composer Robert Schumann's music shows that he was most prolific during periods of mania. In contrast, his output dropped off drastically during periods of depression (see Figure 5). On the other hand, the high output associated with mania does not necessarily lead to higher quality: Some of Schumann's greatest works were created outside his periods of mania (Szegedy Maszak, 2003; Kyaga et al., 2013).

Although creativity may be increased when someone is experiencing mania, persons who experience this disorder often show a recklessness that produces emotional and sometimes physical self-injury. They may alienate people with their talkativeness, inflated self-esteem, and indifference to the needs of others (Simonton, 2014).

bipolar disorder A disorder in which a person alternates between periods of euphoric feelings of mania and periods of depression. (Module 47)

CAUSES OF MOOD DISORDERS

Because they represent a major mental health problem, mood disorders—and, in particular, depression—have received a good deal of study. Several approaches have been used to explain the disorders.

Genetic and biological factors. Some mood disorders clearly have genetic and biological roots. In fact, most evidence suggests that bipolar disorders are caused primarily by biological factors. For instance, bipolar disorder (and some forms of major depression) clearly runs in some families, pointing to a genetic cause. Furthermore, researchers

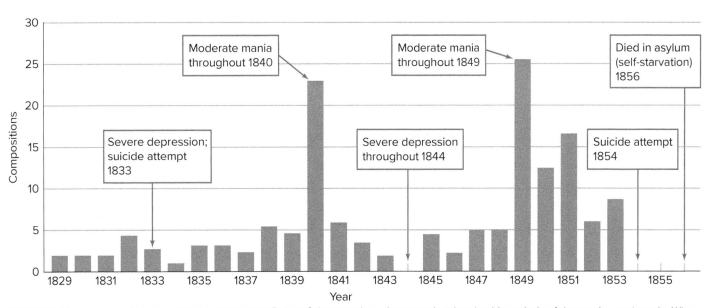

FIGURE 5 The number of pieces written by composer Robert Schumann in a given year is related to his periods of depression and mania. Why do you think mania might be associated with creative productivity in some people?

Source: Slater, E., & Meyer, A. (1959). Contributions to a pathography of the musicians: Robert Schumann. *Confinia Psychiatrica*. Reprinted in K. R. Jamison, *Touched with fire: Manic-depressive illness and the artistic temperament*. New York: Free Press; reprinted in Jamison, K. R. (1995). *An unquiet mind: A memoir of moods and madness*. New York: Knopf. .

have found that several neurotransmitters play a role in depression. For example, alterations in the functioning of serotonin and norepinephrine in the brain are related to the disorder.

In addition, research on neuroimaging suggests that a brain structure called *area 25* is related to depression: When area 25 is smaller than normal, it is associated with a higher risk of depression. Furthermore, the right anterior insula, a region of the brain related to self-awareness and interpersonal experience, also appears to be related to depression (Insel, 2010; Cisler et al., 2013; Serretti, 2017).

Internal, unconscious conflicts. Supporters of psychoanalytic perspectives see depression as the result of feelings of loss (real or potential) or of anger directed inwardly at oneself. However, there is little research evidence to support this explanation (Vanheule et al., 2006; Sa, 2015).

Environmental factors. Some explanations of depression take a behavioral approach, looking to influences outside the person. For example, behavioral theories of depression argue that the stresses of life produce a reduction in positive reinforcers. As a result, people begin to withdraw, which only reduces positive reinforcers further. In addition, people receive attention for their depressive behavior, which further reinforces the depression (Lewinsohn & Essau, 2002; Lewinsohn et al., 2003; Domschke, 2013).

Cognitive and emotional factors. Some explanations for mood disorders attribute them to cognitive factors. For example, psychologist Martin Seligman suggests that depression is largely a response to learned helplessness. *Learned helplessness* is a learned expectation that events in one's life are uncontrollable and that one cannot escape from the situation. As a consequence, people simply give up fighting aversive events and submit to them, which thereby produces depression. Other theorists go a step further and suggest that depression results from hopelessness, a combination of learned helplessness and an expectation that negative outcomes in one's life are inevitable (Bjornstad, 2006; Li et al., 2011; Shirayama & Hashimoto, 2017).

Clinical psychologist Aaron Beck has proposed that faulty cognitions underlie people's depressed feelings. Specifically, his cognitive theory of depression suggests that depressed individuals typically view themselves as life's losers and blame themselves whenever anything goes wrong. By focusing on the negative side of situations, they feel inept and unable to act constructively to change their environment. In sum, their negative cognitions lead to feelings of depression (Newman et al., 2002).

Brain imaging studies suggest that people with depression experience a general blunting of emotional reactions. For example, one study found that the brains of people with depression showed significantly less activation when they viewed photos of human faces displaying strong emotions than did those without the disorder (Gotlib et al., 2004).

DEPRESSION IN WOMEN

The various theories of depression have not provided a complete answer to an elusive question that has dogged researchers: Why does depression occur in approximately twice as many women as men—a pattern that is similar across a variety of cultures?

One explanation suggests that the stress women experience may be greater than the stress men experience at certain points in their lives—such as when a woman must simultaneously earn a living and be the primary caregiver for her children. In addition, women have a higher risk for physical and sexual abuse, typically earn lower wages than men, report greater unhappiness with their marriages, and generally experience chronic negative circumstances. Furthermore, women and men may respond to stress with different coping mechanisms. For instance, men may abuse drugs, whereas women respond with depression (Hyde, Mezulis, & Abramson, 2008; Komarovskaya et al., 2011; Sun et al., 2017).

Biological factors may also explain some women's depression. For example, the rate of female depression begins to rise during puberty, so some psychologists believe that hormones make women more vulnerable to the disorder. In addition, 25–50% of women who take oral contraceptives report symptoms of depression, and depression that occurs after the birth of a child is linked to hormonal changes. Finally, structural differences in men's and women's brains may be related to gender differences in depression (Silverstein et al., 2013; Jones et al., 2017; Yang et al., 2017).

Ultimately, it is clear that researchers have discovered no definitive solutions to the puzzle of depression, and there are many alternative explanations. Most likely, a complex interaction of several factors causes mood disorders.

Schizophrenia

> Things that relate, the town of Antelope, Oregon, Jonestown, Charlie Manson, the Hillside Strangler, the Zodiac Killer, Watergate, King's trial in L.A., and many more. In the last 7 years alone, over 23 Star Wars scientists committed suicide for no apparent reason. The AIDS cover-up, the conference in South America in 87 had over 1,000 doctors claim that insects can transmit it. To be able to read one's thoughts and place thoughts in one's mind without the person knowing it's being done. Realization is a reality of bioelectromagnetic control, which is thought transfer and emotional control, recording individual brainwave frequencies of thought, sensation, and emotions. (Nolen-Hoeksema, 2007)

This excerpt illustrates the efforts of a person with schizophrenia, one of the more severe forms of mental disturbance, to communicate. People with schizophrenia account for by far the largest percentage of those hospitalized for psychological disorders. They are also in many respects the least likely to recover from their difficulties.

Schizophrenia refers to a class of disorders in which severe distortion of reality occurs. Thinking, perception, and emotion may deteriorate; the individual may withdraw from social interaction; and the person may display bizarre behavior. The symptoms displayed by persons with schizophrenia may vary considerably over time. Nonetheless, a number of characteristics reliably distinguish schizophrenia from other disorders. They include the following:

schizophrenia A class of disorders in which severe distortion of reality occurs. (Module 47)

- *Decline from a previous level of functioning.* An individual can no longer carry out activities he or she was once able to do.

- *Disturbances of thought and speech.* People with schizophrenia use logic and language in a peculiar way. Their thinking often does not make sense, and their logic is frequently faulty, which is referred to as a *formal thought disorder*. They also do not follow conventional linguistic rules (Penn et al., 1997). Consider, for example, the following response to the question "Why do you think people believe in God?"

> Uh, let's, I don't know why, let's see, balloon travel. He holds it up for you, the balloon. He don't let you fall out, your little legs sticking down through the clouds. He's down to the smokestack, looking through the smoke trying to get the balloon gassed up you know. Way they're flying on top that way, legs sticking out. I don't know, looking down on the ground, heck, that'd make you so dizzy you just stay and sleep you know, hold down and sleep there. I used to be sleep outdoors, you know, sleep outdoors instead of going home. (Chapman & Chapman, 1973)

As this selection illustrates, although the basic grammatical structure may be intact, the substance of thinking that is characteristic of schizophrenia is often illogical, garbled, and lacking in meaningful content (Holden, 2003; Heinrichs, 2005).

- *Delusions.* People with schizophrenia often have delusions—firmly held, unshakable beliefs with no basis in reality. Among the common delusions people with schizophrenia experience are the beliefs that they are being controlled by someone else, they are being persecuted by others, and their thoughts are being broadcast so that others know what they are thinking (Coltheart, Langdon, & McKay, 2007; Startup, Bucci, & Langdon, 2009; Phalen et al., 2017).

FIGURE 6 This unusual art was created by an individual suffering from a severe psychological disorder.

©Science Source

- *Hallucinations and perceptual problems.* People with schizophrenia sometimes do not perceive the world as most other people do. For example, they may have *hallucinations,* the experience of perceiving things that do not actually exist. Furthermore, they may see, hear, or smell things differently from others (see Figure 6). In fact, they may not even have a sense of their bodies in the way that others do, having difficulty determining where their bodies stop and the rest of the world begins (Botvinick, 2004; Thomas et al., 2007Bauer, Schwab, & McAdams, 2011).

- *Inappropriate emotions.* People with schizophrenia sometimes show a lack of emotion in which even the most dramatic events produce little or no emotional response. Alternately, they may display strong bursts of emotion that are inappropriate to a situation. For example, a person with schizophrenia may laugh uproariously at a funeral or react with rage when being helped by someone.

- *Withdrawal.* People with schizophrenia tend to have little interest in others. They tend not to socialize or hold real conversations with others, although they may talk at another person. In the most extreme cases, they do not even acknowledge the presence of other people and appear to be in their own isolated worlds.

Usually, the onset of schizophrenia occurs in early adulthood, and the symptoms follow one of two primary courses. In *process schizophrenia,* the symptoms develop slowly and subtly. There may be a gradual withdrawal from the world, excessive daydreaming, and a blunting of emotion until eventually the disorder reaches the point where others cannot overlook it. In other cases, known as *reactive schizophrenia,* the onset of symptoms is sudden and conspicuous. The treatment outlook for reactive schizophrenia is relatively favorable, but process schizophrenia has proved more difficult to treat.

DSM-5 classifies the symptoms of schizophrenia into two types. *Positive-symptom schizophrenia* is indicated by the presence of disordered behavior such as hallucinations, delusions, and emotional extremes. Those with positive-symptom schizophrenia clearly lose touch with reality.

In contrast, those with *negative-symptom schizophrenia* show disruptions to normal emotions and behaviors. For example, there may be an absence or loss of normal functioning, such as social withdrawal or blunted emotions (Levine & Rabinowitz, 2007; Tandon et al., 2013; Lauriello & Rahman, 2015).

The distinction between positive and negative symptoms of schizophrenia is important because it suggests that two different kinds of causes might trigger schizophrenia. Furthermore, it has implications for predicting treatment outcomes.

SOLVING THE PUZZLE OF SCHIZOPHRENIA: BIOLOGICAL CAUSES

Although schizophrenic behavior clearly departs radically from normal behavior, its causes are less apparent. It does appear, however, that schizophrenia has both biological and environmental origins (Sawa & Snyder, 2002; Pavão, Tort, & Amaral, 2015).

Let's first consider the evidence pointing to a biological cause. Because schizophrenia is more common in some families than in others, genetic factors seem to be involved in producing at least a susceptibility to or readiness for developing schizophrenia. For example, the closer the genetic link between a person with schizophrenia and another individual, the greater the likelihood that the other person will experience the disorder (see Figure 7; Plomin & McGuffin, 2003; Gottesman & Hanson, 2005; Rodrigues-Amorim et al., 2017).

However, if genetics alone were responsible for schizophrenia, the chance of both of two identical twins having schizophrenia would be 100% instead of just under 50% because identical twins have the same genetic makeup. Moreover, attempts to find a link between schizophrenia and a particular gene have been only partly successful.

Risk of Developing Schizophrenia, Based on Genetic Relatedness to a Person with Schizophrenia		
Relationship	**Genetic Relatedness, %**	**Risk of Developing Schizophrenia, %**
Identical twin	100	48
Child of two schizophrenic parents	100	46
Fraternal twin	50	17
Offspring of one schizophrenic parent	50	17
Sibling	50	9
Nephew or niece	25	4
Spouse	0	2
Unrelated person	0	1

FIGURE 7 The closer the genetic links between two people, the greater the likelihood that if one experiences schizophrenia, so will the other sometime during his or her lifetime. However, genetics is not the full story; if it were, the risk of identical twins having schizophrenia would be 100% and not the 48% shown in this figure.
Source: Adapted from Gottesman, I. I. (1991). *Schizophrenia genesis: The origins of madness.* New York: Freeman.

Apparently, genetic factors alone do not produce schizophrenia (Lenzenweger & Dworkin, 1998).; Abel & Nicki-Jochschat, 2016).

Some researchers suggest that epigenetics are involved in schizophrenia. *Epigenetics* looks at the way in which genes are expressed and influenced by the environment. In this view, genes by themselves do not invariably lead a person to display schizophrenia. Instead, they are affected by the environment. Furthermore, genes can be altered in a way that then passes on the behavior to future generations. An epigenetic explanation of schizophrenia, then, suggests that changes in gene expression may produce the disorder and that subsequently it can be passed on genetically (Alelú-Paz et al., 2017; Whitton et al., 2017).

Despite advances in our understanding of genetic and epigenetic causes of schizophrenia, most researchers agree that no single gene is responsible for the disorder. Consequently, scientists have looked to other possible biological causes (Balter, 2017).

Another biological explanation suggests that the brains of people with schizophrenia may have a biochemical imbalance. For example, the *dopamine hypothesis* suggests that schizophrenia results from excess activity in the areas of the brain that use dopamine as a neurotransmitter. This explanation came to light after the discovery that drugs that block dopamine action in brain pathways can be effective in reducing the symptoms of schizophrenia. Other research suggests that glutamate, another neurotransmitter, may contribute to the disorder, and drugs that reduce the release of glutamate in the brain show promise in alleviating symptoms of schizophrenia (Kendler & Schaffner, 2011; Beck, Javitt, & Howes, 2016; Howes et al., 2017).

Another biological explanation relates to structural abnormalities in the brains of people with schizophrenia. For example, researchers have found abnormalities in the neural circuits of the cortex and limbic systems, as well as reduced amounts of gray matter, in the brains of those with schizophrenia. Furthermore, differences exist in the way the brain functions (see *Neuroscience in Your Life;* Reichenberg & Harvey, 2007; Reichenberg et al., 2009; Bustillo et al., 2017).

Further evidence for the importance of biological factors shows that when people with schizophrenia hear voices during hallucinations, the parts of the brain responsible for hearing and language processing become active. When they have visual hallucinations, the parts of the brain involved in movement and color are active. At the same time, people with schizophrenia often have unusually low activity in the brain's frontal lobes—the parts of the brain involved with emotional regulation, insight, and the evaluation of sensory stimuli (Stern & Silbersweig, 2001; Lavigne et al., 2015).

SITUATIONAL CAUSES OF SCHIZOPHRENIA

Biological factors provide important pieces of the puzzle of schizophrenia. However, we also need to consider past and current experiences of people who develop the disturbance.

AP| NEUROSCIENCE IN YOUR LIFE: BRAIN NETWORKS RELATED TO MEMORY DEFICITS IN SCHIZOPHRENIA

1. Describe the type of schizophrenia symptoms measured in this study.
2. Describe the control group and its purpose

Psychological disorders are well known for their psychological symptoms, but they are also marked by significant cognitive declines. For example, patients with schizophrenia suffer from hallucinations, but they also suffer from memory deficits that can greatly impact their lives. In a recent study, neuroscientists scanned the brains of patients with schizophrenia and healthy control participants while each group attempted to memorize and later recall pictures. As you can see from the images below, healthy control participants (left) showed more activity in certain brain regions of the prefrontal cortex (indicated by more yellow) than patients with schizophrenia (right) in both the left hemisphere (top) and the right hemisphere (bottom) (Ragland et al., 2015).

Source: Adapted from Ragland, J. D., Ranganath, C., Harms, M. P., Barch, D. M., Gold, J. M., Layher, E., . . . Carter, C. S. (2015). Functional and neuroanatomic specificity of episodic memory dysfunction in schizophrenia: A functional magnetic resonance imaging study of the relational and item-specific encoding task. *JAMA Psychiatry, 72*(9), 909-916. doi: 10.1001/jamapsychiatry.2015.0276

For instance, psychoanalytic explanations suggest that schizophrenia occurs when people experience regression to earlier stages of life. Specifically, Freud believed that people with schizophrenia lack egos that are strong enough to cope with their unacceptable impulses. They regress to the oral stage–a time when the id and ego are not yet separated. Therefore, individuals with schizophrenia essentially are presumed to act out impulses without concern for reality.

However, little research evidence supports psychoanalytic explanations. More plausible theories suggest that the emotional and communication patterns of the families of people with schizophrenia are to blame for the disorder. For instance, some researchers suggest that schizophrenia is related to a family interaction style known as expressed emotion.

Expressed emotion is an interaction style characterized by high levels of criticism, hostility, and emotional intrusiveness within a family. Other researchers suggest that faulty communication patterns lie at the heart of schizophrenia (Lobban, Barrowclough, & Jones, 2006; Nader et al., 2013).

Psychologists who take a cognitive perspective on schizophrenia suggest that the problems in thinking that people with the disorder experience point to a cognitive cause. Some suggest that schizophrenia results from *overattention* to stimuli in the environment. Rather than being able to screen out unimportant or inconsequential stimuli and focus on the most important things in the environment, people with schizophrenia may be excessively receptive to virtually everything in their environment. As a consequence of their inability to screen out noncritical information, their information-processing capabilities become overloaded and eventually break down.

Other cognitive experts argue that schizophrenia results from *underattention* to certain stimuli. According to this explanation, people with schizophrenia fail to focus sufficiently on important stimuli and pay attention to other, less important information in their surroundings (Cadenhead & Braff, 1995; Remington et al., 2014).

Although it is plausible that overattention and underattention are related to different forms of schizophrenia, these phenomena do not explain the origins of such information-processing disorders. Consequently, cognitive approaches–like other environmental explanations–do not provide a full explanation of the disorder.

PREDISPOSITIONAL MODEL OF SCHIZOPHRENIA: THE DISORDER'S MULTIPLE CAUSES

Most scientists now believe that schizophrenia is caused by biological as well as situational factors. Specifically, the *predisposition model of schizophrenia* suggests that individuals may inherit a predisposition or an inborn sensitivity to develop schizophrenia. This genetic predisposition makes them particularly vulnerable to stressors in their lives, such as social rejection, dysfunctional family communication patterns, or severe economic stress.

The stressors in people's lives may vary, but if they are strong enough and are coupled with a genetic predisposition, they result in the appearance of schizophrenia. Furthermore, a strong genetic predisposition may lead to the onset of schizophrenia even when the environmental stressors are relatively weak. On the other hand, someone with a genetic predisposition to develop schizophrenia may avoid developing the disorder if that person experiences relatively few life stressors.

In short, schizophrenia is related to several kinds of biological and situational factors. It is increasingly clear, then, that no single factor but rather a combination of interrelated variables produces schizophrenia (Opler et al., 2008; Balter, 2017).

Study Alert
Remember that the multiple causes of schizophrenia include biological and environmental factors.

Personality Disorders

I had always wanted lots of things; as a child I can remember wanting a bullet that a friend of mine had brought in to show the class. I took it and put it into my school bag and when my friend noticed it was missing, I was the one who stayed after school with him and searched the room, and I was the one who sat with him and bitched about the other kids and how one of them took his bullet. I even went home with him to help him break the news to his uncle, who had brought it home from the war for him.

But that was petty compared with the stuff I did later. I wanted a Ph.D. very badly, but I didn't want to work very hard–just enough to get by. I never did the experiments I reported; hell, I was smart enough to make up the results. I knew enough about statistics to make anything look plausible. I got my master's degree without even spending one hour in a laboratory. I mean, the professors believed anything. I'd stay out all night drinking and being with my friends, and the next day I'd get in just before them and tell 'em I'd been in the lab all night. They'd actually feel sorry for me. (Duke & Nowicki, 1979)

This excerpt provides a graphic first-person account of a person with a personality disorder. A **personality disorder** is characterized by a set of inflexible, maladaptive behavior patterns that keep a person from functioning appropriately in society.

Unlike the other disorders we have discussed, people with personality disorders typically have little sense of personal distress. Moreover, people with personality disorders frequently lead seemingly normal lives. However, just below the surface lies a set of inflexible, maladaptive personality traits that prevent them from functioning effectively as members of society (Clarkin & Lenzenweger, 2004; Friedman, Oltmanns, & Turkheimer, 2007; Anderson et al., 2015).

The best-known type of personality disorder, illustrated by the case above, is the **antisocial personality disorder** (sometimes referred to as a sociopathic personality). Individuals with this disturbance show no regard for the moral and ethical rules of society or the rights of others. Although they can appear quite intelligent and likable (at least at first), upon closer examination they turn out to be manipulative and deceptive. Moreover, they lack any guilt or anxiety about their wrongdoing. When those

personality disorder A disorder characterized by a set of inflexible, maladaptive behavior patterns that keep a person from functioning appropriately in society. (Module 47)

antisocial personality disorder A disorder in which individuals show no regard for the moral and ethical rules of society or the rights of others. (Module 47)

Study Alert

Unlike most psychological disorders, personality disorders produce little or no personal distress.

with antisocial personality disorder behave in a way that injures someone else, they understand intellectually that they have caused harm but feel no remorse (Hilarski, 2007; Bateman, 2011; Rosenström et al., 2017).

People with antisocial personality disorder are often impulsive and lack the ability to withstand frustration. They can be extremely manipulative. They also may have excellent social skills; they can be charming, engaging, and highly persuasive. Some of the best con artists have antisocial personalities.

What causes such an unusual constellation of problem behaviors? A variety of factors have been suggested ranging from an inability to experience emotions appropriately to problems in family relationships. For example, in many cases of antisocial behavior, the individual has come from a home in which a parent has died or left or one in which there is a lack of affection, a lack of consistency in discipline, or outright rejection. Other explanations concentrate on sociocultural factors because an unusually high proportion of people with antisocial personalities come from lower socioeconomic groups. Still, no one has been able to pinpoint the specific causes of antisocial personalities, and it is likely that some combination of factors is responsible (Rosenstein & Horowitz, 1996; Costa & Widiger, 2002; Chen et al., 2011).

borderline personality disorder
A disorder characterized by problems regulating emotions and thoughts, displaying impulsive and reckless behavior, and having unstable relationships with others. (Module 47)

People with **borderline personality disorder** have problems regulating emotions and thoughts, display impulsive and reckless behavior, and have unstable relationships with others. They also have difficulty in developing a clear understanding of who they are. As a consequence, they tend to rely on relationships with others to define their identity. The problem with this strategy is that even minor rejection by others is devastating to those with borderline personality disorder. Furthermore, they generally distrust others and have difficulty controlling their anger. Their emotional volatility leads to impulsive and self-destructive behavior.

Individuals with borderline personality disorder often feel empty and alone, and they have difficulty cooperating with others. They may form intense, sudden, one-sided relationships in which they demand the attention of another person and then feel angry when they don't receive it. One reason for this behavior is that they may have a background in which others discounted or criticized their emotional reactions, and they may not have learned to regulate their emotions effectively (King-Casas et al., 2008; Hopwood et al., 2009; Samuel et al., 2013).

narcissistic personality disorder A personality disturbance characterized by an exaggerated sense of self-importance. (Module 47)

The narcissistic personality disorder is another type of personality disorder. The **narcissistic personality disorder** is characterized by an exaggerated sense of self-importance. Those with the disorder expect special treatment from others while also disregarding others' feelings, showing little or no sense of empathy for them.

There are several other categories of personality disorder that range in severity from individuals who may simply be regarded by others as eccentric, obnoxious, or difficult to people who act in a manner that is criminal and dangerous to others. Although they are not out of touch with reality like people with schizophrenia, people with personality disorders often lead lives that put them on the fringes of society (Trull & Widiger, 2003; Wright et al., 2016).

From the perspective of...

A Social Worker Because people with personality disorders often appear from the outside to function well in society, should you try to address their problems?

Disorders That Impact Childhood

We typically view childhood as a time of innocence and relative freedom from stress. In reality, though, almost 20% of children and 40% of adolescents experience significant emotional or behavioral disorders (Romano et al., 2001; Broidy, Nagin, & Tremblay, 2003; Nolen-Hoeksema, 2007).

For example, although major depression is more prevalent in adults, around 2.5% of children and more than 8% of adolescents suffer from the disorder. In fact, by the time they reach age 20, between 15–20% of children and adolescents will experience an episode of major depression. Ten percent of adolescents will have had an episode of major depression in the previous year (Garber & Horowitz, 2002; Substance Abuse and Mental Health Services Administration, 2014; Frodl et al., 2017).

Children do not always display depression the same way adults do. Rather than showing the expression of profound sadness or hopelessness, childhood depression may produce the expression of exaggerated fears, clinginess, or avoidance of everyday activities. In older children, the symptoms may be sulking, school problems, and even acts of delinquency (Koplewicz, 2002; Seroczynski, Jacquez, & Cole, 2003).

A considerably more common childhood disorder is **attention-deficit hyperactivity disorder, or ADHD,** a disorder marked by inattention, impulsiveness, a low tolerance for frustration, and generally a great deal of inappropriate activity. Although all children show such behavior some of the time, it is so common in children diagnosed with ADHD that it interferes with their everyday functioning (Barkley, Knouse, & Murphy, 2011; Walton, Murphy, & Bartram, 2017).

ADHD is surprisingly widespread, with estimates ranging between 3–5% of the school-age population—or some 3.5 million children under the age of 18 in the United States. Children diagnosed with the disorder are often exhausting to parents and teachers, and even their peers find them difficult to deal with.

The cause of ADHD is not known, although most experts feel that it is produced by dysfunctions in the nervous system. For example, one theory suggests that unusually low levels of arousal in the central nervous system cause ADHD. To compensate, children with ADHD seek out stimulation to increase arousal. Still, such theories are speculative. Furthermore, because many children occasionally show behaviors characteristic of ADHD, it often is misdiagnosed or in some cases overdiagnosed. Only the frequency and persistence of the symptoms of ADHD allow for a correct diagnosis, which only a trained professional can do (Barkley, 2000; Sciutto & Eisenberg, 2007; Ketisch & Jones, 2013).

Autism spectrum disorder, a severe developmental disability that impairs one's ability to communicate and relate to others, is another disorder that usually appears in the first 3 years and typically continues throughout life. Children with autism have difficulties in both verbal and nonverbal communication, and they may avoid social contact. About 1 in 88 children are now thought to have the disorder, and its prevalence has risen significantly in the last decade. Whether the increase is the result of an actual rise in the incidence of autism or is due to better reporting is a question of intense debate among researchers (Rice, 2009; Neal, Matson, & Belva, 2013).

Other Disorders

It's important to keep in mind that the various forms of psychological disorders described in DSM-5 cover much more ground than we have been able to discuss in this module. Some relate to topics considered in other chapters. For example, *psychoactive substance use disorder* relates to problems that arise from the use and abuse of drugs. Furthermore, *alcohol use disorders* are among the most serious and widespread problems. Both psychoactive substance use disorder and alcohol use disorder co-occur with many other psychological disorders, such as mood disorders, trauma- and stressor-related disorders, and schizophrenia, which complicate treatment considerably (Salgado, Quinlan, & Zlotnick, 2007).

attention-deficit hyperactivity disorder (ADHD) A disorder marked by inattention, impulsiveness, a low tolerance for frustration, and a great deal of inappropriate activity. (Module 47)

autism spectrum disorder A severe developmental disability that impairs children's ability to communicate and relate to others. (Module 47)

In the most severe cases of autism spectrum disorder, children display self-injurious behavior and must wear protective head gear.
©Tony Freeman/PhotoEdit

Another widespread problem is *eating disorders*. They include such disorders as *anorexia nervosa* and *bulimia*, which we considered in the chapter on motivation and emotion, as well as *binge-eating disorder*, characterized by binge eating without behaviors designed to prevent weight gain. Finally, *sexual disorders*, in which one's sexual activity is unsatisfactory, are another important class of problems. They include *sexual desire disorders, sexual arousal disorders*, and *paraphilic disorders*, atypical sexual activities that may include nonhuman objects or nonconsenting partners.

Another important class of disorders is *neurocognitive disorders*, problems with a biological cause that affect thinking and behavior. We considered some of them earlier, such as Alzheimer's disease and some types of developmental disabilities that are fully the consequence of biological issues. Furthermore, there are many other disorders that we have not mentioned at all, and each of the categories of disorder we have discussed can be divided into several subcategories (Pratt et al., 2003; Reijonen et al., 2003; American Psychiatric Association, 2013).

AP| MODULE 47: THE MAJOR PSYCHOLOGICAL DISORDERS

AP SUMMARY

- The predisposition model of schizophrenia suggests a genetic predisposition makes individuals vulnerable to stressors in their lives. Biological and situational factors may result in the emergence of schizophrenia.
- Schizophrenia is a more severe form of mental illness, in which reality is distorted. Symptoms include: declines in functioning, thought and language disturbances, delusions, hallucinations, inappropriate emotions, and withdrawal from others. Symptoms of schizophrenia are classified as either positive or negative. Strong evidence links schizophrenia to genetic, biochemical, cognitive, and environmental factors.
- Neurodevelopmental disorders include: ADHD and autism spectrum disorder.
- Neurocognitive disorders are problems with a biological cause that affect thinking and behavior. A specific type is Alzheimer's disease.
- Anxiety disorders are present when a person experiences so much anxiety that it affects daily functioning. Specific types include: phobic disorders, panic disorder, and generalized anxiety disorder. Phobic disorders consist of agoraphobia, social phobia, and 4 specific phobias. Causes may be biological, behavioral, or cognitive.
- Obsessive-compulsive disorder is characterized by unwanted thoughts and behaviors. Causes may be biological, such as specific differences in the brain.
- Mood disorders are characterized by disturbances in emotional states that interfere with everyday living. Specific types include: major depression and bipolar. Major depression is a common mood disorder and diagnosed more often in women. Bipolar alternates between depression and mania and is associated with creativity. Mood disorders have been explained by

genetic and biological factors, unconscious conflicts, environmental factors, and cognitive and emotional factors.
- Somatic symptom disorders are psychological difficulties that take on a physical form, but there is no medical cause. Specific types include: illness anxiety disorder and conversion disorders.
- Dissociative disorders are marked by the separation of different facets of a person's personality that are usually integrated. This allows people to escape an anxiety-producing situation. Specific types include: dissociative identity disorder, dissociative amnesia, and dissociative fugue.
- Personality disorders are characterized by inflexible, maladaptive behavior patterns that prevent proper functioning in society. Specific types include: antisocial, borderline, and narcissistic.
- Psychoactive substance use disorders relate to the use and abuse of drugs. One of the most serious and widespread problems is alcohol use disorder.
- Eating disorders include: anorexia nervosa, bulimia, and binge-eating disorder.
- Sexual disorders include: sexual desire disorders, sexual arousal disorders, and paraphilic disorders.

AP KEY TERMS

anxiety disorder
specific phobias
panic disorder
generalized anxiety disorder
obsessive-compulsive disorder (OCD)
obsession
compulsion
somatic symptom disorders

illness anxiety disorder
conversion disorder
dissociative disorders
dissociative identity disorder (DID)
dissociative amnesia
dissociative fugue
mood disorder
major depressive disorder
mania
bipolar disorder
schizophrenia
personality disorder
antisocial personality disorder
borderline personality disorder
narcissistic personality disorder
attention-deficit hyperactivity disorder (ADHD)
autism spectrum disorder

AP TEST PRACTICE

Section I: Multiple Choice

1. Learned helplessness is one of the explanations for which disorder?
   A. Obsessive-compulsive disorder
   B. Major depression
   C. Antisocial personality disorder
   D. Specific phobia
   E. Dissociative amnesia

2. Which disorder is associated with hallucinations or delusions?
   A. Antisocial personality disorder
   B. Dissociative identity disorder
   C. Schizophrenia
   D. Conversion disorder
   E. Obsessive-compulsive disorder

3. Rayna has been experiencing a lot of stress at work. One day she wakes up and cannot see. She is probably experiencing
   A. conversion disorder
   B. major depression
   C. schizophrenia
   D. illness anxiety disorder
   E. generalized anxiety disorder

Section II: Free Response

Disorders can easily be confused. Describe how the following disorders can be differentiated.

- Generalized anxiety disorder and specific phobia
- Major depression and bipolar
- Schizophrenia and dissociative identity disorder

Module 48

Psychological Disorders in Perspective

Study Alert

Remember that the incidence of various psychological disorders in the general population is surprisingly high, particularly in terms of depression and alcohol dependence.

How common are the kinds of psychological disorders we've been discussing? Here's one answer: One out of two people in the United States is likely to experience a psychological disorder at some point in their lives.

That's the conclusion drawn from the most comprehensive study on the prevalence of psychological disorders conducted. In that study, researchers conducted face-to-face interviews with more than 8,000 men and women between the ages of 15 and 54. The sample was designed to be representative of the population of the United States.

According to results of the study, 48% of those interviewed had experienced a disorder at some point in their lives. In addition, 30% experienced a disorder in any particular year. Furthermore, many people experience comorbidity. *Cormobidity* is the appearance of multiple, simultaneous psychological disorders in the same person (Welkowitz et al., 2000; Merikangas et al., 2007; Kessler & Wang, 2008).

The most common disorder reported in the study was depression. Some 17% of those surveyed reported at least one major episode. Ten percent had suffered from depression during the current year. The next most common disorder was alcohol dependence, which occurred at a lifetime incidence rate of 14%. In addition, 7% of those interviewed had experienced alcohol dependence in the previous year. Other frequently occurring psychological disorders were drug dependence, disorders involving panic (such as an overwhelming fear of talking to strangers or terror of heights), and posttraumatic stress disorder.

Although some researchers think the estimates of severe disorders may be too high (Narrow et al., 2002), the national findings are consistent with studies of college students and their psychological difficulties. For example, in one study of the problems of students who visited a college counseling center, more than 40% of students reported being depressed (see Figure 1). These figures include only students who sought help from the counseling center and not those who did not seek treatment. Consequently, the figures are not representative of the entire college population (Benton et al., 2003; also see *Applying Psychology in the 21st Century*).

From the perspective of...

A College Counselor What indicators might be most important in determining whether a college student is experiencing a psychological disorder?

©Chris Ryan/age fotostock

The significant level of psychological disorders is a problem not only in the United States; according to the World Health Organization, mental health difficulties are also a global concern. Throughout the world, psychological disorders are widespread.

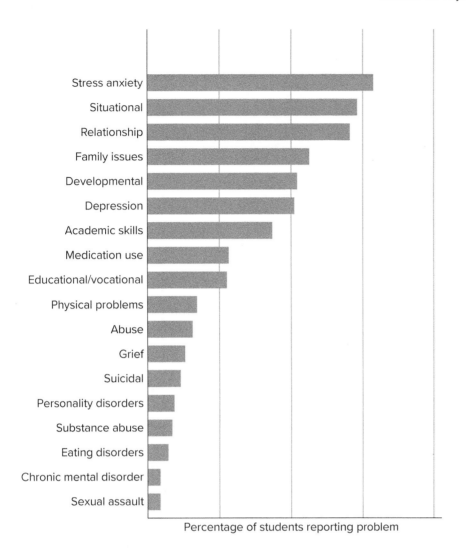

Stress anxiety
Situational
Relationship
Family issues
Developmental
Depression
Academic skills
Medication use
Educational/vocational
Physical problems
Abuse
Grief
Suicidal
Personality disorders
Substance abuse
Eating disorders
Chronic mental disorder
Sexual assault

Percentage of students reporting problem

FIGURE 1 The problems reported by students visiting a college counseling center. Would you have predicted this pattern of psychological difficulties?

Source: Adapted from Benton, S. A., Robertson, J. M., Tseng, W., Newton, F. B., & Benton, S. L. (2003). Changes in counseling center client problems across 13 years. *Professional Psychology: Research and Practice, 34*(1), 66–72.

Furthermore, there are economic disparities in treatment; more affluent people with mild disorders receive more and better treatment than do poor people who have more severe disorders. In fact, psychological disorders make up 14% of global illness, and 90% of people in developing countries receive no care at all for their disorders (see Figure 2; WHO World Mental Health Survey Consortium, 2004; Jacob et al., 2007; Wang et al., 2007).

Also, keep in mind that the incidence of specific disorders varies significantly in other cultures. For instance, cross-cultural surveys show that the incidence of major depression varies significantly from one culture to another. The probability of having at least one episode of depression is only 1.5% in Taiwan and 2.9% in Korea, compared with 11.6% in New Zealand and 16.4% in France. Such notable differences underscore the importance of considering the cultural context of psychological disorders (Weissman et al., 1997; Tseng, 2003).

The Social and Cultural Context of Psychological Disorders

In considering the nature of the psychological disorders described in DSM-5, it's important to keep in mind that the disorders that were included in the manual are a reflection of Western culture at the start of the 21st century. The classification system

IS THE NEWEST GENERATION OF COLLEGE STUDENTS MORE PSYCHOLOGICALLY DISORDERED THAN THEIR PREDECESSORS?

If you are feeling stressed out, anxious, and maybe even depressed, you're not alone. According to the most recent annual report of the Center for Collegiate Mental Health (2017), which summarizes data provided by 139 college and university counselling centers, demand for mental health services has increased dramatically along with an ongoing increase in rates of "threat to self" incidents (including self-injury and suicidal thoughts). In fact, within the past 5 years, the average level of counseling center usage grew 30%–six times more than overall enrollment grew over the same time period.

The most common concerns for students who go in for counselling are anxiety and depression. Moreover, students' self-reported distress levels for depression and anxiety have slowly increased over recent years. Meanwhile, counselling centers are providing nearly 30% more rapid-access service hours and over 7% fewer routine

©Ingram Publishing

service hours during the past 6 years. These statistics illustrate the increase in demand by students with psychological issues.

Several reasons underlie the increase in demand for psychological services. One is that the stigma of psychological disorders is decreasing: Whereas students once may have kept their mental health concerns to themselves, they now feel more empowered to seek treatment (Itkowitz, 2016).

Another reason for the increase in demand for services relates, ironically, to advances in treating psychological disorders generally. Whereas previously, people with more severe disorders would not even consider enrolling in college, better treatment now allows them to start college and attempt to receive treatment while enrolled. Furthermore, colleges may be doing a better job of helping distressed students recognize their need for mental health services and get treatment (Center for Collegiate Mental Health, 2017).

In short, it doesn't appear that the increase in students with self-reported psychological disorders represents an increase in the incidence of those disorders. Instead, it may well be that the willingness of students to report and seek treatment for those disorders is at the root of the apparent increase (Wilson, 2015; Auerbach et al., 2016).

AP SKILL: EXPLAIN BEHAVIOR IN AUTHENTIC CONTEXT

1. The prevalence rate for depression and anxiety is not increasing, but students are more willing to report and seek treatment. Why are students accessing psychological services?
2. Why might the stigma associated with mental illness be decreasing?

---

provides a snapshot of how its authors viewed mental disorder when it was published. In fact, the development of the most recent version of the DSM was a source of great debate, which in part reflects issues that divide society.

One specific, newly classified disorder that was added to DSM-5 and that has caused controversy is known as disruptive mood dysregulation disorder. This particular diagnosis is characterized by temperamental outbursts grossly out of proportion to the situation, both verbally and physically, in children between the ages of 6 and 18. Some practitioners argue these symptoms simply define a child having a temper tantrum rather than a disorder (Marchand & Phillips, 2012; Frances, 2013).

Similarly, someone who overeats 12 times in 3 months can be considered to be suffering from the new classification of binge-eating disorder, which seems to some critics to be overly inclusive. Finally, hoarding behavior is now placed in its own category of psychological disorder. Some critics suggest this change is more a reflection of the rise of reality shows focusing on hoarding rather than reflecting a distinct category of psychological disturbance (Hudson et al., 2012; Racine et al., 2017; Moulding et al., 2017).

Such controversies underline the fact that our understanding of abnormal behavior reflects the society and culture in which we live. Future revisions of DSM may include a different catalog of disorders. Even now, other cultures might include a list of disorders that are very different from the list that appears in the current DSM, as we discuss next.

Study Alert
It is important to understand that the DSM is a living document that presents a view of disorders that reflects the culture and historical context of its authors.

Developed Countries

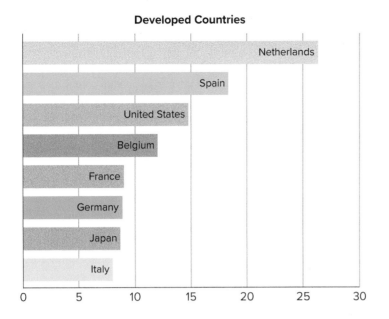

FIGURE 2 According to a global survey conducted by the World Health Organization, the prevalence of psychological disorders is widespread. These figures show the percentage of people who have experienced any psychological disorder within the prior 12-month period.

Source: Adapted from WHO World Mental Health Survey Consortium. (2004). Prevalence, severity, and unmet need for treatment of mental disorders in the World Health Organization World Mental Health Surveys. *Journal of the American Medical Association, 291,* 2581–2590.

Less-Developed Countries

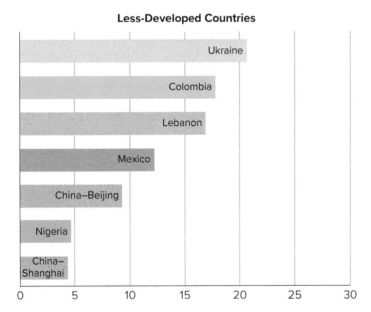

Exploring Diversity

DSM and Culture—and the Culture of DSM

To most people raised in the United States, a person who hears voices of the recently deceased is probably a victim of a psychological disturbance. Yet some Plains Indians routinely hear the voices of the dead calling to them from the afterlife, and in their culture, that's considered perfectly normal.

The voices Plains Indians hear are only one example of the role of culture in determining what behavior should be labeled as "abnormal." In fact, among all the major adult disorders included in the DSM categorization, just a minority are found across all cultures of the world. Most others only are prevalent in North America and Western Europe (Kleinman, 1996; López & Guarnaccia, 2000; Jacob, 2014).

For instance, take anorexia nervosa, the disorder in which people become obsessed with their weight and sometimes stop eating, ultimately starving to death in the process.

It turns out that anorexia nervosa occurs most frequently in cultures that hold the societal standard that slender female bodies are the most desirable. In most of the world, where such a standard does not exist, anorexia nervosa is rare. Furthermore, the disorder may appear in specific ways in a particular culture. For instance, in Hong Kong, symptoms of one form of anorexia relate to complaints of bloated stomachs, rather than fears of becoming fat (Watters, 2010; Munro, Randell, & Lawrie, 2017).

Similarly, dissociative identity (multiple personality) disorder makes sense as a problem only in societies in which a sense of self is fairly concrete. In India, the self is based more on external factors that are relatively independent of the person. There, when an individual displays symptoms of what people in a Western society would call dissociative identity disorder, Indians assume that that person is possessed either by demons (which they view as a malady) or by gods (which does not require treatment).

Furthermore, even though disorders such as schizophrenia are found throughout the world, cultural factors influence the specific symptoms of the disorder. Hence, catatonic schizophrenia, in which unmoving patients appear to be frozen in the same position (sometimes for days), is rare in North America and Western Europe. In contrast, in India, 80% of those with schizophrenia are catatonic.

Other cultures have disorders that do not appear in the West. For example, in Malaysia, a behavior called *amok* is characterized by a wild outburst in which a usually quiet and withdrawn person kills or severely injures another. *Koro* is a condition found in Southeast Asian males who develop an intense panic that their penis is about to withdraw irretrievably into their abdomens. Finally, *ataque de nervios* is a disorder found most often among Latinos from the Caribbean. It is characterized by trembling, crying, uncontrollable screams, and incidents of verbal or physical aggression (Cohen, Slomkowski, & Robins, 1999; Adams & Dzokoto, 2007; Ebigbo, Lekwas, & Chukwunenyem, 2015).

Explanations for psychological disorders also differ among cultures. For example, in China, psychological disorders are commonly viewed as weaknesses of the heart, a concept that derives from thousands of years of traditional Chinese medicine. Chinese people are more likely than people in Western cultures to express their emotional anguish in terms of physical symptoms such as heart pain, "heart panic," or "heart vexed." They also may focus more on the effects that their symptoms have on their relationships with friends and family members than on themselves (Miller, 2006; Lee, Kleinman, & Kleinman, 2007; Watters, 2010).

In sum, we should not assume that the DSM provides the final word on psychological disorders. The disorders it includes are very much a creation and function of Western cultures at a particular moment in time, and its categories should not be seen as universally applicable (Tseng, 2003).

BECOMING AN INFORMED CONSUMER
of Psychology

Deciding When You Need Help

After you've considered the range and variety of psychological disturbances that can afflict people, you may begin to feel that you suffer from one (or more) of the problems we have discussed. In fact, this perception has a name: *medical student's disease*. Although in this case it might more aptly be labeled "psychology student's disease," the basic symptoms are the same: feeling that you suffer from the same sorts of problems you are studying.

Most often, of course, your concerns will be unwarranted. As we have discussed, the differences between normal and abnormal behavior are often so fuzzy that it is easy to jump to the conclusion that you might have the same symptoms that are involved in serious forms of mental disturbance.

Before coming to such a conclusion, though, keep in mind that from time to time, we all experience a wide range of emotions, and it is not unusual to feel deeply unhappy, fantasize about bizarre situations, or feel anxiety about life's circumstances. It is the persistence, depth, and consistency of such behavior that set normal reactions apart from abnormal ones. If you have not previously had serious doubts about the normality of your behavior, it is unlikely that reading about others' psychological disorders will prompt you to re-evaluate your earlier conclusion.

On the other hand, many people do have problems that merit concern, and in such cases, it is important to consider the possibility that professional help is warranted. The following list of symptoms can serve as a guideline to help you determine whether outside intervention might be useful (Engler & Goleman, 1992; APA, 2018).

- Long-term feelings of distress that interfere with your sense of well-being, competence, and ability to function effectively in daily activities
- Occasions in which you experience overwhelmingly high stress accompanied by feelings of inability to cope with the situation
- Prolonged depression or feelings of hopelessness, especially when they do not have any clear cause (such as the death of someone close)
- Withdrawal from other people
- Thoughts of inflicting harm on oneself or suicide
- A chronic physical problem for which no physical cause can be determined
- A fear or phobia that prevents you from engaging in everyday activities
- Feelings that other people are out to get you or are talking about and plotting against you
- Inability to interact effectively with others, preventing the development of friendships and loving relationships

This list offers a rough set of guidelines for determining when the normal problems of everyday living have escalated beyond your ability to deal with them by yourself. In such situations, the *least* reasonable approach would be to pore over the psychological disorders we have discussed in an attempt at self-diagnosis. A more reasonable strategy is to consider seeking professional help.

AP¹ MODULE 48: PSYCHOLOGICAL DISORDERS IN PERSPECTIVE

AP SUMMARY

- The *DSM-5* includes disorders that are reflective of Western culture, but other cultures have disorders that do not appear in the West. The *DSM* is not the final word on disorders.
- About half the people in the United States are likely to experience a psychological disorder at some point in their lives; 30% experience a disorder in any specific year.
- Our understanding of abnormal behavior reflects the culture we live in.

AP TEST PRACTICE

Section I: Multiple Choice

1. Amok and koro are considered disorders connected to one's
   A. social class
   B. hormone levels
   C. economic status
   D. culture
   E. childhood

2. Approximately what percent of individuals experience a disorder in any given year?
   A. 1%
   B. 5%
   C. 30%
   D. 50%
   E. 75%

3. The major disorders listed in the *DSM* are reflective of what type of culture?
   A. Western
   B. Eastern
   C. African
   D. Southern
   E. Cross-cultural

Section II: Free Response

The *Diagnostic and Statistical Manual of Mental Disorders (DSM)* is the most widely used system to classify and define psychological disorders. Explain how the following concepts relate to the *DSM*.

- Culture
- Comborbidity
- Diagnostic labels

LOOKING *Back*

EPILOGUE

We've discussed some of the many types of psychological disorders to which people are prone, noted the difficulty psychologists and physicians have in clearly differentiating normal from abnormal behavior, and looked at some of the approaches mental health professionals have taken to explain and treat psychological disorders. We considered today's most commonly used classification scheme, categorized in the DSM-5, and examined some of the more prevalent forms of psychological disorders. To gain a perspective on the topic of psychological disorders, we discussed the surprisingly broad incidence of psychological disorders in U.S. society and the cultural nature of such disorders.

VISUAL SUMMARY 15 Psychological Disorders

MODULE 46 Normal Versus Abnormal: Making the Distinction

Defining Abnormality

- Deviation from the average
- Deviation from the ideal
- Sense of personal discomfort
- Inability to function effectively
- Legal concept

Perspectives on Abnormality

Perspectives on Psychological Disorders		
Perspective	**Description**	**Possible Application of Perspective to Chris' Case**
Medical	Assumes that physiological causes are at the root of psychological disorders	Examine Chris for medical problems, such as brain tumor, chemical imbalance in the brain, or disease
Psychoanalytic	Argues that psychological disorders stem from childhood conflicts	Seek out information about Chris' past, considering possible childhood conflicts
Behavioral	Assumes that abnormal behaviors are learned responses	Concentrate on rewards and punishments for Chris' behavior, and identify environmental stimuli that reinforce his behavior
Cognitive	Assumes that cognitions (people's thoughts and beliefs) are central to psychological disorders	Focus on Chris' perceptions of self and his environment
Humanistic	Emphasizes people's responsibility for their own behavior and the need to self-actualize	Consider Chris' behavior in terms of his choices and efforts to reach his potential
Sociocultural	Assumes that behavior is shaped by family, society, and culture	Focus on how societal demands contributed to Chris' disorder

Classifying Abnormal Behavior: DSM-5 attempts to provide comprehensive and relatively precise definitions for more than 200 disorders

MODULE 47 Major Psychological Disorders

Anxiety Disorders: Anxiety without external justification

- Phobic disorder
- Panic disorder
- Generalized anxiety disorder
- Causes of anxiety disorders

Obsessive-Compulsive Disorder

Somatic Symptom Disorders: Psychological difficulties that take on a physical form with no medical cause

Dissociative Disorders: Separation of different facets of a person's personality that normally work together

Mood Disorders: Disturbances in emotional experience

- Major depressive disorder
- Mania and bipolar disorder
- Causes of mood disorders
  - Genetics
  - Psychological: feelings of loss or anger
  - Behavioral: stress
  - Cognitive: learned helplessness and no hope

Schizophrenia Spectrum: A class of disorders in which distortion of reality occurs

- Decline from a previous level of functioning
- Disturbances of thought and language
- Delusions
- Hallucinations and perceptual disorders
- Emotional disturbances

Personality Disorders: A set of inflexible, maladaptive behavior patterns

- Antisocial personality disorder
- Borderline personality disorder
- Narcissistic personality disorder

Childhood Disorders: Start during childhood or adolescence

- Attention-deficit hyperactivity disorder
- Autism spectrum disorder

MODULE 48 Psychological Disorders in Perspective

Social and Cultural Context: Our understanding of abnormal behavior reflects the society and culture in which we live

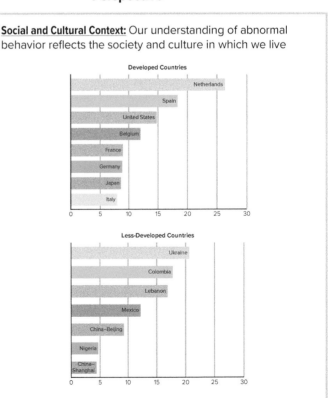

(MODULE 46) (top photo): ©Brett Coomer, Pool/AP Images; (book): ©H.S. Photos/Alamy Stock Photo; Source: Adapted from Nolen-Hoeksema, S. (2007). *Abnormal psychology* (4th ed.). New York: McGraw-Hill; (MODULE 47) (China glass): ©Imaginechina/AP Images; Source: Adapted from WHO World Mental Health Survey Consortium. (2004). Prevalence, severity, and unmet need for treatment of mental disorders in the World Health Organization World Mental Health Surveys. *Journal of the American Medical Association, 291,* 2581–2590.

©urbancow/Getty Images

CHAPTER 16
Treatment of Psychological Disorders

AP'I ESSENTIAL QUESTIONS

• How are psychological disorders treated?

AP'I LEARNING TARGETS FOR CHAPTER 16

MODULE 49

• Identify the contributions of major figures in psychological treatment.

• Describe major treatment orientations used in therapy and how those orientations influence therapeutic planning.

PSYCHOTHERAPY: PSYCHODYNAMIC, BEHAVIORAL, AND COGNITIVE APPROACHES TO TREATMENT

Psychodynamic Approaches to Therapy

Behavioral Approaches to Therapy

Cognitive Approaches to Therapy

AP'I **Neuroscience in Your Life:** How Cognitive Behavioral Therapy Changes Your Brain

MODULE 50

• Describe the central characteristics of psychotherapeutic intervention.

• Identify the contributions of major figures in psychological treatment.

• Describe major treatment orientations used in therapy and how those orientations influence therapeutic planning.

• Summarize effectiveness of specific treatments used to address specific problems.

• Discuss how cultural and ethnic context influence choice and success of treatment.

• Compare and contrast different treatment methods.

PSYCHOTHERAPY: HUMANISTIC, INTERPERSONAL, AND GROUP APPROACHES TO TREATMENT

Humanistic Therapy

Interpersonal Therapy

AP'I **Applying Psychology in the 21st Century:** Click Here for Therapy

Group Therapies

Evaluating Psychotherapy: Does Therapy Work?

Exploring Diversity: Racial and Ethnic Factors in Treatment: Should Therapists Be Color-Blind?

- Describe prevention strategies that build resilience and promote competence.

- Summarize effectiveness of specific treatments used to address specific problems from a biological perspective.

PROLOGUE *GOING DEEP TO TREAT*

Deep brain stimulation (DBS) was originally developed to treat movement disorders such as Parkinson's but is still experimental for the treatment of depression. Vito Randazzo underwent a day-long operation that involved threading tiny electrodes into a mood-related part of the brain and then connecting the electrodes to a pacemaker-like device in his chest. The implant uses electrical currents to correct abnormal brain signals associated with depression.

"It's not as if DBS was a magic bullet," said Randazzo's neurosurgeon, Sameer Sheth. "Vito still had to work hard to fight through the depression, but the therapy helped him actually succeed this time." Randazzo said the operation was transformative: "I can laugh again and really enjoy life with my family" (Columbia Neurosurgery, 2017; Garcia, 2017).

LOOKING *Ahead*

Deep brain stimulation surgery is just one way in which people suffering from psychological disorders—in this instance, severe depression—can be treated. The variety of treatments available to relieve psychological pain share a common objective: to enable individuals to achieve richer, more meaningful, and more fulfilling lives.

For Vito Randazzo, the transition from a life of dark, desperate depression was by no means sudden or miraculous, but by working hard with the DBS team to confront and overcome his depression, Randazzo—while not entirely symptom-free—created a life of laughter and enjoyment with his family.

Despite their diversity, approaches to treating psychological disorders fall into two main categories: psychologically based and biologically based therapies. **Psychotherapy** is psychologically based treatment in which a trained professional—a therapist—uses psychological techniques to help someone overcome psychological difficulties and disorders, resolve problems in living, or bring about personal growth. The goal of psychotherapy is to produce lasting psychological change in a person (called a *client* or *patient*) through discussions and interactions with the therapist. In contrast, **biomedical therapy** is biologically based and relies on drugs and medical procedures to improve psychological functioning.

As we describe the various approaches to therapy, keep in mind that although the distinctions may seem clear-cut, the classifications and procedures overlap a good deal. In fact, many therapists today take an *eclectic approach* to therapy, which means they use a variety of methods with an individual patient. Assuming that psychological as well as biological processes often produce psychological disorders, eclectic therapists may draw from several perspectives simultaneously to address the psychological as well as the biological aspects of a person's problems.

psychotherapy Psychologically based treatment in which a trained professional—a therapist—uses psychological techniques to help a person overcome psychological difficulties and disorders, resolve problems in living, or bring about personal growth. (Module 49)

biomedical therapy Biologically based therapy that relies on drugs and other medical procedures to improve psychological functioning. (Module 49)

Module 49

Psychotherapy: Psychodynamic, Behavioral, and Cognitive Approaches to Treatment

- Describe the central characteristics of psychotherapeutic intervention.
- Identify the contributions of major figures in psychological treatment.
- Describe major treatment orientations used in therapy and how those orientations influence therapeutic planning.
- Summarize effectiveness of specific treatments used to address specific problems.
- Compare and contrast different treatment methods.

FIGURE 1 A variety of professionals provide therapy and counseling. Each could be expected to give helpful advice and direction. However, the nature of the problem a person is experiencing may make one or another therapist more appropriate.

There are about 400 varieties of psychotherapy. Although the methods are diverse, all psychological approaches have a common perspective: They seek to solve psychological problems by modifying people's behavior and helping them obtain a better understanding of themselves and their past, present, and future.

In light of the variety of psychological approaches, it is not surprising that the people who provide therapy vary considerably in educational background and training (see Figure 1). Many have doctoral degrees in psychology, having attended graduate school, learned clinical and research techniques, and held an internship in a facility that treats people with psychological disorders. But therapy is also provided by people in fields allied with psychology, such as psychiatrists (who have a medical degree with a specialization in psychological disorders) and social workers (who have a master's degree and have specialized in psychological disorders).

The nature of the problem a person is experiencing often makes one type of therapist more appropriate than others. For example, a person who is suffering from a severe disturbance and who has lost touch with reality may typically require some sort of biologically based drug therapy. In that case, a psychiatrist—who is a physician—would be the professional of choice. In contrast, those suffering from milder disorders,

---

Getting Help from the Right Person

Clinical Psychologists

Psychologists with a PhD or PsyD with about 5 years of training and who have also completed a postgraduate internship. They specialize in assessment and treatment of psychological difficulties, providing psychotherapy and, in some U.S. states, can prescribe drugs.

Counseling Psychologists

Psychologists with a PhD or EdD who typically treat day-to-day adjustment problems, often in a university mental health clinic

Psychiatrists

MDs with postgraduate training in psychological disorders. Because they can prescribe medication, they often treat the most severe disorders.

Psychoanalysts

Either MDs or psychologists who specialize in psychoanalysis, the treatment technique first developed by Freud

Licensed Professional Counselors or Clinical Mental Health Counselors

Professionals with a master's degree who provide therapy to individuals, couples, and families and who hold a national or state certification

Clinical or Psychiatric Social Workers

Professionals with a master's degree and specialized training who may provide therapy, usually regarding common family and personal problems such as difficulty adjusting to the death of a family member, have a broader choice that might include other types of professionals listed in Figure 1.

Regardless of their specific training, all psychotherapists employ one of four major approaches to therapy that we'll consider next: psychodynamic, behavioral, cognitive, and humanistic treatment approaches. These approaches grow out of the perspectives of personality and psychological disorders developed by psychologists.

Psychodynamic Approaches to Therapy

Psychodynamic therapy seeks to bring unresolved past conflicts and unacceptable impulses from the unconscious into the conscious, where patients may deal with the problems more effectively. Although psychodynamic approaches originally derived from Freud's psychoanalytic theories of personality, today they encompass a wider range of therapies. The common assumptions behind psychodynamic therapies are that unconscious forces affect our behavior and that the goal of therapy is to try to identify and control them.

Psychodynamic approaches hold that people employ *defense mechanisms*, psychological strategies to protect themselves from unacceptable unconscious impulses. The most common defense mechanism is *repression*, which pushes threatening and unpleasant thoughts and impulses back into the unconscious. However, because people cannot completely bury their unacceptable thoughts and impulses, anxiety associated with them can produce abnormal behavior.

How do we rid ourselves of the anxiety produced by unconscious, unwanted thoughts and impulses? To Freud, the answer was to confront the conflicts and impulses by bringing them out of the unconscious part of the mind and into the conscious part. Freud assumed that this technique would reduce anxiety stemming from past conflicts and that the patient could then participate in his or her daily life more effectively.

A psychodynamic therapist, then, faces the challenge of finding a way to assist patients' attempts to explore and understand the unconscious. The technique that has evolved has a number of components, but basically it consists of guiding patients to consider and discuss their past experiences in explicit detail from the time of their first memories. This process assumes that patients will eventually stumble upon long-hidden crises, traumas, and conflicts that are producing anxiety in their adult lives. They will then be able to "work through"–understand and rectify–those difficulties.

PSYCHOANALYSIS: FREUD'S THERAPY

Psychoanalysis is Freud's specific version of psychodynamic therapy. The goal of psychoanalysis is to release hidden thoughts and feelings from the unconscious part of our mind in order to reduce their power in controlling behavior.

In traditional psychoanalysis, which tends to be a lengthy and expensive process, patients may meet with a therapist with considerable frequency, sometimes as much as 50 minutes a session, 4 to 5 days a week, for several years. In their sessions, therapists and patients typically use a technique developed by Freud called *free association*. Patients using free association say aloud whatever comes to mind, regardless of its apparent irrelevance or senselessness. The psychoanalyst then attempts to recognize and label the connections between what a patient says and the patient's unconscious.

Therapists also use *dream interpretation*, examining dreams to find clues to unconscious conflicts and problems. Moving beyond the surface description of a dream (called the *manifest content*), therapists seek its underlying meaning (the *latent content*), which supposedly reveals the true unconscious meaning of the dream (Blum, 2011; Hill et al., 2013; Sandford, 2017).

The processes of free association and dream interpretation do not always move forward easily. The same unconscious forces that initially produced repression may

psychodynamic therapy Therapy that seeks to bring unresolved past conflicts and unacceptable impulses from the unconscious into the conscious, where patients may deal with the problems more effectively. (Module 49)

psychoanalysis Freud's form of psychotherapy in which the goal is to release hidden thoughts and feelings from the unconscious part of our minds in order to reduce their power in controlling behavior. (Module 49)

 Study Alert

To better understand how psychodynamic therapy works, review Freud's psychoanalytic theory discussed in the chapter on personality.

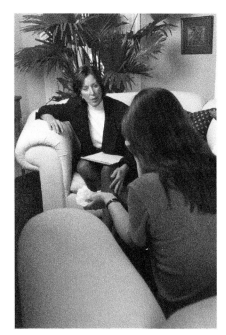

The close and intense relationship between therapist and patient may become highly complex.
©David Buffington/Getty Images

transference The transfer of feelings to a psychoanalyst of love or anger that had been originally directed to a patient's parents or other authority figures. (Module 49)

keep past difficulties out of the conscious mind, which produces resistance. *Resistance* is an inability or unwillingness to discuss or reveal particular memories, thoughts, or motivations.

Patients can show resistance in many ways. For instance, they may be discussing a childhood memory and suddenly forget what they were saying, or they may abruptly change the subject completely. It is the therapist's job to discern instances of resistance and interpret their meaning. The therapists also need to try to make patients return to the subject they are trying to avoid–which is likely to hold difficult or painful memories for the patients.

Because of the close, almost intimate interaction between patient and psychoanalyst, the relationship between the two often becomes emotionally charged and takes on a complexity unlike most other relationships. Patients may eventually think of the analyst as a symbol of a significant other in their past, perhaps a parent or a lover, and apply some of their feelings for that person to the analyst–a phenomenon known as transference. **Transference** is the transfer of feelings to a psychoanalyst of love or anger that had been originally directed to a patient's parents or other authority figures (Steiner, 2008; Høglend et al., 2011; Turri, 2015).

A therapist can use transference to help a patient recreate past relationships that were psychologically difficult. For instance, if a patient undergoing transference views her therapist as a symbol of her father–with whom she had a difficult relationship–the patient and therapist may "redo" an earlier interaction, this time including more positive aspects. Through this process, the patient may resolve conflicts regarding her real father–something that is beginning to happen in the following therapy session:

Sandy: My father . . . never took any interest in any of us. . . . It was my mother–rest her soul–who loved us, not our father. He worked her to death. Lord, I miss her. . . . I must sound angry at my father. Don't you think I have a right to be angry?

Therapist: Do you think you have a right to be angry?

Sandy: Of course, I do! Why are you questioning me? You don't believe me, do you?

Therapist: You want me to believe you.

Sandy: I don't care whether you believe me or not. . . . I know what you're thinking–you think I'm crazy–you must be laughing at me–I'll probably be a case in your next book! You're just sitting there–smirking–making me feel like a bad person–thinking I'm wrong for being mad, that I have no right to be mad.

Therapist: Just like your father.

Sandy: Yes, you're just like my father.–Oh my God! Just now–I–I–thought I was talking to him. (Sue & Sue, 1990)

CONTEMPORARY PSYCHODYNAMIC APPROACHES

Few people have the time, money, or patience to participate in years of traditional psychoanalysis. Even more important, no conclusive evidence shows that psychoanalysis, as Freud originally conceived it in the 19th century, works better than other, more recent forms of psychodynamic therapy.

Today, psychodynamic therapy tends to be of shorter duration, usually lasting no longer than 3 months or 20 sessions. Psychodynamic therapists take a more active role than Freud would have prescribed, and they prod and advise the patient with considerable directness. Finally, contemporary psychodynamic therapists put less emphasis on a patient's past history and childhood. Instead, they concentrate on an individual's current relationships and specific concerns (Wolitzky, 2006; Brafman, 2011; Dreissen et al., 2017).

EVALUATING PSYCHODYNAMIC THERAPY

Even with its current modifications, psychodynamic therapy has its critics. In its longer versions, it can be time-consuming and expensive, especially in comparison with other forms of psychotherapy, such as behavioral and cognitive approaches. Furthermore, less articulate patients may not do as well as more articulate ones.

Ultimately, the most important concern about psychodynamic treatment is whether it actually works, and there is no simple answer to this question. Psychodynamic treatment techniques have been controversial since Freud introduced them. Part of the problem is the difficulty in establishing whether patients have improved after psychodynamic therapy. Determining effectiveness depends on reports from the therapist or the patients themselves—reports that are obviously open to bias and subjective interpretation.

Furthermore, critics have questioned the entire theoretical basis of psychodynamic theory; they maintain that constructs such as the unconscious have not been scientifically confirmed. Despite the criticism, though, the psychodynamic treatment approach has remained viable. For some people, it provides solutions to difficult psychological issues, provides effective treatment for psychological disturbance, and permits the potential development of an unusual degree of insight into one's life (Anestis, Anestis, & Lilienfeld, 2011; Thase, 2013; Sell, Möller, & Taubner, 2017).

Behavioral Approaches to Therapy

Perhaps, when you were a child, your parents rewarded you with an ice cream cone when you were especially good . . . or sent you to your room if you misbehaved. Sound principles back up such a child-rearing strategy: Good behavior is maintained by reinforcement, and unwanted behavior can be eliminated by punishment.

These principles represent the basic underpinnings of behavioral treatment approaches. **Behavioral treatment approaches** use the principles of learning, such as reinforcement and extinction, to reduce or eliminate maladaptive behavior. These approaches are built on a fundamental assumption: Both abnormal behavior and normal behavior are *learned.*

In this view, people who act abnormally either have failed to learn the skills they need to cope with problems of living, or they have acquired faulty skills and patterns that are being maintained through some form of reinforcement. To modify abnormal behavior, then, proponents of these approaches propose that people must learn new behavior to replace the faulty skills they have developed, and they need to unlearn their maladaptive behavior patterns (Norton & Price, 2007; Kowalik et al., 2011; Kivlighan et al., 2015).

Behavioral psychologists do not need to delve into people's pasts or their psyches. Rather than viewing abnormal behavior as a symptom of an underlying problem, they consider the abnormal behavior as the problem in need of modification. The goal of therapy is to change people's behavior to allow them to function more effectively. In this view, then, there is no problem other than the maladaptive behavior itself; if you can change that behavior, treatment is successful.

CLASSICAL CONDITIONING TREATMENTS

Suppose you bite into your favorite candy bar and find that not only is it infested with ants, but you've also swallowed a bunch of them. You immediately become sick to your stomach and throw up. Your long-term reaction? You never eat that kind of candy bar again, and it may be months before you eat any type of candy. You have learned through the basic process of classical conditioning to avoid candy so that you will not get sick and throw up.

Aversive Conditioning This simple example illustrates how a person can be classically conditioned to modify behavior. Behavior therapists use this principle in **aversive conditioning,** which aims to reduce the frequency of undesired behavior by pairing an unpleasant stimulus with undesired behavior. For example, behavior therapists might use aversive conditioning by pairing alcohol with a drug that causes severe nausea and vomiting. After the two have been paired a few times, the person associates the alcohol alone with vomiting and finds alcohol less appealing.

behavioral treatment approaches Treatment approaches that make use of the basic principles of learning, such as reinforcement and extinction, to reduce or eliminate maladaptive behavior. (Module 49)

aversive conditioning A form of therapy that reduces the frequency of undesired behavior by pairing an aversive, unpleasant stimulus with undesired behavior. (Module 49)

Behavioral approaches to treatment would seek to modify the behavior of this couple rather than to focus on the underlying causes of the behavior.
©metinkiyak/Getty Images

Aversion therapy works reasonably well with some specific kinds of disorders, including substance-abuse problems such as alcoholism and certain kinds of sexual disorders. On the other hand, critics question the long-term effectiveness of aversion therapy because rates of relapse are significant (Waters et al., 2017).

In addition, important ethical concerns surround aversion techniques such as electric shock, even though therapists use such potent stimuli only in the most extreme cases, such as with patients who harm themselves. Clearly, though, aversion therapy offers an important procedure for eliminating maladaptive responses for some period of time—a respite that provides, even if only temporarily, an opportunity to encourage more adaptive behavior patterns (Delgado, Labouliere, & Phelps, 2006; Pautassi et al., 2011; Twining et al., 2015).

Systematic Desensitization Another treatment that grew out of the classical conditioning is systematic desensitization. **Systematic desensitization** is a behavioral technique in which exposure to an anxiety-producing stimulus is paired with deep relaxation in order to reduce an anxiety response. The idea is to learn to associate relaxation with a stimulus that previously produced anxiety (Choy, Fyer, & Lipsitz, 2007; Dowling, Jackson, & Thomas, 2008; Triscari et al., 2011).

Suppose, for instance, you were extremely afraid of flying. The very thought of being in an airplane would make you begin to sweat and shake, and you couldn't get yourself near enough to an airport to know how you'd react if you actually had to fly somewhere. Using systematic desensitization to treat your problem, you would first be trained in relaxation techniques by a behavior therapist and learn to relax your body fully—a highly pleasant state, as you might imagine (see Figure 2).

The next step would involve constructing a *hierarchy of fears*—a list in order of increasing severity of the things you associate with your fears. For instance, your hierarchy might resemble this one:

1. Watching a plane fly overhead
2. Going to an airport
3. Buying a ticket
4. Stepping into the plane
5. Seeing the plane door close
6. Having the plane taxi down the runway
7. Taking off
8. Being in the air

systematic desensitization A behavioral technique based on classical conditioning in which exposure to an anxiety-producing stimulus is paired with deep relaxation to reduce or eliminate anxiety. (Module 49)

©Picturenet/Blend Images LLC

To achieve a state of relaxation, follow these steps once or twice a day.

Step 1. Choose a word or phrase that you can repeat to achieve calm. This might be a yoga mantra (*Om* or *Om Mani Padme Hum*, for instance), a word like *Peace* or *Shalom*, or any word or phrase that sounds soft and resonant to you (such as *Peace to my heart*).

Step 2. Find a quiet and comfortable place and sit down.

Step 3. Close your eyes and try to see and feel the darkness.

Step 4. Relax your muscles one by one, starting from your toes and moving slowly up to your scalp.

Step 5. Keep your breathing steady and natural, neither deep nor shallow, and repeat your word or phrase continuously.

Step 6. Do not monitor yourself, but become passive and accepting. If outside thoughts arrive, dismiss them lightly with a smile and return to your repeated word or phrase.

Step 7. Keep this up for 15 minutes. Do not set an alarm; just open your eyes when you feel it is right. If you fall asleep, that is fine.

Step 8. When you have finished, sit quietly, eyes closed, for a minute or two, then stand up.

FIGURE 2 Following these basic steps will help you achieve a sense of calmness by employing the relaxation response.

Source: Adapted from Benson, H., Kornhaber, A., Kornhaber, C., LeChanu, M. N., Zuttermeister, P. C., Myers, P,, & Friedman R. (1994). Increases in positive psychological characteristics with a new relaxation-response curriculum in high school students. *Journal of Research and Development in Education, 27,* 226–231.

From the perspective of...

A Child-Care Provider How might you use systematic desensitization to help children overcome their fears?

©Rubberball/Getty Images

Once you had developed this hierarchy and learned relaxation techniques, you would learn to associate the two sets of responses. To do this, your therapist might ask you to put yourself into a relaxed state and then imagine yourself in the first situation identified in your hierarchy. Once you could consider that first step while remaining relaxed, you would move on to the next situation. Eventually, you would move up the hierarchy in gradual stages until you could imagine yourself being in the air without experiencing anxiety. Ultimately, you would be asked to make a visit to an airport and later to take a flight.

The newest form of exposure therapy makes use of virtual reality technology. In *virtual reality exposure therapy*, clients wear virtual reality goggles that provide highly realistic depictions of stimuli that trigger anxiety. For example, someone who fears heights might be taken virtually to the top of a skyscraper. Or a person who has developed anxiety about driving after a car crash could be taken virtually to the intersection where the crash occurred. Once at the (virtual) site of the source of their anxiety, clients can be treated with traditional systematic desensitization techniques.

The extreme realism of virtual reality ensures that clients face their fears in a highly impactful manner, yet one that can be controlled more precisely than traditional means permit. The treatment is promising, although it is so new that the long-term effectiveness is not yet clear (Metz, 2017; McClay et al., 2017; North & North, 2017).

flooding A behavioral treatment for anxiety in which people are suddenly confronted with a stimulus that they fear. (Module 49)

Flooding Treatments Although systematic desensitization has proven to be a successful treatment, today it is often replaced with a less-complicated form of therapy called flooding. **Flooding** is a behavioral treatment for anxiety in which people are suddenly confronted with a stimulus that they fear. However, unlike systematic desensitization, relaxation training is not included. The goal behind flooding is to allow the maladaptive response of anxiety or avoidance to become extinct (Havermans et al., 2007; Hofmann, 2007; Bush, 2008).

For example, a patient who has a deep fear of germs may be made to soil her hands in dirt and to keep them dirty for hours. For a person with a fear of germs, initially this is a highly anxiety-producing situation. After a few hours, however, the anxiety will decline, leading to extinction of the anxiety.

Flooding has proved to be an effective treatment for a number of problems, including phobias, anxiety disorders, and even impotence and fear of sexual contact. Through this technique, people can learn to enjoy the things they once feared (Franklin, March, & Garcia, 2007; Powers & Emmelkamp, 2008; Tuerk et al., 2011).

OPERANT CONDITIONING TECHNIQUES

Some behavioral approaches make use of the operant conditioning principles that we discussed in the chapter on learning. These

Virtual reality exposure therapy immerses clients in highly realistic depictions of stimuli that trigger anxiety.
©Monika Wisniewska/Alamy Stock Photo

approaches are based on the notion that we should reward people for carrying out desirable behavior and extinguish undesirable behavior by either ignoring it or punishing it.

One example of the systematic application of operant conditioning principles is the *token system,* which rewards a person for desired behavior with a token such as a poker chip or some kind of play money. The person can later exchange the chip or play money for an actual reward, such as real money or food.

Token systems are most frequently used in institutions for people with relatively serious problems and sometimes with children as a classroom-management technique. The system resembles what parents do when they give children money for being well behaved–money that the children can later exchange for something they want. The desired behavior may range from simple things such as keeping one's room neat to personal grooming and interacting with other people. In institutions, patients can exchange tokens for some object or activity, such as snacks, new clothes, or, in extreme cases, sleeping in one's own bed rather than in a sleeping bag on the floor.

Contingency contracting is a variant of the token system that has proved quite effective in modifying behavior. In *contingency contracting,* the therapist and client prepare a written agreement, known as a contract. The contract states a series of behavioral goals the client hopes to achieve. It also specifies positive consequences for the client if she or he reaches those goals–usually an explicit reward such as money or privileges.

Contingency contracts also may state negative consequences if clients do not meet their goals. For example, clients who are trying to quit smoking might write out a check to a cause they have no interest in supporting (for instance, the National Rifle Association if they are strong supporters of gun control). If the client smokes on a given day, the therapist will mail the check.

Behavior therapists also use observational learning to systematically teach people new skills and ways of handling their fears and anxieties. *Observational learning* occurs through observing the behavior of others. For example, for clients who are socially fearful, a therapist may model and teach basic social skills, such as maintaining eye contact during conversation and acting assertively. Similarly, children with dog phobias have been able to overcome their fears by watching another child–called the "Fearless Peer"–repeatedly walk up to a dog, touch it, pet it, and finally play with it. Observational learning, then, can play a role in resolving some kinds of behavior difficulties, especially if the person being observed receives a reward for his or her behavior (Bandura, Grusec, & Menlove, 1967; Helsen, Goubert, & Vlaeyen, 2013; Waismeyer & Meltzoff, 2017).

EVALUATING BEHAVIOR THERAPY

Behavior therapy works especially well for eliminating anxiety disorders, treating phobias and compulsions, establishing control over impulses, and learning complex social skills to replace maladaptive behavior. More than any of the other therapeutic techniques, it provides methods that nonprofessionals can use to change their own behavior. Moreover, it is efficient because it focuses on solving carefully defined problems (Richard & Lauterbach, 2006; Barlow, 2007; Kertz et al., 2015).

Critics of behavior therapy believe that because it emphasizes changing external behavior, it ignores people's inner life–their thoughts and anxieties. Consequently, people do not necessarily gain insight into thoughts and expectations that may be fostering their maladaptive behavior.

On the other hand, neuroscientific evidence shows that behavioral treatments can produce actual changes in brain functioning, which suggests that behavioral treatments can produce changes beyond external behavior. For example, one experiment looked at the neurological reactions of patients with borderline personality disorder who participated in a 12-week behavioral therapy program. Compared with a control group composed of people who did not have the disorder, the patients showed significant changes in their reactions to highly arousing, emotion-evoking stimuli. Following therapy, the patients' neurological functioning was more similar to those without the disorder than it was prior to therapy (Schnell & Herpertz, 2007).

Cognitive Approaches to Therapy

If you assumed that illogical thoughts and beliefs lie at the heart of psychological disorders, wouldn't the most direct treatment route be to teach people new, more adaptive modes of thinking? The answer is yes, according to psychologists who take a cognitive approach to treatment.

Cognitive treatment approaches teach people to think in more adaptive ways by changing their dysfunctional cognitions about the world and themselves. In contrast to behavior therapists, who primarily focus on modifying external behavior, cognitive therapists focus on changing the way people think. Because they often use basic principles of learning, the methods they employ are sometimes referred to as the **cognitive-behavioral approach** (Beck & Rector, 2005; Kalodner, 2011; Sivec et al., 2017).

Although cognitive treatment approaches take many forms, they all share the assumption that anxiety, depression, and negative emotions develop from maladaptive thinking. Accordingly, cognitive treatments seek to change the thought patterns that lead to getting "stuck" in dysfunctional ways of thinking. Therapists systematically teach clients to challenge their assumptions and adopt new approaches to old problems.

Cognitive therapy is relatively short term and usually lasts a maximum of 20 sessions. Therapy tends to be highly structured and focused on concrete problems. Therapists often begin by teaching the theory behind the approach and then continue to take an active role throughout the course of therapy by acting as a combination of teacher, coach, and partner.

One example of cognitive therapy is rational-emotive behavior therapy. **Rational-emotive behavior therapy** attempts to restructure a person's belief system into a more realistic, rational, and logical set of views. By adopting more accurate thought patterns, it is assumed that people will lead more psychologically healthy lives.

Building on these views, psychologist Albert Ellis (**2004**) suggests that many people lead unhappy lives and suffer from psychological disorders because they harbor irrational, unrealistic ideas such as these:

- We need the love or approval of virtually every significant other person for everything we do.
- We should be thoroughly competent, adequate, and successful in all possible respects in order to consider ourselves worthwhile.
- It is horrible when things don't turn out the way we want them to.

Such irrational beliefs trigger negative emotions, which in turn support the irrational beliefs and lead to a self-defeating cycle. Ellis calls it the A-B-C model in which negative activating conditions (A) lead to the activation of an irrational belief system (B), which in turn leads to emotional consequences (C). For example, if a person experiences the breakup of a close relationship (A) and holds the irrational belief (B) that "I'll never be loved again," this triggers negative emotions (C) that in turn feed back into support of the irrational belief (see Figure 3).

The goal of rational-emotive therapy is to help clients eliminate maladaptive thoughts and beliefs and adopt more effective thinking. To accomplish this goal, therapists take an active, directive role during therapy and openly challenge patterns of thought that appear to be dysfunctional. Consider this example:

Martha: The basic problem is that I'm worried about my family. I'm worried about money. And I never seem to be able to relax.

Therapist: Why are you worried about your family? . . . What's to be concerned about? They have certain demands which you don't want to adhere to.

Martha: I was brought up to think that I mustn't be selfish.

cognitive treatment approaches Treatment approaches that teach people to think in more adaptive ways by changing their dysfunctional cognitions about the world and themselves. (Module 49)

cognitive-behavioral approach A treatment approach that incorporates basic principles of learning to change the way people think. (Module 49)

rational-emotive behavior therapy A form of therapy that attempts to restructure a person's belief system into a more realistic, rational, and logical set of views by challenging dysfunctional beliefs that maintain irrational behavior. (Module 49)

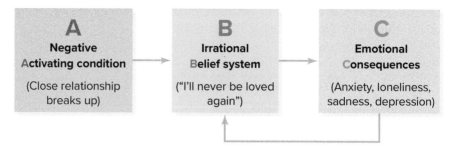

FIGURE 3 In the A-B-C model of rational-emotive behavior therapy, negative activating conditions (A) lead to the activation of an irrational belief system (B), which leads to emotional consequences (C). Those emotional consequences then feed back and support the belief system. At what steps in the model could change occur as a result of rational-emotive behavior therapy?

Source: Ellis, A. (1974). *Growth through reason*. Hollywood, CA: Wilshire Books.

Therapist: Oh, we'll have to knock that out of your head!

Martha: My mother feels that I shouldn't have left home—that my place is with them. There are nagging doubts about what I should—

Therapist: Why are there doubts? Why should you?

Martha: I think it's a feeling I was brought up with that you always have to give of yourself. If you think of yourself, you're wrong.

Therapist: That's a belief. Why do you have to keep believing that—at your age? You believed a lot of superstitions when you were younger. Why do you have to retain them? Your parents indoctrinated you with this nonsense, because that's their belief. . . . Who needs that philosophy? All it's gotten you, so far, is guilt. (Ellis, 1974)

By poking holes in Martha's reasoning, the therapist is attempting to help her adopt a more realistic view of herself and her circumstances (Ellis, 2002; Dryden & David, 2008).

Another influential form of therapy that builds on a cognitive perspective is that of Aaron Beck (Beck, 2004; Beck, Davis, & Freeman, 2015). Like rational-emotive behavior therapy, Beck's *cognitive behavior therapy* aims to change people's illogical thoughts about themselves and the world.

However, cognitive behavior therapy is considerably less confrontational and challenging than rational-emotive behavior therapy is. Instead of the therapist actively arguing with clients about their dysfunctional cognitions, cognitive behavior therapists more often play the role of teacher. Therapists urge clients to obtain information on their own that will lead them to discard their inaccurate thinking through a process of cognitive appraisal.

In *cognitive appraisal*, clients are asked to evaluate situations, themselves, and others in terms of their memories, values, beliefs, thoughts, and expectations. During the course of treatment, therapists help clients discover ways of thinking more appropriately about themselves and others (Beck, Freeman, & Davis, 2004; Moorey, 2007; Leaper, Brown, & Ayres, 2013; also see *Neuroscience in Your Life*).

Cognitive appraisal can also be used to help change students' attributions about the causes of their academic success or failure. For example, rather than attributing academic failure to a lack of intelligence, students can be helped to see that their performance is related to the amount of hard work and perseverance they invest in academic tasks (Elliot, Dweck, & Yeager, 2017).

EVALUATING COGNITIVE APPROACHES TO THERAPY

Cognitive approaches to therapy have proved successful in dealing with a broad range of disorders, including anxiety disorders, depression, substance abuse, and eating disorders. Furthermore, the willingness of cognitive therapists to incorporate additional treatment approaches (e.g., combining cognitive and behavioral techniques in cognitive

AP NEUROSCIENCE IN YOUR LIFE: HOW COGNITIVE BEHAVIORAL THERAPY CHANGES YOUR BRAIN

Psychotherapy has been shown to be effective for multiple psychological disorders. But does it show measurable changes in the brain? Recent research examining the effects of psychotherapy on brain structure and function suggests that it does. Specifically, neuroscientists compared the structure and function of the amygdala, the brain area involved in fear and anxiety, in patients with social anxiety disorder before and after 9 weeks of online cognitive behavioral therapy (CBT). Compared to those who had alternative treatments, the patients who had CBT were less anxious and showed changes in brain volume and activity (see images). These results highlight the fact that psychological therapies have an impact on the brain related to the reduction of symptoms of psychological disorders (Mansson et al., 2016).

AP SKILL: SCIENTIFIC INVESTIGATION

1. What is the sample in this study?

2. What is the independent and dependent variable in this study?

The images show that the CBT group had smaller left amygdala (shown in blue in the left image) and less active right amygdala (shown in blue in the right image) after CBT than the alternative treatment group.

Source: Adapted from Mansson, K. N., Salami, A., Frick, A., Carlbring, P., Andersson, G., Furmark, T., & Boraxbekk, C. J. (2016). Neuroplasticity in response to cognitive behavior therapy for social anxiety disorder. *Translational Psychiatry, 6*, e727. doi: 10.1038/tp.2015.218

behavior therapy) has made this approach a particularly effective form of treatment (Mitte, 2005; Ishikawa et al., 2007; Bhar et al., 2008).

At the same time, critics have pointed out that the focus on helping people to think more rationally ignores the fact that life is in reality sometimes irrational. Changing one's assumptions to make them more reasonable and logical thus may not always be helpful–even assuming it is possible to bring about true cognitive change. Still, the success of cognitive approaches has made it one of the most frequently employed therapies (Beck & Rector, 2005; Fresco, 2013).

PsychTech

Psychologist David Mohr found that an Internet-based treatment for depression in which patients logged into a website and also received e-mail and telephone support was effective in reducing depressive episodes.

AP MODULE 49: PSYCHOTHERAPY: PSYCHODYNAMIC, BEHAVIORAL, AND COGNITIVE APPROACHES TO TREATMENT

AP SUMMARY

- Psychotherapy approaches share the goal of resolving psychological problems by modifying people's behaviors and providing better self-understanding.
- A variety of professionals provide therapy and counseling. A psychiatrist is a physician who has a MD and can prescribe medication.
- Major figures in psychological treatment include: Aaron Beck, Albert Ellis, Sigmund Freud, Mary Cover Jones, B.F. Skinner, and Joseph Wolpe.

- Behavioral approaches view abnormal behavior as learned and use the principles of learning to change maladaptive behavior. Behaviorists use aversive conditioning, systematic desensitization, flooding, token systems, contingency contracting, and observational learning.
- Cognitive approaches help a person restructure their faulty belief system into more adaptive ways. Cognitivists use rational-emotive behavior therapy and the A-B-C model.

- Psychodynamic approaches seek to bring unresolved past conflicts and unacceptable impulses into consciousness. Therapists guide patients to consider and discuss their past experiences in order to understand and work through current anxiety.
- According to Freud, psychoanalysis releases hidden thoughts from the unconscious. Therapists use free association and dream interpretation.
- According to Beck, the cognitive-behavioral approach aims to change people's illogical thoughts and uses basic principles of learning.
- Cognitive therapy is effective for anxiety, depression, substance abuse, and eating disorders.
- The behavioral method works well for eliminating anxiety disorders, treating phobias and compulsions, establishing control over impulses, and learning complex skills to replace maladaptive behaviors.
- Aversive therapy works well for treating substance-abuse problems, such as alcoholism, and certain kinds of sexual disorders.
- Systematic desensitization works well for treating phobias.
- Flooding is effective for phobias, anxiety disorders, and even impotence and fear of sexual contact.
- According to Ellis, the rational-emotive behavior therapy (REBT) restructures a person's belief system into a more realistic, rational, and logical set of views. Therapists take an active, direct role in therapy and openly challenge dysfunctional thoughts.
- Psychoanalysis can be time-consuming and expensive. Patients can have resistance and transference. Critics question the entire theory and determining effectiveness has been challenging.
- Contemporary psychodynamic approaches tend to be shorter, the therapist takes a more active role, and the emphasis is on current relationships and concerns.
- Cognitive therapy is one of the most used therapies. It tends to be short and highly structured. Critics point out that training individuals to be rational ignores the fact that life is sometimes irrational.
- The behavioral method provides strategies useful for nonprofessionals and solves carefully defined problems. Critics argue it ignores thoughts and anxieties; however, there is evidence that behavior treatments produce changes in brain functioning.
- The cognitive-behavioral method is less confrontational, and therapists tend to play the teacher role. Therapists encourage clients to obtain information on their own and discard faulty thinking through cognitive appraisal.

AP KEY TERMS

psychotherapy
biomedical therapy
psychodynamic therapy
psychoanalysis
transference
behavioral treatment
  approaches
aversive conditioning

systematic desensitization
flooding
cognitive treatment
  approaches
cognitive-behavioral
  approach
rational-emotive behavior
  therapy

AP TEST PRACTICE

Section I: Multiple Choice

1. Who created the therapy technique that changes inaccurate thinking through cognitive appraisal?
  A. Mary Cover Jones
  B. Joseph Wolpe
  C. B.F. Skinner
  D. Albert Ellis
  E. Aaron Beck

2. To reduce her patient's drinking behavior, Dr. Krentz paired alcohol with a drug that causes severe nausea and vomiting. Which therapy technique was used?
  A. Aversion
  B. Flooding
  C. Observational learning
  D. Systematic desensitization
  E. Token economy

3. A therapist uses systematic desensitization to treat a specific phobia. Which perspective is the therapist using?
  A. Psychoanalytic
  B. Psychodynamic
  C. Cognitive
  D. Biomedical
  E. Behavioral

Section II: Free Response

Kate has an irrational fear of bridges and has avoided them for many years. She has decided to seek therapy and is exploring her options.
- Explain the difference between a psychologist and a psychiatrist.

Identify what perspective the following therapeutic techniques belong to and explain how a therapist could use the techniques to treat Kate's phobia of bridges.
- Systematic Desensitization
- Flooding
- Rational-emotive behavior therapy

Module 50

Psychotherapy: Humanistic, Interpersonal, and Group Approaches to Treatment

Humanistic Therapy

As you know from your own experience, a student cannot master the material covered in a course without some hard work, no matter how good the teacher and the textbook are. *You must* take the time to study, memorize the vocabulary, and learn the concepts. Nobody else can do it for you. If you choose to put in the effort, you'll succeed; if you don't, you'll fail. The responsibility is primarily yours.

Humanistic therapy draws on this philosophical perspective of self-responsibility in developing treatment techniques. The many different types of therapy that fit into this category have a similar rationale: We have control of our own behavior, we can make choices about the kinds of lives we want to live, and it is up to us to solve the difficulties we encounter in our daily lives.

Humanistic therapists believe that people naturally are motivated to strive for self-actualization. As we discussed in the chapter on motivation, *self-actualization* is the term that clinical psychologist Abraham Maslow used to describe the state of self-fulfillment in which people realize their highest potentials in their own unique way.

Instead of acting in the more directive manner of some psychodynamic and behavioral approaches, humanistic therapists view themselves as guides or facilitators. Therapists using humanistic techniques seek to help people understand themselves and find ways to come closer to the ideal they hold for themselves. In this view, psychological disorders result from the inability to find meaning in life, from feelings of loneliness, and from a lack of connection to others (Watson, Goldman, & Greenberg, 2011; Lewis & Umbreit, 2015).

Humanistic approaches have produced many therapeutic techniques. Among the most important is person-centered therapy.

PERSON-CENTERED THERAPY

Consider the following therapy session excerpt:

> Alice: I was thinking about this business of standards. I somehow developed a sort of a knack, I guess, of–well–habit–of trying to make people feel at ease around me, or to make things go along smoothly. . . .
>
> Therapist: In other words, what you did was always in the direction of trying to keep things smooth and to make other people feel better and to smooth the situation.
>
> Alice: Yes. I think that's what it was. Now the reason why I did it probably was–I mean, not that I was a good little Samaritan going around making other people happy, but that was probably the role that felt easiest for me to play. . . .
>
> Therapist: You feel that for a long time you've been playing the role of kind of smoothing out the frictions or differences or what not. . . .
>
> Alice: M-hm.
>
> Therapist: Rather than having any opinion or reaction of your own in the situation. Is that it? (Rogers, 1951)

AP¹ LEARNING TARGETS

- Describe the central characteristics of psychotherapeutic intervention.
- Identify the contributions of major figures in psychological treatment.
- Describe major treatment orientations used in therapy and how those orientations influence therapeutic planning.
- Summarize effectiveness of specific treatments used to address specific problems.
- Discuss how cultural and ethnic context influence choice and success of treatment (e.g., factors that lead to premature termination of treatment).
- Compare and contrast different treatment methods.

humanistic therapy Therapy in which the underlying rationale is that people have control of their behavior, can make choices about their lives, and are essentially responsible for solving their own problems. (Module 50)

Humanistic therapy focuses on self-responsibility.

©Don Hammond/Design Pics/Getty Images

person-centered therapy Therapy in which the goal is to reach one's potential for self-actualization. (Module 50)

Study Alert

To better remember the concept of unconditional positive regard, try offering it to a friend during a conversation by showing your support, acceptance, and understanding no matter what thought or attitude your friend expresses.

The therapist does not interpret or answer the questions the client has raised. Instead, the therapist clarifies or reflects back what the client has said (e.g., "In other words, what you did. . . ."; "You feel that. . . ."; "Is that it?"). This therapeutic technique, known as *nondirective counseling*, is at the heart of person-centered therapy, which was first practiced by Carl Rogers in the mid-20th century (Raskin & Rogers, 1989).

Person-centered therapy (also called *client-centered therapy*) aims to enable people to reach their potential for self-actualization. By providing a warm and accepting environment, therapists hope to motivate clients to air their problems and feelings. In turn, this enables clients to make realistic and constructive choices and decisions about the things that bother them in their current lives (Bohart, 2006; Cooper & McLeod, 2011; McLean et al., 2017).

Instead of directing the choices clients make, therapists provide what Rogers calls unconditional positive regard. *Unconditional positive regard* involves providing wholehearted acceptance, support, and understanding, and no disapproval, no matter what feelings and attitudes a client expresses. By doing this, therapists hope to create an atmosphere that enables clients to come to decisions that can improve their lives (Vieira & Freire, 2006; Patterson & Joseph, 2013).

Furnishing unconditional positive regard does not mean that therapists must approve of everything their clients say or do. Rather, therapists need to communicate that they are caring, nonjudgmental, and *empathetic*—that is, understanding of a client's emotional experiences (Fearing & Clark, 2000).

Today, therapists using person-centered therapy techniques are more directive with their clients. Rather than merely reflecting back their clients' statements, therapists actively nudge clients toward insights. However, therapists still view their clients' insights as central to the therapeutic process.

EVALUATING HUMANISTIC APPROACHES TO THERAPY

The notion that psychological disorders result from restricted growth potential appeals philosophically to many people. Furthermore, when humanistic therapists acknowledge that the freedom we possess can lead to psychological difficulties, clients find an unusually supportive environment for therapy. In turn, this atmosphere can help clients discover solutions to difficult psychological problems (Cooper, 2007).

However, humanistic treatments lack specificity, a problem that has troubled their critics. Humanistic approaches are not very precise and are probably the least scientifically and theoretically developed type of treatment. Moreover, this form of treatment works best for the same type of highly verbal client who profits most from psychoanalytic treatment.

Interpersonal Therapy

interpersonal therapy (IPT) Short-term therapy designed to help patients control their moods and emotions by focusing on the context of their current social relationships. (Module 50)

Interpersonal therapy (IPT) is short-term therapy designed to help patients control their moods and emotions by focusing on the context of their current social relationships. Although its roots stem from psychodynamic approaches, interpersonal therapy concentrates more on the here and now with the goal of improving a client's existing relationships. It typically focuses on interpersonal issues such as conflicts with others, social skills issues, role transitions (such as divorce), or grief (Weissman, Markowitz, & Klerman, 2007; Stangier et al., 2011; Dimaggio et al., 2015).

Interpersonal therapy is more active and directive than are traditional psychodynamic approaches, and sessions are more structured. The approach makes no assumptions about the underlying causes of psychological disorders but focuses on the interpersonal context in which a disorder is developed and maintained. It also tends to be shorter than traditional psychodynamic approaches and typically lasts only 12–16 weeks. During those sessions, therapists make concrete suggestions on improving relations with others and actively offer recommendations and advice.

CLICK HERE FOR THERAPY

You probably have an app for music, an app for ride sharing, even an app for banking. So why not one for therapy? While it may seem to trivialize the process, online therapy is real. Despite some clear limitations and potential pitfalls, it's proving to be a useful and effective channel for delivering mental health services (Novotney, 2017).

The potential benefits for online therapy clients are considerable. Therapy sessions can be scheduled with ease for convenient times, and transportation isn't an issue. Therapy is also more available to clients who work odd hours or travel frequently. Furthermore, depending on their psychological problem, some clients may lack the emotional strength to bring themselves to a real-world therapy session, in which case online therapy brings the therapist to them. Sessions can be conducted in real-time teleconferencing style, by text-based chat, or even asynchronously–that is, not in real time but, for example, by exchanging emails (Reynolds et al., 2013).

Another advantage of online therapy is that it normalizes mental health care by

©Agenturfotografin/Shutterstock

removing many of the traditional barriers and integrating it into people's daily lives. Indeed, online therapy can even act as a gateway to broader mental health services: some research shows that when clients see that therapy can be a force for positive change in their lives, they are more likely to seek out further mental health care if they need it (Jones et al., 2014).

On the other hand, online therapy has some significant limitations. For one thing, it's not the best channel for treating clients with serious mental disorders who may have difficulty adequately connecting with a therapist. Furthermore, some clients find it cold and impersonal, and therapists may find it difficult to assess clients accurately without direct face-to-face contact. Finally, conducting therapy via telecommunications companies may not be in full compliance with privacy laws and other codes of conduct for therapists (Novotney, 2017).

Despite these limitations, online therapy clearly holds great promise for making mental health services more accessible. But more research needs to be done to determine the answer to the bottom-line question: Does online therapy alleviate psychological disorders as well as more traditional, face-to-face therapy (Rozental et al., 2017)?

> **AP SKILL: SCIENTIFIC INVESTIGATION/ APPLY THEORIES AND PERSPECTIVES IN AUTHENTIC CONTEXT**
>
> 1. What type of research should be done before concluding that online therapy alleviates disorders as well as traditional therapy?
> 2. What would be an advantage of using both types of therapy?

Considerable research supports the effectiveness of interpersonal therapy. It is especially effective in dealing with depression, anxiety, addictions, and eating disorders (Miller et al., 2008; Bohn et al., 2013; Dimaggio et al., 2017; also see *Applying Psychology in the 21st Century*).

Group Therapies

Although most treatment takes place between a single individual and a therapist, some forms of therapy involve groups of people seeking treatment. In **group therapy,** several unrelated people meet with a therapist to discuss some aspect of their psychological functioning.

People typically discuss with the group their problems, which often center on a common difficulty, such as alcoholism or a lack of social skills. The other members of the group provide emotional support and dispense advice on ways they have coped effectively with similar problems (Scaturo, 2004; Rigby & Waite, 2007; Schachter, 2011).

Groups vary greatly in terms of the particular model they employ; there are psychoanalytic groups, humanistic groups, and groups corresponding to the other therapeutic approaches. Furthermore, groups also differ with regard to the degree of guidance the therapist provides. In some, the therapist is quite directive; in others, the members

group therapy Therapy in which people meet in a group with a therapist to discuss problems. (Module 50) of the group set their own agenda and determine how the group will proceed (Beck & Lewis, 2000; Stockton, Morran, & Krieger, 2004; Arlo, 2017).

Because several people are treated simultaneously in group therapy, it is a much more economical means of treatment than individual psychotherapy is. On the other hand, critics argue that group settings lack the individual attention inherent in one-to-one therapy and that especially shy and withdrawn individuals may not receive the attention they need in a group setting.

FAMILY THERAPY

family therapy An approach that focuses on the family and its dynamics. (Module 50)

One specialized form of group therapy is family therapy. As the name implies, **family therapy** involves two or more family members, one (or more) of whose problems led to treatment. But rather than focusing simply on the members of the family who present the initial problem, family therapists consider the family as a unit to which each member contributes. By meeting with the entire family simultaneously, family therapists try to understand how the family members interact with one another (Strong & Tomm, 2007; Bischoff et al., 2011).

Family therapists view the family as a system, and they assume that individuals cannot improve without understanding the conflicts that exist among family members. Thus, therapists expect each member of a family to contribute to the resolution of the problem being addressed (Wretman, 2016).

Family therapists believe that family members often fall into rigid roles or patterns of behavior. For example, one person may act as the victim, another as a bully, and so forth. In their view, that system of roles supports and perpetuates family disturbances. One goal of family therapy, then, is to get family members to adopt new, more constructive patterns of behavior and to get members of the family to view others in new ways (Sori, 2006; Conoley et al., 2015).

SELF-HELP THERAPY

In self-help therapy, people with similar problems get together to discuss their shared feelings and experiences, sometimes without any formal therapist participating. For example, people who have recently experienced the death of a spouse might meet in a *bereavement support group*, or college students may get together to discuss their adjustment to college.

One of the best-known self-help groups is Alcoholics Anonymous (AA), designed to help members deal with alcohol-related problems. AA prescribes 12 steps that alcoholics must pass through on their road to recovery. Alcoholics begin with an admission that they are alcoholics and powerless over alcohol and move through additional steps in the process of recovery by attending frequent AA meetings. Proponents of AA believe that no one is fully cured of alcoholism and that members should permanently think of themselves as recovering alcoholics (Greenfield & Tonigan, 2013; Best, 2017).

Alcoholics Anonymous does not work for everyone. For one thing, there is a strong spiritual component and emphasis on the need for a higher power that do not appeal to some people. More important, some critics say that AA's requirement of total abstinence from alcohol may not be an effective or realistic approach (Kelly et al., 2012).

Still, AA provides more treatment for alcoholics than does any other therapy. Furthermore, research studies show that AA and other 12-step programs (such as Narcotics Anonymous) can be as successful in treating alcohol and other substance-abuse problems as traditional types of therapy (Galanter, 2007; Gossop, Stewart, & Marsden, 2008; Pagano et al., 2013).

In group therapy, people with psychological difficulties meet with a therapist to discuss their problems.
©Jon Bradley/The Image Bank/Getty Images

Evaluating Psychotherapy: Does Therapy Work?

Your best friend, Ben, comes to you because he just hasn't been feeling right about things lately. He's upset because he and his girlfriend aren't getting along, but his difficulties go beyond that. He can't concentrate on his studies, has a lot of trouble getting to sleep, and–this is what really bothers him–has begun to think that people are ganging up on him, talking about him behind his back. It seems that no one really cares about or understands him or makes any effort to see why he's become so miserable.

Ben knows that he ought to get *some* kind of help, but he is not sure where to turn. He is fairly skeptical of psychologists and thinks that a lot of what they say is just mumbo-jumbo, but he's willing to put his doubts aside and try anything to feel better. He also knows there are many different types of therapy, and he doesn't have a clue about which would be best for him. He turns to you for advice because he knows you are taking a psychology course. He asks, "Which kind of therapy works best?"

IS THERAPY EFFECTIVE?

This question requires a complex response. In fact, identifying the single most appropriate form of treatment is a controversial and still unresolved task for psychologists specializing in psychological disorders. In fact, even before considering whether one form of therapy works better than another, we need to determine whether therapy in any form effectively alleviates psychological disturbances.

Until the 1950s, most people simply assumed that therapy was effective. But in 1952, psychologist Hans Eysenck published an historically important study challenging that assumption. He claimed that people who received psychodynamic treatment and related therapies were no better off at the end of treatment than were people who were placed on a waiting list for treatment but never received it. Eysenck concluded that people would go into **spontaneous remission,** recovery without formal treatment, if they were simply left alone–certainly a cheaper and simpler process.

Although other psychologists quickly challenged Eysenck's conclusions, his review stimulated a continuing stream of better controlled, more carefully crafted studies on the effectiveness of psychotherapy. Today most psychologists agree: Therapy does work. Several comprehensive reviews indicate that therapy brings about greater improvement than no treatment at all, with the rate of spontaneous remission being fairly low. In most cases, then, the symptoms of abnormal behavior do not go away by themselves if left untreated–although the issue continues to be hotly debated (Lutz et al., 2006; Gaudiano & Miller, 2013; Abbass et al., 2017).

WHICH KIND OF THERAPY WORKS BEST?

Almost all psychologists agree that psychotherapeutic treatment *in general* is more effective than no treatment at all. However, the question of what specific *kind* of treatment is superior to others has not been answered definitively (Westen, Novotny, & Thompson-Brenner, 2004; Abboud, 2005; Tryer et al., 2015).

For instance, one classic study comparing the effectiveness of various approaches found that although success rates vary somewhat by treatment form, most treatments show fairly equal success rates. As Figure 1 indicates, the rates ranged from about 75-80% greater success for treated compared with untreated individuals. Behavioral and cognitive approaches tended to be slightly more successful, but that result may have been due to differences in the severity of the cases treated (Smith, Glass, & Miller, 1980; Orwin & Condray, 1984).

Other research, which relies on *meta-analysis* in which data from a large number of studies are statistically combined, yields similar general conclusions. Furthermore, a large survey of 186,000 individuals found that respondents felt they had benefited

 Study Alert
Pay special attention to the discussion of (1) whether therapy is effective in general and (2) what specific types of therapy are effective because these are key issues for therapists.

spontaneous remission Recovery without formal treatment. (Module 50)

FIGURE 1 Estimates of the effectiveness of types of treatment, in comparison to control groups of untreated people. The percentage scores show how much more effective a specific type of treatment is for the average patient compared with those who have had no treatment. For example, people given psychodynamic treatment score, on average, more positively on outcome measures than do about 80% of untreated people.

Source: Adapted from Smith, M. L., Glass, G. V., & Miller, T. I. (1980). *The benefits of psychotherapy.* Baltimore: The Johns Hopkins University Press.

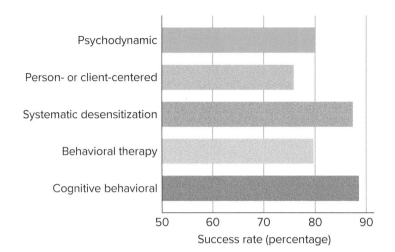

substantially from psychotherapy. However, there was little difference in "consumer satisfaction" on the basis of the specific type of treatment they had received (Seligman, 1995; Cuijpers et al., 2008; Dakin & Areán, 2013).

In short, converging evidence allows us to draw several conclusions about the effectiveness of psychotherapy:

- *For most people, psychotherapy is effective.* This conclusion holds over different lengths of treatment, specific kinds of psychological disorders, and various types of treatment. Thus, the question, "Does psychotherapy work?" appears to have been answered convincingly: It does (Westen, Novotny, & Thompson-Brenner, 2004; Payne & Marcus, 2008; Gaudiano & Miller, 2013).

- *On the other hand, psychotherapy doesn't work for everyone.* As many as 10% of people treated show no improvement—or actually deteriorated (Pretzer & Beck, 2005; Coffman et al., 2007; Lilienfeld, 2007).

- *No single form of therapy works best for every problem, and certain specific types of treatment are better, although not invariably, for specific types of problems.* For example, cognitive therapy works especially well for panic disorders, and flooding therapy relieves specific phobias effectively. However, there are exceptions to these generalizations, and often the differences in success rates for different types of treatment are not substantial (Miller & Magruder, 1999; Westen, Novotny, & Thompson-Brenner, 2004).

- *Most therapies share several basic similar elements.* Despite the fact that the specific methods used in different therapies are very different from one another, there are several common themes that lead them to be effective. These elements include the opportunity for a client to develop a positive relationship with a therapist, an explanation or interpretation of a client's symptoms, and confrontation of negative emotions. The fact that these common elements exist in most therapies makes it difficult to compare one treatment against another (Norcross, 2002; Norcross, Beutler, & Levant, 2006).

Consequently, there is no single, definitive answer to the broad question, "Which therapy works best?" because of the complexity in sorting out the various factors that enter into successful therapy. Recently, however, clinicians and researchers have reframed the question by focusing on evidence-based psychotherapy practice. *Evidence-based psychotherapy practice* seeks to use research findings to determine the best practices for treating a specific disorder. To determine best practices, researchers use clinical interviews, client self-reports of improvement in quality of life, reductions in symptoms, observations of behavior, and other outcomes to compare different therapies. By using objective research findings, clinicians are increasingly able to determine the most effective treatment for a specific disorder (American Psychological Association Presidential Task Force, 2006; Kazdin, 2008; Gaudiano & Miller, 2013).

Because no single type of psychotherapy is invariably effective for every individual, some therapists use an eclectic approach to therapy. In an *eclectic approach to therapy,* therapists use a variety of techniques, thus integrating several perspectives, to treat a person's problems. By employing more than one approach, therapists can choose the appropriate mix of evidence-based treatments to match the individual's specific needs. Furthermore, therapists with certain personal characteristics may work better with particular individuals and types of treatments, and–as we consider next–even racial and ethnic factors may be related to the success of treatment (Chambless et al., 2006; Hays, 2008; Kertz et al., 2015).

 # Exploring Diversity

Racial and Ethnic Factors in Treatment: Should Therapists Be Color-Blind?

Consider the following case report written by a school counselor about Jimmy Jones, a 12-year-old student who was referred to a counselor because of his lack of interest in schoolwork:

> Jimmy does not pay attention, daydreams often, and frequently falls asleep during class. There is a strong possibility that Jimmy is harboring repressed rage that needs to be ventilated and dealt with. His inability to directly express his anger had led him to adopt passive-aggressive means of expressing hostility, i.e., inattentiveness, daydreaming, falling asleep. It is recommended that Jimmy be seen for intensive counseling to discover the basis of the anger. (Sue & Sue, 1990)

The counselor was wrong, however. Rather than suffering from "repressed rage," Jimmy lived in a poverty-stricken and disorganized home. Because of overcrowding at his house, he did not get enough sleep and consequently was tired the next day. Frequently, he was also hungry. In short, the stresses arising from his environment and not any deep-seated psychological disturbances caused his problems.

This incident underscores the importance of taking people's environmental and cultural backgrounds into account during treatment for psychological disorders. In particular, members of racial and ethnic minority groups, especially those who are also poor, may behave in ways that help them deal with a society that discriminates against them. As a consequence, behavior that may signal psychological disorder in middle-class and upper-class whites may simply be adaptive in people from other racial and socio-economic groups. For instance, characteristically suspicious and distrustful people may be displaying a survival strategy to protect themselves from psychological and physical injury rather than suffering from a psychological disturbance (Paniagua, 2000; Tseng, 2003; Pottick et al., 2007).

In fact, therapists must question some basic assumptions of psychotherapy when dealing with racial, ethnic, and cultural minority group members. For example, compared with the dominant culture, Asian and Latino cultures typically place much greater emphasis on the group, family, and society. When an Asian or Latino faces a critical decision, the family helps make it—a cultural practice suggesting that family members should also play a role in psychological treatment. Similarly, the traditional Chinese recommendation for dealing with depression or anxiety is to urge people who experience such problems to avoid thinking

Therapists' interpretation of their clients' behavior is influenced by racial, ethnic, cultural, and social class backgrounds of the clients. For example, this man could be seen as lazy, drunk, or merely exhausted, depending on the context.
©Arts Illustrated Studios/Shutterstock

about whatever is upsetting them. Consider how this advice contrasts with treatment approaches that emphasize the value of insight (Ponterotto, Gretchen, & Chauhan, 2001; McCarthy, 2005; Leitner, 2007).

Clearly, therapists *cannot* be "color-blind." Instead, they must take into account the racial, ethnic, cultural, and social class backgrounds of their clients in determining the nature of a psychological disorder and the course of treatment (Pedersen et al., 2002; Hays, 2008; Moodley, Gielen, & Wu, 2013).

From the perspective of...

A Social Worker How might the types of therapies you employ vary depending on a client's cultural and socioeconomic background?

©Sam Edwards/age fotostock

AP MODULE 50: PSYCHOTHERAPY: HUMANISTIC, INTERPERSONAL, AND GROUP APPROACHES TO TREATMENT

AP SUMMARY

- Most therapies share basic elements: opportunity to develop a positive relationship with a therapist, an explanation or interpretation of a client's symptoms, and confrontation of negative emotions.
- According to Rogers, humanistic therapists should provide unconditional positive regard to help patients improve their lives. Therapists must be caring, nonjudgmental, and empathetic.
- Humanistic therapy is based on the premise that people have control of their behavior, that they can make choices about their lives, and that it is up to them to solve their own problems. Humanistic therapies, which take a nondirective approach, include person-centered therapy.
- Interpersonal therapy (IPT) focuses on current social relationships. It has roots in psychodynamic therapy but concentrates on the here and now. IPT is more active and structured, with the therapist offering advice. It is shorter in duration and does not makes assumptions of underlying causes.
- Most research suggests that therapy is more effective in resolving conflict than no therapy; however, it does not work for everyone.
- It is hard to say which therapy works best, but behavioral and cognitive therapies tend to be slightly more successful.

- Because no single type of psychotherapy is invariably effective, eclectic approaches in which a therapist uses a variety of techniques and, thus, integrates several perspectives are sometimes used.
- Therapists must take into consideration the racial, ethnic, cultural, and social class of their clients when determining the nature of a disorder and the course of treatment.
- Therapy is impacted by cultural practices, such as emphasizing the group or avoiding upsetting thoughts.
- Most therapies take place between a single individual and a therapist.
- In group therapy, several unrelated people meet with a therapist to discuss a common problem. Specialized types include family and self-help.
- Client-centered (person-centered) therapy aims to enable people to reach their potential for self-actualization. The therapist is nondirective and provides a supportive atmosphere. It works well for verbal patients, but the treatments are unscientific and lack specificity.

AP KEY TERMS

humanistic therapy	group therapy
person-centered therapy	family therapy
interpersonal therapy (IPT)	spontaneous remission

Section I: Multiple Choice

1. All of the following are advantages of group therapy EXCEPT
   A. It is economical compared to individual therapy
   B. Patients can provide emotional support to one another
   C. Patients can offer advice to one another
   D. Successful coping strategies are modeled in the group
   E. The proper amount of attention is provided for each member

2. What therapy is based on providing unconditional positive regard?
   A. Interpersonal therapy
   B. Aversive conditioning
   C. Client-centered therapy
   D. Systematic desensitization
   E. Rational-emotive behavior therapy

3. Most therapies share what basic element?
   A. Changing irrational thought patterns
   B. Preventing comorbid disorders
   C. Prescribing drugs to reduce symptoms
   D. Exploring unconscious childhood conflicts
   E. Developing a positive therapist/client relationship

Section II: Free Response

Hannah plans to see a humanistic therapist. Explain how the following could relate to her experience.
- Nondirective counseling
- Person-centered therapy
- Empathy
- Advantage of the humanistic perspective
- Criticism of the humanistic perspective

Module 51

Biomedical Therapy: Biological Approaches to Treatment

- Describe prevention strategies that build resilience and promote competence.

- Summarize effectiveness of specific treatments used to address specific problems from a biological perspective.

drug therapy Treatment of psychological disorders through the use of drugs that alter the operation of neurons and neurotransmitters in the brain and body. (Module 51)

antipsychotic drugs Drugs that temporarily reduce psychotic symptoms such as agitation, hallucinations, and delusions. (Module 51)

If you get a kidney infection, your doctor gives you an antibiotic; with luck, your kidneys should be as good as new about a week later. If your appendix becomes inflamed, a surgeon removes it, and your body functions normally once more. Could a comparable approach that focuses on the body's physiology be effective for psychological disturbances?

According to biological approaches to treatment, the answer is yes. Therapists routinely use biomedical therapies that rely on drugs and medical procedures to improve psychological functioning.

The biomedical approach focuses treatment directly on altering brain chemistry or other neurological factors rather than concentrating on a patient's psychological conflicts, past traumas, or other issues of daily life that may produce psychological disorder. To do this, therapists provide treatment with drugs, electric shock, or surgery, as we will discuss.

Drug Therapy

Drug therapy is the treatment of psychological disorders using drugs. Drug therapy works by altering the operation of neurons and neurotransmitters in the brain.

Some drugs operate by *inhibiting* neurotransmitters or receptor neurons, which reduces activity at particular synapses. (Recall from our discussion of neurons in the neuroscience chapter that synapses are the gaps where nerve impulses travel from one neuron to another.) Thus, particular neurons are inhibited from firing.

Other drugs do just the opposite: They *increase* the activity of certain neurotransmitters or neurons, which allows particular neurons to fire more frequently (see Figure 1).

ANTIPSYCHOTIC DRUGS

Probably no greater change has occurred in mental hospitals than the successful introduction in the mid-1950s of **antipsychotic drugs**—drugs used to reduce severe symptoms of disturbance, such as loss of touch with reality and agitation. Previously, the typical mental hospital wasn't very different from the stereotypical 19th-century insane asylum; it gave mainly custodial care to screaming, moaning, clawing patients who displayed bizarre behaviors. However, in just a matter of days after hospital staff members administered antipsychotic drugs, the wards became considerably calmer environments in which professionals could do more than just try to get patients through the day without causing serious harm to themselves or others.

This dramatic change came about through the introduction of the drug *chlorpromazine*. Along with other similar drugs, chlorpromazine rapidly became the most popular and successful treatment for schizophrenia. Today, drug therapy is typically the preferred treatment for most cases of severely abnormal behavior and is used for most patients hospitalized with psychological disorders. The newest generation of antipsychotics, referred to as *atypical antipsychotics*, have fewer side effects; they include *risperidone, olanzapine,* and *paliperidone* (Nasrallah et al., 2008; Hattori et al., 2017).

How do antipsychotic drugs work? Most block dopamine receptors at the brain's synapses, the space between pairs of neurons that communicate via chemical messengers.

Drug Treatments			
Class of Drug	**Effects of Drug**	**Primary Action of Drug**	**Examples**
Antipsychotic Drugs, Atypical Antidepressant Drugs	Reduction in loss of touch with reality, agitation	Block dopamine receptors	Antipsychotic: chlorpromazine (Thorazine), clozapine (Clozaril), haloperidol (Haldol) Atypical antipsychotic: risperidone, olanzapine
Antipsychotic Drugs Tricyclic antidepressants	Reduction in depression	Permit rise in neurotransmitters such as norepinepherine	Trazodone (Desyrel), amitriptyline (Elavil), desipramine (Norpamin)
MAO inhibitors	Reduction in depression	Prevent MAO from breaking down neurotransmitters	Phenelzine (Nardil), tranylcypromine (Parnate)
Selective serotonin reuptake inhibitors (SSRIs)	Reduction in depression	Inhibit reuptake of serotonin	Fluoxetine (Prozac), Luvox, Paxil, Celexa, Zoloft, nefazodone (Serzone)
Mood Stabilizers Lithium	Mood stabilization	Can alter transmission of impulses within neurons	Lithium (Lithonate), Depakote, Tegretol
Antianxiety Drugs	Reduction in anxiety	Increase activity of neurotransmitter GABA	Benzodiazepines (Valium, Xanax)

FIGURE 1 The major classes of drugs used to treat psychological disorders have different effects on the brain and nervous system.

Atypical antipsychotics affect both serotonin and dopamine levels in the brain, particularly those related to planning and goal-directed activity (Sawa & Snyder, 2002; Advokat, 2005; Mizrahi et al., 2011).

Despite the effectiveness of antipsychotic drugs, they do not produce a "cure" in the same way that, say, penicillin cures an infection. Most of the time, the symptoms reappear when the drug is withdrawn. Furthermore, such drugs can have long-term side effects, such as dryness of the mouth and throat, dizziness, and sometimes tremors and loss of muscle control, which may continue after drug treatments are stopped (Voruganti et al., 2007; Pijnenborg et al., 2015).

ANTIDEPRESSANT DRUGS

As their name suggests, **antidepressant drugs** are a class of medications used in cases of severe depression to improve a patient's mood and feeling of well-being. They are also sometimes used for other disorders, such as anxiety disorders and bulimia (Walsh et al., 2006; Hedges et al., 2007; Deacon & Spielmans, 2017).

Most antidepressant drugs work by changing the concentration of specific neurotransmitters in the brain. For example, *tricyclic drugs* increase the availability of norepinephrine at the synapses of neurons, whereas *MAO inhibitors* prevent the enzyme monoamine oxidase (MAO) from breaking down neurotransmitters. Newer antidepressants—such as Lexapro—are *selective serotonin reuptake inhibitors (SSRIs)*. SSRIs target the neurotransmitter serotonin and permit it to linger at the synapse. Some antidepressants produce a combination of effects. For instance, nefazodone (Serzone) blocks serotonin at some receptor sites but not others, whereas bupropion (Wellbutrin and Zyban) affects the norepinephrine and dopamine systems (see Figure 2; Dhillon, Yang, & Curran, 2008; Harmer, Duman, & Cowen, 2017).

Finally, there are some newer drugs on the horizon. For instance, scientists have found that the anesthetic *ketamine* blocks the neural receptor NMDA, which affects the neurotransmitter *glutamate*. Glutamate plays an important role in mood regulation and the ability to experience pleasure, and researchers believe that ketamine blockers

antidepressant drugs Medications that improve a severely depressed patient's mood and feeling of well-being. (Module 51)

Study Alert

To help organize your study of different drugs used in therapy, review Figure 1, which classifies them according to the categories of antipsychotic, atypical antipsychotic, antidepressant, mood-stabilizing, and antianxiety drugs.

FIGURE 2 In (a), selective serotonin reuptake inhibitors (SSRIs) reduce depression by permitting the neurotransmitter serotonin to remain in the synapse. In (b), a newer antidepressant, nefazodone (Serzone), operates more selectively to block serotonin at some sites but not others, which helps to reduce the side effects of the drug.

Source: Adapted from Mischoulon, D. (2000, June). Anti-depressants: Choices and controversy. *HealthNews,* 4.

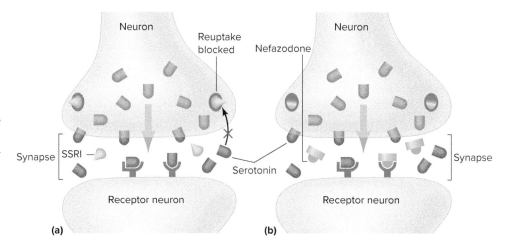

The drug fluoxetine, commonly known as Prozac, is a widely prescribed antidepressant.

©McGraw-Hill Education/Jill Braaten, photographer

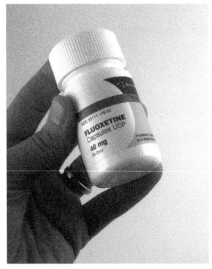

may prove to be useful in the treatment of depression (Skolnick, Popik, & Trullas, 2009; Schwartzmant, Alexander, & Grothusen, 2011).

Overall, the success rates of antidepressant drugs are quite good. In fact, antidepressants can produce lasting, long-term recovery from depression. In many cases, even after patients stop taking the drugs, their depression does not return. On the other hand, antidepressant drugs may produce side effects such as drowsiness and cognitive deficits such as memory loss. Evidence also suggests that SSRI antidepressants can increase the risk of suicide in children and adolescents—clearly a significant concern (Prus et al., 2015; Shehab, Brent, & Maalouf, 2016).

Consumers spend billions of dollars each year on antidepressant drugs. Ten percent of Americans now take antidepressants, and for women in their 40s and 50s, the figure is 25%. In particular, the antidepressant *fluoxetine,* sold under the trade name *Prozac,* has been highlighted on magazine covers and has been the topic of best-selling books (Rabin, 2013).

Does Prozac deserve its acclaim? In some respects, yes. It is effective and has relatively few side effects. Furthermore, many people who do not respond to other types of antidepressants do well on Prozac. On the other hand, 20–30% of users report experiencing nausea and diarrhea, and a smaller number report sexual dysfunctions (Brambilla et al., 2005; Fenter, 2006).

Another substance that has received a great deal of publicity is *St. John's wort,* an herb that some have called a "natural" antidepressant. Although it is widely used in Europe for the treatment of depression, the U.S. Food and Drug Administration considers it a dietary supplement, and therefore, the substance is available here without a prescription.

Despite the popularity of St. John's wort, definitive clinical tests have found that the herb is ineffective in the treatment of depression. However, because some research shows that the herb successfully reduces certain psychological symptoms, some proponents argue that using it is reasonable. In any case, people should not use St. John's wort to medicate themselves without consulting a mental health-care professional (Thachil, Mohan, & Bhugra, 2007; Rapaport et al., 2011; Ng, Venkatanarayanan, & Ho, 2017).

MOOD STABILIZERS

mood stabilizers Drugs used to treat mood disorders characterized by intense mood swings, especially manic episodes in bipolar disorder. (Module 51)

Mood stabilizers are used to treat mood disorders characterized by intense mood swings, especially manic episodes in bipolar disorder. For example, the drug *lithium,* a form of mineral salts, has been used very successfully in patients with bipolar disorders. Although no one knows definitely why, lithium and other mood stabilizers such as divalproex sodium (*Depakote*) and carbamazepine (*Tegretol*) effectively reduce manic episodes. However, they do not effectively treat depressive phases of bipolar disorder, so antidepressants are usually prescribed during those phases (Smith et al., 2007; Salvi et al., 2008; Inoue et al., 2011).

Lithium and similar drugs have a quality that sets them apart from other drug treatments: They can be a *preventive* treatment that blocks future episodes of manic depression. Often, people who have had episodes of bipolar disorder can take a daily dose of lithium to prevent a recurrence of their symptoms. Most other drugs are useful only when symptoms of psychological disturbance occur.

ANTIANXIETY DRUGS

As the name implies, **antianxiety drugs** reduce the level of anxiety a person experiences and increase feelings of well-being. They are prescribed not only to reduce general tension in people who are experiencing temporary difficulties but also to aid in the treatment of more serious anxiety disorders.

Antianxiety drugs such as alprazolam and Valium are among the medications physicians most frequently prescribe. In fact, more than half of all U.S. families have someone who has taken such a drug at one time or another.

Although the popularity of antianxiety drugs suggests that they hold few risks, they can produce a number of potentially serious side effects. For instance, they can cause fatigue, and long-term use can lead to dependence. Moreover, when taken in combination with alcohol, some antianxiety drugs can be lethal. But a more important issue concerns their use to suppress anxiety. Almost every therapeutic approach to psychological disturbance views continuing anxiety as a signal of some other sort of problem. Thus, drugs that mask anxiety may simply be hiding other difficulties. Consequently, rather than confronting their underlying problems, people may be hiding from them through the use of antianxiety drugs.

antianxiety drugs Drugs that reduce the level of anxiety a person experiences and increase feelings of well-being. (Module 51)

Electroconvulsive Therapy (ECT)

First introduced in the 1930s, **electroconvulsive therapy (ECT)** is a procedure used in the treatment of severe depression. In the procedure, an electric current of 70-150 volts is briefly administered to a patient's head, which causes a loss of consciousness and often causes seizures. Typically, health-care professionals sedate patients and give them muscle relaxants before administering the current; such preparations help reduce the intensity of muscle contractions produced during ECT. The typical patient receives about 10 ECT treatments in the course of a month, but some patients continue with maintenance treatments for months afterward (Greenberg & Kellner, 2005; Stevens & Harper, 2007; Glass, Forester, & Hermida, 2017).

ECT is a controversial technique. Apart from the obvious distastefulness of a treatment that evokes images of electrocution, side effects occur frequently. For instance, after treatment patients often experience disorientation, confusion, and sometimes memory loss that may remain for months. Furthermore, ECT often does not produce long-term improvement; one study found that without follow-up medication, depression returned in most patients who had undergone ECT treatments. Finally, even when ECT does work, we do not know why, and some critics believe it may cause permanent brain damage (Gardner & O'Connor, 2008; Kato, 2009; Weiner & Falcone, 2011).

In light of the drawbacks to ECT, why do therapists use it at all? Basically, they use it because in many severe cases of depression, it offers the only quickly effective treatment. For instance, it may prevent depressed, suicidal individuals from committing suicide, and it can act more quickly than antidepressive medications.

The use of ECT has risen in the last decade, with more than 100,000 people undergoing it each year. Still, ECT tends to be used only when other treatments have proved ineffective, and researchers continue to search for alternative treatments (Eranti & McLoughlin, 2003; Pandya, Pozuelo, & Malone, 2007; Tokutsu et al., 2013).

One new and promising alternative to ECT is **transcranial magnetic stimulation (TMS).** TMS creates a precise magnetic pulse in a specific area of the brain. By activating particular neurons, TMS has been effective in relieving the symptoms of major depression in a number of controlled experiments. However, the therapy can produce side effects, such as seizures and convulsions, and it is still considered experimental (Kim, Pesiridou, & O'Reardon, 2009; Bentwich et al., 2011).

electroconvulsive therapy (ECT) A procedure used in the treatment of severe depression in which an electric current of 70-150 volts is briefly administered to a patient's head. (Module 51)

transcranial magnetic stimulation (TMS) A depression treatment in which a precise magnetic pulse is directed to a specific area of the brain. (Module 51)

Another promising therapy, still in the early stages of development, is the use of implants placed deep inside the brain to provide a short jolt of electrical stimulation, a method called *deep brain stimulation (DBS)*. Unlike ECT, which involves the entire brain, DBS (the treatment described in the chapter prologue) pinpoints specific, tiny regions of the brain and delivers a short burst of electrical stimulation to provide relief from major depression (Lipsman, Giacobbe, & Lozano, 2015; Lozano & Mayberg, 2015; Sun et al., 2015).

Because DBS treatment is so new, researchers are still trying the stimulation in different regions of the brain and fine-tuning the exact placement within given regions to get the best results. The location may vary depending on the specific symptoms the patient is experiencing. Furthermore, the optimal level, frequency, and duration of stimulation are also being explored, as are the long-term effects. Still, initial results are promising (deGusmao, Pollak, & Sharma, 2017).

Psychosurgery

psychosurgery Brain surgery once used to reduce the symptoms of mental disorder but rarely used today. (Module 51)

If ECT strikes you as a questionable procedure, the use of **psychosurgery**–brain surgery in which the object is to reduce symptoms of mental disorder–probably appears even more dubious. A technique used exceedingly rarely today, psychosurgery was introduced as a "treatment of last resort" in the 1930s.

The first form of psychosurgery to be developed was the prefrontal lobotomy. *Prefrontal lobotomy* consists of surgically destroying or removing parts of a patient's frontal brain lobes, which surgeons thought controlled emotionality. In the 1930s and 1940s, surgeons performed the procedure on thousands of patients, often with little precision. For example, in one common technique, surgeons jabbed an ice pick under a patient's eyeball and swiveled it back and forth; in other cases, they drilled into the patient's skull (Phillips, 2013; Chodakiewitz et al., 2015; Carroll, 2017).

Psychosurgery sometimes did improve a patient's behavior–but not without drastic side effects. Along with remission of the symptoms of the mental disorder, patients sometimes experienced personality changes and became bland, colorless, and unemotional. In other cases, patients became aggressive and unable to control their impulses. In the worst cases, treatment resulted in the patient's death.

With the introduction of effective drug treatments–and the obvious ethical questions regarding the appropriateness of forever altering someone's personality–psychosurgery became nearly obsolete. However, it is still used in very rare cases when all other procedures have failed and the patient's behavior presents a high risk to the patient and others. For example, surgeons sometimes use a more precise form of psychosurgery called a *cingulotomy* in rare cases of obsessive-compulsive disorder in which they destroy tissue in the *anterior cingulate* area of the brain. In another technique, *gamma knife surgery*, beams of radiation are used to destroy areas of the brain related to obsessive-compulsive disorder (Lopes et al., 2009; Wilkinson, 2009; Eljamel, 2015).

Occasionally, dying patients with severe, uncontrollable pain also receive psychosurgery. Still, even these cases raise important ethical issues, and psychosurgery remains a highly controversial treatment (Mashour, Walker, & Martuza, 2005; Steele et al., 2007; Garfield, 2014).

From the perspective of...

A Politician How would you go about regulating the use of electroconvulsive therapy and psychosurgery?

©Exactostock/SuperStock

Biomedical Therapies in Perspective

In some respects, no greater revolution has occurred in the field of mental health than biological approaches to treatment. As previously violent, uncontrollable patients have been calmed by the use of drugs, mental hospitals have been able to concentrate more on actually helping patients and less on custodial functions. Similarly, patients whose lives have been disrupted by depression or bipolar episodes have been able to function normally, and other forms of drug therapy have also shown remarkable results.

Furthermore, new forms of biomedical therapy are promising. For example, the newest treatment possibility—which remains experimental at this point—is gene therapy. Specific genes may be introduced to particular regions of the brain. These genes then have the potential to reverse or even prevent biochemical events that give rise to psychological disorders (Tuszynski, 2007; Valenzuela et al., 2016).

Another new treatment, now in its infancy, addresses disorders such as depression and anxiety using brain scan neurofeedback. In *brain scan neurofeedback*, patients are exposed to real-time brain scans showing brain activity as they recall emotion-laden memories or triggers for anxiety. By attempting to modify their brain activity, they seem to better cope with their symptoms (McDonald et al., 2017; Young et al., 2017).

Despite their current usefulness and future promise, biomedical therapies do not represent a complete cure for psychological disorders. For one thing, critics charge that biomedical therapies merely provide temporary relief of the symptoms, given that in most cases, symptoms return as soon as the drugs are withdrawn. Consequently, biomedical treatment may not solve the underlying problems that led a patient to therapy in the first place.

Second, critics note that drugs may produce side effects that range from minor to serious physical reactions. In the worst case, biomedical therapies may lead to the development of new symptoms of abnormal behavior.

Finally, an overreliance on biomedical therapies may lead therapists to overlook alternative forms of treatment, such as psychotherapy, that may be helpful. In fact, new research demonstrates that adding psychotherapy involving talk sessions with a therapist to drug treatments is preferable in even severe psychological disorders such as schizophrenia (Carey, 2015; Kane et al., 2016; Browne et al., 2017).

Thus, biomedical therapies—sometimes alone and more often in conjunction with psychotherapy—have permitted millions of people to function more effectively. Furthermore, although biomedical therapy and psychotherapy appear distinct, research shows that biomedical therapies ultimately may not be as different from talk therapies as one might imagine, at least in terms of their consequences.

Specifically, measures of brain functioning as a result of drug therapy compared with psychotherapy show little difference in outcomes. For example, one study compared the reactions of patients with major depression who received either an antidepressant drug or psychotherapy. After 6 weeks of either therapy, activity in the portion of the brain related to the disorder—the basal ganglia—had changed in similar ways, and that area appeared to function more normally. Although such research is not definitive, it does suggest that at least for some disorders, psychotherapy may be just as effective as biomedical interventions—and vice versa. Research also makes it clear that no single treatment is effective universally and that each type of treatment has advantages as well as disadvantages (Greenberg & Goldman, 2009; Gaudiano & Miller, 2013).

> **Study Alert**
> Remember that biomedical treatments have benefits as well as drawbacks.

Community Psychology:
Focus on Prevention

Each of the treatments we have reviewed has a common element: It is a "restorative" treatment aimed at alleviating psychological difficulties that already exist. However, an approach known as **community psychology** has a different aim: to prevent or minimize the incidence of psychological disorders.

community psychology A branch of psychology that focuses on the prevention and minimization of psychological disorders in the community. (Module 51)

While deinstitutionalization has had many successes, it has also contributed to the release of mental patients into the community with little or no support. As a result, many have become homeless.
©McGraw-Hill Education/Gary He, photographer

Deinstitutionalization: The process of transferring patients who have been hospitalized for long periods into less-isolated community mental health settings. (Module 51)

Community psychology came of age in the 1960s, when mental health professionals developed plans for a nationwide network of community mental health centers. The hope was that those centers would provide low-cost mental health services, including short-term therapy and community educational programs. In another development, the population of mental hospitals has plunged as drug treatments made physical restraint of patients unnecessary.

The community psychology movement encouraged deinstitutionalization. **Deinstitutionalization** is the process of transferring patients who have been hospitalized for long periods into less-isolated community mental health settings (see Figure 3). Proponents of deinstitutionalization wanted to ensure not only that deinstitutionalized patients received proper treatment but also that their civil rights were maintained (St. Dennis et al., 2006; Henckes, 2011; Pow et al., 2015).

Unfortunately, the promise of deinstitutionalization has not been met largely because insufficient resources are provided to deinstitutionalized patients. What started as a worthy attempt to move people out of mental institutions and into the community ended, in many cases, with former patients being dumped into the community without any real support. Many became homeless–between 15–35% of all homeless adults are thought to have a major psychological disorder–and some became involved in illegal acts caused by their disorders. In short, many people who need treatment do not get it, and in some cases, care for people with psychological disorders has simply shifted from one type of treatment site to another. In fact, for many people, the only form of mental health treatment comes in emergency rooms of hospitals, with little or no follow-up care (Dumont & Dumont, 2008; Whitaker, 2009; Searight, 2013).

On the other hand, the community psychology movement has had some positive outcomes. Its emphasis on prevention has led to new approaches to psychological disorders. Furthermore, telephone "hot lines" are now common. At any time of the day or night, people experiencing acute stress can call a trained, sympathetic listener who can provide immediate–although obviously limited–treatment (Cauce, 2007; Jarrett, 2015; Nelson & MacLeod, 2017).

College and high school crisis centers are another innovation that grew out of the community psychology movement. Modeled after suicide prevention hot-line centers, crisis centers give callers an opportunity to discuss life crises with a sympathetic listener, who is often a volunteer.

FIGURE 3 As deinstitutionalization has become prevalent over the years, the number of patients being treated in state mental hospitals declined significantly, while the number of patients being treated in outpatient facilities increased.
Source: Adapted from Doyle, R. (2002). Deinstitutionalization. *Scientific American, 287,* 38.

Choosing the Right Therapist

If you decide to seek therapy, you're faced with a daunting task. Choosing a therapist is not a simple matter. One place to begin the process of identifying a therapist is at the "Help Center" of the American Psychological Association at http://www.apa.org/helpcenter. And if you start therapy, several general guidelines can help you determine whether you've made the right choice:

You and your therapist should agree on the goals for treatment. They should be clear, specific, and attainable.

- *You should feel comfortable with your therapist.* You should not be intimidated by or in awe of a therapist. Rather, you should trust the therapist and feel free to discuss the most personal issues without fearing a negative reaction. In sum, the "personal chemistry" should be right.

- *Therapists should have appropriate training and credentials and should be licensed by appropriate state and local agencies.* Check therapists' membership in national and state professional associations. In addition, the cost of therapy, billing practices, and other business matters should be clear. It is not a breach of etiquette to put these matters on the table during an initial consultation.

- *You should feel that you are making progress after therapy has begun, despite occasional setbacks.* If you have no sense of improvement after repeated visits, you and your therapist should discuss this issue frankly. Although there is no set timetable, the most obvious changes resulting from therapy tend to occur relatively early in the course of treatment. For instance, half of patients in psychotherapy improve by the 8th session and three-fourths by the 26th session. The average number of sessions with college students is just five (Lazarus, 1997; Taibbi, 2018).

Be aware that you will have to put in a great deal of effort in therapy. Although our culture promises quick cures for any problem, in reality, solving difficult problems is not easy. You must be committed to making therapy work and should know that it is you, not the therapist, who must do most of the work to resolve your problems. The effort has the potential to pay off handsomely—as you experience a more positive, fulfilling, and meaningful life.

AP SUMMARY

- The community psychology approach aims to prevent or minimize disorders. Positive outcomes include: "hot lines" and crisis centers.
- Community psychology encouraged deinstitutionalization, but the program lacked sufficient resources and many individuals ended up homeless.
- Biomedical treatment approaches suggest that therapy should focus on the physiological causes of abnormal behavior. Therapists use drugs, electric shock, or surgery.

- Drug therapy has brought about dramatic reductions in the symptoms of mental disturbance. Antipsychotic drugs, such as *chlorpromazine*, effectively reduce psychotic symptoms but have various side effects. Antidepressant drugs, such as *Prozac*, are used for depression, anxiety, and eating disorders. Specific types include: tricyclics, MAO inhibitors, and SSRIs. Mood stabilizers, such as *lithium*, are used to treat bipolar. Antianxiety drugs, such as *Valium*, are used for general tension and anxiety disorders. They are widely used but have serious side effects.

- ECT is a procedure in which a patient receives a brief electric current. It is used in cases of severe depression and possible side effects include disorientation and memory loss. Newer and promising alternatives include TMS and DBS.
- Psychosurgery typically consists of surgically destroying or removing certain parts of a patient's brain, often leading to drastic side effects. The first type was the prefrontal lobotomy. Effective drug treatments decreased the use of this biomedical technique.
- New forms of biomedical therapy are promising, such as gene therapy and brain scan neurofeedback.
- Biomedical therapies revolutionized mental health treatments, but they have been criticized.

AP KEY TERMS

drug therapy
antipsychotic drugs
antidepressant drugs
mood stabilizers
antianxiety drugs
electroconvulsive therapy (ECT)
transcranial magnetic stimulation (TMS)
psychosurgery
community psychology
deinstitutionalization

AP TEST PRACTICE

Section I: Multiple Choice

1. Community psychologists try to
   A. reduce the number of symptoms
   B. slow the spread of disorders
   C. find new therapy techniques
   D. treat current problems at epidemic levels
   E. prevent or minimize the incidence of disorders

2. Electroconvulsive therapy is used to effectively treat which disorder?
   A. Generalized anxiety disorder
   B. Schizophrenia
   C. Major depression
   D. Specific phobias
   E. Personality disorders

3. *Lithium*, a mineral salt, has been found effective for treating which disorder?
   A. Bipolar
   B. Anxiety disorders
   C. Eating disorders
   D. Major depression
   E. Schizophrenia

Section II: Free Response

Cameron is researching biomedical therapies. Explain how the following types of drugs relate to neurotransmitters and provide an example of each.
- SSRI
- Antipsychotic
- Antianxiety

LOOKING *Back*

EPILOGUE

We have examined how psychological professionals treat people with psychological disorders. We have considered a range of approaches that include both psychologically based and biologically based therapies. Clearly, the field has made substantial progress in recent years both in treating the symptoms of mental disorders and in understanding their underlying causes.

MODULE 49 Psychotherapy: Psychodynamic, Behavioral, and Cognitive Approaches

Psychodynamic Therapy

- Psychoanalysis
  - Free association: say aloud whatever comes to mind
  - Dream interpretation: looking for clues to unconscious conflicts and problems in dreams
  - Frequent sessions for a long time
- Contemporary psychodynamic approaches
  - Sessions are of shorter duration
  - Therapist takes more active role: focus is more in the present

Behavioral Treatment Approaches: Help modify behavior rather than find underlying causes

- Classical conditioning treatments
  - Aversive conditioning
  - Systematic desensitization
  - Flooding
- Operant conditioning techniques
  - Token system
  - Contingency contracting
  - Observational learning

Cognitive Approaches: Teach people to think in adaptive ways

- Rational-emotive behavior therapy

A	B	C
Negative Activating condition	**Irrational Belief system**	**Emotional Consequences**
(Close relationship breaks up)	("I'll never be loved again")	(Anxiety, loneliness, sadness, depression)

MODULE 50 Psychotherapy: Humanistic, Interpersonal, and Group Approaches

Humanistic Therapy: Focuses on self-responsibility in treatment techniques

- Person-centered therapy: helps people to reach their potential for self-actualization using unconditional positive regard

Interpersonal Therapy: Focuses on interpersonal relationships and improvement through short-term therapy

Group Therapy: Several people meet with a therapist to discuss psychological functioning

- Family therapy
- Self-help therapy

Does Psychotherapy Work?

- More effective than no treatment for most people
- Certain types of therapy work better for particular problems
- Most therapy approaches share basic elements

MODULE 51 Biomedical Therapy: Biological Approaches to Treatment

Drug Therapy: Controlling psychological disorders with drugs

Drug Treatments			
Class of Drug	**Effects of Drug**	**Primary Action of Drug**	**Examples**
Antipsychotic Drugs, Atypical Antidepressant Drugs	Reduction in loss of touch with reality, agitation	Block dopamine receptors	Antipsychotic: chlorpromazine (Thorazine), clozapine (Clozaril), haloperidol (Haldol)
			Atypical antipsychotic: risperidone, olanzapine
Antipsychotic Drugs Tricyclic antidepressants	Reduction in depression	Permit rise in neurotransmitters such as norepinepherine	Trazodone (Desyrel), amitriptyline (Elavil), desipramine (Norpamin)
MAO inhibitors	Reduction in depression	Prevent MAO from breaking down neurotransmitters	Phenelzine (Nardil), tranylcypromine (Parnate)
Selective serotonin reuptake inhibitors (SSRIs)	Reduction in depression	Inhibit reuptake of serotonin	Fluoxetine (Prozac), Luvox, Paxil, Celexa, Zoloft, nefazodone (Serzone)
Mood Stabilizers Lithium	Mood stabilization	Can alter transmission of impulses within neurons	Lithium (Lithonate), Depakote, Tegretol
Antianxiety Drugs	Reduction in anxiety	Increase activity of neurotransmitter GABA	Benzodiazepines (Valium, Xanax)

Electroconvulsive Therapy: Used as the only quickly effective treatment for severe depression

Psychosurgery: Brain surgery to reduce symptoms of mental disorders

Community Psychology: Prevention of the incidence of psychological disorders

- Deinstitutionalization: transfer of mental patients into the community where they may not receive necessary treatment

(MODULE 49) Source: Ellis, A. (1974). *Growth through reason*. Hollywood, CA: Wilshire Books; (MODULE 50) (photo): ©Jon Bradley/The Image Bank/Getty Images; Source: Adapted from Smith, M. L., Glass, G. V., & Miller, T. I. (1980). *The benefits of psychotherapy*. Baltimore: The Johns Hopkins University Press; (MODULE 51) ©McGraw-Hill Education/Gary He, photographer

©Ingram Publishing/SuperStock

CHAPTER 17
Social Psychology

AP'I LEARNING TARGETS FOR CHAPTER 17

MODULE 52

- Apply attribution theory to explain motives

- Articulate the impact of social and cultural categories.

- Identify important figures and research in attitude formation and change.

- Discuss attitude formation and change, including persuasion strategies and cognitive dissonance.

ATTITUDES AND SOCIAL COGNITION

Persuasion: Changing Attitudes

Social Cognition: Understanding Others

Exploring Diversity: Attribution Biases in a Cultural Context: How Fundamental Is the Fundamental Attribution Error?

MODULE 53

- Identify the contributions of key researchers in the areas of conformity, compliance, and obedience.

- Explain how individuals respond to expectations of others.

- Describe the structure and function of group behavior.

- Predict the impact of the presence of others

SOCIAL INFLUENCE AND GROUPS

Conformity: Following What Others Do

Compliance: Submitting to Direct Social Pressure

Obedience: Following Direct Orders

MODULE 54

- Define intelligence and list characteristics of how psychologists measure intelligence.

- Anticipate the impact of self-fulfilling prophecy on behavior.

PREJUDICE AND DISCRIMINATION

The Foundations of Prejudice

AP'I Neuroscience in Your Life: The Prejudiced Brain

Measuring Prejudice and Discrimination: The Implicit Association Test

- Describe processes that contribute to differential treatment of group members.

- Predict the impact of the presence of others on individual behavior.

- Describe the variables that contribute to altruism and aggression.

- Describe the variables that contribute to attraction.

PROLOGUE *AN AMERICAN TERRORIST*

On a warm summer evening, Dylann Roof walked into Charleston, South Carolina's Emanuel AME Church—the South's oldest black church. The 12 church members present at that time welcomed Roof, handed him a Bible, and invited him to join their prayer meeting.

What the church members—all black—did not know was that Roof had arrived with a heart full of hate and a weapon, a Glock .45. Forty-five minutes later, during the final prayer, Roof opened fire, shooting some of his victims multiple times. Only three survived.

The 21-year-old Roof showed no remorse for his crime either at the time of his arrest or later in the courtroom. He did tell FBI agents he hoped the shootings would bring back segregation, maybe even start a race war.

Roof maintained throughout his trial (in which he acted as his own attorney during sentencing) that he was not mentally ill. "Anyone who hates anything in their mind has a good reason for it," he told the jurors. The jury responded by convicting Roof of all 33 federal charges. He became the first person to be given the death penalty for a federal hate crime (Tribune News Services, 2017).

LOOKING *Ahead*

Dylann Roof never clearly explained why he targeted the church members. He did claim to be a white supremacist and had posed with the Confederate flag in photographs. At his sentencing, he told jurors, "I still feel like I had to do it" (Tribune News Services, 2017).

What drives people like Roof to hate and distrust others of a different religion, race, or ethnicity? And conversely, why do others celebrate human diversity? More broadly, how can we improve social attitudes so that people live together in harmony?

We can fully answer these questions only by taking into account findings from the field of social psychology, the branch that focuses on the aspects of human behavior that unite—and separate—us from one another. **Social psychology** is the scientific study of how people's thoughts, feelings, and actions are affected by others. Social psychologists consider the kinds and causes of the individual's behavior in social situations. They examine how the nature of situations in which we find ourselves influences our behavior in important ways.

The broad scope of social psychology is conveyed by the kinds of questions social psychologists ask, such as: How can we convince people to change their attitudes or adopt new ideas and values? In what ways do we come to understand what others are like? How are we influenced by what others do and think? Why do some people display so much violence, aggression, and cruelty toward others that people throughout the world live in fear of annihilation at their hands? And why, in comparison, do some people place their own lives at risk to help others? In exploring these and other questions, we also discuss strategies for confronting and solving a variety of problems and issues that all of us face—ranging from achieving a better understanding of persuasive tactics to forming more accurate impressions of others.

We begin with a look at how our attitudes shape our behavior and how we form judgments about others. We'll discuss how we are influenced by others, and we will consider prejudice and discrimination by focusing on their roots and the ways we can reduce them. After examining what social psychologists have learned about the ways people form friendships and relationships, we'll conclude with a look at the determinants of aggression and helping—two opposing sides of human behavior.

social psychology The scientific study of how people's thoughts, feelings, and actions are affected by others. (Module 52)

Module 52
Attitudes and Social Cognition

attitudes Evaluations of people, objects, ideas, and behavior. (Module 52)

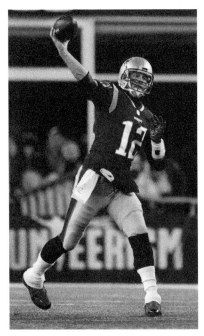

Do celebrities such as Patriot quarterback Tom Brady influence attitudes? Advertisers certainly believe this is true, investing millions of dollars in endorsement fees.
©John Cetrino/EPA-EFE/REX/Shutterstock/Shutterstock

What do Rachael Ray and Tom Brady have in common? Both have appeared in advertisements designed to mold or change our attitudes. Such commercials are part of the barrage of messages we receive each day from sources as varied as politicians, sales staff in stores, and celebrities–all of which are meant to influence us.

Persuasion: Changing Attitudes

Attitudes are one of the central concepts of social psychology. **Attitudes** are evaluations of people, objects, ideas, and behavior. We have all sorts of attitudes, ranging from those about others ("I think the president is great"), to attitudes about behavior ("I hate it when people are late for appointments"), to attitudes toward more abstract concepts ("I support affirmative action") (Hegarty & Massey, 2007; Simon & Hoyt, 2008).

Persuasion involves changing attitudes. The ease with which attitudes can be changed depends on a number of factors, including:

- *Message source.* The characteristics of a person who delivers a persuasive message, known as an *attitude communicator,* have a major impact on the effectiveness of that message. Communicators who are physically and socially attractive produce greater attitude change than do those who are less attractive. Moreover, the communicator's expertise and trustworthiness are related to the impact of a message–except in situations in which the audience believes the communicator has an ulterior motive (MMessner, Reinhard, & Sporer, 2008; Bebermeier et al., 2015).

- *Characteristics of the message.* It is not just *who* delivers a message but what the message is like that affects attitudes. Generally, two-sided messages–which include both the communicator's position and the one he or she is arguing against–are more effective than one-sided messages, given the assumption that the arguments for the other side can be effectively refuted and the audience is knowledgeable about the topic. In addition, fear-producing messages ("If you don't practice safer sex, you'll get AIDS") are generally effective when they provide the audience with a means for reducing the fear. However, if the fear that is aroused is too strong, messages may evoke people's defense mechanisms and be ignored (Keer et al., 2013; Bigsby, Monahan, & Ewoldsen, 2017).

- *Characteristics of the target.* Once a communicator has delivered a message, characteristics of the *target* of the message may determine whether the message will be accepted. For example, intelligent people are more resistant to persuasion than are those who are less intelligent. Gender differences in persuadability also seem to exist. In public settings, women are somewhat more easily persuaded than men, particularly when women have less knowledge about the message's topic. However, they are as likely as men to change their private attitudes. In fact, the magnitude of the differences in resistance to persuasion between men and women is not large (Wood, 2000; Guadagno & Cialdini, 2002).

ROUTES TO PERSUASION

Recipients' receptiveness to persuasive messages relates to the type of information-processing they use. Social psychologists have discovered two primary information-processing routes to persuasion: central route and peripheral route processing. **Central route processing** occurs when the recipient thoughtfully considers the issues and arguments involved in persuasion. In central route processing, people are swayed in their judgments by the logic, merit, and strength of arguments.

In contrast, **peripheral route processing** occurs when people are persuaded on the basis of factors unrelated to the nature or quality of the content of a persuasive message. Instead, factors that are irrelevant or extraneous to the issue, such as who is providing the message, how long the arguments are, or the emotional appeal of the arguments, influence them (Warden, Wu, & Tsai, 2006; Kao, 2011; Xie & Johnson, 2015).

In general, people who are highly involved and motivated use central route processing to comprehend a message. However, if a person is disinterested, unmotivated, bored, or distracted, the characteristics of the message become less important, and peripheral factors become more influential (see Figure 1). Although both central route and peripheral route processing lead to attitude change, central route processing generally leads to stronger, more lasting attitude change.

Are some people more likely than others to habitually use central route processing rather than peripheral route processing? The answer is yes. *Need for cognition* is someone's typical level of thoughtfulness and cognitive activity. Those who have a high need for cognition are more likely to employ central route processing. In contrast, those with a low need for cognition are more likely to use peripheral route processing. See Figure 2 to get a sense of your own need for cognition (Dai & Wang, 2007; Hill et al., 2013; Luttrell, Petty, & Xu, 2017).

People who have a high need for cognition enjoy thinking, philosophizing, and reflecting on the world. Because they are more likely to reflect on persuasive messages by using central route processing, they are persuaded by complex, logical, and detailed messages. In contrast, those who have a low need for cognition become impatient when forced to spend too much time thinking about an issue. Consequently, they usually use peripheral route processing and are persuaded by factors other than the quality and detail of messages (Dollinger, 2003; Van Overwalle & Siebler, 2005).

central route processing The type of mental processing that occurs when a persuasive message is evaluated by thoughtful consideration of the issues and arguments used to persuade. (Module 52)

peripheral route processing The type of mental processing that occurs when a persuasive message is evaluated on the basis of irrelevant or extraneous factors. (Module 52)

Study Alert
Central route processing involves the content of the message; peripheral route processing involves how the message is provided.

From the perspective of...

A Sales Specialist Suppose you were selling an automobile to a customer who walked in the door. What strategies might you use to be persuasive?

©Amos Morgan/Getty Images

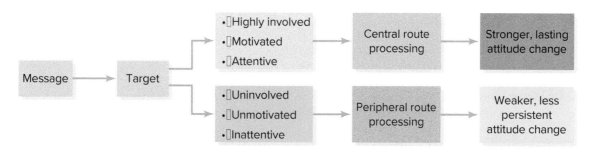

FIGURE 1 Routes to persuasion. Targets who are highly involved, motivated, and attentive use central route processing when they consider a persuasive message, which leads to a more lasting attitude change. In contrast, uninvolved, unmotivated, and inattentive targets are more likely to use peripheral route processing, and attitude change is likely to be less enduring. Can you think of specific advertisements that try to produce central route processing?

FIGURE 2 This simple questionnaire will give you a general idea of the level of your need for cognition.

Source: Adapted from Cacioppo, J. T., Berntson, G. G., & Crites, S. L., Jr. (1996). Social neuroscience: Principles of psychophysiological arousal and response. In E. T. Higgins & A. W. Kruglanski (Eds.), *Social psychology: Handbook of basic principles.* New York: Guilford.

The Need for Cognition

Which of the following statements apply to you?

1. I really enjoy a task that involves coming up with new solutions to problems.

2. I would prefer a task that is intellectual, difficult, and important to one that is somewhat important but does not require much thought.

3. Learning new ways to think doesn't excite me very much.

4. The idea of relying on thought to make my way to the top does not appeal to me.

5. I think only as hard as I have to.

6. I like tasks that require little thought once I've learned them.

7. I prefer to think about small, daily projects rather than long-term ones.

8. I would rather do something that requires little thought than something that is sure to challenge my thinking abilities.

9. I find little satisfaction in deliberating hard and for long hours.

10. I don't like to be responsible for a situation that requires a lot of thinking.

Scoring: The more you agree with statements 1 and 2, and disagree with the rest, the greater the likelihood that you have a high need for cognition.

THE LINK BETWEEN ATTITUDES AND BEHAVIOR

Not surprisingly, attitudes influence behavior. The strength of the link between particular attitudes and behavior varies, of course, but generally, people strive for consistency between their attitudes and their behavior. Furthermore, people hold fairly consistent attitudes. For instance, you would probably not hold the attitude that eating meat is immoral and still have a positive attitude toward hamburgers (Levi, Chan, & Pence, 2006; Elen et al., 2013; Rodrigues & Girandola, 2017).

Ironically, the consistency that leads attitudes to influence behavior sometimes works the other way around; in some cases, our behavior shapes our attitudes. Consider, for instance, the following incident:

> You've just spent what you feel is the most boring hour of your life turning pegs for a psychology experiment. Just as you finally finish and are about to leave, the experimenter asks you to do him a favor. He tells you that he needs a helper for future experimental sessions to introduce subsequent participants to the peg-turning task. Your specific job will be to tell them that turning the pegs is an interesting, fascinating experience. Each time you tell this tale to another participant, you'll be paid $1.

If you agree to help the experimenter, you may be setting yourself up for a state of psychological tension called cognitive dissonance. **Cognitive dissonance** occurs when a person holds two contradictory attitudes or thoughts (referred to as *cognitions;* Festinger, 1957).

If you participate in the situation just described, you are left with two contradictory thoughts: (1) I believe the task is boring, but (2) I said it was interesting with little justification ($1). These two thoughts should arouse cognitive dissonance.

How can you reduce the cognitive dissonance? You cannot deny having said that the task is interesting, because you just said it. On the other hand, it is relatively easy to change your attitude toward the task—and thus, the theory predicts that participants will reduce dissonance by adopting more positive attitudes toward the task (Rydell, McConnell, & Mackie, 2008; Dickinson & Oxoby, 2011; Harmon-Jones, Harmon-Jones, & Levy, 2015).

cognitive dissonance The mental conflict that occurs when a person holds two contradictory attitudes or thoughts (referred to as cognitions). (Module 52)

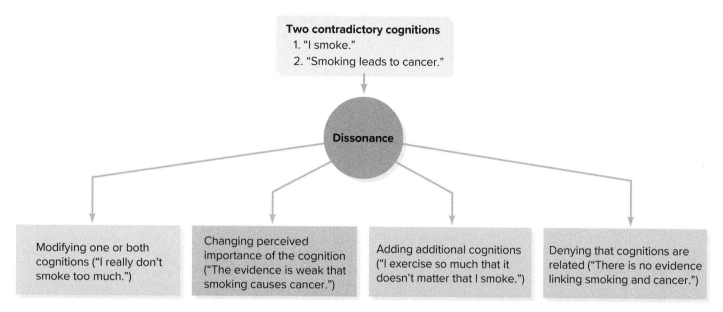

FIGURE 3 Cognitive dissonance. The simultaneous presence of two contradictory cognitions ("I smoke." and "Smoking leads to cancer.") produces dissonance, which can be reduced through several methods. What are additional ways in which dissonance can be reduced?

A classic experiment (Festinger & Carlsmith, 1959) confirmed this prediction. The experiment followed essentially the same procedure outlined earlier in which a participant was offered $1 to describe a boring task as interesting. In addition, in a comparison condition, some participants were offered $20 to say that the task was interesting. The reasoning behind this condition was that $20 was so much money that participants in this condition had a good reason to be conveying incorrect information; dissonance would not be aroused, and less attitude change would be expected. The results supported this notion. More of the participants who were paid $1 changed their attitudes (becoming more positive toward the peg-turning task) than did participants who were paid $20.

Cognitive dissonance explains many everyday events involving attitudes and behavior. For example, smokers who know that smoking leads to lung cancer hold contradictory cognitions: (1) I smoke, and (2) smoking leads to lung cancer. The theory predicts that these two thoughts will lead to a state of cognitive dissonance. More important, it predicts that smokers will be motivated to reduce their dissonance.

There are four ways to reduce the dissonance in this case:

- Modifying one or both of the cognitions (e.g., "I really don't smoke that much.")

- Changing the perceived importance of one cognition ("The link between cancer and smoking is weak.")

- Adding cognitions ("I exercise so much that I'm really a healthy person.")

- Denying that the two cognitions are related to each other ("There's no compelling evidence linking smoking and cancer.")

Whichever strategy the smoker uses results in reduced dissonance (see Figure 3).

Social Cognition: Understanding Others

Regardless of Bill Clinton's personal transgressions and impeachment trial in the late 1990s, many Americans continued to find him extremely likable throughout his presidency, and even today he is among the most popular U.S. politicians. Cases like this illustrate the power of our impressions and attest to the importance of determining how people develop an understanding of others. One of the dominant areas in social psychology during the last few years has focused on learning how we come to understand what others are like and how we explain the reasons underlying others' behavior.

social cognition The cognitive processes by which people understand and make sense of others and themselves. (Module 52)

schemas Organized bodies of information stored in memory that bias the way new information is interpreted, stored, and recalled. (Modules 21, 52)

UNDERSTANDING WHAT OTHERS ARE LIKE

Consider for a moment the enormous amount of information about other people to which we are exposed. How can we decide what is important and what is not and make judgments about the characteristics of others? Social psychologists interested in this question study **social cognition**–the way people understand and make sense of others and themselves. Those psychologists have learned that individuals have highly developed **schemas,** sets of cognitions about people and social experiences. Those schemas organize information stored in memory; represent in our minds the way the social world operates; and give us a framework to recognize, categorize, and recall information relating to social stimuli such as people and groups (Amodio & Ratner, 2011; Leahy, 2015; Kitayama, 2017).

We typically hold schemas for specific types of people. Our schema for "teacher," for instance, generally consists of a number of characteristics: knowledge of the subject matter he or she is teaching, a desire to impart that knowledge, and an awareness of the student's need to understand what is being said. Or we may hold a schema for "mother" that includes the characteristics of warmth, nurturance, and caring. Regardless of their accuracy, schemas are important because they organize the way in which we recall, recognize, and categorize information about others. Moreover, they help us predict what others are like on the basis of relatively little information because we tend to fit people into schemas even when we do not have much concrete evidence to go on (Ruscher, Fiske, & Schnake, 2000; Yamada & Itsukushima, 2013).

FORMING IMPRESSIONS OF OTHERS

How do we decide that Sayreeta is a flirt, Jacob is obnoxious, or Hector is a really nice guy? The earliest work on social cognition examined *impression formation,* the process by which an individual organizes information about another person to form an overall impression of that person. In a classic study, for instance, students learned that they were about to hear a guest lecturer (Kelley, 1950). Researchers told one group of students that the lecturer was "a rather warm person, industrious, critical, practical, and determined" and told a second group that he was "a rather cold person, industrious, critical, practical, and determined."

The simple substitution of "cold" for "warm" caused drastic differences in the way the students in each group perceived the lecturer even though he gave the same talk in the same style in each condition. Students who had been told he was "warm" rated him considerably more positively overall than did students who had been told he was "cold."

central traits The major traits considered in forming impressions of others. (Module 52)

The findings from this experiment led to additional research on impression formation that focused on the way in which people pay particular attention to certain unusually important traits–known as **central traits**–to help them form an overall impression of others. According to this work, the presence of a central trait alters the meaning of other traits. Hence, the description of the lecturer as "industrious" presumably meant something different when it was associated with the central trait "warm" than it meant when it was associated with "cold" (Glicksohn & Nahari, 2007; McCarthy & Skowronski, 2011; Huang, Sacchi, & Sherman, 2017).

Some researchers have used information-processing approaches to develop mathematical models of how we combine individual personality traits to develop an overall impression of others. Generally, we calculate a kind of psychological "average" of the individual traits we see in a person to form an overall judgment, just as we would find the mathematical average of several numbers (Mignon & Mollaret, 2002).

We also form impressions remarkably quickly. In just a few seconds, using what have been called "thin slices of behavior," we are able to make judgments of people. Interestingly, these quick impressions are surprisingly accurate and typically match those of people who make judgments based on longer samples of behavior (Pavitt, 2007; Holleran, Mehl, & Levitt, 2009; Pretsch et al., 2013).

Of course, as we gain more experience with people and see them exhibiting behavior in a variety of situations, our impressions of them become more complex. However, because our knowledge of others usually has gaps, we still tend to fit individuals into personality schemas that represent particular "types" of people. For instance, we may hold a "gregarious person" schema made up of the traits of friendliness, aggressiveness, and openness. The presence of just one or two of those traits may be sufficient to make us assign a person to a particular schema.

However, our schemas are susceptible to error. For example, mood affects how we perceive others. Happy people form more favorable impressions and make more positive judgments than do people who are in a bad mood (Forgas & Laham, 2005; Human & Biesanz, 2011).

Even when schemas are not entirely accurate, they serve an important function: They allow us to develop expectations about how others will behave. Those expectations permit us to plan our interactions with others more easily and serve to simplify a complex social world.

ATTRIBUTION PROCESSES: UNDERSTANDING THE CAUSES OF BEHAVIOR

When Barbara Washington, a new employee at the Ablex Computer Company, completed a major staffing project 2 weeks early, her boss, Yolanda, was delighted. At the next staff meeting, she announced how pleased she was with Barbara and explained that *this* was an example of the kind of performance she was looking for in her staff. The other staff members looked on resentfully, trying to figure out why Barbara had worked night and day to finish the project not just on time but 2 weeks early. She must be an awfully compulsive person, they decided.

At one time or another, most of us have puzzled over the reasons behind someone's behavior. Perhaps it was in a situation similar to the one above, or it may have been in more formal circumstances, such as being a judge on a student judiciary board in a cheating case. **Attribution theory** considers how we decide, on the basis of samples of a person's behavior, what the specific causes of that behavior are. Unlike impression formation, which focuses on how people develop an overall impression of others' personality traits, attribution theory asks the "why" question: Why is someone acting in a particular way?

In seeking an explanation for behavior, we must answer one central question: Is the cause situational or dispositional? **Situational causes** are causes of behavior that are external to a person. For instance, someone who knocks over a quart of milk and then cleans it up probably does the cleaning not because he or she is necessarily a neat person but because the *situation* requires it. In contrast, a person who spends hours shining the kitchen floor probably does so because he or she is an unusually neat person. Hence, the behavior has a dispositional cause. **Dispositional causes** are causes of behavior brought about by a person's traits or personality characteristics.

In our example involving Barbara Washington, her fellow employees attributed her behavior to her disposition rather than to the situation. But from a logical standpoint, it is equally plausible that something about the situation caused the behavior. If asked, Barbara might attribute her accomplishment to situational factors and explain that she had so much other work to do she just had to get the project out of the way or that the project was not all that difficult and was easy to complete ahead of schedule. To her, then, the reason for her behavior might not be dispositional at all; it could be situational.

attribution theory The theory that considers how we decide, on the basis of samples of a person's behavior, what the specific causes of that behavior are. (Module 52)

situational causes (of behavior) Causes of behavior that are external to a person. (Module 52)

dispositional causes (of behavior) Perceived causes of behavior brought about by a person's traits or personality characteristics. (Module 52)

ATTRIBUTION BIASES: TO ERR IS HUMAN

If we always processed information in the rational manner that attribution theory suggests, the world might run a lot more smoothly. Unfortunately, although attribution theory generally makes accurate predictions, people do not always process information

Study Alert
The central question in making an attribution is whether the cause of behavior is due to situational or dispositional factors.

about others as logically as the theory seems to suggest. In fact, research reveals consistent biases in the ways people make attributions. Typical biases include the following:

- *The halo effect.* Harry is intelligent, kind, and loving. Is he also conscientious? If you were to guess, your most likely response probably would be yes. Your guess reflects the **halo effect,** a phenomenon in which an initial understanding that a person has positive traits is used to infer other uniformly positive characteristics. The opposite would also hold true. Learning that Harry was unsociable and argumentative would probably lead you to assume that he was lazy as well. However, few people have either uniformly positive or uniformly negative traits, so the halo effect leads to misperceptions of others (Dennis, 2007; Park, Park, & Dubinsky, 2011; Forgas & Laham, 2017).

- *Assumed-similarity bias.* How similar to you–in terms of attitudes, opinions, likes, and dislikes–are your friends and acquaintances? Most people believe that their friends and acquaintances are fairly similar to themselves. But this feeling goes beyond just people we know to a general tendency–known as the **assumed-similarity bias**–to think of people as being similar to oneself even when meeting them for the first time. Given the range of people in the world, this assumption often reduces the accuracy of our judgments (Lemay, Clark, & Feeney, 2007; Lemay & Clark, 2008).

- *The self-serving bias.* When their teams win, coaches usually feel that the success is due to their coaching. But when their teams lose, coaches may think it's due to their players' poor skills. Similarly, if you get an A on a test, you may think it's due to your hard work, but if you get a poor grade, it's due to the professor's inadequacies. The reason is the **self-serving bias,** the tendency to attribute success to personal factors (skill, ability, or effort) and attribute failure to factors outside oneself (Shepperd, Malone, & Sweeny, 2008; Ferring, Tournier, & Mancini, 2015).

- *The fundamental attribution error.* One of the more common attribution biases is the **fundamental attribution error,** which is the tendency to overattribute others' behavior to dispositional causes and the corresponding failure to recognize the importance of situational causes. The fundamental attribution error is prevalent in Western cultures. We tend to exaggerate the importance of personality characteristics (dispositional causes) in producing others' behavior and minimize the influence of the environment (situational factors). For example, we are more likely to jump to the conclusion that someone who is often late to work is lazy or a routinely tardy person (dispositional causes) than to assume that, perhaps, the subway they take to work frequently runs behind schedule, causing them to be late (a situational cause).

halo effect A phenomenon in which an initial understanding that a person has positive or negative traits is used to infer other uniformly positive or negative characteristics. (Module 52)

assumed-similarity bias The tendency to think of people as being similar to oneself even when meeting them for the first time. (Module 52)

self-serving bias The tendency to attribute personal success to personal factors (skill, ability, or effort) and to attribute failure to factors outside oneself. (Module 52)

fundamental attribution error A tendency to overattribute others' behavior to dispositional causes and minimize the importance of situational causes. (Module 52)

The assumed-similarity bias leads us to believe that others hold similar attitudes, opinions, and likes and dislikes.
©PhotoAlto/SuperStock

Why is the fundamental attribution error so common? One reason pertains to the nature of information available to the people making an attribution. When we view another person's behavior in a particular setting, the most conspicuous information is the person's behavior. Because the individual's immediate surroundings remain relatively unchanged and less attention grabbing, we center our attention on the person whose behavior we're considering. Consequently, we are more likely to make attributions based on personal dispositional factors and less likely to make attributions relating to the situation (Follett & Hess, 2002; Langdridge & Butt, 2004; Tal-Or & Papirman, 2007).

Social psychologists' awareness of attribution biases has led, in part, to the development of a new branch of economics called behavioral economics. *Behavioral economics* is concerned with how economic conditions are affected by individuals' biases and irrationality. Rather than viewing people as rational, thoughtful decision makers who are impartially weighing choices to draw conclusions, behavioral economists focus on the irrationality of judgments (Ariely & Norton, 2009).

 # Exploring Diversity

Attribution Biases in a Cultural Context: How Fundamental Is the Fundamental Attribution Error?

Attribution biases do not affect all of us in the same way. The culture in which we are raised clearly plays a role in the way we attribute others' behavior.

Take, for example, the fundamental attribution error: the tendency to overestimate the importance of personal, dispositional factors and underattribute situational factors in determining the causes of others' behavior. The error is pervasive in Western cultures and not in Eastern societies. For instance, adults in India were more likely to use situational attributions than to use dispositional ones in explaining events. These findings are the opposite of those for the United States, and they contradict the fundamental attribution error (Miller, 1984; Lien et al., 2006).

One reason for the difference may lie in the values of Eastern society, which emphasize social responsibility and societal obligations to a greater extent than Western societies do. In addition, the language spoken in a culture may lead to different sorts of attributions. For instance, a tardy person using English may say, "I am late"; this suggests a personal, dispositional cause ("I am a tardy person"). In contrast, speakers of Spanish who are late say, "The clock caused me to be late." Clearly, the statement in Spanish implies that the cause is situational (Macduff, 2006; Alon & Brett, 2007).

Cultural differences in attributions affect subsequent behavior. For example, parents in Asia tend to attribute good academic performance to effort and hard work (situational factors). In contrast, parents in Western cultures tend to de-emphasize the role of effort and attribute school success to innate ability (a dispositional factor). As a result, Asian students in general may strive harder to achieve and ultimately outperform U.S. students in school (Stevenson, Lee, & Mu, 2000; Lien et al., 2006).

The difference in thinking between people in Asian and Western cultures is a reflection of a broader difference in the way the world is perceived. Asian societies generally have a *collectivistic orientation*, a worldview that promotes the notion of interdependence. People with a collectivistic orientation generally see themselves as parts of a larger, interconnected social network and as responsible to others. In contrast, people in Western cultures are more likely to hold an *individualist orientation* that emphasizes personal identity and the uniqueness of the individual. They focus more on what sets them apart from others and what makes them special (Markus & Kitayama, 2003; Wang, 2004; Markus, 2007).

AP MODULE 52: ATTITUDES AND SOCIAL COGNITION

AP SUMMARY

- Social cognition involves the way people understand and make sense of others and themselves. People develop schemas that organize information in memory and allow them to interpret and categorize information about others.
- People form impressions of others in part through the use of central traits. We tend to average together sets of traits to form an overall impression.
- Attribution theory tries to explain how we understand the causes of behavior, particularly with respect to situational and dispositional factors.
- Attribution is prone to error. For instance, people are susceptible to the halo effect, assumed-similarity bias, self-serving bias, and fundamental attribution error.
- Attributional biases are influenced by culture.
- Festinger discovered that participants who were paid $1 to do a boring task changed their attitude in order to reduce cognitive dissonance.
- Attitudes change based on the message of the source, characteristics of the message, and characteristics of the target.
- There are two primary routes of persuasion: central route and peripheral route.
- Cognitive dissonance occurs when an individual simultaneously holds two attitudes or thoughts that contradict each other. There are four ways to reduce the dissonance.

AP KEY TERMS

social psychology
attitudes
central route processing
peripheral route processing
cognitive dissonance
social cognition
schemas
central traits
attribution theory
situational causes (of behavior)
dispositional causes (of behavior)
halo effect
assumed-similarity bias
self-serving bias
fundamental attribution error

AP TEST PRACTICE

Section I: Multiple Choice

1. Having a famous celebrity promote a new car is using what type of persuasion?
   A. Peripheral route
   B. Central route
   C. Cognitive dissonance
   D. Dispositional
   E. Situational

2. Beau stopped suddenly while walking down the hallway. The tendency to attribute his behavior to a dispositional cause is known as the
   A. assumed-similarity bias
   B. fundamental attribution error
   C. self-serving bias
   D. halo-effect
   E. ingroup bias

3. In Festinger's study on cognitive dissonance, two groups were paid to describe a boring task as interesting to other participants. One group was paid $1 and the other group was paid $20. Which group was the experimental group?
   A. Participants who told the truth
   B. Participants who received $20
   C. Participants who received $1
   D. Participants who did a boring task
   E. Participants who were lied to

Section II: Free Response

Sonya wants to start a new mental health club at school. She needs to start by finding an advisor who is organized. Immediately she thinks of her psychology teacher who is always happy and outgoing. To promote the club, she plans to use posters with famous celebrities who are willing to share their story about mental health.

Explain how the following concepts relate to Sonya starting the new mental health club.
- Fundamental attribution error
- Culture and attribution errors
- Halo effect
- Peripheral route to persuasion

Module 53
Social Influence and Groups

You have just transferred to a new college and are attending your first class. When the professor enters, your fellow classmates instantly rise, bow to the professor, and then stand quietly with their hands behind their backs. You've never encountered such behavior, and it makes no sense to you. Is it more likely that you will (1) jump up to join the rest of the class or (2) remain seated?

Most people would probably choose the first option. As you undoubtedly know from your own experience, pressures to conform to others' behavior can be painfully strong and can bring about changes in behavior that otherwise never would have occurred.

Conformity pressures are just one type of social influence. **Social influence** is the process by which social groups and individuals exert pressure on an individual, either deliberately or unintentionally.

Social influence is so powerful in part because groups and other people generally play a central role in our lives. As defined by social psychologists, **groups** consist of two or more people who (1) interact with one another; (2) perceive themselves as part of a group; and (3) are interdependent—that is, the events that affect one group member affect other members, and the behavior of members has significant consequences for the success of the group in meeting its goals.

Groups develop and hold *norms*, informal beliefs, expectations, and standards about what is appropriate behavior for group members. Norms not only tell us how people in a group should behave ("wearing pink is fashionable this year") but also what members shouldn't do ("under no circumstances wear black"). Group members understand that not adhering to group norms can result in retaliation from other group members, ranging from being ignored to being overtly derided or even being rejected or excluded by the group. Thus, people conform to meet the beliefs and expectations of the group (Miles, Schaufeli, & van den Bos, 2011; Becker, Brackbill, & Centola, 2017).

Groups exert considerable social pressure over individuals. We'll consider three types of social pressure: conformity, compliance, and obedience.

Conformity: Following What Others Do

Conformity is a change in behavior or attitudes brought about by a desire to follow the beliefs or standards of other people. Subtle or even unspoken social pressure results in conformity.

The classic demonstration of pressure to conform comes from a series of studies carried out in the 1950s by Solomon Asch (Asch, 1951). In the experiments, the participants thought they were taking part in a test of perceptual skills with six other people. The experimenter showed the participants one card with three lines of varying length and a second card that had a fourth line that matched one of the first three (see Figure 1). The task was seemingly straightforward: Each of the participants had to announce aloud which of the first three lines was identical in length to the "standard" line on the second card. Because the correct answer was always obvious, the task seemed easy to the participants.

Indeed, because the participants all agreed on the first few trials, the procedure appeared to be simple. But then something odd began to happen. From the perspective of the participant in the group who answered last on each trial, all the answers of the

AP® LEARNING TARGETS

- Identify the contributions of key researchers in the areas of conformity, compliance, and obedience.

- Explain how individuals respond to expectations of others, including groupthink, conformity, and obedience to authority.

- Describe the structure and function of different kinds of group behavior.

- Predict the impact of the presence of others on individual behavior.

social influence The process by which social groups and individuals exert pressure on an individual, either deliberately or unintentionally. (Module 53)

group Two or more people who interact with one another, perceive themselves as part of a group, and are interdependent. (Module 53)

Study Alert
The distinction between the three types of social pressure—conformity, compliance, and obedience—depends on the nature and strength of the social pressure brought to bear on a person.

conformity A change in behavior or attitudes brought about by a desire to follow the beliefs or standards of other people. (Module 53)

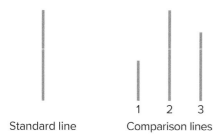

Standard line   Comparison lines

FIGURE 1 Which of the three comparison lines is the same length as the "standard" line?

status The social standing of someone in a group. (Module 53)

social supporter A group member whose dissenting views make nonconformity to the group easier. (Module 53)

first six participants seemed to be wrong–in fact, unanimously wrong. And this pattern persisted. Over and over again, the first six participants provided answers that contradicted what the last participant believed to be correct. The last participant faced the dilemma of whether to follow his or her own perceptions or follow the group by repeating the answer everyone else was giving.

As you might have guessed, this experiment was more contrived than it appeared. The first six participants were actually confederates (paid employees of the experimenter) who had been instructed to give unanimously erroneous answers in many of the trials. And the study had nothing to do with perceptual skills. Instead, the issue under investigation was conformity.

Asch found that in about one-third of the trials, the participants conformed to the unanimous but erroneous group answer; about 75% of all participants conformed at least once. However, he found strong individual differences. Some participants conformed nearly all the time, whereas others never did.

CONFORMITY CONCLUSIONS

Since Asch's pioneering work, literally hundreds of studies have examined conformity, and we now know a great deal about the phenomenon. Significant findings focus on:

- *The characteristics of the group.* The more attractive a group appears to its members, the greater its ability to produce conformity. Furthermore, a person's relative **status,** the social standing of someone within a group, is critical: The lower a person's status in the group, the greater groups' power over that person's behavior (Hogg & Hains, 2001).

- *The situation in which the individual is responding.* Conformity is considerably higher when people must respond publicly than it is when they can do so privately, as the founders of the United States noted when they authorized secret ballots in voting.

- *The kind of task.* People working on ambiguous tasks and questions (those with no clear answer) are more susceptible to social pressure. When asked to give an opinion on something, such as what type of clothing is fashionable, a person will more likely yield to conformist pressures than he or she will if asked a question of fact. In addition, tasks at which an individual is less competent than others in the group make conformity more likely. For example, a person who is an infrequent computer user may feel pressure to conform to an opinion about computer brands when in a group of experienced computer users.

- *Unanimity of the group.* Groups that unanimously support a position show the most pronounced conformity pressures. But what about the case in which people with dissenting views have an ally in the group, known as a **social supporter,** who agrees with them? Having just one person present who shares the minority point of view is sufficient to reduce conformity pressures (Goodwin, Costa, & Adonu, 2004; Levine & Moreland, 2006).

GROUPTHINK: CAVING IN TO CONFORMITY

Although we usually think of conformity in terms of our individual relations with others, in some instances, conformity pressures in organizations can lead to disastrous effects with long-term consequences. One classic example from 2003 concerns the space shuttle *Columbia* and the engineers who had to consider whether insulation that slammed into the space shuttle during takeoff would pose danger during landing. In fact, despite misgivings on the part of some engineers, a strong consensus emerged among them that the insulation would not impair the landing. Ultimately, that consensus proved wrong: The shuttle came apart as it attempted to land, killing all the astronauts on board (Schwartz & Wald, 2003; Mintz & Wayne, 2014).

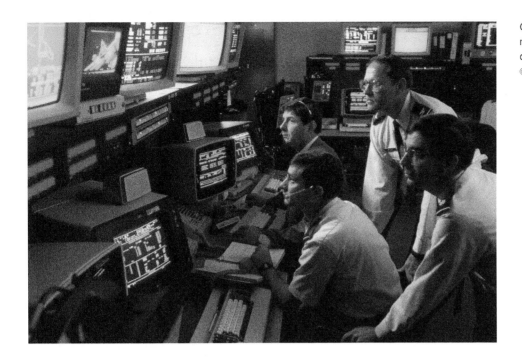

Groupthink may explain the poor decision making of NASA engineers that led to the destruction of the space shuttle *Columbia*.
©Jim Sugar/Corbis/Getty Images

How could they have made such a poor decision?

A phenomenon known as groupthink may provide an explanation. **Groupthink** is a type of thinking in which group members share such a strong motivation to achieve consensus that they lose the ability to critically evaluate alternative points of view. Groupthink is most likely to occur when a popular or powerful leader is surrounded by people of lower status—which is obviously the case with any U.S. president and his advisers but is also true for leaders in a variety of other organizations.

Groupthink may have been a partial cause of numerous questionable decisions and conclusions in the political and business worlds. For example, the United States invading Iraq or the consensus among media experts that Hilary Clinton would beat Donald Trump in the 2016 presidential election can be seen at least in part as a result of groupthink (Henningsen, Henningsen, & Eden, 2006; Baumeister, Ainsworth, & Vohs, 2015).

Groupthink typically leads to poor decisions. Groups limit the list of possible solutions to just a few, and they spend relatively little time considering any alternatives once the leader seems to be leaning toward a particular solution. In addition, groups may fall prey to *entrapment*, a circumstance in which commitments to a failing point of view or course of action are increased to justify investments in time and energy that have already been made (Turner, Pratkanis, & Struckman, 2007; Willis, 2017).

Ultimately, group members may completely ignore information that challenges a developing consensus. Because historical research suggests that many disastrous decisions reflect groupthink, it is important for groups to be on guard (Chapman, 2006; Packer, 2009).

groupthink A type of thinking in which group members share such a strong motivation to achieve consensus that they lose the ability to critically evaluate alternative points of view. (Module 53)

PsychTech

Through the use of Facebook, Twitter, and other social media, social norms can develop and be rapidly communicated to others.

CONFORMITY TO SOCIAL ROLES

Another way in which conformity influences behavior is through social roles. *Social roles* are the expectations for people who occupy a given social position. For example, we expect that the role of "student" comprises behaviors such as studying, listening to an instructor, and attending class. Similarly, we expect that taxi drivers will know their way around a city and be able to find the quickest route to where we are going. Like a theatrical role, social roles tell us what behavior is associated with a given position.

In some cases, though, social roles influence us so profoundly that we engage in behavior in ways that are atypical for us. This fact was brought home in a classic experiment conducted by Philip Zimbardo and colleagues. In the study, the researchers set up a mock prison complete with cells, solitary confinement cubicles, and a small recreation area. The researchers then advertised for participants who were willing to spend 2 weeks in a study of prison life. Once they identified the study participants, a flip of a coin designated who would be prisoners and who would be prison guards. Neither prisoners nor guards were told how to fulfill their roles (Zimbardo, Maslach, & Haney, 2000; Zimbardo, 2007).

After just a few days in this mock prison, the students assigned to be guards became abusive to the prisoners by waking them at odd hours and subjecting them to arbitrary punishment. They withheld food from the prisoners and forced them to perform hard labor. On the other hand, the students assigned to the prisoner role soon became docile and submissive to the guards. They became extremely demoralized, and one slipped into a depression so severe he was released after just a few days. In fact, after only 6 days of captivity, the remaining prisoners' reactions became so extreme that the study was ended.

The experiment (which, it's important to note, drew criticism on both methodological and ethical grounds) provided a clear lesson: Conforming to a social role can have a powerful consequence on the behavior of even normal, well-adjusted people and induce them to change their behavior in sometimes undesirable ways. This phenomenon may explain how the situation in 2004 in which U.S. Army guards at the Iraqi Abu Ghraib prison found themselves could have led to their abusive behavior toward the prisoners (Haney & Zimbardo, 2009; Post, 2011; Coultas & van Leeuwen, 2015).

Compliance: Submitting to Direct Social Pressure

When we refer to conformity, we usually mean a phenomenon in which the social pressure is subtle or indirect. But in some situations, social pressure is much more obvious with direct, explicit pressure to endorse a particular point of view or behave in a certain way. **Compliance** is behavior that occurs in response to direct social pressure.

Several specific techniques represent attempts to gain compliance. Those frequently employed include:

compliance Behavior that occurs in response to direct social pressure. (Module 53)

- *Foot-in-the-door technique.* The use of the *foot-in-the-door technique* begins when someone asks a target to comply with a small, trivial request. Because such a request is easy to fulfill, the likelihood that the target of the request will comply is high. Later, though, the target is asked to comply with a significantly larger request related to the first one. It turns out that compliance with the second request increases substantially when the target has first agreed to the initial, smaller request.

  Researchers first demonstrated the foot-in-the-door phenomenon in a study in which experimenters went door to door asking residents to sign a petition in favor of safe driving (Freedman & Fraser, 1966). Almost everyone complied with that small, easy-to-agree-to request. However, a few weeks later, different experimenters contacted the residents and made a request that took considerably more effort, asking residents to erect a huge sign on their front lawns that read, "Drive Carefully." The results were clear: 55% of those who had initially signed the petition agreed to the request to put up a sign, whereas only 17% of those in a control group who initially had not been asked to sign the petition agreed to put up a sign.

  Why does the foot-in-the-door technique work? For one reason, consideration of the small request may lead to an interest in the topic of the request or issue; taking an action—any action—makes the individual more committed to the issue, thereby increasing the likelihood of future compliance. Another explanation revolves around people's self-perceptions. By complying with the initial request, individuals may come to see themselves as people who provide help when asked. Then, when confronted with the larger request, they agree in order to maintain the kind of consistency in attitudes and behavior that we described earlier. Although we don't know which of these two explanations is more accurate, it is clear that the foot-in-the-door strategy is effective (Bloom, McBride, & Pollak, 2006; Guéguen et al., 2008).

The persuasive techniques identified by social psychologists can be seen in practice at auto dealerships.
©kzenon/Getty Images

- *Door-in-the-face technique.* A fund-raiser asks for a $1,000 contribution. You laughingly refuse and tell her that the amount is way out of your league. She then asks for a $10 contribution. How would you react? If you are like most people, you'll probably be a lot more compliant than you would be if she hadn't asked for the huge contribution first. In this tactic, called the *door-in-the-face technique*, someone makes a large request, expects it to be refused, and follows it with a smaller one. This strategy, which is the opposite of the foot-in-the-door approach, has also proved to be effective (Dolinski, 2011; Cantarero, Gamian-Wilk, & Dolinski, 2017).

  In a research study that demonstrates the success of this approach, experimenters stopped college students on the street and asked them to agree to a substantial favor—acting as unpaid counselors for juvenile delinquents 2 hours a week for 2 years (Cialdini et al., 1975). Unsurprisingly, no one agreed to make such an enormous commitment. But when they were later asked the considerably smaller favor of taking a group of delinquents on a 2-hour trip to the zoo, 50% of the people complied. In comparison, only 17% of a control group of participants who had not first received the larger request agreed.

  The use of this technique is widespread. You may have tried it at some point yourself by perhaps by asking your parents for a large increase in your allowance and later settling for less. Similarly, television writers, by sometimes sprinkling their scripts with obscenities that they know network censors will cut out, hope to keep other key phrases intact (Cialdini & Sagarin, 2005).

- *That's-not-all technique.* In this technique, a salesperson offers you a deal at an inflated price. But immediately after the initial offer, the salesperson offers an incentive, discount, or bonus to clinch the deal.

  Although it sounds transparent, this practice can be quite effective. In one study, the experimenters set up a booth and sold cupcakes for 75¢ each. In one condition, the experimenters directly told customers that the price was 75¢. In another condition, they told customers that the price was originally $1 but had been reduced to 75¢. As we might predict, more people bought cupcakes at the "reduced" price—even though it was identical to the price in the other experimental condition (Burger, Reed, & DeCesare, 1999; Pratkanis, 2007).

- *Not-so-free sample.* If you ever receive a free sample, keep in mind that it comes with a psychological cost. Although they may not couch it in these terms, salespeople who provide samples to potential customers do so to bring the norm of reciprocity into play. The *norm of reciprocity* is the social standard that we should treat other people as they treat us. (It's a variant of the Golden Rule we learn as kids: "Do unto others as they will do unto you.") It's a strong cultural standard: When someone does something nice for us, we tend to feel obligated to return the favor. In the case of the *not-so-free sample*, receiving a free sample activates the norm of reciprocity and makes us feel that we should return the favor—in the form of a purchase (Cialdini, 2006; Park & Antonioni, 2007; Burger, 2009).

industrial-organizational (I/O)
psychology The branch of psychology
focusing on work- and job-related issues,
including worker motivation,
satisfaction, safety, and productivity.
(Module 53)

obedience A change in behavior in
response to the commands of others.
(Module 53)

Companies seeking to sell their products to consumers often use the techniques identified by social psychologists for promoting compliance. But employers also use them to bring about compliance and raise employees' productivity in the workplace. In fact, **industrial-organizational (I/O) psychology,** a close cousin to social psychology, considers issues such as worker motivation, satisfaction, safety, and productivity. I/O psychologists also focus on the operation and design of organizations; they ask questions such as how decision making can be improved in large organizations and how the fit between workers and their jobs can be maximized.

Obedience: Following Direct Orders

The compliance techniques that we've been discussing share a common thread: They are used to gently lead people toward agreement with a request. In some cases, however, requests are made in a strong manner. In fact, they're hardly requests at all but rather commands, aimed at producing obedience. **Obedience** is a change in behavior in response to the commands of others. Although obedience is considerably less common than conformity and compliance, it does occur in several specific kinds of relationships. For example, we may show obedience to our bosses, teachers, or parents merely because of the power they hold to reward or punish us.

To acquire an understanding of obedience, consider for a moment how you might respond if a stranger said to you:

I've devised a new way of improving memory. All I need is for you to teach people a list of words and then give them a test. The test procedure requires only that you give learners a shock each time they make a mistake on the test. To administer the shocks, you will use a "shock generator" that gives shocks ranging from 15 to 450 volts. You can see that the switches are labeled from "slight shock" through "danger: severe shock" at the top level, where there are three red Xs. But don't worry; although the shocks may be painful, they will cause no permanent damage.

Presented with this situation, you would be likely to think that neither you nor anyone else would go along with the stranger's unusual request. Clearly, it lies outside the bounds of what we consider good sense.

Or does it? Suppose the stranger asking for your help was a psychologist conducting an experiment. Or suppose the request came from your teacher, your employer, or your military commander—all people in authority with a seemingly legitimate reason for the request.

If you still believe it's unlikely that you would comply, think again. The situation presented above describes a classic experiment conducted by social psychologist Stanley Milgram in the 1960s. In the study, an experimenter told participants to give increasingly stronger shocks to another person as part of a study on learning (see Figure 2). In reality, the experiment had nothing to do with learning; the real issue under consideration was the degree to which participants would comply with the experimenter's requests. In fact, the "learner" supposedly receiving the shocks was a confederate who never really received any punishment (Milgram, 2005; Maher, 2015; Griggs, 2017).

Most people who hear a description of Milgram's experiment feel it is unlikely that *any* participant would give the maximum level of shock—or, for that matter, any shock at all. Even a group of psychiatrists to whom the situation was described predicted that fewer than 2% of the participants would fully comply and administer the strongest shocks.

However, the actual results contradicted both experts' and nonexperts' predictions. Some 65% of the participants eventually used the highest setting on the shock generator—450 volts—to shock the learner. This obedience occurred even though the learner, who had mentioned at the start of the experiment that he had a heart condition, demanded to be released, screaming, "Let me out of here! Let me out of here!

FIGURE 2 This fearsome "shock generator" led participants to believe they were administering electric shocks to another person, who was connected to the generator by electrodes attached to the skin.

(Both): From the film OBEDIENCE © 1968 by Stanley Milgram, © renewed 1993 by Alexandra Milgram. Permission granted by Alexandra Milgram.

My heart's bothering me. Let me out of here!" Despite the learner's pleas, most participants continued to administer the shocks.

Why did so many individuals comply with the experimenter's demands? The participants, who were extensively interviewed after the experiment, said they obeyed primarily because they believed that the experimenter would be responsible for any potential ill effects that befell the learner. The participants accepted the experimenter's orders, then, because they thought that they personally could not be held accountable for their actions–they could always blame the experimenter (Blass, 2004; Kaposi, 2017).

From the perspective of...

An Educator Student obedience in the elementary and secondary classroom is a major issue for many teachers. How might you promote student obedience in the classroom?

©Andersen Ross/Blend Images/Getty Images

Most participants in the Milgram experiment said later they felt the knowledge gained from the study outweighed the discomfort they may have felt. However, the experiment has been criticized for creating an extremely trying set of circumstances for the participants, thereby raising serious ethical concerns. Undoubtedly, the same experiment could not be conducted today because of ethical considerations (Perry, 2013).

Other critics have suggested that Milgram's methods were ineffective in creating a situation that actually mirrored real-world obedience. For example, how often are people placed in a situation in which someone orders them to continue hurting a victim while the victim's protests are ignored (Blass, 2004; Werhane et al., 2013)?

Despite these concerns, Milgram's research remains the strongest laboratory demonstration of obedience. And partial replications of Milgram's work, conducted in an ethically defensible way, find similar results, which adds credence to the original work (Blass, 2009; Burger, 2009; Gibson, 2013).

Study Alert

Because of its graphic demonstration of obedience to authority, the Milgram experiment is one of the most famous and influential studies in social psychology.

Furthermore, we need only consider actual instances of obedience to authority to witness some frightening real-life parallels. For instance, after World War II, the major defense that Nazi officers gave to excuse their participation in atrocities during the war was that they were "only following orders." Milgram's experiment, which was motivated in part by his desire to explain the behavior of everyday Germans during World War II, forces us to ask ourselves this question: Would we be able to withstand the intense power of authority?

AP MODULE 53: SOCIAL INFLUENCE AND GROUPS

AP SUMMARY

- Compliance is behavior that results from direct social pressure. Specific techniques for gaining compliance include: foot-in-the-door, door-in-the-face, that's-not-all, and not-so-free sample.
- Solomon Asch conducted the line experiment and found about 75% of participants conformed at least once.
- Stanley Milgram conducted the shock experiment and found 65% of participants would administer the highest level of shock when told to do so by an authority figure. Ethical concerns have been raised with this experiment.
- Philip Zimbardo conducted the prison experiment to study the power of conforming to social roles. The experiment had to be called off after only 6 days.
- Conformity refers to changes in behavior or attitudes that result from a desire to follow the beliefs or standards of others. Whether individuals conform depends on the characteristics of the group, the situation, the kind of task, and the unanimity of the group.
- Groupthink occurs when group members share such a strong motivation to achieve consensus that they lose the ability to critically evaluate alternative points of view. It often leads to poor decisions.
- Obedience is a change in behavior in response to the commands of others.
- Social influence is the area of social psychology concerned with situations in which the actions of an individual or group affects the behavior of others. Groups can exert social pressure over individuals.
- Groups develop and hold norms. Failure to follow these norms can lead to rejection.
- The norm of reciprocity is the social standard that we should treat other people as they treat us.

AP KEY TERMS

social influence	groupthink
group	compliance
conformity	industrial-organizational
status	(I/O) psychology
social supporter	obedience

AP TEST PRACTICE

Section I: Multiple Choice

1. Who conducted an experiment with significant ethical concerns because participants thought they harmed others?
   A. Philip Zimbardo
   B. Leon Festinger
   C. Solomon Asch
   D. Kitty Genovese
   E. Stanley Milgram

2. Leah doesn't want to see the movie her friends selected. To keep everyone happy she decides to go along with the group without voicing her opinion. This is an example of
   A. compliance
   B. obedience
   C. groupthink
   D. norm of reciprocity
   E. cognitive dissonance

3. Students were asked to sign a petition to start a new club at school. After signing, they were asked to provide a donation to help with the startup of the club. This is an example of the
   A. foot-in-the-door technique
   B. door-in-the-face technique
   C. that's-not-all technique
   D. not-so-free sample
   E. norm of reciprocity

Section II: Free Response

Jay recently moved and will attend a new school where he must wear a uniform that he dislikes. Explain how the following concepts could influence Jay's decision to wear the uniform.
- Compliance
- Conformity
- Obedience
- Cognitive dissonance

Module 54
Prejudice and Discrimination

What do you think when someone says, "He's African American," "She's Chinese," or "That's a woman driver"?

If you're like most people, you'll probably automatically form some sort of impression of what each person is like. Most likely your impression is based on a **stereotype,** a set of generalized beliefs and expectations about a specific group and its members. Stereotypes grow out of our tendency to categorize and organize the vast amount of information we encounter in our everyday lives. All stereotypes share the common feature of oversimplifying the world: We view individuals not in terms of their unique, personal characteristics but also in terms of characteristics we attribute to all the members of a particular group.

Stereotypes can lead to **prejudice,** a negative (or positive) evaluation of a group and its members. For instance, racial prejudice occurs when a member of a racial group is evaluated in terms of race and not because of his or her own characteristics or abilities. Although prejudice can be positive ("I love the Irish"), social psychologists have focused on understanding the roots of negative prejudice ("I hate immigrants").

Common stereotypes and forms of prejudice involve race, religion, ethnicity, and gender. Over the years, various groups have been called "lazy" or "shrewd" or "cruel" with varying degrees of regularity by those who are not members of that group. Even today, despite major progress toward reducing legally sanctioned forms of prejudice, such as school segregation, stereotypes remain (Hunt, Seifert, & Armenta, 2006; Devos, 2011; Bhatia, 2017).

Even people who on the surface appear to be unprejudiced may harbor hidden prejudice. For example, when white participants in experiments are shown faces on a computer screen so rapidly that they cannot consciously perceive the faces, they react more negatively to black than to white faces–an example of what has been called *modern racism* (Pearson, Dovidio, & Pratto, 2007; Blanton, Jaccard, & Burrows, 2015).

Stereotypes can have harmful consequences because acting on stereotypes results in discrimination. **Discrimination** is behavior directed toward individuals on the basis of their membership in a particular group. Discrimination can lead to exclusion from jobs, neighborhoods, and educational opportunities, and it may result in lower salaries and benefits for members of specific groups. Discrimination can also result in more favorable treatment to favored groups–for example, when an employer hires a job applicant of his or her own racial group because of the applicant's race (Pager & Shepherd, 2008; Leskinen, Rabelo, & Cortina, 2015).

Stereotyping not only leads to overt discrimination but also can cause members of stereotyped groups to behave in ways that reflect the stereotype through a phenomenon known as the *self-fulfilling prophecy.* Self-fulfilling prophecies are expectations about the occurrence of a future event or behavior that act to increase the likelihood the event or behavior will occur. For example, if people think that members of a specific group lack ambition, they may treat them in a way that actually brings about a lack of ambition. Furthermore, it can lead to a self-perpetuating phenomenon that we discuss next (Madon, Willard, & Guyll, 2006; Tappin, McKay, & Abrams, 2017).

The Foundations of Prejudice

No one has ever been born disliking a specific racial, religious, or ethnic group. People learn to hate in much the same way that they learn the alphabet.

AP® LEARNING TARGETS

- Define intelligence and list characteristics of how psychologists measure intelligence.

- Anticipate the impact of self-fulfilling prophecy on behavior.

- Describe processes that contribute to differential treatment of group members.

stereotype A set of generalized beliefs and expectations about a particular group and its members. (Module 54)

prejudice A negative (or positive) evaluation of a particular group and its members. (Module 54)

discrimination Behavior directed toward individuals on the basis of their membership in a particular group. (Module 54)

Study Alert
Remember that *prejudice* relates to *attitudes* about a group and its members, whereas *discrimination* relates to *behavior* directed to a group and its members.

According to *observational learning approaches* to stereotyping and prejudice, the behavior of parents, other adults, and peers shapes children's feelings about members of various groups. For instance, bigoted parents may commend their children for expressing prejudiced attitudes. Likewise, young children learn prejudice by imitating the behavior of adult models. Such learning starts at an early age: Children as young as 6 months judge others according to their skin color, and by 3 years of age, they begin to show preferences for members of their own race (Dovidio & Gaertner, 2006; Ponterotto, Utsey, & Pedersen, 2006; Bronson & Merryman, 2009).

The mass media also provide information about stereotypes not just for children but for adults as well. Even today, some television shows and movies portray Italians as Mafia-like mobsters, Jews as greedy bankers, and African Americans as promiscuous or lazy. When such inaccurate portrayals are the primary source of information about minority groups, they can lead to the development and maintenance of unfavorable stereotypes (Do, 2006; Scharrer & Ramasubramanian, 2015).

Other explanations of prejudice and discrimination focus on how being a member of a specific group helps to magnify one's sense of self-esteem. According to *social identity theory*, we use group membership as a source of pride and self-worth. Social identity theory suggests that people tend to be ethnocentric, viewing the world from their own perspective and judging others in terms of their group membership. Slogans such as "gay pride" and "Black is beautiful" illustrate that the groups to which we belong give us a sense of self-respect (Tajfel & Turner, 2004; Hogg, 2006; Kahn et al., 2017).

However, the use of group membership to provide social respect produces an unfortunate outcome. In an effort to maximize our sense of self-esteem, we may come to think that our own group (our *ingroup*) is better than groups to which we don't belong (our *outgroups*). Consequently, we inflate the positive aspects of our ingroup— and, at the same time, devalue outgroups. Ultimately, we come to view members of outgroups as inferior to members of our ingroup (Tajfel & Turner, 2004). The end result is prejudice toward members of groups of which we are not a part.

Neither the observational learning approach nor the social identity approach provides a full explanation for stereotyping and prejudice. For instance, some psychologists argue that prejudice results when there is perceived competition for scarce societal resources. Thus, when competition exists for jobs or housing, members of majority groups may believe (however unjustly or inaccurately) that minority group members are hindering their efforts to attain their goals; this belief can lead to prejudice. In addition, other explanations for prejudice emphasize human cognitive limitations that

Like father, like son: Social learning approaches to stereotyping and prejudice suggest that attitudes and behaviors toward members of minority groups are learned through the observation of parents and other individuals. How can this cycle be broken?
©Barbara Burnes/Science Source

lead us to categorize people on the basis of visually conspicuous physical features such as race, sex, and ethnic group. Such categorization can lead to the development of stereotypes and, ultimately, to discriminatory behavior (Weeks & Lupfer, 2004; Hugenberg & Sacco, 2008; Yoo & Pituc, 2013).

The most recent approach to understanding prejudice comes from an increasingly important area in social psychology: social neuroscience. **Social neuroscience** seeks to identify the neurological basis of social behavior. It looks at how we can illuminate our understanding of groups, interpersonal relations, and emotions by understanding their neuroscientific underpinnings (Harmon-Jones & Winkielman, 2007; Todorov, Fiske, & Prentice, 2011; Kasemsap, 2017).

In one example of the value of social neuroscience approaches, researchers examined activation of the *amygdala,* the structure in the brain that relates to emotion-evoking stimuli and situations, while people viewed white and black faces. Because the amygdala is especially responsive to threatening, unusual, or highly arousing stimuli, the researchers hypothesized greater activation of the amygdala during exposure to black faces due to negative cultural associations with racial minorities (Lieberman, 2007; Nelson, 2013).

As you can see in *Neuroscience in Your Life,* the hypothesis was confirmed: The amygdala showed more activation when participants saw a black face than when they saw a white one. Because both blacks and whites were participants in the study, it is unlikely that the amygdala activation was simply the result of the novelty of viewing members of a racial minority. Instead, the findings suggest that culturally learned societal messages about race led to the brain activation.

social neuroscience The subfield of social psychology that seeks to identify the neurological basis of social behavior. (Module 54)

AP NEUROSCIENCE IN YOUR LIFE: THE PREJUDICED BRAIN

Problems related to racial prejudice are ongoing in the United States. To provide insight into these problems, social neuroscientists have begun to examine how we process social information in the brain and how that processing relates to stereotypes and prejudice.

To examine a potential relationship between racial differences and threat detection, social neuroscientists scanned participants' brains while asking them to look at photos of black or white individuals, determine whether the person in the photo had a weapon, and respond by "shooting" the person in the photo if they thought a gun was present. Participants, who were white, Asian, Hispanic, and of unknown races. more quickly decided to shoot and showed greater brain activity in the parietal and visual cortexes for armed blacks than for armed whites.

In addition, as shown in the images below, greater connectivity occurred (shown in purple) between the amygdala, parietal cortex, visual cortex, and other areas when participants viewed armed blacks than when they viewed armed whites. These results demonstrate possible neural correlates contributing to the greater likelihood of treating blacks as more dangerous than whites (Senholzi et al., 2015).

AP SKILL: EXPLAIN BEHAVIOR IN AUTHENTIC CONTEXT / SCIENTIFIC INVESTIGATION

1. What types of employment might benefit from using brain scans to identify prejudice?

2. What questions do you have about the sample besides race?

Source: Adapted from Senholzi, K. B., Depue, B. E., Correll, J., Banich, M. T., & Ito, T. A. (2015). Brain activation underlying threat detection to targets of different races. *Society for Neuroscience, 10*(6), 651–662. doi: 10.1080/17470919.2015.1091380

Measuring Prejudice and Discrimination: The Implicit Association Test

Could you be prejudiced and not even know it? Probably yes, according to the researchers who developed a test that reveals hidden prejudice.

The *Implicit Association Test*, or *IAT*, is an ingenious measure of prejudice that permits a more accurate assessment of people's discrimination between members of different groups.

The IAT uses the fact that people's automatic, instant reactions often provide the most valid indicator of what they actually believe. The test asks people questions that assess the degree to which they associate members of target groups (say, African Americans versus whites) with positive stimuli (such as a puppy) versus negative stimuli (such as a funeral). The test is based on the fact that growing up in a particular culture teaches us to unconsciously associate members of particular groups with positive or negative qualities, and we tend to absorb associations about those groups that reflect the culture without even being aware of it (Aikawa & Fujii, 2011; Blanton, Jaccard, & Burrows, 2015; Roberts, Neate, & Gierasch, 2017).

The results of the IAT show that almost 90% of test-takers have an implicit prowhite bias, and more than two-thirds of non-Arab, non-Muslim volunteers display implicit biases against Arab Muslims. Moreover, more than 80% of heterosexuals display an implicit bias against gays and lesbians (Lane et al., 2007).

So, of course, having an implicit bias does not mean that people will overtly discriminate, which is a criticism that has been made of the test. Yet it does mean that the cultural lessons to which we are exposed have a considerable unconscious influence on us. (If you would like to try a version of the IAT yourself, there is a sample test at https://implicit.harvard.edu/implicit. You may well be surprised at the results.)

Study Alert
Remember that the IAT allows measurement of attitudes about which people might not be consciously aware as well as attitudes they wish to keep hidden from others.

Reducing the Consequences of Prejudice and Discrimination

How can we diminish the effects of prejudice and discrimination? Psychologists have developed several strategies that have proved effective.

- *Increasing contact between the target of stereotyping and the holder of the stereotype.* Research consistently shows that increasing the amount of interaction between people can reduce negative stereotyping. But only certain kinds of contact are likely to reduce prejudice and discrimination. Situations in which contact is relatively intimate, the individuals are of equal status, or participants must cooperate with one another or are dependent on one another are more likely to reduce stereotyping. On the other hand, even virtual contact via social media may be sufficient to improve intergroup relations (Tropp & Pettigrew, 2005; Pettigrew & Tropp, 2006; White, Harvey, & Abu-Rayya, 2015).

- *Making values and norms against prejudice more conspicuous.* Sometimes just reminding people about the values they already hold regarding equality and fair treatment of others is enough to reduce discrimination. Similarly, people who hear others making strong, vehement antiracist statements are subsequently more likely to strongly condemn racism. Furthermore, one study found that even a short, 10-minute conversation with voters asking them to recall a time when they were judged negatively and unfairly was sufficient to reduce prejudice toward transgender people that lasted 3 months (Tropp & Bianchi, 2006; Rutland & Killen, 2015; Broockman & Kalla, 2016).

- *Providing information about the targets of stereotyping.* Probably the most direct means of changing stereotypical and discriminatory attitudes is education: teaching people to be more aware of the positive characteristics of targets of stereotyping. For instance, when the meaning of puzzling behavior is explained to people who hold stereotypes, they may come to appreciate the actual significance of the behavior (Isbell & Tyler, 2003; Banks, 2006; Nagda, Tropp, & Paluck, 2006).

- *Reducing stereotype threat.* Social psychologist Claude Steele suggests that many African Americans suffer from *stereotype vulnerability*, obstacles to performance that stem from their awareness of society's stereotypes regarding minority group members. He argues that African American students too often receive instruction from teachers who doubt their students' abilities and who set up remedial programs to assist their students. As a result of their teachers' (as well as society's) low expectations for their performance, African American students may come to accept society's stereotypes and come to believe that they are likely to fail (Aronson & Steele, 2005; Nussbaum & Steele, 2007; Aronson & Dee, 2012).

  Such beliefs can have devastating effects. When confronted with an academic task, African American students may fear that their performance will simply confirm society's negative stereotypes. The immediate consequence of this fear is anxiety that hampers performance. But the long-term consequences may be even worse: Doubting their ability to perform successfully in academic environments, African Americans may decide that the risks of failure are so great it is not worth the effort even to attempt to do well. Ultimately, they may "disidentify" with academic success by minimizing the importance of academic endeavors (Stone, 2002; Lombaard & Naudé, 2017).

  However, Steele's analysis suggests that African Americans may be able to overcome their predicament. Specifically, schools can design intervention programs to train minority group members about their vulnerability to stereotypes and provide them with self-affirmation that reinforces their confidence in their abilities and thereby inoculates them against the fear and doubt triggered by negative stereotypes (Cohen et al., 2006; Wilson, 2006; Shnabel et al., 2013).

- *Increasing the sense of social belonging of ethnic minority students.* Although almost every college student faces feelings of inadequacy and uncertainty about belonging at the start of college, such feelings are especially strong for members of groups who are underrepresented and have been the targets of prejudice and discrimination. However, research shows that a simple intervention in which members of minority groups are made to understand that feelings of inadequacy are not unique to them—and that such feelings usually diminish with time—can help minority students increase their sense of social belonging (Walton & Cohen, 2011; also see *Applying Psychology in the 21st Century*).

From the perspective of...

A Corrections Officer How might overt forms of prejudice and discrimination toward disadvantaged groups (such as African Americans) be reduced in a state or federal prison?

HELPING MORE WOMEN SUCCEED AS ENGINEERS

Majoring in a science, technology, engineering, or math (STEM) field is challenging for anyone but particularly so for women—not because women are less capable than men in these fields but because they face many additional obstacles that men don't. Chief among these is the stereotype that STEM fields are a male domain.

Female STEM students often encounter sexism, harassment, and hostility from their peers and even from their professors. In ways that are subtle and sometimes not so subtle, they are treated as if they are less capable than men and don't belong in their chosen field. Often women come to implicitly believe in these stereotypes themselves and to lose confidence in their own abilities. The result too often is that capable female students end up leaving STEM majors behind (Nosek, Banaji, & Greenwald, 2002; Dennehy et al., 2018).

Finding ways to overcome these obstacles and retain talented female students in STEM majors has therefore become an important priority of many colleges and universities. Compelling new research establishes how a relatively simple intervention is remarkably effective at achieving this goal: Pairing female STEM majors with female peer mentors. In the research, 150 incoming female engineering students were randomly paired with a female peer mentor, a male peer mentor, or no mentor for 1 year. The mentors received some training and kept a diary of their mentoring conversations, establishing that the male

©YinYang/Getty Images

mentors were as available and supportive as the female mentors. But they weren't equally effective. The female students paired with female (but not male) mentors reported a greater sense of belonging in engineering, self-efficacy, motivation, and intentions to pursue a career in engineering. They were also more likely to remain in the engineering major. Whereas 11% of the students without a mentor dropped out within that first year, *all* the students with a female mentor remained in the major—an astounding difference (Dennehy & Dasgupta, 2017).

The researchers emphasize that the key contribution of the female peer mentors was helping new female STEM undergraduates feel that they fit in and belonged. It's not about their ability; grades were in fact

not related to retention or career aspirations in their study. Feelings of belonging and confidence were, and this is what the female peer mentors reinforced. Moreover, the benefits persisted well beyond the conclusion of the mentoring period, showing up in the researchers' follow-ups throughout the second year. And these benefits are crucial, as women are most likely to withdraw from a STEM major during the first 2 years, so even a relatively short-term intervention of female peer mentoring can inoculate female students throughout this critical period.

What makes female peer mentors particularly effective at retaining female STEM students? It's not that they give better advice or care more or show greater empathy; the researchers found no evidence that their mentoring quality was better than that of men. Rather, the female mentors acted as role models. They reinforced to the incoming female STEM students that women do indeed belong in this field and that they could succeed. Beyond its important practical applications, this research provides a clear example of how social factors can be just as important determinants of success as native ability (Dennehy & Dasgupta, 2017; Dennehy et al., 2018).

> ### AP SKILL: SCIENTIFIC INVESTIGATION / DEFINE AND/OR APPLY CONCEPTS
>
> 1. What is the independent variable?
> 2. What terms are associated with lowering one's performance due to a negative belief?

AP SUMMARY

- Stereotype threat is the perceived risk of confirming a stereotype, which leads to lowered performance.
- Stereotypes for gender, race, and ethnic groups can lead to a self-fulfilling prophecy and lower performance.
- Prejudice is the negative (or positive) evaluation of a particular group and its members.

- Stereotypes are generalized beliefs and expectations about a group and its members.
- Discrimination is behavior directed toward individuals based on their membership in a particular group.
- According to observational learning approaches, children learn stereotyping and prejudice by observing the behavior of parents, other adults, and peers.

- Social identity theory suggests that group membership is used as a source of pride and self-worth, and this may lead people to be ethnocentric.
- To maximize our self-esteem, we may come to think that our own group (ingroup) is better than groups to which we don't belong (outgroup). We have a bias for our ingroup.
- Social neuroscientists examine the functioning of the brain and nervous system to understand the basis of prejudice.
- The Implicit Association Test (IAT) measures implicit (hidden) bias.
- Among the ways of reducing prejudice and discrimination are increasing contact, education, reducing stereotype threat, and increasing social belonging.

AP KEY TERMS

stereotype
prejudice
discrimination
social neuroscience

AP TEST PRACTICE

Section I: Multiple Choice

1. If people believe a certain group of people are lazy, they may treat them a particular way that brings out lazy behavior. This is an example of
   A. fundamental attribution error
   B. self-serving bias
   C. self-fulfilling prophecy
   D. stereotype
   E. obedience

2. What is the term for negative behavior directed toward someone based on their membership in a particular group?
   A. Implicit bias
   B. Ingroup bias
   C. Stereotype
   D. Discrimination
   E. Self-fulfilling prophecy

3. Cherry loves her school and attends lots of extracurricular events. She believes her school has the best fans in the area. Cherry's favoritism for her own school is an example of
   A. confirmation bias
   B. contact theory
   C. implicit bias
   D. ingroup bias
   E. rationalization

Section II: Free Response

A. A researcher has a hypothesis that biased expectations can influence others. Students were given an IQ test before school started. Then, the researcher randomly selected one class in which teachers were told they had "gifted" students (even though they didn't) and a second class in which teachers were given no information about their students. At the end of the school year students were given another IQ test. The researcher found that students in the class labeled as "gifted" had greater increases in their IQ scores.
   - What conclusion can researchers draw from this study?
   - Operationally define the dependent variable.
   - What makes the study experimental rather than correlational?

B. Explain how the following concepts could impact an individual student's test results.
   - Stereotype threat
   - Self-fulfilling prophecy
   - Circadian rhythm
   - Mnemonics

Module 55
Positive and Negative Social Behavior

AP® LEARNING TARGETS

- Predict the impact of the presence of others on individual behavior.

- Describe the variables that contribute to altruism and aggression.

- Describe the variables that contribute to attraction.

interpersonal attraction (or close relationship) Positive feelings for others; liking and loving. (Module 55)

Like philosophers and theologians, social psychologists have pondered the basic nature of humanity. Is it represented mainly by the violence and cruelty we see throughout the world, or does something special about human nature permit loving, considerate, unselfish, and even noble behavior as well?

We turn to two routes that social psychologists have followed in seeking answers to these questions. We first consider what they have learned about the sources of our attraction to others; we end with a look at two opposite sides of human behavior: aggression and helping.

Liking and Loving: Interpersonal Attraction and the Development of Relationships

Nothing is more important in most people's lives than their feelings for others. Consequently, it is not surprising that liking and loving have become a major focus of interest for social psychologists. Known more formally as the study of **interpersonal attraction or close relationships,** this area addresses the factors that lead to positive feelings for others.

HOW DO I LIKE THEE? LET ME COUNT THE WAYS

By far the greatest amount of research has focused on liking, probably because it is easier for investigators conducting short-term experiments to produce states of liking in strangers who have just met than to instigate and observe loving relationships over long periods. Consequently, research has given us a good deal of knowledge about the factors that initially attract two people to each other. The important factors social psychologists consider are the following:

- *Proximity.* If you live in a residence hall or an apartment, consider the friends you made when you first moved in. Chances are that you became friendliest with those who lived geographically nearest to you. In fact, this is one of the more firmly established findings in the research on interpersonal attraction: Proximity leads to liking (Burgoon et al., 2002; Smith & Weber, 2005; Semin & Garrido, 2013).

- *Mere exposure.* Repeated exposure to a person is often sufficient to produce attraction. Interestingly, repeated exposure to *any* stimulus–a person, picture, tweet, or virtually anything–usually makes us like the stimulus more. Becoming familiar with a person can evoke positive feelings; we then transfer the positive feelings stemming from familiarity to the person him- or herself. Of course, there are exceptions: In cases of strongly negative initial encounters, repeated exposure is unlikely to cause us to like a person more. Instead, the more we are exposed to the person, the more we are likely to dislike the individual (Zajonc, 2001; Butler & Berry, 2004).

- *Similarity.* Folk wisdom tells us that birds of a feather flock together. However, folk wisdom also maintains that opposites attract. Which is right? Social psychologists have come up with a clear verdict regarding which of the two statements is correct: We tend to like those who are similar to us. Discovering that others have similar attitudes, values, or traits promotes our liking for them. Furthermore, the more similar others are, the more we like them. One reason similarity increases the likelihood of interpersonal attraction is that we assume people with similar attitudes will evaluate us positively. Because we experience a strong **reciprocity-of-liking effect,** a tendency to like those who like us, knowing that someone evaluates us positively promotes our attraction to that person. In addition, if *we* like someone else, we tend to assume that person likes us in return (Heffernan & Fraley, 2015; Wróbel & Królewiak, 2017).

reciprocity-of-liking effect A tendency to like those who like us. (Module 55)

- *Physical attractiveness.* For most people, the equation *beautiful = good* is quite true. As a result, physically attractive people are more popular than are physically unattractive ones, if all other factors are equal. This finding, which contradicts the values that most people say they hold, is apparent even in childhood (preschoolers' popularity is related to their attractiveness) and continues into adulthood. Indeed, physical attractiveness may be the single most important element promoting initial liking in college dating situations, although its influence eventually decreases when people get to know each other better (Little, Burt, & Perrett, 2006; Luo & Zhang, 2009).

These factors alone, of course, do not account for liking. For example, in one experiment that examined the desired qualities in a friendship, the top-rated qualities in a same-sex friend included sense of humor, warmth and kindness, expressiveness and openness, an exciting personality, and similarity of interests and leisure activities. In addition, our friendships and social networks may be related to neurological factors (Sprecher & Regan, 2002).

PsychTech

Research on Facebook and other social media sites indicates that social networking provides a less-intimidating social outlet for students who otherwise have trouble making and keeping friendships, such as those who are introverted or have low self-esteem.

Friendship and Social Networking The newest forms of friendship are found on social network sites. One out of 10 people *worldwide* belongs to Facebook, and the concentration of college students using the social network site is more than 90 percent.

For college students, the primary motivation in using social network sites is to keep in touch with their friends. In addition, younger college students use Facebook to explore their developing identities. Because users can control how they present themselves to the world on a social network profile, it is easy for college students to "try on" identities by posting selected photos of themselves, revealing specific tastes and interests, or otherwise presenting themselves in new and different ways. The feedback they get from others may help them decide which identities and forms of self-presentation suit them best (Subrahmanyam et al., 2008; Pempek, Yermolayeva, & Calvert, 2009; Phua, Jin, & Kim, 2017).

But how do social network sites affect users' nonvirtual social lives? Maintaining social connections that might otherwise have withered and died seems like a good thing, but it may be detrimental if someone spends so much time maintaining online distant or superficial friendships that they sacrifice time spent on intimate, face-to-face interactions with close friends (Steinfeld, Ellison, & Lampe, 2008).

It turns out, though, that intensity of Facebook use is positively related to college students' life satisfaction, social trust, and civic engagement. In short, research suggests that users of social network sites are not disengaged from the real world and that the benefits of social networking may outweigh the costs to real-world social lives (Valenzuela, Park, & Kee, 2009; Brandtzæg, Lüders, & Skjetne, 2010).

HOW DO I LOVE THEE? LET ME COUNT THE WAYS

Whereas our knowledge of what makes people like one another is extensive, our understanding of love is more limited in scope and recently acquired. For some time, many social psychologists believed that love was too difficult to observe and study in a controlled, scientific way. However, love is such a central issue in most people's lives that eventually social psychologists could not resist its allure.

As a first step, researchers tried to identify the characteristics that distinguish between mere liking and full-blown love. They discovered that love is not simply a greater quantity of liking but a qualitatively different psychological state. For instance, at least in its early stages, love includes relatively intense physiological arousal, an all-encompassing interest in the other individual, fantasizing about the other, and relatively rapid swings of emotion. Similarly, love, unlike liking, includes elements of passion, closeness, fascination, exclusiveness, sexual desire, and intense caring. We idealize partners by exaggerating their good qualities and minimizing their imperfections (Murray, Holmes, & Griffin, 2004; Tamini, Bojhd, & Yazdani, 2011).

Other researchers have theorized that there are two main types of love: passionate love and companionate love. **Passionate (or romantic) love** represents a state of intense absorption in someone. It includes intense physiological arousal, psychological interest, and caring for the needs of another. In contrast, **companionate love** is the strong affection we have for those with whom our lives are deeply involved. The love we feel for parents, other family members, and even some close friends falls into the category of companionate love (Regan, 2006; Loving, Crockett, & Paxson, 2009; Yildirim & Barnett, 2017).

Psychologist Robert Sternberg makes an even finer differentiation between types of love. He proposes that love consists of three parts (see Figure 1):

- *Decision/commitment*, the initial thoughts that one loves someone and the longer-term feelings of commitment to maintain love
- *Intimacy component*, feelings of closeness and connectedness
- *Passion component*, the motivational drives relating to sex, physical closeness, and romance

According to Sternberg, these three components combine to produce the different types of love. He suggests that different combinations of the three components vary over the course of relationships. For example, in strong, loving relationships, the level of commitment peaks and then remains stable. Passion, on the other hand, peaks quickly and then declines and levels off relatively early in most relationships. In addition, relationships are happiest in which the strength of the various components are similar between the two partners (Sternberg, Hojjat, & Barnes, 2001; Sternberg, 2004, 2006).

Is love a necessary ingredient in a good marriage? Yes, if you live in the United States. In contrast, it's considerably less important in other cultures. Although mutual attraction (love) is the most important characteristic men and women in the United States desire in a mate, men in China rated good health as most important, and women there rated emotional stability and maturity as most important. Among the Zulu in South Africa, men rated emotional stability first and women rated dependable character first (see Figure 2; Buss, Abbott, & Angleitner, 1990).

passionate (or romantic) love A state of intense absorption in someone that includes intense physiological arousal, psychological interest, and caring for the needs of another. (Module 55)

companionate love The strong affection we have for those with whom our lives are deeply involved. (Module 55)

FIGURE 1 According to Sternberg, love has three main components: intimacy, passion, and decision/commitment. Different combinations of these components can create other types of love. Nonlove contains none of the three components.
Source: Adapted from Sternberg, R. J. (1986). A triangular theory of love. *Psychological Review, 93*(2), 119–135.

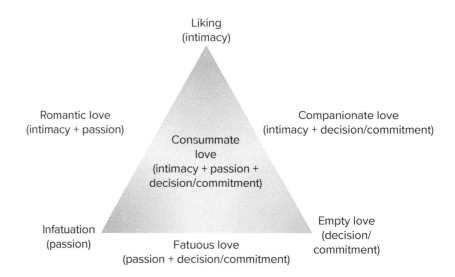

	Rank Ordering of Five Desired Characteristics in a Mate					
	United States		China		South Africa Zulu	
	Females	**Males**	**Females**	**Males**	**Females**	**Males**
Mutual attraction—love	1	1		4	5	
Emotional stability and maturity	2	2	1	5	2	1
Dependable character	3	3			1	3
Pleasing disposition	4	4			3	4
Education and intelligence	5	5	4			
Good health			3	1	4	5
Desire for home and children			2	2		
Ambition and industriousness			5			
Good cook and housekeeper						2
Chastity (no prior sexual intercourse)				3		

FIGURE 2 Although love may be an important factor in choosing a marriage partner if you live in the United States, other cultures place less importance on it.

Source: Adapted from Buss, D. M., Abbott, M., & Angleitner, A. (1990). International preferences in selecting mates: A study of 37 cultures. *Journal of Cross-Cultural Psychology, 21,* 5–47.

How we meet our romantic partners and spouses has changed drastically over the years. In the 1940s, heterosexual Americans met their future family members most often through family. Now friends and the Internet are much more frequent matchmakers (see Figure 3). The likelihood of meeting online is even greater for same-sex couples today; some 70% of gay couples report meeting online (Rosenfeld & Thomas, 2012).

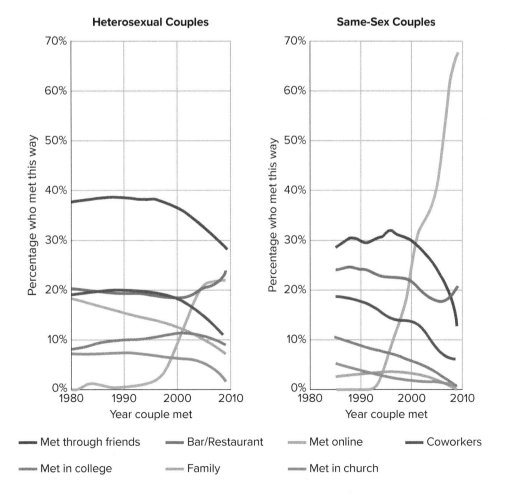

FIGURE 3 Couples are considerably more likely to meet online today than were couples in earlier generations, a change that holds true for heterosexual as well as same-sex couples.

Source: Rosenfeld, M. J., & Thomas, R. J. (2012). Searching for a mate: The rise of the Internet as a social intermediary. *American Sociological Review, 77,* 523–547.

Liking and loving clearly show a positive side of human social behavior. Now we turn to behaviors that are just as much a part of social behavior: aggression and helping behavior.

Aggression and Prosocial Behavior: Hurting and Helping Others

Drive-by shootings, carjackings, and abductions are just a few examples of the violence that seems all too common today. Yet we also find examples of generous, unselfish, thoughtful behavior that suggest a more optimistic view of humankind. Consider, for instance, people such as Mother Teresa, who ministered to the poor in India. Or contemplate the simple kindnesses of life: lending class lecture notes, stopping to help a child who has fallen off a bicycle, or merely sharing a candy bar with a friend. Such instances of helping are no less characteristic of human behavior than are the distasteful examples of aggression.

HURTING OTHERS: AGGRESSION

We need look no further than the daily news cycle to be bombarded with examples of aggression on both a societal level (war, invasion, assassination) and an individual level (crime, child abuse, and the many petty cruelties humans are capable of inflicting on one another). Is such aggression an inevitable part of the human condition? Or is aggression primarily a product of particular circumstances that, if changed, could lead to its reduction?

The difficulty of answering such knotty questions becomes apparent as soon as we consider how best to define the term *aggression*. Depending on the way we define the word, many examples of inflicted pain or injury may or may not qualify as aggression (see Figure 4). For instance, a rapist is clearly acting with aggression toward his victim. On the other hand, it is less certain that a physician carrying out an emergency medical procedure without an anesthetic, thereby causing incredible pain to the patient, should be considered aggressive.

Most social psychologists define aggression in terms of the intent and the purpose behind the behavior. **Aggression** is intentional injury of or harm to another person. By this definition, the rapist is clearly acting aggressively, whereas the physician causing pain during a medical procedure is not (Berkowitz, 2001).

Also, the aggression we encounter in our daily lives can take many forms. Not only do we hurt others through direct physical or verbal attacks, but we also can hurt people indirectly by doing such things as spreading rumors or purposely ignoring someone. In fact, some research finds that *microaggressions*–small, daily slights, put-downs, and insults, often perpetrated against members of marginalized groups based on race, gender, and sexual orientation–may be more harmful in the long run than are highly visible acts of aggression. However, the research findings on mircroaggressions are mixed, and more research needs to be done to understand how the daily experience of small acts of prejudice impacts recipients (Richardson, 2014; Lilienfeld, 2017; Sue, 2017).

We turn now to several approaches to understanding aggressive behavior developed by social psychologists.

aggression The intentional injury of, or harm to, another person. (Module 55)

INSTINCT APPROACHES: AGGRESSION AS A RELEASE

If you have ever punched an adversary in the nose, you may have experienced a certain satisfaction despite your better judgment. Instinct theories, which note the prevalence of aggression not only in humans but in animals as well, propose that aggression is primarily the outcome of innate–or inborn–urges.

Sigmund Freud was one of the first to suggest, as part of his theory of personality, that aggression is a primary instinctual drive. Konrad Lorenz, an ethologist (a scientist who studies animal behavior), expanded Freud's notions by arguing that humans, along

FIGURE 4 What is aggression? It depends on how the word is defined and in what context it is used.

Source: Adapted from Benjamin, L. T., Jr. (1985). Defining aggression: An exercise for classroom discussion. *Teaching of Psychology, 12*(1), 40–42.

Is This Aggression?

Defining aggression can be difficult. To see the challenges it raises, read each of the following scenarios and consider whether it describes an aggressive act—according to your own definition of aggressive behavior.

1. A dog chases a rabbit and kills it. Yes _____ No _____

2. A man places a live lobster into boiling water to prepare it for dinner. Yes _____ No _____

3. A war pilot bombs a village, killing both enemy soldiers and civilians. Yes _____ No _____

4. A man repairing a roof accidentally drops a hammer. The hammer hits a child in the yard below, causing permanent brain damage. Yes _____ No _____

5. A boy repeatedly yanks the leash sharply as he walks his dog, ignoring the dog's cries of pain. Yes _____ No _____

6. Mrs. X, hoping to get her son's teacher fired, spreads nasty rumors about the teacher to other parents. Yes _____ No _____

7. A woman continually threatens to spank her toddler for "acting up" while they are shopping for groceries. Yes _____ No _____

8. A man does nothing to help a drowning person at the beach, even though he is an excellent swimmer. Yes _____ No _____

9. A rock star trashes his hotel room while celebrating the success of his latest CD. Yes _____ No _____

10. A woman throws herself under a train. Yes _____ No _____

with members of other species, have a fighting instinct, which in earlier times ensured protection of food supplies and weeded out the weaker of the species (Lorenz, 1974). Lorenz's instinct approach led to the controversial notion that aggressive energy constantly builds up in an individual until the person finally discharges it in a process called **catharsis.** The longer the energy builds up, said Lorenz, the greater the amount of the aggression displayed when it is discharged.

Lorenz believed that society should offer people acceptable ways of permitting catharsis. For example, he suggested that participation in aggressive sports and games would prevent the discharge of aggression in less socially desirable ways. However, little research has found evidence for the existence of a pent-up reservoir of aggression that needs to be released. In fact, some studies flatly contradict the notion of catharsis, which leads psychologists to look for other explanations for aggression (Bushman, Wang, & Anderson, 2005; Verona & Sullivan, 2008; Richardson & Hammock, 2011).

catharsis The process of discharging built-up aggressive energy. (Module 55)

FRUSTRATION-AGGRESSION APPROACHES: AGGRESSION AS A REACTION TO FRUSTRATION

Suppose you've been working on a paper that is due for a class early the next morning, and your computer printer runs out of ink just before you can print out the paper. You rush to the store to buy more ink only to find the sales clerk locking the door for the day. Even though the clerk can see you gesturing and begging him to open the door, he refuses, shrugs his shoulders, and points to a sign that indicates when the store will open the next day. At that moment, the feelings you experience toward the sales clerk probably place you on the verge of real aggression, and you are undoubtedly seething inside.

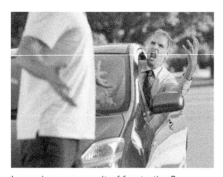

Is road rage a result of frustration? According to frustration-aggression approaches, frustration is a likely cause.

©Chris Ryan/age fotostock

Frustration-aggression approaches explain how the frustration one might feel standing at that closed door could lead to aggression. According to these approaches, frustration (the experience of having one's goals thwarted or blocked) produces anger, which in turn produces a readiness to act aggressively.

But anger doesn't always lead to aggression. Whether actual aggression occurs depends on the presence of *aggressive cues*, stimuli that have been associated in the past with actual aggression or violence and that will trigger aggression again (Berkowitz, 2001; Burton et al., 2013).

What kinds of stimuli act as aggressive cues? They can range from the most explicit, such as the presence of weapons, to more subtle cues, such as the mere mention of the name of an individual who behaved violently in the past. For example, angered participants in experiments behave significantly more aggressively when in the presence of a gun than in a comparable situation in which no guns are present. Similarly, frustrated participants who view a violent movie are more physically aggressive toward a confederate with the same name as the star of the movie than they are toward a confederate with a different name (Berkowitz, 2001; Jovanović, Stanojević, & Stanojević, 2011; Wang & Zhong, 2015).

It appears, then, that frustration does lead to aggression—at least when aggressive cues are present. However, psychologists have come to realize that frustration is not the only trigger of aggression. For example, physical pain, verbal insults, and unpleasant experiences in general can also lead to aggression. Similarly, violent behavior increases when the temperature rises—suggesting that one consequence of global warming may be an increase in aggression and intergroup conflict (Barash & Lipton, 2011; Van Damme et al., 2017; Plante & Anderson, 2017).

OBSERVATIONAL LEARNING APPROACHES: LEARNING TO HURT OTHERS

Do we learn to be aggressive? The *observational learning* (sometimes called *social learning*) approach to aggression says that we do. Taking an almost opposite view from instinct theories, which focus on innate explanations of aggression, observational learning theory emphasizes that social and environmental conditions can teach individuals to be aggressive. The theory sees aggression not as inevitable but rather as a learned response that can be understood in terms of rewards and punishments.

Observational learning theory pays attention to the direct rewards and punishments that people receive for acting aggressively. For example, a father may tell his son how glad he was that he "stood up for himself" after getting into a fight, thereby rewarding aggressive behavior.

More frequently, though, people learn aggression through watching others' behavior. According to the *observational learning approach*, we learn to be aggressive by viewing the rewards and punishments that models provide. *Models* are individuals who provide a guide to appropriate behavior through their own behavior. According to observational learning theory, people observe the behavior of models and the subsequent consequences of that behavior. If the consequences are positive, the behavior is likely to be imitated when observers find themselves in a similar situation.

Suppose, for instance, a girl hits her younger brother when he damages one of her new toys. Whereas instinct theory would suggest that the aggression had been pent up and was now being discharged, and frustration-aggression theory would examine the girl's frustration at no longer being able to use her new toy, observational learning theory would look to previous situations in which the girl had viewed others being rewarded for their aggression. For example, perhaps she had watched a friend get to play with a toy after he painfully twisted it out of the hand of another child.

Observational learning theory has received wide research support. For example, children of nursery school age who have watched an adult model behave aggressively and then receive reinforcement for it later display similar behavior themselves if they have been angered, insulted, or frustrated after exposure. Furthermore, a significant

Study Alert

Understand the distinction between the instinctual, frustration-aggression, and observational learning approaches to aggression.

amount of research links watching television shows containing violence with subsequent viewer aggression (Greer, Dudek-Singer, & Gautreaux, 2006; Carnagey, Anderson, & Bartholow, 2007).

From the perspective of...

A Criminal Justice Worker How would proponents of the three main approaches to the study of aggression—instinct approaches, frustration-aggression approaches, and observational learning approaches—interpret the aggression of the killer in the Sandy Hook Elementary School shooting, in which 26 children and adults were killed?

©Deposit Photos/
Glow Images

Helping Others: The Brighter Side of Human Nature

Turning away from aggression, we move now to the opposite—and brighter—side of human nature: how we provide aid to others. **Prosocial behavior,** which is the term that psychologists use for helping behavior, has been considered under many different conditions. However, the question that psychologists have looked at most closely relates to bystander intervention in emergency situations. What are the factors that lead someone to help a person in need?

One critical factor related to helping in emergency situations is the number of other individuals present. When multiple people witness an emergency situation, a sense of diffusion of responsibility can arise among the bystanders. **Diffusion of responsibility** is the belief that responsibility for intervening is shared, or diffused, among those present. The more people present in an emergency, the less personally responsible each individual feels—and therefore the less help he or she provides (Blair, Thompson, & Wuensch, 2005; Gray, 2006; Martin & North, 2015).

For example, think back to the classic case of Kitty Genovese that we described when discussing the topic of research. Genovese was stabbed multiple times, and—according to some accounts of the event—no one offered help, despite the fact that allegedly close to 40 people who lived in nearby apartments heard her screams for help. The lack of help has been attributed to diffusion of responsibility: The fact that there were so many potential helpers led each individual to feel diminished personal responsibility (Fischer et al., 2011; Gallo, 2015; Griggs, 2015).

Although most research on helping behavior supports the diffusion-of-responsibility explanation, other factors are clearly involved in helping behavior. The decision to give aid involves four basic steps (see Figure 5; Latané & Darley, 1970; Garcia et al., 2002; López-Pérez et al., 2017):

- *Noticing a person, event, or situation that may require help.* If we are to provide help, we first have to perceive that a situation is one that potentially requires our help and intervention.

- *Interpreting the event as one that requires help.* Even if we notice an event, it may be sufficiently ambiguous for us to interpret it as a nonemergency situation that requires no help. Thus, we make an interpretation as to whether or not the event requires help.

- *Assuming responsibility for helping.* It is at this key point that diffusion of responsibility is likely to occur if others are present. Moreover, a bystander's particular expertise is likely to play a role in determining whether he or she helps. For instance, if people with training in medical aid or lifesaving techniques are

prosocial behavior Helping behavior. (Module 55)

diffusion of responsibility The belief that responsibility for intervening is shared, or diffused, among those present. (Module 55)

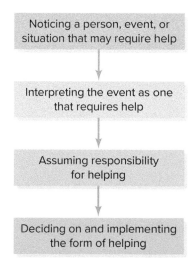

FIGURE 5 The basic steps of helping.
Source: Adapted from Latané, B., & Darley, J. M. (1970). *The unresponsive bystander: Why doesn't he help?* New York: Appleton-Century-Crofts.

present, untrained bystanders are less likely to intervene because they feel they have less expertise.

- *Deciding on and implementing the form of helping.* After we assume responsibility for helping, we must decide how to provide assistance. Helping can range from very indirect forms of intervention, such as calling the police, to more direct forms, such as giving first aid or taking the victim to a hospital. Most social psychologists use a *rewards-costs approach* for helping to predict the nature of the assistance a bystander will choose to provide. The general notion is that the bystander's perceived rewards for helping must outweigh the costs if helping is to occur, and most research tends to support this notion (Koper & Jaasma, 2001; Bartlett & DeSteno, 2006; Lin & Lin, 2007).

altruism Behavior meant to help another person without regard for self-interest. (Module 55)

After determining the nature of the assistance needed, the actual help must be implemented. A rewards-costs analysis suggests that we are most likely to use the least costly form of implementation. However, this is not always the case: In some situations, the help that is provided shows altruism. **Altruism** is behavior meant to help another without regard for self-interest. It is putting the welfare of others above oneself. For example, we can see altruism in soldiers who risk their own lives to save another soldier who is wounded; a woman who jumps into an icy pond to save a drowning stranger; and everyday people who put themselves at mortal risk to help strangers escape from the burning World Trade Center towers during the 9/11 terrorist attack (Manor & Gailliot, 2007; Marshall, 2011; Xi, et al., 2017).

People who intervene in emergency situations tend to possess certain personality characteristics that differentiate them from nonhelpers. For example, helpers are more self-assured, sympathetic, emotionally understanding, and empathetic (empathy is a personality trait in which someone observing another person experiences the emotions of that person) than are nonhelpers (Walker & Frimer, 2007; Stocks, Lishner, & Decker, 2009; Batson, 2011).

Still, most social psychologists agree that no single set of attributes differentiates helpers from nonhelpers. For the most part, temporary situational factors (such as the mood we're in) determine whether we will intervene in a situation requiring aid (Dovidio et al., 2006; Sallquist et al., 2009; Snyder & Dwyer, 2013).

More generally, what leads people to make moral decisions? Clearly, situational factors make a difference. For example, one study asked people to judge the morality of plane crash survivors cannibalizing an injured boy to avoid starvation. Participants in the study were more likely to condemn the behavior if they were placed

Altruism is often the only bright side of a natural disaster.
©John Glaser/CSM/REX/Shutterstock

in an emotional state than if they were less emotional (Schnall et al., 2008; Broeders et al., 2011).

Other psychologists, using a neuroscience perspective, believe that there's a kind of tug-of-war between emotion and rational thinking in the brain. If the rational side wins out, we're more likely to take a logical view of moral situations (if you're at risk for starving, go ahead and eat the injured boy). On the other hand, if the emotional side prevails, we're more likely to condemn the cannibalism, even if it means we may be harmed. In support of such reasoning, researchers have found that different areas of the brain are involved in moral decisions (Miller, 2008; Greene & Paxton, 2009).

Evidence also exists that our brains are hardwired to help us feel empathy for others. In this view, helping others in some ways is just as natural as other, more negative behaviors. The question becomes, then, how we balance the positive and negative behaviors that are equally the result of the functioning of the brain (Pfaff, 2014; de Waal, 2014; Fedyk, 2017).

Study Alert

The distinction between *prosocial behavior* and *altruism* is important. Prosocial behavior does not need to have a self-sacrificing component; altruism, by definition, contains an element of self-sacrifice.

BECOMING AN INFORMED CONSUMER
of Psychology

Dealing Effectively with Anger

At one time or another, almost everyone feels angry. The anger may result from a frustrating situation, or it may be due to another individual's behavior. The way we deal with anger may determine the difference between a promotion and a lost job or a broken relationship and one that mends itself.

Social psychologists who have studied the topic suggest several good strategies to deal with anger that maximize the potential for positive consequences (Nelson & Finch, 2000; Bernstein, 2011; Faupel, Herrick, & Sharp, 2018). Among the most useful strategies are the following:

- *Calm down.* Take a walk or engage in some other physical activity in order to cool down your emotional arousal.
- *Look again at the anger-provoking situation from the perspective of others.* By taking others' points of view, you may be able to understand the situation better, and with increased understanding, you may become more tolerant of the apparent shortcomings of others.
- *Minimize the importance of the situation.* Does it really matter that someone is driving too slowly and that you'll be late to an appointment as a result? Reinterpret the situation in a way that is less bothersome.
- *Use language effectively by saying "I," not "you."* Don't say *"You did _____ wrong."* Instead, say *"I felt hurt when you did _____."* When you accuse people of being wrong, they are likely to feel the need to fight back.
- *Fantasize about getting even—but don't act on it.* Fantasy provides a safety valve. In your fantasies, you can yell at that unfair professor all you want and suffer no consequences at all. However, don't spend too much time brooding: Fantasize, but then move on.
- *Relax.* By teaching yourself the relaxation techniques used in systematic desensitization (discussed in the module on treatment of psychological disorders), you can help reduce your reactions to anger. In turn, your anger may dissipate.

No matter which of these strategies you try, above all, don't ignore your anger. People who always try to suppress their anger may experience a variety of consequences, such as self-condemnation, frustration, and even physical illness (Quartana & Burns, 2007; Gardner & Moore, 2008).

AP' MODULE 55: POSITIVE AND NEGATIVE SOCIAL BEHAVIOR

AP SUMMARY

- Prosocial behavior, or helping behavior, in emergencies is determined in part by diffusion of responsibility. Bystanders are less likely to help if there are more people present because they don't feel responsible.
- Deciding to help is the outcome of a four-stage process that consists of noticing a possible need for help, interpreting the situation as requiring aid, assuming responsibility to act, and deciding on and implementing a form of assistance.
- According to the mere-exposure effect, repeated exposure to a stimulus will produce positive feelings for that stimulus.
- Aggression is intentional injury of or harm to another person.
- Explanations of aggression include instinct approaches, frustration-aggression theory, and observational learning.
- Altruism is behavior meant to help another without regard for self-interest.
- The primary determinants of interpersonal attraction include: proximity, exposure, similarity, reciprocity-of-liking, and physical attractiveness.
- Love can be categorized as passionate or companionate. According to Sternberg, love has several components: intimacy, passion, and decision/commitment.

AP KEY TERMS

interpersonal attraction (or close relationship)
reciprocity-of-liking effect
passionate (or romantic) love
companionate love
aggression
catharsis
prosocial behavior
diffusion of responsibility
altruism

AP TEST PRACTICE

Section I: Multiple Choice

1. You hated a new song but after hearing it multiple times you've grown to like it. This is an example of
   A. mere exposure
   B. proximity
   C. reciprocity
   D. ingroup bias
   E. social desirability

2. Sydney went to a rage room where she could throw dishes to release her anger. What theory explains her behavior?
   A. Catharsis
   B. Altruism
   C. Observational learning
   D. Prosocial behavior
   E. Diffusion of responsibility

3. All of the following are important factors that lead to positive feelings for others EXCEPT
   A. similarity
   B. proximity
   C. reciprocity
   D. physical attraction
   E. distance

Section II: Free Response

A. Jacob spent Friday night babysitting for his neighbors who have three children under the age of five. The children are known to be a handful by other babysitters in the neighborhood, but Jacob liked the kids and they behaved very well for him.

   Explain how the following concepts influenced Jacob's experience.
   - Mere exposure
   - Self-fulfilling prophecy

B. Saturday night Jacob decided to hang out with his friends. As they were crossing the street he tripped on the curb and fell into the busy street.

   Explain how the following concepts might influence Jacob's receiving assistance from others.
   - Diffusion of responsibility
   - Altruism
   - Ingroup bias

LOOKING *Back*

EPILOGUE

We have touched on some of the major ideas, research topics, and experimental findings of social psychology. We examined how people form, maintain, and change attitudes and how they form impressions of others and assign attributions to them. We also saw how groups, through conformity and tactics of compliance, can influence individuals' actions and attitudes. Finally, we discussed interpersonal relationships, including both liking and loving, and looked at aggression and prosocial behavior, the two sides of a coin that represent the extremes of social behavior.

MODULE 52 Attitudes and Social Cognition

Persuasion: Attitudes: Evaluations of a particular person, behavior, belief, or concept

— Routes to persuasion

— Attitude-behavior link

Social Cognition: How people understand what others and themselves are like

— Forming impressions of others: Central traits help us form impressions of others

— Attribution theory: How we decide the specific causes of a person's behavior

- Situational causes: of behavior that are external to a person

- Dispositional causes: of behavior brought about by a person's traits or internal personality characteristics

- Attribution biases

MODULE 53 Social Influence and Groups

Conformity: A desire to follow the beliefs or standards of other people

— Groupthink: Group members want to achieve consensus and lose the ability to evaluate alternative points of view

— Social roles: Behaviors associated with people in a given position

Compliance: Social pressure to behave in a certain way

— Foot-in-the-door technique

— Door-in-the-face technique

— That's-not-all technique

— Not-so-free sample

Obedience: Behavior change in response to the commands of others

MODULE 54 Prejudice and Discrimination

Prejudice: A negative or positive evaluation of a group

Discrimination: Behavior directed toward individuals on the basis of their membership in a particular group

Stereotype: Generalized beliefs and expectations about a specific group that arise when we categorize information

Reducing Prejudice and Discrimination

— Increase contact between the target of stereotyping and the holder of the stereotype

— Make values and norms against prejudice more conspicuous

— Provide information about the targets of stereotyping

— Reduce stereotype threat

— Increase a sense of belonging

MODULE 55 Positive and Negative Social Behavior

Liking and Loving

— Determinants of liking

- Proximity

- Mere exposure

- Similarity

- Physical attractiveness

— What is love?

- Qualitatively different from liking

- Three components of love

Aggression: Intentional injury of or harm to another person

— Instinct approaches

— Frustration-aggression approach

— Observational learning approaches

Helping (Prosocial) Behavior: Actions intended to provide aid to others

(MODULE 52) Source: Adapted from Sternberg, R. J. (1986). A triangular theory of love. *Psychological Review, 93*(2), 119–135; (MODULE 53) photo (top): ©Jim Sugar/Corbis/Getty Images; (bottom): From the film OBEDIENCE ©1968 by Stanley Milgram, ©renewed 1993 by Alexandra Milgram. Permission granted by Alexandra Milgram; (MODULE 54) (photo): ©Barbara Burnes/Science Source

©Shutterstock/Rawpixel.com

EPILOGUE
Diversity, Culture, Conflict, and Cooperation

AP'I LEARNING TARGETS FOR EPILOGUE

- Discuss the interaction of nature and nurture (including cultural variations), specifically social development, in the determination of behavior.

- Describe how cultural influences shape emotional expression, including variations in body language.

- Speculate how cultural context can facilitate or constrain personality develop, especially as if relates to self-concept.

- Articulate the impact of social and cultural categories on self-concept and relations with others.

- Describe the variables that contribute to altruism and aggression.

DIVERSITY AND CULTURE
The Language of Diversity
Culture
Collectivism and Individualism: The Group Versus the Individual
Our View of Ourselves: Looking Inward
Exploring Diversity: The Culture of Aggression
Immigrants: The Newest Americans

- Discuss how experience and culture can influence perceptual processes.

- Identify and apply basic motivational concepts to understand the behavior of humans and other animals.

- Articulate the impact of social and cultural categories on self-concept and relations with others.

CONFLICT AND COOPERATION: STRIVING FOR A JUST AND PEACEFUL WORLD
The Roots of Conflict
Misperceiving Our Enemies
Genocidal Violence and Mass Killing: Explaining the Inexplicable

- Articulate the impact of social and cultural categories on self-concept and relations with others.

- Explain how individuals respond to expectations of others, including groupthink, conformity, and obedience to authority.

- Predict the impact of the presence of others on individual behavior.

- Describe the variables that contribute to altruism and aggression.

BRIDGING THE DIVIDE OF DIFFERENCE

Haifa Staiti made a friend beside a lake at a summer camp in Maine. Sitting under a canopy of trees, she spoke to another camper who, it turned out, shared many of her dreams and basic values. "I felt I was being heard, and I felt comfortable about sharing my experiences," she said (Epatko, 2018).

What made the exchange unusual was that Staiti was a Palestinian and her fellow camper was an Israeli. Although the two came from cultures that are in a perpetual state of undeclared war, they found they had much in common.

The interchange was possible due to a program called Seeds of Peace, designed to bring Israelis and Palestinians together in a neutral and supportive environment. Staiti's childhood had been difficult, with curfews and repeated imprisonment of her politically active father by the Israeli government.

Initially, the camp experience was not easy for Staiti, who was a shy 14-year-old when she began the program. But by the time her stay at the camp was over, both Staiti and her Israeli acquaintance realized that they had much in common, and they remain friends today (Epatko, 2018).

LOOKING *Ahead*

What is it about racial, ethnic, and cultural differences that evoke strong, and sometimes even deadly, responses? Why do such differences lead to prejudice, discrimination, and violence, both in the United States and across the world? And can programs such as Seeds of Peace bridge the differences that divide the diverse world in which we all live?

No principle of psychology leads us to expect that we are destined to live in constant discord. Indeed, in some communities, minorities and majorities live in tranquility, building societies that both acknowledge and welcome the differences between people.

In this module, we examine issues that shed light on psychology's role in understanding diversity and fostering a better world. In the first section, we look at how diversity and culture affect thinking and behavior in fundamental ways. In the second section, we explore issues of conflict, war, and peace. We consider why conflicts occur between people, groups, and nations. We then look at factors that sustain conflicts, such as the views people develop of enemies, and we explore some of the most extreme forms conflict can take: genocide and nuclear war. We end this epilogue on an optimistic note, considering psychological techniques for promoting peace.

Diversity and Culture

No matter where we live, we are increasingly likely to encounter people who differ from us racially, ethnically, and culturally. Technology is bringing people from across the globe into our homes, as close to us as the phone in our hand or the computer on our desk. Businesses now operate globally, so coworkers are likely to come from many countries and cultures. Being comfortable with people whose backgrounds and beliefs differ from our own is not only a social necessity, but also a requirement for career success.

Moreover, by the mid-21st century, the percentage of people in the United States of African, Latin American, Asian, and Arabic ancestry will be greater than the percentage of those of Western European ancestry—a profound statistical, and social, shift. College enrollments will mirror these changes, as populations that were minority become the majority (Alba & Barbosa, 2016; Cohn & Caumont, 2016).

More specifically, consider the following population trends (Cohn & Caumont, 2016; U.S. Census Bureau, 2017):

- By 2055, the United States will not have any single racial or ethnic majority. Put another way, we will all be members of minority groups.
- Almost 60 million immigrants have come to the United States since 1970.
- Most population growth in the United States is projected to be related to Hispanic and Asian immigration.
- Around 14% of the U.S. population is foreign-born.
- Twenty percent of U.S. residents speak a language other than English at home.

Furthermore, diversity is not just based in racial, ethnic, and cultural characteristics. The world's population is also diverse in terms of sex, gender identity, sexual orientation, age, and mental and physical abilities. Then, layer on factors such as education, religion, and income level, and you can see that each person is a complex mix of identities. The way those diverse identities overlap or interact is known as *intersectionality*. One can be, for instance, a hearing-impaired lesbian African-American woman and

Increasingly, many workplaces will include staff from a wide variety of countries and cultures, and with a wide range of customs and beliefs. What are your experiences with people who differ from you culturally?
©monkeybusinessimages/Getty Images

evoke responses from others that reflect any, all, or none of those identities (DeBlaere, Watsonk, & Langrehr, 2018; Mays & Ghavami, 2018).

The Language of Diversity

The language we use to describe others and their diversity is important, and social-cultural norms often determine what labels are appropriate. For example, should one say African American or black? Caucasian, white, or Euro-American? Hispanic or Latino? American Indian or Native American? Gay, lesbian, straight, or queer? Transgender, cisgender, male, or female? Physically challenged, differently abled, or disabled? The choice of labels matters. The subtleties of language affect how people think about members of particular groups, and how they think about themselves (Forson, 2018).

One difficulty in understanding diversity is that many of the terms we use are ill-defined and often overlapping. For example, the term **race** generally refers to obvious physical differences that set one group apart from others. But depending on how race is defined, there are between 3 and 300 races, with no race genetically distinct. And the reality is that 99.9% of our genetic makeup is similar across all human beings. Because of this, race is generally thought of as a *social construction*, something that is defined by people's attitudes and beliefs (Zuberi, Patterson, & Stewart, 2015; Gross & Weiss, 2018).

Ethnicity refers to shared national origins or cultural patterns. In the United States, for example, Puerto Rican, Irish, and Italian American typically are categorized as ethnic groups. However, ethnicity–like race–is very much in the eye of the beholder. For instance, a Cuban American who is a third-generation citizen of the United States

race Generally refers to obvious physical differences that set one group apart from others.

ethnicity Shared national origins or cultural patterns.

The term *race* is generally used to refer to obvious physical differences between groups of people. However, as you can see from these images, skin tone, hair texture, and facial features come in many varieties and combinations, so the lines between groups can't be clearly drawn.
©Shutterstock/Rawpixel.com

may feel few ties or associations to Cuba or Cuban culture. Yet whites may view her as "Hispanic," and blacks may view her as "white."

Race and ethnicity shape each of us to an enormous degree, profoundly influencing our view of others as well as ourselves. They affect how others treat us and how we treat them in turn. They can also determine a broad range of behaviors, ranging from whether we look people in the eye when we meet them (in some cultures, direct eye contact is viewed as disrespectful, so it is avoided) or how much food we eat when we're invited to dinner at a friend's house (in some cultures, it is considered impolite to leave food on one's plate (Mannarini, Talò, & Rochira, 2017; Park et al., 2018).

Even the words we use to describe others reflect our beliefs and values. For instance, the term *African American* is a label that has historical, geographical, and sociological implications. On the other hand, *black* focuses primarily on skin color.

Similarly, we do not yet have clear rules about the language to use for the varieties of gender identities and sexualities individuals may hold. For example, *transgender* refers to individuals whose sense of whether they are male or female (their *gender identity*) does not match the sex they were assigned at birth. Transgender people may refer to themselves as trans, transexual, agender, demigender, or genderqueer, and some prefer the use of gender-neutral pronouns, such as *ze, zir,* or *they.*

Furthermore, gender identity is not the same as *sexual orientation*, which describes a person's physical and emotional attraction to another person. For example, people may consider themselves straight, lesbian, gay, bisexual–or something else–depending on who they are attracted to sexually..

Culture

As a graduate student from Korea, Jung felt she was adjusting well to her psychology program in the United States. She got along well with her professors, and her officemates seemed cordial and friendly. But she felt uneasy in one area. Every Friday afternoon, other graduate students would gather at a local bar for what they called "Happy Hour," which–although Jung didn't know it–was a long-standing tradition among students in the psychology program. No one extended a personal invitation to Jung, and although she wished she could go with the other students, she felt it would be presumptuous to attend without an invitation. Since they never invited her to go along, she wondered if she had somehow insulted them.

How would you respond to Jung about her concerns? Most people familiar with the social customs of the United States would probably tell her that she needs no invitation to join her fellow students at the bar. Such gatherings are informal, and U.S. natives would neither expect nor routinely offer personal invitations to them.

Jung's confusion over the customs of public gatherings is just one example of the way in which habits differ from one culture to another. Although this problem appears to be relatively trivial, variations in such everyday behaviors indicate fundamental differences between people of diverse cultures. Furthermore, such misunderstandings may lead to stereotyping and prejudice. For example, Jung's classmates might think she was standoffish or unfriendly, and they might generalize such a view to something about Koreans. Learning about culture is essential to understanding the differences between people.

Culture comprises the learned behaviors, beliefs, and attitudes that are characteristic of an individual society or population. Culture is transmitted from one generation to another in both written and spoken form. Culture also encompasses people's creations, such as art, music, literature, and architecture. In sum, culture both shapes and reflects a society's behavior, understanding of the world, attitudes, and values (Kasser, 2011; Wan & Chiu, 2011; Han & Ma, 2015).

Despite their broad impact on people, cultural factors have traditionally received little attention from psychologists. One reason is that many psychologists have instead focused on broad universal principles of human behavior. Presumably, the thinking went, such principles should apply to all people, regardless of their culture.

culture The learned behaviors, beliefs, and attitudes that characterize an individual society or population.

Cultures vary in multiple ways, including their funeral ceremonies. In this colorful procession, family and friends accompany a loved one to burial grounds in the Vietnamese countryside. What is the funeral tradition in your culture or religion?
©Jimmy Tran/Shutterstock

Today, however, psychologists increasingly appreciate the importance of culture. Rather than considering it an obstacle to finding universal psychological principles, psychologists now view culture as a major factor in shaping our behavior. In fact, explanations for many central aspects of behavior remain elusive without an understanding of the consequences of culture. Indeed, psychologists can identify broad, universal principles of behavior only by determining which ones apply across cultures and which are specific to particular cultures. For example, a psychologist studying grief as a universal emotion would want to determine what a festive New Orleans jazz funeral has in common with a more conventional funeral at a graveside (Triandis, 2011; Rosenblatt, 2013).

Understanding the role of culture has also become increasingly important due to the growing diversity of U.S. society. The fabric of society is changing to reflect the contributions of people of diverse ethnic, racial, and religious backgrounds. We can understand the similarities and differences around us only when we consider culture. Furthermore, when we are aware of the effects of cultural differences, we may overcome our prejudices and better understand the roots of discrimination.

Furthering interest in culture is the concept of multiculturalism, which has both psychological and political implications for how members of racial, ethnic, religious, and other demographic groups are perceived. **Multiculturalism** is the view that members of all cultures deserve equal respect and that their contributions to society should be recognized. This concept not only acknowledges differences among subcultural groups, it also furthers the argument that society is stronger due to the presence of multiple groups and cultures.

Let's examine some primary psychological considerations related to culture, including differing cultural orientations and how people in different cultures vary in their view of themselves.

multiculturalism The view that members of all cultures deserve equal respect and that their contributions to society should be recognized.

Collectivism and Individualism: The Group Versus the Individual

Do you think teenagers should take their parents' views into account when choosing a career? Do you think you ought to help a neighbor who is in financial distress? Do you have an obligation to lend your class notes to a fellow student who missed a class?

If you answer yes to these questions, your responses represent values similar to those found in many Eastern cultures. On the other hand, if you reply no to these questions, your value orientation is more like that fostered in Western cultures.

These two orientations are known as *collectivism* and *individualism*. Cultures that support **collectivism** promote the idea that the well-being of the group or society is more important than that of the individual. People in collectivistic societies place the welfare of the group above their own personal well-being (Nguyen, Le, & Boles, 2010; Arpaci, Baloğlu, & Kesici, 2018).

In contrast, societies that encourage **individualism** hold as a primary value the personal identity, uniqueness, freedom, and worth of the individual person. In individualistic cultures, personal goals are viewed as more important than goals relating to society in general.

The individualistic and collectivistic tendencies of these cultures influence the way people interpret and understand behavior. For example, students and teachers in the United States tend to attribute their scholastic success to stable, internal characteristics. Consequently, a student who does well is seen as being smart, which is a stable, internal trait and is an outgrowth of an individualistic view of the world. In contrast, in China and Japan, both countries that have a more collectivistic culture than the United States, people see scholastic performance in terms of temporary, situational factors, such as how hard a student works.

The varying cultural perceptions that underlie academic success lead to different levels of scholastic motivation. Because Chinese and Japanese students are more apt to assume that academic success results from hard work, they are likely to put greater effort into their studies. U.S. students may exert less effort because they believe that their stable, unvarying level of ability underlies their school performance. After all, students who assume that their internal ability is the primary cause of their performance may not understand that studying harder may bring better results. In other words, they may feel they can't do much to change the outcome (Chen & Zhang, 2011; Fetvadjiev et al., 2018; Wu et al., 2018).

Whether a culture is collectivistic or individualistic also influences people's willingness to share scarce resources with others. For instance, people living in collectivistic cultures primarily employ the *norm of equality* to determine how rewards should be granted. The norm of equality suggests that all people ought to be rewarded equally, regardless of who they are or how competent or successful they are. In this case, an

collectivism The concept that the well-being of the group or society is more important than that of the individual.

individualism The concept that holds as a primary value the personal identity, uniqueness, freedom, and worth of the individual person.

In Eastern collectivist cultures, students are more likely to view academic achievement as tied to situational factors, such as how hard they work. In contrast, those in Western individualistic cultures tie achievement to more stable characteristics, such as how smart they think they are. How do you view academic success?
©Paul Burns/Blend Images LLC

equality norm would mean that all students working on a project together as a group would receive the same grade.

In contrast, people living in individualistic societies tend to distribute resources according to a *norm of equity,* in which rewards are based on the size of the contribution people make or the quality of their performance. Those who receive the most are the ones who have made the greatest contribution, whereas those who receive the least have made the smallest contribution. In an individualistic society, then, workers are paid according to their perceived merit. As a consequence, great discrepancies exist in the amount of rewards people receive (Boarini, Laslier, & Robin, 2009; Okely, Weiss, & Gale, 2018).

Our View of Ourselves: Looking Inward

In Western cultures, "the squeaky wheel gets the grease." In Asian cultures, "the nail that stands out gets pounded down."

The differences in these two sayings reflect profound cultural variations between the West and East in how people see themselves. In the Western perspective, people tend to differentiate themselves, making their voices heard and letting others know what their individual needs are in a situation. The Asian perspective suggests that the best approach is to blend in, to avoid being noticed (Krassner et al., 2017).

These divergent points-of-view exemplify how people in Eastern and Western cultures view the **self,** the way in which we look inward and define ourselves as individuals. Research suggests that people raised in Asian societies have an **interdependent** view of themselves, in part reflective of their collectivistic orientation. They think of themselves as members of a larger society, working together with others to achieve social harmony. In this view, people strive to fit in, to behave in a way that coincides with how others think, feel, and act (Markus & Kitayama, 2003, 2010; Levine et al., 2016).

People in Western societies, however, see themselves as **independent** of others, reflecting in part their individualistic orientation. Rather than striving to fit in, they may compete rather than cooperate with others. In many cases, they pride themselves on their uniqueness, distinctiveness, and above all, individuality.

These distinct views of the self are revealed on many levels and in all aspects of individualistic cultures. Even the languages people speak reflect the differences. For instance, the English language has more words for emotions focused on oneself, such as jealousy and anger, than the Japanese language. In contrast, the Japanese language contains many more terms for emotions involving others, such as sympathy, than the English language. In fact, the Japanese language contains words for some emotions that do not have similar words in English. *Oime,* for instance, refers to being indebted to another individual–a word for which English has nothing comparable (Markus & Kitayama, 2010; Andersen, 2017).

People in Eastern cultures also view achievement very differently than people in Western cultures. For example, Westerners assess achievement in terms of personal gains. They look at how well they are doing relative to others, comparing whether they are better or worse off. Grades, salaries, and the size of one's home or office are things that people may use to compare and measure achievements. Thus, the value they place on their success is relative to what others achieve.

In contrast, people in interdependent societies tend to measure success in terms of group achievement. Rewards are thought to be appropriate in terms of how well one's group does, rather than how one does as an individual. For example, a student's success on a group project would be measured in terms of how well the overall project turns out, rather than in terms of each student's individual contribution. Similarly, salary raises in a business might be based on the performance of the company as a whole.

Most aspects of a culture, such as the degree of its individualism and collectivism, are neither inherently good nor bad. In an absolute sense, neither individualism nor collectivism is preferable to the other. But elements in some cultures are clearly harmful. One such element is the aggressiveness of a given society, which we consider next.

self A person's essential being distinguishing themselves from others; how we define ourselves as individuals.

interdependent (view of self) To view oneself as a member of a larger society, working together with others to achieve social harmony.

independent (view of self) To view oneself as behaving independently, competing rather than cooperating with others.

Exploring Diversity

The Culture of Aggression

Violence is as American as apple pie. At least that's the conclusion of some observers of society in the United States, who point to the grim quantity of violence that occurs. For example, the homicide rate in the United States is four times greater than in comparable countries such as France and the United Kingdom. Even within the United States, certain segments of the population are at extraordinary risk: African Americans account for nearly half of all murder victims, yet make up only about 13% of the population. And big-city homicides rose substantially in both 2015 and 2016 (Lepore, 2009; Associated Press, 2011; Rosenfeld et al., 2017).

The United States is also an outlier when it comes to the magnitude of school violence. Since the Columbine High School shooting in 1999, 131 children, educators, and others have been killed in school shootings in 217 schools. Furthermore, 215,000 children have been witnesses to school shootings (Cox et al., 2018).

Do these figures imply that U.S. society is uniquely violent compared to other societies? Before we can answer such a question, we need to consider several factors, because comparing levels of aggression across cultures is no easy matter.

Take, for instance, the difficulty in defining the term *aggression*. Most researchers suggest that for an act to be considered aggressive, it must involve intentional injury or harm to another person; others use broader definitions. The particular definition of aggression becomes critical when comparing statistics collected from a variety of settings in very different cultures.

In addition, even when a specific definition of aggression can be agreed on, labeling a particular behavior as aggressive may prove problematic. Consider this example of observing children: One boy shoves another from behind and knocks him over; both boys laugh about the incident. Should this behavior be labeled as aggressive or as spirited play?

Finally, cultures are not necessarily homogeneous, which adds to why differences exist in the incidence of aggression. For example, there are regional differences in the United States: The rate of murder in the Texas panhandle is four times higher than the murder rate in Nebraska. Generalizing across an entire country or culture, then, may obscure important differences among subgroups (Nisbett & Cohen, 1996; Anwar, Fry, & Grigaitytė, 2018; Hornsveld et al, 2018).

Despite such critical difficulties in comparing rates of violence across cultures, several researchers have attempted to identify differences between cultures in the levels of aggression. As a result, several findings have emerged.

One finding is that cultures have very different views of aggression. For instance, people in some cultures hold extremely positive attitudes about aggression. Among the Simbu of New Guinea, the most admired people are the most aggressive. The more violent a male is, the more followers he is likely to have and the higher his status. These higher-status males often seek fights and urge others to join in fighting. As a consequence, warfare is frequent (Brown, 1986; Dernbach & Marshall, 2001).

In contrast, some cultures are notably nonviolent. For instance, the Semai, who live in the Malaysian rain forest, traditionally hold negative attitudes about aggression (Bonta, 1997). They tend to deride people who are violent and hold nurturance in high esteem. Perhaps because they live in an area rich in natural resources, they generally see less practical value in antagonistic or adversarial behavior.

Other studies have focused on more direct comparisons. In one classic study, cross-cultural psychologist William Lambert (1971) examined aggression in Kenya, India, Mexico, Okinawa, the Philippines, and the United States. He looked at how mothers, the primary child-care providers in each of the cultures, reacted to their own children's aggression toward other children. The results showed that Mexican mothers were the strictest, whereas mothers in the United States showed the greatest leniency toward aggressive behavior. In contrast, mothers responded differently to acts of aggression by their children toward adults. Children who were aggressive toward adults received the greatest punishment in Kenya, the Philippines, and Mexico and the least punishment in India. U.S. children received a relatively moderate degree of punishment (Lopez, Schneider, & Dula, 2002; Stacks et al., 2009; Lansford et al., 2014).

How mothers react to aggression is ultimately reflected in overall rates of societal aggression, although the display of aggression depends on the children's activity level and opportunities for social interaction. For instance, active children who frequently interact with other children seem to learn their culture's lessons about aggression most readily. Thus, active Mexican children are relatively less aggressive than U.S. children because mothers in Mexico tend to react strongly against displays of aggressive behavior. In contrast, active children in the United States show more aggression since their aggression typically earns only a mild rebuke from their mothers.

These findings clearly demonstrate that culture plays a role in providing children with experiences that ultimately result in different levels of social aggression. How a culture trains its children, then, affects their degree of aggressiveness.

Although people in various cultures differ in levels of aggression, at least one common factor bridges across cultures: Males are more aggressive than females. In no culture do females commit more aggressive acts than males, a finding that holds for adults as well as children (Segall, 1988; Slotboom, Hendriks, & Verbruggen, 2011; Bass et al., 2018).

Why should this be true? Although we might attribute the finding to heredity—the idea that males are born with a predisposition to be more aggressive than females—this is not the only possibility. For instance, across cultures, societies may hold similar expectations about the behaviors boys and girls are taught, and it is these expectations that lead to the differences in aggression. In many cultures, boys are explicitly taught to be aggressive, whereas aggression in girls is discouraged. Related explanations suggest that boys act aggressively to accentuate their masculine identity, most likely because their societies value "strong," aggressive males (Whiting, 1965; Pellegrini et al., 2010; Bosson & Vandello, 2011; Aimé et al., 2018).

Although the universal differences in male and female aggression levels are striking, the fact that psychologists find substantial differences in levels of aggression from culture to culture is also noteworthy (Felson & Tedeschi, 1993). It suggests that aggression is not an inevitable aspect of human behavior, and it implies that people may learn to control and reduce violence in the world. In turn, it may be possible to diminish global aggression and to enhance the potential for peace in our time.

Across cultures, males tend to be more aggressive than females. Why might this be true?
©PhotoAlto/Odilon Dimier/Getty Images

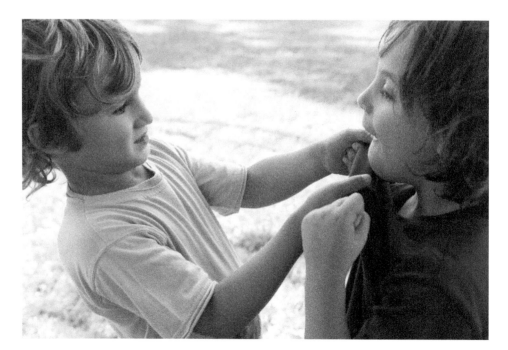

Immigrants: The Newest Americans

Anti-immigrant rhetoric in the United States today describes immigrants as rapists, murderers, and worse, who are straining the prison system, stealing jobs, living on welfare, and contributing little to society. However, the reality, as embodied by statistical evidence, is quite different.

For instance, consider the following data (Lazear, 2017):

- The majority of legal and illegal immigrants ultimately become financially successful. Although initially they have higher rates of poverty than native-born Americans, most immigrants eventually have higher average family incomes than native-born citizens. They have a higher rate of business startups.

- Most of the projected increase in immigration comes from increases in legal immigration, not illegal immigration.

- Few immigrants come to the United States to receive welfare. Instead, most say they come because of opportunities to work and prosper in the United States. Many come to escape political oppression and crippling poverty, and their goal is to work and earn a living. In fact, the unemployment rate for immigrants is about 10% lower than for the native-born population.

- Although they are initially more costly to the government, immigrants become increasingly productive as they get older, paying taxes that outweigh their cost to government.

Why do immigrants so often end up financially successful? One hypothesis is that those immigrants who voluntarily leave their native countries are unusually motivated to become successful, more so than immigrants who choose not to immigrate. Whatever the reason, the evidence suggests that most immigrants eventually become part of the fabric of U.S. life (Giridharadas, 2014; Bruni, 2017; López & Bialik, 2017).

Conflict and Cooperation: Striving for a Just and Peaceful World

Despite their broad cultural differences, the vast majority of the peoples of the world share some fundamental aspirations: They wish to live in peace and harmony with their neighbors and to seek a better life for themselves and their families. Unfortunately, efforts at resolving conflict often fall short of such aspirations, and we inhabit a globe where aggression and war are all too often seen as the solution to problems.

Yet, we can improve our lot. Let's consider why conflicts arise and how we can achieve cooperation and peace.

The Roots of Conflict

Conflict occurs when individuals, groups, or nations perceive that their behavior, goals, or beliefs are incompatible with those of others. What one person—or group or nation—desires, others may see as being potentially damaging. Consider these examples: Community business leaders want to erect a parking garage on land next to a residence for the elderly; the elderly fear that the increased traffic will compromise their safety, the exhaust fumes will harm their health, and the diminished green space will detract from their quality of life. On another scale, Palestinians want to establish an independent country on land currently controlled by Israelis; the Israelis fear this country will threaten their security. In the first example, the conflict may lead to a war of words, petitions, and hurt feelings; in the other, the potential for a war with lethal weapons increases.

In some cases, conflict may arise from competition over scarce resources. **Realistic conflict theory** argues that conflict is the outcome of direct competition over valued, but limited, resources. According to this perspective, the qualities we most desire, such as security, health, a good job, a safe and comfortable environment,

realistic conflict theory The theory that conflict arises from direct competition over valued, but limited, resources.

An estimated **22.5 million** people are now refugees—forced to flee their homes due to ethnic persecution, war, or violence. Many settle in refugee camps, such as the one shown here, that are intended to offer temporary shelter but may house people for decades.
©brianafrica/Alamy Stock Photo

and an adequate standard of living, are limited. Consequently, we compete with others to acquire our fair share (Moghaddam, 2008; Tajfel & Turner, 2010; Densley & Peterson, 2018).

But how do we determine what's a fair share? For many people, a fair share is more than just a minimum level of resources. In reckoning how much more than a minimum level they should have, they consider what others have. According to this view, then, people consider their own level of relative deprivation to determine their level of satisfaction. **Relative deprivation** is the sense that one group lacks a desired amount of resources in comparison to another group, which the first group perceives as having more. For example, even relatively well-paid factory workers may feel underpaid when they compare their compensation to the huge salary the chief executive of the company receives (Raviallion & Lokshin, 2010; Greitemeyer & Sagioglou, 2017).

relative deprivation The sense that one lacks a desired resource in comparison to another group, which is perceived to have more.

In some cases, *perceived* conflict fuels hostility among individuals and groups. Because we use group membership as a source of pride and self-worth, threats to group identity may provoke conflict. For example, the conflict between the Hutu and Tutsi clans in Rwanda in 1994 was based, primarily, on ethnic rivalries. Tragically, the focus on group membership in this situation resulted in the death or displacement of more than 2 million people (Tajfel & Turner, 2004; Staub, 2011, 2018).

Finally, conflict may occur inadvertently, with individuals pursuing a course of action that benefits them as individuals but has quite negative consequences for society as a whole. In such cases, people fall into *social traps*, situations in which individual rewards come into conflict with the optimal outcome for the group. Consider what happened to the people who fished the waters of the Georges Banks off the coast of Massachusetts in the late 1980s. Each individual sought to catch as many fish as possible–a reasonable strategy for a person seeking to maximize each day's profits. Besides, people thought that no one person could catch so many fish that the overall stock of fish would be threatened. When considered collectively, however, the behavior of the many individuals seeking to maximize their catch resulted in such rapid overfishing that the overall supply was devastated. As a consequence, Massachusetts was forced to pass laws to restrict fishing, and many fishermen went bankrupt. Ironically, their pursuit of individual goals ultimately damaged the long-term interests of all parties involved (Urlacher, 2008; Abel, 2015).

Misperceiving Our Enemies

In 2017, during a war of words between U.S. President Donald Trump and North Korean leader Kim Jong-un, Trump called Kim "Rocket Man." In return, the North Korean leader called Trump a "mentally deranged U.S. dotard." This extraordinary public display of name-calling between world leaders illustrated how antagonism can escalate and dehumanize others. In fact, in many situations, our view of our enemies is so distorted that it causes serious strategic miscalculations. For example, psychologists suggest that several distortions in thinking influenced decision-making during the course of the war in Vietnam (White, 2004; Sang-hun, 2017):

- *An image of the enemy as diabolical.* Americans viewed the communist Vietnamese as inscrutable and deceptive, as people who were capable of horrible atrocities and fiendish aggression.

- *A virile self-image.* Americans saw themselves and their military policy as determined, correct, and strong.

- *An overconfident military.* Having never "lost" a war, Americans believed they could win any confrontation in which they participated. It always seemed that just one more battle would bring a final victory.

- *Lack of empathy for the enemy.* Political and military leaders had no clear understanding of what the enemy felt, how it perceived the situation, or even why it was fighting.

- *Selective inattention.* The U.S. government consistently ignored facts and events that might have led it to change its position on or understanding of the war. For example, widespread corruption in the South Vietnamese army, the United States' ally, was ignored, as were South Vietnam's undemocratic government policies.

- *A moral self-image.* The United States viewed itself as superior not only militarily, but morally as well.

Such misperceptions of enemies are not restricted to the war in Vietnam. Citizens and powerful world leaders still tend to mischaracterize the pronouncements of their enemies, and they base their views of other nations on stereotypes regarding national personality traits and other characteristics. Many of the mistakes in perception regarding Vietnam also apply to some degree to the U.S. military interventions in Iraq, Afghanistan, and Syria (Jost, Kay, & Thorisdotter, 2009).

Ironically, a nation's enemies are susceptible to similar misperceptions and stereotyping. Consequently, nations often hold *mirror-image perceptions*, views that duplicate those their opponents hold of them. In other words, each side sees itself as virtuous and morally just, and its enemy as evil and ruthless. Moreover, as conflicts escalate, perceptions of one's enemies grow increasingly simplistic. For example, the complexity of the images that both Israelis and Arabs use to describe each other declined as the level of conflict between them increased (Hirschberger, Pyszczynski, & Ein-Dor, 2010; Fischer, 2011; Fisher & Kelman, 2011).

Genocidal Violence and Mass Killing: Explaining the Inexplicable

The genocide of the Armenians in Turkey during World War I. The Holocaust during World War II. The massacres in Rwanda in 1994. The recent attacks on hundreds of thousands of Rohingya in Myanmar.

All these events, in which collectively *millions* of people were killed because of their religion, ethnicity, or race, represent the worst of humanity: an extinguishing of the caring and altruistic spark in human beings. How do psychologists explain such horrific behavior?

According to Ervin Staub (2018), *genocides*, in which particular demographic groups are targeted for mass killing, share certain features. They typically occur when difficult life conditions stand in the way of fulfilling some basic human needs, such as physical security and a positive social identity. When these difficult conditions occur, one group of people may blame another group of people in an effort to solve their problems, which may unleash several other processes. For example, people may elevate their own group by belittling others. Moreover, one group may identify another group as the source of the problems—the process called scapegoating. Finally, one group may develop an ideology that holds the promise of an improved future and, at the same time, accuses a particular group of blocking the success of the ideology.

Once those in power identify a group as the scapegoat, those in the more powerful group may tolerate minor acts of discrimination against them. Subsequently, these minor acts may escalate into more violent behavior, as bystanders use "just world" reasoning to conclude that the victims are merely getting the treatment they deserve because the bystanders see the world as a just and fair place. As such thinking evolves, people increasingly devalue the victims to the point that they view them as having less moral worth than the perpetrators. At the same time, perpetrators become increasingly committed to their ideology and commit higher levels of violence. Because most bystanders do not intervene, perpetrators reason that they have the tacit approval of the bystanders. Eventually, the level of violence intensifies, and societal norms change. Ultimately, full-blown genocide occurs.

Although difficult life conditions do not lead inevitably to genocide, some cultures have traditions that may increase its likelihood. These cultures have a history of devaluing

When people come together to promote caring and positive relations, they offer hope for a more peaceful world.
©Shutterstock/Rawpixel.com

other groups. Furthermore, conditions are ripe for genocide in cultures with a particularly strong respect for authority, a fairly homogeneous population, a history of aggression, and a dominant culture that sees itself as superior to other cultures.

Staub's analysis, which suggests that situational conditions combine with cultural factors to permit the development of genocide, is sobering. At the same time, though, it suggests two avenues to prevent its development. One is to deal directly with difficult life conditions by striving to help people economically and socially. The other avenue is to change cultural norms from those that permit the devaluation of others to norms that promote caring and positive relations among groups of people (Staub, Pearlman, & Bilali, 2010; Staub, 2011, 2018).

BECOMING AN INFORMED CONSUMER
of Psychology

Reducing War, Promoting Peace, and Creating a Just World

As the violence in Syria, Afghanistan, Gaza, and many other hot spots shows, the world remains a dangerous place. Although the threat of a major, all-out nuclear war has diminished, the danger remains high for smaller, more limited wars. Furthermore, other problems of the world continue unabated, such as environmental degradation, overpopulation, disease, and famine.

Yet, the world's citizens are not powerless. Several strategies, developed as a result of work conducted by psychologists, can help create a world that is safer and more just in the future. Here are some of the most promising possibilities:

cross-cutting relations The links between groups in the areas of work, education, and recreation.

- *Increase cross-cutting relations between people.* **Cross-cutting relations** are the links between groups in the areas of work, education, and recreation. By arranging opportunities for people to interact with one another, as does the Seeds of Peace program we discussed at the beginning of the chapter, cross-cutting relations can allow people to understand the underlying similarities among all the world's peoples. Ultimately, such relationships can lead to feelings of connectedness and the awareness that we all share basic needs and aspirations (Deutsch, 1994; Nowak et al., 2010).

- *Use education to overcome attitudes that devalue outgroups.* One method to reduce violence against members of minority groups and other outgroups is to extend the boundaries that delineate the people who are considered "us" to include those who are considered "them." When people become more accepting of other cultures and better understand their own, they learn that their own culture may not be the standard against which to judge all others (Staub, Pearlman, & Bilali, 2010; Staub, 2011, 2018).

- *Create a robust multicultural society.* Demographic trends show that the white majority in the United States is shrinking. Over the coming decades, the rise in the Hispanic population will be particularly dramatic. Experts estimate that by 2050, nearly one in every three Americans will be Hispanic. Whether or not the United States is prepared, it is about to become an even more deeply multicultural society with direct links to countries throughout the world. Indeed, as international travel becomes increasingly affordable and social networking tools such as Facebook and Twitter become steadily more prominent, people all over the globe will have increasing opportunities to interact (Shrestha & Heisler, 2011; Herskovits, 2018).

Increased intercultural interaction can bring several benefits. For one thing, it can reduce ingroup–outgroup bias, in which people hold more favorable opinions about members of ingroups and less favorable opinions about outgroups. By reducing this bias, people can become more flexible in their thinking and better understand the subtleties of others' behavior (Brewer, 2007; Giannakakis, & Fritsche, 2011; Jacoby-Senghor, Sinclair, & Smith, 2015).

Perhaps more important, direct interaction with people from varied racial, cultural, ethnic, and religious backgrounds, and of various sexual orientations, gender identities, and physical abilities may allow us to see the basic similarities that underlie all human behavior. Throughout this book, we discussed the broad principles that psychologists use to explain behavior. The understanding provided by this knowledge can encourage citizens to become keenly interested in the prospects for a more peaceful and just world for all the globe's inhabitants.

AP EPILOGUE: DIVERSITY, CULTURE, CONFLICT, AND COOPERATION

AP SUMMARY

- Culture comprises the learned behaviors, beliefs, and attitudes that are characteristic of an individual society or population. Culture both shapes and reflects a society's behavior, understanding of the world, attitudes, and values.

- Societies that encourage individualism hold as a primary value the personal identity, uniqueness, freedom, and worth of the individual. In contrast, cultures that support collectivism promote the idea that the well-being of the group or society is more important than that of the individual.

- Culture has an impact on people's view of themselves, meaning the way in which they look inward and define themselves as individuals. People in Eastern societies tend to have an interdependent view, perceiving themselves as members of a larger society and working together with others to achieve social harmony. In comparison, people in Western societies generally see themselves as independent. The emphasis in such societies is on competing rather than cooperating with others.

- Societies and cultures vary significantly in the degree of aggression their members display. However, at least one universal principle crosses cultures: Males are more aggressive than females.

- Despite political rhetoric to the contrary, research shows that most immigrants to the United States are productive and ultimately successful.
- Conflicts occur when individuals, groups, or nations perceive that their behavior, goals, or beliefs are incompatible with those of others. Realistic conflict theory holds that conflict stems from competition over valued, but limited, resources. The notion of relative deprivation–the perception that one group lacks a desired amount of resources in comparison to the amount held by others–adds to the idea that the sense of resource scarcity may be related to a perception of fairness.
- In some cases, perceived conflict can fuel hostility between groups. If the perception exists that group identity is threatened, conflict may occur. Conflict can also result when people fall into social traps, situations in which individual goals conflict with the optimal outcome for the group.
- Psychologists have studied how people's misperceptions about their enemies act as hindrances to peace. Possible distortions include an image of the enemy as diabolical, a virile self-image, an overconfident military, lack of empathy for the enemy, selective inattention to facts, and a moralistic self-image.
- Genocide is a form of collective murder in which particular demographic groups are targeted for killing. Genocides may occur when people's basic needs are unmet because of difficult life conditions and a particular group is first belittled, then singled out as the scapegoat for those difficult conditions. Genocides are often supported by an ideology that promises a bright future and identifies the targeted group as the main obstacle to achieving that future.
- Among the ways to enhance the chances for future peace are to increase cross-cutting relations between people, to use education to overcome attitudes that devalue outgroups, and to create a robust multicultural society.

AP KEY TERMS

race	interdependent (view of self)
ethnicity	independent (view of self)
culture	realistic conflict theory
multiculturalism	relative deprivation
individualism	cross-cutting relations
collectivism	
self	

AP TEST PRACTICE

Section I: Multiple Choice

1. Your friend, Sarah, is throwing a party on Saturday night while her parents are out of town. She was expressly told not to have a party and you feel uncomfortable knowing that Sarah has lied to her parents. You decide to go anyway but don't enjoy the party as much as you'd hoped. What you're experiencing is
   A. realistic conflict theory
   B. cognitive dissonance
   C. mirror-image perceptions
   D. generalized anxiety disorder

2. The term "intersectionality" can be described as
   A. when one has a revelation leading to a solution
   B. the way in which families resolve conflict
   C. when two psychologists with differing opinions reach consensus
   D. the way in which diverse identities overlap or interact

3. What are some of the benefits of increased multicultural interaction?
   A. relative deprivation
   B. mirror-image perceptions
   C. reduction in ingroup-outgroup bias
   D. an increased virile self-image

Section II: Free Response

A. Ezra has an elderly neighbor who has difficulty getting to the store and taking care of her lawn. Many of his classmates live in the neighborhood, and Ezra is trying to set up a rotating schedule with each of them pitching in to help. He has found it interesting that some classmates responded right away and have eagerly signed up to participate while others, although contacted more than once, have never even replied. Explain this scenario as it relates to

- collectivism
- individualism

Glossary

abnormal behavior Behavior that causes people to experience distress and prevents them from functioning in their daily lives. (Module 46)

absolute threshold The smallest intensity of a stimulus that must be present for the stimulus to be detected. (Module 10)

acquired immune deficiency syndrome (AIDS) A sexually transmitted infection caused by a virus that destroys the body's immune system. (Module 34)

action potential An electric nerve impulse that travels through a neuron's axon when it is set off by a "trigger," changing the neuron's charge from negative to positive. (Module 7)

activation-synthesis theory Hobson's theory that the brain produces random electrical energy during REM sleep that stimulates memories stored in the brain. (Module 14)

activity theory of aging The theory that suggests that successful aging is characterized by maintaining the interests and activities of earlier stages of life. (Module 39)

adaptation An adjustment in sensory capacity after prolonged exposure to unchanging stimuli. (Module 10)

addictive drugs Drugs that produce a biological or psychological dependence in the user so that withdrawal from them leads to a craving for the drug that, in some cases, may be nearly irresistible. (Module 16)

adolescence The developmental stage between childhood and adulthood. (Module 38)

age of viability The point at which a fetus can survive if born prematurely. (Module 36)

aggression The intentional injury of, or harm to, another person. (Module 55)

algorithm A rule that, if applied appropriately, guarantees a solution to a problem. (Module 23)

all-or-none law The rule that neurons are either on or off. (Module 7)

altruism Behavior meant to help another person without regard for self-interest. (Module 55)

Alzheimer's disease A progressive brain disorder that leads to a gradual and irreversible decline in cognitive abilities. (Modules 22, 39)

amnesia Memory loss that occurs without other mental difficulties. (Module 22)

anal stage According to Freud, a stage from age 12-18 months to 3 years of age in which a child's pleasure is centered on the anus. (Module 40)

androgens Male sex hormones secreted by the testes. (Module 33)

anorexia nervosa A severe eating disorder in which people may refuse to eat while denying that their behavior and appearance–which can become skeleton-like–are unusual. (Module 30)

anterograde amnesia Amnesia in which memory is lost for events that follow an injury. (Module 22)

antianxiety drugs Drugs that reduce the level of anxiety a person experiences and increase feelings of well-being. (Module 51)

antidepressant drugs Medications that improve a severely depressed patient's mood and feeling of well-being. (Module 51)

antipsychotic drugs Drugs that temporarily reduce psychotic symptoms such as agitation, hallucinations, and delusions. (Module 51)

antisocial personality disorder A disorder in which individuals show no regard for the moral and ethical rules of society or the rights of others. (Module 47)

anxiety disorder The occurrence of anxiety without an obvious external cause that affects daily functioning. (Module 47)

archetypes According to Jung, universal symbolic representations of particular types of people, objects, ideas, or experiences. (Module 40)

archival research Research in which existing data, such as census documents, college records, and newspaper clippings, are examined to test a hypothesis. (Module 5)

arousal approaches to motivation The belief that people try to maintain a steady level of stimulation and activity. (Module 29)

association areas One of the major regions of the cerebral cortex; the site of the higher mental processes, such as thought, language, memory, and speech. (Module 9)

assumed-similarity bias The tendency to think of people as being similar to oneself even when meeting them for the first time. (Module 52)

attachment The positive emotional bond that develops between a child and a particular individual. (Module 37)

attention-deficit hyperactivity disorder (ADHD) A disorder marked by inattention, impulsiveness, a low tolerance for frustration, and a great deal of inappropriate activity. (Module 47)

attitudes Evaluations of people, objects, ideas, and behavior. (Module 52)

attribution theory The theory that considers how we decide, on the basis of samples of a person's behavior, what the specific causes of that behavior are. (Module 52)

authoritarian parents Parents who are rigid and punitive and value unquestioning obedience from their children. (Module 37)

authoritative parents Parents who are firm, set clear limits, reason with their children, and explain things to them. (Module 37)

autism spectrum disorder A severe developmental disability that impairs children's ability to communicate and relate to others. (Module 47)

autobiographical memory Our recollections of our own life experiences. (Module 21)

autonomic division The part of the peripheral nervous system that controls involuntary movement of the heart, glands, lungs, and other organs. (Module 8)

autonomy-versus-shame-and-doubt stage The period during which, according to Erikson, toddlers (ages 1½ to 3 years) develop independence and autonomy if exploration and freedom are encouraged or shame and self-doubt if they are restricted and overprotected. (Module 37)

aversive conditioning A form of therapy that reduces the frequency of undesired behavior by pairing an aversive, unpleasant stimulus with undesired behavior. (Module 49)

axon The part of the neuron that carries messages to other neurons. (Module 7)

babble Meaningless, speechlike sounds made by children from around the age of 3 months through 1 year. (Module 25)

background stressors ("daily hassles") Everyday annoyances, such as being stuck in traffic, that cause minor irritations and may have long-term ill effects if they continue or are compounded by other stressful events. (Module 43)

basilar membrane A vibrating structure that runs through the center of the cochlea, dividing it into an upper chamber and a lower chamber and containing sense receptors for sound. (Module 12)

behavior modification A technique whose goal is to increase the frequency of desirable behaviors and decrease the incidence of unwanted ones. (Module 18)

behavioral assessment Direct measures of an individual's behavior used to describe personality characteristics. (Module 42)

behavioral genetics The study of the effects of heredity on behavior. (Module 8)

behavioral neuroscientists (or biopsychologists) Psychologists who specialize in considering the ways in which the biological structures and functions of the body affect behavior. (Module 7)

behavioral perspective The approach that suggests that observable, external behavior, which can be objectively measured, should be the focus of study. (Module 2)

behavioral perspective The perspective that looks at the rewards and punishments in the environment that determine abnormal behavior. (Module 46)

behavioral treatment approaches Treatment approaches that make use of the basic principles of learning, such as reinforcement and extinction, to reduce or eliminate maladaptive behavior. (Module 49)

biofeedback A procedure in which a person learns to control through conscious thought internal physiological processes such as blood pressure, heart and respiration rate, skin temperature, sweating, and the constriction of particular muscles. (Module 9)

biological and evolutionary approaches to personality Theories that suggest that important components of personality are inherited. (Module 41)

biomedical therapy Biologically based therapy that relies on drugs and other medical procedures to improve psychological functioning. (Module 49)

bipolar disorder A disorder in which a person alternates between periods of euphoric feelings of mania and periods of depression. (Module 47)

bisexuals Persons who are sexually attracted to people of the same sex and the other sex. (Module 34)

borderline personality disorder A disorder characterized by problems regulating emotions and thoughts, displaying impulsive and reckless behavior, and having unstable relationships with others. (Module 47)

bottom-up processing Perception that consists of the progression of recognizing and processing information from individual components of a stimuli and moving to the perception of the whole. (Module 13)

bulimia A disorder in which a person binges on large quantities of food, followed by efforts to purge the food through vomiting or other means. (Module 30)

Cannon-Bard theory of emotion The belief that both physiological arousal and emotional experience are produced simultaneously by the same nerve stimulus. (Module 31)

case study An in-depth, intensive investigation of an individual or small group of people. (Module 5)

cataclysmic events Strong stressors that occur suddenly and typically affect many people at once (e.g., natural disasters). (Module 43)

catharsis The process of discharging built-up aggressive energy. (Module 55)

central core The "old brain," which controls basic functions such as eating and sleeping and is common to all vertebrates. (Module 9)

central nervous system (CNS) The part of the nervous system that includes the brain and spinal cord. (Module 8)

central route processing The type of mental processing that occurs when a persuasive message is evaluated by thoughtful consideration of the issues and arguments used to persuade. (Module 52)

central tendency An index of the central location within a distribution of scores; the most representative score in a distribution of scores (the mean, median, and mode are measures of central tendency). (Module 56)

central traits The major traits considered in forming impressions of others. (Module 52)

cerebellum (ser-uh-BELL-um) The part of the brain that controls bodily balance. (Module 9)

cerebral cortex The "new brain," responsible for the most sophisticated information processing in the brain; contains four lobes. (Module 9)

chromosomes Rod-shaped structures that contain all basic hereditary information. (Module 36)

chunk A group of separate pieces of information stored as a single unit in short-term memory. (Module 20)

circadian rhythms Biological processes that occur regularly on approximately a 24-hour cycle. (Module 14)

classical conditioning A type of learning in which a neutral stimulus comes to bring about a response after it is paired with a stimulus that naturally brings about that response. (Module 17)

cochlea (KOKE-lee-uh) A coiled tube in the ear filled with fluid that vibrates in response to sound. (Module 12)

cognitive approaches to motivation Theories suggesting that motivation is the outcomes of people's thoughts, beliefs, expectations, and goals. (Module 29)

cognitive development The process by which a child's understanding of the world changes due to the child's age and experience. (Module 37)

cognitive dissonance The mental conflict that occurs when a person holds two contradictory attitudes or thoughts (referred to as cognitions). (Module 52)

cognitive learning theory An approach to the study of learning that focuses on the thought processes that underlie learning. (Module 19)

cognitive perspective The approach that focuses on how people think, understand, and know about the world. (Module 2)

cognitive perspective The perspective that suggests that people's thoughts and beliefs are central components of abnormal behavior. (Module 46)

cognitive psychology The branch of psychology that focuses on the study of higher mental processes, including thinking, language, memory, problem solving, knowing, reasoning, judging, and decision making. (Module 23)

cognitive-treatment approaches Treatment approaches that teach people to think in more adaptive ways by changing their dysfunctional cognitions about the world and themselves. (Module 49)

collective unconscious According to Jung, an inherited set of ideas, feelings, images, and symbols that are shared with all humans because of our common ancestral past. (Module 40)

collectivism An idea that the well-being of the group or society is more important than that of the individual.

community psychology A branch of psychology that focuses on the prevention and minimization of psychological disorders in the community. (Module 51)

companionate love The strong affection we have for those with whom our lives are deeply involved. (Module 55)

compliance Behavior that occurs in response to direct social pressure. (Module 53)

compulsion An irresistible urge to repeatedly carry out some behavior that seems strange and unreasonable. (Module 47)

concepts Mental groupings of similar objects, events, or people. (Module 23)

concrete operational stage According to Piaget, the period from 7 to 12 years of age that is characterized by logical thought and a loss of egocentrism. (Module 37)

conditioned response (CR) A response that, after conditioning, follows a previously neutral stimulus (e.g., salivation at the ringing of a bell). (Module 17)

conditioned stimulus (CS) A once-neutral stimulus that has been paired with an unconditioned stimulus to bring about a response formerly caused only by the unconditioned stimulus. (Module 17)

cones Cone-shaped, light-sensitive receptor cells in the retina that are responsible for sharp focus and color perception, particularly in bright light. (Module 11)

confirmation bias The tendency to seek out and weight more heavily information that supports one's initial hypothesis and

to ignore contradictory information that supports alternative hypotheses or solutions. (Module 24)

conformity A change in behavior or attitudes brought about by a desire to follow the beliefs or standards of other people. (Module 53)

consciousness The awareness of the sensations, thoughts, and feelings being experienced at a given moment. (Module 14)

constructive processes Processes in which memories are influenced by the meaning we give to events. (Module 21)

continuous reinforcement schedule A schedule in which behavior is reinforced every time the behavior occurs. (Module 18)

control group A group participating in an experiment that receives no treatment. (Module 5)

convergent thinking Thinking in which a problem is viewed as having a single answer and which produces a solution that is based primarily on knowledge and logic. (Module 24)

conversion disorder A major somatic symptom disorder that involves an actual physical disturbance, such as the inability to use a sensory organ or the complete or partial inability to move an arm or leg. (Module 47)

coping The efforts to control, reduce, or learn to tolerate the threats that lead to stress. (Module 43)

correlation coefficient A numerical measure that indicates the extent of the relationship between two variables. (Module 58)

correlational research Research in which the relationship between two sets of variables is examined to determine whether they are associated, or "correlated." (Module 5)

creativity The ability to generate original ideas or solve problems in novel ways. (Module 24)

cross-cutting relations The links between groups in the areas of work, education, and recreation.

cross-sectional research A research method that compares people of different ages at the same point in time. (Module 35)

crystallized intelligence The accumulation of information, knowledge, and skills that people have learned through experience and education, reflecting the facts that we have learned. (Module 26)

cue-dependent forgetting Forgetting that occurs when there are insufficient retrieval cues to rekindle information that is in memory. (Module 22)

culture The learned behaviors, beliefs, and attitudes that characterize an individual society or population.

culture-fair IQ test A test that does not discriminate against the members of any minority group. (Module 28)

date rape Rape in which the rapist is either a date or a romantic acquaintance. (Module 34)

daydreams Fantasies that people construct while awake. (Module 14)

decay The loss of information in memory through its nonuse. (Module 22)

declarative memory Memory for factual information: names, faces, dates, and the like. (Module 20)

deductive reasoning Reasoning from the general to the specific. (Module 23)

defense mechanisms In Freudian theory, unconscious strategies that people use to reduce anxiety by distorting reality and concealing the source of the anxiety from themselves. (Module 40)

deinstitutionalization The process of transferring patients who have been hospitalized for long periods into less-isolated community mental health settings. (Module 51)

delayed ejaculation disorder A disorder in which it takes an extended period of sexual stimulation for a male to be able to ejaculate (Module 34)

dendrite A cluster of fibers at one end of a neuron that receives messages from other neurons. (Module 7)

dependent variable The variable that is measured in an experiment. It is expected to change as a result of the experimenter's manipulation of the independent variable. (Module 5)

depressants Drugs that slow down the nervous system. (Module 16)

depth perception The ability to view the world in three dimensions and to perceive distance. (Module 13)

descriptive statistics The branch of statistics that provides a means of summarizing data. (Module 56)

determinism The idea that people's behavior is produced primarily by factors outside of their willful control. (Module 3)

developmental psychology The branch of psychology that studies the patterns of growth and change that occur throughout life. (Module 35)

Diagnostic and Statistical Manual of Mental Disorders, Fifth Edition (DSM-5) A system, devised by the American Psychiatric Association, used by most professionals to classify and define psychological disorders. (Module 46)

difference threshold (just noticeable difference) The smallest level of added or reduced stimulation required to sense that a change in stimulation has occurred. (Module 10)

diffusion of responsibility The belief that responsibility for intervening is shared, or diffused, among those present. (Module 55)

discrimination Behavior directed toward individuals on the basis of their membership in a particular group. (Module 54)

disengagement theory of aging The theory that suggests that successful aging is characterized by a gradual withdrawal from the world on physical, psychological, and social levels. (Module 39)

dispositional causes (of behavior) Perceived causes of behavior brought about by a person's traits or personality characteristics. (Module 52)

dissociative amnesia A disorder in which a significant, selective memory loss occurs. (Module 47)

dissociative disorders Psychological dysfunctions characterized by the separation of different facets of a person's personality that are normally integrated. (Module 47)

dissociative fugue A form of amnesia in which a person leaves home and assumes a new identity. (Module 47)

dissociative identity disorder (DID) A disorder in which a person displays characteristics of two or more distinct personalities. (Module 47)

divergent thinking Thinking that generates multiple and unusual, although appropriate, responses to problems or questions. (Module 24)

double standard The view that premarital sex is permissible for males but not for females. (Module 34)

dreams-for-survival theory The theory suggesting that dreams permit information that is critical for our daily survival to be reconsidered and reprocessed during sleep. (Module 14)

drive Motivational tension, or arousal, that energizes behavior to fulfill a need. (Module 29)

drive-reduction approaches to motivation Theories suggesting that a lack of some basic biological need produces a drive to push an organism to satisfy that need. (Module 29)

drug therapy Treatment of psychological disorders through the use of drugs that alter the operation of neurons and neurotransmitters in the brain and body. (Module 51)

eardrum The part of the ear that vibrates when sound waves hit it. (Module 12)

ego The rational, logical part of personality that attempts to balance the desires of the id and the realities of the objective, outside world. (Module 40)

ego-integrity-versus-despair stage According to Erikson, a period from late adulthood until death during which we review life's accomplishments and failures. (Module 38)

egocentric thought A way of thinking in which a child views the world entirely from his or her own perspective. (Module 37)

electroconvulsive therapy (ECT) A procedure used in the treatment of severe depression in which an electric current of 70–150 volts is briefly administered to a patient's head. (Module 51)

embryo A developed zygote that has a heart, a brain, and other organs. (Module 36)

emerging adulthood The period beginning in the late teenage years and extending into the mid-20s. (Module 39)

emotional intelligence The set of skills that underlie the accurate assessment, evaluation, expression, and regulation of emotions. (Module 26)

emotions Feelings that generally have both physiological and cognitive elements and that influence behavior. (Module 31)

endocrine system A chemical communication network that sends messages throughout the body via the bloodstream. (Module 8)

episodic memory Memory for events that occur in a particular time, place, or context. (Module 20)

erectile disorder A male's inability to achieve or maintain an erection. (Module 34)

erogenous zones Areas of the body that are particularly sensitive because of the presence of an unusually rich array of nerve receptors. (Module 33)

estrogens Class of female sex hormones. (Module 33)

ethnicity Shared national origins or cultural patterns.

evolutionary psychology The branch of psychology that seeks to identify behavior patterns that are a result of our genetic inheritance from our ancestors. (Module 8)

excitatory message A chemical message that makes it more likely that a receiving neuron will fire and an action potential will travel down its axon. (Module 7)

excitement phase The period in which an arousing stimulus begins a sequence that prepares the genitals for sexual intercourse. (Module 33)

experiment The investigation of the relationship between two (or more) variables by deliberately producing a change in one variable in a situation and observing the effects of that change on other aspects of the situation. (Module 5)

experimental bias Factors that distort how the independent variable affects the dependent variable in an experiment. (Module 6)

experimental group Any group participating in an experiment that receives a treatment. (Module 5)

experimental manipulation The change that an experimenter deliberately produces in a situation. (Module 5)

explicit memory Intentional or conscious recollection of information. (Module 21)

extinction A basic phenomenon of learning that occurs when a previously conditioned response decreases in frequency and eventually disappears. (Module 17)

extramarital sex Sexual activity between a married person and someone who is not his or her spouse. (Module 34)

facial-affect program The theory that a set of nerve impulses produce a facial display reflecting an emotion that is universal across cultures. (Module 31)

facial-feedback hypothesis The hypothesis that facial expressions not only reflect emotional experience but also help determine how people experience and label emotions. (Module 31)

familial intellectual disability Intellectual disability in which no apparent biological or genetic problems exist, but there is a history of intellectual disability among family members. (Module 27)

family therapy An approach that focuses on the family and its dynamics. (Module 50)

feature detector Specialized neurons that are activated only by visual stimuli having specific features, such as a particular shape or pattern. (Module 11)

female orgasmic disorder A female's lack of orgasm. (Module 34)

fetal alcohol syndrome The most common cause of intellectual disability in newborns, occurring when the mother uses alcohol during pregnancy. (Module 27)

fetus A developing individual from 8 weeks after conception until birth. (Module 36)

fixations Conflicts or concerns that persist beyond the developmental period in which they first occur. (Module 40)

fixed-interval schedule A schedule in which reinforcement is provided for a response only after a fixed time period has elapsed. (Module 18)

fixed-ratio schedule A schedule in which reinforcement is given only after a specific number of responses are made. (Module 18)

flashbulb memories Memories of a specific, important, or surprising emotionally significant event that are recalled easily and with vivid imagery. (Module 21)

flooding A behavioral treatment for anxiety in which people are suddenly confronted with a stimulus that they fear. (Module 49)

fluid intelligence Intelligence that reflects the ability to think logically, reason abstractly, solve problems, and find patterns. (Module 26)

formal operational stage According to Piaget, the period from age 12 to adulthood that is characterized by abstract thought. (Module 37)

free will The idea that behavior is caused primarily by choices that are made freely by the individual. (Module 3)

frequency distribution An arrangement of scores from a sample that indicates how often a particular score is present. (Module 56)

frequency theory of hearing The theory that the entire basilar membrane acts like a microphone, vibrating as a whole in response to a sound. (Module 12)

functional fixedness The tendency to think of an object only in terms of the way it is most frequently or typically used. (Module 24)

functionalism An early approach to psychology that concentrated on what the mind does–the functions of mental activity–and the role of behavior in allowing people to adapt to their environments. (Module 2)

fundamental attribution error A tendency to overattribute others' behavior to dispositional causes and minimize the importance of situational causes. (Module 52)

_g_ or _g_-factor The single, general factor for mental ability assumed to underlie intelligence in some early theories of intelligence. (Module 26)

gate-control theory of pain The theory that particular nerve receptors in the spinal cord lead to specific areas of the brain related to pain. (Module 12)

gender The perception of being male or female. (Module 32)

gender roles The set of expectations, defined by a particular society, that indicate what is appropriate behavior for men and women. (Module 32)

gender schema A mental framework that organizes and guides a child's understanding of information relevant to gender. (Module 32)

general adaptation syndrome (GAS) A theory developed by Selye that suggests that a person's response to a stressor consists of three stages: alarm and mobilization, resistance, and exhaustion. (Module 43)

generalized anxiety disorder The experience of long-term, persistent anxiety and worry. (Module 47)

generativity-versus-stagnation stage According to Erikson, a period in middle adulthood during which we take stock of our contributions to family and society. (Module 38)

genes The parts of the chromosomes through which genetic information is transmitted. (Module 36)

genetic programming theories of aging Theories that suggest that our DNA genetic code includes a built-in time limit to the reproduction of human cells and that they are no longer able to divide after a certain time. (Module 39)

genital stage According to Freud, the period from puberty until death, marked by mature sexual behavior (that is, sexual intercourse). (Module 40)

genitals The male and female sex organs. (Module 33)

Gestalt (geh-SHTALLT) laws of organization A series of principles that describe how we organize bits and pieces of information into meaningful wholes. (Module 13)

Gestalt psychology An approach to psychology that focuses on the organization of perception and thinking in a "whole" sense rather than on the individual elements of perception. (Module 2)

grammar The system of rules that determine how our thoughts can be expressed. (Module 25)

group Two or more people who interact with one another, perceive themselves as part of a group, and are interdependent. (Module 53)

group therapy Therapy in which people meet in a group with a therapist to discuss problems. (Module 50)

groupthink A type of thinking in which group members share such a strong motivation to achieve consensus that they lose the ability to critically evaluate alternative points of view. (Module 53)

habituation The decrease in the response to a stimulus that occurs after repeated presentations of the same stimulus. (Module 37)

hair cells Tiny cells covering the basilar membrane that, when bent by vibrations entering the cochlea, transmit neural messages to the brain. (Module 12)

hallucinogens Drugs that are capable of producing alterations in perception, thoughts, and feelings. (Module 16)

halo effect A phenomenon in which an initial understanding that a person has positive or negative traits is used to infer other uniformly positive or negative characteristics. (Module 52)

hardiness A personality trait characterized by a sense of commitment, the perception of problems as challenges, and a sense of control. (Module 43)

health psychology The branch of psychology that investigates the psychological factors related to wellness and illness, including the prevention, diagnosis, and treatment of medical problems. (Module 43)

hemispheres Symmetrical left and right halves of the brain that control the side of the body opposite to their location. (Module 9)

heritability The degree to which a characteristic is related to inherited genetic factors. (Module 28)

heterosexuality Sexual attraction and behavior directed to the other sex. (Module 34)

heuristic A thinking strategy that may lead us to a solution to a problem or decision but–unlike algorithms–may sometimes lead to errors. (Module 23)

histogram Bar graph. (Module 56)

homeostasis The body's tendency to maintain a steady internal state. (Module 29)

homosexuals Persons who are sexually attracted to members of their own sex. (Module 34)

hormones Chemicals that circulate through the blood and regulate the functioning or growth of the body. (Module 8)

humanistic approaches to personality Theories that emphasize people's innate goodness and desire to achieve higher levels of functioning. (Module 41)

humanistic perspective The approach that suggests that all individuals naturally strive to grow, develop, and be in control of their lives and behavior. (Module 2)

humanistic perspective The perspective that emphasizes the responsibility people have for their own behavior, even when such behavior is abnormal. (Module 46)

humanistic therapy Therapy in which the underlying rationale is that people have control of their behavior, can make choices about their lives, and are essentially responsible for solving their own problems. (Module 50)

hypnosis A trancelike state of heightened susceptibility to the suggestions of others. (Module 15)

hypothalamus A tiny part of the brain, located below the thalamus, that maintains homeostasis and produces and regulates vital behavior, such as eating, drinking, and sexual behavior. (Module 9)

hypothesis A prediction, stemming from a theory, stated in a way that allows it to be tested. (Module 4)

id The instinctual and unorganized part of personality whose sole purpose is to reduce tension created by primitive drives related to hunger, sex, aggression, and irrational impulses. (Module 40)

identical twins Twins who are genetically identical. (Module 35)

identification The process of wanting to be like another person as much as possible, imitating that person's behavior and adopting similar beliefs and values. (Module 40)

identity The distinguishing character of the individual: who each of us is, what our roles are, and what we are capable of. (Module 38)

identity-versus-role-confusion stage According to Erikson, a time in adolescence of major testing to determine one's unique qualities. (Module 38)

illness anxiety disorder A somatic symptom disorder in which people have a constant fear of illness and a preoccupation with their health. (Module 47)

implicit memory Memories of which people are not consciously aware but that can affect subsequent performance and behavior. (Module 21)

incentive approaches to motivation Theories suggesting that motivation stems from the desire to attain external rewards, known as incentives. (Module 29)

independent (view of self) To view oneself as behaving independently, competing rather than cooperating with others.

independent variable The variable that is manipulated by an experimenter. (Module 5)

individualism The idea that holds as a primary value the personal identity, uniqueness, freedom, and worth of the individual person.

inductive reasoning Reasoning from the specific to the general. (Module 23)

industrial-organizational (I/O) psychology The branch of psychology focusing on work- and job-related issues, including worker motivation, satisfaction, safety, and productivity. (Module 53)

industry-versus-inferiority stage According to Erikson, the last stage of childhood, during which children ages 6 to 12 years may develop positive social interactions with others or may feel inadequate and become less sociable. (Module 37)

inferential statistics The branch of statistics that uses data from samples to make predictions about the larger population from which the sample is drawn. (Module 58)

information processing The way in which people take in, use, and store information. (Module 37)

informed consent A document signed by participants affirming that they have been told the basic outlines of the study and are aware of what their participation will involve. (Module 6)

inhibitory message A chemical message that prevents or decreases the likelihood that a receiving neuron will fire. (Module 7)

initiative-versus-guilt stage According to Erikson, the period during which children ages 3 to 6 years experience conflict between independence of action and the sometimes negative results of that action. (Module 37)

insight A sudden awareness of the relationships among various elements that had previously appeared to be independent of one another. (Module 24)

instinct approaches to motivation The explanation of motivation that suggests people and animals are born preprogrammed with sets of behaviors essential to their survival. (Module 29)

instincts Inborn patterns of behavior that are biologically determined rather than learned. (Module 29)

intellectual disability A disability characterized by significant limitations in both intellectual functioning and in adaptive behavior, which covers many everyday social and practical skills. (Module 27)

intellectually gifted The 2%-4% segment of the population who have IQ scores greater than 130. (Module 27)

intelligence The capacity to understand the world, think rationally, and use resources effectively when faced with challenges. (Module 26)

intelligence quotient (IQ) A score that takes into account an individual's mental and chronological ages. (Module 26)

intelligence tests Tests devised to quantify a person's level of intelligence. (Module 26)

interactionist approach (to language development) The view that language development is determined by genetic and social factors, produced through a combination of genetically determined predispositions and the social world in which one is raised. (Module 25)

interdependent (view of self) To view oneself as a member of a larger society, working together with others to achieve social harmony.

interference The phenomenon by which information in memory disrupts the recall of other information. (Module 22)

interpersonal attraction (or close relationship) Positive feelings for others; liking and loving. (Module 55)

interpersonal therapy (IPT) Short-term therapy designed to help patients control their moods and emotions by focusing on the context of their current social relationships. (Module 50)

intimacy-versus-isolation stage According to Erikson, a period during early adulthood that focuses on developing close relationships. (Module 38)

introspection A procedure used to study the structure of the mind in which a person is asked to describe in detail what they are experiencing when they are exposed to a stimulus. (Module 2)

James-Lange theory of emotion The belief that emotional experience is a reaction to bodily events occurring as a result of an external situation ("I feel sad because I am crying"). (Module 31)

Korsakoff's syndrome A disease that afflicts long-term alcoholics, leaving some abilities intact but including hallucinations and a tendency to repeat the same story. (Module 22)

language The communication of information through symbols arranged according to systematic rules. (Module 25)

latency period According to Freud, the period between the phallic stage and puberty during which children's sexual concerns are temporarily put aside. (Module 40)

latent learning Learning in which a new behavior is acquired but is not demonstrated until some incentive is provided for displaying it. (Module 19)

lateralization The dominance of one hemisphere of the brain in specific functions, such as language. (Module 9)

learned helplessness A state in which people conclude that unpleasant or aversive stimuli cannot be controlled–a view of the world that becomes so ingrained that they cease trying to remedy the aversive circumstances even if they actually can exert some influence on the situation. (Module 43)

learning A relatively permanent change in behavior brought about by experience. (Module 17)

learning-theory approach (to language development) The theory that language acquisition follows the principles of reinforcement and conditioning. (Module 25)

levels-of-processing theory The theory of memory that emphasizes the degree to which new material is mentally analyzed. (Module 21)

life review The process by which people examine and evaluate their lives. (Module 39)

limbic system The part of the brain that controls eating, aggression, and reproduction. (Module 9)

linguistic-relativity hypothesis The hypothesis that language shapes and helps determine the way people perceive and understand the world. (Module 25)

lobes The four major sections of the cerebral cortex: frontal, parietal, temporal, and occipital. (Module 9)

long-term memory Memory that stores information on a relatively permanent basis, although it may be difficult to retrieve. (Module 20)

longitudinal research A research method that investigates behavior as participants get older. (Module 35)

major depressive disorder A severe form of depression that interferes with concentration, decision making, and sociability. (Module 47)

mania An extended state of intense, wild elation. (Module 47)

masturbation Sexual self-stimulation. (Module 34)

mean The average of all scores, arrived at by adding scores together and dividing by the number of scores. (Module 56)

means-ends analysis A strategy in which a problem-solver considers the ultimate goal (the end) and determines the best strategy for attaining the goal. (Module 24)

median The point in a distribution of scores that divides the distribution exactly in half when the scores are listed in numerical order. (Module 56)

medical perspective The perspective that suggests that when an individual displays symptoms of abnormal behavior, the root cause will be found in a physical examination of the individual, which may reveal a hormonal imbalance, a chemical deficiency, or a brain injury. (Module 46)

meditation A learned technique for refocusing attention that brings about an altered state of consciousness. (Module 15)

memory The process by which we encode, store, and retrieve information. (Module 20)

menopause The period during which women stop menstruating and are no longer fertile. (Module 39)

mental age The age for which a given level of performance is average or typical. (Module 26)

mental images Representations in the mind of an object or event. (Module 23)

metabolism The rate at which food is converted to energy and expended by the body. (Module 30)

metacognition An awareness and understanding of one's own cognitive processes. (Module 37)

Minnesota Multiphasic Personality Inventory-2-Restructured Form (MMPI-2-RF) A widely used self-report test that identifies people with psychological difficulties and is employed to predict some everyday behaviors. (Module 42)

mirror neurons Specialized neurons that fire not only when a person enacts a particular behavior but also when a person simply observes *another* individual carrying out the same behavior. (Module 7)

mode The most frequently occurring score in a set of scores. (Module 56)

mood disorder A disturbance in emotional experience that is strong enough to interfere with everyday living. (Module 47)

mood stabilizers Drugs used to treat mood disorders characterized by intense mood swings, especially manic episodes in bipolar disorder. (Module 51)

motivation The factors that direct and energize the behavior of humans and other organisms. (Module 29)

motor area The part of the cortex that is largely responsible for the body's voluntary movement. (Module 9)

motor (efferent) neurons Neurons that communicate information from the brain and nervous system to muscles and glands. (Module 8)

multiculturalism The view that members of all cultures deserve equal respect and that their contributions to society should be recognized.

myelin sheath A protective coat of fat and protein that wraps around the axon. (Module 7)

narcissistic personality disorder A personality disturbance characterized by an exaggerated sense of self-importance. (Module 47)

narcotics Drugs that increase relaxation and relieve pain and anxiety. (Module 16)

nativist approach (to language development) The theory that humans are genetically prewired to learn language at certain times and in particular ways. (Module 25)

naturalistic observation Research in which an investigator simply observes some naturally occurring behavior and does not make a change in the situation. (Module 5)

nature–nurture issue The issue of the degree to which environment and heredity influence behavior. (Module 35)

need for achievement A person's desire to strive for and achieve challenging accomplishments. (Module 30)

need for affiliation An interest in establishing and maintaining relationships with other people. (Module 30)

need for power A tendency to seek impact, control, or influence over others and to be seen as a powerful individual. (Module 30)

negative reinforcer An unpleasant stimulus whose removal leads to an increase in the probability that a preceding response will be repeated in the future. (Module 18)

negative relationship A relationship established by data that shows high values of one variable corresponding with low values of the other. (Module 58)

neo-Freudian psychoanalysts Psychoanalysts who were trained in traditional Freudian theory but who later rejected some of its major points. (Module 40)

neonate A newborn child. (Module 37)

neurons Nerve cells, the basic elements of the nervous system. (Module 7)

neuroplasticity The brain's ability to change throughout the life span through the addition of new neurons, new interconnections between neurons, and the reorganization of information-processing areas. (Module 9)

neuroscience perspective The approach that views behavior from the perspective of the brain, the nervous system, and other biological functions. (Module 2)

neurotransmitters Chemicals that communicate messages from one neuron to another neuron across the synapse. (Module 7)

neutral stimulus A stimulus that, before conditioning, does not naturally bring about the response of interest. (Module 17)

normal distribution A distribution of scores that produces a symmetrical, bell-shaped curve in which the right half mirrors the left half and in which the mean, median, and mode all have the same value. (Module 56)

norms Standards of test performance that permit the comparison of one person's

score on a test with the scores of other individuals who have taken the same test. (Module 26)

obedience A change in behavior in response to the commands of others. (Module 53)

obesity Body weight that is more than 20% above the average weight for a person of a particular height. (Module 30)

object permanence The awareness that objects—and people—continue to exist even if they are out of sight. (Module 37)

observational learning Learning by observing the behavior of another person, or model. (Module 19)

obsession A persistent, unwanted thought or idea that keeps recurring. (Module 47)

obsessive-compulsive disorder (OCD) A disorder characterized by obsessions or compulsions. (Module 47)

Oedipal conflict A child's intense, sexual interest in his or her opposite-sex parent. (Module 40)

operant conditioning Learning in which a voluntary response is strengthened or weakened, depending on the response's favorable or unfavorable consequences. (Module 18)

operational definition The translation of a hypothesis into specific, testable procedures that can be measured and observed in an experiment. (Module 4)

opponent-process theory of color vision The theory that receptor cells for color are linked in pairs, working in opposition to each other. (Module 11)

optic nerve A bundle of ganglion axons that carry visual information to the brain. (Module 11)

oral stage According to Freud, a stage from birth to age 12-18 months in which an infant's center of pleasure is the mouth. (Module 40)

orgasm The peak of sexual excitement, during which rhythmic muscular contractions occur in the genitals. (Module 33)

overgeneralization The phenomenon by which children over-apply a language rule, thereby making a linguistic error. (Module 25)

ovulation The point at which an egg is released from the ovaries. (Module 33)

panic disorder Anxiety disorder that takes the form of panic attacks lasting from a few seconds to several hours. (Module 47)

parasympathetic division The part of the autonomic division of the nervous system that acts to calm the body after an emergency has ended. (Module 8)

partial (or intermittent) reinforcement schedule Reinforcing of a behavior some but not all of the time. (Module 18)

passionate (or romantic) love A state of intense absorption in someone that includes intense physiological arousal, psychological interest, and caring for the needs of another. (Module 55)

perception The sorting out, interpretation, analysis, and integration of stimuli by the sense organs and brain. (Module 10)

perceptual constancy Our understanding that physical objects are consistent and do not vary, even though sensory input about them may vary. (Module 13)

peripheral nervous system The part of the nervous system that includes the autonomic and somatic subdivisions; made up of neurons with long axons and dendrites, it branches out from the spinal cord and brain and reaches the extremities of the body. (Module 8)

peripheral route processing The type of mental processing that occurs when a persuasive message is evaluated on the basis of irrelevant or extraneous factors. (Module 52)

permissive parents Parents who give their children relaxed or inconsistent direction and, although they are warm, require little of them. (Module 37)

person-centered therapy Therapy in which the goal is to reach one's potential for self-actualization. (Module 50)

personal stressors Major life events, such as the death of a family member, that have immediate negative consequences that generally fade with time. (Module 43)

personality The pattern of enduring characteristics that produce consistency and individuality in a given person. (Module 40)

personality disorder A disorder characterized by a set of inflexible, maladaptive behavior patterns that keep a person from functioning appropriately in society. (Module 47)

phallic stage According to Freud, a period beginning around age 3 during which a child's pleasure focuses on the genitals. (Module 40)

phonemes The smallest units of speech. (Module 25)

phonology The study of the smallest units of speech, called phonemes. (Module 25)

pituitary gland The major component of the endocrine system, or "master gland," that secretes hormones that control growth and other parts of the endocrine system. (Module 8)

place theory of hearing The theory that different areas of the basilar membrane respond to different frequencies. (Module 12)

placebo A false treatment, such as a pill, "drug," or other substance, without any significant chemical properties or active ingredient. (Module 6)

plateau phase The period in which the maximum level of arousal is attained, the penis and clitoris swell with blood, and the body prepares for orgasm. (Module 33)

population All the members of a group of interest. (Module 58)

positive reinforcer A stimulus added to the environment that brings about an increase in a preceding response. (Module 18)

positive relationship A relationship established by data that shows high values of one variable corresponding with high values of another and low values of the first variable corresponding with low values of the other. (Module 58)

posttraumatic stress disorder (PTSD) A phenomenon in which victims of major catastrophes or strong personal stressors feel long-lasting effects that may include re-experiencing the event in vivid flashbacks or dreams. (Module 43)

practical intelligence According to Sternberg, intelligence related to overall success in living. (Module 26)

prejudice A negative (or positive) evaluation of a particular group and its members. (Module 54)

premature (early) ejaculation A male's inability to delay orgasm as long as he wishes. (Module 34)

preoperational stage According to Piaget, the period from 2 to 7 years of age that is characterized by language development. (Module 37)

priming A phenomenon that occurs when exposure to a word or concept (called a *prime*) later makes it easier to recall information related to the prime. (Module 21)

principle of conservation The understanding that quantity is unrelated to the arrangement and physical appearance of objects. (Module 37)

proactive interference Interference in which information learned earlier disrupts the recall of material learned later. (Module 22)

procedural memory Memory for skills and habits, such as riding a bike or hitting a baseball; sometimes referred to as *nondeclarative memory* or *implicit memory*. (Module 20)

projective personality test A test in which a person is shown an ambiguous stimulus and asked to describe it or tell a story about it in order to infer information about their personality. (Module 42)

prosocial behavior Helping behavior. (Module 55)

prototypes Typical, highly representative examples of a concept. (Module 23)

psychoactive drugs Drugs that influence a person's emotions, perceptions, and behavior. (Module 16)

psychoanalysis Freud's form of psychotherapy in which the goal is to release hidden thoughts and feelings from the unconscious part of our minds in order to reduce their power in controlling behavior. (Module 49)

psychoanalytic perspective The perspective that suggests that abnormal behavior stems from childhood conflicts over opposing wishes regarding sex and aggression. (Module 46)

psychoanalytic theory Freud's theory that unconscious forces act as determinants of personality. (Module 40)

psychodynamic approaches to personality Approaches that assume that personality is primarily unconscious and motivated by inner forces and conflicts about which people have little awareness. (Module 40)

psychodynamic perspective The approach based on the view that behavior is motivated by unconscious inner forces over which the individual has little control. (Module 2)

psychodynamic therapy Therapy that seeks to bring unresolved past conflicts and unacceptable impulses from the unconscious into the conscious, where patients may deal with the problems more effectively. (Module 49)

psychological tests Standard measures devised to assess behavior objectively; used by psychologists to help people make decisions about their lives and understand more about themselves. (Module 42)

psychology The scientific study of behavior and mental processes. (Module 1)

psychoneuroimmunology (PNI) The study of the relationship among psychological factors, the immune system, and the brain. (Module 43)

psychophysics The study of the relationship between the physical aspects of stimuli and our psychological experience of them. (Module 10)

psychophysiological disorders Medical problems influenced by an interaction of psychological, emotional, and physical difficulties. (Module 43)

psychosexual stages Developmental periods that children pass through during which they encounter conflicts between the demands of society and their own sexual urges. (Module 40)

psychosocial development Development of individuals' interactions and understanding of each other and of their knowledge and understanding of themselves as members of society. (Module 37)

psychosurgery Brain surgery once used to reduce the symptoms of mental disorder but rarely used today. (Module 51)

psychotherapy Psychologically based treatment in which a trained professional–a therapist–uses psychological techniques to help a person overcome psychological difficulties and disorders, resolve problems in living, or bring about personal growth. (Module 49)

puberty The period at which maturation of the sexual organs occurs, beginning at about age 11 or 12 for girls and 13 or 14 for boys. (Module 38)

punishment A stimulus that decreases the probability that a previous behavior will occur again. (Module 18)

race Generally refers to obvious physical differences that set one group apart from others.

random assignment to condition A procedure in which participants are assigned to different experimental groups or "conditions" on the basis of chance and chance alone. (Module 5)

range The difference between the highest score and the lowest score in a distribution. (Module 57)

rape The act by which one person forces another person to submit to sexual activity. (Module 34)

rapid eye movement (REM) sleep Sleep occupying 20% of an adult's sleeping time, characterized by increased heart rate, blood pressure, and breathing rate; erections; eye movements; and the experience of dreaming. (Module 14)

rational-emotive behavior therapy A form of therapy that attempts to restructure a person's belief system into a more realistic, rational, and logical set of views by challenging dysfunctional beliefs that maintain irrational behavior. (Module 49)

realistic conflict theory The theory that conflict arises from direct competition over valued, but limited, resources.

recall Memory task in which specific information must be retrieved. (Module 21)

reciprocity-of-liking effect A tendency to like those who like us. (Module 55)

recognition Memory task in which individuals are presented with a stimulus and asked whether they have been exposed to it in the past or to identify it from a list of alternatives. (Module 21)

reflex An automatic, involuntary response to an incoming stimulus. (Module 8)

reflexes Unlearned, involuntary responses that occur automatically in the presence of certain stimuli. (Module 37)

refractory period A temporary period that follows the resolution stage and during which the male cannot develop an erection again. (Module 33)

rehearsal The repetition of information that has entered short-term memory. (Module 20)

reinforcement The process by which a stimulus increases the probability that a preceding behavior will be repeated. (Module 18)

reinforcer Any stimulus that increases the probability that a preceding behavior will occur again. (Module 18)

relative deprivation The sense that one lacks a desired resource in comparison to another group, which is perceived to have more.

reliability The consistency of a test in measuring what it is trying to measure. (Module 26)

replicated research Research that is repeated, sometimes using other procedures, settings, and groups of participants, to increase confidence in prior findings. (Module 5)

repression The defense mechanism in which the ego pushes unacceptable or unpleasant thoughts and impulses out of consciousness but maintains them in the unconscious. (Module 40)

resilience The ability to withstand, overcome, and actually thrive after profound adversity. (Module 43)

resolution stage The interval after orgasm in which the body returns to its unaroused state, reversing the changes brought about by arousal. (Module 33)

resting state The state in which there is a negative electrical charge of about −70 millivolts within a neuron. (Module 7)

reticular formation The part of the brain extending from the medulla through the pons; it is related to changes in the level of arousal of the body. (Module 9)

retina The part of the eye that converts the electromagnetic energy of light to electrical impulses for transmission to the brain. (Module 11)

retroactive interference Interference in which material that was learned later disrupts the retrieval of information that was learned earlier. (Module 22)

retrograde amnesia Amnesia in which memory is lost for occurrences prior to a certain event but not for new events. (Module 22)

reuptake The reabsorption of neurotransmitters by a terminal button. (Module 7)

rods Thin, cylindrical receptor cells in the retina that are highly sensitive to light. (Module 11)

Rorschach test A test that involves showing a series of symmetrical visual stimuli to people who then are asked what the figures represent to them. (Module 42)

sample A representative subgroup of a population of interest. (Module 58)

Schachter-Singer theory of emotion The belief that emotions are determined jointly by a nonspecific kind of physiological arousal and its interpretation, based on environmental cues. (Module 31)

schedule of reinforcement The pattern of frequency and timing of reinforcement following desired behavior. (Module 18)

schemas Organized bodies of information stored in memory that bias the way new information is interpreted, stored, and recalled. (Modules 21, 52)

schizophrenia A class of disorders in which severe distortion of reality occurs. (Module 47)

scientific method The approach through which psychologists systematically acquire knowledge and understanding about behavior and other phenomena of interest. (Module 4)

self The way in which we look inward and define ourselves as individuals.

self-actualization A state of self-fulfillment in which people realize their highest potential in their own unique way. (Modules 29, 41)

self-efficacy The belief that we can master a situation and produce positive outcomes. (Module 41)

self-esteem The component of personality that encompasses our positive and negative self-evaluations. (Module 41)

self-report measures A method of gathering data about people by asking them questions about their own behavior and traits. (Module 42)

self-serving bias The tendency to attribute personal success to personal factors (skill, ability, or effort) and to attribute failure to factors outside oneself. (Module 52)

semantic memory Memory for general knowledge and facts about the world, as well as memory for the rules of logic that are used to deduce other facts. (Module 20)

semantic networks Mental representations of clusters of interconnected information. (Module 20)

semantics The aspect of language referring to the meaning of words and sentences. (Module 25)

semicircular canals Three tube-like structures of the inner ear containing fluid that sloshes through them when the head moves, signaling rotational or angular movement to the brain. (Module 12)

sensation The activation of the sense organs by a source of physical energy. (Module 10)

sensorimotor stage According to Piaget, the stage from birth to 2 years, during which a child has little competence in representing the environment by using images, language, or other symbols. (Module 37)

sensory (afferent) neurons Neurons that transmit information from the perimeter of the body to the nervous system and brain. (Module 8)

sensory area The site in the brain of the tissue that corresponds to each of the senses, with the degree of sensitivity related to the amount of tissue. (Module 9)

sensory memory The initial, momentary storage of information, lasting only an instant. (Module 20)

sexism Negative attitudes and behavior toward a person based on that person's gender. (Module 32)

sexual interest/arousal disorder A sexual dysfunction in which the motivation for sexual activity is restrained or lacking entirely. (Module 34)

sexually transmitted infection (STI) A disease acquired through sexual contact. (Module 34)

shaping The process of teaching a complex behavior by rewarding closer and closer approximations of the desired behavior. (Module 18)

short-term memory Memory that holds information for 15 to 25 seconds. (Module 20)

significant outcome An outcome in which the observed outcome would be expected to have occurred by chance with a probability of .05 or less. (Module 58)

significant outcome Meaningful results that make it possible for researchers to feel confident that they have confirmed their hypotheses. (Module 5)

situational causes (of behavior) Causes of behavior that are external to a person. (Module 52)

skin senses The senses of touch, pressure, temperature, and pain. (Module 12)

social cognition The cognitive processes by which people understand and make sense of others and themselves. (Module 52)

social cognitive approaches to personality Theories that emphasize the influence of a person's cognitions–thoughts, feelings, expectations, and values–as well as observation of others' behavior, in determining personality. (Module 41)

social influence The process by which social groups and individuals exert pressure on an individual, either deliberately or unintentionally. (Module 53)

social neuroscience The subfield of social psychology that seeks to identify the neurological basis of social behavior. (Module 54)

social psychology The scientific study of how people's thoughts, feelings, and actions are affected by others. (Module 52)

social support A mutual network of caring, interested others. (Module 43)

social supporter A group member whose dissenting views make nonconformity to the group easier. (Module 53)

sociocultural perspective The perspective that assumes that society and culture shape abnormal behavior (Module 46)

somatic division The part of the peripheral nervous system that specializes in the control of voluntary movements and the communication of information to and from the sense organs. (Module 8)

somatic symptom disorders Psychological difficulties that take on a physical (somatic) form for which there is no medical cause. (Module 47)

sound The movement of air molecules brought about by a source of vibration. (Module 12)

specific phobia Intense, irrational fear of specific objects or situations. (Module 47)

spinal cord A bundle of neurons that leaves the brain and runs down the length of the back and is the main means for transmitting messages between the brain and the body. (Module 8)

spontaneous recovery The reemergence of an extinguished conditioned response after a period of rest and with no further conditioning. (Module 17)

spontaneous remission Recovery without formal treatment. (Module 50)

stage 1 sleep The state of transition between wakefulness and sleep, characterized by relatively rapid, low-amplitude brain waves. (Module 14)

stage 2 sleep A sleep deeper than that of stage 1, characterized by a slower, more regular wave pattern, along with momentary interruptions of "sleep spindles." (Module 14)

stage 3 sleep The deepest stage of sleep, characterized by slow brain waves, with greater peaks and valleys in the wave pattern than in stage 2 sleep. (Module 14)

standard deviation An index of the average deviation of a set of scores from the center of the distribution. (Module 57)

statistics The branch of mathematics concerned with collecting, organizing, analyzing, and drawing conclusions from numerical data. (Module 56)

status The social standing of someone in a group. (Module 53)

stereotype A set of generalized beliefs and expectations about a particular group and its members. (Module 54)

stimulants Drugs that have an arousal effect on the central nervous system, causing a rise in heart rate, blood pressure, and muscular tension. (Module 16)

stimulus Energy that produces a response in a sense organ. (Module 10)

stimulus discrimination The process that occurs if two stimuli are sufficiently distinct from one another such that one evokes a conditioned response but the other does not; the ability to differentiate between stimuli. (Module 17)

stimulus generalization A process in which after a stimulus has been conditioned to produce a particular response, stimuli that are similar to the original stimulus produce the same response. (Module 17)

stress A person's response to events that are threatening or challenging. (Module 43)

structuralism Wundt's approach, which focuses on understanding the fundamental mental components of consciousness, thinking, and other kinds of mental states and activities. (Module 2)

subjective well-being People's sense of their happiness and satisfaction with their lives. (Module 45)

superego The part of personality that harshly judges the morality of our behavior. (Module 40)

survey research Research in which people chosen to represent a larger population are asked a series of questions about their behavior, thoughts, or attitudes. (Module 5)

sympathetic division The part of the autonomic division of the nervous system that acts to prepare the body for action in stressful situations, engaging all the organism's resources to respond to a threat. (Module 8)

synapse The space between two neurons where the axon of a sending neuron communicates with the dendrites of a receiving neuron by using chemical messages. (Module 7)

syntax Ways in which words and phrases can be combined to form sentences. (Module 25)

systematic desensitization A behavioral technique based on classical conditioning in which exposure to an anxiety-producing stimulus is paired with deep relaxation to reduce or eliminate anxiety. (Module 49)

telegraphic speech Sentences in which only essential words are used, typically including only nouns and verbs. (Module 25)

temperament A basic, inborn characteristic way of responding and behavioral style. (Module 37)

temperament An individual's behavioral style and characteristic way of responding that emerges early in life. (Module 41)

teratogens Environmental agents such as a drug, chemical, virus, or other factor that produce a birth defect. (Module 36)

terminal buttons The part of the axon that sends messages to other neurons. They look like a small bulge at the end of the axon. (Module 7)

test standardization A technique used to validate questions in personality tests by studying the responses of people with known diagnoses. (Module 42)

thalamus The part of the brain located in the middle of the central core that acts primarily to relay information about the senses. (Module 9)

Thematic Apperception Test (TAT) A test consisting of a series of pictures about which a person is asked to write a story. (Module 42)

theories Broad explanations and predictions concerning phenomena of interest. (Module 4)

theory of multiple intelligences Gardner's intelligence theory that proposes that there are eight distinct spheres of intelligence. (Module 26)

thinking Brain activity in which people mentally manipulate information, including words, visual images, sounds, or other data. (Module 23)

tip-of-the-tongue phenomenon The inability to recall information that one realizes one knows–a result of the difficulty of retrieving information from long-term memory. (Module 21)

top-down processing Perception that is guided by higher-level knowledge, experience, expectations, and motivations. (Module 13)

trait theory A model of personality that seeks to identify the basic traits necessary to describe personality. (Module 41)

traits Consistent, habitual personality characteristics and behaviors that are displayed across different situations. (Module 41)

transcranial magnetic stimulation (TMS) A depression treatment in which a precise magnetic pulse is directed to a specific area of the brain. (Module 51)

transference The transfer of feelings to a psychoanalyst of love or anger that had been originally directed to a patient's parents or other authority figures. (Module 49)

transgender An umbrella term for persons whose gender identity, gender expression, or behavior does not conform to that typically associated with the sex to which they were assigned at birth. (Module 34)

treatment The manipulation implemented by the experimenter. (Module 5)

trichromatic theory of color vision The theory that there are three kinds of cones in the retina, each of which responds primarily to a specific range of wavelengths. (Module 11)

trust-versus-mistrust stage According to Erikson, the first stage of psychosocial development, occurring from birth to age 1½ years, during which time infants develop feelings of trust or lack of trust. (Module 37)

Type A behavior pattern A cluster of behaviors involving hostility, competitiveness, time urgency, and feeling driven. (Module 44)

Type B behavior pattern A cluster of behaviors characterized by a patient, cooperative, noncompetitive, and nonaggressive manner. (Module 44)

unconditional positive regard An attitude of acceptance and respect on the part of an observer, no matter what a person says or does. (Module 41)

unconditioned response (UCR) A response that is natural and needs no training (e.g., salivation at the smell of food). (Module 17)

unconditioned stimulus (UCS) A stimulus that naturally brings about a particular response without having been learned. (Module 17)

unconscious A part of the personality that contains the memories, knowledge, beliefs, feelings, urges, drives, and instincts of which the individual is not aware. (Module 40)

unconscious wish fulfillment theory Sigmund Freud's theory that dreams represent unconscious wishes that dreamers desire to see fulfilled. (Module 14)

uninvolved parents Parents who show little interest in their children and are emotionally detached. (Module 37)

validity The degree to which a test actually measures what it is supposed to measure. (Module 26)

variability The spread, or dispersion, of scores in a distribution. (Module 57)

variable-interval schedule A schedule by which the time between reinforcements varies around some average rather than being fixed. (Module 18)

variable-ratio schedule A schedule in which reinforcement occurs after an average number of responses, but the reinforcement schedule is unpredictable. (Module 18)

variables Behaviors, events, or other characteristics that can change, or vary, in some way. (Module 5)

visual illusions Physical stimuli that consistently produce errors in perception. (Module 13)

wear-and-tear theories of aging Theories that suggest that the mechanical functions of the body simply stop working efficiently. (Module 39)

Weber's law A basic law of psychophysics stating that a just noticeable difference is a constant proportion to the intensity of an initial stimulus (rather than a constant amount). (Module 10)

weight set point The particular level of weight that the body strives to maintain. (Module 30)

working memory A memory system that holds information temporarily while actively manipulating and rehearsing that information. (Module 20)

zone of proximal development (ZPD) According to Vygotsky, the gap between what children already are able to accomplish on their own and what they are not quite ready to do by themselves. (Module 37)

zygote The new cell formed by the union of an egg and sperm. (Module 36)

References

Aazh, H., & Moore, B. C. J. (2007). Dead regions in the cochlea at 4 kHz in elderly adults: Relation to absolute threshold, steepness of audiogram, and pure-tone average. *Journal of the American Academy of Audiology, 18*, 97-106.

Abbass, A., Town, J., Ogrodniczuk, J., Joffres, M., & Lilliengren, P. (2017). Intensive short-term dynamic psychotherapy trial therapy: Effectiveness and role of "unlocking the unconscious". *Journal of Nervous and Mental Disease, 205*, 453-457.

Abboud, L. (2005, July 27). The next phase in psychiatry. *Wall Street Journal*, pp. D1, D5.

Abel, D. (2015, June 16.) Panel votes to reopen Georges Bank. *Boston Globe*. Retrieved from https://www.bostonglobe.com/metro/2015/06/16/fishing-industry-body-votes-open-parts-georges-bank/c8UBRJ6zsD-Jbdps19Gu6VN/story.html.

Abel, T., & Nickl-Jockschat, T. (2016). *The neuro biology of schizophrenia*. San Diego, CA, US: Elsevier Academic Press.

Abelman, R. (2007). Fighting the war on indecency: Mediating TV, Internet, and video-game usage among achieving and underachieving gifted children. *Roeper Review, 29*, 100-112.

Abraham, A., Thybusch, K., Pieritz, K., & Hermann, C. (2013). Gender differences in creative thinking: Behavioral and fMRI findings. *Brain Imaging and Behavior, 8*(1), 39-51.

Abramowitz, J. S., Olatunji, B. O., & Deacon, B. J. (2007). Health anxiety, hypochondriasis, and the anxiety disorders. *Behavior Therapy, 38*, 86-94.

Accardi, M., & Milling, L. (2009). The effectiveness of hypnosis for reducing procedure-related pain in children and adolescents: A comprehensive methodological review. *Journal of Behavioral Medicine, 32*, 328-339.

Ackard, D. M., & Neumark-Sztainer, D. (2002). Date violence and date rape among adolescents: Associations with disordered eating behaviors and psychological health. *Child Abuse and Neglect, 26*, 455-473.

Ackerman, P. L. (2011). Intelligence and expertise. In R. J. Sternberg & S. Kaufman (Eds.), *The Cambridge handbook of intelligence*. New York: Cambridge University Press.

Acuna, D. E., Berniker, M., Fernandes, H. L., & Kording, K. P. (2015). Using psychophysics to ask if the brain samples or maximizes. *Journal of Vision, 15*, 7-18.

Adams, G., & Dzokoto, V. A. (2007). Genital-shrinking panic in Ghana: A cultural psychological analysis. *Culture & Psychology, 13*, 83-104.

Adams, K. B. (2004). Changing investment in activities and interests in elders' lives: Theory and measurement. *International Journal of Aging and Human Development, 58*, 87-108.

Adams, M., Bell, L. A., & Griffin, P. (2007). *Teaching for diversity and social justice* (2nd ed.). New York: Routledge/Taylor & Francis Group.

Adams-Byers, J., Squilkr, S., & Moon, S. M. (2004). Gifted students' perceptions of the academic and social/emotional effects of homogeneous and heterogeneous grouping. *Gifted Child Quarterly, 48*, 7-20.

Addison, A. (2017). Jung's psychoid concept: An hermeneutic understanding. *International Journal of Jungian Studies, 9*, 1-16.

Adler, M. (2013). Hunger and longing: A developmental regulation model for exploring core relational needs. In S. P. Gantt & B. Badenoch (Eds.), *The interpersonal neurobiology of group psychotherapy and group process*. London: Karnac Books.

Adolph, K. E., & Berger, S. E. (2011). Physical and motor development. In M. H. Bornstein & M. E. Lamb (Eds.), *Cognitive development: An advanced textbook*. New York: Psychology Press.

Advokat, C. (2005). Differential effects of clozapine versus other antipsychotics on clinical outcome and dopamine release in the brain. *Essential Psychopharmacology, 6*, 73-90.

Ahrens, S., Pirschel, I., & Snower, D. J. (2017). A theory of price adjustment under loss aversion. *Journal of Economic Behavior & Organization, 134*, 78-95.

Aiello, R. J. (2006). Hypermasculinity and psychosocial development as predictors of potential date-rape perpetration on campus. *Dissertation Abstracts International: Section B: The Sciences and Engineering, 67*(2-B), 1178.

Aikawa, A., & Fujii, T. (2011). Using the Implicit Association Test (IAT) to measure implicit shyness. *Japanese Journal of Psychology, 82*, 41-48.

Aiken, L. (2000). *Dying, death, and bereavement* (4th ed.). Mahwah, NJ: Erlbaum.

Aimé, C., Paquette, D., Déry, M., & Verlaan, P. (2018). Predictors of childhood trajectories of overt and indirect aggression: An interdisciplinary approach. *Aggressive Behavior*, doi:10.1002/ab.21759.

Ainsworth, M. D. S., Blehar, M. C., Waters, E., & Wall, S. (1978). *Patterns of attachment: A psychological study of the strange situation*. Hillsdale, NJ: Erlbaum.

Airuehia, E., Walker, L. Y., & Nittler, J. (2015). A review of "bath salts": Evolving designer drugs of abuse. *Journal of Child & Adolescent Substance Abuse, 24*, 186-190.

Akil, H., & Morano, M. I. (1996). The biology of stress: From periphery to brain. In S. J. Watson (Ed.), *Biology of schizophrenia and affective disease*. Washington, DC: American Psychiatric Press.

Alampay, L. P., Godwin, J., Lansford, J. E., Bombi, A. S., Bornstein, M. H., Chang, L., . . . Bacchini, D. (2017). Severity and justness do not moderate the relation between corporal punishment and negative child outcomes: A multicultural and longitudinal study. *International Journal of Behavioral Development, 41*, 491-502.

Alba, R., & Barbosa, G. Y. (2016). Room at the top? Minority mobility and the transition to demographic diversity in the USA. *Ethnic and Racial Studies, 39*(6), 917-938. doi:10.1080/01419870.2015.1081966.

Albanese, M., & Case, S. M. (2015). Progress testing: Critical analysis and suggested practices. *Advances in Health Sciences Education, 21*, 221-234.

Alberts, A., Elkind, D., & Ginsberg, S. (2007). The personal fable and risk-taking in early adolescence. *Journal of Youth and Adolescence, 36*, 71-76.

Alboni, S., Di Bonaventura, M. M., Benatti, C., Giusepponi, M. E., Brunello, N., & Cifani, C. (2017). Hypothalamic expression of inflammatory mediators in an animal model of binge eating. *Behavioural Brain Research, 320*, 420-430.

Alderson-Day, B., Weis, S., McCarthy-Jones, S., Moseley, P., Smailes, D., & Fernyhough, C. (2016). The brain's conversation with itself: Neural substrates of dialogic inner speech. *Social Cognitive and Affective Neuroscience, 11*(1), 110-120.

Aleksander, I. (2013, June 23). Molly: Pure, but not so simple. *The New York Times*, p. ST1.

Alelú-Paz, R., Carmona, F. J., Sanchez-Mut, J. V., Cariaga-Martínez, A., González-Corpas, A., Ashour, N., . . . Ropero, S. (2016). Epigenetics in schizophrenia: A pilot study of global DNA methylation in different brain regions associated with higher cognitive functions. *Frontiers In Psychology, 7*, 1496.

Alexandersen, P., Karsdal, M. A., & Christiansen, C. (2009). Long-term prevention with hormone-replacement therapy after the menopause: Which women should be targeted? *Women's Health, 5,* 637-647.

Alfaro, A., Bernabeu, Á., Agulló, C., Parra, J., & Fernández, E. (2015). Hearing colors: An example of brain plasticity. *Frontiers in Systems Neuroscience, 9,* 42-50.

Alho, K., Vorobyev, V. A., Medvedev, S. V., Pakhomov, S. V., Starchenko, M. G., Terganiemi, M., . . . Näätänen, R. (2006). Selective attention to human voice enhances brain activity bilaterally in the superior temporal sulcus. *Brain Research, 1075,* 142-150.

Allport, G. W. (1966). Traits revisited. *American Psychologist, 21,* 1-10.

Allport, G. W., & Postman, L. J. (1958). The basic psychology of rumor. In E. D. Maccoby, T. M. Newcomb, & E. L. Hartley (Eds.), *Readings in social psychology* (3rd ed.). New York: Holt, Rinehart and Winston.

Allwood, M. A. (2007). The relations of violence exposure, trauma symptoms and aggressive cognitions to youth violent behavior. *Dissertation Abstracts International: Section B: The Sciences and Engineering, 67,* 5387.

Alon, I., & Brett, J. M. (2007). Perceptions of time and their impact on negotiations in the Arabic-speaking Islamic world. *Negotiation Journal, 23,* 55-73.

Alter, A. (2017). *Irresistible.* New York: Penguin.

Altman, N., & Stile, J. (2015). Staying alive: Freud for a new generation. *PsycCRITIQUES, 60,* 25-32.

Alzheimer's Association. (2017). *2017 Alzheimer's disease: Facts and figures.* Chicago, IL: Author.

American Academy of Pediatrics Council on Communications and Media. (2016). Virtual violence. *Pediatrics, 138,* e20161298.

American Association of Intellectual and Developmental Disabilities. (2015). Frequently asked questions on intellectual disability and the AAIDD definition. Retrieved from http://aaidd.org/docs/default-source/sis-docs/aaiddfaqonidtemplate.pdf?sfvrsn=2.

American Association of University Women (AAUW). (2012). *Hostile hallways: Bullying, teasing and sexual harassment in school.* Washington, DC: Author.

American College Health Association. (2006). *Acquaintance and date rape: What everyone should know.* Baltimore, MD: Author.

American Psychiatric Association. (2013). *Diagnostic and Statistical Manual of Mental Disorders* (5th ed.). Washington, DC: Author.

American Psychiatric Association. (2018). Warning signs of mental illness. Retrieved from https://www.psychiatry.org/patients-families/warning-signs-of-mental-illness.

American Psychological Association (2015). *Demographics of the U.S. psychology workforce: Findings from the American Community Survey.* Washington, DC: Author.

American Psychological Association Presidential Task Force on Evidence-Based Practice. (2006). Evidence-based practice in psychology. *American Psychologist, 61,* 271-285.

American Psychological Association. (2002). *APA ethics code, 2002.* Washington, DC: Author.

American Psychological Association. (June, 2016). What do people do with their psychology degrees? *Monitor on Psychology,* p. 12.

Amid, P. K., & Chen, D. C. (2011). Surgical treatment of chronic groin and testicular pain after laparoscopic and open preperitoneal inguinal hernia repair. *Journal of the American College of Surgeons, 213,* 531-536.

Amodio, D. M., & Ratner, K. G. (2011). A memory systems model of implicit social cognition. *Current Directions in Psychological Science, 20,* 143-148.

Anastasi, A., & Urbina, S. (1997). *Psychological testing* (7th ed.). Englewood Cliffs, NJ: Prentice Hall.

Andersen, B. (2017). Careful words: Nursing, language, and emotion in Papua New Guinea. *Medical Anthropology, 36*(8), 758-771. doi:10.1080/01459740.2017.1317771.

Anderson, C. A., Lazard, D. S., & Hartley, D. H. (2017). Plasticity in bilateral superior temporal cortex: Effects of deafness and cochlear implantation on auditory and visual speech processing. *Hearing Research, 343,* 138-149.

Anderson, C., & Home, J. A. (2006). Sleepiness enhances distraction during monotonous task. *Sleep: Journal of Sleep and Sleep Disorders Research, 29,* 573-576.

Anderson, C., Andrighetto, L., Bartholow, B. D., Bègue, L., Boxer, P., Brockmyer, J. F., . . . Warburton, W. (2015). Consensus on media violence effects: Comment on Bushman, Gollwitzer, and Cruz. *Psychology of Popular Media Culture, 4,* 215-221.

Anderson, J. L., Sellbom, M., Pymont, C., Smid, W., De Saeger, H., & Kamphuis, J. H. (2015). Measurement of DSM-5 section II personality disorder constructs using the MMPI-2-RF in clinical and forensic samples. *Psychological Assessment, 27,* 786-800.

Anderson, K. B., Cooper, H., & Okamura, L. (1997). Individual differences and attitudes toward rape: A meta-analytic review. *Personality and Social Psychology Bulletin, 23,* 295-315.

Anderson, L. B., Paul, L. K., & Brown, W. S. (2017). Emotional intelligence in agenesis of the corpus callosum. *Archives of Clinical Neuropsychology, 32,* 267-279.

Andrasik, F. (2006). Psychophysiological disorders: Headache as a case in point. In F. Andrasik, *Comprehensive handbook of personality and psychopathology, Vol. 2: Adult psychopathology.* Hoboken, NJ: John Wiley & Sons.

Andrasik, F. (2007). What does the evidence show? Efficacy of behavioural treatments for recurrent headaches in adults. *Neurological Science, 28, Supplement,* S70-S77.

Anestis, M. D., Anestis, J. C., & Lilienfeld, S. O. (2011). When it comes to evaluating psychodynamic therapy, the devil is in the details. *American Psychologist, 66,* 149-151.

Anker, A. E., & Feeley, T. (2011). Are nonparticipants in prosocial behavior merely innocent bystanders? *Health Communication, 26,* 13-24.

Antonini, A., & Barone, P. (2008). Dopamine agonist-based strategies in the treatment of Parkinson's disease. *Neurological Sciences, 29,* S371-SS374.

Anwar, F., Fry, D. P., & Grigfaityte, I. (2018). Aggression prevention and reduction in diverse cultures and contexts. *Current Opinion in Psychology, 19,* 49-54. doi:10.1016/j.copsyc.2017.03.029.

Apanovich, A. M., McCarthy, D., & Salovey, P. (2003). Using message framing to motivate HIV testing among low-income, ethnic minority women. *Health Psychology, 22,* 88-94.

Appel, H., Gerlach, A. L., & Crusius, J. (2016). The interplay between Facebook use, social comparison, envy, and depression. *Current Opinion in Psychology, 9* 44-49.

Appelbaum, P. S., Scurich, N., & Raad, R. (2015). Effects of behavioral genetic evidence on perceptions of criminal responsibility and appropriate punishment. *Psychology, Public Policy, and Law, 21,* 134-144.

Apple, D. M., Fonseca, R. S., & Kokovay, E. (2017). The role of adult neurogenesis in psychiatric and cognitive disorders. *Brain Research, 1655,* 270-276.

Arafat, I., & Cotton, W. L. (1974). Masturbation practices of males and females. *Journal of Sex Research, 10,* 293-307.

Arbuthnott, A., & Sharpe, D. (2009). The effect of physician-patient collaboration on patient adherence in non-psychiatric medicine. *Patient Education and Counseling, 77,* 60-67.

Arcaro, M. J., Schade, P. F., Vincent, J. L., Ponce, C. R., & Livingstone, M. S. (2017). Seeing faces is necessary for face-domain formation. *Nature Neuroscience, 20,* 1404-1412.

Arcelus, J., Mitchell, A. J., Wales, J., & Nielsen, S. (2011). Mortality rates in patients with anorexia nervosa and other eating disorders: A meta-analysis of 36 studies. *Archives of General Psychiatry, 68,* 724-731.

Ardila, A. (2015). A proposed neurological interpretation of language evolution. *Behavioural Neurology, 20,* 15-22.

Ariely, D., & Norton, M. I. (2009). Conceptual consumption. *Annual Review of Psychology, 60,* 475-499.

Arimoto, M., Shiomi, T., Sasanabe, R., Inagawa, S., Ueda, H., & Inafuku, S. (2011). A sheet-type device for home-monitoring sleep apneas in children. *Sleep and Biological Rhythms, 9,* 103-111.

Arlo, C. (2017). Group therapy and dialectical behavior therapy: An integrative response to a clinical case. *International Journal of Group Psychotherapy, 67*(Supp1), S13-S23.

Armbruster, D., Mueller, A., Strobel, A., Lesch, K., Kirschbaum, C., & Brocke, B. (2011). Variation in genes involved in dopamine clearance influence the startle response in older adults. *Journal of Neural Transmission, 118,* 1281-1292.

Arnett, J. (2008). The neglected 95%: Why American psychology needs to become less American. *American Psychologist, 63,* 602-614.

Arnett, J. (2011). Emerging adulthood(s): The cultural psychology of a new life stage. In L. Jensen (Ed.), *Bridging cultural and* developmental approaches to psychology: New syntheses in theory, research, and policy. New York: Oxford University Press.

Arnett, J. J. (2000). Emerging adulthood. *American Psychologist, 55,* 469-480.

Arnett, J. J. (2006). *Emerging adulthood: The winding road from the late teens through the twenties.* New York: Oxford University Press.

Arnett, J. J. (2007). Afterword: Aging out of care–Toward realizing the possibilities of emerging adulthood. *New Directions for Youth Development, 113,* 151-161.

Aronson, J., & Dee, T. (2012). Stereotype threat in the real world. In M. Inzlicht & T. Schmader (Eds.), *Stereotype threat: Theory, process, and application.* New York: Oxford University Press.

Aronson, J., & Steele, Claude M. (2005). Stereotypes and the fragility of academic competence, motivation, and self-concept. In A. J. Elliot & C. S. Dweck (Eds.), *Handbook of competence and motivation.* New York, NY: Guilford Publications.

Arpaci, I., Baloğlu, M., & Kesici, Ş. (2018). The relationship among individual differences in individualism-collectivism, extraversion, and self-presentation. *Personality and Individual Differences, 121,* 89-92. doi:10.1016/j.paid.2017.09.034.

Arshamian, A., Iannilli, E., Gerber, J. C., Willander, J., Persson, J., Seo, H., . . . Larsson, M. (2013). The functional neuroanatomy of odor evoked auto-biographical memories cued by odors and words. *Neuropsychologia, 51,* 123-131.

Artistico, D., Pinto, A., Douek, J., Black, J., & Pezzuti, L. (2013). The value of removing daily obstacles via everyday problem-solving theory: Developing an applied novel procedure to increase self-efficacy for exercise. *Frontiers in Psychology, 4.* Retrieved from http://www.ncbi.nlm.nih.gov/pubmed/23372560.

Asch, S. E. (1951). Effects of group pressure upon the modification and distortion of judgments. In H. Guetzkow (Ed.), *Groups, leadership, and men.* Pittsburgh: Carnegie Press.

Aspinwall, L. G., & Taylor, S. E. (1997). A stitch in time: Self-regulation and proactive coping. *Psychological Bulletin, 121,* 417-436.

Associated Press (2011, September 27). Study: Murder victims disproportionately black. Accessed May 2, 2018 from http://www.msnbc.msn.com/id/20203888/ns/us news-life/t/study-murder-victims-disproportionately-black/.

Atkinson, H. (Ed.). (1997, January 21). Understanding your diagnosis. *HealthNews,* p. 3.

Atkinson, R. C., & Shiffrin, R. M. (1968). Human memory: A proposed system and its control processes. In K. W. Spence & J. T. Spence (Eds.), *The psychology of learning and motivation: Advances in research and theory* (Vol. 2). New York: Academic Press.

Auerbach, R. P., Alonso, J., Axinn, W. G., Cuijpers, P., Ebert, D. D., Green, J. G., . . . Bruffaerts, R. (2016). Mental disorders among

college students in the World Health Organization World Mental Health Surveys. *Psychological Medicine, 46,* 2955-2970.

Aujoulat, I., Luminet, O., & Deccache, A. (2007). The perspective of patients on their experience of powerlessness. *Quality Health Research, 17,* 772-785.

Aussilloux, C., & Bagdadli, A. (2006). Handicap mental et société: Soigner, éduquer, intégrer. Mental handicap and society. *Neuropsychiatrie de l'Enfance et de l'Adolescence, 54,* 336-340.

Averill, J. R. (1975). A semantic atlas of emotional concepts. *Catalog of Selected Documents in Psychology, 5,* 330.

Ayling, K., Bowden, T., Tighe, P., Todd, I., Dilnot, E. M., Negm, O. H., . . . Vedhara, K. (2017). The application of protein microarray assays in psychoneuroimmunology. *Brain, Behavior, and Immunity, 59,* 62-66.

Bacchiochi, J. R. (2006). Development and validation of the Malingering Discriminant Function Index (M-DFI) for the Minnesota Multiphasic Personality Inventory-2 (MMPI-2). *Dissertation Abstracts International: Section B: The Sciences and Engineering, 66*(10-B), 5673.

Baczyńska, A., & Thornton, G. C. (2017). Relationships of analytical, practical, and emotional intelligence with behavioral dimensions of performance of top managers. *International Journal of Selection and Assessment, 25,* 171-182.

Baddeley, A. D., Allen, R. J., & Hitch, G. J. (2011). Binding in visual working memory: The role of the episodic buffer. *Neuropsychologia, 49,* 1393-1400.

Baddeley, A., & Wilson, B. (1985). Phonological coding and short-term memory in patients without speech. *Journal of Memory and Language, 24,* 490-502.

Badke, M. B., Sherman, J., Boyne, P., Page, S., & Dunning, K. (2011). Tongue-based biofeedback for balance in stroke: Results of an 8-week pilot study. *Archives of Physical and Medical Rehabilitation, 92,* 1364-1370.

Bagattini, C., Mele, S., Brignani, D., & Savazzi, S. (2015). No causal effect of left hemisphere hyperactivity in the genesis of neglect-like behavior. *Neuropsychologia, 72,* 12-21.

Bagge, C., & Sher, K. (2008). Adolescent alcohol involvement and suicide attempts: Toward the development of a conceptual framework. *Clinical Psychology Review, 28,* 1283-1296.

Bagnall, D. (2010). The use of spinal cord stimulation and intrathecal drug delivery in the treatment of low back-related pain. *Physical Medicine & Rehabilitation Clinics of North America, 21,* 851-858.

Bahrick, L. E., Lickliter, R., & Castellanos, I. (2013). The development of face perception in infancy: Intersensory interference and unimodal visual facilitation. *Developmental Psychology, 49,* 1919-1930.

Bai, L. (2005). Children at play: A childhood beyond the Confucian shadow. *Childhood: A Global Journal of Child Research, 12,* 9-32.

Bailey, J. M., Vasey, P. L., Diamond, L. M., Breedlove, S. M., Vilain, E., & Epprecht, M. (2016). Sexual orientation, controversy, and science. *Psychological Science in the Public Interest, 17*(2), 45-101.

Baker, J., & Berenbaum, H. (2007). Emotional approach and problem-focused coping: A comparison of potentially adaptive strategies. *Cognition and Emotion, 21,* 95-118.

Baker, S. E., Johnson, P. J., & Slater, D. (2007). Learned food aversion with and without an odour cue for protecting untreated baits from wild mammal foraging [Special issue: Conservation, enrichment, and animal behavior]. *Applied Animal Behaviour Science, 102,* 410-428.

Balaban, C. D., McBurney, D. H., & Affeltranger, M. A. (2005). Three distinct categories of time course of pain produced by oral capsaicin. *The Journal of Pain, 6,* 315-322.

Balconi, M., Bortolotti, A., & Crivelli, D. (2013). Self-report measures, facial feedback, and personality differences (BEES) in cooperative vs. noncooperative situations: Contribution of the mimic system to the sense of empathy. *International Journal of Psychology, 48,* 631-640.

Ball, D. (2004). Genetic approaches to alcohol dependence. *British Journal of Psychiatry, 185,* 449-451.

Balon, R. (2017). Burden of sexual dysfunction. *Journal of Sex & Marital Therapy, 43,* 49-55.

Balter, M. (2017). Schizophrenia's unyielding mysteries. *Scientific American, 316*(5), 54-61.

Bandura, A. (1986). *Social foundations of thought and action: A social cognitive theory.* Englewood Cliffs, NJ: Prentice Hall.

Bandura, A. (1994). Social cognitive theory of mass communication. In J. Bryant & D. Zillmann (Eds.), *Media effects: Advances in theory and research: LEA's communication series.* Hillsdale, NJ: Erlbaum.

Bandura, A. (1999). Social cognitive theory of personality. In D. Cervone & Y. Shod (Eds.), *The coherence of personality.* New York: Guilford.

Bandura, A. (2000). Self-efficacy: The foundation of agency. In W. J. Perrig & A. Grob (Eds.), *Control of human behavior, mental processes, and consciousness: Essays in honor of the 60th birthday of August Flammer.* Mahwah, NJ: Erlbaum.

Bandura, A. (2004). Swimming against the mainstream: The early years from chilly tributary to transformative mainstream. *Behavior Research and Therapy, 42,* 613-630.

Bandura, A. (2009). Social cognitive theory goes global. *The Psychologist, 22,* 504-506.

Bandura, A., & Locke, E. A. (2003). Negative self-efficacy and goal effects revisited. *Journal of Applied Psychology, 88,* 87-99.

Bandura, A., Grusec, J. E., & Menlove, F. L. (1967). Vicarious extinction of avoidance behavior. *Journal of Personality and Social Psychology, 5,* 16-23.

Bandura, A., Ross, D., & Ross, S. (1963a). Imitation of film-mediated aggressive models. *Journal of Abnormal and Social Psychology, 66,* 3-11.

Bandura, A., Ross, D., & Ross, S. (1963b). Vicarious reinforcement and imitative learning. *Journal of Abnormal and Social Psychology, 67,* 601-607.

Banks, J. A. (2006). Improving race relations in schools: From theory and research to practice. *Journal of Social Issues, 62,* 607-614.

Banks, J. B., & Boals, A. (2017). Understanding the role of mind wandering in stress-related working memory impairments. *Cognition and Emotion, 31,* 1023-1030.

Barandiaran, A. A., Pascual, A. C., & Samaniego, C. M. (2006). A criticism of the Kohlberg theory: The moral development in adults and educative implications. *Revista de Psicologia General y Aplicada, 59,* 165-182.

Barash, D. P., & Lipton, J. E. (2011). *Payback: Why we retaliate, redirect aggression, and take revenge.* New York: Oxford University Press.

Barbaro, N., Boutwell, B. B., Barnes, J. C., & Shackelford, T. K. (2017). Rethinking the transmission gap: What behavioral genetics and evolutionary psychology mean for attachment theory: A comment on Verhage et al. (2016). *Psychological Bulletin, 143,* 107-113.

Barcott, B., & Scherer, M. (2015, May 25). The great pot experiment. *Time,* pp. 38-44.

Bargh, J. A. (2014). Our unconscious mind. *Scientific American, 310,* 30-37.

Barke, D. B. (2011). Self-selection for stressful experiences. *Stress and Health: Journal of the International Society for the Investigation of Stress, 27,* 194-205.

Barker, J., & Jones, M. (2008). The effects of hypnosis on self-efficacy, affect, and soccer performance: A case study. *Journal of Clinical Sport Psychology, 2,* 127-147.

Barkley, R. (2000). *Taking charge of ADHD* (rev. ed.). New York: Guilford Press.

Barkley, R. A., Knouse, L. E., & Murphy, K. R. (2011). Correspondence and disparity in the self- and other ratings of current and childhood ADHD symptoms and impairment in adults with ADHD. *Psychological Assessment, 23,* 437-446.

Barlow, D. H. (2007). *Clinical handbook of psychological disorders: A step-by-step treatment manual* (4th ed.). New York: Guilford Press.

Barmeyer, C. I. (2004). Learning styles and their impact on cross-cultural training: An international comparison in France, Germany and Quebec. *International Journal of Intercultural Relations, 28,* 577-594.

Barnes, J. C., & Jacobs, B. A. (2013). Genetic risk for violent behavior and environmental exposure to disadvantage and violent crime: The case for gene-environment interaction. *Journal of Interpersonal Violence, 28,* 92-120.

Barnes, T., & Eardley, I. (2007). Premature ejaculation: The scope of the problem. *Journal of Sex & Marital Therapy, 33,* 151-170.

Barnett, J. E., Wise, E. H., & Johnson-Greene, D. (2007). Informed consent: Too much of a good thing or not enough? *Professional Psychology: Research and Practice, 38,* 179-186.

Barnett, R. C. (2004). Woman and work: Where are we, where did we come from, and where are we going? [Preface]. *Journal of Social Issues, 60,* 667-674.

Barnett, S. M., Rindermann, H., Williams, W. M., & Ceci, S. J. (2011). Society and intelligence. In R. J. Sternberg & S. Kaufman (Eds.), *The Cambridge handbook of intelligence.* New York: Cambridge University Press.

Barrada, J., Abad, F., & Olea, J. (2011). Varying the valuating function and the presentable bank in computerized adaptive testing. *The Spanish Journal of Psychology, 14,* 500-508.

Barresi, J. (2007). Consciousness and intentionality. *Journal of Consciousness Studies, 14, Special issue: Concepts of Consciousness: Integrating an Emerging Science,* 77-93.

Barrett, L. (2011). *Beyond the brain: How body and environment shape animal and human minds.* Princeton, NJ: Princeton University Press.

Barrett, L. F., & Russell, J. A. (2015). An introduction to psychological construction. In L. F. Barrett & J. A. Russell (Eds.), *The psychological construction of emotion.* New York: Guilford Press.

Barrett, L. F., & Salovey, P. (Eds.). (2002). *The wisdom in feeling: Psychological processes in emotional intelligence.* New York: Guilford Press.

Barron, F. (1990). *Creativity and psychological health: Origins of personal vitality and creative freedom.* Buffalo, NY: Creative Education Foundation.

Barry, C. T., Doucette, H., Loflin, D. C., Rivera-Hudson, N., & Herrington, L. L. (2017). "Let me take a selfie": Associations between self-photography, narcissism, and self-esteem. *Psychology of Popular Media Culture, 6,* 48-60.

Barson, J. R., Morganstern, I., & Leibowitz, S. F. (2011). Similarities in hypothalamic and mesocorticolimbic circuits regulating the overconsumption of food and alcohol. *Physiology & Behavior, 104,* 128-137.

Bartlett, F. (1932). *Remembering: A study in experimental and social psychology.* Cambridge, England: Cambridge University Press.

Bartlett, M. Y., & DeSteno, D. (2006). Gratitude and prosocial behavior: Helping when it costs you. *Psychological Science, 17,* 319-325.

Bartocci, G. (2004). Transcendence techniques and psychobiological mechanisms underlying religious experience. *Mental Health, Religion and Culture, 7,* 171-181.

Bartone, P., Roland, R., Picano, J., & Williams, T. (2008). Psychological hardiness predicts success in U.S. Army Special Forces candidates. *International Journal of Selection and Assessment, 16,* 78-81.

Baruss, I. (2003). *Alterations of consciousness: An empirical analysis for social scientists.* Washington, DC: American Psychological Association.

Barzilay, S., Feldman, D., Snir, A., Apter, A., Carli, V., Hoven, C. W., & . . . Wasserman, D. (2015). The interpersonal theory of suicide and adolescent suicidal behavior. *Journal of Affective Disorders, 183,* 68-74.

Basak, C., Boot, W., Voss, M., & Kramer, A. (2008). Can training in a real-time strategy video game attenuate cognitive decline in older adults? *Psychology and Aging, 23,* 765-777.

Bass, E. C., Saldarriaga, L., Cunha, J., Chen, B., Santo, J. B., & Bukowski, W. M. (2018). A cross-cultural analysis of the relations of physical and relational aggression with peer victimization. *International Journal of Behavioral Development, 42*(1), 132-142.

Bassett, A. M., & Baker, C. (2015). Normal or abnormal? "Normative uncertainty" in psychiatric practice. *Journal of Medical Humanities, 36,* 89-111.

Bassotti, G., & Villanacci, V. (2011). Can "functional" constipation be considered as a form of enteric neuro-gliopathy? *Glia, 59,* 345-350.

Basten, U., Hilger, K., & Fiebach, C. J. (2015). Where smart brains are different: A quantitative meta-analysis of functional and structural brain imaging studies on intelligence. *Intelligence, 51,* 10-17.

Bastian, B., Jetten, J, Hornsey, M. J., & Leknes, S. (2014). The positive consequences of pain: A biopsychosocial approach. *Personality and Social Psychology Review, 18,* 256-279.

Bateman, A. W. (2011). Commentary on "Minding the difficult patient": Mentalizing and the use of formulation in patients with borderline personality disorder comorbid with antisocial personality disorder. *Personality and Mental Health, 5,* 85-90.

Bates, E. (2005). Plasticity, localization, and language development. In S. T. Parker & J. Langer (Eds.), *Biology and knowledge revisited: From neurogenesis to psychogenesis.* Mahwah, NJ: Lawrence Erlbaum Associates.

Bates, J. E., & Pettit, G. S. (2015). Temperament, parenting, and social development. In J. E. Grusec & P. D. Hastings (Eds.), *Handbook of socialization: Theory and research* (2nd ed.). New York: Guilford Press.

Batson, C. (2011). *Altruism in humans.* New York: Oxford University Press.

Bauer, J. J., Schwab, J. R., & McAdams, D. P. (2011). Self-actualizing: Where ego development finally feels good? *Humanistic Psychologist, 39,* 121-136.

Bauer, P. (2008). Toward a neuro-developmental account of the development of declarative memory. *Developmental Psychobiology, 50,* 19-31.

Baum, A., Lorduy, K., & Jenkins, F. J. (2011). The molecular biology of stress: Cellular defense, immune response, and aging. In R. J. Contrada & A. Baum (Eds.), *The handbook of stress science: Biology, psychology, and health.* New York: Springer Publishing Co.

Baumeister, R. F., & Stillman, T. (2006). Erotic plasticity: Nature, culture, gender, and sexuality. In R. D. McAnulty & M. M. Burnette (Eds.), *Sex and sexuality, Vol 1: Sexuality today: Trends and controversies.* Westport, CT: Praeger Publishers/Greenwood Publishing.

Baumeister, R. F., Ainsworth, S. E., & Vohs, K. D. (2015). Are groups more or less than the sum of their members? The moderating role of individual identification. *Behavioral and Brain Sciences.* Accessed at http://www.ncbi.nlm.nih.gov/pubmed/25936575.

Baumgartner, F. (2002). The effect of hardiness in the choice of coping strategies in stressful situations. *Studia Psychologica, 44,* 69-75.

Baumrind, D. (1971). Current patterns of parental authority. *Developmental Psychology, 4*, 1-104.

Baumrind, D. (2005). Patterns of parental authority and adolescent autonomy. *New Directions for Child and Adolescent Development, 108*, 61-69.

Baumrucker, S., Mingle, P., Harrington, D., Stolick, M., Carter, G. T., & Oertli, K. A. (2011). Medical marijuana and organ transplantation: Drug of abuse, or medical necessity? *American Journal of Hospice & Palliative Medicine, 28*, 130-134.

Bautista, D. M., Wilson, S. R., & Hoon, M. A. (2014). Why we scratch an itch: The molecules, cells and circuits of itch. *Nature Neuroscience, 17*(2), 175-182.

Bavelier, Daphne and C. Shawn Green (2016). The brain-boosting power of video games. *Scientific American, 315*, 26-31.

Bayliss, D. M., Jarrold, C., Baddeley, A. D., & Gunn, D. M. (2005). The relationship between short-term memory and working memory: Complex span made simple? *Memory, 13*, 414-421.

Bazalakova, M. H., Wright, J., Schneble, E. J., McDonald, M. P., Heilman, C. J., Levey, A. I., . . . Blakely, R. D. (2007). Deficits in acetylcholine homeostasis, receptors and behaviors in choline transporter heterozygous mice. *Genes, Brain & Behavior, 6*, 411-424.

Beam, A. (2014, August 21). Four-bit recall. *Boston Globe*, p. 1.

Beam, C. R., & Turkheimer, E. (2013). Phenotype-environment correlations in longitudinal twin models. *Development and Psychopathology, 25*, 7-16.

Bearman, C. R., Ball, L. J., & Ormerod, T. C. (2007). The structure and function of spontaneous analogising in domain-based problem solving. *Thinking & Reasoning, 13*, 273-294.

Beaudry, J. L., Lindsay, R. C. L., Leach, A., Mansour, J. K., Bertrand, M. I., & Kalmet, N. (2015). The effect of evidence type, identification accuracy, line-up presentation, and line-up administration on observers' perceptions of eyewitnesses. *Legal and Criminological Psychology, Vol 20*, 343-364.

Bebermeier, S., Echterhoff, G., Bohner, G., & Hellmann, J. H. (2015). The generalization of shared reality: When communication about one target shapes evaluations of other targets. *European Journal of Social Psychology, 45*, 623-640.

Bechara, A., Damasio, A. R., Damasio, H., & Anderson, S. (1994). Insensitivity to future consequences following damage to human prefrontal cortex. *Cognition, 50*, 7-15.

Beck, A. P., & Lewis, C. M. (Eds.). (2000). *The process of group psychotherapy: Systems for analyzing change.* Washington, DC: American Psychological Association.

Beck, A. T. (1995). Cognitive therapy: Past, present, and future. In M. J. Mahoney (Ed.), *Cognitive and constructive psychotherapies: Theory, research, and practice.* New York: Springer.

Beck, A. T. (2004). Cognitive therapy, behavior therapy, psychoanalysis, and pharmacotherapy: A cognitive continuum. In A. Freeman, M. J. Mahoney, P. Devito, & D. Martin (Eds.), *Cognition and Psychotherapy* (2nd ed.). New York: Springer Publishing Co.

Beck, A. T., & Rector, N. A. (2005). Cognitive approaches to schizophrenia: Theory and therapy. *Annual Review of Clinical Psychology, 1*, 577-606.

Beck, A. T., Davis, D. D., & Freeman, A. (2015). *Cognitive therapy of personality disorders* (3rd ed.). New York: Guilford Press.

Beck, A. T., Freeman, A., & Davis, D. D. (2004). *Cognitive therapy of personality disorders* (2nd ed.). New York: Guilford Press.

Beck, K., Javitt, D. C., & Howes, O. D. (2016). Targeting glutamate to treat schizophrenia: Lessons from recent clinical studies. *Psychopharmacology, 233*, 2425-2428.

Beck, M. (2015, June 2). Your body's witching hours. *Wall Street Journal*, pp. D1-D2.

Becker, J., Brackbill, D., & Centola, D. (2017). Network dynamics of social influence in the wisdom of crowds. *PNAS Proceedings of the National Academy of Sciences of the United States of America, 114*, 70-76.

Becker, T. (2003). Is emotional intelligence a viable concept? *Academy of Management Review, 28*, 192-195.

Beersma, D. G. M., & Gordijn, M. C. M. (2007). Circadian control of the sleep-wake cycle. *Physiology & Behavior, 90*.

Begeny, J. C., & Martens, B. K. (2007). Inclusionary education in Italy: A literature review and call for more empirical research. *Remedial and Special Education, 28*, 80-94.

Begg, D., & Langley, J. (2001). Changes in risky driving behavior from age 21 to 26 years. *Journal of Safety Research, 32*, 491-499.

Beghetto, R. A., & Kaufman, J. C. (Eds.). (2010). *Nurturing creativity in the classroom.* New York: Cambridge University Press.

Behrendt, R. (2011). *Neuroanatomy of social behaviour: An evolutionary and psychoanalytic perspective.* London England: Karnac Books.

Behrens, M., Lendon, C., & Roe, C. (2009). A common biological mechanism in cancer and Alzheimer's disease? *Current Alzheimer Research, 6*, 196-204.

Beidel, D. C., & Turner, S. M. (2007). Etiology of social anxiety disorder. In D. C. Beidel & S. M. Turner (Eds.), *Shy children, phobic adults: Nature and treatment of social anxiety disorders* (2nd ed.). Washington, DC: American Psychological Association.

Beitel, M., Wald, L. M., Midgett, A., Green, D., Cecero, J. J., Kishon, R., & Barry, D. T. (2015). Humanistic experience and psychodynamic understanding: Empirical associations among facets of self-actualization and psychological mindedness. *Person-Centered and Experiential Psychotherapies, 14*, 137-148.

Belasen, A. T., & Fortunato, M. V. (2013). Situational motivation: Challenge the binary. In M. A. Paludi (Ed.), *Psychology for business success, Vol 1: Juggling, balancing, and integrating work and family roles and responsibilities, Vol 2: Institutional equity and compliance, Vol 3: Managing, leading, and developing employees, Vol 4: Implementing best practices in human resources.* Santa Barbara, CA: Praeger/ABC-CLIO.

Bem, D. (2012). ESP is not a psychological anomaly. *PsychCRITIQUES, 57*, 2012.

Ben-Porath, Y. S., Corey, D. M., & Tarescavage, A. M. (2017). Using the MMPI-2-RF in pre-employment evaluations of police officer candidates. In C. L. Mitchell & E. H. Dorian (Eds.), *Police psychology and its growing impact on modern law enforcement.* Hershey, PA: Information Science Reference/IGI Global.

Bench, S. W., Lench, H. C., Liew, J., Miner, K., & Flores, S. A. (2015). Gender gaps in overestimation of math performance. *Sex Roles, 72*, 536-546.

Benderly, B. L. (2004). Looking beyond the SAT. *American Psychological Society, 17*, 12-18.

Benet-Martinez, V., Lee, F., & Leu, J. (2006). Biculturalism and cognitive complexity: Expertise in cultural representations. *Journal of Cross-Cultural Psychology, 37*, 386-407.

Benham, G., Woody, E. Z., & Wilson, K. S. (2006). Expect the unexpected: Ability, attitude, and responsiveness to hypnosis. *Journal of Personality and Social Psychology, 91*, 342-350.

Benitez, P., de Carvalho Gomes, M. L., Bondioli, R., & Domeniconi, C. (2017). Mapping of inclusive strategies for students with intellectual disabilities and autism. *Psicologia Em Estudo, 22*, 81-93.

Benson, E. (2003, April). The science of sexual arousal. *Monitor on Psychology*, 50-56.

Benton, S. A., Robertson, J. M., Tseng, W., Newton, F. B., & Benton, S. L. (2003) Changes in counseling center client problems across 13 years. *Professional Psychology: Research and Practice 34*(1) 66-72.

Bentwich, J., Dobronevsky, E., Aichenbaum, S., Shorer, R., Peretz, R., Khaigrekht, M., . . . Rabey, J. M. (2011). Beneficial effect of repetitive transcranial magnetic stimulation combined with cognitive training for the treatment of Alzheimer's disease: A proof of concept study. *Journal of Neural Transmission, 118*, 463-471.

Beran, M. J., Smith, J., & Perdue, B. M. (2013). Language-trained chimpanzees (*Pan troglodytes*) name what they have seen but look first at what they have not seen. *Psychological Science, 24*, 660-666.

Berecki-Gisolf, J., McKenzie, S. J., Dobson, A. J., McFarlane, A., & McLaughlin, D. (2013). A history of comorbid depression and anxiety predicts new onset of heart disease. *Journal of Behavioral Medicine, 36*, 347-353.

Beresnevaité, M., Taylor, G. J., & Bagby, R. M. (2007). Assessing alexithymia and type A behavior in coronary heart disease patients: A multimethod approach. *Psychotherapy and Psychosomatics, 76*, 186-192.

Berk, L. E. (2005). Why parenting matters. In S. Olfman (Ed.), *Childhood lost: How American culture is failing our kids.* Westport, CT: Praeger Publishers/Greenwood Publishing Group.

Berke, D. S., Reidy, D. E., Miller, J. D., & Zeichner, A. (2017). Take it like a man: Gender-threatened men's experience of gender role discrepancy, emotion activation, and pain tolerance. *Psychology of Men & Masculinity, 18*, 62-69.

Berkman, L. F., Ertel, K. A., & Glymour, M. M. (2011). Aging and social intervention: Life course perspectives. In R. H. Binstock & L. K. George (Eds.), *Handbook of aging and the social sciences* (7th ed.). San Diego, CA: Elsevier Academic Press.

Berkowitz, L. (2001). On the formation and regulation of anger and aggression: A cognitive-neoassociationistic analysis. In W. G. Parrott (Ed.), *Emotions in social psychology: Essential readings.* New York: Psychology Press.

Bernard, L. L. (1924). *Instinct: A study in social psychology.* New York: Holt.

Bernstein, D., & Loftus, E. (2009a). How to tell if a particular memory is true or false. *Perspectives on Psychological Science, 4*, 370-374.

Bernstein, D., & Loftus, E. (2009b). The consequences of false memories for food preferences and choices. *Perspectives on Psychological Science, 4*, 135-139.

Bernstein, E. (2011, April 19). Friendly fight: A smarter way to say "I'm angry." *Wall Street Journal*, pp. D1, D4.

Berntsen, D., & Rubin, D. C. (2004). Cultural life scripts structure recall from autobiographical memory. *Memory and Cognition, 32*, 427-442.

Berridge, K. C. (2004). Motivation concepts in behavioral neuroscience. *Physiology and Behavior, 81*, 179-209.

Bertakis, K. (2009). The influence of gender on the doctor-patient interaction. *Patient Education and Counseling, 76*, 356-360.

Bertakis, K., Franks, P., & Epstein, R. (2009). Patient-centered communication in primary care: Physician and patient gender and gender concordance. *Journal of Women's Health, 18*, 539-545.

Berthoud, H. R. (2002). Multiple neural systems controlling food intake and body weight. *Neuroscience and Biobehavioral Reviews, 26*, 393-428.

Best, D. (2017). Why the mechanisms of 12-step behaviour change should matter to clinicians. *Addiction, 112*, 938-939.

Betley, J. N., Xu, S., Cao, Z. H., Gong, R., Magnus, C. J., Yu, Y., . . . Sternson, S. M. (2015). Neurons for hunger and thirst transmit a negative-valence teaching signal. *Nature, 521*, 180-185.

Betterton, R. T., Broad, L. M., Tsaneva-Atanasova, K., & Mellor, J. R. (2017). Acetylcholine modulates gamma frequency oscillations in the hippocampus by activation of muscarinic M1 receptors. *European Journal of Neuroscience, 45*, 1570-1585.

Beyene, Y., Gilliss, C., & Lee, K. (2007). "I take the good with the bad, and I moisturize": Defying middle age in the new millennium. *Menopause, 14*, 734-741.

Bhar, S., Gelfand, L., Schmid, S., Gallop, R., DeRubeis, R., Hollon, S., . . . Beck, A. T. (2008). Sequence of improvement in depressive symptoms across cognitive therapy and pharmacotherapy. *Journal of Affective Disorders, 110*, 161-166.

Bhatia, S. (2017). The semantic representation of prejudice and stereotypes. *Cognition, 164*, 46-60.

Bialystok, E. (2011). Reshaping the mind: The benefits of bilingualism. *Canadian Journal of Experimental Psychology, 65*, 229-235.

Bialystok, E., & Craik, F. I. M. (2011). Cognitive and linguistic processing in the bilingual mind. *Current Directions in Psychological Science, 19*, 19-23.

Bialystok, E., Barac, R., Blaye, A., & Poulin-Dubois, D. (2010). Word mapping and executive functioning in young monolingual and bilingual children. *Journal of Cognition and Development, 11*, 485-508.

Bian, L., Leslie, S., & Cimpian, A. (2017). Gender stereotypes about intellectual ability emerge early and influence children's interests. *Science, 355*, 389-391.

Bianchi, S. M., & Casper, L. M. (2000). American families. *Population Bulletin, 55*(4).

Bieberstein, A., & Roosen, J. (2015). Gender differences in the meanings associated with food hazards: A means-end chain analysis. *Food Quality and Preference, 42*, 165-176.

Bienvenu, O. J., Davydow, D. S., & Kendler, K. S. (2011). Psychiatric "diseases" versus behavioral disorders and degree of genetic influence. *Psychological Medicine: A Journal of Research in Psychiatry and the Allied Sciences, 41*, 33-40.

Bigsby, E., Monahan, J. L., & Ewoldsen, D. R. (2017). An examination of adolescent recall of anti-smoking messages: Attitudes, message type, and message perceptions. *Health Communication, 32*, 409-419.

Billiard, M. (2008). Narcolepsy: Current treatment options and future approaches. *Neuropsychiatric Disease and Treatment, 4*, 557-566.

Binet, A., & Simon, T. (1916). *The development of intelligence in children (The Binet-Simon Scale).* Baltimore: Williams & Wilkins.

Bingenheimer, J. B., Brennan, R. T., & Earls, E. J. (2005). Firearm violence exposure and serious violent behavior. *Science, 308*, 1323-1327.

Bischoff, R. J., Springer, P. R., Felix, D. S., & Hollist, C. S. (2011). Finding the heart of medical family therapy: A content analysis of medical family therapy casebook articles. *Families, Systems, & Health, 29*, 184-196.

Bitterman, M. E. (2006). Classical conditioning since Pavlov. *Review of General Psychology, 10*, 365-376.

Bittles, A. H., Bower, C., & Hussain, R. (2007). The four ages of Down syndrome. *European Journal of Public Health, 17*, 121-225.

Bjork, R. A. (2015). Forgetting as a friend of learning. In D. S. Lindsay, A. P. Yonelinas, H. I. Roediger, D. S. Lindsay, A. P. Yonelinas, & H. I. Roediger (Eds.), *Remembering: Attributions, processes, and control in human memory: Essays in honor of Larry Jacoby.* New York: Psychology Press.

Bjornsdottir, E., Keenan, B. T., Eysteinsdottir, B., Arnardottir, E. S., Janson, C., Gislason, T., . . . Benediktsdottir, B. (2015). Quality of life among untreated sleep apnea patients compared with the general population and changes after treatment with positive airway pressure. *Journal of Sleep Research, 24*, 328-338.

Bjornstad, R. (2006). Learned helplessness, discouraged workers, and multiple unemployment equilibria. *Journal of Socio-Economics, 35*, 458-475.

Black, A. L., & McCafferty, D. (1998, July 3-5). The age of contentment. *USA Weekend*, 4-6.

Black, B. M., & Weisz, A. N. (2004). Dating violence: A qualitative analysis of Mexican American youths' views. *Journal of Ethnic and Cultural Diversity in Social Work, 13*, 69-90.

Blackwell, L. S., Rodriguez, S., & Guerra-Carrillo, B. (2015). Intelligence as a malleable construct. In S. Goldstein, D. Princiotta, & J. A. Naglieri (Eds.), *Handbook of intelligence: Evolutionary theory, historical perspective, and current concepts.* New York: Springer Science + Business Media.

Blair, C. A., Thompson, L. F., & Wuensch, K. L. (2005). Electronic helping behavior: The virtual presence of others makes a difference. *Basic and Applied Social Psychology, 27*, 171-178.

Blakeslee, S. (1992, September 29). Radical brain surgery, the earlier the better, offers epileptics hope. *The New York Times*, p. C3.

Blanton, H., Jaccard, J., & Burrows, C. N. (2015). Implications of the Implicit Association Test D-transformation for psychological assessment. *Assessment, 22*, 429-440.

Blass, T. (1996). Attribution of responsibility and trust in the Milgram obedience experiment. *Journal of Applied Social Psychology, 26*, 1529-1535.

Blass, T. (2004). *The man who shocked the world: The life and legacy of Stanley Milgram.* New York: Basic Books.

Blass, T. (2009). From New Haven to Santa Clara: A historical perspective on the Milgram obedience experiments. *American Psychologist, 64*, 37-45.

Blatter, K., & Cajochen, C. (2007). Circadian rhythms in cognitive performance: Methodological constraints, protocols, theoretical underpinnings. *Physiology & Behavior, 90*, 196-208.

Blechner, M. J. (2013). New ways of conceptualizing and working with dreams. *Contemporary Psychoanalysis, 49*, 259-275.

Bloom, P. N., McBride, C. M., & Pollak, K. I. (2006). Recruiting teen smokers in shopping malls to a smoking-cessation program using the foot-in-the-door technique. *Journal of Applied Social Psychology, 36*, 1129-1144.

Blum, D. (2002). *Love at goon park: Harry Harlow and the science of affection.* Cambridge, MA: Perseus.

Blum, H. P. (2011). To what extent do you privilege dream interpretation in relation to other forms of mental representations? *International Journal of Psychoanalysis, 92*, 275-277.

Blumen, H. M., Rajaram, S., & Henkel, L. (2013). The applied value of collaborative memory research in aging: Considerations for broadening the scope. *Journal of Applied Research in Memory and Cognition, 2,* 133-135.

Blumenthal, H., Leen-Feldner, E. W., Babson, K. A., Gahr, J. L., Trainor, C. D., & Frala, J. L. (2011). Elevated social anxiety among early maturing girls. *Developmental Psychology, 47,* 1133-1140.

Boag, S. (2015). Repression, defence, and the psychology of science. In S. Boag, L. W. Brakel, & V. Talvitie (Eds.), *Philosophy, science, and psychoanalysis: A critical meeting.* London: Karnac Books.

Boag, S. (2017). On dreams and motivation: Comparison of Freud's and Hobson's views. *Frontiers in Psychology, 7,* 1-13.

Boag, S., Brakel, L. W., & Talvitie, V. (2015). *Philosophy, science, and psychoanalysis: A critical meeting.* London, England: Karnac Books.

Boahen, K. (2005). Neuromorphic microchips. *Scientific American, 292*(5), 56-64.

Boake, C. (2008). Clinical neuropsychology. *Professional Psychology: Research and Practice, 39,* 234-239.

Boarini, R., Laslier, J., & Robin, S. (2009). Interpersonal comparisons of utility in bargaining: Evidence from a transcontinental ultimatum game. *Theory and Decision, 67,* 341-373.

Bode, C., de Ridder, D. T., Kuijer, R. G., & Bensing, J. M. (2007). Effects of an intervention promoting proactive coping competencies in middle and late adulthood. *Gerontologist, 47,* 42-51.

Boden, J. M., Fergusson, D. M., & Horwood, L. J. (2007). Anxiety disorders and suicidal behaviours in adolescence and young adulthood: Findings from a longitudinal study. *Psychological Medicine, 37,* 431-440.

Boeve-de Pauw, J., Donche, V., & Van Petegem, P. (2011). Adolescents' environmental worldview and personality: An explorative study. *Journal of Environmental Psychology, 31,* 109-117.

Bogaert, A. F., Visser, B. A., & Pozzebon, J. A. (2015). Gender differences in object of desire self-consciousness sexual fantasies. *Archives of Sexual Behavior, 44*(8), 2299-2310.

Bogart, R. K., McDaniel, R. J., Dunn, W. J., Hunter, C., Peterson, A. L., & Write, E. E. (2007). Efficacy of group cognitive behavior therapy for the treatment of masticatory myo-fascial pain. *Military Medicine, 172,* 169-174.

Bohart, A. C. (2006). Understanding person-centered therapy: A review of Paul Wilkins' person-centered therapy in focus. *Person-Centered and Experiential Psychotherapies, 5,* 138-143.

Bohn, A., & Berntsen, D. (2007). Pleasantness bias in flashbulb memories: Positive and negative flashbulb memories of the fall of the Berlin Wall among East and West Germans. *Memory and Cognition, 35,* 565-577.

Bohn, C., Aderka, I. M., Schreiber, F., Stangier, U., & Hofmann, S. G. (2013). Sudden gains in cognitive therapy and interpersonal therapy for social anxiety disorder. *Journal of Consulting and Clinical Psychology, 81,* 177-182.

Boles, D. B. (2005). A large-sample study of sex differences in functional cerebral lateralization. *Journal of Clinical and Experimental Neuropsychology, 27,* 759-768.

Bolger, N., & Amarel, D. (2007). Effects of social support visibility on adjustment to stress: Experimental evidence. *Journal of Personality and Social Psychology, 92,* 458-475.

Bolkan, S. (2015). Intellectually stimulating students' intrinsic motivation: The mediating influence of affective learning and student engagement. *Communication Reports, 28,* 80-91.

Boller, F. (2004). Rational basis of rehabilitation following cerebral lesions: A review of the concept of cerebral plasticity. *Functional Neurology: New Trends in Adaptive and Behavioral Disorders, 19,* 65-72.

Bonanno, G. A. (2004). Loss, trauma, and human resilience: Have we underestimated the human capacity to thrive after extremely aversive events? *American Psychologist, 59,* 20-28.

Bonezzi, A., Brendl, C., & De Angelis, M. (2011). Stuck in the middle: The psychophysics of goal pursuit. *Psychological Science, 22,* 607-612.

Bonham, V. L., Warshauer-Baker, E., & Collins, F. S. (2005). Race and ethnicity in the genome era: The complexity of the constructs. *American Psychologist, 60,* 9-15.

Bonini, L. (2017). The extended mirror neuron network: Anatomy, origin, and functions. *The Neuroscientist, 23,* 56-67.

Bonta, B., D. (1997). Cooperation and competition in peaceful societies. *Psychological Bulletin, 121,* 299-320.

Borghuis, J., Denissen, J. A., Oberski, D., Sijtsma, K., Meeus, W. J., Branje, S., . . . Bleidorn, W. (2017). Big Five personality stability, change, and codevelopment across adolescence and early adulthood. *Journal of Personality and Social Psychology, 113*(4), 641-657.

Bornstein, R. F. (2003). Psychodynamic models of personality. In T. Millon & M. J. Lerner (Eds.), *Handbook of psychology: Personality and social psychology* (Vol. 5). New York: Wiley.

Boroditsky, L. (2010, July 24-25). Lost in translation. *Wall Street Journal,* p. W3.

Boser, U. (2017). *Learn better: Mastering the skills for success in life, business, and school, or, how to become an expert in just about anything.* Emmaus, PA: Rodale Books.

Bosma, H., van Boxtel, M. P. J., Ponds, R. W. H. M., Houx, P. J. H., & Jolles, J. (2003). Education and age-related cognitive decline: The contribution of mental workload. *Educational Gerontology, 29,* 165-173.

Bossarte, R. M., & Swahn, M. H. (2011). The associations between early alcohol use and suicide attempts among adolescents with a history of major depression. *Addictive Behaviors, 36.*

Bosse, T., Gerritsen, C., & Treur, J. (2011). Combining rational and biological factors in virtual agent decision making. *Applied Intelligence, 34,* 87-101.

Bosson, J. K., & Vandello, J. A. (2011). Precarious manhood and its links to action and aggression. *Current Directions in Psychological Science, 20,* 82-86.

Botvinick, M. (2004). Probing the neural basis of body ownership. *Science, 305,* 782-783.

Bouchard, T. J., Jr. (2004). Genetic influence on human psychological traits: A survey. *Current Directions in Psychological Science, 13,* 148-151.

Bouchard, T. J., Jr., Segal, N. L, Tellegen, A., McGue, M., Keyes, M., & Krueger, R. (2004). Genetic influence on social attitudes: Another challenge to psychology from behavior genetics. In L. F. DiLalla (Ed.), *Behavior genetics principles: Perspectives in development, personality, and psychopathology.* Washington, DC: American Psychological Association.

Bourne, L. E., Dominowski, R. L., Loftus, E. F., & Healy, A. F. (1986). *Cognitive processes* (2nd ed.). Englewood Cliffs, NJ: Prentice Hall.

Bouton, C., Shaikhouni, A., Annetta, N., Bockbrader, M., Friedenberg, D. A., Nielson, D. M., . . . Rezai, A. R. (2016). Restoring cortical control of functional movement in a human with quadriplegia. *Nature, 533,* 247-250.

Bouton, M. E., Todd, T. P., Vurbic, D., & Winterbauer, N. E. (2011). Renewal after the extinction of free operant behavior. *Learning & Behavior, 39,* 57-67.

Bouvard, M., & Roulin, J. (2017). Exploratory factor analysis of the French version of the Big Five Questionnaire for Children (BFQ-C). *Swiss Journal of Psychology, 76,* 125-130.

Bouvard, M., Fournet, N., Denis, A., Sixdenier, A., & Clark, D. (2017). Intrusive thoughts in patients with obsessive compulsive disorder and non-clinical participants: A comparison using the International Intrusive Thought Interview Schedule. *Cognitive Behaviour Therapy, 46,* 287-299.

Boxer, P., Huesmann, L., Bushman, B., O'Brien, M., & Moceri, D. (2009). The role of violent media preference in cumulative developmental risk for violence and general aggression. *Journal of Youth and Adolescence, 38,* 417-428.

Boyd-Wilson, B. M., McClure, J., & Walkey, E. H. (2004). Are well-being and illusory perceptions linked? The answer may be yes, but. . . . *Australian Journal of Psychology, 56,* 1-9.

Boylan, J. M., & Ryff, C. D. (2015). Psychological well-being and metabolic syndrome: Findings from the Midlife in the United States national sample. *Psychosomatic Medicine, 77,* 548-558.

Boyle, G. J., Goldman, R., Svoboda, J. S., & Fernandez, E. (2002). Male circumcision: Pain, trauma and psychosexual sequelae. *Journal of Health Psychology, 7,* 329-343.

Boyle, S. H., Williams, R. B., Mark, D. B., Brummett, B. H., Siegler, I. C., & Barefoot, J. C. (2005). Hostility, age, and mortality in a sample of cardiac patients. *American Journal of Cardiology, 96,* 64-72.

Bradford, A. C., & Bradford, W. D. (2017). Factors driving the diffusion of medical marijuana legalisation in the United States. *Drugs: Education, Prevention & Policy, 24,* 75-84.

Brafman, A. H. (2011). *Fostering independence: Helping and caring in psychodynamic therapies.* London: Karnac Books.

Brambilla, P., Cipriani, A., Hotopf, M., & Barbui, C. (2005). Side-effect profile of fluoxetine in comparison with other SSRIs, tricyclic and newer antidepressants: A meta-analysis of clinical trial data. *Pharmacopsychiatry, 38,* 69-77.

Brandao, T., Tavares, R., Schulz, M. S., & Matos, P. M. (2015). Measuring emotion regulation and emotional expression in breast cancer patients: A systematic review. *Clinical Psychology Review, 43,* 114-127 .

Brandon, M., & Saffran, J. R. (2011). Apparent motion enhances visual rhythm discrimination in infancy. *Attention, Perception, & Psychophysics, 73,* 1016-1020.

Brandtzaeg, P. B., Lüders, M., Skjetne, J. H. (2010). Too many Facebook "friends"? Content sharing and sociability versus the need for privacy in social network sites. *International Journal of Human-Computer Interaction, 26,* 1006-1030.

Brang, D., Rouw, R., Ramachandran, V. S., & Coulson, S. (2011). Similarly shaped letters evoke similar colors in grapheme-color synesthesia. *Neuropsychologia, 49,* 1355-1358.

Brant, A. M., Munakata, Y., Boomsma, D. I., DeFries, J. C., Haworth, C. A., Keller, M. C., . . . Hewitt, J. K. (2013). The nature and nurture of high IQ: An extended sensitive period for intellectual development. *Psychological Science, 24,* 1487-1495.

Brasic, J. R. (2002). Conversion disorder in childhood. *German Journal of Psychiatry, 5,* 54-61.

Brausch, A. M., & Gutierrez, P. M. (2009). Differences in non-suicidal self-injury and suicide attempts in adolescents. *Journal of Youth and Adolescence, 21,* 46-51.

Brazelton, T. B. (1969). *Infants and mothers: Differences in development.* New York: Dell.

Breland, K., & Breland, M. (1966). *Animal behavior.* New York: Macmillan.

Brennan, P. (2011). Pheromones: Fact or fantasy? *Ethology, 117,* 265-266.

Brennen, T., Vikan, A., & Dybdahl, R. (2007). Are tip-of-the-tongue states universal? Evidence from the speakers of an unwritten language. *Memory, 15,* 167-176.

Breslin, C. W., & Safer, M. A. (2011). Effects of event valence on long-term memory for two baseball championship games. *Psychological Science, 20,* 1-5.

Brewer, M. B. (2007). The social psychology of intergroup relations: Social categorization, ingroup bias, and outgroup prejudice. In A. W. Kruglanski & E. Higgins (Eds.), *Social psychology: Handbook of basic principles* (2nd ed.). New York: Guilford Press.

Bright, P., Buckman, J., & Fradera, A. (2006). Retrograde amnesia in patients with hippocampal, medial temporal, temporal lobe, or frontal pathology. *Learning & Memory, 13,* 545-557.

Brody, J. (2008, May 20). Trying to break nicotine's grip. *The New York Times,* p. E9.

Brody, S., & Costa, R. M. (2017). Vaginal orgasm is associated with indices of women's better psychological, intimate relationship, and psychophysiological function. *Canadian Journal of Human Sexuality, 26,* 1-4.

Brody, S., & Weiss, P. (2015). Erectile dysfunction and premature ejaculation: Interrelationships and psychosexual factors. *Journal of Sexual Medicine, 12,* 398-404.

Broeders, R., van den Bos, K., Müller, P. A., & Ham, J. (2011). Should I save or should I not kill? How people solve moral dilemmas depends on which rule is most accessible. *Journal of Experimental Social Psychology, 47,* 923-934.

Broidy, L. M., Nagin, D. S., & Tremblay, R. E. (2003). Developmental trajectories of childhood disruptive behaviors and adolescent delinquency: A six-site, cross-national study. *Developmental Psychology, 39,* 222-245.

Bronson, P., & Merryman, A. (2009). *NurtureShock.* New York: Twelve.

Broockman, D., & Kalla, J. (2016). Durably reducing transphobia: A field experiment on door-to-door canvassing. *Science, 352,* 220-224.

Brown, E. (2001, September 17). The World Health Organization takes on big tobacco (but don't hold your breath): Anti-smoking advocates are mounting a global campaign: It's going to be a long, hard fight. *Forbes,* pp. 37-41.

Brown, M. W., & Banks, P. J. (2015). In search of a recognition memory engram. *Neuroscience and Biobehavioral Reviews, 50,* 12-28.

Brown, M., Chodzen, G., Mihelicova, M., & Collins, K. (2017). Applying a time-patterned typology of homelessness among individuals with mental illness. *American Journal of Community Psychology, 59,* 306-315.

Brown, P. (1986). Simbu aggression and the drive to win. *Anthropolitical Quarterly, 59,* 165-170.

Brown, P. K., & Wald, G. (1964). Visual pigments in single rod and cones of the human retina. *Science, 144,* 45-52.

Brown, R. (1958). How shall a thing be called? *Psychological Review, 65,* 14-21.

Brown, R. D., Goldstein, E., & Bjorklund, D. F. (2000). The history and zeitgeist of the repressed-false-memory debate: Scientific and sociological perspectives on suggestibility and childhood memory. In D. F. Bjorklund (Ed.), *False-memory creation in children and adults: Theory, research, and implications.* Mahwah, NJ: Lawrence Erlbaum.

Brown, R. J. (2006). Different types of "dissociation" have different psychological mechanisms. *Journal of Trauma Dissociation, 6,* 7-28.

Brown, S., Martinez, M. J., & Parsons, L. M. (2006). Music and language side by side in the brain: A PET study of the generation of melodies and sentences. *European Journal of Neuroscience, 23,* 2791-2803.

Browne, J., Penn, D. L., Meyer-Kalos, P. S., Mueser, K. T., Estroff, S. E., Brunette, M. F., . . . Kane, J. M. (2017). Psychological well-being and mental health recovery in the NIMH RAISE early treatment program. *Schizophrenia Research, 185,* 167-172.

Brucker, B., Ehlis, A., Häußinger, F. B., Fallgatter, A. J., & Gerjets, P. (2015). Watching corresponding gestures facilitates learning with animations by activating human mirror-neurons: An fNIRS study. *Learning and Instruction, 36,* 27-37.

Bruehl, S., Burns, J. W., Gupta, R., Buvanendran, A., Chont, M., Orlowska, D., . . . France, C. R.. (2017). Do resting plasma β-endorphin levels predict responses to opioid analgesics? *Clinical Journal of Pain, 33,* 12-20.

Bruggeman, H., Yonas, A., & Konczak, J. (2007). The processing of linear perspective and binocular information for action and perception. *Neuropsychologia, 45,* 1420-1426.

Bruni, F. (2017, September 24). Want geniuses? Welcome immigrants. *The New York Times,* p. SR3.

Bruno, D. (2016, November 23). An electric shock therapy stops self-harm among the autistic, but at what cost? *Washington Post Magazine.* Accessed from https://www.washingtonpost.com/lifestyle/magazine/an-electric-shock-therapy-stops-self-harm-among-the-autistic-but-at-what-cost/2016/11/21/b9b06c44-8f2c-11e6-9c85-ac42097b8cc0_story.html?utm_term=.1b9a9a3266b4.

Bryant, R. M., Coker, A. D., Durodoye, B. A., McCollum, V. J., Pack-Brown, S. P., Constantine, M. G., & O'Bryant, B. J. (2005). Having our say: African American women, diversity, and counseling. *Journal of Counseling and Development, 83,* 313-319.

Bub, K. L., Buckhalt, J. A., & El-Sheikh, M. (2011). Children's sleep and cognitive performance: A cross-domain analysis of change over time. *Developmental Psychology, 47(6),* 1504-1514.

Buchanan, T., & Selmon, N. (2008). Race and gender differences in self-efficacy: Assessing the role of gender role attitudes and family background. *Sex Roles, 58,* 822-836.

Buchert, R., Thomasius, R., Wilke, F., Petersen, K., Nebeling, B., Obrocki, J., . . . Clausen, M. (2004). A voxel-based PET investigation of the long-term effects of "ecstasy" consumption on brain serotonin transporters. *American Journal of Psychiatry, 161,* 1181-1189.

Buckner, J. D., & Shah, S. M. (2015). Fitting in and feeling fine: Conformity and coping motives differentially mediate the relationship between social anxiety and drinking problems for men and women. *Addiction Research & Theory, 23,* 231-237.

Buerkle, C. (2011). Masters of their domain: Seinfeld and the discipline of mediated men's sexual economy. In E. Watson & M. E. Shaw (Eds.), *Performing American masculinities: The 21st-century man in popular culture.* Bloomington, IN: Indiana University Press.

Bukobza, G. (2009). Relations between rebelliousness, risk-taking behavior, and identity status during emerging adulthood. *Identity, 9,* 159-177.

Bulf, H., Johnson, S. P., & Valenza, E. (2011). Visual statistical learning in the newborn infant. *Cognition, 121,* 127-132.

Bunce, J. A. (2015). Incorporating ecology and social system into formal hypotheses to guide field studies of color vision in primates. *American Journal of Primatology, 77,* 516-526.

Bunting, M. (2006). Proactive interference and item similarity in working memory. *Journal of Experimental Psychology: Learning, Memory, and Cognition, 32,* 183-196.

Buon, M., Habib, M., & Frey, D. (2017). Moral development: Conflicts and compromises. In J. A. Sommerville & J. Decety (Eds.), *Social cognition: Development across the life span.* New York: Routledge/Taylor & Francis Group.

Burbach, M. E., Matkin, G. S., & Fritz, S. M. (2004). Teaching critical thinking in an introductory leadership course utilizing active learning strategies: A confirmatory study. *College Student Journal, 38,* 482-493.

Burchinal, M. R., Roberts, J. E., & Riggins, R., Jr. (2000). Relating quality of center-based child care to early cognitive and language development longitudinally. *Child Development, 71,* 338-357.

Bureau of Labor Statistics, U.S. Department of Labor. (2017, March 8). Women's median earnings 82 percent of men's in 2016. *The Economics Daily.* Accessed at https://www.bls.gov/opub/ted/2017/womens-median-earnings-82-percent-of-mens-in-2016.htm.

Bureau, J., Martin, J., Yurkowski, K., Schmiedel, S., Quan, J., Moss, E., . . . Pallanca, D. (2017). Correlates of child-father and child-mother attachment in the preschool years. *Attachment & Human Development, 19,* 130-150.

Burger, J. M. (2009). Replicating Milgram: Would people still obey today? *American Psychologist, 64,* 1-11.

Burger, J. M., Reed, M., & DeCesare, K. (1999). The effects of initial request size on compliance: More about the that's-not-all technique. *Basic and Applied Social Psychology, 21,* 243-249.

Burgoon, J. K., & Bacue, A. E. (2003). Nonverbal communication skills. In J. O. Greene & B. R. Burleson (Eds.), *Handbook of communication and social interaction skills.* Mahwah, NJ: Lawrence Erlbaum.

Burgoon, J. K., Bonito, J. A., Ramirez, A. J. R., Dunbar, N. E., Kam, K., & Fischer, J. (2002). Testing the interactivity principle: Effects of mediation, propinquity, and verbal and nonverbal modalities in interpersonal interaction [Special Issue: Research on the relationship between verbal and nonverbal communication: Emerging integrations]. *Journal of Communication, 52,* 657-677.

Burns, G. W. (2017). *101 stories for enhancing happiness and well-being: Using metaphors in positive psychology and therapy.* New York: Routledge/Taylor & Francis Group.

Burns, N. R., Bryan, J., & Nettelbeck, T. (2006). Ginkgo biloba: No robust effect on cognitive abilities or mood in healthy young or older adults. *Human Psychopharmacology: Clinical and Experimental, 21,* 27-37.

Burri, A., Spector, T., & Qazi, R. (2015). Common genetic factors among sexual orientation, gender nonconformity, and number of sex partners in female twins: Implications for the evolution of homosexuality. *Journal of Sexual Medicine, 12,* 1004-1011.

Burton, L., Bensimon, E., Allimant, J., Kinsman, R., Levin, A., Kovacs, L., . . . Bahrami, J. (2013). Relationship of prosody perception to personality and aggression. *Current Psychology: A Journal for Diverse Perspectives on Diverse Psychological Issues, 32,* 275-280.

Busch, A. J., Morey, L. C., & Hopwood, C. J. (2017). Exploring the assessment of the DSM-5 alternative model for personality disorders with the personality assessment inventory. *Journal of Personality Assessment, 99,* 211-218.

Bush, J. (2008). Viability of virtual reality exposure therapy as a treatment alternative. *Computers in Human Behavior, 24,* 1032-1040.

Bushman, B. J., Wang, M. C., & Anderson, C. (2005). Is the curve relating temperature to aggression linear or curvilinear? Assaults and temperature in Minneapolis reexamined. *Journal of Personality and Social Psychology, 89,* 62-66.

Buss, A. H. (2011). *Pathways to individuality: Evolution and development of personality traits.* Washington, DC: American Psychological Association.

Buss, D. (2003). *Evolutionary psychology.* Boston: Allyn & Bacon.

Buss, D. (2009). How can evolutionary psychology successfully explain personality and individual differences? *Perspectives on Psychological Science, 4,* 359-366.

Buss, D. M. (2001). Human nature and culture: An evolutionary psychological perspective. *Journal of Personality, 69,* 955-978.

Buss, D. M. (2004). Sex differences in human mate preferences: Evolutionary hypotheses tested in 37 cultures. In H. T. Reis & C. E. Rusbult (Eds.), *Close relationships: Key readings.* Philadelphia: Taylor & Francis.

Buss, D. M., Abbott, M., & Angleitner, A. (1990). International preferences in selecting mates: A study of 37 cultures. *Journal of Cross-Cultural Psychology, 21,* 5-47.

Bustillo, J. R., Jones, T., Chen, H., Lemke, N., Abbott, C., Qualls, C., . . . Gasparovic, C. (2017). Glutamatergic and neuronal dysfunction in gray and white matter: A spectroscopic imaging study in a large schizophrenia sample. *Schizophrenia Bulletin, 43,* 611-619.

Butcher, J. N. (2011). *A beginner's guide to the MMPI-2* (3rd ed.). Washington, DC: American Psychological Association.

Butler, L. T., & Berry, D. C. (2004). Understanding the relationship between repetition priming and mere exposure. *British Journal of Psychology, 95,* 467-487.

Buysse, D. J., Germain, A., Moul, D. E., Franzen, P. L., Brar, L. K., Fletcher, M. E., . . . Monk, T. H. (2011). Efficacy of brief behavioral treatment for chronic insomnia in older adults. *Archives of Internal Medicine, 171,* 887-895.

Buzi, R., Weinman, M., & Smith, P. (2007). The relationship between adolescent depression and a history of sexual abuse. *Adolescence, 42*(168), 679-688.

Bylund, E., & Athanasopoulos, P. (2017). The Whorfian time warp: Representing duration through the language hourglass. *Journal of Experimental Psychology: General, 146,* 911-916.

Byne, W. (1996). Biology and homosexuality: Implications of neuroendocrinological and neuroanatomical studies. In R. P. Cabaj & T. S. Stein (Eds.), *Textbook of homosexuality and mental health.* Washington, DC: American Psychiatric Press.

Byrne, B. M., & Watkins, D. (2003). The issue of measurement invariance revisited. *Journal of Cross-Cultural Psychology, 34,* 155-175.

Cabioglu, M., Ergene, N., & Tan, Ü. (2007). Smoking cessation after acupuncture treatment. *International Journal of Neuroscience, 117,* 571-578.

Cachelin, F. M., & Regan, P. C. (2006). Prevalence and correlates of chronic dieting in a multiethnic U.S. community sample. *Eating and Weight Disorders, 11,* 91-99.

Cacioppo, J. T., & Decety, J. (2009). What are the brain mechanisms on which psychological processes are based? *Perspectives on Psychological Science, 4,* 10-18.

Cadenhead, K., & Braff, D. L. (1995). Neurophysiology of schizophrenia: Attention, information processing, and inhibitory processes in schizophrenia. In J. A. Den Boer, H. G. M. Westenberg, & H. M. van Praag (Eds.), *Advances in the neurobiology of schizophrenia.* Oxford, England: John Wiley & Sons.

Caelian, C. F. (2006). The role of perfectionism and stress in the suicidal behaviour of depressed adolescents. *Dissertation Abstracts International: Section B: The Sciences and Engineering, 66*(12-B), 6915.

Calvert, S. L., Appelbaum, M., Dodge, K. A., Graham, S., Nagayama Hall, G. C., Hamby, S., . . . Hedges, L. (2017). The American Psychological Association Task Force assessment of violent video games: Science in the service of public interest. *American Psychologist, 72,* 126-143.

Camerer, C., Babcock, L., Loewenstein, G., & Thaler, R. (1997). Labor supply of New York City cabdrivers: One day at a time. *Quarterly Journal of Economics, 112*(2), 407-441.

Cameron, C. D., Spring, V. L., & Todd, A. R. (2017). The empathy impulse: A multinomial model of intentional and unintentional empathy for pain. *Emotion, 17,* 395-411.

Cameron, O. G. (2002). *Visceral sensory neuroscience: Interoception.* London: Oxford University Press.

Campbell, R. (2008). The psychological impact of rape victims. *American Psychologist, 63,* 702-717.

Campos, R. C. (2011). "It might be what I am": Looking at the use of Rorschach in psychological assessment. *Journal of Projective Psychology & Mental Health, 18,* 28-38.

Cannon, W. B. (1929). Organization for physiological homeostatics. *Physiological Review, 9,* 280-289.

Cantarero, K., Gamian-Wilk, M., & Dolinski, D. (2017). Being inconsistent and compliant: The moderating role of the preference for consistency in the door-in-the-face technique. *Personality and Individual Differences, 115,* 54-57.

Cao, R., Nosofsky, R. M., & Shiffrin, R. M. (2017). The development of automaticity in short-term memory search: Item-response learning and category learning. *Journal of Experimental Psychology: Learning, Memory, and Cognition, 43*, 669-679.

Caplan, D., Waters, G., & Dede, G. (2007). A study of syntactic processing in aphasia I: Behavioral (psycholinguistic) aspects. *Brain and Language, 101*, 103-150.

Capraro, V., & Sippel, J. (2017). Gender differences in moral judgment and the evaluation of gender-specified moral agents. *Cognitive Processing, 18*(4), 399-405.

Carbon, C., & Ditye, T. (2011). Sustained effects of adaptation on the perception of familiar faces. *Journal of Experimental Psychology: Human Perception and Performance, 37*, 615-625.

Carciofo, R., Song, N., Du, F., Wang, M. M., & Zhang, K. (2017). Metacognitive beliefs mediate the relationship between mind wandering and negative affect. *Personality and Individual Differences, 107*, 78-87.

Card, N. A. (2017). Developmental methodology: I. Developmental methodology as a central subdiscipline of developmental science. *Monographs of the Society for Research in Child Development, 82*, 7-12.

Card, N. A. (2017). Developmental methodology: VII. Replication, research accumulation, and meta-analysis in developmental science. *Monographs of the Society for Research in Child Development, 82*, 105-121.

Cardemil, E. V., Pinedo, T. M., & Miller, I. W. (2005). Developing a culturally appropriate depression prevention program: The family coping skills program. *Cultural Diversity and Ethnic Minority Psychology, 11*, 99-112.

Carels, R. A., Young, K. M., Koball, A., Gumble, A., Darby, L. A., Oehlhof, M., . . . Hinman, N. (2011). Transforming your life: An environmental modification approach to weight loss. *Journal of Health Psychology, 16*, 430-438.

Carey, B. (2015, October 20). New approach may alleviate schizophrenia. *The New York Times*, p. A1.

Carey, B. (2016, April 14). Quadriplegic gets use of hand from chip placed in his brain. *The New York Times*, A1.

Carey, B. (2016, May 30). After thriving in combat tours, veterans are struggling at home. *The New York Times*, pp. A1, A3.

Carhart-Harris, R. (2007). Speed > Ecstasy > Ritalin: The science of amphetamines. *Journal of Psychopharmacology, 21*, 225.

Carleton, R. N., Duranceau, S., Freeston, M. H., Boelen, P. A., McCabe, R. E., & Antony, M. M. (2014). "But it might be a heart attack": Intolerance of uncertainty and panic disorder symptoms. *Journal of Anxiety Disorders, 28*, 463-470.

Carlstedt, R. A. (2017). Sports performance. In G. R. Elkins, G. R. Elkins (Eds.), *Handbook of medical and psychological hypnosis: Foundations, applications, and professional issues*. New York: Springer Publishing Co.

Carnagey, N., Anderson, C. A., & Bushman, B. J. (2007). The effect of video game violence on physiological desensitization to real-life violence. *Journal of Experimental Social Psychology, 43*, 489-496.

Carnagey, N., Anderson, C., & Bartholow, B. (2007). Media violence and social neuroscience: New questions and new opportunities. *Current Directions in Psychological Science, 16*, 178-182.

Carnevale, M., Luna, D., & Lerman, D. (2017). Brand linguistics: A theory-driven framework for the study of language in branding. *International Journal of Research in Marketing, 34*(2), 572-591.

Carpenter, S. (2002). What can resolve the paradox of mental health disparities? *APA Monitor, 33*, 18.

Carr, P., & Steele, C. (2009). Stereotype threat and inflexible perseverance in problem solving. *Journal of Experimental Social Psychology, 45*, 853-859.

Carrillo, M., Ricci, L., Coppersmith, G., & Melloni, R. (2009). The effect of increased serotonergic neurotransmission on aggression: A critical meta-analytical review of preclinical studies. *Psychopharmacology, 205*, 349-368.

Carroll, D. W. (2017). The ethics of memory research. *PsycCRITIQUES, 62*, 15-22.

Carter, R. T. (2003). Becoming racially and culturally competent: The racial-cultural counseling laboratory. *Journal of Multicultural Counseling and Development, 31*, 20-30.

Cartwright, R. (2006). A neuroscientist looks at how the brain makes up our minds. *PsycCRITIQUES, 51*, 35-41.

Cartwright, R., Agargum, M. Y., & Kirkby, J. (2006). Relation of dreams to waking concerns. *Psychiatry Research, 141*, 261-270.

Caruso, E. (2008). Use of experienced retrieval ease in self and social judgments. *Journal of Experimental Social Psychology, 44*, 148-155.

Carvalho, J., & Nobre, P. (2011). Biopsychosocial determinants of men's sexual desire: Testing an integrative model. *Journal of Sexual Medicine, 8*, 754-763.

Carver, C., & Scheier, M. (2002). Coping processes and adjustment to chronic illness. In A. Christensen & M. Antoni (Eds.), *Chronic physical disorders: Behavioral medicine's perspective*. Malden: Blackwell Publishers.

Casad, B. J. (2007). Gender stereotype violation among job applicants: An examination of theory and measurement. *Dissertation Abstracts International: Section B: The Sciences and Engineering, 67*(7-B), 4154.

Casasola, M. (2011). Infant spatial categorization from an information processing approach. In L. M. Oakes, C. H. Cashon, M. Casasola, & D. H. Rakison (Eds.), *Infant perception and cognition: Recent advances, emerging theories, and future directions*. New York: Oxford University Press.

Case, R., & Okamoto, Y. (1996). The role of central conceptual structures in the development of children's thought. *Monographs of the Society for Research in Child Development, 61*, v-265.

Cassells, J. V. S. (2007). The virtuous roles of truth and justice in integral dialogue: Research, theory, and model practice of the evolution of collective consciousness. *Dissertation Abstracts International Section A: Humanities and Social Sciences, 67*(10-A), 4005.

Catalano, S. M. (2006, September). Criminal victimization, 2005. *Bureau of Justice Statistics Bulletin*. Washington, DC: Bureau of Justice Statistics.

Cattell, R. B., Cattell, A. K., & Cattell, H. E. P. (2000). *The sixteen personality factor™ (16PF®) questionnaire*. Champaign, IL: Institute for Personality and Ability Testing.

Cauce, A. M. (2007). Bringing community psychology home: The leadership, community and values initiative. *American Journal of Community Psychology, 39*, 1-11.

Cavallini, E., Pagnin, A., & Vecchi, T. (2003). Aging and everyday memory: The beneficial effect of memory training. *Archives of Gerontology & Geriatrics, 37*, 241-257.

Celi, L.A.G., Fraser, H.S.F., Nikore, V., Osorio, J.S., & Paik, K. (2017). *Global health informatics: Principles of eHealth and mHealth to improve quality of care*. Cambridge, MA: MIT Press.

Center for Collegiate Mental Health. (2017, January). *2016 Annual Report* (Publication No. STA 17-74).

Centers for Disease Control and Prevention. (2013). Adult cigarette smoking in the United States: Current estimate. Retrieved from http://www.cdc.gov/tobacco/data_statistics/fact sheets/adult data/cig smoking/.

Centers for Disease Control and Prevention. (2000). *Suicide prevention fact sheet*. Atlanta: National Center for Injury Prevention and Control.

Centers for Disease Control and Prevention. (2004). Suicide and attempted suicide. *Morbidity and Mortality Weekly Report, 53*, 471.

Centers for Disease Control and Prevention. (2015, April 16). E-cigarette use triples among middle and high school students in just one year. Press release. Retrieved from http://www.cdc.gov/media/releases/2015/p0416-e-cigarette-use.html.

Centers for Disease Control and Prevention. (2011). *The national Intimate Partner and Sexual Violence Survey*. Washington, DC: CDC.

Centers for Disease Control and Prevention. (2013). *HIV in the United States: At a Glance*. Atlanta: CDC.

Centers for Disease Control and Prevention. (2013). *STD surveillance tables*. Atlanta: CDC.

Centers for Disease Control and Prevention Vitalsigns. (2010). *Binge drinking*. Atlanta, GA: CDC.

Cerami, C., Dodich, A., Lettieri, G., Iannaccone, S., Magnani, G., Marcone, A., . . . Perani, D. (2016). Different FDG-PET metabolic patterns at single-subject level in the behavioral variant of fronto-temporal dementia. *Cortex: A Journal Devoted to the Study of the Nervous System and Behavior, 83* 101-112.

Chamberlain, K., & Zika, S. (1990). The minor events approach to stress: Support for the use of daily hassles. *British Journal of Psychology, 81*, 469-481.

Chamberlain, S. R., Menzies, L., Hampshire, A., Suckling, J., Fineberg, N. A., del Campo, N., . . . Sahakian, B. J. (2008). Orbitofrontal dysfunction in patients with obsessive-compulsive disorder and their unaffected relatives. *Science, 321,* 421-422.

Chambless, D. L., Crits-Christoph, P., Wampold, B. E., Norcross, J. C., Lambert, M. J., Bohart, A. C., . . . Johannsen, B. E. (2006). What should be validated? In J. C. Norcross, L. E. Beutler, & R. E Levant (Eds.). *Evidence-based practices in mental health: Debate and dialogue on the fundamental questions.* Washington, DC: American Psychological Association.

Chandler, D. R. (2011). Proactively addressing the shortage of blacks in psychology: Highlighting the school psychology subfield. *Journal of Black Psychology, 37,* 99-127.

Chandran, S., & Menon, G. (2004). When a day means more than a year: Effects of temporal framing on judgments of health risk. *Journal of Consumer Research, 31,* 375-389.

Chang, L., & Geary, D. C. (2007). The future of psychology: Evolutionary approach to scientific psychology [Special issue: Evolutionary psychology]. *Acta Psychologica Sinica, 39,* 381-382.

Chao, M. M., Takeuchi, R., & Farh, J. (2017). Enhancing cultural intelligence: The roles of implicit culture beliefs and adjustment. *Personnel Psychology, 70,* 257-292.

Chao, R. (2011). Managing stress and maintaining well-being: Social support, problem-focused coping, and avoidant coping. *Journal of Counseling & Development, 89,* 338-348.

Chapman, J. (2006). Anxiety and defective decision making: An elaboration of the group-think model. *Management Decision, 44,* 1391-1404.

Chapman, L. J., & Chapman, J. P. (1973). *Disordered thought in schizophrenia* (p. 3). New York: Appleton-Century-Crofts.

Chapman, S. C., & Wu, L. (2015). Epidemiology and demography of illicit drug use and drug use disorders among adults aged 50 and older. In I. Crome, L. Wu, R. Rao, & P. Crome, (Eds.), *Substance use and older people.* New York: Wiley-Blackwell.

Chavez, P. R., Nelson, D. E., Naimi, T. S., & Brewer, R. D. (2011). Impact of a new gender-specific definition for binge drinking on prevalence estimates for women. *American Journal of Preventive Medicine, 40,* 468-471.

Chen, C., & Stevenson, H. W. (1995). Motivation and mathematics achievement: A comparative study of Asian-American, Caucasian-American, and East Asian high school students. *Child Development, 66,* 1215-1234.

Chen, C., & Zhang, L. (2011). Temperament, personality and achievement goals among Chinese adolescent students. *Educational Psychology, 31,* 339-359.

Chen, T., Yue, G. H., Tian, Y., & Jiang, C. (2017). Baduanjin mind-body intervention improves the executive control function. *Frontiers in Psychology, 7,* 72-81.

Chen, Z., Fu, L., Peng, Y., Cai, R., & Zhou, S. (2011). The relationship among childhood abuse, parenting styles, and antisocial personality disorder tendency. *Chinese Journal of Clinical Psychology, 19,* 212-214.

Cheng, C., & Cheung, M. L. (2005). Cognitive processes underlying coping flexibility: Differentiation and integration. *Journal of Personality, 73,* 859-886.

Cheng, S., & Kwan, K. (2008). Attachment dimensions and contingencies of self-worth: The moderating role of culture. *Personality and Individual Differences, 45,* 509-514.

Cheng, Y., Diao, Q., & Behrens, J. T. (2017). A simplified version of the maximum information per time unit method in computerized adaptive testing. *Behavior Research Methods, 49,* 502-512.

Chi, R. P., Fregni, F., & Snyder, A. W. (2010). Visual memory improved by non-invasive brain stimulation. *Brain Research, 1353* 168-175.

Chin, J. (2013). Eastern and Western learning styles: The paradox of Asian learners. *PsycCRITIQUES, 58,* 102-111.

Chin, T. (2015). Harmony and organizational citizenship behavior in Chinese organizations. *International Journal of Human Resource Management, 26,* 1110-1129.

Chiodo, D., Wolfe, D., Crooks, C., Hughes, R., & Jaffe, P. (2009). Impact of sexual harassment victimization by peers on subsequent adolescent victimization and adjustment: A longitudinal study. *Journal of Adolescent Health, 45,* 246-252.

Chiu, Y., Lo, S., & Hsieh, A. (2017). How colour similarity can make banner advertising effective: Insights from Gestalt theory. *Behaviour & Information Technology, 36,* 606-619.

Cho, S., Holyoak, K. J., & Cannon, T. D. (2007). Analogical reasoning in working memory: Resources shared among relational integration, interference resolution, and maintenance. *Memory & Cognition, 35,* 1445-1455.

Chodakiewitz, Y., Williams, J., Chodakiewitz, J., & Cosgrove, G. R. (2015). Ablative surgery for neuropsychiatric disorders: Past, present, future. In B. Sun & A. De Salles (Eds.), *Neurosurgical treatments for psychiatric disorders.* New York: Springer Science + Business Media.

Choi, H., Kensinger, E. A., & Rajaram, S. (2013). Emotional content enhances true but not false memory for categorized stimuli. *Memory & Cognition, 41,* 403-415.

Choi, H., Kensinger, E. A., & Rajaram, S. (2017). Mnemonic transmission, social contagion, and emergence of collective memory: Influence of emotional valence, group structure, and information distribution. *Journal of Experimental Psychology: General, 146,* 1247-1265.

Choi, H., Van Ouytsel, J., & Temple, J. R. (2016). Association between sexting and sexual coercion among female adolescents. *Journal of Adolescence, 53,* 164-168.

Choma, B. L., Jagayat, A., Hodson, G., & Turner, R. (2018). Prejudice in the wake of terrorism: The role of temporal distance, ideology, and intergroup emotions. *Personality and Individual Differences, 123,* 65-75.

Chomsky, N. (1978). On the biological basis of language capacities. In G. A. Miller & E. Lennenberg (Eds.), *Psychology and biology of language and thought.* New York: Academic Press.

Chomsky, N. (1991). Linguistics and cognitive science: Problems and mysteries. In A. Kasher (Ed.), *The Chomskyan turn.* Cambridge, MA: Blackwell.

Chou, K. (2005). Everyday competence and depressive symptoms: Social support and sense of control as mediators or moderators? *Aging and Mental Health, 9,* 177-183.

Choubsaz, Y., & Gheitury, A. (2017). Is semantics affected by missing a critical period? Evidence from the Persian deaf. *Journal of Psycholinguistic Research, 46,* 77-88.

Choy, Y., Fyer, A. J., & Lipsitz, J. D. (2007). Treatment of specific phobia in adults. *Clinical Psychology Review, 27,* 266-286.

Christakis, N. A., & Fowler, J. H. (2008). The collective dynamics of smoking in a large social network. *The New England Journal of Medicine, 358,* 2249-2258.

Christensen, K. A., Aldao, A., Sheridan, M. A., & McLaughlin, K. A. (2017). Habitual reappraisal in context: Peer victimisation moderates its association with physiological reactivity to social stress. *Cognition and Emotion, 31,* 384-394.

Christian, C. J., Lencz, T., Robinson, D. G., Burdick, K. E., Ashtari, M., Malhotra, A. K., . . . Szeszko, P. R. (2008). Gray matter structural alterations in obsessive-compulsive disorder: Relationship to neuropsychological functions. *Neuroimaging, 164,* 123-131.

Christoffels, I. K., de Haan, A. M., Steenbergen, L., van den Wildenberg, W. M., & Colzato, L. S. (2015). Two is better than one: Bilingual education promotes the flexible mind. *Psychological Research, 79,* 371-379.

Cialdini, R. B. (2006). *Influence: The psychology of persuasion.* New York: Collins.

Cialdini, R. B., & Sagarin, B. J. (2005). Principles of interpersonal influence. In T. C. Brock & M. C. Green (Eds.), *Persuasion: Psychological insights and perspectives* (2nd ed.). Thousand Oaks, CA: Sage Publications.

Cialdini, R. B., Schaller, M., Houlihan, D., Arps, K., Fultz, J., & Beaman, A. L. (1975). Reciprocal concessions procedure for inducing compliance: The door-in-the-face technique. *Journal of Personality and Social Psychology, 31,* 206-215.

Cisler, J. M., James, G. A., Tripathi, S., Mletzko, T., Heim, C., Hu, X. P., . . . Kilts, C. D. (2013). Differential functional connectivity within an emotion regulation neural network among individuals resilient and susceptible to the depressogenic effects of early life stress. *Psychological Medicine, 43,* 507-518.

Clark, D. A. (2007). Obsessions and compulsions. In N. Kazantzis & L. L'Abate (Eds.), *Handbook of homework assignments in psychotherapy: Research, practice, prevention.* New York: Springer Science + Business Media.

Clarkin, J. F., & Lenzenweger, M. F. (Eds.). (2004). *Major theories of personality disorders* (2nd ed.). New York: Guilford.

Clay, R. A. (2017, July/August). Women outnumber men in psychology, but not in the field's top echelons. *Monitor on Psychology,* pp. 18–19.

Clements, A. M., Rimrodt, S. L., & Abel, J. R. (2006). Sex differences in cerebral laterality of language and visuospatial processing. *Brain, 8,* 150–158.

Clemons, T. L. (2006). Underachieving gifted students: A social cognitive model. *Dissertation Abstracts International Section A: Humanities and Social Sciences, 66*(9-A), 3208.

Clément-Guillotin, C., & Fontayne, P. (2011). Situational malleability of gender schema: The case of the competitive sport context. *Sex Roles, 64,* 426–439.

Coan, J. A., Schaefer, H. S., & Davidson, R. J. (2006). Lending a hand: Social regulation of the neural response to threat. *Psychological Science, 17*(12), 1032–1039.

Coats, E. J., & Feldman, R. S. (1996). Gender differences in nonverbal correlates of social status. *Personality and Social Psychology Bulletin, 22,* 1014–1022.

Cobos, P., Sanchez, M., Garcia, C., Vera, M. N., & Vila, J. (2002). Revisiting the James versus Cannon debate on emotion: Startle and autonomic modulation in patients with spinal cord injuries. *Biological Psychology, 61,* 251–269.

Coderre, T. J. (2011). Complex regional pain syndrome: What's in a name? *The Journal of Pain, 12,* 2–12.

Coffman, S. J., Martell, C. R., Dimidjian, S., Gallop, R., & Holon, S. D. (2007). Extreme non-response in cognitive therapy: Can behavioral activation succeed where cognitive therapy fails? *Journal of Consulting Clinical Psychology, 75,* 531–545.

Cohen, G. L., Garcia, J., Apfel, N., & Master, A. (2006). Reducing the racial achievement gap: A social-psychological intervention. *Science, 313,* 1307–1310.

Cohen, L., & Cashon, C. (2003). Infant perception and cognition. In R. Lerner & M. Easterbrooks (Eds.), *Handbook of psychology: Developmental psychology* (Vol. 6). New York: Wiley.

Cohen, P., Slomkowski, C., & Robins, L. N. (Eds.). (1999). *Historical and geographical influences on psychopathology.* Mahwah, NJ: Erlbaum.

Cohn, D., & Caumont, A. (2016, March 31). 10 demographic trends that are shaping the U.S. and the world. *FactTank: News in the Numbers.* Retrieved from http://www.pewresearch.org/fact-tank/2016/03/31/10-demographic-trends-that-are-shaping-the-u-s-and-the-world/.

Cole, S. W., Arevalo, J. M., Takahashi, R., Sloan, E. K., Lutgendorf, S. L., Sood, A. K., . . . Seeman, T. E. (2010). Computational identification of gene-social environment interaction at the human IL6 locus. *Proceedings of the National Academy of Sciences of the USA, 107,* 5681–5686.

Coles, R., & Stokes, G. (1985). *Sex and the American teenager.* New York: Harper & Row.

Colland, V. T., Van Essen-Zandvliet, L. E. M., Lans, C., Denteneer, A., Westers, P., & Brackel, H. J. L. (2004). Poor adherence to self-medication instructions in children with asthma and their parents. *Patient Education and Counseling, 55,* 416–421.

Colom, R., Haier, R. J., Head, K., Alvarez-Linera, J., Quiroga, M. A., Shih, P. C., . . . Jung, R. E. (2009). Gray matter correlates of fluid, crystallized, and spatial intelligence: Testing the P-FIT model. *Intelligence, 37,* 124–135.

Coltheart, M., Langdon, R., & McKay, R. (2007). Schizophrenia and monothematic delusions. *Schizophrenia Bulletin, 33,* 642–647.

Columbia Neurosurgery. (2017, April). Pioneering surgical treatment for depression. Columbia Doctors: Neurological Surgery. Retrieved from http://www.columbianeurosurgery.org/2017/04/pioneering-depression-surgical-treatment/.

Colwell, M. J., & Lindsey, E. W. (2005). Preschool children's pretend and physical play and sex of play partner: Connections to peer competence. *Sex Roles, 52,* 497–509.

Commons, M. L., Adhikari, D., Giri, S., Weinberg, M., Baran, J. J., & Malik, E. (2017). Measuring developmental outcomes in autism spectrum disorder (ASD). *Behavioral Development Bulletin, 22*(1), 197–208.

Compagni, A., & Manderscheid, R. W. (2006). A neuroscientist-consumer alliance to transform mental health care. *Journal of Behavioral Health Services & Research, 33,* 265–274.

Connolly, A. C. (2007). Concepts and their features: Can cognitive science make good on the promises of concept empiricism? *Dissertation Abstracts International: Section B: The Sciences and Engineering, 67*(7-B), 4125.

Conoley, C. W., Plumb, E. W., Hawley, K. J., Spaventa-Vancil, K. Z., & Hernández, R. J. (2015). Integrating positive psychology into family therapy: Positive family therapy. *The Counseling Psychologist, 43,* 703–733.

Conway, M. A. (Ed.). (2002). *Levels of processing 30 years on: Special issue of memory.* Hove, UK: Psychology Press.

Cook, L. (2015, August 19). The heroin epidemic in 9 graphs. *US News & World Report.* Accessed from http://www.usnews.com/news/blogs/data-mine/2015/08/19/the-heroin-epidemic-in-9-graphs.

Cook, M. (2013). *Levels of personality* (3rd ed.). New York: Cambridge University Press.

Cook-Cottone, C., & Smith, A. (2013). Eating disorders. In C. A. Noggle & R. S. Dean (Eds.), *The neuropsychology of psychopathology.* New York: Springer Publishing Co.

Coolidge, F. L., Segal, D. L., Estey, A. J., & Neuzil, P. J. (2011). Preliminary psychometric properties of a measure of Karen Horney's Tridimensional Theory in children and adolescents. *Journal of Clinical Psychology, 67,* 383–390.

Cooper, J. (2007). *Cognitive dissonance: Fifty years of a classic theory.* Thousand Oaks, CA: Sage Publications.

Cooper, M., & McLeod, J. (2011). Person-centered therapy: A pluralistic perspective. *Person-Centered and Experiential Psychotherapies, 10,* 210–223.

Cooper, Z., & Shafran, R. (2008). Cognitive behaviour therapy for eating disorders. *Behavioural and Cognitive Psychotherapy, 36,* 713–722.

Cope, D. (2001). *Virtual music.* Cambridge, MA: MIT.

Cope, D. (2003). Computer analysis of musical allusions. *Computer Music Journal, 27,* 11–28.

Coplan, R., Reichel, M., & Rowan, K. (2009). Exploring the associations between maternal personality, child temperament, and parenting: A focus on emotions. *Personality and Individual Differences, 46,* 241–246.

Cordnoldi, C., De Beni, R., & Helstrup, T. (2007). Memory sensitivity in auto-biographical memory. In S. Magnussen & T. Helstrup (Eds.), *Everyday memory.* New York: Psychology Press.

Coren, S. (2004). Sensation and perception. In I. B. Weiner (Ed.), *Handbook of Psychology* (Vol. 1). Hoboken, NJ: John Wiley & Sons.

Cornelis, M. C., Tordoff, M. G., El-Sohemy, A., & van Dam, R. M. (2017). Recalled taste intensity, liking and habitual intake of commonly consumed foods. *Appetite, 109,* 182–189.

Cornell, C. B. (2006). A graduated scale for determining mental age. *Dissertation Abstracts International: Section B: The Sciences and Engineering, 66*(9-B), 5121.

Cornier, M. (2011). Is your brain to blame for weight regain? *Physiology & Behavior, 104,* 608–612.

Corsello, A. (2005). The wronged man. In *The best American magazine writing, 2005.* New York: Columbia University Press.

Cosmides, L., & Tooby, J. (2004). Social exchange: The evolutionary design of a neurocognitive system. In M. S. Gazzaniga (Ed.), *Cognitive neurosciences* (3rd ed.). Cambridge, MA: MIT.

Costa, P. T., Jr., & Widiger, T. A. (Eds.). (2002). *Personality disorders and the Five-Factor Model of personality* (2nd ed.). Washington, DC: American Psychological Association.

Costa, R., & Figueiredo, B. (2011). Infant's psychophysiological profile and temperament at 3 and 12 months. *Infant Behavior & Development, 34,* 270–279.

Cottencin, O., Rolland, B., & Karila, L. (2013). New designer drugs (synthetic cannabinoids and synthetic cathinones): review of literature. *Current Pharmaceutical Design.* Accessed from http://www.ncbi.nlm.nih.gov/pubmed/24001292.

Coulson, D., & Harvey, M. (2013). Scaffolding student reflection for experience-based learning: A framework. *Teaching in Higher Education, 18,* 401–413.

Coultas, J. C., & van Leeuwen, E. C. (2015). Conformity: Definitions, types, and evolutionary grounding. In V. Zeigler-Hill, L. M. Welling, & T. K. Shackelford (Eds.), *Evolutionary perspectives on social psychology.* Cham, Switzerland: Springer International Publishing.

Council of National Psychological Associations for the Advancement of Ethnic Minority Interests. (2000, January). *Guidelines for research in ethnic minority communities.* Washington, DC: American Psychological Association.

Couturier, J., & Lock, J. (2006). Eating-disorders: Anorexia nervosa, bulimia nervosa, and binge eating disorder. In T. G. Plante (Ed.), *Mental disorders of the new millennium: Biology and function* (Vol. 3). Westport, CT: Praeger Publishers/Greenwood Publishing.

Coventry, K. R., Venn, S. F., Smith, G. D., & Morley, A. M. (2003). Spatial problem solving and functional relations. *European Journal of Cognitive Psychology, 15,* 71-99.

Cowan, N. (2001). The magical number 4 in short-term memory: A reconsideration of mental storage capacity. *Behavioral and Brain Sciences, 24,* 97-185.

Cox, J. (2003, May 6). How far would you go to save your life? *Denver Post,* p. F1.

Cox, J. C., Green, E. P., & Hennig-Schmidt, H. (2016). Experimental and behavioral economics of healthcare. *Journal of Economic Behavior & Organization, 131*(Part B), A1-A4.

Cox, J. W., Rich, S., Chui, A., Muyskens, J., & Ulmanu, M. (2018). Database: The number of children impacted by school shootings. *Washington Post.* Retrieved from https://www.washingtonpost.com/graphics/2018/local/school-shootings-database/.

Cox, R., Baker, S. E., Macdonald, D. W., & Berdoy, M. (2004). Protecting egg prey from carrion crows: The potential of aversive conditioning. *Applied Animal Behaviour Science, 87,* 325-342.

Coyle, N. (2006). The hard work of living in the face of death. *Journal of Pain and Symptom Management, 32,* 266-274.

Craig, P. L. (2017). Clinical neuropsychologists. In R. J. Sternberg, (Ed.) , *Career paths in psychology: Where your degree can take you* (3rd ed.). Washington, DC: American Psychological Association.

Craighero, L., Leo, I., Umilta, C., & Simion, F. (2011). Newborns' preference for goal-directed actions. *Cognition, 120,* 26-32.

Craik, F., & Lockhart, R. (2008). Levels of processing and Zinchenko's approach to memory research. *Journal of Russian & East European Psychology, 46,* 52-60.

Crano, W. D., Brewer, M. B., & Lac, A. (2015). *Principles and methods of social research* (3rd ed.). New York: Routledge/Taylor & Francis Group.

Cranston, C. C., Miller, K. E., Davis, J. L., & Rhudy, J. L. (2017). Preliminary validation of a brief measure of the frequency and severity of nightmares: The Trauma-Related Nightmare Survey. *Journal of Trauma & Dissociation, 18,* 88-99.

Creasey, G. L. (2005). *Research methods in lifespan development* (6th ed.). Boston: Allyn & Bacon.

Creel, S. C., & Bregman, M. R. (2011). How talker identity relates to language processing. *Language and Linguistics Compass, 5,* 190-204.

Crespo, R., & Mesurado, B. (2015, August). Happiness economics, eudaimonia and positive psychology: From happiness economics to flourishing economics. *Journal of Happiness Studies, 16*(4), 931-946.

Criswell, H., Ming, Z., Kelm, M., & Breese, G. (2008). Brain regional differences in the effect of ethanol on GABA release from presynaptic terminals. *Journal of Pharmacology and Experimental Therapeutics, 326,* 596-603.

Critelli, J., & Bivona, J. (2008). Women's erotic rape fantasies: An evaluation of theory and research. *Journal of Sex Research, 45,* 57-70.

Crockford, C., Wittig, R. M., & Zuberbühler, K. (2015). An intentional vocalization draws others' attention: A playback experiment with wild chimpanzees. *Animal Cognition, 18,* 581-591.

Croom, A. M. (2015). Aristotelian moral psychology and the situationist challenge. *Polish Psychological Bulletin, 46,* 262-277.

Crosnoe, R., & Elder, G. H., Jr. (2002). Successful adaptation in the later years: A life course approach to aging. *Social Psychology Quarterly, 65,* 309-328.

Cross, C. P., & Campbell, A. (2011). Women's aggression. *Aggression and Violent Behavior, 16,* 390-398.

Crowne, K. (2013). Cultural exposure, emotional intelligence, and cultural intelligence: An exploratory study. *International Journal of Cross-Cultural Management, 13*(1), 5-22.

Crum, A. J., & Langer, E. J. (2007). Mind-set matters: Exercise and the placebo effect. *Psychological Science, 18,* 165-171.

Cuddy, A. J. C., Fiske, S. T., & Glick, P. (2004). When professionals become mothers, warmth doesn't cut the ice. *Journal of Social Issues, 60,* 701-718.

Cuijpers, P., van Straten, A., Andersson, G., & van Oppen, P. (2008). Psychotherapy for depression in adults: A meta-analysis of comparative outcome studies. *Journal of Consulting and Clinical Psychology, 76,* 909-922.

Culhane-Pera, K. A., Borkan, J. M., & Patten, S. (2007). Culture and ethnicity. In O. J. Z. Sahler & J. E. Carr (Eds.), *The behavioral sciences and health care* (2nd rev. and updated ed.). Ashland, OH: Hogrefe & Huber Publishers.

Cullinane, C. A., Chu, D. Z. J., & Mamelak, A. N. (2002). Current surgical options in the control of cancer pain. *Cancer Practice, 10,* s21-s26.

Cummings, A., Ceponiene, R., & Koyama, A. (2006). Auditory semantic networks for words and natural sounds. *Brain Research, 1115,* 92-107.

Cunningham, P. (2006). Early years teachers and the influence of Piaget: Evidence from oral history. *Early Years: An International Journal of Research and Development, 26,* 5-16.

Curthoys, I. S. (2017). The new vestibular stimuli: Sound and vibration–anatomical, physiological and clinical evidence. *Experimental Brain Research, 235,* 957-972.

Cynkar, A. (2007). The changing gender composition of psychology. *Monitor on Psychology, 38,* 46-48.

Daftary, F., & Meri, J. W. (2002). *Culture and memory in medieval Islam.* London: I. B. Tauris.

Dai, D. Y., & Wang, X. (2007). The role of need for cognition and reader beliefs in text comprehension and interest development. *Contemporary Educational Psychology, 32,* 332-347.

Dakin, E. K., & Areán, P. (2013). Patient perspectives on the benefits of psychotherapy for late-life depression. *American Journal of Geriatric Psychiatry, 21,* 155-163.

Dalal, A. K., & Misra, G. (2006). Psychology of health and well-being: Some emerging perspectives [Special issue: Psychology of health and well-being]. *Psychological Studies, 51,* 91-104.

Damaske, S. (2011). A "major career woman"? How women develop early expectations about work. *Gender & Society, 25,* 409-430.

Damjanovic, L., Meyer, M., & Sepulveda, F. (2017). Raising the alarm: Individual differences in the perceptual awareness of masked facial expressions. *Brain and Cognition, 114,* 1-10.

Dani, J. A., & Montague, P. (2007). Disrupting addiction through the loss of drug-associated internal states. *Nature Neuroscience, 10,* 403-404.

Daniels, C. W., & Sanabria, F. (2017). Interval timing under a behavioral microscope: Dissociating motivational and timing processes in fixed-interval performance. *Learning & Behavior, 45,* 29-48.

Danner, D., Hagemann, D., Schankin, A., Hager, M., & Funke, J. (2011). Beyond IQ: A latent state-trait analysis of general intelligence, dynamic decision making, and implicit learning. *Intelligence, 39,* 323-334.

Dare, J. S. (2011). Transitions in midlife women's lives: Contemporary experiences. *Health Care for Women International, 32,* 111-133.

Das, A. (2007). Masturbation in the United States. *Journal of Sex & Marital Therapy, 33,* 301-317.

Das, A., Parish, W., & Laumann, E. (2009). Masturbation in urban China. *Archives of Sexual Behavior, 38,* 108-120.

Das, J. P. (2015). Search for intelligence by PASSing g. *Canadian Psychology/Psychologie Canadienne, 56,* 39-45.

Dasborough, M., & Harvey, P. (2017). Schadenfreude: The (not so) secret joy of another's misfortune. *Journal of Business Ethics, 141,* 693-707.

Datar, A. (2017). The more the heavier? Family size and childhood obesity in the U.S. *Social Science & Medicine, 180,* 143-151.

Davern, M. (2013). Nonresponse rates are a problematic indicator of nonresponse bias in survey research. *Health Services Research, 48,* 905-912.

David, E. R., & Derthick, A. O. (2018). *The psychology of oppression.* New York: Springer Publishing Co.

Davidson, J. (2016, August 11). With 500,000 female genital mutilation survivors or at risk in U.S., it's not just someone else's problem. *Washington Post.* Accessed from https://www.washingtonpost.com/news/powerpost/wp/2016/08/11/with-500000-female-genital-mutilation-survivors-or-at-risk-in-u-s-its-not-just-someone-elses-problem/?utm_term=.1fa2e2862173.

Davidson-Kelly, K., Schaefer, R. S., Moran, N., & Overy, K. (2015). "Total inner memory": Deliberate uses of multimodal musical imagery during performance preparation. *Psychomusicology: Music, Mind, and Brain, 25,* 83-92.

Davies, S., Jackson, P., Lewis, G., Hood, S., Nutt, D., & Potokar, J. (2008). Is the association of hypertension and panic disorder explained by clustering of autonomic panic symptoms in hypertensive patients? *Journal of Affective Disorders, 111,* 344-350.

Davis, K., Christodoulou, J., Seider, S., & Gardner, H. (2011). The theory of multiple intelligences. In R. J. Sternberg & S. Kaufman (Eds.), *The Cambridge handbook of intelligence.* New York: Cambridge University Press.

Davis, L. J. (2009, June 15). Sotomayor and the New Haven firefighters case: More myths than facts. *Washington Times,* p. A04.

Davis, O., Haworth, C., & Plomin, R. (2009). Learning abilities and disabilities: Generalist genes in early adolescence. *Cognitive Neuropsychiatry, 14,* 312-331.

Davis, S. R. (2007). The nose knows best. *PsycCRITIQUES, 52,* 22-31.

Dawson, S. J., Fretz, K. M., & Chivers, M. L. (2017). Visual attention patterns of women with androphilic and gynephilic sexual attractions. *Archives of Sexual Behavior, 46,* 141-153.

Day, A. L., & Livingstone, H. A. (2003). Gender differences in perceptions of stressors and utilization of social support among university students. *Canadian Journal of Behavioural Science, 35,* 73-83.

Day, R. D., & Lamb, M. E. (2004). *Conceptualizing and measuring father involvement.* Mahwah, NJ: Lawrence Erlbaum Associates.

de Abreu, C. N., & Filho, R. C. (2017). Anorexia nervosa and bulimia nervosa—A psychotherapeutic cognitive-constructivist approach. *International Review of Psychiatry, 29,* 248-253.

De Bini, R., Pazzaglia, F., & Gardini, S. (2007). The generation and maintenance of visual mental images: Evidence from image type and aging. *Brain and Cognition, 63,* 271-278.

De Brigard, F., Brady, T. F., Ruzic, L., & Schacter, D. L. (2017). Tracking the emergence of memories: A category-learning paradigm to explore schema-driven recognition. *Memory & Cognition, 45,* 105-120.

De Dreu, C. W., Greer, L. L., Van Kleef, G. A., Shalvi, S., & Handgraaf, M. J. (2011). Oxytocin promotes human ethnocentrism. *PNAS Proceedings of the National Academy of Sciences of the United States of America, 108,* 1262-1266.

de Gusmao, C. M., Pollak, L. E., & Sharma, N. (2017). Neuropsychological and psychiatric outcome of GPi-deep brain stimulation in dystonia. *Brain Stimulation, 10,* 994-996.

de Visser, E. J., Monfort, S. S., Goodyear, K., Lu, L., O'Hara, M., Lee, M. R., . . . Krueger, F. (2017). A little anthropomorphism goes a long way: Effects of oxytocin on trust, compliance, and team performance with automated agents. *Human Factors, 59,* 116-133.

de Vivo, L., Bellesi, M., Marshall, W., Bushong, E. A., Ellisman, M. H., Tononi, G., & Cirelli, C. (2017). Ultrastructural evidence for synaptic scaling across the wake/sleep cycle. *Science, 355,* 507-510.

de Voogd, L. D., Klumpers, F., Fernández, G., & Hermans, E. J. (2017). Intrinsic functional connectivity between amygdala and hippocampus during rest predicts enhanced memory under stress. *Psychoneuroendocrinology, 75,* 192-202.

de Waal, F. B. M. (2014). Hard-wired for good? *Science, 347,* 379.

Deacon, B. J., & Spielmans, G. I. (2017). Is the efficacy of "antidepressant" medications overrated?. In S. O. Lilienfeld & I. D. Waldman (Eds.), *Psychological science under scrutiny: Recent challenges and proposed solutions.* Hoboken, NJ: Wiley-Blackwell.

DeAngelis, D., & Monahan, J. (2008). Professional credentials and professional regulations: Social work professional development. In B. W. White, K. M. Sowers, & C. N. Dulmus (Eds.), *Comprehensive handbook of social work and social welfare, Vol. 1: The profession of social work.* Hoboken, NJ: John Wiley & Sons.

DeAngelis, T. (2016). Behavioral therapy works best for insomnia. *Monitor on Psychology, 47,* 18-19.

DeAngelis, T. (2016, September). Preventing medical errors. *Monitor on Psychology,* pp. 48-52.

Dearing, E., McCartney, K., & Taylor, B. (2009). Does higher quality early child care promote low-income children's math and reading achievement in middle childhood? *Child Development, 80,* 1329-1349.

Deater-Deckard, K., Ivy, L., & Smith, J. (2005). Resilience in gene-environment transactions. In S. Goldstein & R. B. Brooks (Eds.), *Handbook of resilience in children.* New York: Kluwer Academic/Plenum Publishers.

DeBlaere, C., Watson, L. B., & Langrehr, K. J. (2018). Intersectionality applied: Intersectionality is as intersectionality does. In C. B. Travis & J. W. White (Eds.), *APA handbook of the psychology of women: Volume 1: History, theory, and battlegrounds* (pp. 567-584). Washington, DC: American Psychological Association.

DeBord, K. A., Fischer, A. R., Bieschke, K. J., & Perez, R. M. (2017). *Handbook of sexual orientation and gender diversity in counseling and psychotherapy.* Washington, DC: American Psychological Association.

DeGaton, J. F., Weed, S., & Jensen, L. (1996). Understanding gender differences in adolescent sexuality. *Adolescence, 31,* 217-231.

deGroot, A. (1978). *Thought and choice in chess.* Paris: Mouton de Gruyter.

deGroot, A. D. (1966). Perception and memory versus thought: Some old ideas and recent findings. In B. Kleinmuntz (Ed.), *Problem solving: Research, method, and theory.* New York: Wiley.

Deisseroth, K. (2016). A look inside the brain. *Scientific American, 315,* 32-37.

Del Giudice, M. (2011). Alone in the dark? Modeling the conditions for visual experience in human fetuses. *Developmental Psychobiology, 53,* 214-219.

del Rosal, E., Alonso, L., & Moreno, R. (2006). Simulation of habituation to simple and multiple stimuli. *Behavioural Processes, 73,* 272-277.

Delacollette, N., Dumont, M., Sarlet, M., & Dardenne, B. (2013). Benevolent sexism, men's advantages and the prescription of warmth to women. *Sex Roles, 68,* 296-310.

DeLamater, J. D., & Sill, M. (2005). Sexual desire in later life. *Journal of Sex Research, 42,* 138-149.

Delcourt, M. A. B., Cornell, D. G., & Goldberg, M. D. (2007). Cognitive and affective learning outcomes of gifted elementary school students. *The Gifted Child Quarterly, 51,* 359-382.

Delgado, M. R., Labouliere, C. D., & Phelps, E. A. (2006). Fear of losing money? Aversive conditioning with secondary reinforcers [Special issue: Genetic, comparative and cognitive studies of social behavior]. *Social Cognitive and Affective Neuroscience, 1,* 250-259.

Dell, P. F. (2013). Three dimensions of dissociative amnesia. *Journal of Trauma & Dissociation, 14,* 25-39.

DeLoache, J., & LoBue, V. (2009). The narrow fellow in the grass: Human infants associate snakes and fear. *Developmental Science, 12,* 201-207.

Demaree, H. A., & Everhart, D. E. (2004). Healthy high-hostiles: Reduced para-sympathetic activity and decreased sympathovagal flexibility during negative emotional processing. *Personality and Individual Differences, 36,* 457-469.

DeMaris, A. (2013). Burning the candle at both ends: Extramarital sex as a precursor of marital disruption. *Journal of Family Issues, 34,* 1474-1499.

Dement, W. C., & Wolpert, E. A. (1958). The relation of eye movements, body mobility, and external stimuli to dream content. *Journal of Experimental Psychology, 55,* 543-553.

Dender, A., & Stagnitti, K. (2011). Development of the Indigenous Child-Initiated Pretend Play Assessment: Selection of play materials and administration. *Australian Occupational Therapy Journal, 58,* 34-42.

Deng, C., & Georgiou, G. K. (2015). Establishing measurement invariance of the cognitive assessment system across cultures. In T. C. Papadopoulos, R. K. Parrila, & J. R. Kirby (Eds.), *Cognition, intelligence, and achievement: A tribute to J. P. Das.* San Diego, CA: Elsevier Academic Press.

Denmark, G. L., & Fernandez, L. C. (1993). Historical development of the psychology of women. In F. L. Denmark & M. A. Paludi (Eds.), *A handbook of issues and theories.* Westport, CT: Greenwood Press.

Dennehy, T. C., & Dasgupta, N. (2017). Female peer mentors early in college increase women's positive academic experiences and retention in engineering. *PNAS Proceedings of the National Academy of Sciences of the United States of America, 114,* 5964-5969.

Dennehy, T. C., Smith, J. S., Moore, C., & Dasgupta, N. (2018). Stereotype threat and stereotype inoculation for underrepresented students in the first year of college. In R. S. Feldman (Ed.), *The first year of college: Research, theory, and practice on improving the student experience and increasing retention.* Cambridge, England: Cambridge University Press.

Dennis, I. (2007). Halo effects in grading student projects. *Journal of Applied Psychology, 92,* 1169-1176.

Dennis, S. (2011). Smoking causes creative responses: On state antismoking policy and resilient habits. *Critical Public Health, 21,* 25-35.

Denollet, J., & Pedersen, S. S. (2011). Type D personality in patients with cardiovascular disorders. In R. Allan & J. Fisher (Eds.), *Heart and mind: The practice of cardiac psychology* (2nd ed.) (pp. 219-247). Washington, DC: American Psychological Association.

Densley, J., & Peterson, J. (2018). Group aggression. *Current Opinion in Psychology, 19*43-48. doi:10.1016/j.copsyc.2017.03.031.

Denworth, L. (2017). Is there a "female" brain? *Scientific American, 317,* 38-43.

Deregowski, J. B. (1973). Illusion and culture. In R. L. Gregory & G. H. Combrich (Eds.), *Illusion in nature and art.* New York: Scribner.

Dernbach, K., & Marshall, M. (2001). Pouring beer on troubled waters: Alcohol and violence in the Papua New Guinea Highlands during the 1980s. *Contemporary Drug Problems: An Interdisciplinary Quarterly, 28,* 3-47.

Deroy, O., & Spence, C. (2013). Are we all born synaesthetic? Examining the neonatal synaesthesia hypothesis. *Neuroscience and Biobehavioral Reviews, 37,* 1240-1253.

Deshields, T., Tibbs, T., Fan, M. Y., & Taylor, M. (2006). Differences in patterns of depression after treatment for breast cancer. *Psycho-Oncology, 15*(5), 398-406.

Després, O., Lithfous, S., Tromp, D., Pebayle, T., & Dufour, A. (2017). Gamma oscillatory activity is impaired in episodic memory encoding with age. *Neurobiology of Aging, 52,* 53-65.

Deutsch, M. (1994). Constructive conflict resolution: Principles, training, and research. *Journal of Social Issues, 50,* 13-32.

Devos, T. (2011). The role of race in American politics: Lessons learned from the 2008 presidential election. In G. S. Parks & M. W. Hughey (Eds.), *The Obamas and a (post) racial America?* New York: Oxford University Press.

Dhillon, S., Yang, L., & Curran, M. (2008). Spotlight on bupropion in major depressive disorder. *CNS Drugs, 22,* 613-617.

Di Fabio, A., & Palazzeschi, L. (2009). An in-depth look at scholastic success: Fluid intelligence, personality traits or emotional intelligence? *Personality and Individual Differences, 46,* 581-585.

Di Ieva, A., Esteban, F. J., Grizzi, F., Klonowski, W., & Martín-Landrove, M. (2015). Fractals in the neurosciences, part II: Clinical applications and future perspectives. *The Neuroscientist, 21,* 30-43.

Diamond, M. (2009). Human intersexuality: Difference or disorder? *Archives of Sexual Behavior, 38,* 172.

Dias, A. M., & van Deusen, A. (2011). A new neurofeedback protocol for depression. *Spanish Journal of Psychology, 14,* 374-384.

Diaz, A., & Bell, M. (2011). Information processing efficiency and regulation at five months. *Infant Behavior & Development, 34,* 239-247.

Dickinson, D. L., & Oxoby, R. J. (2011). Cognitive dissonance, pessimism, and behavioral spillover effects. *Journal of Economic Psychology, 32,* 295-306.

Diemand-Yauman, C., Oppenheimer, D. M., & Vaughan, E. B. (2010), Fortune favors the bold (and the italicized): Effects of disfluency on educational outcomes. *Cognition, 118*(1), 111-115.

Diener, E., & Clifton, D. (2002). Life satisfaction and religiosity in broad probability samples. *Psychological Inquiry, 13,* 206-209.

Diener, E., & Seligman, M. E. P. (2004). Beyond money: Toward an economy of well-being. *Psychological Science in the Public Interest, 5,* 1-31.

Diener, E., Lucas, R. E., & Scollon, C. N. (2006). Beyond the hedonic treadmill: Revising the adaptation theory of well-being. *American Psychologist, 61,* 305-314.

Diener, M., Isabella, R., Behunin, M., & Wong, M. (2008). Attachment to mothers and fathers during middle childhood: Associations with child gender, grade, and competence. *Social Development, 17,* 84-101.

Dienst, J., Schreiber, K., & Valiquette, J. (2016, May 23). FBI's newest K-9 sniffs out digital evidence. Retrieved from http://www.nbcnewyork.com/news/local/New-Jersey-FBI-Dog-Electronics-Sniffing-Dog-NJ-Police-380560881.html.

Diering, G. H., Nirujogi, R. S., Roth, R. H., Worley, P. F., Pandey, A., & Huganir, R. L. (2017). Homer1a drives homeostatic scaling-down of excitatory synapses during sleep. *Science, 355,* 511-515.

Dierolf, A. M., Fechtner, J., Böhnke, R., Wolf, O. T., & Naumann, E. (2017). Influence of acute stress on response inhibition in healthy men: An ERP study. *Psychophysiology, 54,* 684-695.

Digdon, N. (2017). The Little Albert controversy: Intuition, confirmation bias, and logic. *History of Psychology.* Accessed from https://www.ncbi.nlm.nih.gov/pubmed/28125246.

DiGiovanna, A. G. (1994). *Human aging: Biological perspectives.* New York: McGraw-Hill.

Dijksterhuis, A., Chartrand, T. L., & Aarts, H. (2007). Effects of priming and perception on social behavior and goal pursuit. *Frontiers of Social Psychology, 17,* 33-40.

DiJulio, B., Norton, M., Craighill, P., Clement, P., & Brodie, M. (2015, June 12). Survey of current and recent college students on sexual assault. Henry J. Kaiser Foundation.

Dill, K., & Thill, K. (2007). Video game characters and the socialization of gender roles: Young people's perceptions mirror sexist media depictions. *Sex Roles, 57,* 851-864.

Dillard, J. P., & Shen, L. (2007). Self-report measures of discrete emotions. In R. A. Reynolds, R. Woods, & J. D. Baker (Eds.), *Handbook of research on electronic surveys and measurements.* Hershey, PA: Idea Group Reference/IGI Global, 2007.

Diller, L. (2017, January 17). The United States of Adderall. *Huffington Post.* Accessed from http://www.huffingtonpost.com/larry-diller/the-united-states-of-adderall_b_8914480.html.

Dimaggio, G., D'Urzo, M., Pasinetti, M., Salvatore, G., Lysaker, P. H., Catania, D., & Popolo, R. (2015). Metacognitive interpersonal therapy for co-occurrent avoidant personality disorder and substance abuse. *Journal of Clinical Psychology, 71,* 157-166.

Dimaggio, G., Salvatore, G., MacBeth, A., Ottavi, P., Buonocore, L., & Popolo, R. (2017). Metacognitive interpersonal therapy for personality disorders: A case study series. *Journal of Contemporary Psychotherapy, 47,* 11-21.

Dingfelder, S. (2011). Reflecting on narcissism. *Monitor on Psychology, 42,* 64-68.

Diniz, B. S., Butters, M. A., Albert, S. M., Dew, M., & Reynolds, C. (2013). Late-life depression and risk of vascular dementia and Alzheimer's disease: Systematic review and meta-analysis of community-based cohort studies. *British Journal of Psychiatry, 202,* 329-335.

Dirie, W. (2011). *Desert flower.* NY: William Morrow.

Dittrich, W. H., Johansen, T., & Fineberg, N. A. (2011). Cognitive Assessment Instrument of Obsessions and Compulsions (CAIOV-13)–A new 13-item scale for evaluating functional impairment associated with OCD. *Psychiatry Research, 187,* 283-290.

Dixon, R. A., & Cohen, A. L. (2003). Cognitive development in adulthood. In R. M. Lerner, M. A. Easterbrooks, & J. Mistry (Eds.), *Handbook of psychology: Developmental psychology* (Vol. 6). New York: Wiley.

Dixon, R. A., McFall, G., Whitehead, B. P., & Dolcos, S. (2013). Cognitive development in adulthood and aging. In R. M. Lerner, M. Easterbrooks, J. Mistry, & I. B. Weiner (Eds.), *Handbook of psychology, Vol. 6: Developmental psychology* (2nd ed.). Hoboken, NJ: John Wiley & Sons Inc.

Dixon, R. A., Rust, T. B., & Feltmate, S. E. (2007). Memory and aging: Selected research directions and application issues. *Canadian Psychology Psychologie Canadienne, 48,* 67-76.

Djamba, Y. K. (2013). Sexual practices in Africa. In A. K. Baumle (Ed.), *International handbook on the demography of sexuality.* New York: Springer Science + Business Media.

Djapo, N., Kolenovic-Djapo, J., Djokic, R., & Fako, I. (2011). Relationship between Cattell's 16PF and fluid and crystallized intelligence. *Personality and Individual Differences, 51,* 63-67.

Do, V. T. (2006). Asian American men and the media: The relationship between ethnic identity, self-esteem, and the endorsement of stereotypes. *Dissertation Abstracts International: Section B: The Sciences and Engineering, 67*(6-B), 3446.

Dockrell, J. E., & Marshall, C. R. (2015). Measurement issues: Assessing language skills in young children. *Child and Adolescent Mental Health, 20,* 116-125.

Dodge, K. A. (2004). The nature-nurture debate and public policy [Special issue: 50th anniversary issue, part 2: The maturing of the human development sciences–Appraising past, present, and prospective agendas]. *Merrill-Palmer Quarterly: Journal of Developmental Psychology, 50,* 418-427.

Dohnke, B., Weiss-Gerlach, E., & Spies, C. D. (2011). Social influences on the motivation to quit smoking: Main and moderating effects of social norms. *Addictive Behaviors, 36,* 286-293.

Doi, T. (1990). The cultural assumptions of psychoanalysis. In J. W. Stigler, R. A. Shweder, & G. Herdt (Eds.), *Cultural psychology: Essays on comparative human development.* New York: Cambridge University Press.

Dolan, R. J. (2002). Emotion, cognition, and behavior. *Science, 298,* 1191-1194.

Dolbier, C. L., Smith, S. E., & Steinhardt, M. A. (2007). Relationships of protective factors to stress and symptoms of illness. *American Journal of Health Behavior, 31,* 423-433.

Dolinski, D. (2011). A rock or a hard place: The foot-in-the-face technique for inducing compliance without pressure. *Journal of Applied Social Psychology, 41,* 1514-1537.

Dollinger, S. J. (2003). Need for uniqueness, need for cognition and creativity. *Journal of Creative Behavior, 37,* 99-116.

Domhoff, G. W. (2011). The neural substrate for dreaming: Is it a subsystem of the default network? *Consciousness and Cognition, 20,* 1163-1174.

Domschke, K. (2013). Clinical and molecular genetics of psychotic depression. *Schizophrenia Bulletin, 39,* 766-775.

Donahoe, J. W., & Vegas, R. (2004). Pavlovian Conditioning: The CSUR Relation. *Journal of Experimental Psychology: Animal Behavior Processes, 30,* 17-33.

Doty, R. L., Green, P. A., Ram, C., & Yankell, S. L. (1982). Communication of gender from human breath odors: Relationship to perceived intensity and pleasantness. *Hormones and Behavior, 16,* 13-22.

Doty, R. L., Tourbier, I., Ng, V., Neff, J., Armstrong, D., Battistini, M., . . . Sondheimer, S. J. (2015). Influences of hormone replacement therapy on olfactory and cognitive function in postmenopausal women. *Neurobiology of Aging, 36,* 2053-2059.

Douthit, K. Z., & Russotti, J. (2017). Biology of marginality: A neurophysiological exploration of the social and cultural foundations of psychological health. In T. A. Field, L. K. Jones, & L. A. Russell-Chapin (Eds.), *Neurocounseling: Brain-based clinical approaches.* Alexandria, VA: American Counseling Association.

Dovidio, J. F., Piliavin, J. A., Schroeder, D. A., & Penner, L. A. (2006). *The social psychology of prosocial behavior.* Mahwah, NJ: Lawrence Erlbaum Associates.

Dowling, N., Jackson, A., & Thomas, S. (2008). Behavioral interventions in the treatment of pathological gambling: A review of activity scheduling and desensitization. *International Journal of Behavioral Consultation and Therapy, 4,* 172-187.

Dresler, M., Shirer, W. R., Konrad, B. N., Muller, N. C., Wagner, I. C., Fernandez, G., . . . Greicius, M. D. (2017). Mnemonic training reshapes brain networks to support superior emory. *Neuron, 93*(5), 1227-1235.

Dresler, T., Guhn, A., Tupak, S. V., Ehlis, A., Herrmann, M. J., Fallgatter, A. J., . . . Domschke, K. (2013). Revise the revised? New dimensions of the neuroanatomical hypothesis of panic disorder. *Journal of Neural Transmission, 120,* 3-29.

Drewes, A. A. (2005). Play in selected cultures: Diversity and universality. In E. Gil & A. A. Drewes (Eds.), *Cultural issues in play therapy.* New York: Guilford Press.

Driessen, E., Van, H. L., Peen, J., Don, F. J., Twisk, J. R., Cuijpers, P., & Dekker, J. M. (2017). Cognitive-behavioral versus psychodynamic therapy for major depression: Secondary outcomes of a randomized clinical trial. *Journal of Consulting and Clinical Psychology, 85,* 653-663.

Dryden, W., & David, D. (2008). Rational emotive behavior therapy: Current status. *Journal of Cognitive Psychotherapy, 22,* 195-209.

Dudai, Y. (2011). The engram revisited: On the elusive permanence of memory. In S. Nalbantian, P. M. Matthews, & J. L. McClelland (Eds.), *The memory process: Neuroscientific and humanistic perspectives.* Cambridge, MA: MIT Press.

Dugger, C. W. (1996, December 28). Tug of taboos: African genital rite vs. U.S. law. *The New York Times,* pp. 1, 9.

Dugger, C. W. (2013, July 22). Genital cutting found in decline in many nations. *The New York Times,* p. A1.

Duke, M., & Nowicki, S., Jr. (1979). *Abnormal psychology: Perspectives on being different.* Monterey, CA: Brooks/Cole.

Dumont, M., & Dumont, D. (2008). Deinstitutionalization in the United States and Italy: A historical survey. *International Journal of Mental Health, 37,* 61-70.

Duncker, K. (1945). On problem solving. *Psychological Monographs, 58* (5, whole no. 270).

Dunkley, D. M., Lewkowski, M., Lee, I. A., Preacher, K. J., Zuroff, D. C., Berg, J., . . . Westreich, R. (2017). Daily stress, coping, and negative and positive affect in depression: Complex trigger and maintenance patterns. *Behavior Therapy, 48,* 349-365.

Dunlop, W. L., Beatty, D. J., & Beauchamp, M. R. (2011). Examining the influence of other-efficacy and self-efficacy on personal performance. *Journal of Sport & Exercise Psychology, 33,* 586-593.

Dunlop, W. L., Guo, J., & McAdams, D. P. (2016). The autobiographical author through time: Examining the degree of stability and change in redemptive and contaminated personal narratives. *Social Psychological and Personality Science, 7,* 428-436.

Dweck, C. S. (2017). Is psychology headed in the right direction? Yes, no, and maybe. *Perspectives on Psychological Science, 12,* 656-659.

Diaz, E., & De la Casa, L. G. (2011). Extinction, spontaneous recovery and renewal of flavor preferences based on taste-taste learning. *Learning and Motivation, 42,* 64-75.

Eagly, A. H., & Wood, W. (2013). The nature-nurture debates: 25 years of challenges in understanding the psychology of gender. *Perspectives on Psychological Science, 8,* 340-357.

Eagly, A. H., Beall, A., & Sternberg, R. S. (Eds.). (2004). *The psychology of gender* (2nd ed.). New York: Guilford Press.

Eagly, A. S. (2016). Psychology of gender: Nature and nurture working together. In R. J. Sternberg, S. T. Fiske, & D. J. Foss (Eds.), *Scientists making a difference: One hundred eminent behavioral and brain scientists talk about their most important contributions* (pp. 365-368). New York: Cambridge University Press.

Eaker, E. D., Sullivan, L. M., Kelly-Hayes, M., D'Agostino, R. B., Sr., & Benjamin, E. J. (2004). Anger and hostility predict the development of atrial fibrillation in men in the Framingham Offspring Study. *Circulation, 109,* 1267-1271.

Ebigbo, P. O., Lekwas, E. C., & Chukwunenyem, N. F. (2015). Brain fag: New perspectives from case observations. *Transcultural Psychiatry, 52,* 311-330.

Ebrahimian, Z., Karimi, Z., Khoshnoud, M. J., Namavar, M. R., Daraei, B., & Haidari, M. R. (2017). Behavioral and stereological analysis of the effects of intermittent feeding diet on the orally administrated MDMA ('ecstasy') in mice. *Innovations in Clinical Neuroscience, 14,* 40-52.

Ecenbarger, W. (1993, April 1). America's new merchants of death. *Reader's Digest,* p. 50.

Eckardt, M. H. (2005). Karen Horney: A portrait: The 120th anniversary, Karen Horney, September 16, 1885. *American Journal of Psychoanalysis, 65,* 95-101.

Ecker, U. H., Tay, J., & Brown, G. A. (2015). Effects of prestudy and poststudy rest on memory: Support for temporal interference accounts of forgetting. *Psychonomic Bulletin & Review, 22,* 772-778.

Edoka, I. P., Petrou, S., & Ramchandani, P. G. (2011). Healthcare costs of paternal depression in the postnatal period. *Journal of Affective Disorders, 133,* 356-360.

Edwards, M. S., Moore, P., Champion, J. C., & Edwards, E. J. (2015). Effects of trait anxiety and situational stress on attentional shifting are buffered by working memory capacity. *Anxiety, Stress & Coping: An International Journal, 28,* 1-16.

Efklides, A., & Moraitou, D. (2013). *A positive psychology perspective on quality of life.* New York: Springer Science + Business Media.

Egan, K. (2005). Students' development in theory and practice: The doubtful role of research. *Harvard Educational Review, 75,* 25-41.

Egan, K. J., Knutson, K. L., Pereira, A. C., & von Schantz, M. (2017). The role of race and ethnicity in sleep, circadian rhythms and cardiovascular health. *Sleep Medicine Reviews, 33,* 70-78.

Egervari, G., Ciccocioppo, R., Jentsch, J. D., & Hurd, Y. L. (2017). Shaping vulnerability to addiction - the contribution of behavior, neural circuits and molecular mechanisms. *Neuroscience and Biobehavioral Reviews.* Accessed from http://www.sciencedirect.com/science/article/pii/S0149763417300866.

Ehde, D. M., Dillworth, T. M., & Turner, J. A. (2014). Cognitive-behavioral therapy for individuals with chronic pain: Efficacy, innovations, and directions for research. *American Psychologist, 69,* 153-177.

Einarsson, C., & Granstroem, K. (2002). Gender-biased interaction in the classroom: The influence of gender and age in the relationship between teacher and pupil. *Scandinavian Journal of Educational Research, 46,* 117-127.

Eizenberg, M. M., & Zaslavsky, O. (2004). Students' verification strategies for combinatorial problems. *Mathematical Thinking and Learning, 6,* 15-36.

Ekman, P. (1972). Universals and cultural differences in facial expressions of emotion. In J. Cole (Ed.), *Darwin and facial expression: A century of research in review.* New York: Academic Press.

Ekman, P. (1994b). Strong evidence for universals in facial expressions: A reply to Russell's mistaken critique. *Psychological Bulletin, 115,* 268-287.

Ekman, P. (2003). *Emotions revealed: Recognizing faces and feelings to improve communication and emotional life.* New York: Times Books.

Ekman, P. (2007). *Emotions revealed* (2nd ed.). New York: Holt.

Ekman, P., Levenson, R. W., & Friesen, W. V. (1983). Autonomic nervous system activity distinguishes among emotions. *Science, 223,* 1208-1210.

Ekonomou, A., Savva, G. M., Brayne, C., Forster, G., Francis, P. T., Johnson, M., . . . Ballard, C. G. (2015). Stage-specific changes in neurogenic and glial markers in Alzheimer's disease. *Biological Psychiatry, 77,* 711-719.

Ekroll, V., & Scherzer, T. R. (2009). Apparent visual motion of the observer's own limbs. *Perception, 38,* 778-780.

Elen, M., D'Heer, E., Geuens, M., & Vermeir, I. (2013). The influence of mood on attitude-behavior consistency. *Journal of Business Research, 66,* 917-923.

Elfhag, K., Tynelius, P., & Rasmussen, F. (2007). Sugar-sweetened and artificially sweetened soft drinks in association to restrained, external and emotional eating. *Physiology & Behavior, 91,* 191-195.

Elias, V. L., Fullerton, A. S., & Simpson, J. M. (2015). Long-term changes in attitudes toward premarital sex in the United States: Re-examining the role of cohort replacement. *Journal of Sex Research, 52,* 129-139.

Eljamel, S. (2015). Ablative surgery for depression. In B. Sun & A. De Salles (Eds.), *Neurosurgical treatments for psychiatric disorders.* New York: Springer Science + Business Media.

Elkins, D. (2009). Why humanistic psychology lost its power and influence in American psychology: Implications for advancing humanistic psychology. *Journal of Humanistic Psychology, 49,* 267-291.

Elkins, G., Marcus, J., Bates, J., Hasan, R. M., & Cook, T. (2006). Intensive hypnotherapy for smoking cessation: a prospective study. *International Journal of Clinical Experimental Hypnosis, 54,* 303-315.

Ellins, E., Halcox, J., Donald, A., Field, B., Brydon, L., Deanfield, J., & Steptoe, A. (2008). Arterial stiffness and inflammatory response to psychophysiological stress. *Brain, Behavior, and Immunity, 22,* 941-948.

Elliot, A. J., Dweck, C. S., & Yeager, D. S. (2017). *Handbook of competence and motivation: Theory and application* (2nd ed.). New York: Guilford Press.

Elliott, J., Berman, H., & Kim, S. (2002). Critical ethnography of Korean Canadian women's menopause experience. *Health Care for Women International, 23,* 377-388.

Ellis, A. (1974). *Growth through reason* (pp. 223-286). Hollywood, CA: Wilshire Books.

Ellis, A. (2002). *Overcoming resistance: A rational emotive behavior therapy integrated approach* (2nd ed.). New York: Springer.

Ellis, A. (2004). *Expanding the ABCs of rational emotive behavior therapy.* In A. Freeman, M. J. Mahoney, P. Devito, & D. Martin (Eds.), *Cognition and psychotherapy* (2nd ed.). New York: Springer Publishing Co.

Emmett, J., & McGee, D. (2013). Extrinsic motivation for large-scale assessments: A case study of a student achievement program at one urban high school. *The High School Journal, 96,* 116-137.

Endendijk, J. J., Groeneveld, M. G., van der Pol, L. D., van Berkel, S. R., Hallers-Haalboom, E. T., Bakermans-Kranenburg, M. J., . . . Messman, J. (2017). Gender differences in child aggression: Relations with gender-differentiated parenting and parents' gender-role stereotypes. *Child Development, 88,* 299-316.

Enge, L. R., Lupo, A. K., & Zárate, M. A. (2015). Neurocognitive mechanisms of prejudice formation: The role of time-dependent memory consolidation. *Psychological Science, 26,* 964-971.

Engel, U., Jann, B., Lynn, P., Scherpenzeel, A., & Sturgis, P. (2015). *Improving survey methods: Lessons from recent research.* NY: Routledge/Taylor & Francis Group.

Engen, T. (1987). Remembering odors and their names. *American Scientist, 75,* 497-503.

Engler, J., & Goleman, D. (1992). *The consumer's guide to psychotherapy.* New York: Simon & Schuster.

Epatko, L. (2018, April 16). This summer camp helps kids reach across the Israeli-Palestinian divide. *PBS News Hour.* Accessed May 2, 2018, from https://www.pbs.org/newshour/world/seeds-of-peace-empowers-its-young-leaders-to-confront-conflict-around-the-world.

Eranti, S. V., & McLoughlin, D. M. (2003). Electroconvulsive therapy: State of the art. *British Journal of Psychiatry, 182,* 8-9.

Erb, J., Henry, M. J., Eisner, F., & Obleser, J. (2013). The brain dynamics of rapid perceptual adaptation to adverse listening conditions. *Journal of Neuroscience, 33,* 10688-10697.

Erickson, R. (2008). A study of the science of taste: On the origins and influence of the core ideas. *Behavioral and Brain Sciences, 31,* 59-75.

Erikson, E. H. (1963). *Childhood and society.* New York: Norton.

Ervik, S., Abdelnoor, M., & Heier, M. S. (2006). Health-related quality of life in narcolepsy. *Acta Neurologica Scandinavica, 114,* 198-204.

Espinola, M., DeVinney, H., & Steinberg, A. (. (2017). Women at midlife. In K. A. Kendall-Tackett, L. M. Ruglass, K. A. Kendall-Tackett, & L. M. Ruglass (Eds.), *Women's mental health across the lifespan: Challenges, vulnerabilities, and strengths.* New York: Routledge/Taylor & Francis Group.

Etienne, J. (2013). Thoughts on how to regulate behaviours: An overview of the current debate. *British Journal of Guidance & Counselling, 41,* 36-45.

Etzrodt, C. M. (2013). Ethical considerations of therapeutic hypnosis and children. *American Journal of Clinical Hypnosis, 55,* 370-377.

Euler, M. J., Weisend, M. P., Jung, R. E., Thoma, R. J., & Yeo, R. A. (2015). Reliable activation to novel stimuli predicts higher fluid intelligence. *Neuroimage, 114,* 311-319.

Evans, D. E., & Rothbart, M. K. (2007). Developing a model for adult temperament. *Journal of Research in Personality, 41,* 868-888.

Evans, D., & Rothbart, M. (2009). A two-factor model of temperament. *Personality and Individual Differences, 47,* 565-570.

Evcik, D., Kavuncu, V., Cakir, T., Subasi, V., & Yaman, M. (2007). Laser therapy in the treatment of carpal tunnel syndrome: A randomized controlled trial. *Photomedical Laser Surgery, 25,* 34-39.

Everette, M. (2008). Gestational weight and dietary intake during pregnancy: Perspectives of African American women. *Maternal & Child Health Journal, 12,* 718-724.

Everly, G. S., Jr., & Lating, J. M. (2007). Psychotherapy: A cognitive perspective. In A. Monat, R. S. Lazarus, & G. Reevy (Eds.), *The Praeger handbook on stress and coping* (Vol. 2). Westport, CT: Praeger Publishers/Greenwood Publishing.

Eysenck, H. J. (1995). *Eysenck on extraversion.* New York: Wiley.

Fagan, J. F., & Holland, C. R. (2002). Equal opportunity and racial differences in IQ. *Intelligence, 30,* 361-387.

Fagan, J. F., & Holland, C. R. (2007). Racial equality in intelligence: Predictions from a theory of intelligence as processing. *Intelligence, 35,* 319-334.

Fagan, J. F., & Holland, C. R. (2009). Culture-fair prediction of academic achievement. *Intelligence, 37,* 62-67.

Fagan, J., & Press, J. (2008). Father influences on employed mothers' work-family balance. *Journal of Family Issues, 29,* 1136-1160.

Fairfield, H. (2012, February 4). Clues to a troubling gap. *The New York Times,* p. S1.

Falasca, N. W., D'Ascenzo, S., Di Domenico, A., Onofrj, M., Tommasi, L., Laeng, B., . . . Franciotti, R. (2015). Hemispheric lateralization in top-down attention during spatial relation processing: A Granger causal model approach. *European Journal of Neuroscience, 41,* 912-922.

Faniko, K., Ellemers, N., Derks, B., & Lorenzi-Cioldi, F. (2017). Nothing changes, really: Why women who break through the glass ceiling end up reinforcing it. *Personality and Social Psychology Bulletin, 43,* 638-651.

Farnsworth, D. L. (2015). Identical twins raised apart. *Teaching Statistics, 37,* 1-6.

Farrell, A. K., Simpson, J. A., Carlson, E. A., Englund, M. M., & Sung, S. (2017). The impact of stress at different life stages on physical health and the buffering effects of maternal sensitivity. *Health Psychology, 36,* 35-44.

Faupel, A., Herrick, E., & Sharp, P. M. (2018). *Anger management: A practical guide for teachers,* (3rd ed.) New York: Routledge/Taylor & Francis Group.

Fayek, A. (2017). *Understanding classical psychoanalysis: Freudian concepts in contemporary practice.* New York: Routledge/Taylor & Francis Group.

Fearing, V. G., & Clark, J. (Eds.). (2000). *Individuals in context: A practical guide to client-centered practice.* Chicago: Slack Publishing.

Fedeli, A., Braconi, S., Economidou, D., Cannella, N., Kallupi, M., Guerrini, R., . . . Ciccocioppo, R. (2009). The paraventricular nucleus of the hypothalamus is a neuroanatomical substrate for the inhibition of palatable food intake by neuropeptide S. *European Journal of Neuroscience, 30,* 1594-1602.

Fedyk, M. (2017). *The social turn in moral psychology.* Cambridge, MA: MIT Press.

Feldman, D. H. (2003). Cognitive development in childhood. In R. M. Lerner, M. A. Easterbrooks, & J. Mistry (Eds.), *Handbook of psychology: Developmental psychology* (Vol. 6). New York: Wiley.

Feldman, D. H. (2004). Piaget's stages: The unfinished symphony of cognitive development. *New Ideas in Psychology, 22,* 175-231.

Feldman, R. S. (2013). *P.O.W.E.R. learning: Foundations of student success.* New York: McGraw-Hill.

Feldman, R. S. (2017). *P.O.W.E.R. learning: Strategies for success in college and life.* New York: McGraw-Hill.

Felson, R. B., & Tedeschi, J.T. (Eds.). (1993). *Aggression and violence: Social interactionist perspectives.* Washington, DC: American Psychological Association.

Feng, B., Bell, R. A., Jerant, A. F., & Kravitz, R. L. (2011). What do doctors say when prescribing medications? An examination of medical recommendations from a communication perspective. *Health Communication, 26,* 286-296.

Fenter, V. L. (2006). Concerns about Prozac and direct-to-consumer advertising of prescription drugs. *International Journal of Risk & Safety in Medicine, 18,* 1-7.

Ferguson, C. J. (2010). Blazing angels or resident evil? Can violent video games be a force for good? *Review of General Psychology, 14,* 68-81.

Ferguson, C. J. (2011). Video games and youth violence: A prospective analysis in adolescents. *Journal of Youth and Adolescence, 40,* 377-391.

Ferguson, C. J. (2015a). Does media violence predict societal violence? It depends on what you look at and when. *Journal of Communication, 65,* E1-E22.

Ferguson, C. J. (2015b). Do angry birds make for angry children? A meta-analysis of video game influences on children's and adolescents' aggression, mental health, prosocial behavior, and academic performance. *Psychological Science,* 1-22.

Ferguson, C. J. (2015c). "Everybody knows psychology is not a real science": Public perceptions of psychology and how we can improve our relationship with policymakers, the scientific community, and the general public. *American Psychologist, 70,* 527-542.

Ferguson, C. J., & Beresin, E. (2017). Social science's curious war with pop culture and how it was lost: The media violence debate and the risks it holds for social science. *Preventive Medicine: An International Journal Devoted to Practice and Theory, 99,* 69-76.

Ferguson, M., & Ogloff, J. P. (2011). Criminal responsibility evaluations: Role of psychologists in assessment. *Psychiatry, Psychology and Law, 18,* 79-94.

Fernald, R. D. (2015). Social behaviour: Can it change the brain? *Animal Behaviour, 103,* 259-265.

Fernyhough, C. (2017). Talking to ourselves. *Scientific American, 317,* 74-79.

Ferring, D., Tournier, I., & Mancini, D. (2015). "The closer you get . . .": Age, attitudes and self-serving evaluations about older drivers. *European Journal of Ageing, 12*(3), 229-238.

Festinger, D., Marlowe, D., Croft, J., Dugosh, K., Arabia, P., & Benasutti, K. (2009). Monetary incentives improve recall of research consent information: It pays to remember. *Experimental and Clinical Psychopharmacology, 17,* 99-104.

Festinger, L. (1957). *A theory of cognitive dissonance.* Stanford, CA: Stanford University Press.

Festinger, L., & Carlsmith, J. M. (1959). Cognitive consequences of forced compliance. *Journal of Abnormal and Social Psychology, 58,* 203-210.

Festini, S. B., & Reuter-Lorenz, P. A. (2017). Rehearsal of to-be-remembered items is unnecessary to perform directed forgetting within working memory: Support for an active control mechanism. *Journal of Experimental Psychology: Learning, Memory, and Cognition, 43,* 94-108.

Fetvadjiev, V. H., Meiring, D., van de Vijver, F. R., Nel, J. A., Sekaja, L., & Laher, S. (2018). Personality and behavior prediction and consistency across cultures: A multimethod study of Blacks and Whites in South Africa. *Journal of Personality and Social Psychology, 114*(3), 465-481. doi:10.1037/pspp0000129.

Fevang, S. E., Hysing, M., Sommerfelt, K., & Elgen, I. (2017). Mental health assessed by the strengths and difficulties questionnaire for children born extremely preterm without severe disabilities at 11 years of age: A Norwegian, national population-based study. *European Child & Adolescent Psychiatry.* Accessed from https://www.ncbi.nlm.nih.gov/pubmed/28585081.

Fichtenberg, C. M., & Glantz, S. A. (2006). Association of the California tobacco control program with declines in cigarette consumption and mortality from heart disease. In K. E. Warner (Ed.), *Tobacco control policy.* San Francisco, CA: Jossey-Bass.

Figen, A. (2011). The relationship between test anxiety and learned helplessness. *Social Behavior and Personality, 39,* 101-112.

Filippello, P., Sorrenti, L., Buzzai, C., & Costa, S. (2015). Perceived parental psychological control and learned helplessness: The role of school self-efficacy. *School Mental Health, 7*(4), 298-310.

Filippi, C. A., Cannon, E. N., Fox, N. A., Thorpe, S. G., Ferrari, P. F., & Woodward, A. L. (2016). Motor system activation predicts goal imitation in 7-month-old infants. *Psychological Science, 27*(5), 675-684.

Finan, P. H., Zautra, A. J., & Wershba, R. (2011). The dynamics of emotion in adaptation to stress. In R. J. Contrada & A. Baum (Eds.), *The handbook of stress science: Biology, psychology, and health.* New York: Springer Publishing Co.

Fine, C. (2010). *Delusions of gender: How our minds, society, and neurosexism create difference.* New York: W. W. Norton & Co.

Fine, R., & Fine, L. (2003). *Basic chess endings.* New York: Random House.

Fingelkurts, A., Fingelkurts, A. A., & Kallio, S. (2007). Hypnosis induces a changed composition of brain oscillations in EEG: A case study. *Contemporary Hypnosis, 24,* 3-18.

Fink, B., Manning, J. T., & Williams, J. H. G. (2007). The 2nd to 4th digit ratio and developmental psychopathology in school-aged children. *Personality and Individual Differences, 42,* 369-379.

Fink, S. (2017, July 28). Two C.I.A. psychologists can face trial, judge rules. *The New York Times,* p. A18.

Finke, M. S., Howe, J. S., & Huston, S. J. (2017). Old age and the decline in financial literacy. *Management Science, 63,* 213-230.

Finkelhor, D., & Jones, L. M. (2004, January). Explanations for the decline in child sexual abuse cases. *Juvenile Justice Bulletin.*

Finkelhor, D., Ormrod, R., & Turner, H. (2005). The victimization of children and youth: A comprehensive, national survey. *Child Maltreatment: Journal of the American Professional Society on the Abuse of Children, 10,* 5-25.

Finkelstein, M. (2009). Intrinsic vs. extrinsic motivational orientations and the volunteer process. *Personality and Individual Differences, 46,* 653-658.

Finkler, K. (2004). Traditional healers in Mexico: The effectiveness of spiritual practices. In U. P. Gielen, J. M. Fish, & J. G. Draguns (Eds.), *Handbook of culture, therapy, and healing.* Mahwah, NJ: Lawrence Erlbaum Associates.

Finlay, F. O., Jones, R., & Coleman, J. (2002). Is puberty getting earlier? The views of doctors and teachers. *Child: Care, Health and Development, 28,* 205-209.

Finley, C. L., & Cowley, B. J. (2005). The effects of a consistent sleep schedule on time taken to achieve sleep. *Clinical Case Studies, 4,* 304-311.

Finn, A. (2011). Jungian analytical theory. In D. Capuzzi & D. R. Gross (Eds.), *Counseling and psychotherapy* (5th ed.). Alexandria, VA: American Counseling Association.

Finn, K. (2015). Sequelae of cannabis as medicine. *Pain Medicine, 16,* 1447-1449.

Firestein, B. A. (Ed.). (1996). *Bisexuality: The psychology and politics of an invisible minority.* Thousand Oaks, CA: Sage.

Fischer, I. (2011). Several eyes for an eye: The impact of biased perceptions and noise on conflict escalation patterns. *Peace and Conflict: Journal of Peace Psychology, 17,* 77-84.

Fischer, P., Krueger, J. I., Greitemeyer, T., Vogrincic, C., Kastenmüller, A., Frey, D., & Kainbacher, M. (2011). The bystander-effect: A meta-analytic review on bystander intervention in dangerous and non-dangerous emergencies. *Psychological Bulletin, 137,* 517-537.

Fischetti, M. (2016). Fatter still. *Scientific American, 315,* 80.

Fishbach, A., Dhar, R., & Zhang, Y. (2006). Subgoals as substitutes or complements: The role of goal accessibility. *Journal of Personality and Social Psychology, 91,* 232-242.

Fisher, A. K., Moore, D. J., Simmons, C., & Allen, S. C. (2017). Teaching social workers about microaggressions to enhance understanding of subtle racism. *Journal of Human Behavior in the Social Environment, 27*(4), 346-355.

Fisher, C. B. (2003). *Decoding the ethics code: A practical guide for psychologists.* Thousand Oaks, CA: Sage.

Fisher, G. G., & Barnes-Farrell, J. L. (2013). Use of archival data in occupational health psychology research. In R. R. Sinclair, M. Wang, & L. E. Tetrick (Eds.), *Research methods in occupational health psychology: Measurement, design, and data analysis.* New York: Routledge/Taylor & Francis Group.

Fisher, R. J., & Kelman, H. C. (2011). Perceptions in conflict. In D. Bar-Tal, (Ed.), *Intergroup conflicts and their resolution: A social psychological perspective.* New York: Psychology Press.

Fiske, S. T. (2017). Going in many right directions, all at once. *Perspectives on Psychology, 12,* 652-655.

Flannelly, K. J. (2017). *Religious beliefs, evolutionary psychiatry, and mental health in America: Evolutionary threat assessment systems theory.* Cham, Switzerland: Springer International Publishing.

Fleck, J. I., Green, D. L., Payne, L., Stevenson, J. L., Bowden, E. M., Jung-Beeman, M., . . . Kounios, J. (2008). The transliminal brain at rest: Baseline EEG, unusual experiences, and access to unconscious mental activity. *Cortex, 44,* 1353-1363.

Fleming, J. (2000). Affirmative action and standardized test scores. *Journal of Negro Education, 69,* 27-37.

Flohr, E. R., Erwin, E., Croy, I., & Hummel, T. (2017). Sad man's nose: Emotion induction and olfactory perception. *Emotion, 17,* 369-378.

Flynn, J. R. (2009). *What is intelligence? Beyond the Flynn effect* (Expanded paperback ed.). Cambridge, England: Cambridge University Press.

Foderaro, L. W. (2006, February 16). Westchester lawyer, his memory lost, is found in Chicago shelter after 6 months. *The New York Times,* p. B3.

Foell, J., Bekrater-Bodmann, R., Diers, M., & Flor, H. (2014). Mirror therapy for phantom limb pain: Brain changes and the role of body representation. *European Journal of Pain, 18,* 729-739.

Folk, C., & Remington, R. (2008). Bottom-up priming of top-down attentional control settings. *Visual Cognition, 16,* 215-231.

Folkman, S., & Moskowitz, J. T. (2000). Stress, positive emotion, and coping. *Current Directions in Psychological Science, 9,* 115-118.

Folkman, S., & Moskowitz, J. T. (2004). Coping: Pitfalls and promise. *Annual Review of Psychology, 55,* 745-774.

Follett, K., & Hess, T. M. (2002). Aging, cognitive complexity, and the fundamental attribution error. *Journal of Gerontology: Series B: Psychological Sciences and Social Sciences, 57B,* P312-P323.

Forbus, K. D., Liang, C., & Rabkina, I. (2017). Representation and computation in cognitive models. *Topics in Cognitive Science, 9*(3), 694-718.

Forer, B. (1949). The fallacy of personal validation: A classroom demonstration of gullibility. *Journal of Abnormal and Social Psychology, 44,* 118-123.

Forgas, J. P., & Laham, S. M. (2005). The interaction between affect and motivation in social judgments and behavior. In J. P. Forgas, K. P. Williams, & S. M. Laham (Eds.), *Social motivation: Conscious and unconscious processes.* New York: Cambridge University Press.

Forgas, J. P., & Laham, S. M. (2017). Halo effects. In R. F. Pohl (Ed.), *Cognitive illusions: Intriguing phenomena in thinking, judgment and memory.* New York: Routledge/Taylor & Francis Group.

Forson, T.S. (2018, February 21.) Who is African-American? Definition evolves as USA does. *USA Today,* Retrieved from https://www.usatoday.com/story/news/nation-now/2018/02/21/black-history-african-american-definition/1002344001/.

Fost, J. (2015). Are there psychological species? *Review of Philosophy and Psychology, 6,* 293-315.

Foster, K. M. (2005). Introduction: John Uzo Ogbu (1939-2003): How do you ensure the fair consideration of a complex ancestor? Multiple approaches to assessing the work and legacy of John Uzo Ogbu. *International Journal of Qualitative Studies in Education, 18,* 559-564.

Fothergill, E., Guo, J., Howard, L., Kerns, J. C., Knuth, N. D., Brychta, R., . . . Hall, K. D. (2016). Persistent metabolic adaptation 6 years after "The Biggest Loser" competition. *Obesity, 24,* 1612-1619.

Foulds, J., Gandhi, K. K., Steinberg, M. B., Richardson, D. L., Williams, J. M., Burke, M. V., & Rhoads, G. G. (2006). Factors associated with quitting smoking at a tobacco dependence treatment clinic. *American Journal of Health Behavior, 30,* 400-412.

Fountas, K. N., & Smith, J. R. (2007). Historical evolution of stereotactic amygdalotomy for the management of severe aggression. *Journal of Neurosurgery, 106,* 716-713.

Fox, S., & Spector, P. E. (2000). Relations of emotional intelligence, practical intelligence, general intelligence, and trait affectivity with interview outcomes: It's not all just "G." *Journal of Organizational Behavior, 21,* 203-220.

Frances, A. (2013). *Saving normal: An insider's revolt against out-of-control psychiatric diagnosis, DSM-5, Big Pharma, and the medicalization of ordinary life.* New York: Morrow.

Frank, K., & Hou, F. (2015). Source-country gender roles and the division of labor within immigrant families. *Journal of Marriage and Family, 77,* 557-574.

Frank, S., Goldwater, S., & Keller, F. (2013). Adding sentence types to a model of syntactic category acquisition. *Topics in Cognitive Science, 5,* 495-521.

Franklin, A., Pilling, M., & Davies, I. (2005). The nature of infant color categorization: Evidence from eye movements on a target decision task. *Journal of Experimental Child Psychology, 91,* 227-248.

Franklin, M. E., March, J. S., & Garcia, A. (2007). Treating obsessive-compulsive disorder in children and adolescents. In C. Purdon, M. M. Antony, & L. J. Summerfeldt (Eds.), *Psychological treatment of obsessive-compulsive disorder: Fundamentals and beyond.* Washington, DC: American Psychological Association.

Franklin, T. B., & Mansuy, I. M. (2011). The involvement of epigenetic defects in mental retardation. *Neurobiology of Learning and Memory, 96,* 61-67.

Franko, D. L., & Roehrig, J. P. (2011). African American body images. In T. F. Cash & L. Smolak (Eds.), *Body image: A handbook of science, practice, and prevention (2nd ed.).* New York: Guilford Press.

Frawley, T. (2008). Gender schema and prejudicial recall: How children misremember, fabricate, and distort gendered picture book information. *Journal of Research in Childhood Education, 22,* 291-303.

Freedberg, D. (2011). Memory in art: History and the neuroscience of response. In S. Nalbantian, P. M. Matthews, & J. L. McClelland (Eds.), *The memory process: Neuroscientific and humanistic perspectives.* Cambridge, MA: MIT Press.

Freedman, J. L., & Fraser, S. C. (1966). Compliance without pressure: The foot-in-the-door technique. *Journal of Personality and Social Psychology, 4,* 195-202.

Freedman, M. R., & Waldrop, J. (2011). Freshman orientation sessions can teach incoming students about healthful lifestyles. *Journal of Nutrition Education and Behavior, 43,* 69-70.

Freeman, J. (2013). The long-term effects of families and educational provision on gifted children. *Educational and Child Psychology, 30*(2), 7-17.

Freeman, J. E. (2006). Psychology of race and ethnicity. In W. Buskit & S. F. Davis (Eds.), *Handbook of the teaching of psychology.* Malden, MA: Blackwell Publishing.

French, S., Coleman, B., & DiLorenzo, M. (2013). Linking racial identity, ethnic identity, and racial-ethnic socialization: A tale of three race-ethnicities. *Identity: An International Journal of Theory and Research, 13,* 1-45.

Fresco, D. M. (2013). Tending the garden and harvesting the fruits of behavior therapy. *Behavior Therapy, 44,* 177-179.

Freud, S. (1922/1959). *Group psychology and the analysis of the ego.* London: Hogarth.

Friborg, O., Barlaug, D., Martinussen, M., Rosenvinge, J. H., & Hjemdal, O. (2005). Resilience in relation to personality and intelligence. *International Journal of Methods in Psychiatric Research, 14,* 29-42.

Friborg, O., Hjemdal, O., & Rosenvinge, J. H. (2006). Resilience as a moderator of pain and stress. *Journal of Psychosomatic Research, 61,* 213-219.

Friedman, J. N. W., Oltmanns, T. F., & Turkheimer, E. (2007). Interpersonal perception and personality disorders: Utilization of a thin slice approach. *Journal of Research in Personality, 41,* 667-688.

Frijda, N. H. (2005). Emotion experience. *Cognition and Emotion, 19,* 473-497.

Frodl, T., Janowitz, D., Schmaal, L., Tozzi, L., Dobrowolny, H., Stein, D. J., . . . Grabe, H. J. (2017). Childhood adversity impacts on brain subcortical structures relevant to depression. *Journal of Psychiatric Research, 86,* 58-65.

Frosch, A. (2011). The effect of frequency and duration on psychoanalytic outcome: A moment in time. *Psychoanalytic Review, 98,* 11-38.

Fryling, M. J. (2017). The functional independence of Skinner's verbal operants: Conceptual and applied implications. *Behavioral Interventions, 32,* 70-78.

Fuhrman, O., McCormick, K., Chen, E., Jiang, H., Shu, D., Mao, S., . . . Boroditsky, L. (2011). How linguistic and cultural forces shape conceptions of time: English and Mandarin time in 3D. *Cognitive Science: A Multidisciplinary Journal, 7,* 1305-1328.

Fujita, K., Nakamura, N., Watanabe, S., & Ushitani, T. (2017). Comparative visual illusions: Evolutionary, cross-cultural, and developmental perspectives. In J. Call, G. M. Burghardt, I. M. Pepperberg, C. T. Snowdon, & T. Zentall (Eds.), *APA handbook of comparative psychology: Perception, learning, and cognition.* Washington, DC: American Psychological Association.

Fuller, A. (2006). Hypnosis and ideomotor compliance in the treatment of smoking tobacco and cannabis. *Australian Journal of Clinical Hypnotherapy and Hypnosis, 27,* 14-18.

Furnham, A., & Swami, V. (2007). Perception of female buttocks and breast size in profile. *Social Behavior and Personality, 35,* 1-8.

Furumoto, L., & Scarborough, E. (2002). Placing women in the history of psychology: The first American women psychologists. In W. E. Pickren (Ed.), *Evolving perspectives on the history of psychology.* Washington, DC: American Psychological Association.

Fusari, A., & Ballesteros, S. (2008). Identification of odors of edible and nonedible stimuli as affected by age and gender. *Behavior Research Methods, 40,* 752-759.

Gaab, J., Rohleder, N., Nater, U. M., & Ehlert, U. (2005). Psychological determinants of the cortisol stress response: The role of anticipatory cognitive appraisal. *Psychoneuroendocrinology, 30,* 599-610.

Gabbiadini, A., & Greitemeyer, T. (2017). Uncovering the association between strategy video games and self-regulation: A correlational study. *Personality and Individual Differences, 104,* 129-136

Gadbois, S. A., & Sturgeon, R. D. (2011). Academic self-handicapping: Relationships with learning specific and general self-perceptions and academic performance over time. *British Journal of Educational Psychology, 81,* 207-222.

Gade, M., Souza, A. S., Druey, M. D., & Oberauer, K. (2017). Analogous selection processes in declarative and procedural working memory: N-2 list-repetition and task-repetition costs. *Memory & Cognition, 45,* 26-39.

Gaffney, K. F., & Henry, L. L. (2007). Identifying risk factors for postpartum tobacco use. *Journal of Nursing Scholarship, 39,* 126-132.

Gafner, G. (2013). Review of *Subliminal: How your unconscious mind rules your behavior. American Journal of Clinical Hypnosis, 56,* 192-193.

Galambos, N. L., Fang, S., Krahn, H. J., Johnson, M. D., & Lachman, M. E. (2015). Up, not down: The age curve in happiness from early adulthood to midlife in two longitudinal studies. *Developmental Psychology, 51*(11), 1664-1671.

Galanter, M. (2007). Spirituality and recovery in 12-step programs: An empirical model. *Journal of Substance Abuse Treatment, 33,* 265-272.

Galdi, G. (2015). Celebrating the 75th anniversary of the *American Journal of Psychoanalysis. American Journal of Psychoanalysis, 75,* 1-2.

Galef, D. (2001). The information you provide is anonymous, but what was your name again? *Chronicle of Higher Education, 47,* p. B5.

Gallese, V., Gernsbacher, M. A., Heyes, C., Hickok, G., & Iacoboni, M. (2011). Mirror neuron forum. *Perspectives on Psychological Science, 6,* 369-407.

Gallo, M. M. (2015). "No one helped": Kitty Genovese, New York City, and the myth of urban apathy. New York: Cornell University Press.

Gandolphe, M., & El Haj, M. (2017). Flashbulb memories of the Paris attacks. *Scandinavian Journal of Psychology, 58,* 199-204.

Gangestad, S. W., Simpson, J. A., Cousins, A. J., Garver-Apgar, C. E., & Christensen, P. N. (2004). Women's preferences for male behavioral displays change across the menstrual cycle. *Psychological Science, 15,* 203-207.

Gao, Y., Schneider, B., & Li, L. (2017). The effects of the binocular disparity differences between targets and maskers on visual search. *Attention, Perception, & Psychophysics, 79,* 459-472.

Garber, J., & Horowitz, J. L. (2002). Depression in children. In I. H. Gotlib & C. L. Hammen (Eds.), *Handbook of depression.* New York: Guilford Press.

Garcia, J. (2003). Psychology is not an enclave. In R. J. Sternberg (Ed.), *Psychologists defying the crowd: Stories of those who battled the establishment and won.* Washington, DC: American Psychological Association.

Garcia, L. (2017, May 31). State of mind episode 5: Out of the depths. *CBS News.* Accessed at https://www.cbsnews.com/news/depression-neurosurgery-dbs-mental-health-uncharted-state-of-mind-episode-5/.

Garcia, S. M., Weaver, K., Moskowitz, G. B., & Darley, J. M. (2002). Crowded minds: The implicit bystander effect. *Journal of Personality and Social Psychology, 83,* 843-853.

García-Herrero, S., Mariscal, M. A., Gutiérrez, J. M., & Ritzel, D. O. (2013). Using Bayesian networks to analyze occupational stress caused by work demands: Preventing stress through social support. *Accident Analysis and Prevention, 57,* 114-123.

Gardini, S., Cornoldi, C., De Beni, R., & Venneri, A. (2009). Cognitive and neuronal processes involved in sequential generation of general and specific mental images. *Psychological Research/Psychologische Forschung, 73,* 633-643.

Gardner, B., & O'Connor, D. (2008). A review of the cognitive effects of electroconvulsive therapy in older adults. *Journal of ECT, 24,* 68-80.

Gardner, E. P., & Kandel, E. R. (2000). Touch. In E. R. Kandel, J. H. Schwartz, & T. M. Jessell (Eds.), *Principles of neural science* (4th ed.). New York: McGraw-Hill.

Gardner, F., & Moore, Z. (2008). Understanding clinical anger and violence: The anger avoidance model. *Behavior Modification, 32,* 897-912.

Gardner, H. (1999). *Intelligence reframed: Multiple intelligences for the 21st century.* New York: Basic Books.

Gardner, H. (2000). The giftedness matrix: A developmental perspective. In R. C. Friedman & B. M. Shore (Eds.), *Talents unfolding: Cognition and development.* Washington, DC: American Psychological Association.

Garfield, J. (2014). Sad psychosurgery. *Brain: A Journal of Neurology, 137,* 1262-1265.

Garfin, D. R., Holman, E. A., & Silver, R. C. (2015). Cumulative exposure to prior collective trauma and acute stress responses to the Boston marathon bombings. *Psychological Science, 26,* 675-683.

Garlow, S. J., Purselle, D. C., & Heninger, M. (2007). Cocaine and alcohol use preceding suicide in African American and White adolescents. *Journal of Psychiatric Research, 41,* 530-536.

Garrigan, P., & Kellman, P. (2008). Perceptual learning depends on perceptual constancy. *PNAS Proceedings of the National Academy of Sciences of the United States of America, 105,* 2248-2253.

Garwick, G. B. (2007). Intelligence-related terms in mental retardation, learning disability, and gifted/talented professional usage, 1983–2001: The 1992 mental retardation redefinition as natural experiment. *Dissertation Abstracts International Section A: Humanities and Social Sciences, 67*(9-A), 3296.

Gatchel, R. J., & Weisberg, J. N. (2000). *Personality characteristics of patients with pain.* Washington, DC: APA Books.

Gaudiano, B. A., & Miller, I. W. (2013). The evidence-based practice of psychotherapy. *Clinical Psychology Review, 33,* 813-824.

Gazzaniga, M. S., Ivry, R. B., & Mangun, G. R. (2002). *Cognitive neuroscience: The biology of the mind* (2nd ed.). New York: W. W. Norton.

Gelbard-Sagiv, H., Mukamel, R., Harel, M., Malach, R., & Fried, I. (2008). Internally generated reactivation of single neurons in human hippocampus during free recall. *Science, 322,* 96-101.

Gelfand, M. M. (2000). Sexuality among older women. *Journal of Women's Health and Gender Based Medicine, 9*(Suppl. 1), S15-S20.

Geller, E. S. (2011). Psychological science and safety: Large-scale success at preventing occupational injuries and fatalities. *Psychological Science, 20,* 109-114.

Gelman, R., & Baillargeon, R. (1983). A review of some Piagetian concepts. In J. H. Flavell & E. M. Markman (Eds.), *Handbook of child psychology, Vol. 3: Cognitive development* (4th ed.). New York: Wiley.

Gelstein, S., Yeshurun, Y., Rozenkrantz, L., Shusha, S., Frumin, I., Roth, Y., . . . Sobel, N. (2011). Human tears contain a chemosignal. *Science, 331,* 226-230.

Gennaro, R. J. (2004). *Higher-order theories of consciousness: An anthology.* Amsterdam, Netherlands: John Benjamins.

Genovese, J. E. C. (2006). Piaget, pedagogy, and evolutionary psychology. *Evolutionary Psychology, 4,* 2127-2137.

Genter, D. (2016). Language as cognitive tool kit: How language supports relational thought. *American Psychologist, 71,* 650-657.

Gentile, B., Grabe, S., Dolan-Pascoe, B., Twenge, J., Wells, B., & Maitino, A. (2009). Gender differences in domain-specific self-esteem: A meta-analysis. *Review of General Psychology, 13,* 34-45.

Gentner, D., Goldin, S., & Goldin-Meadow, S. (Eds.). (2003). *Language in mind: Advances in the study of language and cognition.* Cambridge, MA: MIT.

Gerdes, A., Uhl, G., & Alpers, G. (2009). Spiders are special: Fear and disgust evoked by pictures of arthropods. *Evolution and Human Behavior, 30,* 66-73.

Gershkoff-Stowe, L., Connell, B., & Smith, L. (2006). Priming overgeneralizations in two- and four-year-old children. *Journal of Child Language, 33,* 461-486.

Gerstel, N. (2005). In search of time. *Science, 308,* 204-205.

Getner, D., & Holyoak, K. J. (1997). Reasoning and learning by analogy. *American Psychologist, 52,* 32-34.

Geurten, M., Willems, S., Germain, S., & Meulemans, T. (2015). Less is more: The availability heuristic in early childhood. *British Journal of Developmental Psychology, 33,* 405-410 .

Geyer, T., Gokce, A., & Müller, H. J. (2011). Reinforcement of inhibitory positional priming by spatial working memory contents. *Acta Psychologica, 137,* 235-242.

Ghahramani, Z. (2015). Probabilistic machine learning and artificial intelligence. *Nature, 521*(7553), 452-459.

Ghavami, N., & Peplau, L. (2013). An intersectional analysis of gender and ethnic stereotypes: Testing three hypotheses. *Psychology of Women Quarterly, 37,* 113-127.

Giacobbi, P. R. Jr., Lynn, T. K., Wetherington, J. M., Jenkins, J., Bodendorf, M., & Langley, B. (2004). Stress and coping during the transition to university for first-year female athletes. *Sports Psychologist, 18,* 1-20.

Giacomini, M., Baylis, F., & Robert, J. (2007). Banking on it: Public policy and the ethics of stem cell research and development. *Social Sciences Medicine, 22,* 88-84.

Gialopsos, B. M. (2017). Sexual violence in academia: Policy, theory, and prevention considerations. *Journal of School Violence, 16,* 141-147.

Gianaros, P. J., & Wager, T. D. (2015). Brain-body pathways linking psychological stress and physical health. *Current Directions in Psychological Science, 24,* 313-321.

Giannakakis, A., & Fritsche, I. (2011). Social identities, group norms, and threat: On the malleability of ingroup bias. *Personality and Social Psychology Bulletin, 37,* 82-93.

Giannopoulos, V. L., & Vella-Brodrick, D. A. (2011). Effects of positive interventions and orientations to happiness on subjective well-being. *Journal of Positive Psychology, 6,* 95-105.

Gibb, K., Tunbridge, D., Chua, A., & Frederickson, N. (2007). Pathways to inclusion: Moving from special school to mainstream. *Educational Psychology in Practice, 23,* 109-127.

Gibbs, N. (2005, August 8). Being 13. *Time,* pp. 41-55.

Gibbs, W. W. (2002). From mouth to mind. *Scientific American, 287.* 26.

Gibson, S. (2013). Milgram's obedience experiments: A rhetorical analysis. *British Journal of Social Psychology, 52,* 290-309.

Giedd, J., Stockman, M., Weddle, C., Liverpool, M., Alexander-Bloch, A., Wallace, G., . . . Lenroot, R. K. (2010). Anatomic magnetic resonance imaging of the developing child and adolescent brain and effects of genetic variation. *Neuropsychology Review, 20,* 349-361.

Gilbert, P. D. (2007). Spirituality and mental health: A very preliminary overview. *Current Opinions in Psychiatry, 20,* 594-598.

Gilboa, A., Winocur, G., & Rosenbaum, R. S. (2006). Hippocampal contributions to recollection in retrograde and anterograde amnesia. *Hippocampus, 16,* 966-980.

Gillam, B., Palmisano, S. A., & Govan, D. G. (2011). Depth interval estimates from motion parallax and binocular disparity beyond interaction space. *Perception, 40,* 39-49.

Gillan, C. M., & Sahakian, B. J. (2015). Which is the driver, the obsessions or the compulsions, in OCD? *Neuropsychopharmacology, 40,* 247-248.

Gillespie, L. K., Brooks, P.J., Someki, F., Obeid, R., Shane-Simpson, C., Kapp, S. K., . . . Smith, D. S. (2015). Changing college students' conceptions of autism: An online training to increase knowledge and decrease stigma. *Journal of Autism Development and Disorders, 45,* 2553-2566.

Gilligan, C. (1996). The centrality of relationships in psychological development: A puzzle, some evidence, and a theory. In G. G. Noam & K. W. Fischer (Eds.), *Development and vulnerability in close relationships.* Hillsdale, NJ: Erlbaum.

Gilligan, C. (2004). Recovering psyche: Reflections on life-history and history. *Annual of Psychoanalysis, 32,* 131-147.

Gingrich, J.A., Malm, H., Ansorge, M.S., Brown, A., Sourander, A., Suri, D., . . . Weissman, M. M. (2017). New insights into how serotonin selective reuptake inhibitors shape the developing brain. *Brain Defects Research, 109,* 924-932.

Giovenco, D.P., & Delnevo, C.D. (2018). Prevalence of population smoking cessation by electronic cigarette use status in a national sample of recent smokers. *Addictive Behaviors, 76,* 129-134.

Giridharadas, A. (2014, May 24). The immigrant advantage. *The New York Times,* p. SR1.

Gizer, I. R., Ehlers, C. L., Vieten, C., Seaton-Smith, K. L., Feiler, H. S., Lee, J. V., . . . Wilhelmsen, K. C. (2011). Linkage scan of alcohol dependence in the UCSF Family Alcoholism Study. *Drug and Alcohol Dependence, 113,* 125-132.

Gladwell, M. (2004, September 20). Annals of psychology: Personality, plus how corporations figure out who you are. *The New Yorker,* 42-45.

Glass, K., Flory, K., Hankin, B., Kloos, B., & Turecki, G. (2009). Are coping strategies, social support, and hope associated with psychological distress among Hurricane Katrina survivors? *Journal of Social and Clinical Psychology, 28,* 779-795.

Glass, O. M., Forester, B. P., & Hermida, A. P. (2017). Electroconvulsive therapy (ECT) for treating agitation in dementia (major neurocognitive disorder)—A promising option. *International Psychogeriatrics, 29,* 717-726.

Glick, P., Lameiras, M., Fiske, S. T., Eckes, T., Masser, B., Volpato, C., . . . Glick, P. (2004). Bad but bold: Ambivalent attitudes toward men predict gender inequality in 16 nations. *Journal of Personality and Social Psychology, 86,* 713-728.

Glicksohn, J., & Nahari, G. (2007). Interacting personality traits? Smoking as a test case. *European Journal of Personality, 21,* 225-234.

Glisky, E. L. (2007). Changes in cognitive function in human aging. In D. R. Riddle (Ed.), *Brain aging: Models, methods, and mechanisms.* Boca Raton, FL: CRC Press.

Golden, W. L. (2006). Hypnotherapy for anxiety, phobias and psychophysiological disorders. In R. A. Chapman (Ed.), *The clinical use of hypnosis in cognitive behavior therapy: A practitioner's casebook.* New York: Springer Publishing.

Golder, S. A., & Macy, M. W. (2011). Diurnal and seasonal mood vary with work, sleep, and day length across diverse cultures. *Science, 333,* 1878-1881.

Goldey, K. L., & van Anders, S. M. (2011). Sexy thoughts: Effects of sexual cognitions on testosterone, cortisol, and arousal in women. *Hormones and Behavior, 59,* 754-764.

Goldman, B. (2017, February 21). Brain-computer interface advance allows fast, accurate typing by people with paralysis. Retrieved from https://med.stanford.edu/news/all-news/2017/02/brain-computer-interface-allows-fast-accurate-typing-by-people-with-paralysis.html.

Goldstein, I. (2000). Female sexual arousal disorder: New insights. *International Journal of Impotence Research, 12*(Suppl. 4), S152-S157.

Goldstein, S. N. (2006). The exploration of spirituality and identity status in adolescence. *Dissertation Abstracts International: Section B: The Sciences and Engineering, 67*(6-B), 3481.

Golimbet, V. E., Alfimova, M. V., Gritsenko, I. K., & Ebstein, R. P. (2007). Relationship between dopamine system genes and extraversion and novelty seeking. *Neuroscience Behavior and Physiology, 37,* 601-606.

Gontkovsky, S. T. (2005). Neurobiological bases and neuropsychological correlates of aggression and violence. In J. P. Morgan (Ed.), *Psychology of aggression.* Hauppauge, NY: Nova Science Publishers.

González-Torres, M. A., & Fernandez-Rivas, A. (2015). Self-identity and gender differences. In M. Sáenz-Herrero (Ed.), *Psychopathology in women: Incorporating gender perspective into descriptive psychopathology.* Cham, Switzerland: Springer International Publishing.

Goode, E. (1999, April 13). If things taste bad, "phantoms" may be at work. *The New York Times,* pp. D1-D2.

Goodman, G., & Quas, J. (2008). Repeated interviews and children's memory: It's more than just how many. *Current Directions in Psychological Science, 17,* 386-390.

Goodwin, R., Costa, P., & Adonu, J. (2004). Social support and its consequences: "Positive" and "deficiency" values and their implications for support and self-esteem. *British Journal of Social Psychology, 43,* 465-474.

Gooren, L. (2006). The biology of human psychosexual differentiation. *Hormones and Behavior, 50,* 589-601.

Gopie, N., Craik, F. M., & Hasher, L. (2011). A double dissociation of implicit and explicit memory in younger and older adults. *Psychological Science, 22,* 634-640.

Gopnik, A. (2017). Making AI more human. *Scientific American, 316,* 60-65.

Gopnik, A., & Griffiths, T. (2017, August 20). What happens to creativity as we age? *The New York Times,* p. SR9.

Gopnik, A., Griffiths, T. L., & Lucas, C. G. (2015). When younger learners can be better (or at least more open-minded) than older ones. *Current Directions in Psychological Science, 24*(2), 87-92.

Gorton, R. N., & Erickson-Schroth, L. (2017). Hormonal and surgical treatment options for transgender men (female-to-male). *Psychiatric Clinics of North America, 40,* 79-97.

Gossop, M., Stewart, D., & Marsden, J. (2008). Attendance at Narcotics Anonymous and Alcoholics Anonymous meetings, frequency of attendance and substance use outcomes after residential treatment for drug dependence: A 5-year follow-up study. *Addiction, 103,* 119-125.

Goswami, I., & Urminsky, O. (2017). The dynamic effect of incentives on postreward task engagement. *Journal of Experimental Psychology: General, 146,* 1-19.

Gotlib, I. H., Krasnoperova, E., Yue, D. N., & Joorman, J. (2004). Attentional biases for negative interpersonal stimuli in clinical depression. *Journal of Abnormal Psychology, 113,* 127-135.

Goto, T., Ishibashi, Y., Kajimura, S., Oka, R., & Kusumi, T. (2015). Development of free will and determinism scale in Japanese. *Japanese Journal of Psychology, 86,* 32-41.

Gottesman, I. I., & Hanson, D. R. (2005). Human development: Biological and genetic processes. *Annual Review of Psychology, 56,* 263-286.

Gotts, S. J., Jo, H., Wallace, G. L., Saad, Z. S., Cox, R. W., & Martin, A. (2013). Two distinct forms of functional lateralization in the human brain. *PNAS Proceedings of the National Academy of Sciences of the United States of America, 110,* E3435-E3444.

Gould, R. L. (1978). *Transformations.* New York: Simon & Schuster.

Gowaty, P. A. (2003). Power asymmetries between the sexes, mate preferences, and components of fitness. In C. B. Travis (Ed.), *Evolution, gender, and rape.* Cambridge, MA: MIT.

Grady, C. L., St-Laurent, M., & Burianová, H. (2015). Age differences in brain activity related to unsuccessful declarative memory retrieval. *Brain Research, 161,* 230-47.

Grady, D., & Altman, L. K. (2008, December 29). Lessons for other smokers in Obama's efforts to quit. *The New York Times,* p. A12.

Grahek, N. (2007). *Feeling pain and being in pain* (2nd ed.). Cambridge, MA: MIT Press.

Granic, I., Hollenstein, T., & Dishion, T. (2003). Longitudinal analysis of flexibility and reorganization in early adolescence: A dynamic systems study of family interactions. *Developmental Psychology, 39,* 606-617.

Granic, I., Lobel, A., & Engels, R. E. (2014). The benefits of playing video games. *American Psychologist, 69,* 66-78.

Grann, J. D. (2007). Confidence in knowledge past: An empirical basis for a differential decay theory of very long-term memory monitoring. *Dissertation Abstracts International Section A: Humanities and Social Sciences, 67,* 2462.

Grant, A. (2008). Does intrinsic motivation fuel the prosocial fire? Motivational synergy in predicting persistence, performance, and productivity. *Journal of Applied Psychology, 93,* 48-58.

Grant, D. M., & Wingate, L. R. (2011). Cognitive-behavioral therapy. In C. Silverstein (Ed.), *The initial psychotherapy interview: A gay man seeks treatment.* Amsterdam, Netherlands: Elsevier.

Gray, G. C. (2006). The regulation of corporate violations: Punishment, compliance, and the blurring of responsibility. *British Journal of Criminology, 46,* 875-892.

Gray, J. R., Chabris, C. F., & Braver, T. S. (2003). Neural mechanisms of general fluid intelligence. *Nature: Neurosciences, 6*(3), 316-322.

Green, J., Lynn, S., & Montgomery, G. (2008). Gender-related differences in hypnosis-based treatments for smoking: A follow-up meta-analysis. *American Journal of Clinical Hypnosis, 50,* 259-271.

Greenberg, G., & Rosenheck, R. (2008). Jail incarceration, homelessness, and mental health: A national study. *Psychiatric Services, 59,* 170-177.

Greenberg, L. S. (2015). Working with primary emotions. In L. S. Greenberg, *Emotion-focused therapy: Coaching clients to work through their feelings* (2nd ed.). Washington, DC: American Psychological Association.

Greenberg, R. M., & Kellner, C. H. (2005). Electroconvulsive therapy: A selected review. *American Journal of Geriatric Psychiatry, 13,* 268-281.

Greenberg, R., & Goldman, E. (2009). Antidepressants, psychotherapy or their combination: Weighing options for depression treatments. *Journal of Contemporary Psychotherapy, 39,* 83-91.

Greene, J. D., & Paxton, J. M. (2009). Patterns of neural activity associated with honest and dishonest moral decisions. *PNAS Proceedings of the National Academy of Sciences of the United States of America, 106*(30), 12506-12511.

Greene, K. M., & Maggs, J. L. (2017). Academic time during college: Associations with mood, tiredness, and binge drinking across days and semesters. *Journal of Adolescence, 56,* 24-33.

Greenfield, B. L., & Tonigan, J. S. (2013). The general Alcoholics Anonymous tools of recovery: The adoption of 12-step practices and beliefs. *Psychology of Addictive Behaviors, 27,* 553-561.

Greenfield, S. (2002). Mind, brain and consciousness. *British Journal of Psychiatry, 181,* 91-93.

Greenspan, S. (2006). Functional concepts in mental retardation: Finding the natural essence of an artificial category. *Exceptionality, 14,* 205-224.

Greenwald, A. G., Nosek, B. A., & Sriram, N. (2006). Consequential validity of the implicit association test: Comment on Blanton and Jaccard. *American Psychologist, 61,* 56-61.

Greer, R. D., Dudek-Singer, J., & Gautreaux, G. (2006). Observational learning. *International Journal of Psychology, 41,* 486-499.

Gregory, R. L. (1978). *The psychology of seeing* (3rd ed.). New York: McGraw-Hill.

Gregory, R. L. (2008). Emmert's Law and the moon illusion. *Spatial Vision, 21,* 407-720.

Gregory, S. (1856). *Facts for young women.* Boston: George Gregory.

Gregory, S. S. (1994, March 21). At risk of mutilation. *Time,* pp. 45-46.

Greitemeyer, T., & Sagioglou, C. (2017). Increasing wealth inequality may increase interpersonal hostility: The relationship between personal relative deprivation and aggression. *Journal of Social Psychology, 157*(6), 766-776.

Grenfell-Essam, R., Ward, G., & Tan, L. (2013). The role of rehearsal on the output order of immediate free recall of short and long lists. *Journal of Experimental Psychology: Learning, Memory, and Cognition, 39,* 317-347.

Grigg-Damberger, M. M. (2017). Ontogeny of sleep and its functions in infancy, childhood, and adolescence. In S. Nevšímalová, & O. Bruni (Eds.), *Sleep disorders in children.* Cham, Switzerland: Springer International Publishing.

Griggs, R. A. (2015a). Psychology's lost boy: Will the real Little Albert please stand up? *Teaching of Psychology, 42,* 14-18.

Griggs, R. A. (2015b). The Kitty Genovese story in introductory psychology textbooks: Fifty years later. *Teaching of Psychology, 42,* 149-152.

Griggs, R. A. (2017). Milgram's obedience study: A contentious classic reinterpreted. *Teaching of Psychology, 44,* 32-37.

Grigorenko, E. (2009). Speaking genes or genes for speaking? Deciphering the genetics of speech and language. *Journal of Child Psychology and Psychiatry, 50,* 116-125.

Grigorenko, E. L., & Dozier, M. (2013). Introduction to the special section on genomics. *Child Development, 84,* 6-16.

Grimm, J. W. (2011). Craving. In M. C. Olmstead (Ed.), *Animal models of drug addiction.* Totowa, NJ: Humana Press.

Gronholm, P., Rinne, J. O., Vorobyev, V., & Laine, M. (2005). Naming of newly learned objects: A PET activation study. *Brain Research and Cognitive Brain Research, 14,* 22-28.

Gross, D. M. (2006). *The secret history of emotion: From Aristotle's rhetoric to modern brain science.* Chicago: University of Chicago Press.

Gross, G., & Weiss, E. L. (2018). A call to the helping disciplines to deconstruct diversity and race: An essay on the social constructions of the "other." *International Journal for the Advancement of Counselling,* doi:10.1007/s10447-018-9344-0.

Grossberg, S. (2013). Adaptive Resonance Theory: How a brain learns to consciously attend, learn, and recognize a changing world. *Neural Networks, 47,* 88-94.

Grossmann, T., Striano, T., & Friederici, A. D. (2007). Developmental changes in infants' processing of happy and angry facial expressions: A neurobehavioral study. *Brain and Cognition, 64,* 30-41.

Grosso, M. (2015). The "transmission" model of mind and body: A brief history. In E. F. Kelly, A. Crabtree, & P. Marshall (Eds.), *Beyond physicalism: Toward reconciliation of science and spirituality.* Lanham, MD: Rowman & Littlefield.

Groves, C. L., & Anderson, C. A. (2015). Video game violence and offline aggression. In E. Aboujaoude & V. Starcevic (Eds.), *Mental health in the digital age: Grave dangers, great promise.* New York: Oxford University Press.

Groves, R. M., Singer, E., Lepkowski, J. M., Heeringa, S. G., & Alwin, D. F. (2004). Survey methodology. In S. J. House, F. T. Juster, R. L. Kahn, H. Schuman, & E. Singer (Eds.), *A telescope on society: Survey research and social science at the University of Michigan and beyond.* Ann Arbor, MI: University of Michigan Press.

Gruber, R. P., & Block, R. A. (2017). Perception of scenes in different sensory modalities: A result of modal completion. *American Journal of Psychology, 130,* 23-34.

Gruber, T. R. (2013). Nature, nurture, and knowledge acquisition. *International Journal of Human-Computer Studies, 71,* 191-194.

Grundy, D. (2015). Principles and standards for reporting animal experiments in the *Journal of Physiology* and *Experimental Physiology. Journal of Physiology, 593,* 2547-2549.

Grünbaum, A. (2015). Critique of psychoanalysis. In S. Boag, L. W. Brakel, & V. Talvitie (Eds.), *Philosophy, science, and psychoanalysis: A critical meeting.* London: Karnac Books.

Grünert, U., Jusuf, P. R., Lee, S. S., & Nguyen, D. (2011). Bipolar input to melanopsin containing ganglion cells in primate retina. *Visual Neuroscience, 28,* 39-50.

Gu, C., Warkentin, S., Mais, L. A., & Carnell, S. (2017). Ethnic differences in parental feeding behaviors in UK parents of preschoolers. *Appetite, 113,* 398-404.

Guadagno, R. E., & Cialdini, R. B. (2002). Online persuasion: An examination of gender differences in computer-mediated interpersonal influence [Special issue: Groups and Internet]. *Group Dynamics, 6,* 38-51.

Guastella, A., Mitchell, P., & Dadds, M. (2008, January). Oxytocin increases gaze to the eye region of human faces. *Biological Psychiatry, 63,* 3-5.

Guiard, B. P., Chenu, F., Mansari, M., & Blier, P. (2011). Characterization of the electrophysiological properties of triple reuptake inhibitors on monoaminergic neurons. *International Journal of Neuropsychopharmacology, 14,* 211-223.

Guida, A., Tardieu, H., Le Bohec, O., & Nicolas, S. (2013). Are schemas sufficient to interpret the personalization effect? Only if long-term working memory backs up. *European Review of Applied Psychology/Revue Européenne De Psychologie Appliquée, 63,* 99-107.

Guidelines for the treatment of animals in behavioural research and teaching. (2017). *Animal Behaviour, 123,* i-ix.

Gupta, A., Love, A., Kilpatrick, L. A., Labus, J. S., Bhatt, R., Chang, L., . . . Mayer, E. A. (2017). Morphological brain measures of cortico-limbic inhibition related to resilience. *Journal of Neuroscience Research, 95*(9), 1760-1775. doi: 10.1002/jnr.24007.

Gupta, M. A. (2013). Review of somatic symptoms in post-traumatic stress disorder. *International Review of Psychiatry, 25,* 86-99.

Guttmacher Institute (2012). Facts on American teens' sources of information about sex. Accessed at http://www. guttmacher.org/pubs/FB-Teen-Sex-Ed.html.

Guéguen, N., Marchand, M., Pascual, A., & Lourel, M. (2008). Foot-in-the-door technique using a courtship request: A field experiment. *Psychological Reports, 103,* 529-534.

Haas, H. S., Fuerst, M. P., Tönz, P., & Gubser-Ernst, J. (2015). Analyzing the psychological and social contents of evidence–Experimental comparison between guessing, naturalistic observation, and systematic analysis. *Journal of Forensic Sciences, 60,* 659-668.

Haberstick, B. C., Schmitz, S., Young, S. E., & Hewitt, J. K. (2005). Contributions of genes and environments to stability and change in externalizing and internalizing problems during elementary and middle school. *Behavior Genetics, 35,* 381-396.

Hadad, B., Maurer, D., & Lewis, T. L. (2017). The role of early visual input in the development of contour interpolation: The case of subjective contours. *Developmental Science, 20,* 25-32.

Hadiwijaya, H., Klimstra, T. A., Vermunt, J. K., Branje, S. T., & Meeus, W. J. (2017). On the development of harmony, turbulence, and independence in parent-adolescent relationships: A five-wave longitudinal study. *Journal of Youth and Adolescence, 46,* 1772-1788.

Hagelskamp, C., Hughes, D., Yoshikawa, H., & Chaudry, A. (2011). Negotiating motherhood and work: A typology of role identity associations among low-income, urban women. *Community, Work & Family, 14,* 335-366.

Haier, R. J. (2003). Brain imaging studies of intelligence: Individual differences and neurobiology. In R. J. Sternberg & J. Lautrey (Eds.), *Models of intelligence: International perspectives.* Washington, DC: American Psychological Association.

Haier, R. J. (2011). Biological basis of intelligence. In R. J. Sternberg & S. Kaufman (Eds.), *The Cambridge handbook of intelligence.* New York: Cambridge University Press.

Haier, R. J., Colom, R., Schroeder, D. H., Condon, C. A., Tang, C., Eaves, E., . . . Head, K. (2009). Gray matter and intelligence factors: Is there a neuro-g? *Intelligence, 37,* 136-144.

Halford, S. (2006). Collapsing the boundaries? Fatherhood, organization and home-working. *Gender, Work & Organization, 13,* 383-402.

Halkitis, P. (2009). *Methamphetamine addiction: Biological foundations, psychological factors, and social consequences.* Washington, DC: American Psychological Association.

Hall, G. C. N. (1996). *Theory-based assessment, treatment, and prevention of sexual aggression.* New York: Oxford University Press.

Hall, P. J., Chong, C., McNaughton, N., & Corr, P. J. (2011). An economic perspective on the reinforcement sensitivity theory of personality. *Personality and Individual Differences, 51*, 242-247.

Halpern, D. F. (2010). How neuromythologies support sex role stereotypes. *Science, 330*, 1320-1322.

Halpern, D. F. (2011). *Sex differences in cognitive abilities* (4th ed.). New York: Psychology Press.

Halpert, J. (2003, April 28). What do patients want? *Newsweek*, pp. 63-64.

Hamani, Y., Sciaki-Tamir, Y., Deri-Hasid, R., Miller-Pogrund, T., Milwidsky, A., & Haimov-Kochman, R. (2007). Misconceptions about oral contraception pills among adolescents and physicians. *Human Reproduction, 22*, 3078-3083.

Hamann, S. B., Ely, T. D., Hoffman, J. M., & Kilts, C. D. (2002). Ecstasy and agony: Activation of human amygdala in positive and negative emotion. *Psychological Science, 13*, 135-141.

Hambleton, R. K. (2006). Psychometric models, test designs and item types for the next generation of educational and psychological tests. In D. Bartram & R. K. Hambleton (Eds.), *Computer-based testing and the Internet: Issues and advances*. New York: John Wiley & Sons.

Hambleton, R. K., & Zenisky, A. L. (2013). Reporting test scores in more meaningful ways: A research-based approach to score report design. In K. F. Geisinger, B. A. Bracken, J. F. Carlson, J. C. Hansen, N. R. Kuncel, S. P. Reise, & M. C. Rodriguez (Eds.), *APA handbook of testing and assessment in psychology, Vol. 3: Testing and assessment in school psychology and education*. Washington, DC: American Psychological Association.

Hamer, M., Taylor, A., & Steptoe, A. (2006). The effect of acute aerobic exercise on stress-related blood pressure responses: A systematic review and meta-analysis. *Bi Psychology, 71*, 183-190.

Hamilton, A. C., & Martin, R. C. (2007). Semantic short-term memory deficits and resolution of interference: A case for inhibition? In D. S. Gorfein & C. M. Macleod (Eds.), *Inhibition in cognition*. Washington, DC: American Psychological Association.

Hamilton, L. K., Joppé, S. E., Cochard, L. M., & Fernandes, K. L. (2013). Aging and neurogenesis in the adult forebrain: What we have learned and where we should go from here. *European Journal of Neuroscience, 37*, 1978-1986.

Hammond, D. C. (2007). Review of the efficacy of clinical hypnosis with headaches and migraines [Special issue: Evidence-based practice clinical hypnosis–part 1]. *International Journal of Clinical and Experimental Hypnosis 55*, 207-219.

Han, S., & Ma, Y. (2014). Cultural differences in human brain activity: A quantitative meta-analysis. *NeuroImage, 99*, 293-300.

Han, S., & Ma, Y. (2015). A culture-behavior-brain loop model of human development. *Trends in Cognitive Sciences, 19*(11), 666-676.

Haney, C., & Zimbardo, P. (2009). Persistent dispositionalism in interactionist clothing: Fundamental attribution error in explaining prison abuse. *Personality and Social Psychology Bulletin, 35*, 807-814.

Hangya, B., Tihanyi, B. T., Entz, L., Fabo, D., Erőss, L., Wittner, L., . . . Ulbert, I. (2011). Complex propagation patterns characterize human cortical activity during slow-wave sleep. *Journal of Neuroscience, 31*, 8770-8779.

Hanna-Pladdy, B., Pahwa, R., & Lyons, K. E. (2015). Paradoxical effect of dopamine medication on cognition in Parkinson's disease: Relationship to side of motor onset. *Journal of the International Neuropsychological Society, 21*, 259-270.

Hao Z., Mumphrey M., Townsend R., Morrison, C. D., Münzberg , H., Ye, J., & Berthoud, H. R. (2016). Reprogramming of defended body weight after Roux-En-Y gastric bypass surgery in diet-induced obese mice. *Obesity, 24*, 654-660.

Harden, R., Oaklander, A., Burton, A. W., Perez, R. M., Richardson, K., Swan, M., . . . Bruehl, S. (2013). Complex regional pain syndrome: Practical diagnostic and treatment guidelines, 4th edition. *Pain Medicine, 14*, 180-229.

Harding, D. J., & Jencks, C. (2003). Changing attitudes toward premarital sex: Cohort, period, and aging effects. *Public Opinion Quarterly, 67*, 211-226.

Hardison, D. M. (2006). Review of phonetics and phonology in language comprehension and production: Differences and similarities. *Studies in Second Language Acquisition, 28*, 138-140.

Hardt, J., Sidor, A., Nickel, R., Kappis, B., Petrak, P., & Egle, U. (2008). Childhood adversities and suicide attempts: A retrospective study. *Journal of Family Violence, 23*, 713-718.

Hardt, O., Nader, K., & Nadel, L. (2013). Decay happens: The role of active forgetting in memory. *Trends in Cognitive Sciences, 17*, 111-120.

Hardy, L. T. (2007). Attachment theory and reactive attachment disorder: Theoretical perspectives and treatment implications. *Journal of Child and Adolescent Psychiatric Nursing, 20*, 27-39.

Haridi, M., Weyn Banningh, S., Clé, M., Leu-Semenescu, S., Vidailhet, M., & Arnulf, I. (2017). Is there a common motor dysregulation in sleepwalking and REM sleep behaviour disorder? *Journal of Sleep Research. 26*(5), 614-622.

Hariri, A. R. (2015). *Looking inside the disordered brain: An introduction to the functional neuroanatomy of psychopathology*. Sunderland, MA: Sinauer Associates.

Harlow, H. F., & Zimmerman, R. R. (1959). Affectional responses in the infant monkey. *Science, 130*, 421-432.

Harlow, J. M. (1869). Recovery from the passage of an iron bar through the head. *Massachusetts Medical Society Publication, 2*, 329-347.

Harmer, C. J., Duman, R. S., & Cowen, P. J. (2017). How do antidepressants work? New perspectives for refining future treatment approaches. *The Lancet Psychiatry, 4*, 409-418.

Harmon-Jones, E., & Winkielman, P. (2007). *Social neuroscience: Integrating biological and psychological explanations of social behavior*. New York, NY: Guilford Press.

Harmon-Jones, E., Harmon-Jones, C., & Levy, N. (2015). An action-based model of cognitive-dissonance processes. *Current Directions in Psychological Science, 24*, 184-189.

Harper, T. (1978, November 15). It's not true about people 65 or over. *Green Bay Press-Gazette* (Wisconsin), p. D-1.

Hart, B., & Risley, T. R. (1997). Use of language by three-year-old children. Courtesy of Drs. Betty Hart and Todd Risley, University of Kansas.

Hartshorne, J., & Germine, L. (2015). When does cognitive functioning peak? The asynchronous rise and fall of different cognitive abilities across the life span. *Psychological Science, 26*, 433-443.

Harvey, J. H., Wenzel, A., & Sprecher, S. (Eds.). (2004). *The handbook of sexuality in close relationships*. Mahwah, NJ: Lawrence Erlbaum Associates.

Harvie, D. S., Moseley, G. L., Hillier, S. L., & Meulders, A. (2017). Classical conditioning differences associated with chronic pain: A systematic review. *The Journal of Pain, 18*(8), 889-898.

Hasnain, N. N., Ansari, S., & Sethi, S. (2011). Life satisfaction and self esteem in married and unmarried working women. *Journal of the Indian Academy of Applied Psychology, 37*, 316-319.

Hass, R. W. (2017). Tracking the dynamics of divergent thinking via semantic distance: Analytic methods and theoretical implications. *Memory & Cognition, 45*, 233-244.

Hassouneh, D., Alcala-Moss, A., & McNeff, E. (2011). Practical strategies for promoting full inclusion of individuals with disabilities in community-based participatory intervention research. *Research in Nursing & Health, 34*, 253-265.

Hastings, R. P., & Oakford, S. (2003). Student teachers' attitudes towards the inclusion of children with special needs. *Educational Psychology, 23*, 87-94.

Hattori, S., Kishida, I., Suda, A., Miyauchi, M., Shiraishi, Y., Fujibayashi, M., . . . Hirayasu, Y. (2017). Effects of four atypical antipsychotics on autonomic nervous system activity in schizophrenia. *Schizophrenia Research.* Accessed at https://www.ncbi.nlm.nih.gov/pubmed/28709776.

Hauke, C. (2006). The unconscious: Personal and collective. In R. K. Papadopoulos (Ed.), *The handbook of Jungian psychology: Theory, practice and applications*. New York: Routledge.

Havermans, R. C., Mulkens, S., Nederkoorn, C., & Jansen, A. (2007). The efficacy of cue exposure with response prevention in extinguishing drug and alcohol cue reactivity. *Behavioral Interventions, 22*, 121-135.

Haviland-Jones, J. M., & Wilson, P. J. (2008). A "nose" for emotion: Emotional information and challenges in odors and semiochemicals. In M. Lewis, J. M. Haviland-Jones, & L. G. Barrett (Eds.), *Handbook of emotions* (3rd ed.). New York: Guilford Press.

Hayes, S. C. (2015). Humanistic psychology and contextual behavioral perspectives. In K. J. Schneider, J. F. Pierson, & J. T. Bugental (Eds.), *The handbook of humanistic psychology: Theory, research, and practice* (2nd ed.). Thousand Oaks, CA: Sage Publications, Inc.

Hayflick, L. (2007). Biological aging is no longer an unsolved problem. *Annals of the New York Academy of Sciences, 1100*, 1-13.

Hays, P. A. (2008). *Addressing cultural complexities in practice: Assessment, diagnosis, and therapy* (2nd ed.). Washington, DC: American Psychological Association.

Hayward, R., & Elliott, M. (2011). Subjective and objective fit in religious congregations: Implications for well-being. *Group Processes & Intergroup Relations, 14*, 127-139.

Heath, M., & Manzone, J. (2017). Manual estimations of functionally graspable target objects adhere to Weber's law. *Experimental Brain Research, 235*, 1701-1707.

Heathcote, A., Coleman, J. R., Eidels, A., Watson, J. M., Houpt, J., & Strayer, D. L. (2015). Working memory's workload capacity. *Memory & Cognition, 43*, 973-989.

Heatherton, T., & Sargent, J. (2009). Does watching smoking in movies promote teenage smoking? *Current Directions in Psychological Science, 18*, 63-67.

Hecht, J. M. (2007). *The happiness myth: Why what we think is right is wrong. A history of what really makes us happy.* New York: HarperSanFrancisco/HarperCollins.

Hedges, D. W., Brown, B. L., Shwalk, D. A., Godfrey, K., & Larcher, A. M. (2007). The efficacy of selective serotonin reuptake inhibitors in adult social anxiety disorder: A meta-analysis of double-blind, placebo-controlled trials. *Journal of Psychopharmacology, 21*, 102-111.

Heffernan, M. E., & Fraley, R. C. (2015). How early experiences shape attraction, partner preferences, and attachment dynamics. In V. Zayas & C. Hazan (Eds.), *Bases of adult attachment: Linking brain, mind and behavior.* New York: Springer Science + Business Media.

Hegarty, P. (2007). From genius inverts to gendered intelligence: Lewis Terman and the power of the norm [Special issue: Power matters: Knowledge politics in the history of psychology]. *History of Psychology, 10*, 132-155.

Hegarty, P., & Massey, S. (2007). Anti-homosexual prejudice . . . as opposed to what? Queer theory and the social psychology of anti-homosexual attitudes. *Journal of Homosexuality, 52*, 47-71.

Heilman, K. M. (2005). *Creativity and the brain.* New York: Psychology Press.

Heilman, R. M., & Kusev, P. (2017). The gender pay gap: Can behavioral economics provide useful insights? *Frontiers in Psychology, 8*, 22-32.

Heinrichs, R. W. (2005). The primacy of cognition in schizophrenia. *American Psychologist, 60*, 229-242.

Heintz, M. M., Brander, S. M., & White, J. W. (2015). Endocrine disrupting compounds alter risk-taking behavior in guppies (Poecilia reticulata). *Ethology, 121*, 480-491.

Heitzmann, C. A., Merluzzi, T. V., Jean-Pierre, P., Roscoe, J. A., Kirsh, K. L., & Passik, S. D. (2011). Assessing self-efficacy for coping with cancer: Development and psychometric analysis of the brief version of the Cancer Behavior Inventory (CBI-B). *Psycho-Oncology, 20*, 302-312.

Helgeson, V. S. (2015). Gender and personality. In M. Mikulincer, P. R. Shaver, M. L. Cooper, & R. J. Larsen (Eds.), *APA handbook of personality and social psychology, Volume 4: Personality processes and individual differences.* Washington, DC: American Psychological Association.

Helgeson, V. S., & Zajdel, M. (2017). Adjusting to chronic health conditions. *Annual Review of Psychology, 68*, 545-571.

Heller, H. C., Ruby, N. F., Rolls, A., Makam, M., & Colas, D. (2014). Adaptive and pathological inhibition of neuroplasticity associated with circadian rhythms and sleep. *Behavioral Neuroscience, 128*, 273-282.

Helsen, K., Goubert, L., & Vlaeyen, J. S. (2013). Observational learning and pain-related fear: Exploring contingency learning in an experimental study using colored warm water immersions. *The Journal of Pain, 14*, 676-688.

Henckes, N. (2011). Reforming psychiatric institutions in the mid-twentieth century: A framework for analysis. *History of Psychiatry, 22*, 164-181.

Hennessy, M. B., & Shair, H. N. (2017). Filial attachment: Development, mechanisms, and consequences. In J. Call, G. M. Burghardt, I. M. Pepperberg, C. T. Snowdon, & T. Zentall (Eds.), *APA handbook of comparative psychology: Basic concepts, methods, neural substrate, and behavior.* Washington, DC: American Psychological Association.

Hennig-Fast, K., Meister, F., Frodl, T., Beraldi, A., Padberg, F., Engel, R., . . . Meindl, T. (2008). The case of persistent retrograde amnesia following a dissociative fugue: Neuropsychological and neurofunctional underpinnings of loss of autobiographical memory and self-awareness. *Neuropsychologia, 46*(12), 2993-3005.

Henningsen, D. D., Henningsen, M. L., & Eden, J. (2006). Examining the symptoms of groupthink and retrospective sensemaking. *Small Group Research, 37*, 36-64.

Henrich, J., Heine, S., and Norenzayan, A. (2010). The weirdest people in the world? *Behavioral and Brain Sciences, 33*, 61-83.

Henry, D., McClellen, D., Rosenthal, L., Dedrick, D., & Gosdin, M. (2008). Is sleep really for sissies? Understanding the role of work in insomnia in the US. *Social Science & Medicine, 66*, 715-726.

Herbenick, D., Reece, M., Sanders, S., Dodge, B., Ghassemi, A., & Fortenberry, J. (2009). Prevalence and characteristics of vibrator use by women in the United States: Results from a nationally representative study. *Journal of Sexual Medicine, 6*, 1857-1866.

Herbert, W. (2011). *On second thought: Outsmarting your mind's hard-wired habits.* New York: Broadway.

Hernández-Orallo, J. (2017). *The measure of all minds: Evaluating natural and artificial intelligence.* New York: Cambridge University Press.

Herrnstein, R. J., & Murray, D. (1994). *The bell curve.* New York: Free Press.

Herskovits, M. (2018). *Acculturation: A study of culture contact.* New York: Moat Portultis.

Herting, M. M., & Sowell, E. R. (2017). Puberty and structural brain development in humans. *Frontiers in Neuroendocrinology, 44*, 122-137.

Hertlein, K. M., Weeks, G. R., & Gambescia, N. (2007). The treatment of hypoactive sexual desire disorder: An intersystem approach. In L. VandeCreek, F. L. Peterson, Jr., & J. W. Bley (Eds.), *Innovations in clinical practice: Focus on sexual health.* Sarasota, FL: Professional Resource Press/Professional Resource Exchange.

Hertzog, C., Kramer, A., Wilson, R., & Lindenberger, U. (2008). Enrichment effects on adult cognitive development: Can the functional capacity of older adults be preserved and enhanced? *Psychological Science in the Public Interest, 9*, 1-65.

Herzberg, L. (2009). Direction, causation, and appraisal theories of emotion. *Philosophical Psychology, 22*, 167-186.

Herzog, H. (2017). The ethics of behavioral research using animals: A classroom exercise. In J. R. Stowell & W. E. Addison (Eds.), *Activities for teaching statistics and research methods: A guide for psychology instructors.* Washington, DC: American Psychological Association.

Heshka, S., Anderson, J. W., Atkinson, R. L., Greenway, F. L., Hill, J. O., Phinney, S. D., . . . Pi-Sunyer, F. X. (2003). Weight loss with self-help compared with a structured commercial program: A randomized trial. *Journal of the American Medical Association, 289*, 1792-1798.

Hess, M. J., Houg, S., & Tammaro, E. (2007). The experience of four individuals with paraplegia enrolled in an outpatient interdisciplinary sexuality program. *Sexuality and Disability, 25*, 189-195.

Hetzel-Riggin, M. D. (2017). A study of the impact of informed consent procedures on participant responses in trauma-related research. *Journal of Loss and Trauma, 22*, 36-46.

Heward, W. L., & Orlansky, M. D. (1988). *Exceptional children* (3rd ed.). Columbus, OH: Merrill.

Hewitt, E. (2017, June 4). Fentanyl takes a deadly toll on Vermont. Retrieved from https://vtdigger.org/2017/06/04/hollywood-heroin-hits-vermont/.

Hickok, G. (2015, May 10). Rhythms of the brain. *The New York Times*, p. SR 9.

Higgs, S. (2015). Social norms and their influence on eating behaviours. *Appetite, 86*, 38-44.

Hilarski, C. (2007). Antisocial personality disorder. In B. A. Thyer & J. S. Wodarski (Eds.), *Social work in mental health: An evidence-based approach.* Hoboken, NJ: John Wiley & Sons.

Hilbert, S., Schwaighofer, M., Zech, A., Sarubin, N., Arendasy, M., & Bühner, M. (2017). Working memory tasks train working memory but not reasoning: A material- and operation-specific investigation of transfer from working memory practice. *Intelligence, 61,* 102-114.

Hill, B. D., Foster, J. D., Elliott, E. M., Shelton, J., McCain, J., & Gouvier, W. (2013). Need for cognition is related to higher general intelligence, fluid intelligence, and crystallized intelligence, but not working memory. *Journal of Research in Personality, 47,* 22-25.

Hilton, R. C., Rengasamy, M., Mansoor, B., He, J., Mayes, T., Emslie, G. J., . . . Brent, D. A. (2013). Impact of treatments for depression on comorbid anxiety, attentional, and behavioral symptoms in adolescents with selective serotonin reuptake inhibitor-resistant depression. *Journal of the American Academy of Child & Adolescent Psychiatry, 52,* 482-492.

Hines, M. (2004). *Brain gender.* New York: Oxford University Press.

Hines, M., & Alexander, G. (2008). Monkeys, girls, boys and toys: A confirmation letter regarding sex differences in toy preferences: Striking parallels between monkeys and humans. *Hormones and Behavior, 54,* 478-479.

Hinterberger, T., Schöner, J., & Halsband, U. (2011). Analysis of electrophysiological state patterns and changes during hypnosis induction. *International Journal of Clinical and Experimental Hypnosis, 59,* 165-179.

Hipp, T. N., Bellis, A. L., Goodnight, B. L., Brennan, C. L., Swartout, K. M., & Cook, S. L. (2017). Justifying sexual assault: Anonymous perpetrators speak out online. *Psychology of Violence, 7,* 82-90.

Hirschberger, G., Pyszczynski, T., & Ein-Dor, T. (2010). An ever-dying people: The existential underpinnings of Israelis' perceptions of war and conflict. *Cahiers Internationaux de Psychologie Sociale, 87*(3), 443-457. doi:10.3917/cips.087.0443.

Hirsh, I. J., & Watson, C. S. (1996). Auditory psychophysics and perception. *Annual Review of Psychology, 47,* 461-484.

Hirst, W., Phelps, E. A., Meksin, R., Vaidya, C. J., Johnson, M. K., Mitchell, K. J., . . . Olsson, A. (2015). A ten-year follow-up of a study of memory for the attack of September 11, 2001: Flashbulb memories and memories for flashbulb events. *Journal of Experimental Psychology: General, 144,* 604-623.

Ho, S. M. Y., Saltel, P., Machavoine, J., Rapoport-Hubschman, N., & Spiegel, D. (2004). Cross-cultural aspects of cancer care. In National Institutes of Health and Stanford University School of Medicine, *Cancer, culture, and communication.* New York: Kluwer Academic/Plenum Publishers.

Hobson, J. A. (2005). In bed with Mark Solms? What a nightmare! A reply to Domhoff (2005). *Dreaming, 15,* 21-29.

Hobson, J. A. (2007). States of conciseness: Normal and abnormal variation. In P. D. Zelazo, M. Moscovitch, & E. Thompson (Eds.), *The Cambridge Handbook of Consciousness.* London: Cambridge University Press.

Hobson, K. (2011, March 28). How can you help the medicine go down? *Wall Street Journal,* p. R10.

Hochschild, A. (2001, February). A generation without public passion. *Atlantic Monthly,* pp. 33-42.

Hoenen, M., Lübke, K. T., & Pause, B. M. (2017). Sensitivity of the human mirror neuron system for abstract traces of actions: An EEG-study. *Biological Psychology, 124,* 57-64.

Hofeditz, M., Nienaber, A., Dysvik, A., & Schewe, G. (2017). "Want to" versus "have to": Intrinsic and extrinsic motivators as predictors of compliance behavior intention. *Human Resource Management, 56,* 25-49.

Hofer, J., Busch, H., Raihala, C., Šolcová, I. P., & Tavel, P. (2017). The higher your implicit affiliation-intimacy motive, the more loneliness can turn you into a social cynic: A cross-cultural study. *Journal of Personality, 85,* 179-191.

Hoff, E. (2003). Language development in childhood. In R. M. Lerner, M. A. Easterbrooks, & J. Mistry. (Eds.), *Handbook of psychology: Developmental psychology* (Vol. 6). New York: Wiley.

Hoff, E. (2008). *Language development.* New York: Wadsworth.

Hofmann, S. G. (2007). Enhancing exposure-based therapy from a translational research perspective. *Behaviour Research and Therapy, 45,* 1987-2001.

Hofmann, W., Gschwendner, T., Castelli, L., & Schmitt, M. (2008). Implicit and explicit attitudes and interracial interaction: The moderating role of situationally available control resources. *Group Processes & Intergroup Relations, 11,* 69-87.

Hogan, J., Davies, S., & Hogan, R. (2007). Generalizing personality-based validity evidence. In S. M. McPhail (Ed.), *Alternative validation strategies: Developing new and leveraging existing validity evidence.* Hoboken, NJ: John Wiley & Sons.

Hogg, M. A. (2006). Social identity theory. In P. J. Burke (Ed.), *Contemporary social psychological theories.* Palo Alto, CA: Stanford University Press.

Hogg, M. A., & Hains, S. C. (2001). Intergroup relations and group solidarity: Effects of group identification and social beliefs on depersonalized attraction. In M. A. Hogg & D. Abrams (Eds.), *Intergroup relations: Essential readings.* New York: Psychology Press.

Holden, C. (2003). Deconstructing schizophrenia. *Science, 299,* 333-335.

Holden, C. (2007). Embryonic stem cells. Stem cell science advances as politics stall. *Science, 316,* 1825.

Holland, J. C., & Lewis, S. (2001). *The human side of cancer: Living with hope, coping with uncertainty.* New York: Quill.

Holleran, S., Mehl, M., & Levitt, S. (2009). Eavesdropping on social life: The accuracy of stranger ratings of daily behavior from thin slices of natural conversations. *Journal of Research in Personality, 43,* 660-672.

Hollingworth, H. L. (1943/1990). *Leta Stetter Hollingworth: A biography.* Boston: Anker.

Hollins, K. (2007). Consequences of antenatal mental health problems for child health and development. *Current Opinions on Obstetric Gynecology, 19,* 568-573.

Holloway, L. (2000, December 16). Chief of New York City schools plans to revamp bilingual study. *The New York Times,* p. A1.

Holmes, A. (2017). Drug addictions: New insight into causes, comorbidity and potential treatments. *Genes, Brain & Behavior, 16,* 5-7.

Holowka, S., & Petitto, L. A. (2002). Left hemisphere cerebral specialization for babies while babbling. *Science, 297,* 1515.

Holtyn, A. F., & Lattal, K. A. (2013). Briefly delayed reinforcement effects on variable "ratio and yoked" interval schedule performance. *Journal of the Experimental Analysis of Behavior, 100,* 198-210.

Holtz, J. (2011). *Applied clinical neuropsychology: An introduction.* New York: Springer Publishing Co.

Holzhauer, C. G., Wemm, S., & Wulfert, E. (2017). Distress tolerance and physiological reactivity to stress predict women's problematic alcohol use. *Experimental and Clinical Psychopharmacology, 25,* 156-165.

Hongchun, W., & Ming, L. (2006). About the research on suggestibility and false memory. *Psychological Science (China), 29,* 905-908.

Hoobler, J. M., Lemmon, G., & Wayne, S. J. (2011). Women's underrepresentation in upper management: New insights on a persistent problem. *Organizational Dynamics, 40,* 151-156.

Hopkins, W., & Cantalupo, C. (2008). Theoretical speculations on the evolutionary origins of hemispheric specialization. *Current Directions in Psychological Science, 17,* 233-237.

Hopper, J., & Lisak, D. (2014, December 9). Why rape and trauma survivors have fragmented and incomplete memories. *Time.* Accessed from http://time.com/3625414/rape-trauma-brain-memory/.

Hopwood, C., Newman, D., Donnellan, M., Markowitz, J., Grilo, C., Sanislow, C., . . . Morey, L. C. (2009). The stability of personality traits in individuals with borderline personality disorder. *Journal of Abnormal Psychology, 118,* 806-815.

Horesh, D., Solomon, Z., Zerach, G., & Ein-Dor, T. (2011). Delayed-onset PTSD among war veterans: The role of life events throughout the life cycle. *Social Psychiatry and Psychiatric Epidemiology, 46,* 863-870.

Hori, H., Teraishi, T., Sasayama, D., Matsuo, J., Kawamoto, Y., Kinoshita, Y., & Kunugi, H. (2011). Relationships between season of birth, schizotypy, temperament, character and neurocognition in a non-clinical population. *Psychiatry Research, 189,* 388-397.

Horiguchi, H., Winawer, J., Dougherty, R. F., & Wandell, B. A. (2013). Human trichromacy revisited. *Proceedings of the National Academy of Sciences, 110,* 199-106.

Horney, K. (1937). *Neurotic personality of our times.* New York: Norton.

Hornsveld, R. J., Zwets, A. J., Leenaars, E. M., Kraaimaat, F. W., Bout, R., Lagro-Janssen, T. M., & Kanters, T. (2018). Violent female offenders compared with violent male offenders on psychological determinants of aggressive behavior. *International Journal of*

Offender Therapy and Comparative Criminology, 62(2), 450-467. doi:10.1177/0306624X16648109.

Horton, C. L. (2011). Recall and recognition of dreams and waking events: A diary paradigm. *International Journal of Dream Research*, 4, 8-16.

Horton, K. D., Wilson, D. E., Vonk, J., Kirby, S. L., & Nielsen, T. (2005). Measuring automatic retrieval: A comparison of implicit memory, process dissociation, and speeded response procedures. *Acta Psychologica*, 119, 235-263.

Houghtalen, R. P., & Talbot, N. (2007). Dissociative disorders and cognitive disorders. In O. J. Z. Sahler & J. E. Carr (Eds.), *The behavioral sciences and health care* (2nd rev. and updated ed.). Ashland, OH: Hogrefe & Huber Publishers, 2007.

Hounkpatin, H. O., Wood, A. M., Boyce, C. J., & Dunn, G. (2015). An existential-humanistic view of personality change: Co-occurring changes with psychological well-being in a 10 year cohort study. *Social Indicators Research*, 121, 455-470.

Howe, M. L. (2011). The adaptive nature of memory and its illusions. *Psychological Science*, 20, 312-315.

Howell, E. F. (2011). *Understanding and treating dissociative identity disorder: A relational approach.* New York: Routledge/Taylor & Francis Group.

Howes, O. D., McCutcheon, R., Owen, M. J., & Murray, R. M. (2017). The role of genes, stress, and dopamine in the development of schizophrenia. *Biological Psychiatry*, 81(1), 9-20.

Howes, O., & Kapur, S. (2009). The dopamine hypothesis of schizophrenia: Version III–The final common pathway. *Schizophrenia Bulletin*, 35, 549-562.

Hu, E. B., Li, T. Y., Colditz, G. A., Willett, W. C., & Manson, J. E. (2003). Television watching and other sedentary behaviors in relation to risk of obesity and type 2 diabetes mellitus in women. *Journal of the American Medical Association*, 289, 1785-1791.

Huang, H., & Kashubeck-West, S. (2015). Exposure, agency, perceived threat, and guilt as predictors of posttraumatic stress disorder in veterans. *Journal of Counseling & Development*, 93, 3-13.

Huang, L. M., Sacchi, D. M., & Sherman, J. W. (2017). On the formation of context-based person impressions. *Journal of Experimental Social Psychology*, 68, 146-156.

Huang, S., Etkin, J., & Jin, L. (2017). How winning changes motivation in multiphase competitions. *Journal of Personality and Social Psychology*, 112, 813-837.

Hubbard, K., O'Neill, A., & Cheakalos, C. (1999, April 12). Out of control. *People*, pp. 52-72.

Hubel, D. H., & Wiesel, T. N. (2004). *Brain and visual perception: The story of a 25-year collaboration.* New York: Oxford University Press.

Hudson, J. I., Coit, C. E., Lalonde, J. K., & Pope, H. G. (2012). By how much will the proposed new DSM-5 criteria increase the prevalence of binge eating disorder? *International Journal of Easting Disorders*, 45, 139-141.

Hudson, W. (1960). Pictorial depth perception in subcultural groups in Africa. *Journal of Social Psychology*, 52, 183-208.

Hudspeth, A. J. (2000). Hearing. In E. R. Kandel, J. H. Schwartz, & T. M. Jessell (Eds.), *Principles of neural science* (4th ed.). New York: McGraw-Hill.

Huerta, M., Cortina, L. M., & Pang, J. S. (2006). Sex and power in the academy: Modeling sexual harassment in the lives of college women. *Personality and Social Psychology Bulletin*, 32, 616-628.

Huesmann, L., Dubow, E. F., & Boxer, P. (2011). The transmission of aggressiveness across generations: Biological, contextual, and social learning processes. In P. R. Shaver & M. Mikulincer (Eds.), *Human aggression and violence: Causes, manifestations, and consequences.* Washington, DC: American Psychological Association.

Hugdahl, K., Thomsen, T., & Ersland, L. (2006). Sex differences in visuo-spatial processing: An fMRI study of mental rotation. *Neuropsychologia*, 44, 1575-1583.

Hugenberg, K., & Sacco, D. (2008). Social categorization and stereotyping: How social categorization biases person perception and face memory. *Social and Personality Psychology Compass*, 2, 1052-1072.

Hull, C. L. (1943). *Principles of behavior.* New York: Appleton-Century-Crofts.

Human, L. J., & Biesanz, J. C. (2011). Through the looking glass clearly: Accuracy and assumed similarity in well-adjusted individuals' first impressions. *Journal of Personality and Social Psychology*, 100, 349-364.

Hummer, T. A., & McClintock, M. K. (2009). Putative human pheromone androstadienone attunes the mind specifically to emotional information. *Hormones and Behavior*, 55, 548-559.

Humphrey, N., Curran, A., & Morris, E. (2007). Emotional intelligence and education: A critical review. *Educational Psychology*, 27, 235-254.

Hunt, E. (1994). Problem solving. In R. J. Sternberg (Ed.), *Thinking and problem solving: Handbook of perception and cognition* (2nd ed.). San Diego, CA: Academic Press.

Hunt, J. S. (2017). Studying the effects of race, ethnicity, and culture on jury behavior. In M. B. Kovera & M. B. Kovera (Eds.), *The psychology of juries.* Washington, DC: American Psychological Association.

Hunt, J. S., Seifert, A. L., & Armenta, B. E. (2006). Stereotypes and prejudice as dynamic constructs: Reminders about the nature of inter-group bias from the hurricane Katrina relief efforts. *Analyses of Social Issues and Public Policy*, 6, 237-253.

Hunt, M. (1974). *Sexual behaviors in the 1970s.* New York: Dell.

Huprich, S. K., & Nelson, S. M. (2015). Advancing the assessment of personality pathology with the Cognitive-Affective Processing System. *Journal of Personality Assessment*, 97, 467-477.

Hurley, D. B., & Kwon, P. (2013). Savoring helps most when you have little: Interaction between savoring the moment and uplifts on positive affect and satisfaction with life. *Journal of Happiness Studies*, 14, 1261-1271.

Hurschler, M. A., Liem, F., Oechslin, M., Stämpfli, P., & Meyer, M. (2015). fMRI reveals lateralized pattern of brain activity modulated by the metrics of stimuli during auditory rhyme processing. *Brain and Language*, 14, 741-750.

Husain, O. (2015). From persecution to depression: A case of chronic depression–Associating the Rorschach, the TAT, and Winnicott. *Journal of Personality Assessment*, 97, 230-240.

Huston, J. P., Silva, M., Komorowski, M., Schulz, D., & Topic, B. (2013). Animal models of extinction-induced depression: Loss of reward and its consequences. *Neuroscience and Biobehavioral Reviews*, 37(9A), 2059-2070.

Hwang, E., Kim, H., Lee, S., Kim, M., Lee, S., Han, S., . . . Park, J. (2017). Loganin enhances long-term potentiation and recovers scopolamine-induced learning and memory impairments. *Physiology & Behavior*, 171, 243-248.

Hyde, J. S. (2005). The gender similarities hypothesis. *American Psychologist*, 50, 581-592.

Hyde, J. S., & Mertz, J. E. (2009). Gender, culture, and mathematics performance. *Proceedings of the National Academy of Sciences of the United States of America*, 106, 8801-8807.

Hyde, J. S., Lindberg, S. M., Linn, M. C., Ellis, A. B., & Williams, C. C. (2008). Gender similarities characterize math performance. *Science*, 321, 494-495

Hyde, J., Mezulis, A. H., & Abramson, L. Y. (2008). The ABCs of depression: Integrating affective, biological, and cognitive models to explain the emergence of the gender difference in depression. *Psychological Review*, 115, 291-313.

Hyman, B. T. (2011). Amyloid-dependent and amyloid-independent stages of Alzheimer disease. *Archives of Neurology*, 68, 1662-1664.

Høglend, P. P., Dahl, H. S., Hersoug, A. G., Lorentzen, S. S., & Perry, J. C. (2011). Long-term effects of transference interpretation in dynamic psychotherapy of personality disorders. *European Psychiatry*, 26, 419-424.

Ibbotson, P. , & Tomasello, M. (2016). Language in a new key. *Scientific American*, 315, 70-75.

Iglesias, A. (2005). Awake-alert hypnosis in the treatment of panic disorder: A case report. *American Journal of Clinical Hypnosis*, 47, 249-257.

Igo, S. E. (2006). Review of a telescope on society: Survey research and social science at the University of Michigan and beyond. *Journal of the History of the Behavioral Sciences*, 42, 95-96.

Iliceto, P., D'Antuono, L., Cassarà, L., Giacolini, T., Sabatello, U., & Candilera, G. (2017). Obsessive-compulsive tendencies, self/other perception, personality, and suicidal ideation in a non-clinical sample. *Psychiatric Quarterly*, 88, 411-422.

Imamura, M., & Nakamizo, S. (2006). An empirical test of formal equivalence between Emmert's Law and the size-distance invariance hypothesis. *Spanish Journal of Psychology*, 9(2), 295-299.

Innocenti, G. M. (2007). Subcortical regulation of cortical development: Some effects of early, selective deprivations. *Progressive Brain Research, 164,* 23–37.

Inoue, T., Abekawa, T., Nakagawa, S., Suzuki, K., Tanaka, T., Kitaichi, Y., . . . Koyama, T. (2011). Long-term naturalistic follow-up of lithium augmentation: Relevance to bipolarity. *Journal of Affective Disorders, 129,* 64–67.

Insel, T. R. (2010). Faulty circuits. *Scientific American, 302*(4), 44–51.

International Human Genome Sequencing Consortium. (2003). *International Consortium completes Human Genome Project.* Bethesda, MD: National Human Genome Research Institute.

Irwin, M. (2008). Human psychoneuroimmunology: 20 years of discovery. *Brain, Behavior, and Immunity, 22,* 129–139.

Irwin, R. R. (2006). Spiritual development in adulthood: Key concepts and models. In C. Hoare (Ed.), *Handbook of adult development and learning.* New York: Oxford University Press.

Isay, R. A. (1994). *Being homosexual: Gay men and their development.* Lanham, MD: Jason Aronson.

Isbell, L. M., & Tyler, J. M. (2003). Teaching students about in-group favoritism and the minimal groups paradigm. *Teaching of Psychology, 30,* 127–130.

Ishikawa, S., Okajima, I., Matsuoka, H., & Sakano, Y. (2007). Cognitive behavioural therapy for anxiety disorders in children and adolescents: A meta-analysis. *Child and Adolescent Mental Health, 12,* 164–172.

Itkowitz, C. (2016, June 1). Unwell and unashamed. *Washington Post.* Retrieved from http://www.washingtonpost.com/sf/local/wp/2016/06/01/unwell-and-unashamed.

Iversen, S., & Iversen, L. (2007). Dopamine: 50 years in perspective. *Trends in Neurosciences, 30,* 188–193.

Iverson, P., Kuhl, P. K., Reiko, A. Y., Diesch, E., Tohkura, Y., Ketterman, A., . . . Siebert, C. (2003). A perceptual interference account of acquisition difficulties for non-native phonemes. *Cognition, 87,* B47–B57.

Ivtzan, I., Gardner, H. E., Bernard, I., Sekhon, M., & Hart, R. (2013). Wellbeing through self-fulfilment: Examining developmental aspects of self-actualization. *The Humanistic Psychologist, 41,* 119–132.

Izard, C. E. (1994). Innate and universal facial expressions: Evidence from developmental and cross-cultural research. *Psychological Bulletin, 115,* 288–299.

Jablonka, E. (2017). The evolution of linguistic communication: Piagetian insights. In N. Budwig, E. Turiel, P. D. Zelazo, N. Budwig, E. Turiel, & P. D. Zelazo (Eds.), *New perspectives on human development.* New York: Cambridge University Press.

Jack, R. E., & Schyns, P. G. (2017). Toward a social psychophysics of face communication. *Annual Review of Psychology, 68,* 269–297.

Jackson, J. D. (2006). Trauma, attachment, and coping: Pathways to resilience. *Dissertation Abstracts International: Section B: The Sciences and Engineering, 67*(1-B), 547.

Jackson, M. L., Gunzelmann, G., Whitney, P., Hinson, J. M., Belenky, G., Rabat, A., . . . Van Dongen, H. P. (2013). Deconstructing and reconstructing cognitive performance in sleep deprivation. *Sleep Medicine Reviews, 17,* 215–225.

Jacob, B. C. (2011). Testosterone replacement therapy in males with erectile dysfunction. *Journal of Pharmacy Practice, 24,* 298–306.

Jacob, K. S. (2014). DSM-5 and culture: The need to move towards a shared model of care within a more equal patient-physican partnership. *Asian Journal of Psychiatry, 7,* 89–91.

Jacob, K. S., Kumar, P. S., Gayathri, K., Abraham, S., & Prince, M. J. (2007). The diagnosis of dementia in the community [Special issue: Focus on psychogeriatrics in the developing world]. *International Psychogeriatrics, 19,* 669–678.

Jacobs, A., & Richtel, M. (2017, September 18). How big business got Brazil hooked on junk foods. *The New York Times.* Accessed from https://www.nytimes.com/interactive/2017/09/16/health/brazil-obesity-nestle.html?emc=edit_ta_20170917&nl=top-stories&nlid=15802952&ref=headline&_r=0.

Jacobs, E. G., Kroenke, C., Lin, J., Epel, E. S., Kenna, H. A., Blackburn, E. H., . . .Rasgon, N. L. (2013). Accelerated cell aging in female APOE-4 carriers: Implications for hormone therapy use. *Plos ONE, 8,* 103–111.

Jacobs, J. A., & Gerson, K. (2004). *The time divide: Work, family, and gender inequality.* Cambridge, MA: Harvard University Press.

Jacobs, M., Roesch, S., Wonderlich, S., Crosby, R., Thornton, L., Wilfley, D., . . . Bulik, C. M. (2009). Anorexia nervosa trios: Behavioral profiles of individuals with anorexia nervosa and their parents. *Psychological Medicine, 39,* 451–461.

Jacobson, S. W., Stanton, M. E., Dodge, N. C., Pienaar, M., Fuller, D. S., Molteno, C. D., . . . Jacobson, J. L. (2011). Impaired delay and trace eyeblink conditioning in school-age children with fetal alcohol syndrome. *Alcoholism: Clinical and Experimental Research, 35,* 250–264.

Jacoby, J., & Schwartz, G. W. (2017). Three small-receptive-field ganglion cells in the mouse retina are distinctly tuned to size, speed, and object motion. *Journal of Neuroscience, 37,* 610–625.

Jacoby, L. L., & Wahlheim, C. N. (2013). On the importance of looking back: The role of recursive reminders in recency judgments and cued recall. *Memory & Cognition, 41,* 625–637.

Jacoby, L. L., Bishara, A. J., Hessels, S., & Hughes, A. (2007). Probabilistic retroactive interference: The role of accessibility bias in interference effects. *Journal of Experimental Psychology: General, 136,* 200–216.

Jacoby-Senghor, D. S., Sinclair, S., & Smith, C. T. (2015). When bias binds: Effect of implicit outgroup bias on ingroup affiliation. *Journal of Personality and Social Psychology, 109*(3), 415–433.

James, W. (1890). *The principles of psychology.* New York: Holt.

James, W. (2015). The principles of psychology (excerpt). In T. Alter & Y. Nagasawa (Eds.), *Consciousness in the physical world: Perspectives on Russellian monism.* New York: Oxford University Press.

Jamieson, G. A. (2007). *Hypnosis and conscious states: The cognitive neuroscience perspective.* New York: Oxford University Press.

Jamison, K. R. (1995). *An unquiet mind: A memoir of moods and madness.* New York: Knopf.

Jang, H., Reeve, J., Ryan, R. M., & Kim, A. (2009). Can self-determination theory explain what underlies the productive, satisfying learning experiences of collectivistically oriented Korean students? *Journal of Educational Psychology, 101,* pp. 644–661.

Jannini, E. A., McMahon, C. G., & Waldinger, M. D. (2013). *Premature ejaculation: From etiology to diagnosis and treatment.* New York: Springer-Verlag Publishing.

Jarlais, D. C. D., Arasteh, K., & Perlis, T. (2007). The transition from injection to non-injection drug use: Long-term outcomes among heroin and cocaine users in New York City. *Addiction, 102,* 778–785.

Jarrett, S. (2015). The meaning of "community" in the lives of people with intellectual disabilities: An historical perspective. *International Journal of Developmental Disabilities, 61,* 107–112.

Jarrold, C., & Tam, H. (2011). Rehearsal and the development of working memory. In P. Barrouillet & V. Gaillard (Eds.), *Cognitive development and working memory: A dialogue between neo-Piagetian theories and cognitive approaches.* New York: Psychology Press.

Jeffery, A. J. (2015). Two behavioral hypotheses for the evolution of male homosexuality in humans. In T. K. Shackelford & R. D. Hansen (Eds.), *The evolution of sexuality.* Cham, Switzerland: Springer International Publishing.

Jenkins, S. R. (1994). Need for power and women's careers over 14 years: Structural power, job satisfaction, and motive change. *Journal of Personality and Social Psychology, 66,* 155–165.

Jennings, D. J., Alonso, E., Mondragón, E., Franssen, M., & Bonardi, C. (2013). The effect of stimulus distribution form on the acquisition and rate of conditioned responding: Implications for theory. *Journal of Experimental Psychology: Animal Behavior Processes, 39,* 233–248.

Jensen, A. R. (2002). Galton's legacy to research on intelligence. *Journal of Biosocial Science, 34,* 145–172.

Jensen, M. P., & Patterson, D. R. (2014). Hypnotic approaches for chronic pain management: Clinical implications of recent research findings. *American Psychologist, 69,* 167–177.

Jensen, M. P., & Turk, D. C. (2014). Contributions of psychology to the understanding and treatment of people with chronic pain: Why it matters to ALL psychologists. *American Psychologist, 69,* 105–118.

Jequier, E. (2002). Pathways to obesity. *International Journal of Obesity and Related Metabolic Disorders, 26*, S12-S17.

Jia, C., & Hegg, C. C. (2015). Effect of IP3R3 and NPY on age-related declines in olfactory stem cell proliferation. *Neurobiology of Aging, 36*, 1045-1056.

Jia, H., Zack, M. M., & Thompson, W. W. (2011). State quality-adjusted life expectancy for U.S. adults from 1993 to 2008. *Quality of Life Research: An International Journal of Quality of Life Aspects of Treatment, Care & Rehabilitation, 20*, 853-863.

Jiang, S., Miao, B., & Chen, Y. (2017). Prolonged duration of isoflurane anesthesia impairs spatial recognition memory through the activation of JNK1/2 in the hippocampus of mice. *Neuroreport: For Rapid Communication of Neuroscience Research, 28*, 386-390.

Jin, B., & Kim, J. (2017). Grit, basic needs satisfaction, and subjective well-being. *Journal of Individual Differences, 38*(1), 29-35.

Joe, G. W., Flynn, P. M., & Broome, K. M. (2007). Patterns of drug use and expectations in methadone patients. *Addictive Behaviors, 32*, 1640-1656.

Joel, D., & McCarthy, M.M. (2017). Incorporating sex as a biological variable in neuropsychiatric research: Where are we now and where should we be. *Neuropsychopharmacology, 42*, 379-385.

John-Steiner, V., & Mahn, H. (2003). Sociocultural contexts for teaching and learning. In W. M. Reynolds & G. E. Miller (Eds.), *Handbook of psychology: Educational psychology* (Vol. 7). New York: Wiley.

Johnsdotter, S., & Essén, B. (2005). It is only a tradition: Making sense of Swedish Somalis' narratives of female circumcision and avoiding submission to hegemonic political discourse. *Critical Social Policy, 25*, 577-589.

Johnson, C. Y. (2014, January 17). Finding a way to erase harmful memories. *Boston Globe*, p. 1.

Johnson, G. (1997, July 29). To test a powerful computer, play an ancient game. *The New York Times*, p. C3.

Johnson, G. B. (2000). *The Living World* (p. 600). Boston: McGraw-Hill.

Johnson, H. D. (2004). Gender, grade and relationship differences in emotional closeness within adolescent friendships. *Adolescence, 39*, 243-255.

Johnson, R., Stewart, C., & Bachman, C. (2015). What drives students to complete online courses? What drives faculty to teach online? Validating a measure of motivation orientation in university students and faculty. *Interactive Learning Environments, 23*, 528-543.

Johnson, W., & Deary, I. J. (2011). Placing inspection time, reaction time, and perceptual speed in the broader context of cognitive ability: The VPR model in the Lothian Birth Cohort 1936. *Intelligence, 39*, 405-417.

Johnson-Laird, P. N. (2006). *How we reason.* Oxford, England: Oxford University Press.

Johnston, E., & Olson, L. (2015). *The feeling brain: The biology and psychology of emotions.* New York: W. W. Norton & Co.

Johnston, L. D., Miech, R. A., O'Malley, P. M., Bachman, J. G., & Schulenberg, J. E. (2016, December 13). Teen use of any illicit drug other than marijuana at new low, same true for alcohol. University of Michigan News Service. Accessed from http://www.monitoring-thefuture.org.

Johnston, L. D., O'Malley, P. M., Bachman, J. G., & Schulenberg, J. E. (2009). *Monitoring the future–National results on adolescent drug use; overview of key findings, 2008* (NIH Publication No. 09-7401). Bethesda, MD: National Institute on Drug Abuse.

Johnston, M. V. (2004). Clinical disorders of brain plasticity. *Brain and Development, 26*, 73-80.

Jokela, M., Pekkarinen, T., Sarvimäki, M., Terviö, M., & Uusitalo, R. (2017). Secular rise in economically valuable personality traits. *PNAS Proceedings of the National Academy of Sciences of the United States of America, 114*, 6527-6532.

Jones, A. L. (2006). The contemporary psychoanalyst: Karen Horney's theory applied in today's culture. *PsycCRITIQUES, 51*, 127-134.

Jones, D. (2010). A WEIRD view of human nature skews psychologists' studies. *Science, 328*, 1627.

Jones, J. E., & Corp, E. S. (2003). Effect of naltrexone on food intake and body weight in Syrian hamsters depends on metabolic status. *Physiology and Behavior, 78*, 67-72.

Jones, J. M. (2007). Exposure to chronic community violence: Resilience in African American children. *Journal of Black Psychology, 33*, 125-149.

Jones, M., Kass, A. E., Trockel, M., Glass, A. I., Wilfley, D. E., & Taylor, C. B. (2014). A population-wide screening and tailored intervention platform for eating disorders on college campuses: The Healthy Body Image program. *Journal of American College Health, 62*, 351-356.

Jones, R. K., Darroch, J. E., & Singh, S. (2005). Religious differentials in the sexual and reproductive behaviors of young women in the United States. *Journal of Adolescent Health, 36*, 279-288.

Jones, S. W., Weitlauf, J., Danhauer, S. C., Qi, L., Zaslavsky, O., Wassertheil-Smoller, S., . . . LaCroix, A. Z. (2017). Prospective data from the Women's Health Initiative on depressive symptoms, stress, and inflammation. *Journal of Health Psychology, 22*, 457-464.

Jordan-Young, R. M. (2010). *Brain storm: The flaws in the science of sex differences.* Cambridge, MA: Harvard University Press.

Jost, J. T., Kay, A. C., & Thorisdottir, H. (2009). *Social and psychological bases of ideology and system justification.* New York: Oxford University Press.

Jovanović, D., Stanojević, P., & Stanojević, D. (2011). Motives for, and attitudes about, driving-related anger and aggressive driving. *Social Behavior and Personality, 39*, 755-764.

Joyce, J. (1934). *Ulysses.* New York: Random House.

Julien, R. M. (2001). *A primer of drug action* (9th ed.). New York: Freeman.

Jung, C. G. (1961). *Freud and psychoanalysis.* New York: Pantheon.

Jung, J. (2002). *Psychology of alcohol and other drugs: A research perspective.* Thousand Oaks, CA: Sage.

Jung, J., & Chang, D. (2017). Types of creativity–Fostering multiple intelligences in design convergence talents. *Thinking Skills and Creativity, 23*, 101-111.

Juster, E. T., Ono, H., & Stafford, E. (2002). *Report on housework and division of labor.* Ann Arbor, MI: Institute for Social Research.

Justman, S. (2011). From medicine to psychotherapy: The placebo effect. *History of the Human Sciences, 24*, 95-107.

Kadosh, R., Henik, A., & Walsh, V. (2009). Synaesthesia: Learned or lost? *Developmental Science, 12*, 484-491.

Kahn, K. B., Lee, J. K., Renauer, B., Henning, K. R., & Stewart, G. (2017). The effects of perceived phenotypic racial stereotypicality and social identity threat on racial minorities' attitudes about police. *Journal of Social Psychology, 157*, 416-428.

Kahn, R. E., Frick, P. J., Youngstrom, E. A., Kogos Youngstrom, J., Feeny, N. C., & Findling, R. L. (2013). Distinguishing primary and secondary variants of callous-unemotional traits among adolescents in a clinic-referred sample. *Psychological Assessment, 25*, 966-978.

Kai-hsiang, Y. and Wu, L. (2017, July 10). *13-year-old Taiwanese student becomes youngest admitted by NYU.* Retrieved from http://focustaiwan.tw/news/aedu/201707100015.aspx.

Kaiser Family Foundation. (2014, April). *The HIV/AIDS epidemic in the United States.* Menlo Park, CA: Kaiser Family Foundation.

Kaiser, B. L., Thomas, G. R., & Bowers, B. J. (2017). A case study of engaging hard-to-reach participants in the research process: Community Advisors on Research Design and Strategies (CARDS)®. *Research in Nursing & Health, 40*, 70-79.

Kalanthroff, E., Anholt, G. E., Keren, R., & Henik, A. (2013). What should I (not) do? Control over irrelevant tasks in obsessive-compulsive disorder patients. *Clinical Neuropsychiatry: Journal of Treatment Evaluation, 10*, Suppl. 1, 61-64.

Kalb, C. (2003, May 19). Taking a new look at pain. *Newsweek*, pp. 51-52.

Kalka, D. (2016). Quality of life and proactive coping with stress in a group of middle adulthood women with type 2 diabetes. *Polish Psychological Bulletin, 47*, 327-337.

Kaller, C. P., Unterrainer, J. M., Rahm, B., & Halsband, U. (2004). The impact of problem structure on planning: Insights from the Tower of London task. *Cognitive Brain Research, 20*, 462-472.

Kalodner, C. R. (2011). Cognitive-behavioral theories. In D. Capuzzi & D. R. Gross (Eds.), *Counseling and psychotherapy* (5th ed.). Alexandria, VA: American Counseling Association.

Kamens, S. R. (2011). On the proposed sexual and gender identity diagnoses for DSM-5: History and controversies. *Humanistic Psychologist, 39*, 37-59.

Kamimori, G. H., McLellan, T. M., Tate, C. M., Voss, D. M., Niro, P., & Lieberman, H. R. (2015). Caffeine improves reaction time, vigilance and logical reasoning during extended periods with restricted opportunities for sleep. *Psychopharmacology, 232*, 2031-2042.

Kandler, C., Riemann, R., & Angleitner, A. (2013). Patterns and sources of continuity and change of energetic and temporal aspects of temperament in adulthood: A longitudinal twin study of self- and peer reports. *Developmental Psychology, 49*, 1739-1753.

Kane, J. M., Robinson, D. G., Schooler, N. R., Mueser, K. T., Penn, D. L., Rosenheck, R. A., . . . Heinssen, R. K. (2016). Comprehensive versus usual community care for first-episode psychosis: 2-year outcomes from the NIMH RAISE Early Treatment Program. *American Journal of Psychiatry, 173*, 362-372.

Kanoski, S. E., Hayes, M. R., Greenwald, H. S., Fortin, S. M., Gianessi, C. A., Gilbert, J. R., . . . Grill, H. J. (2011). Hippocampal leptin signaling reduces food intake and modulates food-related memory processing. *Neuropsychopharmacology, 36*, 1859-1870.

Kantrowitz, B., & Underwood, A. (2007, June 25). The teen drinking dilemma. *Newsweek*, pp. 36-37.

Kao, D. (2011). Message sidedness in advertising: The moderating roles of need for cognition and time pressure in persuasion. *Scandinavian Journal of Psychology, 52*, 329-340.

Kaposi, D. (2017). The resistance experiments: Morality, authority and obedience in Stanley Milgram's account. *Journal for the Theory of Social Behaviour*. Accessed from http://onlinelibrary.wiley.com/doi/10.1111/jtsb.12137/abstract.

Karama, S., Ad-Dab'bagh, Y., Haier, R. J., Deary, I. J., Lyttelton, O. C., Lepage, C., . . . Evans, A. C. (2009). Positive association between cognitive ability and cortical thickness in a representative US sample of healthy 6 to 18 year-olds. *Brain Development Cooperative Group; Intelligence, 37*, 145-155.

Karaszewski, B. (2008). Sub-neocortical brain: A mechanical tool for creative generation? *Trends in Cognitive Sciences, 12*, 171-172.

Karlson, C. W., Gallagher, M. W., Olson, C. A., & Hamilton, N. A. (2013). Insomnia symptoms and well-being: Longitudinal follow-up. *Health Psychology, 32*, 311-319.

Kasemsap, K. (2017). Mastering cognitive neuroscience and social neuroscience perspectives in the information age. In M. A. Dos Santos (Ed.), *Applying neuroscience to business practice*. Hershey, PA: Business Science Reference/IGI Global.

Kasof, J. (2009). Cultural variation in seasonal depression: Cross-national differences in winter versus summer patterns of seasonal affective disorder. *Journal of Affective Disorders, 115*, 79-86.

Kassam, K. S., Gilbert, D. T., Swencionis, J. K., & Wilson, T. D. (2009). Misconceptions of memory: The Scooter Libby effect. *Psychological Science, 20*, 551-552.

Kassel, J. D., Evatt, D. P., Greenstein, J. E., Wardle, M. C., Yates, M. C., & Veilleux, J. C. (2007). The acute effects of nicotine on positive and negative affect in adolescent smokers. *Journal of Abnormal Psychology, 116*, 543-553.

Kasser, T. (2011). Cultural values and the well-being of future generations: A cross-national study. *Journal of Cross-Cultural Psychology, 42*, 206-215.

Kassin, S. M. (2017). The killing of Kitty Genovese: What else does this case tell us? *Perspectives on Psychological Science, 12*, 374-381.

Kassin, S. M., Redlich, A. D., Alceste, F., & Luke, T. J. (2018). On the general acceptance of confessions research: Opinions of the scientific community. *American Psychologist, 73*, 63-80.

Kato, K., & Pedersen, N. L. (2005). Personality and coping: A study of twins reared apart and twins reared together. *Behavior Genetics, 35*, 147-158.

Kato, N. (2009). Neurophysiological mechanisms of electroconvulsive therapy for depression. *Neuroscience Research, 64*, 3-11.

Katsiyannis, A., Zhang, D., & Woodruff, N. (2005). Transition supports to students with mental retardation: An examination of data from the national longitudinal transition study 2. *Education and Training in Developmental Disabilities, 40*, 109-116.

Katz, J. (2017, June 15). Drug deaths in America are rising faster than ever. *The New York Times*. Accessed from https://www.nytimes.com/interactive/2017/06/05/upshot/opioid-epidemic-drug-overdose-deaths-are-rising-faster-than-ever.html.

Katz, M. (2001). The implications of revising Freud's empiricism for drive theory. *Psychoanalysis and Contemporary Thought, 24*, 253-272.

Kaufman, A., Johnson, C., & Liu, X. (2008). A CHC theory-based analysis of age differences on cognitive abilities and academic skills at ages 22 to 90 years. *Journal of Psychoeducational Assessment, 26*, 350-381.

Kaufman, J. C., & Baer, J. (2006). *Creativity and reason in cognitive development*. New York: Cambridge University Press.

Kaufman, J. C., & Plucker, J. A. (2011). Intelligence and creativity. In R. J. Sternberg & S. Kaufman (Eds.), *The Cambridge handbook of intelligence*. New York: Cambridge University Press.

Kaufman, J. C., Kaufman, S., & Plucker, J. A. (2013). Contemporary theories of intelligence. In D. Reisberg (Ed.), *The Oxford handbook of cognitive psychology*. New York: Oxford University Press.

Kauten, R. L., Lui, J. L., Stary, A. K., & Barry, C. T. (2015). "Purging my friends list. Good luck making the cut": Perceptions of narcissism on Facebook. *Computers in Human Behavior, 51*, 244-254.

Kawakami, N., & Miura, E. (2015). Image or real? Altering the mental imagery of subliminal stimuli differentiates explicit and implicit attitudes. *Imagination, Cognition and Personality, 34*, 259-269.

Kawasaki, C., Nugent, J. K., Miyashita, H., Miyahara, H., & Brazelton, T. B. (1994). The cultural organization of infants' sleep [Special issue: Environments of birth and infancy]. *Children's Environment, 11*, 135-141.

Kawashima, H., Izaki, Y., & Grace, A. A. (2006). Cooperativity between hippocampal-prefrontal short-term plasticity through associative long-term potentiation. *Brain Research, 1109*, 37-44.

Kazantseva, A., Gaysina, D., Kutlumbetova, Y., Kanzafarova, R., Malykh, S., Lobaskova, M., . . . Khusnutdinova, E. (2015). Brain derived neurotrophic factor gene (BDNF) and personality traits: The modifying effect of season of birth and sex. *Progress in Neuro-Psychopharmacology & Biological Psychiatry, 56*, 58-65.

Kazar, D. B. (2006). Forensic psychology: Did we leave anything out? *PsycCRITIQUES, 51*, 88-97.

Kazdin, A. (2008). Evidence-based treatment and practice: New opportunities to bridge clinical research and practice, enhance the knowledge base, and improve patient care. *American Psychologist, 63*, 146-159.

Keating, D. P., & Clark, L. V. (1980). Development of physical and social reasoning in adolescence. *Developmental Psychology, 16*, 23-30.

Keer, M., van den Putte, B., Neijens, P., & de Wit, J. (2013). The influence of affective and cognitive arguments on message judgement and attitude change: The moderating effects of meta-bases and structural bases. *Psychology & Health, 28*, 895-908.

Keillor, J. M., Barrett, A. M., Crucian, G. P., Kortenkamp, S., & Heilman, K. M. (2002). Emotional experience and perception in the absence of facial feedback. *Journal of the International Neuropsychological Society, 8*, 130-135.

Keller, J. (2007). Stereotype threat in classroom settings: The interactive effect of domain identification, task difficulty and stereotype threat on female students' math performance. *British Journal of Educational Psychology, 77*, 323-338.

Kelley, H. (1950). The warm-cold variable in first impressions of persons. *Journal of Personality and Social Psychology, 18*, 431-439.

Kelly, J. B. (2000). Children's adjustment in conflicted marriage and divorce: A decade review of research. *Journal of the American Academy of Child & Adolescent Psychiatry, 39*, 963-973.

Kelly, J. F., Hoeppner, B., Stout, R. L., & Pagano, M. (2012). Determining the relative importance of the mechanisms of behavior change within Alcoholics Anonymous: A multiple mediator analysis. *Addiction, 107*, 289-299.

Keltikangas-Järvinen, L., Räikkönen, K., Ekelund, J., & Peltonen, L. (2004). Nature and nurture in novelty seeking. *Molecular Psychiatry, 9*, 308-311.

Kempermann, G. (2011). Seven principles in the regulation of adult neurogenesis. *European Journal of Neuroscience, 33*, 1018-1024.

Kemps, E., & Tiggemann, M. (2007). Reducing the vividness and emotional impact of distressing autobiographical memories: The importance of modality-specific interference. *Memory, 15,* 412-422.

Kendler, K. S., & Schaffner, K. F. (2011). The dopamine hypothesis of schizophrenia: An historical and philosophical analysis. *Philosophy, Psychiatry, & Psychology, 18,* 41-63.

Kendler, K. S., Aggen, S. H., Gillespie, N., Neale, M. C., Knudsen, G. P., Krueger, R. F., . . . Reichborn-Kjennerud, T. (2017). The genetic and environmental sources of resemblance between normative personality and personality disorder traits. *Journal of Personality Disorders, 31,* 193-207.

Kendler, K., Halberstadt, L., Butera, F., Myers, J., Bouchard, T., & Ekman, P. (2008). The similarity of facial expressions in response to emotion-inducing films in reared-apart twins. *Psychological Medicine, 38*(10), 1475-1483.

Kenett, Y. N., Levi, E., Anaki, D., & Faust, M. (2017). The semantic distance task: Quantifying semantic distance with semantic network path length. *Journal of Experimental Psychology: Learning, Memory, and Cognition, 43,* 1470-1489.

Kennedy, C. E., Moore, P. J., Peterson, R. A., Katzman, M. A., Vermani, M., & Charmak, W. D. (2011). What makes people anxious about pain? How personality and perception combine to determine pain anxiety responses in clinical and non-clinical populations. *Anxiety, Stress & Coping: An International Journal, 24,* 179-200.

Kennedy, D. O., & Haskell, C. F. (2011). Cerebral blood flow and behavioural effects of caffeine in habitual and non-habitual consumers of caffeine: A near infrared spectroscopy study. *Biological Psychology, 86,* 296-305.

Kennedy, J. E. (2004). A proposal and challenge for proponents and skeptics of psi. *Journal of Parapsychology, 68,* 157-167.

Kennison, S. M., & Bowers, J. (2011). Illustrating brain lateralisation in a naturalistic observation of cell-phone use. *Psychology Learning & Teaching, 10,* 46-51.

Keppler, J. (2017, May 3). Shedding light on the fundamental mechanism underlying hypnotic analgesia. *Annals of Palliative Medicine,* pii: apm.2017.04.03. doi: 10.21037/apm.2017.04.03.

Kertz, S. J., Koran, J., Stevens, K. T., & Björgvinsson, T. (2015). Repetitive negative thinking predicts depression and anxiety symptom improvement during brief cognitive behavioral therapy. *Behaviour Research and Therapy, 68,* 54-63.

Keränen, T., Halkoaho, A., Itkonen, E., & Pietilä, A. (2015). Placebo-controlled clinical trials: How trial documents justify the use of randomisation and placebo. *BMC Medical Ethics, 16,* 88-96.

Kesebir, P., & Diener, E. (2008). In pursuit of happiness: Empirical answers to philosophical questions. *Perspectives on Psychological Science, 3,* 117-125.

Keshavarz, M. (2017). Glial cells as key elements in the pathophysiology and treatment of bipolar disorder. *Acta Neuropsychiatrica, 29,* 140-152.

Kessler, R. C., & Wang, P. S. (2008). The descriptive epidemiology of commonly occurring mental disorders in the United States. *Annual Review of Public Health, 29,* 115-129.

Ketisch, T., & Jones, R. A. (2013). Review of "ADHD diagnosis & management." *American Journal of Family Therapy, 41,* 272-274.

Key, W. B. (2003). Subliminal sexuality: The fountainhead for America's obsession. In T. Reichert & J. Lambaiase (Eds.), *Sex in advertising: Perspectives on the erotic appeal. LEA's communication series.* Mahwah, NJ: Lawrence Erlbaum.

Khazaal, Y., Chatton, A., Claeys, F., Ribordy, F., Zullino, D., & Cabanac, M. (2008). Antipsychotic drug and body weight set-point. *Physiology & Behavior, 95,* 157-160.

Khedr, E. M., Omran, E. A., Ismail, N. M., El-Hammady, D. H., Goma, S. H., Kotb, H., . . . Ahmed, G. A. (2017). Effects of transcranial direct current stimulation on pain, mood and serum endorphin level in the treatment of fibromyalgia: A double blinded, randomized clinical trial. *Brain Stimulation, 10*(5), 893-890.

Kidd, E., & Lum, J. (2008). Sex differences in past tense overregularization. *Developmental Science, 11,* 882-889.

Kiecolt, J. K. (2003). Satisfaction with work and family life: No evidence of a cultural reversal. *Journal of Marriage and Family, 65,* 23-35.

Kihlstrom, J. F. (2005a). Dissociative disorders. *Annual Review of Clinical Psychology, 1,* 227-253.

Kihlstrom, J. F. (2005b). Is hypnosis an altered state of consciousness or what? Comment. *Contemporary Hypnosis, 22,* 34-38.

Kim, D. R., Pesiridou, A., & O'Reardon, J. P. (2009). Transcranial magnetic stimulation in the treatment of psychiatric disorders. *Current Psychiatry Reports, 11,* 447-452.

Kim, H., Clark, D., & Dionne, R. (2009). Genetic contributions to clinical pain and analgesia: Avoiding pitfalls in genetic research. *The Journal of Pain, 10,* 663-693.

Kim, N. (2008). The moon illusion and the size-distance paradox. In S. Cummins-Sebree, M. A. Riley, & K. Shockley (Eds.), *Studies in perception and action IX: Fourteenth International Conference on Perception and Action.* Mahwah, NJ: Lawrence Erlbaum Associates.

Kim, S., Polari, A., Melville, F., Moller, B., Kim, J., Amminger, P., & . . . Nelson, B. (2017). Are current labeling terms suitable for people who are at risk of psychosis? *Schizophrenia Research, 188,* 172-177.

Kim, Y., & Yoon, H. (2017). Common and distinct brain networks underlying panic and social anxiety disorders. *Progress In Neuro-Psychopharmacology & Biological Psychiatry.* Accessed from https://www.ncbi.nlm.nih.gov/pubmed/28642079.

Kim-Cohen, J., Caspi, A., & Moffitt, T. E. (2003). Prior juvenile diagnoses in adults with mental disorder: Developmental follow-back of a prospective-longitudinal cohort. *Archives of General Psychiatry, 60,* 709-717.

Kim-Cohen, J., Moffitt, T. E., Taylor, A., Pawlby, S. J., & Caspi, A. (2005). Maternal depression and children's antisocial behavior: Nature and nurture effects. *Archives of General Psychiatry, 62,* 173-181.

Kimbrel, N. A. (2007). A model of the development and maintenance of generalized social phobia. *Clinical Psychological Review, 8,* 69-75.

King-Casas, B., Sharp, C., Lomax-Bream, L., Lohrenz, T., Fonagy, P., & Montague, P. R. (2008). The rupture and repair of cooperation in borderline personality disorder. *Science, 321,* 806-810.

Kinsey, A. C., Pomeroy, W. B., & Martin, C. E. (1948). *Sexual behavior in the human male.* Philadelphia: Saunders.

Kinsey, A. C., Pomeroy, W. B., Martin, C. E., & Gebhard, P. H. (1953). *Sexual behavior in the human female.* Philadelphia: Saunders.

Kirk, E. P., Jacobsen, D. J., Gibson, C., Hill, J. O., & Donnelly, J. E. (2003). Time course for changes in aerobic capacity and body composition in overweight men and women in response to long-term exercise: The Midwest exercise trial (MET). *International Journal of Obesity, 27,* 912-919.

Kirsch, I., Lynn, S. J., Vigorito, M., & Miller, R. R. (2004). The role of cognition in classical and operant conditioning. *Journal of Clinical Psychology, 60,* 369-392.

Kisely, S., Chang, A., Crowe, J., Galletly, C., Jenkins, P., Loi, S., . . . Macfarlane, S. (2015). Getting started in research: Systematic reviews and meta-analyses. *Australasian Psychiatry, 23,* 16-21.

Kish, S., Fitzmaurice, P., Boileau, I., Schmunk, G., Ang, L., Furukawa, Y., . . . Tong, J. (2009). Brain serotonin transporter in human methamphetamine users. *Psychopharmacology, 202,* 649-661.

Kitayama, S. (2017). Journal of Personality and Social Psychology: Attitudes and social cognition. *Journal of Personality and Social Psychology, 112,* 357-360.

Kivipelto, M. & Hakansson, K. (2017). A rare success against Alzheimer's. *Scientific American, 316,* 32-37.

Kivlighan, D. M., Goldberg, S. B., Abbas, M., Pace, B. T., Yulish, N. E., Thomas, J. G., . . . Wampold, B. E. (2015). The enduring effects of psychodynamic treatments vis-à-vis alternative treatments: A multilevel longitudinal meta-analysis. *Clinical Psychology Review, 40,* 1-14.

Kizilirmak, J. M., Galvao Gomes da Silva, J., Imamoglu, F., & Richardson-Klavehn, A. (2015). Generation and the subjective feeling of "aha!" are independently related to learning from insight. *Psychological Research, 80*(6), 1059-1074.

Klein, K. M., Apple, K. J., & Kahn, A. S. (2011). Attributions of blame and responsibility in sexual harassment: Reexamining a psychological model. *Law and Human Behavior, 35,* 92-103.

Kleinman, A. (1996). How is culture important for DSM-IV? In J. E Mezzich, A. Kleinman, H.

Fabrega, Jr., & D. L. Parron (Eds.), *Culture and psychiatric diagnosis: A DSM-IV perspective.* Washington, DC: American Psychiatric Press.

Kleinplatz, P. J., Moser, C., & Lev, A. (2013). Sex and gender identity disorders. In G. Stricker, T. A. Widiger, & I. B. Weiner (Eds.), *Handbook of psychology, Vol. 8: Clinical psychology* (2nd ed.). Hoboken, NJ: John Wiley & Sons Inc.

Kluck, A. (2008). Family factors in the development of disordered eating: Integrating dynamic and behavioral explanations. *Eating Behaviors, 9,* 471-483.

Kluger, J. (2001, April 2). Fear not! *Time,* pp. 51-62.

Kluger, J. (2006, December 4). Why we worry about the things we shouldn't and ignore the things we should. *Time,* pp. 64-71.

Kluger, J. (2013, July 29). The power of the bilingual brain. *Time,* 42-47.

Knight, S. C., & Meyer, R. G. (2007). Forensic hypnosis. In A. M. Goldstein (Ed.), *Forensic psychology: Emerging topics and expanding roles.* Hoboken, NJ: John Wiley & Sons.

Knoblich, G., & Sebanz, N. (2006). The social nature of perception and action. *Current Directions in Psychological Science, 15,* 99-111.

Kobayashi, F., Schallert, D. L., & Ogren, H. A. (2003). Japanese and American folk vocabularies for emotions. *Journal of Social Psychology, 143,* 451-478.

Koch, C., & Greenfield, S. (2007). How does consciousness happen? *Scientific American, 297*(4), 76-83.

Koch, J. (2003). Gender issues in the classroom. In W. M. Reynolds & G. E. Miller (Eds.), *Handbook of psychology: Educational psychology* (Vol. 7). New York: Wiley.

Kochli, D. E., Thompson, E. C., Fricke, E. A., Postle, A. F., & Quinn, J. J. (2015). The amygdala is critical for trace, delay, and contextual fear conditioning. *Learning & Memory, 22,* 92-100.

Kogstad, R. E., Ekeland, T. J., & Hummelvoll, J. K. (2011). In defence of a humanistic approach to mental health care: Recovery processes investigated with the help of clients' narratives on turning points and processes of gradual change. *Journal of Psychiatric and Mental Health Nursing, 18,* 479-486.

Koh, E., Stauss, K., Coustaut, C., & Forrest, C. (2017). Generational impact of single-parent scholarships: Educational achievement of children in single-parent families. *Journal of Family Issues, 38,* 607-632.

Kohlberg, L. (1984). *The psychology of moral development: Essays on moral development* (Vol. 2). San Francisco: Harper & Row.

Kohlberg, L., & Ryncarz, R. A. (1990). Beyond justice reasoning: Moral development and consideration of a seventh stage. In C. N. Alexander & E. J. Langer (Eds.), *Higher stages of human development: Perspectives on adult growth.* New York: Oxford University Press.

Kojima, M., & Kangawa, K. (2008). Structure and function of ghrelin. *Results & Problems in Cell Differentiation, 46,* 89-115.

Kolata, G. (2002, December 2). With no answers on risks, steroid users still say "yes." *The New York Times,* p. 1A.

Kolb, B., Gibb, R., & Robinson, T. E. (2003). Brain plasticity and behavior. *Current Directions in Psychological Science, 12,* 1-5.

Komarovskaya, I., Loper, A., Warren, J., & Jackson, S. (2011). Exploring gender differences in trauma exposure and the emergence of symptoms of PTSD among incarcerated men and women. *Journal of Forensic Psychiatry & Psychology, 22,* 395-410.

Koper, R. J., & Jaasma, M. A. (2001). Interpersonal style: Are human social orientations guided by generalized interpersonal needs? *Communications Reports, 14,* 117-129.

Koplewicz, H. (2002). *More than moody: Recognizing and treating adolescent depression.* New York: Putnam.

Korcha, R. A., Polcin, D. L., Bond, J. C., Lapp, W. M., & Galloway, G. (2011). Substance use and motivation: A longitudinal perspective. *American Journal of Drug and Alcohol Abuse, 37,* 48-53.

Korotkov, D., Perunovic, M., Claybourn, M., Fraser, I., Houlihan, M., Macdonald, M., & Korotkov, K. (2011). The Type B behavior pattern as a moderating variable of the relationship between stressor chronicity and health behavior. *Journal of Health Psychology, 16,* 397-409.

Korur F, Toker S, Eryılmaz A. (2016). Effects of the integrated online advance organizer teaching materials on students' science achievement and attitude. *Journal of Science Education and Technology* [serial online], *25*(4), 628-640.

Kosambi, D. D. (1967). The Vedic "Five Tribes." *American Oriental Society, 14,* 5-12.

Kosinski, M., Matz, S. C., Gosling, S. D., Popov, V., & Stillwell, D. (2015). Facebook as a research tool for the social sciences. *American Psychologist, 70,* 543-556.

Kosinski, M., Matz, S. C., Gosling, S. D., Popov, V., & Stillwell, D. (2015). Facebook as a research tool for the social sciences: Opportunities, challenges, ethical considerations, and practical guidelines. *American Psychologist, 70*(6), 543-556.

Kosinski, M., Matz, S. C., Gosling, S. D., Popov, V., & Stillwell, D. (2016). Facebook as a research tool. *Monitor on Psychology, 47*(3), 70.

Koslowski, B. (2013). Scientific reasoning: Explanation, confirmation bias, and scientific practice. In G. J. Feist & M. E. Gorman (Eds.), *Handbook of the psychology of science.* New York: Springer Publishing Co.

Koss, M. P. (1993). Rape: Scope, impact, interventions, and public policy responses. *American Psychologist, 48,* 1062-1069.

Koss, M. P. (2011). Hidden, unacknowledged, acquaintance, and date rape: Looking back, looking forward. *Psychology of Women Quarterly, 35,* 348-354.

Kosslyn, S. M., & Miller, G. W. (2013). *Top brain, bottom brain: Surprising insights into how you think.* New York: Simon & Schuster.

Kotre, J., & Hall, E. (1990). *Seasons of life.* Boston: Little, Brown.

Kounios, J., Fleck, J. I., Green, D. L., Payne, L., Stevenson, J. L., Bowden, E. M., . . . Jung-Beeman, M. (2008). The origins of insight in resting-state brain activity. *Neuropsychologia, 46,* 281-291.

Kovacs, A. M., & Mehler, J. (2009). Flexible learning of multiple speech structures in bilingual infants. *Science, 325,* 611-612.

Kowalik, J., Weller, J., Venter, J., & Drachman, D. (2011). Cognitive behavioral therapy for the treatment of pediatric posttraumatic stress disorder: A review and meta-analysis. *Journal of Behavior Therapy and Experimental Psychiatry, 42,* 405-413.

Kozulin, A., Gindis, B., Ageyev, V. S., & Miller, S. M. (2003). *Vygotsky's educational theory in cultural context.* New York: Cambridge University Press.

Koçak, O., Özpolat, A., Atbaşoğlu, C., & Çiçek, M. (2011). Cognitive control of a simple mental image in patients with obsessive-compulsive disorder. *Brain and Cognition, 76,* 390-399.

Krassner, A. M., Gartstein, M. A., Park, C., Dragan, W. Ł., Lecannelier, F., & Putnam, S. P. (2017). East-west, collectivist-individualist: A cross-cultural examination of temperament in toddlers from Chile, Poland, South Korea, and the U.S. *European Journal of Developmental Psychology, 14*(4), 449-464. doi:10.1080/17405629.2016.1236722.

Kreher, D., Holcomb, P., Goff, D., & Kuperberg, G. (2008). Neural evidence for faster and further automatic spreading activation in schizophrenic thought disorder. *Schizophrenia Bulletin, 34,* 473-482.

Kreppner, J., Rutter, M., Marvin, R., O'Connor, T., & Sonuga-Barke, E. (2011). Assessing the concept of the 'insecure-other' category in the Cassidy-Marvin scheme: Changes between 4 and 6 years in the English and Romanian adoptee study. *Social Development, 20,* 1-16.

Kreuger, A. (2007). Are we having fun yet? Categorizing and evaluating changes in time allocation. *Brookings Papers on Economic Activity,* (Vol. 2), 38, 193-218.

Krueger, K., & Dayan, P. (2009). Flexible shaping: How learning in small steps helps. *Cognition, 110,* 380-394.

Krumhuber, E. G., & Scherer, K. R. (2011). Affect bursts: Dynamic patterns of facial expression. *Emotion, 11,* 825-841.

Krüger, O., Korsten, P., & Hoffman, J. I. (2017). The rise of behavioral genetics and the transition to behavioral genomics and beyond. In J. Call, G. M. Burghardt, I. M. Pepperberg, C. T. Snowdon, &T. Zentall (Eds.), *APA handbook of comparative psychology: Basic concepts, methods, neural substrate, and behavior.* Washington, DC: American Psychological Association.

Kubanek, J., Snyder, L. H., & Abrams, R. A. (2015). Reward and punishment act as distinct factors in guiding behavior. *Cognition, 139,* 154-167.

Kulik, L., & Sadeh, I. (2015). Explaining fathers' involvement in childcare: An ecological approach. *Community, Work & Family, 18,* 19-40.

Kumari, S., & Joshi, S. (2013). Neonatal outcomes in women with depression during pregnancy. *Journal of Projective Psychology & Mental Health, 20,* 141-145.

Kuncel, N. R., & Beatty, A. S. (2013). Thinking at work: Intelligence, critical thinking, job knowledge, and reasoning. In K. F. Geisinger, B. A. Bracken, J. F. Carlson, J. C. Hansen, N. R. Kuncel, S. P. Reise, & M. C. Rodriguez (Eds.), *APA handbook of testing and assessment in psychology, Vol. 1: Test theory and testing and assessment in industrial and organizational psychology.* Washington, DC: American Psychological Association.

Kuo, L. J. (2007). Effects of bilingualism on development of facets of phonological competence (China). *Dissertation Abstracts International Section A: Humanities and Social Sciences, 67*(11-A), 4095.

Kupfer, D. J., Kuhl, E. A., & Regier, D. A. (2013). DSM-5–The future arrived. *JAMA: Journal of the American Medical Association, 309,* 1691-1692.

Kuppens, P., Ceulemans, E., Timmerman, M. E., Diener, E., & Kim-Prieto, C. (2006). Universal intracultural and intercultural dimensions of the recalled frequency of emotional experience. *Journal of Cross Cultural Psychology, 37,* 491-515.

Kurdziel, L., Duclos, K., & Spencer, R. M. C. (2013). Sleep spindles in midday naps enhance learning in preschool children. *PNAS Early Edition,* 1-6.

Kuriyama, K., Stickgold, R., & Walker, M. P. (2004). Sleep-dependent learning and motor-skill complexity. *Learning and Memory, 11,* 705-713.

Kushlev, K., Dunn, E. W., & Lucas, R. E. (2015). Higher income is associated with less daily sadness but not more daily happiness. *Social Psychological and Personality Science, 6,* 483-489.

Kuther, T. L. (2003). *Your career in psychology: Psychology and the law.* New York: Wadsworth.

Kwang, T., Crockett, E. E., Sanchez, D. T., & Swann, W. B., Jr. (2013). Men seek social standing, women seek companionship: Sex differences in deriving self-worth from relationships. *Psychological Science, 24,* 1142-1150.

Kwon, K., Bingham, G., Lewsader, J., Jeon, H., & Elicker, J. (2013). Structured task versus free play: The influence of social context on parenting quality, toddlers' engagement with parents and play behaviors, and parent–toddler language use. *Child & Youth Care Forum, 42,* 207-224.

Kwon, P. (2013). Resilience in lesbian, gay, and bisexual individuals. *Personality and Social Psychology Review, 17,* 371-383.

Kyaga, S., Landén, M., Boman, M., Hultman, C. M., Långström, N., & Lichtenstein, P. (2013). Mental illness, suicide and creativity: 40-year prospective total population study. *Journal of Psychiatric Research, 47,* 83-90.

Kyllonen, P., & Kell, H. (2017). What is fluid intelligence? Can it be improved? In M. Rosén, K. Yang Hansen, U. Wolff, M. Rosén, K. Yang Hansen, & U. Wolff (Eds.), *Cognitive abilities and educational outcomes: A festschrift in honour of Jan-Eric Gustafsson.* Cham, Switzerland: Springer International Publishing.

Köhler, W. (1927). *The mentality of apes.* London: Routledge & Kegan Paul.

Kübler-Ross, E. (1969). *On death and dying.* New York: Macmillan.

LaBar, K. (2007). Beyond fear: Emotional memory mechanisms in the human brain. *Current Directions in Psychological Science, 16,* 173-177.

Labrecque, L. T., & Whisman, M. A. (2017). Attitudes toward and prevalence of extramarital sex and descriptions of extramarital partners in the 21st century. *Journal of Family Psychology, 31*(7), 952-957.

Labrecque, N., & Cermakian, N. (2015). Circadian clocks in the immune system. *Journal of Biological Rhythms, 30,* 277-290.

Laddis, A., Dell, P. F., & Korzekwa, M. (2017). Comparing the symptoms and mechanisms of "dissociation" in dissociative identity disorder and borderline personality disorder. *Journal of Trauma & Dissociation, 18,* 139-173.

Laederach-Hofmann, K., & Messerli-Buergy, N. (2007). Chest pain, angina pectoris, panic disorder, and Syndrome X. In J. Jordan, B. Barde, & A. M. Zeiher (Eds.), *Contributions toward evidence-based psychocardiology: A systematic review of the literature.* Washington, DC: American Psychological Association.

LaFrance, M., & Harris, J. L. (2004). Gender and verbal and nonverbal communication. In M. A. Paludi (Ed.), *Praeger guide to the psychology of gender.* Westport, CT: Praeger Publishers/Greenwood Publishing Group.

Lagacé-Séguin, D. G., & d'Entremont, M. L. (2006). The role of child negative affect in the relations between parenting styles and play. *Early Child Development and Care, 176,* 461-477.

Lahti, J., Räikkönen, K., Ekelund, J., Peltonen, L., Raitakari, O. T., & Keltikangas-Järvinen, L. (2005). Novelty seeking: Interaction between parental alcohol use and dopamine D4 receptor gene exon III polymorphism over 17 years. *Psychiatric Genetics, 15,* 133-139.

Lal, S. (2002). Giving children security: Mamie Phipps Clark and the racialization of child psychology. *American Psychologist, 57,* 20-28.

Lalasz, C. B., & Weigel, D. J. (2011). Understanding the relationship between gender and extradyadic relations: The mediating role of sensation seeking on intentions to engage in sexual infidelity. *Personality and Individual Differences, 50,* 1079-1083.

LaLumiere, R. T., & Kalivas, P. W. (2013). Motivational systems: Rewards and incentive value. In R. J. Nelson, S. Y. Mizumori, & I. B. Weiner (Eds.), *Handbook of psychology, Vol. 3: Behavioral neuroscience* (2nd ed.). New York: John Wiley & Sons Ltd.

Lambert, W. W. (1971). *Comparative perspectives on social psychology.* Boston: Little, Brown.

Lamborn, S. D., & Groh, K. (2009). A four-part model of autonomy during emerging adulthood: Associations with adjustment. *International Journal of Behavioral Development, 33,* 393-401.

Lampard, A. M., Byrne, S. M., McLean, N., & Fursland, A. (2011). An evaluation of the enhanced cognitive-behavioural model of bulimia nervosa. *Behaviour Research and Therapy, 49,* 529-535.

Lanciano, T., Curci, A., Mastandrea, S., & Sartori, G. (2013). Do automatic mental associations detect a flashbulb memory? *Memory, 21,* 482-493.

Lancy, D. F. (2015). *The anthropology of childhood: Cherubs, chattel, changelings* (2nd ed.). New York: Cambridge University Press.

Landro, L. (2010, May 11). New ways to treat pain. *Wall Street Journal,* p. D1-D2.

Landro, L. (2011, April 26). "Use only as directed" isn't easy. *Wall Street Journal,* pp. D1-D2.

Landry, S. H., Zucker, T. A., Taylor, H. B., Swank, P. R., Williams, J. M., Assel, M., . . . School Readiness Research Consortium. (2013). Enhancing early child care quality and learning for toddlers at risk: The responsive early childhood program. *Developmental Psychology, 50*(2), 526-541.

Lane, K. A., Banaji, M. R., Nosek, B. A., & Greenwald, A. G. (Eds.). (2007). Understanding and using the implicit association test: IV: What we know (so far) about the method. In B. Wittenbrink & N. Schwarz (Eds.), *Implicit measures of attitudes.* New York: Guilford Press.

Lane, S. D., Cherek, D. R., & Tcheremissine, O. V. (2007). Response perseveration and adaptation in heavy marijuana-smoking adolescents. *Addictive Behaviors, 32,* 977-990.

Lang, A. J., Sorrell, J. T., & Rodgers, C. S. (2006). Anxiety sensitivity as a predictor of labor pain. *European Journal of Pain, 10,* 263-270.

Lang, P. J., & Bradley, M. M. (2013). Appetitive and defensive motivation: Goal-directed or goal-determined? *Emotion Review, 5,* 230-234.

Langan-Fox, J., & Grant, S. (2006). The Thematic Apperception Test: Toward a standard measure of the big three motives. *Journal of Personality Assessment, 87,* 277-291.

Langdridge, D., & Butt, T. (2004). The fundamental attribution error: A phenomenological critique. *British Journal of Social Psychology, 43,* 357-369.

Langley, Liz. (2016, March 19). How dogs can sniff out diabetes and cancer. *National Geographic.* Retrieved from http://news.nationalgeographic.com/2016/03/160319-dogs-diabetes-health-cancer-animals-science/.

Langlois, F., Langlois, M., Carpentier, A. C., Brown, C., Lemieux, S., & Hivert, M. (2011). Ghrelin levels are associated with hunger as measured by the Three-Factor Eating Questionnaire in healthy young adults. *Physiology & Behavior, 104,* 373-377.

Langreth, R. (2000, May 1). Every little bit helps: How even moderate exercise can have a big impact on your health. *Wall Street Journal,* p. R5.

Lankov, A. (2004). The dawn of modern Korea: Changes for better or worse. *The Korea Times,* p. A1.

Lansford, J. E., Sharma, C., Malone, P. S., Woodlief, D., Dodge, K. A., Oburu, P., . . . Di Giunta, L. (2014). Corporal punishment, maternal warmth, and child adjustment: A longitudinal study in eight countries. *Journal of Clinical Child and Adolescent Psychology, 43*(4), 670-685.

Lanza, S. T., & Collins, L. M. (2002). Pubertal timing and the onset of substance use in females during early adolescence. *Prevention Science, 3*, 69-82.

LaPointe, L. L. (2013). *Paul Broca and the origins of language in the brain.* San Diego, CA: Plural Publishing.

Larsen, E. F. (2014). Good teens turned addicts. *Choices.* Accessed from http://www.huffingtonpost.com/2014/09/24/teens-turned-drug-addicts n 5877306.html.

Larsen, R. J., & Buss, D. M. (2006). *Personality psychology: Domains of knowledge about human nature with PowerWeb* (2nd ed.). New York: McGraw-Hill.

Lasalvia, A. (2015). DSM-5 two years later: Facts, myths and some key open issues. *Epidemiology and Psychiatric Sciences, 24*, 185-187.

Lascaratos, G., Ji, D., & Wood, J. P. (2007). Visible light affects mitochondrial function and induces neuronal death in retinal cell cultures. *Vision Research, 47*, 1191-1201.

Latané, B., & Darley, J. M. (1970). *The unresponsive bystander: Why doesn't he help?* New York: Appleton-Century-Crofts.

Lattal, K. A., Cançado, C. X., Cook, J. E., Kincaid, S. L., Nighbor, T. D., & Oliver, A. C. (2017). On defining resurgence. *Behavioural Processes, 141*(Part 1), 85-91.

Laugharne, J., Janca, A., & Widiger, T. (2007). Posttraumatic stress disorder and terrorism: 5 years after 9/11. *Current Opinion in Psychiatry, 20*, 36-41.

Lauriello, J., & Rahman, T. (2015). Schizophrenia spectrum and other psychotic disorders. In L. W. Roberts & A. K. Louie (Eds.), *Study Guide to DSM-5®.* Arlington, VA: American Psychiatric Publishing, Inc.

Lavazza, A., & Manzotti, R. (2013). An externalist approach to creativity: Discovery versus recombination. *Mind & Society, 12*, 61-72.

Lavenex, P., & Lavenex, P. (2009). Spatial memory and the monkey hippocampus: Not all space is created equal. *Hippocampus, 19*, 8-19.

Lavigne, K. M., Rapin, L. A., Metzak, P. D., Whitman, J. C., Jung, K., Dohen, M., . . . Woodward, T. S. (2015). Left-dominant temporal-frontal hypercoupling in schizophrenia patients with hallucinations during speech perception. *Schizophrenia Bulletin, 41*, 259-267.

Lazarus, A. A. (1997). *Brief but comprehensive psychotherapy: The multimodal way.* New York: Springer.

Lazarus, R. S. (1995). Emotions express a social relationship, but it is an individual mind that creates them. *Psychological Inquiry, 6*, 253-265.

Lazear, E.P. (2017, June 26). The surprising factor for immigrant success. *Wall Street Journal.* Accessed from https://www.wsj.com/articles/the-surprising-factor-for-immigrant-success-1498517898.

Le Maner-Idrissi, G., & Renault, L. (2006). Développement du 'schéma de genre': Une asymétrie entre filles et garçons? Are there

sex differences in the acquisition of a gender schema? *Enfance, 58*, 251-265.

Leahy, R. L. (2015). Emotional schema therapy. In N. C. Thoma & D. McKay (Eds.), *Working with emotion in cognitive-behavioral therapy: Techniques for clinical practice.* New York: Guilford Press.

Leaper, C., & Ayres, M. (2007). A meta-analytic review of gender variations in adults' language use: Talkativeness, affiliative speech, and assertive speech. *Personality and Social Psychology Review, 11*, 328-363.

Leaper, C., & Friedman, C. K. (2007). The socialization of gender. In J. E. Grusec & P. D. Hastings (Eds.), *Handbook of socialization: Theory and research.* New York: Guilford Press.

Leaper, C., Brown, C., & Ayres, M. M. (2013). Adolescent girls' cognitive appraisals of coping responses to sexual harassment. *Psychology in the Schools, 50*, 969-986.

Leclair-Visonneau, L., Oudiette, D., Gaymard, B., Leu-Semenescu, S., & Arnulf, I. (2011). Do the eyes scan dream images during rapid eye movement sleep? Evidence from the rapid eye movement sleep behaviour disorder model: Corrigendum. *Brain: A Journal of Neurology, 134*, 88-97.

Lee, A. Y., & Aaker, J. L. (2004). Bringing the frame into focus: The influence of regulatory fit on processing fluency and persuasion. *Journal of Personality and Social Psychology, 86*, 205-218.

Lee, A., Isaac, M., & Janca, A. (2007). Posttraumatic stress disorder and terrorism. In A. Monat, R. S. Lazarus, & G. Reevy (Eds.), *The Praeger handbook on stress and coping* (Vol. 1). Westport, CT: Praeger Publishers/Greenwood Publishing Group.

Lee, D., Kleinman, J., & Kleinman, A. (2007). Rethinking depression: An ethnographic study of the experiences of depression among Chinese. *Harvard Review of Psychiatry, 15*, 1-8.

Lee, E., & Troop-Gordon, W. (2011). Peer processes and gender role development: Changes in gender atypicality related to negative peer treatment and children's friendships. *Sex Roles, 64*, 90-102.

Lee, F. H., & Raja, S. N. (2011). Complementary and alternative medicine in chronic pain. *Pain, 152*, 28-30.

Lee, K-F. (2017, June 25). The real threat of artificial intelligence. *The New York Times*, p. SR4.

Lee-Chiong, T. L. (2006). *Sleep: A comprehensive handbook.* New York: Wiley-Liss.

Leeman, R. F., Fischler, C., & Rozin, P. (2011). Medical doctors' attitudes and beliefs about diet and health are more like those of their lay countrymen (France, Germany, Italy, UK and USA) than those of doctors in other countries. *Appetite, 56*, 558-563.

Lehman, D. R., & Taylor, S. E. (1988). Date with an earthquake: Coping with a probable, unpredictable disaster. *Personality and Social Psychology Bulletin, 13*, 546-555.

Lehrer, J. (2012, April 13). When memory commits an injustice. *Wall Street Journal*, p. C18.

Lehrman, S. (2007). Going beyond X and Y. *Scientific American, 296*, 40-41.

Leib, J. R., Gollust, S. E., Hull, S. C., & Wilfond, B. S. (2005). Carrier screening panels for Ashkenazi Jews: Is more better? *Genetic Medicine, 7*, 185-190.

Leiblum, S. R., & Chivers, M. L. (2007). Normal and persistent genital arousal in women: New perspectives. *Journal of Sex & Marital Therapy, 33*, 357-373.

Leigh, J. H., Zinkhan, G. M., & Swaminathan, V. (2006). Dimensional relationships of recall and recognition measures with selected cognitive and affective aspects of print ads. *Journal of Advertising, 35*, 105-122.

Leising, D., Scharloth, J., Lohse, O., & Wood, D. (2014). What types of terms do people use when describing an individual's personality? *Psychological Science, 25*, 1787-1794.

Leiter, S., & Leiter, W. M. (2003). *Affirmative action in antidiscrimination law and policy: An overview and synthesis. SUNY series in American constitutionalism.* Albany: State University of New York Press.

Leitner, L. M. (2007). Diversity issues, postmodernism, and psychodynamic therapy. *PsycCRITIQUES, 52*, n.p.

Lemay, E. P., Jr., Clark, M. S., & Feeney, B. C. (2007). Projection of responsiveness to needs and the construction of satisfying communal relationships. *Journal of Personality and Social Psychology, 92*, 834-853.

Lemay, E., & Clark, M. (2008). How the head liberates the heart: Projection of communal responsiveness guides relationship promotion. *Journal of Personality and Social Psychology, 94*, 647-671.

Lemogne, C., Consoli, S. M., Geoffroy-Perez, B., Coeuret-Pellicer, M., Nabi, H., Melchior, M., & . . . Cordier, S. (2013). Personality and the risk of cancer: A 16-year follow-up study of the GAZEL cohort. *Psychosomatic Medicine, 75*, 262-271.

Lenzenweger, M. F., & Dworkin, R. H. (Eds.). (1998). *The origins and development of schizophrenia: Advances in experimental psychopathology.* Washington, DC: American Psychological Association.

Leong, C., Alessi-Severini, S., Enns, M. W., Nie, Y., Sareen, J., Bolton, . . . Chateau, D. (2017). Cerebrovascular, cardiovascular, and mortality events in new users of selective serotonin reuptake inhibitors and serotonin norepinephrine reuptake inhibitors: A propensity score-matched population-based study. *Journal of Clinical Psychopharmacology, 37*, 332-340.

Lepore, J. (2009, November 9). Why is American history so murderous? *The New Yorker.*

Leppänen, J. M., Moulson, M. C., Vogel-Farley, V. K., & Nelson, C. A. (2007). An ERP study of emotional face processing in the adult and infant brain. *Child Development, 78*, 232-245.

Leskinen, E. A., Rabelo, V. C., & Cortina, L. M. (2015). Gender stereotyping and harassment: A "catch-22" for women in the workplace. *Psychology, Public Policy, and Law, 21*, 192-204.

Lester, K. J., Coleman, J. I., Roberts, S., Keers, R., Breen, G., Bögels, S., . . . Eley, T. C. (2017). Genetic variation in the endocannabinoid system and response to cognitive behavior therapy for child anxiety disorders. *American Journal of Medical Genetics Part B: Neuropsychiatric Genetics, 174*, 144-155.

Leung, A. K., & Chiu, C. (2010). Multicultural experience, idea receptiveness, and creativity. *Journal of Cross-Cultural Psychology, 41*(5-6), 723-741.

LeVay, S. (1993). *The sexual brain.* Cambridge, MA: MIT.

LeVay, S. (2011). *Gay, straight, and the reason why: The science of sexual orientation.* New York: Oxford University Press.

Levi, A., Chan, K. K., & Pence, D. (2006). Real men do not read labels: The effects of masculinity and involvement on college students' food decisions. *Journal of American College Health, 55*, 91-98.

Levin, R. J. (2007). Sexual activity, health and well-being–the beneficial roles of coitus and masturbation. *Sexual and Relationship Therapy, 22*, 135-148.

Levine, C. S., Miyamoto, Y., Markus, H. R., Rigotti, A., Boylan, J. M., Park, J., & . . . Ryff, C. D. (2016). Culture and healthy eating: The role of independence and interdependence in the United States and Japan. *Personality and Social Psychology Bulletin, 42*(10), 1335-1348.

Levine, J. M., & Moreland, R. L. (2006). Small groups: An overview. In J. M. Levine & R. L. Moreland (Eds.), *Small groups.* New York: Psychology Press.

Levine, L. E., & Munsch, J. (2011). *Child development: An active learning approach.* Thousand Oaks, CA: Sage Publications, Inc.

Levine, S. Z. (2011). Elaboration on the association between IQ and parental SES with subsequent crime. *Personality and Individual Differences, 50*, 1233-1237.

Levine, S. Z., & Rabinowitz, J. (2007). Revisiting the 5 dimensions of the Positive and Negative Syndrome Scale. *Journal of Clinical Psychopharmacology, 27*, 431-436.

Levinson, D. (1992). *The seasons of a woman's life.* New York: Knopf.

Levinson, D. J. (1990). A theory of life structure development in adulthood. In C. N. Alexander & E. J. Langer (Eds.), *Higher stages of human development: Perspectives on adult growth.* New York: Oxford University Press.

Levy, B. (1996). Improving memory in old age through implicit self-stereotyping. *Journal of Personality and Social Psychology, 71*, 1092-1107.

Levy, B. R., & Myers, L. M. (2004). Preventive health behaviors influenced by self-perceptions of aging. *Preventive Medicine: An International Journal Devoted to Practice and Theory, 39*, 625-629.

Levy, B. R., Slade, M. D., Kunkel, S. R., & Kasl, S. V. (2002). Longevity increased by positive self-perceptions of aging. *Journal of Personality & Social Psychology, 83*, 261-270.

Lewin, T. (2003, December 22). For more people in their 20s and 30s, going home is easier because they never left. *The New York Times*, p. A27.

Lewinsohn, P. M., & Essau, C. A. (2002). Depression in adolescents. In I. H. Gotlib & C. L. Hammen (Eds.), *Handbook of depression.* New York: Guilford Press.

Lewinsohn, P. M., Petit, J. W., Joiner, T. E., Jr., & Seeley, J. R. (2003). The symptomatic expression of major depressive disorder in adolescents and young adults. *Journal of Abnormal Psychology, 112*, 244-252.

Lewis, C. E., Thomas, K. F., Dodge, N. C., Molteno, C. D., Meintjes, E. M., Jacobson, J. L., . . . Jacobson, S. W. (2015). Verbal learning and memory impairment in children with fetal alcohol spectrum disorders. *Alcoholism: Clinical and Experimental Research, 39*, 724-732.

Lewis, C., & Lamb, M. (2011). The role of parent-child relationships in child development. In M. E. Lamb & M. H. Bornstein (Eds.), *Social and personality development: An advanced textbook.* New York: Psychology Press.

Lewis, D. G., Al-Shawaf, L., Conroy-Beam, D., Asao, K., & Buss, D. M. (2017). Evolutionary psychology: A how-to guide. *American Psychologist, 72*(4), 353-373.

Lewis, T., & Umbreit, M. (2015). A humanistic approach to mediation and dialogue: An evolving transformative practice. *Conflict Resolution Quarterly, 33*(1), 3-17.

Li, A., Bagger, J., & Cropanzano, R. (2017). The impact of stereotypes and supervisor perceptions of employee work-family conflict on job performance ratings. *Human Relations, 70*, 119-145.

Li, B., Piriz, J., Mirrione, M., Chung, C., Proulx, C. D., Schulz, D., . . . Malinow, R. (2011). Synaptic potentiation onto habenula neurons in learned helplessness model of depression. *Nature, 470*, 535-539.

Li, M. D., Cheng, R., Ma, J. Z., & Swan, G. E. (2003). A meta-analysis of estimated genetic and environmental effects on smoking behavior in male and female adult twins. *Addiction, 98*, 23-31.

Li, M. D., Lou, X., Chen, G., Ma, J. Z., & Elston, R. C. (2008). Gene-gene interactions among CHRNA4, CHRNB2, BDNF, and NTRK2 in nicotine dependence. *Biological Psychiatry, 64*, 951-957.

Li, T. K., Volkow, N. D., & Baler, R. D. (2007). The biological bases of nicotine and alcohol co-addiction. *Biological Psychiatry, 61*, 1-3.

Li, Y., Hofstetter, C. R., Wahlgren, D., Irvin, V., Chhay, D., & Hovell, M. F. (2015). Social networks and immigration stress among first-generation mandarin-speaking Chinese immigrants in Los Angeles. *International Journal of Social Welfare, 24*, 170-181.

Li, Y., Zuo, Y., Yu, P., Ping, X., & Cui, C. (2015). Role of basolateral amygdala dopamine D2 receptors in impulsive choice in acute cocaine-treated rats. *Behavioural Brain Research, 287*, 187-195.

Liang, K. A. (2007). Acculturation, ambivalent sexism, and attitudes toward women who engage in premarital sex among Chinese American young adults. *Dissertation Abstracts International: Section B: The Sciences and Engineering, 67*(10-B), 6065.

Libedinsky, C., & Livingstone, M. (2011). Role of prefrontal cortex in conscious visual perception. *Journal of Neuroscience, 31*, 64-69.

Liben, L. S., & Bigler, R. S. (2002). The development course of gender differentiations: Conceptualizing, measuring, and evaluation constructs and pathways. *Monographs of the Society for Research in Child Development, 67*, 148-167.

Licis, A. K., Desruisseau, D. M., Yamada, K. A., Duntley, S. P., & Gurnett, C. A. (2011). Novel genetic findings in an extended family pedigree with sleepwalking. *Neurology, 76*, 49-52.

Lick, D. J., Durso, L. E., & Johnson, K. L. (2013). Minority stress and physical health among sexual minorities. *Perspectives on Psychological Science, 8*, 521-548.

Lieberman, M. D. (2007). Social cognitive neuro-science: A review of core processes. *Annual Review of Psychology, 58*, 259-289.

Lieberman, P. (2015). A tangled tale of circuits, evolution, and language. *PsycCRITIQUES, 60*, 88-97.

Liechti, M. E., Dolder, P. C., & Schmid, Y. (2017). Alterations of consciousness and mystical-type experiences after acute LSD in humans. *Psychopharmacology, 234*, 1499-1510.

Liedl, A., Müller, J., Morina, N., Karl, A., Denke, C., & Knaevelsrud, C. (2011). Physical activity within a CBT intervention improves coping with pain in traumatized refugees: Results of a randomized controlled design. *Pain Medicine, 12*, 138-145.

Liem, G. D. (2015). Academic and social achievement goals: Their additive, interactive, and specialized effects on school functioning. *British Journal of Educational Psychology, 86*, 37-56.

Lien, Y. W., Chu, R. L., Jen, C. H., & Wu, C. H. (2006). Do Chinese commit neither fundamental attribution error nor ultimate attribution error? *Chinese Journal of Psychology, 48*, 163-181.

Lilienfeld, S. O. (2007). Psychological treatments that cause harm. *Perspectives on Psychological Science, 2*, 53-58.

Lilienfeld, S. O. (2012). Further sources of our field's embattled public reputation. *American Psychologist*, 808-809.

Lilienfeld, S. O. (2017). Microaggressions: Strong claims, inadequate evidence. *Perspectives on Psychological Science, 12*, 138-169.

Lillard, A. S., & Woolley, J. D. (2015). Grounded in reality: How children make sense of the unreal. *Cognitive Development, 34*, 111-114.

Lim, A., & Okuno, H. G. (2015). A recipe for empathy: Integrating the mirror system, insula, somatosensory cortex and motherese. *International Journal of Social Robotics, 7*, 35-49.

Limberg, B. (2015). Nature vs. nurture . . . again: Examining the interplay between genetics and the environment. *PsycCRITIQUES, 60*, 88-98.

Lin, C. H., & Lin, H. M. (2007). What price do you ask for the "extra one"? A social value orientation perspective. *Social Behavior and Personality, 35,* 9-18.

Lin, I., Wang, S., Chu, I., Lu, Y., Lee, C., Lin, T., & Fan, S. (2017). The association of Type D personality with heart rate variability and lipid profiles among patients with coronary artery disease. *International Journal of Behavioral Medicine, 24,* 101-109.

Lin, J., Arthurs, J., & Reilly, S. (2017). Conditioned taste aversions: From poisons to pain to drugs of abuse. *Psychonomic Bulletin & Review, 24,* 335-351.

Lin, L., McCormack, H., Kruczkowski, L., & Berg, M. B. (2015). How women's perceptions of peer weight preferences are related to drive for thinness. *Sex Roles, 72,* 117-126.

Lin, Y., Li, K., Sung, W., Ko, H., Tzeng, O. L., Hung, D. L., . . . Juan, C. H. (2011). The relationship between development of attention and learning in children: A cognitive neuroscience approach. *Bulletin of Educational Psychology, 42,* 517-542.

Lindblad, F., Lindahl, M., & Theorell, T. (2006). Physiological stress reactions in 6th and 9th graders during test performance. *Stress and Health: Journal of the International Society for the Investigation of Stress, 22,* 189-195.

Lindemann, O., & Bekkering, H. (2009). Object manipulation and motion perception: Evidence of an influence of action planning on visual processing. *Journal of Experimental Psychology: Human Perception and Performance, 35,* 1062-1071.

Lindley, L. D. (2006). The paradox of self-efficacy: Research with diverse populations. *Journal of Career Assessment, 14,* 143-160.

Lindorff, M. (2005). Determinants of received social support: Who gives what to managers? *Journal of Social and Personal Relationships, 22,* 323-337.

Lindsay, P. H., & Norman, D. A. (1977). *Human information processing* (2nd ed.). New York: Academic Press.

Lindsey, E., & Colwell, M. (2003). Preschoolers' emotional competence: Links to pretend and physical play. *Child Study Journal, 33,* 39-52.

Linley, P. (2013). Human strengths and well-being: Finding the best within us at the intersection of eudaimonic philosophy, humanistic psychology, and positive psychology. In A. S. Waterman (Ed.), *The best within us: Positive psychology perspectives on eudaimonia.* Washington, DC: American Psychological Association.

Lips, H. M. (2003). *A new psychology of women: Gender, culture, and ethnicity.* New York: McGraw-Hill.

Lipsman, N., Giacobbe, P., & Lozano, A. M. (2015). Deep brain stimulation for the management of treatment-refractory major depressive disorder. In B. Sun & A. De Salles (Eds.), *Neurosurgical treatments for psychiatric disorders* (pp. 95-104). New York: Springer Science + Business Media.

Little, A., Burt, D. M., & Perrett, D. I. (2006). What is good is beautiful: Face preference reflects desired personality. *Personality and Individual Differences, 41,* 1107-1118.

Little, K., Ramssen, E., Welchko, R., Volberg, V., Roland, C., & Cassin, B. (2009). Decreased brain dopamine cell numbers in human cocaine users. *Psychiatry Research, 168,* 173-180.

Liu, J., Ying, Z., & Zhang, S. (2015). A rate function approach to computerized adaptive testing for cognitive diagnosis. *Psychometrika, 80,* 468-490

Liu, L., He, S-Z., & Wu, Y. (2007). An analysis of the characteristics of single parent families with different structures and their children. *Chinese Journal of Clinical Psychology, 15,* 68-70.

Livingstone, A. G., Spears, R., Manstead, A. R., Bruder, M., & Shepherd, L. (2011). We feel, therefore we are: Emotion as a basis for self-categorization and social action. *Emotion, 11,* 754-767.

Llorca-Mestre, A., Samper-García, P., Malonda-Vidal, E., & Cortés-Tomás, M. T. (2017). Parenting style and peer attachment as predictors of emotional instability in children. *Social Behavior and Personality, 45,* 677-694.

Lobato, M. I., Koff, W. J., & Manenti, C. (2006). Follow-up of sex reassignment surgery in transsexuals: A Brazilian cohort. *Archives of Sexual Behavior, 35,* 711-715.

Lobban, F., Barrowclough, C., & Jones, S. (2006). Does expressed emotion need to be understood within a more systemic framework? An examination of discrepancies in appraisals between patients diagnosed with schizophrenia and their relatives. *Social Psychiatry and Psychiatric Epidemiology, 41,* 50-55.

Lobo, I., & Harris, R. (2008). GABAa receptors and alcohol. *Pharmacology, Biochemistry and Behavior, 90,* 90-94.

Lockl, K., & Schneider, W. (2007). Knowledge about the mind: Links between theory of mind and later metamemory. *Child Development, 78,* 148-167.

Loehlin, J. C., Bartels, M., Boomsma, D. I., Bratko, D., Martin, N. G., Nichols, R. C., . . . Wright, M. J. (2015). Is there a genetic correlation between general factors of intelligence and personality? *Twin Research and Human Genetics, 18,* 234-242.

Lofholm, N. (2003, May 6). Climber's kin share relief: Ralston saw 4 options, they say; death wasn't one of them. *Denver Post,* p. A1.

Loftus, E. F., & Palmer, J. C. (1974). Reconstruction of automobile destruction: An example of the interface between language and memory. *Journal of Verbal Learning and Verbal Behavior, 13,* 585-589.

Loitfelder, M., Fazekas, F., Petrovic, K., Fuchs, S., Ropele, S., Wallner-Blazek, M., . . . Ensinger, C. (2011). Reorganization in cognitive networks with progression of multiple sclerosis: Insights from fMRI. *Neurology, 76,* 526-533.

Lombaard, N., & Naudé, L. (2017). "Breaking the cycle": Black adolescents' experiences of being stereotyped during identity development. *Journal of Psychology in Africa, 27,* 185-190.

London, B. (2013, October 16). From a child bride who was circumcised at five to woman of the year: Extraordinary story of Somali supermodel who starred in James Bond film. *Mail Online.* Retrieved from http://www.dailymail.co.uk/femail/article-2461477/Waris-Dirie-fights-female-circumcision-receives-Woman-Year-Campaigning-award.html.

Longo, M. R., Trippier, S., Vagnoni, E., & Lourenco, S. F. (2015). Right hemisphere control of visuospatial attention in near space. *Neuropsychologia, 70,* 350-357.

Lopes, A. C., Greenberg, B. D., Noren, G., Canteras, M. M., Busatto, G. F. de Mathis, . . . Miguel, E. C. (2009). Treatment of resistant obsessive-compulsive disorder with ventral capsular/ventral striatal gamma capsulotomy: A pilot prospective study. *Journal of Neuropsychiatry and Clinical Neurosciences, 21,* 381-392.

Lopez, N. L., Schneider, H. G., & Dula, C. S. (2002). Parent Discipline Scale: Discipline choice as a function of transgression type. *North American Journal of Psychology, 4,* 381-393.

Lorenz, K. (1966). *On aggression.* New York: Harcourt Brace Jovanovich.

Lorenz, K. (1974). *Civilized man's eight deadly sins.* New York: Harcourt Brace Jovanovich.

Loriedo, C., & Di Leone, F. G. (2017). Conversion disorder. In G. R. Elkins (Ed.), *Handbook of medical and psychological hypnosis: Foundations, applications, and professional issues.* New York: Springer Publishing Co.

Loving, T., Crockett, E., & Paxson, A. (2009). Passionate love and relationship thinkers: Experimental evidence for acute cortisol elevations in women. *Psychoneuroendocrinology, 34,* 939-946.

Lowe, P., Humphreys, C., & Williams, S. J. (2007). Night terrors: Women's experiences of (not) sleeping where there is domestic violence. *Violence against Women, 13,* 549-561.

Lozano, A., & Mayberg, H. (2015). Treating depression at the source: Electrical stimulation deep within the brain may alleviate devastating mood. *Scientific American, 312,* 68-73.

Lu, S. (2015, February.) Erasing bad memories. *Monitor on Psychology,* pp. 41-45.

Lubell, K. M., Swahn, M. H., Crosby, A. E., & Kegler, S. R. (2004). Methods of suicide among persons aged 10-19 years–United States, 1992-2001. *Morbidity and Mortality Weekly Report, 53,* 471-473.

Lucas, W. (2008). Parents' perceptions of the Drug Abuse Resistance Education program (DARE). *Journal of Child & Adolescent Substance Abuse, 17,* 99-114.

Luchins, A. S. (1946). Classroom experiments on mental set. *American Journal of Psychology, 59,* 295-298.

Luders, E., Narr, K. L., Thompson, P. M., & Toga, A. W. (2009). Neuroanatomical correlates of intelligence. *Intelligence, 37,* 156-163.

Lun, V. M., & Bond, M. H. (2006). Achieving relationship harmony in groups and its consequence for group performance. *Asian Journal of Social Psychology, 9,* 195-202.

Luo, S., & Zhang, G. (2009). What leads to romantic attraction: Similarity, reciprocity, security, or beauty? Evidence from a speed-dating study. *Journal of Personality, 77*, 933-964.

Luong, G., Rauers, A., & Fingerman, K. L. (2015). The multifaceted nature of late-life socialization: Older adults as agents and targets of socialization. In J. E. Grusec & P. D. Hastings (Eds.), *Handbook of socialization: Theory and research* (2nd ed.). New York: Guilford Press.

Luria, A. R. (1968). *The mind of a mnemonist.* Cambridge, MA: Basic Books.

Lurie, K., Robinson, A., & Pecsenye, M. (2005). *Cracking the GRE 2006.* New York: Random House.

Lutgendorf, S. K., & Andersen, B. L. (2015). Biobehavioral approaches to cancer progression and survival: Mechanisms and interventions. *American Psychologist, 70*, 186-197.

Luttrell, A., Petty, R. E., & Xu, M. (2017). Replicating and fixing failed replications: The case of need for cognition and argument quality. *Journal of Experimental Social Psychology, 69*, 178-183.

Lutz, C. K., & Novak, M. A. (2005). Environmental enrichment for nonhuman primates: Theory and application. *ILAR Journal, 46*, 178-191.

Lutz, W., Lambert, M. J., Harmon, S. C., Tschitsaz, A., Schurch, E., & Stulz, N. (2006). The probability of treatment success, failure and duration–What can be learned from empirical data to support decision making in clinical practice? *Clinical Psychology & Psychotherapy, 13*, 223-232.

Luxton, D. D. (Ed.) (2016). *Artificial intelligence in behavioral and mental health care.* San Diego, CA: Elsevier Academic Press.

Lynn, S. J., Kirsch, I., Barabasz, A., Cardena, E., & Patterson, D. (2000). Hypnosis as an empirically supported clinical intervention: The state of the evidence and a look to the future. *International Journal of Clinical and Experimental Hypnosis, 48*, 239-259.

Lynn, S. J., Krackow, E., Loftus, E. F., Locke, T. G., & Lilienfeld, S. O. (2015). Constructing the past: Problematic memory recovery techniques in psychotherapy. In S. O. Lilienfeld, S. J. Lynn, & J. M. Lohr (Eds.), *Science and pseudoscience in clinical psychology* (2nd ed.). New York: Guilford Press.

Lynn, S. J., Laurence, J., & Kirsch, I. (2015). Hypnosis, suggestion, and suggestibility: An integrative model. *American Journal of Clinical Hypnosis, 57*, 314-329.

Lyons, H., Giordano, P. C., Manning, W. D., & Longmore, M. A. (2011). Identity, peer relationships, and adolescent girls' sexual behavior: An exploration of the contemporary double standard. *Journal of Sex Research, 48*, 437-449.

López, G., & Bialik, K. (2017, May 3.). Key findings about U.S. immigrants. *Fact Tank: News in the Numbers.* http://www.pewresearch.org/fact-tank/2017/05/03/key-findings-about-u-s-immigrants/.

López, S. R., & Guarnaccia, P. J. J. (2000). Cultural psychopathology: Uncovering the social

world of mental illness. *Annual Review of Psychology, 51*, 571-598.

López-Pérez, B., & Ambrona, T. (2015). The role of cognitive emotion regulation on the vicarious emotional response. *Motivation and Emotion, 39*, 299-308.

López-Pérez, B., Carrera, P., Oceja, L., Ambrona, T., & Stocks, E. (2017). Sympathy and tenderness as components of dispositional empathic concern: Predicting helping and caring behaviors. *Current Psychology: A Journal for Diverse Perspectives on Diverse Psychological Issues.* Accessed from https://link.springer.com/article/10.1007/s12144-017-9615-7.

Macaluso, E., & Driver, J. (2005). Multisensory spatial interactions: a window onto functional integration in the human brain. *Trends in Neurosciences, 28, Issue 5*, 264-271.

Macaluso, E., Frith, C. D., & Driver, J. (2000). Modulation of human visual cortex by crossmodal spatial attention. *Science, 289*, 1206-1208.

Maccoby, E. E., & Jacklin, C. N. (1974). *The psychology of sex differences.* Palo Alto, CA: Stanford University Press.

Macduff, I. (2006). Your pace or mine? Culture, time and negotiation. *Negotiation Journal, 22*, 31-45.

Mace, J. H., Bernas, R. S., & Clevinger, A. (2015). Individual differences in recognising involuntary autobiographical memories: Impact on the reporting of abstract cues. *Memory, 23*, 445-452.

Mack, J. (2003). *The museum of the mind.* London: British Museum Publications.

Mack, M. L., Love, B. C., & Preston, A. R. (2016). Dynamic updating of hippocampal object representations reflects new conceptual knowledge. *PNAS Proceedings of the National Academy Of Sciences of the United States of America, 113*, 13203-13208.

Mackay, J., & Eriksen, M. (2002). *The tobacco atlas.* Geneva, Switzerland: World Health Organization.

Mackey, A. P., Finn, A. S., Leonard, J. A., Jacoby-Senghor, D. S., West, M. R., Gabrieli, C. F. O., . . . Gabrieli, J. D. (2015). Neuroanatomical correlates of the income-achievement gap. *Psychological Science*, 1-9.

MacLennan, A. (2009). Evidence-based review of therapies at the menopause. *International Journal of Evidence-Based Healthcare, 7*, 112-123.

MacLennan, B. J. (2017). Neural networks, learning, and intelligence. In J. Call, G. M. Burghardt, I. M. Pepperberg, C. T. Snowdon, & T. Zentall (Eds.), *APA handbook of comparative psychology: Basic concepts, methods, neural substrate, and behavior.* Washington, DC: American Psychological Association.

MacNeilage, P. F., Rogers, L. J., & Vallortigara, G. (2009). Origins of the left & right brain. *Scientific American, 301*, 60-67.

Macur, J. (2017, July 18). Honest tour analysis from a familiar, though hardly trusted, voice. *The New York Times*, p. B7.

Madden, D. J. (2007). Aging and visual attention. *Current Directions in Psychological Science, 16*, 70-74.

Maddi, S. R. (2007). The story of hardiness: Twenty years of theorizing, research, and practice. In A. Monat, R. S. Lazarus, & G. Reevy (Eds.), *The Praeger handbook on stress and coping* (Vol. 2). Westport, CT: Praeger Publishers/Greenwood Publishing.

Maddi, S. R., Khoshaba, D. M., Harvey, R. H., Fazel, M., & Resurreccion, N. (2011). The personality construct of hardiness, V: Relationships with the construction of existential meaning in life. *Journal of Humanistic Psychology, 51*, 369-388.

Maddock, R. J., Buonocore, M. H., Miller, A. R., Yoon, J. H., Soosman, S. K., & Unruh, A. M. (2013). Abnormal activity-dependent brain lactate and glutamate + glutamine responses in panic disorder. *Biological Psychiatry, 73*, 1111-1119.

Mader, S. S. (2000). *Biology* (6th ed.). Boston: McGraw-Hill.

Madon, S., Willard, J., & Guyll, M. (2006). Self-fulfilling prophecy effects of mothers' beliefs on children's alcohol use: Accumulation, dissipation, and stability over time. *Journal of Personality and Social Psychology, 90*, 911-926.

Magee, S. R., Bublitz, M. H., Orazine, C., Brush, B., Salisbury, A., Niaura, R., . . . Stroud, L. R. (2013). The relationship between maternal-fetal attachment and cigarette smoking over pregnancy. *Maternal and Child Health Journal, 18*(4), 1017-1022.

Magida, A. J. (2006). *Opening the doors of wonder: Reflections on religious rites of passage.* Berkeley, CA: University of California Press.

Magis, D., & Schoenen, J. (2011). Treatment of migraine: update on new therapies. *Current Opinions in Neurology, 24*, 203-210.

Magley, V. J. (2002). Coping with sexual harassment: Reconceptualizing women's resistance. *Journal of Personality and Social Psychology, 83*, 930-946.

Magoni, M., Bassani, L., Okong, P., Kituuka, P., Germinario, E. P., Giuliano, M., . . . Vella, S. (2005). Mode of infant feeding and HIV infection in children in a program for prevention of mother-to-child transmission in Uganda. *AIDS, 19*, 433-437.

Magoon, M., & Critchfield, T. (2008). Concurrent schedules of positive and negative reinforcement: Differential-impact and differential-outcomes hypotheses. *Journal of the Experimental Analysis of Behavior, 90*, 1-22.

Magruder, K., & Yeager, D. (2009). The prevalence of PTSD across war eras and the effect of deployment on PTSD: A systematic review and meta-analysis. *Psychiatric Annals, 39*, 778-788.

Maher, B. (2015). The anatomy of obedience. *Nature, 523*, 408-409.

Majeres, R. L. (2007). Sex differences in phonological coding: Alphabet transformation speed. *Intelligence, 35*, 335-346.

Major, J. T., Johnson, W., & Bouchard, T. J. (2011). The dependability of the general factor of intelligence: Why small, single-factor models do not adequately represent g. *Intelligence, 39*, 418-433.

Majorano, M., & D'Odorico, L. (2011). The transition into ambient language: A longitudinal study of babbling and first word production of Italian children. *First Language, 31*, 47-66.

Malamuth, N. M., Linz, D., Heavey, C. L., & Barnes, G. (1995). Using the confluence model of sexual aggression to predict men's conflict with women: A 10-year follow-up study. *Journal of Personality and Social Psychology, 69*, 353-369.

Malin, D. H., Schaar, K. L., Izygon, J. J., Nghiem, D. M., Jabitta, S. Y., Henceroth, M. M., . . . Ward, C. P. (2015). Validation and scopolamine-reversal of latent learning in the water maze utilizing a revised direct platform placement procedure. *Pharmacology, Biochemistry and Behavior, 13*, 590-96.

Malloy, L. C., Brubacher, S. P., & Lamb, M. E. (2011). Expected consequences of disclosure revealed in investigative interviews with suspected victims of child sexual abuse. *Applied Developmental Science, 15*, 8-19.

Malouff, J. M., & Rooke, S. E. (2013). Expert-recommended warnings for medical marijuana. *Substance Abuse, 34*, 92-93.

Mancinelli, R., Binetti, R., & Ceccanti, M. (2007). Woman, alcohol and environment: Emerging risks for health. *Neuroscience & Biobehavioral Reviews, 31*, 246-253.

Manjhi, A., & Purty, S. (2017). Response to the blank card of Thematic Apperception Test (TAT) and its correlation with personality factors. *Journal of Projective Psychology & Mental Health, 24*, 52-56.

Manly, J. J. (2005). Advantages and disadvantages of separate norms for African Americans. *Clinical Neuropsychologist, 19*, 270-275.

Manly, J., & Echemendia, R. (2007). Race-specific norms: Using the model of hypertension to understand issues of race, culture, and education in neuropsychology. *Archives of Clinical Neuropsychology, 22*, 319-325.

Mann, R. E., & Hollin, C. R. (2007). Sexual offenders' explanations for their offending. *Journal of Sexual Aggression, 13*, 3-9.

Mannarini, T., Talò, C., & Rochira, A. (2017). How diverse is this community? Sense of community, ethnic prejudice, and perceived ethnic heterogeneity. *Journal of Community and Applied Social Psychology, 27*(3), 181-195.

Manni, R., & Terzaghi, M. (2013). Dreaming and enacting dreams in nonrapid eye movement and rapid eye movement parasomnia: A step toward a unifying view within distinct patterns? *Sleep Medicine, 14*, 387-388.

Manor, J. K., & Gailliot, M. T. (2007). Altruism and egoism: Prosocial motivations for helping depend on relationship context. *European Journal of Social Psychology, 37*, 347-358.

Mansson, K. N., Salami, A., Frick, A., Carlbring, P., Andersson, G., Furmark, T., & Boraxbekk, C. J. (2016). Neuroplasticity in response to cognitive behavior therapy for social anxiety disorder. *Translational Psychiatry, 6*, e727. doi: 10.1038/tp.2015.218.

Manstead, A. S. R., & Wagner, H. L. (2004). *Experience emotion.* Cambridge, England: Cambridge University Press.

Manstead, A. S. R., Frijda, N., & Fischer, A. H. (Eds.). (2003). *Feelings and emotions: The Amsterdam Symposium.* Cambridge, England: Cambridge University Press.

Manzo, L., Gómez, M. J., Callejas-Aguilera, J. E., Fernández-Teruel, A., Papini, M. R., & Torres, C. (2015). Partial reinforcement reduces vulnerability to anti-anxiety self-medication during appetitive extinction. *International Journal of Comparative Psychology, 28*, 22-30.

Marchand, S., & Phillips, G. E. (2012). Hoarding's place in the DSM-5: Another symptom, or a newly listed disorder? *Issues in Mental Health Nursing, 33*, 591-597.

Marks, I. M. (2004). The Nobel prize award in physiology to Ivan Petrovich Pavlov-1904. *Australian and New Zealand Journal of Psychiatry, 38*, 674-677.

Markus, H. R. (2007). Sociocultural psychology: The dynamic interdependence among self systems and social systems. In S. Kitayama & D. Cohen (Eds.), *Handbook of cultural psychology.* New York: Guilford Press.

Markus, H. R., & Kitayama, S. (2003). Models of agency: Sociocultural diversity in the construction of action. In V. Murphy-Berman & J. J. Berman (Eds.), *Cross-cultural differences in perspectives on the self.* Lincoln, NE: University of Nebraska Press.

Markus, H., & Kitayama, S. (2003). Culture, self, and the reality of the social. *Psychological Inquiry, 14*, 277-283.

Markus, H., & Kitayama, S. (2010). Cultures and selves: A cycle of mutual constitution. *Perspectives on Psychological Science, 5*, 420-430.

Markus, K. A., & Borsboom, D. (2013). *Frontiers of test validity theory: Measurement, causation, and meaning.* New York: Routledge/Taylor & Francis Group.

Marques, A. H., Bjørke-Monsen, A., Teixeira, A. L., & Silverman, M. N. (2015). Maternal stress, nutrition and physical activity: Impact on immune function, CNS development and psychopathology. *Brain Research, 161*, 728-746.

Marsh, B. (2008, February 24). A growing cloud over the planet. *The New York Times,* p. WK4.

Marsh, H. W., Hau, K. T., & Sung, R. Y. T. (2007). Childhood obesity, gender, actual-ideal body image discrepancies, and physical self-concept in Hong Kong children: Cultural differences in the value of moderation. *Developmental Psychology, 43*, 647-662.

Marshall, J. R. (2011). Ultimate causes and the evolution of altruism. *Behavioral Ecology and Sociobiology, 65*, 503-512.

Marshall, K., Laing, D. G., & Jinks, A. L. (2006). The capacity of humans to identify components in complex odor-taste mixtures. *Chemical Senses, 31*, 539-545.

Marshall, L., & Born, J. (2007). The contribution of sleep to hippocampus-dependent memory consolidation. *Trends in Cognitive Sciences, 11*(10), 442-450.

Marshall, M. K. (2007). The critical factors of coaching practice leading to successful coaching outcomes. *Dissertation Abstracts International: Section B: The Sciences and Engineering, 67*(7-B), 4092.

Marshall, R. D., Bryant, R. A., Amsel, L., Suh, E. J., Cook, J. M., & Neria, Y. (2007). The psychology of ongoing threat: Relative risk appraisal, the September 11 attacks and terrorism-related fears. *American Psychologist, 62*, 304-316.

Martelle, S., Hanley, C., & Yoshino K. (2003, January 28). "Sopranos" scenario in slaying? *Los Angeles Times,* p. B1.

Martin, E. A., & Kerns, J. G. (2011). The influence of positive mood on different aspects of cognitive control. *Cognition and Emotion, 25*, 265-279.

Martin, K. K., & North, A. C. (2015). Diffusion of responsibility on social networking sites. *Computers in Human Behavior, 44*, 124-131.

Martin, L., & Pullum, G. K. (1991). *The great Eskimo vocabulary hoax.* Chicago: University of Chicago Press.

Marwha, D., Halari, M., & Eliot, L. (2017). Meta-analysis reveals a lack of sexual dimorphism in human amygdala volume. *NeuroImage, 147*, 282-288.

Mashour, G. A., Walker, E. E., & Martuza, R. L. (2005). Psychosurgery: Past, present, and future. *Brain Research Reviews, 48*, 409-419.

Masi, S., Asselain, N., Robelin, L., Bourgeois, A., Hano, C., Dousseau, G., . . . Krief, S. (2013). Response to bitter substances in primates: Roles of diet tendency and weaning age. *Cognitive, Affective & Behavioral Neuroscience, 13*(4), 916-929.

Maslow, A. H. (1970). *Motivation and personality.* New York: Harper & Row.

Maslow, A. H. (1987). *Motivation and personality* (3rd ed.). New York: Harper & Row.

Mason, M. (1995). *The making of Victorian sexuality.* New York: Oxford University Press.

Mason, T. B., Maduro, R. S., Derlega, V. J., Hacker, D. S., Winstead, B. A., & Haywood, J. E. (2017). Individual differences in the impact of vicarious racism: African American students react to the George Zimmerman trial. *Cultural Diversity and Ethnic Minority Psychology, 23*, 174-184.

Massadi, O. A., López, M., Tschöp, M., Diéguez, C., & Nogueiras, R. (2017). Current understanding of the hypothalamic ghrelin pathways inducing appetite and adiposity. *Trends In Neurosciences, 40*, 167-180.

Massé-Alarie, H., Beaulieu, L., Preuss, R., & Schneider, C. (2017). The side of chronic low back pain matters: Evidence from the primary motor cortex excitability and the postural adjustments of multifidi muscles. *Experimental Brain Research, 235*, 647-659.

Mast, F. W., & Kosslyn, S. M. (2002). Visual mental images can be ambiguous: Insights from individual differences in spatial transformation abilities. *Cognition, 86*, 57-70.

Masters, W. H., & Johnson, V. E. (1966). *Human sexual response.* Boston: Little, Brown.

Masters, W. H., & Johnson, V. E. (1979). *Homosexuality in perspective.* Boston: Little, Brown.

Matchock, R. L., & Mordkoff, J. T. (2009). Chronotype and time-of-day influences on the alerting, orienting, and executive components of attention. *Experimental Brain Research, 192,* 189-198.

Mathews, H. L., & Janusek, L. (2011). Epigenetics and psychoneuroimmunology: Mechanisms and models. *Brain, Behavior, and Immunity, 25,* 25-39.

Matlin, M. W. (1996). *The psychology of women* (3rd ed.). Orlando, FL: Harcourt Brace College Publishers.

Maton, K. I., Kohout, J. L., Wicherski, M., Leary, G. E., & Vinokurov, A. (2006). Minority students of color and the psychology graduate pipeline. *American Psychologist, 61,* 117-131.

Matsumoto, D. (2002). Methodological requirements to test a possible in-group advantage in judging emotions across cultures: Comment on Elfenbein and Ambady (2002) and evidence. *Psychological Bulletin, 128,* 236-242.

Mattan, B. D., Kubota, J. T., & Cloutier, J. (2017). How social status shapes person perception and evaluation: A social neuroscience perspective. *Perspectives on Psychological Science, 12,* 468-507.

Mattys, S. L., Seymour, F. F., Attwood, A. S., & Munafò, M. R. (2013). Effects of acute anxiety induction on speech perception: Are anxious listeners distracted listeners? *Psychological Science, 24,* 1606-1608.

Maturana, M. J., Pudell, C., Targa, A. S., Rodrigues, L. S., Noseda, A. D., Fortes, . . . Lima, M. (2015). REM sleep deprivation reverses neurochemical and other depressive-like alterations induced by olfactory bulbectomy. *Molecular Neurobiology, 51,* 349-360.

Maurer, D., Lewis, T. L., Brent, H. P., & Levin, A. V. (1999). Rapid improvement in the acuity of infants after visual input. *Science, 286,* 108-110.

Maxson, S. C. (2013). Behavioral genetics. In R. J. Nelson, S. Y. Mizumori, & I. B. Weiner (Eds.), *Handbook of psychology, Vol. 3: Behavioral neuroscience* (2nd ed.). New York: John Wiley & Sons Ltd.

Maxwell, S. E., Lau, M. Y., & Howard, G. S. (2015). Is psychology suffering from a replication crisis? *American Psychologist, 70,* 487-498.

Mayer, D., Simetin, I. P., Rodin, U., Benjak, T., Puntarić, E., & Puntarić, I. (2015). The impacts of media messaging and age and sex variance on adolescent smoking habits in Croatia. *Journal of Addiction Medicine, 9,* 147-154.

Mayer, J. D., Salovey, P., & Caruso, D. R. (2004). Emotional intelligence: Theory, findings, and implications. *Psychological Inquiry, 15,* 197-215.

Mayer, J. D., Salovey, P., & Caruso, D. R. (2008). Emotional intelligence: New ability or eclectic traits? *American Psychologist, 63,* 503-517.

Mayer, R. E. (2013). Problem solving. In D. Reisberg (Ed.), *The Oxford handbook of cognitive psychology.* New York: Oxford University Press.

Maynard, A. E., & Martini, M. I. (2005). *Learning in cultural context: Family, peers, and school.* New York: Kluwer Academic/Plenum Publishers.

Mays, V. M., & Ghavami, N. (2018). History, aspirations, and transformations of intersectionality: Focusing on gender. In C. B. Travis & J. W. White (Eds.), *APA handbook of the psychology of women: Volume 1: History, theory, and battlegrounds* (pp. 541-566). Washington, DC: American Psychological Association.

McAdams, D. P., Diamond, A., de St. Aubin, E., & Mansfield, E. (1997). Stories of commitment: The psychosocial construction of generative lives. *Journal of Personality and Social Psychology, 72,* 678-694.

McCabe, C., & Rolls, E. T. (2007). Umami: A delicious flavor formed by convergence of taste and olfactory pathways in the human brain. *European Journal of Neuroscience, 25,* 1855-1864.

McCabe, M. (2009). Anorgasmia in women. *Journal of Family Psychotherapy, 20,* 177-197.

McCann, J. T., Lynn, S. J., Lilienfeld, S. O., Shindler, K. L., & Hammond Natof, T. R. (2015). The science and pseudoscience of expert testimony. In S. O. Lilienfeld, S. J. Lynn, & J. M. Lohr (Eds.), *Science and pseudoscience in clinical psychology* (2nd ed.). New York: Guilford Press.

McCarrey, A. C., & Resnick, S. M. (2015). Postmenopausal hormone therapy and cognition. *Hormones and Behavior, 74,* 167-172.

McCarthy, J. (2005). Individualism and collectivism: What do they have to do with counseling? *Journal of Multicultural Counseling and Development, 33,* 108-117.

McCarthy, J., & Brown, A. (2015, March 2). Getting more sleep linked to higher well-being. Gallup Poll. Accessed from http://www.gallup.com/poll/1181583/getting-sleep-linked-higher.aspx.

McCarthy, R. J., & Skowronski, J. J. (2011). You're getting warmer: Level of construal affects the impact of central traits on impression formation. *Journal of Experimental Social Psychology, 47,* 1304-1307.

McCaul, K. D., Johnson, R. J., & Rothman, A. J. (2002). The effects of framing and action instructions on whether older adults obtain flu shots. *Health Psychology, 21,* 624-628.

McCauley, R. N., & Henrich, J. (2006). Susceptibility to the Müller-Lyer illusion, theory-neutral observation, and the diachronic penetrability of the visual input. *Philosophical Psychology, 19,* 79-101.

McClelland, D. C. (1985). How motives, skills, and values determine what people do. *American Psychologist, 40,* 812-825.

McClelland, D. C., Atkinson, J. W., Clark, R. A., & Lowell, E. L. (1953). *The achievement motive.* New York: Appleton-Century-Crofts.

McClure, J., Sutton, R. M., & Sibley, C. G. (2007). Listening to reporters or engineers? How instance-based messages about building design affect earthquake fatalism. *Journal of Applied Social Sciences, 37,* 1956-1973.

McCrae, R. R., & Costa, P. T. (1994). The stability of personality: Observation and evaluations. *Current Directions in Psychological Science, 3,* 173-175.

McCrae, R. R., Kurtz, J. E., Yamagata, S., & Terracciano, A. (2011). Internal consistency, retest reliability, and their implications for personality scale validity. *Personality and Social Psychology Review, 15,* 28-50.

McCrink, K., & Wynn, K. (2007). Ratio abstraction by 6-month-old infants. *Psychological Science, 18,* 740-745.

McCulloch, K., Lachner Bass, N., Dial, H., Hiscock, M., & Jansen, B. (2017). Interaction of attention and acoustic factors in dichotic listening for fused words. *Laterality: Asymmetries of Body, Brain and Cognition, 22,* 473-494.

McDaniel, M. A., Maier, S. F., & Einstein, G. O. (2002). "Brain specific" nutrients: A memory cure? *Psychological Science in the Public Interest, 3,* 12-18.

McDermott, M. S., Beard, E., Brose, L. S., West, R., & McEwen, A. (2013). Factors associated with differences in quit rates between "specialist" and "community" stop-smoking practitioners in the English stop-smoking services. *Nicotine & Tobacco Research, 15,* 1239-1247.

McDonald, A. R., Muraskin, J., Van Dam, N. T., Froehlich, C., Puccio, B., Pellman, J., . . . Craddock, R. C. (2017). The real-time fMRI neurofeedback based stratification of Default Network Regulation Neuroimaging data repository. *Neuroimage, 146,* 157-170.

McDonald, H. E., & Hirt, E. R. (1997). When expectancy meets desire: Motivational effects in reconstructive memory. *Journal of Personality and Social Psychology, 72,* 5-23.

McDougall, W. (1908). *Introduction to social psychology.* London: Methuen.

McElreath, R., Wallin, A., & Fasolo, B. (2013). The evolutionary rationality of social learning. In R. Hertwig & U. Hoffrage (Eds.), *Simple heuristics in a social world.* New York: Oxford University Press.

McEwen, B. S. (1998). Protective and damaging effects of stress mediators [Review article]. *New England Journal of Medicine, 338,* 171-179.

McGaugh, J. L, & LePort, A. (2014). Remembrance of all things past. *Scientific American, 310,* 41-45.

McGilvray, J. (Ed.). (2004). *The Cambridge companion to Chomsky.* Oxford, England: Cambridge University Press.

McGinn, D. (2003, June 9). Testing, testing: The new job search. *Time,* pp. 36-38.

McGregor, K. K., & Capone, N. C. (2004). Genetic and environmental interactions in determining the early lexicon: Evidence from a set of tri-zygotic quadruplets. *Journal of Child Language, 31,* 311-337.

McIntyre, K., Korn, J., & Matsuo, H. (2008). Sweating the small stuff: How different types of hassles result in the experience of stress. *Stress and Health: Journal of the International Society for the Investigation of Stress, 24,* 383-392.

McKinley, J. C. Jr. (2013, September 12). Overdoses of "Molly" led to Electric Zoo deaths. *The New York Times.* Accessed from http://artsbeat.blogs.nytimes.com/2013/09/12/overdoses-of-molly-led-to-electric-zoo-deaths/.

McLay, R. N., Baird, A., Webb-Murphy, J., Deal, W., Tran, L., Anson, H., . . . Johnston, S. (2017). A randomized, head-to-head study of virtual reality exposure therapy for posttraumatic stress disorder. *Cyberpsychology, Behavior, and Social Networking, 20*, 218-224.

McLean, C. P., Su, Y., Carpenter, J. K., & Foa, E. B. (2017). Changes in PTSD and depression during prolonged exposure and client-centered therapy for PTSD in adolescents. *Journal of Clinical Child And adolescent Psychology, 46*, 500-510.

McLeod, J. (2015). Happiness, wellbeing and self-esteem: Public feelings and educational projects. In K. Wright & J. McLeod (Eds.), *Rethinking youth wellbeing: Critical perspectives.* New York: Springer Science + Business Media.

McMurtray, A. M., Licht, E., Yeo, T., Krisztal, E., Saul, R. E., & Mendez, M. F. (2007). Positron emission tomography facilitates diagnosis of early-onset Alzheimer's disease. *European Neurology, 59*, 31-37.

McNamara, T. P. (2013). Semantic memory and priming. In A. F. Healy, R. W. Proctor, & I. B. Weiner (Eds.), *Handbook of psychology, Vol. 4: Experimental psychology* (2nd ed.). Hoboken, NJ: John Wiley & Sons Inc.

McRobbie, L. R. (2017, February 8). Total recall: The people who never forget. *The Guardian.* Retrieved from https://www.theguardian.com/science/2017/feb/08/total-recall-the-people-who-never-forget.

McSpadden, K. (2015, May 14). You now have a shorter attention span than a goldfish. *Time.*

McTeague, L. M., Lang, P. J., Laplante, M., & Bradley, M. M. (2011). Aversive imagery in panic disorder: Agoraphobia severity, comorbidity, and defensive physiology. *Biological Psychiatry, 70*, 415-424.

Medeiros, R., Prediger, R. D. S., Passos, G. F., Pandolfo, P., Duarte, F. S., Franco, J. L., . . . Calixto, J. B. (2007). Connecting TNF-alpha signaling pathways to iNOS expression in a mouse model of Alzheimer's disease: Relevance for the behavioral and synaptic deficits induced by amyloid beta protein. *Journal of Neuroscience, 27*, 5394-5404.

Meeter, M., & Murre, J. M. J. (2004). Consolidation of long-term memory: Evidence and alternatives. *Psychological Bulletin, 130*, 843-857.

Megill, J. (2013). Emotion, cognition and artificial intelligence. *Minds and Machines, 24*, 189-199.

Mehl, M. R., Vazire, S., Ramirez-Esparza, N., Slatcher, R. B., & Pennebaker, J. W. (2007). Are women really more talkative than men? *Science, 317*, 82.

Meier, B., & Rothen, N. (2015). Developing synaesthesia: A primer. *Frontiers in Human Neuroscience, 9*, 211.

Meltzer, A. L., Makhanova, A., Hicks, L. L., French, J. E., McNulty, J. K., & Bradbury, T. N. (2017). Quantifying the sexual afterglow: The lingering benefits of sex and their implications for pair-bonded relationships. *Psychological Science, 28*(5), 587-598.

Meltzoff, A. N. (1996). The human infant as imitative generalist: A 20-year progress report on infant imitation with implications for comparative psychology. In C. M. Heyes & B. G. Galef, Jr. (Eds.), *Social learning in animals: The roots of culture.* San Diego, CA: Academic Press.

Meltzoff, J., & Cooper, H. (2018). *Critical thinking about research: Psychology and related fields., 2nd ed.* Washington, DC: American Psychological Association.

Melzack, R., & Katz, J. (2001). The McGill Pain Questionnaire: Appraisal and current status. In D. Turk & R. Melzack (Eds.), *Handbook of pain assessment* (2nd ed.). New York: Guilford Press.

Melzack, R., & Katz, J. (2004). *The gate control theory: Reaching for the brain.* Mahwah, NJ: Lawrence Erlbaum Associates.

Mendle, J., Moore, S. R., Briley, D. A., & Harden, K. P. (2016). Puberty, socioeconomic status, and depression in girls: Evidence for gene × environment interactions. *Clinical Psychological Science, 4*(1), 3-16.

Mensah, F. K., Bayer, J. K., Wake, M., Carlin, J. B., Allen, N. B., & Patton, G. C. (2013). Early puberty and childhood social and behavioral adjustment. *Journal of Adolescent Health, 53*, 118-124.

Mercadillo, R. E., Díaz, J., Pasaye, E. H., & Barrios, F. A. (2011). Perception of suffering and compassion experience: Brain gender disparities. *Brain and Cognition, 76*, 5-14.

Mercier, H. (2017). Confirmation bias–Myside bias. In R. F. Pohl (Ed.), *Cognitive illusions: Intriguing phenomena in thinking, judgment and memory.* New York: Routledge/Taylor & Francis Group.

Merikangas, K. R., Ames, M., Cui, L., Stang, P. E., Ustun, T. B., VonKorff, M., & Kessler, R. C. (2007). The impact of comorbidity of mental and physical conditions on role disability in the US adult household population. *Archives of General Psychiatry, 64*, 1180-1188.

Merrill, Everett. (2016, June 26). Meet Iris the FBI dog. Retrieved from http://www.mycentral-jersey.com/story/news/crime/jersey-may-hem/2016/06/26/meet-iris-fbi-dog/84770556/.

Mesoudi, A. (2011). Evolutionary psychology meets cultural psychology. *Journal of Evolutionary Psychology, 9*, 83-87.

Messner, M., Reinhard, M., & Sporer, S. (2008). Compliance through direct persuasive appeals: The moderating role of communicator's attractiveness in interpersonal persuasion. *Social Influence, 3*, 67-83.

Meston, C. M. (2003). Validation of the female sexual function index (FSFI) in women with female orgasmic disorder and in women with hypoactive sexual desire disorder. *Journal of Sex and Marital Therapy, 29*, 39-46.

Metz, C. (2017, July 31). Therapy in a dose of illusion. *The New York Times*, pp. B1, B4.

Meyer-Bahlburg, H. (1997). The role of prenatal estrogens in sexual orientation. In L. Ellis & L. Ebertz (Eds.), *Sexual orientation: Toward biological understanding.* Westport, CT: Praeger.

Michael, R. T., Gagnon, J. H., Laumann, E. O., & Kolata, G. (1994). *Sex in America: A definitive survey.* Boston: Little, Brown.

Micheau, J., & Marighetto, A. (2011). Acetylcholine and memory: A long, complex and chaotic but still living relationship. *Behavioural Brain Research, 221*, 424-429.

Midanik, L. T., Tam, T. W., & Weisner, C. (2007). Concurrent and simultaneous drug and alcohol use: Results of the 2000 national alcohol survey. *Drug and Alcohol Dependence, 90*, 72-80.

Mifflin, L. (1998, January 14). Study finds a decline in TV network violence. *The New York Times*, p. A14.

Šmigelskas, K., Žemaitienė, N., Julkunen, J., & Kauhanen, J. (2015). Type A behavior pattern is not a predictor of premature mortality. *International Journal of Behavioral Medicine, 22*, 161-169.

Mignon, A., & Mollaret, P. (2002). Applying the affordance conception of traits: A person perception study. *Personality and Social Psychology Bulletin, 28*, 1327-1334.

Miguez, G., Witnauer, J. E., & Miller, R. R. (2011). The role of contextual associations in producing the partial reinforcement acquisition deficit. *Journal of Experimental Psychology: Animal Behavior Processes, 37*, 88-97.

Mihalca, L., Mengelkamp, C., & Schnotz, W. (2017). Accuracy of metacognitive judgments as a moderator of learner control effectiveness in problem-solving tasks. *Metacognition and Learning.* Accessed from https://link.springer.com/article/10.1007/s11409-017-9173-2.

Mika, V. S., Wood, P. R., Weiss, B. D., & Trevino, L. (2007). Ask Me 3: Improving communication in a Hispanic pediatric outpatient practice. *American Journal of Behavioral Health, 31*, S115-S121.

Miles, P., Schaufeli, W. B., & van den Bos, K. (2011). When weak groups are strong: How low cohesion groups allow individuals to act according to their personal absence tolerance norms. *Social Justice Research, 24*, 207-230.

Milgram, S. (2005). *Obedience to authority.* Pinter & Martin: New York.

Miller, C., & Williams, A. (2011). Ethical guidelines in research. In J. C. Thomas & M. Hersen (Eds.), *Understanding research in clinical and counseling psychology* (2nd ed.). New York: Routledge/Taylor & Francis Group.

Miller, G. (2006). A spoonful of medicine–and a steady diet of normalcy. *Science, 311*, 464-465.

Miller, G. (2008). The roots of morality. *Science, 320*, 734-737.

Miller, G. E., Chen, E., & Parker, K. J. (2011). Psychological stress in childhood and susceptibility to the chronic diseases of aging: Moving toward a model of behavioral and biological mechanisms. *Psychological Bulletin, 137*, 959-997.

Miller, J. A., & Leffard, S. A. (2007). Behavioral assessment. In S. R. Smith & L. Handler (Eds.), *The clinical assessment of children and adolescents: A practitioner's handbook.* Mahwah, NJ: Lawrence Erlbaum Associates.

Miller, J. G. (1984). Culture and the development of everyday social explanation. *Journal of Personality and Social Psychology, 46*, 961-978.

Miller, L. A., McIntire, S. A., & Lovler, R. L. (2011). *Foundations of psychological testing: A practical problem* (3rd ed.). Thousand Oaks, CA: Sage Publications, Inc.

Miller, L., Gur, M., Shanok, A., & Weissman, M. (2008). Interpersonal psychotherapy with pregnant adolescents: Two pilot studies. *Journal of Child Psychology and Psychiatry, 49*, 733-742.

Miller, N. E., & Magruder, K. M. (Eds.). (1999). *Cost-effectiveness of psychotherapy: A guide for practitioners, researchers, and policymakers.* New York: Oxford University Press.

Miller, Naseem S. (2016, January 18). Doctors learn how to give bad news to patients. *Orlando Sentinel.* Retrieved from http://www.orlandosentinel.com/health/os-breaking-bad-news-residents-ormc-20160118-story.html.

Miller-Perrin, C., Perrin, R., & Kocur, J. (2009). Parental physical and psychological aggression: Psychological symptoms in young adults. *Child Abuse & Neglect, 33*, 1-11.

Mills, J. (2013). Jung's metaphysics. *International Journal of Jungian Studies, 5*, 19-43.

Mills, M. J. (2011). Associations among achievement measures and their collective prediction of work involvement. *Personality and Individual Differences, 50*, 360-364.

Milner, B. (1966). Amnesia following operation on temporal lobes. In C. W. M. Whitty & P. Zangwill (Eds.), *Amnesia.* London: Butterworth.

Milner, B. (2005). The medial temporal-lobe amnesic syndrome. *Psychiatric Clinics of North America, 28*, 599-611.

Milos, G., Baur, V., Schumacher, S., Kuenzli, C., Schnyder, U., Mueller-Pfeiffer, C., . . . Martin-Soelch, C. (2017). How fat will it make me? Estimation of weight gain in anorexia nervosa. *Appetite, 114*, 368-373.

Miner, J., & Clarke-Stewart, K. (2008). Trajectories of externalizing behavior from age 2 to age 9: Relations with gender, temperament, ethnicity, parenting, and rater. *Developmental Psychology, 44*, 771-786.

Miner-Rubino, K., & Cortina, L. M. (2007). Beyond targets: Consequences of vicarious exposure to misogyny at work. *Journal of Applied Psychology, 92*, 1254-1269.

Miner-Rubino, K., Winter, D. G., & Stewart, A. J. (2004). Gender, social class, and the subjective experience of aging: Self-perceived personality change from early adulthood to late midlife. *Personality and Social Psychology Bulletin, 30*, 1599-1610.

Minică, C. C., Mbarek, H., Pool, R., Dolan, C. V., Boomsma, D. I., & Vink, J. M. (2017). Pathways to smoking behaviours: Biological insights from the Tobacco and Genetics Consortium meta-analysis. *Molecular Psychiatry, 22*, 82-88.

Mintz, A., & Wayne, C. (2014). Group decision making in conflict: From groupthink to polythink in the war in Iraq. In P. T. Coleman, M. Deutsch, & E. C. Marcus (Eds.), *The handbook of conflict resolution: Theory and practice* (3rd ed.). San Francisco, CA: Jossey-Bass.

Miquel, J. (2006). Integración de teorías del envejecimiento (parte I). Integration of theories of aging. *Revista Espanola de Geriatria y Gerontologia, 41*, 55-63.

Mirzairad, R., Haydari, A., Pasha, R., Ehteshamzadeh, P., & Makvandi, B. (2017). The relationship between perfectionism and psychological distress with the mediation of coping styles and self-esteem. *International Journal of Mental Health and Addiction, 15*, 614-620.

Mischel, W. (2004). Toward an integrative science of the person. *Annual Review of Psychology, 55*, 1-22.

Mischel, W. (2009). From Personality and Assessment (1968) to Personality Science, 2009. *Journal of Research in Personality, 43*, 282-290.

Mischel, W., & Shoda, Y. (2008). Toward a unified theory of personality: Integrating dispositions and processing dynamics within the cognitive-affective processing system. In O. P. Oliver, R. W. Robins, & L. A. Pervin (Eds.), *Handbook of personality psychology: Theory and research* (3rd ed.). New York: Guilford Press.

Mitchell, D. B., & Schmitt, F. A. (2006). Short- and long-term implicit memory in aging and Alzheimer's disease. *Neuropsychological Development and Cognition, B, Aging and Neuropsychological Cognition, 13*, 611-635.

Mitte, K. (2005). Meta-analysis of cognitive-behavioral treatments for generalized anxiety disorder: A comparison with pharmacotherapy. *Psychological Bulletin, 131*, 785-795.

Mizrahi, R., Agid, O., Borlido, C., Suridjan, I., Rusjan, P., Houle, S., . . . Kapur, S. (2011). Effects of antipsychotics on D3 receptors: A clinical PET study in first episode antipsychotic naive patients with schizophrenia using [^{11}C]-(+)-PHNO. *Schizophrenia Research, 131*, 63-68.

Moen, K. C., Miller, J. K., & Lloyd, M. E. (2017). Selective attention meets spontaneous recognition memory: Evidence for effects at retrieval. *Consciousness and Cognition: An International Journal, 49*, 181-189.

Moen, P. (2015). An institutional/organizational turn: Getting to work-life quality and gender equality. *Work and Occupations, 42*, 174-182.

Moffitt, T. E., Caspi, A., & Rutter, M. (2006). Measured gene-environment interactions in psychopathology: Concepts, research strategies, and implications for research, intervention, and public understanding of genetics. *Perspectives on Psychological Science, 1*, 5-27.

Moghaddam, F. M. (2008). The materialist view: From realistic conflict theory to evolutionary psychology. In F. M. Moghaddam (Ed.), *Multiculturalism and intergroup relations: Psychological implications for democracy in global.* Washington, DC: American Psychological Association.

Mograss, M., Guillem, F., Brazzini-Poisson, V., & Godbout, R. (2009). The effects of total sleep deprivation on recognition memory processes: A study of event-related potential. *Neurobiology of Learning and Memory, 91*, 343-352.

Mohan, A., Sharma, R., & Bijlani, R. L. (2011). Effect of meditation on stress-induced changes in cognitive functions. *Journal of Alternative and Complementary Medicine, 17*, 207-212.

Moher, C., Gould, D., Hegg, E., & Mahoney, A. (2008). Non-generalized and generalized conditioned reinforcers: Establishment and validation. *Behavioral Interventions, 23*, 13-38.

Mohr, C., & Messina, S. (2015). Brain dysfunctions, psychopathologies, and body image distortions: Propositions for a possible common cause. *European Psychologist, 20*, 72-81.

Mokdad, A. H., Brewer, R. D., & Naimi, T. (2007). Binge drinking is a problem that cannot be ignored. *Preventive Medicine: An International Journal Devoted to Practice and Theory, 44*, 303-304.

Molina, M., Sann, C., David, M., Touré, Y., Guillois, B., & Jouen, F. (2015). Active touch in late-preterm and early-term neonates. *Developmental Psychobiology, 57*, 322-335.

Mollen, S., Engelen, S., Kessels, L. E., & van den Putte, B. (2017). Short and sweet: The persuasive effects of message framing and temporal context in antismoking warning labels. *Journal of Health Communication, 22*, 20-28.

Monk, T. H., Buysse, D. J., Billy, B. D., Fletcher, M. E., Kennedy, K. S., Schlarb, J. E., & Beach, S. R. (2011). Circadian type and bed-timing regularity in 654 retired seniors: Correlations with subjective sleep measures. *Sleep, 34*, 235-239.

Monteleone, P., Martiadis, V., & Maj, M. (2011). Circadian rhythms and treatment implications in depression. *Progress in Neuro-Psychopharmacology & Biological Psychiatry, 35*, 1569-1574.

Montgomery, K. L. (2011). Living with panic, worry, and fear: Anxiety disorders. In C. Franklin & R. Fong (Eds.), *The church leader's counseling resource book: A guide to mental health and social problems.* New York: Oxford University Press.

Moodley, R., Gielen, U. P., & Wu, R. (2013). *Handbook of counseling and psychotherapy in an international context.* New York: Routledge/Taylor & Francis Group.

Moody, R. L., Starks, T. J., Grov, C., & Parsons, J. T. (2017). Internalized homophobia and drug use in a national cohort of gay and bisexual men: Examining depression, sexual anxiety, and gay community attachment as mediating factors. *Archives of Sexual Behavior.* Accessed from https://www.ncbi.nlm.nih.gov/pubmed/28608294.

Moon, C., Lagercrantz, H., & Kuhl, P. (2013). Language experienced in utero affects vowel perception after birth: A two-country study. *Acta Paediatrica, 102*, 156-160.

Moore, D. G., Goodwin, J. E., & George, R. (2007). Infants perceive human point-light displays as solid forms. *Cognition, 104*, 377-396.

Moore, D. W. (2005, June 16). Three in four Americans believe in paranormal. *Gallup News Service.*

Moore, E. S., Wilkie, W. L., & Desrochers, D. M. (2017). All in the family? Parental roles in the epidemic of childhood obesity. *Journal of Consumer Research, 43*, 824-859.

Moorey, S. (2007). Cognitive therapy. In W. Dryden (Ed.), *Dryden's handbook of individual therapy* (5th ed.). Thousand Oaks, CA: Sage Publications.

Mora-Giral, M., Raich-Escursell, R. M., Segues, C. V., Torras-Claras, A. J., & Huon, G. (2004). Bulimia symptoms and risk factors in university students. *Eating and Weight Disorders, 9,* 163-169.

Morad, Y., Barkana, Y., Zadok, D., Hartstein, M., Pras, E., & Bar-Dayan, Y. (2009). Ocular parameters as an objective tool for the assessment of truck drivers fatigue. *Accident Analysis and Prevention, 41,* 856-860.

Moran, A. (2009). Cognitive psychology in sport: Progress and prospects. *Psychology of Sport and Exercise, 10,* 420-426.

Morcom, A. M., & Friston, K. J. (2011). Decoding episodic memory in ageing: A Bayesian analysis of activity patterns predicting memory. *Neuroimage, 33,* 88-91.

Moreno-Gómez, F. N., Véliz, G., Rojas, M., Martínez, C., Olmedo, R., Panussis, F., . . . Delano, P. H. (2017). Music training and education slow the deterioration of music perception produced by presbycusis in the elderly. *Frontiers in Aging Neuroscience, 9,* 1-10.

Moretz, M., & McKay, D. (2009). The role of perfectionism in obsessive-compulsive symptoms: "Not just right" experiences and checking compulsions. *Journal of Anxiety Disorders, 23,* 640-644.

Morgan, A. A., Marsiske, M., & Whitfield, K. E. (2008). Characterizing and explaining differences in cognitive test performance between African American and European American older adults. *Experimental Aging Research, 34,* 80-100.

Morone, N. E., & Greco, C. M. (2007). Mind-body interventions for chronic pain in older adults: A structured review. *Pain Medicine, 8,* 359-375.

Morris, S. Y. (2017, May 25). What does it mean to have hyperthymesia or highly superior autobiographical memory (HSAM)? *HealthLine.* Retrieved from http://www.healthline.com/health/hyperthymesia#overview1.

Morrone, A. S., & Pintrich, P. R. (2006). Achievement motivation. In G. G. Bear & K. M. Minke (Eds.), *Children's needs III: Development, prevention, and intervention.* Washington, DC: National Association of School Psychologists.

Moscoso, S. C., Chaves, S. S., & Argilaga, M. T. A. (2013). Reporting a program evaluation: Needs, program plan, intervention, and decisions. *International Journal of Clinical and Health Psychology, 13,* 58-66.

Mosher, C. E., Winger, J. G., Given, B. A., Helft, P. R., & O'Neil, B. H. (2015). Mental health outcomes during colorectal cancer survivorship: A review of the literature. *Psycho-Oncology, 25*(11), 1261-1270.

Moshman, D. (2011). *Adolescent rationality and development: Cognition, morality, and identity* (3rd ed.). New York: Psychology Press.

Moskowitz, D. S., Sutton, R., Zuroff, D. C., & Young, S. N. (2015). Fetal exposure to androgens, as indicated by digit ratios (2D:4D), increases men's agreeableness with women. *Personality and Individual Differences, 75,* 97-101.

Motley, M. T. (1987, February). What I meant to say. *Psychology Today,* pp. 25-28.

Moulding, R., Nedeljkovic, M., Kyrios, M., Osborne, D., & Mogan, C. (2017). Short-term cognitive-behavioural group treatment for hoarding disorder: A naturalistic treatment outcome study. *Clinical Psychology & Psychotherapy, 24,* 235-244.

Moynihan, A. B., Igou, E. R., & van Tilburg, W. P. (2017). Free, connected, and meaningful: Free will beliefs promote meaningfulness through belongingness. *Personality and Individual Differences, 107,* 54-65.

Muammar, O. M. (2007). An integration of two competing models to explain practical intelligence. *Dissertation Abstracts International: Section B: The Sciences and Engineering, 67*(7-B), 4128.

Mueller, C. E. (2009). Protective factors as barriers to depression in gifted and nongifted adolescents. *Gifted Child Quarterly, 53,* 3-14.

Mullane, M. P., Martens, B. K., Baxter, E. L., & Steeg, D. V. (2017). Children's preference for mixed-versus fixed-ratio schedules of reinforcement: A translational study of risky choice. *Journal of the Experimental Analysis of Behavior, 107,* 161-175.

Mungan, E., Peynircioğlu, Z. F., & Halpern, A. R. (2011). Levels-of-processing effects on 'remember' responses in recognition for familiar and unfamiliar tunes. *The American Journal of Psychology, 124,* 37-48.

Munjiza, J., Britvic, D., Radman, M., & Crawford, M. J. (2017). Severe war-related trauma and personality pathology: A case-control study. *BMC Psychiatry, 17,* 22-28.

Munro, C., Randell, L., & Lawrie, S. M. (2017). An integrative bio-psycho-social theory of anorexia nervosa. *Clinical Psychology & Psychotherapy, 24,* 1-21.

Murayama, K., & Kitagami, S. (2013). Consolidation power of extrinsic rewards: Reward cues enhance long-term memory for irrelevant past events. *Journal of Experimental Psychology: General, 143,* 15-20.

Murray, B. (2002, June). Good news for bachelor's grads. *Monitor on Psychology,* pp. 30-32.

Murray, R., Lappin, J., & Di Forti, M. (2008). Schizophrenia: From developmental deviance to dopamine dysregulation. *European Neuropsychopharmacology, 18,* S129-SS134.

Murray, S. L., Holmes, J. G., & Griffin, D. W. (2004). The benefits of positive illusions: Idealization and the construction of satisfaction in close relationships. In H. T. Reis & C. E. Rusbult (Eds.), *Close relationships: Key readings.* Philadelphia, PA: Taylor & Francis.

Murthy, P., Kudlur, S., George, S., & Mathew, G. (2009). A clinical overview of fetal alcohol syndrome. *Addictive Disorders & Their Treatment, 8,* 1-12.

Myers, L. L. (2007). Anorexia nervosa, bulimia nervosa, and binge eating disorder. In B. A. Thyer & J. S. Wodarski (Eds.), *Social work in mental health: An evidence-based approach.* Hoboken, NJ: John Wiley & Sons.

Myrtek, M. (2007). Type A behavior and hostility as independent risk factors for coronary heart disease. In J. Jordan, B. Barde, & A. M. Zeiher (Eds.), *Contributions toward evidence-based psychocardiology: A systematic review of the literature.* Washington, DC: American Psychological Association.

Møller, A. R. (2011). Anatomy and physiology of the auditory system. In A. R. Møller, B. Langguth, D. DeRidder, & T. Kleinjung (Eds.), *Textbook of tinnitus.* New York: Springer Science + Business Media.

Müller, M., Bosy-Wesphal, A., & Heymsfield, S. B. (2010). Is there evidence for a set point that regulates human body weight? *F1000 Medicine Reports, 2,* 59.

Nabi, R. L., Prestin, A., & So, J. (2013). Facebook friends with (health) benefits? Exploring social network site use and perceptions of social support, stress, and well-being. *Cyberpsychology, Behavior, and Social Networking, 16,* 721-727.

Nader, E. G., Kleinman, A., Gomes, B., Bruscagin, C., Santos, B., Nicoletti, M., & Caetano, S. C. (2013). Negative expressed emotion best discriminates families with bipolar disorder children. *Journal of Affective Disorders, 148,* 418-423.

Nagda, B. A., Tropp, L. R., & Paluck, E. L. (2006). Looking back as we look ahead: Integrating research, theory, and practice on intergroup relations. *Journal of Social Research, 62,* 439-451.

Nagesh, Ashitha. (2017, July 9). Instagram star's "healthy food" obsession was actually a dangerous eating disorder. *Metro.co.uk.* Retrieved from http://metro.co.uk/2017/07/09/instagram-stars-healthy-food-obsession-was-actually-a-dangerous-eating-disorder-6766434/.

Naglieri, J. A., LeBuffe, P. A., & Ross, K. M. (2013). Measuring resilience in children: From theory to practice. In S. Goldstein & R. B. Brooks (Eds.), *Handbook of resilience in children* (2nd ed.). New York: Springer Science + Business Media.

Nagy, T. F. (2011). Informed consent. In T. F. Nagy (Ed.), *Essential ethics for psychologists: A primer for understanding and mastering core issues.* Washington, DC: American Psychological Association.

Najman, J. M., Aird, R., Bor, W., O'Callaghan, M., Williams, G. M., & Shuttlewood, G. J. (2004). The generational transmission of socioeconomic inequalities in child cognitive development and emotional health. *Social Science and Medicine, 58,* 1147-1158.

Nakamura, Y., Goto, T. K., Tokumori, K., Yoshiura, T., Kobayashi, K., Nakamura, Y., . . . Yoshiura, K. (2011). Localization of brain activation by umami taste in humans. *Brain Research, 1390,* 156-163.

Nalbantian, S. (2011). Autobiographical memory in modernist literature and neuroscience. In S. Nalbantian, P. M. Matthews, & J. L. McClelland (Eds.), *The memory process: Neuroscientific and humanistic perspectives.* Cambridge, MA: MIT Press.

Narrow, W. E., Rae, D. S., Robins, L. N., & Regier, D. A. (2002). Revised prevalence estimates of mental disorders in the United States: Using a clinical significance criterion to reconcile 2 surveys' estimates. *Archives of General Psychiatry, 59*, 115-123.

Nasrallah, H., Black, D., Goldberg, J., Muzina, D., & Pariser, S. (2008). Issues associated with the use of atypical antipsychotic medications. *Annals of Clinical Psychiatry, 20*, S24-S29.

National Adolescent Health Information Center. (2003). *Fact sheet on demographics: Adolescents.* San Francisco: University of California, San Francisco.

National Association for the Education of Young Children. (2005). *Position statements of the NAEYC.* Retrieved from https://www.naeyc.org/resources/pubs/tyc/about.

National Institute of Child Health and Human Development (NICHD) Early Child Care Research Network. (1999). Child care and mother-child interaction in the first 3 years of life. *Psychology, 35*, 1399-1413.

National Institute of Child Health and Human Development (NICHD) Early Child Care Research Network. (2001). Child-care and family predictors of preschool attachment and stability from infancy. *Development Psychology, 37*, 847-862.

National Institute of Child Health and Human Development (NICHD) Early Child Care Research Network. (2002). Child-care structure–process–outcome: Direct and indirect effects of child-care quality on young children's development. *Psychological Science, 13*, 199-206.

National Institute of Child Health and Human Development (NICHD) Early Child Care Research Network. (2006). Child-care effect sizes for the NICHD study of early child care and youth development. *American Psychologist, 61*, 99-116.

National Institute on Drug Abuse. (2000). *Monitoring the future study.* Bethesda, MD: National Institutes of Health.

National Institute on Drug Abuse. (2018). What is the scope of cocaine use in the United States? Downloaded from https://www.drugabuse.gov/publications/research-reports/cocaine/what-scope-cocaine-use-in-united-states.

National Institutes of Health. (2015, November 24). Talking to your doctor. Retrieved from https://www.nih.gov/institutes-nih/nih-office-director/office-communications-public-liaison/clear-communication/talking-your-doctor.

National Prevention Information Network. (2011). *STDs today.* Retrieved from http://www.cdcnpin.org/scripts/std/std.asp.

National Research Council. (2001). *Eager to learn: Educating our preschoolers.* Washington, DC: National Academy Press.

Natsuaki, M. N., Samuels, D., & Leve, L. D. (2015). Puberty, identity, and context: A biopsychosocial perspective on internalizing psychopathology in early adolescent girls. In K. C. McLean & M. Syed (Eds.), *The Oxford handbook of identity development.* New York: Oxford University Press.

Naveh-Benjamin, M., Guez, J., & Sorek, S. (2007). The effects of divided attention on encoding processes in memory: Mapping the locus of interference. *Canadian Journal of Experimental Psychology, 61*, 1-12.

Neal, D., Matson, J. L., & Belva, B. C. (2013). An examination of the reliability of a new observation measure for Autism spectrum disorders: The autism spectrum disorder observation for children. *Research in Autism Spectrum Disorders, 7*, 29-34.

Nedelec, J. L. (2017). A multi-level analysis of the effect of interviewer characteristics on survey respondents' reports of sensitive topics. *Personality and Individual Differences, 107*, 96-101.

Nelson, D. L., Kitto, K., Galea, D., McEvoy, C. L., & Bruza, P. D. (2013). How activation, entanglement, and searching a semantic network contribute to event memory. *Memory & Cognition, 41*, 797-819.

Nelson, G., & MacLeod, T. (2017). The evolution of housing for people with serious mental illness. In J. Sylvestre, G. Nelson, & T. Aubry (Eds.), *Housing, citizenship, and communities for people with serious mental illness: Theory, research, practice, and policy perspectives.* New York: Oxford University Press.

Nelson, T. D. (2013). The neurobiology of stereotyping and prejudice. In D. D. Franks & J. H. Turner (Eds.), *Handbook of neurosociology.* New York: Springer Science + Business Media.

Nelson, W. M., III, & Finch, A. J., Jr. (2000). Managing anger in youth: A cognitive-behavioral intervention approach. In P. C. Kendall (Ed.), *Child & adolescent therapy: Cognitive-behavioral procedures* (2nd ed.). New York: Guilford Press.

Nepi, L. D., Fioravanti, J., Nannini, P., & Peru, A. (2015). Social acceptance and the choosing of favourite classmates: A comparison between students with special educational needs and typically developing students in a context of full inclusion. *British Journal of Special Education, 42*(3), 320-337.

Neria, Y., DiGrande, L., & Adams, G. G. (2011). Postraumatic stress disorder following the September 11, 2001, terrorist attacks. *American Psychologist, 66*, 429-446.

Nesheim, S., Henderson, S., Lindsay, M., Zuberi, J., Grimes, V., Buehler, J., . . . Bulterys, M. (2004). *Prenatal HIV testing and antiretroviral prophylaxis at an urban hospital-Atlanta, Georgia, 1997-2000.* Atlanta: Centers for Disease Control and Prevention.

Nestler, E. J., & Malenka, R. C. (2004). The addicted brain. *Scientific American, 290*(3), 78-83.

Nestoriuc, Y., Martin, A., Rief, W., & Andrasik, F. (2008). Biofeedback treatment for headache disorders: A comprehensive efficacy review. *Applied Psychophysiology and Biofeedback, 33*, 125-140.

Newby-Clark, I. R., & Ross, M. (2003). Conceiving the past and future. *Personality and Social Psychology Bulletin, 29*, 807-818.

Newman, C. F., Leahy, R. L., Beck, A. T., Reilly-Harrington, N. A., & Gyulai, L. (2002). *Bipolar disorder: A cognitive therapy approach.* Washington, DC: American Psychological Association.

Newman, M., & Bakay, R. (2008). Therapeutic potentials of human embryonic stem cells in Parkinson's disease. *Neurotherapeutics, 5*, 237-251.

Newman, S. D., Willoughby, G., & Pruce, B. (2011). The effect of problem structure on problem-solving: An fmri study of word versus number problems. *Brain Research, 30*, 88-96.

Ng, Q. X., Venkatanarayanan, N., & Ho, C. X. (2017). Clinical use of Hypericum perforatum (St. John's wort) in depression: A meta-analysis. *Journal of Affective Disorders, 210*, 211-221.

Nguyen, H. D., Le, H., & Boles, T. (2010). Individualism-collectivism and co-operation: A cross-society and cross-level examination. *Negotiation and Conflict Management Research, 3*, 179-204.

Niccols, A. (2007). Fetal alcohol syndrome and the developing socio-emotional brain. *Brain Cognition, 65*, 135-142.

Nichols, S. (2011). Experimental philosophy and the problem of free will. *Science, 331*, 1401-1403.

Niedenthal, P. M. (2007). Embodying emotion. *Science, 316*, 1002-1005.

Nielsen, T., O'Reilly, C., Carr, M., Dumel, G., Godin, I., Solomonova, E., . . . Paquette, T. (2015). Overnight improvements in two REM sleep-sensitive tasks are associated with both REM and NREM sleep changes, sleep spindle features, and awakenings for dream recall. *Neurobiology of Learning and Memory, 122*, 88-97.

Nijboer, T. C. W., te Pas, S. F., & van der Smagt, M. J. (2011). Detecting gradual visual changes in colour and brightness agnosia: A double dissociation. *NeuroReport: For Rapid Communication of Neuroscience Research, 22*, 175-180.

Nimrod, G., & Kleiber, D. A. (2007). Reconsidering change and continuity in later life: Toward an innovation theory of successful aging. *International Journal of Human Development, 65*, 1-22.

Nisbet, E. K., Zelenski, J. M., & Murphy, S. A. (2011). Happiness is in our nature: Exploring nature relatedness as a contributor to subjective well-being. *Journal of Happiness Studies, 12*, 303-322.

Nisbett, R. E. (2007, December 9). All brains are the same color. *The New York Times*, p. E11.

Nisbett, R. E. (2009). All brains are the same color. *Association for Psychological Science Observer, 22*(3), 20-21.

Nisbett, R.E., & Cohen, D. (1996). *Culture of honor: The psychology of violence in the South.* Boulder, CO: Westview Press.

Nishida, M., Pearsall, J., Buckner, R., & Walker, M. (2009). REM sleep, prefrontal theta, and the consolidation of human emotional memory. *Cerebral Cortex, 19*, 1158-1166.

Nishimura, T., Kawamura, S., & Sakurai, S. (2011). Autonomous motivation and meta-cognitive strategies as predictors of academic performance: Does intrinsic motivation predict academic performance? *Japanese Journal of Educational Psychology, 59*, 77-87.

Nishino, S. (2007). Clinical and neurobiological aspects of narcolepsy. *Sleep Medicine, 8*, 373-399.

Nittrouer, S., & Lowenstein, J. H. (2007). Children's weighting strategies for word-final stop voicing are not explained by auditory sensitivities. *Journal of Speech, Language, and Hearing Research, 50,* 58-73.

Nolen-Hoeksema, S. (2007). *Abnormal psychology* (4th ed.). New York: McGraw-Hill.

Norcia, A. M., Pei, F., Bonneh, Y., Hou, C., Sampath, V., & Petter, M. W. (2005). Development of sensitivity to texture and contour information in the human infant. *Journal of Cognitive Neuroscience, 17,* 569-579.

Norcross, J. C. (2002). Empirically supported therapy relationships. In J. C. Norcross (Ed.), *Psychotherapy relationships that work: Therapist contributions and responsiveness to patients.* New York: Oxford University Press.

Norcross, J. C., Beutler, L. E., & Levant, R. F. (2006). *Evidence-based practices in mental health: Debate and dialogue on the fundamental questions.* Washington, DC: American Psychological Association.

Norlander, T., Von Schedvin, H., & Archer, T. (2005). Thriving as a function of affective personality: Relation to personality factors, coping strategies and stress. *Anxiety, Stress & Coping: An International Journal, 18,* 105-116.

North, M. M., & North, S. M. (2017). Virtual reality therapy for treatment of psychological disorders. In M. M. Maheu, K. P. Drude, & S. D. Wright (Eds.), *Career paths in telemental health* (pp. 263-268). Cham, Switzerland: Springer International Publishing.

Norton, D., Heath, D., & Ventura, D. (2013). Finding creativity in an artificial artist. *Journal of Creative Behavior, 47,* 106-124.

Norton, P. J., & Price, E. C. (2007). A meta-analytic review of adult cognitive-behavioral treatment outcome across the anxiety disorders. *Journal of Nervous and Mental Disease, 195,* 521-531.

Nosek, B. A., Banaji, M. R., & Greenwald, A. G. (2002). Math = male, me = female, therefore math ≠ me. *Journal of Personality and Social Psychology, 83,* 44-59.

Nosek, C. L., Kerr, C. W., Woodworth, J., Wright, S. T., Grant, P. C., Kuszczak, S. M., . . . Depner, R. M. (2015). End-of-life dreams and visions: A qualitative perspective from hospice patients. *American Journal of Hospice & Palliative Medicine, 32,* 269-274.

Nourouzpour, N., Salomonczyk, D., Cressman, E. K., & Henriques, D. Y. (2015). Retention of proprioceptive recalibration following visuomotor adaptation. *Experimental Brain Research, 233,* 1019-1029.

Nouwens, P. G., Lucas, R., Embregts, P. M., & van Nieuwenhuizen, C. (2017). In plain sight but still invisible: A structured case analysis of people with mild intellectual disability or borderline intellectual functioning. *Journal of Intellectual and Developmental Disability, 42,* 36-44.

Novotney, A. (2017). A growing wave of online therapy. *Monitor on Psychology, 48*(2), 48.

Nowak, A., Deutsch, M., Bartkowski, W., & Solomon, S. (2010). From crude law to civil relations: The dynamics and potential resolution of intractable conflict. *Peace and Conflict: Journal of Peace Psychology, 16,* 189-209.

Noy, V. M. (2006). A psychoneuroimmunology program for Hispanic women with stage I–H breast cancer. *Dissertation Abstracts International: Section B: The Sciences and Engineering, 66*(11-B), 6287.

Nurnberger, J. I., Jr., & Bierut, L. J. (2007). Seeking the connections: Alcoholism and our genes. *Scientific American, 296*(4), 46-53.

Nussbaum, A. D., & Steele, C. M. (2007). Situational disengagement and persistence in the face of adversity. *Journal of Experimental Social Psychology, 43,* 127-134.

Nyaradi, A., Li, J., Hickling, S., Foster, J., & Oddy, W. H. (2013). The role of nutrition in children's neurocognitive development, from pregnancy through childhood. *Frontiers in Human Neuroscience, 7,* 97.

Nygaard, E., Slinning, K., Moe, V., & Walhovd, K. B. (2017). Cognitive function of youths born to mothers with opioid and poly-substance abuse problems during pregnancy. *Child Neuropsychology, 23,* 159-187.

Nærland, T., Bakke, K. A., Storvik, S., Warner, G., & Howlin, P. (2017). Age and gender-related differences in emotional and behavioural problems and autistic features in children and adolescents with Down syndrome: A survey-based study of 674 individuals. *Journal of Intellectual Disability Research, 61,* 594-603.

O'Leary, A. P., & Sloutsky, V. M. (2017). Carving metacognition at its joints: Protracted development of component processes. *Child Development, 88,* 1015-1032.

Oberauer, K., Awh, E., & Sutterer, D. W. (2017). The role of long-term memory in a test of visual working memory: Proactive facilitation but no proactive interference. *Journal of Experimental Psychology: Learning, Memory, and Cognition, 43,* 1-22.

Occhionero, M. (2004). Mental processes and the brain during dreams. *Dreaming, 14,* 54-64.

Occhionero'Brien, K. M., & LeBow, M. D. (2007). Reducing maladaptive weight management practices: Developing a psychoeducational intervention program. *Eating Behaviors, 8,* 195-210.

Occhionero'Brien, W. H., & Young, K. M. (2013). Assessment of psychopathology: Behavioral approaches. In J. R. Graham, J. A. Naglieri, & I. B. Weiner (Eds.), *Handbook of psychology, Vol. 10: Assessment psychology* (2nd ed.). Hoboken, NJ: John Wiley & Sons Inc.

Offer, D., Kaiz, M., Howard, K. I., & Bennett, E. S. (2000). The altering of reported experiences. *Journal of the American Academy of Child & Adolescent Psychiatry, 39,* 735-742.

Ogbu, J. U. (2003). *Black American students in an affluent suburb: A study of academic disengagement.* New Jersey: Lawrence Erlbaum.

Ogden, C. L., Carroll, M. D, Kit, B. K., & Flegal, K. M. (2014). Prevalence of childhood and adult obesity in the United States, 2011-2012. *Journal of the American Medical Association, 311,* 806-814.

Ogletree, S. M., Martinez, C. N., & Turner, T. R. (2004). Pokémon: Exploring the role of gender. *Sex Roles, 50,* 851-859.

Ohira, T., Hozawa, A., Iribarren, C., Daviglus, M. L., Matthews, K. A., Gross, M. D., & Jacobs, D. R. Jr. (2007). Longitudinal association of serum carotenoids and tocopherols with hostility: The CARDIA study. *American Journal of Epidemiology, 18,* 235-241.

Ojha, H., & Pramanick, M. (2009). Effects of age on intensity and priority of life needs. *Journal of the Indian Academy of Applied Psychology, 35,* 131-136.

Okada, K., Nakao, T., Sanematsu, H., Murayama, K., Honda, S., Tomita, M., . . . Kanba, S. (2015). Biological heterogeneity of obsessive-compulsive disorder: A voxel-based morphometric study based on dimensional assessment. *Psychiatry and Clinical Neurosciences, 69,* 411-421

Okely, J. A., Weiss, A., & Gale, C. R. (2018). The interaction between individualism and well-being in predicting mortality: Survey of Health Ageing and Retirement in Europe. *Journal of Behavioral Medicine, 41*(1), 1-11. doi:10.1007/s10865-017-9871-x.

Olatunji, B. (2008). New directions in research on health anxiety and hypochondriasis: Commentary on a timely special series. *Journal of Cognitive Psychotherapy, 22,* 183-190.

Oliver, M. B., & Hyde, J. S. (1993). Gender differences in sexuality: A meta-analysis. *Psychological Bulletin, 114,* 29-51.

Olson, D. H., & DeFrain, J. (2005). *Marriages and families: Intimacy, diversity, and strengths with PowerWeb.* New York: McGraw-Hill.

Ong, J. C. (2017). Insomnia: The problem of sleeplessness. In J. C. Ong, *Mindfulness-based therapy for insomnia.* Washington, DC: American Psychological Association.

Open Science Collaboration. (2015, August 28). Estimating the reproducibility of psychological science. *Science, 349.*

Opendak, M., Gould, E., & Sullivan, R. (2017). Early life adversity during the infant sensitive period for attachment: Programming of behavioral neurobiology of threat processing and social behavior. *Developmental Cognitive Neuroscience, 25,* 145-159.

Opler, M., Perrin, M., Kleinhaus, K., & Malaspina, D. (2008). Factors in the etiology of schizophrenia: Genes, parental age, and environment. *Primary Psychiatry, 15,* 37-45.

Ornat, S. L., & Gallo, P. (2004). Acquisition, learning, or development of language? Skinner's "Verbal behavior" revisited. *Spanish Journal of Psychology, 7,* 161-170.

Orwin, R. G., & Condray, D. S. (1984). Smith and Glass' psychotherapy conclusions need further probing: On Landman and Dawes' re-analysis. *American Psychologist, 39,* 71-72.

Otake, K., Shimai, S., & Tanaka-Matsumi, J. (2006). Happy people become happier through kindness: A counting kindnesses intervention. *Journal of Happiness Studies, 7,* 361-375.

Otgaar, H., Howe, M. L., & Muris, P. (2017). Maltreatment increases spontaneous false memories but decreases suggestion-induced false memories in children. *British Journal of Developmental Psychology, 35*(3), 376-391.

Otters, R. V., & Hollander, J. F. (2015). Leaving home and boomerang decisions: A family simulation protocol. *Marriage & Family Review, 51,* 39-58.

Ouimet, A., Gawronski, B., & Dozois, D. (2009). Cognitive vulnerability to anxiety: A review and an integrative model. *Clinical Psychology Review, 29,* 459-470.

Oviedo-Joekes, E., Brissette, S., Marsh, D. C., Lauzon, P., Guh, D., Anis, A., . . . Schechter, M. T. (2009). Diacetylmorphine versus methadone for the treatment of opioid addiction. *New England Journal of Medicine, 361,* 777-786.

Özdemir, V., Dove, E. S., Gürsoy, U. K., Şardaş, S., Yıldırım, A., Yılmaz, Ş. G., . . . Srivastava, S. (2017). Personalized medicine beyond genomics: Alternative futures in big data—Proteomics, environtome and the social proteome. *Journal of Neural Transmission, 124,* 25-32.

Paciorek, A., & Williams, J. N. (2015). Semantic generalization in implicit language learning. *Journal of Experimental Psychology: Learning, Memory, and Cognition, 41,* 989-1002.

Packer, D. (2009). Avoiding groupthink: Whereas weakly identified members remain silent, strongly identified members dissent about collective problems. *Psychological Science, 20,* 546-548.

Padgett, D. K., Stanhope, V., & Henwood, B. F. (2011). Housing-first services for homeless adults with co-occurring disorders: An evidence-based practice. In M. Roberts-DeGennaro & S. J. Fogel (Eds.), *Using evidence to inform practice for community and organizational change.* Chicago: Lyceum Books.

Pagano, M. E., White, W. L., Kelly, J. F., Stout, R. L., & Tonigan, J. S. (2013). The 10-year course of Alcoholics Anonymous participation and long-term outcomes: A follow-up study of outpatient subjects in Project MATCH. *Substance Abuse, 34,* 51-59.

Pager, D., & Shepherd, H. (2008). The sociology of discrimination: Racial discrimination in employment, housing, credit, and consumer markets. *Annual Review of Sociology, 34,* 181-209.

Pagonis, T. A., Angelopoulos, N., & Koukoulis, G. N. (2006). Psychiatric side effects induced by supraphysiological doses of combinations of anabolic steroids correlate to the severity of abuse. *European Psychiatry, 21,* 551-562.

Pahlke, E., Hyde, J., & Mertz, J. E. (2013). The effects of single-sex compared with coeducational schooling on mathematics and science achievement: Data from Korea. *Journal of Educational Psychology, 105,* 444-452.

Pallanti, S., & Bernardi, S. (2009, July). Neurobiology of repeated transcranial magnetic stimulation in the treatment of anxiety: A critical review. *International Clinical Psychopharmacology, 24,* 163-173.

Palmiter, R. (2015). Hunger logic. *Nature Neuroscience, 18,* 789-791.

Pandya, M., Pozuelo, L., & Malone, D. (2007). Electroconvulsive therapy: What the internist needs to know. *Cleveland Clinic Journal of Medicine, 74,* 679-685.

Paniagua, F. A. (2000). *Diagnosis in a multicultural context: A casebook for mental health professionals.* Thousand Oaks, CA: Sage.

Papoiu, A., Nattkemper, L., Sanders, K., Kraft, R., Chan, Y-H, Coghill, R., . . . Yosipovitch, G. (2013). Brain's reward circuits mediate itch relief. A functional MRI study of active scratching. *PLoS ONE 8*(12): e82389.

Pardini, D., White, H. R., Xiong, S., Bechtold, J., Chung, T., Loeber, R., . . . Hipwell, A. (2015). Unfazed or dazed and confused: Does early adolescent marijuana use cause sustained impairments in attention and academic functioning? *Journal of Abnormal Child Psychology, 43*(7), 1203-1217.

Parish, C. L., & Arenas, E. (2007). Stem-cell-based strategies for the treatment of Parkinson's disease. *Neurodegenerative Disease, 4,* 339-347.

Park, A. (2011, March 7). Healing the hurt. *Time,* 64-71.

Park, A. (2015, May 7). Exclusive: Meet the world's first baby born with an assist from stem cells. *Time.* Retrieved from http://time.com/3849127/baby-stem-cells-augment-ivf/.

Park, D. C. (2007). Eating disorders: A call to arms. *American Psychologist, 62,* 158.

Park, E., McCoy, T. P., Erausquin, J. T., & Bartlett, R. (2018). Trajectories of risk behaviors across adolescence and young adulthood: The role of race and ethnicity. *Addictive Behaviors, 76,* 1-7.

Park, H., & Antonioni, D. (2007). Personality, reciprocity, and strength of conflict resolution strategy. *Journal of Research in Personality, 41,* 110-125.

Park, H., & Raymo, J. M. (2013). Divorce in Korea: Trends and educational differentials. *Journal of Marriage and Family, 75,* 110-126.

Park, H., Yun, I., & Walsh, A. (2017). Early puberty, school context, and delinquency among South Korean girls. *International Journal of Offender Therapy and Comparative Criminology, 61*(7), 795-818.

Park, J., Park, K., & Dubinsky, A. J. (2011). Impact of retailer image on private brand attitude: Halo effect and summary construct. *Australian Journal of Psychology, 63,* 173-183.

Parke, B. N. (2003). *Discovering programs for talent development.* Thousand Oaks, CA: Corwin Press.

Parke, M. R., Seo, M., & Sherf, E. N. (2015). Regulating and facilitating: The role of emotional intelligence in maintaining and using positive affect for creativity. *Journal of Applied Psychology, 100,* 917-934.

Parker-Pope, T. (2003, April 22). The diet that works. *Wall Street Journal,* pp. R1, R5.

Parkinson, J., Garfinkel, S., Critchley, H., Dienes, Z., & Seth, A. K. (2017). Don't make me angry, you wouldn't like me when I'm angry: Volitional choices to act or inhibit are modulated by subliminal perception of emotional faces. *Cognitive, Affective & Behavioral Neuroscience, 17,* 252-268.

Parra, A., & Argibay, J. C. (2007). Comparing psychics and non-psychics through a 'token-object' forced-choice ESP test. *Journal of the Society for Psychical Research, 71,* 80-90.

Parris, B. A. (2017). The role of frontal executive functions in hypnosis and hypnotic suggestibility. *Psychology of Consciousness: Theory, Research, and Practice, 4,* 211-229.

Parrott, A. C., Downey, L. A., Roberts, C. A., Montgomery, C., Bruno, R., & Fox, H. C. (2017). Recreational 3,4-methylenedioxymethamphetamine or 'ecstasy': Current perspective and future research prospects. *Journal of Psychpharmacology, 269881117711922.* doi: 10.1177/0269881117711922.

Passos, V. L., Berger, M. P. F., & Tan, F. E. (2007). Test design optimization in CAT early stage with the nominal response model. *Applied Psychological Measurement, 31,* 213-232.

Paterson, H. M., Kemp, R. I., & Ng, J. R. (2011). Combating co-witness contamination: Attempting to decrease the negative effects of discussion on eyewitness memory. *Applied Cognitive Psychology, 25,* 43-52.

Patten, S. B., Williams, J. A., Lavorato, D. H., Bulloch, A. M., Fiest, K. M., Wang, J. L., . . . Sajobi, T. T. (2017). Seasonal variation in major depressive episode prevalence in Canada. *Epidemiology and Psychiatric Sciences, 26,* 169-176.

Patterson, T. G., & Joseph, S. (2013). Unconditional positive self-regard. In M. E. Bernard (Ed.), *The strength of self-acceptance: Theory, practice and research.* New York: Springer Science + Business Media.

Paul, A. M. (2004). *Cult of personality: How personality tests are leading us to miseducate our children, mismanage our companies and misunderstand ourselves.* New York: Free Press.

Paulmann, S., Jessen, S., & Kotz, S. A. (2009). Investigating the multimodal nature of human communication: Insights from ERPs. *Journal of Psychophysiology, 23,* 63-76.

Pautassi, R., Myers, M., Spear, L., Molina, J., & Spear, N. E. (2011). Ethanol induces second-order aversive conditioning in adolescent and adult rats. *Alcohol, 45,* 45-55.

Pavitt, C. (2007). Impression formation. In B. B. Whaley & W. Samter (Eds.), *Explaining communication: Contemporary theories and exemplars.* Mahwah, NJ: Lawrence Erlbaum Associates.

Pavot, W., & Diener, E. (2013). Happiness experienced: The science of subjective well-being. In S. A. David, I. Boniwell, & A. Conley Ayers (Eds.), *The Oxford handbook of happiness.* New York: Oxford University Press.

Pavão, R., Tort, A. L., & Amaral, O. B. (2015). Multifactoriality in psychiatric disorders: A computational study of schizophrenia. *Schizophrenia Bulletin, 41,* 980-988.

Payne, K., & Marcus, D. (2008). The efficacy of group psychotherapy for older adult clients:

A meta-analysis. *Group Dynamics: Theory, Research, and Practice, 12,* 268-278.

Pearce, R. R., & Lin, Z. (2007). Chinese American post-secondary achievement and attainment: A cultural and structural analysis. *Educational Review, 59,* 19-36.

Pearson, A. R., Dovidio, J. F., & Pratto, E. (2007). Racial prejudice, intergroup hate, and blatant and subtle bias of whites toward blacks in legal decision making in the United States. *International Journal of Psychology & Psychological Therapy, 7,* 125-134.

Pedersen, P. B., Draguns, J. G., Lonner, W. J., & Trimble, J. E. (Eds.). (2002). *Counseling across cultures* (5th ed.). Thousand Oaks, CA: Sage.

Pedraza, O., & Mungas, D. (2008). Measurement in cross-cultural neuropsychology. *Neuropsychology Review, 18,* 184-193.

Pekrun, R. (2017). Emotion and achievement during adolescence. *Child Development Perspectives, 11,* 215-222.

Pell, M. D., Monetta, L., Paulmann, S., & Kotz, S. A. (2009). Recognizing emotions in a foreign language. *Journal of Nonverbal Behavior, 33,* 107-120.

Pellegrini, A. D., Bohn-Gettler, C. M., Dupuis, D., Hickey, M., Roseth, C., & Solberg, D. (2010). An empirical examination of sex differences in scoring preschool children's aggression. *Journal of Experimental Child Psychology, 109,* 232-238.

Pellis, S. M., & Pellis, V. C. (2007). Rough-and-tumble play and the development of the social brain. *Current Directions in Psychological Science, 16,* 95-97.

Pelphrey, K., & Shultz, S. (2013). Brain mechanisms for social perception: Moving toward an understanding of autism. In K. L. Johnson & M. Shiffrar (Eds.), *People watching: Social, perceptual, and neurophysiological studies of body perception.* New York: Oxford University Press.

Pempek, T., Yermolayeva, Y., & Calvert, S. (2009). College students' social networking experiences on Facebook. *Journal of Applied Developmental Psychology, 30,* 227-238.

Pendyam, S., Bravo-Rivera, C., Burgos-Robles, A., Sotres-Bayon, F., Quirk, G. J., & Nair, S. S. (2013). Fear signaling in the prelimbic-amygdala circuit: A computational modeling and recording study. *Journal of Neurophysiology, 110,* 844-861.

Penhollow, T. M., Young, M., & Nnaka, T. (2017). Alcohol use, hooking-up, condom use: Is there a sexual double standard? *American Journal of Health Behavior, 41,* 92-103.

Penley, J. A., Tomaka, J., & Wiebe, J. S. (2002). The association of coping to physical and psychological health outcomes: A meta-analytic review. *Journal of Behavioral Medicine, 25,* 551-603.

Penn, D. L., Corrigan, P. W., Bentall, R. P., Racenstein, J. M., & Newman, L. (1997). Social cognition in schizophrenia. *Psychological Bulletin, 121,* 114-132.

Perogamvros, L., & Schwartz, S. (2015). Sleep and emotional functions. In P. Meerlo, R. M. Benca, & T. Abel (Eds.), *Sleep, neuronal plasticity and brain function.* New York: Springer-Verlag Publishing.

Perovic, S., & Radenovic, L. (2011). Fine-tuning nativism: The "nurtured nature" and innate cognitive structures. *Phenomenology and the Cognitive Sciences, 10,* 399-417.

Perrier, M., & Ginis, K. M. (2017). Narrative interventions for health screening behaviours: A systematic review. *Journal of Health Psychology, 22,* 375-393.

Perry, G. (2013). *Behind the shock machine.* New York: New Press.

Perry, J., Presniak, M. D., & Olson, T. R. (2013). Defense mechanisms in schizotypal, borderline, antisocial, and narcissistic personality disorders. *Psychiatry: Interpersonal and Biological Processes, 76,* 32-52.

Pert, C. B. (2002). The wisdom of the receptors: Neuropeptides, the emotions, and body-mind. *Advances in Mind-Body Medicine, 18,* 30-35.

Pervin, L. A. (2003). *The science of personality* (2nd ed.). London: Oxford University Press.

Pesmen, C. (2006). Health and wealth techniques to help keep chronic pain from taking over. *Money Builder, 35,* 48.

Pessoa, L. (2011). Reprint of: Emotion and cognition and the amygdala: From "what is it?" to "what's to be done?" *Neuropsychologia, 49,* 681-694.

Peterfi, Z., McGinty, D., Sarai, E., & Szymusiak, R. (2010). Growth hormone-releasing hormone activates sleep regulatory neurons of the rat preoptic hypothalamus. *American Journal of Physiology: Regulatory, Integrative and Comparative Physiology, 298,* R147-R156.

Peters, E. N., Rosenberry, Z. R., Schauer, G. L., O'Grady, K. E., & Johnson, P. S. (2017). Marijuana and tobacco cigarettes: Estimating their behavioral economic relationship using purchasing tasks. *Experimental and Clinical Psychopharmacology, 25*(3), 208-215.

Peters, E., Hess, T. M., Västfjäll, D., & Auman, C. (2007). Adult age differences in dual information processes. *Perspectives on Psychological Science, 2,* 1-23.

Peters, J., Suchan, B., Koster, O., & Daum, I. (2007). Domain-specific retrieval of source information in the medial temporal lobe. *European Journal of Neuroscience, 26,* 1333-1343.

Petersen, A. (2011, August 23). A sleep battle of the sexes. *Wall Street Journal,* pp. D1, D4.

Petersen, A. (2017, April 28). My escape from anxiety. *Wall Street Journal.* Retrieved from https://www.wsj.com/articles/my-escape-from-anxiety-1493391641.

Peterson, C. (2000). The future of optimism. *American Psychologist, 55,* 44-55.

Peterson, L. R., & Peterson, M. J. (1959). Short-term retention of individual items. *Journal of Experimental Psychology, 58,* 193-198.

Petersson, K. M., Silva, C., Castro-Caldas, A., Ingvar, M., & Reis, A. (2007). Literacy: A cultural influence on functional left-right differences in the inferior parietal cortex. *European Journal of Neuroscience, 26,* 791-799.

Petrill, S. A., & Deater-Deckard, K. (2004). The heritability of general cognitive ability: A within-family adoption design. *Intelligence, 32,* 403-409.

Pettigrew, T. F., & Tropp, L. R. (2006). A meta-analytic test of intergroup contact theory. *Journal of Personality and Social Psychology, 90,* 751-783.

Pettito, L. A. (1993). On the ontogenetic requirements for early language acquisition. In B. de Boysson-Bardies, S. de Schonen, P. W. Jusczyk, P. McNeilage, & J. Morton (Eds.), *Developmental neurocognition: Speech and face processing in the first year of life. NATO ASI series D: Behavioural and social sciences* (Vol. 69). Dordrecht, Netherlands: Kluwer Academic.

Pezoulas, V. C., Zervakis, M., Michelogiannis, S., & Klados, M. A. (2017). Resting-state functional connectivity and network analysis of cerebellum with respect to crystallized IQ and gender. *Frontiers in Human Neuroscience, 11,* 1-10.

Pfaff, D. W. (2014). *The altruistic brain: How we are naturally good.* Oxford: Oxford University Press.

Phalen, P. L., Dimaggio, G., Popolo, R., & Lysaker, P. H. (2017). Aspects of Theory of Mind that attenuate the relationship between persecutory delusions and social functioning in schizophrenia spectrum disorders. *Journal of Behavior Therapy and Experimental Psychiatry, 56,* 65-70.

Phillips, M. (2013, December 12). The lobotomy files. *Wall Street Journal,* p. A1.

Phinney, J. S. (2003). Ethnic identity and acculturation. In K. M. Chun, O. Balls, & P. Organista (Eds.), *Acculturation: Advances in theory, measurement, and applied research.* Washington, DC: American Psychological Association.

Phua, J., Jin, S. V., & Kim, J. (. (2017). Uses and gratifications of social networking sites for bridging and bonding social capital: A comparison of Facebook, Twitter, Instagram, and Snapchat. *Computers in Human Behavior, 72,* 115-122.

Pi-Sunyer, X. (2003). A clinical view of the obesity problem. *Science, 299,* 859-860.

Piaget, J. (1970). Piaget's theory. In P. H. Mussen (Ed.), *Carmichael's manual of child psychology* (3rd ed., Vol. I). New York: Wiley.

Piaget, J., & Inhelder, B. (1958). *The growth of logical thinking from childhood to adolescence* (A. Parsons & S. Seagrin, Trans.). New York: Basic Books.

Pickel, K. (2009). The weapon focus effect on memory for female versus male perpetrators. *Memory, 17,* 664-678.

Pickering, G. J., & Gordon, R. (2006). Perception of mouthfeel sensations elicited by red wine are associated with sensitivity to 6-N-propylthiouracil. *Journal of Sensory Studies, 21,* 249-265.

Pickrell, J. E., McDonald, D., Bernstein, D. M., & Loftus, E. F. (2017). Misinformation effect. In R. F. Pohl (Ed.), *Cognitive illusions: Intriguing phenomena in thinking, judgment and memory* (pp. 406-423). New York: Routledge/Taylor & Francis Group.

Pietarinen, A.-V. (2006). The evolution of semantics and language-games for meaning. *Interaction Studies: Social Behaviour and Communication in Biological and Artificial Systems, 7,* 79-104.

Pietromonaco, P., & Collins, N.L. (2017). Interpersonal mechanisms linking close relationships to health. *American Psychologist, 72,* 531-542.

Pietschnig, J., & Voracek, M. (2015). One century of global IQ gains: A formal meta-analysis of the Flynn effect (1909-2013). *Perspectives on Psychological Science, 10*(3), 282-306.

Pijnenborg, G. M., Timmerman, M. E., Derks, E. M., Fleischhacker, W. W., Kahn, R. S., & Aleman, A. (2015). Differential effects of antipsychotic drugs on insight in first episode schizophrenia: Data from the European First-Episode Schizophrenia Trial (EUFEST). *European Neuropsychopharmacology, 25,* 808-816.

Pillay, S. S., Rogowska, J., Gruber, S. A., Simpson, N., & Yurgelun-Todd, D. A. (2007). Recognition of happy facial affect in panic disorder: an fMRI study. *Journal of Anxiety Disorders, 21,* 381-393.

Pina, A., Gannon, T., & Saunders, B. (2009). An overview of the literature on sexual harassment: Perpetrator, theory, and treatment issues. *Aggression and Violent Behavior, 14,* 126-138.

Pinal, D., Zurrón, M., & Díaz, F. (2015). Age-related changes in brain activity are specific for high order cognitive processes during successful encoding of information in working memory. *Frontiers in Aging Neuroscience, 7,* 88-97.

Pincus, T., & Morley, S. (2001). Cognitive processing bias in chronic pain: A review and integration. *Psychological Bulletin, 127,* 599-617.

Pinker, S. (1994). *The language instinct.* New York: William Morrow.

Pinker, S. (2004). Clarifying the logical problem of language acquisition. *Journal of Child Language, 31,* 949-953.

Pinker, S., & Jackendoff, R. (2005). The faculty of language: What's special about it? *Cognition, 96,* 201-236.

Pinkerton, S. D., Bogart, L. M., Cecil, H., & Abramson, P. R. (2002). Factors associated with masturbation in a collegiate sample. *Journal of Psychology and Human Sexuality, 14,* 103-121.

Pinquart, M., & Kauser, R. (2017). Do the associations of parenting styles with behavior problems and academic achievement vary by culture? Results from a meta-analysis. *Cultural Diversity and Ethnic Minority Psychology.* Accessed from https://www.ncbi.nlm.nih.gov/pubmed/28394165.

Pisarik, C. T., Rowell, P., & Currie, L. K. (2013). Work-related daydreams: A qualitative content analysis. *Journal of Career Development, 40,* 87-106.

Plante, C., & Anderson, C.A. (2017). Global warming and violent behavior. *APS Observer,* pp. 29-32.

Plomin, R. (2003). 50 years of DNA: What it has meant to psychological science. *American Psychological Society, 16,* 7-8.

Plomin, R. (2005). Finding genes in child psychology and psychiatry: When are we going to be there? *Journal of Child Psychology and Psychiatry, 46,* 1030-1038.

Plomin, R. (2009). The nature of nurture. In K. McCartney & R. A. Weinberg (Eds.), *Experience and development: A festschrift in honor of Sandra Wood Scarr.* New York: Psychology Press.

Plomin, R., & McGuffin, P. (2003). Psychopathology in the postgenomic era. *Annual Review of Psychology, 54,* 205-228.

Pluess, M., & Belsky, J. (2009). Differential susceptibility to rearing experience: The case of childcare. *Journal of Child Psychology and Psychiatry, 50,* 396-404.

Plötner, M., Over, H., Carpenter, M., & Tomasello, M. (2015). Young children show the bystander effect in helping situations. *Psychological Science, 26*(4), 499-506.

Poirier, M., Saint-Aubin, J., Mair, A., Tehan, G., & Tolan, A. (2015). Order recall in verbal short-term memory: The role of semantic networks. *Memory & Cognition, 43,* 489-499.

Pole, N. (2007).The psychophysiology of post-traumatic stress disorder: A meta-analysis. *Psychological Bulletin, 133,* 34-45.

Polgár, Z., Kinnunen, M., Újváry, D., Miklósi, Á., & Gácsi, M. (2016). A test of canine olfactory capacity: Comparing various dog breeds and wolves in a natural detection task. *Plos ONE, 11*(5).

Polivy, J., Herman, C. P., & Boivin, M. (2005). Eating disorders. In J. E. Maddux & B. A. Winstead (Eds.), *Psychopathology: Foundations for a contemporary understanding.* Mahwah, NJ: Lawrence Erlbaum Associates.

Polonsky, D. C. (2006). Review of the big book of masturbation: From angst to zeal. *Journal of Sex & Marital Therapy, 32,* 75-78.

Ponterotto, J. G., Gretchen, D., & Chauhan, R. V. (2001). Cultural identity and multicultural assessment: Quantitative and qualitative tools for the clinician. In L. A. Suzuki & J. G. Ponterotto (Eds.), *Handbook of multicultural assessment: Clinical, psychological, and educational applications* (2nd ed.). San Francisco: Jossey-Bass/Pfeiffer.

Ponterotto, J. G., Utsey, S. O., & Pedersen, P. B. (2006). *Preventing prejudice: A guide for counselors, educators, and parents.* Thousand Oaks, CA: Sage Publications.

Pontzer, H. (2017). Exercise paradox. *Scientific American, 316,* 28-31.

Pool, E., Rehme, A. K., Fink, G. R., Eickhoff, S. B., & Grefkes, C. (2013). Network dynamics engaged in the modulation of motor behavior in healthy subjects. *Neuroimage, 88,* 68-76.

Popa, D., Lena, C., Alexandre, C., & Adrien, J. (2008). Lasting syndrome of depression produced by reduction in serotonin uptake during postnatal development: Evidence from sleep, stress, and behavior. *Journal of Neuroscience, 28,* 88-97.

Popp, D., Donovan, R. A., & Crawford, M. (2003). Gender, race, and speech style stereotypes. *Sex Roles, 48,* 317-325.

Porcerelli, J. H., Bornstein, R. F., Porcerelli, D., & Arterbery, V. E. (2015). The complex role of personality in cancer treatment: Impact of dependency-detachment on health status, distress, and physician-patient relationship. *Journal of Nervous and Mental Disease, 203,* 264-268.

Porkka-Heiskanen, T. (2013). Sleep homeostasis. *Current Opinion in Neurobiology, 23,* 799-805.

Porkka-Heiskanen, T., & Kalinchuk, A. V. (2011). Adenosine, energy metabolism and sleep homeostasis. *Sleep Medicine Reviews, 15,* 123-135.

Posada, G., & Trumbell, J. M. (2017). Universality and cultural specificity in child-mother attachment relationships: In search of answers. In S. Gojman-de-Millan, C. Herreman, & L. A. Sroufe (Eds.), *Attachment across clinical and cultural perspectives: A relational psychoanalytic approach.* New York: Routledge/Taylor & Francis Group.

Post, J. M. (2011). Crimes of obedience: "Groupthink" at Abu Ghraib. *International Journal of Group Psychotherapy, 61,* 49-66.

Post, J. M. (2015, April). Terrorism and right-wing extremism: The changing face of terrorism and political violence in the 21st century: The virtual community of hatred. (Special issue: Violence in America: Part II.) *International Journal of Group Psychotherapy, 65*(2), 243-271.

Potash, J. S. (2015). Archetypal aesthetics: Viewing art through states of consciousness. *International Journal of Jungian Studies, 7,* 139-153.

Pottick, K. J., Kirk, S. A., Hsieh, D. K., & Tian, X. (2007). Judging mental disorder in youths: Effects of client, clinician, and contextual differences. *Journal of Consulting Clinical Psychology, 75,* 1-8.

Pow, A. M., & Cashwell, C. S. (2017). Posttraumatic stress disorder and emotion-focused coping among disaster mental health counselors. *Journal of Counseling & Development, 95*(3), 322-331.

Pow, J. L., Baumeister, A. A., Hawkins, M. F., Cohen, A. S., & Garand, J. C. (2015). Deinstitutionalization of American public hospitals for the mentally ill before and after the introduction of antipsychotic medications. *Harvard Review of Psychiatry, 23,* 176-187.

Powell, L. H. (2006). Review of marital and sexual lifestyles in the United States: Attitudes, behaviors, and relationships in social context. *Family Relations, 55,* 149.

Powell, L. H., Shahabi, L., & Thoresen, C. E. (2003). Religion and spirituality: Linkages to physical health. *American Psychology, 58,* 36-52.

Powell, R. A., Digdon, N., Harris, B., & Smithson, C. (2014). Correcting the record on Watson, Rayner, and Little Albert: Albert Barger as "Psychology's Lost Boy." *American Psychologist, 69,* 600-611.

Powers, K. D. (2006). An analysis of Kohlbergian moral development in relationship to biblical factors of morality in seminary students (Lawrence Kohlberg). *Dissertation Abstracts International: Section B: The Sciences and Engineering, 67*(6-B), 3485.

Powers, K. L., Brooks, P. J., Aldrich, N. J., Palladino, M. A., & Alfieri, L. (2013). Effects of video-game play on information processing: A meta-analytic investigation. *Psychonomic Bulletin & Review, 20*, 1055-1079.

Powers, M., & Emmelkamp, P. (2008). Virtual reality exposure therapy for anxiety disorders: A meta-analysis. *Journal of Anxiety Disorders, 22*, 561-569.

Pozzan, L., & Valian, V. (2017). Asking questions in child English: Evidence for early abstract representations. *Language Acquisition: A Journal of Developmental Linguistics, 24*, 209-233.

Praisner, C. L. (2003). Attitudes of elementary school principals toward the inclusion of students with disabilities. *Exceptional Children, 69*, 135-145.

Prasser, J., Schecklmann, M., Poeppl, T. B., Frank, E., Kreuzer, P. M., Hajak, G., . . . Langguth, B. (2015). Bilateral prefrontal rTMS and theta burst TMS as an add-on treatment for depression: A randomized placebo controlled trial. *World Journal of Biological Psychiatry, 16*, 57-65.

Pratkanis, A. R. (2007). Social influence analysis: An index of tactics. In A. R. Pratkanis (Ed.), *The science of social influence: Advances and future progress*. New York: Psychology Press.

Pratkanis, A. R., Epley, N., & Savitsky, K. (2007). Issue 12: Is subliminal persuasion a myth? In J. A. Nier (Ed.), *Taking sides: Clashing views in social psychology* (2nd ed.). New York: McGraw-Hill.

Pratt, H. D., Phillips, E. L., Greydanus, D. E., & Patel, D. R. (2003). Eating disorders in the adolescent population: Future directions [Special issue: Eating disorders in adolescents]. *Journal of Adolescent Research, 18*, 297-317.

Pratto, F., Lee, I., Tan, J. Y., & Pitpitan, E. Y. (2011). Power basis theory: A psychoecological approach to power. In D. Dunning (Ed.), *Social motivation*. New York: Psychology Press.

Pretsch, J., Heckmann, N., Flunger, B., & Schmitt, M. (2013). Agree or disagree?: Influences on consensus in personality judgments. *European Journal of Psychological Assessment*. Retrieved from http://psycnet.apa.org/psycinfo/2013-30588-001/.

Pretzer, J. L., & Beck, A. T. (2005). A cognitive theory of personality disorders. In M. F. Lenzenweger & J. F. Clarkin (Eds.), *Major theories of personality disorder* (2nd ed.). New York: Guilford Press.

Price, M. (2008, September). Against doctors' orders. *Monitor on Psychology*, pp. 34-36.

Priester, J. R., & Petty, R. E. (2011). The potholed path to happiness, possibly paved with money: A research dialogue. *Journal of Consumer Psychology, 21*, 113-114.

Prince, C. V. (2005). Homosexuality, transvestism and transsexuality: Reflections on their etymology and differentiation. *International Journal of Transgenderism, 8*, 15-18.

Prinz, J. J. (2007). Emotion: Competing theories and philosophical issues. In P. Thagard (Ed.), *Philosophy of psychology and cognitive science*. Amsterdam, Netherlands: North Holland/Elsevier.

Prior, K. N., & Bond, M. J. (2017). Patterns of "abnormal" illness behavior among healthy individuals. *American Journal of Health Behavior, 41*, 139-146.

Proffitt, D. R. (2006). Distance perception. *Current Directions in Psychological Science, 15*, 131-139.

Prohovnik, I., Skudlarski, P., Fulbright, R. K., Gore, J. C., & Wexler, B. E. (2004). Functional MRI changes before and after onset of reported emotions. *Psychiatry Research: Neuroimaging, 132*, 239-250.

Proudfoot, D. (2009). Meaning and mind: Wittgenstein's relevance for the "does language shape thought?" debate. *New Ideas in Psychology, 27*, 163-183.

Proyer, R. T., Gander, F., Wellenzohn, S., & Ruch, W. (2013). What good are character strengths beyond subjective well-being? The contribution of the good character on self-reported health-oriented behavior, physical fitness, and the subjective health status. *Journal of Positive Psychology, 8*, 222-232.

Prus, A. J., Mooney-Leber, S. M., Berquist, M. I., Pehrson, A. L., Porter, N. P., & Porter, J. H. (2015). The antidepressant drugs fluoxetine and duloxetine produce anxiolytic-like effects in a schedule-induced polydipsia paradigm in rats: Enhancement of fluoxetine's effects by the α_2 adrenoceptor antagonist yohimbine. *Behavioural Pharmacology, 26*, 489-494.

Puca, R. M. (2005). The influence of the achievement motive on probability estimates in pre- and post-decisional action phases. *Journal of Research in Personality, 39*, 245-262.

Purdy, S. C., Sharma, M. M., Munro, K. J., & Morgan, C. A. (2013). Stimulus level effects on speech-evoked obligatory cortical auditory evoked potentials in infants with normal hearing. *Clinical Neurophysiology, 124*, 474-480.

Putnam, E. W. (2000). Dissociative disorders. In A. J. Sameroff & M. Lewis (Eds.), *Handbook of developmental psychopathology* (2nd ed.). Dordrecht, Netherlands: Kluwer Academic Publishers.

Pérez-Leroux, A. T., Pirvulescu, M., & Roberge, Y. (2011). Topicalization and object omission in child language. *First Language, 31*, 280-299.

Qu, C., Zhang, A., & Chen, Q. (2013). Monetary effects on fear conditioning. *Psychological Reports, 112*, 353-364.

Quartana, P. J., & Burns, J. W. (2007). Painful consequences of anger suppression. *Emotion, 7*, 400-414.

Quinn, K., Pacella, M. L., Dickson-Gomez, J., & Nydegger, L. A. (2017). Childhood adversity and the continued exposure to trauma and violence among adolescent gang members. *American Journal of Community Psychology, 59*, 36-49.

Quinn, T. C., & Overbaugh, J. (2005). HIV/AIDS in women: An expanding epidemic. *Science, 308*, 1582-1583.

Quintana, S. M., Aboud, F. E., & Chao, R. K. (2006). Race, ethnicity, and culture in child development: Contemporary research and future directions. *Child Development, 77*, 1129-1141.

Rabin, J. (2004). Quantification of color vision with cone contrast sensitivity. *Visual Neuroscience, 21*, 483-485.

Rabin, R. C. (2013, August 13). A glut of antidepressants. *The New York Times*, p. D4.

Racine, S. E., VanHuysse, J. L., Keel, P. K., Burt, S. A., Neale, M. C., Boker, S., & Klump, K. L. (2017). Eating disorder-specific risk factors moderate the relationship between negative urgency and binge eating: A behavioral genetic investigation. *Journal of Abnormal Psychology, 126*, 481-494.

Radvansky, G. A. (2010). *Human memory*. N.Y.: Psychology Press.

Radvansky, G. A., Pettijohn, K. A., & Kim, J. (2015). Walking through doorways causes forgetting: Younger and older adults. *Psychology and Aging, 30*, 259-265.

Raffin, E., Richard, N., Giraux, P., & Reilly, K. T. (2016). Primary motor cortex changes after amputation correlate with phantom limb pain and the ability to move the phantom limb. *Neuroimage, 130*, 134-144.

Ragins, B., & Winkel, D. E. (2011). Gender, emotion and power in work relationships. *Human Resource Management Review, 21*, 377-393.

Ragland, J. D., Layher, E., Hannula, D. E., Niendam, T.A., Lesh, T.A., Solomon, M., Carter, C. S., & Ranganath, C. (2015). Impact of schizophrenia on anterior and posterior hippocampus during memory for complex scenes. *Neuroimage Clinics, 13*, 82-88.

Rahman, Q., & Yusuf, S. (2015). Lateralization for processing facial emotions in gay men, heterosexual men, and heterosexual women. *Archives of Sexual Behavior, 44*, 1405-1413.

Rahman, Q., Kumari, V., & Wilson, G. D. (2003). Sexual orientation-related differences in prepulse inhibition of the human startle response. *Behavioral Neuroscience, 117*, 1096-1102.

Rajagopal, S. (2006). The placebo effect. *Psychiatric Bulletin, 30*, 185-188.

Rajecki, D. W., & Borden, V. M. H. (2011). Psychology degrees: Employment, wage, and career trajectory consequences. *Perspectives on Psychological Science, 6*, 321-335.

Rajsic, J., Wilson, D. E., & Pratt, J. (2015). Confirmation bias in visual search. *Journal of Experimental Psychology: Human Perception and Performance. 41*(5), 1353-1364.

Ramachandra, V. (2009, February). On whether mirror neurons play a significant role in processing affective prosody. *Perceptual and Motor Skills, 108*, 30-36.

Ramachandran, V. S., & Hubbard, E. M. (2006). Hearing colors, tasting shapes. *Scientific American, 16*, 76-83

Ramos, R. A., Ferguson, C. J., Frailing, K., & Romero-Ramirez, M. (2013). Comfortably numb or just yet another movie? Media violence exposure does not reduce viewer empathy for victims of real violence among primarily Hispanic viewers. *Psychology of Popular Media Culture, 2*, 2-10.

Ramus, F. (2006). Genes, brain, and cognition: A roadmap for the cognitive scientist. *Cognition, 101*, 247-269.

Randall, D. K. (2012, August 4–5). Decoding the science of sleep. *Wall Street Journal*, pp. C1–C2.

Randolph-Seng, B., & Nielsen, M. E. (2009). Opening the doors of perception: Priming altered states of consciousness outside of conscious awareness. *Archiv für Religionspsychologie/Archive for the Psychology of Religions, 31*, 237–260.

Rangell, L. (2007). *The road to unity in psychoanalytic theory.* Lanham, MD: Jason Aronson.

Rapaport, M., Nierenberg, A. A., Howland, R., Dording, C., Schettler, P. J., & Mischoulon, D. (2011). The treatment of minor depression with St. John's wort or citalopram: Failure to show benefit over placebo. *Journal of Psychiatric Research, 45*, 931–941.

Raskin, N. J., & Rogers, C. R. (1989). Person-centered therapy. In R. J. Corsini & D. Wedding (Eds.), *Current psychotherapies* (4th ed.). Itasca, IL: F. E. Peacock.

Rassin, E., & Muris, P. (2007). Abnormal and normal obsessions: A reconsideration. *Behaviour Research and Therapy, 45*, 1065–1070.

Ravallion, M., & Lokshin, M. (2010). Who cares about relative deprivation? *Journal of Economic Behavior & Organization, 73*(2), 171–185. doi:10.1016/j.jebo.2009.08.008.

Ravicz, M.M., Perdue, K.L., Westerlund, A., Vanderwert, R.E. and Nelson, C.A. (2015). Infants' neural responses to facial emotion in the prefrontal cortex are correlated with temperament: A functional near-infrared spectroscopy study. *Frontiers in Psychology. 6*, 922.

Ray, J. V., Thornton, L. C., Frick, P. J., Steinberg, L., & Cauffman, E. (2015). Impulse control and callous-unemotional traits distinguish patterns of delinquency and substance use in justice involved adolescents: Examining the moderating role of neighborhood context. *Journal of Abnormal Child Psychology, 43*(9), 1190–1203.

Ray, L. A., & Hutchison, K. E. (2007). Effects of naltrexone on alcohol sensitivity and genetic moderators of medication response: a double-blind placebo-controlled study. *Archives of General Psychiatry, 64*, 1069–1077.

Ray, L., Bryan, A., MacKillop, J., McGeary, J., Hesterberg, K., & Hutchison, K. (2009). The dopamine D4 receptor gene exon III polymorphism, problematic alcohol use and novelty seeking: Direct and mediated genetic effects. *Addiction Biology, 14*, 238–244.

Ray, R., Loughead, J., Wang, Z., Detre, J., Yang, E., Gur, R., . . . Lerman, C. (2008). Neuroimaging, genetics and the treatment of nicotine addiction. *Behavioural Brain Research, 193*, 159–169.

Raz, A. (2007). Suggestibility and hypnotizability: Mind the gap. *American Journal of Clinical Hypnosis, 49*, 205–210.

Raznahan, A., Lee, Y., Stidd, R., Long, R., Greenstein, D., Clasen, L., . . . Giedd, J. N. (2010). Longitudinally mapping the influence of sex and androgen signaling on the dynamics of human cortical maturation in adolescence. *Proceedings of the National Academy of Sciences, 107*, 16988–16993.

Rea, L.M., & Parker, R.A. (2014). *Designing and Conducting Survey Research: A Comprehensive Guide* (4th Edition.) . NY: Jossey-Bass.

Reddy, S. (2013, March 19). People who taste too much. *Wall Street Journal*, p. D1.

Reddy, S. (2013, September 3). A field guide to the perfect nap. *Wall Street Journal*, pp. D1–D2.

Reddy, S. (2015, May 19.) How doctors break bad news. *Wall Street Journal*, pp. D1, D4.

Reddy, S. (2016, May 10). When daydreaming becomes a problem. *Wall Street Journal*, pp. D1, D4.

Reddy, S. (2017, January 17.) A disorder that blurs the senses. *Wall Street Journal*, pp. A13–A14.

Redford, M. A. (2017). Sound categories or phonemes? *British Journal of Psychology, 108*, 34–36.

Redish, A. D. (2004). Addiction as a computational process gone awry. *Science, 306*, 1944–1947.

Redshaw, M., & Martin, C. (2013). Babies, "bonding" and ideas about parental "attachment". *Journal of Reproductive and Infant Psychology, 31*, 219–221.

Reece, M., Herbenick, D., Sanders, S., Dodge, B., Ghassemi, A., & Fortenberry, J. (2009). Prevalence and characteristics of vibrator use by men in the United States. *Journal of Sexual Medicine, 6*, 1867–1874.

Reed, P. (2007). Response rate and sensitivity to the molar feedback function relating response and reinforcement rate on VI + schedules of reinforcement. *Journal of Experimental Psychology: Animal Behavior Processes, 33*, 428–439.

Reed, P., & Morgan, T. (2008). Effect on subsequent fixed-interval schedule performance of prior exposure to ratio and interval schedules of reinforcement. *Learning & Behavior, 36*, 82–91.

Reed, S. K. (2017). Problem solving. In S. F. Chipman, (Ed.) , *The Oxford handbook of cognitive science.* New York: Oxford University Press.

Rees, P., & Seaton, N. (2011). Psychologists' response to crises: International perspectives. *School Psychology International, 32*, 73–94.

Regan, P. C. (2006). Love. In R. D. McAnulty & M. M. Burnette (Eds.), *Sex and sexuality, Vol. 2: Sexual function and dysfunction.* Westport, CT: Praeger Publishers/Greenwood Publishing.

Regnerus, M., Price, J., & Gordon, D. (2017). Masturbation and partnered sex: Substitutes or complements? *Archives of Sexual Behavior, 46*(7), 2111–2121.

Reichenberg, A., & Harvey, P. D. (2007). Neuro-psychological impairments in schizophrenia: Integration of performance-based and brain imaging findings. *Psychological Bulletin, 133*, 212–223.

Reichenberg, A., Harvey, P., Bowie, C., Mojtabai, R., Rabinowitz, J., Heaton, R., & Bromet, E. (2009). Neuropsychological function and dysfunction in schizophrenia and psychotic affective disorders. *Schizophrenia Bulletin, 35*, 1022–1029.

Reid, J. L., Martin, A., & Brooks-Gunn, J. (2017). Low-income parents' adult interactions at childcare centres. *Early Child Development and Care, 187*, 138–151.

Reid, J. R., MacLeod, J., & Robertson, J. R. (2010). Cannabis and the lung. *Journal of the Royal College of Physicians, 40*, 328–334.

Reijonen, J. H., Pratt, H. D., Patel, D. R., & Greydanus, D. E. (2003). Eating disorders in the adolescent population: An overview [Special issue: Eating disorders in adolescents]. *Journal of Adolescent Research, 18*, 209–222.

Reilly, E. D., Rackley, K. R., & Awad, G. H. (2017). Perceptions of male and female STEM aptitude: The moderating effect of benevolent and hostile sexism. *Journal of Career Development, 44*, 159–173.

Reilly, M. T., Noronha, A., Goldman, D., & Koob, G. F. (2017). Genetic studies of alcohol dependence in the context of the addiction cycle. *Neuropharmacology, 12*, 23–21.

Reilly, T., & Waterhouse, J. (2007). Altered sleep-wake cycles and food intake: The Ramadan model. *Physiology & Behavior, 90*, 219–228.

Reiner, R. (2008). Integrating a portable biofeedback device into clinical practice for patients with anxiety disorders: Results of a pilot study. *Applied Psychophysiology and Biofeedback, 33*, 55–61.

Reinisch, J. M., Mortensen, E. L., & Sanders, S. A. (2017). Prenatal exposure to progesterone affects sexual orientation in humans. *Archives of Sexual Behavior, 46*(5), 1239–1249.

Reisberg, D. (1997). *Cognition: Exploring the science of the mind.* New York: Norton.

Reisberg, D. (2009). *Cognition: Exploring the science of the mind.* New York: Norton.

Reisberg, D. (2013). Mental images. In D. Reisberg (Ed.), *The Oxford handbook of cognitive psychology.* New York: Oxford University Press.

Reisner, A. D., Piel, J., & Makey, M. (2013). Competency to stand trial and defendants who lack insight into their mental illness. *Journal of the American Academy of Psychiatry and the Law, 41*, 85–91.

Reks, S., Sheaves, B., & Freeman, D. (2017, July 15.) Nightmares in the general population: Identifying potential causal factors. *Social Psychiatry and Psychiatric Epidemiology.* doi: 10.1007/s00127-017-1408-7.

Remington, G., Foussias, G., Fervaha, G., & Agid, O. (2014). Schizophrenia, cognition, and psychosis. *JAMA Psychiatry, 71*, 336–337.

Ren, X., Wang, T., & Jarrold, C. (2016). Individual differences in frequency of inner speech: Differential relations with cognitive and non-cognitive factors. *Frontiers in Psychology, 7*, 1675.

Renshaw, D. C. (2006). Male and female circumcision today. *The Family Journal, 14*, 283–285.

Repp, B. H., & Knoblich, G. (2007). Action can affect auditory perception. *Psychological Science, 18*, 6–7.

Reynolds, C. A., & Maughan, E. D. (2015). Telehealth in the school setting: An integrative review. *Journal of School Nursing, 31*, 44–53.

Reynolds, C. R., & Ramsay, M. C. (2003). Bias in psychological assessment: An empirical review and recommendations. In J. R. Graham & J. A. Naglieri (Eds.), *Handbook of psychology: Assessment psychology* (Vol. 10). New York: Wiley.

Reynolds, d. J., Stiles, W. B., Bailer, A. J., & Hughes, M. R. (2013). Impact of exchanges and client-therapist alliance in online-text psychotherapy. *Cyberpsychology, Behavior, and Social Networking, 16,* 370-377.

Reznikova, T. N., Seliverstova, N. A., Kataeva, G. V., Aroev, R. A., Ilves, A. G., & Kuznetsova, A. K. (2015). Functional activity of brain structures and predisposition to aggression in patients with lingering diseases of the CNS. *Human Physiology, 41,* 27-33.

Riccelli, R., Toschi, N., Nigro, S., Terracciano, A. & Passamonti, L. (2017). Surface-based morphometry reveals the neuroanatomical basis of the five-factor model of personality. *Social Cognitive and Affective Neuroscience, 12,* 671-684

Rice, C. (2009). Prevalence of autism spectrum disorders–Autism and Developmental Disabilities Monitoring Network, United States, 2006. *MMWR, 58*(SS10), 1-20.

Richard, D. C. S., & Lauterbach, D. (Eds.). (2006). *Handbook of exposure therapies.* New York: Academic Press.

Richards, C. (2011). Transsexualism and existentialism. *Existential Analysis, 22*(2), 272-279.

Richards, R. (2006). Frank Barron and the study of creativity: A voice that lives on. *Journal of Humanistic Psychology, 46,* 352-370.

Richardson, D. S. (2014). Everyday aggression takes many forms. *Current Directions in Psychological Science, 23,* 220-224.

Richardson, D., & Hammock, G. S. (2011). Is it aggression? Perceptions of and motivations for passive and psychological aggression. In J. P. Forgas, A. W. Kruglanski, & K. D. Williams (Eds.), *The psychology of social conflict and aggression.* New York: Psychology Press.

Richmond, A. S., Broussard, K. A., Sterns, J. L., Sanders, K. K., & Shardy, J. C. (2015). Who are we studying? Sample diversity in teaching of psychology research. *Teaching of Psychology, 42,* 218-226.

Rieber, R. W., & Robinson, D. K. (2006). Review of the essential Vygotsky. *Journal of the History of the Behavioral Sciences, 42,* 178-180.

Rigby, L., & Waite, S. (2007). Group therapy for self-esteem: Using creative approaches and metaphor as clinical tools. *Behavioural and Cognitive Psychotherapy, 35,* 361-364.

Rimmele, J. M., Sussman, E., & Poeppel, D. (2015). The role of temporal structure in the investigation of sensory memory, auditory scene analysis, and speech perception: A healthy-aging perspective. *International Journal of Psychophysiology, 95,* 175-183.

Rinaman, L., Banihashemi, L., & Koehnle, T. J. (2011). Early life experience shapes the functional organization of stress-responsive visceral circuits. *Physiology & Behavior, 104,* 632-640.

Rindermann, H., Becker, D., & Coyle, T. R. (2017). Survey of expert opinion on intelligence: The Flynn effect and the future of intelligence. *Personality and Individual Differences, 106,* 242-247.

Rindone, H. G. (2015). Methamphetamine addiction. In R. L. Smith (Ed.), *Treatment strategies for substance and process addictions.* Alexandria, VA: American Counseling Association.

Riniolo, T. C., Koledin, M., Drakulic, G. M., & Payne, R. A. (2003). An archival study of eyewitness memory of the Titanic's final plunge. *Journal of General Psychology, 130,* 89-95.

Rinn, W. E. (1984). The neuropsychology of facial expression: A review of neurological and psychological mechanisms for producing facial expressions. *Psychological Bulletin, 95,* 52-77.

Rinn, W. E. (1991). Neuropsychology of facial expression. In R. S. Feldman & B. Rimé (Eds.), *Fundamentals of non-verbal behavior.* Cambridge, England: Cambridge University Press.

Ripley, A. (2005, March 7). Who says a woman can't be Einstein? *Time,* pp. 51-60.

Risen, J. (2015, August 8). Association bars psychologists from ties to U.S. national security interrogations. *The New York Times,* p. A11.

Rivera-Gaxiola, M., Klarman, L., Garcia-Sierra, A., & Kuhl, P. K. (2005). Neural patterns to speech and vocabulary growth in American infants. *Neuroreport: For Rapid Communication of Neuroscience Research, 16,* 495-498.

Rizzi, T. S., & Posthuma, D. (2013). Genes and intelligence. In D. Reisberg (Ed.), *The Oxford handbook of cognitive psychology.* New York: Oxford University Press.

Robert, S. (2006). Deictic space in Wolof: Discourse, syntax and the importance of absence. In M. Hickman & S. Robert (Eds.), *Space in languages: Linguistic systems and cognitive categories.* Amsterdam, Netherlands: John Benjamins.

Roberts, M. E., Moore, S. D., & Beckham, J. C. (2007). Post-traumatic stress disorder and substance use disorders. In M. Al'bsi (Ed.), *Stress and addiction: Biological and psychological mechanisms.* San Diego, CA: Elsevier Academic Press.

Roberts, R. M., Neate, G. M., & Gierasch, A. (2017). Implicit attitudes towards people with visible difference: Findings from an Implicit Association Test. *Psychology, Health & Medicine, 22,* 352-358.

Robinson, D. N. (2007). Theoretical psychology: What is it and who needs it? *Theory & Psychology, 17,* 187-198.

Robinson, N. M. (2003). Two wrongs do not make a right: Sacrificing the needs of gifted students does not solve society's unsolved problems. *Journal for the Education of the Gifted, 26,* 251-273.

Robinson-Papp, J., George, M. C., Dorfman, D., & Simpson, D. M. (2015). Barriers to chronic pain measurement: A qualitative study of patient perspectives. *Pain Medicine, 16,* 1256-1264.

Robson, H., Grube, M., Lambon Ralph, M. A., Griffiths, T. D., & Sage, K. (2013). Fundamental deficits of auditory perception in Wernicke's aphasia. *Cortex: A Journal Devoted to the Study of the Nervous System and Behavior, 49,* 1808-1822.

Rock, A. (1999, January). Quitting time for smokers. *Money,* pp. 139-141.

Rodrigues, L., & Girandola, F. (2017). Self-prophecies and cognitive dissonance: Habit, norms and justification of past behavior. *North American Journal of Psychology, 19,* 65-86.

Rodrigues-Amorim, D., Rivera-Baltanás, T., López, M., Spuch, C., Olivares, J. M., & Agís-Balboa, R. C. (2017). Schizophrenia: A review of potential biomarkers. *Journal of Psychiatric Research, 93,* 37-49.

Rodriguez, D. N., & Strange, D. (2015). False memories for dissonance inducing events. *Memory, 23,* 203-212.

Roediger, H. L., III, & McCabe, D. P. (2007). Evaluating experimental research: Critical issues. In R. J. Sternberg, H. L. Roediger, III, & D. F. Halpern (Eds.), *Critical thinking in psychology.* New York: Cambridge University Press.

Roets, A., & Van Hiel, A. (2011). An integrative process approach on judgment and decision making: The impact of arousal, affect, motivation, and cognitive ability. *The Psychological Record, 61,* 497-520.

Roffman, R. A. (2013). Legalization of marijuana: Unraveling quandaries for the addiction professional. *Frontiers in Psychiatry, 4,* 88-93.

Rogalsky, C., Love, T., Driscoll, D., Anderson, S. W., & Hickok, G. (2011). Are mirror neurons the basis of speech perception? Evidence from five cases with damage to the purported human mirror system. *Neurocase, 17,* 178-187.

Rogers, B., & Naumenko, O. (2015). The new moon illusion and the role of perspective in the perception of straight and parallel lines. *Attention, Perception, & Psychophysics, 77,* 249-257.

Rogers, C. R. (1951). *Client-centered therapy.* Boston: Houghton-Mifflin.

Rogers, C. R. (1971). A theory of personality. In S. Maddi (Ed.), *Perspectives on personality.* Boston: Little, Brown.

Rogers, C. R. (1995). *A way of being.* Boston: Houghton Mifflin.

Rogers, J. M. (2009). Tobacco and pregnancy: Overview of exposures and effects. *Birth Defects Res. C. Embryo Today, 84,* 152-160.

Rogers, S. (2007). The underlying mechanisms of semantic memory loss in Alzheimer's disease and semantic dementia. *Dissertation Abstracts International: Section B: The Sciences and Engineering, 67*(10-B), 5591.

Roid, G., Nellis, L., & McLellan, M. (2003). Assessment with the Leiter International Performance Scale–Revised and the S-BIT. In R. S. McCallum & R. Steve (Eds.), *Handbook of nonverbal assessment.* New York: Kluwer Academic/Plenum Publishers.

Rolls, E. T. (2011). Functions of human emotional memory: The brain and emotion. In S. Nalbantian, P. M. Matthews, & J. L. McClelland (Eds.), *The memory process: Neuroscientific and humanistic perspectives.* Cambridge, MA: MIT Press.

Rom, S. A., Miller, L., & Peluso, J. (2009). Playing the game: Psychological factors in surviving cancer. *International Journal of Emergency Mental Health, 11,* 25-36.

Romani, C., Palermo, L., MacDonald, A., Limback, E., Hall, S. K., & Geberhiwot, T. (2017). The impact of phenylalanine levels on cognitive outcomes in adults with phenylketonuria: Effects across tasks and developmental stages. *Neuropsychology, 31,* 242-254.

Romano, E., Tremblay, R. E., Vitaro, E., Zoccolillo, M., & Pagani, L. (2001). Prevalence of psychiatric diagnoses and the role of perceived impairment: Findings from an adolescent community sample. *Journal of Child Psychology and Psychiatry and Allied Disciplines, 42,* 451-461.

Romero-Guevara, R., Cencetti, F., Donati, C., & Bruni, P. (2015). Sphingosine 1-phosphate signaling pathway in inner ear biology. New therapeutic strategies for hearing loss? *Frontiers in Aging Neuroscience, 7,* 101-111.

Roncero, C., Daigre, C., Gonzalvo, B., Valero, S., Castells, X., Grau-López, L., . . . Casas, M. (2013). Risk factors for cocaine-induced psychosis in cocaine-dependent patients. *European Psychiatry, 28,* 141-146.

Ronconi, L., Casartelli, L., Carna, S., Molteni, M., Arrigoni, F., & Borgatti, R. (2017). When one is enough: Impaired multisensory integration in cerebellar agenesis. *Cerebral Cortex, 27,* 2041-2051

Rooke, S. E., & Hine, D. W. (2011). A dual process account of adolescent and adult binge drinking. *Addictive Behaviors, 36,* 341-346.

Roos, V., & Zaaiman, R. (2017). Active ageing as positive intervention: Some unintended consequences. In C. Proctor (Ed.), *Positive psychology interventions in practice.* Cham, Switzerland: Springer International Publishing.

Rorschach, H. (1924). *Psychodiagnosis: A diagnostic test based on perception.* New York: Grune & Stratton.

Rose, N., & Blackmore, S. (2002). Horses for courses: Tests of a psychic claimant. *Journal of the Society for Psychical Research, 66,* 29-40.

Rosellini, A. J., Stein, M. B., Colpe, L. J., Heeringa, S. G., Petukhova, M. V., Sampson, N. A., . . . Army STARRS Collaborators. (2015). Approximating a DSM-5 diagnosis of PTSD using DSM-IV criteria. *Depression and Anxiety, 32,* 493-501.

Rosenberg, L., & Park, S. (2002). Verbal and spatial functions across the menstrual cycle in healthy young women. *Psychoneuroendocrinology, 27,* 834-841.

Rosenblat, A., & Stark, L. (2016). Algorithmic labor and information assymetries: A case study of Uber's drivers. *International Journal of Communication, 10,* 3758-3784.

Rosenblatt, P. C. (2013). The concept of complicated grief: Lessons from other cultures. In M. Stroebe, H. Schut, & J. van den Bout (Eds.), *Complicated grief: Scientific foundations for health care professionals* (pp. 27-39). New York: Routledge/Taylor & Francis Group.

Rosenbloom, T., & Wolf, Y. (2002). Sensation seeking and detection of risky road signals: A developmental perspective. *Accident Analysis and Prevention, 34,* 569-580.

Rosenfeld, , R., Gaston, S., Spivak, H., & Irazola, S. (2017, November.) Assessing and responding to the recent homicide rise in the United States. Washington, DC: National Institute of Justice.

Rosenfeld, M. J., & Thomas, R. J. (2012). Searching for a mate: The rise of the Internet as a social intermediary. *American Sociological Review, 77,* 523-547.

Rosenhan, D. L. (1973). On being sane in insane places. *Science, 179,* 250-258.

Rosenstein, D. S., & Horowitz, H. A. (1996). Adolescent attachment and psychopathology. *Journal of Consulting and Clinical Psychology, 64,* 244-253.

Rosenström, T., Ystrom, E., Torvik, F. A., Czajkowski, N. O., Gillespie, N. A., Aggen, S. H., . . . Reichborn-Kjennerud, T. (2017). Genetic and environmental structure of DSM-IV criteria for antisocial personality disorder: A twin study. *Behavior Genetics, 47,* 265-277.

Rosenthal, N. F. (2003). *The emotional revolution: How the new science of feeling can transform your life.* New York: Citadel.

Rosenthal, R. (2002). Covert communication in classrooms, clinics, courtrooms and cubicles. *American Psychologist, 57,* 838-849.

Rosenthal, R. (2003). Covert communication in laboratories, classrooms, and the truly real world. *Current Directions in Psychological Science, 12,* 151-154.

Rosner, H. (2001, April 30). The science of O. *New York Magazine,* 25-31.

Ross, C. A. (2015). When to suspect and how to diagnose dissociative identity disorder. *Journal of EMDR Practice and Research, 9,* 114-120.

Ross, J. (2006). Sleep on a problem . . . It works like a dream. *The Psychologist, 19,* 738-740.

Ross, L. A., Molholm, S., Blanco, D., Gomez-Ramirez, M., Saint-Amour, D., & Foxe, J. J. (2011). The development of multisensory speech perception continues into the late childhood years. *European Journal of Neuroscience, 33,* 2329-2337.

Ross, P. E. (2004). Draining the language out of color. *Scientific American, 290*(4), 46-51.

Rossato, M., Pagano, C., & Vettor, R. (2008). The cannabinoid system and male reproductive functions. *Journal of Neuroendocrinology, 20,* 90-93.

Rossi-Arnaud, C., Cestari, V., Marques, V. S., Gabrielli, G. B., & Spataro, P. (2017). Collaboration in implicit memory: Evidence from word-fragment completion and category exemplar generation. *Psychological Research, 81,* 55-65.

Rotan, L. W., & Ospina-Kammerer, V. (2007). *Mindbody medicine: Foundations and practical applications.* New York: Routledge/Taylor & Francis Group.

Rouder, J. N., Morey, R. D., & Province, J. M. (2013). A Bayes factor meta-analysis of recent extrasensory perception experiments: Comment on Storm, Tressoldi, and Di Risio (2010). *Psychological Bulletin, 139,* 241-247.

Roughton, R. E. (2002). Rethinking homosexuality: What it teaches us about psychoanalysis. *Journal of the American Psychoanalytic Association, 50,* 733-763.

Routtenberg. A., & Lindy, J. (1965). Effects of the availability of rewarding septal and hypothalamic stimulation on bar pressing for food under conditions of deprivation. *Journal of Comparative and Physiological Psychology, 60,* 158-161.

Royzman, E. B., Cassidy, K. W., & Baron, J. (2003). "I know, you know": Epistemic egocentrism in children and adults. *Review of General Psychology, 7,* 38-65.

Rozental, A., Shafran, R., Wade, T., Egan, S., Nordgren, L. B., Carlbring, P., . . . Andersson, G. (2017). A randomized controlled trial of Internet-Based Cognitive Behavior Therapy for perfectionism including an investigation of outcome predictors. *Behaviour Research and Therapy, 95*79-86.

Rozin, P., Kabnick, K., Pete, E., Fischler, C., & Shields, C. (2003). The ecology of eating: Smaller portion sizes in France than in the United States help explain the French paradox. *Psychological Science, 14,* 450-454.

Rubichi, S., Ricci, F., Padovani, R., & Scaglietti, L. (2005). Hypnotic susceptibility, baseline attentional functioning, and the Stroop task. *Consciousness and Cognition: An International Journal, 14,* 296-303.

Rubin, D. C., Schrauf, R. W., Gulgoz, S., & Naka, M. (2007). Cross-cultural variability of component processes in autobiographical remembering: Japan, Turkey, and the USA. *Memory, 15,* 536-547.

Ruiz, M. R. (2015). Behaviourisms: Radical behaviourism and critical inquiry. In I. Parker & I. Parker (Eds.), *Handbook of critical psychology.* NY: Routledge/Taylor & Francis Group.

Rulison, K. L., & Loken, E. (2009). I've fallen and I can't get up: Can high-ability students recover from early mistakes in CAT? *Applied Psychological Measurement, 33,* 83-101.

Ruscher, J. B., Fiske, S. T., & Schnake, S. B. (2000). The motivated tactician's juggling act: Compatible vs. incompatible impression goals. *British Journal of Social Psychology, 39,* 241-256.

Rushton, J. P., & Jensen, A. R. (2006). The totality of available evidence shows the race IQ gap still remains. *Psychological Science, 17,* 921-922.

Russo, N. (1981). Women in psychology. In L. T. Benjamin, Jr. & K. D. Lowman (Eds.), *Activities handbook for the teaching of psychology.* Washington, DC: American Psychological Association.

Rutherford, B., Rose, S., Sneed, J., & Roose, S. (2009, April). Study design affects participant expectations: A survey. *Journal of Clinical Psychopharmacology, 29,* 179-181.

Rutland, A., & Killen, M. (2015). A developmental science approach to reducing prejudice and social exclusion: Intergroup processes, social-cognitive development, and moral reasoning. *Social Issues and Policy Review, 9,* 121-154.

Rutter, M. (2002). Nature, nurture, and development: From evangelism through science toward policy and practice. *Child Development, 73,* 1-21.

Ryan, R. M., & Deci, E. L. (2011). A self-determination theory perspective on social, institutional, cultural, and economic supports for autonomy and their importance for well-being. In V. I. Chirkov, R. M. Ryan, & K. M. Sheldon (Eds.), *Human autonomy in cross-cultural context: Perspectives on the psychology of agency, freedom, and well-being.* New York: Springer Science + Business Media.

Ryan, R. M., & Deci, E. L. (2017). *Self-determination theory: Basic psychological needs in motivation, development, and wellness.* New York: Guilford Press.

Rydell, R., McConnell, A., & Mackie, D. (2008). Consequences of discrepant explicit and implicit attitudes: Cognitive dissonance and increased information processing. *Journal of Experimental Social Psychology, 44,* 1526-1532.

Rymer, R. (1994). *Genie: A scientific tragedy.* New York: Penguin.

Sa, M. (2015). Mood and personality disorders. In G. M. Kapalka (Ed.), *Treating disruptive disorders: A guide to psychological, pharmacological, and combined therapies.* New York: Routledge/Taylor & Francis Group.

Saarimäki, H., Gotsopoulos, A., Jaaskelainen, I. P., Lampinen, J., Vuilleumier, P., Hari, R., . . . Nummanmaa, L. (2016). Discrete neural signatures of basic emotions. *Cerebral Cortex, 26*(6), 2563-2573.

Sachs-Ericsson, N., Joiner, T., Plant, E. A., & Blazer, D. G. (2005). The influence of depression on cognitive decline in community-dwelling elderly persons. *American Journal of Geriatric Psychiatry, 13,* 402-408.

Sachse, P., Beermann, U., Martini, M., Maran, T., Domeier, M., & Furtner, M. R. (2017). "The world is upside down"–The Innsbruck Goggle Experiments of Theodor Erismann (1883-1961) and Ivo Kohler (1915-1985). *Cortex: A Journal Devoted to the Study of the Nervous System and Behavior, 92,* 222-232.

Sachser, R. M., Haubrich, J., Lunardi, P. S., & de Oliveira Alvares, L. (2017). Forgetting of what was once learned: Exploring the role of postsynaptic ionotropic glutamate receptors on memory formation, maintenance, and decay. *Neuropharmacology, 112*(Part A), 94-103.

Sacks, O. (2003, July 28). The mind's eye. *The New Yorker,* pp. 48-59.

Sadeghi-Nejad, H., & Watson, R. (2008). Premature ejaculation: Current medical treatment and new directions. *Journal of Sexual Medicine, 5,* 1037-1050.

Sado, M., Yamauchi, K., Kawakami, N., Ono, Y., Furukawa, T. A., Tsuchiya, M., . . . Kashima, H. (2011). Cost of depression among adults in Japan in 2005. *Psychiatry and Clinical Neurosciences, 65,* 442-450.

Safdar, S., & Kosakowska-Berezecka, N. (2015). *Psychology of gender through the lens of culture: Theories and applications.* Cham, Switzerland: Springer International Publishing.

Salazar, L. F., Crosby, R. A., & DiClemente, R. J. (2015). Experimental research designs. In L. F. Salazar, R. A. Crosby, & R. J. DiClemente (Eds.), *Research methods in health promotion* (2nd ed.). San Francisco: Jossey-Bass.

Salgado, D. M., Quinlin, K. J., & Zlotnick, C. (2007). The relationship of lifetime polysubstance dependence to trauma exposure, symptomatology, and psychosocial functioning in incarcerated women with comorbid PTSD and substance use disorder. *Journal of Trauma Dissociation, 8,* 9-26.

Sallquist, J., Eisenberg, N., Spinrad, T. L., Eggum, N. D., & Gaertner, B. (2009). Assessment of preschoolers' positive empathy: Concurrent and longitudinal relations with positive emotion, social competence, and sympathy. *Journal of Positive Psychology, 4,* 223-233.

Salmon, C. (2017). Long-term romantic relationships: Adaptationist approaches. *Evolutionary Behavioral Sciences, 11,* 121-130.

Salvi, V., Fagiolini, A., Swartz, H., Maina, G., & Frank, E. (2008). The use of antidepressants in bipolar disorder. *Journal of Clinical Psychiatry, 69,* 1307-1318.

Sammut, G., & Buhagiar, L. J. (2017). The sociocultural determination of planned behaviour. *Integrative Psychological & Behavioral Science, 51,* 164-170.

Samoilov, V., & Zayas, V. (2007). Ivan Petrovich Pavlov (1849-1936). *Journal of the History of the Neurosciences, 16,* 74-89.

Sampson, S., & Moore, L. (2008). Is there a glass ceiling for women in development? *Nonprofit Management and Leadership, 18,* 321-339.

Samuel, D. B., & Widiger, T. A. (2006). Differentiating normal and abnormal personality from the perspective of the DSM. In S. Strack (Ed.), *Differentiating normal and abnormal personality* (2nd ed.). New York: Springer Publishing.

Samuel, D. B., Carroll, K. M., Rounsaville, B. J., & Ball, S. A. (2013). Personality disorders as maladaptive, extreme variants of normal personality: Borderline personality disorder and neuroticism in a substance using sample. *Journal of Personality Disorders, 27,* 625-635.

Sanders, C., Sadoski, M., van Walsum, K., Bramson, R., Wiprud, R., & Fossum, T. (2008). Learning basic surgical skills with mental imagery: Using the simulation centre in the mind. *Medical Education, 42,* 607-612.

Sandford, S. (2017). Freud, Bion and Kant: Epistemology and anthropology in The Interpretation of Dreams. *International Journal of Psychoanalysis, 98,* 91-110.

Sandman, C. A. (2015). Mysteries of the human fetus revealed. *Monographs of the Society for Research in Child Development, 80,* 124-137.

Sandomir, R. (2007, July 17). W. W. E.'s testing is examined after Bennoit murder-suicide. *The New York Times,* p. S3.

Sanes, J. R., & Masland, R. H. (2015). The types of retinal ganglion cells: Current status and implications for neuronal classification. *Annual Review of Neuroscience, 38,* 221-246.

Sang-hun, C. (2017, September 21). Kim's rejoinder to Trump's rocket man: "Mentally deranged U.S. dotard." *The New York Times.* Retrieved from https://www.nytimes.com/2017/09/21/world/asia/kim-trump-rocketman-dotard.html.

Santarnecchi, E., Rossi, S., & Rossi, A. (2015). The smarter, the stronger: Intelligence level correlates with brain resilience to systematic insults. *Cortex: A Journal Devoted to the Study of the Nervous System and Behavior, 64,* 293-309.

Santelli, J., Carter, M., Orr, M., & Dittus, P. (2009). Trends in sexual risk behaviors, by nonsexual risk behavior involvement, U.S. high school students, 1991-2007. *Journal of Adolescent Health, 44,* 372-379.

Santos, B. G., Carey, R. J., & Carrera, M. P. (2017). The acquisition, extinction and spontaneous recovery of Pavlovian drug conditioning induced by post-trial dopaminergic stimulation/inhibition. *Pharmacology, Biochemistry and Behavior, 156,* 24-29.

Santtila, P., Wager, I., Witting, K., Harlaar, N., Jern, P., Johansson, A., . . . Sandnabba, N. K. (2008). Discrepancies between sexual desire and sexual activity: Gender differences and associations with relationship satisfaction. *Journal of Sex & Marital Therapy, 34,* 31-44.

Saper, C. B. (2013). The neurobiology of sleep. *CONTINUUM: Lifelong Learning in Neurology, 19,* 19-31.

Sarmiento, I. (2011). Rape stereotypes and labeling: Awareness of victimization and trauma. *Psychological Reports, 108,* 141-148.

Sarsour, K., Sheridan, M., Jutte, D., Nuru-Jeter, A., Hinshaw, S., & Boyce, W. (2011). Family socioeconomic status and child executive functions: The roles of language, home environment, and single parenthood. *Journal of the International Neuropsychological Society, 17,* 120-132.

Sarubin, N., Hilbert, S., Naumann, F., Zill, P., Wimmer, A., Nothdurfter, C., . . . Schüle, C. (2017). The sex-dependent role of the glucocorticoid receptor in depression: Variations in the NR3C1 gene are associated with major depressive disorder in women but not in men. *European Archives of Psychiatry and Clinical Neuroscience, 267,* 123-133.

Saucier, G., & Srivastava, S. (2015). What makes a good structural model of personality? Evaluating the big five and alternatives. In M. Mikulincer, P. R. Shaver, M. L. Cooper, & R. J. Larsen (Eds.), *APA handbook of personality and social psychology, Volume 4: Personality processes and individual differences.* Washington, DC: American Psychological Association.

Saunders, B. T., Yager, L. M., & Robinson, T. E. (2013). Preclinical studies shed light on individual variation in addiction vulnerability. *Neuropsychopharmacology, 38,* 249-250.

Sauter, S. L., & Hurrell, J. J. (2017). Occupational health contributions to the development and promise of occupational health psychology. *Journal of Occupational Health Psychology, 22,* 251-258.

Savage, J., & Yancey, C. (2008). The effects of media violence exposure on criminal aggression: A meta-analysis. *Criminal Justice and Behavior, 35,* 772-791.

Savage-Rumbaugh, E. S., Toth, N., & Schick, K. (2007). Kanzi learns to knap stone tools. In D. A. Washburn (Ed.), *Primate perspectives on behavior and cognition.* Washington, DC: American Psychological Association.

Savazzi, S., Fabri, M., Rubboli, G., Paggi, A., Tassinari, C. A., & Marzi, C. A. (2007). Interhemispheric transfer following callosotomy in humans: Role of the superior colliculus. *Neuropsychologia, 45,* 2417-2427.

Saville, B. (2009). Performance under competitive and self-competitive fixed-interval schedules of reinforcement. *The Psychological Record, 59,* 21-38.

Sawa, A., & Snyder, S. H. (2002). Schizophrenia: Diverse approaches to a complex disease. *Science, 296,* 692-695.

Scalzo, S., Bowden, S., & Hillbom, M. (2015). Wernicke-Korsakoff syndrome. In J. Svanberg, A. Withall, B. Draper, & S. Bowden (Eds.) , *Alcohol and the adult brain.* New York: Psychology Press.

Scarr, S., & Weinberg, R. A. (1976). I.Q. test performance of black children adopted by white families. *American Psychologist, 31,* 726-739.

Scaturo, D. J. (2004). Fundamental clinical dilemmas in contemporary group psychotherapy. *Group Analysis, 37,* 201-217.

Scelfo, J. (2007, February 26). Men & depression: Facing darkness. *Newsweek,* pp. 43-50.

Scelfo, J. (2015, February 8). They. *The New York Times,* p. ED18.

Schachter, R. (2011). Using the group in cognitive group therapy. *Group, 35,* 135-149.

Schachter, S., & Singer, J. E. (1962). Cognitive, social, and physiological determinants of emotional state. *Psychological Review, 69,* 379-399.

Schachter, S., & Singer, J. E. (2001). Cognitive, social, and psychological determinants of emotional state. In W. G. Parrott, (Ed.), *Emotions in social psychology: Essential readings* (pp. 76-93). New York: Psychology Press.

Schacter, D. L., Dobbins, I. G., & Schnyer, D. M. (2004). Specificity of priming: A cognitive neuroscience perspective. *Nature Reviews Neuroscience, 5,* 853-862.

Schacter, D. L., Guerin, S. A., & St. Jacques, P. L. (2011). Memory distortion: An adaptive perspective. *Trends in Cognitive Sciences, 15,* 467-474.

Schaefer, E. G., Halldorson, M. K., & Dizon-Reynante, C. (2011). TV or not TV? Does the immediacy of viewing images of a momentous news event affect the quality and stability of flashbulb memories? *Memory, 19,* 251-266.

Schaie, K. W. (2005b). What can we learn from longitudinal studies of adult development? *Research in Human Development, 2,* 133-158.

Schaller, M., & Crandall, C. S. (Eds.). (2004). *The psychological foundations of culture.* Mahwah, NJ: Lawrence Erlbaum Associates.

Scharrer, E., & Ramasubramanian, S. (2015). Intervening in the media's influence on stereotypes of race and ethnicity: The role of media literacy education. *Journal of Social Issues, 71,* 171-185.

Schepers, P., & van den Berg, P. T. (2007). Social factors of work-environment creativity. *Journal of Business and Psychology, 21,* 407-428.

Schermer, J., Johnson, A. M., Vernon, P. A., & Jang, K. L. (2011). The relationship between personality and self-report abilities: A behavior-genetic analysis. *Journal of Individual Differences, 32,* 47-53.

Schieber, E. (2006). Vision and aging. In J. E. Birren & K. W. Schaire (Eds.), *Handbook of the psychology of aging* (6th ed.). Amsterdam, Netherlands: Elsevier.

Schiff, R., & Vakil, E. (2015). Age differences in cognitive skill learning, retention and transfer: The case of the Tower of Hanoi Puzzle. *Learning and Individual Differences, 39,* 164-171.

Schilling, O. K., & Diehl, M. (2015). Psychological vulnerability to daily stressors in old age: Results of short-term longitudinal studies. *Zeitschrift Für Gerontologie Und Geriatrie, 48,* 517-523.

Schlinger, H. D. (2015). Behavior analysis and behavioral neuroscience. *Frontiers in Human Neuroscience, 9,* 98-105

Schlinger, H. R. (2011). Skinner as missionary and prophet: A review of Burrhus F. Skinner: Shaper of behaviour. *Journal of Applied Behavior Analysis, 44,* 217-225.

Schmidt, J. P. (2006). The discovery of neurotransmitters: A fascinating story and a scientific object lesson. *PsycCRITIQUES, 61,* 101-115.

Schmidt, J., Klusmann, U., Lüdtke, O., Möller, J., & Kunter, M. (2017). What makes good and bad days for beginning teachers? A diary study on daily uplifts and hassles. *Contemporary Educational Psychology, 48,* 85-97.

Schnall, S., Haidt, J., Clore, G. L., & Jordan, A. H. (2008). Disgust as embodied moral judgment. *Personality and Social Psychology Bulletin, 34,* 1096-1109.

Schneider, D. W., & Logan, G. D. (2015). Chunking away task-switch costs: A test of the chunk-point hypothesis. *Psychonomic Bulletin & Review, 22,* 884-889.

Schnell, K., & Herpertz, S. C. (2007). Effects of dialectic-behavioral-therapy on the neural correlates of affective hyperarousal in borderline personality disorder. *Journal of Psychiatric Research, 41,* 837-847.

Schnupp, J., Nelken, I., & King, A. (2011). *Auditory neuroscience: Making sense of sound.* Cambridge, MA: MIT Press.

Schofield, W., & Vaughan-Jackson, P. (1913). *What a boy should know.* New York: Cassell.

Schoofs, H., Hermans, D., Griffith, J. W., & Raes, F. (2013). Self-discrepancy and reduced autobiographical memory specificity in ruminating students and depressed patients. *Cognition and Emotion, 27,* 245-262.

Schooler, L. J., & Hertwig, R. (2012). How forgetting aids heuristic inference. In G. Gigerenzer, R. Hertwig, & T. Pachur (Eds.), *Heuristics: The foundations of adaptive behavior.* New York: Oxford University Press.

Schredl, M., & Piel, E. (2005). Gender differences in dreaming: Are they stable over time? *Personality and Individual Differences, 39,* 309-316.

Schredl, M., & Reinhard, I. (2011). Gender differences in nightmare frequency: A meta-analysis. *Sleep Medicine Reviews, 15,* 115-121.

Schreurs, B. G., Smith-Bell, C. A., & Burhans, L. B. (2011). Classical conditioning and conditioning-specific reflex modification of rabbit heart rate as a function of unconditioned stimulus location. *Behavioral Neuroscience, 125,* 604-612.

Schroers, M., Prigot, J., & Fagen, J. (2007). The effect of a salient odor context on memory retrieval in young infants. *Infant Behavior & Development, 30,* 685-689.

Schrotenboer, B. (2016, July 12). Feds call Lance Armstrong "a doper, dealer and liar" in scathing new rebuke. *USA Today.* Retrieved from https://www.usatoday.com/story/sports/cycling/2016/07/12/feds-lance-armstrong-rebuke-doper-dealer-liar/86978852/.

Schubert, T., & Koole, S. (2009). The embodied self: Making a fist enhances men's power-related self-conceptions. *Journal of Experimental Social Psychology, 45,* 828-834.

Schultheiss, O. C., & Schiepe-Tiska, A. (2013). The role of the dorsoanterior striatum in implicit motivation: The case of the need for power. *Frontiers in Human Neuroscience, 7.* Retrieved from http://www.ncbi.nlm.nih.gov/pubmed/23626531.

Schurger, A., Sarigiannidis, I., Naccache, L., Sitt, J. D., & Dehaene, S. (2015). Cortical activity is more stable when sensory stimuli are consciously perceived. *PNAS Proceedings of the National Academy of Sciences of the United States of America, 112,* E2083-E2092.

Schwartz, B. (2008). Working memory load differentially affects tip-of-the-tongue states and feeling-of-knowing judgments. *Memory & Cognition, 36,* 9-19.

Schwartz, B. L. (2002). The phenomenology of naturally-occurring tip-of-the-tongue states: A diary study. In S. P. Shohov (Ed.), *Advances in psychology research* (Vol. 8). Huntington, NY: Nova.

Schwartz, B. L., & Metcalfe, J. (2011). Tip-of-the-tongue (TOT) states: Retrieval, behavior, and experience. *Memory & Cognition, 39,* 737-749.

Schwartz, J. M., & Begley, S. (2002). *The mind and the brain: Neuroplasticity and the power of mental force.* New York: Regan Books/Harper Collins.

Schwartz, J., & Wald, M. L. (2003). NASA's curse? "Groupthink" is 30 years old, and still going strong. *The New York Times,* p. C1.

Schwartz, P., Maynard, A., & Uzelac, S. (2008). Adolescent egocentrism: A contemporary view. *Adolescence, 43(171),* 441-448.

Schwartz, S. J., Donnellan, M., Ravert, R. D., Luyckx, K., & Zamboanga, B. L. (2013). Identity development, personality, and well-being in adolescence and emerging adulthood: Theory, research, and recent advances. In R. M. Lerner, M. Easterbrooks, J. Mistry, & I. B. Weiner (Eds.), *Handbook of psychology, Vol. 6: Developmental psychology* (2nd ed.). Hoboken, NJ: John Wiley & Sons Inc.

Schwartzmant, R. J., Alexander, G. M., & Grothusen, J. R. (2011). The use of ketamine in complex regional pain syndrome: Possible mechanisms. *Expert Review of Neurotherapeutics, 11,* 719-734.

Schwarzer, R., & Luszczynska, A. (2013). Stressful life events. In A. M. Nezu, C. Nezu, P. A. Geller, & I. B. Weiner (Eds.), *Handbook of psychology, Vol. 9: Health psychology* (2nd ed.). Hoboken, NJ: John Wiley & Sons Inc.

Schwenkreis, P., El Tom, S., Ragert, P., Pleger, B., Tegenthoff, M., & Dinse, H. (2007). Assessment of sensorimotor cortical representation asymmetries and motor skills in violin players. *European Journal of Neuroscience, 26,* 3291-3302.

Sciutto, M., & Eisenberg, M. (2007). Evaluating the evidence for and against the overdiagnosis of ADHD. *Journal of Attention Disorders, 11*, 106-113.

Scull, A. (2015). *Madness in civilization: A cultural history of insanity, from the Bible to Freud, from the madhouse to modern medicine.* Princeton, NJ: Princeton University Press.

Searight, H. (2013). Deinstitutionalization of people with mental illness: A failed policy that could have succeeded. *PsycCRITIQUES, 58*, 88-94.

Searls, D. (2017). *The inkblots: Hermann Rorschach, his iconic test, and the power of seeing.* New York: Crown Publishers/Random House.

Sebastiani, L., Castellani, E., & D'Alessandro, L. (2011). Emotion processing without awareness: Features detection or significance evaluation? *International Journal of Psychophysiology, 80*, 150-156.

Sebel, P. S., Bonke, B., & Winograd, E. (Eds.). (1993). *Memory and awareness in anesthesia.* Englewood Cliffs, NJ: Prentice-Hall.

Seeman, P. (2011). All roads to schizophrenia lead to dopamine supersensitivity and elevated dopamine D2(high) receptors. *CNS Neuroscience & Therapeutics, 17*, 118-132.

Sefcek, J. A., Brumbach, B. H., & Vasquez, G. (2007). The evolutionary psychology of human mate choice: How ecology, genes, fertility, and fashion influence mating strategies. *Journal of Psychology & Human Sexuality, 18*, 125-182.

Segall, M. H. (1988). Cultural roots of aggressive behavior. In M. Bond (Ed.), *The cross-cultural challenge to social psychology.* Newbury Park, CA: Sage.

Segall, M. H., Campbell, D. T., & Herskovits, M. J. (1966). *The influence of culture on visual perception.* New York: Bobbs-Merrill.

Seligman, M. E. (2007). *What you can change . . . and what you can't: The complete guide to successful self-improvement.* New York: Vintage.

Seligman, M. E. P. (1995). The effectiveness of psychotherapy: The *Consumer Reports* study. *American Psychologist, 50*, 965-974.

Sell, C., Möller, H., & Taubner, S. (2017). Effectiveness of integrative Imagery- and trance-based psychodynamic therapies: Guided imagery psychotherapy and hypnopsychotherapy. *Journal of Psychotherapy Integration.* Accessed at http://psycnet.apa.org/record/2017-07863-001.

Sellbom, M., Fischler, G., & Ben-Porath, Y. (2007). Identifying MMPI-2 predictors of police officer integrity and misconduct. *Criminal Justice and Behavior, 34*, 985-1004.

Sells, R. (1994, August). *Homosexuality study.* Paper presented at the annual meeting of the American Statistical Association, Toronto.

Selove, R. (2007). The glass is half full: Current knowledge about pediatric cancer and sickle cell anemia. *PsycCRITIQUES, 52*, 88-99.

Selsky, A. (1997, February 16). African males face circumcision rite. *The Boston Globe*, p. C7.

Selye, H. (1976). *The stress of life.* New York: McGraw-Hill.

Selye, H. (1993). History of the stress concept. In L. Goldberger & S. Breznitz (Eds.), *Handbook of stress: Theoretical and clinical aspects* (2nd ed.). New York: Free Press.

Semin, G. R., & Garrido, M. V. (2013). A systemic approach to impression formation: From verbal to multimodal processes. In J. P. Forgas, K. Fiedler, & C. Sedikides (Eds.), *Social thinking and interpersonal behavior.* New York: Psychology Press.

Semler, C. N., & Harvey, A. G. (2005). Misperception of sleep can adversely affect daytime functioning in insomnia. *Behaviour Research and Therapy, 43*, 843-856.

Semykina, A., & Linz, S. J. (2007). Gender differences in personality and earnings: Evidence from Russia. *Journal of Economic Psychology, 28*, 387-410.

Senholzi, K. B., Depue, B. E., Correll, J., Banich, M. T., & Ito, T. A. (2015). Brain activation underlying threat detection to targets of different races. *Social Neuroscience, 10*, 651-662.

Seroczynski, A. D., Jacquez, F. M., & Cole, D. A. (2003). Depression and suicide during adolescence. In G. R. Adams & M. D. Berzonsky (Eds.), *Blackwell handbook of adolescence.* Malden, MA: Blackwell Publishers.

Serpell, R. (2000). Intelligence and culture. In R. Sternberg (Ed.), *Handbook of intelligence.* Cambridge, England: Cambridge University Press.

Serretti, A. (2017). Genetics and pharmacogenetics of mood disorders. *Psychiatria Polska, 51*, 197-203.

Servick, K. (2014). New support for "gay gene." *Science, 346*, 900.

Seymour, B. (2006). Carry on eating: Neural pathways mediating conditioned potentiation of feeding. *Journal of Neuroscience, 26*, 1061-1062.

Sezgin, F., & Erdogan, O. (2015). Academic optimism, hope and zest for work as predictors of teacher self-efficacy and perceived success. *Kuram Ve Uygulamada Eğitim Bilimleri, 15*, 7-19.

Shafer, V. L., & Garrido-Nag, K. (2007). The neurodevelopmental bases of language. In E. Hoff & M. Shatz (Eds.), *Blackwell handbook of language development.* Malden, MA: Blackwell Publishing.

Shah, A. S., Young, J., & Vieira, K. (2014). Long-term Suboxone treatment and its benefit on long-term remission for opiate dependence. *African Journal of Psychiatry, 17*, 1-4.

Shaikholeslami, R., & Khayyer, M. (2006). Intrinsic motivation, extrinsic motivation, and learning English as a foreign language. *Psychological Reports, 99*, 813-818.

Shaked, A., & Clore, G. (2017). Breaking the world to make it whole again: Attribution in the construction of emotion. *Emotion Review, 9*(1), 27-35.

Shakya, H., & Christakis, N. (2017). Association of Facebook use with compromised well-being: A longitudinal study. *American Journal of Epidemiology, 185*, 203-211.

Shanahan, L., Copeland, W. E., Worthman, C. M., Erkanli, A., Angold, A., & Costello, E. (2013). Sex-differentiated changes in C-reactive protein from ages 9 to 21: The contributions of BMI and physical/ sexual maturation. *Psychoneuroendocrinology, 38*, 2209-2217.

Shaner, L., Kelly, L., Rockwell, D., & Curtis, D. (2017). Calm abiding: The lived experience of the practice of long-term meditation. *Journal of Humanistic Psychology, 57*, 98-121.

Sharpe, L. (2013, November 1). U.S. obesity rate climbing in 2013. Gallup Poll.

Shea, A., & Steiner, M. (2008). Cigarette smoking during pregnancy. *Nicotine & Tobacco Research, 10*, 267-278.

Sheahan, C. L., Pozzulo, J. D., Reed, J. E., & Pica, E. (2017). The role of familiarity with the defendant, type of descriptor discrepancy, and eyewitness age on mock jurors' perceptions of eyewitness testimony. *Journal of Police and Criminal Psychology.* Accessed from https://link.springer.com/article/10.1007/s11896-017-9232-2.

Shehab, A. S., Brent, D., & Maalouf, F. T. (2016). Neurocognitive changes in selective serotonin reuptake inhibitors–Treated adolescents with depression. *Journal of Child and Adolescent Psychopharmacology, 26*, 713-720.

Shehata-Dieler, W., Ehrmann-Mueller, D., Wermke, P., Voit, V., Cebulla, M., & Wermke, K. (2013). Pre-speech diagnosis in hearing-impaired infants: How auditory experience affects early vocal development. *Speech, Language and Hearing, 16*, 99-106.

Shellenbarger, S. (2012, August 22). Are you a hero or a bystander? *Wall Street Journal*, p. D1.

Shellenbarger, S. (2013, April 3). Tactics to spark creativity. *Wall Street Journal*, pp. D1-D2.

Shepperd, J., Malone, W., & Sweeny, K. (2008). Exploring causes of the self-serving bias. *Social and Personality Psychology Compass, 2*, 895-908.

Sherblom, S. (2008). The legacy of the "care challenge": Re-envisioning the outcome of the justice-care debate. *Journal of Moral Education, 37*, 81-98.

Sherman, S. L., Allen, E. G., Bean, L. H., & Freeman, S. B. (2007). Epidemiology of Down syndrome [Special issue: Down syndrome]. *Mental Retardation and Developmental Disabilities Research Reviews, 13*, 221-227.

Shibata, K., Sasaki, Y., Bang, J. W., Walsh, E. G., Machizawa, M. G., Tamaki, M., . . . Watanabe, T. (2017). Overlearning hyperstabilizes a skill by rapidly making neurochemical processing inhibitory-dominant. *Nature Neuroscience, 20*, 470-475.

Shiffman, S. (2007). Use of more nicotine lozenges leads to better success in quitting smoking. *Addiction, 102*, 809-814.

Shimono, K., & Wade, N. J. (2002). Monocular alignment in different depth planes. *Vision Research, 42*, 1127-1135.

Shin, D. W., Roter, D. L., Roh, Y. K., Hahm, S. K., Cho, B., & Park, H. (2015). Physician gender and patient centered communication: The moderating effect of psychosocial and biomedical case characteristics. *Patient Education and Counseling, 98*, 55-60.

Shin, H. B., & Kominski, R. A. 2010. *Language Use in the United States: 2007.* American Community Survey Reports, ACS-12. Washington, DC: U.S. Census Bureau.

Shirai, F., & Hayashi-Takagi, A. (2017). Optogenetics: Applications in psychiatric research. *Psychiatry and Clinical Neurosciences, 71*, 363-372.

Shirayama, Y., & Hashimoto, K. (2017). Effects of a single bilateral infusion of R-ketamine in the rat brain regions of a learned helplessness model of depression. *European Archives of Psychiatry and Clinical Neuroscience, 267*, 177-182.

Shnabel, N., Purdie-Vaughns, V., Cook, J. E., Garcia, J., & Cohen, G. L. (2013). Demystifying values-affirmation interventions: Writing about social belonging is a key to buffering against identity threat. *Personality and Social Psychology Bulletin, 39*, 663-676.

Shogren, K. A., & Wehmeyer, M. L. (2017). Problem solving. In M. L. Wehmeyer, K. A. Shogren, T. D. Little, & S. J. Lopez (Eds.), *Development of self-determination through the lifecourse.* New York: Springer Science + Business Media.

Shors, T. J. (2009). Saving new brain cells. *Scientific American, 500*, 47-54.

Shrestha, L. B., & Heisler, E. J. (2011). The changing demographic profile of the United States. Congressional Research Service. Retrieved from www.fas.org/sgp/crs/misc/RL32701.pdf.

Shulman, J. L., & Horne, S. G. (2006). Guilty or not? A path model of women's sexual force fantasies. *Journal of Sex Research, 43*, 368-377.

Shultz, S. K., Scherman, A., & Marshall, L. J. (2000). Evaluation of a university-based date rape prevention program: Effect on attitudes and behavior related to rape. *Journal of College Student Development, 41*, 193-201.

Shurkin, J. N. (1992). *Terman's kids: The groundbreaking study of how the gifted grow up.* Boston: Little, Brown.

Shweder, R. A. (1994). You're not sick, you're just in love: Emotion as an interpretive system. In P. Ekman & R. J. Davidson (Eds.), *The nature of emotion: Fundamental questions.* New York: Oxford.

Sibunruang, H., Capezio, A., & Restubog, S. D. (2015). In pursuit of success: The differential moderating effects of political skill on the relationships among career-related psychological needs and ingratiation. *Journal of Career Assessment, 23*, 336-348.

Sidman, M. (2006). The distinction between positive and negative reinforcement: Some additional considerations. *Behavior Analyst, 29*, 135-139.

Sielski, R., Rief, W., & Glombiewski, J. A. (2017). Efficacy of biofeedback in chronic back pain: A meta-analysis. *International Journal of Behavioral Medicine, 24*, 25-41.

Siemer, M., Mauss I., & Gross, J. J. (2007). Same situation–different emotions: How appraisals shape our emotions. *Emotion, 7*, 592-600.

Sifrit, K. J. (2006). The effects of aging and cognitive decrements on simulated driving performance. *Dissertation abstracts international: Section B: The Sciences and Engineering, 67*, 2863.

Sikka, P., Revonsuo, A., Sandman, N., Tuominen, J., & Valli, K. (2017). Dream emotions: A comparison of home dream reports with laboratory early and late REM dream reports. *Journal of Sleep Research.* Accessed from https://www.ncbi.nlm.nih.gov/pubmed/28568911.

Sikkema, K. J., Ranby, K. W., Meade, C. S., Hansen, N. B., Wilson, P. A., & Kochman, A. (2013). Reductions in traumatic stress following a coping intervention were mediated by decreases in avoidant coping for people living with HIV/AIDS and childhood sexual abuse. *Journal of Consulting and Clinical Psychology, 81*, 274-283.

Silva, M. T. A., Gonçalves, E. L., & Garcia-Mijares, M. (2007). Neural events in the reinforcement contingency. *Behavior Analyst, 30*, 17-30.

Silverstein, B., Edwards, T., Gamma, A., Ajdacic-Gross, V., Rossler, W., & Angst, J. (2013). The role played by depression associated with somatic symptomatology in accounting for the gender difference in the prevalence of depression. *Social Psychiatry and Psychiatric Epidemiology, 48*, 257-263.

Silverstein, M. L. (2007). Rorschach test findings at the beginning of treatment and 2 years later, with a 30-year follow-up. *Journal of Personality Assessment, 88*, 131-143.

Simon, E. B., Maron-Katz, A., Lahav, N., Shamir, R., & Hendler, T. (2017). Tired and misconnected: A breakdown of brain modularity following sleep deprivation. *Human Brain Mapping, 38*, 3300-3314.

Simon, E. B., Oren, N., Sharon, H., Kirschner, A., Goldway, N., Okon-Singer, H., . . . Hendler, T. (2015). Losing neutrality: The neural basis of impaired emotional control without sleep. *Journal of Neuroscience, 35*(38), 13194-13205.

Simon, G., Ludman, E., Unützer, J., Operskalski, B., & Bauer, M. (2008). Severity of mood symptoms and work productivity in people treated for bipolar disorder. *Bipolar Disorders, 10*, 718-725.

Simon, S., & Hoyt, C. (2008). Exploring the gender gap in support for a woman for president. *Analyses of Social Issues and Public Policy, 8*, 157-181.

Simonton, D. K. (2009). Varieties of (scientific) creativity: A hierarchical model of domain-specific disposition, development, and achievement. *Perspectives on Psychological Science, 4*, 441-452.

Simonton, D. K. (2014). The mad-genius paradox: Can creative people be more mentally healthy but highly creative people more mentally ill? *Perspectives on Psychological Science, 9*, 470-480.

Sinclair, R. R., Waitsman, M. C., Oliver, C. M., & Deese, M. (2013). Personality and psychological resilience in military personnel. In R. R. Sinclair & T. W. Britt (Eds.), *Building psychological resilience in military personnel: Theory and practice.* Washington, DC: American Psychological Association.

Singer, B. F., Bryan, M. A., Popov, P., Robinson, T. E., & Aragona, B. J. (2017). Rapid induction of dopamine sensitization in the nucleus accumbens shell induced by a single injection of cocaine. *Behavioural Brain Research, 324*, 66-70.

Singer, J. L. (2006). Why imagery, personal memories, and daydreams matter. In J. L. Singer (Ed.), *Imagery in psychotherapy.* Washington, DC: American Psychological Association.

Singer, L. T., & Richardson, G. A. (2011). Introduction to "understanding developmental consequences of prenatal drug exposure: Biological and environmental effects and their interactions." *Neurotoxicology and Teratology, 33*, 5-8.

Singh, R. D., Jimerson, S. R., Renshaw, T., Saeki, E., Hart, S. R., Earhart, J., . . . Stewart, K. (2011). A summary and synthesis of contemporary empirical evidence regarding the effects of the Drug Abuse Resistance Education Program (D.A.R.E.). *Contemporary School Psychology, 15*, 93-102.

Singh, S., Wulf, D., Samara, R., & Cuca, Y. P. (2000). Gender differences in the timing of first intercourse: Data from 14 countries. *International Family Planning Perspectives, 26*, 21-28, 43.

Sininger, Y. S., & Cone-Wesson, B. (2004). Asymmetric cochlear processing mimics hemispheric specialization. *Science, 305*, 1581.

Sininger, Y. S., & Cone-Wesson, B. (2006). Lateral asymmetry in the ABR of neonates: evidence and mechanisms. *Hearing Research, 212*, 203-211.

Sivec, H. J., Montesano, V. L., Skubby, D., Knepp, K. A., & Munetz, M. R. (2017). Cognitive behavioral therapy for psychosis (CBT-p) delivered in a community mental health setting: A case comparison of clients receiving CBT informed strategies by case managers prior to therapy. *Community Mental Health Journal, 53*, 134-142.

Skinner, B. F. (1957). *Verbal behavior.* New York: Appleton-Century-Crofts.

Skinner, B. F. (1975). The steep and thorny road to a science of behavior. *American Psychologist, 30*, 42-49.

Skolnick, P., Popik, P., & Trullas, R. (2009). Glutamate-based antidepressants: 20 years on. *Trends in Pharmacological Science, 30*, 563-569.

Slocombe, K. E., Waller, B. M., & Liebal, K. (2011). The language void: The need for multimodality in primate communication research. *Animal Behaviour, 81*, 919-924.

Slotboom, A., Hendriks, J., & Verbruggen, J. (2011). Contrasting adolescent female and male sexual aggression: A self-report study on prevalence and predictors of sexual aggression. *Journal of Sexual Aggression, 17*, 15-33.

Smart, R. G. (2007). Review of introduction to addictive behaviours. *Addiction, 102*, 831.

Smetana, J. B. (2007). Strategies for understanding archetypes and the collective unconscious of an organization. *Dissertation Abstracts International Section A: Humanities and Social Sciences, 67* (12-A), 4714.

Smetana, J. G. (2005). Adolescent-parent conflict: Resistance and subversion as developmental process. In L. Nucci (Ed.), *Conflict, contradiction, and contrarian elements in moral development and education.* Mahwah, NJ: Lawrence Erlbaum Associates.

Smetana, J., Daddis, C., & Chuang, S. (2003). "Clean your room!" A longitudinal investigation of adolescent-parent conflict and conflict resolution in middle-class African American families. *Journal of Adolescent Research, 18,* 631-650.

Smith, C. (2006). Symposium V–Sleep and learning: New developments [Special issue: Methods and learning in functional MRI]. *Brain and Cognition, 60,* 331-332.

Smith, C. A., & Lazarus, R. S. (2001). Appraisal components, core relational themes, and the emotions. In W. G. Parrott (Ed.), *Emotions in social psychology: Essential readings* (pp. 94-114). Philadelphia: Psychology Press.

Smith, C. D., Chebrolu, J., Wekstein, D. R., Schmitt, F. A., & Markesbery, W. R. (2007). Age and gender effects on human brain anatomy: A voxel-based morphometric study in healthy elderly. *Neurobiology of Aging, 28,* 1057-1087.

Smith, D. E., Springer, C. M., & Barrett, S. (2011). Physical discipline and socioemotional adjustment among Jamaican adolescents. *Journal of Family Violence, 26,* 51-61.

Smith, E. P., Witherspoon, D. P., Hart, M., & Davidson, W. S. (2017). The dynamic and interactive role of theory in community psychology research, practice, and policy. In M. A. Bond, I. Serrano-García, C. B. Keys, & M. Shinn (Eds.), *APA handbook of community psychology: Methods for community research and action for diverse groups and issues.* Washington, DC: American Psychological Association.

Smith, E. S., Geissler, S. A., Schallert, T., & Lee, H. J. (2013). The role of central amygdala dopamine in disengagement behavior. *Behavioral Neuroscience, 127,* 164-174.

Smith, M. L., Glass, G. V., & Miller, T. I. (1980). *The benefits of psychotherapy.* Baltimore: The Johns Hopkins University Press.

Smith, N. A., Folland, N. A., Martinez, D. M., & Trainor, L. J. (2017). Multisensory object perception in infancy: 4-month-olds perceive a mistuned harmonic as a separate auditory and visual object. *Cognition, 164,* 1-7.

Smith, R. A., & Weber, A. L. (2005). Applying social psychology in everyday life. In F. W. Schneider, J. A. Gruman, & L. M. Coutts (Eds.), *Applied social psychology: Understanding and addressing social and practical problems.* Thousand Oaks, CA: Sage Publications.

Smith, T. W., & Son, J. (2013). *Trends in public attitudes about sexual morality.* Chicago: NORC at the University of Chicago.

Smith, W. B. (2007). Karen Horney and psychotherapy in the 21st century. *Clinical Social Work Journal, 35,* 57-66.

Smrtnik-Vitulić, H., & Zupančič, M. (2011). Personality traits as a predictor of academic achievement in adolescents. *Educational Studies, 37,* 127-140.

Snowdon, C. T. (2017). Learning from monkey "talk." *Science, 355,* 1120-1122.

Snyder, J., Cramer, A., & Afrank, J. (2005). The contributions of ineffective discipline and parental hostile attributions of child misbehavior to the development of conduct problems at home and school. *Developmental Psychology, 41,* 30-41.

Snyder, M. (2002). Applications of Carl Rogers' theory and practice to couple and family therapy: A response to Harlene Anderson and David Bott. *Journal of Family Therapy, 24,* 317-325.

Snyder, M. D., & Dwyer, P. C. (2013). Altruism and prosocial behavior. In H. Tennen, J. Suls, & I. B. Weiner (Eds.). *Handbook of psychology, Vol. 5: Personality and social psychology* (2nd ed.). Hoboken, NJ: John Wiley & Sons.

Society for Personality Assessment. (2005). The status of Rorschach in clinical and forensic practice: An official statement by the board of trustees of the Society for Personality Assessment. *Journal of Personality Assessment, 85,* 219-237.

Sodian, B. (2011). Theory of mind in infancy. *Child Development Perspectives, 5,* 39-43.

Sohr-Preston, S. L., & Scaramella, L. V. (2006). Implications of timing of maternal depressive symptoms for early cognitive and language development. *Clinical Child and Family Psychology Review, 9,* 65-83.

Šolcová, I. P., & Lačev, A. (2017). Differences in male and female subjective experience and physiological reactions to emotional stimuli. *International Journal of Psychophysiology, 117,* 75-82.

Solesio-Jofre, E., Lorenzo-López, L., Gutiérrez, R., López-Frutos, J., Ruiz-Vargas, J., & Maestú, F. (2011). Age effects on retroactive interference during working memory maintenance. *Biological Psychology, 88,* 72-82.

Solomonia, R. O., & McCabe, B. J. (2015). Molecular mechanisms of memory in imprinting. *Neuroscience and Biobehavioral Reviews, 50,* 56-69.

Somers, T. J., Moseley, G., Keefe, F. J., & Kothadia, S. M. (2011). Neuroimaging of pain: A psychosocial perspective. In R. A. Cohen & L. H. Sweet (Eds.), *Brain imaging in behavioral medicine and clinical neuroscience.* New York: Springer Science + Business Media.

Sood, A. B., & Linker, J. (2017). Proximal influences on the trajectory of suicidal behaviors and suicide during the transition from adolescence to young adulthood. *Child and Adolescent Psychiatric Clinics of North America, 26,* 235-251.

Soorya, L. V., Carpenter, L., & Romanczyk, R. G. (2011). Applied behavior analysis. In E. Hollander, A. Kolevzon, & J. T. Coyle (Eds.), *Textbook of autism spectrum disorders.* Arlington, VA: American Psychiatric Publishing, Inc.

Sori, C. E. (Ed.). (2006). *Engaging children in family therapy: Creative approaches to integrating theory and research in clinical practice.* New York: Routledge/Taylor & Francis Group.

Source: Adapted from Olulade, O. A., Jamal, N. I., Koo, D. S., Perfetti, C. A., LaSasso, C., & Eden, G. F. (2016). Neuroanatomical evidence in support of the bilingual advantage theory. *Cerebral Cortex, 26*(7), 3196-3204.

Soussignan, R. (2002). Duchenne smile, emotional experience, and automatic reactivity: A test of the facial feedback hypothesis. *Emotion, 2,* 52-74.

South, S. C., Reichborn-Kjennerud, T., Eaton, N. R., & Krueger, R. F. (2013). Genetics of personality. In H. Tennen, J. Suls, & I. B. Weiner (Eds.), *Handbook of psychology, Vol. 5: Personality and social psychology* (2nd ed.). Hoboken, NJ: John Wiley & Sons Inc.

South, S., & Krueger, R. (2008). An interactionist perspective on genetic and environmental contributions to personality. *Social and Personality Psychology Compass, 2,* 929-948.

Spackman, M. P., Fujiki, M., & Brinton, B. (2006). Understanding emotions in context: The effects of language impairment on children's ability to infer emotional reactions. *International Journal of Language & Communication Disorders, 41,* 173-188.

Spangler, W. D. (1992). Validity of questionnaire and TAT measures of need for achievement: Two meta-analyses. *Psychological Bulletin, 112,* 140-154.

Sparks, S. D. (2007). Foundation: Gifted poor students given short shrift. *Education Daily, 40,* 3.

Sparrow, B., Liu, J., & Wegner, D. M. (2011). Google effects on memory: cognitive consequences of having information at our fingertips. *Science, 333,* 776-778.

Spaulding, S. (2013). Mirror neurons and social cognition. *Mind & Language, 28,* 233-257.

Special issue: The dopamine hypothesis of schizophrenia. (2017). *Biological Psychiatry, 81*(1), 1.

Speirs-Neumeister, K. L., & Finch, H. (2006). Perfectionism in high-ability students: Relational precursors and influences on achievement motivation. *Gifted Child Quarterly, 50,* 238-251.

Spence, C., Auvray, M., & Smith, B. (2015). Confusing tastes with flavours. In D. Stokes, M. Matthen, & S. Biggs (Eds.), *Perception and its modalities.* New York: Oxford University Press.

Spence, M. J., & DeCasper, A. J. (1982, March). *Human fetuses perceive maternal speech.* Paper presented at the meeting of the International Conference on Infant Studies, Austin, TX.

Spence-Cochran, K., & Pearl, C. (2006). Moving toward full inclusion. In P. Wehman (Ed.), *Life beyond the classroom: Transition strategies for young people with disabilities* (4th ed.). Baltimore: Paul H. Brookes Publishing.

Spencer, S. J., Fein, S., Zanna, M. P., & Olson, J. M. (Eds.). (2003). *Motivated social perception: The Ontario Symposium* (Vol. 9). Mahwah, NJ: Erlbaum.

Sperling, G. (1960). The information available in brief visual presentation. *Psychological Monographs, 74,* pp. 29.

Sperner-Unterweger, B., & Fuchs, D. (2015). Schizophrenia and psychoneuroimmunology: An integrative view. *Current Opinion in Psychiatry, 28,* 201-206.

Sperry, R. (1982). Some effects of disconnecting the cerebral hemispheres. *Science, 217,* 1223-1226.

Spiegel, D. (2014). Minding the body: Psychotherapy and cancer survival. *British Journal of Health Psychology, 19,* 465-485.

Spiegel, D. (2015). Hypnosis and pain control. In T. R. Deer, M. S. Leong, & A. L. Ray (Eds.), *Treatment of chronic pain by integrative approaches: The American Academy of Pain Medicine textbook on patient management.* New York: Springer Science + Business Media.

Spitzer, R. L., Skodol, A. E., Gibbon, M., & Williams, J. B. W. (1983). *Psychopathology: A case book.* New York: McGraw-Hill.

Sprecher, S., & Hatfield, E. (1996). Premarital sexual standards among U.S. college students: Comparison with Russian and Japanese students. *Archives of Sexual Behavior, 25,* 261-288.

Sprecher, S., & Regan, P. C. (2002). Liking some things (in some people) more than others: Partner preferences in romantic relationships and friendships. *Journal of Social and Personal Relationships, 19,* 436-481.

Sprecher, S., Treger, S., & Sakaluk, J. K. (2013). Premarital sexual standards and sociosexuality: Gender, ethnicity, and cohort differences. *Archives of Sexual Behavior, 42*(8), 1395-1405.

Squire, L. R., Clark, R. E., & Bayley, P. J. (2004). Medial temporal lobe function and memory. In M. S. Gazzaniga (Ed.), *Cognitive neurosciences* (3rd ed.). Cambridge, MA: MIT.

Srinivasan, M., Al-Mughairy, S., Foushee, R., & Barner, D. (2017). Learning language from within: Children use semantic generalizations to infer word meanings. *Cognition, 159,* 11-24.

St. Dennis, C., Hendryx, M., Henriksen, A. L., Setter, S. M., & Singer, B. (2006). Postdischarge treatment costs following closure of a state geropsychiatric ward: Comparison of 2 levels of community care. *Primary Care Companion Journal of Clinical Psychiatry, 8,* 279-284.

St. Jacques, P. L., & Levine, B. (2007). Ageing and autobiographical memory for emotional and neutral events. *Memory, 15,* 129-144.

Stacks, A., Oshio, T., Gerard, J., & Roe, J. (2009). The moderating effect of parental warmth on the association between spanking and child aggression: A longitudinal approach. *Infant and Child Development, 18,* 178-194.

Stainton, T., & Clare, I. C. H. (2012). Human rights and intellectual disabilities: An emergent theoretical paradigm? *Journal of Intellectual Disability Research, 56,* 1011-1013.

Staley, J. K., Sanacora, G., & Tamagnan, G. (2006). Sex differences in diencephalon serotonin transporter availability in major depression. *Biological Psychiatry, 59,* 40-47.

Stam, G. (2015). Changes in thinking for speaking: A longitudinal case study. *Modern Language Journal, 99*(Suppl 1), 83-99.

Stam, K., Verbakel, E., & Graaf, P. M. (2013). Do values matter? The impact of work ethic and traditional gender role values on female labour market supply. *Social Indicators Research, 116,* 593-610.

Stangier, U., Schramm, E., Heidenreich, T., Berger, M., & Clark, D. M. (2011). Cognitive therapy vs. interpersonal psychotherapy in social anxiety disorder: A randomized controlled trial. *Archives of General Psychiatry, 68,* 692-700.

Stankov, L. (2003). Complexity in human intelligence. In R. J. Sternberg, J. Lautrey, & T. I. Lubart (Eds.), *Models of intelligence: International perspectives.* Washington, DC: American Psychological Association.

Stanley, M. L., Henne, P., Iyengar, V., Sinnott-Armstrong, W., & De Brigard, F. (2017). I'm not the person I used to be: The self and autobiographical memories of immoral actions. *Journal of Experimental Psychology: General, 146,* 884-895.

Stanojevic, S., Mitic, K., & Vujic, V. (2007). Exposure to acute physical and psychological stress alters the response of rat macrophages to corticosterone, neuropeptide Y and beta-endorphin. *International Journal on the Biology of Stress, 10,* 65-73.

Stanton, A. L., Danoff-Burg, S., Cameron, C. L., Bishop, M., Collins, C. A., Kirk, S. B., . . . Twillman, R. (2000). Emotionally expressive coping predicts psychological and physical adjustment to breast cancer. *Journal of Consulting and Clinical Psychology, 68,* 875-882.

Stapleton, P., Crighton, G. J., Carter, B., & Pidgeon, A. (2017). Self-esteem and body image in females: The mediating role of self-compassion and appearance contingent self-worth. *The Humanistic Psychologist, 45*(3), 238-257.

Starcevic, V., Berle, D., Milicevic, D., Hannan, A., Pamplugh, C., & Eslick, G. D. (2007). Pathological worry, anxiety disorders and the impact of co-occurrence with depressive and other anxiety disorders. *Journal of Anxiety Disorders, 21,* 1016-1027.

Startup, M., Bucci, S., & Langdon, R. (2009). Delusions of reference: A new theoretical model. *Cognitive Neuropsychiatry, 14,* 110-126.

Staub, E. (2011). *Overcoming evil: Genocide, violent conflict, and terrorism.* New York: Oxford University Press.

Staub, E. (2018). Preventing violence and promoting active bystandership and peace: My life in research and applications. *Peace and Conflict: Journal of Peace Psychology, 24*(1), 95-111.

Staub, E., Pearlman, L., & Bilali, R. (2010). Understanding the roots and impact of violence and psychological recovery as avenues to reconciliation after mass violence and intractable conflict: Applications to national leaders, journalists, community groups, public education through radio, and children. In G. Salomon & E. Cairns (Eds.), *Handbook on peace education.* New York: Psychology Press.

Steele, C. M., Spencer, S. J., & Aronson, J. (2002). Contending with group image. The psychology of stereotype and social identity threat. In M. P. Zanna (Ed.), *Advances in experimental social psychology* (Vol. 34). San Diego: Academic Press.

Steele, J. D., Christmas, D., Eljamel, M. S., & Matthews, K. (2007). Anterior cingulotomy for major depression: clinical outcome and relationship to lesion characteristics. *Biological Psychiatry, 12,* 127-134.

Steiger, A. (2007). Neurochemical regulation of sleep. *Journal of Psychiatric Research, 41,* 537-552.

Stein, L. A. R., & Graham, J. R. (2005). Ability of substance abusers to escape detection on the Minnesota Multiphasic Personality Inventory- Adolescent (MMPI-A) in a juvenile correctional facility. *Assessment, 12,* 28-39.

Steinbeis, N., Crone, E., Blakemore, S., & Kadosh, K. C. (2017). Development holds the key to understanding the interplay of nature versus nurture in shaping the individual. *Developmental Cognitive Neuroscience, 25,* 1-4.

Steinberg, L. (2007). Risk taking in adolescence: New perspectives from brain and behavioral science. *Current Directions in Psychological Science, 16,* 55-59.

Steinberg, L. (2016). Commentary on special issue on the adolescent brain: Redefining adolescence. *Neuroscience and Biobehavioral Reviews, 70,* 343-346.

Steiner, J. (2008). Transference to the analyst as an excluded observer. *International Journal of Psychoanalysis, 89,* 39-54.

Steinfeld, C., Ellison, N., & Lampe, C. (2008). Social capital, self-esteem, and use of online social network sites: A longitudinal analysis. *Journal of Applied Developmental Psychology, 29,* 434-445.

Steinhubl, S. R., Wineinger, N. E., Patel, S., Boeldt, D. L., Mackellar, G., Porter, V., . . . Topol, E. J. (2015). Cardiovascular and nervous system changes during meditation. *Frontiers in Human Neuroscience, 9,* 88-97.

Steinmetz, K. (2071, March, 27). Infinite identities. *Time,* pp. 49-54.

Steinmetz, Katy. (2015, March 6). States battle over bathroom access for transgender people. *Time.* Accessed from http://time.com/3734714/transgender-bathroom-bills-lgbtdiscrimination/.

Stemler, S. E., & Sternberg, R. J. (2006). Using situational judgment tests to measure practical intelligence. In J. A. Weekley & R. E. Ployhart (Eds.), *Situational judgment tests: Theory, measurement, and application.* Mahwah, NJ: Lawrence Erlbaum Associates.

Stemler, S. E., Sternberg, R. J., Grigorenko, E. L., Jarvin, L., & Sharpes, K. (2009). Using the theory of successful intelligence as a framework for developing assessments in AP physics. *Contemporary Educational Psychology, 34,* 195-209.

Stenbacka, L., & Vanni, S. (2007). fMRI of peripheral visual field representation. *Clinical Neurophysiology, 108,* 1303-1314.

Stern, E., & Silbersweig, D. A. (2001). Advances in functional neuroimaging methodology for the study of brain systems underlying human neuropsychological function and dysfunction. In D. A. Silbersweig & E. Stern (Eds.), *Neuropsychology and functional neuroimaging: Convergence, advances and new directions.* Amsterdam, Netherlands: Swets and Zeitlinger.

Sternberg, R. J. (1998). *Successful intelligence: How practical and creative intelligence determine success in life.* New York: Plume.

Sternberg, R. J. (2000). Intelligence and wisdom. In R. J. Sternberg et al. (Eds.), *Handbook of intelligence.* New York: Cambridge University Press.

Sternberg, R. J. (2004). A triangular theory of love. In H. T. Reis & C. E. Rusbult (Eds.), *Close relationships: Key readings*. Philadelphia, PA: Taylor & Francis.

Sternberg, R. J. (2006). A duplex theory of love. In R. J. Sternberg (Ed.), *The new psychology of love*. New Haven, CT: Yale University Press.

Sternberg, R. J. (2011). Individual differences in cognitive development. In U. Goswami (Ed.), *The Wiley-Blackwell handbook of childhood cognitive development* (2nd ed.). New York: Wiley-Blackwell.

Sternberg, R. J. (2013). What is cognitive education? *Journal of Cognitive Education and Psychology, 12*(1), 45-58.

Sternberg, R. J. (2015). Multiple intelligences in the new age of thinking. In S. Goldstein, D. Princiotta, & J. A. Naglieri (Eds.), *Handbook of intelligence: Evolutionary theory, historical perspective, and current concepts*. New York: Springer Science + Business Media.

Sternberg, R. J. (2017). *Career paths in psychology: Where your degree can take you* (3rd ed.). Washington, DC: American Psychological Association.

Sternberg, R. J., & Jarvin, L. (2003). Alfred Binet's contributions as a paradigm for impact in psychology. In R. J. Sternberg (Ed.), *The anatomy of impact: What makes the great works of psychology great*. Washington, DC: American Psychological Association.

Sternberg, R. J., & Pretz, J. E. (2005). *Cognition and intelligence: Identifying the mechanisms of the mind*. New York: Cambridge University Press.

Sternberg, R. J., Grigorenko, E. L., & Kidd, K. K. (2005). Intelligence, race, and genetics. *American Psychologist, 60*, 46-59.

Sternberg, R. J., Hojjat, M., & Barnes, M. L. (2001). Empirical aspects of a theory of love as a story. *European Journal of Personality, 15*, 1-20.

Sternberg, R. J., Jarvin, L., & Grigorenko, E. L. (2011). *Explorations in giftedness*. New York: Cambridge University Press.

Sternberg, R. J., Kaufman, J. C., & Pretz, J. E. (2004). A propulsion model of creative leadership [Special issue: Creativity in the workplace]. *Creativity and Innovation Management, 13*, 145-153.

Sternson, S. M., Betley, J., & Cao, Z. (2013). Neural circuits and motivational processes for hunger. *Current Opinion in Neurobiology, 23*, 353-360.

Stettler, N., Stallings, V. A., Troxel, A. B., Zhao, J. Z., Schinnar, R., Nelson, S. E., . . . Strom, B. L. (2005). Weight gain in the first week of life and overweight in adulthood. *Circulation, 111*, 1897-1903.

Stevens, C. F. (2015). Novel neural circuit mechanism for visual edge detection. *PNAS Proceedings of the National Academy of Sciences of the United States of America, 112*, 875-880.

Stevens, G. (2015). Black psychology: Resistance, reclamation, and redefinition. In I. Parker & I. Parker (Eds.), *Handbook of critical psychology.*

New York: Routledge/Taylor & Francis Group.

Stevens, P., & Harper, D. J. (2007). Professional accounts of electroconvulsive therapy: A discourse analysis. *Social Science & Medicine, 64*, 1475-1486.

Stevens, S. S., & Pashler, H. E. (2002). *Steven's handbook of experimental psychology: Learning, motivation, and emotion*. New York: Wiley.

Stevens, T., Brevers, D., Chambers, C. D., Lavric, A., McLaren, I. L., Mertens, M., . . . Verbruggen, F. (2015). How does response inhibition influence decision making when gambling? *Journal of Experimental Psychology: Applied, 21*, 15-36.

Stevenson, H. W., Lee, S., & Mu, X. (2000). Successful achievement in mathematics: China and the United States. In C. F. M. van Lieshout & P. G. Heymans (Eds.), *Developing talent across the life span*. New York: Psychology Press.

Stewart, C. E., Lee, S. Y., Hogstrom, A., & Williams, M. (2017). Diversify and conquer: A call to promote minority representation in clinical psychology. *Behavior Therapist, 40*, 74-79.

Stey, P. C., Lapsley, D., & McKeever, M. O. (2013). Moral judgement in adolescents: Age differences in applying and justifying three principles of harm. *European Journal of Developmental Psychology, 10*, 206-220.

Stickgold, R. (2015). Why we sleep. *Scientific American, 313*(4), 52-57.

Stickgold, R., Hobson, J. A., Fosse, R., & Fosse, M. (2001). Sleep, learning, and dreams: Off-line memory reprocessing. *Science, 294*, 1052-1057.

Stickley, T., & Nickeas, R. (2006). Becoming one person: Living with dissociative identity disorder. *Journal of Psychiatric and Mental Health Nursing, 13*, 180-187.

Stifter, C. A., Dollar, J. M., & Cipriano, E. A. (2011). Temperament and emotion regulation: The role of autonomic nervous system reactivity. *Developmental Psychobiology, 53*, 266-279.

Stix, G. (2011). The neuroscience of true grit. *Scientific American, 304*, 28-33.

Stockdale, M. S., & Sagrestano, L. M. (2011). Resources for targets of sexual harassment. In M. A. Paludi, C. R. Paludi, & E. R. DeSouza (Eds.), *Praeger handbook on understanding and preventing workplace discrimination* (Vols 1 & 2). Santa Barbara, CA: Praeger/ABC-CLIO.

Stocks, E., Lishner, D., & Decker, S. (2009). Altruism or psychological escape: Why does empathy promote prosocial behavior? *European Journal of Social Psychology, 39*, 649-665.

Stockton, R., Morran, D. K., & Krieger, K. (2004). An overview of current research and best practices for training beginning group leaders. In J. L. DeLucia-Waack, D. A. Gerrity, C. R. Kalodner, & M. T. Riva (Eds.), *Handbook of group counseling and psychotherapy*. Thousand Oaks, CA: Sage Publications.

Stolorow, R. D., & Stolorow, B. A. (2013). Blues and emotional trauma. *Clinical Social Work Journal, 41*, 5-10.

Stone, D. L., & Rosopa, P. J. (2017). The advantages and limitations of using meta-analysis in human resource management research. *Human Resource Management Review, 27*, 1-7.

Stone, J. (2002). Battling doubt by avoiding practice: The effects of stereotype threat on self-handicapping in white athletes. *Personality and Social Psychology Bulletin, 28*, 1667-1678.

Stopa, L., Denton, R., Wingfield, M., & Taylor, K. (2013). The fear of others: A qualitative analysis of interpersonal threat in social phobia and paranoia. *Behavioural and Cognitive Psychotherapy, 41*, 188-209.

Stoppelbein, L., McRae, E., & Greening, L. (2017). A longitudinal study of hardiness as a buffer for posttraumatic stress symptoms in mothers of children with cancer. *Clinical Practice in Pediatric Psychology, 5*, 149-160.

Storm, L., & Ertel, S. (2001). Does psi exist? Comments on Milton and Wiseman's (1999) meta-analysis of Ganzfeld's research. *Psychological Bulletin, 127*, 424-433.

Storm, L., & Rock, A. J. (2015). Dreaming of psi: A narrative review and meta-analysis of dream-ESP studies at the Maimonides Dream Laboratory and beyond. In J. A. Davies & D. B. Pitchford (Eds.), *Stanley Krippner: A life of dreams, myths, and visions: Essays on his contributions and influence*. New York: University Professors Press.

Stowell, J. R., Robles, T. F., & Kane, H. S. (2013). Psychoneuroimmunology: Mechanisms, individual differences, and interventions. In A. M. Nezu, C. Nezu, P. A. Geller, & I. B. Weiner (Eds.), *Handbook of psychology, Vol. 9: Health psychology* (2nd ed.). Hoboken, NJ: John Wiley & Sons Inc.

Strange, D., Clifasefi, S., & Garry, M. (2007). False memories. In M. Garry & H. Hayne (Eds.), *Do justice and let the sky fall: Elizabeth Loftus and her contributions to science, law, and academic freedom*. Mahwah, NJ: Lawrence Erlbaum Associates.

Strassberg, D. S., Cann, D., & Velarde, V. (2017). Sexting by high school students. *Archives of Sexual Behavior, 46*(6), 1667-1672.

Strathern, A., & Stewart, P. J. (2003). *Landscape, memory and history: Anthropological perspectives*. London: Pluto Press.

Strayer, D. L., & Drews, F. A. (2007). Cell-phone-induced driver distraction. *Current Directions in Psychological Science, 16*, 128-131.

Strenze, T. (2015). Intelligence and success. In S. Goldstein, D. Princiotta, & J. A. Naglieri (Eds.), *Handbook of intelligence: Evolutionary theory, historical perspective, and current concepts* (pp. 405-413). New York: Springer Science + Business Media.

Striano, T., & Vaish, A. (2006). Seven- to 9-month-old infants use facial expressions to interpret others' actions. *British Journal of Developmental Psychology, 24*, 753-760.

Striegel, R. H., Bedrosian, R., Wang, C., & Schwartz, S. (2011). Why men should be included in research on binge eating: Results from a comparison of psychosocial impairment in men and women. *International Journal of Eating Disorder, 45*, 233-240.

Striegel-Moore, R., & Bulik, C. M. (2007). Risk factors for eating disorders. *American Psychologist, 62*, 181-198.

Strohmaier, H., Murphy, M., & DeMatteo, D. (2014). Youth sexting: Prevalence rates, driving motivations, and the deterrent effect of legal consequences. *Sexuality Research & Social Policy: A Journal of the NSRC, 11*(3), 245-255.

Strong, T., & Tomm, K. (2007). Family therapy as re-coordinating and moving on together. *Journal of Systemic Therapies, 26*, 42-54.

Stålhammar, J., Nordlund, A., & Wallin, A. (2015). An example of exceptional practice effects in the verbal domain. *Neurocase, 21*, 162-168.

Subrahmanyam, K., Reich, S., Waechter, N., & Espinoza, G. (2008). Online and offline social networks: Use of social networking sites by emerging adults. *Journal of Applied Developmental Psychology, 29*, 420-433.

Substance Abuse and Mental Health Services Administration. (2014). *Results from the 2013 National Survey on Drug Use and Health: Mental Health Findings*, NSDUH Series H-49, HHS Publication No. (SMA) 14-4887. Rockville, MD: Author.

Sue, D. W. (2017). Microaggressions and "evidence": Empirical or experiential reality? *Perspectives on Psychological Science, 12*, 170-172.

Sue, D. W., & Sue, D. (1990). *Counseling the culturally different: Theory and practice* (2nd ed.) (pp. 514-515). Oxford, England: John Wiley & Sons.

Suh, E. M. (2002). Culture, identity consistency, and subjective well-being. *Journal of Personality & Social Psychology, 83*, 1378-1391.

Suhail, K., & Chaudhry, H. R. (2004). Predictors of subjective well-being in an Eastern Muslim culture. *Journal of Social and Clinical Psychology, 23*, 359-376.

Suizzo, M.-A., & Bornstein, M. H. (2006). French and European American child-mother play: Culture and gender considerations. *International Journal of Behavioral Development, 30*, 498-508.

Sullivan, E. L., Smith, S. M., & Grove, K. L. (2011). Perinatal exposure to high-fat diet programs energy balance, metabolism and behavior in adulthood. *Neuroendocrinology, 93*, 1-8.

Sullivan, J., Riccio, C., & Reynolds, C. (2008). Variations in students' school- and teacher-related attitudes across gender, ethnicity, and age. *Journal of Instructional Psychology, 35*, 296-305.

Summa, K. C., & Turek, F. W. (2015). The clocks within us. *Scientific American, 312*, 51-55.

Summers, M. (2000). *Everything in its place.* New York: Putnam.

Summers, S. J., Schabrun, S. M., Marinovic, W., & Chipchase, L. S. (2017). Peripheral electrical stimulation increases corticomotor excitability and enhances the rate of visuomotor adaptation. *Behavioural Brain Research, 322* (Part A), 42-50.

Sun, X., Niu, G., You, Z., Zhou, Z., & Tang, Y. (2017). "Gender, negative life events and coping on different stages of depression severity: A cross-sectional study among Chinese university students": Corrigendum. *Journal of Affective Disorders, 215*, 102.

Sun, Y., Giacobbe, P., Tang, C. W., Barr, M. S., Rajji, T., Kennedy, S. H., . . . Daskalakis, Z. J. (2015). Deep brain stimulation modulates gamma oscillations and theta-gamma coupling in treatment resistant depression. *Brain Stimulation, 6*, 1033-1042.

Super, C. M. (1980). Cognitive development: Looking across at growing up. In C. M. Super & S. Harakness (Eds.), *New directions for child development: Anthropological perspectives on child development.* San Francisco: Jossey-Bass.

Sutherland, S. (2016). The maddening sensation of itch. *Scientific American, 314*, 39-43.

Sutin, A. R., & Robins, R. W. (2007). Phenomenology of autobiographical memories: The Memory Experiences Questionnaire. *Memory, 15*, 390-411.

Suzuki, L. A., Short, E. L., & Lee, C. S. (2011). Racial and ethnic group differences in intelligence in the United States: Multicultural perspectives. In R. J. Sternberg & S. Kaufman (Eds.), *The Cambridge handbook of intelligence.* New York: Cambridge University Press.

Swain, P. I. (2006). *New developments in eating disorders research.* Hauppauge, NY: Nova Science Publishers.

Swain, R. A., Kerr, A. L., & Thompson, R. F. (2011). The cerebellum: A neural system for the study of reinforcement learning. *Frontiers in Behavioral Neuroscience, 18*, 89-96.

Szasz, T. S. (2011). *The myth of mental illness: Foundations of a theory of personal conduct.* New York: HarperCollins.

Szegedy Maszak, M. (2003, January 13). The sound of unsound minds. *U.S. News & World Report*, pp. 45-46.

Sørensen, S. Ø. (2017). The performativity of choice: Postfeminist perspectives on work-life balance. *Gender, Work and Organization, 24*(3), 297-313.

Ślusarczyk, E., & Niedzwienska, A. (2013). A naturalistic study of prospective memory in preschoolers: The role of task interruption and motivation. *Cognitive Development, 28*, 179-192.

Tadmor, C. T. (2007). Biculturalism: The plus side of leaving home? The effects of second-culture exposure on integrative complexity and its consequences for overseas performance. *Dissertation Abstracts International Section A: Humanities and Social Sciences, 67*(8-A), 3068.

Taibbi, R. (2018). *Brief therapy with couples and families in crisis.* New York: Routledge/Taylor & Francis Group.

Tajfel, H., & Turner, J. C. (2004). The social identity theory of intergroup behavior. In J. T. Jost & J. Sidanius (Eds.), *Political psychology: Key readings.* New York: Psychology Press.

Tajfel, H., & Turner, J. C. (2010). An integrative theory of intergroup conflict. In T. Postmes & N. R. Branscombe (Eds.), *Rediscovering social.* New York: Psychology Press.

Takahashi, M., Nakata, A., Haratani, T., Ogawa, Y., & Arito, H. (2004). Post-lunch nap as a worksite intervention to promote alertness on the job. *Ergonomics, 47*, 1003-1013.

Taki, Y., Thyreau, B., Kinomura, S., Sato, K., Goto, R., Wu, K., . . .Fukuda, H. (2013). A longitudinal study of age and gender related annual rate of volume changes in regional gray matter in healthy adults. *Human Brain Mapping, 34*, 2292-2301.

Takizawa, T., Kondo, T., & Sakihara, S. (2007). Stress buffering effects of social support on depressive symptoms in middle age: Reciprocity and community mental health: Corrigendum. *Psychiatry and Clinical Neurosciences, 61*, 336-337.

Takooshian, H., Gielen, U. P., Plous, S., Rich, G. J., & Velayo, R. S. (2016). Internationalizing undergraduate psychology education: Trends, techniques, and technologies. *American Psychologist, 71*, 136-147.

Tal-Or, N., & Papirman, Y. (2007). The fundamental attribution error in attributing fictional figures' characteristics to the actors. *Media Psychology, 9*, 331-345.

Talarico, J. (2009). Freshman flashbulbs: Memories of unique and first-time events in starting college. *Memory, 17*, 256-265.

Talarico, J., & Rubin, D. (2007). Flashbulb memories are special after all; in phenomenology, not accuracy. *Applied Cognitive Psychology, 21*, 557-578.

Talmi, D., Anderson, A., Riggs, L., Caplan, J., & Moscovitch, M. (2008). Immediate memory consequences of the effect of emotion on attention to pictures. *Learning & Memory, 15*, 172-182.

Talukdar, S., & Shastri, J. (2006). Contributory and adverse factors in social development of young children. *Psychological Studies, 51*, 294-303.

Tam, S. E., Bonardi, C., & Robinson, J. (2015). Relative recency influences object-in-context memory. *Behavioural Brain Research, 281*, 250-257.

Tamini, B., Bojhd, F., & Yazdani, S. (2011). Love types, psychological well-being and self-concept. *Journal of the Indian Academy of Applied Psychology, 37*, 169-178.

Tan, G., Rintala, D. H., Jensen, M. P., Richards, J. S., Holmes, S. A., Parachuri, R., . . . Price, L. R. (2011). Efficacy of cranial electrotherapy stimulation for neuropathic pain following spinal cord injury: a multi-site randomized controlled trial with a secondary 6-month open-label phase. *Journal of Spinal Cord Medicine, 34*, 285-296.

Tan, L., Chan, A., Kay, P., Khong, P., Yip, L., & Luke, K. (2008). Language affects patterns of brain activation associated with perceptual decision. *PNAS Proceedings of the National Academy of Sciences of the United States of America, 105*(10), 4004-4009.

Tan, L., Yu, J., & Tan, L. (2015). Causes and consequences of microRNA dysregulation in neurodegenerative diseases. *Molecular Neurobiology, 51*, 1249-1262.

Tandon, R., Gaebel, W., Barch, D. M., Bustillo, J., Gur, R. E., Heckers, S., . . . Carpenter, W. (2013). Definition and description of schizophrenia in the DSM-5. *Schizophrenia Research, 150*(1), 3-10.

Tappin, B. M., McKay, R. T., & Abrams, D. (2017). Choosing the right level of analysis: Stereotypes shape social reality via collective action. *Behavioral and Brain Sciences, 40.* Accessed from https://www.ncbi.nlm.nih.gov/pubmed/28327226.

Tasker, F. (2005). Lesbian mothers, gay fathers, and their children: A review. *Journal of Developmental and Behavioral Pediatrics, 26,* 224–240.

Tavernise, S. (2015, April 17). Teenagers pick up e-cigarettes as old-school smoking declines. *The New York Times,* p. A1.

Taylor, F., & Bryant, R. A. (2007). The tendency to suppress, inhibiting thoughts, and dream rebound. *Behaviour Research and Therapy, 45,* 163–168.

Taylor, S. (2003). Anxiety sensitivity and its implications for understanding and treating PTSD. *Journal of Cognitive Psychotherapy, 17,* 179–186.

Taylor, S. (2015). *Health psychology* (9th ed.). New York: McGraw-Hill.

Taylor, S. E. (1995). Quandary at the crossroads: Paternalism versus advocacy surrounding end-of-treatment decisions. *American Journal of Hospital Palliatory Care, 12,* 43–46.

Taylor, S. E., Kemeny, M. E., Reed, G. M., Bower, J. E., & Gruenewald, T. L. (2000). Psychological resources, positive illusions, and health. *American Psychologist, 55,* 99–109.

Teague, R. (2013). The American view of Freud's couch. *PsycCRITIQUES, 58,* 12–21.

Tedeschi, R. G., Blevins, C. L., & Riffle, O. M. (2017). Posttraumatic growth: A brief history and evaluation. In M. A. Warren & S. I. Donaldson (Eds.), *Scientific advances in positive psychology* (pp. 131–163). Santa Barbara, CA: Praeger/ABC-CLIO.

Temple, J. R., & Choi, H. (2014). Longitudinal association between teen sexting and sexual behavior. *Pediatrics, 134,* e1287–e1292.

ten Cate, C. (2017). Assessing the uniqueness of language: Animal grammatical abilities take center stage. *Psychonomic Bulletin & Review, 24,* 91–96.

Tenenbaum, H. R., & Leaper, C. (2002). Are parents' gender schemas related to their children's gender-related cognitions? A meta-analysis. *Developmental Psychology, 38,* 615–630.

Teodorov, E., Salzgerber, S. A., Felicio, L. F., Varolli, F. M. F., & Bernardi, M. M. (2002). Effects of perinatal picrotoxin and sexual experience on heterosexual and homosexual behavior in male rats. *Neurotoxicology and Teratology, 24,* 235–245.

Teovanović, P., Knežević, G., & Stankov, L. (2015). Individual differences in cognitive biases: Evidence against one-factor theory of rationality. *Intelligence, 50,* 75–86.

Thachil, A. F., Mohan, R., & Bhugra, D. (2007). The evidence base of complementary and alternative therapies in depression. *Journal of Affective Disorders, 97,* 23–35.

Thaler, L. (2015). Using sound to get around: Discoveries in human echolocation. *APS Observer, 28,* 24–27.

Thaler, N. S., Thames, A. D., Cagigas, X. E., & Norman, M. A. (2015). IQ testing and the African

American client. In L. T. Benuto & B. D. Leany (Eds.), *Guide to psychological assessment with African Americans.* New York: Springer Science + Business Media.

Thanos, P. K., Robison, L. S., Robinson, J. K., Michaelides, M., Wang, G., & Volkow, N. D. (2013). Obese rats with deficient leptin signaling exhibit heightened sensitivity to olfactory food cues. *Synapse, 67,* 171–178.

Tharp, R. G. (1989). Psychocultural variables and constants: Effects on teaching and learning in schools [Special issue: Children and their development: Knowledge base, research agenda, and social policy application]. *American Psychologist, 44,* 349–359.

Thase, M. E. (2013). Comparative effectiveness of psychodynamic psychotherapy and cognitive-behavioral therapy: It's about time, and what's next? *American Journal of Psychiatry, 170,* 953–956.

Thatcher, D. L., & Clark, D. B. (2006). Adolescent alcohol abuse and dependence: Development, diagnosis, treatment and outcomes. *Current Psychiatry Reviews, 2,* 159–177.

Theriault, J., Krause, P., & Young, L. (2017). Know thy enemy: Education about terrorism improves social attitudes toward terrorists. *Journal of Experimental Psychology: General, 146*(3), 305–317.

Thomas, P., Mathur, P., Gottesman, I. I., Nagpal, R., Nimgaonkar, V. L., & Deshpande, S. N. (2007). Correlates of hallucinations in schizophrenia: A cross-cultural evaluation. *Schizophrenia Research, 92,* 41–49.

Thompson, A. K., & Wolpaw, J. R. (2015). Restoring walking after spinal cord injury: Operant conditioning of spinal reflexes can help. *The Neuroscientist, 21*(2), 203–215.

Thompson, M. (2015, April 6.) Unlocking the secrets of PTSD. *Time,* pp. 41–43.

Thorkildsen, T. A. (2006). An empirical exploration of language and thought. *PsycCRITIQUES, 51,* n.p.

Thorndike, E. L. (1932). *The fundamentals of learning.* New York: Teachers College.

Thornton, A., & Young-DeMarco, L. (2001). Four decades of trends in attitudes toward family issues in the United States: The 1960s through the 1990s. *Journal of Marriage and the Family, 63,* 1009–1017.

Thrailkill, E. A., & Bouton, M. E. (2017). Effects of outcome devaluation on instrumental behaviors in a discriminated heterogeneous chain. *Journal of Experimental Psychology: Animal Learning and Cognition, 43,* 88–95.

Thrash, T. M., & Elliot, A. J. (2002). Implicit and self-attributed achievement motives: Concordance and predictive validity. *Journal of Personality, 70,* 729–755.

Thurman, S. M., & Lu, H. (2013). Physical and biological constraints govern perceived animacy of scrambled human forms. *Psychological Science, 24,* 1133–1141.

Tien, L., Davis, A., Arnold, T. H., & Benjamin, G. H. (2012). *Ethics for psychologists: A casebook approach.* Thousand Oaks, CA, US: Sage Publications.

Tingley, K. (2016, March 20). Sixth sense. *The New York Times Magazine,* p. MM52.

Tippin, J., Sparks, J., & Rizzo, M. (2009). Visual vigilance in drivers with obstructive sleep apnea. *Journal of Psychosomatic Research, 67,* 143–151.

Tirri, K., & Nokelainen, P. (2008). Identification of multiple intelligences with the Multiple Intelligence Profiling Questionnaire III [Special issue: High-ability assessment]. *Psychology Science, 50,* 206–221.

Todorov, A., Fiske, S., & Prentice, D. (Eds.). (2011). *Social neuroscience: Toward understanding the underpinnings of the social mind.* New York: Oxford University Press.

Toft, A., Tome, M., Barnett, S. C., & Riddell, J. S. (2013). A comparative study of glial and non-neural cell properties for transplant mediated repair of the injured spinal cord. *Glia, 61,* 513–528.

Tokutsu, Y., Umene-Nakano, W., Shinkai, T., Yoshimura, R., Okamoto, T., Katsuki, A., . . . Nakamura, J. (2013). Follow-up study on electroconvulsive therapy in treatment-resistant depressed patients after remission: A chart review. *Clinical Psychopharmacology and Neuroscience, 11,* 34–38.

Tolman, E. C., & Honzik, C. H. (1930). Introduction and removal of reward and maze performance in rats. *University of California Publications in Psychology, 4,* 257–275.

Tolnai, S., Beutelmann, R., & Klump, G. M. (2017). Effect of preceding stimulation on sound localization and its representation in the auditory midbrain. *European Journal of Neuroscience, 45,* 460–471.

Tommasi, L. (2009). Mechanisms and functions of brain and behavioural asymmetries. *Philosophical Transactions of the Royal Society B, 364,* 855–859.

Tonidandel, S., Quinones, M. A., & Adams, A. A. (2002). Computer-adaptive testing: The impact of test characteristics on perceived performance and test takers' reactions. *Journal of Applied Psychology, 87,* 320–332.

Tononi, G., & Cirelli, C. (2013). Perchance to prune. *Scientific American, 309*(2), 34–39.

Tononi, G., & Koch, C. (2008). The neural correlates of consciousness: An update. In A Kingstone & M. B. Miller (Eds.), *The year in cognitive neuroscience.* Malden, MA: Blackwell Publishing.

Tosto, M. G., Hayiou-Thomas, M. E., Harlaar, N., Prom-Wormley, E., Dale, P. S., & Plomin, R. (2017). The genetic architecture of oral language, reading fluency, and reading comprehension: A twin study from 7 to 16 years. *Developmental Psychology, 53,* 1115–1129.

Toth, J. P., & Daniels, K. A. (2002). Effects of prior experience on judgments of normative word frequency: Automatic bias and correction. *Journal of Memory and Language, 46,* 845–874.

Touhara, K. (2007). Molecular biology of peptide pheromone production and reception in mice. *Advanced Genetics, 59,* 147–171.

Towns, C. R. (2017). The science and ethics of cell-based therapies for Parkinson's disease. *Parkinsonism & Related Disorders, 34*, 1-6.

Tracy, J. L., & Robins, R. W. (2004). Show your pride: Evidence for a discrete emotion expression. *Psychological Science, 15*, 194-197.

Trafton, A. (2015). It's not all downhill after 20. *MIT Technology Review, 118*(4), 8-9.

Tramontana, J. (2011). *Sports hypnosis in practice: Scripts, strategies and case examples.* Norwalk, CT: Crown House Publishing Limited.

Tranter, L. J., & Koutstaal, W. (2008). Age and flexible thinking: An experimental demonstration of the beneficial effects of increased cognitively stimulating activity on fluid intelligence in healthy older adults. *Neuropsychology and Cognition, 15*, 184-207.

Travis, F. (2006). From I to I: Concepts of self on a object-referral/self-referral continuum. In A. P. Prescott (Ed.), *The concept of self in psychology.* Hauppauge, NY: Nova Science Publishers.

Travis, F., Haaga, D. A., Hagelin, J., Tanner, M., Nidich, S., Gaylord-King, C., . . . Schneider, R. H. (2009). Effects of transcendental meditation practice on brain functioning and stress reactivity in college students. *International Journal of Psychopathy, 71*, 170-176.

Treffert, D. (2014). Accidental genius. *Scientific American, 311*(2), 52-57.

Tremblay, A. (2004). Dietary fat and body weight set point. *Nutrition Review, 62*(7, Pt 2), S75-S77.

Triandis, H. C. (2011). Culture and self-deception: A theoretical perspective. *Social Behavior and Personality, 39*, 3-14.

Tribune News Services. (2017, January 10). Dylann Roof sentenced to death for killing 9 black church members in South Carolina. *Chicago Tribune.* Retrieved from http://www.chicagotribune.com/news/nation-world/ct-dylann-roof-sentencing-20170110-story.html.

Triscari, M., Faraci, P., D'Angelo, V., Urso, V., & Catalisano, D. (2011). Two treatments for fear of flying compared: Cognitive behavioral therapy combined with systematic desensitization or eye movement desensitization and reprocessing (EMDR). *Aviation Psychology and Applied Human Factors, 1*, 9-14.

Tropp, L. R., & Bianchi, R. A. (2006). Valuing diversity and interest in intergroup contact. *Journal of Social Issues, 62*, 533-551.

Tropp, L. R., & Pettigrew, T. F. (2005). Differential relationships between intergroup contact and affective and cognitive dimensions of prejudice. *Personality and Social Psychology Bulletin, 31*, 1145-1158.

Trujillo-Pisanty, I., Hernandez, G., Moreau-Debord, I., Cossette, M. P., Conover, K., Cheer, J. F., & Shizgal P. (2011). Cannabinoid receptor blockade reduces the opportunity cost at which rats maintain operant performance for rewarding brain stimulation. *Journal of Neuroscience, 31*, 5426-5430.

Trull, T. J., & Widiger, T. A. (2003). Personality disorders. In G. Stricker, T. A. Widiger, & I. B. Wiener (Eds.), *Handbook of psychology: Clinical psychology* (Vol. 8). New York: Wiley.

Tsaousis, I., Nikolaou, I., & Serdaris, N. (2007). Do the core self-evaluations moderate the relationship between subjective well-being and physical and psychological health? *Personality and Individual Differences, 42*, 1441-1452.

Tschentscher, N., & Hauk, O. (2017). Frontal cortex supports the early structuring of multiple solution steps in symbolic problem-solving. *Journal of Cognitive Neuroscience, 29*, 114-124.

Tseng, W. S. (2003). *Clinician's guide to cultural psychiatry.* San Diego: Elsevier Publishing.

Tsenkova, V., Boylan, J., & Ryff, C. (2013). Stress eating and health. Findings from MIDUS, a national study of US adults. *Appetite, 69*, 151-155.

Tsuchida, K., Ueno, K., & Shimada, S. (2015). Motor area activity for action-related and nonaction-related sounds in a three-dimensional sound field reproduction system. *Neuroreport: For Rapid Communication of Neuroscience Research, 26*, 291-295.

Tsukasaki, T., & Ishii, K. (2004). Linguistic-cultural relativity of cognition: Rethinking the Sapir- Whorf hypothesis. *Japanese Psychological Review, 47*, 173-186.

Tucker, C. M., & Herman, K. C. (2002). Using culturally sensitive theories and research to meet the academic needs of low-income African American children. *American Psychologist, 57*, 762-773.

Tuckey, M. R., Searle, B. J., Boyd, C. M., Winefield, A. H., & Winefield, H. R. (2015). Hindrances are not threats: Advancing the multidimensionality of work stress. *Journal of Occupational Health Psychology, 20*, 131-147.

Tuerk, P. W., Yoder, M., Grubaugh, A., Myrick, H., Hamner, M., & Acierno, R. (2011). Prolonged exposure therapy for combat-related post-traumatic stress disorder: An examination of treatment effectiveness for veterans of the wars in Afghanistan and Iraq. *Journal of Anxiety Disorders, 25*, 397-403.

Tuerlinckx, F., De Boeck, P., & Lens, W. (2002). Measuring needs with the Thematic Apperception Test: A psychometric study. *Journal of Personality and Social Psychology, 82*, 448-461.

Tugay, N., Akbayrak, T., Demirtürk, F., Karakaya, I. C., Kocaacar, O., Tugay, U., . . . Demirtürk, F. (2007). Effectiveness of transcutaneous electrical nerve stimulation and interferential current in primary dysmenorrhea. *Pain Medicine, 8*, 295-300.

Tulving, E. (2002). Episodic memory and common sense: How far apart? In A. Baddeley & J. P. Aggleton (Eds.), *Episodic memory: New directions in research.* London: Oxford University Press.

Tummala-Narra, P. (2016). *Psychoanalytic theory and cultural competence in psychotherapy.* Washington, DC: American Psychological Association.

Tunstall, B. J., Verendeev, A., & Kearns, D. N. (2013). Outcome specificity in deepened extinction may limit treatment feasibility: Co-presentation of a food cue interferes with extinction of cue-elicited cocaine seeking. *Drug and Alcohol Dependence.* Retrieved from http://www.ncbi.nlm.nih.gov/pubmed/24071568.

Turner, M. E., Pratkanis, A. R., & Struckman, C. K. (2007). Groupthink as social identity maintenance. In C. K. Struckman (Ed.), *The science of social influence: Advances and future progress.* New York: Psychology Press.

Turner, S., Taillieu, T., Cheung, K., & Afifi, T. O. (2017). The relationship between childhood sexual abuse and mental health outcomes among males: Results from a nationally representative United States sample. *Child Abuse & Neglect, 66*, 64-72.

Turri, M. G. (2015). Transference and katharsis, Freud to Aristotle. *International Journal of Psychoanalysis, 96*, 369-387.

Tuszynski, M. H. (2007). Nerve growth factor gene therapy in Alzheimer's disease. *Alzheimer's Disease and Associated Disorders, 21*, 179-189.

Tutwiler, S., Lin, M., & Chang, C. (2013). The use of a gesture-based system for teaching multiple intelligences: A pilot study. *British Journal of Educational Technology, 44*, E133-E138.

Tversky, A., & Kahneman, D. (1987). Rational choice and the framing of decisions. In R. Hogarth & M. Reder (Eds.), *Rational choice: The contrast between economics and psychology.* Chicago: University of Chicago Press.

Twenge, J. M. (2013). Does online social media lead to social connection or social disconnection? *Journal of College and Character, 14*, 11-20.

Twenge, J. M., & Kasser, T. (2013). Generational changes in materialism and work centrality, 1976-2007: Associations with temporal changes in societal insecurity and materialistic role-modeling. *Personality and Social Psychology Bulletin, 34*, 17-31.

Twenge, J. M., Campbell, W. K., & Gentile, B. (2013). Changes in pronoun use in American books and the rise of individualism, 1960-2008. *Journal of Cross-Cultural Psychology, 44*, 406-415.

Twining, R. C., Wheeler, D. S., Ebben, A. L., Jacobsen, A. J., Robble, M. A., Mantsch, J. R., & Wheeler, R. A. (2015). Aversive stimuli drive drug seeking in a state of low dopamine tone. *Biological Psychiatry, 77*, 895-902.

Tydgat, I., & Grainger, J. (2009). Serial position effects in the identification of letters, digits, and symbols. *Journal of Experimental Psychology: Human Perception and Performance, 35*, 480-498.

Tyrer, H., Tyrer, P., Lisseman-Stones, Y., McAllister, S., Cooper, S., Salkovskis, P., . . . Wang, D. (2015). Therapist differences in a randomised trial of the outcome of cognitive behaviour therapy for health anxiety in medical patients. *International Journal of Nursing Studies, 52*, 686-694.

U.S. Bureau of Labor Statistics. (2007). *American time use survey.* Washington, DC: Author.

U.S. Bureau of Labor Statistics. (2013, April 26). Employment characteristics of families–2012. Washington, DC: Author.

U.S. Bureau of the Census. (2000). *Census 2000.* Washington, DC: Author.

U.S. Census Bureau. (2017, September 14). New American community survey statistics for income, poverty and health insurance available for states and local areas. Release Number CB17-157. Retrieved from https://www.census.gov/newsroom/press-releases/2017/acs-single-year.html?CID=CBSM+ACS16.

U.S. Department of Health and Human Services. (2016). E-cigarette use among youth and young adults. A report of the Surgeon General. Atlanta, GA: U.S. Department of Health and Human Services, Centers for Disease Control and Prevention, National Center for Chronic Disease Prevention and Health Promotion, Office on Smoking and Health.

U.S. Senate Select Committee on Intelligence. (2004, July 7). Report of the U.S. intelligence community's prewar intelligence assessments on Iraq. Retrieved from https://www.hsdl.org/?abstract&did=448158.

Uchino, B. N. (2006). Social support and health: A review of physiological processes potentially underlying links to disease outcomes. Journal of Behavioral Medicine, 29, 377-387.

Ullman, S. E., & Townsend, S. M. (2007). Barriers to working with sexual assault survivors: A qualitative study of rape crisis center workers. Violence Against Women, 13, 412-443.

UNAIDS. (December 2013). 2013 AIDS epidemic update. Geneva, Switzerland: United Nations Programme on HIV/AIDS.

Underwood, A. (2005, October 3). The good heart. Newsweek, p. 49.

United Nations Children's Fund. (2013). Female genital mutilation/cutting: A statistical overview and exploration of the dynamics of change. New York: UNICEF.

Unsworth, N., & Engle, R. W. (2005). Individual differences in working memory capacity and learning: Evidence from the serial reaction time task. Memory and Cognition, 33, 213-220.

Unsworth, N., Redick, T. S., McMillan, B. D., Hambrick, D. Z., Kane, M. J., & Engle, R. W. (2015). Is playing video games related to cognitive abilities? Psychological Science, 26(6), 759-774.

Updegraff, K. A., Helms, H. M., McHale, S. M., Crouter, A. C., Thayer, S. M., & Sales, L. H. (2004). Who's the boss? Patterns of perceived control in adolescents' friendships. Journal of Youth & Adolescence, 33, 403-420.

Urlacher, B. R. (2008). Walking out of two-level social traps (with a little help from my friends). Simulation & Gaming, 39, 453-464.

Ursprung, W. W., Sanouri, A., & DiFranza, J. R. (2009). The loss of autonomy over smoking in relation to lifetime cigarette consumption. Addictive Behaviors, 22, 12-19.

Uylings, H. B. M. (2006). Development of the human cortex and the concept of "critical" or "sensitive" periods. Language Learning, 56, 59-90.

Vagianos, A. (2015, February 19). 1 in 3 women has been sexually harassed at work, according to survey. Huffington Post. Accessed at http://www.huffingtonpost.com/2015/02/19/1-in-3-women-sexually-harassed-work-cosmopolitan n 6713814.html.

Vaillant, G. E., & Vaillant, C. O. (1990). Natural history of male psychological health: XII. A 46-year study of predictors of successful aging at age 65. American Journal of Psychiatry, 147, 31-37.

Valencia, R. R., & Suzuki, L. A. (2003). Intelligence testing and minority students: Foundations, performance factors, and assessment issues. Thousand Oaks, CA: Sage.

Valenzuela, S., Park, N., & Kee, K. F. (2009). Is there social capital in a social network site? Facebook use and college students' life satisfaction, trust, and participation. Journal of Computer-Mediated Communications, 14, 875-901.

Valenzuela, V., Martínez, G., Duran-Aniotz, C., & Hetz, C. (2016). Gene therapy to target ER stress in brain diseases. Brain Research, 1648(Part B), 561-570.

Valois, R. F., Zullig, K. J., & Hunter, A. A. (2013). Association between adolescent suicide ideation, suicide attempts and emotional self-efficacy. Journal of Child and Family Studies, 24, 237-248.

Valsecchi, M., Caziot, B., Backus, B. T., & Gegenfurtner, K. R. (2013). The role of binocular disparity in rapid scene and pattern recognition. I-Perception, 4(2), 254-262.

Valyear, M. D., Villaruel, F. R., & Chaudhri, N. (2017). Alcohol-seeking and relapse: A focus on incentive salience and contextual conditioning. Behavioural Processes, 141(Part 1), 26-32.

Van Belle, V., Pelckmans, K., Suykens, J. A. K., & Van Huffel, S. (2011). Learning transformation models for ranking and survival analysis. Journal of Machine Learning Research, 12, 819-862.

Van Damme, C., Deschrijver, E., Van Geert, E., & Hoorens, V. (2017). When praising yourself insults others: Self-superiority claims provoke aggression. Personality and Social Psychology Bulletin, 43, 1008-1019.

Van den Wildenberg, W. P. M., & Van der Molen, M. W. (2004). Developmental trends in simple and selective inhibition of compatible and incompatible responses. Journal of Experimental Child Psychology, 87, 201-220.

Van der Zee, E. A., Platt, B. B., & Riedel, G. G. (2011). Acetylcholine: Future research and perspectives. Behavioural Brain Research, 221, 583-586.

van Dijk, W. W., Ouwerkerk, J. W., Wesseling, Y. M., & van Koningsbruggen, G. M. (2011). Towards understanding pleasure at the misfortunes of others: The impact of self-evaluation threat on schadenfreude. Cognition and Emotion, 25, 360-368.

van Hooren, S. A. H., Valentijn, A. M., & Bosma, H. (2007). Cognitive functioning in healthy older adults aged 64-81: A cohort study into the effects of age, sex, and education. Aging, Neuropsychology, and Cognition, 14, 40-54.

van Marle, K., & Wynn, K. (2009). Infants' auditory enumeration: Evidence for analog magnitudes in the small number range. Cognition, 111, 302-316.

van Nieuwenhuijzen, M., Vriens, A., Scheepmaker, M., Smit, M., & Porton, E. (2011). The development of a diagnostic instrument to measure social information processing in children with mild to borderline intellectual disabilities. Research in Developmental Disabilities, 32, 358-370.

Van Overwalle, F., & Siebler, F. (2005). A connectionist model of attitude formation and change. Personality and Social Psychology Review, 9, 231-274.

Van Rosmalen, L., Van der Veer, R., & Van der Horst, F. (2015). Ainsworth's strange situation procedure: The origin of an instrument. Journal of the History of the Behavioral Sciences, 51, 261-284.

van Soelen, I. C., Brouwer, R. M., van Leeuwen, M., Kahn, R. S., Pol, H., & Boomsma, D. I. (2011). Heritability of verbal and performance intelligence in a pediatric longitudinal sample. Twin Research and Human Genetics, 14, 119-128.

van Wesel, F., Boeije, H., & Hoijtink, H. (2013). Use of hypotheses for analysis of variance models: Challenging the current practice. Quality & Quantity: International Journal of Methodology, 47, 137-150.

Vanasse, A., Niyonsenga, T., & Courteau, J. (2004). Smoking cessation within the context of family medicine: Which smokers take action? Preventive Medicine: An International Journal Devoted to Practice and Theory, 38, 330-337.

Vandell, D. L., Burchinal, M. R., Belsky, J., Owen, M. T., Friedman, S. L., Clarke-Stewart, . . . Weinraub, M. (2005). Early child care and children's development in the primary grades: Follow-up results from the NICHD Study of Early Child Care. Paper presented at the biennial meeting of the Society for Research in Child Development, Atlanta, GA.

Vandervert, L. R., Schimpf, P. H., & Liu, H. (2007). How working memory and the cerebellum collaborate to produce creativity and innovation. Creativity Research Journal, 19, 1-18.

Vandierendonck, A., & Szmalec, A. (Eds.). (2011). Spatial working memory. New York: Psychology Press.

Vanheule, S., Desmet, M., Rosseel, Y., & Meganck, R. (2006). Core transference themes in depression. Journal of Affective Disorders, 91, 71-75.

Varma, S. (2007). A computational model of Tower of Hanoi problem solving. Dissertation Abstracts International: Section B: The Sciences and Engineering, 67(8-B), 4736.

Vasudeva, K., Vodovotz, Y., Azhar, N., Barclay, D., Janjic, J. M., & Pollock, J. A. (2015). In vivo and systems biology studies implicate IL-18 as a central mediator in chronic pain. Journal of Neuroimmunology, 28, 343-49.

Vecchione, M., Schoen, H., Castro, J., Cieciuch, J., Pavlopoulos, V., & Caprara, G. (2011). Personality correlates of party preference: The Big Five in five big European countries. Personality and Individual Differences, 51, 737-742.

Vega, C. P. (2006). The effects of therapeutic components on at-risk middle school children's grades and attendance: An archival study of an after-school prevention program. Dissertation Abstracts International: Section B: The Sciences and Engineering, 66, 4504.

Velentzas, K., Heinen, T., & Schack, T. (2011). Routine integration strategies and their effects on volleyball serve performance and players' movement mental representation. *Journal of Applied Sport Psychology, 23,* 209-222.

Vellacott, J. (2007). Resilience: A psychoanalytic exploration. *British Journal of Psychotherapy, 23,* 163-170.

Veltman, M. W. M., & Browne, K. D. (2001). Three decades of child maltreatment research: Implications for the school years. *Trauma Violence and Abuse, 2,* 215-239.

Vera-Estay, E., Dooley, J. J., & Beauchamp, M. H. (2015). Cognitive underpinnings of moral reasoning in adolescence: The contribution of executive functions. *Journal of Moral Education, 44,* 17-33.

Verdejo, A., Toribio, I., & Orozco, C. (2005). Neuropsychological functioning in methadone maintenance patients versus abstinent heroin abusers. *Drug and Alcohol Dependence, 78,* 283-288.

Verdon, B. (2011). The case of thematic tests adapted to older adults: On the importance of differentiating latent and manifest contents in projective tests. *Rorschachiana, 32,* 46-71.

Verfaellie, M., & Keane, M. M. (2002). Impaired and preserved memory processes in amnesia. In L. R. Squire & D. L. Schacter (Eds.), *Neuropsychology of memory* (3rd ed.). New York: Guilford Press.

Verhaeghen, P., Aikman, S. N., & Van Gulick, A. E. (2011). Prime and prejudice: Co-occurrence in the culture as a source of automatic stereotype priming. *British Journal of Social Psychology, 50,* 501-518.

Verona, E., & Sullivan, E. (2008). Emotional catharsis and aggression revisited: Heart rate reduction following aggressive responding. *Emotion, 8,* 331-340.

Verschueren, M., Rassart, J., Claes, L., Moons, P., & Luyckx, K. (2017). Identity statuses throughout adolescence and emerging adulthood: A large-scale study into gender, age, and contextual differences. *Psychologica Belgica, 57,* 32-42.

Vesely, A. K., Saklofske, D. H., & Leschied, A. W. (2013). Teachers—The vital resource: The contribution of emotional intelligence to teacher efficacy and well-being. *Canadian Journal of School Psychology, 28,* 71-89.

Vicari, S., Pontillo, M., & Armando, M. (2013). Neurodevelopmental and psychiatric issues in Down's syndrome: Assessment and intervention. *Psychiatric Genetics, 23,* 95-107.

Vieira, E. M., & Freire, J. C. (2006). Alteridade e psicologia humanista: Uma leitura ética da abordagem centrada na pessoa. Alterity and humanistic psychology: An ethical reading of the person-centered approach. *Estudos de Psicologia, 23,* 425-432.

Villarosa, L. (2002, December 3). To prevent sexual abuse, abusers step forward. *The New York Times,* B1.

Villemure, C., Slotnick, B. M., & Bushnell, M. C. (2003). Effects of odors on pain perception: Deciphering the roles of emotion and attention. *Pain, 106,* 101-108.

Vincus, A. A., Ringwalt, C., Harris, M. S., & Shamblen, S. R. (2010). A short-term,

quasi-experimental evaluation of D.A.R.E.'s revised elementary school curriculum. *Journal of Drug Education, 40,* 37-49.

Vitaro, F., Brendgen, M., & Arseneault, L. (2009). Methods and measures: The discordant MZ-twin method: One step closer to the holy grail of causality. *International Journal of Behavioral Development, 33,* 376-382.

Vitello, P. (2006, June 12). A ring tone meant to fall on deaf ears. *The New York Times,* A1.

Vitiello, A. L., Bonello, R. P., & Pollard, H. P. (2007). The effectiveness of ENAR® for the treatment of chronic neck pain in Australian adults: A preliminary single-blind, randomised controlled trial. *Chiropractic Osteopathology, 9,* 9.

Vlassova, A., & Pearson, J. (2013). Look before you leap: Sensory memory improves decision making. *Psychological Science, 24,* 1635-1643.

Vleioras, G., & Bosma, H. A. (2005). Are identity styles important for psychological well-being? *Journal of Adolescence, 28,* 397-409.

Vogt, D., Rizvi, S., Shipherd, J., & Resick, P. (2008). Longitudinal investigation of reciprocal relationship between stress reactions and hardiness. *Personality and Social Psychology Bulletin, 34,* 61-73.

Volterra, V., Caselli, M. C., Capirci, O., Tonucci, F., & Vicari, S. (2003). Early linguistic abilities of Italian children with Williams syndrome [Special issue: Williams syndrome]. *Developmental Neuropsychology, 23,* 33-58.

Voruganti, L. P., Awad, A. G., Parker, B., Forrest, C., Usmani, Y., Fernando, M. L. D., . . . Senthilal, S. (2007). Cognition, functioning and quality of life in schizophrenia treatment: Results of a one-year randomized controlled trial of olanzapine and quetiapine. *Schizophrenia Research, 96,* 146-155.

Vrieze, S. I., McGue, M., Miller, M. B., Hicks, B. M., & Iacono, W. G. (2013). Three mutually informative ways to understand the genetic relationships among behavioral disinhibition, alcohol use, drug use, nicotine use/dependence, and their co-occurrence: Twin biometry, GCTA, and genome-wide scoring. *Behavior Genetics, 43,* 97-107.

Vukasović, T., & Bratko, D. (2015). Heritability of personality: A meta-analysis of behavior genetic studies. *Psychological Bulletin, 141,* 769-785.

Vygotsky, L. S. (1926/1997). *Educational psychology.* Delray Beach, FL: St. Lucie Press.

Vöhringer, I. A., Kolling, T., Graf, F., Poloczek, S., Fassbender, I., Freitag, C., . . . Knopf, M. (2017). The development of implicit memory from infancy to childhood: On average performance levels and interindividual differences. *Child Development.* Accessed from https://www.ncbi.nlm.nih.gov/pubmed/28220933.

Wabitsch, M., Funcke, J., Lennerz, B., Kuhnle-Krahl, U., Lahr, G., Debatin, K., & Fischer-Posovszky, P. (2015). Biologically inactive leptin and early-onset extreme obesity. *The New England Journal of Medicine, 372,* 48-54.

Waddell, J., & Shors, T. J. (2008). Neurogenesis, learning and associative strength. *European Journal of Neurosciences, 27,* 3020-3028.

Wagemans, J., Elder, J. H., Kubovy, M., Palmer, S. E., Peterson, M. A., Singh, M., . . . von der Heydt, R. (2012). A century of Gestalt psychology in visual perception: I. Perceptual grouping and figure–ground organization. *Psychological Bulletin, 138,* 1172-1217.

Wagner, R. K. (2002). Smart people doing dumb things: The case of managerial incompetence. In R. J. Sternberg (Ed.), *Why smart people can be so stupid.* New Haven, CT: Yale University Press.

Wagner, R. K. (2011). Practical intelligence. In R. J. Sternberg & S. Kaufman (Eds.), *The Cambridge handbook of intelligence.* New York: Cambridge University Press.

Wagstaff, G. (2009). Is there a future for investigative hypnosis? *Journal of Investigative Psychology and Offender Profiling, 6,* 43-57.

Wagstaff, G. F., Wheatcroft, J. M., & Jones, A. (2011). Are high hypnotizables especially vulnerable to false memory effects? A socio-cognitive perspective. *International Journal of Clinical and Experimental Hypnosis, 59,* 310-326.

Wain, H. J., Grammer, G. G., & Stasinos, J. (2006). Psychiatric intervention for medical and surgical patients following traumatic injuries. In E. C. Ritchie, P. J. Watson, & M. J. Friedman (Eds.), *Interventions following mass violence and disasters: Strategies for mental health practice.* New York: Guilford Press.

Waismeyer, A., & Meltzoff, A. N. (2017). Learning to make things happen: Infants' observational learning of social and physical causal events. *Journal of Experimental Child Psychology, 162,* 58-71.

Wakefield, J. C. (2013). DSM-5: An overview of changes and controversies. *Clinical Social Work Journal, 41,* 139-154.

Walker, L. J., & Frimer, J. A. (2007). Moral personality of brave and caring exemplars. *Journal of Personality and Social Psychology, 93,* 845-860.

Walker, L., & Frimer, J. (2009). The song remains the same: Rebuttal to Sherblom's re-envisioning of the legacy of the care challenge. *Journal of Moral Education, 38,* 53-68.

Walker, M. P., & van der Helm, E. (2009). Overnight therapy? The role of sleep in emotional brain processing. *Psychological Bulletin, 135,* 731-748.

Walker, W. R., Skowronski, J. J., & Thompson, C. P. (2003). Consolidation of long-term memory: Evidence and alternatives. *Review of General Psychology, 7,* 203-210.

Wallace, L. S., Chisolm, D. J., Abdel-Rasoul, M., & DeVoe, J. E. (2013). Survey mode matters: Adults' self-reported statistical confidence, ability to obtain health information, and perceptions of patient-health-care provider communication. *Journal of Health Psychology, 18,* 1036-1045.

Wallen, K., & Lloyd, E. A. (2011). Female sexual arousal: genital anatomy and orgasm in intercourse. *Hormonal Behavior, 59,* 780-792.

Wallerstein, J. S., Lewis, J., Blakeslee, S., & Lewis, J. (2000). *The unexpected legacy of divorce.* New York: Hyperion.

Walsh, B. T., Kaplan, A. S., Attia, E., Olmstead, M., Parides, M., Carter, J. C., . . . Rockert, W. (2006). Fluoxetine after weight restoration in anorexia nervosa: A randomized controlled trial. *JAMA: Journal of the American Medical Association, 295,* 2605-2612.

Walsh, R., & Shapiro, S. L. (2006). The meeting of meditative disciplines and Western psychology. *American Psychologist, 61,* 227-239.

Walton, G. M., & Cohen, G. L. (2011). A brief social-belonging intervention improves academic and health outcomes of minority students. *Science, 331,* 1447-1451.

Walton, J. R., Murphy, C., & Bartram, L. (2017). Childhood behavioral problems–Attention-deficit/hyperactivity disorder (ADHD). In W. O'Donohue, L. James, & C. Snipes (Eds.), *Practical strategies and tools to promote treatment engagement.* Cham, Switzerland: Springer International Publishing.

Wan, C., & Chiu, C. (2011). Culture as intersubjective representations of values. In A. Y. Leung, C. Chiu, & Y. Hong (Eds.), *Cultural processes: A social psychological perspective.* New York: Cambridge University Press.

Wang, A., & Clark, D. A. (2002). Haunting thoughts: The problem of obsessive mental intrusions [Special issue: Intrusions in cognitive behavioral therapy]. *Journal of Cognitive Psychotherapy, 16,* 193-208.

Wang, F., Kameda, M., Yasuhara, T., Tajiri, N., Kikuchi, Y., Liang, H. B., . . . Agari, T. (2011). GDNF-pretreatment enhances the survival of neural stem cells following transplantation in a rat model of Parkinson's disease. *Neuroscience Research, 18,* 202-211.

Wang, J. X., Rogers, L. M., Gross, E. Z., Ryals, A. J., Dokucu, M. E., Brandstatt, Hermiller, M. S., . . . Voss, J. L. (2014). Targeted enhancement of cortical-hippocampal brain networks and associative memory. *Science, 345*(6200), 1054-1057.

Wang, M. T., & Kenny, S. (2013). Longitudinal links between fathers' and mothers' harsh verbal discipline and adolescents' conduct problems and depressive symptoms. *Child Development, 85*(3), 908-923.

Wang, M., Chen, W., Zhang, C., & Deng, X. (2017). Personality types and scholarly creativity in undergraduate students: The mediating roles of creative styles. *Personality and Individual Differences, 105,* 170-174.

Wang, P. S., Aguilar-Gaxiola, S., Alonso, J., Angermeyer, M. C., Borges, G., Bromet, E. J., . . .Wells, J. E. (2007). Use of mental health services for anxiety, mood, and substance disorders in 17 countries in the WHO world mental health surveys. *Lancet, 370,* 841-850.

Wang, Q. (2004). The emergence of cultural self-constructs: Autobiographical memory and self-description in European American and Chinese children. *Developmental Psychology, 40,* 3-15.

Wang, Q., & Conway, M. A. (2006). Autobiographical memory, self, and culture. In L-G.

Nilsson & N. Ohta, *Memory and society: Psychological perspectives.* New York: Psychology Press.

Wang, R., Liu, H., Jiang, J., & Song, Y. (2017). Will materialism lead to happiness? A longitudinal analysis of the mediating role of psychological needs satisfaction. *Personality and Individual Differences, 105,* 312-317.

Wang, V. O., & Sue, S. (2005). In the eye of the storm: Race and genomics in research and practice. *American Psychologist, 60,* 37-45.

Wang, X., Lu, T., Snider, R. K., & Liang, L. (2005). Sustained firing in auditory cortex evoked by preferred stimuli. *Nature, 435,* 341-346.

Wang, Y., & Zhong, Z. (2015). Effects of frustration situation and resilience on implicit aggression. *Chinese Journal of Clinical Psychology, 23,* 209-212.

Wannez, S., Heine, L., Thonnard, M., Gosseries, O., & Laureys, S. (2017). The repetition of behavioral assessments in diagnosis of disorders of consciousness. *Annals of Neurology, 81,* 883-889.

Ward, L. M. (2011). The thalamic dynamic core theory of conscious experience. *Consciousness and Cognition: An International Journal, 20,* 464-486.

Ward-Baker, P. D. (2007). The remarkable oldest old: A new vision of aging. *Dissertation Abstracts International Section A: Humanities and Social Sciences, 67*(8-A), 3115.

Warden, C. A., Wu, W. Y., & Tsai, D. (2006). Online shopping interface components: Relative importance as peripheral and central cues. *CyberPsychology & Behavior, 9,* 285-296.

Wark, B., Lundstrom, B., & Fairhall, A. (2007). Sensory adaptation. *Current Opinion in Neurobiology, 17,* 423-429.

Warmbold-Brann, K., Burns, M. K., Preast, J. L., Taylor, C. N., & Aguilar, L. N. (2017). Meta-analysis of the effects of academic interventions and modifications on student behavior outcomes. *School Psychology Quarterly, 32*(3), 291-305.

Warne, R. T., & Liu, J. K. (2017). Income differences among grade skippers and non-grade skippers across genders in the Terman sample, 1936-1976. *Learning and Instruction, 47,* 1-12.

Waters, A. M., Theresiana, C., Neumann, D. L., & Craske, M. G. (2017). Developmental differences in aversive conditioning, extinction, and reinstatement: A study with children, adolescents, and adults. *Journal of Experimental Child Psychology, 159,* 263-278.

Watkins, C. (2007). *Date rape.* Farmington Hills, MI: Greenhaven Press.

Watson, J. B. (1924). *Behaviorism.* New York: Norton.

Watson, J. C., Goldman, R. N., & Greenberg, L. S. (2011). Humanistic and experiential theories of psychotherapy. In J. C. Norcross, G. R. VandenBos, & D. K. Freedheim (Eds.), *History of psychotherapy: Continuity and change* (2nd ed.). Washington, DC: American Psychological Association.

Watson, P. J., Brymer, M. J., & Bonanno, G. A. (2011). Postdisaster psychological intervention since 9/11. *American Psychologist, 66,* 482-494.

Watters, E. (2010, January 10). The Americanization of mental illness. *The New York Times,* p. C2.

Waxman, S. (2009). Learning from infants' first verbs. *Monographs of the Society for Research in Child Development, 74,* 127-132.

Weber, L., & Dwoskin, E. (2014, September 30). As personality tests multiply, employers are split. *Wall Street Journal,* pp. A1, A12.

Wechsler, H., Lee, J. E., Nelson, T. F., & Kuo, M. (2002). Underage college students' drinking behavior, access to alcohol, and the influence of deterrence policies. *Journal of American College Health, 50,* 223-236.

Weck, F., Bleichhardt, G., Witthöft, M., & Hiller, W. (2011). Explicit and implicit anxiety: Differences between patients with hypochondriasis, patients with anxiety disorders, and healthy controls. *Cognitive Therapy and Research, 35,* 317-325.

Weeks, M., & Lupfer, M. B. (2004). Complicating race: The relationship between prejudice, race, and social class categorizations. *Personality and Social Psychology Bulletin, 30,* 972-984.

Wehrle, R., Kaufmann, C., Wetter, T. C., Holsboer, F., Auer, D. P., Pollmacher, T., . . . Czisch, M. (2007). Functional microstates within human REM sleep: First evidence from fMRI of a thalamocortical network specific for phasic REM periods. *European Journal of Neuroscience, 25,* 863-871.

Wehrum, S., Klucken, T., Kagerer, S., Walter, B., Hermann, A., Vaitl, D., . . . Stark, R. (2013). Gender commonalities and differences in the neural processing of visual sexual stimuli. *Journal of Sexual Medicine, 10,* 1328-1342.

Weimann, J., Knabe, A., & Schöb, R. (2015). *Measuring happiness: The economics of well-being.* Cambridge, MA: MIT Press.

Weinberg, M. S., Williams, C. J., & Pryor, D. W. (1991, February 27). Personal communication. Indiana University, Bloomington.

Weiner, R. D., & Falcone, G. (2011). Electroconvulsive therapy: How effective is it? *Journal of the American Psychiatric Nurses Association, 17,* 217-218.

Weinstein, L. (2007). Selected genetic disorders affecting Ashkenazi Jewish families. *Family & Community Health, 30,* 50-62.

Weinstein, M., Glei, D. A., Yamazaki, A., & Ming-Cheng, C. (2004). The role of intergenerational relations in the association between life stressors and depressive symptoms. *Research on Aging, 26,* 511-530.

Weir, K. (2016). The science of naps. *Monitor on Psychology, 47,* 48-51.

Weir, K. (2016, April). New insights on eating disorders. *Monitor on Psychology,* pp. 36-40.

Weir, K. (2016, March). The risks of earlier puberty. *Monitor on Psychology,* pp. 41-44.

Weiss, A., Bates, T., & Luciano, M. (2008). Happiness is a personal(ity) thing: The genetics of personality and well-being in a representative sample. *Psychological Science, 19,* 205-210.

Weissman, M. M., Bland, R. C., Canino, G. J., Faravelli, C., Greenwald, S., Hwu, H. G., . . . Yeh, E. K.

(1997). Cross-national epidemiology of major depression and bipolar disorder. *Journal of the American Medical Association, 276,* 293-299.

Weissman, M., Markowitz, J., & Klerman, G. L. (2007). *Clinician's quick guide to interpersonal psychotherapy.* New York: Oxford University Press.

Welkowitz, L. A., Struening, E. L., Pittman, J., Guardino, M., & Welkowitz, J. (2000). Obsessive-compulsive disorder and comorbid anxiety problems in a national anxiety screening sample. *Journal of Anxiety Disorders, 14,* 471-482.

Weller, P. D., Anderson, M. C., Gomez-Ariza, C. J., & Bajo, M. T. (2013). On the status of cue independence as a criterion for memory inhibition. *Journal of Experimental Psychology: Learning, Memory, and Cognition, 39,* 1232-1245.

Wells, R., Phillips, R. S., & McCarthy, E. P. (2011). Patterns of mind-body therapies in adults with common neurological conditions. *Neuroepidemiology, 36,* 46-51.

Wen, M., Butler, L. T., & Koutstaal, W. (2013). Improving insight and non-insight problem solving with brief interventions. *British Journal of Psychology, 104,* 97-118.

Wenzel, A. (2011). Obsessions and compulsions. In A. Wenzel & S. Stuart (Eds.), *Anxiety in childbearing women: Diagnosis and treatment.* Washington, DC: American Psychological Association.

Wenzel, A., Zetocha, K., & Ferraro, R. F. (2007). Depth of processing and recall of threat material in fearful and nonfearful individuals. *Anxiety, Stress & Coping: An International Journal, 20,* 223-237.

Werhane, P. H., Pincus Hartman, L., Archer, C., Englehardt, E. E., & Pritchard, M. S. (2013). *Obstacles to ethical decision-making: Mental models, Milgram and the problem of obedience.* New York: Cambridge University Press.

Werker, J. F., & Tees, R. C. (2005). Speech perception as a window for understanding plasticity and commitment in language systems of the brain. *Developmental Psychobiology, 46,* 233-234.

Werner, J. S., Pinna, B., & Spillmann, L. (2007). Illusory color and the brain. *Scientific American, 296,* 90-96.

Wertheimer, M. (1923). Untersuchungen zur Lehre von der Gestalt, II. *Psychol. Forsch., 5,* 301-350. In R. Beardsley & M. Wertheimer (Eds.) (1958), *Readings in perception.* New York: Van Nostrand.

West, D. S., Harvey-Berino, J., & Raczynski, J. M. (2004). Behavioral aspects of obesity, dietary intake, and chronic disease. In J. M. Raczynski & L. C. Leviton (Eds.), *Handbook of clinical health psychology: Vol. 2. Disorders of behavior and health.* Washington, DC: American Psychological Association.

West, R. L., Bagwell, D. K., & Dark-Freudeman, A. (2007). Self-efficacy and memory aging: The impact of a memory intervention based on self-efficacy. *Neuropsychological Development and Cognition, B, Aging and Neuropsychological Cognition, 14,* 1-28.

Westen, D., Novotny, C. M., & Thompson-Brenner, H. (2004). The empirical status of empirically supported psychotherapies:

Assumptions, findings, and reporting in controlled clinical trials. *Psychological Bulletin, 130,* 631-663.

Wester, A. J., van Herten, J. C., Egger, J. M., & Kessels, R. C. (2013). Applicability of the Rivermead Behavioural Memory Test-Third Edition (RBMT-3) in Korsakoff's syndrome and chronic alcoholics. *Neuropsychiatric Disease and Treatment, 9,* 202-212.

Westerhausen, R., Moosmann, M., Alho, K., Medvedev, S., Hämäläinen, H., & Hugdahl, K. (2009). Top-down and bottom-up interaction: Manipulating the dichotic listening ear advantage. *Brain Research, 1250,* 183-189.

Westerterp, K. R. (2006). Perception, passive overfeeding and energy metabolism. *Physiology & Behavior, 89,* 62-65.

Westmarland, N., & Alderson, S. (2013). The health, mental health, and well-being benefits of rape crisis counseling. *Journal of Interpersonal Violence, 28,* 3265-3282.

Whillans, A.V., Dunn, E.W., Smeets, Pl., Bekkers, R., & Norton, M.I. (2017). Buying time promotes happiness, *PNAS, 114,* 8523-8527.

Whisman, M., & Snyder, D. (2007). Sexual infidelity in a national survey of American women: Differences in prevalence and correlates as a function of method of assessment. *Journal of Family Psychology, 21,* 14-154.

Whitaker, R. (2009). Deinstitutionalization and neuroleptics: The myth and reality. In Y. O. Alanen, M. González de Chávez, A. S. Silver, B. Martindale, Y. O. Alanen, M. González de Chávez, . . . B. Martindale (Eds.) , *Psychotherapeutic approaches to schizophrenic psychoses: Past, present and future.* New York: Routledge/Taylor & Francis Group.

Whitbourne, S. (2010). *The search for fulfillment.* New York: Ballantine.

Whitbourne, S. K. (2000). The normal aging process. In S. K. Whitbourne & S. Krauss (Eds.), *Psychopathology in later adulthood.* New York: Wiley.

Whitbourne, S. K., Zuschlag, M. K., Elliot, L. B., & Waterman, A. S. (1992). Psychosocial development in adulthood: A 22-year sequential study. *Journal of Personality and Social Psychology, 63,* 260-271.

White, F. A., Harvey, L. J., & Abu-Rayya, H. M. (2015). Improving intergroup relations in the Internet Age: A critical review. *Review of General Psychology, 19,* 129-139.

White, L. (2013). Remembering and forgetting. In G. J. Madden, W. V. Dube, T. D. Hackenberg, G. P. Hanley, & K. A. Lattal (Eds.), *APA handbook of behavior analysis, Vol. 1: Methods and principles.* Washington, DC: American Psychological Association.

White, L. (2007). Linguistic theory, universal grammar, and second language acquisition. In B. Van Patten & J. Williams (Eds.), *Theories in second language acquisition: An introduction.* Mahwah, NJ: Lawrence Erlbaum Associates.

White, R. G., Jain, S., Orr, D. R., & Read, U. M. (2017). *The Palgrave handbook of sociocultural perspectives on global mental health.* New York: Palgrave Macmillan.

White, R. K. (2004). Misperception and war. *Peace and Conflict: Journal of Peace Psychology, 10,* 399-409.

Whitebread, D., Coltman, P., Jameson, H., & Lander, R. (2009). Play, cognition and self-regulation: What exactly are children learning when they learn through play? *Educational and Child Psychology, 26,* 40-52.

Whitehouse, W. G., Orne, E. C., Dinges, D. F., Bates, B. L., Nadon, R., & Orne, M. T. (2005). The cognitive interview: Does it successfully avoid the dangers of forensic hypnosis? *American Journal of Psychology, 118,* 213-234.

Whiting, B. B. (1965). Sex identity conflict and physical violence: A comparative study. *American Anthropologist, 67,* 123-140.

Whitney, P. G., & Green, J. A. (2011). Changes in infants' affect related to the onset of independent locomotion. *Infant Behavior & Development, 34,* 459-466.

Whitton, L., Cosgrove, D., Clarkson, C., Harold, D., Kendall, K., Richards, A., . . . Morris, D. W. (2016). Cognitive analysis of schizophrenia risk genes that function as epigenetic regulators of gene expression. *American Journal of Medical Genetics Part B: Neuropsychiatric Genetics, 171,* 1170-1179.

WHO World Mental Health Survey Consortium. (2004). Prevalence, severity, and unmet need for treatment of mental disorders in the World Health Organization World Mental Health Surveys. *Journal of the American Medical Association, 291,* 2581-2590.

Whorf, B. L. (1956). *Language, thought, and reality.* New York: Wiley.

Wickelgren, E. A. (2004). Perspective distortion of trajectory forms and perceptual constancy in visual event identification. *Perception and Psychophysics, 66,* 629-641.

Widaman, K. (2009). Phenylketonuria in children and mothers: Genes, environments, behavior. *Current Directions in Psychological Science, 18,* 48-52.

Widiger, T. A. (2015). Assessment of DSM-5 personality disorder. *Journal of Personality Assessment, 97,* 456-466.

Wiech, K. (2016). Deconstructing the sensation of pain: The influence of cognitive processes on pain perception. *Science, 354,* 584-587.

Wiederman, M. W. (2011). Body image and sexual functioning. In T. F. Cash & L. Smolak (Eds.), *Body image: A handbook of science, practice, and prevention* (2nd ed.). New York: Guilford Press.

Wieth, M., & Zacks, R. (2011). Time of day effects on problem solving: When the non-optimal is optimal. *Thinking & Reasoning, 17,* 387-401.

Wiggins, J. S. (2003). *Paradigms of personality assessment.* New York: Guilford Press.

Wilcox, C. E., Calhoun, V. D., Rachakonda, S., Claus, E. D., Littlewood, R. A., Mickey, J., . . . Hutchinson, K. E. (2017). Functional network connectivity predicts treatment outcome during treatment of nicotine use disorder. *Psychiatry Research: Neuroimaging, 26,* 545-53.

Wildavsky, B. (2000, September 4). A blow to bilingual education. *U.S. News & World Report,* pp. 22-28.

Wilde, D. J. (2011). *Jung's personality theory quantified.* New York: Springer-Verlag Publishing.

Wiley, J., & Jarosz, A. F. (2012). Working memory capacity, attentional focus, and problem solving. *Current Directions in Psychological Science, 21,* 258-262.

Wilkin, L., & Haddock, B. (2011). Functional fitness of older adults. *Activities, Adaptation & Aging, 35,* 197-209.

Wilkinson, H. A. (2009). Cingulotomy. *Journal of Neurosurgery, 110,* 607-611.

Wilkinson, L., & Olliver-Gray, Y. (2006). The significance of silence: Differences in meaning, learning styles, and teaching strategies in cross-cultural settings [Special issue: Child language]. *Psychologia: An International Journal of Psychology in the Orient, 49,* 74-88.

Willander, J., & Larsson, M. (2006). Smell your way back to childhood: Autobiographical odor memory. *Psychonomic Bulletin & Review, 13,* 240-244.

Williams, C. L., & Butcher, J. N. (2011). The nuts and bolts: Administering, scoring, and augmenting MMPI-A assessments. In C. L. Williams & J. N. Butcher (Eds.), *A beginner's guide to the MMPI–A.* Washington, DC: American Psychological Association.

Williams, J. E., & Best, D. L. (1990). *Measuring sex stereotypes: A multinational study.* Newbury Park, CA: Sage.

Williams, J. E., Paton, C. C., Siegler, I. C., Eigenbrodt, M. L., Nieto, F. J., & Tyroler, H. A. (2000). Anger proneness predicts coronary heart disease risk: Prospective analysis from the Atherosclerosis Risk in Communities (ARIC) Study. *Circulation, 101,* 2034-2039.

Williams, R. L. (2013). Overview of the Flynn effect. *Intelligence, 41,* 753-764.

Williamson, P., McLeskey, J., & Hoppey, D. (2006). Educating students with mental retardation in general education classrooms. *Exceptional Children, 72,* 347-361.

Willis, J. (2017). Moving toward extremism: Group polarization in the laboratory and the world. In S. C. Cloninger & S. A. Leibo, S. C. (Eds.), *Understanding angry groups: Multidisciplinary perspectives on their motivations and effects on society.* Santa Barbara, CA: Praeger/ABC-CLIO.

Wills, K. E. (2013). Sickle cell disease. In I. Baron & C. Rey-Casserly (Eds.), *Pediatric neuropsychology: Medical advances and lifespan outcomes.* New York: Oxford University Press.

Wills, T., Sargent, J., Stoolmiller, M., Gibbons, F., & Gerrard, M. (2008). Movie smoking exposure and smoking onset: A longitudinal study of mediation processes in a representative sample of U.S. adolescents. *Psychology of Addictive Behaviors, 22,* 269-277.

Willyard, C. (2011). Men: A growing minority? Women earning doctoral degrees in psychology outnumber men three to one. What does this mean for the future of the field? *GradPsych, 40.*

Wilson, J. H., & Joye, S. W. (2017). Demonstrating interobserver reliability in naturalistic settings. In J. R. Stowell & W. E. Addison (Eds.),

Activities for teaching statistics and research methods: A guide for psychology instructors. Washington, DC: American Psychological Association.

Wilson, Michael (2017, May 9). A cry for help as a witness recounts a man's fall onto the subway tracks. *The New York Times,* p. A19.

Wilson, R. (2015, August 31). An epidemic of anguish: overwhelmed by demand for mental-health care, colleges face conflicts in choosing how to respond. *Chronicle of Higher Education,* p. 38.

Wilson, T. D. (2006). The power of social psychological interventions. *Science, 313,* 1251-1252.

Wilson, T. G., Grilo, C. M., & Vitousek, K. M. (2007). Psychological treatment of eating disorders [Special issue: Eating disorders]. *American Psychologist, 62,* 199-216.

Wimmer, M. C., Maras, K. L., Robinson, E. J., & Thomas, C. (2016). The format of children's mental images: Evidence from mental scanning. *Cognition, 154,* 49-54.

Winner, E. (2003). Creativity and talent. In M. H. Bornstein & L. Davidson (Eds.), *Well-being: Positive development across the life course.* Mahwah, NJ: Lawrence Erlbaum.

Winstead, B. A., & Sanchez, A. (2005). Gender and psychopathology. In J. E. Maddux & B. A. Winstead (Eds.), *Psychopathology: Foundations for a contemporary understanding.* Mahwah, NJ: Lawrence Erlbaum Associates.

Winston, C. N., Maher, H., & Easvaradoss, V. (2017). Needs and values: An exploration. *The Humanistic Psychologist, 45*(3), 295-311.

Winter, D. G. (2007). The role of motivation, responsibility, and integrative complexity in crisis escalation: Comparative studies of war and peace crises. *Journal of Personality and Social Psychology, 92,* 920-937.

Winter, D. G. (2016). Taming power: Generative historical consciousness. *American Psychologist, 71,* 160-174.

Winters, B. D., & Bussey, T. J. (2005). Glutamate receptors in perirhinal cortex mediate encoding, retrieval, and consolidation of object recognition memory. *Journal of Neuroscience, 25,* 4243-4251.

Wiseman, R., & Greening, E. (2002). The mind machine: A mass participation experiment into the possible existence of extra-sensory perception. *British Journal of Psychology, 93,* 487-499.

Wishart, D., Somoray, K., & Rowland, B. (2017). Role of thrill and adventure seeking in risky work-related driving behaviours. *Personality and Individual Differences, 104,* 362-367.

Witelson, S., Kigar, D., Scamvougeras, A., Kideckel, D., Buck, B., Stanchev, P., . . . Black, S. (2008). Corpus callosum anatomy in right-handed homosexual and heterosexual men. *Archives of Sexual Behavior, 37,* 857-863.

Witt, C. M., Jena, S., & Brinkhaus, B. (2006). Acupuncture for patients with chronic neck pain. *Pain, 125,* 98-106.

Wittchen, H., Nocon, A., Beesdo, K., Pine, D., Hofler, M., Lieb, R., & Gloster, A. T. (2008).

Agoraphobia and panic. *Psychotherapy and Psychosomatics, 77,* 147-157.

Wixted, J. T., & Carpenter, S. K. (2007). The Wickelgren power law and the Ebbinghaus savings function. *Psychological Science, 18,* 133-134.

Wixted, J. T., & Wells, G. L. (2017). The relationship between eyewitness confidence and identification accuracy: A new synthesis. *Psychological Science in the Public Interest, 18*(1), 10-65.

Wixted, J. T., Mickes, L., Clark, S. E., Gronlund, S. D., & Roediger, H. L., III. (2015, September). Initial eyewitness confidence reliably predicts eyewitness identification accuracy. *American Psychologist, 70*(6), 515-526.

Wlodarczyk, A., Basabe, N., Páez, D., Villagrán, L., & Reyes, C. (2017). Individual and collective posttraumatic growth in victims of natural disasters: A multidimensional perspective. *Journal of Loss and Trauma, 22*(5), 371-384.

Wojciechowska, L. (2017). Subjectivity and generativity in midlife. *Polish Psychological Bulletin, 48,* 38-43.

Wolf, A. J., Guyer, M. J., & Sharpe, L. (2010). Repressed memories in a controversial conviction. *Journal of the American Academy of Psychiatry Law, 38,* 607-609.

Wolfe, D. A. (1999). *Child abuse: Implications for child development and psychopathology.* Thousand Oaks, CA: Sage.

Wolitzky, D. L. (2006). Psychodynamic theories. In J. C. Thomas, D. L. Segal, & M. Hersen (Eds.), *Comprehensive handbook of personality and psychopathology, Vol. 1: Personality and everyday functioning.* Hoboken, NJ: John Wiley & Sons.

Wolk, D. A., Das, S. R., Mueller, S. G., Weiner, M. W., & Yushkevich, P. A. (2017). Medial temporal lobe subregional morphometry using high resolution MRI in Alzheimer's disease. *Neurobiology of Aging, 49,* 204-213.

Wolman, D. (2012, March 15). The split brain: A tale of two halves. *Nature, 483,* 260-263.

Wong, N., Sarver, D. E., & Beidel, D. C. (2011). Quality of life impairments among adults with social phobia: The impact of subtype. *Journal of Anxiety Disorders, 14,* 88-95.

Wood, E., Desmarais, S., & Gugula, S. (2002). The impact of parenting experience on gender stereotyped toy play of children. *Sex Roles, 47,* 39-49.

Wood, W. (2000). Attitude change: Persuasion and social influence. *Annual Review of Psychology, 51,* 539-570.

Wood, W., & Eagly, A. H. (2002). A cross-cultural analysis of the behavior of women and men: Implications for the origins of sex differences. *Psychological Bulletin, 128,* 699-727.

Wood, W., & Eagly, A. H. (2015). Two traditions of research on gender identity. *Sex Roles, 73,* 461-473.

Woodruff, S. I., Conway, T. L., & Edwards, C. C. (2007). Sociodemographic and smoking-related psychosocial predictors of smoking behavior change among high school smokers. *Addictive Behaviors, 33,* 354-358.

Woods, S. C., Schwartz, M. W., Baskin, D. G., & Seeley, R. J. (2000). Food intake and the regulation of body weight. *Annual Review of Psychology, 51,* 255–277.

Woodson, S. R. J. (2006). Relationships between sleepiness and emotion experience: An experimental investigation of the role of subjective sleepiness in the generation of positive and negative emotions. *Dissertation Abstracts International: Section B: The Sciences and Engineering, 67*(5-B), 2849.

Woollett, K., & Maguire, E. (2009). Navigational expertise may compromise anterograde associative memory. *Neuropsychologia, 47,* 1088–1095.

World Health Organization. (2017, May). Smoking fact sheet. Retrieved from http://www.who.int/mediacentre/factsheets/fs339/en/.

Wretman, C. J. (2016). Saving Satir: Contemporary perspectives on the change process model. *Social Work, 61,* 61–68.

Wright, A. C. (2017). The current state and future of factor analysis in personality disorder research. *Personality Disorders: Theory, Research, and Treatment, 8,* 14–25.

Wright, A. C., Zalewski, M., Hallquist, M. N., Hipwell, A. E., & Stepp, S. D. (2016). Developmental trajectories of borderline personality disorder symptoms and psychosocial functioning in adolescence. *Journal of Personality Disorders, 30,* 351–372.

Wright, D. S., Nash, R. A., & Wade, K. A. (2015). Encouraging eyewitnesses to falsely corroborate allegations: Effects of rapport-building and incriminating evidence. *Psychology, Crime & Law, 21,* 648–660.

Wrosch, C., Bauer, I., & Scheier, M. (2005). Regret and quality of life across the adult life span: The influence of disengagement and available future goals. *Psychology and Aging, 20,* 657–670.

Wrzesniewski, K., & Chylinska, J. (2007). Assessment of coping styles and strategies with school-related stress. *School Psychology International, 28,* 179–194.

Wróbel, M., & Królewiak, K. (2017). Do we feel the same way if we think the same way? Shared attitudes and the social induction of affect. *Basic and Applied Social Psychology, 39,* 19–37.

Wu, L.-T., Schlenger, W. E., & Galvin, D. M. (2006). Concurrent use of methamphetamine, MDMA, LSD, ketamine, GHB, and flunitrazepam among American youths. *Drug and Alcohol Dependence, 84,* 102–113.

Wu, N., Hou, Y., Wang, Q., & Yu, C. (2018). Intergenerational transmission of educational aspirations in Chinese families: Identifying mediators and moderators. *Journal of Youth and Adolescence,* doi:10.1007/s10964-018-0820-y.

Wu, Y. (2013). An empirical study of narrative imagery in implicit and explicit contexts. *Computers in Human Behavior, 29,* 1580–1589.

Wynn, K., Bloom, P., & Chiang, W. C. (2002). Enumeration of collective entities by 5-month-old infants. *Cognition, 83,* B55–B62.

Wyra, M., Lawson, M. J., & Hungi, N. (2007). The mnemonic keyword method: The effects of bidirectional retrieval training and of ability to image on foreign language vocabulary recall. *Learning and Instruction, 17,* 360–371.

Xi, J., Lee, M., LeSuer, W., Barr, P., Newton, K., & Poloma, M. (2017). Altruism and existential well-being. *Applied Research in Quality of Life, 12,* 67–88.

Xiang, J., & Stanley, S. J. (2017). From online to offline: Exploring the role of e-health consumption, patient involvement, and patient-centered communication on perceptions of health care quality. *Computers in Human Behavior, 70,* 446–452.

Xiao, N. G., Quinn, P. C., Liu, S., Ge, L., Pascalis, O., & Lee, K. (2015). Eye tracking reveals a crucial role for facial motion in recognition of faces by infants. *Developmental Psychology, 51,* 744–757.

Xiao, Z., Yan, H., Wang, Z., Zou, Z., Xu, Y., Chen, J., . . . Keyes, B. B. (2006). Trauma and dissociation in China. *American Journal of Psychiatry, 163,* 1388–1391.

Xie, G., & Johnson, J. Q. (2015). Examining the third-person effect of baseline omission in numerical comparison: The role of consumer persuasion knowledge. *Psychology & Marketing, 32,* 438–449.

Yadav, R., Yadav, R. K., Sarvottam, K. & Netam, R. (2017). Framingham Risk Score and estimated 10-year cardiovascular disease risk reduction by a short-term yoga-based lifestyle intervention. *Journal of Alternative Complement Medicine, 23*(9), 730–737.

Yagi, M., Hirano, Y., Nakazato, M., Nemoto, K., Ishikawa, K., Sutoh, C., . . . Nakagawa, A. (2017). Relationship between symptom dimensions and white matter alterations in obsessive-compulsive disorder. *Acta Neuropsychiatrica, 29,* 153–163.

Yamada, R., & Itsukushima, Y. (2013). The schema provokes a disparity of false recollection between actions and objects in an everyday scene. *Scandinavian Journal of Psychology, 54,* 276–282.

Yamawaki, N., Darby, R., & Queiroz, A. (2007). The moderating role of ambivalent sexism: The influence of power status on perception of rape victim and rapist. *Journal of Social Psychology, 147,* 41–56.

Yang, C., Crain, S., Berwick, R. C., Chomsky, N., & Bolhuis, J. J. (2017). The growth of language: Universal grammar, experience, and principles of computation. *Neuroscience and Biobehavioral Reviews.* Accessed from http://www.sciencedirect.com/science/article/pii/S0149763416305656.

Yang, D., Bushnell, E. W., Buchanan, D. W., & Sobel, D. M. (2013). Infants' use of contextual cues in the generalization of effective actions from imitation. *Journal of Experimental Child Psychology , 116,* 510–531.

Yang, J., Hou, C., Ma, N., Liu, J., Zhang, Y., Zhou, J., . . . Li, L. (2007). Enriched environment treatment restores impaired hippocampal synaptic plasticity and cognitive deficits induced by prenatal chronic stress. *Neurobiology of Learning and Memory, 87,* 257–263.

Yang, N., Gelaye, B., Zhong, Q., Rondon, M. B., Sanchez, S. E., & Williams, M. A. (2016). Serum brain-derived neurotrophic factor (BDNF) concentrations in pregnant women with post-traumatic stress disorder and comorbid depression. *Archives of Women's Mental Health, 19,* 979–986.

Yang, Q., Song, D., & Qing, H. (2017). Neural changes in Alzheimer's disease from circuit to molecule: Perspective of optogenetics. *Neuroscience and Biobehavioral Reviews, 79,* 110–118.

Yapko, M. D. (2006). Utilizing hypnosis in addressing ruminative depression-related insomnia. In M. D. Yapko (Ed.), *Hypnosis and treating depression: Applications in clinical practice.* New York: Routledge/Taylor & Francis Group.

Yardley, L., & Moss-Morris, R. (2009, January). Current issues and new directions in psychology and health: Increasing the quantity and quality of health psychology research. *Psychology & Health, 24,* 1–4.

Yarkoni, T. (2015). Neurobiological substrates of personality: A critical overview. In M. Mikulincer, P. R. Shaver, M. L. Cooper, & R. J. Larsen (Eds.), *APA handbook of personality and social psychology, Volume 4: Personality processes and individual differences.* Washington, DC: American Psychological Association.

Ybarra, M. L., & Mitchell, K. J. (2014). "Sexting" and its relation to sexual activity and sexual risk behavior in a national survey of adolescents. *Journal of Adolescent Health, 55*(6), 757–764.

Yelderman, L. A., & Miller, M. K. (2017). Religious fundamentalism, religiosity, and priming: Effects on attitudes, perceptions, and mock jurors' decisions in an insanity defense case. *Psychology, Crime & Law, 23,* 147–170.

Yeomans, M. R., Tepper, B. J., & Ritzschel, J. (2007). Human hedonic responses to sweetness: Role of taste genetics and anatomy. *Physiology & Behavior, 91,* 264–273.

Yesilyaprak, B., Kisac, I., & Sanlier, N. (2007). Stress symptoms and nutritional status among survivors of the Marmara region earthquakes in Turkey. *Journal of Loss & Trauma, 12,* 1–8.

Yi, X., Plucker, J. A., & Guo, J. (2015). Modeling influences on divergent thinking and artistic creativity. *Thinking Skills and Creativity, 16,* 62–68.

Yildirim, F., & Barnett, R. V. (2017). Comparing the effects of specific variables on passionate love among young people: A cross-cultural study. In N. R. Silton (Ed.), *Family dynamics and romantic relationships in a changing society.* Hershey, PA: Information Science Reference/IGI Global.

Yim, D., & Rudoy, J. (2013). Implicit statistical learning and language skills in bilingual children. *Journal of Speech, Language, and Hearing Research, 56,* 310–322.

Yoder, R. M., Goebel, E. A., Köppen, J. R., Blankenship, P. A., Blackwell, A. A., & Wallace, D. G. (2015). Otolithic information is required for homing in the mouse. *Hippocampus, 25,* 890–899.

Yoo, H., & Castro, K. S. (2011). Does nativity status matter in the relationship between perceived racism and academic performance of Asian American college students? *Journal of College Student Development, 52,* 234-245.

Yoo, H., & Pituc, S. T. (2013). Assessments of perceived racial stereotypes, discrimination, and racism. In K. F. Geisinger, B. A. Bracken, J. F. Carlson, J. C. Hansen, N. R. Kuncel, S. P. Reise, & M. C. Rodriguez (Eds.), *APA handbook of testing and assessment in psychology, Vol. 2: Testing and assessment in clinical and counseling psychology.* Washington, DC: American Psychological Association.

Yost, M. R., & Zurbriggen, E. L. (2006). Gender differences in the enactment of sociosexuality: An examination of implicit social motives, sexual fantasies, coercive sexual attitudes, and aggressive sexual behavior. *Journal of Sex Research, 43,* 163-173.

Young, G. (2017). *Revising the APA ethics code.* Cham, Switzerland: Springer International Publishing.

Young, K. D., Misaki, M., Harmer, C. J., Victor, T., Zotev, V., Phillips, R., . . . Bodurka, J. (2017). Real-time functional magnetic resonance imaging amygdala neurofeedback changes positive information processing in major depressive disorder. *Biological Psychiatry, 82*(8), 578-586.

Young, N. L., Kuss, D. J., Griffiths, M. D., & Howard, C. J. (2017). Passive Facebook use, Facebook addiction, and associations with escapism: An experimental vignette study. *Computers In Human Behavior, 71,* 24-31.

Young, R., Subramanian, R., Miles, S., Hinnant, A., & Andsager, J. L. (2017). Social representation of cyberbullying and adolescent suicide: A mixed-method analysis of news stories. *Health Communication, 32*(9), 1082-1092.

Zacks, J. (2008). Neuroimaging studies of mental rotation: A meta-analysis and review. *Journal of Cognitive Neuroscience, 20,* 1-19.

Zahn, N., Sellbom, M., Pymont, C., & Schenk, P. W. (2017). Associations between MMPI-2-RF scale scores and self-reported personality disorder criteria in a private practice sample. *Journal of Psychopathology and Behavioral Assessment, 39*(4), 723-741.

Zahnow, R., McVeigh, J., Ferris, J., & Winstock, A. (2017). Adverse effects, health service engagement, and service satisfaction among anabolic androgenic steroid users. *Contemporary Drug Problems: An Interdisciplinary Quarterly, 44,* 69-83.

Zaitsu, W. (2007). The effect of fear on eyewitness' retrieval in recognition memory. *Japanese Journal of Psychology, 77,* 504-511.

Zajonc, R. B. (2001). Mere exposure: A gateway to the subliminal. *Current Directions in Psychological Science, 10,* 224-228.

Zamarian, L., Högl, B., Delazer, M., Hingerl, K., Gabelia, D., Mitterling, T., . . . Frauscher, B. (2015). Subjective deficits of attention, cognition and depression in patients with narcolepsy. *Sleep Medicine, 16,* 45-51.

Zeigler, D. W., Wang, C. C., Yoast, R. A., Dickenson, B. D., McCaffree, M. A., Robinowitz, C. B., . . . Council on Scientific Affairs, AMA. (2005). The neurocognitive effects of alcohol on adolescents and college students. *Preventive Medicine: An International Journal Devoted to Practice and Theory, 40,* 23-32.

Zell, E., Krizan, Z., & Teeter, S. R. (2015). Evaluating gender similarities and differences using metasynthesis. *American Psychology, 50,* 10-20.

Zeng, L., Proctor, R. W., & Salvendy, G. (2011). Can traditional divergent thinking tests be trusted in measuring and predicting real-world creativity? *Creativity Research Journal, 23,* 24-37.

Zhang, D., He, Z., Chen, Y., & Wei, Z. (2016). Deficits of unconscious emotional processing in patients with major depression: An ERP study. *Journal of Affective Disorders, 199,* 13-20.

Zhang, W., & Guo, B. (2017). Resolving defence mechanisms: A perspective based on dissipative structure theory. *International Journal of Psychoanalysis, 98,* 457-472.

Zhao, K., & Smillie, L. D. (2015). The role of interpersonal traits in social decision making: Exploring sources of behavioral heterogeneity in economic games. *Personality and Social Psychology Review, 19,* 277-302.

Zhou, Y., Li, H., Siddiqui, N., Caudle, Y., Zhang, H., Elgazzar, M., & Yin, D. (2017). Hematopoietic stem progenitor cells prevent chronic stress-induced lymphocyte apoptosis. *Journal of Neuroimmunology, 309*72-76.

Zhou, Z., & Buck, L. B. (2006). Combinatorial effects of odorant mixes in olfactory cortex. *Science, 311,* 1477-1481.

Zhou, Z., Liu, Q., & Davis, R. L. (2005). Complex regulation of spiral ganglion neuron firing patterns by neurotrophin-3. *Journal of Neuroscience, 25,* 7558-7566.

Zickar, M. J. (2015). Digging through dust: Historiography for the organizational sciences. *Journal of Business and Psychology, 30,* 1-14.

Zigler, E., Bennett-Gates, D., Hodapp, R., & Henrich, C. (2002). Assessing personality traits of individuals with mental retardation. *American Journal on Mental Retardation, 107,* 181-193.

Zilbergeld, B., & Ellison, C. R. (1980). Desire discrepancies and arousal problems in sex therapy. In S. R. Leiblum & L. A. Pervin (Eds.), *Principles and practices of sex therapy.* New York: Guilford.

Zimbardo, P. (2007). *The Lucifer effect: Understanding how good people turn evil.* New York: Random House.

Zimbardo, P. G. (1973). On the ethics of intervention in human psychological research: With special reference to the Stanford Prison Experiment. *Cognition, 2,* 243-256.

Zimbardo, P. G., Maslach, C., & Haney, C. (2000). Reflections on the Stanford Prison Experiment: Genesis, transformations, consequences. In T. Blass (Ed.), *Obedience to authority: Current perspectives on the Milgram Paradigm.* Mahwah, NJ: Lawrence Erlbaum Associates.

Zizzari, Z. V., Engl, T., Lorenz, S., van Straalen, N. M., Ellers, J., & Groot, A. T. (2017). Love at first sniff: A spermatophore-associated pheromone mediates partner attraction in a collembolan species. *Animal Behaviour, 124,* 221-227.

Zuberi, T., Patterson, E. J., & Stewart, Q. T. (2015). Race, methodology, and social construction in the genomic era. *Annals of the American Academy of Political and Social Science, 661*(1), 109-127.

Zuger, A. (2005, November 10). Doctors learn how to say what no one wants to hear. *The New York Times,* p. S1.

Zvyagintsev, M., Clemens, B., Chechko, N., Mathiak, K. A., Sack, A. T., & Mathiak, K. (2013). Brain networks underlying mental imagery of auditory and visual information. *European Journal of Neuroscience, 37,* 1421-1434.

Zyoud, S. H., Sweileh, W. M., Awang, R., & Al-Jabi, S. W. (2018). Global trends in research related to social media in psychology: Mapping and bibliometric analysis. *International Journal of Mental Health Systems, 12,* doi:10.1186/s13033-018-0182-6.

Name Index

Subject Index

Note: Page numbers followed by *f* indicate figures.

AP Practice Exam

Section I

Time: 1 hour and 10 minutes
Number of questions: 100

1. Creativity seems to be associated with
   A. divergent thinking.
   B. old age.
   C. narrowed focus.
   D. high intelligence.
   E. extrinsic motivation.

2. The defense mechanism called sublimation protects us from painful emotions by
   A. allowing us to pretend certain events never happened.
   B. enabling us to attribute to others embarrassing feelings we have.
   C. enabling us to bury deep in our memory painful events of the past.
   D. enabling us to retreat to an earlier stage of life when life was simpler.
   E. allowing us to transform negative energy into positive and useful outcomes.

3. Which of the following produces a graph that displays wave patterns?
   A. an fMRI image
   B. an electro-encephalogram device
   C. a CAT scan
   D. a PET scan using radioactive sugar molecules
   E. lesioning

4. In his Stanford Prison Experiment, Philip Zimbardo discovered that his subjects
   A. suffered from schizophrenia, because some experienced hallucinations.
   B. provided evidence for the existence of the mere exposure effect.
   C. assumed stereotypical social roles.
   D. assumed gender roles more appropriate for the opposite sex.
   E. exhibited post-conventional moral reasoning.

5. Mark's retired grandmother decided to study art history at a university, as she put it, "just for fun." She is demonstrating
   A. extrinsic motivation.
   B. intrinsic motivation.
   C. social-cognitive theory.
   D. drive-reduction theory.
   E. the James-Lange theory.

6. Francesca wanted to make an apple-cinnamon cake, but her recipe was smudged and she could not read how much cinnamon to put in the mix. To resolve this problem, she added one teaspoon of cinnamon to the mix, then tasted it. It wasn't quite right so continued to add one teaspoon at a time, tasting after each addition, until she had a cake that tasted right. Which problem solving technique was she using?
   A. Heuristic
   B. Algorithm
   C. Insight
   D. State-dependent
   E. Confirmation bias

7. The ability to read a word despite it missing letters is related to the concept of
   A. top-down processing.
   B. bottom-up processing.
   C. difference threshold.
   D. depth perception.
   E. perceptual constancy.

8. Stress has all of the following direct physiological effects EXCEPT
   A. elevated blood pressure.
   B. decreased immune functioning.
   C. decreased fatigue.
   D. increased hormonal activity.
   E. psychophysiological conditions.

9. Since environment generally has little effect on eye color, we can say that eye color has a high degree of
   A. variability.
   B. reliability.
   C. introspection.
   D. heritability.
   E. determinism.

10. The type of reinforcement schedule likely to produce the longest-lasting behavior is a(n)
    A. interval schedule.
    B. ratio schedule.
    C. intensity schedule.
    D. variable schedule.
    E. implied schedule.

11. Conversion disorder and illness anxiety disorder are classified as
    A. mood disorders because they all have an element of depression.
    B. somatic symptom disorders because they are all caused by neurotransmitter deficits.
    C. anxiety disorders because they all feature impaired reality testing.
    D. mood disorders because they all include an element of mania.
    E. somatic symptom disorders because they all have physical features that are not caused by medical conditions.

12. Conditioning is most effective if the neutral stimulus
    A. precedes the unconditioned stimulus.
    B. precedes the conditioned stimulus.
    C. follows the unconditioned stimulus.
    D. follows the conditioned stimulus.
    E. occurs at the same time as the conditioned stimulus.

13. The ability to "bounce back" from life's problems, disappointments, and failures is termed
    A. resilience.
    B. self-efficacy.
    C. self-serving bias.
    D. competence.
    E. psychotherapeutic efficacy.

14. If a weightlifter can distinguish 50 lbs. from 55 lbs half of the time, then, according to Weber's Law, she
    A. will be able to distinguish 20 lbs. from 21 lbs. 50% of the time.
    B. will be able to distinguish 70 lbs. from 77 lbs. 50% of the time.
    C. will not be able to 20 lbs. from 25 lbs. 50% of the time
    D. will be able to distinguish 90 lbs. from 95 lbs. 50% of the time.
    E. will not be able to distinguish 60 lbs. from 67 lbs. 50% of the time.

15. An individual who displays an exaggerated sense of self-importance is exhibiting symptoms of
   A. an antisocial personality disorder.
   B. a narcissistic personality disorder.
   C. a borderline personality disorder.
   D. an attention-deficit hyperactivity disorder.
   E. an autism spectrum disorder.

16. Place theory provides a better explanation for the sensing of
   A. low-frequency sounds.
   B. high-frequency sounds.
   C. medium-frequency sounds.
   D. loud sounds.
   E. soft sounds.

17. Developmental psychologists use this term to describe the biologically programmed process by which infants develop motor skills such as rolling over, sitting, standing, and walking.
   A. Growth spurts
   B. Attachment
   C. Developmental graduation
   D. Maturation
   E. Motor skills learning

18. A therapist working from the cognitive perspective would likely
   A. be most concerned about the patient's family relationships.
   B. focus on incentives that motivate the patient's current behavior.
   C. help the patient identify and change dysfunctional thoughts.
   D. analyze a patient's dreams in order to explain the patient's unconscious conflicts.
   E. assist the patient in meeting his social and ego needs.

19. Giving a test or assessment to a group of students, and, one month later, giving it to them again is a method of establishing that the test has
   A. norms.
   B. adaptive testing.
   C. mental age.
   D. validity.
   E. reliability.

20. Which theory provides a neuroscience explanation of dreams?
   A. Unconscious wish fulfillment
   B. Activation-synthesis
   C. Dreams-for-survival
   D. Circadian rhythm
   E. Memory consolidation

21. Which of the following methods of brain research involves placing sensors on the skull to record brain activity?
   A. PET scan
   B. fMRI
   C. EEG
   D. CAT scan
   E. Lesioning

22. In Erikson's theory of social development individuals who fail to successfully resolve trust and identity issues may have difficulty later in
   A. earning a living.
   B. having children.
   C. making moral decisions.
   D. forming intimate relationships.
   E. thinking abstractly.

23. Jeffrey does poorly in school because he works until midnight every night to help support his family. When a teacher accuses him of being "just plain lazy," the teacher
   A. is probably using reciprocal determinism.
   B. has committed the fundamental attribution error.
   C. is using a peripheral route to persuasion to motivate Jeffrey.
   D. is using variable reinforcement on Jeffrey.
   E. is using the self-serving bias to cover up her poor teaching skills.

24. In Freud's terms, material that is easily recalled to the conscious mind is stored in
   A. the unconscious.
   B. as collective unconscious.
   C. the preconscious.
   D. the superego.
   E. the tranference conscious.

25. In late adulthood, individuals often show declines in what type of intelligence?
   A. Crystallized intelligence
   B. Fluid intelligence
   C. Practical intelligence
   D. Emotional intelligence
   E. Interpersonal intelligence

26. One's vestibular sense is in his or her
   A. ears.
   B. nose.
   C. eyes.
   D. skin.
   E. mouth.

27. Split-brain patients have undergone surgery to sever the
   A. optic chiasm.
   B. cerebellum.
   C. corpus callosum.
   D. optic nerve.
   E. sensory cortex.

28. A concept is
   A. an example of habituation.
   B. an example of bottom-up processing.
   C. the equilavent of feature abstraction.
   D. a collection of items that fit a schema.
   E. a heuristic algorithm.

29. A charitable organization tries to solicit contributions by showing TV commercials with celebrities endorsing the organization. The organization is using
   A. the celebrity heuristic.
   B. confirmation bias.
   C. the peripheral route to persuasion.
   D. an algorithm.
   E. the self-serving bias.

30. Incoming math majors at a university are given a math aptitude test. The university found a strong positive correlation between the incoming scores and the students' math GPA after two years. The university concluded that
   A. the test has predictive validity.
   B. the test has internal reliability.
   C. the test has adaptive testing.
   D. the test has mental age.
   E. the test has norms.

31. Unconditional positive regard is generally associated with
   A. Freud's psychoanalysis.
   B. Beck's cognitive therapy.
   C. Jones's behavior therapy.
   D. Rogers's person-centered therapy.
   E. psychopharmacology.

32. When children first begin to babble, at only a few months of age, they voice
   A. phonemes that are found only in the language spoken in the home.
   B. only a few, easily-pronounced phonemes.
   C. most of the morphemes found in the home language.
   D. phonemes from almost every language in the world.
   E. only phonemes from the correct language "family" – such European Romance languages.

33. As Megan anxiously prepares to step onstage to deliver the commencement speech, her heart is racing, her mouth is dry, and her pupils are fully dilated. Which part of her nervous system is in control?
   A. Endocrinatic
   B. Parasympathetic
   C. Skeletal
   D. Sympathetic
   E. Muscular

34. A highly skilled architect or sculptor probably has, according to Howard Gardner's theory of intelligence, a high level of
   A. spatial intelligence.
   B. 3-D intelligence.
   C. intrapersonal intelligence.
   D. naturalistic intelligence.
   E. bodily kinesthetic intelligence.

35. If a dog learns to associate a tone with being fed, the dog will salivate when it hears the tone. If the dog later hears a slightly higher pitched tone and salivates in response to the second tone, then a researcher can say that which of the following has occurred?
   A. Stimulus discrimination
   B. Spontaneous recovery
   C. Operant conditioning
   D. Stimulus deferment
   E. Stimulus generalization

36. As long as sales remain above the daily quota, a sales manager rewards his staff using the variable interval reinforcement schedule by
   A. giving each employee a $10 bill on Friday.
   B. giving the best seller of the week an extra $20 on Friday.
   C. occasionally buying lunch, once every week or so.
   D. giving the employees $10 every time sales exceed quota for five consecutive days.
   E. firing the least productive employee every month.

37. A student watched patrons at a sporting event and noted whether they more often went to the food concession stands during time-outs or when there was action on the field. Which type of research is this?
   A. Survey
   B. Correlational
   C. Naturalistic observation
   D. Clinical observation
   E. Experimental

38. Most professionals use the APA's DSM for what purpose?
   A. Define different therapy techniques
   B. Classify and define psychological disorders
   C. Establish the history of the different disorders
   D. List causes of psychological disorders
   E. Explain the theoretical basis of different therapies

39. Cognitive psychologists are likely to be interested in how
    A. you choose a college major.
    B. you feel about your college's football team.
    C. you process fear in your brain.
    D. you use your sense of depth perception.
    E. your heart rate changes when an attractive person walks by.

40. An individual who has a male body but views their gender identity as female may consider themselves
    A. transgender.
    B. androgynous.
    C. bisexual.
    D. feministic.
    E. intersexual.

41. A reuptake inhibitor is likely to have the effect of
    A. raising the threshold for firing a neuron.
    B. increasing the amount of a neurotransmitter in the synapse.
    C. increasing the intensity of a neuron's firing.
    D. decreasing the amount of a transmitter in the synapse.
    E. lowering the threshold for firing a neuron.

42. Jennifer noticed that her husband, who snored heavily, often stopped breathing as he slept and then, after 30 to 45 seconds of not breathing, gasped for breath. She is concerned that he may be suffering from
    A. night terrors.
    B. insomnia.
    C. excessive REM sleep.
    D. sleep apnea.
    E. sleep tremors.

43. One reason that the validity of projective personality tests is questioned is that
    A. projective tests always have objective scoring criteria.
    B. psychologists who administer projective tests have extensive training in scoring them.
    C. projective tests are administered only by psychiatrists.
    D. most projective tests require some subjective scoring.
    E. an individual may score differently on two separate administrations of a projective test.

44. Because Celia's absolute threshold for hearing is eight decibels, it is likely that she will hear what percentage of sounds that are exactly eight decibels?
    A. 100%
    B. 0%
    C. 10%
    D. 90%
    E. 50%

45. When group members share such a strong motivation to achieve consensus that they lose the ability to critically evaluate alternative points of view, this is known as
    A. group polarization.
    B. gate control theory.
    C. prejudice.
    D. groupthink.
    E. ingroup bias.

46. When a four-year-old was asked to decide whether a row of four narrowly-spaced pennies or a row of four widely-spaced pennies had more coins, he said the widely-spaced row had more. This indicates that he has not yet developed
    A. egocentrism.
    B. conservation of number.
    C. telegraphic speech.
    D. conservation of length.
    E. the Babinski reflex.

47. Roger Sperry is primarily known for his work in
  A. split-brain research.
  B. personality.
  C. reuptake processes.
  D. feature detection in vision.
  E. social facilitation.

48. What type of memory is an episodic memory?
  A. Implicit memory
  B. Explicit memory
  C. Procedural memory
  D. Sensory memory
  E. Semantic memory

49. The Rosenhan study, in which normal people reported briefly experiencing a single symptom of schizophrenia, illustrated the fact that
  A. schizophrenia is a pervasive disorder in modern society.
  B. schizophrenia is easily treated with modern therapeutic methods.
  C. a mental set can interfere with proper diagnosis.
  D. many schizophrenics lie about their symptoms.
  E. older people are more likely than younger people to report symptoms of schizophrenia.

50. Before engaging in animal psychology research, a university professor would likely have to
  A. design his research so that no animal suffered any pain in the research.
  B. obtain approval from the Federal Psychology Licensing Board.
  C. provide the animals a comfortable retirement when he finished.
  D. ensure that he used only male animals in his research.
  E. obtain approval of his research from an Institutional Review Board or similar body.

51. The motor cortex devotes the most resources to which parts of the body?
  A. Muscles requiring very fine movement, such as in the lips and fingers
  B. The most important muscles, such as the heart and lungs
  C. The largest and strongest muscles
  D. The muscles furthest from the brain, such as those in the legs and feet
  E. The autonomic muscles

52. The area of central focus on the retina is called the
  A. cornea.
  B. aqueous humor.
  C. blind spot.
  D. fovea.
  E. ganglion cell.

53. Henry has a crush on a girl in his school, but she did not know him and never seemed to notice him. Because Henry understood the mere exposure effect, he decided to
  A. look up her online profile.
  B. join the swim team.
  C. join a club in which she is active.
  D. send her an anonymous note.
  E. work out to improve his physique.

54. In the basement of their home, a toddler and mother see a spider. The toddler is curious about the spider until the mother screams in terror, grabs the child tightly, and runs from the home, screaming, her heart beating wildly as she pants for breath between screams and sobs. Because of the mother's terror, the child also becomes terribly afraid of spiders. Assuming this phobia is established in the child by classical conditioning, what is the unconditioned stimulus in this scenario?
  A. The spider
  B. The basement
  C. The child's fear
  D. The toddler's curiosity
  E. The mother's fearful behavior

55. As people age, their resting metabolism tends to
    A. remain relatively constant.
    B. increase for men, and decrease for women.
    C. increase for women, and decrease for men.
    D. increase for both men and women.
    E. decrease for both men and women.

56. Which of the following drugs may produce mild euphoria and general relaxation, and in some cases, hallucinations, delusions and paranoia, though it is usually not physically addicting?
    A. Amphetamines
    B. Morphine
    C. Marijuana
    D. Stimulants
    E. Barbiturates

57. What does it mean if the results of an experiment are statistically significant?
    A. No difference was found between conditions
    B. The research was very important
    C. The research was conducted by a famous researcher
    D. Researchers are confident that they have confirmed their hypothesis
    E. The results have not been replicated

58. Which of the following research results regarding adolescent maturation is true?
    A. Menopause is associated with the start of puberty
    B. Sex characteristics develop at the end of puberty
    C. Puberty for boys is usually earlier than girls
    D. Early maturation is favorable for boys
    E. Early maturation is favorable for girls

59. The Big 5 personality traits consist of the following traits EXCEPT
    A. conscientiousness.
    B. neuroticism.
    C. optimism.
    D. extraversion.
    E. agreeableness.

60. According to the Cannon-Bard theory, which of the following is true?
    A. Arousal and the emotion are simultaneous
    B. The emotion precedes the arousal
    C. The arousal precedes the emotion
    D. Arousal of sufficient intensity inhibits the emotion
    E. Arousal includes a simultaneously-occurring cognitive event

61. Angela wanted to try a new restaurant. She went to the restaurant's website, where she found dozens of glowing reviews from other patrons. She decided that the restaurant must be good, and she quickly made a reservation. It appears that Angela used
    A. self-serving bias.
    B. an algorithm.
    C. confirmation bias.
    D. expectations bias.
    E. hindsight bias.

62. In Hans Selye's theory of stress, the highest level of reaction to stress occurs in the
    A. initiation stage.
    B. the exhaustion stage.
    C. the resistance stage.
    D. the alarm stage.
    E. the extinction stage.

63. Though he hadn't ridden a bicycle in many tears, George's grandfather quickly regained the skill of doing so when he began riding for exercise in his 70s. George's grandfather apparently has a functioning
   A. state memory.
   B. flashbulb memory.
   C. eidetic memory.
   D. iconic memory.
   E. procedural memory.

64. In Freudian theory, the process of projecting onto one's therapist the emotions felt earlier in life, especially toward parents, is called
   A. accommodation.
   B. the Electra Complex.
   C. identification.
   D. insight maintenance.
   E. transference.

65. Which of the following is a true statement?
   A. The hypothesis generally predicts that the dependent variable is affected by the independent variable.
   B. The dependent variable and the independent variable are interchangeable in most research.
   C. The random variable is the cause of both the independent variable and the dependent variable.
   D. Dependent variables are generally not used in psychology research.
   E. The independent variable is always affected by the dependent variable.

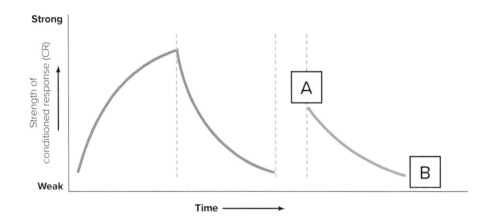

66. In the graph above illustrating the strength of a classically conditioned response, which of the following shows the conditioning process that is occurring in the phase from point A to point B?
   A. Spontaneous recovery
   B. Acquisition
   C. Extinction
   D. Variable reinforcement
   E. Generalization

67. The scores on a national psychology test are normally distributed. The mean of the test is 75 and the standard deviation is 15. What percentage of the test-takers scored between 60 and 90?
   A. less than 1%
   B. About 2.5 %
   C. About 34%
   D. About 57%
   E. About 68%

68. The fact that children who are blind from birth can make facial expressions appropriate to the emotional situation is reason to believe that
   A. expressions of basic emotions are attributable to social learning.
   B. facial expressions differ dramatically across cultures.
   C. facial expressions are subject to the James-Lange theory.
   D. expression of basic emotions is genetic in nature, not learned.
   E. such children cannot be representative of all children and therefore we cannot generalize about their abilities.

69. Three of Suzanne's friends know a lot about cell phones. When Suzanne purchases her phone, she buys the same brand that her friends have purchased. This is an example of
   A. obedience.
   B. deindividuation.
   C. groupthink.
   D. social facilitation.
   E. conformity.

70. A way to treat bed-wetting in older children is to provide a special pad for the child to sleep on. The pad sounds an alarm and wakes the child if the child wets it. This method, which uses classical conditioning, has proven successful. What is the unconditioned response in this method?
   A. The alarm
   B. Bed-wetting
   C. Waking up
   D. Ending the habit of bed-wetting
   E. The feeling of a full bladder

71. Which endocrine gland produces Human Growth Hormone?
   A. Testes
   B. Hypothalamus
   C. Adrenal
   D. Pituitary
   E. Parathyroid

72. Students who continually fail in school classes and have difficulty forming personal relationships might
   A. suffer from deindividuation.
   B. be excessively optimistic.
   C. have an internal locus of control.
   D. experience learned helplessness.
   E. have high expectations of themselves.

73. Which of the following variables could not be used in correlational research?
   A. Age
   B. Gender
   C. Income
   D. Height
   E. Weight

74. An individual diagnosed with autism spectrum disorder who displays extraordinary memory skills would be known as
   A. conscientious.
   B. intellectually disabled.
   C. a prodigy.
   D. a savant.
   E. a genius.

75. The Freudian process by which a child incorporates the behavior and attitudes of the same-sex parent into his or her own personality is called
   A. transference.
   B. imitation.
   C. imprinting.
   D. identification.
   E. unconscious development.

76. The afterimage effect is explained by
    A. the opponent-process theory.
    B. accommodation.
    C. Weber's Law.
    D. the trichomatic theory.
    E. Helmholtz's Law.

77. Professor O'Doyle is conducting an experiment to determine whether or not drinking pomegranate juice before a test has an effect on students' scores on the test. Which of the following describes an operational definition for the dependent variable in this research?
    A. The amount of juice consumed before the test
    B. The students' post-test estimates of their scores
    C. The mean of the students' scores
    D. The difficulty of the test
    E. 6 oz. of juice consumed 40 minutes before the test

78. This researcher conducted a number of studies in which a mother and small child were left in a room. A stranger then entered the room and the mother left for a short period, before returning. The researcher was
    A. Mary Cover Jones.
    B. Mary Ainsworth.
    C. John Garcia.
    D. Robert Rescorla.
    E. Aaron Beck.

79. When a teacher gives her young students gold stars for good scores on a spelling test, she is using the principle of
    A. negative reinforcement.
    B. stimulus identification.
    C. stimulus generalization.
    D. reverse punishment.
    E. positive reinforcement.

80. Which classic experiment researched the concept of obedience?
    A. Zimbardo's prison study
    B. Milgram's shock study
    C. Asch's line study
    D. Ainsworth's strange situation study
    E. Pavlov's dog study

81. Antipsychotic drugs work by blocking what type of receptors at the brain's synapses?
    A. Serotonin
    B. Glutamate
    C. GABA
    D. Dopamine
    E. Norepinephrine

82. In a study conducted in the 1930s, a psychologist surveyed hotel and restaurant owners in California, asking them if they would serve Chinese immigrants to California. Nearly all said they would not serve the Chinese. Later, the psychologist sent a Chinese-American couple who spoke fluent English and dressed in American clothes to the establishments. Nearly all served the couple. The psychologist concluded from this study
    A. that racism was common in California in the 1930s.
    B. that confirmation bias had affected the couple's treatment.
    C. that the fundamental attribution error affected the couple's treatment.
    D. that there was no discrimination in California in the 1930s.
    E. that attitudes do not always predict behavior.

83. For an experiment in how U.S. high school students learn best, Mr. Abercrombie gave the girls in his class written material on Freud to read. He gave the boys the same written material to read plus a video to watch on the same material. Later, he tested both groups, and when the boys scored higher on the test, he concluded that U.S. high school students learn best with two forms of study materials. One problem with this experiment is that
   A. he used neither random sampling nor random selection.
   B. he had too many dependent variables.
   C. he had too many independent variables.
   D. he used random sampling, but not random selection.
   E. he included no random variables.

84. The rooting reflex in infants occurs when
   A. the infant's cheek is stroked.
   B. the infant is preparing to walk.
   C. strangers interrupt the child's caregiver.
   D. an infant is tired.
   E. the caregiver leaves the room.

85. Young parents who hope to raise confident, self-reliant, independent children might do well to adopt
   A. an authoritarian parenting style.
   B. an authoritative parenting style.
   C. a permissive parenting style.
   D. an uninvolved parenting style.
   E. a "helicopter" parenting style.

86. One advantage of group therapy over individual therapy is
   A. most patients prefer it.
   B. that many styles of therapy are more effective in groups.
   C. that patients' tendencies to conform make it likely that all in the group will improve.
   D. that the therapist can exploit the self-serving bias more effectively in a group.
   E. that it is more cost effective, because the therapist can work with more patients each day.

87. Phineas Gage has been of interest to psychologists because it appears that
   A. his thalamus was damaged, thus accounting for his vision problems.
   B. the connection between his amygdala and frontal cortex was damaged, thus accounting for his emotional problems.
   C. he became, as a result of his injury, a split-brain patient.
   D. his sensory cortex was damaged, thus accounting for his inability to smell after the accident.
   E. his temporal lobe was damaged, accounting for his inability to speak after the accident.

88. Which of the following is likely to become a flashbulb memory?
   A. What you had for lunch yesterday
   B. The title of your 8th grade math textbook
   C. Your first kiss
   D. The capital of Montana
   E. Part of a song you heard today on the car radio

89. According to Robert Sternberg's theory of intelligence, a person with high creative intelligence is likely to be able to
   A. adjust quickly to novel situations.
   B. solve simple addition and subtraction problems easily.
   C. recall the capitals of all 50 states.
   D. make friends easily.
   E. achieve a high score in Conscientiousness on a Big 5 test.

90. Forensic psychology is the field in which psychologists
   A. investigate and solve crimes.
   B. profile serial killers.
   C. interact with the legal system.
   D. train FBI agents in profiling techniques.
   E. interpret lie detector tests in criminal investigations.

91. Penny is a young infant who is irritable, easy to upset, and difficult to soothe. She would be best described as having a difficult
   A. excitement phase.
   B. attitude.
   C. temperament.
   D. attachment.
   E. gender identity.

92. Who was known for looking at head size to measure intelligence?
   A. Alfred Binet
   B. Howard Gardner
   C. David Wechsler
   D. Lewis Terman
   E. Francis Galton

93. In a correlation study comparing daily yogurt intake with blood sugar levels, the results showed an r value of −.12. This indicates
   A. that yogurt causes increased blood sugar level.
   B. that yogurt causes decreased blood sugar level.
   C. that there is a slight negative relationship between yogurt intake and blood sugar level.
   D. that there is a slight positive relationship between yogurt intake and blood sugar level.
   E. that there is no relationship at all between the two.

94. Which statistic represents the strongest relationship between two variables?
   A. $r = 0$
   B. $r = .75$
   C. $r = -.90$
   D. $p = 1$
   E. $p = .05$

95. A student who frequently enrolls in difficult courses because he finds them challenging and therefore rewarding to master exhibits a high level of
   A. extrinsic motivation.
   B. self-efficacy.
   C. reciprocal determinism.
   D. neuroticism.
   E. extraversion.

96. In Chomsky's theory of language acquisition, children's ability to make sense of language
   A. is acquired through classical conditioning.
   B. is voluntarily developed cognitive ability.
   C. is rarely affected by genetics.
   D. is acquired through operant conditioning.
   E. is a facility humans are born with.

97. If a culture generally expects males to be more aggressive and less overtly emotional than females, then boys who are more aggressive and less emotional can be said to be conforming to
   A. gender roles.
   B. gender identities.
   C. sexual typing.
   D. sexual scripting.
   E. cultural identities.

98. He showed that an important feature of a conditioned stimulus is the extent to which it predicts the likelihood of the unconditioned stimulus's appearance, as, for example, in taste aversions.
   A. Robert Rescorla
   B. Edward Tolman
   C. B.F. Skinner
   D. John Garcia
   E. Albert Bandura

99. A psychologist who studies ways that the elderly adapt to physical limitations in their lives is probably working in which of the following domains of psychology?

A. Clinical

B. I/O

C. Developmental

D. Psychometric

E. Experimental

100. In drive-reduction theory, drives are always associated with

A. instincts.

B. emotional arousal.

C. physiological needs.

D. psychological needs.

E. stress levels.

Section II

Time: 50 minutes
Number of questions: 2

Directions: You have 50 minutes to answer both of the following questions. It is not enough to answer a question merely listing facts. You should present a cogent argument based on your critical analysis of the question posed.

1. Mary is planning a trip to Europe after her first year of college. She plans to fly to Europe from her home in Chicago. She will travel by train in Europe and stay in hostels. She is excited that she will be able to experience new cultures and see the museums and tourist sights of Europe.

For each of the following concepts, define (or describe) the concept AND explain how the concept would affect Mary's enjoyment of her trip.

- Stereotype
- Diffusion of responsibility
- Conformity
- Altruism
- Motion parallax
- Top-down processing
- Place theory
- Circadian rhythm

2. Explain how the first term in the following pairs causes, affects, facilitates, or improves the second. Definitions alone are not enough to score a point; you must address the relationship between the terms.

- practice – self-efficacy
- assimilation – schema
- latent content – insight
- refractory period – neuron
- interneuron – reflex
- operational definition – dependent variable
- feature detection – perception
- evolutionary psychology – mate selection